COUNTRY MUSIC

COUNTRY MUSIC

A BIOGRAPHICAL DICTIONARY

RICHARD CARLIN

Routledge
NEW YORK AND LONDON

Published in 2003 by
Routledge
29 West 35th Street
New York, NY 10001
www.routledge-ny.com

Published in Great Britain by
Routledge
11 New Fetter Lane
London EC4P 4EE
www.routledge.co.uk

Portions of this work were originally issued as *The Big Book of Country Music* (Penguin, 1995), although most of these articles were revised and expanded for this new work.

Library of Congress Cataloging-in-Publication Data

Carlin, Richard.
    Country music : a biographical dictionary / Richard Carlin.
        p. cm.
''Portions of this book originally appeared as The big book of country music: a biographical encyclopedia, by Richard Carlin (Penguin, 1995)''—T.p. verso.
Includes bibliographical references (p.   ) and discographies.
    ISBN 0-415-93802-3 (alk. paper)
    1. Country music—Bio-bibliography—Dictionaries.   I. Carlin, Richard.
Big book of country music. II. Title.
    ML102.C7 C28 2002
    781.642′092′2—dc20

                                                           2002003451

10 9 8 7 6 5 4 3 2 1

Contents

To Bob Carlin
Who Taught Me How to Love Country Music

To Richard Kostelanetz
Who Taught Me How to Write Dictionaries

And To Benson Carlin, 1915–1996
With Love and Affection

Introduction: An Apology

Since the publication of the original version of this work, titled by Penguin *The Big Book of Country Music*, in 1995, I have had the chance to be humbled and supported by many readers who have offered their emendations and corrections to my original work. I use the term "apology" here not to mean that I am disowning my work, but in the original meaning of the word, as an explanation of my rationale for revising, expanding, and updating this work.

In the period since I completed the original edition of this book, country music's dominance of the pop charts has subsided. Acts that once held the #1 spot are gone; others have faded badly. New "superstars" have crossed over into the mainstream, while a renewed return-to-roots movement has also blossomed. As in all areas of popular music, the pendulum continues to swing, the traditionalists holding steadily to their acoustic roots while the would-be megastars look toward middle-of-the-road pop sounds for their pot of gold.

Despite the fading of country's chart dominance, the music remains vital and strong. The core country audience—which has never been given much respect by either the music business or academics—remains as strongly devoted to the music as ever. And the music continues to interact and feed into mainstream pop music and culture. All of the issues raised by country's success still remain unanswered, and the artists themselves continue to straddle the line between serving their audience and achieving fame and fortune.

When revising a work that is itself now a document of its time, I was faced with the question of what to do with entries on onetime major stars who are now mostly forgotten. In a strange way these entries have increased in value, insofar as it's difficult to find information on singers who held the #1 spot on the charts just a few years ago—a telling commentary on the transience of popular success. I decided not to eliminate these entries, or even to cut them down, but rather to admit that the work will have a mid-1990s bias in its coverage, because comparable performers from earlier years may not be covered.

As for the revision itself, many new entries have been written on artists who have arisen since the mid-1990s, as well as on early pioneers. Other entries have been reviewed, some simply expanded to cover the balance of a career, others completely reworked as my opinions and ideas have matured. I hope these additions further demonstrate the range of country music and its huge impact on American cultural life.

My inclination, albeit somewhat perverse, is to give more coverage to earlier recording artists who may be almost entirely forgotten to most listeners today. Again, the value of this coverage should be that these are the artists who are least likely to be found in other, mainstream, reference works—or even other dictionaries of country music. Similarly, the history of country music is underrepresented in the general histories of twentieth-century American popular music, so it seems appropriate to focus on these artists.

To the many historians, archivists, and dogged collectors who have unearthed this information, I owe more than I can express. The leaders in the field—Charles Wolfe, Colin Escott, Rich Kienzle, Doug Green, Bill Malone, Tony Russell—have inspired me in my own (admittedly much more limited) research. There are many others who have focused on a single artist or genre whose books have inspired me (and are listed in the bibliography). I have particular respect for the determined field researchers, including Alan Lomax, Mike Seeger, Ray Alden, Art Rosenbaum, Carl Fleischauer, and others who have recorded and preserved the music itself. And for the record collectors and researchers, unsung heroes in unearthing rare and early recordings, such as Dick Spottswood and Richard Nevins. It would be impossible for me to create a volume of this scope based entirely on my own research; and I have attempted to give credit whenever I am aware of the source of the original research. For those I have unintentionally slighted in my borrowing of information, I offer my sincere apologies.

My other biases should be readily apparent, as they were to reviewers and critics of the first edition. To those critics I am most appreciative of the many suggestions for changes and corrections of fact. Any work compiled by a single author, despite all due vigilance, is bound to suffer from some errors. The source material itself is often contradictory; and the artists are not above misrepresenting their exact ages and the "facts" of their lives and careers. The "official" biography is often written to support the image that an artist (or his/her handlers) hopes to project. I have made a greater effort to be watchful for my own lapses in spelling and memory, but I'm sure that in adding to the work I've added new material that will, in turn, need correcting in the future.

The great Nicolas Slonimsky, the model for all music lexicographers (as he liked to call himself), wrote many essays on the impossibilities of uncovering the entire "truth" about a life or career. A dogged researcher, he would dig up birth certificates to prove, once and for all, that an operatic diva had subtracted five years from her age; weather records to show that Mozart was buried on a sunny day (and not during a snowstorm, as often was reported); and other ephemera to the point where all admired his command of the basic information. But, even given this diligence, it was the quality of his writing that distinguished his work, his humorous and sometimes controversial opinions, anecdotes, and asides being the heart of his fact-filled entries. I do not claim to come near to touching the hem of his lexicographical garment; rather, in my humble way, I have tried to emulate his better qualities.

Dictionary makers are necessarily obsessive, cranky, and opinionated. As an editor I have worked with some of the best and crankiest. Again, I do not hold myself up as deserving to be in that elite class, because my own need for information is sometimes limited by my admitted weakness for the juicy anecdote or the telling aside. I invite all of my readers to be also my proofreaders; and I appreciate in advance your corrections and criticisms.

As for having strong opinions about country music, I can only plead guilty. My attempts to describe how the music sounds, and where it falls within the spectrum of popular styles, must of necessity reflect my own opinions about the state of popular culture. And, in a way, these opinions are more valuable than the retelling of facts, because the reader can at least get some notion about the musical achievement of the artists, as well as the basic nuts-and-bolts information (that, admittedly, can be found in other sources as well). "Just the facts" works for *Dragnet*, but unfortunately not for dictionary makers.

A Short History of Country Music

It is tempting in this time of its greatest popularity to pronounce country music dead and buried. After all, what's the difference between 1970s soft-pop-rock and 1990s country-corn-kitsch? If Garth Brooks outsells Guns 'n' Roses, maybe it's heavy metal that should be called "folk music" and country, "mainstream pop." When everybody wants to be a hunk in a hat or a cowgirl in a gingham dress, maybe it's time to forget about the history of one of America's few indigenous musics and move on.

Country music is not America's only indigenous music—there are jazz and blues and rock 'n' roll to contend for the crown. But country music has never garnered the critical respect or intellectual prestige of even rock, perhaps because it is so closely associated with "hillbilly" or "red-neck" roots. But, like jazz, country music has a century-old tradition, with myriad styles evolving (and coexisting) over the decades. Like jazz it is constantly turning back and renewing itself at the source; flirting with mainstream success; crossing over into pop; going into lengthy periods of exile; and ultimately bubbling forth again like an irrepressible voice of the earth.

Country music, like all great American art forms, has its roots in commerce; that is to say, it took commercial recording companies and radio stations to nurture the country style. There were settlers both black and white in the Appalachians from time immemorial, and they brought with them two distinct traditions: the European tradition of Anglo-American balladry, story songs, and dance music based on four-square harmonies and fixed forms; and the African-American tradition of blues, work songs, and field hollers, featuring often improvisatory melodies and words accompanied by polyrhythmic instrumental virtuosity. And like all great American musics, country music is a blending of these black and white elements, with each tradition tipping its hat in the other's direction so that it is impossible to cleanly unravel one from the other.

The first commercialization of America's backwoods sounds came in the mid-nineteenth century, thanks to the minstrel and traveling tent shows. Minstrel show music was built around the popularity of a new musical instrument, the banjo, whose roots were in Africa. But while the banjo was African in its origins, the music played by the minstrels—whether black or white—was an amalgam of traditional English dance tunes and the popular composed songs of the day. While originally the minstrel show was created by whites imitating/parodying black manners, and thus could be viewed as an elevation of racism to a form of mass entertainment, it must be admitted that the minstrel shows were entertaining, and in a backward kind of way proved the value of black culture to a larger audience (just as Pat Boone singing "Tutti Fruiti" helped introduce white-bread America in the late 1950s to the real thing, Little Richard).

Minstrel shows gave birth to two distinct forms of American entertainment. The large, successful troops managed to make a mark in Northern cities like Baltimore, Philadelphia, and New York, and eventually toured Europe; they began to incorporate other ethnic types found in the nation's large cities—such as stage Irishmen and Germans—eventually maturing into what would be known as vaudeville, with music provided by the composers of Tin Pan Alley. Meanwhile, the backwoods traveling shows continued to tour the South, nurturing hundreds of wanna-be banjo and fiddle players, country rube comedians, and assorted semiprofessional entertainers.

A second seedbed for country music was, oddly enough, the rural church. Music was an integral part of church services both black and white; many churches founded singing schools to teach the rudiments of harmony through the "shape-note" system. (Shape notes use different shapes—such as squares, triangles, and so on—to differentiate the scale tones, so that it's not necessary to "read music" to sing from the hymnal.)

While the black church evolved an ecstatic, semi-improvised, and highly emotional take on the tradition of Protestant hymn singing, the white church evolved its own sound, a blend of primitive harmonizing with the nasal twang of backwoods singing. Each tradition would cross-pollinate and ultimately fertilize the other, so eventually a blues-influenced, tightly harmonized music called "blue-grass" would become the ultimate melding of black and white music making.

But it took new technologies and the coming of mass marketing in the twentieth century to really launch country music. In the early days of recording, when heavy and primitive equipment was used to capture sound, almost all sessions were held in the large Northern cities, and were limited to the sounds and styles that record executives knew—such as light opera, comedic stage vocalists, or watered-down dance bands. Occasionally a fiddle player or vocalist would work his way north—such as the great Texas champion fiddler Eck Robertson, who made some of the first solo fiddle recordings in 1922—but there was little understanding of or appetite for recording this music.

However, as local dealers began selling phonographs in the South and the West, they reported back to the home office about artists who were popular in their area. One influential dealer was Polk Brockman, working out of Atlanta; he knew what his customers wanted, and was important enough to the home base to be able to suggest that local artists be recorded. One artist whom Brockman recommended was a fifty-plus-year-old fiddler and sometime house painter named Fiddlin' John Carson; the Okeh label dutifully made a custom record of Carson singing the late-nineteenth-century popular song "The Little Old Log Cabin in the Lane" for Brockman to sell, but didn't even bother to assign a master number or affix a label to the 500 records pressed for him. It was only after the record became a regional hit that the light bulb of commerce lit up in the executives' heads, and suddenly they were scouring the countryside for entertainers.

Recording technology was so improved by the late 1920s that portable equipment was finally available, and studios could be set up closer to the musicians. In 1927 Victor recording executive Ralph Peer made a famous trip to Bristol, Tennessee, near the Virginia border, where he set up a makeshift studio in a local hotel. There he "discovered" two of country's greatest acts—The Carter Family, a Virginia-based trio who specialized in songs of hearth and home, and Jimmie Rodgers, a blues-influenced yodeler who sang hard and died young—the first great country stars. Through the Carters came the sound of the white country church, with songs derived from the Anglo-American traditions of balladry; Rodgers was a more progressive voice, a Jazz Era-influenced vocalist who somehow brought together the lonesome sound of the blues and Swiss yodeling to create something altogether new. Even in imagery the two pioneers represented diametric poles: the Carters were marketed as the ultimate embodiment of the home, while Rodgers was promoted as the "yodeling brakeman," a rambling hell-raiser who lived hard and died young.

These two strands—home harmonizers versus bluesy barroom singers—would become the model for much country music that followed in the 1930s. This was the era of the brother act, beginning with The Blue Sky Boys, Earl and Bill Bolick. In their simple harmonizing and sedate instrumental accompaniments, the Boys sounded like they were just "sittin' and pickin' " on their back porch. Their songs focused on mother, home, and religion; they were the good sons who dutifully plowed the fields and attended church. Meanwhile, Jimmie Rodgers's legacy was also brewing, but on the other side of the tracks. The outlaw railroad man gave birth to hundreds of singing cowboys, from Gene Autry through Roy Rogers and countless others. Although Autry sentimentalized and diluted the power of Rodgers's music and image, his music maintained a vital connection with jazz and blues roots.

Many of the stars of the 1930s got their start on the radio, not records. Originally country music got onto the radio because it was easily accessible and cheap for rural programmers to use local talent. Local announcers could ferret out popular performers and interview them on the air to fill the dead time between network broadcasts. George

Hay, a news reader and radio programmer for station WSM in Nashville in the early 1920s, brought a local fiddler named Uncle Jimmy Thompson to the studios to perform on his program; the listener response was so great that Thompson became a regular feature of the weekly show. This program immediately followed the national NBC broadcast of the Metropolitan Opera out of New York; Hay, taking on the character of a backwoods "solemn old judge," parodied the previous broadcast by extemporizing, "You've just heard Grand Opera; get ready for the Grand Ole Opry." The name stuck.

Soon a slew of barn-dance programs were operating out of the South and Midwest. Each program had its own personality, although most were modeled after the traveling tent shows that were still popular in backwoods America. Many country stars got their start on the radio, where they could establish their unique sound and style, sell songbooks (often in the thousands), and promote personal appearances. The producer John Lair, who worked for Chicago's *National Barn Dance* and later the *Renfro Valley Barn Dance* out of Kentucky, carefully nurtured the images of his star performers, and thus was among the first to sell an image as well as a sound.

One of the most unusual progressive movements of the 1930s was a new style brewing in Texas and Oklahoma that would become known as Western Swing. Like all the great country styles, it is an amalgam of different influences: old-style Texas fiddling (always jazz-influenced in its elaborate, syncopated variations) meeting the sound of the big bands. Vocalists such as Tommy Duncan sounded like they had their ears glued to Bing Crosby's popular recordings and broadcasts, singing a mixture of blues, pop, and sentimental songs. The Western Swing bands were the first country groups to feature drums, barrelhouse piano, and amplified "steel" guitars. The voice of the Jazz Age crossed with a country kick crackles forth from the classic recordings of bands like Bob Wills's Texas Playboys.

Social changes in the 1930s also would have an impact on the growth of country music. The dust storms in Oklahoma and Texas would influence a mass migration of poor farmers looking for increased job opportunities in southern California. Meanwhile, black and white Southerners in search of better job possibilities were migrating farther north, settling in Cincinnati, Cleveland, Detroit, and Chicago, bringing with them their mixture of country and blues musics. World War II would increase the forces of displacement; from family farms it drew thousands of Southerners who, after the war, were deposited back in major ports like New York and San Francisco, many never to return to the rural life.

In the postwar years country music would take two radically different directions. The old string-band tradition would be gussied up and energized into something entirely new that would be known as "bluegrass," created by fiery mandolinist and high-tenor vocalist Bill Monroe and his classic, late-1940s band featuring the revolutionary banjo work of Earl Scruggs, Chubby Wise's swing-influenced fiddling, and guitarist/vocalist Lester Flatt's modern, relaxed style of singing. Although Monroe would record for major labels—first Columbia and then, through the 1950s, Decca (later MCA)—and was a regular on *The Grand Ole Opry*, bluegrass was viewed as, at best, a nostalgic reminder of the old days, and its audience was small, compared to mainstream country.

Meanwhile, a new style was brewing in the small neighborhood bars in the South and Southwest known as honky-tonks. These bars were often located on the edge of town, and had a somewhat seedy, disreputable atmosphere; they were places where men could go after work to do some serious drinking. To be heard over the considerable racket, musicians began using electrified instruments, as well as performing in small ensembles featuring guitar, bass, and drums as well as, occasionally, fiddle and steel guitar. No longer would songs about mother, home, and church be acceptable to an audience drenched in beer and lusting after loose women; a new subject matter needed to be created to suit the new circumstances.

The first great honky-tonk star was Hank Williams, whose short, troubled life served as both a cautionary tale and a role model for hundreds of wanna-be honky-tonkers. Like Jimmie Rodgers before him, Williams was influenced by black music, learning his first songs from a black street entertainer in Montgomery, Alabama, known as "Tee-Tot." His first hit, "Lovesick Blues," was a revival of a Jazz Age song, right down to its short yodeling breaks. But Williams would be best remembered for the searing songs he composed, songs that addressed firsthand issues like drinking ("Tear in My Beer," "Honky-Tonkin' ") and love gone wrong ("Your Cheatin' Heart"). His songs were told in the first person, and dealt head-on with topics, such as adultery and alcoholism, that were only peripherally dealt with in previous country music. Williams's songs were cannily marketed by Nashville power broker Fred Rose, and so were among the first to be "covered" by mainstream pop acts, furthering popularizing country music.

The growth of Nashville as a center of country-music making was intense in the years following World War II. Previously recording companies had visited the city occasionally for field recording; now, major labels established their country-music home bases in the city. The continued influence and success of *The Grand Ole Opry* kept major acts tied to the city, while it also allowed backup musicians to find steady, profitable work there. Recognizing the value of country music, performer Roy Acuff teamed with veteran music-industry professional Fred Rose to form Acuff-Rose Publishers; they were the first to employ professional songwriters to create country songs for the market, and among the first to craft a recognizable "country sound," supervising the production of their artists' recordings and selection of material.

In the mid-1950s the Nashville Sound grew around two major studios: one was led by Owen Bradley, who worked as a pianist for radio station WSM (the home of the *Opry*) and became the leading producer for the Decca label; the other was headed by Chet Atkins, a talented guitarist who worked for RCA. Both men were fans of contemporary jazz and pop, and wanted to see country music viewed as the equal of these more socially accepted musics. Both downplayed the presence of traditional instruments—such as banjos, fiddles, and even steel guitars—for what they viewed as more modern instrumentation, such as tinkling piano, purling electric guitar, bass, and drums. Atkins used vocal groups like The Anita Kerr Singers or The Jordanaires as backups to his country artists, again to give them a slicker, more contemporary sound. By the mid-1960s there was little to distinguish country music from mainstream pop, which was the Nashville Sound's ultimate triumph (or tragedy, depending on your point of view).

The effect of the Nashville Sound could be seen in the stories of hundreds of acts, and is exemplified in the career of Virginia Hensley, aka Patsy Cline. Cline began as a pure country vocalist, appearing in cowgirl getup and performing classic honky-tonk hanky strainers like "Walking After Midnight." However, after she came under the guiding hand of producer Owen Bradley, she increasingly began to perform and record songs that could easily fit into the mainstream pop repertoire. By the time of her tragic death in an airplane crash, Cline was a full-throated chanteuse, belting out songs that were country in their weepy contents but otherwise were the equivalent of the pop ballads that could be found on the mainstream charts.

Meanwhile, on the edges of the country-music empire, another musical revolution was brewing. Memphis, Tennessee, located miles from Nashville philosophically and musically, was becoming a hotbed for the marriage of black R&B and white country. In the early 1950s the city was home to influential disc jockey and later performer Riley B. (B. B.) King, as well as a number of small labels specializing in the new rhythm and blues sounds. At Sun Records radio engineer Sam Phillips produced many of these black acts, and realized their appeal went beyond the African-American community. If only a white artist could capture the sound, he was certain he'd have a monster act on his hands. That artist materialized in the form of a teenager who came to his studios to record a custom disc of a sentimental song for his mother: Elvis Presley. In late 1954 Phillips brought him into the studio to record his first single, which interestingly enough paired a reworked R&B song ("That's All Right, Mama") with a reworked bluegrass number ("Blue Moon of Kentucky"), representing in miniature the polarities of a new musical style, rockabilly.

Although Elvis began his career as a country performer, working the same circuit of small-time bars, clubs, and fairs as well as appearing on *The Grand Ole Opry* and *Louisiana Hayride* radio programs, just like any other country act, he soon outgrew his country roots to enter the pantheon of mainstream pop. In his wake hundreds of Elvis imitators and admirers sprang up in the South, some recording just a few songs, others refining and expanding on the rockabilly style (like Carl Perkins, Jerry Lee Lewis, and Buddy Holly) to create a truly unique music.

The late 1950s saw the beginnings of the "folk boom" on the pop charts, with The Kingston Trio's surprise hit recording of "Tom Dooley." Johnny Horton's recording of "The Battle of New Orleans," set to the old fiddle tune "The Eighth of January," was another surprise hit on both country and pop charts, and a new trend, "the saga song," swept country music. These songs were narrative, pseudo folk songs (newly composed) celebrating tales of the Civil War or the Old West. They were perfect for the go-go optimism of the turn of the decade, when the Kennedys were re-creating an epic Camelot for a nation newly proud and young.

Mainstream Nashville was becoming increasingly conservative politically and as a musical force. With the Nashville Sound fully entrenched, any artist could be transformed from a rough "hillbilly" into a smooth pop crooner. The machinery of Nashville, well oiled, perfectly in tune with the conservative tastes of the average listener, needed only to be activated to turn country ham into high-quality bologna. The only problem was that the music was soulless; like all good assembly-line products, the heart was ripped out to make the music inoffensive, attractive but not alluring.

While mainstream Nashville became increasingly conservative through the 1960s, a quiet revolution was brewing along the sidelines. Singer/songwriter Willie Nelson was frustrated and disappointed by his record label, RCA, which tried to mold him into the homogeneous Nashville Sound with little success. Nelson knew that his music could have appeal if he were allowed to perform it on record the way he did for his live shows, but the Nashville power brokers were not convinced that anything that "country" would sell.

At the same time a new generation of singer/songwriters was coming to town, influenced equally by the legacy of Hank Williams and the new music of folk-rockers like Bob Dylan. Dylan proved that an idiosyncratic, highly personal style of performing his songs could be more successful than a more polished approach. This lesson was not lost on country songwriters like Nelson, Waylon Jennings, and Kris Kristofferson, all of whom felt that their individual voices were being stifled by the Nashville establishment.

In the 1970s Nelson and friends would abandon Nashville, many heading to the hinterlands of Texas, there establishing what would become known as "outlaw" music. Meanwhile, the Nashville Sound matured into what has been called "countrypolitan" music, personified by bland mainstream pop-type acts like Barbara Mandrell and Kenny Rogers. These performers were just as comfortable in a Vegas lounge as they were on the Opry stage, if not more comfortable, and for many it seemed that country music had lost all contact with its roots.

Meanwhile, way off on the edges of country music, there were some fledgling signs of rebirth developing. One was a revival of interest in bluegrass music, beginning with the urban folk revival in the 1960s but then growing deeper in the 1970s with the founding of new bands. Young musicians, including Ricky Skaggs and Keith Whitley, began performing with both traditional and more progressive bands, and their interest in bluegrass blossomed into a wider interest in older country styles. Many of the house musicians of today's Nashville—including Dobroist Jerry Douglas and fiddler Mark O'Connor—came out of this movement.

In the late 1960s a number of rock bands began flirting with country sounds, forming the short-lived but influential country-rock movement. The spiritual leader of the movement was Gram Parsons, who performed with his own International Submarine Band, then with a revitalized Byrds, and cofounded The Flying Burrito Brothers, before embarking on a short-lived solo career, cut off by his death due to drugs. The legacy of his music cast a long shadow through the 1970s, and his torch was carried by his partner and sometime backup singer Emmylou Harris. Harris began as a Linda Ronstadt-styled singer whose music turned increasingly country, thanks to members of her backup band, including Albert Lee, Rodney Crowell, and Ricky Skaggs.

Skaggs was probably the first bluegrass star to cross over into mainstream country success in the early 1980s, paving the way for countless others, including his past partner Keith Whitley, Vince Gill, Kathy Mattea, and Alison Krauss. But the first true megastar of the new country, back-to-roots movement of the 1980s was Randy Travis, who created a unique vocal style that hauntingly recalled many of the greatest stars of the 1950s. Unlike others who strain to sound country, Travis seems to feel it in his bones (or at least down to the threads of his vocal cords), so that even on his least-inspired recordings he still sounds disarmingly authentic.

Travis's success opened the floodgates to the "hunks in hats," hundreds of would-be country crooners who flooded the airwaves with music that blended rockabilly, honky-tonk, and sentimental pop in an increasingly mechanical way. Still, there were blips of originality among the cowpoke stars, some talented, some simply artfully promoted. Garth Brooks successfully blurred the lines between singer/songwriter, arena rocker, and good ol' boy in his hit recordings and energetic stage show. While Brooks has talent, there were others, like Billy Ray Cyrus, whose astonishing lack of talent along with their great success showed that, as the saying goes, the proof is in the packaging.

While new country began as a revolt against the homogenized, mainstream country-pop of the 1970s and early 1980s, it is now in danger of itself becoming a stylistic cliché. The use of similar backing musicians, songwriters, and producers, all neatly packaged, has meant that many of today's new acts sound generically like all others. And yet what makes country great is the personality, the undeniable recognizability of its best performers. Performers like Travis Tritt break through by sounding unique, performing material that is different from the pack; but too often, like Tritt, they are sucked into the mainstream, so that their music and presentation begin to take on the sheen of a product rather than a personal message.

But, just as the Nashville Sound collapsed under its own weight, so, too, will this Stepford-new-country music disappear when the next generation discovers that it has become hollow and lifeless. Country music in some guise, under some new form, will survive; and its survival depends on understanding where it's been, why it's been there, and where it's going. This book attempts to trace that route, celebrating the unique voices while condemning those who stood in the way.

Listening to new-country starlet Faith Hill schmooze her way through "Piece of My Heart," replete with whining steel guitars and wheezing fiddles, it seemed to me that, culturally speaking, an era had ended. After all, twenty-five years ago, when Janis Joplin ached this same song in all of its original glory, country fans were not lining up to purchase tickets to see her show. It's almost as if 1,001 strings cut the songs (perhaps they have, and I mercifully just don't know it). Imagine lying back in the dentist's chair and hearing an orchestra purr its way through "Ball and Chain," and you'll realize the extent to which pop culture has co-opted the revolutionary, original music of years ago.

This being said, there will always be "pop-country" to go along with "pop-rock" and even "pop-avant-garde" (Laurie Anderson, are you wearing a cowgirl outfit, too?) These diluted, ghost versions of the real thing will be sold to the masses, who live on a diet of Diet Coke and Wonder Bread, oblivious to the joys of alternative foods. Occasionally the real thing is so powerful that it breaks through into mass conscious-ness, only to be eaten alive or spit out again. It's the classic American dichotomy: we are awed by the young "I'm-Creating-a-New-Sound" Elvis, but we end up with the old "I'm-So-Doped-Up-I-Could-Cry" Elvis.

This book traces the ups and downs, celebrating the innovators as well as the popularizers; both have their place in the history of any musical form. It is an attempt to map out the territory of country music, to take an eclectic, as much as possible all-encompassing look at the great artists, genres, and musical instruments that have made up the country sound. One of my main goals is to capture the sound—or at least the personality—of the artist in the entry; not just to provide names, dates, and facts, but also to talk about styles, influences, and contributions. Like all personal selections this book suffers from a high degree of subjectivity; at least it should be clear to the canny reader where opinion begins and ends. If this work is not always reliable on its facts, I hope it is very reliable on its "feels": a collection of essential thumbnail portraits of the personalities who are country.

Acknowledgments

Thanks to my agent, John Wright, for advice and operatic interludes; to all the researchers and scholars who did the legwork that made this book possible including manuscript reviewers Ronnie Pugh, Charles Wolfe, and W.S. McNeil; and to my Penguin editors, David Stanford and Kris Poppolo, for careful line reading. For this new edition, I also acknowledge Sylvia Miller for agreeing to publish it; Mark O'Malley for carefully shepherding the work to completion; and to Jeanne Shu for care in its typesetting and production. Thanks also to ace photographer Raeanne Rubenstein for graciously providing her wonderful portraits taken over the last 25 years, and to Bob Carlin and the staff of the University of North Carolina's Southern Folklife Center for historic photographs.

A Note About the Recommended Recordings

I have made an attempt only to list in-print, currently available recordings; all are CDs. All discographies are selected ones; I have not attempted to list all recordings by every artist, a gigantic task that should be undertaken in a separate, "complete" country listing. For some artists it was necessary to list out-of-print items, because nothing is currently available. Some of these out-of-print items may be available in used record stores or libraries, and they may also be reissued eventually on CD or cassette. Folkways recordings are technically all still available, although they must be ordered directly from the Smithsonian Institution and can be had on custom-made cassette or CD, with the exception of those listed as "Smithsonian/Folkways," which are sold commercially through regular stores.

As always, record labels come and go; catalog numbers may change; and what is available today in one format may be available tomorrow only in a different format.

A

ACUFF, ROY (b. Maynardville, Tenn., September 15, 1903; d. Nashville, Tenn., November 23, 1992)

One of the most important and influential members of THE GRAND OLE OPRY, as well as a country music performer and businessman, Acuff helped pave the way for the transformation of old-time country music into modern pop-styled country. In addition to his success as a country singer, Acuff left a lasting mark as a business executive.

The son of a middle-class farmer who was also the town's postmaster and, on Sundays, a Baptist preacher, Acuff originally hoped to be a professional ballplayer. A case of severe sunstroke left him bedridden for two years, during which time he took up the FIDDLE. His first band, The Crazy Tennesseans, formed in the early 1930s, performed on Knoxville radio. In 1936 they were signed by ARC, for which they recorded their first hit, "The Great Speckled Bird," as well as Acuff's biggest hit, "The Wabash Cannonball." He made his first appearance on *The Grand Ole Opry* in 1938.

At this time Acuff, at the suggestion of *Opry* management, changed the name of his backup band to The Smoky Mountain Boys. The band prominently featured the Dobro, thus popularizing the instrument in country music; the most famous Dobro player associated with Acuff is "Bashful Brother Oswald" (Pete Kirby). Despite the fact that he performed holding a fiddle, the slight twang in Acuff's voice was the only hint that he came from country roots. 1942 brought his last big hit, the bathetic car-wreck ballad "Wreck on the Highway."

In the same year, recognizing the value of country songs, Acuff formed a music-publishing partnership with songwriter FRED ROSE. In 1948 the young publishing company scored a major coup when it signed SINGER/SONGWRITER HANK WILLIAMS to its list. Fred Rose worked closely with Williams until his death, getting him a major-label recording contract and helping him shape his material.

The late 1940s were difficult years for Acuff. Country music had changed, with a new emphasis on songs of drinkin', lovin', and losin', and Acuff's style and repertoire seemed old-fashioned. He briefly left the *Opry* in 1946–1947 because he felt he wasn't being paid enough for his appearances. In 1948 he tried his hand at politics, running as the Republican candidate for governor of Tennessee, a testimony to his popularity among rural voters. He lost, however, and returned to performing.

Although he continued to record during the 1950s, Acuff focused more of his attention on the music business, making Acuff-Rose into the leading publisher of country music. In 1953 the partners founded the Hickory label, which became Acuff's home as a recording artist four years later. In 1962 he became the first living inductee into the Country Music Hall of Fame. Three years later a bad car accident sidelined Acuff's performing career, although he continued to make some personal appearances outside of Nashville through the early 1970s.

In 1974, with the opening of the theme park Opryland USA, Acuff retired from active touring. Despite increasingly poor health he continued to perform at the Opry through the late 1980s and early 1990s, appearing at a show honoring the career of country comedienne MINNIE PEARL just a month before his death.

Acuff's son, Roy, Jr. (b. July 25, 1943), recorded for his father's Hickory label in the mid-1960s, enjoying some success, and continued to tour and perform until 1976, when he retired to work as an executive for Hickory.

Select Discography

Columbia Historic Edition, Columbia 39998. The best overview of Acuff's classic recordings, including four from his first 1936 session.

Steamboat Whistle Blues, Rounder 23/*Fly Birdie Fly*, Rounder 24. For true Acuff fans, this is a more com-

Roy Acuff with fiddle in appropriate countrified dress, c. 1938. Photo: University of North Carolina, Southern Historical Collection, Southern Folklife Collection, University Archives

plete overview of his classic recordings, including pop ballads and jazzy numbers along with the country standards.

King of Country Music, Bear Family 15652. Acuff's mid-1950s recordings cut for a variety of labels, including gospel numbers and remakes of his earlier hits.

ADKINS, TRACE (b. Tracy Darrell A., Springhill, La., January 13, 1962)

Adkins, a bass-voiced, big-hatted country hunk star of the late 1990s, is the son of a paper-mill worker in rural Louisiana, where Adkins was raised in the town of Sarepta. He performed in a local GOSPEL group, The New Commitment, while still in high school, singing bass and appearing on two locally issued albums. After graduation Adkins attended Louisiana Tech to study petroleum engineering and played on the university's football team. Although a knee injury ended his sports ambitions, he continued to study and eventually worked on oil rigs for about ten years in the Gulf region. He continued to perform semiprofessionally, including a stint with a local band called Bayou, which played in the Gulf region and enjoyed some success.

In 1992 Adkins resettled in Nashville, determined to pursue a musical career. While working local bars, he was "discovered" by SCOTT HENDRICKS, then president of Capitol Nashville, and signed to the label. His debut album appeared in mid-1996 and quickly produced hits; his own upbeat love song "There's a Girl in Texas" reached the Top 20, then the more syrupy ballad "There's a Light in the House" climbed to the Top 5. In 1997 he reached #1 on the country charts for the first time with "(This Ain't No) Thinkin' Thing."

Marketed as both a rowdy good old boy and a sensitive hunk in a hat, Adkins continued to enjoy great success with his second album, *Big Time*, released in the autumn of 1997. It yielded more hits, primarily tear-straining ballads, including the classic HONKY-TONK weeper "Lonely Won't Leave Me Alone." Meanwhile, Adkins's success led to a predictable shower of awards, including the Academy of Country Music's Best New Male Vocalist title in 1997, and a nomination for the Country Music Association's Horizon Award in 1998.

Perhaps fearing he was going to drown in the treacle of tearful ballads, Adkins decided to go in a slightly more macho direction on his 1999 album, *More....* It included a clever, WESTERN SWING-flavored anthem, "All Hat, No Cattle," as well as a standard-issue "I'm just a working guy like y'all" anthem, "Working Man's Wage." Adkins's own PR brags about his various work-related injuries ("he had to have a finger sewn back on following an industrial accident. His nose had to be reattached after a highway crash. He was run down by a bulldozer . . ."), in a further attempt to position him as "just a hardworkin', hard-livin' country boy."

Adkins farms outside of Nashville (in 1991 he sustained a knee injury after falling into a sinkhole on his farm). He is also one of the nation's greatest proponents of Spam, making the annual pilgrimage to Austin, Minnesota, to celebrate the annual Spamfest.

Select Discography

Dreamin' Out Loud, Capitol 37222. 1996 debut album, which some feel is still his best.
Big Time, Capitol 55856. 1997 release.
More . . ., Capitol 91668. Released in 1999, slightly harder-edged than his previous releases.

ALABAMA (c. 1975–present: Randy Yuell Owen [voc, gtr]; Jeffrey Alan Cook [voc, gtr]; Teddy Wayne

Gentry [voc, b]; Jackie Owen [1975–1979: drms]; Mark Joel Herndon [1979–present: drms])

Alabama is a pop-rock-influenced vocal group that was most popular in the early and mid-1980s. They were one of the first vocal bands to introduce a harder, rocking style to country music while they continued to project a good-time, nostalgic message through their music.

Originally formed around a quartet of cousins, the group worked as a bar band from the mid-1970s to about 1979, first under the name Young Country, then Wildcountry, and finally, in 1977, Alabama, when they recorded their first hit, "I Wanna Come Over," for MDJ Records of Dallas, operated by their manager. This was followed by "My Home's in Alabama," written by group members/first cousins Randy Owen and Teddy Gentry, which became their first theme song and a Top 20 hit in 1980. That same year they signed with RCA, which released the follow-up "Tennessee River" and the pop-country "Why, Lady, Why."

Alabama was notable for its three-person lead (most other country acts focused on a soloist accompanied by an anonymous band); their for-the-time long hair (and even beards), which would have been unacceptable to country audiences just ten years earlier; and their prominent use of electric bass and drums, giving their music a rocking kick that was unlike the middle-of-the-road country of the day. Not surprisingly their appeal was to a younger audience, although their wholesome good looks and "just country folks" stage presence did help sell them to the more conservative, older country audience.

The group's biggest hit was "Play Me Some Mountain Music," notable for its sunny harmonies and "down-home" content. Still, this was basically an uptempo pop song, one that could have as easily been recorded by Three Dog Night.

By the mid-1980s the group was moving increasingly in a pop-rock direction, going for splashier productions with a more heavily amplified sound. By the early 1990s their sunny harmonies, a vestige of 1970s pop, were beginning to sound a bit dated, particularly compared to the more hard-driving groups and soloists then working in country. Nonetheless they have continued to record and tour, and maintain a strong fan base. Unlike many other 1970s performers they continue to release new albums on a regular basis, and even have attempted to "stay relevant" by cutting a vocal number with pop group 'N Sync in 1999.

Select Discography

Greatest Hits, RCA Nashville 61040. 1991 collection of their chart toppers.
Mountain Music, RCA 4229. One of their earlier, less glitzy albums, giving a good sampling of their sound.

When It All Goes South, RCA 69337. 2001 release featuring an all-star cast of guests.

ALGER, PAT (b. Patrick J. A., LaGrange, Ga., September 23, 1947)

A friend of folksingers Happy and Artie Traum, Alger was a leading writer of new country hits of the 1980s and 1990s.

Alger first emerged as a guitarist/songwriter/vocalist in several different Traum projects, including the various incarnations of The Woodstock Mountains Revue, a loosely knit group of musicians from the greater Woodstock area including bluegrasser John Herald, the Traums, Maria Muldaur, and others. Alger contributed some of the more country-flavored songs to the group's repertoire, including "Old Time Music" and "Southern Crescent Line." Alger hooked up with folk/country singer NANCI GRIFFITH in the mid-1980s, cowriting several of her hits, including "Once in a Very Blue Moon" and "Lone Star State of Mind." In 1988 KATHY MATTEA covered "Goin' Gone," a song he had cowritten for Griffith, which launched his career in New Nashville circles. Alger made three solo albums in the early 1990s, featuring backup by many current Nashville stars, including Griffith, Mattea, and LYLE LOVETT.

Alger's simple GUITAR style and relaxed vocals recall his folkie roots. He is the purest link of the folk-Nashville connection that has produced some of the more eccentric of the 1980s and 1990s new country stars, including Griffith and Lovett.

Select Discography

True Love and Other Short Stories, Sugar Hill 1029. His "comeback" album from 1991.
Seeds, Sugar Hill 1041. 1993 album that features Alger performing some of his hits for other performers, notably "The Thunder Rolls," which was a smash for GARTH BROOKS.

ALLEN BROTHERS (Austin [bnj, lead voc], February 7, 1901–January 5, 1959, and Lee [gtr, kazoo, voc], June 1, 1906–February 24, 1981; both b. Sewanee, Tenn.)

The Allen Brothers were a jazzy duo who specialized in blues and hokum numbers. Their biggest hit was "Salty Dog Blues," with its snappy "hey-hey-hey-hey" chorus.

The Allens were a strange anomaly in country music; they were born and raised in the small city of Sewanee, Tennessee, and they moved to Chattanooga home of the University of the South. They were well educated (Lee attended the city's St. Andrew's Prep School, also attended by the famous Depression-era writer James Agee). They dressed in natty, double-breasted suits and aspired to be vaudeville stars. Chattanooga had its share of blues-oriented acts that the Allens undoubtedly heard, including a GUITAR player named May Bell, who was a popular performer on the riverboats that cruised up and down the Mississippi, and a group known as The Two Poor Boys, familiar street singers originally from Knoxville, Tennessee, who made a few 78s themselves. The brothers were also influenced by Jazz Era orchestras and pop crooners, with their jivey vocals reminiscent of the sis-boom-bah style of pop crooners of the era.

They first recorded for Columbia in Chattanooga under the direction of famed producer FRANK WALKER. Their first record, "Salty Dog Blues," sold well and became their signature number. It led to a second session producing another Jazz Age-influenced number, "Chattanooga Blues," featuring a "wow-wow-wow-wow" chorus echoing their earlier "hey-hey" chant in "Salty Dog"; a ragtime-influenced guitar break by brother Lee; and even some strange vocal interjections by brother Austin (urging his brother to "percolate, mama, percolate," during his guitar solo!). Perhaps because it was called a "blues," and perhaps because Walker returned the master to New York along with recordings of black as well as white artists, the company released the record in its "race" series (reserved for black artists); the brothers were furious, and threatened to sue the label. (Evidence of an actual lawsuit has never come to light. Later, Lee claimed that their suit was not based on racism but rather on their fears that managers would not hire an act to perform in mainstream theaters if they believed its members were black.) This soured their relationship with the label, and soon after, they signed with the rival Victor Company.

The Allens recorded prolifically for Victor and Vocalion through the mid-1930s, again focusing on songs that at least had "blues" in the title. These songs were pop-jazz numbers, many with topical themes, including songs that commented on the plight of the farmer ("Price of Cotton Blues") and the rise of mass-market chain stores that were threatening the local mom-and-pop venues ("Chain Store Blues"). They moved into "hokum" (slightly sexually suggestive) novelty numbers in the second half of their career, including their hit "(Mama Don't Allow) No Low-Down Hanging Around," from 1930, a version of the ever-popular jazz novelty that was widely copied by other country acts. They also rerecorded their first song, now called "New Salty Dog Blues," which helped keep the song in circulation through the late 1930s.

The Depression and the advent of radio conspired to bite into the profitability of many recording labels. The Allens, like many other country acts, saw their sales suffer. In the early 1930s they were performing in vaudeville and eventually ended up in New York, where in 1934 they made their last recordings for the smaller, dimestore label Vocalion-ARC, mostly remakes of their earlier hits. Older brother Austin remained in the city, but his younger sibling returned to Tennessee, where he eventually became an electrician.

Select Discography

Complete Recordings in Chronological Order, Document 1033–1035. Three CDs collecting all of their 78s.

ALLEN, DEBORAH (b. D. Lynn Thurmond, Memphis, Tenn., September 30, 1953)

Deborah Allen is a SINGER/SONGWRITER who straddles the line between new country and power pop.

Allen came to Nashville at age seventeen, looking for work as a singer; instead she took a job as a waitress at the local International House of Pancakes. Fate intervened when singer ROY ORBISON stopped in for a short stack; Allen served him and convinced him that she could sing, and so he hired her as a backup singer for his next session. She then worked as a singer/dancer at Opryland, where Jim Stafford heard her and hired her to be a part of his touring company. She worked with him from 1974 to 1977, during which time she was based in Los Angeles, the home of Stafford's syndicated television program.

On her return to Nashville in 1977, Allen began writing songs, hitting it big with "Don't Worry 'Bout Me," recorded by JANIE FRICKE in 1980. The song was the first #1 hit for both the composer and the singer. Soon after, Allen married songwriter/producer Raf van Hoy, and the duo wrote hits for a number of traditional and new country stars.

Allen's recording career got off to a slow start. She made a critically acclaimed LP for Capitol in 1979 that combined country, GOSPEL, and folk sounds, but it failed on the charts and her follow-up LP was never released. Four years later she was signed by RCA, and her husband produced her first album, which yielded the hits "Baby, I Lied," "Cheat the Night," "I Hurt for You," and "I've Been Wrong Before."

Guided by her husband, Allen took a more commercial orientation through the mid- and later 1980s. The two began to work as songwriters with a variety of up-and-comers, including a young singer named Kix Brooks; Van Hoy produced his debut album, which went nowhere, although Brooks later became one of the mega-duo BROOKS AND DUNN. In 1993 Allen separated from her husband, making an attempt at a comeback with the album *Delta Dreamland*, which had a more hard-rocking sound. She followed up with another harder-edged collection, *All That I Am*, in 1994.

Though Allen continued to perform, she became better known as a songwriter in the later 1990s. Several of her songs were dance and pop hits when recorded by mainstream artists, including Mary Griffin's version of "We Can Get There," which Allen composed with MIKE CURB. It appeared on the sound track of the popular film *Coyote Ugly* in 2000.

Select Discography

Special Look, MCA 6317. 1989 recordings in a pop-country mold.
Delta Dreamland, Giant 24485. 1993 "comeback" with a tougher sound.

ALLEN, JULES VERNE (b. Waxahachie, Tex., April 1, 1883–1945)

An early COWBOY recording star and folklorist who was the real thing—a rodeo star who genuinely loved cowboy lore and song—Allen began ranch work at the age of ten, and was soon an accomplished horseman. During the 1890s he worked on several cattle drives in the plains and into Mexico, earning his cowboy stripes. He also performed at local rodeos and sang occasionally on an amateur basis. After serving in World War I, Allen briefly returned to ranching, but the growth of radio led him to believe he could make a living as a performer. He landed his first radio work in the early 1920s in Dallas, and was also employed in San Antonio and Los Angeles through the 1920s. He took various nicknames, including "Longhorn Luke" (after the Longhorn Cement Company, his San Antonio sponsor) and "The Original Singing Cowboy."

During 1928–1929, Allen made twenty-four recordings for Victor Records that have come to be viewed as classic examples of "real" cowboy singing. These included such evergreen cowboy favorites as his first record, "Little Joe the Wrangler," and classics like "The Dying Cowboy" and "The Days of '49." In 1933 Allen published a book of cowboy stories and songs that was printed in Texas. After that he faded from the scene, although he continued to play at rodeos and on local radio.

ALLEN, RED (b. Harley A.; February 12, 1930–April 3, 1993)

Red Allen was a BLUEGRASS guitarist/vocalist who was quite influential on the first generation of bluegrass revivalists in the 1960s.

Allen first came to prominence as the lead singer and guitarist for The OSBORNE BROTHERS in the mid-1950s. He soon broke away, however, and formed his own band, The Kentuckians. In the early 1960s he recorded and performed with innovative mandolinist Frank Wakefield and also with a new young revival mandolinist, DAVID GRISMAN. At this time his band was a little more progressive than traditional outfits, although not as far out as some of the younger players.

In the early 1970s Allen hooked up with progressive banjo player J. D. CROWE to sing lead in the first version of The New South. He performed through the 1970s and 1980s, guiding the careers of his three sons, who formed The Allen Brothers band in the mid-1970s. They recorded a couple of albums of more contemporary country and bluegrass compositions in tight three-part harmonies.

Select Discography

And the Kentuckians, County 710. 1990 CD reissue of 1966 Melodeon LP (7325).
1964–83, Smithsonian/Folkways 40127. Reissue of out-of-print early 1960s album, produced by David Grisman, that was quite influential on the first generation of bluegrass revivalists, plus additional tracks from the late 1970s and early 1980s.

ALLEN, REX (b. Willcox, Ariz., December 21, 1920; d. Tucson, Ariz., December 17, 1999)

Allen was a COWBOY actor/singing star who was most active from the mid-1940s through the late 1960s. He is as well known for his TV appearances and work as a narrator of Disney documentaries as he is for his musical skills.

Born in rural Arizona, Allen was already working the amateur rodeo circuit in his early teens; at the same time he took up GUITAR and FIDDLE playing as a sideline. His smooth, modern singing style won him many fans through radio appearances and at fairs. In his late teens he traveled west to California on the rodeo circuit; he then crossed the country to take a job as a performer on radio stations in Trenton, New Jersey, and Philadelphia that led to a role on Chicago's popular NATIONAL BARN DANCE from 1945 to 1949.

In 1949 Allen returned to California to host his own radio show and appear in the first of a series of Westerns for the famous C-grade Republic studio. Like GENE AUTRY and ROY ROGERS before him, Allen became a popular star of these horse operas, always accompanied by his horse/sidekick, Koko. He also helped to pioneer the Western genre on television in *Frontier Doctor*, broadcast in 1949–1950 on CBS TV.

In the early 1950s Allen signed with Decca Records, producing a string of Western hits including 1953's "Crying in the Chapel." He moved to Mercury in 1961, immediately hitting with the slightly bizarre "Don't Go Near the Indians." He continued to record through the 1960s, drawing heavily on cowboy standards like "On Top of Old Smoky" along with Western epics he had written.

Allen pretty much retired from music in the early 1970s, just when his son, REX ALLEN, JR., began to achieve some success. Allen died in a bizarre accident when his companion accidentally backed his Cadillac

5

over him while he was standing in his driveway. He may have collapsed before the accident, or have been knocked down by the car.

Select Discography

Voice of the West, Bear Family 15284. Nicely produced sessions from the early 1970s cut by JACK CLEMENT, including Western standards as well as modern country numbers. No mushy strings or swelling choruses!

ALLEN, REX, JR. (b. Chicago, Ill., August 23, 1947)

This second Rex Allen was a popular baritone-voiced crooner of the 1970s who pretty much continued the tradition of COWBOY-themed hits that were first purveyed by his father.

Raised in southern California, the young singer often traveled with his father on the rodeo/county fair circuit, performing with him from the age of six. After forming amateur bands in high school, and serving in the military, he relocated to Nashville in search of success as a country singer. Allen had his first break in 1973, when he signed with Warner Brothers. His first hits were in the popular COUNTRYPOLITAN style of the day, including "Goodbye," a country version of the reggae hit "I Can See Clearly Now," and "Lyin' in My Arms." He recorded an album of Western standards in 1975, many associated with his father, including the hoary old chestnut "Streets of Laredo," BOB WILLS'S "San Antonio Rose," and his own composition "I Gotta Remember to Forget You" (an obvious allusion to the old country warhorse "I Forgot to Remember to Forget About You").

1976 brought his first big hit with "Can You Hear Those Pioneers?," which he cowrote, firmly in the Western vein. He continued to produce minor hits, alternating Western-flavored numbers with more standard mid-1970s country. His career pretty much faded out during the new-country movement of the early 1980s, although he recorded for a while in a new-country vein at that time.

Select Discography

Best of, Warners 45766. 1994 CD compilation featuring most of Allen's mid-1970s/early 1980s hits.

ALLEN, ROSALIE (b. Julie Marlene Bedra, Old Forge, Pa., July 27, 1924)

Rosalie Allen was one of the most successful cowgirl yodelers of the 1930s. She recorded both as a solo act and in partnership with ELTON BRITT from the late 1930s through the 1950s.

Allen's pedigree is hardly what you'd call classic Western cowgirl; she was the daughter of a Polish im-

migrant chiropractor who lived in rural Pennsylvania. But, like many of her peers, she was bitten by the cowgirl bug early in her career, and was performing on DENVER DARLING'S New York-based pseudo-Western radio show by the time she was in her mid-teens. Like other cowgirls the big draw of her act was her spectacular YODELING, featured on her remake of PATSY MONTANA'S "I Want to Be a Cowboy's Sweetheart," one of her first hits for Victor. The label paired her with cowpoke Elton Britt, and the two recorded some of the greatest harmony yodeling on disc, including "The Yodel Blues" and "Beyond the Sunset."

In the late 1950s Allen tired of touring and took a job as a disc jockey; in the 1960s she opened a New Jersey-based country record shop. By the 1980s she had retired to rural Alabama, her performing days long behind her.

Select Discography

Queen of the Yodelers, Cattle 46. Out-of-print reissue collection of Victor recordings from 1946 to 1951. Includes CHET ATKINS on GUITAR and Jethro Burns (of HOMER AND JETHRO fame) on MANDOLIN on some cuts.

ALLEN, TERRY (b. Wichita, Kan., May 7, 1943)

Terry Allen is a SINGER/SONGWRITER/pianist who gained a cult following in Europe during the late 1970s and 1980s for his offbeat, original compositions and gruff vocal style.

Trained as an architect and a sometime art teacher, Allen recorded a number of concept LPs in the 1970s and early 1980s, collaborated with David Byrne on the sound track for his movie *True Stories*, and accompanied JOE ELY and BUTCH HANCOCK on their recordings. His most interesting LPs are *Juarez*, a 1975 song cycle that relates the story of four Californians who migrate to Mexico in search of a better life, and *Lubbock on Everything*, a double-LP set peopled with archetypal Texan misfits and desperadoes. His best-known songs are "New Delhi Freight Train," covered by Little Feat, and the slightly skewed "Cocktail Desperado," which he performed in Byrne's film. He also scored Wolf Echart's film on the American impact on Southeast Asia during the Vietnam War, called *Amerasia*, which is probably the world's only country-*Eastern* record, because it features Allen accompanied by traditional Thai instrumentalists! Allen is also a painter whose work has been shown around the world.

In the mid-1990s, after a period of recording inactivity, Allen cut two records for the Sugar Hill label. His most recent to date, 1999's *Salvation*, took a skewed look at religion.

Select Discography

Lubbock on Everything, Sugar Hill 1047. Reissue of what many feel is Allen's best album, originally on the Fate label.

AMAZING RHYTHM ACES (c. 1973–1981: Russell Smith [lead voc, gtr]; Barry "Byrd" Burton [gtr, Dobro]; Billy Earheart III [kybds]; Jeff Davis [b]; Butch McDade [drms])

Somewhat ahead of their time, The Amazing Rhythm Aces combined rock, Memphis soul, and country in their sound, predicting 1980s hybrid bands like SAWYER BROWN.

Formed in the early 1970s, the group grew out of the rhythm section of folksinger Jesse Winchester's road band, led by SINGER/SONGWRITER Russell Smith. He supplied their first hit, the up-tempo "Third Rate Romance," in 1975, charting on both pop and country lists. However, they were unable to duplicate this pop success, so turned their attention to country with follow-up singles including "Amazing Grace (Used to Be Her Favorite Song)" and "The End Is Not in Sight." Smith left to pursue a solo career in 1981 with little success, and also wrote songs in the early 1980s for mainstream country stars like CONWAY TWITTY and GEORGE JONES.

Although the group featured some country instrumentation (including Burton's DOBRO), they basically had a sound similar to mainstream pop acts of the era, including the far more successful EAGLES.

ANDERSON, BILL (b. Columbia, S.C., November 1, 1937)

Anderson is a songwriter and recording artist whose late 1950s and early 1960s compositions brought a new realism to Nashville songwriting. Known as "Whispering Bill" because of his famous half-recited vocals on his 1963 hit "Still" (and the general limitations of his vocal style), Anderson later redirected his career toward being an "all-around entertainer," working in TV, B movies, and game shows.

Growing up in suburban Atlanta, Anderson was already leading his own country band and writing songs while in high school. With a B.A. from the University of Georgia and experience as a working journalist, he was hardly just "one of the folks." He pursued a part-time career as a songwriter and performer. His 1958 recording of "City Lights" was caught on local radio by RAY PRICE, who covered it and made it a gold record; Price followed it with another Anderson composition, "That's What It's Like to Be Lonesome." Anderson abandoned journalism and began writing for many of the big Nashville recording stars of the day, including JIM REEVES, HANK LOCKLIN, and PORTER WAGONER.

Anderson achieved his greatest success in the early 1960s, joining THE GRAND OLE OPRY in 1961. He first topped the country charts with 1962's "Mama Sang a Sad Song," and then crossed over into the lucrative pop market with "Still" in 1963. Other HONKY-TONK classics from this period include "I've Enjoyed as Much of This as I Can Stand," "My Name Is Mud," and "8 × 10." The taste of pop glory encouraged Anderson to direct his career in a more pop-oriented direction by seeking success on TV and in the movies while continuing to record country hits. In the late 1960s he recorded some popular duets with JAN HOWARD, and then in the early 1970s with Mary Lou Turner, whom he discovered. Mid-1970s hits with Turner included "More Than a Bedroom Thing," "That's What Made Me Love You," and a reworking of the traditional "Where Are You Going, Billy Boy?" He even tried to cash in on the disco market with his "country-disco" recordings of "I Can't Wait Any Longer" and "Three Times a Lady."

In the early 1980s, as his country career waned, Anderson launched two ill-fated game shows, *Mister and Mrs.* and *Funzapoppin*, while recording for his own Southern Tracks label. He also authored a history of Nashville's golden years. He continues to tour, appealing primarily to an older, more conservative audience who remember his bygone hitmaking days. In 2001 he was inducted into the Country Music Hall of Fame.

Select Discography

Bright Lights, Longhorn 3005. Cassette-only reissue of the 1965 album, the only thing currently available from this period.

A Lot of Things Different, Varese 066262. 2001 release, featuring STEVE WARINER and other New Nashville stars.

ANDERSON, JOHN (b. Apopka, Fla., December 13, 1954)

One of the first "new traditionalists" in country music, Anderson scored some early 1980s hits before lapsing into pop-country obscurity. He returned with a vengeance with his 1992 megahit, "Seminole Wind."

Anderson performed in a high-school rock band and then moved to Nashville immediately following his graduation to pursue a music career, performing with his sister Donna. They signed with the tiny Ace of Hearts label, recording a GOSPEL number, "Swoop Down, Sweet Jesus," in 1974. Anderson worked for a couple of years as a songwriter, and then signed with Warner Brothers in 1977. He began recording in the late 1970s, featuring a hard-core, Texas HONKY-TONK sound. He wrote a number of traditional rockin' country numbers with Lionel Delmore, son of one half of the famous DELMORE BROTHERS, including the big hit

"Swingin'," as well as covering country favorites like BILLY JOE SHAVER'S "I'm Just an Old Hunk of Coal."

However, mismanagement of his career led him to detour into a more mainstream pop sound in the mid-1980s. In 1988 he returned to his roots with the excellent *10* album, emphasizing his world-weary vocals against simple, tasteful, traditional accompaniments, and his original compositions. Still, Anderson looked like he had missed the boat to younger performers like RANDY TRAVIS, until 1992 brought his comeback hit, "Seminole Wind," the kind of Western-myth, COWBOY-flavored number that the country charts love. The hits dried up by the mid-1990s, although in 2000 he signed with Sony Columbia, which released "Nobody's Got It All," a minor chart hit.

Despite his years of ups and downs, Anderson's sound remains pretty much unchanged. Although he is unlikely to make it back to the top in the new century, his loyal fans will continue to enjoy his recordings and tours.

Select Discography

Greatest Hits, Warner Bros. 25169. His chart-toppers from his late 1970s–early 1980s prime recordings.
10, MCA 42218. Cassette-only reissue of this important 1988 album.
Seminole Wind, BNA 61029. His 1992 "comeback," with the title hit track.
Nobody's Got It All, Sony 63990. 2001 album featuring the minor hit title track.

ANDERSON, LIZ (b. Elizabeth Jane Haaby, Roseau, Minn., March 13, 1930)

Anderson is a SINGER/SONGWRITER best known for her hits penned for MERLE HAGGARD, including the bad-guy classics "Lonesome Fugitive" and "My Friends Are Gonna Be Strangers." She also had a brief recording career in the late 1960s, during the time of her daughter LYNN's greatest success.

Born in Minnesota near the Canadian border, Anderson took an early interest in music, singing on street corners with her older brother. In the early 1940s the family relocated to Grand Forks, North Dakota, where she met her future husband, Casey Anderson. They married in 1946, and their daughter was born a year later. In 1951 the family moved to California in search of better times, and Casey got a job selling cars. Meanwhile, Liz began writing songs and attracted the attention of Casey's coworker Jack McFadden, who later became BUCK OWENS's manager. He pitched her song "I Watched You Walking" to DEL REEVES; it had some local success and was followed by Reeves's and Anderson's first national hit, 1961's "Be Quiet, Mind."

In the mid-1960s, Anderson wrote songs for many California-based country stars. BONNIE OWENS picked up her "Just Between the Two of Us" and recorded it as a duet with Merle Haggard. It was at this time that Haggard heard the song "My Friends Are Gonna Be Strangers," which became a signature tune for him. In 1966 Liz and her husband went to Nashville, where she was signed by CHET ATKINS at RCA Records. Her back-home sound married to her many well-known songs led to a string of moderately successful albums on RCA through the late 1960s. After that the pair settled in Hendersonville, Tennessee, where Casey became a song publisher and also wrote further hits with his wife.

ANDERSON, LYNN (b. L. Rene A., Grand Forks, N.Dak, September 26, 1947)

Lynn Anderson is a smooth-voiced vocalist whose 1970 hit "Rose Garden" influenced the nascent "COUNTRYPOLITAN" movement.

The daughter of HONKY-TONK tunesmith LIZ ANDERSON, Lynn was raised in California, and first found success as an equestrian on the local horse-show circuit

Lynn Anderson, c. mid-1970s. Photo: Raeanne Rubenstein

while also working as a singer on *The Lawrence Welk Show*. She signed with tiny Chart records in 1966, scoring a hit with the peppy "Ride, Ride, Ride," written by her mother. In 1966 she moved to Nashville and, a year later, had a country hit with "That's a No-No." She wed producer/songwriter R. Glenn Sutton, who in 1970 produced her biggest hit, which hardly sounds like a country song at all. The title song of a successful film, "Rose Garden" brought Anderson widespread exposure to a middle-of-the-road audience. A string of pop-country hits followed. Anderson split from her husband in the mid-1970s, and by the early 1980s she had returned to a career as a horsewoman, although she did make an abortive comeback attempt in 1989 with a cover of The Drifters' pop hit "Under the Boardwalk."

Select Discography

Greatest Hits, Columbia 31641. Cassette-only reissue of her early-to-mid-1970s goldies.

Live at Billy Bob's Texas, Smith Music Group 2010. Undated live concert, probably recorded shortly before its 2000 release, featuring most of her hits. Her vocals sound relatively unchanged despite the passing years.

AREA CODE 615 (c. 1969–1971: Ken Buttrey [drms, voc]; Wayne Moss [gtr]; David Briggs [kybds]; Mac Gayden [gtr, French horn]; Charlie McCoy [hca]; Weldon Myrick [steel gtr]; Norman Putnam [b, cello]; Buddy Spicher [fdl, viola, cello]; Bobby Thompson [bnj, gtr])

Area Code 615 was the first Nashville supergroup made up primarily of younger session players. They were noteworthy for their tasteful instrumental work, far from the sanitized strings and reverb-laden choirs heard on much of 1960s Nashville work.

The leader of the group was guitarist Wayne Moss. Like the other players, he had a varied background in country, pop, and R&B. For many years he worked for BRENDA LEE in her backing band, before joining The Escorts, led by harmonica player CHARLIE McCOY and also featuring Gayden and Buttrey. Later they became the nucleus of the house band at Nashville's Monument label, taking the name The Music City Five.

Area Code 615, named for the Nashville phone area code, was formed in 1969 and gained a good deal of attention from the pop press because of their more progressive outlook. In the same year many of these musicians worked on BOB DYLAN's *Nashville Skyline* sessions, one of the first COUNTRY-ROCK albums. The core group was joined by the fine BLUEGRASS fiddler Buddy Spicher, along with banjoist Bobby Thompson; they featured unusual instrumentation including cello,

viola, and even occasional French horn. They recorded two albums, the first all instrumental, the second featuring vocals by Buttrey, before they disbanded. Most have returned to session work; Spicher also has recorded an occasional solo album, particularly working with jazz-styled steel guitarist BUDDY EMMONS.

Moss, along with another Nashville session player, steel guitarist Russ Hicks, formed Barefoot Jerry to continue the progressive country-rock style of Area Code 615. The group also included Jim Colvard (guitar), Warren Hartman (keyboards), Terry Dearmore (bass, vocals), and Si Edwards (drums). They stayed together for about five years, recording for a variety of labels with limited success. Unlike the country-rock groups out of California, this Nashville-based band had a hard time gaining respect either from the conservative country audience or from the mainstream rock press.

ARKIE THE ARKANSAS WOODCHOPPER (b. Luther William Ossenbrik, near Knob Noster, Mo., September 21, 1915–June 23, 1981)

A radio personality and square-dance caller, Arkie was a longtime favorite country performer in the Chicago area.

Born and raised in rural Missouri, Arkie performed as a boy guitarist/fiddler/dance caller. In 1928 he made his debut on Kansas City radio, and a year later joined the prestigious NATIONAL BARN DANCE program broadcast out of Chicago. One of its longest-running stars, Arkie continued on air with the program until the original show was canceled in 1960, and for a further decade on a revived version of the show.

His colorful name and handle—"Country boy from the Ozarks"—was given to him by WLS staff, who cared little that he was not from the Ozark region at all! He made a few country-novelty recordings for ARC and Columbia in the 1930s and 1940s, but was best loved for his on-air monologues about country life. In 1940 Chicago-based M. M. Cole published a book of his square-dance calls, and a year later he recorded an album of 78s with calls and music. This helped spur further interest in square dancing among urban listeners, as did Arkie's tours as a caller.

After 1970, when the second incarnation of *National Barn Dance* went off the air, Arkie retired from active performing.

ARMSTRONG TWINS (Lloyd [voc., mdln] and Floyd [voc, gtr], b. DeWitt, Ark., January 24, 1930)

Childhood stars and excellent harmonizers, the Armstrong Twins were one of the later great brother acts.

Born in rural Arkansas but raised in Little Rock, the twins were performing professionally by age nine.

Influenced by the BLUE SKY BOYS and the Monroe Brothers, BILL and CHARLIE, they developed a tight harmony sound with a modern, slightly jazz-influenced bounce to their accompaniments. Besides being young, cute, and brothers, the boys had the added attraction of being twins, so they soon had quite a strong following. They remained local favorites on various Little Rock-based radio shows through 1947, when they decided to relocate to southern California, which had a growing country music scene.

They quickly established themselves in California, becoming favorites on CLIFFIE STONE'S radio show, performing regularly as a featured act with popular groups like SPADE COOLEY'S band, and hosting their own radio spot. They also made their first recordings, mostly of well-known songs, although they also cut some original MANDOLIN instrumentals and a few novelty numbers.

In 1952 they left California for Odessa, Texas, where they had their own radio and TV shows. They began touring with HONKY-TONK star JOHNNY HORTON and performing on the prestigious LOUISIANA HAYRIDE radio program. During a brief return to California toward the end of the 1950s, they were featured on the popular *Town Hall Party* show out of Compton.

By the early 1960s the brothers had retired to their home state because their musical style was out of fashion. In 1979 a selection of their earlier recordings was reissued, bringing them a new audience in the old-time music revival. They toured through the 1980s, until Floyd's health began to fail, forcing them to curtail their activities.

Select Discography

Old Timey Mandolin, Old Timey 118. 1979 LP reissue of 78 recordings, now out of print.
Just Country Boys, Arhoolie 5022. 1981 new recordings by the Twins, now out of print. Some tracks have been reissued on various Arhoolie CD compilations.

ARNOLD, EDDY (b. Richard Evert A., near Henderson, Tenn., May 15, 1918)

Originally a HONKY-TONK crooner, Arnold became one of the most successful crossover artists of the 1960s, championing the NASHVILLE SOUND on a series of middle-of-the-road hits.

The son of an old-time fiddler father and a guitar-playing mother, Arnold took up the GUITAR at age ten, abandoning his schooling soon after to help on his family's farm during the Depression years. After playing at local dances, Arnold was hired to perform on local radio, which in turn led to further radio jobs in Memphis and St. Louis. A job fronting PEE WEE KING'S Golden West Cowboys led to nationwide exposure on

THE GRAND OLE OPRY. From his early experiences on the farm, Arnold took the nickname "The Tennessee Ploughboy."

In 1944 he signed as a solo act with RCA, and had his first string of hits with honky-tonk and COWBOY numbers for RCA between the late 1940s and early 1950s, including 1948's sentimental "Bouquet of Roses," 1951's slightly racy "I Wanna Play House with You," and 1955's Western epic, "Cattle Call." Many of his early hits were written or cowritten by Arnold, including the bathetic "I'm Throwing Rice at the Girl I Love" and "Will Santa Claus Come to Shanty Town?" Much of his early success can be ascribed to his wily manager, COLONEL TOM PARKER, who later helped another Southern boy (ELVIS PRESLEY) make it big.

Up to the mid-1950s Arnold's accompaniments were fairly spare, featuring the fine steel guitar of Roy Wiggins, who was influenced by Hawaiian artists like Sol Hoopi. However, by the mid-1950s he was coming increasingly under the influence of RCA's house style, molded by producer CHET ATKINS, and his originally plaintive vocal style became increasingly smooth and bland. He also hosted his own syndicated TV program and, because of his mainstream good looks and smooth vocals, was invited to guest on many of the popular 1950s variety programs aimed at a general audience.

It was in the mid-1960s that Arnold really hit pay dirt with a series of string-smothered recordings made for the country charts that had broad-based appeal. In hits like "Make the World Go Away," "Lonely Again," and "Turn the World Around," Arnold successfully wed blue-and-lonesome subject matter with mainstream schmaltz. He proved that a country artist could have broad appeal, encouraging others to take a similar middle-of-the-road approach. His career flagged a little in the early 1970s and then picked up steam again in 1976 when he re-signed with RCA.

Although Arnold continued to chart on the country scene into the early 1980s, he survived primarily as a nostalgic reminder of mid-1960s pop-country. His legacy was that he proved a country artist could appeal to a mass audience, something that the New Nashville crowd would discover again in the late 1980s and early 1990s.

Select Discography

My World, DCC 146. 1997 CD reissue of 1965 album featuring "Make the World Go Away."
Cattle Call/Thereby Hangs a Tail, Bear Family 15441. CD reissue of two LPs issued to cash in on the Western/folk revival in the late 1950s. Includes his tasteful cover of "Tennessee Stud." Among Arnold's better later work.
Pure Gold, RCA 58398. One of many budget CDs featuring the hits from the 1960s.

ARTHUR, CHARLINE (b. C. Highsmith, Henrietta, Tex., September 2, 1929–November 27, 1987)

Arthur was a pioneering country-boogie and ROCKA-BILLY singer, full of spunk and sass, who helped clear the path for the next generation of spunky songstresses.

Charline's family was dirt-poor; she was said to have been born in a boxcar. Her father rambled around Texas, working as a Pentecostal preacher and performing on the harmonica, accompanied by his guitarist/wife. Impressed by the music of ERNEST TUBB, Charline bought a $4.95 guitar, and wrote her first song "I've Got the Boogie Blues," when she was twelve (she recorded the song seven years later for Nashville's Bullet Records). She formed a duo with her sister to perform at community functions, and in 1945 was hired by a traveling medicine show. Three years later she married bassist Jack Arthur, who performed with the show; he became her manager, taking her to Nashville a year later and booking her into HONKY-TONKS as a sultry diva.

After recording for the small Bullet label, Charline attracted the attention of HANK SNOW's manager, Colonel TOM PARKER (who would later take another fireball, ELVIS PRESLEY, and make him famous). Parker got her a contract with RCA, but she was unhappy with their attempt to change her into a demure country chanteuse. Charline refused to wear the standard-issue gingham dress that all country women were meant to don; instead she appeared in pant suits years before these outfits were considered acceptable, particularly by the conservative country audience. Arthur's stage show featured lots of theatrics, and she loved best to shout the bluesy numbers that drove small-town bar audiences wild. Her best RCA recordings were of up-tempo material, including "I'm Having a Party All by Myself," the husband-stealer's warning "Just Look, Don't Touch, He's Mine," and the proto-rockabilly recordings "Honey Bun" and "Burn That Candle."

In the mid-1950s she really raised eyebrows with the for-the-time racy titles "The Good and the Bad" (in which bluesy Charline has a "dialogue" with her more sweet-voiced alter ego; naturally the bad girl wins out!) and "Kiss the Baby Good Night," which could not be performed in its original, unedited version on THE GRAND OLE OPRY. In 1957, after continuing battles with her producer, CHET ATKINS, Arthur was dropped by RCA and fell into obscurity as a performer. She died penniless and forgotten some thirty years later.

Select Discography

Welcome to the Club, Bear Family 16279. Reissue of Arthur's mid-1950s RCA recordings, with vintage photographs and complete notes.

ARTHUR, EMRY (b. Elk Spring Valley, Wayne County, Ky., c. 1900–August 1966)

An early country artist best known for first recording "I Am a Man of Constant Sorrow," Arthur was raised on a small farm in southern Kentucky, where both his brothers, Sam and Henry, were musicians. A hunting accident damaged one of his hands, so Emry, a talented singer, was a rather limited musician. Around 1925 the brothers moved to Indianapolis in search of work; there, two years later, they were heard by a talent scout from the Vocalion label. In early 1928 Henry and Emry cut ten songs in Chicago for Vocalion, recording traditional play-party songs and ballads, GOSPEL numbers, and even the odd pop tune.

Also cut during this session was the first recording of "I Am a Man of Constant Sorrow." The song was native to Kentucky; Dick Burnett (of BURNETT AND RUTHERFORD), who lived close to the Arthur family farm, had published the song in one of his songbooks in 1913, and that may have been Emry's source for it. His recording was a source for traditional singers Sarah Ogan Gunning (who renamed it "Girl of Constant Sorrow") and, eventually, the STANLEY BROTHERS. The song got a considerable boost in 2000 when it was featured in the film *O Brother, Where Art Thou?*, as performed by "The Soggy Bottom Boys."

Emry recorded through the summer of 1929, but then seems to have faced a life crisis. His wife left him, and the Depression struck; he eventually moved to Wisconsin, where he was hired by the Wisconsin Chair Company. The company owned a well-known record label, Paramount, and when they discovered that their employee was the same Emry Arthur who had previously had hits on Vocalion, recorded him again in the early 1930s. These recordings did not fare well, and sessions for a smaller label followed. In 1934 Arthur made his last recordings for Decca, including country blues and novelty numbers, along with remakes of some of his earlier hits. He died in Indianapolis in 1966.

ASCH, MOSES (b. Russia, December 2, 1905–October 19, 1986)

For thirty-nine years Moses Asch ran Folkways Records, the main (and for many years the only) source for folk and country music available to an urban audience.

The son of the noted novelist Sholem Asch, he began his career as a sound engineer, working on the sound for Broadway shows like the original *Hellzapoppin'*. His father was friendly with many leading intellectuals of the day, and Asch claimed he took his inspiration to start a record company from Albert Einstein, who suggested that with his background in sound recording, he could make a valuable contribution to documenting the twentieth century.

Asch founded the Disc and Asch labels in the early '40s, recording jazz and folk and blues revivalists like PETE SEEGER, WOODY GUTHRIE, and Josh White. During World War II, when the shellac used in making 78 rpm records was rationed and only established labels could get records pressed, he joined forces with the Stinson label for a while. In 1947 he started Folkways Records as a means of documenting all types of music and speech.

From the beginning Folkways played a central role in the revival of interest in old-time music. In 1952 the eccentric filmmaker/record collector Harry Smith approached Asch about issuing a six-record set of recordings from the 1920s and 1930s that he called *The Anthology of American Folk Music*. Smith, who had an excellent collection and peerless taste, selected a number of key country artists for representation on this set (many of their recordings were long unavailable, or had never been available in urban areas). These six records were highly prized by the first generation of FOLK REVIVALISTS, who in turn passed along the songs to another generation of performers. Meanwhile, Asch was recording Pete Seeger throughout the 1950s when Seeger was blacklisted for his "Communist" sympathies, as well as issuing albums by traditional artists like BASCOM LAMAR LUNSFORD and Woody Guthrie, to name just two.

In 1959 the young folklorist MIKE SEEGER approached Asch about issuing an album he called *Mountain Music Blue Grass Style*; this was the first album of BLUEGRASS MUSIC issued for a city audience. Seeger's group, THE NEW LOST CITY RAMBLERS, were the first old-time string band revivalists, and they recorded for Folkways throughout the 1960s. Meanwhile, group members Seeger and JOHN COHEN produced albums of traditional country musicians, both rediscovered artists from the 1920s and 1930s like DOCK BOGGS and newly found masters such as ROSCOE HOLCOMB. Folkways also issued albums by the traditional banjo players WADE WARD and Pete Steele.

In the mid-1960s Asch entered into a distribution agreement with MGM Records, which was anxious to cash in on the folk-music craze, and then into a second deal with the educational publisher Scholastic. By 1971 he had resurfaced on his own, issuing records on the revived Asch label, and by 1973 he had taken control of the Folkways back catalog. He continued to issue records until his death thirteen years later, although by then other labels, like Rounder, County, and Arhoolie, had become more important in issuing new recordings of folk and country figures.

Because Asch believed that all of his records should remain in print, even if they sold only a few copies each year, all of this material remained available until the time of his death in 1986, influencing many generations of musicians. The Smithsonian Institution, under

ex–GREENBRIAR BOY Ralph Rinzler, took over the label after his death, and has been slowly reissuing the better material on compact disc while keeping everything available through special-order cassettes and CDs.

ASHLEY, TOM (b. Clarence Earl McCurry, Bristol, Tenn., September 29, 1895–June 2, 1967)

Ashley was a spirited performer on BANJO and GUITAR, and one of the finest of the classic country artists who were rediscovered during the FOLK REVIVAL of the 1960s.

Clarence was raised by his maternal grandfather, Enoch Ashley, in the Mountain City area of northeastern Tennessee (he later legally took his grandfather's surname). He was already playing banjo and guitar in local medicine shows around 1910, and remained active on the informal tent-show circuit through World War II. He performed on records, usually as guitarist, with a number of bands, including the famed old-time trio THE CAROLINA TAR HEELS, Byrd Moore and His Hotshots, and The Blue Ridge Mountain Entertainers.

The Tar Heels recorded many sides in the late 1920s and early 1930s, usually featuring Ashley on guitar and lead vocals; either Gwen or Garley Foster (they weren't related) on harmonica, guitar, and tenor vocals; and Doc Walsh on banjo and baritone vocal. For the group Ashley "composed" the folk ballad "My Home's Across the Blue Ridge Mountains," which became popular in the folk-revival repertoire after BASCOM LAMAR LUNSFORD recorded it for the Library of Congress. In 1928 Ashley also cut solo play-party songs on the banjo, most notably his versions of "The Coo Coo Bird" and "The House Carpenter," which were much copied during the early days of the folk revival in the 1950s and 1960s.

Ashley was "rediscovered" at the Galax, Virginia, fiddlers' convention in 1960 by folklorist Ralph Rinzler, who encouraged him to take up banjo playing again. (He had stopped playing in the early 1940s due to a hand injury.) Ashley had discovered and tutored a number of younger musicians in northwestern North Carolina, where he had been living, including guitarists Clint Howard and Arthel "Doc" WATSON, and fiddler Fred Price. The quartet was brought to New York City by Rinzler in 1961–1962 to record a series of influential albums as well as to perform for folk-revival audiences. Watson was such a standout that he was quickly performing as a solo act and recording for the then major folk label Vanguard Records. Ashley continued to appear at folk festivals and in concerts, and made one further album, before he died in 1967.

Although not as flamboyant a performer as UNCLE DAVE MACON, Ashley had a fine singing voice, a good memory for traditional and sentimental tunes, and a simple but clean playing style on the five-string banjo. His many years as a performer made him an ideal figure to introduce old-time sounds to a new, younger audience.

Select Discography

Greenback Dollar, 1929-33, County 3620. Reissue of Ashley's early solo recordings, along with band recordings by The Carolina Tar Heels and The Blue Ridge Mountain Entertainers.

Old Time Music at Clarence Ashley's, Smithsonian/Folkways 40029/40030. Wonderful early-1960s recordings by Ralph Rinzler, featuring Doc Watson, Clint Howard, and Fred Price.

ASHWORTH, ERNIE (b. Huntsville, Ala., December 15, 1928)

Ashworth was a typical mainstream songsmith of the 1950s who developed a successful career as a pop-influenced crooner through the mid-1960s.

Raised in a midsized Alabama community, Ashworth performed his own material on GUITAR on local radio while still in his teens. His success prompted him to take a chance on a career as a songwriter, and in the mid-1950s he moved to Nashville, where he placed songs with stars CARL SMITH and "LITTLE" JIMMY DICKENS, among others, while performing on radio. He signed with powerful song publisher WESLEY ROSE, who got him a contract with MGM, for which he recorded under his own name and also under the nom-de-disc of Billy Worth. These recordings were duds, however, and by 1957 Ashworth had returned, discouraged, to his Alabama home.

In 1960 Rose lured him back to Nashville with a promise of a contract with Decca Records. Ashworth hit it big with his first release, "Each Moment (Spent with You)," laying the groundwork for drippy follow-ups "You Can't Pick a Rose in December" and "Forever Gone." In 1962 Rose moved him to Rose's new record label, Hickory, and the hits kept coming with more hanky-strainin' weepers including "Talk Back, Trembling Lips" (his one and only #1 hit), "A Week in the Country," "The DJ Cried," and "Sad Face." In 1965 his big break in Hollywood came with an appearance in the "memorable" film *The Farmer's Other Daughter*.

By the late 1960s Ashworth had fallen off the charts, and taken to constant touring on the back roads of the country circuit and performing on THE GRAND OLE OPRY into the twenty-first century. In the early 1980s he performed at DOLLY PARTON'S Dollywood theme park in Pigeon Forge, Tennessee. During the 1990s he built his popularity in Europe (his Web site invites readers of Spanish, French, Portuguese, Italian, and Norwegian), scoring a few minor country hits there, as well as cutting country and GOSPEL numbers on his own B&E label.

Select Discography

Greatest Hits, Curb 77483. Reissue of 1960s recordings.

ASLEEP AT THE WHEEL (c. 1970–present. Original lineup: Ray Benson [gtr, voc]; Lucky Oceans [steel gtr]; Chris O'Connell [vcl, gtr]; Jim "Floyd Domino" Haber [pno]; LeRoy Preston [drms, voc])

Asleep at the Wheel is a rockin' WESTERN SWING revival band that was most popular in the mid-1970s; it is said to have employed over seventy-five musicians in its thirty-plus years of existence. Leader guitarist/vocalist Ray Benson is the motivating force behind this band that will not die, and the only original member left.

Benson's love of Western Swing music began when he was a teenager in suburban Philadelphia, playing music with his friend, steel guitarist Reuben Gosfield (aka Lucky Oceans). The duo, along with pianist Danny Levin and drummer/vocalist LeRoy Preston, moved in 1970 to a farm in West Virginia, where they formed the nucleus of the original band. Soon they were playing rock and Western Swing (but never mixing the styles) at local clubs.

Around 1971 the band was beginning to make waves as an opening act in the Washington, D.C., area. They were heard by George Frayne (aka Commander Cody) at a local gig, and he urged them to move to San Francisco later that year. Through 1973 the band was headquartered on the West Coast, continuing to grow in personnel, and finally landed a record contract with United Artists. By this time Levin had been replaced by pianist Jim Haber, who took the nickname Floyd Domino in honor of his idols, country tinkler FLOYD CRAMER and R&B stylist Fats Domino.

A 1974 tour of Texas, then a hotbed of progressive country music, led the band to move to Austin, where they signed a one-album deal with Epic. In 1975 they finally scored a hit with "The Letter That Johnny Walker Read" on Capitol Records, the label where they had their greatest success. The band ballooned to eleven members, creating a sound that mixed BOB WILLS'S styled Western Swing with a little Count Basie and a little Commander Cody. A hardworking touring band, they developed a large following in Europe while occasionally scoring minor hits. They also had a devoted following on the college circuit, where their nouveau Western style appealed to the latter-day hippie audience.

In the early 1980s Benson cut the size of the outfit, for financial and artistic reasons. The band had grown so big that it was hard to control and expensive to take on tour. Through the 1980s and 1990s the band soldiered on, with Benson leading a pack of musicians through Western Swing, CAJUN, and country styles. Although no longer the darlings of FM college radio, they found a steady audience on the road, where they had always made their best music. Benson is one of those rare true believers who has been able to keep his band going against the odds, and will probably be performing with some version of Asleep at the Wheel for many years to come.

Select Discography

Collision Course, EMI 53127. Reissue of 1978 Capitol album (11726), the only album from this period currently on CD.

A Tribute to Bob Wills and The Texas Playboys, Liberty/Capitol 81470. 1993 CD featuring New Nashville vocalists (GARTH BROOKS, DOLLY PARTON, MARTY STUART, etc.) performing Wills's hits backed by the band.

ATCHER, BOB (b. James Robert Owen A., Hardin County, Ky., May 11, 1914–October 31, 1993)

An early COWBOY actor/performer, Atcher was long associated with Chicago's NATIONAL BARN DANCE.

Although he was born in Kentucky, Atcher was raised in North Dakota, the heart of Western song and lore. His father was a champion fiddler, and many other members of the family picked and sang, so he was exposed to both Southern folksongs and songs of the West from an early age. By his late teens he had moved to Chicago, which at the time had a thriving country-music scene, primarily centering around a number of popular radio shows. Atcher, with his smooth tenor voice and good looks, was a natural for the role of singing cowboy; he appeared on a number of Chicago-based radio shows from 1931 on, and signed with Columbia Records in 1937 (he remained there for twenty-one years).

Atcher's fame grew after he joined the *National Barn Dance* in 1948, performing both as a soloist and in duet with a string of partners all going by the name of "Bonnie Blue Eyes." He remained with the *Barn Dance* for twenty-two years, until it went off the air, a vital link to the 1930s cowboy style that otherwise had disappeared from popular music. Toward the end of his career Atcher turned his attention to local politics, serving as mayor of Schaumburg, Illinois (a Chicago suburb), for sixteen years.

ATKINS, CHET (b. Chester Burton A., Lutrell, Tenn., June 20, 1924–June 20, 2001)

Chet Atkins was one of those maddeningly professional Nashville musicians who, while undoubtedly a great talent on the GUITAR, recorded his share of

Chet Akins (center with guitar) with Mother Maybelle Carter and her three daughters, c. 1950. Photo: University of North Carolina, Southern Historical Collection, Southern Folklife Collection, University Archives

schlock over the years. And, as house producer for RCA, he is credited with creating the late 1950s/1960s NASHVILLE SOUND, the mainstream trivialization of country music that drove many traditionalists to despair.

Atkins came from a musical line; his grandfather was a well-known fiddler, and his father scraped out a living teaching music, tuning pianos, and working as a revivalist preacher. His parents divorced when he was young, and he got his first guitar from his stepfather, Willie Strevel, when he was about nine years old. He already was playing a homemade BANJO, and had learned the basics of ukulele and FIDDLE. The young Atkins played for the occasional local dance or party. He had two stepbrothers who were also guitarists. (His half brother Jim worked in the LES PAUL Trio as rhythm guitarist through the 1930s.)

Because he suffered from asthma, when he was eleven years old Atkins relocated to Columbus, Georgia, where his father lived with his new wife. Two years later he got a job working with the National Youth Administration in Mountain Hill, Georgia. He continued to play music for parties and small gatherings.

Atkins's guitar style is rooted in the playing of MERLE TRAVIS, the legendary finger-picker who developed a style in which he played the melody with a flat pick while picking out an accompanying bass line with his thumb. He first heard Travis playing electric guitar on the radio in the late 1930s, and soon was saving money for electrifying his own guitar. Without seeing Travis play, Atkins developed his own version of "Travis picking," using a thumb pick as Travis did, but picking the other strings with three fingers, rather than just one.

At age seventeen Atkins got his first radio work, not as a guitarist but playing fiddle on the Bill Carlisle–Archie Campbell show, then broadcasting out of Knoxville, Tennessee. After the show was canceled, the station manager hired Atkins as staff guitarist. Through the mid-1940s he moved from station to station, working wherever he could.

Starting in the mid-1940s, Atkins worked as an accompanist for various country acts (including THE CARTER FAMILY and country comedians HOMER AND JETHRO) on radio and on the road, and began recording as a soloist in the late 1940s. In the late 1940s he appeared on *The Carter Family and Chet Atkins Show*, broadcasting out of Springfield, Missouri, which was so successful that it was picked up for national syndication. He also joined the Carters when they appeared on THE GRAND OLE OPRY. His best work was done in this period through the early 1950s, when his electric-guitar instrumentals set new standards for performance, including 1947's "Canned Heat," 1949's "Galloping on the Guitar," through his best-known composition, "Country Gentlemen," in 1953. (Atkins would help design a guitar for the Gretsch Company that was named after this, his most popular solo recording.)

An appointment as manager of A&R at RCA's new Nashville studios in the mid-1950s spelled the end of Atkins's creative career as an instrumentalist. In choosing a house band he selected pop-oriented players, including the famous pianist FLOYD CRAMER, whose "slip-note" style epitomized the new mainstream orientation of the Nashville Sound. Atkins also employed vocal groups like THE JORDANAIRES and The ANITA KERR Singers, along with string sections to give his productions a slicker sound. Atkins gave a new professionalism to Nashville's recordings, and he helped mold the careers of ELVIS PRESLEY, THE EVERLY BROTHERS, THE BROWNS, and SKEETER DAVIS.

Atkins's later recordings are best when he is paired with a musician who inspires him to do his finest work, such as Les Paul, DOC WATSON, JERRY REED, Merle Travis, or even Scottish rock guitarist Mark Knopfler. In the late 1970s he retired from working for RCA as a producer to return to his first love, performing, although his 1980s and early 1990s output varied from the sublime to the saccharine. His last work was with singer SUZY BOGGUSS, whose smooth, pop singing style he admired greatly.

Atkins was elected to the Country Music Hall of Fame in 1973. From the mid-1990s he suffered from cancer, undergoing brain surgery in 1997 and finally succumbing to complications from the disease in 2001.

Select Discography

Galloping Guitars: The Early Years, Bear Family 15174. Multi-CD boxed set of Atkins's classic recordings made before he became the king of the Nashville Sound.

The RCA Years, RCA 61095. A double-CD set with some gems among the dross. Hear Chet pick with the Boston Pops under Arthur Fiedler! When you've recovered, there are some decent tracks with Jerry Reed and Merle Travis, along with cuts accompanying DOLLY PARTON.

AUTRY, GENE (b. Orvon G. A., Tioga Springs, Tex., September 29, 1907–October 2, 1998)

The most famous singing COWBOY, Autry transformed the image of the country singer with his introduction of Western garb and mannerisms into his stage persona. In the 1930s he was a star of radio, records, and films; from the end of World War II on, he was primarily a canny businessman who invested in enterprises ranging from real estate to baseball to oil. Besides performing many venerable cowboy hits, he

Early publicity shot for Gene Autry, before he got his cowboy gear. Photo: University of North Carolina, Southern Historical Collection, Southern Folklife Collection, University Archives

wrote or cowrote songs in sentimental ("That Silver-Haired Daddy of Mine"), cowboy ("Tumblin' Tumbleweeds," "South of the Border"), and blues ("I Hang My Head and Cry") styles, as well as famous Christmas/children's songs ("Frosty the Snowman," "Rudolph the Red-Nosed Reindeer," "Here Comes Santa Claus," and "Peter Cottontail").

Autry was the son of a Texas dirt farmer. He began his musical career as a member of the choir in the church where his grandfather was the preacher. Like many other rural musicians, he got his first mail-order guitar from Sears in his early teens and began playing at local events. The family moved to Oklahoma when he was in his late teens, and he found a job with a local railroad line as a telegraph operator. There he befriended an older, part-time musician, who encouraged him to pursue his career.

Autry began his career as a JIMMIE RODGERS imitator; like so many country performers of the late 1920s and early 1930s, he was enamored with the Rodgers sound, which he shamelessly copied. In 1928, supposedly on the advice of famous radio comedian Will Rogers, he traveled to New York in search of radio work. After making the rounds of the music industry bigwigs, he quickly returned to Oklahoma and radio work on the local station (KVOO, in Tulsa), billed as "Oklahoma's Yodeling Cowboy."

In October 1929 Autry returned to New York and finally broke into the recording world, albeit for the many budget "dimestore" labels that then existed. By the early 1930s many of these labels had failed due to the Depression, and were consolidated into the American Recording Company (ARC) label. There talent scout and producer ART SATHERLEY recorded the young singer. Their first hit collaboration was a sentimental number called "That Silver-Haired Daddy of Mine," released in 1931. This led to a radio contract with the influential and powerful station WLS out of Chicago, where he would remain through mid-1934.

At WLS, Autry began downplaying his rural-farm upbringing while emphasizing his (nonexistent) roots as a cowboy, perhaps influenced by the increasing popularity of movie cowboys such as Ken Maynard. In 1934 Autry gained his first movie role, supporting Maynard in *In Old Santa Fe*; the next year he starred in his first serial, the unusual *Phantom Empire*, which featured a bizarre mix of science fiction and cowboy antics! He would go on to appear in almost a hundred horse operas, usually accompanied by his favorite horse, Champion. From 1939 to 1956 he starred on radio in *Gene Autry's Melody Ranch*, further underscoring his cowboy image.

Autry recorded dozens of Western-flavored songs during this period that became major hits and have entered American folklore as "standards" in the cowboy repertoire. These include the evergreen "Tumbling Tumbleweeds," "Back in the Saddle Again," and "The Last Roundup." Autry sang them straight—no matter how clichéd the sentiments or lyrics, he sang 'em like he meant 'em—and his audience loved 'em.

After serving in the Army Air Corps in World War II, Autry returned to civilian life to find himself supplanted in the public imagination by another civilian-turned-cowpoke, ROY ROGERS. His last successes came with kids-oriented records, including the wintertime perennials "Rudolph, the Red-Nosed Reindeer," "Frosty the Snowman," and "Here Comes Santa Claus." Branching out to more moderate-weather holidays, he also cut "(Here Comes) Peter Cottontail." Besides continuing to make films, Autry became an early TV star, appearing on his popular program for six years beginning in 1950.

Autry pretty much retired from music making in the mid-1950s to focus on his lucrative business ventures. In 1960 he purchased the Los Angeles major league baseball team. In 1969 he was inducted into the Country Music Hall of Fame.

Autry's main importance was not his style, which was a mix of country mannerisms with the crooning popularized by Bing Crosby. Rather, it was his image, with the complete Western garb, that helped spread the myth of the cowboy as the last American pioneer. Country stars, who had previously appeared in overalls to emphasize their rural background, suddenly began appearing in cowboy hats and chaps. The romance of the West joined with the sentimentality of heart-tugging songs to produce an unbeatable combination. It's no surprise that GARTH BROOKS, country's latest superstar, always appears in a ten-gallon hat.

Select Discography

Blues Singer, Columbia/Legacy 64987. 1929–1931 recordings, made while Autry was still emulating the great Jimmie Rodgers.
The Essential, Columbia/Legacy 48957. Fine 1933–1946 recordings, featuring swingin' Western accompaniments, and including previously unissued alternate takes for the collector.

AXTON, HOYT (b. Comanche, Okla., March 25, 1938–October 26, 1999)
Axton was a 1970s singer/songwriter who had more success placing hits for other artists than scoring them on his own. He worked in a number of styles, from blues to folk-rock to pure country.

Son of noted pop tunesmith Mae Boren Axton (who wrote ELVIS PRESLEY's early hit "Heartbreak Hotel"), Axton was raised in rural Oklahoma, and was greatly influenced by the topical music of fellow Oklahoman WOODY GUTHRIE. His first big hit was a rewrite of "I Don't Want Your Millions, Mister," a Depression-era song popularized by Guthrie; his version, called "Greenback Dollar," was written with Ken Ramsey of the FOLK-REVIVAL group The Kingston Trio. Through the 1960s he placed other countryesque songs with mainstream Nashville acts, including FARON YOUNG, JEAN SHEPARD, and HANK SNOW.

Axton's big break into pop music came when the rock group Steppenwolf recorded his "The Pusher" in 1969; it was featured on the sound track of every hippie biker's favorite movie, *Easy Rider*. The song did little to endear him to country audiences, however, who failed to realize that its message was that drug dealers are evil. Thanks to this success he was signed by Columbia in the same year, and released an album in a soft, singer-songwriter style.

Axton next penned the ultimate 1970s feel-good anthem, "Joy to the World," a megahit for Three Dog Night in 1971; this was followed by the silly "No-No Song" for Ringo Starr four years later, another #1 pop hit. Axton recorded two more folk-country discs in the mid-1970s, scoring minor hits with 1974's "When the Morning Comes" and 1976's "Flash of Fire." By 1977 he had moved to a new label, where he recorded another anti-drug tune, "Snow Blind Friend," about the evils of cocaine, and produced the hit satire "You're the Hangnail in My Life." Unable to do much on the pop charts, Axton recorded a pure country album in 1979, with minor success on the story songs "Delta and the Dealer" and "Rusty Old Halo"; however, the new country movement had not yet been born, and his career stalled out.

In the 1980s Axton worked as a film actor, appearing in a number of Steven Spielberg-produced films, including *Gremlins* and *E.T.* Axton suffered a stroke in 1995, and although he made a few appearances and attempted to make some recordings, he passed away four years later.

Select Discography

Gotta Keep Rollin': The Jeremiah Years, Raven 91. CD reissue of 1979–1981 fine recordings that Axton did for his own Jeremiah label.

B

BAILES BROTHERS (Homer, b. H. Abraham B., Jr., May 8, 1922 [fdl, voc]; Johnny, b. John Jacob B., June 24, 1918–December 21, 1989 [gtr, voc]; Kyle, b. May 7, 1915 [b, voc]; Walter, b. W. Butler B., January 17, 1920–November 27, 2000 [gtr, voc]; all born near Charleston, W. Va.)

The Bailes Brothers were a family group centering on Johnny and Walter, whose classic GOSPEL songs (the ever-popular "Dust on the Bible") and sentimental numbers ("Remember Me") have become country standards.

Hailing from a West Virginia farming community, the boys performed together at home and church, where they learned the classic SHAPE-NOTE style of harmony singing that would be echoed in their recordings. Their father was a Baptist preacher, and two of the four sons would eventually follow him into this profession. Johnny was the first successful musician, working with RED SOVINE in 1937 and then hooking up with Skeets and Laverne Williamson (Laverne later gained fame as MOLLY O'DAY) and Little" JIMMY DICKENS, working out of Beckley, West Virginia, on radio. He also began performing with brother Kyle as a brother vocal duo; soon after, Walter had replaced Kyle, and The Bailes Brothers were born.

In 1942 ROY ACUFF brought the two brothers to THE GRAND OLE OPRY, where they remained popular performers for six years. They were signed by Columbia, where they recorded many of their classic compositions, including "I Want to Be Loved (But Only by You)," "Oh, So Many Years," and "Give Mother My Crown." All of these recalled the vocal sound and accompaniment of recordings of a decade earlier; in fact their vocal style resonated with the age-old mountain ballad singing style, as it was filtered through rural churches.

In 1948 the duo switched to the rival LOUISIANA HAYRIDE program, performing for one more year before the act dissolved. Although Johnny and Walter continued to work sporadically as a gospel duo through the early 1950s, Walter curtailed his performing to focus on the ministry. In the late 1970s Johnny ended up managing one of WEBB PIERCE's country radio stations, and Walter, while still a minister, was also performing. Homer followed Walter into the ministry; Kyle went into the air-conditioning business.

Select Discography

Early Radio, Vols. 1–3, Old Homestead 103, 104, 109. 1930s and 1940s radio broadcasts reissued on this series of out-of-print LPs.

BAILEY, DEFORD (b. Bellwood, Tenn., December 14, 1899–July 2, 1982)

One of the most popular performers on the original GRAND OLE OPRY, Bailey is one of those tragic pioneers who never received the recognition that he deserved and spent much of his life in a bitter retirement from music making. In his day he revolutionized harmonica playing, and his 1928 recordings, including the famous "Pan American Blues" with its myriad train sound effects, influenced generations of musicians. For years he was the sole black performer on the *Opry* stage.

Bailey's growth was stunted by polio, and he suffered all his life from back pain. Bailey was discovered by another early harmonica whiz, DR. HUMPHREY BATE, who had broadcast over WSM prior to the formal beginnings of the *Opry*. Bate brought him to the *Opry*'s announcer and motivating force, GEORGE HAY, for an audition, and Hay was so impressed he made Bailey the first act on the new *Opry* program. His talents on the harmonica were awesome, and besides being hired to perform on the *Opry*, he was among the first artists to be recorded in Nashville in 1928.

Although Bailey continued to perform on the *Opry*, the novelty of his few numbers began to wear thin in the 1930s, and he was phased off the program by 1941. Bailey blamed racism for his failure to build on his career; Hay blamed Bailey for his failure to learn new material. Whatever the case, Bailey spent the final decades of his life an embittered man, turning down recording offers and most other opportunities to play. He operated a shoeshine stand in Nashville until his retirement in the 1970s. Befriended by a local housing authority worker, David Morton, he made a series of recordings during the mid-1970s that showed his harmonica skills still very much intact, along with his memories of his days as a country star. Morton assembled Bailey's biography from these tapes, working with folklorist Charles Wolfe.

Select Discography

Harmonica Showcase, Matchbox 218. Out-of-print LP reissue of all eleven of Bailey's original recordings, plus five by D. H. "Bert" Bilbro, a white contemporary of his.

The Legendary, Revenant 208. 1974–1976 recordings featuring new versions of his legendary harmonica pieces, plus a few pieces played on five-string BANJO and GUITAR.

BAILEY, RAZZY (b. Rasie Michael B., Five Points, Ala., February 14, 1939)

Bailey is a soul-flavored country vocalist whose big hit was "9,999,999 Tears," covered by DICKEY LEE in 1976. Although he was initially a COUNTRYPOLITAN hitmaker, Bailey's natural affinity for soul music led him to pursue a career as a blue-eyed soulster.

Bailey was raised in rural Alabama on a farm with no running water or electricity. His father's name was Erastus and his nickname, "Rasie," the name he gave his son. As a teenager young Bailey formed his first band, sponsored by the local branch of the Future Farmers of America. He continued to play music part-time as he pursued careers as a truck driver, insurance and furniture salesman, and finally a butcher. His first recordings, made for the tiny Peach label under the producing hand of Joe South in the mid-1960s, were followed by two further stabs at recording in the early 1970s while continuing in his day jobs.

His big break came in 1976 when Dickey Lee covered his song "9,999,999 Tears"; two years later he was signed by RCA and had a number of Top 20 hits through the mid-1980s with his original compositions in a pop-country vein, including his first single, "What Time Do You Have to Be Back in Heaven?," through 1980's "Loving Up a Storm." In 1981 he had his first #1 country hit in a more R&B vein with "I Keep Coming Back," followed by the TRUCK-DRIVING anthem "Midnight Hauler." In the mid-1980s he hooked up with soul legend Steve Cropper (of Booker T. & The

MGs fame), cutting remakes of Wilson Pickett's "In the Midnight Hour" and Eddie Floyd's "Knock on Wood" along with his own compositions in an R&B vein.

Select Discography

Anthology, Renaissance 214. Collection of Bailey's hits from the 1970s and 1980s reissued on his own label.

BAKER, KENNY (b. Kenneth B., Jenkins, Ky., June 26, 1926)

Baker, longtime fiddler for BILL MONROE and one of the most influential of all BLUEGRASS fiddlers who still maintains links with older traditions, was born to a line of coal miners and fiddlers; he is said to have first taken up the FIDDLE at age eight, but his father apparently did not feel he had sufficient potential to handle the instrument. Consequently he switched to GUITAR in his high-school years, then returned to the fiddle in his early twenties. After serving in World War II he returned home to work in the mines. However, in 1953 country singer DON GIBSON hired him as the fiddler for his backup band. Three years later, when Bill Monroe heard him playing with Gibson, he immediately offered Baker a job.

Baker joined Monroe's band at a time when bluegrass music had gone underground. Monroe had difficulty meeting the band's payroll, so Baker often returned to mining in order to support his family. He first worked with Monroe from 1956 to 1959; during this period he shared fiddle duties with Bobby Hicks, and the two were featured on Monroe's classic instrumentals "Scotland" and "Panhandle County," recorded in 1958. Baker then left the band but briefly returned in 1962–1963, appearing on Monroe's recording of "Sailor's Hornpipe," featuring Monroe's latest discovery, Boston-born banjo player BILL KEITH. Baker then went back to mining, but the pull of a musical career was too strong, and in 1967 he finally returned to Monroe for good.

A year later Baker made the first in a series of solo albums for County Records. County appealed to the old-time music revivalists, who were taken with Baker's great technique. Although he showed elements of bluegrass, WESTERN SWING, and jazz in his playing, his general approach had such a strong old-time flavor that he could appeal to fans of both bluegrass and old-time music (groups who usually did not have much truck with each other). His long-bow, smooth style recalled earlier legendary Kentucky fiddlers, from "FIDDLIN' " DOC ROBERTS and Ed Haley to J. P. Fraley. Baker also composed new tunes in an older style, many of which would enter the bluegrass revival repertoire.

In 1969 Monroe issued his classic album *Uncle Pen*, a tribute to his fiddle-playing uncle. Baker played an important role in this work; Monroe felt that only Baker had the necessary roots in traditional styles to honor his uncle's music. *Uncle Pen* was a landmark in Monroe's career and further enhanced Baker's reputation as a premier bluegrass fiddler. Baker returned the favor by recording an album of Monroe instrumentals for County in 1976.

Baker became a fixture in Monroe's later bands, remaining with the master until 1986, when he began an association with DOBRO player BUCK GRAVES. The two recorded and performed as a duo, and also as part of a "supergroup" called The Masters, which also featured Eddie Adcock on BANJO and Jesse McReynolds of JIM AND JESSE fame on MANDOLIN. Baker has continued to record as a solo artist as well, and regularly tours the bluegrass circuit. In 1999 he was inducted into the International Bluegrass Music Hall of Fame.

Selected Discography

Puritan Sessions, Rebel 1108. With Buck Graves.

Master Fiddler, County 2705. Reissue of 1968–1983 tracks from various County albums; a good introduction to Baker's music.

Plays Bill Monroe, County 2708. Featuring the big man himself, this is Baker's homage to Monroe; it includes many standards by the father of bluegrass music.

BAKERSFIELD SOUND (c. 1955–1965)

About a hundred miles north of Los Angeles lies the oil-boom town of Bakersfield. In the late 1940s many displaced Midwesterners, particularly from Oklahoma, came to the town in search of work. The oil industry provided good jobs that paid well, and soon a local club scene was thriving to cater to the tastes of the displaced Okies. One of the first stars from the area was Okie TOMMY COLLINS, who featured a stripped-down HONKY-TONK sound in his band and recordings, thanks to lead guitarist BUCK OWENS, another Okie. Owens was soon a star on his own, leading a hot country combo from the late 1950s through the 1960s that featured lead GUITAR parts and vocal harmonies by Don Rich, who played the newly introduced Fender Telecaster (favored by country rockers like BUDDY HOLLY for its twangy sound), as well as steel guitarist TOM BRUMLEY. A Bakersfield native named MERLE HAGGARD furthered the roots-oriented style, performing songs about his real-life experiences.

The Bakersfield Sound was first captured on records by tiny labels that sprang up in the area, but was really given a boost when Los Angeles-based Capitol Records hooked into it. Capitol was not a country label in the early 1950s, but soon they had signed Collins, and then his protégé Owens, and finally Merle Haggard. A continent away from Nashville, the Capitol producers pretty much let the Bakersfield groups record without adding the deadening strings and sickly choruses that were a key part of the then popular NASHVILLE SOUND. The result was some of the finest roots country recordings of the 1950s and 1960s.

The Bakersfield Sound has been revived by new country stars like DWIGHT YOAKAM, who have taken the blend of rock, honky-tonk, and traditional country to a new audience.

BANDY, MOE (b. Marion B., Meridian, Miss., February 12, 1944)

Bandy, who hailed from the same town as JIMMIE RODGERS, was instrumental in launching the mid-1970s revival of HONKY-TONK songs, from his first hit, 1973's "I Just Started Hatin' Cheatin' Songs Today," through "Hank Williams, You Wrote My Life." At the decade's end he teamed with JOE STAMPLEY to form the influential country duo Moe and Joe, who performed a mix of honky-tonk and humorous numbers. They gained some attention in 1984 with their parody of Boy George's stage attire in "Where's the Dress?," complete with a video showing the two performers in MINNIE PEARL-type getups. Bandy's later solo material suffered from pop-rock flavorings that softened his original honky-tonk edge.

Moe was born in Mississippi, but his family relocated to San Antonio, Texas, when he was just six years old, and his musical legacy is pure Texas honky-tonk. Both of his parents were musical, particularly his father, who had his own country band for a while. He encouraged his son to learn FIDDLE and GUITAR, but Moe was more interested in pursuing a career as a rodeo rider. After several years of hard knocks and little pay, he abandoned the rodeo life to take a job as a sheet-metal worker during the day and a honky-tonk singer at night. He formed his first band, Moe and the Mavericks, in 1962, and for the next decade recorded sporadically for many small Texas labels.

In 1972 Moe met record producer Ray Baker, who took an interest in his career. He gave Bandy the song "I Just Started Hatin' Cheatin' Songs Today" to record; it was released a year later on GRC Records out of Atlanta. The song shot to #5 on the country charts, and was followed by similar honky-tonk anthems, including "Honky-Tonk Amnesia" and "Don't Anyone Make Love at Home Anymore." In 1975 Bandy and LEFTY FRIZZELL wrote a song recalling his rodeo days, "Bandy the Rodeo Clown," his last hit for GRC.

In that same year Bandy, still under Baker's guiding hand, signed with Columbia. They continued their string of beer-soaked laments through the early 1980s, including "Here I Am Drunk Again," "She Just Loved the Cheatin' out of Me," "Barstool Mountain," and 1979's duet with JANIE FRICKE, "It's a Cheatin' Situation." Also in 1979 Moe made his first recording with Joe Stampley, "Just Good Ol' Boys," the beginning of a string of successful duets with a good-natured, humorous tone that culminated in 1981's Top 10 "Hey Joe, Hey Moe."

Although Moe continued to tour (accompanied by his backup band, The Rodeo Clowns) and record, he more or less faded from the charts during the onslaught of New Nashville artists in the mid-1980s. Since the early 1990s he has made his home in Branson, Missouri, where he appears at his own theater.

Select Discography

Honky-Tonk Amnesia: The Best of, Razor and Tie 2096. Comprehensive career retrospective of the Columbia years, including solo hits and the Moe and Joe tracks.

BANJO, FIVE-STRING (c. 1840)

The five-string banjo, developed in the mid-nineteenth century, was probably derived from earlier African instruments. White minstrel star Joel Walker Sweeney is generally credited with adding the short fifth or drone string to the banjo, which previously had been made in four-, six-, eight-, and ten-string models. Early banjos generally had wooden bodies and rims, a fretless neck, and a skin head. The original banjo playing style has been variously called clawhammer, frailing, rapping, or knocking. It involves brushing the back of the hand across the strings while catching the thumb on the fifth string. There are many different varieties of clawhammer styles, from highly melodic to highly percussive.

Around the turn of the twentieth century, ragtime players like Fred van Epps and Vess L. Ossmann popularized a picked style using three fingers; this style is known as "classical" or "ragtime" banjo. Improved instrument designs helped increase the banjo's popularity. Makers like the Vega Company in Boston introduced new metal tone rings that helped project the instrument's sound, so it could be heard in a band setting. The famous instruments of the 1910s and 1920s, such as Vega's Whyte Laydie and Tubaphone models, were favored by banjoists working as soloists or in a band.

In the mid-1940s a new style of playing the banjo helped transform it from a background (or accompaniment) instrument to a new prominence as a melody instrument. Two-finger and three-finger picking styles had existed among folk banjoists at least since the turn of the century, particularly in North Carolina and the upper South. These evolved into BLUEGRASS-style picking, originally introduced by Earl Scruggs (later of FLATT AND SCRUGGS) when he was a member of BILL MONROE's Blue Grass Boys. Here three fingers are used, with metal picks, to play rapid chord rolls and melody parts. Bluegrass musicians began playing a newly styled banjo, called the Mastertone, marketed by the Gibson Company; it featured further improvements in the design of the tone ring, including a raised head, as well as a full resonator to further increase the instrument's sound.

Five-string banjo club at Princeton University, c. 1890s. The banjo enjoyed a short popularity around the turn of the 20th century among the educated elite, and several Ivy League universities had their own clubs. Photo: Author's collection

Although old-time styles continue to be performed, particularly among urban revivalists, bluegrass-styled banjo dominates commercial Nashville music. The mid-1970s progressive bluegrass movement helped introduce jazz and rock techniques into the banjoist's repertoire; some of the leading practitioners of this latest banjo style include TONY TRISCHKA and BELA FLECK, who leads the jazz-pop band The Flecktones.

BANNON, R. C. (b. Daniel Shipley, Dallas, Tex., May 2, 1945)

Bannon is a SINGER/SONGWRITER in the countrypolitan style who was upstaged on the charts by his then-wife, LOUISE MANDRELL.

Bannon grew up in Texas, where he first sang in his church choir. He moved on to playing rock and roll in local teen groups, and then worked the Texas club circuit as a guitarist for a couple of years. He moved to Seattle in the late 1960s, taking the name R. C. Bannon after he became a professional deejay in 1968. Five years later Bannon signed with Marty Robbins' backup band, and eventually worked his way to Nashville. In 1976 he became the deejay at a popular Music City hangout, The Smugglers Inn, where he befriended songwriter Harlan Sanders, who put him in touch with Warner Music.

In 1977 Bannon was signed by Columbia Records, but produced only a minor stir on the charts. Two years later he married Louise Mandrell, and they recorded the hit duet "Reunited" written by Bannon with John Bettis, followed a year later by "We Love Each Other." Bannon then returned to recording on his own, scoring minor success with 1981's "Where There's Smoke, There's Fire" and "Our Wedding Band" a year later. He also supplied more hit songs for wife Louise, and with Louise's sister BARBARA MANDRELL wrote "One-of-a-Kind Pair of Fools" in 1983.

Like that of the Mandrell sisters, Bannon's work represented the kind of mainstream, glitzy pop-country that was popular in the late 1970s and early 1980s. Never achieving their success, he pretty much faded into the woodwork after his early 1980s recording career fizzled. In 1991 he divorced Louise, although he continued to work as a musician in her show.

BARE, BOBBY (b. Robert Joseph B., Ironton, Ohio, April 7, 1935)

A longtime SINGER/SONGWRITER, Bare has passed through many career phases, from country to folk to R&B-shaded rock and back to country again. He is best known for his mid-1970s hit "Detroit City."

Bare was raised in relative poverty on a farm by his father (his mother had died when he was five years old). He began working as a farm laborer when he

Bobby Bare and clan, c. mid-1970s. Photo: Raeanne Rubenstein

was fifteen, and eventually landed a job in a clothing factory.

He joined in a local country band, recording his first solo song, "All-American Boy," in 1958. The song was a hit when it was released by the Fraternity label a year later as by "Bill Parsons," but Bare did not profit much from it, because he had sold his rights to the number for $50.00. The record was so successful that Fraternity sent a stand-in "Bill Parsons" out on the road; he lip-synched to Bare's recording!

Soon after, Bare signed with RCA Records, for which he had minor hits with his own "Shame on Me" and "Detroit City" in 1962–1963. He recorded an arrangement of the traditional folk song, "500 Miles Away from Home" that Bare, folksinger Hedy West, and Charles Williams took credit for as "arrangers." He continued to score minor hits on the country and pop charts through the 1960s. He moved to Mercury in the early 1970s, then returned to RCA in a more rockin' mood in 1972, having country hits with "Daddy, What If" and "Marie Laveau," both penned by Shel Silverstein. (Bare would collaborate again with Silverstein in 1980 and 1982.) He was an early fan of then-progressive country songwriters like BILLY JOE SHAVER, KRIS KRISTOFFERSON, and MICKEY NEWBURY.

In the late 1970s Bare was heavily promoted by rock entrepreneur Bill Graham, who got him a contract with Columbia Records, hailing him as the "Bruce Springsteen of country music." The label tried to market him as a more mainstream star. His career fizzled, however, and he ended up back in country music by the mid-1980s, hosting his own show on the then fledgling Nashville Network. After some years off the country radar, Bare returned as part of the (aged) supergroup The Old Dogs, which included JERRY REED, MEL TILLIS, and WAYLON JENNINGS for an album of new songs by Shel Silverstein; it was Silverstein's last major work, for he died soon after it was released.

Select Discography

Best of, Razor and Tie 2043. His 1960s and early 1970s hits, including "Detroit City," collected on CD.
Sings Lullabies, Legends and Lies, Bear Family 15683. Reissue of 1973 RCA LP consisting entirely of Shel Silverstein compositions.

BARNETT, MANDY (b. Amanda Carol B., Crossville, Tenn., September 28, 1975)

Barnett is best known for portraying PATSY CLINE in the biographical show *Always . . . Patsy Cline* that has been staged sporadically at Nashville's Ryman Auditorium since 1994. She has also attempted to establish herself as a contemporary country singer.

The child of a building contractor father and bookkeeper mother, Barnett began singing at age five, making her first "appearances" a year later at her local church. Her parents drove her career almost immediately, encouraging her to sing locally in GOSPEL choirs and on her own. When she was just nine years old, her father bankrolled a professional recording session for her that produced a cassette of gospel material that the family sold at shows. A year later she was hired to sing at Dollywood, DOLLY PARTON's theme park, where Barnett worked for the next two years. She won a Dollywood-sponsored talent contest that led to the chance to record a demo in Nashville when she was twelve.

Barnett's mother began a campaign to get her daughter on ERNEST TUBB's legendary post–GRAND OLD OPRY radio show, broadcast from his downtown Nashville record shop. Persistence paid off, and the youngster was soon belting her lungs out over the airwaves. At age thirteen, she was signed to a contract with producer JIMMY BOWEN, which led to a frustrating three years of recording demos with various producers, none of which led to an album. Eventually Bowen

teamed her with the talented SINGER/SONGWRITER GAIL DAVIES, but even these recordings were rejected. Meanwhile, Mandy led a relatively normal life; in high school (her official bio proudly notes) "she was voted both the Secretary of the Future Farmers of America chapter, and the school Prom Queen."

The same year Mandy graduated from high school, her parents divorced. She moved to Nashville in an attempt to revive her career, working in various jobs before auditioning successfully to portray Patsy Cline in a new biographical revue to be staged at the longtime home of *The Grand Ole Opry*, the Ryman Auditorium. First appearing in April–September 1994, Mandy received strong reviews for her interpretation of Cline and again attracted the attention of recording executives. She was quickly signed by Asylum Records, which released her debut album in 1996. Handled by pop-oriented producers, the recording straddled country and soft rock; despite good reviews, it didn't produce strong sales, and the label subsequently dropped her.

Through the late 1990s and into the new century, Mandy has continued to appear in *Always . . . Patsy Cline* for various periods at the Ryman while pursuing an independent career. She has guested on other artists' albums, and also has provided songs for film sound tracks. Her second album, the more roots-country-oriented *I've Got a Right to Cry*, was initially to be produced by legendary Patsy Cline producer OWEN BRADLEY, but he died during the preliminary sessions. The album was completed under other hands and released in 1999. Despite a more country orientation, it failed to make much impact on the charts. During 1999–2000 Barnett toured extensively to promote the album, in between returns to the Ryman for more Patsy Cline shows.

BATE, DR. HUMPHREY, AND THE POSSUM HUNTERS (Dr. Humphrey Bate, b. Castallian Springs, Tenn., May 25, 1875–June 12, 1936 [hca]; Alcyone Bate [Beasley] [voc, uke, pno]; Buster Bate [gtr, tipple, hca, Jew's harp]; Burt Hutcherson [gtr]; Walter Leggett [bnj]; Oscar Stone [fdl]; Staley Walton [gtr]; Oscar Albright [b])

The Possum Hunters, one of the first old-time string bands featured on THE GRAND OLE OPRY, were led by the harmonica-playing physician Dr. Humphrey Bate.

Bate, a Vanderbilt-educated doctor, led several old-time bands in the Nashville area. He was already performing on Nashville radio in 1925, before *The Grand Ole Opry* was first broadcast, and he was immediately invited to perform on the *Opry* as a representative not only of one of Tennessee's finer string bands but also as a respected member of the community. Soon after their *Opry* debut the band recorded for Brunswick Records. Bate's two children—Alcyone, who began performing with her father when she was thirteen and continued to play with various versions of the band through the early 1960s, and Buster—were prominent members of the group, with other members floating in and out as recording sessions or radio work came their way. After Bate's death the band continued until the late 1940s under the lead of fiddler Oscar Stone, and then into the early 1960s led by Alcyone and guitarist Staley Walton. In the early 1960s the band merged with THE CROOK BROTHERS, another old-time string band long resident on the *Opry*.

The sound of The Possum Hunters was fairly typical of middle Tennessee string bands. They were not as wild as The SKILLET LICKERS in their approach to traditional dance tunes, and favored a repertoire of old-time songs mixed with the sentimental favorites of the day. In a publicity photo taken in the 1920s, Dr. Bate is pictured in a rumpled hat and work shirt, holding his favorite hunting dog; other band members are dressed in typical "country" getups (banjoist Leggett is wearing a loosely fitted tie, but his shirtsleeves are rolled up and his baggy pants reach only to the knees). Obviously, despite Bate's educated background, the idea was to promote the band as just "down-home" folks.

Though not the greatest of the classic string bands of the late 1920s and early 1930s, The Possum Hunters had wide exposure through their residence on *The Grand Ole Opry*, and they continued to represent an important aspect of country music history for *Opry* listeners for many decades. Their recordings reveal that Dr. Bate was indeed an able harmonica player who propulsively played the popular old-time dance tunes of the day.

BEE, MOLLY (b. M. Beachboard [some sources give Beechwood], Oklahoma City, Okla., August 18, 1939)

A country comedian-singer-actress, Molly Bee has been a popular performer since her preteen years, reaching her greatest success in the late 1950s and early 1960s.

Born in Oklahoma, Bee was raised on a farm in the colorfully named town of Bell Buckle, Tennessee. The family relocated to Tucson, Arizona, when she was ten, and her mother brashly introduced her to singer REX ALLEN, for whom she performed "Lovesick Blues," leading him to recommend her to a local radio station. A year later the family moved to southern California, where the young singer/comedian was signed to CLIFFIE STONE's *Hometown Jamboree* radio show, and was a regular on it through her teenage years. At the same time she signed with the California-based Capitol label, and began performing on television, working three years with Pinky Lee, followed by two years on TENNESSEE ERNIE FORD's daytime show. She

then moved to Ford's more prestigious nighttime program, and also guested on a slew of 1950s TV variety shows.

In the 1960s Bee took to the glitzy Vegas trail, as did many other contemporary country stars, performing regularly at the city's hot spots. She also toured as a musical-comedy actress, and appeared as a solo act at country fairs, rodeos, and clubs. She switched from Capitol to MGM in the 1960s, continuing to produce a smattering of hits in country WEEPER and light comedy styles.

After two failed marriages, Bee took time off in the 1970s to try to make her marriage with husband number three work out a little better. But by mid-decade she was recording and performing again, this time for Cliffie Stone's tiny Granite label, for which she produced the modest hit "She Kept on Talkin'." After that, however, she pretty much disappeared from the charts, although she continued to perform into the 1980s.

BELLAMY BROTHERS (b. Derby, Fla.; David [keybds, voc], b. September 16, 1950, and Howard [gtr, voc], b. February 2, 1946)

The Bellamy Brothers are sweet-voiced harmonizers whose music is an amalgam of country, rock, and mainstream pop.

The brothers were born in rural Florida; their father was a farmer who played DOBRO and FIDDLE in an amateur BLUEGRASS band. David was the first to make it into the musical big time, in the mid-1960s, as a member of an R&B band called The Accidents that backed such stars as Percy Sledge and Little Anthony and The Imperials. The brothers began performing together in a COUNTRY-ROCK band called Jericho in the late 1960s, playing the Southern club circuit through 1971, when they disbanded. The Bellamys then went to work writing jingles and songs.

Their big break came in 1975 when Jim Stafford scored a hit with David's composition "Spiders and Snakes." They were signed by Warner Brothers, and had a minor hit with 1975's "Nothin' Heavy." In 1976 they covered the Neil Diamond–Larry Williams pop anthem "Let Your Love Flow," replete with their sugary harmonies and jangling acoustic guitars. The record was an enormous hit on country and pop charts. The Bellamys continued to record in this acoustic-rock amalgam through the 1970s, scoring minor hits with songs like "If I Said You Had a Beautiful Body, Would You Hold it Against Me?" in 1979.

In the 1980s they turned to more mainstream country sounds, recording a number of minor hits, most of them written by David, including 1982's "Redneck Girl," 1983's "Dancing Cowboys," and 1986's "Too Much Is Not Enough." In 1987 they recorded "Kids of the Baby Boom" with THE FORESTER SISTERS, a nostalgic look at growing up in the 1950s that had broad appeal. They continued to perform through the 1990s, releasing their work after 1991 on their own Bellamy Brothers and other small labels.

Select Discography

The Best of, Curb/CEMA 77554. Reissues cuts from the 1980s originally on MCA.
25 Year Collection, Vols. 1–2, Delta Disc 7002/7003. Remastered versions of the big hits of a quarter-century issued on the Bellamys' own label.

BERLINE, BYRON (b. Caldwell, Kan., July 6, 1944)

Berline is a flashy fiddler credited with introducing Texas or show-style fiddling into the BLUEGRASS repertoire. He has had a distinguished career in bluegrass, newgrass, and COUNTRY-ROCK.

A country boy with a college education, Berline was the son of an old-time fiddling father and a piano-playing mother. His father, Luke, was a big fan of Texas or contest-style fiddling, and the boy picked up this style when he began to play at age five. He beat his father in a local contest when he was ten, and soon was taking many regional titles. Meanwhile, an athletic scholarship took him to the University of Oklahoma, where he began to perform in a college band.

At college he heard bluegrass music for the first time when the progressive band THE DILLARDS performed on campus. He met BANJO player Doug Dillard after the concert, and they soon discovered that their fathers shared a love of old-time fiddling. Berline was invited to perform on the Dillards' next album, an homage to traditional fiddling called *Pickin' and Fiddlin'*. On this album the band performed many Texas favorites in the ornate competition style that Berline had picked up playing at countless fiddlers' conventions.

After finishing college in 1967, Berline performed briefly with BILL MONROE before joining the Army; during his stint with Monroe he recorded "Sally Goodin," first recorded by ECK ROBERTSON in 1922, complete with the many variations that have made the piece a competition favorite. After he was discharged from the Army, Berline rejoined Doug Dillard on the West Coast as a member of the country-rock outfit Dillard and Clark, and also sessioned with many bands, including playing the FIDDLE part on The Rolling Stones' "Country Honk," the first version of "Honky-Tonk Women." In the early 1970s he also performed with a reconstituted version of THE FLYING BURRITO BROTHERS that soon after became the first version of COUNTRY GAZETTE.

Thanks to the mid-1970s bluegrass revival, Berline was able to return to playing acoustic music in a variety of formats. As a bandleader he recorded bluegrass, newgrass, and jazz-influenced music with his group,

Sundance; as a member of the trio Crary, Hickman, and Berline, he recorded in a more straightforward traditional vein (the group added bassist Steve Spurgin and MANDOLIN player John Moore in 1988 and 1990, respectively, and toured under the name California through 1995). Since the mid-1990s he has led his own Byron Berline Band, continuing to play in a variety of styles. Berline's jazz-tinged, highly ornamented, and richly improvised fiddle style influenced an entire generation of fiddlers, particularly those who helped create the newgrass style, such as Sam Bush.

Select Discography

Dad's Favorites, Rounder 0100. 1979 album featuring tunes Berline learned from his father; includes a slew of young bluegrass stars, among them VINCE GILL before he became a country superstar.
Berline-Crary-Hickman, Sugar Hill 3720. 1981 album, the first for the superpicker trio. They would record three more albums for Sugar Hill through the mid-1980s.

BERRY, JOHN (b. Aiken, S.C., September 14, 1959)

Berry, a 1990s hitmaker whose performances are best described as "if Meat Loaf sang country music . . .," was born in South Carolina but raised in Georgia. He began playing GUITAR as a teenager, performing locally while pursuing an interest in sports. However, at age twenty-two he suffered a major setback when his legs were crushed in a motorcycle accident. Berry at this time was living in Athens, Georgia, and he began playing in local clubs, attracting a following as a "country singer for people who don't like country music." Besides his own songs and country standards, a typical set might include covers of The Doobie Brothers or Bruce Springsteen, thus widening his appeal. He twice won the Marlboro Country Music Roundup contest for his region, and released six albums independently from the late 1970s through 1990.

In 1992 Berry began traveling to Nashville, hoping for a major label deal. Two years later he was signed by Liberty. His first single did well, but it was the second release, "Your Love Amazes Me," that took him to #1 and immediate country superstardom. Ironically, the day the song hit #1, Berry was hospitalized for emergency surgery following the discovery of a cyst on his brain. However, he soon bounced back, and continued to chart with a series of arena-rock-styled ballads, including "You and You Only" and "If I Had Any Pride Left at All." If you closed your eyes, and ignored the cowboy hat and twang, you might think you were reliving the glory days of mid-1970s power rock.

Berry continued to record and tour prolifically through the late 1990s. Besides his rock-flavored country ballads, he has recorded several Christmas and GOS-PEL albums. He counts among his fans ex-president George H. W. Bush, who asked him to sing at a private birthday celebration in 1999. That same year Berry moved from Liberty/Curb to Lyric Street Records.

Select Discography

Greatest Hits, Capitol 24740. Compilation of his big 1990s hits.

BEVERLY HILL BILLIES (Original lineup: Zeke Manners (aka Leo Mannes) [acc]; Tom "Pappy" Murray [gtr]; Ezra Longnecker (aka Cyprian Paulette) [lead voc]; and "Hank Skillet" (Henry Blaeholder) [fdl]), 1930s COWBOY-Western group who enjoyed great popularity on California radio and on recordings.

During the late 1920s and early 1930s the Depression and Dust Bowl sent hundreds of thousands of Southwesterners scrambling into southern California in search of a better life. They brought with them a hunger for authentic country music that California radio stations, record producers, and showmen quickly capitalized on. The station manager at KMPC in Los Angeles, Glen Rice, recognized the potential audience, and decided to launch a country program. Taking the name "Mr. Tallfeller," he announced that a group of "hillbillies" had been discovered living in Beverly Hills, and he had convinced them to come to the studio to sing a few numbers. At the time it wasn't unusual to find "hillbilly" families living in makeshift villages around Los Angeles (ROSE MADDOX and her family, originally from Alabama, camped out in a drainpipe because they couldn't find affordable housing), so the loopy notion of discovering backwoodsmen in the Hollywood hills was initially taken at face value.

The group was assembled from local performers, who were given colorful "country" names. Like many of the pop-Western outfits of the day, the Beverly Hill Billies combined slick, pop-flavored harmonies with corn-pone humor and a dose of jazz-influenced stringbending and accordion pumping. Their repertoire stayed close to the saddle-and-sagebrush, with an occasional nod to "dear old mother" or a heartfelt nod to the old home. An immediate radio sensation, they were signed by Brunswick Records, for which they recorded from mid-1930 through the fall of 1932. During this period they also began to appear in the Hollywood horse operas featuring "cowboys" GENE AUTRY, TEX RITTER, and others.

The group soldiered on with various members through the outbreak of World War II, although their popularity had been greatly diminished by the more prolific SONS OF THE PIONEERS (who had the advantage of a close association with ROY ROGERS). Groups like today's cowboy revivalists RIDERS IN THE SKY draw heavily on the repertoire and stage presentation that made the Beverly Hill Billies so popular.

The Hill Billies had no relationship to the successful mid-1960s TV comedy show of the same name. Whether the producers came up with the name independently was at issue when some surviving band members sued; they subsequently won a settlement from the TV producers for the use of the name.

BINKLEY BROTHERS DIXIE CLODHOPPERS (1926–1939: Gale Binkley [fdl]; Amos Binkley [bnj]; (Tom Andrews [gtr])

Not much is known about this early rural string band made famous by their appearances on THE GRAND OLE OPRY. The Binkleys were Nashville natives who eventually owned and operated a successful watch-repair business, which was still in business as late as 1960. Andrews was from nearby Franklin, Tennessee, and was said to be an associate of the musical McGee brothers, who accompanied UNCLE DAVE MACON and also worked in various bands and on their own.

The Binkley band was originally called the Binkley Barn Dance Orchestra, and appeared under that name for the first time on the *Opry* on October 10, 1926. GEORGE HAY, the *Opry* announcer, gave them the more rural-sounding Dixie Clodhoppers name. From 1929 to 1931 they appeared on both the *Opry* and Nashville's other major country show, broadcast over rival station WLAC. In 1932 they became official *Opry* members, playing on the show every other week until they were dropped in 1939. Various members came and went, but the basic old-time style of the band remained unchanged. Probably this is the reason they were summarily dropped in 1939; their music was, by then, considerably out of date. They were replaced by a more modern string band, BILL MONROE's Blue Grass Boys.

The Binkleys were among the first bands to record in Nashville, during the famous September 1928 sessions held by the Victor label. However, when they arrived at the studios, the engineers were unhappy with their singing. They quickly enlisted the help of singer/guitarist Jack Jackson. Jackson was a Lebanon, Tennessee, native known as "the Singing Yodeler" (this before JIMMIE RODGERS had made YODELING an integral part of country blues recording). He provided the vocals on the ten numbers the Binkleys recorded, including their "hit" version of "I'll Rise When the Rooster Crows," a song popularized by Uncle Dave Macon thanks to his 1925 recording on Vocalion. Gale Binkley's smooth fiddling was a perfect complement to Jackson's modern singing style, and the record enjoyed wide success. However, the Binkleys never recorded again.

After they left the *Opry*, the two brothers apparently were happy to pursue their jewelry business and leave music making to others.

BLACK, CLINT (b. C. Patrick B., Long Branch, N.J., February 4, 1962)

One of the superstars of late 1980s country, Black began as an honest-to-God Texas HONKY-TONKER but has gone Hollywood with his marriage to soap-opera cutie Lisa Hartmann.

Born in New Jersey, Black was raised in Houston, Texas, from the age of six months. As a teenager he played bass in his brother's band and began working local clubs soon after. He hooked up with guitarist Hayden Nicholas, who had been working in Los Angeles but returned to Houston in the mid-1980s. Nicholas and Black began writing songs together, as well as working at Nicholas's studio to produce a demo tape. The tape landed Black an audition with Z Z Top's manager, Bill Ham, who was able to get him a contract with RCA. Black's first single, "A Better Man," written with Nicholas, hit #1, a rare feat for a first recording. It was followed by another chart-buster, "Killin' Time."

Black's career was cleverly managed. He paid homage to old country by recording a COWBOY duet with ROY ROGERS and followed that with a rowdier-than-thou duo recording with HANK WILLIAMS, JR., on the boozy "Hotel Whiskey." Meanwhile, he kept on racking up the solo hits, including "Put Yourself in My Shoes," an updating of the WESTERN SWING sound in modern cowpoke clothing. He reached the apex of his popularity around 1994–1995 (along with country music in general).

During the mid-through-late 1990s Black was more noticeable for his appearances on *Entertainment Tonight*, escorting his glitzy wife, than for his country recordings. Like GARTH BROOKS and other megastars of new country, his later recordings show the influence of 1970s arena-rock and middle-of-the-road pop, veering away from his honky-tonk roots. He attempted a "return to roots" with his 1999 album, *D'Lectrified*, but by then he was remembered only by his dedicated fans.

Select Discography

Killin' Time, RCA 9668. 1989 major-label debut.

Put Yourself in My Shoes, RCA 2372. His best-known recording, glitzier than his debut.

The Hard Way, RCA 66003. Actually, the easy way. Clint stalls out on his third album.

D'Lectrified, RCA 67893. 1999 CD that Clint produced himself, an eclectic mix of acoustic country, WESTERN SWING, and contemporary country sounds. His most musical album, but not a popular hit.

BLACKHAWK (Original lineup: Henry Paul [mdln, gtr, voc]; David Ray Robbins [kybds, bass harmony voc]; Van Stephenson [gtr, high harmony voc])

A Southern COUNTRY-ROCK trio, founded in 1994, BlackHawk scored several Top 10 country hits in the late 1990s, propelled by the band's strong songwriting and sweet harmonies. Henry Paul had a long background in performing in rock and country-rock ensembles, and Stephenson and Robbins were two highly successful Nashville-based songwriters when they got together in the early 1990s. Paul had begun his musical career playing with two Southern rock-styled bands, The Outlaws, who recorded and toured in the mid-1970s, and his own Henry Paul Band; he then reunited in a new Outlaws for touring in the mid-1980s. Stephenson and Robbins met in 1981, when they began working together as songwriters. Stephenson also enjoyed a brief solo career in the early 1980s, scoring a minor hit with "Modern-Day Delilah" on the Top 40 pop charts. Stephenson and Robbins paired up with producer/songwriter TIM DUBOIS to write several top country hits of the mid-to-late 1980s, including their biggest hit, "Bluest Eyes in Texas," which went to #1 on the country charts for the group RESTLESS HEART.

At Dubois's suggestion Stephenson and Robbins began to perform with Paul, who had settled in Nashville in 1990. The trio began writing together, and DuBois signed on to produce their first record for Arista. They were successful right out of the box with their mix of hard-rocking melodies and refined harmonies. Their first album, *BlackHawk*, was released in the fall of 1993, and the trio hit #1 in 1994 with the track "Every Once in a While," which they also composed. By 1995 their debut had gone platinum, and the band released a second album, *Strong Enough*. The "hits kept coming," with the album producing several more Top 5 singles, including the title track and "Like There Ain't No Yesterday."

In 1997 the trio released their third album, *Love and Gravity*, a more rock-oriented affair than their previous efforts, which marked the beginning of a slide in their popularity. Scoring only low-chart hits, they tried to win back their country audience with 1998's *The Sky's the Limit*, although some longtime fans were put off by the more countrified sound. To complicate matters, harmony vocalist and songwriter Van Stephenson was diagnosed with cancer, and decided to quit the group in early 2000. At that point Arista put together a *Greatest Hits* album, including songs that weren't exactly big hits but nonetheless were fan favorites, such as 1997's "Postmarked in Birmingham." New guitarist Chris Anderson—formerly in Henry Paul's Outlaws band—replaced Stephenson on the road in 2000. Arista, dropped the group, however, and their future as a recording unit was up in the air in early 2001.

Select Discography

Greatest Hits, Arista 18907. The big hits from the Arista years.

BLACKWOOD BROTHERS (Original lineup: Roy E. B., b. Fentress, Miss., December 24, 1900–March 21, 1971 [baritone voc]; Doyle J. B., b. Ackerman, Miss., August 22, 1911 [bass voc]; James Weber B., b. Ackerman, Miss., August 4, 1919–February 3, 2002 [lead voc]; Ronald Winston [R. W.] B., b. Ackerman, Miss., October 23, 1921–June 24, 1954 [tenor voc])

A long-lived Southern GOSPEL group, The Blackwood Brothers had a great influence, particularly on the young ELVIS PRESLEY.

The Blackwood family were sharecroppers in the Mississippi Delta. Like many others they were caught up in the gospel fervor that swept the South, propelled by traveling revivalists. At one such revival the brothers' mother was "saved," inspiring her sons also to follow the Lord. Sometime around the mid-1920s Roy became a traveling preacher while brothers Doyle and James began performing religious material at local revival meetings and schoolhouses. Around 1933 they joined with a local singing school teacher to form the Choctaw County Jubilee Singers. Doyle briefly traveled to Birmingham to work with another professional gospel group, but by early 1935 Doyle, James, Roy, and Roy's son R. W. were all back in Mississippi. The first quartet was born around this time.

After broadcasting on several small stations, the group got its big break when it began a daily program on the powerful KWKH station out of Shreveport, Louisiana. With its strong signal the station could be heard through much of the South and Midwest. The group expanded its repertoire to include country and pop songs as well as gospel numbers around this time. The Stamps-Baxter Publishing Company, which specialized in gospel music, was impressed by their radio broadcasts, and hired the Blackwoods to travel to promote their songbooks. Stamps arranged for them to broadcast out of Shenandoah, Iowa, where the group spent the early 1940s. The group briefly disbanded during the height of World War II.

In 1946 the group broke with Stamps-Baxter and formed their own publishing company. Between 1946 and 1948, Doyle left the group, and was replaced by the first nonfamily member, Don Smith. The group moved increasingly toward pop material, gaining such popularity that by 1948 they formed a separate unit, The Blackwood Gospel Quartet, to focus on religious material. Doyle returned to lead this group.

In 1950 Doyle and eldest brother Roy decided to retire. James and R. W. took the group to Memphis, where they had their own radio show that was broadcast twice a day. They also signed with RCA Records,

where they scored several hits, beginning in 1952 with "Rock My Soul," reflecting the influence of black gospel groups. During this period Roy's son Cecil (October 28, 1934–November 13, 2000) formed a "junior" quartet for the younger family members and friends, called the Songfellows. It was this group that a young Elvis Presley hoped to join, but was turned down after an audition. In 1954 the senior group seemed poised for greater success after appearing on the *Arthur Godfrey Show*, but R. W. and group member Bill Lyles were killed in a plane crash following a performance.

After a period of mourning the group re-formed and became even more popular in Memphis. Cecil and James's son James, Jr. (b. July 31, 1943), came on board, along with bass singer J. D. Sumner. During this period the group became a prime force in the gospel music industry, founding or buying several gospel publishing houses, including the Stamps-Baxter Company that had originally sponsored them. In 1956 the group organized the National Quartet Convention, which has become an important annual event in Memphis, and the Gospel Music Association, which brought greater organization to the field.

The Blackwoods continued to record and perform through the end of the twentieth century, with varying personnel. James, the last of the original brothers, continued to be the group's guiding force through the 1970s. He was inducted into the Gospel Music Hall of Fame in 1974, and won numerous Dove Awards as best male gospel singer from the late 1960s through the late 1970s; he died in early 2002. In 1998 the group was inducted into the Gospel Music Hall of Fame. Cecil was the de facto leader for the last quarter-century, until his death in 2000; his son Mark continues to sing with the group.

Select Discography

Gospel Classic Series, RCA 67624. Budget reissue of ten of the group's best-known recordings.

BLAKE, NORMAN (b. Chattanooga, Tenn., March 10, 1938)

Blake is a pleasant-voiced SINGER/SONGWRITER who was most popular in the mid-1970s for his country-esque songs and superb instrumental skills.

Blake was born in Tennessee but raised in Georgia, and could play a number of instruments by his teen years. In the mid-to-late 1950s he played MANDOLIN with a number of BLUEGRASS-flavored bands, including the Lonesome Travelers, who made two albums for RCA. After serving with the Army in the Panama Canal Zone, Blake returned to Georgia in the mid-1960s to discover that traditional music was on the wane. Determined not to shortchange his talents, he took to teaching guitar while playing in a local dance band on the side.

Blake was "discovered" by June Carter, wife of JOHNNY CASH, who invited him to join her road show in the late 1960s. He began performing with both husband and wife, and moved to Nashville in the spring of 1969. He was one of the young pickers featured on BOB DYLAN's *Nashville Skyline* album, further enhancing his reputation as both a guitarist and a DOBRO player. He toured with KRIS KRISTOFFERSON's band in 1970, and then hooked up with JOHN HARTFORD's seminal country-bluegrass band of the early 1970s, which featured fiddler VASSAR CLEMENTS, Dobroist TUT TAYLOR, and bassist RANDY SCRUGGS. They recorded the highly influential *Aeroplane* album and toured widely. By 1972 the rest of the band had dispersed, but Hartford and Blake continued as a duo, recording *Morning Bugle*.

Blake's solo career began with a number of low-key albums featuring both original material and re-creations of traditional bluegrass, country, and old-time songs. His song "Last Train from Poor Valley," featured on his 1974 album *The Fields of November*, was widely covered in bluegrass circles. Blake also showed he was no laggard when it came to hot GUITAR licks, issuing the all-instrumental *Whiskey Before Breakfast* LP in the mid-1970s.

Blake often performed as a duo with his wife, Nancy, a classically trained cellist, from the later 1970s through the mid-1980s; after a period of separation they have been performing together again since the later 1990s. With the addition of bluegrass fiddler James Bryan, who had previously played with BILL MONROE, they formed a trio called The Rising Fawn String Ensemble. Although the name didn't stick, the group continued to perform together informally through the 1980s. Bryan was the perfect foil for Blake; not a flashy fiddler, but a very talented one, he had an almost cerebral approach to bluegrass fiddling that matched Blake's own increasingly soft-edged approach.

Blake's approach softened in the 1990s as he returned to solo performing and recording. While still a fleet-fingered guitarist, he sounded increasingly mellow and laid-back, the onetime energy of his playing seemingly gone. He was one of many country players who was featured on the 2000 film sound track of *O Brother, Where Art Thou?*, which helped revive interest in his music.

Select Discography

Back Home in Sulphur Springs, Rounder 0012. Cassette-only reissue of early 1970s debut solo album.
Slow Train Through Georgia, Rounder 11526. CD compilation drawn from various Rounder releases.

Natasha's Waltz, Rounder 11530. CD compilation taken from various albums cut with wife Nancy and fiddler James Bryan.
Blake & Rice, Rounder 0233/0266. Two albums cut with hot picker TONY RICE, from 1988 and 1990, respectively, both available on CD.
Flower from the Field of Alabama, Shanachie 6053. 2001 album that draws on traditional country numbers.

BLANCHARD, JACK, AND MISTY MORGAN
(Blanchard: b. Buffalo, N.Y., May 8, 1942; Morgan: b. Mary M., Buffalo, N.Y., May 23, 1945)

One-hit wonders of the 1970s, Blanchard and Morgan are best remembered for the novelty song "Tennessee Birdwalk."

Although they were both born in Buffalo, and both were child prodigies on the keyboards, Blanchard and Morgan didn't meet until they were working in clubs located a block apart in Hollywood, Florida. By then Blanchard had become an adept performer on slide guitar, DOBRO, and lap steel, as well as keyboards and synthesizer, while Morgan mostly stuck to the keyboards and vocal work. Blanchard had recorded a couple of country singles on his own, with little success, before meeting and marrying Morgan. The two formed a duo after Blanchard's band dissolved, more or less out of desperation, hitting it big in 1970 with the screwball "Tennessee Birdwalk." They followed this with the even stranger novelty "Humphrey the Camel" and the more straightforward country "You've Got Your Troubles, I've Got Mine," both in the same year as their original megahit.

Although they continued to place hits on the charts until the mid-1970s, they were never able to equal their first fluky successes. Blanchard increasingly turned to writing humorous pieces for newspapers, as well as drawing his own comic strip, and the two continued to write songs individually and together, occasionally placing a number with another country artist.

BLUEGRASS MUSIC (c. 1946–present)

Sometimes called "country music in overdrive," bluegrass music is often characterized as high-speed, high-pitched, high-energy music. Taking its name from the legendary band (The Blue Grass Boys) led by mandolinist BILL MONROE in the late 1940s, bluegrass actually is more than just fancy pickin' and breathless singing. It is a music of great emotional power that borrows from country, GOSPEL, HONKY-TONK, and, more recently, jazz and rock to form a unique musical union.

All bluegrass bands owe a debt to Bill Monroe, who brought together a group of five musicians to form the first classic lineup of his Blue Grass Boys in 1946.

These included Lester Flatt and Earl Scruggs on lead GUITAR and BANJO, respectively, fiddler Chubby Wise, Monroe on MANDOLIN and high tenor vocals, and bass player Cedric Rainwater. Scruggs had evolved a unique method of playing the five-string banjo, a three-finger picking style that changed the instrument from primarily an accompaniment to a melodic lead instrument. Flatt developed a new way of playing guitar accompaniments, using bass runs rather than chords as "fills" to bridge the gaps between chord progressions. Monroe was, of course, a fire-breathing mandolin player, and Wise was a fiddler influenced as much by WESTERN SWING as by old-time styles. Vocally the group offered a strong contrast between the relaxed, almost crooning lead vocals of Flatt and the intense, high-pitched harmonies and leads of Monroe. They also recorded as a gospel quartet, dropping the banjo, and were perhaps the first band to borrow from traditional SHAPE-NOTE, backwoods church singing to record gospel in an entirely new way. It is not an exaggeration to say that Monroe's band—vocally and instrumentally—not only invented bluegrass but also became the model that every other band has emulated.

When this band performed on THE GRAND OLE OPRY, their effect was immediate and revolutionary. Bands like THE STANLEY BROTHERS, who had been playing in a more traditional style, immediately switched to bluegrass; FLATT AND SCRUGGS left the Monroe fold to form a less mandolin-oriented ensemble. Monroe continued to work through the 1990s, composing many classic bluegrass tunes and songs while refining the overall sound.

In 1959 MIKE SEEGER recorded a number of groups for an anthology for Folkways Records called *Mountain Music: Bluegrass Style*. While a few urban players had been aware of bluegrass before this LP was issued, it opened the floodgates, with many groups forming in urban centers including New York, Boston, Baltimore, Washington, San Francisco, and Los Angeles. "Progressive" bluegrass was born, a wedding of traditional bluegrass instrumentation with a broader palette of material. Banjoist BILL KEITH, who briefly performed with Monroe, introduced "melodic" bluegrass banjo, almost eliminating accompaniment chords from his playing. Bands like Washington's COUNTRY GENTLEMEN, Boston's Charles River Valley Boys (who recorded an LP of Beatles songs redone in bluegrass arrangements), Los Angeles's KENTUCKY COLONELS (with Clarence and Roland White), and New York's GREENBRIAR BOYS all represented a new approach to the bluegrass style.

The older acts, like Monroe, the Stanleys, and Flatt and Scruggs, had eked out a living through the 1950s, existing somewhere on the edge of country music. The FOLK REVIVAL, along with the growth of progressive bluegrass, helped them gain a larger audience, al-

though they still remained definitely on the fringes. Flatt and Scruggs came the closest to widespread popularity, thanks to their appearance on TV's *Beverly Hillbillies* and the sound track of the film *Bonnie and Clyde*. By the end of the decade Scruggs was pursuing a COUNTRY-ROCK audience, performing with his sons, while Flatt formed a more traditional bluegrass band.

The 1970s brought a second wave of bluegrass innovators. These bands and solo acts tended to emphasize flashy instrumental work over vocals. COUNTRY COOKING, out of Ithaca, New York, featured the twin banjos of TONY TRISCHKA and Pete Wernick on original bluegrass-flavored instrumentals (the band never recorded vocals). DAVID GRISMAN, once a mandolinist with RED ALLEN, began recording what he called "dawg" music, a synthesis of swing and bluegrass. NEW GRASS REVIVAL, under the leadership of mandolinist Sam Bush, combined the energy of rock (and the lack of subtlety of heavy metal) with bluegrass instrumentation.

In the 1980s Bill Monroe began to gain the wide acceptance that his being the "father of bluegrass music" deserved. Meanwhile, progressive bluegrassers began returning to more traditional material, while traditionalists showed the influence of the influx of the progressive crowd. The new country explosion featured many ex-bluegrassers, most prominently RICKY SKAGGS, KATHY MATTEA, and VINCE GILL. They brought traditional bluegrass songs and instrumentation into mainstream country music. Bands like THE JOHNSON MOUNTAIN BOYS arose as virtual clones of traditional bluegrass outfits, re-creating the look, style, and sound of a generic 1950s bluegrass ensemble. Meanwhile, THE NASHVILLE BLUEGRASS BAND and others continued to broaden the bluegrass repertoire while remaining true to the roots of the music.

The later 1990s saw yet another bluegrass revival. Singer/fiddle player ALISON KRAUSS achieved remarkable success, both as a solo performer and with her band, Union Station. The group won even more attention thanks to their appearance on the sound track of the hit film *O Brother, Where Art Thou?* in 2000, and the subsequent "Down from the Mountain" tours featuring music from the film. Krauss in turn discovered the band Nickel Creek, a highly photogenic group of young bluegrass players who recorded a less aggressive form of the music. They have become a popular act on the country charts and Country Music Television (CMT). Ricky Skaggs, who had previously "crossed over" to mainstream country, returned to the bluegrass fold in the later 1990s with his group, Kentucky Thunder. Earlier bluegrass stars like DEL MCCOURY also began to enjoy wider followings, thanks to broadening their repertoire to include contemporary SINGER/SONGWRITER material along with more traditional bluegrass staples. Bluegrass achieved such high visibility that in early 2002 CMT broadcast

31

a "Bluegrass Rules" weekend featuring concerts and videos.

BLUE SKY BOYS, THE (Bill Bolick, b. Hickory, N.C., October 28, 1917; Earl Bolick, b. Hickory, N.C., November 16, 1919–April 19, 1998)

One of the archetypal "brother" acts of the 1930s, The Blue Sky Boys were perhaps the purest vocal-harmony duo ever. Lacking the bluesy style of THE ALLEN BROTHERS, THE CARLISLE BROTHERS, or THE DELMORE BROTHERS, or the raw excitement of The Monroe Brothers, The Blue Sky Boys performed a combination of sentimental and traditional songs in tight harmonies that would have a lasting impact on country music (through THE LOUVIN BROTHERS and JOHNNIE AND JACK) and early rock and roll (THE EVERLY BROTHERS).

The boys were raised on a small family farm in mountainous western North Carolina. They learned their repertoire of traditional songs from family members, GOSPEL hymns from the local church and mail-order hymnals, and sentimental songs from the recordings of 1920s country artists like KARL AND HARTY, RILEY PUCKETT, and BRADLEY KINCAID.

Their major period of recording and performing was the late 1930s, beginning with a radio slot out of Asheville, North Carolina, in 1935, along with fiddler Homer Sherrill, as The Good Coffee Boys (after their sponsor, JFG coffee), followed by a stint in Atlanta as The Blue Ridge Entertainers. It is said that Victor scout Eli Oberstein gave the brothers their new name, The Blue Sky Boys, taking the "blue" from the Blue Ridge Mountains and "sky" from "Land of the Sky," a nickname for the region where the boys were born. The brothers recorded prolifically for Bluebird beginning in 1936, their close harmonies and slightly nasal voices

Bill (left) and Earl Bollick, c. 1950, The Blue Sky Boys. Photo: University of North Carolina, Southern Historical Collection, Southern Folklife Collection, University Archives

a trademark of their recordings. Although Bill played MANDOLIN, he was no hot picker, mostly limiting himself to a few fills between verses; Earl's GUITAR playing was equally sedate.

On their best songs their carefully worked-out harmony arrangements often made for breathtaking effects. On "The Sweetest Gift (a Mother's Smile)" the interplay on the chorus has each of the two voices echoing the other's part for a truly unique sound; a similar effect can be heard on their popular "Sunny Side of Life."

Although they lacked the overt blues influence of other duos, the Bolicks did have a lonesome, yearning sound that at least implied a blues style. Their classic "Short Life of Trouble" is perhaps the most plaintive recording in the country repertoire, and they managed to imbue such pure country bathos as "The Little Paper Boy" with deep feeling. Even on happy numbers like "Are You from Dixie?," their radio theme song, they managed to capture the "high, lonesome" mountain sound.

The brothers were more or less inactive in the 1950s, returned to recording in the early 1960s for Starday, and then retired again until the old-time music revival of the mid-1970s brought them back to the studio. Even though Starday added a fuller country band to the accompaniment, the sound and style of the Bolicks' music never really changed. The closest vocal style to the Bolicks' is that of The Everly Brothers, who in both tone and style sound remarkably like the earlier duo, although their choice of material obviously is far different.

Select Discography

On Radio, Vols. 1–4, Copper Creek 120–121, 146–147. 1946–1947 radio shows, including colorful skits and talk as well as songs.
Farm & Farm Time Favorites, 1–2, Copper Creek 125–126. Radio shows from 1949, without the patter.
In Concert, 1964, Rounder 11536. Live recording from their first reunion.

BOGGS, DOCK (b. Moran Lee B., Dooley, Va., February 7, 1898–February 7, 1971)

Boggs was a blues-influenced BANJO player and vocalist who recorded in the 1920s and was "rediscovered" during the FOLK REVIVAL of the 1960s by MIKE SEEGER.

Raised in a traditional mountain community, Boggs was part of a musical family that was particularly fond of the banjo. Boggs began playing the instrument at the age of twelve, the same year he was introduced to coal mining, work he would pursue for the next forty-one years. Originally he played in the traditional "frailing" or "clawhammer" style; however, he was impressed by the bluesy playing of a local black banjoist who picked the strings with two fingers and a thumb. This would become Boggs's mature style, perfectly suited to his repertoire of blues-flavored songs, including his adaptations of traditional songs like "Country Blues" and "Mean Mistreatin' Mama."

After his wedding in 1918 Boggs continued to play the banjo, despite the fact that his religious wife frowned on what she considered to be "the devil's music." His fame spread locally, and in 1927 he was approached by a scout from Brunswick Records to make some recordings. He recorded twenty-four songs in 1927–1928 but, discouraged by his wife's continued disapproval, he abandoned the banjo soon after, not picking it up again until his retirement from mining in the early 1950s.

In the early 1960s folklorist Mike Seeger came to the mountains, looking for some of the older recording artists. By this time Boggs was a legendary figure, thanks to his unusual recordings that were more blues-oriented than those of most other white pickers. However, no one knew if he was still alive or active until Seeger found him still living in Norton, Virginia, where he had made his original recordings. A series of albums of music and interviews followed, and Boggs was also soon performing at the Newport Folk Festival and on the folk-revival circuit.

Boggs was a unique musician for a number of reasons. His picking style was more modern than that of many mountain players of his generation, although not as advanced as Scruggs-style or BLUEGRASS picking. The intensity of his singing and his choice of material were unique in that he avoided almost entirely the dance music and upbeat songs usually associated with the banjo, preferring blues numbers that expressed the troubles he had experienced as a coal miner. Although some younger pickers emulated his style, Boggs's playing and singing remained his own, and he made no concessions to build a bigger audience. His music was like that of blues great Skip James, also rediscovered in the 1960s: difficult, thorny, and definitely an acquired taste.

Boggs's career was highlighted by culture/music critic Greil Marcus in his influential 1997 book, *Invisible Republic: Bob Dylan and the Basement Tapes*. Marcus singled him out as a unique American musician who embodied the heart and soul of the country sound. Thanks to this book his Folkways recordings were reissued on CD, as were his original 1928 recordings.

Select Discography

Country Blues: Complete Early Recordings 1927–29, Revenant 205. Beautifully packaged CD reissue of his classic recordings, with extensive booklet.

Folkways Years 1963–68, Smithsonian/Folkways 40108. Recordings made by Mike Seeger, originally issued on three separate Folkways albums, with complete annotation.

BOGGUSS, SUZY (b. Susan Kay B., Aledo, Ill., December 30, 1956)

Bogguss is a perky, well-scrubbed singer who got her big break singing at DOLLY PARTON's Dollywood theme park.

Bogguss seems to have stepped out of Norman Rockwell America; her father was a machinist and her mother a secretary, and in her teen years she passed through the rituals of scouting, cheerleading, and, yes, she was even homecoming queen in high school. She took up GUITAR and singing as a teenager, a hobby she carried with her to college, where she studied art. After graduation in 1978 Bogguss hit the road with some friends, performing informally throughout the Western states. She made an abortive trip to Nashville in 1981, then returned in 1984 to try to break into music making. Two years later she was the lead attraction at Dollywood; offstage she sold a cassette she had made herself that attracted the attention of Capitol Records, which signed her in 1987.

Bogguss's first hits were remakes, beginning with 1987's redo of the pop standard "I Don't Want to Set the World on Fire," followed by a rather tepid reading of PATSY MONTANA's classic "I Want to Be a Cowboy's Sweetheart." Her best-selling effort so far is her 1991 collection *Aces*, featuring the title hit along with covers of Ian Tyson's (of IAN AND SYLVIA fame) "Someday Soon" and NANCI GRIFFITH's "Outbound Plane." She also released a duet recording with LEE GREENWOOD, "Hopelessly Yours," a two-hanky WEEPER.

Bogguss is one of those eternally well-scrubbed singers you can't help but like, despite the fact that she has a thin voice and limited vocal capabilities. Listening to her 1992 rendition of JOHN HIATT's "Drive South" was a truly painful experience; she was able to reduce his gritty Southern-roots anthem into harmless cotton candy—a trick that, unfortunately, seems to be her forte as an artist. In 1994 she paired for a laid-back album with GUITAR legend CHET ATKINS, who admired her mainstream vocal style. Although she continued to record through the late 1990s, Bogguss could not repeat her chart success.

Select Discography

Aces, Liberty 95847. Her third, and still best, album.
Simpatico, Liberty 29606. 1994 duet album with Chet Atkins.
Country Classics, EMI 856038. Budget-priced hits compilation.

BOND, JOHNNY (b. Cyrus Whitfield B., Enville, Okla., June 1, 1915–June 22, 1978)

Author of over 500 songs, many of them country and COWBOY standards, Bond was a sidekick to singing cowboys GENE AUTRY and TEX RITTER in hundreds of horse operas on the big and small screens.

Raised on a number of small Oklahoma farms, Bond could remember listening to his parents' Victrola, and was particularly fond of "The Prisoner's Song" and "The Death of Floyd Collins," both tremendously popular recordings by urban country crooner VERNON DALHART. Bond was a member of his high-school brass band, where he learned the rudiments of music. He invested 98 cents in a Montgomery Ward ukulele, then quickly graduated to the GUITAR, and was playing locally during his high school years.

At age nineteen Bond made his radio debut out of Oklahoma City, and three years later he was hired by JIMMY WAKELY, who led a Western trio called The Bell Boys. Also in 1937 Bond made his first solo recordings for Columbia Records, including his classic cowboy ballad "Cimarron" and the country WEEPER "Divorce Me C.O.D." In 1940 Wakely's group was hired to back popular cowboy star Gene Autry on film and his *Melody Ranch* radio show, a relationship that lasted sixteen years. Meanwhile, in 1943 Bond hooked up with Tex Ritter, with whom he would star in numerous horse epics, tour, and form a music-publishing company, Vidor Publications.

In 1953 Bond and Ritter were hired to host the syndicated *Town Hall Party* TV show, which gave them national exposure for the next seven years, while Bond continued to work on TV and radio with Autry, SPADE COOLEY, and Wakely. He also began writing prolifically, adding to his catalog many country classics such as "I Wonder Where You Are Tonight," "Gone and Left Me Blues," and "Tomorrow Never Comes." In 1960 his "Hot Rod Lincoln" was a major rock-and-roll hit for him on Autry's Republic record label, and he had one further hit, 1965's tongue-in-cheek classic "Ten Little Bottles," issued by Starday.

In the 1970s he retired from active performing to focus on music publishing. He also wrote two books, a biography of Ritter and his own memoirs. In 2000 he was elected to the Country Music Hall of Fame.

Select Discography

That Wild, Wicked but Wonderful West, King 147. Reissue of 1961 album of cowpoke songs, his first for Starday and among his best.

Ten Little Bottles, Richmond 2155. Cassette-only reissue of Starday 333, from 1965, featuring the title hit.

Singing Cowboy Rides Again, CMH 8001. 1976 recordings with THE WILLIS BROTHERS featuring covers of hits by Gene Autry, ROY ROGERS, and other cowboy stars. Bond's singing is a little stiff, perhaps reflecting his advanced age. Reissued on CD in 1994.

BONNIE LOU (b. Mary Kath, Towanda, Ill., October 27, 1924)

Bonnie Lou, a minor hitmaker of the 1950s, is remembered for her powerful voice and cowgirl-styled YODELING.

Raised in rural Illinois, she credited her Swiss grandmother for her interest in yodeling, although she probably also heard a popular group, THE GIRLS OF THE GOLDEN WEST, who broadcast regularly on Chicago's WLS. After learning GUITAR and snagging a talent-contest ribbon, she began appearing on local radio, graduating to the big time, KMBC out of Kansas City, in 1942. She was given the name "Sally Carson" and added to the station's house band, The Rhythm Rangers.

In 1945 promoter Bill McCluskey of Cincinnati's WLW station heard a radio transcription of Kath/Sally Carson yodeling her heart out on "Freight Train Blues." He lured the singer to his station, but she had to leave the Carson name behind. Newly minted as "Bonnie Lou," she was given a prime spot on the *Midwestern Hayride* radio show and tours, paired with a backup band called The Trailblazers. Except for a brief stint in Bloomington, Indiana, in 1947, she remained in Cincinnati for the rest of her career.

The local King label, which specialized in country and R&B acts, signed her in 1953, and she quickly scored two hits, "Seven Lonely Nights" and, her best-known disc, "Tennessee Wig Walk." Her follow-up recordings did not see much chart action, but she remained a solid star on Cincinnati radio, continuing with *Midwestern Hayride* until the last bale of hay was broadcast in 1966.

Meanwhile, Bonnie Lou began singing in a more mainstream pop style on local television, and gaining exposure on a series of daytime talk shows, starting in the early 1960s. She continued to perform on TV until 1974, when she retired from show business to spend more time with her entrepreneur husband. She is not to be confused with the country singer who performs as part of the duo BONNIE LOU AND BUSTER.

Select Discography

Doin' the Tennessee Wig Walk, West Side 102. CD reissue of King recordings, including all her 1950s hits.

BONNIE LOU AND BUSTER (Bonnie Lou: b. Margaret Bell, Asheville, N.C., June 4, 1927; Buster: b. Hubert R. Moore, Bybee, Tenn., October 28, 1920)

This old-style husband-and-wife country duo are well established as leaders of *Smoky Mountain Hayride*, a tourist-oriented country radio show broadcast from Pigeon Forge, Tennessee.

Buster, so called because of his large size at birth ("He's a real Buster!" was a common description of a large baby), began playing MANDOLIN as a child in rural Tennessee. After completing high school he found work in a grocery store in Knoxville and also performed on local radio. He briefly played with BLUE-GRASS pioneer CARL STORY in the mid-1940s out of Asheville, N.C. The brother-and-sister act of Lloyd and Margaret Bell was also a favorite on Asheville radio; Margaret would soon become Buster's wife.

After serving in the Army, Buster briefly returned to Asheville to work again for Story before forming his own band and moving back to Knoxville. His wife began appearing with the group, and was so popular that she was quickly made a permanent member and given the stage name Bonnie Lou. They continued to work at various radio stations in Tennessee and the Carolinas before returning to Knoxville in 1948, when they cut their first records.

The couple had a hard time keeping their act going in the 1950s. Their musical style was by then very old-fashioned, and they could find employment only in the small radio town of Johnson City, Tennessee, where they remained through the early 1960s. A break came in 1963 when radio station owner/promoter Jim Walter hired them to play on his syndicated TV show, *The Jim Walter Jubilee*, which ran for years in many small markets. They also began performing GOSPEL music in the early 1960s, and it has remained an important part of their act and recorded repertoire.

In 1972 they helped establish *Smoky Mountain Hayride*, based in Pigeon Forge, Tennessee. This "old-style" radio show was purposely formed to appeal to tourists who wanted to relive the world of country radio in the 1930s and 1940s. Bonnie Lou and Buster were perfect ambassadors for this style, combining her sweet voice and a repertoire of sentimental and old-style songs with country comedy and onstage antics. They have released a number of records on various small labels, mostly sold at their own shows.

BOONE, DEBBIE (b. Deborah Ann B., Hackensack, N.J., September 22, 1956)

Sure, go ahead and laugh. But face it, this clean-scrubbed diva was one of the biggest country and pop stars of the late 1970s and early 1980s, showing once again that, in America, anyone can be famous (even if it is only for fifteen minutes).

The daughter of Pat "Isn't That a Shame" Boone, Debbie comes by her musical "talents" naturally; her grandfather was legendary country showman RED FOLEY, which just adds to her musical pedigree. Pat ripped off some of the greatest rock songs of the late 1950s and sanitized them for white-bread America before becoming a born-again Bible-thumper. Young Debbie followed in Dad's footsteps, first shooting up the charts in 1977 with "You Light Up My Life," which at least isn't as grotesque as KENNY ROGERS's later variation on the theme, "You Decorated My Life." She had a couple more country hits, including the #1 1980 ode "Are You on the Road to Lovin' Me Again" (ironically, written and produced by the same team that created "You Decorated My Life"!) before she found Christ in 1982 and began cutting religious albums for the Word label. Since there is a God, we can thank him (or her) for taking both Debbie and Pat into the fold and pulling them (mercifully) off commercial radio.

Select Discography

The Best of, Curb/CEMA 77258. All the hits (that you can stand) in one place at a low, low price . . .

BOWEN, JIMMY (b. James Albert B., Santa Rita, N.Mex., November 30, 1937)

Onetime ROCKABILLY star Bowen has become one of Nashville's most successful producers, molding the career of REBA MCENTIRE and discovering and shaping GARTH BROOKS.

Bowen started out as a musician, working with famed guitarist Buddy Knox in a group known as The Rhythm Orchids, which they formed in 1955, while still in college at West Texas State. They made some recordings for Norman Petty (the same fellow who recorded and produced BUDDY HOLLY) that were leased to Roulette in 1957. The pair had a two-sided hit: "Party Doll," credited to Knox, and "I'm Stickin' with You," credited to Bowen. Bass-playing Bowen was only a marginal singer, however, and after he recorded one album for Roulette, his career as a performer ended.

By the mid-1960s Bowen had relocated to Los Angeles, where he became a house producer for Reprise Records, then owned by crooner Frank Sinatra. He produced big hits for the label, including Dean Martin's mellow classic "Everybody Loves Somebody Sometime." Following this work he ended up at MGM in the mid-1970s, but by the time that label fizzled out, he was tiring of the fast-paced Los Angeles lifestyle. He moved to Nashville in 1977, and a year later was running MCA's country division. He went from there to Elektra, where he shaped the career of EDDIE RABBITT and the resurgence of HANK WILLIAMS, JR.

In 1984 he was persuaded by music whiz kid Irving Azoff to return to MCA. He played a central role in molding Reba McEntire into the glitzy, and more mainstream, act that she became. In the early 1990s he moved to Capitol Records, which had few, if any, country performers. He immediately discovered and nurtured Garth Brooks, building him into a megastar who topped both pop and country charts.

Bowen's background in country, rockabilly, mainstream pop, and rock shows the diverging styles that have come to be called today's "new country." His talent for identifying new stars and for carefully grooming and marketing them reveals that country is, just like pop, a megadollar business, one that depends as much on shrewd marketing and packaging as it does on musical ability.

BOXCAR WILLIE (b. Lecil Travis Martin, Sterrett, Tex., September 1, 1931–April 12, 1999)

Boxcar Willie was a pseudo hobo who was, frankly, not much of a musician. However, he made a reputation, first in England and Europe and then in the U.S., mainly off of his carefully crafted stage character.

Although his father was a railroad worker (and a part-time fiddler), Willie never rode the rails, despite his colorful name. He had a number of professions while pursuing his love of music, ranging from deejay to mechanic to refrigeration engineer and flight engineer. In the mid-1970s he decided to scrap it all for the life of an entertainer, relocating from his native Texas to Nashville and taking on his hobo persona. Scottish agent Drew Taylor caught him performing at a local club, and arranged for several English tours; the locals were wowed by his repertoire of train sound effects. In 1979 he returned triumphantly to the U.S., premiering on THE GRAND OLE OPRY and receiving a standing ovation for his kitschy act. He had a minor hit in 1980 with "Train Medley." He followed this with a number of half-sung, half-spoken novelty numbers, including 1982's European hit "Bad News," which charted on the lower ends of the U.S. country charts. He also was a regular performer on the syndicated version of *Hee Haw* in the early 1980s.

Willie established himself as a prime draw at the new country capital of BRANSON, MISSOURI, in the 1980s. He often performed six shows a day at his own theater, which was one of the first and most successful in town. When he died of leukemia at his Branson home in 1999, flags were flown at half-staff throughout the town.

Willie's act was a combination of hokey renditions of hoary old chestnuts and "stories" of his life as a "rambling hobo." He always appeared in a calculated costume including a floppy hat, ratty overalls, and a smudged face. As such he represented the ultimate triumph of image over substance, and for those who prefer to enjoy the myth of country life (rather than its reality), Willie certainly filled the bill.

Select Discography

King of the Freight Train, MCA 20544. 1992 album, with guest WILLIE NELSON on vocals.

BOYD, BILL (b. William Lemuel B., near Ladonia, Tex., September 28, 1910–December 7, 1977)

Boyd was a WESTERN SWING pioneer who led The Cowboy Ramblers along with his brothers. Boyd's music focused on bluesy and novelty numbers, often with a COWBOY theme. He later appeared in many Hollywood-produced, B-grade horse operas, and ended his career in the 1960s as a country deejay.

Boyd was one of thirteen children born to Lemuel and Molly Jared Boyd, both originally from Tennessee. The family migrated to Texas around 1902, settling on a large ranch. There the young Boyds were exposed to hard work and music; both parents were singers and many of the ranch hands played music in the evening. Bill got his first GUITAR through a mail-order catalog, and was soon performing with his younger brother Jim (September 28, 1914–March 11, 1993). When the Depression hit Texas, the family relocated to Dallas, where Bill began working odd jobs ranging from laborer to salesman while pursuing music on the side. Brother Jim enrolled in Technical High School, where he met Art (b. Audrey) Davis, a talented musician who played clarinet, FIDDLE, and MANDOLIN, and would become a key member of The Cowboy Ramblers.

While Jim and Art were getting their act together, Bill got his first radio job as a member of a trio known as The Alexanders Daybreakers, for a local early-morning show. By 1932 The Daybreakers had become The Cowboy Ramblers and moved to station WRR, and the brothers were reunited. They were signed by the Victor budget label, Bluebird, in 1934, and would continue to perform together for nearly twenty years.

Through the 1930s the Boyds made classic Western Swing recordings for Bluebird, including blues like "Fan It" and "I've Got Those Oklahoma Blues," instrumentals like "Beaumont Rag" and "New Steel Guitar Rag" (picking up on the popularity of BOB WILLS's recording of "Steel Guitar Rag"), and novelties like the silly "Wah Hoo," complete with animal sound effects. Their recording of "Under the Double Eagle" remained in print for more than twenty-five years, making it one of the best-loved of all Western Swing recordings. They also recorded the obligatory cowboy numbers, including "The Strawberry Roan" and "The Windswept Desert." The band was a small, tight unit focusing on Davis's fine swinging fiddle and the brothers on guitar and bass, along with piano, tenor banjo, and, on later recordings, accordion and steel guitar. Younger brother John played steel guitar on several of their later recordings, and also formed his own band,

The Southerners, in the late 1930s. He continued to perform until his death in 1942.

During the 1940s the two brothers relocated to Hollywood, following in the footsteps of other swing bands who found lucrative work in southern California. They also appeared in a number of the inane, comic-book Westerns that small Hollywood studios produced by the bushel during this period. In the late 1940s and early 1950s Jim formed his own band, The Men of the West, to cash in on the cowboy craze.

In the 1950s live music on the radio was gradually edged out by records, and the two brothers switched to working as deejays. Bill retired in the early 1970s, and his brother Jim was still working part-time as late as 1975.

Select Discography

Bill Boyd and His Cowboy Ramblers, RCA/Bluebird 5503. Mid-1970s two-LP reissue of classic sides, now out of print.

BR5-49 (1996–present: Gary Bennett [voc, gtr]; Chuck Mead [voc, gtr]; Don Herron [fdl, mndln, Dobro, lap steel gtr]; "Smilin' " Jay McDowell [b]; "Hank" Shaw Wilson [drms, voc])

A Nashville-based neo HONKY-TONK group who have garnered great press if few hits, the band was formed in 1996, taking their hip name from an obscure reference from *Hee Haw*. (BR5-49 was the phone number for comedian Junior Samples's fictional used-car dealership.) From their name to their retro honky-tonk garb, the group appealed to a young, cool set who were attuned to inside jokes and the back rooms of country music history, from GOSPEL and BLUEGRASS to 1950s ROCKABILLY. Even their choice of regular venue—Robert's Western World, a retailer of Western clothing located next to the historic Ryman Auditorium—was a clever choice. Their first EP, *Live from Robert's*, which they produced, was released in 1996 and garnered them attention primarily among Europeans, who are longtime fans of retro country. It was followed by a full album, also independently released.

Their garnering of buzz among Nashville's hippest audience led to a record deal for the young band with Arista, which rereleased their 1996 album. *Big Backyard Beat Show* followed in 1998, and the band toured extensively through the U.S. and Europe. But no hits were forthcoming, and Arista's Nashville label was dissolved in a corporate reorganization, leaving the band labelless for a while.

In 2001 the band returned, now christened BR549, with a third album released on Sony. With the loss of the hyphen came a more mainstream sound, and also more conventional garb. The band claimed that this did not signal a change for their longtime fan base, but it is obvious that both band and label are hoping for greater commercial success; Paul Worley, a New Nashville producer, came on board to handle the record. Whether this approach will simply alienate the old without gaining any new following is yet to be seen.

Select Discography

BR5-49, Arista 18818. Reissue of the band's first album.
Big Backyard Beat Show, Arista 18862.
This is BR549, Sony Nashville 85466. Oddly, despite the title, this 2001 album veers more in a new country direction and away from the band's original retro image.

BRADDOCK, BOBBY (b. Lakeland, Fla., August 5, 1940)

Braddock is a country songwriter most famous for cowriting TAMMY WYNETTE's tear-jerkin' hit "D-I-V-O-R-C-E," as well as for a sporadic solo career.

Born in Florida, Braddock began his career as a pianist working in local bars and clubs before moving to Nashville, where he gained work as a studio musician. He hooked up with MARTY ROBBINS in the early 1960s, writing "While You're Dancin'," a 1965 hit for him. He left Robbins soon after, signing with Tree Publishing, run by session musician/Music City mogul Buddy Killen.

Working with partners including Sonny Throckmorton and Curly Putman, he wrote numerous hits, including 1967's "Ruthless," recorded by THE STATLER BROTHERS; Wynette's 1968 hit "D-I-V-O-R-C-E"; "Golden Ring," a 1976 GEORGE JONES–Tammy Wynette duet; and Jones's 1980 solo hit, "He Stopped Loving Her Today." He also wrote early 1980s hits for T. G. SHEPPHARD, 1981's "I Feel Like Loving You Again" and a duet with KAREN BROOKS, "Faking Love." Most of these songs were in the classic HONKY-TONK, tears-in-my-beer style.

Braddock had a minor recording career, initially recording for MGM between 1967 and 1969 with the hits "I Know How to Do It" and "Girls in Country Music," but didn't return to wax until 1979, when he signed with Elektra, then moved briefly in the early 1980s to RCA. His style of country heart-draggers fell out of favor in the new-country era. Nonetheless, he scored big as a songwriter in 2002 with "Talk About Me" for Toby Keith.

BRADLEY, OWEN (b. Westmoreland, Tenn., October 21, 1915–January 7, 1998)

Along with CHET ATKINS, Bradley was the man most responsible for the growth of the NASHVILLE SOUND, moving country away from its roots toward bland, middle-of-the-road pop. As owner of the famous Bradley's Barn studio and house producer for Decca in the 1950s and 1960s, Bradley was responsible for some of country's biggest hits in this smoother, more commercial style.

Bradley began his career as a piano and GUITAR player in various pop pickup bands in and around Nashville. In 1947 he was selected to be the orchestra leader for radio station WSM, home of THE GRAND OLE OPRY. In that same year he was approached by Paul Cohen of Decca Records, who wanted to establish a presence in country music. Cohen agreed to guarantee Bradley a hundred sessions a year if he would build a studio meeting Decca's specifications. Bradley built three different studios between 1952 and 1955, the last being the most famous, a Quonset hut that was the first studio on Music Row. In 1962 Columbia Records purchased the studio when they opened their Nashville recording operation.

Although Bradley recorded everything from BILL MONROE's traditional BLUEGRASS to ERNEST TUBB's original HONKY-TONK sessions, he is most famous for his late 1950s and early 1960s recordings of crossover artists like BRENDA LEE and PATSY CLINE. Traditional instruments—like FIDDLES, GUITARS, and PEDAL STEEL GUITAR—were downplayed, if they were used at all on these sessions, replaced by tinkling pianos, soothing strings, and walls of backup singers (usually provided by the JORDANAIRES or the ANITA KERR Singers). In 1962 he was promoted to chief staff producer for MCA (now the parent company of Decca). Through the 1960s he was country's premier producer, toning down the rural roots of singers like CONWAY TWITTY and LORETTA LYNN and bathing their productions in mainstream-pop arrangements. After retiring in the early 1970s Bradley occasionally returned to the studio to work with acts ranging from Elvis Costello to K.D. LANG.

Although best known as a producer, Bradley also had a recording career with Decca from 1949 through the 1950s. He led an all-instrumental quintet that played everything from instrumental versions of country hits to pop-schlock. His biggest hits came with covers of rock numbers, particularly 1958's "Big Guitar"; he even produced two albums of rock covers in the late 1950s.

Bradley's younger brother Harold (b. Nashville, Tenn., January 2, 1926) worked as a guitarist on many of his brother's sessions, as well as in the WSM house band, before serving as musical director for the JIMMY DEAN TV show in the mid-1960s. In the 1980s he toured with SLIM WHITMAN, and more recently he has limited himself to working as a music publisher.

BRANSON, MISSOURI A formerly sleepy town that was best known for its natural springs, Branson has become a center for (mostly older) country and pop performers who have built lavish theaters there to present their music.

The Branson story is oft-told. This town of some 3,700 inhabitants, nestled in the foothills of the Ozarks, was first put on the map by Harold Bell Wright in his 1907 best-selling romance, *The Shepherd of the Hills*. Things heated up a little further when a minor-league theme park, Silver Dollar City, opened there in 1960, followed by a couple of music clubs, most notably Presley's Mountain Music Jubilee, said to be the first country-music attraction in town, which opened its doors in 1967.

In the old days country acts continued to perform for their core audience long after their hits dried up, primarily by hitting the road for a grueling round of one-nighters. Many wished they could stay put in one place and let their core audience come to them. ROY CLARK had often vacationed in the Branson area, and figured it would be as good a place as any to open a year-round music theater. He set up shop in 1983 and continues to offer one of the better music shows in the area. Soon Clark brought other older country stars to the area, including MEL TILLIS. Both had long been off the country charts, but they proved to be major draws in Branson. They opened their own palatial theaters, with architecture and floor shows reminiscent of the best (or worst, depending on your taste) of Las Vegas. A second wave of musical immigrants, such as Andy Williams and Wayne Newton, came from other mainstream musical genres and discovered that Branson was hospitable to their talents as well. The number of theaters multiplied, and the town's main drag became a glittering strip of marquees and neon.

A featured segment on *60 Minutes*, hosted by a bemused Morley Safer in 1989, cemented the town's growing reputation as middle America's country entertainment mecca. A highlight of Safer's report was his interview with Japanese violin virtuoso Shoji Tabuchi, who became one of the town's major attractions. Tabuchi didn't just play Mozart—from Mozart to Broadway tunes to high-speed BLUEGRASS standards—he put on a spectacular show, including lasers, smoke bombs, genies emerging from bottles, and magic carpets. Tabuchi's wife served as the show's genial emcee, and his teenage daughter entertained as a singer and dancer. Tabuchi's show was typical of the redneck-Vegas mix that made Branson such an enormous success; when WILLIE NELSON opened a theater there simply to play music, it was a financial failure.

Another Branson standout is The Baldknobbers, a rural hayseed comedy troupe reminiscent of the tradition of "kountry korn komedy" immortalized by TV's *Hee Haw*. The Baldknobbers had been performing in Branson long before the town ascended to its legendary status. And, of course, their show featured leggy chorus girls along with the backwoods rubes, to appeal to everyone in the family.

Branson stands apart from such prepackaged amusement attractions as Dollywood (the theme park built by DOLLY PARTON in rural Tennessee) and even Nashville's Opryland USA, in that it was a real town and simply grew like Topsy. As such, it gives strong testimony to the dedication of country music's core audience, and it has continued to prosper even with the decline of new country since the later 1990s. Branson has become America's second favorite vacation destination off the interstates. Don't be surprised when the GARTH BROOKS and New Kids on the Block pavilions open there in the year 2015!

BRITT, ELTON (b. James E. Baker, Zack, Ark., June 27, 1913–June 23, 1972)

An amazing YODELER, Britt was a singing COWBOY who appeared in B movies and on early TV as well as working as a radio and recording artist.

Baker/Britt, the son of a champion fiddler/small-time farmer, learned to play GUITAR on a $5.00 Sears-Roebuck model. At age fourteen he was discovered after playing in a local amateur show, and was hired to perform on radio station KMPC out of Los Angeles, fronting the pseudo-country band The BEVERLY HILL BILLIES, and given his stage name. He began recording almost immediately with this group and as a soloist. In 1937 he broke with the band to sign a contract with RCA that would last for over twenty years.

Britt's best recordings, from the late 1930s through the late 1940s, were made primarily in New York. RCA had yet to establish a studio in Nashville, so it was not unusual for the country star to record in the Northern music capital. Many of his recordings feature some of the city's finest sidemen, including pop/jazz instrumentalists, which gives them an unusual quality for country sides of the era.

Britt's 1942 patriotic ballad, "There's a Star-Spangled Banner Waving Somewhere," was the first country recording to be awarded a gold record, although it took two years to achieve this feat. (Previously, PATSY MONTANA's "I Want to Be a Cowboy's Sweetheart" had sold a million copies in 1935, but this was before gold record awards were made.) This led to an invitation from President Franklin Roosevelt to perform at the White House. Other popular recordings include 1948's "Chime Bells," where Britt yodels up a storm, including a final high falsetto note that is held for a breathtakingly long time. He also recorded many duets with ROSALIE ALLEN, including 1949's "Quicksilver."

Britt's recording career continued through the 1950s, but was upstaged somewhat by his film and TV work. He retired from active performing from 1954 to 1968, then returned to perform occasionally during the last four years of his life.

Select Discography

Ridin' with Elton, Soundies 4121. CD reissue of late 1930s and early 1940s 78s.

BROOKS AND DUNN (Leon Eric "Kix" B., b. Shreveport, La., May 12, 1955 [lead gtr, voc]; and Ronnie Dunn, b. Tulsa, Okla., June 1, 1953 [gtr, voc])

Brooks and Dunn have been called country music's answer to Hall and Oates, and indeed there are many similarities between them: front man Ronnie Dunn is the looker of the two, sings most of the lead vocals, and writes much of their material, while lower-profile (and shorter) Kix Brooks romps across the stage in a modified Chuck Berry duckwalk, strumming his Stratocaster. And like Hall and Oates in the mid-1970s through early 1980s, these guys are a veritable hitmaking machine, churning out country anthems from the get-go.

Both were frustrated performers struggling to get their careers on track when a canny producer at Arista Records, SCOTT HENDRICKS, brought them together to form a duo. Brooks was a Louisiana-born SINGER/SONGWRITER who had spent some time working in Alaska on the pipeline before settling in Nashville to start a career as a successful songmaker. He had written a number of country hits, beginning with JOHN CONLEE's 1983 "I'm Only in It for Love," which he wrote with the team of Rafe van Hoy and his singing/songwriter wife, DEBORAH ALLEN; in 1988 Van Hoy produced Brooks's debut album for Capitol, which did nothing on the charts. Meanwhile Brooks continued to write with a variety of partners, including Dan Tyler (with whom he wrote "Modern Day Romance," a 1985

Kix Brooks and Ronnie Dunn enjoying yet more recognition at the CMA award show, 1998. Photo: Raeanne Rubenstein

hit for THE NITTY GRITTY DIRT BAND), while (unsuccessfully) pursuing a solo career.

Dunn came out of Oklahoma, a hotbed of country performers (home of GARTH BROOKS, REBA McENTIRE, and ALAN JACKSON, to mention a few). Originally pursuing a career as a Baptist minister, he was led astray by the local HONKY-TONKS where he performed on guitar. The lanky Westerner won a Marlboro Talent Contest in 1988 (he does resemble the Marlboro man); one of the contest's judges was Hendricks, who brought Dunn together with Brooks to write some songs for a solo album. The pair clicked, and they debuted with the mega dance hit, "Boot Scootin' Boogie," in 1990.

Through the mid-1990s the duo were rarely off the charts with nouveau honky-tonk anthems like "Brand New Man" and 1992's "Hard Working Man." They also dominated the award shows, winning Best Country Duo nods from nearly all sources. However, the hits dried up somewhat in the later 1990s as tastes changed, and it looked like Brooks and Dunn would never return to their top-of-the-charts glory. But in 2001 they came back strongly with "Ain't Nothin' 'Bout You," promoted with a sexy (for country, anyway) video.

Select Discography

Brand New Man, Arista 18658. 1991 debut album.
Greatest Hits, Arista 18852. Just like the title says: the major hits through the mid-1990s.
Steers and Stripes, Arista 67003. 2001 comeback album, a return to harder-edged material.

BROOKS, GARTH (b. Luba, Okla., February 7, 1963)

Brooks's phenomenal success in the early 1990s was a combination of genuine talent, shrewd marketing, and being "in the right place at the right time (with the right act)." His new-country act draws so much on mid-1970s folk-rock and even arena-rock (in its staging) that it's hard to think of him as a pure country artist. The fact that his early '90s albums shot to the top of the pop charts, outgunning Michael Jackson, Guns 'n' Roses, and Bruce Springsteen, underscores the fact that Brooks is a pop artist dressed in a cowboy hat. Still, Brooks draws on genuine country traditions, particularly the HONKY-TONK sound of GEORGE JONES, and he's managed to popularize country music without diluting the sound.

Brooks's mother, Coleen, was a small-time country singer who worked sporadically on recordings and radio in their native Oklahoma. Brooks grew up interested in sports, playing football, basketball, and track in high school, and entering Oklahoma State on a track-and-field scholarship, with a specialty in javelin throw-

ing. His GUITAR-playing career began in high school and continued in college, where he worked area clubs, performing a mix of James Taylor folk-pop and country. He made his first trip to Nashville in 1985, without success, and returned home with his college-sweetheart wife, Sandy Mahl. Back in Nashville in 1987, Brooks attracted the attention of Capitol Records and producer Allen Reynolds.

His first album was successful, but the follow-up, *No Fences*, really began Garthmania. It sold 700,000 copies in its first ten days of release, and stayed on the pop charts for over a year. His third album, *Ropin' the Wind*, entered the pop charts in the #1 position, the first country album ever to do so. Brooks's hit singles from these albums combined country bathos ("If Tomorrow Never Comes," a ten-hanky WEEPER about a husband's realization of the value of his marriage), with neo honky-tonk ("Friends in Low Places," a cleverly humorous song with its tip-of-the-hat bass vocals recalling GEORGE JONES), and even the feminist "The Thunder Rolls," a story of a cheating husband (whose message is made graphic in a video that ruffled quite a few conservative Nashville feathers with its depiction of a physically abusive husband).

Brooks's performing style captured the attention of the major media. Learning a lesson from the arena-rock stars of his youth, Brooks built a special set featuring large ramps enclosing the band (enabling him to dramatically charge up and down around his backup musicians), and even installed a rope so he could swing out over the audience—shades of Ozzy Osbourne-like theatrics! With his portable mike neatly hooked to his ten-gallon hat, Brooks is one of the most mobile and energetic of all country performers, although recently he has descended to such schmaltzy tactics as waving and winking at the audience, and blowing air kisses at his fans.

Brooks's 1992 album, *The Chase*, reflects a further nudging toward mainstream pop, particularly in the anthemic single "We Shall Be Free," whose vaguely liberal politics sent shivers of despair through the conservative Nashville musical community. Less successful than his previous releases (although still selling several million copies), it was followed by 1993's *In Pieces*, featuring a safer selection of high-energy honky-tonk numbers and even the odd "American Honky-Tonk Bar Association," in which Brooks beats up on welfare recipients, a shameless attempt to cater to country's traditionally conservative audience.

Brooks's career sagged in the mid-1990s as he pursued a lifelong ambition to be the first artist to sell more records than The Beatles. This led to a series of shameless repackagings of earlier work while he fought with his label over what he felt was a lack of commitment to promoting his songs. He held up the release of his 1997 album, *Sevens*, until Capitol changed its country management to restore his lack of faith in their marketing efforts. The album, returning him to his earlier country sound, was a major success. Then, in 1999, Brooks decided to appear in a film portraying a 1970s pop SINGER/SONGWRITER named Chris Gaines. He decided to record an album of "greatest hits" by his alter ego, with rock producer Don Was at the controls. The result was a major career fiasco; despite a TV special and heavy promotion, the album was a major flop, and Brooks's fan base was greatly confused. The film never appeared (although during his comeback in the fall of 2001, rumors were spread that it might be salvaged and eventually released). Brooks withdrew from the public eye in 2000, amid announcements that his longtime storybook marriage was coming to an end.

Never one to give up easily, Brooks came roaring back with his album *Scarecrow* in the autumn of 2001. Announced as his "last" album, it returned him to the sound and style of his earlier country outings, and the fans responded by making it a major hit. To promote the album Brooks undertook his "Coast-to-Coast" tour, including three dates that were broadcast live on CBS. As of early 2002 the album had already topped 4 million in sales, propelled by its first single, "Wrapped Up in You." Despite his assurances that this would be his "last" album, Brooks was already hinting in press conferences that an album of outtakes might be forthcoming, and the possibility of new recording certainly exists. For an artist as competitive as Brooks, it is highly unlikely that he will retire quietly.

Select Discography

Garth Brooks, Liberty 90897. Debut LP from 1989.
No Fences, Liberty 93866. The big kahuna that put Garth on the charts.
Ropin' the Wind, Liberty 96330.
The Chase, Liberty 98743. Garth as soulful singer/songwriter.
In Pieces, Liberty 80857. A return to Garth form and another megaseller.
Sevens, Capitol 56599. Not as strong as his earlier outings, but an attempt to return to his country roots.
Chris Gaines: Greatest Hits, Capitol 20051. The "big hits" of the mythical 1970s singer/songwriter, featuring a bewigged Garth singing a mushy collection of pop ballads.

BROOKS, KAREN (b. Dallas, Tex., April 29, 1954)
A talented SINGER/SONGWRITER, Brooks enjoyed minor chart success in the mid-1980s, but never has had the following that she really deserves.

With a voice midway between EMMYLOU HARRIS and ROSANNE CASH, Brooks has had a strong following among other country performers. A graduate of the Texas/alternative school of country songwriting, Brooks cut her teeth in the Austin, Texas, country-folk scene that also nurtured JERRY JEFF WALKER, TOWNES VAN ZANDT, and Gary P. Nunn, a producer/performer who was briefly her husband. RODNEY CROWELL heard her performing in Austin and hired her as a backup vocalist for his band in the late 1970s.

She left Texas for a farm outside of Nashville in 1981, and was signed to a contract with Warner Brothers a year later. She had a minor hit with "New Way Out," her first single, followed by more solid success with 1983's "If That's What You're Thinking" and "Walk On," and 1984's "Born to Love You" and "Tonight I'm Here with Someone Else." A year later she cut a duet with JOHNNY CASH on "I Will Dance with You," but after that the hits pretty much dried up. Soulmates Harris and Rosanne Cash had hits with her compositions "Tennessee Rose" and "Couldn't Do Nothing Right," respectively.

Brooks retired to raise quarter horses and cattle on her Tennessee farm, although she returned to the recording studio to make a duet LP with Randy Sharp in 1992.

Select Discography

That's Another Story, Mercury 512232. Duet LP with Randy Sharp.

BROWN, "JUNIOR" (b. Jamieson B., Cottonwood, Ariz., June 12, 1952)
"Junior" Brown, a deep-voiced retro guitar twanger, reintroduced into 1990s country-pop the sounds of 1950s HONKY-TONK, with a dash of surf-era twangy GUITAR, to make his own unique stylistic and musical statement. Although some might discount him as purely a "retro" act, Brown manages to give his music a contemporary, often tongue-in-cheek twist. He also designed the Guit-Steel, a twin-necked guitar that combines the tonal qualities of both conventional electric and steel guitars. Guitar maker Michael Stevens made the first Guit-Steel to Brown's specifications in 1985.

Brown's unique style owes much to his eclectic upbringing. The son of a pianist, he took up guitar early in life, and counts among his influences everything from country to Jimi Hendrix. Although born in Arizona, he was raised primarily in rural Indiana. After a stint playing clubs in the Albuquerque, New Mexico, area in the mid-1970s, he settled in Austin, Texas, in 1979, just as alt-country was beginning to develop. He worked as a guitarist in several local bands, and then taught guitar and pedal steel guitar at Rodgers State College in Oklahoma in the mid-1980s. There he met guitarist-vocalist Tanya Rae, whom he wed in 1988, and the duo were off and running. Brown himself released his first album, *12 Shades of Brown*, which was

Junior Brown, 1995. Photo: Raeanne Rubenstein

licensed by a British label, Demon Records, in 1990. Two years later he made a stunning and well-received debut at Austin's South-by-Southwest conference, and was signed by Curb Records.

In 1993 Curb reissued Brown's debut album and also issued *Guit with It*. It featured a remake of Red Simpson's 1950s road epic, "Highway Patrol," which—in a remixed version and repromoted with a humorous video—became a chart hit in 1995. Another minor hit was the humorous "My Wife Thinks You're Dead," also promoted with a clever video (it won an Academy of Country Music award for best country video of 1995). The loping country beat of the tune perfectly suits the somewhat tongue-in-cheek lyrics. He followed with his third album, *Semi Crazy*, in 1996, but it did not produce any further hits. On it Brown paid homage to twangy surf guitarists like the legendary Duane Eddy with his own "Surf Medley."

Besides his traditional-sounding baritone vocals, Brown is a very talented guitarist. He mixes into his lead guitar work traditional country licks along with references to Jimi Hendrix and acid rock. His steel work is more traditional-sounding, and his Guit-Steel hybrid guitar allows him to move effortlessly between twangy lead work and sliding steel licks.

Brown issued *Long Walk Back* and *Mixed Bag* in 1998 and 2001, respectively, both featuring a more eclectic mix of music. *Long Walk Back* included two tracks with Hendrix drummer Mitch Mitchell. However, it failed to win any new fans for him. Nonetheless, Brown continued to write and perform. He has suffered a fate somewhat similar to Dwight Yoakam: once categorized as a retro hillbilly act, he has had a hard time breaking out of the mold. Meanwhile, the twangy sound, once a novelty for him, has grown a little tiresome while others on the mainstream country charts have managed to stretch the rockabilly genre more successfully. Nonetheless, underneath the Bryllcream, Brown is a talented performer who should not be dismissed as a mere novelty.

Select Discography

Guit with It, Curb 77622. 1993 major-label debut, with many of his best-known songs.
Long Walk Back, Curb 77897.
Mixed Bag, Curb 78719. 2001 release that offers an eclectic mix of honky-tonk, rock, and country.

BROWN, MILTON (b. Stephensville, Tex., September 8, 1903–April 18, 1936)

One of the fathers of WESTERN SWING, Brown was a vocalist who combined jazz-styled phrasings with the popular manner of a crooner.

Brown began his career as a cohort of BOB WILLS, in 1931 forming a band known originally as The Aladin Laddies, which became the famous Forth Worth Doughboys (later LIGHT CRUST DOUGHBOYS) in 1932. Brown soon struck out on his own, as did Wills. From 1934 until his death he led one of the first and hottest bands in Western Swing, The Musical Brownies, who were far more hard-edged than Wills's band at the time. The band featured a swinging fiddler (originally Cecil Brower, who was replaced in 1936 by Cliff Bruner); a jazz-styled pianist, Fred Calhoun; and legendary steel guitarist BOB DUNN, whose rapid-fire, staccato bursts of sound were unequaled at the time. Dunn is said to have been the first player to use an electric instrument on a country recording, and certainly his unique playing style made the instrument stand out. The group further capitalized on this novelty by doubling the fiddle lead with the steel guitar, an effect that was often imitated on other Western Swing and later country recordings.

The band's repertoire was heavy on blues, jazz, and pop standards, with the occasional country number thrown in. They avoided ballads, perhaps because they worked primarily as a dance band, and probably also because Brown's vocal style, a combination of Cab Calloway-styled jive and Bing Crosby-styled smooch, was ill-suited to slower numbers. After Brown died in a car accident, his brother, guitarist Durwood, managed to keep the band going for a few years, but most of the key members soon defected to join other outfits or to lead their own ensembles.

BROWN, T. GRAHAM (b. Anthony G. B., Arabi, Ga., October 30, 1954)

Motown-influenced hitmaker of the mid-1980s, Brown brought a younger audience to country in the days before GARTH BROOKS.

Brown formed his group, playfully called Rack of Spam, when he was still at the University of Georgia, originally as a soul-flavored R&B outfit. They were also strongly influenced by the soft pop-rock of THE EAGLES, spiritual granddaddies of most of today's new-country artists. After coming to Nashville in 1982, Brown was soon in demand for cutting jingles (when he became a star, he continued to perform the Taco Bell theme in concert) as well as country-flavored demos. He signed with Capitol in 1984, first charting in 1985 with his own "I Tell It Like It Used to Be," which he describes as a cross between GEORGE JONES and Otis Redding. His first #1 was "Hell and High Water" (1986), written with Alex Harvey, a top Nashville tunesmith famous for writing early 1970s COUNTRYPOLITAN hits like "Delta Dawn." Brown followed up with two other #1 songs, "Don't Go to Strangers" and "Darlene," and a remake of Redding's "(Sittin' on the) Dock of the Bay." He also enjoyed a movie career as a character actor in Hollywood.

Brown's career was sidetracked by his increased dependence on alcohol. In the early 1990s, he attempted a comeback after drying out. He continued to record and perform through the 1990s, without much commercial success (at least not on the level of his original chart days). In 2001 he issued an album, *Lives!* (perhaps for those fans who might think that he had disappeared off the planet), on a small label.

Select Discography

Super Hits, Columbia/Sony 67134. Budget-priced compilation of his best-known songs.

BROWN, TONY (b. Greensboro, N.C., December 11, 1946)

Brown was one of the most influential recording executives in 1980s–1990s Nashville. He was raised in the GOSPEL tradition; his family had their own non-denominational group that performed spiritual songs at churches throughout the South. He began playing piano on stage as a teenager, and after completing high school went "professional" when he joined The Stamps Gospel Quartet. Next he worked with THE OAK RIDGE BOYS when they were still performing gospel material, and then joined Voice, which became the official backup vocal group for none other than ELVIS PRESLEY. Brown eventually became Presley's pianist, accompanying him during his last, King-sized years, from 1975 to 1977. After Presley's death he worked briefly with EMMYLOU HARRIS's Hot Band.

In 1978 Brown took his first job as a record producer. Two years later he joined RCA's Nashville offices. His first signing was the country-harmony group ALABAMA, who became one of the biggest hitmakers of the early 1980s. Brown went back on the road briefly with RODNEY CROWELL and Crowell's wife, ROSANNE CASH, before returning to RCA in 1983. His next signing would be one of country's all-time biggest hitmakers, vocalist VINCE GILL (another ex-Crowell backing-band member). A year later MCA's president, an ex-musician named JIMMY BOWEN, lured Brown to that company. In 1988, when Bowen left MCA, Brown became the label's president.

Unlike many other industry executives, Brown has remained active, not only signing artists but also producing their recordings. He has also steered the careers of many artists, and created groups and duos by suggesting that they work together. In the mid-1980s he brought to MCA more progressive country figures, like STEVE EARLE and NANCI GRIFFITH, but in the 1990s he became associated with the country mainstream, signing such megastars as THE MAVERICKS, MARK CHESNUTT, and TRISHA YEARWOOD. He also continued to produce, working with old friend Gill and newcomer LYLE LOVETT. He helped launch the solo career of Wynonna Judd (of THE JUDDS), and revitalized the career of longtime hitmaker REBA MCENTIRE in the early 1990s. He also shaped the early careers of important new-country artists such as PATTY LOVELESS.

Brown's production style borrows heavily from Los Angeles COUNTRY-ROCK of the 1970s and 1980s; in the mid-1990s he even produced a country-homage album to the ultimate 1970s country rockers, THE EAGLES. Brown's production style is perfectly geared to mainstream pop radio; although with some more country-oriented artists he allows more traditional stylings to creep in, he generally uses a soft-rock backup for up-tempo numbers, and a high-sheen pop accompaniment for ballads.

Through the 1990s Brown held his position at MCA and consolidated his power. He was regularly listed as a Nashville power broker in annual surveys by the likes of *Entertainment Weekly* and *Billboard* magazine, and in 1996 was profiled in the *Los Angeles Times Magazine* in an article headlined "The King of Nashville."

BROWNS, THE (Ella Maxine, b. Samti, La., April 27, 1932; James Edward [Jim Ed], b. Sparkman, Ark., April 1, 1934; Bonnie, b. Sparkman, Ark., July 31, 1937)

The Browns were a popular 1950s country trio who performed a mix of light country and pop schmaltz (their big hit was a cover of Edith Piaf's "Les Trois Cloches"), and later jumped on the early 1960s FOLK-REVIVAL bandwagon. Their smooth harmonies and re-fined good looks made them natural crossover artists in the great NASHVILLE SOUND era; many of their re-cordings can hardly be distinguished from mainstream pop of the 1950s and 1960s.

The Browns were not dirt-poor country folks; their father operated a sawmill, and for a while Jim Ed stud-ied forestry with the idea that he would take over the family business. However, his sister Maxine was ambi-tious and longed for a career as an entertainer. The two had been singing together since junior high school, and began performing as a duo in the early 1950s on Little Rock radio station KLRA after winning a talent contest sponsored by the station. They eventually worked their way up to being featured on the larger KWKH's *Hayride*, also originating out of Little Rock. They made some early recordings for the local Abbott label in 1954–1955 that feature some nice country har-mony singing, including their own composition, "Looking Back to See," along with lots of country novelty songs. Their backup on these sessions included JIM REEVES on GUITAR (he would later encourage RCA to sign the group) and slip-note pianist FLOYD CRAMER.

In 1955 younger sister Bonnie joined the act, and the group toured as headliners with The *Ozark Jubilee*. Thanks to Reeves they got a contract with RCA, and the group had a hit with a cover of the LOUVIN BROTH-ERS' "I Take a Chance" in 1956. They were inactive on the recording scene for a few years while Jim Ed served in the Army (although another sibling, Norma, temporarily joined to help out with touring), but scored a big pop and country hit in 1959 on his return with the saccharine "The Three Bells," a cover of Edith Piaf's French-language "Les Trois Cloches."

Some more pop-country hits followed, as well as covers of traditional folk songs, such as 1961's "Groundhog," performed in the manner of the popular folk-revival groups of the day (such as The Kingston Trio and Peter, Paul, and Mary). In 1963 they were invited to join THE GRAND OLE OPRY, but internal dis-agreements in the group, sparked by the marriages of the two women, led to their career's end in 1967. Jim Ed had already recorded successfully as a soloist in 1965, and continued his solo career on RCA through the early 1980s, appearing regularly in the late 1960s at Lake Tahoe as a lounge singer. He also scored as a partner with HELEN CORNELIUS from 1976 to 1981. His first hit with Cornelius was the slightly racy "I Don't

Want to Have to Marry You," followed by other coun-try-pop heartache numbers (even a cover of Neil Dia-mond's three-hanky WEEPER "You Don't Bring Me Flowers"). Maxine made a successful solo single in 1968 ("Sugar Cane Country," issued by Chart), but soon retired from performing.

Select Discography

The Three Bells, Bear Family 15665. Eight CDs of their prime recordings, everything they did for RCA from the late 1950s through the late 1960s.
Rockin' Rollin' Browns, Bear Family 15104. Out-of-print LP reissue of cuts from 1957 through 1964; exactly why they called this collection of mushy pop-folk "rockin' rollin' " beats me.

BRUCE, ED (b. William Edwin B., Jr., Kaiser, Ark., December 29, 1939)

A SINGER/SONGWRITER with a long career, Bruce began with ROCKABILLY-filled 1950s recordings for Sun Records; became a country songwriter in the 1960s and 1970s (including the classic "Mama, Don't Let Your Babies Grow Up to Be Cowboys," a 1978 hit for WAYLON JENNINGS and WILLIE NELSON); and then scored his own #1 country hit with "You're the Best Break This Old Heart Ever Had" in 1982.

Arkansas-born Bruce made his first recordings in the then-popular rockabilly style for Sun Records in the late 1950s; he next recorded teen pop for Sceptre in the early 1960s. Moving to Nashville, he placed his first country hit on a duet with Charlie Louvin on 1965's "See the Big Man Cry." Thanks to his enterpris-ing wife/manager, Bruce picked up a good deal of work doing jingles, his down-home voice gracing ads for everything from burgers to coffee to military service. During the later 1960s he recorded for RCA, performing a mix of country and pop covers and origi-nals.

By the mid-1970s Bruce was recording country ma-terial for United Artists, including the first version of "Mama" (the song originally warned young girls against marrying guitar players, but then Bruce real-ized that "cowboys" was even better). He also penned "The Man that Turned My Mama On" and "Texas (When I Die)," both mid-1970s recordings by TANYA TUCKER. In the early 1980s he signed with MCA, scor-ing his sole #1 country hit in 1982. At the same time he enjoyed minor success portraying cowpokes on TV, including the short-run return of the classic *Maverick* program.

In the late 1980s the rockabilly revival brought re-newed interest in Bruce's first recordings; many of these listeners were unaware of his more mainstream country career. However, by the early 1990s Bruce was focusing his attention on trying to establish himself as a television actor; in 1997 he appeared (along with Levon Helm, RANDY TRAVIS, and TRAVIS TRITT) in the Steven Seagal action film *Fire Down Below*.

Select Discography

Puzzles, Bear Family 15830. All of Bruce's late 1960s RCA recordings, not as well known as his 1980s hits but perhaps his best recordings.

Best of, Varese 5566. CD reissue of earlier hits, originally issued on LP in 1982 (MCA 3142).

BRUMLEY, ALBERT E. (b. A. Edward B., Spiro, Okla., October 29, 1905–November 15, 1977)

A noted GOSPEL songwriter whose many compositions have become standards in the country repertoire, Brumley was trained by the best of the gospel songwriters from an early age. He attended many local singing schools and conventions on the Oklahoma/Arkansas border. But most important, as a teenager he enrolled at the Hartford (Arkansas) Music Institute, where he encountered, among others, Virgil O. Stamps, the founder of The Stamps Quartet and Stamps Publishing Company. The Institute served as a training ground for songwriters, and had its own affiliated publishing arm to take advantage of the school's output. After his marriage in 1931, Brumley settled in the small town of Powell, Missouri, in the rural Ozarks; that same year he wrote his first (and perhaps most famous) gospel classic, "I'll Fly Away" (recorded hundreds of times, and revived most recently in the 2000 film *O Brother, Where Art Thou?*).

Brumley eventually penned over 800 songs, many of them standards in the country and BLUEGRASS repertoires. Among his classics are "Rank Stranger to Me" (1942), which became one of the favorites in THE STANLEY BROTHERS' repertoire, and "Turn Your Radio On" (1938), revived in 1971 by JOHN HARTFORD on his groundbreaking "newgrass" album, Aereo-Plain. Other favorites include 1933's "Jesus, Hold My Hand," 1937's "There's a Little Pine Log Cabin," and 1939's "I've Found a Hiding Place." Brumley's songs were recorded by a wide range of gospel and country artists, including RED FOLEY, THE CHUCK WAGON GANG, and BILL MONROE.

Brumley also became a gospel publishing mogul with his Albert E. Brumley Music Company, which published gospel songbooks beginning in the 1930s. These books helped spread his songs throughout the South and West, and many artists used them as resources for their radio or record work. In the late 1940s Brumley purchased the Hartford Music Company, which owned the rights to his earliest songs. He continued to live in Powell, Missouri, until his death.

Brumley's children have all been active in the music business. His son Al, Jr., began his performing career

in HONKY-TONK music, working primarily in California. However, since the 1980s he has made a career out of performing his father's songs on the gospel circuit. Tom Brumley is perhaps the most famous of Albert's children; he played steel guitar with BUCK OWENS's Buckaroos in the mid-1960s and then cofounded one of the first COUNTRY-ROCK bands, The Stone Canyon Band, with singer RICK NELSON later that decade. Both Tom and Al are involved with *The Brumley Music Show*, which is staged in the family theater in BRANSON, MISSOURI, as are their children. Brumley's other children are active in the music-publishing business that he founded.

Brumley's songs mix gospel fervor with down-home, catchy melodies and simple-to-understand images. His songs are similar in spirit and style to the contemporary country music being produced at the time; this is probably one reason they enjoyed such great popularity. Thanks to his publishing and promotion, he became the best-known of his generation of gospel composers.

BRYANT, BOUDELEAUX AND FELICE (Bryant: b. Shellman, Ga., February 13, 1920–June 25, 1987; Felice: b. Matilda Genevieve Scaduto, Milwaukee, Wis., August 7, 1925)

The Bryants, the most famous of all country songwriting duos, penned hundreds of country classics, including the perennial BLUEGRASS favorite "Rocky Top," along with most of THE EVERLY BROTHERS' late 1950s hits.

Boudeleaux Bryant's first love was classical music; as a classical violinist he played for a year with the Atlanta Symphony before turning to jazz and leading a series of small combos. While touring the Midwest he met and befriended Felice Scaduto, an elevator attendant at Milwaukee's Shrader Hotel; the couple were married soon after World War II. At about the same time he joined HANK PENNY's band as a country-style fiddler, and he began writing country songs with his young wife.

Their first hit was "Country Boy," recorded by "LITTLE" JIMMY DICKENS in 1949, which led to a contract with FRED ROSE of the powerful Acuff-Rose Publishing Company. They produced hits for both pop crooners (Tony Bennett's "Have a Good Time") and mainstream country acts (CARL SMITH's "Hey Joe," later covered by Frankie Laine, and a number of hits for EDDY ARNOLD, including "I've Been Thinking" and "The Richest Man," both released in 1955).

Fred Rose's son Wesley introduced the Bryants to an up-and-coming country duo called The Everly Brothers in 1957, asking them to come up with some teen-styled hits for the pair. They quickly produced "Bye-Bye, Love," the Everlys' first hit, followed by

"Wake Up, Little Susie" in the same year; 1958's "All I Have to Do Is Dream," "Bird Dog," and "Problems"; and 1959's "Take a Message to Mary" and "Poor Jenny." Their success with the Everlys led to other teen popsters covering their material, including BUDDY HOLLY ("It's Raining in My Heart") and BOB LUMAN ("Let's Think About Living"). In these songs the Bryants combined classic country sentiments of love gone wrong with teen angst; even the nonhits, like The Everlys' "Love Hurts" (later covered by ROY ORBISON and GRAM PARSONS), have had a long shelf life because of this classic combination of teen-pop sentiments with good ol' country WEEPER feelings.

In the 1960s, with the growth of power and influence of the New York-based Brill Building songwriters, the Bryants returned to writing primarily for country performers, including SONNY JAMES's 1964 hit, "Baltimore," and ROY CLARK's 1973 hit, "Come Live with Me." They made their first recording, with the unusual title *Surfin' on a New Wave*, in 1979 on the tiny DB label.

BRYANT, JIMMY (b. Ivy James B., Moutlrie, Ga., March 5, 1925–September 22, 1980)

Bryant was one of the hottest country-jazz guitarists of the 1950s, often recording with steel guitarist SPEEDY WEST.

Originally a child prodigy fiddler, Bryant took up the guitar to amuse himself while recuperating from a wound he received in World War II. He settled in Los Angeles after the war, working in the vibrant country bar and club scene. Singer TEX WILLIAMS heard him perform, and invited him to session on his 1950 recording of "Wild Card." CLIFFIE STONE, the host of the influential Los Angeles *Hometown Jamboree* program, hired Bryant soon after to work in the show's backup band. It was there that he met the talented steel guitarist Speedy West, and the two were soon paired on instrumentals, earning the nickname "The Flaming Guitars." Bryant and West were signed by Capitol, for which they recorded many jazz-influenced instrumentals, including Bryant's original compositions with colorful names like "Frettin' Fingers" and "Stratosphere Boogie"; on "Jammin' with Jimmy," through the miracle of overdubbing, Bryant played a duet with himself on swinging FIDDLE and guitar! Additionally, the two worked on many 1950s West Coast country recordings for Capitol and smaller labels.

West left California in the late 1950s to work in Oklahoma, but Bryant continued to record as a soloist for the West Coast-based Imperial label. He also produced recordings by other country acts, and wrote the country standard "Only Daddy That'll Walk the Line." He died in 1980 of lung cancer.

BUFFALO GALS, THE (1974–1979: Susie Monick [bnj]; Carol Siegel [mdln]; Martha Trachtenberg [gtr, voc]; Sue Raines [fdl]; Nancy Josephson [b])

One of the first all-female revival BLUEGRASS bands, The Buffalo Gals spotlighted progressive banjoist Susie Monick (b. 1952), whose noodling instrumentals recalled the work of her contemporary, TONY TRISCHKA.

The band was formed when Monick, guitarist Debby Gabriel, and dulcimer player Carol Siegel were undergraduates together at Syracuse University. Siegel took up the MANDOLIN, and they formed an old-time/bluegrass trio. Gabriel decided to pursue a career as a painter, and was replaced by vocalist/guitarist Martha Trachtenberg and bassist Nancy Josephson. By 1974 fiddler Sue Raines was on board, and the quintet was playing bluegrass and folk festivals.

The band's notoriety came mostly from their all-female makeup: it was unusual for women to play bluegrass; women were rarely showcased as hot pickers, and the band members could certainly hold their own with any of the other progressive bluegrass bands of the day. By 1976 new members Lainie Lyle on mandolin and fiddler Kristin Wilkinson had replaced Raines and Siegel, and the band relocated to Nashville. At about the same time, Monick released a solo BANJO LP, *Melting Pots*, a mix of far-out instrumentals with Celtic-flavored and other experimental banjo sounds. The band went through more personnel changes before it finally folded in 1979.

During the 1990s Monick performed as a mandolin and button accordion player in State of the Heart, a country-folk ensemble led by Nashville songwriter Richard Dobson. In the later 1990s she began displaying her clay art, including many figures based on traditional musicians.

Another group by the same name, playing in a WESTERN SWING style, has performed on the popular radio show *A Prairie Home Companion*.

BUMGARNER, SAMANTHA (b. S. Biddix, Silva, N.C., c. 1878–December 24, 1960)

Bumgarner was an early country banjoist, fiddler, and vocalist who is best known for twelve recordings made in April 1924 along with guitarist Eva Davis for Okeh records, among the earliest old-time recordings. She was probably the first banjoist, male or female, to record in this style. In 1928 she appeared at the first Mountain Dance and Folk Festival, organized by another legendary banjoist, BASCOM LAMAR LUNSFORD, in Asheville, North Carolina, and continued to be a favorite at this festival for the next thirty-one years, until her death.

The daughter of an old-time fiddler, Bumgarner was a talented performer on both BANJO and FIDDLE who won numerous contests, an unusual feat for a woman at the time. She continued to perform through the 1950s, gaining regional fame as a performer of traditional banjo tunes and songs.

BURNETT AND RUTHERFORD (Burnett: b. Richard D. B., Elk Spring Valley, Ky., October 8, 1883–January 1977; Rutherford: b. Leonard R., Somerset, Ky., c. 1900–1954)

Burnett and Rutherford were an old-time BANJO-and-FIDDLE duo who were prolific and popular recording artists in the mid-to-late 1920s. Their style was somewhat smoother than some of the more backwoods units that recorded at the time, and their repertoire included sentimental and novelty songs along with the older traditional numbers.

Burnett was a talented musician who began playing the dulcimer, banjo, and fiddle at an early age. Both his father and grandfather were dedicated churchgoers, and Burnett remembered singing hymns from the age of four. He also picked up the traditional songs and tunes of the south-central Kentucky region where he was born. Burnett lost both parents by the time he was twelve, a fact he immortalized in his sentimental ballad "The Orphan Boy," which became one of his most popular numbers.

Burnett began working as an oil-field hand around 1901. Six years later, when returning from work one night, he was robbed and shot in the face; the bullet struck his optic nerve, blinding him. Unable to continue to work, he fell back on his musical skills, becoming a wandering performer. Around 1914 he approached a local family, the Rutherfords, to ask if their young son Leonard could serve as his companion and guide. The fourteen-year-old was already proficient on the fiddle, and would be a valuable addition to the street-corner act. The parents agreed, and the Burnett and Rutherford duo was born. Burnett took credit for teaching Rutherford music, and also for training him to play note-for-note along with his banjo. This made their performances much tighter and less "chaotic" than those of many other old-time performers of the day.

By the mid-1920s the duo was in great demand throughout the Kentucky-Tennessee-Virginia area. In 1926 they were performing in Virginia when a local store owner heard them and recommended them to Columbia Records. Their first recordings were made soon after, under the supervision of legendary A&R man FRANK WALKER, who oversaw many of Columbia's "hillbilly" records, including the classic sides made by THE SKILLET LICKERS. Burnett's expressive vocals and Rutherford's smooth fiddling made these records stand out, and they would often record again, first for Columbia and later, with the addition of guitarist Byrd Moore, for Gennett.

Burnett's older style of performing—including a good deal of clowning around on stage (he even worked up a vocal imitation of the sound of the Jew's harp to accompany his banjo playing)—irritated the younger, more serious Rutherford. By the late 1920s they were recording with other musicians, although they continued to perform together sporadically until Rutherford's death. The Depression effectively ended their recording careers, but they were still well-known street performers through the early 1950s. Later Burnett took up chair caning and retired from music.

Burnett and Rutherford's recordings were quite influential throughout the South. Rutherford's fiddling featured many blue notes, slides, and complicated syncopation that forecast the BLUEGRASS fiddle style of some twenty years later. Burnett's energetic banjo playing and singing (and his older-style fiddling, highlighted on recordings made without Rutherford) make their recordings some of the most memorable and enjoyable of the old-time style.

Select Discography

Complete Record Works, 1926–30, Document 8025. CD reissue of all of their 78 recordings, including some Burnett made on his own or with other partners.

BURNETTE, DORSEY (b. Memphis, Tenn., December 28, 1932–August 19, 1979)

Along with his famous brother Johnny, Burnette was one of the pioneers of ROCKABILLY before moving into a more mainstream country career as a songwriter.

The Burnette brothers were raised in a house full of country music, and Dorsey remembered traveling to Nashville with his dad to hear THE GRAND OLE OPRY. Both brothers took up musical instruments at an early age, and by their high-school years were playing in pickup bands of various types throughout the region. Uncertain if music could be a career, they both trained as electricians while still pursuing musical interests; they even traveled to New York in the early 1950s to appear on *Ted Mack's Amateur Hour*, taking first-place honors four times.

By 1954 they were working in Memphis at Crown Electric, which had previously employed another local musician, ELVIS PRESLEY; they befriended another Crown employee, guitarist Paul Burlison, and formed The Burnette Trio, playing for local dances and at bars and clubs. After Elvis hit it big, they recorded a couple of jazzed-up country tunes under the new name of The Rock 'n' Roll Trio for Coral Records, including a swinging version of THE DELMORE BROTHERS' "Blues, Stay Away from Me" and their most famous recording, "Train Kept a-Rollin'," later covered by The Yardbirds in the 1960s and Aerosmith in the 1970s.

Discouraged by their relative lack of success, the brothers relocated to the West Coast. Here they teamed up with young RICKY NELSON, providing him with a number of hits including "Waitin' in School" and "It's Late." Meanwhile they recorded both individually and as a duo, Dorsey having hits with "Hey, Little One" and "Tall Oak Tree" in the early 1960s, while Johnny had solo hits with the teenybopper numbers "You're Sixteen" and "Dreamin' " before dying in a boating accident in 1964.

Dorsey moved from label to label from the late 1960s through the time of his death, while also supplying hit songs for country performers like ROGER MILLER and GLEN CAMPBELL, and befriending COUNTRY-ROCKERS Delaney and Bonnie. He had a couple of minor hits in the country-WEEPER style, and also penned some GOSPEL standards, the best-known being "The Magnificent Sanctuary Band." His biggest hit was 1975's "Molly, I Ain't Getting Any Younger," released by the Melodyland division of Motown Records. In 1979, shortly after issuing "Here I Go Again" on Elektra/Asylum, Dorsey died of a heart attack. His sons Billy and Rocky have performed as rockabilly revivalists, and Billy briefly served as guitarist for Fleetwood Mac after Lindsey Buckingham jumped ship.

Select Discography

Great Shakin' Fever, Bear Family 15545. Compilation of twenty-five 1950s recordings.

BURTON, JAMES (b. Dubberly, La., August 21, 1939)

Burton is a highly influential session guitarist who has had a great impact on country, rock, and pop music in general. His sharp, staccato-picking, and bluesy stylings have made him one of the most loved and most copied of all guitarists. In a long career he has recorded with hundreds of artists, from RICK NELSON and ELVIS PRESLEY to GRAM PARSONS and EMMYLOU HARRIS.

Although originally strictly a country guitarist, Burton first made his mark in 1957's duet with Dale Hawkins on "Suzie Q"; he then signed on with BOB LUMAN, who was briefly recording in a teen-star style (he would later go country). Along with bassist James Kirkland, Burton was hired to accompany the young teen star Ricky Nelson, and played on most of his late 1950s and early 1960s hits, beginning with "Hello, Mary Lou."

In 1964 Burton returned to playing country, accompanying BUCK OWENS and MERLE HAGGARD on many of their classic Capitol recordings, helping to bring a rockabilly edge to the nascent BAKERSFIELD SOUND. In 1969 he was signed by Elvis to be his accompanist, and he remained with the King until his death. Meanwhile, he accompanied Gram Parsons on his two solo albums, and helped form Emmylou Harris's Hot Band following Parsons's death. Along the way he unfortunately made some solo recordings revealing that his personal taste runs to the worst kind of pop-schlock.

Burton's guitar of choice was the Fender Telecaster, and he helped popularize this instrument in both rock and country circles. He used the Telecaster's biting tone to emphasize his own propensity for cleanly played bursts of notes. He was one of the first electric guitarists to work consistently in country, and through his association with Parsons he was also one of the shaping voices of COUNTRY-ROCK.

BUSH, JOHNNY (b. John B. Shin, Houston, Tex., February 17, 1935)

A protégé and sometime accompanist of WILLIE NELSON, Bush had a series of late 1960s and early 1970s hits, primarily with Nelson's songs.

Born in Houston, Bush relocated to San Antonio when he was twenty-seven years old, getting a job performing at a local HONKY-TONK as a singer/guitarist. He switched to drums soon after, playing informally with Nelson before linking up with RAY PRICE, with whom he toured as a member of his backup group, The Cherokee Cowboys, for three years. He returned to working with Nelson in 1966, leading his backup group, The Record Men, and also signing as a singer on the local Stop label. He remained with the label for three years, producing hits with Nelson's "You Ought to Hear Me Cry" and "What a Way to Live" in 1967, followed by "Undo the Right" and "You Gave Me a Mountain" in 1968 and 1969, respectively. In 1972 he signed with RCA and had his biggest hit, a cover of Nelson's "Whiskey River."

However, Bush soon fell out of favor, eventually recording a few more hits for the smaller Starday/Gusto label, a Nashville-based BLUEGRASS-oriented outfit, including a minor 1977 hit with "You'll Never Leave Me Completely." By the late 1970s vocal-cord injuries made it difficult for Bush to speak, and he had to limit himself to performing for only short periods at a time. However, after a period of inactivity he came back full-voiced in 2000, issuing two new albums and showing that he was still able to rock the honky-tonk.

Select Discography

14 Greatest Hits, Power Play 6101. Budget-priced hits compilation.

Lost Highway Saloon, Texas 2001. The sixty-five-year-old singer returns for this 2000 collection of honky-tonk favorites.

BUTLER, CARL AND PEARL (Carl: b. C. Roberts B., Knoxville, Tenn., June 2, 1927–September 4, 1992; Pearl: b. P. Dee Jones, Nashville, Tenn., September 30, 1927–March 3, 1989)

The Butlers were a husband-and-wife team who produced a string of hits in classic country-harmony style in the mid-1960s.

Butler was originally a solo recording artist, first charting in the early 1960s with the HONKY-TONK throwbacks "Honky Tonkitis" (1961) and "Don't Let Me Cross Over" (1962). The second recording featured an uncredited Pearl on harmony vocals. After it hit it big, the duo followed up with a number of similar-sounding WEEPERS, from 1963's "Loving Arms" to 1969's "I Never Got Over You." Most of their recordings were made in typical mid-1960s Nashville style, burdened with schlocky strings and mainstream pop accompaniments that did little to enhance their basically down-home performances. In 1967 the duo appeared in the B-grade epic film *Second Fiddle to a Steel Guitar*. In the 1970s they pretty much retired from performing.

BYRD, JERRY (b. J. Lester B., Lima, Ohio, March 9, 1920)

Byrd was a pioneering Hawaiian-flavored steel guitarist who helped make the instrument a central part of country music in the 1950s.

As a youngster Byrd took up the lap steel guitar, influenced greatly by the Hawaiian style of playing. Although he worked professionally as a painter before enlisting in the Army, he also found time to be a musician on the side, often with The Pleasant Valley Boys. After his discharge from the service at the end of World War II, he joined ERNEST TUBB's Troubadours for two years, and was a regular member of RED FOLEY's band, before signing as a solo artist with Mercury in 1949.

Byrd's recordings became famous for their remarkably clean picking and high level of virtuosity, even though his material tended toward the crassly commercial. Whereas many players bubbled and burbled, Byrd managed to produce clean melodic lines, a warm romantic tone, and flawlessly executed phrases even when performing the kind of "shores-of-old-Waikiki" numbers that make grown folks weep! However, as the 1950s wore on and the newly introduced pedal steel guitar gained popularity in country music, Byrd refused to give up his simpler style and found it increasingly hard to find work. Eventually he retired to Hawaii, where he worked for a while in the mid-1960s as bandmaster for the Bobby Lord TV show. He became a champion of the traditional Hawaiian style of playing, and still occasionally records and performs.

BYRD, TRACY (b. Vidor, Tex., December 18, 1966)

Byrd, another hunk-in-a-hat hitmaker of the mid-1990s, comes from the small Texas town of Vidor, where he was raised on a diet of classic WESTERN SWING records by the likes of BOB WILLS. The nearest

big city was Beaumont, fifteen miles away, where Byrd made his "recording" debut at a local shopping mall, cutting his own version of "Your Cheatin' Heart" to a prerecorded accompaniment. The clerk operating the pay-to-record machine was impressed by Byrd's baritone, and immediately signed him to appear in a local amateur show he sponsored on a monthly basis. Byrd was soon working Beaumont clubs, where he met future country star MARK CHESNUTT; he even took Chesnutt's place at the popular Cutter's nightclub when Chesnutt left town for Nashville in 1990. Chesnutt recommended Byrd to his producer at MCA, hitmaker TONY BROWN, who signed Byrd in 1992.

Byrd's 1993 debut album was fairly successful, producing a #1 hit with the tears-in-my-beer ballad "Holdin' Heaven." But it was 1994's *No Ordinary Man* that launched him big time as a platinum-selling country hitmaker. It featured two novelty hits, "Watermelon Crawl" and "Lifestyles of the Not So Rich and Famous," that remain two of the songs most closely associated with Byrd. Byrd would repeat the formula of pseudo-Western Swing up-tempo numbers mixed with poppish country balladry on his follow-up albums through the 1990s, but his hitmaking slowed toward the decade's end.

In 2000 Byrd left MCA and signed with RCA Nashville. Boldly declaring his independence, he vowed to return to his earlier Western Swing style, feeling that MCA had diluted his personality, trying to make him just another hunky hitmaker. But like many other successful 1990s acts, Byrd is having trouble establishing himself long-term, at least as a chart-topping artist. Like many country acts he will maintain a loyal audience, and could probably make a good living touring the country circuit. But having smelled the big bucks of chart success, a life of lesser honky-tonking may not appeal to him.

Unlike many other country stars, Byrd has resisted the siren call of living in Nashville. He remains in Beaumont, where he has become somewhat of a local booster. He sponsors an annual homecoming weekend, which features an all-star concert, and trout-fishing and golf tournaments. An avid outdoorsman, Byrd hosted a long-running TNN program on the joys of fishing and hunting.

Select Discography

Keepers: Greatest Hits, MCA 70048. His 1990s hits.

BYRDS, THE (1964–1973: original lineup, Roger [Jim] McGuinn [gtr, 12-string gtr, voc]; David Crosby [gtr, voc]; Gene Clark [gtr, voc]; Chris Hillman [b, voc]; Michael Clarke [drms])

The Byrds, one of the most influential folk-rock groups of the 1960s, later helped popularize COUNTRY-ROCK with their classic album *Sweetheart of the Rodeo*.

McGuinn, the leader of the group, had previously been a FOLK REVIVALIST, working as an accompanist for The Chad Mitchell Trio and The Limelighters before settling in Los Angeles. Crosby also had worked in a professional folk band, Les Baxter's Balladeers, while Hillman's background was in BLUEGRASS, as the leader (along with the Gosdin brothers) of The Hillmen. All of the group's members were active in the Los Angeles folk scene, and all were inspired by The Beatles to take up electric instruments. The band was originally called The Beefeaters, and then The Jet Set, before they finally settled on The Byrds.

From the beginning the group's repertoire reflected a folk and country orientation. They were among the first to record and popularize BOB DYLAN's songs on the pop charts, beginning with their first hit, 1965's "Mr. Tambourine Man." The same year they took PETE SEEGER's "Turn, Turn, Turn," a folkie setting of text from the Book of Ecclesiastes, to #1.

Clark left the group in 1966 because of his fear of flying; he hooked up with Doug Dillard soon after to form the country-rock outfit Dillard and Clark. The McGuinn-Crosby-led band took a decided psychedelic turn, scoring with the spacey anthem "Eight Miles High" along with the parody of life as a teen idol, "So You Want to Be a Rock and Roll Star." However, Crosby soon left the group to form the pop trio Crosby, Stills, and Nash, leaving the Byrds a three-member group: McGuinn, Hillman, and Clarke. They recorded their first country-rock tunes for their album *The Notorious Byrd Brothers*, although they were still experimenting with psychedelia.

1968 brought the band's total transformation with the addition of GRAM PARSONS, who had previously performed with The International Submarine Band, an early country-rock group. The new Byrds, with McGuinn, Hillman, Parsons, and drummer Kevin White, along with guests Clarence White and JOHN HARTFORD, recorded *Sweetheart of the Rodeo*. Besides remakes of country classics like "An Empty Bottle, a Broken Heart, and You're Still on My Mind," the group recorded Parsons's neocountry ballad "Hickory Wind," pointing the direction for a new country-rock fusion.

Determined to pursue the country-rock direction, Hillman and Parsons left the band to form THE FLYING BURRITO BROTHERS; session guitarist Clarence White came on board along with bassist John York (later replaced by Skip Battin). This group lasted for four years, producing the hits "Ballad of Easy Rider," a folkie-esque tune sung by McGuinn for the sound track of the film *Easy Rider*, as well as the 1971 minor hit "Chestnut Mare." In 1975 the original five-man Byrds reunited for an album for Asylum Records, but the old group magic was gone.

In the mid-1970s McGuinn went solo, recording a couple of ill-received albums, as well as touring with Bob Dylan's Rolling Thunder Review. In the early 1980s he reunited with Hillman and Gene Clark to form a trio that was plagued by Clark's bouts of depression and continued fears of traveling. Hillman formed THE DESERT ROSE BAND in the mid-1980s; Clark went back to a solo career (and eventually committed suicide); and McGuinn has continued to perform sporadically as a solo artist, hooking up with rocker Tom Petty to record a solo album in 1992. When Columbia issued a boxed set of the Byrds' classic recordings, McGuinn, Hillman, and Crosby reunited to record a couple of new tracks.

Select Discography

The Byrds, Columbia 46773. Four-CD retrospective set.

Twenty Essential Tracks, Columbia 47884. If you can't afford the boxed set, how about buying this single CD and sampling the best of the best?

Sweetheart of the Rodeo, Columbia/Legacy 65610. Hear the record that started it all! CD reissue of the 1968 album (Columbia 9670) with additional tracks.

C

CACKLE SISTERS, THE (c. 1935–c. 1950: Mary Jane [voc], 1917–1981; Carolyn [gtr., voc], 1919; Lorraine [voc]; and Eva DeZurick [voc]; all b. Royalton, Minn.)

The DeZurick sisters were amazing trick YODELERS who specialized in all kinds of barnyard and natural sound effects.

Born on a dairy farm in Royalton, Minnesota, to a Dutch farming family of six girls and a boy, the original duo consisted of elder sisters Mary Jane and Carolyn, who undoubtedly honed their skills while working among the various farm animals. After being signed by the NATIONAL BARN DANCE, their popularity brought them to the attention of feed manufacturer Ralston-Purina, which hired them in the mid-1940s to perform their harmonized chicken-cackling act on THE GRAND OLE OPRY and EDDY ARNOLD's syndicated radio show. In order to maintain their ties with WLS, they took the name The Cackle Sisters for their *Opry* appearances. When the older sisters got married, younger sisters began to fill in; Lorraine came to the fore after World War II, introducing a new element to their act: rapid-fire, staccato vocalizing that was called "machine-gun" or "triple-tongue" yodels, giving the act a final burst of popularity in the early 1950s.

CAJUN MUSIC A revival of interest in the traditional music of southern Louisiana in the 1970s and 1980s led to a "rediscovery" of Cajun music, the songs and dance tunes performed by the descendants of the French Acadians who settled the area. While elements of the Cajun style have been introduced into mainstream country music from time to time, through the influence of radio and recordings country music has also reshaped contemporary Cajun sounds.

The Acadians originally hailed from the island of Acadia, a French colony off of Canada (now known as Nova Scotia); when the French ceded the island to the British in 1713, the settlers moved south to what was then still French territory in Louisiana. There they intermixed with English, Spanish, and African-American settlers while developing their own unique language (known as Louisiana French or Creole) and musical style. Through the nineteenth century the musical styles of Europe—waltzes, quadrilles, cotillions, mazurkas—came to the area and entered the musical repertoire. While in the eighteenth century the FIDDLE and triangle were the primary musical instruments, the nineteenth century brought the newly introduced accordion and its many relatives as well as, later in the century, the GUITAR.

Cajun music was first recorded in the 1920s when the record industry was quickly discovering the commercial potential for musics directed at specific regional groups. Fiddlers Dennis McGee and Saday Courville made the first, legendary twin-fiddle recordings. In the 1930s and 1940s WESTERN SWING and pop styles swept the area, and several Cajun musicians—in the prewar era notably fiddler Leo Soileau, who led the first band to feature drums with a jazzy feeling, and after the war fiddler/bandleader Harry Choates, who wrote the big country and Cajun hit "Jole Blon"—modernized the music to reflect these outside influences.

In the post–World War II era Cajun sounds occasionally crossed over onto the country charts. HANK WILLIAMS had a hit with the Cajunesque "Jambalaya," and Rusty and DOUG KERSHAW began recording for both country and Cajun markets. Meanwhile, the FOLK REVIVAL of the late 1950s and early 1960s led to a renewed interest in more traditional Cajun music. Groups like THE NEW LOST CITY RAMBLERS added Cajun music to their act, and traditional family bands like The Balfa Brothers from Mamou, Louisiana, were successful on the festival and folk-revival trail. Accordionist Nathan Abshire, who had originally recorded in the 1930s without much success, was rediscovered and became a big attraction on the concert scene.

Along with Cajun music its sister sound, known as zodico or zydeco, gained new popularity in the 1970s and 1980s. Zydeco is the wedding of African-American blues and jazz styles with Cajun dance and song; its proponents are mostly African-American Creoles. One of the greatest zydeco musicians was Clifton Chenier, an accordionist who recorded extensively through the 1960s and 1970s.

Revival bands began springing up in the 1970s to cater to a more educated, upscale market. Fiddler Michael Doucet was one of the most active of the younger Cajun musicians; eventually he formed the group Beausoleil, a wedding of Cajun sounds with folk-rock instrumentation. Their music was celebrated in MARY CHAPIN CARPENTER's first big country hit, "Down at the Twist and Shout" (the band also performed on the track). Other popular Cajun and zydeco revivalists include Rockin' Dopsie and the Twisters (who appear on Paul Simon's *Graceland* album), Rockin' Sydney (popularizer of the much-recorded "My Toot Toot"), and Jo-el Sonnier.

CALLAHAN BROTHERS (b. Laurel, N.C.; Walter T. ["Joe," gtr, lead voc], January 27, 1910–September 10, 1971 and Homer C. ["Bill," mdln, gtr, b, harmony voc], March 27, 1912)

A popular brother duo of the 1930s, the Callahans featured both traditional ballads and sentimental songs, and newer blues and jazz-influenced, pop-swing material in their repertoire. Their songbooks and radio broadcasts were quite influential in the South, Midwest, and Southwest through the 1940s.

Born in the mountains of western North Carolina, the brothers absorbed the traditional dance music, ballads, and religious songs that were performed throughout the region. After performing locally for various functions, they made their "professional" debut at the 1933 Asheville, North Carolina, folk festival, emulating the YODELING style of JIMMIE RODGERS. They were immediately signed by a Knoxville radio station, and a year later made their first recordings for the budget American Record Company (ARC) label. In 1935 they made one of the first recordings of the traditional folk blues "The House of the Rising Sun," released under the title "Rounder's Luck." They scored big hits with "Curly Headed Baby" and "St. Louis Blues," also cut at this session. They published a series of songbooks that they promoted through their radio shows and personal appearances, greatly influencing the repertoire of many other traditional musicians.

The Callahans moved throughout the South and West to work for a number of different country radio programs, including a stint with RED FOLEY on Cincinnati's WLW and another with the country musical comedy act THE WEAVER BROTHERS AND ELVIRY, out

of Springfield, Missouri. They finally settled in Texas in the early 1940s, broadcasting out of Dallas and Wichita Falls, where they worked with LEFTY FRIZZELL. After recording a good deal of traditional material in the 1930s, they moved into more blues- and jazz-oriented sounds in the 1940s, expanding their band (now called The Blue Ridge Mountain Folk) into a cross between the sound and style of old-time bands like the J. E. MAINER outfits and more modern WESTERN SWING orchestras. Their recordings included country blues numbers like "Step It Up and Go" and a cover of Bill Carlisle's (of THE CARLISLE BROTHERS) "Rattlesnakin' Daddy."

The Callahans are a link between the old-time country style and the newer COWBOY and Western acts who emphasized bluesier styles. Though they continued to perform through the early 1960s (primarily on radio and in personal appearances), their greatest impact was in the 1930s and 1940s, when this period of transition was occurring.

CAMPBELL, GLEN (b. G. Travis C., Delight, Ark., April 22, 1936)

A country-pop vocalist and guitarist best known for a string of mid-1960s crossover hits, Campbell has soldiered on in the country market, although with diminishing success.

Campbell was encouraged by other musicians in his family to take up the GUITAR at age four; by his teens he was touring with his own country band, The Western Wranglers. At age twenty-four Campbell relocated to Los Angeles, where he quickly found employment as a session guitarist, scoring a minor solo hit in 1961 with "Turn Around, Look at Me." Campbell worked comfortably as a session player in pop, country, and rock, even briefly touring as bassist for The Beach Boys after founder Brian Wilson suffered a nervous breakdown.

In the mid-1960s he was signed by Capitol as a solo artist. The company first tried to promote him as an instrumentalist, releasing an LP of twelve-string guitar instrumentals aimed at a general, pop market. However, it was Campbell's clear tenor, with only a hint of a country twang, that would gain him his hits as a pop crooner. 1967 brought his first hit, a cover of JOHN HARTFORD's "Gentle on My Mind," followed by a string of Jimmy Webb-penned soft-country hits ("By the Time I Get to Phoenix," "Wichita Lineman," and "Galveston"). These songs all had pop arrangements, replete with string sections and choruses, giving them great appeal to a general audience, as well as on the country charts. Campbell's career was furthered by his exposure as the guest-host of a summer replacement program for the popular *Smothers Brothers* TV show,

Glen Campbell, lording it over the Tennessee hills, c. mid-1970s. Photo: Raeanne Rubenstein

followed by his own variety show in 1969, plus film roles, most notably with John Wayne in *True Grit.*

Soon after, the hits stopped. Campbell returned to the charts in the mid-1970s as more of a country-oriented performer with "Rhinestone Cowboy" and "Southern Nights," but then lapsed into obscurity again. Although he continues to perform both as a vocalist and as an instrumentalist, Campbell has failed to capitalize on his earlier success.

Select Discography

Best of the Early Years, Curb 77441. His 1960s Capitol hits.

CANOVA, JUDY (b. Juliette C., Starke, Fla., November 20, 1916–August 5, 1983)

Canova was a hillbilly comedian who first performed in New York nightclubs, then on radio, and finally in a series of C-grade Hollywood comedies.

Canova's character of a backwoods, slightly ditsy, but always lovable RUBE was the prototype for hundreds of country comics who followed. Canova's mother, from a well-to-do Southern family, was a concert singer who managed her performing children's careers. Judy began her career performing with her

family at the age of fourteen, traveling in a musical-comedy revue throughout the South. Known as The Georgia Crackers, Judy, sister Anne (Diana), and brother Zeke (Leon) worked up a novelty act combining verbal and physical comedy with reworkings of country and novelty songs. In mid-1930 they hit New York, and in 1931 became the prime attraction at Greenwich Village's Village Barn, a pseudo-rustic hangout for New York's Bohemia featuring Western-garbed waitresses and a countryesque floor show. From there they went on to play vaudeville, radio, and Broadway, appearing with Martha Raye in *Calling All Stars* in 1934.

The Canovas made their first recordings in 1931, including hammed-up versions of folk songs like "Frog Went a-Courtin' " performed by the two girls and "I Wish I Was a Single Girl Again," Judy's first solo recording. The trio also cut cornball harmony numbers like "Snake-Eyed Killing Dude" along with sentimental favorites such as "When the Sun Goes Down Behind the Hill." Beginning in 1934, they published their own songbooks.

They first went to Hollywood in 1937 to make films for Paramount, with little success. After a tour of England and more radio work, the trio landed back on Broadway in *Yodel Boy,* the show that launched Judy's solo career. In 1940 she returned to Hollywood as a solo act, starring in her first movie, *Scatterbrain*, produced by Republic Pictures, the same schlock studio that brought the world the Western adventures of GENE AUTRY and ROY ROGERS. Canova's Republic hits were top grossers, and she became the studio's one and only female star. Most of these vehicles were thin on plot and broad in humor, and all featured pseudo-Western numbers for Canova to show off her blend of vocal gymnastics (including YODELING and jazzy inflections), all put to the service of broad comedy.

Canova never made many recordings, focusing instead on radio. She did have one hit in 1947 with her pairing of "No Letter Today" and the bluesy girls-listen-up ballad "Never Trust a Man." By the mid-1950s, with her film career and radio days behind her, she recorded one album. Backed by legendary steel guitarist SPEEDY WEST and issued in 1958, it combined well-worn traditional numbers with the hokey composed material she favored in the 1940s.

Canova tried to break into TV in the 1960s, with little success; eventually she retired and, in 1983, died of cancer.

Daughter Diana Canova became a TV comedian, starring on the series *Soap*, as well as in *Throb*, a satire of the pop music business.

CARLIN, BOB (b. Robert Mark C., New York City, March 17, 1953)

Carlin is a traditional-styled BANJO player and record producer who has been active in the revival scene since the mid-1970s.

Originally the bass player with the New York old-time string band The Delaware Watergap, Carlin produced and performed on 1977's *Melodic Clawhammer Banjo* album. Inspired by John Burke, a group of banjoists had begun to play full melody lines while still using the old-time clawhammer style (banjoist BILL KEITH had done a similar thing fifteen years earlier in a BLUEGRASS style). This album was quite popular among young pickers, although Carlin pretty much abandoned the note-for-note style soon after.

In his his first solo album, released in 1980, he played in a more traditionally oriented style. It was followed by a second album with an eclectic mix of old-time banjo numbers, duets with progressive banjoist TONY TRISCHKA, and adaptations of Rolling Stones songs to an old-time style. A third album featured duets with a number of fiddlers, including James Bryant (a relaxed, old-style bluegrass fiddler who works with NORMAN BLAKE) and Brad Leftwich. Carlin and Bruce Molsky released a cassette of old-time songs and instrumentals soon after. His next recording was a FIDDLE-banjo duet album made with JOHN HARTFORD in 1995; Carlin subsequently recorded and toured with The John Hartford String Band until Hartford's death

in June 2001, but also continued to work as a solo act. His self-released *Mr. Spaceman* CD was issued in 1997.

As a producer Carlin has released anthologies of old-time banjo picking as well as a tribute album to fiddler TOMMY JARRELL. He also hosted a traditional music radio program out of Philadelphia for over a decade. During the 1990s he was an artist-in-residence in North Carolina and Virginia while still performing and producing recordings.

Select Discography

Bangin' and Sawin', Rounder 197. Banjo and fiddle duets; CD reissue includes bonus tracks not on original LP.
The Fun of Open Discussion, Rounder 320. Banjo-fiddle duets with John Hartford.
Mr. Spaceman, Cartunes 102.

CARLISLE BROTHERS (Cliff [Dobro, voc], b. Clifford Raymond C., Mount Eden, Ky., March 6, 1904–April 2, 1983; Bill [gtr, voc], b. Wakefield, Ky., December 19, 1908)

The Carlisles performed as a brother duo in the 1930s, but also had careers as solo artists. In their brother-duo days the Carlisles were on the more bluesy end of the spectrum, closer in sound to THE DELMORE BROTHERS, for example, than to THE BLUE SKY BOYS. Cliff Carlisle, one of the first masters of the DOBRO guitar, recorded prolifically as a soloist, accompanist, and in various combinations with other musicians in addition to his brother Bill. After Cliff retired in 1947, Bill had a new career leading his own family band.

The duo was raised in the hills of Kentucky, although the family originally hailed from Tennessee. Their father led singing schools in rural churches, teaching GOSPEL songs in the traditional SHAPE-NOTE style, but his kids were more interested in the sounds coming over the radio from Nashville. Cliff apparently toured the South as a youngster, playing on the Keith vaudeville circuit and specializing in RAILROAD SONGS and Hawaiian numbers. The novelty of playing the guitar with a steel bar to perform pseudo-Hawaiian songs made him an instant success. He signed with the Indiana-based Gennett label when he was twenty-six, initially recording with guitarist Wilbur Ball; inspired by JIMMIE RODGERS, the pair specialized in blues numbers featuring closely harmonized YODELING. In fact, Carlisle sessioned on some of Rodgers's recordings, providing Dobro accompaniment for the famous musician.

The brothers formed their duo in 1931, and they performed together on many recordings for various labels, as well as on radio stations out of Lexington, Kentucky, and Charlotte, North Carolina. They specialized in train songs (such as "Pan American Man" and the hobo numbers "Just a Lonely Hobo" and "Ramblin' Jack"), along with the blue yodeling that Cliff had performed with his first partner; both of these styles showed their debt to Jimmie Rodgers. They also performed comic novelty numbers, including risqué, suggestive songs such as "Tom Cat Blues," and Hawaiian instrumentals, both vestiges of Cliff's vaudeville days (some of Cliff's solo recordings in a more rowdy style were issued under the nom-de-disc "Bob Clifford"). Bill said that as part of the act he portrayed a country hayseed character called "Hotshot Elmer," appearing as a barefoot comedian. Meanwhile, Cliff continued to perform and record with other musicians, including his original partner Ball, and Fred Kirby.

Cliff retired in 1947, and Bill formed a new family group called The Carlisles. Taking the name "Jumpin' Bill Carlisle," he made his GRAND OLE OPRY debut in 1952, introducing the hit comic novelty number "Too Old to Cut the Mustard," a Carlisle original. He also wrote the follow-up hit "No Help Wanted," as well as the novelties "Is That You, Myrtle?" (written with the LOUVIN BROTHERS) and "Rough Stuff." Bill continued to record through the late 1960s, having one more hit with another country comedy number, "What Kinda Deal Is This," in 1966. He appeared on *The Grand Ole Opry* through the 1990s and into the twenty-first century, when he was in his nineties.

Select Discography

Cliff Carlisle, Vols. 1 and 2, Old Timey 103, 104. Two out-of-print LPs reissuing Cliff's solo recordings and duets with his brother and Wilbur Ball.
Busy Body Boogie, Bear Family 15172. 1950s band recordings, mostly led by Bill.

CAROLINA COTTON (b. Helen Hagstrom, Cash, Ark., October 20, 1926–June 10, 1997)

For a period of about ten years following World War II, Cotton was one of the best-loved cowgirl stars of the B-Westerns that were churned out by lesser Hollywood studios such as Republic Pictures.

Her family relocated to San Francisco from a small town in Arkansas when Hagstrom/Carolina was quite young. Encouraged by her parents, she took dancing lessons and began working on local radio. In the early 1940s announcer "Dude" Martin gave her a country nom-de-hertz, "Carolina Cotton." In 1944 she landed her first appearance in a film, Roy Acuff's *Sing, Neighbor, Sing*, which launched her horse-opera career, and she relocated to the Los Angeles area, a hotbed of Western-styled performers.

During the later 1940s Cotton recorded prolifically, her YODELING capabilities much admired; some of her last sessions featured backing by BOB WILLS's famed WESTERN SWING band. During the Korean War she gained new popularity thanks to the regular broadcasts of her show, *Carolina Calls*, on the Armed Forces Radio Network. However, by the mid-1950s her career was fading, and she retired from performing to become an elementary-school teacher in Bakersfield, California. Toward the end of her life she made a few appearances at COWBOY film festivals, before dying of cancer in 1997.

CAROLINA TAR HEELS, THE (c. 1927–1932: Dock [Doctor Coble] Walsh [bnj, gtr, voc], b. Wilkes County, N.C., July 23, 1901–May 1967; Garley Foster [hca, voc], b. Wilkes County, N.C., January 10, 1905–October 1968; Gwen Foster [hca, voc], place and date of birth unknown; Clarence "Tom" Ashley [gtr, voc], b. C. Earl McCurry, Bristol, Tenn., September 29, 1895–June 2, 1967)

A low-key North Carolina-based and -styled string band led by guitarist/banjoist/entertainer Doc Walsh that had some success in the late 1920s as a recording band.

Little is known of Walsh's early life. He was apparently a street singer who worked the mill towns of North Carolina; in 1925 he made his first recordings as a solo artist. A year later he teamed with Gwen Foster, and the two formed a band. In 1927 they were signed by Columbia and given the Carolina Tar Heels name.

During the band's short recording history, they had several different lineups. Gwen Foster appeared on the first three sessions and then left the fold; he was replaced by another friend of Walsh's, also a harmonica player and also with the surname Foster (Garley Foster was no relation to Gwen). Besides playing the harmonica, Garley was billed as "The Human Bird" because of his whistling capabilities.

By the fall of 1928 CLARENCE "TOM" ASHLEY, a popular solo recording artist, had joined the group. Ashley was primarily a BANJO player; however, because Walsh already played banjo and was the group's leader, Ashley switched to GUITAR during his approximately one-year stint with the band. The group's biggest hit, "My Home's Across the Blue Ridge Mountains," came as a trio. After Ashley left, Walsh and Foster were again a duo.

In 1931 an unrelated group, broadcasting out of Atlanta, took the Carolina Tar Heels name. This led the Walsh-Foster duo to bill themselves alternately as The Pine Mountain Boys or The "Original" Carolina Tar Heels. By 1932, with the Depression leading to fewer opportunities for country bands to record and perform, the group made its last recordings, this time with Walsh and original member Gwen Foster.

The 1960s FOLK REVIVAL led many folklorists to try to find stars of the 1920s and 1930s. Gene Earle and Archie Green brought Doc Walsh and Garley Foster back together to form a new Carolina Tar Heels, along with Doc's son, Drake. They recorded an album for the small Folk Legacy label that showed Garley's human bird capabilities were still intact. They also made a few appearances at folk festivals.

CARPENTER, MARY CHAPIN (b. Princeton, N.J., February 21, 1958)

Well-educated, slightly ironic, a feminist, and politically liberal, Carpenter is the last person you'd think would be successful on the country charts. The fact that she's enjoyed success shows much about how the definition of "country" is changing.

The daughter of a *Life* magazine executive, Carpenter was raised in Princeton, New Jersey, for most of her childhood, except for two years during which the family relocated to Japan so her father could oversee the publication of the Asian edition of *Life*. Her mother had picked up the GUITAR during the FOLK REVIVAL of the early 1960s, and gave her instrument to Mary when she expressed interest in learning to play. Her family moved to Washington, D.C., in 1974, and Carpenter spent a year following her high-school graduation traveling through Europe before enrolling as an American Civilization major at Brown University.

After college she began performing in the Washington area, playing a mix of pop and rock standards and SINGER/SONGWRITER material, including her own songs. She hooked up with guitarist John Jennings, and the duo produced a demo tape that they planned to sell as a self-produced cassette at their engagements. This demo led to her audition for Columbia Records, which signed her and released her first LP in 1987.

From 1987 to 1992 Carpenter developed a cult following, although she was difficult to categorize. FM radio, which at one time had been responsive to singer/songwriters, was now oriented toward either hard rock or oldies. Country stations were not very sympathetic to her material, which tended to be soft-acoustic, with an emphasis on women's themes. She did score a minor hit with 1989's "How Do," a brassy flirtation song told from a woman's point of view, followed by "This Shirt," a song that owes as much to Joni Mitchell as it does to LORETTA LYNN.

Carpenter's breakthrough came with the hit 1992 single "Down at the Twist and Shout," immortalizing a Washington-area folk club where the Cajun band Beausoleil often performed. Its snappy Cajun rhythm, well-made performance video, and rocking arrangement sent it shooting up the country charts. She quickly followed up with the 1993 releases "I Feel Lucky," another up-tempo, sassy number, and her cover of LUCINDA WILLIAMS's "Passionate Kisses."

Still, Carpenter's albums have as much acoustic folk on them as country, and her songs often subtly skew traditional country themes. "Going Out Tonight" tells of a woman who is going out to a bar "in search of a friend"; this is almost the polar opposite of the traditional country HONKY-TONK ballad, in which the man is looking to hoist a few brews with a "honky-tonk angel." Of course, Carpenter's audience is largely made up of young, well-educated, professional people (like herself), and so it's not surprising that they are willing to accept these songs that would never have passed muster in country circles just a decade earlier.

Despite her high-powered hits, Carpenter's best material remains her softer, more acoustic-oriented songs. "Come On, Come On" is a near-perfect ballad of lost love and longing memories, and "I Am a Town" is another nostalgic gem that perfectly captures the feeling of long-ago summers spent in sleepy backwaters. When all the boot-scootin' dust settles, these songs will be accepted as her strongest legacy.

Carpenter has struggled to duplicate her commercial success of 1993–1994. Her follow-up albums to *Come On, Come On* have had a quieter, more introspective quality that continues to appeal to her fans, but has not led to country radio hits. Although she continued to be a strong touring act—with a fan base that is older, better-educated, and much more female than the typical country act—Carpenter's follow-up albums of the 1990s were mostly commercial duds.

A combination greatest-hits-live album, *Party Doll*, released in 1999, helped revive her career, although again outside of the country realm. In 2001 she released *Time * Sex * Love*, continuing her move away from country toward more confessional, singer-songwriter-oriented material.

Select Discography

Shooting Straight in the Dark, Columbia 46077. Her third album, featuring the breakthrough hit "Down at the Twist and Shout."

Come On, Come On, Columbia 48881. Fine 1992 album featuring more chart-busters.

Party Doll, Columbia 68751. 1999 compilation album, with live versions of her hits and "rarities."

CARSON, FIDDLIN' JOHN (b. Fannin County, Ga., c. March 23, 1868–December 11, 1949)

Prominent Georgia fiddler, vocalist, and MINSTREL-SHOW performer, Fiddlin' John Carson single-handedly created the country music industry with his 1923 recording of "Little Old Log Cabin in the Lane," backed with "The Old Hen Cackled." This recording is generally acknowledged to be the first country music record that was successfully marketed to a country audience, convincing big-city recording executives that there was money to be made in recording traditional performers.

Carson was born in 1868 on a farm in Fannin County, Georgia; his first recording appeared in 1923, when he was fifty-five years old, with about forty years of fiddling, singing, and entertaining under his belt. He was a professional entertainer, although he did odd jobs as a painter or carpenter, and probably also worked as a subsistence farmer. His music was so popular that he was enlisted by several local politicians, eventually working on the campaign trail with Herman Talmadge, who repaid the performer after his election as Georgia's governor with a job as an elevator operator in the state capitol building.

Atlanta-based furniture dealer Polk Brockman was responsible for launching Carson's recording career. As the local dealer for Okeh records, in 1923 he sent a telegram to New York requesting that Okeh record Carson, because he knew his music would sell well in Georgia. Legendary producer RALPH PEER oversaw the first session, but felt the music was so bad that he had the records pressed without labels, and shipped copies only to Brockman as a favor. When the records quickly sold out, Peer realized his mistake, and signed Carson to the label.

For his first two years of recording, Carson primarily worked as a soloist, using traditional tunings and uneven rhythms in his accompaniments to his own rough-hewn vocals. He also performed as a duo with daughter Rosa Lee Carson (b. 1909; dubbed "MOONSHINE KATE" by executives at the Okeh label), a fine singer in a deadpan country style who also played the BANJO and GUITAR.

Because string bands were becoming increasingly popular in the mid-1920s, Carson formed his own band, The Virginia Reelers, a floating ensemble of musicians who were mostly younger and played in a more modern style than their leader. Chief among the members of this group were fiddlers Earl Johnson and "Bully" Brewer, banjoists Land Norris and Bill White, and guitarists "Peanut" Brown and Rosa Lee Carson. Many of the band's members doubled or even tripled on other instruments (Brewer played FIDDLE, banjo, and guitar), so that they might take a different part if one or another of the others was absent. On his band recordings Carson continued to use the older tunings and his own unique sense of rhythm, the band often struggling to follow his lead. The result was a sometimes chaotic meeting of two traditions, the older, unaccompanied songster matched with a jazzy, driving string-band sound.

Carson's repertoire reached back into the mid-nineteenth century, and was an amalgam of traditional dance tunes, ballads and songs, and recently composed sentimental, comic, and vaudeville numbers. He performed traditional dance tunes like "Cotton-Eyed Joe," "Fire on the Mountain," "Sugar in the Gourd," "Arkansas Traveler," and the like; topical and protest songs such as "The Honest Farmer," "There's a Hard Time Coming," "The Death of Floyd Collins," "Taxes on the Farmer Feeds Them All," and "My Ford Sedan"; nineteenth-century sentimental songs and early-twentieth-century popular and novelty items like his first recording, "Little Old Log Cabin in the Lane" (al-

though Carson typically transformed it into an almost ancient-sounding celebration of life in the backwoods), "The Baggage Coach Ahead," "When You and I Were Young, Maggie," "Bully of the Town," and "I'm Glad My Wife's in Europe"; and traditional songs such as "Bachelor's Hall," "900 Miles Away from Home," "Old Joe Clark," and "Goin' Where the Weather Suits My Clothes" (Carson's title for "Worried Man Blues").

Carson set the stage for later country stars in many crucial ways. He was a unique personality who transformed the material that he performed into his own unique sound. His sense of rhythm and tonality, influenced by his boyhood in rural Georgia and his years of professional performing in tent shows and fiddlers' contests, gave even the most recently composed of his songs a country sound. Finally, Carson's music was often both topical and humorous, commenting on the everyday experiences of his listeners. As a performer Carson came from the people and, although he achieved great celebrity, he never "took on airs" or acted like a star. His popularity encouraged countless others to believe that they, too, could become country performers.

Select Discography

Complete Recorded Works, 1926–34, Document 8014–8020. Seven CDs of everything Carson recorded, with brief notes.

CARSON, MARTHA (b. Irene Amburgey, Neon, Ky., March 19, 1921)

Carson was one of the great fervent GOSPEL singers of the 1950s who also wrote many famous modern religious numbers, most notably "I'm Gonna Walk and Talk with My Lord."

Born in backwoods Kentucky, Amburgey/Carson got her first radio exposure in Bluefield, West Virginia, when she was eighteen years old. Her father was an old-time banjoist and her mother played organ; along with their daughters Bertha and Irene, they formed a sacred quartet that sang at religious revival meetings throughout the South. About 1938 fiddler Bertha and guitarist Irene, along with younger sister Opal, who played BANJO and MANDOLIN, formed The Amburgey Sisters and began performing on Lexington, Kentucky, radio, followed by a stint in Bluefield, West Virginia, and finally with the famous *Renfro Valley Barn Dance*, where they performed with legendary fiddler/banjoist LILY MAY LEDFORD in a later incarnation of The Coon Creek Girls. In 1940 they went to Atlanta's WSB, where their act was renamed Mattie, Marthie, and Minnie (for Opal, Irene, and Bertha, respectively); they performed such patriotic wartime ditties as "I'll Be Back in a Year, Little Darling."

In the early 1940s the trio dissolved as the sisters married and moved on to other careers. Opal wed Salty

Holmes from THE PRAIRIE RAMBLERS, and the two became popular on THE GRAND OLE OPRY, performing as Salty Holmes and Mattie O'Neill; in the 1950s she took the name of Jean Chapel and recorded for Sun Records as a sultry ROCKABILLY artist; SAM PHILLIPS of Sun sold her contract to RCA, and she was billed "The Female Elvis Presley" by the company, for which she had a minor hit with 1956's "Oo-ba-la Baby"! Bertha married a defense plant worker and more or less retired, although she did return to performing with her sisters in the early 1950s.

In the early 1940s Martha married country songster and mandolin player James Carson (Roberts), the son of old-time fiddler DOC ROBERTS, one of the finer old-time recording artists of the late 1920s. The two became known as the Barn Dance Sweethearts when they signed with Atlanta's WSB in the mid-1940s, and had hits with sentimental numbers such as their cover of THE BLUE SKY BOYS' "The Sweetest Gift," as well as the gospelesque "Man of Galilee."

The Carsons split in 1951, and Martha briefly reunited with her sisters. She joined the cast of *The Grand Ole Opry* a year later, bringing her tub-thumping gospel style to the stage of Nashville's premiere radio show. Oddly enough, her fervent singing, a wedding of old-time religious sentiment, black gospel and R&B, and country styles, found a home in the rarefied supper clubs of Northeastern cities in the mid-1950s, so that she became equally in demand for her appearances at tony venues like New York City's Waldorf Astoria hotel. Her solo recordings increasingly took on the trappings of 1950s pop stylings, complete with wall-to-wall orchestrations accompanying Martha's big voice. She even took a stab at rock and roll, covering numbers like Otis Blackwell's "Just Whistle and Call" and "Music Drives Me Crazy (Especially Rock 'n' Roll)," although she sounded less comfortable outside the country milieu. Carson wrote over 100 songs, all in a religious vein, including "Let's Talk About That Old-Time Religion" and "Satisfied."

Although she continued to perform in the 1960s, 1970s, and even 1980s, Carson's career was pretty much confined to her initial successful days in the 1950s.

CARTER, CARLENE (b. Rebecca C. Smith, Madison, Tenn., September 26, 1955)

The daughter of June Carter and CARL SMITH, and thus part of the famous CARTER FAMILY dynasty, Carlene has been somewhat of an iconoclast in country circles, recording in England in the late 1970s and early 1980s in a punk-country style, creating a music that she says was "too rock for country [radio] and too country for rock." An energetic singer, Carter is most at home with up-tempo material that has a rock edge to it.

Her mother and father split when Carlene was just two, but from an early age she was immersed in music thanks to tours with the entire Carter clan led by her grandmother, Mother Maybelle Carter. When Carlene was twelve, her mother married JOHNNY CASH, and Carlene joined the Cash/Carter road show, working as a backup singer along with her stepsister ROSANNE CASH. Two ill-fated marriages, at ages fifteen and nineteen, produced two children before she returned to the road show. When Carlene was twenty-two, she headed to Los Angeles, where she landed a recording contract as a rock singer. The resulting debut album, *Carlene Carter*, was recorded in London with backup by the punk band The Rumour, and her follow-up featured members of The Doobie Brothers. In 1979 she married Nick Lowe, a British punk-country SINGER/SONGWRITER whose musical eclecticism contributed to her unusual style.

The early 1980s brought her innovative LP *Musical Shapes*, featuring many of her original compositions. The album wed country influences with a hard-rocking sound, forecasting the new country boom of the late 1980s, but was a commercial failure on both country and pop charts. By the mid-1980s her career and third marriage were on the skids, and Carlene was increasingly dependent on cocaine and alcohol. Her mother and aunts came to England at about this time to tour, and Carlene joined them to form a quartet, returning to the country-music fold.

Carter returned to Nashville in the late 1980s and recorded her comeback LP, *I Fell in Love*, which was released in 1990. The title track was a minor country hit, and the album combined traditional country songs with Carlene's own brand of confessional songs with an ironic twist. Her follow-up, *Little Love Letters*, featured the clever ROCKABILLY-sounding "Every Little Thing," a perfect example of Carter's ability to honor, while she slightly skews, country traditions. Two years later she issued her last album to date, *Little Acts of Treason*. In mid-2001 Carter was arrested along with her longtime companion, the musician Howie Epstein, on a charge of drug possession; the issue remained unresolved through early 2002.

Select Discography

I Fell in Love, Reprise 26139.
Little Love Letters, Giant 24499.
Hindsight 20/20, Giant 24655. Career retrospective through the mid-1990s.

CARTER, DEANA (b. Nashville, Tenn., January 4, 1966)

Carter, a mid-1990s hitmaker who has had a hard time scoring a follow-up to her out-of-the-box success, is the daughter of Nashville session guitarist Fred Carter, Jr., who played on sessions for about a decade from the mid-1960s. Carter studied physical and rehabilitation therapy at the University of Tennessee in Knoxville, and worked for a while in that field while pursuing a musical career on the side. A demo tape that she made in the early 1990s was given to WILLIE NELSON, who hired the then-unsigned artist to sing at Farm Air VII in 1994. That same year she was signed by Capitol/Liberty Records.

Carter initially recorded her debut album, *Did I Shave My Legs for This?*, with producer JIMMY BOWEN. The domestic label passed on releasing it, and it was heard only in Europe. Two years later—with Liberty now under new management—Carter was brought back to the studio to rerecord the album for the U.S. market. Only two cuts were maintained from the original sessions. The album, finally released in the U.S. in the autumn of 1996, was an immediate sensation. It produced five hit singles, including the humorous title cut (a Best Country Song winner at the Grammys in 1997) and Bowen's original recording of "Strawberry Wine" (the Country Music Association's Single and Song of the Year in 1997). The album continued to sell strongly for two years after its release, eventually going quadruple platinum.

Carter next recorded the song "Once upon a December," featured in the 1997 animated film *Anastasia*, which took her into the realm of pop divahood from her country roots. However, she failed to cross over to pop superstardom. In this age of quickly changing tastes and fads, Carter failed to produce a second album until the fall of 2000, when she finally released *Everything's Gonna Be Alright*. Capitol subsequently dropped her, and Carter later signed with RCA.

Carter's style has always been squarely in the pop-diva form, despite her Nashville upbringing. She lists a wide variety of influences, from Cat Stevens to Led Zeppelin. Her blond good looks put her in the FAITH HILL league of eye-catching performers, but her career—from a purely commercial point of view—has been poorly managed. Whether she can return to chart-topping success is anyone's guess.

Select Discography

Did I Shave My Legs for This?, Capitol Nashville 2249. 1995 debut album.

CARTER FAMILY, THE "ORIGINAL" (Alvin Pleasant [A. P.] C., b. Maces Spring, Va., December 15, 1891–November 7, 1960 [voc]; Sara Dougherty C., b. Flat Woods, Va., July 21, 1898–January 8, 1979 [autoharp, voc]; Maybelle Addington C., b. Nickelsville, Va., May 10, 1909–October 23, 1978 [gtr, voc])

The Carter Family were one of the first and most popular country vocal groups; their unornamented, nasal harmonies, born and bred in rural church music, are probably the closest we can come to a pure "white" Appalachian sound. The group coalesced around Alvin Pleasant (known as "A. P.") Carter, his wife, Sara, and his sister-in-law Maybelle. Sara usually sang lead and played the autoharp, with Alvin on bass vocals and Maybelle on tenor and GUITAR. A. P., a master collector of traditional songs, reworked them into pleasant and memorable melodies that became the first country music hits, including "Keep on the Sunny Side," "The Storms Are on the Ocean," "Wildwood Flower," "Bury Me Beneath the Willow," and their best-known song,

The Carter Family: Maybelle (with guitar and glasses), Sara (autoharp), and A. P. on the family homestead, c. 1928. Photo: University of North Carolina, Southern Historical Collection, Southern Folklife Collection, University Archives

"Will the Circle Be Unbroken," an adaptation of a SHAPE-NOTE hymn.

Their first and greatest success came recording under the supervision of RALPH PEER for RCA Victor from 1927 to 1933. Exact contemporaries of JIMMIE RODGERS, with whom they made a few comedy sketch records, the Carters were almost straitlaced in their approach to their music. Although the trio did record some blues numbers, and Maybelle also played some slide guitar, they showed less African-American influence in their performance style and repertoire than many other white acts. For some this makes their music excruciatingly bland; for others the beauty lies in the simplicity of their four-square harmonies.

The group continued to record through the later 1930s and early 1940s, even though A. P. and Sara's marriage dissolved in 1932. They gained great exposure in the late 1930s while working on XERA, the famous "border" radio station that, because it broadcast out of Mexico, was unregulated in the U.S. and thus had a much more powerful, and far-reaching, signal than U.S. commercial stations. Various Carter daughters were also getting into the act. The last "original" Carter family performance came in 1943.

In the late 1940s Maybelle performed with her daughters (Anita, b. Ina A. C., Maces Spring, Va., March 31, 1933–July 30, 1999 [voc, b, gtr]; June, b. Valerie J. C., Maces Spring, Va., June 23, 1929 [voc, autoharp, gtr]; and Helen, b. H. Myrl C., Maces Spring, Va., September 12, 1927–June 2, 1998 [voc, gtr, autoharp, accordion]) as The Carter Family; the girls also performed as a more modern-sounding country act, The Carter Sisters. Mother and daughters became members of THE GRAND OLE OPRY in 1950. Meanwhile, A. P. recorded in the early 1950s with his children Janette (b. Maces Spring, Va., July 2, 1932) and Joe (b. Maces Spring, Va., February 27, 1927). Maybelle was "rediscovered" during the 1960s FOLK REVIVAL, and became a popular performer on the autoharp, picking melodies on it rather than just strumming chords. She was also prominently featured on the NITTY GRITTY DIRT BAND's homage to country-music celebration, *Will the Circle Be Unbroken?*, in 1971. Although Sara performed with Maybelle at the 1967 Newport Folk Festival, she was mostly inactive after A. P.'s death in 1960. Janette Carter runs the Carter Family Homestead in Virginia, which includes a museum with memorabilia of the family's music career plus a dance/concert hall that features BLUEGRASS and country acts. She recorded a duet album with her brother Joe in the 1970s.

The Carters remain influential for introducing a great number of folk standards into the country repertoire and for popularizing a smooth, tight harmony style. They were neither virtuoso musicians nor vocalists; indeed, they sounded much like the "folks next door," undoubtedly a large part of their appeal. But their down-home harmonies and simple accompaniments made them models for hundreds of other family bands, and changed the shape of country music from rural entertainment to a popular, mainstream sound.

Select Discography

Complete Recordings, Rounder 1064–1072. Following their similar series devoted to Jimmie Rodgers, Rounder is reissuing all of The Carter Family's original Victor recordings in chronological order.
On Border Radio, JEMF 101. Recordings from their days working out of Mexico.
Clinch Mountain Treasures, County 112. Late 1930s/early 1940s recordings of the original Carters.

CARTER, WILF (b. Guysboro, Nova Scotia, Canada, December 18, 1904–December 5, 1996)
Better known in the U.S. as "Montana Slim," Carter was one of the pioneering "yodeling cowboys," Canada's answer to the Western craze.

Carter was one of the few COWBOY-styled performers who was not directly influenced by JIMMIE RODGERS, although he was certainly aware of Rodgers's incredibly successful recordings. He took up YODELING after hearing a Swiss yodeler who was performing on the Canadian vaudeville circuit. He was a real cowboy, too, having actually worked as a trail rider in the Canadian Rockies and performed at local rodeos.

Carter's big break, on Calgary radio in the mid-1930s, led to a contract with Canadian RCA. He began performing in New York later in the decade, taking the stage name of Montana Slim. Although he recorded over 500 numbers for RCA and its budget Camden label, as well as countless smaller labels, Carter's "skills" as a performer were about as slim as his stage name. He makes another slim performer, SLIM WHITMAN, sound positively plump! He's best known for his 1949 recording of "There's a Bluebird on Your Windowsill," the kind of cowboy pop that is treasured as a kitsch classic. In 1952 he left RCA, and then recorded for Decca through 1957. Beginning in 1953 he and his two daughters toured together, billing themselves as "The Family Show with the Folks You Know." He recorded for Starday briefly in the early 1960s, and then for RCA in Canada, continuing to play mostly up North through the late 1980s. He retired during the last years of his life, dying in 1996 after being diagnosed with stomach cancer.

Select Discography

Prairie Legend, Bear Family 197542. A massive four-CD set containing everything he recorded between 1944 and 1959.
Cowboy Songs, Bear Family 15939. A second four-CD set.

CARVER, JOHNNY (b. Jackson, Miss., November 24, 1940)

Carver was a mid-1970s country star best known for covering ersatz pop hits of the era (such as "Tie a Yellow Ribbon") and making them acceptable for country radio.

Born and raised in Jackson, Mississippi, he began performing as a child in his family's GOSPEL group along with his aunts and uncles. High-school years saw him performing in more of a pop mold, and he took up the life of a touring musician after graduation, eventually settling in Milwaukee. In 1965 he left for California, where he became the lead singer for the house band at a famed country nightspot, the Palomino Club. Talent scouts from the local Imperial label caught his show and signed him up, leading to his first late 1960s hits, 1967's "Your Lily White Hands," followed a year later by "Hold Me Tight."

Carver moved to Imperial's parent label, United Artists, and then to Epic, but could not equal his first success until 1973, when he signed with ABC's Dot division. There he recorded a series of countrified covers of middle-of-the-road hits; his slight twang made the songs more accessible for country radio, although his arrangements were hardly breakthroughs, following their pop models fairly closely. After a spate of these cloned hits culminating in 1977's "Livin' Next Door to Alice," Carver moved on to smaller labels, without much success, through the early 1980s. By the early 1990s he was working out of BRANSON, MISSOURI, home to many a onetime country star.

CASH, JOHNNY (b. John Ray C., Kingsland, Ark., February 25, 1932)

Johnny Cash is one of the most distinctive performers in country music and one of the most unique. Drawing on his poor, rural background, Cash created a country-folk music in the early 1960s that commented on the plight of the working poor. His distinctive deep voice, with its slight flutter and twang, and the sparse backup of The Tennessee Three, with their primal, oom-chiga beat, sets Cash's work apart from all other country performers'. Cash at his best had the unique capability of writing songs that, while stark and simple, sound like they've been around for hundreds of years. In his performances he combined the primal energy of WOODY GUTHRIE with a more menacing undertone.

Cash's family, poor cotton farmers who were wiped out in the Depression, relocated to a Federal Resettlement Colony in rural Tennessee. He joined the Air Force in the early 1950s and took up the GUITAR while stationed in Germany. On his return home he borrowed two pickers from his older brother's band, The Delta Rhythm Ramblers, to form the original Tennessee Two (Cash played guitar, backed by a second guitarist, Lu-

Johnny Cash in a characteristic tough-guy pose, c. mid-1970s. Photo: Raeanne Rubenstein

ther Perkins, and bass; later a drummer was added to make the group The Tennessee Three). Signed to SAM PHILLIPS's legendary ROCKABILLY label, Sun Records, Cash scored with his country classic "I Walk the Line" (1956), along with some forgettable more rock-oriented sides.

Disappointed with Phillips's commercial orientation, Cash signed with Columbia Records in 1959, working with producer DON LAW. Law was sympathetic to Cash's folk leanings, and remolded the star to appeal to the nascent FOLK REVIVAL. He emphasized Cash's folk background by having him record topical songs about America's working class, American Indians, legendary figures (such as John Henry), and outlaws. He recorded Cash with the simple backup of his own band rather than adding the strings and choruses typically heard on country recordings of that era.

Cash's big break came with his legendary live concert at California's Folsom Prison (in 1968), including the classic bad-man song "Folsom Prison Blues," in which Cash presents a sympathetic although ultimately tragic portrayal of a condemned murderer. BOB DYLAN enlisted Cash's aid for his country LP, *Nashville Skyline*, in 1969, exposing him to a younger, rock and folk-pop audience. In the same year Cash had his first solid hit with the unlikely choice of "A Boy Named Sue," a comic song written by Shel Silverstein.

Through the 1970s Cash recorded more mainstream pop-country material while also developing an acting career. Following his Folsom Prison performance and his mid-1960s battle with drug addiction, Cash exploited his image as "The Man in Black," emphasizing his years of "hard traveling." He often performed with a large revue, including his wife, June Carter Cash, and members of The CARTER FAMILY, and old friends like CARL PERKINS.

In the 1980s through early 1990s Cash had a varied career. He recorded a series of successful LPs with country "OUTLAWS" WILLIE NELSON, KRIS KRISTOFFERSON, and WAYLON JENNINGS. His own LPs continued in a pop-country vein through the 1980s.

In the 1990s Cash began to receive renewed attention from the rock and country worlds for his many contributions to the music. In 1992 he was inducted into the Rock and Roll Hall of Fame for his early teen-pop recordings. However, Cash was without a record label, having been dropped by Mercury because his records failed to sell on the country charts. This situation was rectified in the mid-1990s when he signed with ex-rap producer Rick Rubin and Rubin's American Records label. With Rubin's guidance Cash recorded an album of traditional songs accompanied just by his own guitar, and filmed a particularly ominous video to accompany his interpretation of the folk-blues song "Delia's Gone"; the album won Cash a Grammy. A second album with band accompaniment, including Tom Petty, featured Cash's interpretations of a wide range of contemporary material. He also made an appearance with Willie Nelson on the popular VH–1 *Storytellers* program, in which the two swapped songs and stories; the sound track was subsequently released on record.

In the fall of 1997, after completing a second autobiography, Cash surprised the country world by announcing he was retiring from performing because he was suffering from Shy-Drager syndrome, a degenerative nerve disease related to Parkinson's disease (this turned out to be a misdiagnosis). Soon afterward he was hospitalized with double pneumonia and was said to be near death. He recovered, although he was hospitalized again a year later, again said to be suffering from pneumonia. Despite these hardships Cash managed to record a third album with producer Rick Rubin, which was released in 2000.

Johnny's younger brother Tommy (b. April 5, 1940) initially worked as a deejay and then for his brother's publishing company before pursuing a solo career in the mid-1960s; he had his greatest success in the late 1960s, leading his band, The Tomcats, on a couple of hits, including a remake of the traditional country-blues song "Six White Horses" in 1970. He recorded sporadically through the 1970s with moderate success.

Johnny's daughter ROSANNE CASH was one of the most innovative and unusual country SINGER/SONGWRITERS of the 1980–1990s. His stepdaughter CARLENE CARTER combines ROCKABILLY and 1970s rock styles with a country sound.

Select Discography

Columbia Recordings 1958–1986, Columbia 40637. Anthology of Cash's biggest hits recorded during his most popular period as a performer.

Complete Live at San Quentin, Columbia/Legacy 66017. Landmark live recording made in the late 1960s that helped give Johnny his tough-guy image. Additional tracks on reissue CD.

The Sun Years, Rhino 70950. Reissue of classic 1950s Sun sessions; a good introduction to his pre–Columbia sound.

Come Along and Ride This Train, Bear Family 15563. Fans of Johnny's "saga songs" will love this set of eighty-seven pseudo-folk numbers cut between 1960 and 1977.

The Man in Black, 1954–1958, Bear Family 15517. Takes Johnny through all of his Sun label recordings to his first Columbia sessions; four CDs with notes by Colin Escott.

Storytellers, American Recordings 69416. Live tracks with Willie Nelson taken from the popular television program.

American Recordings I, Unchained, American Recordings III, American 45520, 43097, 69691. Rick Rubin-produced 1990s sessions in which Johnny tackles everything from traditional ballads (with just his guitar and vocals on volume 1), through Tom Petty, Beck, and Soundgarden songs with full band accompaniments.

CASH, ROSANNE (b. Memphis, Tenn., May 24, 1956)

Daughter of JOHNNY CASH, Rosanne is one of modern country's best SINGER/SONGWRITERS, whose sophisticated take on country music has made her a true innovator, although not a chart-busting hitmaker.

Rosanne was raised by her mother in southern California, and did not come directly in contact with her father's music until after high-school graduation, when she joined his road show, initially working in the laundry. She says that her dad gave her a list of "100 essential country songs" and advised her, "You have to know them if you want to be my daughter." Undecided whether music would be her career, she spent some time studying acting in Nashville and New York, also working as a secretary in CBS's London office in the mid-1970s.

In the late 1970s Cash hooked up with Texas singer/songwriter/bandleader RODNEY CROWELL, and the two were wed in the early 1980s. Crowell served as her producer, recording her debut LP, *Right or Wrong*, with his primal ROCKABILLY band, The Cherry Bombs, as accompanists. This was followed by *Seven Year Ache*, which netted her two #1 country singles and established her as a sophisticated singer/songwriter. Cash has gone on to produce song cycles reflecting her own dialogue with country-music traditions (*King's Record Shop*), while her 1993 album, *The Wheel*, which documents the breakup of her marriage, raises questions about the romantic myths promoted by popular and country music.

After *The Wheel* Cash took a three-year break from recording and touring. She moved to Capitol Records, where she released the critically acclaimed, sparsely produced *10 Song Demo*. Like much of her previous work it was "country" in name only, more in the mode of confessional singer/songwriters of the 1970s. Cash spent much of the later 1990s focusing on a career as a writer of fiction. Capitol announced a new album, *The Rules of Travel*, which was due in 2001, but has yet to appear.

Cash is a thoughtful songwriter who approaches country themes from a new perspective. "Most country songs go something like, 'Oh, honey, you left me and now I'm sad.' But I'm more interested in the hidden agenda, 'Oh, honey, you left me and why did I want you to do that?'" Cash has tackled difficult issues, such as wife abuse, encouraging women to stand up to their abusive spouses in songs like "Rosie Strikes Back."

Like many other new country performers, Cash feels free to move between styles, from driving rockabilly and HONKY-TONK to intense ballads. She shares with her father an ability to express deep feelings through her vocals, and also an honesty and directness that give her work a slightly disturbing edge. Perhaps it is for this reason that mainstream fame eludes her, while critical plaudits greet her work.

Select Discography

Hits 1979–1989, Columbia 45054. All the chart-toppers.

King's Record Shop, Columbia 40777.

Interiors, Columbia 46079. Introspective, singer songwriter material dominates this collection.

The Wheel, Columbia 52579.

10 Song Demo, Capitol 32390. 1996 album, starkly produced; despite the title, it contains eleven songs.

CHARLES, RAY (b. R. C. Robinson, Albany, Ga., September 23, 1930)

Although he's best known to the general listening public as a soul singer, Charles has recorded country music for over a quarter-century, and was one of the first black artists to "cross over" into the country market. Of course, like as is true of many great artists, Charles's music tends to transcend easy categorization, but his deep love for country music shines through all of his best recordings.

It is not surprising that there should be a natural affinity between R&B and C&W artists (besides the fact that both genres are represented by two initials!). In the rural South, black and white musicians have always mixed rather freely, despite segregation, and country music's greatest stars have all been influenced in one way or another by traditional blues, jazz, and R&B. After Charles's trailblazing success in the country arena, many R&B stars of the 1950s turned to the country market as a natural extension of their audience in the 1960s and 1970s. And both R&B and C&W are definitely soulful musics, in that both value deep-felt emotions expressed through lyrics that deal with the real issues faced by the singer and his or her audience.

Charles has always been an eclectic musician. In a Nat King Cole-styled trio, performing as R. C. Robinson, he had his first success in the mid-1950s, recording what would be called "modern soul" music for Atlantic. In 1959 he scored a minor hit with HANK SNOW's "I'm Movin' On," revealing for the first time his unique take on country sounds. Joining ABC in the same year, Charles took control of his recordings and issued a series of LPs in pop-soul, jazz, and country, beginning in 1963 with the hugely successful *Modern Sounds in Country and Western Music*.

Charles's country hits include "I Can't Stop Lovin' You," a cover of the DON GIBSON classic; "Hit the Road Jack"; "Busted"; and HANK WILLIAMS's "Your Cheatin' Heart." Charles transformed the pop classic "Georgia on My Mind" into a slow country blues; his performance was so brilliant that he was invited to sing it for the Georgia legislature when it was made the official state song. Through the 1970s Charles recorded in a variety of styles, but pretty much settled on country sounds for most of the 1980s and early 1990s.

If you haven't heard Ray Charles sing, you've probably been locked in a Skinner box since the 1950s; suffice it to say, his blues-inflected, gritty vocals have influenced scores of country singers, both black and white. And although CHARLEY PRIDE gets more press as a mainstream black country artist of the 1960s, I would argue that it was Charles who really broke the racial and musical barriers between two of America's greatest musical traditions.

Select Discography

Greatest Country & Western Hits, DCC 040. Ray's great 1960s recordings for ABC that launched his country career.
Friendship, Columbia 39415. Duets with country heavy hitters like GEORGE JONES, Hank Williams, Jr., RICKY SKAGGS, MERLE HAGGARD, JOHNNY CASH, and many others. Typical 1980s sound and production.

CHESNUTT, MARK (b. Beaumont, Tex., September 6, 1963)

Deep-voiced, broad-beamed Chesnutt is another in a long line of hunks-of-the-month who tip their ten-gallon hats to GEORGE JONES.

Raised in Beaumont, Texas, Chesnutt came from a musical home; his dad had been a local country crooner before giving up his dreams of making it big to open a used-car lot. At age sixteen Chesnutt began performing locally, filling in with day jobs as necessary. He worked in the Beaumont area for twelve years, releasing his first single on a small Houston label; the song was "Too Cold at Home," written by country songslinger Bobby Harden. After his record was released, he managed to get it to GEORGE STRAIT (Strait's drummer had previously played in his band), who passed it along to producer TONY BROWN at MCA Records. Brown liked what he heard and signed Chesnutt, rerecording the song and releasing it in the summer of 1990. Buoyed by Chesnutt's pleasant voice and he-man looks, the song hit big, and soon Chesnutt was being compared to GARTH BROOKS as "the next big thing."

Actually, his second album was far superior, featuring far more of an individual personality, in such Texas-styled, light-hearted numbers as "Bubba Shot the Jukebox" and traditional WEEPERS like "I'll Think of Something." He followed with another collection of honkers and weepers, including the 1993 hit "Almost Good-bye." Chesnutt proved successful through 1995, with several albums quickly going gold, but then the hits came less frequently, as did the recordings. Nonetheless, he continues to be a popular concert draw.

Chesnutt never seemed to develop on his initial promise. While his recordings were attractive, ultimately they lacked an individual personality that could carry him through his leaner years. In 2002 Chesnutt left MCA to join Columbia Records in an attempt to revive his career; he toured with JOE DIFFIE and TRACY LAWRENCE on The Rockin' Roadhouse Tour through the late winter.

Select Discography

Top Marks, Edsel 646. His first twenty hit songs in one convenient package.

CHILDRE, LEW (b. Opp, Ala., November 1, 1901–December 3, 1961)

Childre was a popular country comedian and Hawaiian-styled guitarist who performed on THE GRAND OLE OPRY for sixteen years.

Originally performing on the Southern backwoods tent show and vaudeville circuit, Childre developed the rural bumpkin physician character of "Doctor Lew," who gave colorful, if slightly outrageous, medical advice to his many "clients." He played guitar with a steel bar, emulating the popular Hawaiian style of the 1920s, and included in his repertoire such hoary old chestnuts as "I'm Looking over a Four-Leaf Clover," displaying just enough string wizardry to wow his audiences. He joined THE GRAND OLE OPRY in 1945, performing with comic-banjoist STRINGBEAN before embarking on a solo career in 1948; he remained with the *Opry* until his death in 1961. Although a popular stage performer, he rarely recorded.

Select Discography

On the Air, Old Homestead 132. Out-of-print LP reissuing radio transcripts from 1946.

CHUCK WAGON GANG (1935–present: original members—D. P. "Dad" Carter [David Parker C.], b. Milltown, Ky., September 25, 1889–April 28, 1963 [tenor voc]; Carrie Brooks Carter; Rose [Rosa Lola Carter], b. Noel, Mo., December 31, 1915 [sop voc]; Anna [Effie Juarita Carter], b. Noel, Mo., February 15, 1917 [alto voc]; Jim [Ernest Ray Carter], b. Tioga, Tex., August 10, 1910–1971 [b voc])

The Chuck Wagon Gang are one of the most enduring and popular country-gospel harmonizing groups; originally a small-town family group, they have blossomed into a big country business.

The Carters were highly religious sharecroppers in West Texas; D. P. met his future wife, Carrie, at a singing school sponsored by the local Baptist church. They raised nine children, including two particularly talented daughters, Rose and Anna, who became the center of the family's informal singing group. Along with brother Jim, the group appeared on radio out of Lubbock in 1935, and a year later won the sponsorship of Fort Worth's Bewley Mills, which named the group The Chuck Wagon Gang; at the same time the group was signed by Columbia.

Although they always featured at least one GOSPEL number in their radio act and in personal appearances, the group started out performing a mix of folksongs, pop, and sentimental numbers, led by the sweet harmonies of the two young daughters. However, listener response was so overwhelmingly strong for their gospel numbers that by 1938 they switched to an all-gospel format. From the traditional backwoods church they took the call-and-response pattern that was typically used by preacher and chorus; and from pop music they borrowed sweet harmonies and slick instrumentation to achieve a more modern sound. They recorded many gospel standards, including "I'll Fly Away" and "We Are Climbing Jacob's Ladder," and also published countless songbooks. A young songster named HANK WILLIAMS borrowed the melody of their 1941 recording of "He Set Me Free" for his own classic gospel song, "I Saw the Light."

In the wake of World War II, country gospel gained new popularity, in part thanks to groups like The Chuck Wagon Gang and also to a return to traditional values that swept the country. The Gang toured extensively, with some personnel changes over the years. The biggest blow to the group came with the retirement of the two lead singers in swift succession in 1965 and 1967 (Rose retired first, and then Anna wed songster/politician JIMMIE DAVIS, leading to her more or less complete withdrawal from the family act). Although family members continue to work in the band today, it has become more of a business than a group, with new members brought in to carry forward the "Chuck Wagon" sound; since 1989 the two lead singers have been professionals recruited specifically to fit the bill.

The Chuck Wagon Gang are an important link connecting the informal past of rural church singing with the modern, glitzy, country-gospel industry. They bridge traditional, unornamented harmony singing with more modern approaches borrowed from pop music in both harmonies and instrumentation. Their many tours, recordings, and publications have kept gospel music alive for a new audience in the postwar world.

Select Discography

Columbia Historic Edition, Columbia 40152. Reissues of their finest recordings from 1936 to 1975.

CLARK, GENE (b. Tipton, Mo., November 17, 1941–May 24, 1991)

Clark was a country-flavored SINGER/SONGWRITER, and one of the founding members of THE BYRDS. He went on to perform with the Gosdin Brothers, Doug Dillard (in the early country-rock band Dillard and Clark), and vocalist Carla Olson.

Clark began his career in the Los Angeles-based folk-rock band The Byrds, contributing some of their better original numbers, including "It Won't Be Wrong," "Set You Free This Time," and "Feel a Whole Lot Better," along with his emotional lead vocals. He quit the band in 1966 due to his fear of flying, and hooked up with the traditional-sounding Gosdin Brothers for an excellent album of original compositions featuring superguitarists Clarence White and GLEN CAMPBELL, as well as arranger/pianist Leon Russell and The Byrds' rhythm section; however, the album stiffed on the charts. With Doug Dillard and future FLYING BURRITO BROTHER and EAGLE Bernie Leadon, he formed Dillard and Clark, a folk-rock outfit that featured country instrumentation (Dillard's BANJO, BYRON BERLINE'S FIDDLE, plus DOBRO and MANDOLIN) as well as some classic psychedelic 1960s touches like electric harpsichord!

In the early 1970s Clark made a number of abortive attempts at solo albums backed by various members of the Byrds, Burrito Brothers, and other West Coast COUNTRY-ROCK regulars. He had a genuine knack for the contemporary country song, but unfortunately was recording about a decade too soon to gain much popular success. Most of these recordings went unreleased at the time.

Early in the 1980s Clark rejoined with ex–Byrdsmen Roger McGuinn and Chris Hillman for two critically acclaimed albums, but again his fear of flying limited the success of the trio. In the late 1980s Clark linked up with former Textones vocalist Carla Olson as an acoustic duo. Always troubled and prone to periods of depression, he took his own life in 1991.

Select Discography

With the Gosdin Brothers, Edsel 529. Resissue of wonderful 1967 LP (Columbia 2618) featuring BLUEGRASS backup by the Gosdins, Clarence White, then-session picker Glen Campbell, and even pianist Leon Russell. This was the first album Clark recorded after leaving The Byrds.

The Fantastic Expedition of Dillard and Clark Plus, Edsel 708. CD reissuing the first LP made by Dillard and Clark in the late 1960s, plus other tracks.

Echoes, Columbia/Legacy 48253. 1970s recordings, many unissued at the time.

So Rebellious a Lover, Razor and Tie 1992. Clark's last recordings, made in duet with Carla Olson.

CLARK, GUY (b. G. C., Jr., Monahans, Tex., November 6, 1941)

Guy Clark is a Texas SINGER/SONGWRITER who, along with JERRY JEFF WALKER and TOWNES VAN ZANDT, wed HONKY-TONK sounds to contemporary lyrics. His songs have been widely covered by 1980s new country stars.

Raised by his grandmother (who ran a run-down hotel), Clark learned to play GUITAR as a youngster, playing primarily Mexican folksongs that he heard in his small Texas hometown. In the 1960s he went to Houston, where he immediately began performing in the vibrant club scene that centered on that city, Austin, and Dallas. Clark moved briefly to Los Angeles in the late 1960s (inspiring his song "L.A. Freeway," which later was a hit for Jerry Jeff Walker), then settled in 1971 in Nashville, where he recorded for RCA in the mid-1970s and for Warners later in the decade. His first album, *Old No. 1*, was critically acclaimed, although it did little on the charts. It featured many of his classic songs, including "Rita Ballou," "That Old-Time Feeling," and "Desperados Waiting for a Train." Clark became a patron saint of the NEW NASHVILLE crowd, recording with and supplying songs for EMMYLOU HARRIS, RICKY SKAGGS, RODNEY CROWELL, WAYLON JENNINGS, and ROSANNE CASH, among others.

In the mid-1980s Clark recorded a comeback, acoustic-tinged album for the country-BLUEGRASS label Sugar Hill. This led to renewed interest in his music, and he signed with major label Arista in 1992, producing two albums for them before returning to recording for Sugar Hill through the rest of the 1990s.

Besides being one of the most prolific and talented of the new Texas songwriters, Clark helped expand the themes of the traditional honky-tonk song beyond boozin', partyin', and cheatin' to more contemporary and literary themes. Many of his songs recount stories from his youth; "Desperados Waitin' for a Train" is based on the reminiscences of an elderly oil-well worker who was a handyman at his grandmother's hotel. Some are nostalgic, like "Texas-1947," which was a minor hit for JOHNNY CASH in 1975. Many of his songs self-consciously refer to and comment on earlier country roots, as in "The Last Gunfighter Ballad."

Select Discography

Old No. 1/Texas Cooking, BMG 58813. Reissues Clark's first two albums from 1975–1976, originally issued by RCA. It features most of his famous songs, including "L.A. Freeway," "Rita Ballou," and "Desperados Waitin' for a Train."

Old Friends, Sugar Hill 1025. 1989 "comeback" album that features a star-studded cast, including ROSANNE CASH, STEVE WARINER, VINCE GILL, and many of the folks who appeared on *Texas Cooking*.

Boats to Build, Asylum 61442. 1992 major-label recording, with lots of New Nashville folks helping out.

Keepers, Sugar Hill 1055. 1996 live recordings, including many favorites as well as a few new songs.

CLARK, ROY (b. R. Linwood C., Meherrin, Va., April 15, 1933)

If ever a musician defined "pickin' and grinnin'," it is the affable Roy Clark, a talented stringbender and star of the oft-maligned country-corn TV show HEE HAW. Despite his considerable skills as a guitarist and banjo player, Clark does not have a definitive style of his own, perhaps because he spent his formative years as a session player.

Clark's father was a tobacco farmer who moved his family to Washington, D.C., when his son was just

Diana Trask (left) and Roy Clark, c. mid-1970s. Photo: Raeanne Rubenstein

eleven. An important center of country music making, Washington turned out to be the ideal place for the young musician to be raised; he soon was performing locally, winning the prestigious Country Music Banjo Championship at age sixteen. Clark spent most of the 1950s as a backup musician, first working with JIMMY DEAN and eventually hooking up with singer WANDA JACKSON, for whom he played GUITAR and wrote arrangements.

Beginning in the late 1950s Clark recorded as a solo artist for a variety of small labels, but success eluded him until he signed with Capitol in 1963. His first hit came the same year with the classic NASHVILLE SOUND instrumental "Tips of My Fingers," featuring the tinkling piano of FLOYD CRAMER, a girly chorus, and acres of strings. Clark was hired to host the short-lived *Swinging Country* TV show, which led to his successful audition for *Hee Haw*. Exposure on this show brought other charting songs, including 1969's schmaltzy "Yesterday When I Was Young" and the clever novelty number "Thank God and Greyhound (You're Gone)." He continued to score hits through the mid-1970s.

A pleasant singer, an affable showman, and a picker who can wow his audiences with his fleet-fingered solos, Clark is a natural for the Las Vegas-dinner club circuit, where he has performed for most of the period since the 1970s. He has become a popular attraction in BRANSON, MISSOURI, country music's new performance capital, where he has his own theater.

Select Discography

The Best of, Curb 77395. Capitol recordings from the 1960s.

CLARK, TERRI (b. T. Sauson, Montreal, Canada, August 5, 1968)

Clark is a big-lunged, big-hatted sensation of 1995–1996 who went underground, only to return again to the charts in 2000.

Born in Montreal and raised in Calgary, Clark is the daughter of a truck driver and a secretary. She moved to Nashville after graduating high school, in search of the proverbial fame and fortune. She ended up singing at a Nashville institution, Tootsie's Orchid Lounge, earning $15.00 a night plus tips.

Clark soon befriended some other up-and-coming performers and singers, and began pitching songs to established acts. Through her songwriting, she was invited to audition for producer Keith Stegall, who had a production deal with Mercury Nashville. He signed her to the label in 1994, and her debut album, *Terri Clark*, was an immediate success. It produced a number of hits, including "When Boy Meets Girl" and "If I Were You"; went gold; and garnered her a Best New Female Artist award from the Academy of Country Music.

Clark's style is toward the more traditional end of the spectrum than other new female artists', and her look is tougher. Rather than relying on little-girl mannerisms, she projects a personality as hard-edged as her songs.

Her 1996 follow-up album, *Just the Same*, was less successful than the first. It featured a hit cover of "Poor, Poor Pitiful Me" by Eric Kaz, first popularized in 1978 by LINDA RONSTADT. After a slight slump in the later 1990s, and a two-year hiatus from recording, Clark returned to the charts with the singles "A Little Gasoline" and "No Fear" from her *Fearless* album.

Select Discography

Terri Clark, Mercury Nashville 526991. 1995 debut album.
Fearless, Polygram 170157. 2000 album that brought her renewed attention.

CLEMENT, "COWBOY" JACK (b. J. Henderson C., Memphis, Tenn., April 5, 1932)

Best known for his production work with SAM PHILLIPS at Memphis's legendary Sun Studios, Clement has worked as a country producer, songwriter, and sometime performer.

Clement is a talented musician who could play in a number of styles, from big-band jazz to BLUEGRASS, and also had an interest in the more technical aspects of music. He took up music while a Marine stationed in Washington, performing locally with another country legend in the making, ROY CLARK. He worked briefly in the early 1950s with Buzz Busby as a duo called Buzz and Jack, The Bayou Boys, then played Hawaiian-style music in the Washington area, and finally returned to Memphis to pursue a degree in English at the local university.

Clement hooked up with legendary studio owner Phillips in the late 1950s and continued to work for him as a producer, engineer, and session player until he was fired in 1959. Phillips was out of town when a young piano pounder named JERRY LEE LEWIS came through the door; Clement was the one who auditioned him and encouraged the singer to return, thus launching his career. He was Sun's house arranger, working with the other musicians to perfect accompaniments for many classic recordings, as well as recording a few singles under his own name that flopped. He also wrote a couple of hits for Sun artists, including the country WEEPER "Guess Things Happen That Way" and the rockin' "Ballad of a Teenage Queen," recorded by JOHNNY CASH, which Sun historians Colin Escott and Martin Hawkins call "arguably the worst song Cash cut at Sun . . . a teen-oriented story song with an ending so sugary it could put a diabetic into a coma."

After leaving Sun, Clement briefly ran his own Summer label, and then relocated to Nashville, where he was hired as an assistant to CHET ATKINS at RCA. He spent a few years running a studio and label in Beaumont, Texas, before returning in 1965 to Nashville, where he opened a successful music-publishing business and recording studio, and discovered some of the top Nashville stars of the era, including CHARLEY PRIDE and DON WILLIAMS. In the early 1970s, he co-owned the record label JMI, which lasted until about 1974. In 1973 he was inducted into the Nashville Songwriters' Hall of Fame. Later in the decade he was a successful producer working with country outlaws Johnny Cash and WAYLON JENNINGS, and also made a solo album for Elektra Records in 1978.

Clement continued to run his studio, working with JOHN HARTFORD in the late 1970s and early 1980s, and still working with Johnny Cash. He was enlisted by Irish rockers U2 to man the boards at some of their sessions for their 1988 album, *Rattle and Hum*. He was still running his studio in the 1990s, working with a variety of artists, including newcomer IRIS DEMENT. Clement was a longtime friend of Georgia Senator Zell Miller, with whom he authored several humorous songs, including "Talking Pickup Truck Blues" in 2001, to support Miller's attempt to extend fuel regulations to these vehicles.

CLEMENTS, VASSAR (b. V. Carlton C., Kinard, Fla., April 25, 1928)

Clements is a BLUEGRASS fiddler of the 1950s and 1960s who gained fame as a jazz-influenced soloist in the 1970s.

Fiddler Vassar Clements in a pensive moment, c. mid-1970s. Photo: Raeanne Rubenstein

Clements worked through the 1950s and 1960s with a number of traditional bluegrass bands, including BILL MONROE'S and JIM AND JESSE'S groups; accompanied country star FARON YOUNG; and was associated for a while in the late 1960s with the bluegrass-rock amalgam the Earl Scruggs Revue. His career was given a big boost by JOHN HARTFORD, who hired him to tour and record with him in the early 1970s; he appeared on Hartford's seminal *Aeroplane* album.

Clements took the jazz and swing elements that were always present in bluegrass fiddling and brought them to the forefront. He also appeared on the landmark *Will the Circle Be Unbroken* album, hosted by the NITTY GRITTY DIRT BAND, that brought together older and younger musicians. In the mid-1970s he made an album with steel guitarist Doug Jerrigan and hot-picker David Bromberg, *Hillbilly Jazz*, for Flying Fish Records; this helped revive the WESTERN SWING style while establishing Clements as a solo artist. He has made a number of albums since the 1970s in a variety of styles, including bluegrass, jazz, swing, blues, and even COUNTRY-ROCK. He has also continued to work as a session musician for a number of artists, and has appeared with various bluegrass "supergroups."

Clements's fiddling has a slightly nasal sound to it, almost a country twang, reflecting his bluegrass roots. Despite attempts to become the Jean-Luc Ponty of crossover country fiddling, Clements is at his best performing traditional bluegrass stylings.

Select Discography

Back Porch Swing, Cedar Glen 4203. 1999 bluegrass-swing session, reprising many tunes from his earlier recordings, including "Hillbilly Jazz."

Full Circle, OMS 25090. 2001 outing that pairs Clements with folks he has worked with before, including Jim and Jesse, RICKY SKAGGS, and other NEW NASHVILLE luminaries.

CLEMENTS, ZEKE (b. near Empire, Ala., September 6, 1911–June 4, 1994)

Zeke Clements was a COWBOY-styled star who had a long career, appearing on all three major country-music radio programs. He also supplied the voice for Bashful, the yodeling dwarf, in Disney's *Snow White and the Seven Dwarfs*.

Zeke's career began at age seventeen, when he was signed to Chicago's NATIONAL BARN DANCE as a part of Otto Gray's Oklahoma Cowboys touring show. Five years later he joined the Bronco Busters, the first cowboy-oriented vocal group on WSM's GRAND OLE OPRY program. From about 1933 to 1939 the band was led by the husky-voiced TEXAS RUBY, one of the great YODELING cowgirl singers of the era; she often performed harmony yodeling with Zeke. In the mid-1930s he made his home on the West Coast, doing radio work, appearing in B-grade Westerns, and recording voice-overs, including his famous role in Disney's *Snow White*.

In 1939 Clements rejoined the *Opry*, becoming a major star in the 1940s thanks to his wholesome cowboy image and hit songs, including some he wrote himself: "Blue Mexico Skies," "There's Poison in Your Heart," and the all-time country classic "Smoke on the Water," which he cowrote and recorded in 1945; it was the #1 country recording of the year, and has since become a standard at Western square dances.

In the late 1940s Clements moved to the LOUISIANA HAYRIDE for a brief period, and then worked a number of smaller Southern radio stations. By the end of the 1950s he was focusing on his business interests in Nashville. At the end of the 1960s he retired to Florida, where he performed locally as the banjoist in a Dixieland band. He returned to Nashville in the 1970s, where he died in 1994.

CLIFTON, BILL (b. William Marburg, Riverdale, Md., April 5, 1931)

Clifton was one of the first BLUEGRASS revivalists who was instrumental in promoting the music of THE CARTER FAMILY and introducing bluegrass styles primarily to an urban folk audience in the U.S., Europe, and even Asia.

Clifton's interest in folk music bloomed at the University of Virginia, where he began performing with another folk revivalist, guitarist Paul Clayton. After graduation the two formed a bluegrass band in 1954, perhaps the first "second-generation" urban group to pick up the bluegrass style. They recorded for Nashville's Starday label, and often included songs from The Carter Family repertoire, which Clinton had enjoyed as a youngster; he began playing the autoharp in the style that the Carters made famous, reintroducing this instrument to folk revivalists like MIKE SEEGER. He also published a songbook including many GOSPEL and old-time songs that had originally been recorded in the 1920s, 1930s, and 1940s, introducing them to a new musically literate audience.

In 1961 Clifton organized the first bluegrass festival for an urban audience, held outside of Washington, D.C. Two years later, at the height of the FOLK REVIVAL, he left the U.S. to settle in England. Besides performing there and throughout Europe in the then largely unknown bluegrass style, he brought over key U.S. performers, including THE NEW LOST CITY RAMBLERS and bluegrass bands led by BILL MONROE and THE STANLEY BROTHERS. In 1967 Clifton took his act to the Philippines when he joined the Peace Corps, and continued to work throughout the Pacific Rim until the

mid-1970s, turning up in such far-flung places as New Zealand.

Clifton returned to Britain in the late 1970s, and toured Europe and the U.S. with bluegrass veterans Red Rector and Don Stover as The First Generation Band in 1978. He continues to record and perform, with many of his records originating in Germany. However, his style remains frozen in the late 1950s style of the early folk revival.

Select Discography

Early Years (1957–58), Rounder 1021. Compilation of 1950s recordings, with sidemen including banjoist Ralph Stanley, mandolin picker Curly Lambert, and ace fiddler Gordon Terry.

Around the World to Poor Valley, Bear Family 16425. A big eight-CD, boxed set from the German reissue label, featuring 225 selections made between 1954 and 1991.

CLINE, PATSY (b. Virginia Patterson Hensley, Winchester, Va., September 8, 1932–March 5, 1963)

Cline is one of country's best-known vocalists, still celebrated almost forty years after her death. She was among the first country stars to make the crossover into mainstream pop, and undoubtedly she would have become a middle-of-the-road chanteuse if she had lived. Whether this would have been a step forward or backward for country music depends very much on your attitude toward the increasing commercialization of Nashville's musical product in the 1960s.

Growing up in Winchester, Virginia, Cline won an amateur talent contest as a tap-dancer at the ripe old age of four; she began singing soon after. Trained on the piano, she performed in the local church choir as well as in school plays. She won an audition with Wally Fowler of THE GRAND OLE OPRY when she was sixteen, and so impressed him that he invited her to Nashville; however, she was unable to obtain a recording contract, and eventually returned to her hometown. She performed throughout her high-school years, eventually signing with the local Four Star label in 1956. Her 1950s recordings were unexceptional, although she did score one hit in 1957 with "Walkin' After Midnight," after performing it on the *Arthur Godfrey Talent Scouts* TV program. It led to a contract with Decca Records.

Cline worked with producer OWEN BRADLEY from 1957 to 1960, originally in a fairly standard country mold, gaining moderate success on the country charts. It wasn't until 1961's "Crazy" (written by WILLIE NELSON), followed by "I Fall to Pieces" (written by HARLAN HOWARD and HANK COCHRAN), that her characteristic, sad-and-lonesome vocal sound fell into place. A brief two-year hitmaking career followed, including

"When I Get Through with You," "Leavin' on Your Mind," "I Fall to Pieces," and the posthumously released "Sweet Dreams."

Cline's death in an airplane accident, along with stars HAWKSHAW HAWKINS and COWBOY COPAS, helped solidify her place in the country-music pantheon. She combined a lonesome country vocal sound with fairly smooth, poppish delivery, thus bridging the gap between HONKY-TONK singer and pop chanteuse. Many country stars cite her as an influence, including LORETTA LYNN, who was befriended by the older performer when she first came to Nashville, and, of course, new country star K. D. LANG, who has ventured into the same big-throated pop style that made Cline famous. (lang's original backup band, the re-clines, was named in homage to the earlier singer.) Cline's lasting impact was reinforced in 1985 by the release of the Hollywood film *Sweet Dreams*, starring Jessica Lange.

Select Discography

Birth of a Star, Razor and Tie 2108. Air checks from the *Arthur Godfrey* show by a then-unknown Cline.

Live at the Cimarron Ballroom, MCA 11579. 1961 concert recording first issued in 1997; although she's not at the peak of her powers, it gives a good idea of what a typical Cline performance was like.

Live at the Opry, Vols. 1 and 2, MCA 42142/42284. Air checks from *The Grand Ole Opry* that find Cline in good voice with minimal, discreet accompaniment (unlike the sometimes heavy-handed studio recordings of the era).

Patsy Cline Story, MCA 4038. Originally a two-LP set released by Decca (176) after Cline's tragic death, this remains a good collection of her best-loved recordings.

CLOWER, JERRY (b. Liberty, Miss., September 28, 1926–August 24, 1998)

Clower was a country comedian specializing in the kind of rural monologues that have long been staples of tent shows, vaudeville acts, and other backwoods entertainments.

After serving in the Army and graduating college with a degree in agriculture, Clower worked for a local chemical company in the sales division. Trying to inspire his coworkers, he developed a series of monologues based on his experiences growing up in the Mississippi woods. Eventually his friends encouraged him to make his first record, *Jerry Clower from Yazoo City Talkin'*, which he released on his own Lemon label; it quickly sold 8,000 copies with no national distribution. Clower was signed by MCA in 1971, and his monologues, most notably his "Coon Hunt Story," were immediate sensations on the country charts, earning him

Jerry Clower, c. mid-1970s. Photo: Raeanne Rubenstein

a regular spot on THE GRAND OLE OPRY in 1973. He also earned a spot as cohost of the syndicated *Nashville on the Road* TV show.

Besides his humorous monologizing, Clower was an ordained Baptist minister out of Yazoo City, and author of the homily-filled book, *Ain't God Good?*, and three other books. He appeared with Billy Graham and other popular fundamentalist preachers as an evangelist. Following heart-bypass surgery, Clower passed away in August 1998.

Select Discography

Live at Dollywood, MCA 11476. Mid-1990s recording that is typical of the many live and studio recordings still available from the popular comic.

COCHRAN, HANK (b. Garland Perry C., Isola, Miss., August 2, 1935)

Cochran has played two roles in American music history, first as a country-rocker and then as a country songwriter. His performance skills have been overshadowed by his contributions to the repertoires of other hitmakers.

Born in a small town near Greenville, Mississippi, Cochran was educated in New Mexico, where he took a job as an oil-field worker, eventually working his way to California in the early 1950s. He continued to work full-time while performing in clubs at night, hooking up with another local singer/guitarist, Eddie Cochran—who, though he had the same last name, was no relation.

The two formed The Cochran Brothers Trio along with songwriter Jerry Capehart, recording for the tiny Ekko label in a country style. Hank's role as backup guitarist was overshadowed by Eddie's famous stringbending, so much so that he remains a footnote in the more famous musician's career. The two split when Eddie and Jerry moved to Nashville and switched to a ROCKABILLY style (and fame), while Hank continued to struggle along in the country arena, performing on local shows like the *California Hayride* TV program out of Stockton.

In 1960 Hank moved to Nashville to pursue a career as a songwriter and performer. Working with legendary tunesmith HARLAN HOWARD, he wrote Patsy Cline's 1961 megahit "I Fall to Pieces," followed up by "Make the World Go Away," which was successfully waxed by both RAY PRICE and EDDY ARNOLD; Arnold also recorded Cochran's "I Want to Go with You." Thanks to these successes he was signed as a solo artist by Liberty in 1961, charting a year later with "Sally Was a Good Old Girl" and "I'd Fight the World." He moved to the smaller Gaylord and Monument labels, where he had a few more hits through the 1960s. In the mid-1960s he married country chanteuse JEANNIE SEELY, producing and writing many of her sultry hits, including her first biggie, 1966's "Don't Touch Me."

In the mid-1970s WILLIE NELSON recorded his song "(Angel) Flying Too Close to the Ground," leading to renewed interest in Cochran's career. He recorded a new album for Capitol in 1978 with many of the OUTLAW COUNTRY musicians in the supporting cast, including Nelson and MERLE HAGGARD, as well as Seely. Two years later Elektra records released new recordings of his classic 1960s country material. Neither album did much to revive Cochran's career. In the 1980s he returned to the charts as a songwriter, now working with Dean Dillon, penning "Ocean Front Property" and "The Chair" for nouveau country hunk GEORGE STRAIT.

COCKERHAM, FRED (b. Round Peak, N.C., November 3, 1905–July 8, 1980)

Cockerham, an influential traditional banjo and fiddle player most closely associated with TOMMY JARRELL, was born in the musically fertile region along the North Carolina–Virginia border, where a unique style of banjo and fiddle playing developed. Key among the musicians who influenced Cockerham was local banjoist Charlie Lowe, who developed a clean, melodically rich style of playing in the traditional drop-thumb or frailing style. Lowe played with local fiddler Ben Jarrell, and then his son Tommy, developing an intertwined style of playing fiddle–banjo duets that was rhythmically and melodically quite sophisticated. Although Cockerham enjoyed playing the banjo in this style, he was also attracted to more modern sounds; hearing fiddler ARTHUR SMITH on the radio, he began to play the fiddle, incorporating the jazz-influenced style of this famed fiddler.

As a teenager Cockerham performed locally with musicians including fiddler Ernest East and banjo player Kyle Creed. Cockerham played with several semiprofessional bands, including The Ruby Tonic Entertainers, a radio group broadcasting out of Charlotte that was bankrolled by Da Costa Waltz, who also financed a band featuring Ben Jarrell (The Southern Broadcasters). Fred won several fiddle contest titles at the famous Galax, Virginia, fiddlers' convention in the mid-1930s, and continued to work professionally through the early 1940s. World War II ended the first phase of Cockerham's musical career, and he turned to doing construction work with his friend Kyle Creed. In 1959, caught in his car during a blizzard, Cockerham nearly died; although he recovered, he had lost his high tenor voice, and from that point sang in a gravelly bass. A year later his vision was seriously impaired during a failed operation to remove cataracts.

During the 1960s, depressed and unable to work, Cockerham began playing music once again. He worked with fiddler Ernest East in The Camp Creek Boys, a sedate old-style string band. But it was when folklorists and record executives Richard Nevins and Charlie Faurot introduced Fred to Tommy Jarrell that he found his best later-life musical partner. The two formed an immediate bond, and their banjo–fiddle duets were a highlight of several albums issued on the County label. Folk festivals and concert tours followed; Cockerham was befriended by old-time revivalists Barry and Sharon Poss, who in 1973 helped finance an operation that restored a good deal of his sight.

Although not as celebrated as Jarrell, Cockerham was every bit his equal as a musician and fount of traditional song and lore. As a banjo player he preserved an older style while modernizing it by adding to its rhythmic complexity; as a fiddler he reflected the strong influence of the jazz and pop stylings of Arthur Smith, Clayton McMichen, and other popular recording artists of his youth. An expressive singer—despite the damage to his vocal cords—Cockerham was one of the finest of the newly "discovered" musicians of the old-time revival.

Select Discography

Tommy and Fred, County 2702. Anthology of recordings made from the mid-1970s through the 1980s,
compiled by folklorist Ray Alden.

COE, DAVID ALLAN (b. Akron, Ohio, September
6, 1939)

Coe is one of the 1970s OUTLAWS who actually has
a prison background, but he tries too hard to live up
to his image.

Coe spent most of his youth in trouble with the law,
ending up in the state penitentiary, where he allegedly
killed another prisoner; only the abolition of the death
penalty saved him from the electric chair. On his release in 1967 he hooked up with legendary country-
pop producer SHELBY SINGLETON, who signed him to
his SSS label, impressed by the bluesy, soulful original
material he had composed while in prison. Two albums
showing a strong soul influence were produced. Coe
then switched to a more countrified format, without
too much success, before he settled into his mature
style, which seems to draw from both streams.

In 1974 he was signed by Columbia, where he remained for over a decade. Many of his songs were
confessional (some might say self-promotional), including the outlaw ballad "Willie, Waylon and Me,"
about you-know-who, and 1983's "The Ride," telling
of a mystical meeting with the ghost of HANK WIL-
LIAMS, SR.! 1984's "Mona Lisa's Lost Her Smile," a
typically enigmatic and self-conscious composition,
was his biggest "hit." Coe has a darker side as well;
in the early 1980s he issued on his own label two albums of songs that featured racist, homophobic, and
obscene lyrics. Although he later disavowed this work,
Coe rereleased the material on CD in the late 1990s,
saying that he felt he (rather than bootleggers) should
profit from the material, which remained popular
among some fans. This material has found a new life
on white supremacist and sexually oriented Web sites.
In 1986, in another bizarre move, he issued an entire
album of meditations on the death of his father, even
featuring a photo of his dad decked out in his coffin
on the inner sleeve.

Through the 1990s he ran the Willie Nelson and
Family general store in BRANSON, MISSOURI. His career
was given a boost in 2000 when young, white hip-hop
star Kid Rock invited him to be his opening act; after
the summer tour the two recorded some songs together
for a forthcoming Kid Rock album.

As a songwriter Coe has placed a number of hits
with mainstream country acts, including 1975's
"Would You Lay With Me (in a Field of Stone),"
recorded by a young TANYA TUCKER, which created
quite a stir (because of its mature theme), and the 1977

megahit, "Take This Job and Shove It," immortalized
by JOHNNY PAYCHECK.

Select Discography

For the Record: The First Ten Years, Columbia 39585.
Compilation of his 1970s Columbia recordings that
gives a good retrospective of the hits.

COHEN, JOHN (b. New York City, 1932)

Cohen is an old-time revivalist, filmmaker, and folklorist who has discovered and recorded many fine traditional musicians.

Born to a well-educated, urban family, Cohen was
introduced to folk music through his older brother
Mike, who was a founding member of The Shan-
tyboys, an early FOLK-REVIVAL band in the late 1940s.
He attended Yale University and then settled into the
burgeoning folk music/coffeehouse scene in New York
in the mid-1950s; there he met another ex-Yalie, Tom
Paley, and MIKE SEEGER, and in 1958 the trio became
THE NEW LOST CITY RAMBLERS, the first, and probably
most influential, of the old-time string-band revivalists.

Cohen performed with The Ramblers through 1972.
He also began making field trips to the South. Focusing
on the coal-mining communities of Kentucky, in 1964
he made a film, *The High Lonesome Sound*, that introduced master BANJO player ROSCOE HOLCOMB to an
urban audience, and also featured footage of BILL
MONROE. He made several other films, including *The
End of an Old Song* (1974), featuring ballad singer
Dillard Chandler from North Carolina, as well as recording and producing a number of records for Folkways.

In 1972 Cohen formed the Putnam String County
Band with fiddler Jay Ungar, guitarist Lynn Hardy
(then Ungar's wife), and cellist Abby Newton. The
band was one of the more innovative of the old-time
revival groups, although it lasted only a year or so.
Since that time Cohen has continued to perform with
The Ramblers at their various reunion concerts, and
teaches filmmaking at the State University of New
York at Purchase. He has also become interested in
traditional Peruvian music, and has produced a film as
well as several recordings of this musical style. In
2002, Cohen published a book of his photographs,
There is No Eye, and Smithsonian/Folkways released
a CD of his field recordings to accompany it (40091).

Select Discography

Stories the Crow Told Me, Acoustic Music 34. Cohen's
first solo album, released in 1998, with Jody Stecher
and DAVID GRISMAN, among others, in the supporting cast.

High Atmosphere, Rounder 1028. Fine 1960s field recordings made by Cohen, with wonderful photographs and notes.

COLLIE, MARK (b. George M. C., Waynesboro, Tenn., January 18, 1956)

Collie is a young SINGER/SONGWRITER who is half-country, half-R&B in his approach.

Born in Waynesboro, Tennessee, a town Collie describes as "halfway between Memphis and Nashville" (musically as well as geographically), Collie originally hoped to join the Army, but found out that he was ineligible because of his diabetes. He ended up in Memphis, looking for a vibrant music scene that had existed twenty or more years earlier; instead, he bummed around with the few local players he could find.

In 1986 his wife encouraged him to move to Nashville and try to become a professional performer. Collie landed a bar job at Nashville's Douglas Corner club, playing for a year before he was "discovered" by MCA producer TONY BROWN. His first few singles didn't move very high up the country charts, but he finally hit pay dirt with the Top 5 single "Even the Man in the Moon Is Crying," released at the end of 1992. Building on that momentum, his third album was released in 1993, and its first single, "Born to Love You," made the Top 10. However, the follow-up recordings were not as successful, showing how quickly a new Nashville player can fall from favor. He moved to Warner/Giant in 1994, releasing *Tennessee Plates* a year later, his last album of new material to date. Collie has continued to tour and compose songs, and a live album with JOHNNY CASH is said to be in the works.

Collie's music combined hard-edged 1950s HONKY TONK with a Memphis twist; his first album was particularly strong, featuring the fine lead guitar of legendary stringbender JAMES BURTON.

Select Discography

Hardin County Line, MCA 42333. His first album.
Born and Raised in Black & White, MCA 10321. 1991 second album.

COLLINS KIDS (Larry, b. Lawrence Albert C., Tulsa, Okla., October 4, 1944 [gtr, voc]; and Lorrie Collins, b. Lawrencine May C., Tahlequah, Okla., May 7, 1942 [voc])

Mid-1950s ROCKABILLY stars, Larry and Lorrie Collins were big stars in the California country scene. Cutie pie Lorrie was a big-throated belter, and Larry picked a mean GUITAR; together their wholesome, all-American looks made them the perfect ambassadors to present the new rockabilly style to a country audience.

Born and raised in Oklahoma, The Collins Kids came with their family to California, like countless other Okies, in search of a better life. Larry and Lorrie began performing together as teens, singing in close harmonies while Larry energetically played his custom, double-necked guitar. The two became immediate sensations on the *Town Hall Party* radio program, the most influential country show out of southern California, where Larry often dueted with country-jazz guitarist JOE MAPHIS.

The Kids were signed by Columbia, where the pair recorded some hot rockers with descriptive titles like "Beetle-Bug-Bop," "Hop, Skip and Jump," "Hoy Hoy," and "Hot Rod"; Columbia also had them commit some teen drivel to wax, including "I Wish" and "Soda Poppin' Around." Lorrie proved she was no shrinking violet on her bluesy covers of standards like "There'll Be Some Changes Made," and Larry showed off his considerable chops on some fine instrumentals. Lorrie even dated RICKY NELSON for a while, and went out with ELVIS, too!

By the early 1960s the Kids were too old to be cute; Larry's voice changed, making their high-pitched duets a thing of the past. Lorrie recorded some solo country material showing her great potential to be a classy chanteuse, but she retired when she got married. Larry continued working in country behind the scenes, writing a couple of 1970s standards (including Tanya Tucker's "Delta Dawn") as well as occasionally acting (he had a cameo in *Every Which Way but Loose*).

Select Discography

Hop, Skip and Jump, Bear Family 15537. Two CDs featuring fifty-nine drawn from Columbia recordings made between 1955 and 1958, as well as some 1961 sessions with Lorrie belting out four great country numbers, and some solo instrumental sessions by brother Larry.

COLLINS, TOMMY (b. Leonard Raymond Sipes, Bethany, Okla., September 28, 1930–May 14, 2000)

One of the pioneers of the "BAKERSFIELD SOUND," Collins is best remembered for his mid-1950s recordings featuring a young BUCK OWENS on lead GUITAR.

Born and raised in Oklahoma, Collins had his first exposure on local radio before relocating to the Bakersfield, California, area, where many displaced Okies moved in search of employment after World War II. He roomed with FERLIN HUSKY, and soon became an important member of the local country scene, appearing on the influential *Town Hall Party* program that featured TEX RITTER, Rose and JOE MAPHIS, THE COLLINS KIDS (no relations), and many other local country acts. He signed with Los Angeles-based Capitol Records, and had his biggest hits in 1954–1955 with "You

Better Not Do That," "Whatcha Gonna Do Now," "You Gotta Have a License," and "High on a Hilltop," all featuring Buck Owens in the backup band. In 1956 Collins "found Jesus" and for a while abandoned his musical career to become a minister. He recorded some GOSPEL material with his wife, Wanda Lucille Shahan, around this period.

Collins managed to return to the charts in the mid-1960s with a couple of singles for Columbia, including 1966's "If You Can't Bite, Don't Growl" and "Birmingham," and "I Made the Prison Band" two years later. In the late 1960s he remained popular in Europe, although his U.S. career was pretty much over. In the later 1980s new country star GEORGE STRAIT covered some of his earlier HONKY-TONK numbers, including the #1 hit "If You Ain't Lovin' (You Ain't Livin')." In 1993 Collins signed with Ricky Skaggs Music as a songwriter, and continued to write material until his death in Ashland City, Tennessee, in 2000.

Select Discography

Leonard, Bear Family 15577. Five-CD set of Capitol, Columbia, and Morgan label recordings, with nicely illustrated booklet.

COLLER, JESSI (b. Miriam Johnson, Phoenix, Ariz., May 25, 1947)

The only female SINGER/SONGWRITER associated with the mid-1970s OUTLAW movement (thanks to her marriage to primo outlaw WAYLON JENNINGS), Colter actually was a rather tame mainstream country chanteuse, an outlaw by association rather than by blood.

Born Miriam Johnson, she was raised in a strict household by her evangelist mother, who had her playing church piano by the time she reached adolescence. By her teen years she was singing professionally; through her sister, who had married producer/songwriter JACK CLEMENT, she was introduced to twangy guitarist Duane Eddy, who was looking to record with a vocalist. The two married when she was just sixteen, and she became part of his road show, performing mostly in Europe (Eddy's rockin' hits had come a few years earlier in the U.S., and by the mid-1960s he was something of a has-been). In 1966 the couple resettled in Los Angeles, where Miriam Eddy (as she was now known) placed some of her original songs with DON GIBSON and DOTTIE WEST before taking the stage name Jessi Colter (after her great-great-uncle, Jess Colter, a small-time Western outlaw and counterfeiter), and was signed to Lee Hazelwood's Jamie label. Her records failed to make much of an impression, and she briefly returned to being a housewife before divorcing Eddy in 1968.

While performing in Phoenix, she met the next man in her life, Waylon Jennings, and the two were married

in 1969. Jennings took her to his label, RCA, and the two issued a couple of duets, although Colter's solo career was slow to get started. She moved to Capitol in 1974, and the following year produced her sole #1 country hit, the treacly "I'm Not Lisa." (*The Billboard Book of Number One Country Hits* points out that "when put to a slightly different rhythmic pattern, [the first four notes of the song] are the same as the notes in Don Ho's Hawaiian version of 'Tiny Bubbles' "; that about sums up this number for the history books!) Despite the fact that this song was an enormous hit, Colter's album tracks from the time were far superior to it, showing her to be an expressive vocalist not limited to sentimental warbling. She followed this with a couple of other hits over the next two years, charting on both rock and pop charts.

In 1976 RCA issued an anthology featuring recordings by Jennings, Colter, WILLIE NELSON, and Tompall Glaser (of THE GLASER BROTHERS), *Wanted: The Outlaws*. This clever marketing ploy gave a name to the 1970s artists who refused to participate in the COUNTRYPOLITAN sounds of the decade, instead producing a rougher, rowdier, more rock-and-roll-oriented sound. The decision to include Colter gave her career a further jolt, and she spent much of the rest of the 1970s touring with her husband and Nelson as part of The Outlaws.

In the late 1970s and early 1980s Colter's career slowed down, and she returned to recording primarily for the country charts. Many of her albums of this period had cowboyesque themes. In 1980 she recorded a second album of duets with husband Jennings, *Leather and Lace*, a rather lackluster affair that was, however, a big seller. She returned to Capitol Records in 1982, but her recording career slowed down; in 1985 she issued an all-GOSPEL album under her real name, Miriam Johnson. A decade later she issued a children's album.

COMMANDER CODY AND HIS LOST PLANET AIRMEN (c. 1970–1976: George Frayne [aka Commander Cody, kybds]; Billy C. Farlow [voc]; Bill Kirchen [gtr, voc]; John Tichy [gtr]; Andy Stein [fdl, ten sax]; Bruce Barlow [b]; Lance Dickerson [drms])

One of the wackiest of all the bands to come out of the psychedelic era, Commander Cody and His Lost Planet Airmen combined traditional country, WESTERN SWING, R&B, TRUCK-DRIVIN' SONGS, and a whole lot more into a musical stew that enlivened many college dorms in the 1970s. And who can argue with the world's only country band that takes its name from a 1952 Republic B-grade science fiction film?

Frayne was an art student at the University of Michigan when he rounded up his first suspects to form the original Lost Planet Airmen; the lineup jelled around 1970, and a year later the band relocated to San Francisco, where they guested on the debut album of another COUNTRY-ROCK outfit, The NEW RIDERS OF THE PURPLE SAGE.

The group was signed by Paramount and released their first and best-known album, *Lost in the Ozone*, featuring their hit remake of Charlie Ryan's "Hot Rod Lincoln." The album consisted of a mix of original material that gently parodied earlier country and swing styles, along with covers of everything from "Twenty Flight Rock" by Eddie Cochran to Ronnie Self's "Home in My Hand." This set the standard for the band's recordings through their Paramount years, including their second album, featuring odd country-styled numbers like "The Kentucky Hills of Tennessee" as well as all-out rockers like "Rip It Up."

By the time the band signed with the bigger Warner Brothers label in the mid-1970s, they had pretty much played out their hand. The band dissolved after issuing a strong live album based on their 1976 tour of England; Frayne went solo, producing a series of rather mediocre recordings. He formed a new backup band with ex-Airmen Kirchen and Barlow, called The Moonglows, around 1980. They had a minor hit with the kitschy "Two Triple Cheese (Side Order Fries)," and recorded and toured sporadically through the 1980s, mostly in England.

Select Discography

Lost in the Ozone, MCA 31185. Their debut LP, featuring many of their best-known numbers, including "Hot Rod Lincoln."

Hot Licks, Cold Steel, & Truckers Favorites, MCA 31186. Affectionate tribute to 1960s truckers' songs.

Too Much Fun: The Best of, MCA 10092. Hits collection.

CONFEDERATE RAILROAD (c. 1987–present: Danny Shirley, b. Chattanooga, Tenn., August 12, 1956 [leader, voc, gtr]; Michael Lamb [lead gtr]; Gates Nichols [pedal steel gtr]; Chris McDaniel [kybds]; Wayne Secrest [b]; Mark Dufresne [drms])

Vocal harmony group with a slight rock edge, specializing in country-pop material.

The group centers around Danny Shirley, a SINGER/SONGWRITER guitarist originally from Tennessee who started playing Southern clubs in the early 1980s. In 1984 he met the then-unknown TRAVIS TRITT; both played in the house band at the Marietta, Georgia, club Miss Kitty's. That same year Shirley signed with the tiny Armor label, recording some singles between 1984 and 1986 that barely dented the lower reaches of the country charts.

By 1987 Shirley and his bandmates, now known as Confederate Railroad, had built a solid following at Miss Kitty's. After sending a demo tape to several labels, they were signed by Atlantic in 1991 and issued their first album a year later. Their third single, "Queen

of Memphis," was a Top 5 hit, and the group was immediately crowned New Vocal Duet/Group of the Year by the Academy of Country Music.

Their next hit was 1993's "Trashy Women," propelled to popularity by its tongue-in-cheek lyric and a flamboyant music video. It was followed by 1994's "Daddy Never Was the Cadillac Kind," a title that cleverly combines family and working-class values. The band took a break between 1995 and 1998, then returned with the *Keep on Rockin'* album, featuring guest STEVE EARLE. After being dropped by Atlantic in 2000, they released a new album in 2001 with the smaller Audium label.

Select Discography

Confederate Railroad, Atlantic 82335. Debut album, featuring "Queen of Memphis" and other hits.

Greatest Hits, Atlantic 82911. The hits to 1996, and two new songs, making for a short (just over thirty minutes) CD.

CONLEE, JOHN (b. Versailles, Ky., August 11, 1946)

Conlee is a smooth balladeer who was most popular in the late 1970s and early 1980s for his middle-of-the-road countryesque performances. He also claims to be the only licensed mortician ever to have a #1 country record!

Conlee was born and raised on a farm in Kentucky. He learned to play the GUITAR at age nine, playing rock, pop, and country music for his own enjoyment. After high school he trained as an undertaker and worked for eight years at the trade (occasionally performing on the guitar at memorial services!). In his mid-twenties he relocated to Nashville, where he was hired by WLAC as a pop-music deejay.

Another deejay at the station got Conlee an audition with ABC/Dot in 1975, and he was signed a year later, recording a couple of singles that had regional success. His big break came in 1978 with his original country weeper "Rose-Colored Glasses," a story of a deluded, hardworking ol' boy who doesn't realize his girl is cheating on him. This was followed by his first two #1 hits, "Lady, Lay Down" and his own composition, "Backside of 30," about a troubled marriage, both from 1979.

Conlee had a few minor hits in the early 1980s, culminating with 1983's "Common Man," one of those God-bless-ordinary-rednecks songs that have immediate appeal to a country audience. He followed it with some up-tempo hits, unusual for this usually laid-back balladeer, including "I'm Only in It for Love," written by DEBORAH ALLEN; her husband, Rafe van Hoy; and a newcomer named Kix Brooks (later of BROOKS AND DUNN). A year later Conlee spotted another talented newcomer, Kieran Kane (later of The O'Kanes), and recorded his "As Long as I'm Rockin' with You."

Conlee left ABC/MCA Records in 1986 after a decade with the label, switching to Columbia while sticking with his producer, Bud Logan. He had a couple of hits in 1988, but then pretty much faded from the scene. His smooth-voiced pop country was beginning to sound old-fashioned as the "new country" sound took hold. Conlee has a pleasant enough voice and often performs with conviction, but the production values of his recordings vary from OK to downright dreadful, in the forgettable style of late-1970s pop.

Select Discography

Greatest Hits, Vols. 1 and 2, MCA 31229, 31230. His best songs from his first decade of recording.

CONLEY, EARL THOMAS (b. West Portsmouth, Ohio, October 17, 1941)

Dubbed "the thinking man's country musician," probably because his songs tend to have a little more depth than the average pop-country hits and feature more unusual chord progressions, Conley (a student of art history and Eastern philosophy) enjoyed a string of hits through the 1980s despite his failure to fit into an established country niche.

Born to an impoverished rural Ohio family, Conley originally studied art, and didn't take up songwriting professionally until he was twenty-six. He began commuting back and forth from his native Portsmouth to Nashville, but with little success, and then in 1970 he relocated to Huntsville, Alabama, where he cut a demo tape with his brother Fred. The two took it to a local insurance salesman and part-time record producer, Nelson Larkin, who signed Conley to his own Prize label; these first recordings were later licensed to GRT. In 1975, after four years of trying, Conley finally dented the country charts with "I Have Loved You, Girl (But Not Like This Before)," and continued to graze the lower ends of the charts through the decade's end. Through the 1970s Conley suffered some from the confusion of deejays and fans, who mixed him up with CONWAY TWITTY and JOHN CONLEE, so he went by a variety of names, including The ETC Band as well as just plain Earl Conley (although his family called him Tom), before settling on using his full name.

After a brief stint at Warner Brothers in 1979, Conley signed with Larkin's Sunbird label, recording an album of original songs called *Blue Pearl*; RANDY SCRUGGS, a musician and producer (as well as the son of legendary banjoist Earl Scruggs, of FLATT AND SCRUGGS), worked on the sessions, beginning a long association with Conley. The album yielded a hit with "Fire and Smoke," and Larkin quickly licensed it to RCA. The producer and songwriter moved to the new

label together, producing a follow-up hit in 1982 with "Somewhere Between Right and Wrong," a song that featured a rocking beat and horns (although RCA tried to placate country audiences by releasing two versions of the song, one with the horns mixed out). Some country stations refused to play the record because it "promoted" promiscuity.

In 1983 Conley scored a string of hits from his next album, *Don't Make It Easy for Me*, all written with Scruggs. Conley claims that he "programmed himself" through Zenlike meditation to produce radio hits before writing with Scruggs; whatever your feelings about Buddha, the scheme seems to have worked, because the album yielded four #1 country hits for the duo.

Into the mid-1980s Conley and producer Larkin continued to move his recordings into a more rock-oriented sound. Always a somewhat sporadic songwriter, Conley increasingly relied on material provided by Nashville's professional hitmaking factory. In 1986 RCA convinced him to cut a duet with Anita Pointer, of the R&B group The Pointer Sisters (the Sisters had had a freak country hit eleven years earlier with "Fairytale"); the result was "Too Many Times," which made it to #2.

In 1988 Conley finally broke with producer Larkin, although he didn't go far in selecting a new guiding hand; Randy Scruggs handled the production duties on his next record, along with Nashville pro and session bass player EMORY GORDY, JR. From these sessions came an odd-couple pairing of Conley with sweet-voiced singer EMMYLOU HARRIS on "Happy Endings." Conley continued rocking Nashville's boat when he chose to release "What'd I Say" as his first 1989 single, a song that featured the phrase "Go to hell" repeated three times!! Despite the fact that coproducer Gordy once edited the word "friggin' " out of a BELLAMY BROTHERS single for fear of evoking the wrath of country deejays, the song was released as it was and became another #1. Conley scored his sixteenth consecutive #1 as a solo artist later that year with "Love Out Loud," the last in his long, unbroken string of good luck (matched only by the pop-schmoozers ALABAMA). Conlee's last album of new material appeared on the small Intersound label in 1998.

Gruff-voiced Conley, with his oddball songs, minor chords, and love-me-or-leave-me attitude, has had less success on the charts of late; but his long reign in the 1980s reveals that you don't have to perform in a rhinestone-crusted leisure suit to make it in country music. In fact, the audience seems to enjoy the occasional misfit, as long as his rugged individualism doesn't overstep the lines of propriety too much.

Select Discography

Best of, RCA 6700. Big numbers from his years at RCA.

76

COOLEY, SPADE (b. Donnell Clyde C., Pack Saddle Creek, Okla., December 17, 1910–November 23, 1969)

Cooley was a pioneering fiddler/bandleader who led one of the biggest and most popular WESTERN SWING bands.

Cooley was descended from two generations of FIDDLE players, so it's not surprising that he played for his first dance at the age of eight. His family relocated from Oklahoma to southern California, where the young Cooley performed with Western-flavored groups, including JIMMY WAKELY's band. In the mid-1930s he began picking up movie work in the many C-grade cowpoke epics of the day, working as a stand-in at Republic Pictures for popular COWBOY star ROY ROGERS and playing fiddle in a number of films.

In the early 1940s Cooley formed his first band, and by the end of World War II they were permanently installed in the Santa Monica Ballroom, which Cooley leased as his home base, drawing several thousand cowboy-swing fans a night. Cooley's classic first band featured vocalist TEX WILLIAMS, as well as Joaquin Murphey's hot steel guitar and Johnny Weiss's guitar leads that were reminiscent of jazz great Charlie Christian. In 1943 they recorded Cooley's composition "Shame, Shame on You," with Williams on lead vocals, which would be the band's biggest hit and become his theme song. The entire band and singer Williams quit in 1946 to go out on their own as The Western Caravan.

In 1948 Cooley was given his own variety show, on a Los Angeles TV station, which introduced country-comic HANK PENNY. In the 1950s Cooley's bands grew in size, sometimes numbering over a dozen members, including full string sections, harp, and accordion, and he slowly gravitated toward a more pop-sounding style. Increasing problems with alcohol led to a decline in his popularity later in the decade, and his personal problems came to a head in 1961 when he shot and killed his wife in front of their teenage daughter. Cooley spent the rest of the 1960s in prison for his crime. He was released to perform at a benefit concert in 1969; following his performance he died backstage of a heart attack.

Although Cooley's recordings on a whole are more pop-flavored than BOB WILLS's, for a period in the mid-to-late 1940s his band defined the Western Swing style, and helped popularize it to a huge audience. True fans of Western Swing find his later bands bloated and too far removed from the jazz influences of his youth, but they should not forget that, for a brief period, he was one of the great innovators in this style.

Select Discography

Spadella: The Essential, Columbia/Legacy 57392. Great, swinging recordings made just after World War II.

COOLIDGE, RITA (b. Nashville, Tenn., May 1, 1944)

Somewhat of a marginal presence in country, Coolidge is best remembered for her 1970s marriage to KRIS KRISTOFFERSON and the duets they recorded together, and her middle-of-the-road hit, 1977's "(Your Love Has Lifted Me) Higher and Higher," a cover of the old pop tune by Jackie Wilson.

Coolidge began performing nearly at birth as a member of her father's GOSPEL choir. Her parents also encouraged her to play gospel-styled piano. When she was a teenager, the family relocated to Florida, and after high school she enrolled at Florida State. There she began performing COUNTRY-ROCK, blues, and pop with a local band. She moved to Memphis to work for the tiny Pepper record label, which released her first material; she also recorded jingles.

In Memphis she met the British country rockers Delaney and Bonnie (Bramlett), along with session pianist Leon Russell, with whom she became romantically involved. The quartet moved to Los Angles, and Coolidge recorded as a backup singer for the Bramletts' first album. Russell got her a job on the (in)famous "Mad Dogs and Englishmen" tour of Joe Cocker from 1969 to 1970, which led to a recording contract with Cocker's label, A&M.

Coolidge's first albums featured a fairly standard mix of pop-rock and countryish material written by the leading SINGER/SONGWRITERS of the day, including NEIL YOUNG, GUY CLARK, Van Morrison, and her soon-to-be-husband, Kristofferson. The duo met in 1973 and recorded two albums together over the next year, again in a mix of country and light 1970s pop styles. Coolidge's career finally took off in 1977 with her cover of "Higher and Higher," in which she transformed Jackie Wilson's exciting sexuality into a cool, almost offhand rendition that made for perfect dentist's-office listening.

She recorded another album with Kristofferson in 1979, but their marriage fell apart a year later. Despite a couple of early 1980s albums, Coolidge was unable to regain her pop momentum, and her new material had even looser ties to country sounds than her original records. She continues to record and perform sporadically.

Select Discography

Greatest Hits, A&M 3238. Her big-selling, easy-listening country fluff from the mid-1970s.

COOPER, WILMA LEE AND STONEY (Stoney, b. Dale Troy C., Harmon, W. Va., October 16, 1918–March 22, 1977; Wilma Lee, b. W. Leigh Leary, Valley Head, W. Va., February 7, 1921)

The Coopers, a well-known COUNTRY/BLUEGRASS duo with deep roots in traditional mountain music, enjoyed minor success on the country charts in the 1950s and renewed success on the bluegrass-revival trail two decades later.

Wilma Lee was born into a performing group, The Leary Family, a GOSPEL singing group who were well known throughout the upper South in the 1930s and 1940s, performing at church-sponsored socials, on radio, and at folk festivals. Her mother was the motivating force behind the group; a talented organist, she arranged the music for her three daughters, and her coal-miner husband sang bass. Beginning at age five, Wilma Lee sang with the family group; by her teens the group had grown beyond the limits of family to incorporate other local singers and musicians, including a young fiddler named Stoney Cooper. The two were wed in the late 1930s.

Although they continued to perform gospel with the Leary group, the duo began to perform secular music on their own, appearing in the early 1940s throughout the upper South and as far west as Nebraska, as well as having a number of jobs on small radio stations. In 1943 Wilma Lee was performing on Chicago radio while husband Stoney worked in a defense plant; four years later their big break came when they were hired to join the *WWVA Jamboree* out of Wheeling, West Virginia, a powerful station that saturated the upper South and West. They also made their first recordings for Rich-R-Tone Records, a label well known for its bluegrass recordings, and were signed two years later by the bigger and more powerful Columbia label. They remained in Wheeling for ten years, performing with their band, The Clinch Mountain Clan. At this time they had their greatest country hits with a number of songs written either by Wilma or by Stoney and Wilma, from 1956's "Cheated Too" through 1959's "There's a Big Wheel"; their last charting country song was a remake of the venerable "Wreck on the Highway" in 1961. They were well known for sentimental WEEPERS like "Willie Roy, the Crippled Boy" and "I Dreamed About Mom Last Night," and introduced Leadbelly's "Midnight Special" to the country charts. They also continued to record and perform gospel material, giving a hard-driving sound to newly composed hymns like "Walking My Lord up Calvary Hill." In 1957 they left Wheeling to join the cast of THE GRAND OLE OPRY.

The 1960s were slower times for the duo as recording artists, although they continued to tour widely. In the early 1970s the renewed interest in traditional mountain music brought their old-style country/bluegrass sound back in vogue, and they remained quite active, although Stoney's health was beginning to deteriorate due to heart problems. After his death in 1977 Wilma Lee kept the band together, continuing to take a more traditional direction, while recording for bluegrass revival labels. Daughter Carol Lee performed with the family band and directed the background singers on *The Grand Ole Opry* stage (known as The Carol Lee Singers). Although Wilma Lee continued to perform through the 1980s, of late she has been less active.

Select Discography

Wilma Lee and Stoney Cooper, Rounder 0066. Bluegrass sessions cut just before Stoney's death. Available now only on cassette.
Classic Early Recordings, County 103. Out-of-print LP reissuing late-1940s recordings originally cut for Columbia.

COPAS, COWBOY (b. Lloyd C., Blue Creek, Ohio, July 15, 1913–March 5, 1963)

One of the great HONKY-TONK singers of the 1950s, Copas is best remembered for singing lead vocal on PEE WEE KING's "Tennessee Waltz," one of the biggest country hits of all time.

Copas grew up in Ohio, despite his later claims to have been raised on a ranch in Muskogee, Oklahoma. By his late teens he was touring as a musician in a novelty duo with a "pureblood Indian" named Natchee (actually Lesley Vernon Stover, who was no more an Indian than Copas was a "cowboy") who played the FIDDLE. In 1940 the duo broke up when Copas was hired as a single act for a Cincinnati-based radio show, *The Boone Country Jamboree*.

In Cincinnati, Copas hooked up with record producer Syd Nathan, who founded King and other labels in the 1940s to produce country and R&B acts. In the mid-1940s Copas recorded a number of hits for King, including "Filipino Baby," "Tragic Romance," "Gone and Left Me Blues," and "Signed, Sealed and Delivered" (not the same as the later R&B hit), early songs in the honky-tonk style that would become increasingly popular after the war. In his performances Copas wed jazz, blues, and pop influences, making for a "hot," high-energy style that predicted not only honky-tonk but also the coming ROCKABILLY craze.

In 1946 Pee Wee King invited Copas to replace the smooth-voiced EDDY ARNOLD in his Golden West Cowboys, which got him his first exposure on THE GRAND OLE OPRY. Copas stayed for two years, singing lead on the legendary 1948 recording of "Tennessee Waltz" and thus securing his position in country history. He then went solo again with a few more hits, including 1949's "Hangman's Boogie" and 1951's "Strange Little Girl."

Copas's career sagged in the 1950s, but was revived toward the decade's end when he signed with Starday, returning to his original, stripped-down sound on a number of hits, including the #1 1960 hit "Alabam' "; "Flat Top" and "Sunny Tennessee" from 1961; and his last hit, "Goodbye Kisses" from 1963. In that year

Copas had the misfortune to play a benefit concert with HAWKSHAW HAWKINS and PATSY CLINE; the trio were tragically killed when their chartered plane crashed on the way back to Nashville.

Select Discography

Tragic Tales of Love and Life, King 714. Reissue of a late-1950s album.

CORNELIUS, HELEN (b. H. Lorene Johnson, Monroe City, Mo., December 6, 1941)

Cornelius is a mainstream country SINGER/SONGWRITER who is best remembered for a series of duets with Jim Ed Brown released in the late 1970s.

She was raised in a musical family; her father was a big GRAND OLE OPRY fan, and her brothers were all amateur country musicians. Cornelius began her career as a child performing in a vocal trio with her sisters on the local country-fair circuit. After a number of years working on the amateur level, she got her big break as a soloist appearing on *The Ted Mack Amateur Hour* in the mid-1960s.

However, it took a while for her career to get in gear. After failing to get very far as a solo artist, she took up songwriting, placing minor hits with other female country stars, including LYNN ANDERSON, JEANNIE C. RILEY, and SKEETER DAVIS. She recorded demos for MCA and Columbia, and finally was signed by RCA in the mid-1970s, producing a minor hit with "We Still Sing Love Songs in Missouri."

RCA producer Bob Ferguson suggested that the young singer might make a good duet partner for Jim Ed Brown. In 1977 the pair recorded "I Don't Want to Have to Marry You" in the sugary COUNTRYPOLITAN style; it was a #1 hit on the C&W charts. Inspired by this success, they recorded together for the next three years, even doing a country cover of the schlock classic "You Don't Bring Me Flowers," originally cut by Neil Diamond and Barbra Streisand.

In 1980 Cornelius and Brown split to pursue solo careers, without too much success. Cornelius toured the dinner-theater circuit for a while, working with another 1970s country has-been, Dave Rowland of the DAVE AND SUGAR duo. In 1988 Brown and Cornelius reunited, but by then their style was hopelessly outdated.

COUNTRY COOKING (c. 1974–1978: Kenny Kosek [fdl]; Tony Trischka [bnj]; Peter Wernick [bnj]; Russ Barenberg [gtr]; John Miller [b])

Country Cooking was an Ithaca, New York-based progressive BLUEGRASS band of the mid-1970s who spawned many other experimental/"newgrass" outfits. They were marked by TRISCHKA'S and Wernick's dual banjos (inspired by The OSBORNE BROTHERS, who used twin banjos on some of their late-1950s and early-1960s recordings), the jazz-influenced FIDDLE of Kosek, and Barenberg's progressive GUITAR work. They recorded two influential albums for Rounder in the mid-1970s, and various members performed under different names (including Breakfast Special and The Extended Playboys) and with different lineups throughout the 1970s.

After the band's demise Trischka became the most influential of the new, progressive banjoists, recording a series of solo albums that mixed his own somewhat spacey improvised compositions with more traditional numbers. Wernick relocated to the Denver area, where he recorded one solo album before forming the influential bluegrass ensemble HOT RIZE. Kosek continued to perform with various bands as a backing musician, as a duo with Matt Glaser, and as a member of Jay Unger's band, FIDDLE FEVER. Barenberg went on to be a solo artist, and Miller pursued an interest in blues and jazz guitar.

Select Discography

Bluegrass Instrumentals, Rounder 006.
Barrel of Fun, Rounder 0033. Their two fine albums, now both out of print.
26 Bluegrass Instrumentals, Rounder 11551. Compilation from their two albums on CD.

COUNTRY GAZETTE (c. 1972–c. 1986; original lineup: Byron Berline [fdl], Kenny Wertz [gtr, voc], Herb Pederson [bnj, voc], Roger Bush [b]; late-1970s lineup: Alan Munde [bnj], Roland White [mdln, voc], Joe Carr [gtr, voc], Michael Anderson [voc, b])

Originally a California-based progressive BLUEGRASS trio, the Gazette became one of the better revival bands of the 1970s thanks to the teaming of EX-KENTUCKY COLONEL Roland White with banjo whiz Alan Munde.

The group got their first break when they were invited to tour with the last original FLYING BURRITO BROTHERS lineup in 1971–1972, as a kind of extension of the band; the original trio of fiddler BERLINE, guitarist Wertz, and banjoist Pederson would play a bluegrass set in the middle of the Burritos' act, and then join the group for their electric COUNTRY-ROCK numbers.

Mandolinist Roland White came on board in late 1973, after the death of his brother Clarence, with whom he had been playing traditional bluegrass. Munde, who gained fame thanks to a solo album titled *Banjo Sandwich* in the mid-1970s, joined in the same year to replace Pederson, and the two became the nucleus of a new band (at one point, they even recorded as a duo under the band name). The group's greatest lineup, in my opinion, came together in the late 1970s, with vocalist Michael Anderson and jazz-flavored guitarist Joe Carr joining Munde and White. They recorded two excellent albums, both including classic bluegrass numbers along with more recent songs. Anderson was a strong lead singer with a lot of personality whose voice blended perfectly with White's idiosyncratic harmonies, while Munde provided rock-solid BANJO playing that was strongly influenced by bluegrass traditions while still pushing forward into more progressive territory.

This band, like most previous lineups, didn't last long, and soon Carr-Bush-White were recording as a trio, producing a couple of rather lame instrumental albums of standards (marketed as *Festival Favorites* because they were the kind of numbers that are played to death at bluegrass conventions). The band petered out by the late 1980s; Munde went back to solo and session work, and White soon after hooked up with THE NASHVILLE BLUEGRASS BAND, one of the most distinguished of the new traditional bands of the 1980s. In the early 1990s Munde assembled a new Country Gazette lineup without White, but it was short-lived.

Select Discography

Strictly Instrumental, Flying Fish 446. Later incarnation of the band with Munde and White joined by talented Dobroist Gene Wooten and fiddler Billy Joe Foster.

Hello Operator . . . This Is Country Gazette, Flying Fish 70112. Compilation of "the best" of the band recorded between 1976 and 1987.

COUNTRY GENTLEMEN, THE (Classic lineup, 1959–1969: Charlie Waller [lead voc, gtr]; John Duffey [tenor voc, mdln]; Eddie Adcock [bar voc, bnj]; Tom Gray [b voc, b])

The Country Gentlemen were Washington, D.C.'s premiere BLUEGRASS band during the first decade of the FOLK REVIVAL; they were also the best-known of the second generation, "progressive" bands who helped broaden the bluegrass style by introducing new material into the repertoire and new instrumental techniques.

The original band was formed out of the pieces of another Washington-area group, Buzz Busby's Bayou Boys. When most of the group's members were injured in an automobile accident, banjoist BILL EMERSON hired local players to finish out their gigs, including guitarist Charlie Waller, MANDOLIN player John Duffey, and bassist Larry Lahey. The pairing of Waller and Duffey proved to be an inspired choice; Waller's laconic lead vocals (in the style of country crooner HANK SNOW) were a perfect match for Duffey's high-energy and unusual tenor harmonies; as a plus, both

were able players on their instruments. The group changed its name to The Country Gentlemen in 1958 and signed with Starday Records, a Nashville-based label that was dedicated to traditional bluegrass.

Emerson soon left the band, and after a brief period during which bluegrass scholar Pete Kuykendall filled his shoes, Eddie Adcock came on board in mid-1959. Adcock had been playing electric guitar in local bars to make a living, but he had previously worked with BILL MONROE and Bill Harrell; Harrell was one of the first performers to venture beyond the bounds of the traditional bluegrass sound. Adcock was also an excellent baritone vocalist, and the trio of Waller-Duffey-Adcock became one of the most powerful and distinctive in all of bluegrass.

MIKE SEEGER, a Washington-area denizen who had come under the spell of bluegrass music, brought the group to Folkways Records, an urban outfit whose sales were mostly concentrated among the fledgling folk revivalists. Seeger oversaw their first recording in 1959 for Folkways, an album that featured primarily older mountain songs in keeping with the label's folk orientation, although the group also covered LEFTY FRIZZELL's country hit of the same year, "Long Black Veil," a bold move for a bluegrass band (the song has since become a bluegrass and COUNTRY-ROCK standard). They would record three more LPs for the label, becoming the best-known of all bluegrass groups among the urban revivalists.

After their first album was released, the band reached its classic lineup with the addition of bassist Tom Gray. An innovative musician like Adcock, Gray avoided the boom-chick patterns of traditional country styles, instead adapting jazz licks and walking bass lines borrowed from bluegrass guitar. The importance of the bass was further emphasized in the band's recordings, particularly when the harmonies came in full force and the other instruments dropped back.

The band was influential for a number of reasons. Unlike traditional bluegrass bands, they did not feature a FIDDLE player, which was a conscious decision to give them more of a chamber-grass feeling (for this reason, many other urban bluegrass bands also went fiddleless). Waller's solid guitar solos were prominently featured, another innovation that would influence future revival bands, such as THE KENTUCKY COLONELS with Clarence White. Duffey's mandolin work combined the high energy of Bill Monroe with a more sophisticated, bluesy feeling; he was among the first to emulate Jesse McReynolds's (of JIM AND JESSE) style of crosspicking. Adcock's BANJO playing went beyond the rolls of Earl Scruggs to include jazzy melodic riffs. Vocally, the band could not be beat; Duffey set the standard for every bluegrass tenor on the revival scene with his highly ornamented harmony and lead vocals. And, in terms of repertoire, the band both expanded the bluegrass realm backward to include folk classics and added to the field with original compositions like "Red Rocking Chair" (written by Duffey and William York).

Gray left the band in 1964, ending their classic era, and although the band continued to be active on the bluegrass circuit, they were less evident on the mainstream folk scene. Duffey retired in 1969 due to an internal management dispute; within a few years he had again joined with Gray to form THE SELDOM SCENE, the best-loved bluegrass band in Washington in the 1970s. In 1970 Adcock left to form The II Generation, a progressive bluegrass band that was more instrumentally oriented, leaving only Waller to carry the Country Gentlemen torch. In the early 1970s the band signed with another urban folk label, Vanguard Records, and began a long period of success with many new members passing through, including the return of Bill Emerson, young RICKY SKAGGS, JERRY DOUGLAS, DOYLE LAWSON (later leader of Doyle Lawson and Quicksilver), and many other soon-to-be progressive bluegrass stars. The band continues to record for Rebel Records today, under Waller's leadership.

Select Discography

Country Songs, Old and New, Smithsonian Folkways 40004.

Folk Songs and Bluegrass, Smithsonian Folkways 40022. These two CDs reissue The Gentlemen's first two Folkways albums from 1960 and 1961, respectively. This is the "classic" group, and these albums were highly influential on the urban folk/bluegrass revival.

Featuring Ricky Skaggs, Vanguard 73123. Reissue of an album originally recorded about 1976. At the time Skaggs was just a young bluegrass fiddler on the rise.

Twenty Five Years, Rebel 1102. Mid-1990s version of the band celebrating a key anniversary.

COUNTRYPOLITAN (c. 1970–1985)

After the pernicious effects of the NASHVILLE SOUND had made country music into a bland reflection of middle-of-the-road pop, the 1970s drove the final nail into country music's coffin with the development of countrypolitan, or crossover, country artists. It was obvious that the influence of rock, pop, and even disco could no longer be ignored by the country music establishment, who were more comfortable with Dean Martin-era crooning. Younger artists were pushing for a more contemporary sound. But, rather than returning to pure country roots, the professional music establishment turned to pop styles and "countrified" them.

The movement began with soft-pop singers who tried to move a little more toward a rock sound. LYNN ANDERSON's upbeat "(I Never Promised You a) Rose Garden" is a good example of a poppish song that came out of the country charts. The instrumentation was pure pop, and Anderson's little-girl mewing was perfect for the soothing sounds of middle-of-the-road radio (despite the fact that the song's message was hardly upbeat). The ultimate lounge-styled hit would have to be CRYSTAL GAYLE's "Don't It Make My Brown Eyes Blue," with its tinkling piano and oh-so-pleasant vocals. Even RITA COOLIDGE, wife of outlaw KRIS KRISTOFFERSON, got in the act with her cover of "Higher and Higher," taking a sexy R&B hit and sucking the life out of it so it would be acceptable to middle America.

In the mid-1970s countrypolitan tried to jump onto the disco-pop bandwagon, often with disastrous results. DOLLY PARTON made a much-noticed attempt to "cross over," releasing the perky dance number "Here I Come Again," as well as posing in leather pants and more "contemporary" clothing. (Remember that in country music image is often part of the message, so that country women were always pictured in gingham dresses until the mid-1960s; Parton's choice of disco clothing to represent her "new" sound was quite controversial in Nashville.) Late 1970s star EDDIE RABBITT represented the perfect blend of pop-rock and country styles, although it's hard to figure out what makes a song like "I Love a Rainy Night" country.

KENNY ROGERS was the ultimate countrypolitan star. Coming from a folk-pop background (he had been lead singer of the 1960s group The First Edition), Rogers had a husky voice, sexy good looks, and a knack for choosing soft-pop ballads that gave the female members of his audience the screaming meemies. His dress style indicated a basic change in the country audience; no NUDIE suits or ten-gallon hats for this cowboy, but ready-to-wear disco clothes, complete with unbuttoned shirts, chains, and bell-bottoms. Rogers's act found a natural home in places like Vegas, where middle-of-the-road America (i.e., "country") audiences come to enjoy sanitized entertainment and just a little sin.

While the countrypolitan movement was in full flower, stirrings of revolt could be felt in two areas. The so-called OUTLAWS turned their backs on Nashville, heading to places like Austin, Texas, to create a new music by focusing on older country styles. Meanwhile, the BLUEGRASS revival was sweeping through the folk community, and many of these younger pickers would become the new country stars of the 1980s and 1990s.

COUNTRY-ROCK (c. 1968)

Country-rock is the granddaddy of today's progressive or new country. In the 1960s many rock acts were rediscovering the joys of real country music, as opposed to the watered-down pop sounds that were coming from Nashville. Even The Beatles helped point the way, in their recording of BUCK OWENS's hit "Act Naturally." (Remember, Liverpool is a seaport, and country music came across the ocean on many merchant ships, so that HANK WILLIAMS was as big an influence on John Lennon and company as Little Richard.)

Several performers have claimed the mantle of the first to meld country and rock into a new style. RICK NELSON, a forgotten teen idol by the mid-1960s, was among the first to cut all-country albums, and formed his Stone Canyon Band to further his country sound in 1969. THE EVERLY BROTHERS—who had true country roots—also sought to jump-start their lagging careers in the mid-through-late 1960s by dabbling in country-rock.

Probably the first and most important country-rock LP was THE BYRDS' 1968 release, *Sweetheart of the Rodeo*. This West Coast group had always included folk and SINGER/SONGWRITER material in their act; many of the original members had performed in FOLK-REVIVAL groups in the early 1960s. In 1968, new member GRAM PARSONS, who had previously helmed The International Submarine Band (a short-lived country-rock experiment), brought with him a love of country material. *Sweetheart* featured country standards, along with compositions by BOB DYLAN and Parsons in a country style, performed by the band along with some of the better, younger Nashville session men. While this version of the Byrds was short-lived, the album they recorded became a model for later country-rock ensembles.

A year later, Bob Dylan gave the movement added legitimacy by releasing his *Nashville Skyline* LP, in which he took on the voice of a mellow-sounding country crooner and dueted with JOHNNY CASH. Young Nashvillians like multiple instrumentalist NORMAN BLAKE and steel guitarist PETE DRAKE were used for these sessions; these musicians knew country roots but were influenced by more progressive sounds. Dylan was universally respected in the rock world, with every twist and turn in his career carefully inspected. Giving his approval to the country-rock movement undoubtedly encouraged others to try out this new style. Another influential LP, oddly enough, was Ringo Starr's *Beaucoups of Blues*, recorded in Nashville in 1971; it was Ringo who had sung "Act Naturally" with The Beatles, and somehow his sad-sack vocals fit mainstream country songs perfectly. Steel guitarist Pete Drake approached Starr with the project, and produced all of the tracks, using Nashville's young talent.

Out of the remnants of the folk/rock group Buffalo Springfield came POCO, featuring Rusty Young on pedal steel guitar, previously heard only on sappy Nashville recordings, along with Jim Messina, Richie Furay, and Randy Meisner. Their theme song, "Pickin' Up the Pieces," on their first LP, stated their mission quite clearly: to "pick up the pieces" of country tradition and modernize them for a new, young, hipper audience. Meisner would soon leave to help form RICK NELSON's Stone Canyon Band, another pioneering countrified ensemble. (Meisner later formed THE EAGLES, who also began their lives in the country-rock style, although they later veered off into a decidedly pop/rock sound.) THE NITTY GRITTY DIRT BAND was another West Coast band that began its life in rock and converted to country-rock in the late 1960s. Another short-lived West Coast country-rock outfit was Nashville West, featuring guitarist Clarence White, lead singer Gib Guilbeau, and drummer Gene Parsons; they lasted from about 1967 to 1968, before White and Parsons went to the Byrds; Guilbeau sessioned with country-popster LINDA RONSTADT and was a member of one of the later incarnations of the FLYING BURRITO BROTHERS.

Gram Parsons and Byrds bassman CHRIS HILLMAN formed the most influential West Coast country-rock band, The Flying Burrito Brothers, in the early 1970s. Their first two LPs, made while Parsons was still with the group, are considered classics today, combining traditional country subject matter and sounds with a decidedly new outlook. When Parsons left the band, he had a short solo career before his untimely death; he helped launch the career of country-rock vocalist EMMYLOU HARRIS, who would "cross over" in the mid-1980s to become a pure country act. Chris Hillman later formed a progressive country band, THE DESERT ROSE BAND.

Even the San Francisco-hippie band The Grateful Dead got in on the act on their early-1970s releases *Workingman's Dead* and *American Beauty*. Both albums featured songs with distinct country flavorings, along with the purest harmonies ever laid down by this usually loud and grungy outfit. Jerry Garcia, who began his career as a bluegrass banjoist and would from time to time return to this format through the 1970s and 1980s with his informal group, OLD AND IN THE WAY, took up the pedal steel guitar at this time to get that true country sound.

The importance of country-rock cannot be understated. It not only opened country music to a new audience, the young, highly literate audience for contemporary rock, but it also helped remind country of its roots, in WESTERN SWING, HONKY-TONK, and BLUEGRASS, while pointing the way to a new music that could be based on these roots. While COUNTRYPOLITAN and even 1970s crossover country tried to "modernize" country music by employing middle-of-the-road choruses and sappy strings, the country-rock crowd was showing that the real strength of country music lay in its strong lyric content and its stripped-down sound. The country-rock revival would lead, in turn, to interest in other types of country music, such as the mid-to-late-1970s revival of ROCKABILLY.

Cousin Emmy (center with banjo) during her radio days in the '30s. Photo: University of North Carolina, Southern Historical Collection, Southern Folklife Collection, University Archives

COUSIN EMMY (b. Cynthia May Carver, near Lamb, Ky., 1903–April 11, 1980)

Cousin Emmy was an audacious and often outrageous singer/instrumentalist who was a major star of country radio of the late 1930s and early 1940s. Emmy made a comeback during the FOLK REVIVAL of the 1960s, performing for a new, urban audience.

The daughter of a fiddling tobacco farmer, Emmy was a born performer who used her talents to her own advantage: "Mama would leave me in the tobacco patch and tell me to do one row, [and] I'd sing and dance and slap my legs and entertain the seven other kids to git them to do my work for me." Taking up the fiddle at an early age, Emmy won the prestigious National Old-Time Fiddlers Contest in Louisville in 1935, the first woman to fetch this award. Helped by her performing cousins, The Carver Brothers, Emmy began performing professionally. Her first radio job was with the powerful *Wheeling* (West Virginia) *Jamboree*, as a member of Frankie Moore's Log Cabin Boys. In 1937 she formed the first Kinfolks Band (a name she used for many years for her backup group), broadcasting out of Louisville. By this time, besides FIDDLE and BANJO-GUITAR, Emmy was playing a slew of popular instruments, and even handsaw and rubber glove! (By slowly releasing air out of an inflated glove, she could play "You Are My Sunshine," a trick she continued to use through the rest of her career.)

Emmy was a loud, raucous performer in the tradition of UNCLE DAVE MACON. She was probably the first female country performer to drop the demure, "gingham-and-lace" image promoted by the male executives of country radio. She dyed her hair platinum blond, wore bright red lipstick, and dressed in an exaggerated country style. She was unafraid to draw attention to herself, and thus forecast the visual style of later performers like DOLLY PARTON.

In 1941 Emmy moved to St. Louis, where her radio broadcasts were heard by a local university professor who invited her to participate in his lectures on ancient balladry! In 1947 she made her first impact on the urban FOLK REVIVAL through recordings supervised by noted folklorist Alan Lomax, introducing several traditional folksongs into the folk-revival repertoire, including "Free Little Bird" and "I Wish I Was a Single Girl Again."

Emmy appeared in a few B-grade COWBOY flicks in the late 1940s and 1950s, and also performed at Disneyland. Her adaptation of the traditional banjo song "Reuben/Train 45," which she called "Ruby (Are You Mad at Your Man?)" was the first hit for THE OSBORNE BROTHERS in 1956, establishing them on the country circuit. In the 1960s Emmy performed on PETE SEEGER's *Rainbow Quest* television program, and made her final LP backed by the old-time revival band THE NEW LOST CITY RAMBLERS in 1967.

Select Discography

With the New Lost City Ramblers, Folkways 31021. Available now on special-order CD/cassette.

COWBOY SONGS Although Western literature has been popular in America since the days of James Fenimore Cooper and Zane Grey (right up to today with Louis L'Amour), cowboy songs were discovered by urban America with the publication of JOHN A. LOMAX's *Cowboy Ballads* in 1910, followed by several other collections. Lomax introduced such classics as "Home on the Range" and "Git Along, Little Doggies," providing the backbone for cowboy singers' repertoires for decades to come, and also solidifying the image of the cowboy as a lonesome songster.

Although not in the cowboy mold per se, JIMMIE RODGERS was influential in developing the cowboy repertoire. His combination of a black, blues-influenced repertoire and vocal style with white sentimental songs and simple GUITAR accompaniments was influential on dozens of country performers, including a young GENE AUTRY, the first "cowboy" star. Rodgers's characteristic "blue yodel" also became an integral part of many cowboy acts.

The mid-to-late 1930s saw a blossoming of cowboy and cowgirl acts, influenced by successful movie serials starring Autry and other "singing cowboys." These "horse operas," so called because they combined hokey music with fanciful plots of the "old West," were hugely popular in rural America because they reinforced images of a simpler, happier time when good guys wore white hats and bad guys were always run out of town. Groups like THE SONS OF THE PIONEERS and THE GIRLS OF THE GOLDEN WEST were two of many who exploited the cowboy imagery and repertoire. These bands took 1930s and 1940s vocal harmonies and wed them to cowboy themes, giving the odd impression that the Andrews Sisters might have felt at home working at the O.K. Corral! Even the WESTERN SWING bands, who had previously dressed in natty, uptown clothing, began emphasizing their cowboy connections; for instance, BOB WILLS starred in a number of C-grade Westerns in the 1940s.

With cowboys came cowgirls, particularly the popular PATSY MONTANA and ROSE MADDOX. Montana wore a full-fringed outfit while singing the popular "I Want to Be a Cowboy's Sweetheart," appealing to both male and female listeners.

ROY ROGERS and TEX RITTER would continue the image of the singing cowboy for a new generation on TV and in films in the 1950s and 1960s. (Rogers's "Happy Trails" was even covered by the 1960s heavy-metal rockers Quicksilver Messenger Service!) The popularity of Walt Disney's Davey Crockett would also further the cowboy myth. Country performers began wearing increasingly flamboyant cowboy garb, culminating in the famous "NUDIE suits" of the 1960s with their garish rhinestones, embroidery, and exaggerated flared pants.

The good-guy cowboy of the 1930s through 1950s gave way to the OUTLAW cowboy of the 1970s, most notably in the music of WILLIE NELSON and WAYLON JENNINGS. Nelson even created a musical tale of the "old West," Red-Headed Stranger, a song cycle that changed the cowboy image to fit the idea that, in fact, the cowboy lived by his own rules, just as Nelson as SINGER/SONGWRITER refused to obey the "rules" of mainstream Nashville. The early 1970s also saw COUNTRY-ROCK bands in a cowboy mold, such as THE NEW RIDERS OF THE PURPLE SAGE, a spin-off from The Grateful Dead who took their name from Roy Rogers's second backup group (who in turn borrowed their name from one of Zane Grey's most popular novels).

Another recent wrinkle in the cowboy myth has been spearheaded by country/cowguy MICHAEL MARTIN MURPHEY. He has been a champion of cowboy song and poetry, and a main mover behind the annual West Fest, a love-in for fans of cowboyana. Poets specializing in reciting epic tales of the West have sprung up around the country.

The "singing cowboy" continues to be popular in folk and country circles, although he is more likely to be seen behind the wheel of a pickup truck than on horseback. Folklorist Doug Green has revived a 1940s-style cowboy combo in the retro band, RIDERS IN THE SKY, who have become popular on THE GRAND OLE OPRY stage. Nearly every male country star appears wearing a cowboy hat as at least a nod to the Western heritage.

COX, BILL (b. William Jennings C., Kanawha County, W.Va., August 4, 1897–December 10, 1968)

Depression-era SINGER/SONGWRITER who performed humorous and topical songs in the style of JIMMIE RODGERS, best remembered for composing the country standard "Sparkling Brown Eyes."

Raised in rural West Virginia, Cox had settled in Charleston by the mid-1920s. A hotel clerk during the day, he worked as an entertainer at night. In 1927 he was signed as a performer by local station WOBU, whose studios were conveniently located in the hotel where he worked. The station arranged for an audition with the budget Gennett label, and he traveled to their Richmond, Indiana, studios in late 1929 to make his first recordings. Accompanying himself on GUITAR and harmonica, he achieved initial success with a series of satirical looks at the "joys" of married life, including his "Rollin' Pin Woman." Although he recorded for Gennett for only two years, his sides remained in print for years, reissued countless times on Gennett's family of dime-store labels.

In the early 1930s, Cox attracted the attention of country producer/manager ART SATHERLEY, who signed him to the American Record Corporation (ARC) label, a slightly higher-quality outfit than Gennett. Satherley gave Cox the nickname "The Dixie Songbird," and encouraged him to find a partner so he could record vocal duets, which were popular at the time thanks to the success of the many "brother" acts. Although he had previously performed with his cousin WOODROW "RED" SOVINE (soon to be a country star on his own), Cox was paired on records with another local singer, Cliff Hobbs, who sang tenor to Cox's lead.

At ARC, Cox continued to record humorous songs, but added to his repertoire a number of topical songs, such as "NRA Blues" and "Franklin D. Roosevelt's Back Again," that were later popularized during the FOLK REVIVAL by THE NEW LOST CITY RAMBLERS. Cox's best-remembered song is the sentimental love ballad "Sparkling Brown Eyes," which has been covered over the decades by artists including WEBB PIERCE (1954) and DICKEY LEE (1973). Cox also revived a turn-of-the-century hit, "Filipino Baby," which he claimed to have authored. Cox's 1937 recording was widely covered during World War II, when the story of an exotic island sweetheart appealed to servicemen assigned to the Pacific, including ERNEST TUBB's hit version.

After 1940 Cox's recording career ended. Some twenty-five years later he was "rediscovered"—broke and forgotten, living in Charleston. Local folklorist Ken Davidson recorded Cox, performing both his hits and some new compositions written in his original style, for his tiny Kanawha label a year before his death.

COX FAMILY, THE (Willard Lawrence Cox [voc]; Evelyn Marie Cox Hobbs [gtr]; Sidney Lawrence Cox, [bnj/Dobro]; Marla Suzanne Cox, [mdln])

Like many traditional country bands the Coxes, a popular country bluegrass group of the 1990s, are a real family, hailing from Springhill, Louisiana. Father Willard was an oil refinery worker and amateur musician since the 1960s; his future wife, Marie, began her career in a sister harmony act. The two met on the local country circuit, and began performing together shortly thereafter. In the early 1970s Willard began training his children, one by one, on different BLUE-GRASS instruments to make up the family band. His eldest daughter, Lynn, was the group's original bass player (she dropped out of the group before they became popular), and was joined in turn by Evelyn on GUITAR, Suzanne on MANDOLIN, and Sidney on BANJO and DOBRO. They recorded a homemade album in 1974 and began working the local bluegrass festival.

However, it would take sixteen years for the Coxes to reach "the big time." A chance encounter with fiddler/singer ALISON KRAUSS at a Texas bluegrass festival in 1988 led to her becoming a champion of the band, particularly of Suzanne's vocals and Sidney's songwriting abilities. Krauss made a minor hit out of one of Sidney's songs, "I've Got That Old Feeling"(the title track of her 1990 album), and convinced her label, Rounder Records, to sign the group in 1993. They recorded two albums for Rounder, and also joined with Krauss on an all-GOSPEL LP, *I Know Who Holds Tomorrow*, in 1994. Suzanne also became a much-in-demand session singer, backing DOLLY PARTON on her bluegrass albums, as well as RANDY TRAVIS and other mainstream country singers. In 1995 they were signed by Asylum Records, as part of that label's attempt to establish itself in the country field. However, their debut album on the label in 1996 disappointed their core fans because of the use of drums and a slightly slicker sound.

The family has not recorded since then, although both Suzanne and Marie sing harmony vocals on Krauss's 1999 album, *Forget About It*. In 2000 the family was featured in the Coen Brothers' film *O Brother, Where Art Thou?*, singing the GOSPEL song "I Am Weary." This led to renewed interest in them, although that July, Willard was sidelined due to a serious automobile accident. In 2001 he returned to performing, although confined to a wheelchair, with his children, appearing as part of the "Down from the Mountain" tour, featuring musicians from the *O Brother* film.

CRADDOCK, BILLY "CRASH" (b. William Wayne C., Greensboro, N.C., June 13, 1939)

Craddock got his start in the 1950s in ROCKABILLY and teen-pop before becoming a country artist in the 1970s. He was dubbed "Mr. Country Rock" in the

Billy "Crash" Craddock, c. mid-1970s. Photo: Raeanne Rubenstein

1970s, not because he played in the style of THE FLYING BURRITO BROTHERS but because he remade 1950s and early 1960s rock-songs in a country style.

Billy was raised in relative poverty on a farm near Greensboro. His older brother began teaching him GUITAR when he was eleven, and he debuted as part of a country duo during his high-school years, playing with another brother, Ronald. Eventually the duo expanded into a foursome, called The Four Rebels, who played rockabilly and upbeat country music. Billy also earned his nickname "Crash" in high school, thanks to his enthusiasm for tackling the opposing team's players on the football field.

In 1959 a field scout for Columbia caught The Four Rebels' act and signed Billy to the label. Columbia brought him to Nashville, but instead of his recording country or even straight rockabilly, they decided to mold him into a teen idol, in the style of pimply crooners like Fabian. The results were far from awe-inspiring, although fans of rockabilly have rediscovered these recordings today. Oddly enough, Billy's greatest success in this phase of his career was in the Australian market, where he was hailed as the new ELVIS.

After his teen-pop career faded, Craddock returned to North Carolina to work in construction. Although he continued to perform locally, he spent most of the 1960s in semiretirement, until a local pharmaceutical manufacturer named Dale Morris caught his act in 1969. Morris enlisted record producer Ron Chancey to engineer Craddock's comeback sessions, founding with him the tiny Cartwheel label. Billy's first hit was a countrified version of the old rocker "Knock Three Times," released in 1971, followed by remakes of "Ain't Nothin' Shakin' (But the Leaves on the Trees)" and the teen-pop ode "Dream Lover."

Craddock's early 1970s success interested ABC Records, which bought out his contract, and released his first #1 country hit, the cutesy "Rub It In," in 1974. (Some country stations refused to play this ode to suntan oil because they thought the lyrics referred to another kind of rubbin'; a few years later Craddock made an answer song, "You Rubbed It in All Wrong," and then remade his original hit as an ad jingle for the muscle-soothing compound Absorbine Junior in 1986!) Recognizing a good thing, ABC had him record more rock remakes, including his next #1, a cover of the Leiber/Stoller classic "Ruby, Baby."

By the mid-1970s the novelty of doing old pop hits in a country style was wearing thin. Craddock began moving into a more mainstream country style, crafting one final hit with the country WEEPER "Broken Down in Tiny Pieces," featuring background vocals by JANIE FRICKE, who was then working as a session singer. In 1977 he left ABC Records for Capitol, and broke off his relationship with long-time producer Chancey. He managed to score a few more late-1970s hits, beginning with 1978's "I Cheated on a Good Woman's

Love" and the saccharine "If I Could Write a Song as Beautiful as You," from a year later. In 1980 he returned to his old pattern of recording rock songs with a remake of "Sea Cruise." He left Capitol in 1982, then recorded an album three years later for Dot. Today he continues to record and perform, focusing primarily on the Australian market, where he remains a living legend.

Select Discography

Boom, Boom Baby, Bear Family 15610. CD reissue of his late-1950s rockabilly recordings for Columbia.
Crashes Smashes, Razor & Tie 2095. His 1970s–1980s hits from ABC, Capitol, and other labels.

CRAMER, FLOYD (b. Sampti, La., October 27, 1933–December 31, 1997)

If one person can be said to be central to the NASHVILLE SOUND, it would have to be pianist Floyd Cramer, whose "slip-note" style of playing virtually defines the

Nashville pianist Floyd Cramer, c. mid-1970s. Photo: Raeanne Rubenstein

easy-listening/pop hybrid that dominated Nashville from the late 1950s through the mid-1960s. Although CHET ATKINS as a producer crafted the sound, Cramer's presence on literally hundreds of sessions, as well as his own solo hits, solidified it.

Learning piano at the age of five, Cramer was raised in tiny Huttig, Arkansas, and first played professionally for local dances while still in high school. He joined the LOUISIANA HAYRIDE radio program as a staff accompanist following his graduation from high school in 1951. He worked briefly for the Abbott label and then teamed up with Chet Atkins as house pianist at RCA, recording behind a young ELVIS PRESLEY, JIM REEVES, and countless others. Influenced by the picking of Mother Maybelle Carter of THE CARTER FAMILY and the piano playing of Don Robertson, he developed his characteristic "slip-note" style of playing, in which he imitates the sliding from note to note that is possible on GUITAR or FIDDLE by hitting one note and almost immediately sliding his finger onto the next key. Like Atkins, Cramer was influenced by the light jazz of 1950s acts like Nat King Cole.

Cramer recorded a number of ROCKABILLY/bluesy titles in the late 1950s, including his first hit, "Flip, Flop and Bop," issued in 1957. He scored his biggest hits in the early 1960s, including 1960's "Last Date," 1961's "San Antonio Rose" (a cover of the BOB WILLS classic) and "On the Rebound," and finally 1967's "Stood Up." In the 1960s he made countless recordings of everything from pop-schlock tunes like "Smile" and "My Melody of Love" to covers of HANK WILLIAMS favorites such as "Lovesick Blues." He reemerged from obscurity in the late 1970s on an album featuring him playing eight different keyboards (through the miracle of overtracking), including synthesizer!

Less active in the 1980s and 1990s, Cramer died in 1997, at the age of sixty-four, after a six-month battle with cancer.

But it is as a studio pianist that Cramer will always be famous. The slightly blue sound of his piano work, which is almost immediately recognizable, is a signature on some of Nashville's best (and, lamentably, also much of its worst).

Select Discography

Piano Magic of, Vols 1–2, Ranwood 8248/8255. Mostly standards from the jazz and pop catalog, including "Unchained Melody," "Mona Lisa," "Danny Boy," and so on, played in a smooth, relaxing style.

CROOK & CHASE (Charles Chase, b. Rogersville, Tenn., October 19, 1952; Lorraine Crook, b. Wichita, Kan., February 19, 1957)

What Mary Hart and John Tesh were to *Entertainment Tonight,* Crook and Chase, popular Nashville deejays and television personalities, are to the Nashville scene: endlessly upbeat purveyors of happy talk and lite news about "your favorite country stars."

Chase has had a long career as a disc jockey, beginning in his hometown when he was just thirteen. After on-air stints in Kingsport and Knoxville, Chase went to Nashville, where, from 1974 to 1983, he helmed the important morning "drive time" slot at prestigious and powerful WSM. He earned his first TV job at WSM in 1982, when he was recruited to host a live daytime entertainment show. That same year producer Jim Owens decided to launch a weekly country news show, and partnered Chase with perky Lorraine Crook. A native of Kansas, Crook had begun her career as a news reporter on KAUZ in Wichita Falls, Texas, in 1980, also working on the station's *PM Magazine* program. A year later she was recruited for a similar slot at Nashville's WKRN-TV. Owens lured her to his program, and a cohost chair with Charlie Chase, for the syndicated *This Week in Country Music* program.

This Week in Country Music was an immediate success; previous country shows had emphasized a down-home look and cornpone humor. Here were two relatively young, fashionably dressed anchors who purveyed the same mix of light chat and celebrity dish that made *Entertainment Tonight* such a success. Crook & Chase drew hungry autograph hounds at Nashville's annual Fan Fair as if they were stars themselves. Crook apparently made a great impression on the show's producer; she and Owens married in 1985, and she is now an executive in his production company.

This Week in Country Music was so successful that Owens decided to expand the franchise. He packaged the program *Crook and Chase* for the fledgling TNN cable network; it premiered in 1986 and remained a staple on the station through 1991. He also spun off *Weekend with Crook & Chase* and a nighttime show for TNN, *Music City Tonight,* which combined live performances with chat. Chase has also pursued somewhat of a solo career, hosting a bloopers program, *Funny Business with Charlie Chase* on TNN and even recording his own album, *My Wife . . . My Life,* in 1993, that went nowhere. The upbeat duo hosted a Top 40 countdown show, *The Nashville Record Review,* from 1988 to 1996; a similar program, *Crook and Chase Country Countdown,* was launched to replace it in 1996. In October 1995 they published a joint autobiography, *Crook and Chase: Our Lives, the Music, and the Stars,* catering to their fan base.

Also in 1996 the duo decided to remake their show into a general lite-entertainment/gossip program, moving production to Universal Studios in Hollywood and syndicating the show to independent stations. However, by the fall of 1997 they were back on familiar turf in Nashville, recognizing that their core audience remained the country-music fan.

CROOK BROTHERS (Herman C., b. Scottsboro, Tenn., December 2, 1898–June 10, 1988 [hca]; Matthew C., b. Scottsdale, Tenn., June 13, 1896–July 1964 [hca]; Lewis Cr., b. Trousdale County, Tenn., May 30, 1909–April 12, 1997 [bnj, gtr, voc])

This long-lived country string band were among the first performers on *The Grand Ole Opry* radio broadcast.

Like DR. HUMPHREY BATE, another early *Opry* star, Herman and Matthew Crook played the harmonica, an instrument that was very popular at the turn of the twentieth century in middle Tennessee. They began performing in the early 1920s in the Nashville area, and were soon broadcasting on local radio. GEORGE HAY, the founder of THE GRAND OLD OPRY, invited them to play on the show during its second year of broadcasting, in 1926. While they were *Opry* regulars, they continued to perform on other local radio shows as well.

In 1927 Lewis Crook (no relation) joined the band on BANJO and GUITAR, giving it more of a traditional string-band sound. However, like Bate's band, they had a more subdued sound than the more raucous Georgia-based SKILLET LICKERS. A year later Victor Records made the first-ever recordings in Nashville, inspired by the success of the *Opry*, and naturally the Crooks participated. They cut four titles, including their best-seller, "My Wife Died on Friday Night." Oddly, the band did not record again until the FOLK REVIVAL of the 1960s.

Matthew Crook retired in the late 1920s to join the Nashville police force. Brother Herman, unable to find another harmonica player to take his place, decided to add a fiddler to the band. For most of the 1930s this spot was occupied by Tennessee native Floyd Etheridge, who played in a simliar style to FIDDLIN' ARTHUR SMITH (Etheridge had performed with Smith as a teenager). The band also expanded beyond its repertoire of instrumentals by adding a number of country favorites, with vocals handled by Lewis.

Amazingly, the band continued to find work on the *Opry* in the 1940s. Still featuring Herman's harmonica leads, the group had once again changed its sound by adding a vocal harmony trio to the mix, including Neil Matthews, Sr. and Jr. (Junior would later be a member of the popular 1950s country-harmony group THE JORDANAIRES.)

In the early 1960s the group was "discovered" by the FOLK REVIVAL and recorded again, this time for the Starday label. Eventually they were limited to an occasional *Opry* spot, although they continued to perform with various members until Herman's death in 1988.

CROWE, J. D. (b. James Dee C., Lexington, Ky., August 27, 1937)

Crowe is a progressive BANJO player who led one of the most influential 1970s BLUEGRASS bands.

Crowe began his career as banjoist for JIMMY MARTIN in Martin's country-bluegrass backup band, The Sunnysiders. He quickly established himself as one of the more innovative bluegrass banjo players, with an interest in rock and roll and blues as well as straight country. After leaving Martin he formed a band, The New South, in the early 1970s, along with brothers Tony and Larry Rice on GUITAR and MANDOLIN, respectively. They signed with Starday in 1973, playing amplified instruments and drawing on contemporary SINGER/SONGWRITERS as well as traditional bluegrass numbers. Crowe's most influential album was his 1975 debut on Rounder Records, when the band featured TONY RICE on guitar, RICKY SKAGGS on mandolin, JERRY DOUGLAS on DOBRO, and Bobby Slone on bass. This album did much to boost Rice's, Skaggs's, and Douglas's career among young bluegrassers, and the band's style influenced countless other "progressive" outfits.

In the late 1970s KEITH WHITLEY, who had previously performed with Skaggs, joined the band as lead vocalist, and the band began to draw more on a HONKYTONK repertoire based on Whitley's ability to re-create the sounds and styles of LEFTY FRIZZELL and Lester Flatt (of FLATT AND SCRUGGS). Other important Crowe alumni of this era are Sam Bush and Jimmy Gaudreau.

Crowe rejoined with Tony Rice, along with bluegrass "superstars" DOYLE LAWSON (guitar, vocal), Bobby Hicks (fiddle), and Todd Phillips (bass), to form an unnamed supergroup that recorded five "bluegrass albums" for Rounder in the mid-to-late 1980s. These were straightforward, return-to-roots efforts for these artists, all of whom had achieved fame and fortune in a more progressive arena. Meanwhile, Crowe continued to lead his own band through the 1990s, although it did not enjoy the same level of influence that it had twenty years earlier.

Select Discography

And the New South, Rounder 0044. This album, featuring Ricky Skaggs and Tony Rice, was an important and influential 1970s release for the progressive bluegrass movement.

Flashback, Rounder 610322. Compilation of various Crowe albums for Rounder made during the 1970s and 1980s.

Come on Down to My World, Rounder 610422. 1998 recording in which the core band is augmented with bluegrass power pickers.

CROWELL, RODNEY (b. Houston, Tex., August 7, 1950)

New country SINGER/SONGWRITER Rodney Crowell combines rock, R&B, and HONKY-TONK influences. For a while the husband of ROSANNE CASH, Crowell has had a spotty career; he's never quite made it as a performer, although his songs have been covered by many new and old country artists, and he's produced a variety of acts.

Crowell performed with his father in a local country bar band when he was growing up. He moved to Nashville in the mid-1970s in search of a recording career; he ended up performing as a lounge singer. In 1975 he was hired by EMMYLOU HARRIS to play in her Hot Band, where he worked for two years not only as a musician but also as an arranger; Harris also recorded several of his songs, including "Leaving Louisiana in Broad Daylight" and "Bluebird Wine." His songs began being covered by country and pop acts, including big names like CRYSTAL GAYLE, JOHNNY CASH, and THE OAK RIDGE BOYS; rocker Bob Seger scored a hit with his "Shame on the Moon," which led to Crowell's solo recording contract in 1977. Two years later he wed Rosanne Cash, with whom he recorded several duets (and for whom he produced several albums) until their marriage ended in the late 1980s.

Crowell's albums have always been a grab bag of musical influences; he's even worked with Booker T. Jones (of the famous Memphis soul group Booker T and the MGs). His music has been described as "country shuffle," and his attitude (as singer and songwriter) is just slightly left of center. Crowell's subjects are typical country ones—loving, losing, leaving, cheating—but are told in a modern, frank way (such as on "I Know You're Married," a flirtatious cheating song). Crowell has also inherited the confessional style of many 1970s pop singer/songwriters, documenting his stormy relationships and difficulties with self-control in songs like "I'll Gain Control Again" and "Things I Wish I'd Said," a ballad lamenting the loss of his father.

Crowell's career slowed after 1995, when he was dropped by Columbia Records. After six years of trying to find a label interested in his songs, Crowell returned in 2001 with the album *The Houston Kid*. A song cycle of original material, it features a somewhat bizarre reworking of the Johnny Cash song "I Walk the Line." In it Crowell tells the story of what the song meant to him, and then Johnny Cash joins on vocals to reprise his most famous hit. Crowell continues to go in his own, sometimes eccentric, direction, but his material is never less than interesting.

Select Discography

Collection, Warner Bros. 25965. Selected from his first solo recordings.

Diamonds & Dirt, Columbia 44076. Honky-tonk classics performed with a beefed-up rocking sound.
Life Is Messy, Columbia 47985. 1992 album inspired by Crowell's breakup with wife Rosanne Cash.
Houston Kid, Sugar Hill 1065. 2001 release that marked Crowell's return to recording after six years away.

CURB, MIKE (b. Savannah, Ga., December 24, 1944)

Curb has been a wunderkind pop producer; the leader of the ersatz Mike Curb Congregation, a Nixon-era vocal combo that took the Ray Coniff approach to new heights (or depths, depending on your point of view); and a successful producer of pop-country acts.

Curb first burst onto the musical scene as the creator of the Honda jingle, "You Meet the Nicest People on a Honda," and formed the ersatz pop group the Hondells to market it as a hit song. He became the "voice of his generation," at least to Madison Avenue and Hollywood types, who discovered he was one of the few young musicians who understood the bucks that could be made out of the craze for youthful sounds. He scored a number of (in)famous Hollywood B-grade youth flicks, including *Wild Angels* and *Riot on Sunset Strip*, before taking over the ailing MGM label in 1970. He immediately dropped innovative acts like Frank Zappa and the Velvet Underground, replacing them with the far more successful (although musically repugnant) Donny and MARIE OSMOND. He also started his Mike Curb Congregation, one of the few young groups that President Nixon actually could enjoy!

When he left MGM in the mid-1970s, Curb established his own production company, signing a string of the less offensive, more pop-oriented country acts, including DEBBIE "You Light Up My Life" BOONE, and THE BELLAMY BROTHERS, and rockin' country acts like Sawyer Brown. In the 1980s he was involved with the megasuccess of THE JUDDS, and set up his own Curb label to promote mainstream country acts. In the later '90s Curb made a large donation to Nashville's Belmont University to establish the Curb Music Program there.

CURLESS, DICK (b. Richard C., Fort Fairfield, Me., March 17, 1932–May 25, 1995)

Curless was a Northeastern-styled country singer who achieved his greatest success in the mid-1960s with his truck-drivin' ode "A Tombstone Every Mile." His career has been rather erratic due to continuing health problems.

The backwoods of Maine have long been strong grounds for country music; like many other Northeasterners, Curless was bitten by the then prevalent COWBOY bug as a youth. His father was a guitarist who taught him his first chords, and he began playing locally when he was a teenager. When the family relocated to Massachusetts, he gained his own radio show as "The Tumbleweed Kid" when he was just sixteen, and used his high-school graduation money to buy a fancy cowboy suit. When he was eighteen, he moved to Bangor, Maine, and formed a country-western group, The Trail Blazers, to play at local bars.

Drafted during the Korean War, Curless entered a new phase of his career, performing on Armed Forces Radio as the "Rice Paddy Ranger," a kind of cowboy-meets-the-Orient character that he created. He even wrote "China Nights," a cowboy ballad about the tough conditions in Korea. On his discharge in 1954 he returned to Maine and performed locally; three years later he got a big break when he sang MERLE TRAVIS's hit "Nine Pound Hammer" on *Arthur Godfrey's Talent Scouts*, which led to some work in Vegas and Hollywood. However, ongoing heart trouble led him to retire to Maine a year later, where he worked as a logger before he set out once again to conquer the music world on the West Coast.

Curless's Hollywood days in the early 1960s were far from successful, and soon he found himself back in Maine, playing the local nightclub circuit. Bangor-based radio personality Dan Fulkerson talked him into recording a truck-drivin' anthem that he had written, "A Tombstone Every Mile," which they issued on their own label, Allagash, in 1965; at the time TRUCK-DRIVING SONGS were all the rage (thanks to the recordings of DAVE DUDLEY). The tune became a regional hit, leading to a contract with Capitol's Tower subsidiary. Curless and Fulkerson produced a series of hits in a similar hard-life-on-the-road-vein, including "Six Times a Day," also in 1965; "Tater Raisin' Man" a year later; and 1967's "Travelin' Man." Capitol hooked him up with BUCK OWENS, and Curless toured as part of Owens's country extravaganza, "The All American Show," performing for two years all across the country.

However, in 1968 his bad health caught up with him, and Curless was forced into retirement again for a year. He returned with yet another truckin' anthem, "Hard, Hard Travelin' Man," a year later, followed through the early 1970s by more gear-crunchin' numbers, including the colorfully titled "Drag 'em Off the Interstate, Sock It to 'em J.P. Blues." Although long off the charts, the baritone-voiced, eye-patch-wearing singer continued to have appeal on the club circuit, particularly in his native New England, through his death in the mid-1990s.

Select Discography

Drag 'em off the Interstate, Sock It to 'em: The Hits of Dick Curless, Razor & Tie 82163. His biggest hits for those who can't afford the seven-CD box set of *all* his classic recordings issued by Bear Family (16171).

Traveling Through, Rounder 3137. His last album, recorded in 1994, presents the singer still in fine form.

CURTIS, SONNY (b. Meadow, Tex., May 9, 1937)

Curtis has been a star in ROCKABILLY and straight country, best known for his stinging lead GUITAR work and the hit rockin'-country anthems that he composed, including "I Fought the Law."

Originally a session musician in Lubbock, Texas, Curtis worked out of Nashville in the late 1950s with SLIM WHITMAN in his backup band. He was called back to Texas by old friends Jerry Allison and Joe Mauldin, the former Crickets who had returned home after breaking up with BUDDY HOLLY. Curtis joined them to continue The Crickets name, along with guitarist Glen D. Hardin, and they continued to work in a light, pop-rock style. The new Crickets broke up in 1965, and Curtis became a busy session guitarist, working with everyone from WILLIE NELSON to CRYSTAL GAYLE and, in the 1980s, RICKY SKAGGS. A re-formed Crickets led by Curtis recorded in the early 1970s, featuring British countrified guitarist ALBERT LEE; the band continues to perform today in various incarnations, often with Curtis at its helm.

TV trivia buffs please note: Curtis also had a career in jingles and TV themes, his most famous composition being "Love Is All Around," the theme from the 1970s hit sitcom, *The Mary Tyler Moore Show*.

Select Discography

The Liberty Years, EMI 95845. Reissue featuring mostly Curtis's teen-pop hits recorded with The Crickets between 1961 and 1971.

CYRUS, BILLY RAY (b. Flatwoods, Ky., August 25, 1961)

Cyrus, the "achy breaky" kid, initially inspired much controversy in country circles, thanks to his hunk-of-the-month looks, gyrating hips, and Michael Bolton-esque hairdo. Attacked by fans of new country as a flash in the pan, Cyrus has proven to be somewhat of a one-hit wonder. But he has also proven that savvy marketing, combined with a clever choice of material, can lead to megasuccess—if not lasting glory.

Cyrus is the grandson of a preacher and began singing in his family's GOSPEL group before attending school. An early enthusiasm for sports led to a baseball scholarship at Georgetown College in Georgetown, Kentucky. He says that, at age twenty, he heard an "inner voice" urging him to take up music. With his brother, he formed a band, Sly Dog, which played in

Billy Ray Cyrus, 1995. Photo: Raeanne Rubenstein

Cyrus's rush up the pop and country charts in 1991 was an example of canny marketing on the part of Mercury's PR department. They decided they would launch his first single, "Achy Breaky Heart," by introducing a new LINE DANCE, the Achy Breaky, in country-dance clubs. These clubs were popular in big cities and small towns alike, and were a natural place to reach country fans. The dance paved the way for the song, which was accompanied by an excellent video that showed Cyrus performing in a torn T-shirt while dancers enthusiastically executed the new steps. Thanks to exposure on VH-1 and other mainstream video channels, Cyrus achieved success on the pop charts as well as in country circles.

Cyrus's rather limited voice, and his often schlocky material, made his debut album an easy shot for critics of the new Nashville's tendency to prepackage any good-looking "singer" into the latest fad. Even other new country stars, like TRAVIS TRITT, attacked Billy Ray's gyrating stage presence (while at the same time Tritt took to wearing tight leather pants) on the basis that he was not a true country star. His patriotic gut-thumper, "Some Gave All," a revisionist look at the Vietnam War, was the album's second minor hit, reminding us that Billy Ray was catering to the more conservative part of the country audience. (The song enjoyed renewed popularity in the autumn of 2001 following the tragedies at the World Trade Center and Pentagon.)

Not surprisingly, Cyrus has struggled to duplicate his initial success. Despite repeated attempts to kick-start his career, he has never been able to regain the momentum that he had when he was the newest country star. In early 2000 his career enjoyed somewhat of a boost thanks to his starring role on the cable TV show *Doc*. Although he continues to record and tour, Cyrus will be best remembered for stirring up country music with his hip-shakin' anthem, and introducing a new level of marketing to the Nashville scene.

Select Discography

Some Gave All, Mercury 510635. The album that started the craze.

bars and small-time clubs in Kentucky and Ohio. In 1984 a fire destroyed their equipment, and Cyrus relocated to Los Angeles in search of a movie career. Eventually he abandoned this plan and relocated to Huntington, West Virginia, where he returned to singing in local clubs. He persistently traveled to Nashville during his free time, visiting every agent and publisher who would give him the time of day. Eventually he hooked up with Jack McFadden, who got him a job opening for REBA MCENTIRE, which led to a contract with Mercury Records.

D

DAFFAN, TED (b. Theron Eugene D., Beauregard, La., September 21, 1912–October 6, 1996)

Daffan, an early steel GUITARIST and HONKY-TONK vocalist and songsmith, is best remembered for his 1939 hit "Truck Drivin' Blues," introducing the trucker as a country-music hero.

Born in Louisiana, Daffan was raised in Houston, Texas, where at a young age he developed a keen interest in electronics, leading him to open one of the first electric-musical-instrument repair shops. The newly introduced electric steel guitar was particularly fascinating to the young musician/engineer; he even formed an amateur Hawaiian-styled band called The Blue Islanders to play local gigs so he could practice. WESTERN SWING star MILTON BROWN, a customer at Daffan's shop, convinced him to become a full-time musician. Daffan first worked with The Blue Ridge Playboys, led by guitarist FLOYD TILLMAN, in 1934.

Daffan's songwriting career got a good start with "Truck Driver's Blues," a big hit for Western Swing bandleader Cliff Bruner, who featured Texas honky-tonk singer MOON MULLICAN as his lead vocalist. This led to a contract for Daffan and his band, The Texans, with Columbia, and the 1940 hit "Worried Mind." It was followed through the 1940s by similar bluesy numbers, mostly on the themes of lovin', losin', and leavin', classic honky-tonk topics. These include 1943's WEEPER "Born to Lose," the good-ol'-boy-gone-bad of 1945's "Headin' Down the Wrong Highway," and the fine jump number "I've Got Five Dollars and It's Saturday Night" from 1950. Right after World War II, Daffan had a steady job at the Venice Pier Ballroom near Los Angeles, but in 1946 he returned to Houston.

In the 1950s Daffan's career as a performer slowed down, even though he continued to write hits in the beer-soaked style that made him famous. In 1958 he joined forces in Nashville with Canadian HANK SNOW to form a publishing company, and turned his attention to the business side of songwriting and promotion. He returned to Houston in 1961 to continue working on the business side of the industry; that same year Joe Barry had a million-selling hit with a remake of his "I'm a Fool to Care," recorded about a decade earlier by Les Paul and Mary Ford.

DAILY, HAROLD "PAPPY" (b. Yoakum, Tex., February 8, 1902–December 5, 1987)

Famed as a country entrepreneur, Daily cofounded Starday Records and helped launch the career of GEORGE JONES.

A successful Houston-based businessman who had served in the Marines in World War I, Daily established a jukebox and pinball distribution and service business in the 1930s. On the side he distributed records for the boxes, recorded local talent and then sold the masters to various small labels, and ran a country radio program. Eventually he came to the conclusion that he was in an excellent position to press his own records, with a ready market of jukebox owners already established in his state. So in 1953 he formed Starday records with Beaumont-based promoter Jack Starnes and his wife, Neva. A few months later producer Don Pierce was made a third partner because of his wide contacts in the country business. (Pierce had previously worked for the West Coast-based 4-Star label.)

While "Pappy" viewed the deal as a sideline to his business, Starnes saw the label as a means of promoting artists appearing at his clubs. Pierce was the only professional among them, and he soon angered Starnes by refusing to release records to correspond with club dates. Starnes left the label in 1954, selling out to Daily, shortly after recording a local singer who was hanging out at his club: George Jones. Jones, under Daily's guidance, would become Starday's greatest asset, scoring big with his first hit, 1955's "Why, Baby, Why."

Mercury Records, a label that Daily already distributed in Texas, was impressed by the performance of Jones's record, and offered Pierce and Daily the opportunity to run Mercury's country division, beginning in early 1957. The deal lasted for a year and a half, and led to a falling out between Pierce and Daily. Daily wanted to stay with Mercury, having befriended label executive Art Talmadge; Pierce wanted to remain independent. The two divided up Starday's publishing and recording assets, and Pierce went back to being an independent. Starday became primarily a bluegrass label, although it continued to record minor country acts and achieve a few chart hits. In 1978 the label was sold to Nashville-based Lin Broadcasting, which combined it with the assets of another leading independent, Syd Nathan's King Records.

While still at Mercury, Daily had formed another side business—D Records—perhaps to keep one hand in that side of the record world. D would be the home of various Texas artists, including a local deejay who performed a funny half-spoken, half-sung routine he called "Chantilly Lace"—The Big Bopper. The record became a massive rock and roll hit after it was leased to Mercury. Daily kept D going through 1979; both WILLIE NELSON and GEORGE STRAIT recorded for it early in their careers.

Daily joined United Artists Records as director of their country division in 1960, following in the footsteps of his buddy Art Talmadge, and bringing George Jones with him. Jones recommended a young female singer named MELBA MONTGOMERY to Daily, and she soon was one of the label's big hitmakers, both in duet with Jones and on her own.

Daily left UA in 1964 to join, again with Art Talmadge, the Musicor label, and again Jones followed. But in 1971 Jones wanted to join his then-wife TAMMY WYNETTE at Epic Records, which offered a far more lucrative deal than Musicor—and greater exposure. Talmadge and Daily were upset, and threatened to sue. Although the matter was eventually resolved, this ended the relationship between Daily and Jones.

After folding D Records in 1979, Daily retired from the music business. He died in 1987.

DALHART, VERNON (b. Marion Try Slaughter, Jefferson, Tex., April 6, 1883–September 15, 1948)

Dalhart was one of country's first superstars, releasing over 5,000 78 rpm records, although his highly trained voice makes him an acquired taste at best for the true fan of country music.

Dalhart was the son of a rancher who worked the rich land of northeastern Texas. Though young Slaughter worked as a cowhand in the region, his true love was light classical and operatic music. He entered the Dallas Conservatory of Music and then moved to New York, landing a job with the Century Opera Company in 1913. He took his stage name from the names of two tiny Texas towns, Vernon and Dalhart, where he had worked as a cowpoke.

Dalhart first recorded as a popular tenor, not a country singer, beginning with the Edison label in 1916 and then moving to Victor, using over a hundred pseudonyms. He did everything from comic novelties to "darkie" dialect discs to light classics, without much success. Then, in 1924 he recorded "The Wreck of the Old 97," which he learned from the rough, backwoodsy recording made a year earlier by blind fiddler HENRY WHITTER. The record would sell more than 25 million copies over the next two decades, becoming country's first certified big hit. It was backed by the sentimental "The Prisoner's Song," which Dalhart would rerecord several more times, earning, it is said, over a million dollars in composer's royalties.

Dalhart's heyday was between 1925 and 1931. He worked with several accompanists, beginning with CARSON ROBISON (who accompanied him on GUITAR and supplied many of his better songs) and fiddler ADELYNE HOOD, and then, when Robison went out on his own, guitarist FRANK LUTHER. His repertoire was made up of "old familiar tunes," that is to say, a smattering of traditional songs along with popular songs of the late nineteenth and early twentieth centuries, along with topical numbers, such as the ever-popular "Death of Floyd Collins" (written by Robison). Dalhart sang with an exaggerated hillbilly twang, although to modern ears he hardly sounds like a country singer; his mainstream training shines through even when he tries to put on an aw-shucks, backwoodsman's act.

The Depression put a crimp in Dalhart's career, although he continued to record through 1939, when he made his final records for the budget Bluebird label. Meanwhile, his earlier records were reissued on various budget labels, sold both by dime stores and the popular mail-order catalogs that reached thousands of rural Americans. In the 1940s Dalhart relocated to Bridgeport, Connecticut, where he eventually became a hotel clerk; he died of a heart attack in 1948.

Select Discography

Inducted into the Hall of Fame, 1981, King 3820. Ten-song reissue of Dalhart's early 78s, with little or no noise reduction (be prepared for lots of hiss and crackles!). Includes most of his "hits."

DALTON, LACY J. (b. Jill Lynne Byrem, Bloomsburg, Pa., October 13, 1946)

A former folk-rocker who has had a long and bumpy career, Dalton wrote and performed music that emphasized her working-class background and the difficulties women face in a man's world.

Lacy came from rural Pennsylvania; her father was a sometimes mechanic, sometimes hunting guide; her mother worked as a beautician and a waitress. Both were active amateur country musicians, thus giving their child an early indoctrination in country balladry. Interested in art during her high school years, Dalton enrolled at Brigham Young University as an art major; she lasted only a year and a half there, and then began performing with a friend in local coffeehouses. She passed through Minnesota for a while, returned home to Pennsylvania, and then headed out to California, where she fronted a folk-rock band called The Office, managed by her future husband, John Croston.

The band never really took off, despite some record-label interest, and Dalton's marriage went on the skids when her husband was paralyzed in a freak accident; after a few painful months he died. Dalton was left pregnant and unemployed in Santa Cruz, California; although she continued to play her music, she had to fill in with many menial jobs.

In 1978 Dalton recorded an album in a friend's garage; she was able to sell about 3,000 copies locally. A local deejay passed a copy along to Columbia Records, where her songwriting abilities impressed veteran country producer BILLY SHERRILL. Sherrill suggested a name change, and Jill Byrem became Lacy J. (for Jill) Dalton; the last name came from a singer she admired, Karen Dalton. With a husky voice somewhat reminiscent of the bluesy style of rocker Janis Joplin, she obviously did not exactly fit into the country mold; but the country charts were ripe for something new, and her first single, 1978's "Crazy Blue Eyes," which she cowrote, was moderately successful. 1980's remake of the hoary old chestnut "Tennessee Waltz" was a bigger hit.

Through the 1980s Dalton produced a body of work centering on a number of concept albums, often dealing with the difficulty that the rural poor, particularly females, face in making a living. This streak began with 1980's "Hard Times" and ran through her 1986 album *Highway Diner* with its hit "Working-Class Man," and 1989's *Survivor* with the title song, "I'm a Survivor." (Between 1986 and 1989 Dalton struggled to overcome a growing problem with alcohol.) It's unusual for country songs, particularly those performed by female performers, to be so directly autobiographical and topical; in this way Dalton considerably broadened the palette of material available to females in country music.

Dalton released her last major-label album to date in 1992. She continued touring and releasing albums independently through the 1990s, appealing to her core audience.

Select Discography

Greatest Hits, Columbia 38883. Billy Sherrill-produced hits from the early 1980s.

DANIELS, CHARLIE (b. C. Edwards D., Wilmington, N.C., October 28, 1936)

Daniels is a flashy fiddler who leads a solid COUNTRY-ROCK band. He is best known for his 1979 country/pop hit "The Devil Went Down to Georgia."

Raised in rural North Carolina, Daniels played FIDDLE and GUITAR in a number of amateur country and BLUEGRASS bands before turning professional at age twenty-one. His first group was a rock-and-roll instrumental ensemble, The Jaguars, who recorded in 1959 under the hand of producer Bob Johnston, later a leading country and folk producer for Columbia Records. The group stayed together in one form or another until 1967, when Johnston urged Daniels to come to Nashville to work as a session musician and songwriter (Daniels had already placed one song, "It Hurts Me," with ELVIS PRESLEY). Daniels sessioned on a number of landmark recordings, including BOB DYLAN's *Nashville Skyline*, as well as touring with folkie poet Leonard Cohen. He also served as producer for the folk-rock group The Youngbloods' *Elephant's Memory* album.

After recording a solo album for Capitol, Daniels formed his Charlie Daniels Band in 1972, inspired by the success of the Allman Brothers. Daniels played lead guitar (and occasional fiddle) along with Don Murray (aping the twin-guitar approach of the Allmans), and Joe DiGregorio on keyboards, Charlie Hayward on bass, and James W. Marshal on drums. Their first big hit was "Uneasy Rider," a 1973 recording that told of a hippie who accidentally strayed into a backcountry bar, with the "rednecks" the butt of the joke (in 1988 Daniels remade the number for his country audience, now casting the hippie as an honest "good old boy" who wanders into a gay bar). A year later they had another hit with the gut-thumping anthem "The South's Gonna Do It."

By the end of the 1970s it was clear that the rock audience was turning away from Southern bands, so Daniels shifted in a more country-oriented direction. His biggest hit in this mold was 1979's "The Devil Went Down to Georgia," full of flashy fiddle effects (not played by Daniels on the record) along with the requisite pounding beat and screeching lead guitar to appeal to his core rock audience. The song was an enormous hit, and remains the number most closely associated with him.

Through the 1980s Daniels increasingly aligned himself with the core country audience, although he failed to produce a follow-up to his megahit. By the end of the decade he was recording such no-brain anthems as songs advocating lynching as a cure for social ills, as well as calling for the assassination of Soviet premier Mikhail Gorbachev. Luckily these numbers received little airplay, even on conservative country radio.

In 1994 Daniels was invited to remake "The Devil" with master fiddler MARK O'CONNOR, featuring TRAVIS TRITT singing the lead role. He continued to tour through the 1990s, without producing any chart hits.

Select Discography

A Decade of Hits, Epic 38795. All the songs you remember, and a bunch you don't.

Roots Remain, Sony 85761. Three-CD career retrospective for true Daniels diehards.

DARBY AND TARLTON (Tom Darby, b. Columbus, Ga., January 7, 1883; d. Dallas, Tex., June 1971 [gtr, voc], and Jimmy Tarlton, b. Johnny James Rimbert T., Chesterfield County, S.C., May 8, 1892–1979 [steel gtr, voc])

Darby and Tarlton, a legendary country duo of the 1920s, were particularly loved for Jimmy Tarlton's expressive and exquisite steel guitar playing, which greatly influenced the next generation of pickers.

The duo came out of South Carolina's textile mills. Tarlton was undoubtedly the more talented of the pair; early on, he took up the BANJO but could play many instruments well. A fine singer with a clear voice, he apparently traveled around the country performing, covering lots of ground between South Carolina, New York, and California. He first began playing guitar with a bottleneck slide in the blues style popular in the South, but then met a Hawaiian guitarist when he was bumming around the West Coast at the time of World War I, and quickly adopted novelty effects from that musical style.

Exactly when and where Darby and Tarlton met and first performed together is unknown. In April 1927 the duo made their first recordings for Columbia Records in New York, with Darby playing guitar and singing lead vocals, and Tarlton on steel guitar providing tenor harmonies. At their second recording session, also held in 1927, the duo recorded two traditional folk blues numbers, both "arranged" by Tarlton: "Birmingham Jail" and "Columbus Stockade Blues." Tarlton received a $75.00 arranger's fee for these two numbers that have since become folk and country standards.

The duo continued to record together through the early 1930s for a variety of labels, until the Depression put a crimp in the country music industry; Tarlton also recorded without Darby. Their brand of bluesy duets was quite influential on later brother acts, from the ALLEN BROTHERS to the DELMORE BROTHERS.

Select Discography

Complete Recordings, Bear Family 15764. All seventy of the surviving recordings of Darby and Tarlton, in a lovingly assembled box set.

DARLING, DENVER (b. Whopock, Ill., April 6, 1909–April 27, 1981)

Darling, a New York-based "urban" cowboy singer/songwriter briefly popular in the 1940s, was born in rural Illinois. The aptly named (for a soon-to-be-cowboy star) Denver Darling grew up in Jewett, Illinois, where he learned the rudiments of the GUITAR. As a teenager he both performed and worked on various radio stations out of the Midwest. He was briefly a member of the popular WLS NATIONAL BARN DANCE radio show, performing with a vocal trio.

Darling's real success came after he moved to New York City in 1937. A popular "country" nightclub in Greenwich Village was the Village Barn, located on West 4th Street. Decked out with saddles and other Western paraphernalia, it was among the first "urban cowboy" spots that catered to a clientele who liked to imagine they might someday rope cattle and ride the range. Darling was soon an established headliner there, which led, in 1941, to a regular radio program on New York's powerful WOR and a recording contract with Decca. He scored big with the patriotic flag-waver, "Cowards over Pearl Harbor," released shortly after the infamous attack in December 1941. Several more songs with similar sentiments followed.

Although he was positioned as a "cowboy," Darling's material had a light swing that presaged the work of Bill Haley in the 1950s. He often recorded with jazz musicians, including trumpeter "Wild" Bill Davison on his later sessions. Darling's other notable songs include "Juke Joint Mama," a minor hit for him in 1945, which—some say—was "borrowed" by Mike Leiber and Jerry Stoller to make their later hit song, 1952's "Kansas City." Also that year Darling coauthored the R&B hit, "Choo Choo Ch'Boogie," soon a major hit for Louis Jordan and often covered since (producer Milt Gabler and Vaughn Horton shared the credit for the song). In 1945 Darling also had the distinction of being the first "country" performer to sing at New York's Carnegie Hall, appearing as part of the Clef Award presentations. After leaving Decca, Darling recorded for various labels, including Deluxe (often under the nom-de-disc of "Tex Grande") and MGM during the mid-1940s.

Despite his success Darling was homesick for small-town Illinois life. He was also having problems with his singing voice, making performing painful and difficult. In late 1947 he returned to Jewett, Illinois, where he was raised. Though continuing to write songs, he never again performed and was soon forgotten.

DAVE AND SUGAR (b. Dave Rowland, Anaheim, Calif.)

Would everybody who remembers Tony Orlando and Dawn please raise their hands? Will everyone who *liked* their music please raise their hands? OK, everyone else can leave the room while we discuss the career of Dave and Sugar, country's answer to these saccharine popsters.

Dave was Dave Rowland, a California-born vocalist who performed with the "memorable" pop vocal quartet The Four Guys. His "background" in country came thanks to some work backing up CHARLEY PRIDE, but he was fired from Pride's touring band due to "personal problems." In 1975 he formed his memorable country-pop trio, with Sugar consisting of vocalists Vicki Hackman and Jackie Franc. Their second record, 1976's "The Door Is Always Open," was a #1 country hit, opening the door (sorry about that) for a string of "classic" waxings, including 1977's "I'm Knee Deep in Loving You" (and, one might add, neck-deep in schmaltz) through their final big number, 1979's "Golden Tears" (the kind true fans of country music shed when they heard this song made #1).

Luckily, there being a God in cowpoke heaven, the hits dried up after they switched to Elektra Records in 1981; a few years later Dave was touring with another country has-been, HELEN CORNELIUS, and can still be heard occasionally on the road. Watch for an announcement of a concert in your area; then hit the road before the curtain goes up.

DAVIES, GAIL (b. Patricia G. Dickerson, Broken Bow, Okla., June 5, 1948)

Davies is a SINGER/SONGWRITER who had her biggest country hits in the late 1970s and early 1980s. Somewhat ahead of her time, Davies brought a California back-to-roots and feminist sensibility to country music that was similar in sound and style to the recordings of LINDA RONSTADT and EMMYLOU HARRIS.

Davies was the daughter of an amateur country singer/guitarist in the ERNEST TUBB vein. Her parents split when she was five due to her father's alcoholism, and her mother took her and her two brothers to Washington state, where her mother married Darby Allan Davies. Along with her brother Ron (later a successful pop songwriter who wrote "Long Hard Climb" for Helen Reddy and Three Dog Night's "It Ain't Easy") Gail began performing in a country-rock vein as a teenager. The duo relocated to Los Angeles and recorded an LP that was never released. In Los Angeles, Davies met and married a jazz musician, and began singing in that style.

In the mid-1970s Davies returned to country songwriting and performing. Encouraged by the more progressive country songwriters, such as HOYT AXTON and movie-star-turned-singer Ronee Blakley, she began performing in the Los Angeles country-club scene.

Deemed "too traditional" for the more progressive Los Angeles clubs, in 1975 she went to Nashville, where her music was rejected as "too pop"! Finally she was signed by Epic/Lifesong in 1978, and released her first LP, a mixture of original compositions and country classics, a year later.

Davies's songs were unusual because they combined a country sensibility with an ambivalence toward the difficulties of growing up in a country household. "Bucket to the South," her best song from this period, relates her ambivalent feelings toward her father, who was both a role model as a guitarist and unreliable as a parent. She also had a hit with her remake of the classic 1950s tearjerker "Poison Love." Further hits followed in the early 1980s, including "Blue Heartache," "It's a Lovely, Lovely World," and "Singin' the Blues." Unlike more mainstream female country acts, who were still dressing in gingham and lace, Davies projected a more relaxed image with a wardrobe that looked like it came out of her closet rather than from a costume studio.

Davies recorded two of the first country-feminist concept LPs, 1982's *Givin' Herself Away* and 1984's *Where Is a Woman to Go?*, again featuring a combination of original songs and covers. These were way ahead of their time in expressing the woman's side of often difficult issues, as well as drawing on a wider repertoire of songwriters, including folk-rocker Joni Mitchell.

In 1985 Davies formed the short-lived Wild Choir, a country-rock band that showed the influence of British punk-country artists like Nick Lowe and Elvis Costello. After their album went belly-up, Davies struggled on as a solo artist before being hired as one of the first female new-country producers.

Although Davies was ahead of her time as an artist, many of the new country stars of the 1990s continued to cite her work as performer and producer as influential on their sound. Too country to be as successful on the pop charts as Ronstadt, and too pop to be successful on the then more conservative country charts, Davies pointed the way for an army of female singers who would more honestly address women's issues in a contemporary vein. She continues to perform, appearing at Opryland and on Country Music Television as well as occasionally touring. In 1995 she issued an album, *Eclectic*, on her own independent label, and three years later rerecorded her best-known songs for the small Koch label.

Select Discography

Greatest Hits, Koch 8006. New recordings of her twenty best-known songs.

DAVIS, DANNY (b. George Nowlan, Randolph, Mass., April 29, 1925)

In the annals of country Muzak, many names must share the shame of taking a sharp detour down the road of crass commercialism. And at the head of the row stands Danny Davis, who created and directed The Nashville Brass, a group who "contributed" to many of the worst excesses of the NASHVILLE SOUND era.

Davis was raised and nurtured on the classics; his mother was an operatic coach, and the family lived in a tony Boston suburb. Young Davis played classical trumpet, earning a place as a soloist in the Massachusetts All-State Symphony at age fourteen. He entered the New England Conservatory of Music a year later, but was lured away from classical music by big-band star Gene Krupa, who offered him a seat in his orchestra. This led to several years of big-band work.

In the 1950s Danny was a session musician, eventually working his way up into record producing. He had a solo hit, the poppish "Trumpet Cha Cha Cha," that highlighted the melodic, vocally oriented style he had developed. In 1965 Davis was hired by RCA Records, where he originally worked with smoky balladeers like Nina Simone. CHET ATKINS, who was head of Nashville A&R, hired Davis as a producer. With his knowledge of brass instruments Davis was soon adding pop, ersatz horn sections to RCA's Nashville product. Enjoying the results, he approached Atkins with the idea of pumping out some all-instrumental albums featuring brass instruments in the lead.

The result was a series of successful albums marketed as by "The Nashville Brass." These horn-blowin' cowpokes had a hit out of the box with 1969's cover of the HANK WILLIAMS classic "I Saw the Light," followed by "The Wabash Cannonball." A blend of harmless Muzak and all-out dreck, The Brass continued to produce hit instrumentals through the 1970s while earning a seat in kitsch heaven as regular visitors to the Vegas lounges.

Luckily the new-country movement has pretty much eradicated this commercial scourge from the Nashville landscape. Still, I wouldn't be surprised if another clever combination of easy-listenin' elevator sounds didn't arise to cash in on this year's crop of hits.

DAVIS, JIMMIE (b. James Houston D., Beech Springs, La., September 11, 1902; d. Baton Rouge, La., November 5, 2000)

Davis was a country SINGER/SONGWRITER and one-time governor of Louisiana who had a career that could happen only in country music; he began as a warmed-over JIMMIE RODGERS imitator, moved into hokum and off-color material, then became a well-known songwriter of sentimental songs ("You Are My Sunshine"), and, in a final twist, took up GOSPEL singing.

Davis came from a rural background but was a highly educated man, with B.A. and M.A. degrees and experience working as a college professor in the 1920s. Because of his country roots and his pleasant voice, in the late 1920s he was invited to sing "old-time" songs by a radio station out of Shreveport; this led to a performing career and recording contract with Victor Records. Davis's first phase of recording, from 1929 to 1934, featured a mix of sentimental "heart" songs and bluesy numbers sung in the manner of Jimmie Rodgers; he also recorded a number of "hokum" blues (double-entendre songs) such as "Tom Cat and Pussy Blues" and "She's a Hum Dum Dinger," often accompanied by black country blues guitarists, including Oscar Woods.

In 1934 Davis moved to Decca and took on a singing COWBOY persona. Davis is said to have cowritten many of his 1930s hits, although some of these claims may be exaggerations, but he certainly was the first artist to record many songs that have become country standards, from 1934's "Nobody's Darlin' but Mine" to 1938's "(I Don't Worry 'Cause) It Makes No Difference Now" to 1940's "You Are My Sunshine."

During World War II, Davis moved into politics, successfully running for governor of Louisiana in 1944 and serving for one term, and then returning to the governor's office in 1960. In between he became increasingly involved in publishing and business concerns; when he did record, he turned to gospel material, although he had a minor hit with the hokey narrative "Suppertime." His 1960s and 1970s recordings were almost entirely gospel. In 1969 he married Anna Carter, an alum of the CHUCK WAGON GANG, a well-known country gospel group. In 1971 he was among the first inductees into the Country Music Hall of Fame. Despite failing health he continued to perform into the 1980s until suffering a heart attack in October 1987. He made a few appearances in the 1990s, and one final recording of "You Are My Sunshine" in 1998.

Select Discography

Nobody's Darling but Mine: 1928–1937, Bear Family 15943. Five-CD set reissuing everything Davis recorded during these years, from hokum blues to more mainstream country.

You Are My Sunshine: 1937–1946, Bear Family 16216. This five-CD set completes Davis's recordings, now in a much smoother country style than his earlier, bluesier records. It even includes his (surprisingly not too unbearable) final two sessions, when he was accompanied by the Lawrence Welk orchestra.

DAVIS, MAC (b. Scott D., Lubbock, Tex., January 21, 1942)

Davis was a country-pop SINGER/SONGWRITER of the early-to-mid-1970s who also enjoyed some success as a TV and movie actor. His good-natured personality made him a natural for a mainstream performing career during the 1970s boom in easy-listening pop-country music known as COUNTRYPOLITAN.

Born in Buddy Holly's hometown, Davis was raised by his uncle on a ranch, and first sang as a member of the church choir. By his teen years he had been bitten by the rock bug, and was performing with friends in local pop-rock groups. In his late teens he moved to Atlanta, where he worked for the Georgia Board of Probation by day while attending college at night, as well as performing rock and roll with local amateur groups. He got into the promotion end of the business when he was hired by the Chicago-based R&B label Vee Jay to be their Atlanta representative in 1962, and then by the country-pop label Liberty in 1965. He moved in 1967 to Liberty's music-publishing arm, Metric Music, based in Los Angeles, where he worked as a song plugger. In this capacity he began pushing his own songs, placing two with Lou Rawls and GLEN CAMPBELL.

Davis's big break came when he placed his "A Little Less Conversation" with ELVIS PRESLEY in 1968; the song enjoyed so much success that Presley requested a follow-up, and Davis delivered what would become his first smash pop hit, "In the Ghetto." This began a string of Davis-penned songs that had a gritty reality, mostly recorded by blue-eyed soulsters, including two more songs for Elvis ("Memories" and "Don't Cry, Daddy"), two songs for O. C. Smith, the maudlin "Watching Scotty Grow" recorded by Bobby Goldsboro, and KENNY ROGERS and The First Edition's "Something's Burning."

In 1970 Davis decided to promote his own performing career, and began to appear on TV talk shows and play Vegas. He was signed by Columbia Records, producing his first album in 1971. He had a string of hits in the early 1970s in what would today be called a middle-of-the-road pop style, from "Beginning to Feel the Pain" and "I Believe in Music" in 1971 through 1973's "Everybody Loves a Love Song."

Davis dropped off the pop charts by the mid-1970s, but continued to have country hits including "I Still Love You (You Still Love Me)" and "Picking Up the Pieces of My Life" in 1977. At the same time he appeared on a number of televised variety-show specials that drew large ratings, mostly thanks to his "aw-shucks" personality. In 1979 he appeared in the movie *North Dallas Forty*, enjoying some critical success, and it looked like a movie career might be on the horizon.

However, Davis's music and movie careers fizzled in the 1980s. Although an affable sidekick in films, he was unable to carry a film by himself as a leading man. His 1983 appearance in the big-budget floparoo *The Sting II* with Jackie Gleason effectively ended his Hollywood career. Meanwhile, his older-styled countrypolitan sound was being displaced by a return-to-roots country. He still had hits, including 1980's "It's Hard to Be Humble" and "Texas in My Rearview Mirror." He remains a popular performer but has rarely cracked the charts, although he made something of a comeback as the author with DOLLY PARTON of her 1990 hit, "White Limozeen." He also appeared in the early 1990s on Broadway as Will Rogers in the popular revue *The Will Rogers Follies*. In 1994 he issued his first new album in over a decade, but it saw little action.

Davis showed one way that country music could survive the bleak pop-music landscape of the 1970s: by emulating pop in a schmaltzy amalgam of pop's excesses and some of the gritty emotions that always made country music powerful. And although his early compositions for other artists stood out thanks to their almost menacing realism, later songs lapsed into the kind of gooey sentimentality and fear of offending that makes for the worst in mainstream commercial music.

Select Discography

Best of Mac Davis, Razor & Tie 82216. His late 1960s and early 1970s recordings; Davis at his best as a singer and songwriter, if not as successful on the charts.

Greatest Hits, Columbia 36317. The mid-1970s hits.

DAVIS, SKEETER (b. Mary Frances Penick, Dry Ridge, Ky., December 30, 1931)

A sometimes controversial GRAND OLE OPRY star of the 1960s, Davis began her career in ROCKABILLY and then became one of the leading purveyors of the NASHVILLE SOUND in the 1960s, often performing the kind of tear-soaked, pathetic numbers that characterized Nashville's view of women in preliberation days.

Davis took her stage name in high school when she performed with a friend named Betty Jack Davis (1932–1953) in a vocal duo known as The Davis Sisters. They were discovered after appearing on the *Kentucky Barn Dance* radio show out of Lexington, which led to further radio work in Detroit and Cincinnati, and finally a contract with RCA in the early 1950s. They scored big with 1953's "I Forgot More Than You'll Ever Know," but in the same year they were involved in a car crash following a performance that took Betty Jack's life and severely injured Skeeter. After her recovery Skeeter worked for a while with Betty Jack's sister Georgia, but then went out on her own.

Skeeter had several early-1960s hits, mostly in the form of the then-popular women's answer songs to hits by male stars. 1960's "(I Can't Help You) I'm Fallin', Too" is, of course, an answer to HANK LOCKLIN's big number "Please Help Me, I'm Falling," and 1961's "My Last Date (with You)" was a vocal version of FLOYD CRAMER's hit "Last Date"; both songs were written by Davis. Her biggest hit came in 1962 with "The End of the World," followed by the crossover pop hit "I Can't Stay Mad at You" a year later. In these songs Skeeter expressed "men-will-ramble-and-women-must-suffer" sentiments that make her the first in a line of long-suffering country women who were not exactly role models of liberation.

In the mid-1960s, after a brief flirtation with the pop charts, Davis had a couple more country hits, including duets with BOBBY BARE on 1965's "A Dear John Letter" and 1971's "Your Husband, Your Wife," and recordings with PORTER WAGONER and GEORGE HAMILTON IV. Always a religious person she began having her agent write into her contracts that she would not perform where liquor was being served (she didn't want her fans tempted to sin). Meanwhile, she established herself as a Nashville OUTLAW by touring with the Rolling Stones during the 1960s and denouncing the Nashville police for brutality from the stage of *The Grand Ole Opry* in 1973.

Davis returned to performing after her marriage to Joey Stampinato, the bass player of the roots rock ensemble NRBQ, with a new emphasis on the harder rockin' side of her personality.

Select Discography

Memories, Bear Family 15722. Two CDs bringing you all sixty recordings made by The Davis Sisters along with live cuts, radio appearances, and alternate takes. Includes a lavishly illustrated booklet by Bob Allen and Colin Escott.

Essential, RCA 66536. Twenty pop and country hits, essentially all of her best-known material from the early to mid-1960s.

She Sings, They Play, Rounder 3092. Recorded in 1986 with backup by NRBQ; a rockin' collection of remakes.

DEAN, BILLY (b. William Harold D., Quincy, Fla., April 1, 1962)

A multiple instrumentalist and SINGER/SONGWRITER, Dean is one of the more talented of the young crop of New Nashville stars.

A native Floridian, Dean began playing guitar at an early age, and was already playing with his father's bar band when he was eight years old. He attended college for a year on a basketball scholarship, then hit the road as a solo artist playing clubs on the Florida, Louisiana, and Texas coasts.

After scoring high in a Wrangler jeans-sponsored talent contest at age seventeen, Dean came to Nashville, where he quickly formed a band. He played local gigs and was an opening act on tours for more established stars, and also peddled his songs around town. His big break came in 1989 when RANDY TRAVIS scored a hit with "Somewhere in My Broken Heart," which Dean wrote with Richard Leigh. This led to a recording contract for Dean with Capitol Nashville.

Aided by his good looks, a clever video, and solid marketing, Dean's first single, "Only Here for a Little While," reached the Top 3 on the country charts in 1991. His second album went gold within a month of its release in 1992, and spawned more hit singles. However, Dean's career slowed somewhat in 1993–1994; although he continued to produce albums and singles, they weren't as successful on the charts. His last "new" album was 1998's *Real Man*, which failed to bring him back to the charts.

Dean is a likable singer, with a good personality and a knack for a catchy melody. His music fit squarely with the sound and themes of current Nashville hits.

Select Discography

Greatest Hits, Liberty C2-28547. His ten biggest hits from the early through mid-1990s.

DEAN, EDDIE (b. Edgar D. Glossup, Posey, Tex., July 9, 1907–March 4, 1999)

Dean was a minor COWBOY star of the 1940s who is best remembered for coauthoring "I Dreamed of a Hillbilly Heaven," still a kitsch classic.

Dean, originally a GOSPEL singer, worked with a number of popular quartets before he hooked up with his brother Jimmy (not to be confused with the sausage maker) to form a 1930s-style brother act. They ended up on the popular NATIONAL BARN DANCE show out of Chicago through the 1930s, and Eddie even enjoyed a stint on the radio soap opera *Modern Cinderella*, which also originated in the Windy City.

The brothers went to Hollywood in 1937 in search of fame and fortune on the B-film circuit, initially hooking up with cowboy star GENE AUTRY; Eddie also performed for a while as a member of JUDY CANOVA's radio company. Between 1946 and 1948 Eddie made some twenty films for one of the lesser assembly-line producers of cowpoke dramas.

In the 1950s Dean pursued a singing career with a number of labels, but big hits eluded him. Besides "Hillbilly Heaven," he cowrote "One Has My Name, the Other Has My Heart," and had minor hits with "On the Banks of the Sunny San Juan" and "No Vacancy." Dean was still active through the 1960s and 1970s on the California country circuit, and occasionally issued a record on small, local labels, but then retired from the business. He died in early 1999 at his home in southern California.

Select Discography

Very Best of, Varese 066136. Sixteen hits recorded for the Shasta label, including his big number, "I Dreamed of a Hillbilly Heaven."

DEAN, JIMMY (b. Seth Ward, near Plainview, Tex., August 10, 1928)

Dean had a series of melodramatic hits in the early 1960s and also a successful career on television. He is now more famous for his sausage than his music.

Dean was born to a poor, one-parent household; his father had abandoned his mother, who managed a local barbershop to make ends meet. As a child Dean worked as a field hand and showed an early interest in music, learning piano, GUITAR, accordion, and harmonica in rapid succession. Like many other rural Southerners, he used the military to escape from his impoverished family life. He also discovered he could make a few extra bucks on the side performing in the many small bars and clubs that catered to servicemen. While in the service in the late 1940s, he formed his first group, The Tennessee Haymakers.

By 1953 Jimmy was in Arlington, Virginia, performing with a new backup band, The Texas Wildcats. They recorded "Bummin' Around," his first single to gain national attention. Two years later he was hosting a local television program that caught the eye of the CBS network. In 1957 CBS launched a morning show hosted by Dean; it died for lack of a national sponsor.

In 1961 Dean signed with Columbia Records, where he enjoyed his greatest success. His first hit was "Big Bad John," a mock ballad he composed that told the story of a hell-raisin' back country coal miner. One year later he scored again with "P.T. 109," a patriotic anthem describing the exploits of John F. Kennedy during World War II.

Dean's good-natured, backwoodsy appeal brought him a second television contract, this time with ABC, where he remained through the mid-1960s. Although he continued to record for various labels through the mid-1970s, his career was moving increasingly toward being a TV personality rather than a country musician. Since the early 1980s he's been best known for his line of country sausage that he personally promotes through radio and TV ads.

Select Discography

Greatest Hits, Columbia 65256. His early-1960s hit platters.

DELMORE BROTHERS (Alton, b. Elkmont, Ala., December 25, 1908–June 8, 1964 [gtr, voc], and Rabon, b. Elkmont, Ala., December 3, 1916–December 4, 1952 [tenor gtr, voc])

One of the greatest of the brother acts of the 1930s and 1940s, the Delmores combined a country-blues approach with innovative GUITAR work. Their 1930s recordings were fairly sparse in approach, but in the late 1940s and early 1950s they produced recordings that forecast the ROCKABILLY sound.

The brothers were raised on a farm where their mother, "Aunt" Mollie Delmore, taught them the rudiments of GOSPEL singing. As a singing duo they won a prize at a fiddlers contest in 1930. The brothers accompanied themselves on guitars, with Rabon playing the tenor guitar (this instrument, with four strings tuned like a tenor banjo, has a smaller body and a sweeter tone than a standard guitar). The brothers began recording for Columbia in 1931 and joined THE GRAND OLE OPRY in 1932, remaining there until 1938. Their first recordings showed great maturity; their close, uninflected harmonies, great bluesy material (including "Brown's Ferry Blues," "Gonna Lay Down My Old Guitar," and "Nashville Blues"), and Rabon's lead guitar work forecast the style of later pickers like DOC WATSON.

In 1944 the brothers began recording in an even bluesier style for King Records out of Cincinnati, often accompanied by electric guitars and string bass. Their 1949 recording of "Blues Stay Away from Me" was a smash country hit, staying on the charts for twenty-three weeks. These recordings were highly influential on the next generation of rockabilly/rockin' country stars, particularly the young CARL PERKINS. The Delmores also worked with MERLE TRAVIS and GRANDPA JONES during this period as The Brown's Ferry Four, concentrating on R&B-influenced music. In the early 1950s they based their act in Houston, but the act began to disintegrate after the death of Alton's daughter, Sharon. He never recovered, and became a heavy drinker. Rabon, meanwhile, contracted lung cancer, and returned to Alabama to die in 1952. Alton later worked as a traveling salesman and part-time guitar teacher before his death from alcoholism twelve years later.

The Delmores, like THE ALLEN BROTHERS before them, were among the first country acts to integrate a blues sound into their performances. Unlike other brother acts of the era, which emphasized sweetly sentimental material, the Delmores dipped heavily into black traditions. Their powerful twin-guitar work also set them apart from other duos, who mostly played in a more laid-back style (and usually featured a mandolin as the melody or lead instrument). Although their vocals sound almost deadpan today, they have a sly sense of humor that shines through even the most maudlin of their recordings. The brothers were inducted into the Country Music Hall of Fame in 2001.

Select Discography

Sand Mountain Blues, County 110. Up-tempo country-boogie recordings originally issued on the King label between 1944 and 1949.

Freight Train Boogie, Ace 455. Their post-World War II King recordings; ha cha!

DeMENT, IRIS (b. Paragould, Ark., 1961)

A kind of backwoods NANCI GRIFFITH, DeMent is another folk-styled SINGER/SONGWRITER who has been lumped into the "new country" category.

DeMent was born in rural Arkansas, to a farm family who moved to southern California when she was just three. Both parents were deeply religious, singing in the church choir and allowing only GOSPEL music to be played around the house. DeMent recalls, "My parents pretty much stuck to gospel music. If JOHNNY CASH did a gospel album, they'd buy that." Her father was also a fiddler, and her older siblings formed a family gospel group called The DeMent Sisters.

DeMent played gospel music on the piano and, like her brothers and sisters, sang in the church choir until she left home at age twenty-five. Relocating to Kansas City, she began playing the GUITAR and writing original songs, many based on her memories of her musical family, including "Mama's Opry," "After They're Gone," and "Our Town." A demo tape of her songs was given to singer/songwriter John Prine, who recommended that she come to Nashville. After a few showcase performances she was signed to Philo/Rounder and recorded her first album with producer JIM ROONEY, who had previously guided Griffith's recording career. DeMent's folk-edged, homespun sound was an immediate hit with critics, and major label Warner Brothers quickly signed her and rereleased the album, beginning a media blitz for the young star.

DeMent followed in 1994 with *My Life*, an album of introspective songs, and then turned in a harder-edged direction with 1996's *The Way I Should*, with many songs featuring social-protest themes. Since then DeMent has continued to tour and compose, although she hasn't issued a new album. In 2001 she appeared in the film *Songcatcher*, which told the story of a folklorist tracking down a traditional Appalachian ballad singer.

Select Discography

Infamous Angel, Philo 1138. This album was originally released in 1992 and reissued by Warner Brothers a year later.

My Life, Warner Brothers 45493.

The Way I Should, Warner Brothers 46188.

DENNY, JIM (b. James Rae Denney, Silver Point, Buffalo Valley, Tenn., February 28, 1911–August 27, 1963)

Denny, a long-time GRAND OLE OPRY employee who became a major country music promoter and publisher, was raised in rural Tennessee but as a teenager moved to Nashville in search of work. As luck would have it, he found a job with National Life and Accident Insurance Company in their mail room; the company owned the powerful WSM radio station, home of the popular *Grand Ole Opry*. Denny rose through the ranks, Horatio Alger-style, working in the accounting department but attracted most to the radio show, where he began to take small jobs.

In the late 1940s Denny became the manager of the *Opry*'s lucrative concessions business, and in 1951 was named head of the influential Grand Ole Opry Artists Bureau (the booking agency operated by the *Opry* to send its acts out on the road). While still working for the *Opry* in 1953, he founded a music publishing company, Cedarwood Music, with singer WEBB PIERCE. Although at first *Opry* management didn't mind, rumors began to spread that pressure was being put on *Opry* acts to perform material supplied by Denny's company. After a showdown between Denny and the *Opry*, he was fired in September 1956.

However, Denny was well connected in the industry, not only with performers but also, more importantly, with deejays, bookers, promoters, and all the middlemen involved in selling country music. After being fired he immediately formed his own talent agency, the Jim Denny Artist Bureau. The young firm got a big boost when, in early 1957, Denny signed an agreement with tobacco giant Philip Morris to be the exclusive promoter/packager booking their country music shows. Denny quickly made contracts with almost all major country stars, and became so powerful that many feared his wrath—which could be inspired by any artist who dared question his "benevolent" management. Nonetheless, he was devoted to his acts and fought tirelessly to get them better pay and more bookings.

Denny's premature death from cancer left a hole in both of his companies. His booking agency was taken over by one of his closest employees, Lucky Moeller, who also had close ties with Webb Pierce dating back to the mid-1950s, when he helped manage the singer. Moeller continued to operate the agency (under the name Moeller-Denny) until he suffered a stroke in 1974, but by then it was a mere shadow of its once powerful self. Meanwhile, Cedarwood Music stayed in Denny family hands, being managed by Denny's two sons until its sale in 1983 to SINGER/SONGWRITER MEL TILLIS.

Denny was an early inductee into the Country Music Hall of Fame, earning a spot there in 1966, the first nonperformer to be so honored.

DENVER, JOHN (b. Henry J. Deutschendorf, Roswell, N.M., December 31, 1943–October 12, 1997)

Denver was a folk-country SINGER/SONGWRITER who had his greatest success in the mid-1970s with his back-to-nature hymns "Rocky Mountain High" and "Thank God I'm a Country Boy." Denver's bland tenor vocals and golly-gosh manners made him popular both in films and as a middle-of-the-road popster.

Denver was the son of a career Air Force pilot. In the early 1960s he performed with The Chad Mitchell Trio, one of the more topically oriented of the FOLK-REVIVAL groups. In 1965 he replaced leader Chad Mitchell in the group, continuing to record with them until the trio dissolved in 1969. Denver was signed by RCA as a solo artist; in his first album he combined his own satirical songs attacking President Nixon and the war in Vietnam with his sentimental pop songs like "(Leaving on a) Jet Plane," which had been a hit for Peter, Paul, and Mary.

Denver's big break came in 1971 with his recording of "Take Me Home, Country Roads," followed by a string of country-flavored pop hits, including the sappy ballad "Annie's Song" and the up-tempo enthusiastic "Thank God I'm a Country Boy." Denver began a film-acting career in 1977, showing himself to be an affable comedian. He continued to record his own material through the mid-1980s with limited success, later forming his own label to promote the 1988 country album *Higher Ground,* featuring the title hit.

Denver died in 1997 while piloting a small plane.

Select Discography

Rocky Mountain Collection, RRAC 66837. Two-CD set offering all the hits and a good career retrospective.

DESERT ROSE BAND, THE (1985–1994: Chris Hillman [voc, gtr, mdln]; Herb Pedersen [voc, gtr, bnj]; John Jorgenson [voc, lead gtr]; Bill Byrson [b]; Jay Dee Maness [pedal steel]; Steve Duncan [drms])

One of the later California COUNTRY-ROCK bands, Desert Rose is the first to enjoy consistent success on the country charts, showing how much country music had caught up with mainstream rock.

CHRIS HILLMAN, the unofficial leader of the group, is almost a living history of California folk-rock; he was a founding member of both THE BYRDS and THE FLYING BURRITO BROTHERS. Invited to make a solo album for the country label Sugar Hill in the mid-1980s, Hillman assembled a group of friends, including Jorgenson and Pedersen, to back him. The album was called *Desert Rose,* and the name stuck for the band. They also were employed to back folk-rocker

Dan Fogelberg on a mid-1980s tour and album, further cementing their sound.

Their first #1 hit came in 1988 with the country-rocker "He's Back and I'm Blue," followed by another #1 with "I Still Believe in You," a midtempo love song cowritten by Hillman. However, in the early 1990s the group was not able to continue producing chart hits, although they were still recording and performing. They went through a variety of personnel changes, although the leaders (Hillman-Pedersen-Jorgenson) were on hand for most of the recordings. In 1994 the band officially broke up, although many members have worked together in various combinations since then.

Although they were true to their California roots, the band had a light country harmony sound not unlike that of many other pop country bands of the 1980s and 1990s. This is not too surprising, because many of these younger bands were influenced by California country-rockers like The Byrds, The Burrito Brothers, and THE EAGLES. However, there is some irony in the fact that Hillman and company enjoyed only minor success, even as groups that copy the sounds these older musicians originated top the charts.

Select Discography

One Dozen Roses—Greatest Hits, Curb 77571. Their first hits, originally issued on MCA.

DEXTER, AL (b. Clarence Albert Poindexter, Jacksonville, Tex., May 4, 1902–January 28, 1984)

Dexter was a popular COWBOY songwriter famous for his "Pistol Packin' Mama," an up-tempo 1940s hit for him and, on the pop charts, Bing Crosby, The Andrews Sisters, and Frank Sinatra.

Dexter's music was a blend of the pop side of WESTERN SWING with cowboy and HONKY-TONK motifs. In fact his "Honky-Tonk Blues" from 1936 is thought to be the first song to use "honky-tonk" in its title or lyrics. However, it was Dexter's modern-styled recording of his "Pistol Packin' Mama"—featuring accordion, steel guitar, and trumpet in the backup band—that was to bring him his greatest success, and also was to influence the more pop-oriented Nashville recordings of the 1950s and 1960s.

Besides "Mama," Dexter wrote the words to BOB WILLS's theme song, "Take Me Back to Tulsa," the ever-popular "Rosalita," the barroom WEEPER "Too Blue to Cry," and the upbeat cowboy number "So Long, Pal." His clever blend of country themes with perky pop lyrics made his songs the ideal bridge between mainstream pop and country.

Dexter spent much of the 1950s and early 1960s performing at his Dallas-based Bridgeport Club and recording for a number of labels, big and small. He later moved into real estate and retired from music making. His "Too Late to Worry" was covered in the 1970s by COUNTRYPOLITAN star RONNIE MILSAP, and his other compositions crop up from time to time in the new-country music repertoire.

Select Discography

Pistol Packin' Mama, ASV/Living Era 5311. Most of his Top 40 hits, recorded 1942–1949. Not the best sound quality, but a bargain at nearly eighty minutes of playing time.

DIAMOND RIO (1990–Ongoing: Marty Roe [lead voc]; Jimmy Olander [lead gtr]; Gene Johnson [mdln, fdl, voc]; Dan Truman [kybds]; Dana Williams [b, voc]; Brian Prout [drms])

What happens when a bunch of talented BLUEGRASS musicians, who also can sing up a storm, are cleverly packaged and promoted by a major label? Unfortunately, the sad answer is Diamond Rio, an example of how the sum of talented parts can be less than inspiring. OK, call me a spoilsport, but who wants to hear an updated ALABAMA spewing out middle-of-the-road fluff, even if these guys can play the hell out of their instruments?

I guess the group's pedigree helps explain their predicament. The group was born at Opryland, USA, the ersatz theme park. Assembled to play "bluegrass" music (or at least what would sound like bluegrass to the park's visitors), the group grew to include three talented vocalists, with a smooth countryish lead provided by Marty Roe. The group's hot pickers—lead guitarist Olander (who previously was a session picker with RODNEY CROWELL and FOSTER AND LLOYD), MANDOLIN/FIDDLE player Johnson (an alum of J. D. CROWE's New South as well as folk-rocker David Bromberg's band), and bassist Williams (the nephew of the famous bluegrass pickers THE OSBORNE BROTHERS)—are indeed impressive, and the group's harmonies blend a bluegrass sensibility with more pop leanings.

They were signed to Arista Records in 1990, and given their truck-lover's name and a splashy new act and look. Right out of the gate they scored big with the hummable "Meet in the Middle," followed by "Norma Jeanne Riley" and three other Top 5 songs. Although many of these numbers were enlivened by the group's instrumental work, the result was a bland, middle-of-the-road likability that is the opposite of cutting-edge music making. The band followed up with a second album in 1993, leaning heavily on love ballads (the upbeat "Calling All Hearts" and the weepy "I Was Meant to Be with You" and "In a Week or Two"), that the group garnered more than country-pop radio play.

While they swept up the awards with their clever blend of just enough bluegrass to win over the new traditionalists and more than enough mushy blandness to appeal to Mr. and Mrs. Middle America.

After the mid-1990s the band's productivity—and hits—slowed. They have released new albums about once every three years since, but have failed to equal their previous success. Nonetheless they remain popular on the road, where fans know exactly what they're going to get at a Diamond Rio show. In 2001 they issued a new album, *One More Day*, which continued the basic style and sound of their earlier recordings. The title track, a soft-pop ballad, was a major hit.

Select Discography

Super Hits, Arista 18884. Skimpy, nine-track compilation of their big 1990s hits.

DICKENS, HAZEL (b. Montcalm, W. Va., June 1, 1935)

Country SINGER/SONGWRITER Hazel Dickens gained great popularity among urban folk-music fans in the early 1970s thanks to her partnership with singer/songwriter ALICE GERRARD. With a distinctive, high-pitched mountain voice reminiscent of great balladeers like AUNT MOLLY JACKSON, Dickens combined elements of traditional balladry, BLUEGRASS, and HONKY-TONK country in her music.

Dickens was the eighth of eleven children of an operator of a small trucking business, who was a fundamental Baptist, and religiously listened to THE GRAND OLE OPRY. Several of her brothers were miners, and some of them played music. At the age of nineteen Hazel followed other family members to Baltimore in search of a better life. There she met FOLK REVIVALIST MIKE SEEGER and became involved with several local bluegrass bands. She made her first professional recordings with revivalist Alice Gerrard (who was then known as Alice Foster) in the mid-1960s for Verve/Folkways. In the early 1970s she continued to work with Gerrard as a duo; the pair also performed with The Strange Creek Singers, who featured Gerrard's then-husband Mike Seeger, Lamar Grier, and Tracy Schwartz.

Dickens continued to perform and record sporadically through the 1970s and 1980s. After two successful duo LPs with Gerrard for Rounder in the early 1970s, she recorded several solo LPs. Her career was given a considerable boost when she provided the sound track for the Oscar-winning documentary *Harlan County, U.S.A.* Her best-known songs include the traditional-sounding coal miner's lament "Black Lung," and an answer song to the many songs disparaging honky-tonk angels, "Don't Put Her Down, You Helped Put Her There." In this song Dickens combines rough mountain common sense with sentiments borrowed from the urban women's liberation movement, surely one of the more unusual country conglomerations!

Select Discography

Pioneering Women of Bluegrass, Smithsonian/Folkways 40065. Reissues two mid-1960s albums cut by Dickens and Gerrard with band accompaniment, including a then new MANDOLIN player, DAVID GRISMAN.

A Few Old Memories, Rounder 11529. CD reissue of tracks taken from her late-1980s albums, mostly with bluegrass band accompaniment.

DICKENS, "LITTLE" JIMMY (b. Bolt, W. Va., December 19, 1920)

"Little" Jimmy is a perennial country hitmaker known for his tiny size, rhinestone-encrusted outfits, and novelty hits, including his big pop crossover, 1965's "May the Bluebird of Paradise Fly up Your Nose."

Dickens was the thirteenth child born to a small-time rancher in rural West Virginia. After attending the small local school, Dickens was accepted by the University of West Virginia, where he also landed a job as a performer on the local radio station. After radio stints in Cincinnati and Michigan, the pint-sized crooner, then billed as "Jimmy the Kid," attracted the attention of ROY ACUFF, who invited him to perform on THE GRAND OLE OPRY. By the late 1940s he was a permanent member of the show, a position he still holds.

Dickens signed with Columbia at the same time, in the late 1940s, recording a string of novelty hits that included his first Top 10 country song, "Take an Old Cold Tater and Wait," earning him a second nickname, "Tater." Other novelty hit numbers included "I'm Little but I'm Loud," "A-Sleeping at the Foot of the Bed," and "Hillbilly Fever."

In the 1950s Dickens led a hot band called The Country Boys, which featured two lead guitars, pedal steel, and drums. At a time when Nashville recordings were soaked with girly choruses and sentimental strings, this band provided spirited accompaniments to many of his recordings, maintaining a true country sound in the face of considerable pressure to go more mainstream. Many of his recordings from this era share the energy of the best of ROCKABILLY. For this alone Dickens deserves the seat in the Country Music Hall of Fame he earned in 1983.

After his big pop hit with the silly "Bluebird of Paradise" in 1965, Dickens more or less faded from the charts, but continued to tour and perform, as well as to appear on the *Opry*. Today his appearances have more nostalgia value than anything else, maintaining a link with country's past.

Select Discography

Country Boy, Bear Family 15848. Four-CD set collecting all of Dickens's Columbia recordings made between 1949 and 1957, including previously unreleased gems.

DIFFIE, JOE (b. J. Logan D., Tulsa, Okla., December 28, 1958)

Diffie is another neo HONKY-TONKER who hopes to cash in on today's craze for barroom-oriented material.

Born in Tulsa, Diffie was raised in rural Duncan, Oklahoma, although his family relocated several times during his early years, moving as far west as Washington state. After attending college briefly, he returned to Duncan to work in an iron foundry while writing songs at night. His mother sent one of his early compositions to singer HANK THOMPSON, who bought it. After nine years of heavy labor, Diffie was laid off due to tough financial times; with nothing to lose, he headed for Nashville to seek work as a songwriter. In the early 1980s he fell in with a group of other wanna-be songwriters, including Lonnie Wilson and Wayne Perry, and the trio produced HOLLY DUNN's hit "There Goes My Heart Again" in 1984.

For the balance of the 1980s, Diffie worked as a demo singer and songwriter. His demos were well received by the Nashville community, and eventually producer Bob Montgomery at Epic Records signed him, although he waited a few years to release Diffie's first album. He had an immediate hit with 1990's "Home," and has followed it up with some spunky honky-tonk numbers, including 1992's "Honky-Tonk Attitude" and 1993's "Prop Me Up (Beside the Jukebox if I Die)." He also recorded a duet with popular folk-country star MARY CHAPIN CARPENTER. Diffie continued to score hits through and beyond the 1990s, including "Texas Sized Heartache" in 1998 and "In Another World" in 2001.

However, Diffie unwittingly spoke the hard truth when he told one interviewer, "Sometimes I turn on the car radio and for a second I'm not sure if it's me or MARK CHESNUTT or ALAN JACKSON or whoever." This is the problem with many of today's hunks-in-hats; blindfolded, you can't tell them apart, because they all are cast in the same mold.

Select Discography

Greatest Hits, Epic 69137. Twelve of his big numbers through 1998.

DILLARDS, THE (Original lineup, c. 1962–1966: Doug Dillard, b. East St. Louis, Ill., March 6, 1937 [bnj]; Rodney Dillard, b. Salem, Mo., 1942 [gtr, voc]; Dean Webb [mdln]; Mitch Jayne [b])

The Dillards, one of the most commercial and influential BLUEGRASS bands of the mid-1960s, later evolved into one of the first COUNTRY-ROCK outfits.

The Dillard brothers were sons of an old-time fiddler who grew up surrounded by traditional dance music. In the mid-1950s a vibrant bluegrass scene developed in metropolitan St. Louis, including the young Dillards along with banjo-picker JOHN HARTFORD. After hooking up with local country deejay Mitch Jayne, who became the group's spokesperson, they made their debut in 1962 performing at Washington University; soon after, they relocated to California, where they signed with Elektra Records, then an urban-folk label (and soon to become a folk-rock label). At the same time they were hired to portray the Darling family on TV's *Andy Griffith Show*, giving the band further exposure. Their first two albums were a mix of traditional country and bluegrass songs along with more contemporary numbers by songwriters like BOB DYLAN.

Because the Dillards were country-born, they brought an authenticity to their music that other FOLK REVIVALISTS could only emulate; and, because they were young and college-educated, they knew how to appeal to a more upscale audience. For this reason they immediately became popular on the college circuit, and their records were marketed primarily to this audience, not to the traditional bluegrass or country-music consumers.

After recording an influential album of fiddle tunes with guest artist BYRON BERLINE, the band split, with Doug leaving to form a folk-rock group with ex-Byrd Gene Clark and Rodney continuing to lead the band with new banjo player Herb Pedersen (later a founding member of THE DESERT ROSE BAND). The Dillards took a more folk-rock direction, recording two concept albums that featured popular songs by The Beatles and folk artists like Tim Hardin.

The Dillards as a band were dormant through much of the early-to-mid-1970s, but reemerged with the bluegrass revival of the latter half of the decade. Rodney and Doug recorded with old friend John Hartford, and Rodney continued to lead the band, now with Dean Webb, Jeff Gilkinson (vocals, bass, cello), banjoist Billy Ray Latham (who was a member of the influential KENTUCKY COLONELS, another California-based bluegrass band), and Paul York (drums). The band recorded sporadically through the 1990s, although they were not as successful or influential as the first incarnation of the group had been.

Select Discography

Best of the Darling Boys, Vanguard 506. Early recordings when the Dillards were portraying this backwoods group on *The Andy Griffith Show*.
There Is a Time, Vanguard 131/132. Classic band recordings originally issued by Elektra between 1963 and 1970.

DILLY AND HIS DILL PICKLES (c. 1926–1930; core group: John Dilleshaw [gtr, voc]; Harry "Bill" Kiker [fdl]; Raymond W. "Shorty" Lindsey [tenor bnj]; "Pink" Lindsey [gtr, bnj, mdln, bass])

This north Georgia string band was led by "Seven Foot Dilly," a unique guitarist/singer whose real name was John Dilleshaw.

Dilleshaw came from northern Georgia, where his family were subsistence farmers. At age seventeen, he accidentally shot himself in the foot. While recuperating he began playing GUITAR, taking informal lessons from a local black player. He became an excellent guitarist, specializing in the classical-styled, finger-picked pieces of the turn of the century, including the well-known "Spanish Fandango" that turns up in the repertoire of country and blues guitarists throughout the South. (It is sometimes called "Spanish Flang-dang," which also refers to the special tuning used to play the piece.)

Around 1922 Dilleshaw settled in Atlanta, where he was hired by the fire department. He worked both with Charles Brook in a guitar duet known as The Gibson Kings, broadcasting on powerful station WSB around 1924–1925, and with The Dixie String Band. Around 1926 Dilleshaw's brother-in-law, eighteen-year-old fiddler Harry Kiker, came to Atlanta and began working with him in various groups. The Dilleshaw string band was completed when the father-son team of Pink and Shorty Lindsey came on board. Pink was a talented multiple instrumentalist who landed his own contract with Columbia in early 1929 (the sides went unissued, however). Shorty had played tenor banjo for FIDDLIN' JOHN CARSON and led his own bands.

Meanwhile, country producer Bill Brown—who had overseen The SKILLET LICKERS' successful mid-to-late-1920s sessions for Columbia—bolted from the label in 1929 and went over to rival Brunswick-Vocalion. Looking for a Georgia string band to record, he brought Dilleshaw and crew in for a session in March 1930. Though it apparently was still a somewhat loose gathering of musicians, Dilleshaw worked with the core band on this session, along with two well-known local fiddle masters, A. A. (Ahaz) Gray and Joe Brown.

A wide range of material was recorded that day, including humorous skits ("A Georgia Barbecue at

Stone Mountain"), hell-raising fiddle tunes, and even two "talking blues," featuring Dilleshaw accompanied only by his own guitar. Dilleshaw did more than just accompany the band on guitar, however. He provided a kind of comic spoken narration as the band worked through the tunes. His loosely structured comic yarns set these records apart from those of competitors.

The records sold well enough, despite the Depression, for a second session to be scheduled in November 1930. According to Kiker, producer Bill Brown brought Dilleshaw back alone, partnering him with studio musicians. However, like other labels, Brunswick suffered a dramatic drop in sales with the coming of the Depression and the popularity of "free music" on the radio. This was Dilleshaw's last session as a leader. He continued to work locally through 1940, when he became ill. He died a year later.

The saga of Dilleshaw and his bands complements those of the better-known Georgia groups of the day, including the Skillet Lickers and the GEORGIA YELLOW HAMMERS. Like the Skillet Lickers, the group emphasized upbeat FIDDLE tunes that showed the influence of jazz and pop musics. And, like both groups, Dilleshaw recorded clever comic skits that included references to local events, people, and places that helped make the group extremely popular in their home region.

DINNING SISTERS (Eugenia ["Jean"] and Virginia ["Ginger"] D., b. 1924; Lucille ["Lou"] D., b. 1920, all born in Kentucky)

Country music's answer to The Andrews Sisters, the Dinnings were popular stars of Chicago's NATIONAL BARN DANCE in the 1940s and later had a minor career in short musical films and C-grade pictures.

Originally from Kentucky, the sisters, three of eight musically inclined children, were raised primarily on a farm near Enid, Oklahoma. Identical twins Jean and Ginger, and elder sister Lucille formed a harmony group in emulation of the popular Andrews Sisters and performed on the local radio station. In 1939 they moved to Chicago, where elder sister Marvis had already begun a career as a big-band singer; two years later, they were hired to perform on the *National Barn Dance* radio show as "The Sweethearts of Sunbonnet Swing." Their mix of down-home sweetness with purling harmonies won them an immediate audience, and soon they had their own radio show, as well as an invitation to come to Hollywood and appear in cameo roles in a number of quickie films.

By 1945 they had signed with the fledgling West Coast Capitol label, and they had a couple of hits with remakes of sugary pop numbers like 1947's "My Adobe Hacienda" (written by cowgirl star LOUISE MASSEY) and "Buttons and Bows" from a year later;

they also recorded novelty numbers in a more swinging style reminiscent of The Boswell Sisters, including 1946's "Iggedy Song." Elder sister Lou married country songsmith Don Robertson in 1946 (he's best known for writing "Please Help Me, I'm Falling") and left the act; she was replaced first by Jayne Bundesen and, in 1949, by younger sister Delores Dinning.

The group's career faded in the 1950s. Jean later became a songwriter, best known for "Teen Angel," the saccharine pop hit of the early 1960s; sister Delores later joined The Nashville Edition, backup singers who appeared regularly on TV's HEE HAW and did session work.

DIXIE CHICKS, THE (Natalie Maines, b. Lubbock, Tex., 1975 [lead voc, gtr]; Martie Erwin Seidel, b. Dallas, Tex., 1970 [fdl, voc]; Emily Erwin Robinson, b. Dallas, Tex., 1973 [bnj, Dobro, gtr, voc])

Take the Coon Creek Girls, add a heavy dose of peroxide and new-country glitz, fast-forward to 1998, and you get The Dixie Chicks.

Originally known as The Dixie Chickens, the group consisted of sisters Martie and Emily Erwin, along with guitarist/vocalist Robin Macy and bassist/vocalist Laura Lynch when it was founded in 1989. All had backgrounds in BLUEGRASS music, but they initially flavored themselves as a retro cowgirl band, recording two independent albums; their first was wittily titled *Thank Heavens for Dale Evans*. By the mid-1990s, however, they had thrown away the gingham and boots and settled on a more contemporary look and style. Macy defected from the group in the early 1990s because she objected to this more contemporary sound and the addition of a drummer to the touring band. The group soldiered on as a trio, but still were unable to get what they really wanted: a contract with a major Nashville label.

Finally, in 1996 the Chicks got a bite from Sony Records, who were reviving the old Monument label

The Dixie Chicks sweep the CMA awards, 1998. Photo: Raeanne Rubenstein

and looking for an exciting act to be their first signing. However, the company questioned the sex appeal and talent of Laura Lynch, suggesting she was too old to draw a wide audience. (Macy was in her late thirties at the time, while the Erwin sisters were about a decade and a half younger.) Vocalist Natalie Maines, the daughter of noted steel guitarist Lloyd Maines, was brought in to replace Lynch. She was considerably younger—and a more dynamic stage personality and singer—so the addition proved to be smart artistically as well as commercially.

The group's debut major-label album, *Wide Open Spaces*, contained mostly New Nashville material, although the Erwin sisters insisted on playing their own instruments on the recording. The album though, focused on Maines's lead vocals, which mixed the sweetness of traditional country crooning with the harder edge of women like Bonnie Raitt. The second single released from the album, "There's Your Trouble," shot to #1, the first trio recording to achieve this distinction on the country charts in over a decade. The title track cleverly mixed COWBOY and country themes in a contemporary setting. The album garnered many awards (as did the group), eventually selling over 10 million copies.

The Chicks did not suffer from a sophomore slump. Their second release, *Fly*, spawned several hit singles and went quadruple platinum. The playful—some might say shocking—"Good-bye, Earl" was the album's centerpiece, a song about an abusive husband who is killed by his long-suffering wife. Although others might have set this as a sob story or morality tale, the Chicks preferred a lighthearted route. The song was supported by a clever video, which (in case any listeners missed it) underscored the dark comedy of the story. They also showed a spunky side in "Sin Wagon," an unusual song for a female country group because it celebrated (rather than lamented) a "sinful" life over the usual "stay-at-home" stereotype. The album also spurred hit ballads including the romantic "Cowboy, Take Me Away." To date the album has sold over seven million copies, making it one of the most successful country discs of the new century. Not surprisingly, this has led the Chicks to a much-publicized falling out with their label—which, they claim, has shorted them on their royalties and held them to a contract they signed when they were unknown. Suits and countersuits were filed by the group and the label through 2001, until a settlement was finally reached in mid-2002. After much delay, a new single "Long Time Gone" was released, with a new album due to follow in late summer 2002.

Much of the Chicks' allure is based on their wholesome good looks, with a winking nod to the over-the-top stylings of country women like DOLLY PARTON who are not known to spare the makeup in their attempts to attract attention. Previously they were a trio

of bottle blonds, but banjoist Emily "shocked" the country world by going brunette in 2000; and fans fretted over Natalie's dietary struggles and vacillating weight. The Chicks continued to veer between sexy and over-the-top tasteless in their wardrobe, much to the delight of their fans.

Though compared to the Spice Girls because of their rapid success and highly visual stage show and videos, the Dixie Chicks have more claims to legitimacy than the made-for-video Brits. And the Chicks have proven stronger than the Brits, outlasting them thanks to their superior material and musicianship. With strong instrumental skills and roots in bluegrass and HONKY-TONK, they combine clever songs, tasteful arrangements, and full-out belting.

Select Discography

Wide Open Spaces, Monument 68195. The album that launched Chick mania.
Fly, Monument 69678.

DIXON BROTHERS, THE (Dorsey, b. Darlington, S.C., October 14, 1897–April 17, 1968 [gtr, fdl, voc], and Howard, b. Darlington, S.C., June 19, 1903–March 24, 1961 [gtr, steel gtr, voc])

The Dixons were cotton mill workers all their life, but for a brief period in the mid-1930s they recorded a number of classic country numbers, mostly written by elder brother Dorsey.

The entire Dixon family, parents and seven children, worked as mill hands; Dorsey entered the mills when he was twelve years old. From his mother he learned traditional ballads, play-party songs, and hymns, and as a young teenager learned to play GUITAR and FIDDLE. He teamed up with his younger brother, Howard, to perform at local movie theaters as a novelty act between screenings.

By the early 1930s the brothers were working in a mill in East Rockingham, North Carolina, where they met legendary steel guitar player Jimmie Tarlton (of DARBY AND TARLTON fame), who was also working in the mills. Tarlton inspired them to become professional musicians, and also to play more bluesy-sounding songs; Howard took up the steel guitar in emulation of Tarlton's mastery of the instrument. The duo got their big break in 1934 when they appeared on a country radio show out of Charlotte, North Carolina, and two years later were signed to RCA's budget Bluebird label. They recorded sixty numbers over the next two years, including many songs commenting on the hard life in the cotton mills ("Weave Room Blues") and the classic country WEEPER "I Didn't Hear Nobody Pray," which ROY ACUFF remade into the megahit "Wreck on the Highway." Although Dorsey wrote both songs, he sold the rights to them to his publisher, and never earned a penny from the many recordings of these standards. After 1938 the brothers returned to textile work and abandoned their professional careers.

In the early 1960s Dorsey Dixon was "rediscovered" by FOLK REVIVALISTS, and he performed at folk festivals and made a couple of new albums of his own material and traditional country songs, as well as recording for the Library of Congress, receiving belated recognition for his contributions to country-music history.

Select Discography

Volumes 1–4, Document 8046–8049. Chronological reissue of their recordings made between 1936 and 1939. Similar material was issued on LP by Old Homestead (151, 164, 178, 179), grouped thematically.

DOBRO (resophonic guitar, c. 1927)

The Dobro is a unique American musical instrument that has become central to the sound of modern BLUEGRASS and country music. It is one of the key forerunners of the PEDAL-STEEL GUITAR.

The Dobro has its roots in the craze for Hawaiian music that swept the country in the 1920s. The classical guitar was introduced by Portuguese settlers in the islands around the 1830s; by the century's end Hawaiian musicians had taken to playing the guitar on their laps, tuning the strings to a full open or partially open chord (known as "slack-key" tuning), and noting the strings with a solid metal bar (hence the name "steel guitar," referring to the bar used to damp the notes, not to the material used in making the guitar). Joseph Kekuku is generally cited as the first great Hawaiian player; he toured the U.S. and Europe at the turn of the twentieth century, influencing hundreds of lesser-known vaudeville and tent-show musicians. One of the most popular recording stars of the 1920s in this style was Sol Hoopi, whose playing was emulated by both country and blues musicians.

Conventional guitars were modified for Hawaiian playing by being fitted with raised nuts (to increase string height), flush frets (so that the bar could be slid easily across the strings), hollow, square necks (to enable the instrument to sit flat on a player's lap), and stronger and larger body construction (to take the extra tension created by the steel strings used on these instruments, and to increase volume). However, it was still difficult to produce a conventional guitar that would have enough power to be heard over an entire band.

One solution was the Dobro, invented by a family of Czechoslovakian immigrant instrument makers, the Dopyera brothers (hence the trade name Dobro used on

some of their instruments). Brother John is generally credited with designing the original resonator used on Dobros, a system that employed a primitive nonelectric pickup mounted on the bridge of the instrument (like the needle used on early acoustic phonographs) which transmitted the sound down into a chamber holding three megaphone-like cones, facing down (or toward the back of the instrument). Dopyera was awarded a patent for his design in 1927, and a year later began producing instruments with his brothers under the National name; one of their first customers was Hawaiian star Hoopi. These instruments had steel bodies, and so are commonly called National steels by today's players. Square-neck models for Hawaiian players and round-neck models for conventional players (highly prized among blues musicians) were both made through the 1930s.

In a complex business history, John Dopyera broke with National in 1929, coming up with a new design for a resonator instrument, the first true Dobro. This featured a single cone facing forward, with an elaborate eight-legged "spider" pickup that projected sound down from the bridge to the edges of the cone. In order to make a cheaper instrument than the National steel, the brothers decided to use a plywood body for their new instrument, which they called the Dobro.

By the early Depression years the National and Dobro companies had united, and were making a wide variety of both steel-bodied and wood-bodied guitars with either the single or the tricone resonator. Soon after, a new technology in the form of electric (or amplified) lap guitars cut seriously into the popularity of these earlier so-called resophonic instruments. The Dobro probably would have disappeared from the musical scene if it had not been for a couple of influential players. "Bashful Brother Oswald" (aka Pete Kirby) played the instrument in ROY ACUFF's influential band from 1939 through the 1950s, appearing weekly on THE GRAND OLE OPRY. In BLUEGRASS music the pioneering FLATT AND SCRUGGS band featured a talented player of the Dobro, "Uncle Josh" (b. Buck) Graves, who took Earl Scruggs's signature banjo roll and adapted it to the instrument.

The Dobro fell out of popularity in mainstream country music recording circles from the mid-1950s to the mid-1980s, when the whine of the pedal-steel guitar dominated recording sessions. It was the bluegrass revival of the 1970s that helped bring the instrument back to the fore, with young players like JERRY DOUGLAS showing that the Dobro was not just a relic of the past. Douglas was one of the most in-demand session musicians of the 1980s and 1990s, and many other players emulated his versatility on the instrument.

DR. HOOK AND THE MEDICINE SHOW
(c.1968–1982: Ray Sawyer, aka Dr. Hook [gtr, voc, percussion]; Dennis Locorriere [gtr, voc]; Rik Elswit [lead gtr, voc]; George Cummings [steel gtr, lead gtr]; Billy Francis [kybds, voc]; Jance Garfat [b, voc]; John David [drms, voc])

Dr. Hook and the Medicine Show were a silly, novelty rockin' country outfit of the late 1960s and early 1970s, led by eye-patch-wearin' Sawyer; their biggest hits were provided by SINGER/SONGWRITER/children's author Shel Silverstein, including the satiric "Cover of the *Rolling Stone*." They later were transformed into a mainstream country-pop band, after several personnel changes.

Hook got his zany nickname from an automobile accident he endured as a youth that left him wearing an eyepatch over his left eye. Originally from Chicksaw, Alabama, he began performing in small Southern bars at the age of fourteen, taking some time off to pursue an abortive career as a logger before forming a duo with keyboardist Billy Francis that played up and down the East Coast. One favorite spot to perform was Transfer Station, near Union City, New Jersey, where a group of small bars catered to travelers who were often stranded at this bus transfer point for several hours. It was here that Hook met guitarist/vocalist Dennis Locorriere, who originally joined the outfit as a bass player and soon became its coleader.

After unsuccessfully shopping around demos to New York labels and producers, the band was introduced to Ron Haffkine, who was working as musical director for the film *Who is Harry Kellerman and Why Is He Saying These Terrible Things About Me?* The film was being scored by Shel Silverstein, who came to New Jersey to hear the band, and invited them to record the movie's theme song, "Last Morning." They were soon signed by Columbia Records, releasing a series of albums mostly of Silverstein's satiric songs, including "Freakin' at the Freakers Ball," "I Got Stoned (and I Missed It)," and their big FM hit, "Cover of the *Rolling Stone*," which in fact did earn them a cover photo on this prestigious rock journal.

The group broke with Silverstein in 1972, recording an album of original material that flopped. Meanwhile, the recession of the next few years, plus years of mismanagement, led the group to declare bankruptcy; trying to dig themselves out of the hole, they spent $400 to produce the album *Bankrupt*, which was picked up by Capitol Records. The record featured a remake of Sam Cooke's "Only Sixteen" that became the group's next big hit.

The band continued to move in a more country/easy-listening direction through the 1970s. Sawyer recorded his first solo album in 1977, scoring a country hit with "If Not You," a syrupy ballad. In 1978–1979 they had their biggest hits, including the middle-of-the-road anthem "When You're in Love with a Beautiful Woman," miles away from their hipper-than-thou

image of just a few years earlier. In 1980 they were signed to the disco label Casablanca, and had a few more hits before fizzling out two years later. Sawyer formed a new Dr. Hook for touring the revival circuit in 1988.

Select Discography

Doctor Hook and the Medicine Show, Columbia 30898. Rerelease of their first album.
Greatest Hits, Columbia 46620.

DOUGLAS, JERRY (b. Gerald Calvin D., Warren, Ohio, May 28, 1956)

One of the great DOBRO players, Douglas has brought this venerable country instrument into new country by working as a bandleader and session performer.

Douglas, from rural Ohio, began his career as a BLUEGRASS player. In the early 1970s he performed with THE COUNTRY GENTLEMEN, where he met another talented young player, RICKY SKAGGS. Late in the decade the duo formed a progressive bluegrass ensemble, called Boone Creek, to perform more contemporary country material in a bluegrass setting. At the same time he recorded his first two solo outings for Rounder, *Fluxology* and *Fluxedo* (after his nickname, "Flux," for his smooth playing), featuring many contemporary-bluegrass musicians, including Skaggs, TONY RICE, Sam Bush, BELA FLECK, and Russ Barenberg.

Douglas relocated to Nashville in the early 1980s, and was in immediate demand for session work accompanying the new-country artists, including his old friend Skaggs. He was signed by MCA's short-lived Instrumental Masters (new acoustic music) label, where he produced two albums under his own name with many of the players from his earlier sessions. Since the mid-1990s he has continued to record solo albums while also working in an acoustic trio with bassist Edgar Meyer and guitarist Russ Barenberg. He has become an in-demand session musician, appearing on just about every bluegrass album recorded in Nashville, including recent bluegrass forays by DOLLY PARTON and PATTY LOVELESS. In 2001 Douglas became an official member of ALISON KRAUSS's band, Union Station.

Although in his own compositions Douglas shows the influence of DAVID GRISMAN's approach to creating a new acoustic/jazz-tinged music, most of his session work is limited to traditional-styled fills and melody work. In fact the demand for the Dobro sound is not for cutting-edge work but rather for just the right touch of nostalgia for today's current hip country artists. Douglas fills the bill to a T because of his ability to perform everything from WESTERN SWING to country WEEPERS.

Select Discography

Everything's Gonna Work Out Fine, Rounder 11535. Compilation of his Rounder solo albums from early 1980s.
Restless on the Farm, Sugar Hill 3875. 1998 solo outing featuring many of Douglas's regular cohorts.

DOWNING, BIG AL (b. Lenapah, Oklahoma, January 9, 1940)

Al Downing, pioneering black pianist/songwriter/vocalist in country, ROCKABILLY, and R&B styles, was born on a small farm in Oklahoma near the Kansas line. His father was a sharecropper who enjoyed listening to THE GRAND OLE OPRY radio program, thus exposing his son to country music at an early age. The large family—Al had nine brothers and two sisters—formed their own GOSPEL choir when he was just entering his teens, and performed locally. At about the same time Al found a piano in a nearby dump; although it only had forty working keys, he began imitating his favorite artists, including Fats Domino. At age fourteen he won a talent contest by performing Domino's "Blueberry Hill" in the tiny town of Cotteyville, Kansas, just across the state line from his home. Soon after, he was working as a truckdriver while pursuing his musical career locally.

In 1957 young, white guitarist Bobby Poe heard Al's credible Domino imitation and invited him to join his new band. Poe figured he could cover the popular white singers of the day, like ELVIS and JERRY LEE LEWIS, and Al could handle the more soulful hitmakers. The band, originally known as The Rhythm Rockers, was one of the first integrated bands in popular music. Soon they took the name The Poe Cats and began recording, working with producer Lelan Rogers, who operated the White Rock label in Dallas. (KENNY ROGERS is his younger sibling.) Al's composition "Down on the Farm," featuring his energetic vocals, became the band's first and most enduring hit. It was licensed by White Rock to the larger Challenge label, which continued to issue the Poe Cats' records through the early 1960s.

Jim Halsey, who was then managing a young ROCKABILLY star named WANDA JACKSON, heard the band's first record and invited them to accompany her on her Capitol recordings. The band toured with Jackson for several years, and also appeared on her classic recordings, including "Let's Have a Party" and "In the Middle of a Heartache." They often opened for more mainstream country acts, and Al would oblige the audience with his repertoire of hanky-staining country ballads during band breaks.

Downing continued to appear on releases that were issued under both his and the Poe Cats names through 1964. In 1963 he cut a duet with Little Esther Phillips in Nashville, but it failed to hit it big on either R&B or country charts. His last Poe Cats outing, 1964's "Georgia Slop," has won fame among diehard rockabilly fans for its rollicking, good-natured energy.

Downing continued to struggle as a country artist through the 1960s, then switched to a more soulful sound with "I'll Be Holding On," a minor R&B hit in 1970. In the mid-1970s he even dabbled in disco, although he never reached true star status. He returned to his original country roots in 1978, signing with Warner Brothers Records. He scored Top 20 country hits in 1979 with his songs "Touch Me (I'll Be Your Fool Once More)" and "Mr. Jones," followed by 1980's "Bring It On Home," all his own compositions. However, Warner Brothers was unwilling to bankroll an entire album by the singer. Prejudice still ran deep in Nashville, and it was feared that if his identity as an African American were known too widely, his music would fail to sell. He even had difficulty placing his songs; music publishers didn't think an African American could write true "country" songs. His last country hit, 1982's "I'll Be Loving You," barely reached the country Top 50; it was released on the tiny Tug Boat label, which continues to record Downing.

However, Downing's fame as a rockabilly pioneer gave him a new audience in Europe, where rockabilly has gained greatly in popularity since the mid-1980s. He has toured and performed extensively in Europe since then, continuing to perform everything from Fats Domino-flavored R&B to country classics. Performance videos and rereleases of his rockabilly work sell strongly to fans of that early COUNTRY-ROCK hybrid style.

DRAKE, PETE (b. Roddis Franklin D., Atlanta, Ga., October 8, 1932–July 29, 1988)

Premier Nashville session player on the PEDAL-STEEL GUITAR, Drake was also a producer noteworthy for his work for everyone from country crooner JIM REEVES to wanna-be country performer Ringo Starr.

Drake was one of the earliest performers to take up the pedal steel guitar, beginning to play when he was nineteen years old. Soon he was leading a band, The Sons of the South, and performing on radio and in small clubs in his native Georgia. He joined the duo of STONEY AND WILMA LEE COOPER, coming to Nashville with them in 1959. After a year and a half struggling to find work, Drake caught the ears of ROY DRUSKY and GEORGE HAMILTON IV, two popular country crooners, who invited him to perform on their next sessions. Drake's career as a session player took off; it is said that Drake could be heard on two-thirds of *Billboard*'s top seventy-five country singles throughout the early 1960s. In 1964 he released a solo recording of the pop novelty "Forever," which charted on both pop and country listings.

Drake moved into the studio/production end of the business in the mid-to-late 1960s, soon becoming a powerhouse producer. It was his idea to invite Ringo Starr to make an all-country album after hearing the singer's cover of BUCK OWENS's hit, "Act Naturally." Drake recorded all of the backgrounds, then had Starr overdub vocals; the result was arguably Starr's best solo album, *Beaucoups of Blues*, released in the early 1970s.

Although Drake's production style was less heavy-handed than many of his Nashville compeers, by the early 1980s he was working primarily with older acts, such as B. J. THOMAS and LINDA HARGROVE, who combined a pop sensibility with country crooning.

DRIFTING COWBOYS, THE (1948–1951, sporadically thereafter: Don Helms [steel gtr]; Bob McNett [elec gtr]; Jerry Rivers [fdl]; Hillous Butram [b])

The backup group that accompanied HANK WILLIAMS on his best-known *Grand Ole Opry* shows and recordings, The Drifting Cowboys became the prototype for hundreds of other HONKY-TONK bands of the 1950s and beyond.

The core of the group was steel guitarist Don Helms, who had performed with Williams since 1943, when both were still living in Alabama. With the exception of a brief period when Hank starred on the LOUISIANA HAYRIDE radio show, Helms remained with the singer until his death. On early live *Opry* shows, the audience goes wild every time the steel guitar takes a solo. Helms's playing was always tasteful and discreet; a less distinctive player than pioneers like BOB DUNN, Helms never sought to overwhelm Williams's singing, but rather to accompany it.

Guitarist McNett was from Pennsylvania and had originally accompanied cowgirl sweetheart PATSY MONTANA before he joined Williams in 1949, when the singer was invited to join the *Opry*; fiddler Jerry Rivers, who had previously played as a duo with future BLUEGRASS great BENNY MARTIN, came on board at the same time, as did session bass player Hillous Butram. This core group played on all of Williams's classic MGM recordings from the late 1940s and early 1950s, as well as touring with him and appearing on his regular *Grand Ole Opry* spots.

Williams's behavior became increasingly erratic as his alcoholism worsened in the early 1950s, leading Butram to jump ship to join HANK SNOW in 1952 (he was replaced by Cedric Rainwater, who had worked in bluegrass bands and also as a session musician), and McNett left soon after, to be replaced by Sammy

Pruett. When Williams died, the band disintegrated, with individual members continuing to work as session musicians.

In 1977 the group was reunited thanks to Butram, who was now working as a music coordinator for country-flavored movies. The group first performed in a Lorne Greene cowflick, *That's Country*, leading to a contract with Epic Records and a hit a year later with a remake of Johnnie Lee Wills's "Ragmop." They continued to perform through 1984, when the group members decided to retire.

DRIFTWOOD, JIMMY (b. James Corbett Morris, Mountain View, Ark., June 21, 1907–July 12, 1998)

An Ozark mountain folklorist and song collector, Driftwood is best remembered for his reworking of the traditional fiddle tune "Eighth of January" into the country hit "The Battle of New Orleans."

Raised in the Ozarks, Morris first learned music from his family; his uncle gave him a handmade GUITAR, and he soon mastered FIDDLE and BANJO as well. Jimmy worked his way through high school, occasionally performing at local dances and gatherings, and became a rural schoolteacher in the late 1930s. He taught for ten years while working toward his B.A. degree in education at the state teachers college in Conway, Arkansas (the town that provided Harold Jenkins with half of his stage name, CONWAY TWITTY).

Contacts with other folklorists through the 1950s brought Jimmy in touch with the urban FOLK REVIVAL, and he performed at many festivals and concerts. He was signed to RCA in 1958 as a folksinger, issuing an album with the academic name *Newly Discovered Early American Folk Songs*. On this album he recorded his version of "The Battle of New Orleans"; country singer JOHNNY HORTON heard it and a year later released his version, which became a massive hit. RCA rushed out a second album, plus a single version of Jimmy performing his song; this was followed by "Tennessee Stud," which was covered by EDDY ARNOLD for a second hit.

Driftwood continued to perform on the folk revival and country circuits through the early 1960s. He remained devoted to the traditional songs and stories of the Ozarks, and became well known for his playing of the mouthbow (sometimes called "diddley bow"), a single-stringed instrument that is played in a manner similar to the Jew's harp (the end of the bow is held up against the player's open jaw, and while the player strums vigorously on the string, different notes can be produced by varying the shape of the sound chamber formed by the open mouth).

Driftwood refurbished a barn on his farm near Mountain View, where he continued to perform for weekend visitors through the 1980s. He died in 1998, at the age of ninety-one.

Select Discography

Americana, Bear Family 15470. Three-CD set rereleasing all of his RCA recordings.

DRUSKY, ROY (b. R. Frank D., Atlanta, Ga., June 22, 1930)

Sometimes called the "Perry Como of country music" (a dubious achievement), Drusky is nonetheless a fine SINGER/SONGWRITER whose 1960s recordings unfortunately suffer from the heavy-handed NASHVILLE SOUND.

Although Drusky's mother was a church pianist who tried to interest him in music, he spent most of his childhood preoccupied with sports. Drusky's interest in country music was born in the Navy, where he befriended some shipmates who played together in their own country band. After leaving the service he enrolled in veterinary school in Atlanta, but by 1951 he had formed his own band, The Southern Ranch Boys. They were hired to play on a small Decatur, Georgia, radio station where Drusky also worked as a deejay. After the band dissolved, Drusky began singing at local clubs; he was signed by Starday Records in the early 1950s and had a hit with 1953's "Such a Fool." In 1958 he was invited to join THE GRAND OLE OPRY, where he remained as a performer for over two decades.

By the early 1960s he was working out of Minneapolis as a deejay and had signed with Decca Records. He wrote his first hits, including the self-penned "Alone with You," "Three Hearts in a Tangle," and "Another" (cowritten with Vic McAlpin), all fine HONKY-TONK ballads although the recordings were drenched in walls of strings and syrupy vocal choruses. In 1963 he signed with Mercury, producing more hits ranging from the novelty of his first Mercury single, "Peel Me a Nanner" through more country heartache songs that had made him famous, like 1969's "Where the Blue and the Lonely Go." He also appeared in two "classic" movies, the C-grade *The Golden Guitar* and *Forty Acre Feud*.

Drusky's natural propensity for crooning, tied with a change in the country market, led him to be only a minor hitmaker in the 1970s. Although he continues to perform on occasion, he is more active today as a songwriter and record producer in Nashville.

DUBOIS, TIM (b. Grove, Okla., May 4, 1948)

DuBois, an accountant-turned-superstar-country-producer, was born and raised in Oklahoma. He earned a master's degree in accounting at Oklahoma State, and his first jobs were in the accounting field, in Texas-based banks. Meanwhile he yearned to be a country songwriter, penning songs on the side. He retired from banking to teach accounting, and finally retired from teaching to take a shot at making it big in Nashville. He arrived in 1977 and immediately placed his songs with major acts, including the HONKY-TONK, tongue-in-cheek ballad "She Got the Goldmine (I Got the Shaft)," recorded by JERRY REED. He then got into personal management, establishing a Nashville office for the West Coast firm Fitzgerald-Hartley. His first major signing was the group Restless Heart, in the mid-1980s; he not only signed the band, he groomed them carefully and helped them select material. In the late 1980s he signed VINCE GILL, and also began songwriting with him; the two scored a #1 country hit with "When I Call Your Name" in 1992.

In 1989 Arista Records, a pop label out of New York run by legendary producer Clive Davis, was looking to open a Nashville office and tapped DuBois to head the label's efforts. DuBois was an active manager, looking for talent and recognizing potential where even the performers themselves didn't see it. In 1991 he suggested to two SINGER/SONGWRITERS that they might be better off working together than trying to go it alone; the result was the hitmaking factory duo of BROOKS AND DUNN, still one of the most successful acts around. The band BLACKHAWK, another DuBois creation, enjoyed several years of success during the 1990s. DuBois also spotted talent in young ALAN JACKSON, quickly signing him after other Nashville labels had turned him down; Jackson has proven to be another durable hitmaker.

DuBois has become an elder statesman of the country industry. At Arista he has branched out to establish an office in Austin, Texas, to dig up emerging talent, and a Latin group for Spanish artists. He was elected president of the board of directors of the Country Music Association in 1996, for a two-year term. Meanwhile, he continued to write songs with many major Nashville songwriters and on his own, often placing them with his acts on Arista.

DuBois's professional life took some roller-coaster-like turns from late 1999 through the end of 2000. In December 1999 Gaylord Entertainment Group—the Nashville-based company that owns *The Grand Ole Opry*, Acuff-Rose Publishing, and other entertainment properties—announced that DuBois would become the head of their new Entertainment Group as soon as his contract with Arista ended. They also hinted that he might start a new record label for them. Meanwhile, Arista President Clive Davis was under attack by Arista's corporate owner, Bertelsmann, which was "encouraging" him to retire. Davis lost his post in early 2000; by midyear, whether because of this or because of Gaylord's previous announcement that DuBois would be joining them, the Arista Nashville label was "consolidated" into RCA Nashville. In June, DuBois joined Gaylord, amid much fanfare. However, by September, Gaylord went through a major reorganization, and DuBois was mysteriously let go.

In January 2002, DuBois was named the joint head, with TONY BROWN, of a new label, Universal South, a division of the Universal Music Group.

DUDLEY, DAVE (b. Spencer, Wis., May 3, 1928)

If one man can be credited with creating the TRUCK-DRIVIN' mystique, it would have to be Dave Dudley, whose 1963 recording "Six Days on the Road" single-handedly created a new genre of country song. He continued to wax odes to the big rigs through the 1960s and 1970s, adding to the repertoires of bar bands everywhere!

Raised in Stevens Point, Wisconsin, Dudley was given his first GUITAR by his dad when he was just eleven, but baseball was his life throughout his teens. An arm injury while playing with the Gainesville, Texas, Owls led to his early retirement. He began working as a deejay at a Texas radio station, playing along with the songs, until the station owner encouraged him to perform on his own. In the early 1950s he moved to Iowa and Idaho, where he continued to perform with a number of groups but with limited success. Dudley was struck by a hit-and-run driver while he was loading his guitar into his car in the early 1960s; his injuries further sidetracked his career. His luck changed soon after, when he released his ultimate trucker's anthem on the tiny Soma label in 1963. The song was a crossover hit on both pop and country charts.

He signed with Mercury in the same year, staying with the label for a dozen years and producing twenty-five country hits. The truck-driving themes continued with odes like "Two Six Packs Away" and "Trucker's Prayer," while he also tried to capture the God, guts, and guns conservative country market with his Vietnam-era waxings of "Mama, Tell Them What We're Fighting For," penned by TOM T. HALL, and KRIS KRISTOFFERSON's "Vietnam Blues." By the early 1970s he was back to the truckin' milieu with "Me and My Ole CB," "One A.M. Alone," and the 1980 hit listing the contents of every trucker's medicine chest—"Rolaids, Doan's Pills and Preparation H," recorded for the revived Sun label. Dudley was less active in the 1980s and 1990s.

Dudley's best recordings combined a ROCKABILLY, up-tempo accompaniment with his swaggering vocals. He not only sang about truckers, he embodied the image of the trucker. Just as the cowboy was a symbol of rural defiance and freedom in the 1930s and 1940s, so the trucker became the "one-man-against-the-

world" image of the 1960s and 1970s. For his contributions to the trucking world, Dave was made a lifetime member of the Teamsters, and presented with a solid gold membership card.

Select Discography

Trucker Classics, Sun 7024. Twelve of his hits.

DUKE OF PADUCAH, THE (b. Benjamin Francis "Whitey" Ford, DeSoto, Mo., May 12, 1901–June 20, 1986)

Ford was a country comedian and BANJO player who was one of the founding members of the *Renfro Valley Barn Dance*.

Raised by his grandmother in Little Rock, Arkansas, Ford had a career typical of many country musicians of his generation; he moved freely through a variety of styles, from Dixieland jazz to vaudeville-pop to COWBOY-Western to straight country. At the end of World War I he joined the Navy, where he learned the banjo, originally playing the tenor (or four-string) banjo in jazz styles. After touring vaudeville with his own dance band, he hooked up with Otto Gray's Oklahoma Cowboys. In the early 1930s he was hired to emcee GENE AUTRY's radio program out of WLS in Chicago, where he acquired his comic persona and new moniker, The Duke of Paducah, and became famous for the closing line "I'm going to the wagon, these shoes are killin' me." He moved to Cincinnati's *Plantation Party* radio show in the mid-1930s, and then to the new *Renfro Valley* show in 1937.

During World War II, Ford toured Army installations as a comedian/musician, then joined THE GRAND OLE OPRY after the war ended, remaining a regular until 1959. In the 1950s and 1960s his homespun humor was so popular that he developed an inspirational talk, "You Can Lead a Happy Life," which he delivered at sales conventions and colleges throughout the country. Although he continued to perform into the 1970s, his act changed little over the years: a combination of likable country corn with just enough musical numbers to carry him along.

DUNCAN, JOHNNY (b. near Dublin, Tex., October 5, 1938)

Duncan is a country SINGER/SONGWRITER who has had a long and varied career, achieving his greatest success in the late 1970s with a COUNTRYPOLITAN approach and hunky, he-man looks reminiscent of KRIS KRISTOFFERSON before he went to seed.

The cousin of guitarists Jimmy and DAN SEALS, Duncan was raised in a musical household. His mother taught him to play electric lead GUITAR when he was twelve, and he pictured himself as an instrumentalist in the MERLE TRAVIS tradition. He began performing with his mother and his Uncle Moroney on FIDDLE, playing local bars and events.

After completing high school Duncan enrolled at Texas Christian University for a short period, then moved to Clovis, New Mexico, where he began working with legendary producer Norman Petty, who had launched the career of another Texan, BUDDY HOLLY. Petty's attempts to turn Duncan into a teen idol went nowhere, despite taking him as far as England to record with what Duncan calls "4,900 violins." He also sang lead with the rockin' instrumental band JIMMIE GILMORE and the Fireballs.

In 1963 Petty gave up trying to promote Duncan, and the singer went to Nashville, where he worked as a deejay. Three years later he was singing on RALPH EMERY's morning radio show, where Columbia A&R man DON LAW heard him and signed him to the label. He became close friends with CHARLEY PRIDE and toured with the singer, but his initial Columbia recordings were not very successful. In 1972 he was going to leave the label when he decided to make one last try at stardom under the hands of producer BILLY SHERRILL. In 1975 they recorded a number that Duncan had written with LARRY GATLIN (of THE GATLIN BROTHERS), "Jo and the Cowboy," prominently featuring backup singer JANIE FRICKE. This led to a series of recordings with Fricke as a duet partner, including a remake of Kris Kristofferson's "Strangers," and #1 hits with "Thinkin' of a Rendezvous" and "It Couldn't Have Been Any Better."

Fricke and Duncan parted company in 1977, and Duncan had one more solo #1 hit, with the slightly risqué "She Can Put Her Shoes Under My Bed (Anytime)" a year later. The death of his father in 1981 led Duncan to return to Texas and take some time off; he signed with the tiny Pharaoh label in 1986 but has failed to return to the charts, though remaining a popular act on the country circuit.

Select Discography

Greatest Hits, Columbia 35628. Cassette-only reissue of his 1960s and 1970s hits.

DUNCAN, TOMMY (b. T. Elmer D., Hillsboro, Tex., January 11, 1911–July 25, 1967)

Lead vocalist for BOB WILLS's Texas Playboys, Duncan defined the WESTERN SWING vocal style: smooth, mellow, almost poppish in a Bing Crosby-influenced sound. He was the natural link between the bluesy vocals of JIMMIE RODGERS and the more modern sound of pop crooners of the 1940s and later.

Duncan teamed up with Wills when both were members of the original LIGHT CRUST DOUGHBOYS in 1932. When Wills left to form his own band a year later, he took Duncan with him, and the two formed the seminal group The Texas Playboys. It is Duncan's vocals that can be heard on most of Wills's classic recordings, including "San Antonio Rose," "Time Changes Everything," "Mississippi Muddy Water Blues" (adapted from Jimmie Rodgers), and hundreds of others. When Wills left for the West Coast during World War II, Duncan went with him; the old friends quarreled, however, and Wills fired Duncan from the band in 1948. Duncan struck out on his own; his early solo recordings were still in a Western Swing style, but failed to catch on without the Wills name attached to them. In 1961–1962 the duo reunited with some triumphant recordings for Liberty. Duncan died of a heart attack in 1967.

Duncan's importance was not only in expanding the repertoire of country music to include the pop songs of the day, but also in emulating the "crooning" vocal style of Crosby and others, introducing a smoother, more uptown sound to country music.

Select Discography

Beneath a Neon Star in Honky-Tonk, Bear Family 159572. 1951–1953 recordings in a more straight-country vein than his earlier work with Wills.
Texas Moon, Bear Family 159072. 1959 Capitol and smaller label recordings, in a latter-day Western Swing style.

DUNN, BOB (b. Robert Lee D., Fort Gibson, Okla., February 8, 1908–May 27, 1971)

Dunn, a legendary, pioneering steel-guitar player was one of the most exciting of all WESTERN SWING steel guitarists, supposedly the first to amplify his instrument. His background in jazz—he had worked in jazz groups as a trombonist while growing up—gave him a unique, syncopated approach to music making. Unlike others who emphasized sliding chords, Brown spit forth notes in a blazing display of technique. His distinctive sound—something like a cross between a buzz saw and a high-powered rifle—makes him immediately recognizable. There simply had never been a sound like this before in country music.

Dunn came from a rural background, and played in a variety of bands from his teen years. He teamed up with singer MILTON BROWN in 1934, when Brown was leading his Musical Brownies band. Dunn would record and tour with the band until Brown's untimely death in April 1936. After Brown died, Dunn moved from band to band, recording with leaders including fiddler Cliff Bruner, another Brown alumnus, and leading his own Tune Wranglers.

After serving in the Navy, he returned to Houston and by 1950 had opened a music store. For the next twenty years he operated the store and taught locally, but never again recorded. A year after closing the store he died of lung cancer.

Although he was legendary in his day, Dunn's long-time influence on steel and PEDAL-STEEL GUITARS is harder to trace. His own sound has never been duplicated; its aggressive, hard-edged tone has more in common with the acid guitar solos of Jimi Hendrix than the typical steel guitar solo. Nonetheless, scores of steel guitarists count Dunn as a spiritual father, and many say his playing influenced them to reach for greater technical virtuosity.

DUNN, HOLLY (b. San Antonio, Tex., August 22, 1957)

Dunn is a SINGER/SONGWRITER who created a flap with her 1991 song "Maybe I Mean Yes," which she withdrew after feminists angrily asserted that the song condoned date rape.

The daughter of a minister, Dunn attended Abilene Christian College, then traveled to Nashville after her graduation to join her brother, Chris Waters, who was already a successful songwriter. She took a job as a receptionist at a music publisher's office, and soon was singing on demos and writing her own material. Some of her first songs were placed with MARIE OSMOND, LOUISE MANDRELL, and THE WHITES.

In 1985 Dunn signed with MTM Records, who tried to market her as a pop singer, with limited success. She talked them into releasing her song "Daddy's Hands," a folk-styled ballad in honor of her father, as a single in a last-ditch attempt to market her. The song was an instant country success, as was the follow-up, a duet with MICHAEL MARTIN MURPHEY called "A Face in the Crowd."

Dunn quickly became known for her strong ballads, most of which she composed, including her late 1980s hits "Strangers Again" and "Someday." She signed with Warner Brothers in 1989, the same year she was invited to join THE GRAND OLE OPRY. The minor flap over her 1991 song, "Maybe I Mean Yes," brought her publicity in the mainstream press, and she earned some brownie points with more progressive listeners when she asked the label to withdraw the song.

However, Dunn's career sagged thereafter. She left Warner Brothers in 1993, and since then has issued two albums of new material, neither of which has seen much chart action.

Dunn is a better songwriter and musician than many of her contemporaries; however, her vocals, while strong, don't have much of a country character. She is more of a pop balladeer than a straight-country singer.

Select Discography

Milestone: Greatest Hits, Warner Brothers. 26630. Her late 1980s hits.

DYLAN, BOB (b. Robert Allan Zimmerman, Duluth, Minn., May 24, 1941)

Although Dylan's major achievements have been in folk/rock and pop music, he has earned a place in an encyclopedia of country music, and not just because of his two late 1960s LPs, the Western-concept LP *John Wesley Harding* and the Nashville excursion of *Nashville Skyline*. Even more important than these two dabblings in country sounds, Dylan is influential because of his breakthroughs as a songwriter, which had a particularly strong impact on country music outlaws like WILLIE NELSON and KRIS KRISTOFFERSON.

Dylan's initial inspiration was SINGER/SONGWRITER WOODY GUTHRIE, whose populist anthems inspired his first social-protest work. The idea that a singer and guitarist who was neither a talented vocalist nor pretty face nor particularly adept instrumentalist could be a "star" performing his own material (which often defied traditional song structures) was radical, to say the least. Dylan also had an annoying habit of creating an image (such as his original, pseudo-folkie stance) and then turning his back on it, even slapping his audience in the face (as in the famous moment at the Newport Folk Festival in 1965 when he "went electric," enraging the assembled folkies).

After a motorcycle accident in 1966, Dylan spent some time holed up in his home in Woodstock, New York, working with The Band in evolving a highly personal, folk-based music that represented the highest flowering of East Coast COUNTRY-ROCK. In their collaborations on *The Basement Tapes*, they felt their way toward this new music, which sounded both ancient and rooted in American traditions, but also modern. Dylan's influence can be felt most strongly on The Band's first two albums, particularly in songs that reflect American themes with a strong undertow of personal, romantic loss ("The Weight" is one of those cryptic personal songs, while "The Night They Drove Old Dixie Down" is one of the group's strongest American anthems, and an homage to Southern pride).

Dylan's firmest foray into country was on 1969's *Nashville Skyline*, recorded with many of the younger musicians who were then gathering in Nashville and who would influence the return-to-roots country music over the next decades. As with much of Dylan's work, it's hard to determine whether this album is an homage to or a satire of Nashville conventions. He radically changed his voice for these recordings, trying hard to remove the raspy, adenoidal quality from his singing, replacing it with a laid-back, crooning style. His duet with JOHNNY CASH on "Girl from the North Country" is the closest the album gets to straight country, although its roots are clearly in folk balladry; most of the other songs continue in the idiomatic Dylan style. The album was enormously influential in pointing other pop/rock performers toward the possibilities of wedding country with rock, although it's a route that Dylan himself did not pursue for long.

From the mid-1970s through the early 1990s, Dylan's career suffered from an often slapdash approach to recording and his restless search for a new style that would equal the impact of the old. In 1989 he teamed with producer Daniel Lanois for the atmospheric *Oh Mercy*, universally hailed as his best work in years. His 1992 release, *Good as I've Been to You*, was widely hailed as a return to his "folk" roots. However, his mostly out-of-tune guitar playing and lackluster singing on this collection of folk standards, plus his failure to credit other performers for arrangements clearly taken note-for-note from their earlier recordings, makes this just another chapter in Dylan's unhappy recent career. A second all-acoustic album, *World Gone Wrong*, appeared in 1993.

In 1997 Dylan made yet another "comeback," this time with a second album produced by Daniel Lanois, *Time out of Mind*. In contrast to *Oh Mercy*, the producer and songwriter were looking for a more roots-oriented sound, and so added lots of echo and backbeat to Dylan's misanthropic lyrics. The album was an unexpected success, winning Dylan a Grammy and once again resurrecting what seemed to be a semidormant career. (As a footnote, singer GARTH BROOKS covered

"Make You Feel My Love" from the album in 1998, reaching #1 on the country charts; this was the first time that a Dylan song was a #1 country hit, yet another career milestone for the gravel-voiced singer.) Dylan's next album, *Love and Theft*, was released in the fall of 2001. It continued in the roots-twang style of *Time out of Mind*, and brought Dylan further strong reviews in the pop press.

As a singer/songwriter writing topical material, and as an expressive, untrained vocalist, Dylan both draws on country traditions and extends them into new areas, pointing the way for other eccentric performers, from Willie Nelson to LYLE LOVETT.

Select Discography

John Wesley Harding, Columbia 09604. Outlaw ballads for a new generation, post motorcycle crash.
Nashville Skyline, Columbia 09825. Smooth-voiced crooning from a suddenly country Bob, with Johnny Cash lending a bass-voiced hand.
Basement Tapes, Columbia 33682. Working with The Band, in Woodstock c. 1968, Dylan created roots-rock without really trying.
Time out of Mind, Columbia 68556. Dylan returns as a rockabilly rebel, singing songs of love gone wrong.

E

EAGLES, THE (1971–1979; original lineup: Don Henley [voc, drms]; Glenn Frey [gtr, voc]; Randy Meisner [b, voc]; Bernie Leadon [gtr, bnj, voc]; Don Felder [slide gtr] added 1974; Joe Walsh [lead gtr] added 1976, Leadon leaves; Timothy B. Schmidt replaces Meisner, 1977)

The 1993 release of an all-Eagles tribute album recorded by new-country artists showed the enduring legacy of this popular 1970s group. They were the most successful COUNTRY-ROCK band, but only because they crossed out of the genre into being basically a mainstream rock outfit. And their influence on 1990s country stars is based on the success of their pop-rock songs, not their more country elements.

The original band was formed out of the Los Angeles folk-rock scene of the late 1960s and early 1970s. Previous outfits like THE BYRDS, The FLYING BURRITO BROTHERS, and Poco were influential on their original sound. The band coalesced around Linda Ronstadt, who hired them individually to be her backup group. The main country influence on the band came from founding member Bernie Leadon, who had played BLUEGRASS BANJO as well as GUITAR in his teenage years, and had worked with a later incarnation of The Flying Burritos. Frey had previously worked in a folk-oriented duo with songwriter J. D. Souther under the name Longbranch Pennywhistle; the two had collaborated on the countryesque song "Take It Easy," later the first hit for the Eagles. Meisner had been the bass player in one of the first country-rock outfits, RICK NELSON's Stone Canyon Band, and Henley, a Texas native, had previously played with a band of fellow Southerners in a country-rock amalgam known as Shiloh.

The first two Eagles albums were solidly in the country-rock tradition of southern California, although both were produced by rock producer Glyn Johns (who had previously worked with The Beatles, The Who, and Led Zeppelin), and recorded in England. The second album was particularly interesting; a concept album telling the story of the Doolin-Dalton gang of outlaws in the old West, it yielded the hit "Desperado." A few years later WILLIE NELSON would make *Red Headed Stranger*, another concept LP rooted in the old West.

The addition of session guitarist Don Felder in 1974 started the band in a more pop-rock direction, although they continued to show their folky side in hits like 1975's "Lyin' Eyes," a kind of HONKY-TONK love song for a new age. However, when Leadon left the band in 1976 and was replaced by songwriter/guitarist Joe Walsh, it was clear that the band was aiming for mainstream pop success. This was achieved on their 1977 album *Hotel California*, followed by 1979's *The Long Run*. Both established them as megaselling arena rockers. However, as the sales increased, so did the tension between the band's primary SINGERS/SONGWRITERS, Henley and Frey. Eventually, these tensions led the band to dissolve after releasing a final, live album. However, by the end of the 1990s, with only Henley enjoying success as a solo artist, the band reunited for a VH-1 concert special, album, and tour. Meanwhile, their *Greatest Hits* album had become the best-selling pop album of all time, an honor it still holds at the time of this writing.

The Eagles' pleasant harmonies, memorable melodies, and songs that often extolled an outlaw lifestyle have been highly influential on the New Nashville artists and songwriters. Many 1990s Nashville bands—from DIAMOND RIO to LITTLE TEXAS—sound like nothing more than Eagles clones. And performers like TRISHA YEARWOOD and TRAVIS TRITT sing the praises of the band and perform its material. This all leads to the uneasy feeling that the New Nashville is really just the Old Hollywood pop-rock in disguise; and there are some who would argue that this in fact is really where country music is headed—at least the more commercial variety that is driving out the traditional sounds.

Select Discography

The Eagles, Asylum 5054.
Desperado, Asylum 5068.
Selected Works, Elektra 62575. 1999 four-CD boxed set that features all of the hits, "and more," in remastered sound.

EANES, JIM (b. Homer Robert E., Jr., Mountain Valley, Va., December 6, 1923)

BLUEGRASS and country vocalist, songwriter, and guitarist, Eanes led a number of groups from the late 1940s through the 1980s, achieving moderate success on the bluegrass circuit.

From about the age of nine, Eanes played GUITAR, accompanying his father, a traditional-styled BANJO player who worked local dances. When he was a teenager, he began working on local radio, and at age sixteen was hired by ROY HALL, who had his own show out of Roanoke, Virginia. Eanes worked with Hall's band for four years before enlisting in the Army.

After World War II, Eanes worked with a band called Uncle Joe and the Blue Mountain Boys, who broadcast over several small Virginia-based stations, before finally landing a radio job in Knoxville, Tennessee. There he met BILL MONROE, and worked with the legendary father of bluegrass for a few months in 1948.

The next year Eanes cut his first records for Capitol, accompanied by bluegrass pioneers Jenkins and Sherrill (Homer Sherrill on FIDDLE and Snuffy Jenkins on banjo). He then formed a permanent band, The Shenandoah Valley Boys, broadcasting out of Danville, Virginia. After recording for small local labels, Eanes was signed in 1952 by Decca, who polished up his sound to appeal to a broader country audience. However, he failed to produce any hits, and the label dropped him in 1955.

Eanes returned to the bluegrass style for the balance of his 1950s and early 1960s recordings, mostly cut for Starday and a variety of smaller labels. On Starday he had a few minor hits, including "I Wouldn't Change You if I Could," which would be covered by RICKY SKAGGS in 1982 for a #1 country hit. In 1956 Eanes made the first recording of "Your Old Standby," which became his theme song.

Eanes continued to work Virginia-area radio and clubs through the 1960s. The bluegrass revival of the late 1960s led to a series of albums cut with Red Smiley's band, The Bluegrass Cut-ups. When Smiley retired in 1970, Eanes took over the band, now called The Shenandoah Cutups, releasing one album on County before the band broke up.

Eanes continued to work through the 1970s, except for taking a year off following a heart attack in 1978. Although he continued to record into the 1990s, he cut back on live appearances.

Eanes is not one of the more intense bluegrass singers. Instead, his relaxed, warm vocals have lent a more contemporary sound to his recordings. Never quite establishing himself as a country star, and only a second-tier name in bluegrass, Eanes nonetheless enjoyed a long career and worked with many influential musicians.

Select Dicography

Complete Decca Recordings, Bear Family 15934. Everything Eanes recorded for Decca between 1952 and 1955.
Your Old Standby, Starday 3507. Complete Starday recordings, featuring Allen Shelton on banjo.
Classic Bluegrass, Rebel 1116. 1970s recordings.

EARLE, STEVE (b. San Antonio, Tex., January 17, 1955)

Earle is a country-rocker who burst on the scene with the release of his now legendary 1986 album, *Guitar Town*.

Born in Texas, Earle comes from a long tradition of OUTLAW SINGER/SONGWRITERS with an attitude. He

Steve Earle, ridin' that train, 1996. Photo: Raeanne Rubenstein

came to Nashville in 1974; landed a bit part in *Nashville*, Robert Altman's film send-up of the country scene; and began hanging out in local clubs with other displaced Texas singer/songwriters, including TOWNES VAN ZANDT AND GUY CLARK. After a brief move to Mexico in 1980, he returned to his native San Antonio and formed his rockin' backup band, The Dukes. A year later he was back with his band in Nashville, working as a songwriter and cutting his first demo recordings in a 1950s ROCKABILLY style. He signed with Epic in 1983, releasing five singles including one minor hit, "Nothin' but You," but these recordings were marred by an imitation Stray Cats sound. After being dropped by the label, he continued to write, and his songs were covered by some of the older outlaws, including JOHNNY CASH and WAYLON JENNINGS.

His 1986 LP *Guitar Town*, his first release for MCA, seemed to come out of nowhere. Earle combined the sensibility of a Bruce Springsteen or John Cougar Mellencamp as a kind of "people's poet" along with a hard-rockin' attitude. The title hit is his best-known song, although the album's slow ballads, including "My Old Friend the Blues" and "Fearless Heart," are perhaps the true high points. He followed this album with *Exit O*, which took him into an even harder-rocking territory, at which point many more conservative Nashvillians (including new-country musicians) began to write him off as a rock-star wanna-be.

Unfortunately, Earle's career from the late '80s through the early '90s was spotty. He moved to MCA's pop/rock label Uni in the late 1980s and released the half-country, half-rock *Copperhead Road*, which failed to please his core audience or to attract new converts; his follow-up *The Hard Way* also fell with a decided thud between two stylistic stools. Critics of the Nashville establishment claim that Earle was too politically left-wing. *Copperhead Road*'s title cut tells the story of a Vietnam vet so traumatized that he lives by himself on a hill, growing his own private stash of marijuana to wash away his painful wartime memories. Some others counter that his music was too rock-influenced to survive in the country capital. Still others point out that the failure of his career to take off may have as much to do with his inability to produce a follow-up to his original breakthrough recording. After a 1990 tour with BOB DYLAN, Earle pretty much faded from both the country and the pop scenes.

Earle made a remarkable comeback, beginning in the mid-1990s with the album *Train a-Comin'*. He produced a series of hard-edged COUNTRY-ROCK albums, as well as an unusual collaboration with DEL MCCOURY on an album of bluegrass-styled originals, *The Mountain*, in 1999. The collaboration quickly ended with a falling out between Earle and McCoury, but nonetheless was probably the most innovative bluegrass-country-rock experiment of the late 1990s.

With 2000's *Transcendental Blues*, Earle stretched his palette to include bluegrass, rock, country, Celtic, and other musical influences.

Select Discography

Early Tracks, Koch 7903. Epic-label recordings made from 1982 to 1985, before Earle's big breakthrough.
Guitar Town, MCA 31305.
The Mountain, E Squared 51064. Features the Del McCoury band as accompaniment to new songs by Earle that reflect traditional sounds and themes.
Transcendental Blues, Artemis 751033.

EAST TEXAS SERENADERS (c. 1925–1930; sporadically thereafter; core members: Daniel Huggins Williams [fdl]; Cloet Hammons [gtr]; D. P. ["John"] Munnerlyn [tenor bnj]; Henry Brogan [cello])

This group, an early string band that straddled the line between old-time music and WESTERN SWING, is remembered for its recordings made primarily in the late 1920s, which emphasized a swinging, ragtime-influenced repertoire, as well as a modern FIDDLE style, that would have a great impact on the nascent Western Swing movement.

The group originated around the Hammons family; father Will was a fiddler, and his son Cloet accompanied him on GUITAR, with various others joining from time to time. By the mid-1920s Will was replaced by Daniel Huggins Williams, a left-handed fiddler who specialized in the long-bow, smooth, and slightly jazz-influenced fiddle style that was developing in the greater Dallas region. The group's name derived from the fact that they often went door to door "serenading" locals; they had very few professional jobs as musicians, and the fact that they were recorded at all is one of the flukes of the history of early country music.

From 1927 to 1930 they recorded a number of influential sides for Columbia and Brunswick, in four different sessions. They recorded only ragtime-influenced instrumentals and waltzes; apparently none of the older, "traditional" square-dance breakdowns were part of their repertoire. The sessions' producers may have requested these more modern dance styles, but other Texas bands of this time also seem to have focused on this repertoire. The band then returned to local work, resurfacing in 1937 for a final session for Decca Records. At this time Shorty Lester took the tenor banjo seat, and his brother Henry was featured on second fiddle.

Fiddler Williams's influence spread to younger players through these recordings and his local teaching. JOHNNY GIMBLE, later one of the legendary fiddlers associated with BOB WILLS, claimed to have taken lessons from Williams. Williams's style wed blue tones (flatted thirds and sevenths) and unusual keys—such as F and B flat, associated with modern popular music—with classical technique (particularly in the waltz selections that the band recorded). The Serenaders' "Beaumont Rag," recorded at their last (1937) session, was quickly picked up by Wills and company, and became one of their major instrumental hits.

Select Discography

Complete Recorded Works in Chronological Order 1927–37, Document 8031.

EDWARDS, DON (b. Boonton, N.J., March 20, 1939)

Although New Jersey-born, Edwards is the prototypical contemporary WESTERN COWBOY poet/songwriter/singing star, achieving great fame as a new voice of the old West. He was raised in rural New Jersey, where his father had retired from vaudeville. Like many others his first exposure to the West was via pulp fiction and pulp films, the B-grade Westerns of the 1940s and 1950s. Inspired by the guitar-totin' horsemen of the movies, Edwards taught himself the instrument and learned many of the popular "Western" hits of the day.

Drawn by the allure of the sagebrush, Edwards moved to Texas in 1958, and three years later was hired as a performer at the Six Flags over Texas theme park. In 1964 he cut his first record, "The Young Ranger." By the 1970s he had settled in Fort Worth, where he worked at the White Elephant Saloon, performing solo two nights a week and on weekends working with his band, The 7-Bar Cowboys. He has also been a mainstay of the Cowboy Poetry Festival, held in Elko, Nevada, since its inception in 1984. He has since worked the growing cowboy poetry circuit.

Edwards's career was greatly boosted when he was signed to Warner Western in the mid-1990s. He produced four albums for the label, including the minor hit "West of Yesterday." He also appeared on NANCI GRIFFITH's Grammy-winning album, *Other Voices, Other Rooms*, in 1993, singing a duet with her. In 1997 he was a featured performer in Robert Redford's film *The Horse Whisperer*. After the Warner Western label closed, Edwards recorded for Western Jubilee; his first album for the new label was 1998's *My Hero, Gene Autry*, which was recorded live at Autry's ninetieth birthday celebration. This album was subsequently re-released on Shanachie, which is the latest home for the singer.

Edwards's combination of cowboy-hatted good looks, baritone voice, and unsentimental but nostalgic poetry about the "old West" has won him a core of fans in the cowboy revival movement. Although occasionally breaking through into mainstream consciousness, this movement is limited primarily to a group of devoted fans and followers who wish to relive the glory days of ropin', ridin', and sittin' tall in the saddle.

Select Discography

Best of, Warner 46892. His best recordings from the mid-1990s for Warner Western.
Kin to the Wind, Shanachie 6051. 2001 album in homage to MARTY ROBBINS.

EDWARDS, JOHN (b. Cremorne, Australia, 1932–December 24, 1960)

Edwards, an Australian country music fan, compiled the largest private collection of country music recordings from the 1920s, along with memorabilia and related material, which became the heart of the John Edwards Memorial Foundation, the first nonprofit organization dedicated to the study of country music history.

It seems odd that an Australian who never visited the U.S. would become a country music fan and scholar, but it shows how it often takes someone outside of a culture to appreciate the true value of an art form that was often dismissed in the U.S. as merely "hillbilly music." When Edwards died in an automobile accident in 1960, he left behind a request that his collection be sent to the U.S. for others to use in the study of country music. American folklorist Eugene W. Earle arranged for the collection to be housed at UCLA and to be maintained by a new nonprofit, educational organization. Folklorists D. K. Wilgus, Ed Kahn, and Archie Green were among the first officers.

From the time of its founding, the John Edwards Memorial Foundation (JEMF, as it was commonly known) built its archive through contributions from other collectors and folklorists. It was among the first to publish a serious scholarly journal on country music (*The JEMF Quarterly*), and reissue early country recordings on record albums, making them accessible to a new generation of scholars and musicians. In 1986 the collection was given a new home in the Southern Folklife Center at the University of North Carolina, Chapel Hill.

EDWARDS, STONEY (b. Frenchy E., Seminole, Okla., December 24, 1929–April 5, 1997)

Edwards was a roots country performer before its time, having some success in the 1970s, when the COUNTRYPOLITAN sound was dominating the airwaves. Like many other country-soul performers, Edwards had a difficult time finding an audience on either R&B or C&W radio.

Of mixed Indian, African-American, and Irish descent, Edwards was raised in rural Oklahoma, where he was introduced to country music through his mother's brothers, who all played in a country style and encouraged him to listen to THE GRAND OLE OPRY. Stoney learned the guitar, fiddle, and piano by his early teens, playing primarily for his own amusement. His father abandoned the family when Stoney was young, and so he had to work at menial jobs to support the family. In his teens he moved to Oklahoma City to rejoin his father, and then went to Texas to live with an uncle. By the mid-1950s he had moved to the West Coast, where he married and began working in the Bay Area shipyards.

Stoney worked in the shipyards for fifteen years, until two accidents—first, carbon monoxide poisoning, then a broken back—ended his career as a laborer. He returned to his first love—playing the guitar—and began composing songs in the mold of his idols, HANK WILLIAMS and LEFTY FRIZZELL. While performing at a BOB WILLS benefit concert in 1970, he was spotted by a talent scout for Capitol Records, who signed him to the label. He made his first album in 1971, and two years later had a minor hit with "Hank and Lefty Raised My Soul." His biggest hit came in 1974 with "Daddy Bluegrass," followed a year later by "Mississippi, You're on My Mind."

Perhaps because he was an African American in a predominantly white field, or perhaps because his music was strongly influenced by 1950s HONKY-TONK stylings that were yet to be repopularized, Edwards's career at Capitol fizzled out. He moved to smaller labels in the late 1970s, with minor success, and then relocated to Texas, where he continued to perform locally during the late 1980s until his death from stomach cancer in 1997.

Select Discography

Poor Folks Stick Together: The Best of Stoney Edwards, Razor & Tie 82169. Twenty tracks, some previously unissued, featuring most of his 1970s hits.

ELY, JOE (b. Amarillo, Tex., September 2, 1947)
Another oddball Texas SINGER/SONGWRITER whose music defies categorization, Ely has enjoyed only sporadic success, much like his friends and onetime bandmates, BUTCH HANCOCK and JIMMIE DALE GILMORE.

Born to a nonmusical farming family, Joe began taking violin lessons at age eight, followed a few years later by steel-guitar lessons (taught by a door-to-door salesman/teacher); by his early teens he had switched to regular GUITAR, and began playing local dates. By his late teens he was a traveling musician, bouncing back and forth from Los Angeles to Texas, searching for work. In 1970 he was back in Texas, and formed a hybrid country-folk-rock group called The Flatlanders with Hancock and Gilmore; in 1971 the trio wound up

in Nashville, where they recorded what was to become a legendary unreleased album (it finally saw the light of day in 1990). Ely also worked for Joseph Papp, the noted New York City-based theatrical impresario, in the early 1970s, providing music for a show that played in New York and then in Europe.

In the mid-1970s a demo tape made by Ely caught the ear of JERRY JEFF WALKER, the elder statesman of Texas singer/songwriters, and Walker recommended him to MCA records. Ely released a couple of albums, most notably 1978's *Honky Tonk Masquerade*, featuring his blend of country, blues, and rock along with elliptical lyrics that were, at best, difficult for both country and rock audiences to follow. Country was still mired in COUNTRYPOLITAN and glitzy Vegas-styled acts at this time, while rock was barely recovering from the assault of disco, so it's not surprising that Ely's music could not be effectively promoted to either audience. In 1980, in another strange twist in a career filled with them, British punk-rock stars The Clash "discovered" Ely, and vigorously promoted his music. He made a few harder-rocking albums, forecasting the sound of rebel rockers like STEVE EARLE by a few years, but again his music bridged so many different styles that it found only cult success.

By the early 1990s Ely had entered the pantheon of legendary Texas OUTLAWS who are venerated as much for their refusal to fit in with the musical mainstream as they are for the music they produced. He continued to record through the decade, without achieving much commercial success. From time to time he reunited with his fellow Flatlanders for reunion tours.

Select Discography

More a Legend Than a Band: The Flatlanders, Rounder 34. This "legendary" album is more famous for its mythic reputation than for the quality of the music on it; an interesting document of its time.
Best of, MCA 151. 1977–1995 recordings for MCA.
Twistin' in the Wind, MCA 70031. Last major-label collection to date, released in 1998.

EMERSON, BILL (b. William Hundley E., Washington, D.C., January 22, 1938)
Celebrated BLUEGRASS banjo player of the 1950s, Emerson was one of the original members of THE COUNTRY GENTLEMEN, although he didn't stay long, and also played with JIMMY MARTIN and RED ALLEN.

Emerson was an influential banjo player in the Washington, D.C.-Virginia-Maryland area in the 1950s, first working with Buzz Busby and The Bayou Boys, a band that featured Charlie Waller. After Busby was injured in an automobile accident in 1957, Waller and Emerson formed the first version of The Country

Gentlemen. Emerson recorded a couple of singles with the group through 1958.

After leaving The Gentlemen, Emerson worked mainly as a sideman, primarily with Jimmy Martin from 1962 to 1964, then spent a year with Red Allen before returning to Martin for another two-year stint. His tasteful single-note picking with Martin was much admired by many younger bluegrass revivalists. After leaving Martin in 1967, he formed a group with Cliff Waldron that recorded for the small Rebel label.

In 1970 Emerson rejoined The Country Gentlemen, staying with the band for three years. He introduced the band to a song that he had learned from Waldron, "Fox on the Run," written by British folk-rocker Manfred Mann. The Country Gentlemen had a great success with the number, and it became a standard for many aspiring bluegrass pickers in the early 1970s.

Emerson left The Country Gentlemen in 1973 to join the Navy, beginning a twenty-year stint with the Navy Band. He appeared as a session musician sporadically through the 1970s and 1980s, making two triumphant "comeback" albums for Rebel as a solo banjo player in the late 1980s. Because of his fame in bluegrass circles, the Stelling Banjo Company issued a special signature instrument for him in 1992.

Emerson left the Navy in 1993, and continues to record and perform on occasion.

Select Discography

Reunion, Webco 140. 1991 recordings made with various accompanists who played with Emerson over the years.

EMERY, RALPH (b. Warren R. E., McEwen, Tenn., March 10, 1933)

An affable country deejay and TV host, known as the "Dick Clark of country music," Emery has become a major Nashville power broker through his long-running presence on the scene as deejay and TV host. However, his career had fairly humble beginnings. His parents divorced while he was a teen, and he worked wherever he could. He briefly studied at Belmont College in Nashville, and also at a local broadcasting school. His first radio job was in the less-than-major-metropolitan-area of Paris, Tennessee, followed by a position in rural Louisiana.

At age twenty-four, back in Nashville and unemployed, Emery applied for a position at the powerful WSM radio station. There was an opening for the "graveyard" shift—10 P.M. to 3 A.M.—paying a grand salary of $50.00 a week. With nothing to lose, Emery encouraged both established stars and up-and-coming acts to stop by, play their records, and sit and chat. The down-home, relaxed atmosphere was greatly appealing, and soon a stop at Emery's show was an important step in record promotion. Because WSM's signal was strong and many other stations were off the air during these hours, Emery's show could be heard in about thirty-eight states—giving him virtually national exposure.

Although he was not particularly talented as a singer, Emery's popularity landed him a brief moment in the country spotlight. His single "Hello, Fool"—an answer record to FARON YOUNG's "Hello, Walls"—was a #4 country hit in the early 1960s. He also parlayed his popularity into appearances in a few C-grade films, mostly with country or Nashville themes. Emery also expanded his radio presence with an afternoon show, *Sixteenth Avenue*, broadcast from 1966 to 1969, and then launched his first nationally syndicated weekly series, *Pop Goes the Country*, which ran from 1974 to 1982. In recognition of his long nighttime service, WSM switched him to the morning-drive slot in 1971.

The 1980s saw Emery make a major move into television. He first appeared on Ted Turner's "superstation" TBS with the *Nashville Alive* show in 1981–1982, but it was his next show, the daily *Nashville Now*, broadcast on TNN, that established him as a major presence in this medium. The show ran from 1983 to 1993 with Emery as its host, and soon was attracting a million viewers a day. Emery left the show to start his own syndicated show, *On the Record*, which ran through the mid-1990s.

In 1991 Emery, virtually unknown outside of country circles, surprised the New York publishing world when his autobiography, *Memories*, became a national best-seller. Emery's fans snatched up the book, and this led to a new career as an author/memoirist. Emery has since published several more volumes, mixing his own life story with stories about the celebrities he has known.

Since the mid-1990s Emery has scaled back his personal workload to focus more on producing specials for cable stations and on occasional radio appearances. He was one of the hosts for THE GRAND OLE OPRY's seventy-fifth birthday celebration in the fall of 2000, and continues to make local appearances in the Nashville area.

EMILIO (b. E. Navaira III, San Antonio, Tex., August 23, 1963)

Along with Selena, Emilio was a major Tejano star of the early 1990s, famed for his Spanish-language recordings with his band, Rio, which sold well in the Hispanic market. In 1995 he made an attempt to cross over into the country market, and has since recorded in both English and Spanish, to try to attract new audiences.

He began playing GUITAR at age five, and sang and played locally as a teen. He won a voice scholarship to Texas State University in San Marcos, but dropped out after three years to pursue a professional music career. In 1973 he began performing with a local group, David Lee Garza y Los Musicales, remaining with them as their lead singer through 1989. At that time he went solo and formed his own band, Rio, prominently featuring his brother, Raul. Raul is a masterful composer, reworking traditional Tex-Mex dance styles such as the polka, mazurka, and waltz into more contemporary sounds. He is also a talented comedian, and his bulky, nearly 300-pound frame makes an excellent visual foil to his older brother's hunky good looks on stage. While performing Hispanic material Emilio used his full name; he dropped his surname when he turned to the country market.

In 1995, backed by several major corporate sponsors who wished to tap the huge Hispanic market, Emilio recorded his first English-language country LP, *Life Is Good*. The lead single, "Not the End of the World," reached a respectable Top 30 position on the country charts. Like BILLY RAY CYRUS, Emilio also attempted to introduce a new dance craze, the Emilio Shuffle. This somewhat comic dance style was created by brother Raul over a number of years, as part of their stage show. The dance was highlighted on Emilio's second video, for the song "Even if I Tried." Despite heavy airplay on Country Music Television, the song and the dance craze were short-lived. Emilio found many corporate sponsors for his tours, and appeared in commercials for everything from soda to blue jeans.

Since then Emilio has primarily retreated to his core Hispanic audience. He has released one further English-language album, 1997's *It's on the House*, which failed to produce any hits. The remainder of his output has been in Spanish, combining Tejano and country styles. In late 2000 he was arrested on drunken-driving charges, but by early 2001 he was back in corporate good graces, being hired as a spokesperson for Wrangler jeans in the Latino markets.

EMMONS, BUDDY (b. B. Gene E., Mishawaka, Ind., January 27, 1937)

Emmons is a pioneer of the PEDAL-STEEL GUITAR and one of the most influential steel guitarists on the Nashville scene, with a thirty-five-year career. He was born in rural Indiana but raised in South Bend. Hearing HANK WILLIAMS on The Grand Ole Opry, he was mesmerized by the sound of steel guitarist Don Helms, a mainstay of Williams's band. His parents got him his first instrument, and by his early teens he was performing locally. By age sixteen he was working small bars and strip joints in Illinois and Missouri, where his playing was heard by touring country artists like WEBB PIERCE and RAY PRICE. When he was seventeen, Emmons moved to Detroit, where he sat in one night with "LITTLE" JIMMY DICKENS, who immediately offered him a job with his band.

In 1955 Emmons followed Dickens to Nashville, where he immediately found session work with many major acts. After Dickens he worked for a while with ERNEST TUBB, and by the early 1960s he was backing Ray Price. In 1963 he went freelance, and has worked ever since on many major Nashville sessions and toured with a wide variety of performers. Also in 1963 Emmons came to New York to record *Amazing Steel Guitar*, a session that wed his playing with a hard-bop jazz rhythm section. The sessions were arranged by jazzman Quincy Jones, and featured several compositions by Sonny Rollins and other contemporary jazz players, along with Emmons's originals. The album has become a cult classic, although at the time few fans appreciated this unusual wedding of jazz and country.

Emmons was an inveterate tinkerer and inventor, always trying to find ways to improve the design and functionality of the pedal-steel guitar. He went into business with SHOT JACKSON, another steel player, to form Sho-Bud Guitars to market their improved instruments. Emmons also made instructional videos and wrote articles on pedal-steel technique, helping to introduce young players to the instrument. In the 1990s he opened Emmons Guitar Company to make and market custom-built instruments.

Emmons began to enjoy increasing visibility in the early 1980s, thanks to several releases on the FOLK-REVIVAL label Flying Fish Records. Since the late 1980s he has recorded a series of albums with bandleader Ray Pennington that combine WESTERN SWING with big-band numbers; these records are accompanied by books of tablature. Most of his recent recordings have been issued on his own label. Besides his studio work and his own recordings, Emmons continues to work on the road. Since 1998 he has been touring as part of THE EVERLY BROTHERS' backup band.

Select Discography

Amazing Steel Guitar, Razor & Tie 2135. Good career retrospective.

ESMERELDY (b. Verna Sherrill, Middleton, Tenn., June 1, 1920)

Like her contemporary JUDY CANOVA, Esmereldy, a "hillbilly" performer who popularized the music in the 1940s in New York City, helped perpetuate the image of the slightly illiterate, comical female hillbilly for audiences in the Northeast. She was born in rural Tennessee but raised in Memphis, where she began her radio career at age eight. Upon moving to New York in the late 1930s, she quickly began performing with ELTON BRITT, Canova, and other transplanted country artists at spots like the Village Barn. She also landed her own radio program on NBC, working as a country disc jockey. In 1941 she was among the first country artists to make a soundie, a short film used to promote her recordings.

Esmereldy is best remembered for her late-1940s "authentic hillbilly" recordings. Many of her songs were comic novelties, including her biggest hit, "Slap 'Er Down Ag'in, Paw." By the early 1950s she was back in Memphis, hosting the *Tennessee Jamboree* syndicated country show and working as a country deejay.

Her daughter, Amy Holland, had a brief career as a pop singer in the mid-1980s. She married pop singer/songwriter Michael McDonald and toured with him as a backup singer through the 1990s.

EVANS, SARA (b. Boonville, Mo., February 5, 1971)

Beginning as a country traditionalist, Evans quickly transformed herself into the next big thing in country music.

Evans was raised on a tobacco farm. She began singing with her family BLUEGRASS band at the age of four and was always the focus of the act. By the time Evans was ten, the family was billed as "The Sara Evans Show," traveling by RV to perform at Grange halls throughout Missouri. In her early twenties Sara made her way to Nashville, to try to establish a career as a singer. Her lucky break came in 1995 when songwriter HARLAN HOWARD heard her singing his "I've Got a Tiger by the Tail" at a demo session. He convinced RCA to sign the singer.

In 1997 Evans released her first album, the widely hailed *Three Chords and the Truth*. Produced by DWIGHT YOAKAM sidekick Pete Anderson, the album was hailed for its HONKY-TONK authenticity. Evans's vocals were praised as combining the best of LORETTA LYNN and PATSY CLINE. However, despite the accolades, sales were dismal and Evans's career appeared to be in danger.

Not surprisingly, Evans's second album, 1998's *No Place That Far*, was a sudden turn toward mainstream pop-country. From the minute you heard the treacly title tune (replete with heartfelt harmonies from VINCE GILL), you knew that Evans had dropped her honky-tonkin' vocals for something more marketable. Although not a major hit, the second album fared far better on the charts, and set the stage for Evans's major breakthrough, 2000's *Born to Fly*. The title track—promoted by a clever video modeled on *The Wizard of Oz*—is the kind of big-lunged ballad that has made FAITH HILL a chart-topper. Although she's not a platinum blond, Evans's chipper good looks were amply on display in the song's video, undoubtedly con-

tributing to its success. The follow-up single, "I Could Not Ask for More," a mainstream love ballad, also fared well on the charts.

As the twenty-first century dawns, Evans is poised to become a crossover success. Her success is further (discouraging) news that country traditionalists still must bow before the commercial necessity of hitmaking—which means conforming to the "new" Nashville Sound. Or, to put it more plainly, it takes pop production and formulaic songs to make a hit in today's Nashville—not honky-tonk credibility.

Select Discography

Three Chords and the Truth, RCA 66955. A strong 1997 debut album, produced by Pete Anderson.
Born to Fly, RCA 67964. 2000 breakthrough album.

EVERLY BROTHERS, THE (Don [Isaac Donald], b. Brownie, Ky., February 1, 1937; Phil [Philip], b. Brownie, Ky., January 19, 1939)

Coming out of a traditional family country-music band, the Everlys revolutionized rock-and-roll music by introducing the plaintive vocal harmonies heard on classic 1930s brother duo recordings to the late-1950s teen-pop market. From the mid-1960s to their first breakup in 1973, they recorded some of the first COUNTRY-ROCK songs, and since 1973, as both solo artists and a duo, they have continued to honor their country roots.

The boys got their start when Don was eight and Phil was six, touring and performing with their parents, Ike and Margaret, and playing on the family's local radio show. Ike was a fine blues-flavored guitarist who was well known in the greater Kentucky region; picker MERLE TRAVIS is said to have learned some licks from him. When Phil graduated from high school, the duo hit the road for Nashville, and Don signed up with Acuff-Rose as a songwriter, penning "Thou Shalt Not Steal" for KITTY WELLS in 1954. Two years later they recorded a country single for Columbia, "Keep on Loving Me," produced by CHET ATKINS, which went nowhere.

A year later they hooked up with producer/Nashville powerhouse WESLEY ROSE, who brought them to Cadence Records and the country songwriting duo FELICE AND BOUDELEAUX BRYANT; they struck gold with the pair's "Bye-Bye, Love." The teen-angst lyrics of the Bryants wed with the brothers' sweet country harmonies (reminiscent of the LOUVIN BROTHERS, who were still performing in Nashville at this time) gave them chart-busting appeal on both country and pop charts. And although they were marketed as teen popsters, the Everlys never really shed their country identities, recording 1958's classic *Songs Our Daddy Taught Us*,

EXILE

a country tribute album, in the midst of their more pop-oriented sessions.

The brothers left Cadence at the height of their popularity for the big bucks offered by Warner Brothers in 1960. Although they lost the services of the Bryants, they revealed themselves to be adequate writers on their own with "(Til I) Kissed You" and "When Will I Be Loved," a classic country-rocker later covered by LINDA RONSTADT. Their string of good luck ended in 1963 during a tour of England; although it was reported at the time that Don had suffered a "nervous breakdown," he now admits that an addiction to prescription pills was the real problem. One year later the British invasion of American pop charts would push their more folksy sound off the playlists. They searched for a new identity through the 1960s; their best work was issued on *Roots*, a nod to their country childhood including a fragment of one of the family's radio shows. They also put out a fine country/pop LP, *Pass the Chicken and Listen*, in the early 1970s, again produced by Atkins.

In 1973 the duo split up during a performance at Knotts Berry Farm. Don spent most of the next ten years recording country material in the U.S. for Hickory and other labels, while Phil went to Europe, where the brothers always had a strong following, to pursue a more pop-oriented career. They reunited in 1983 with the country and pop hit "On the Wings of a Nightingale," written for them by Paul McCartney. Since the late 1980s the duo have reunited for annual tours, including a long-standing engagement in Las Vegas.

The Everly Brothers brought the brother act tradition into the modern era. The two sides of their personalities—Phil's sunniness reflected in his high tenor vocals and Don's more brooding pessimism represented by his baritone leads—represent the tensions in country music itself, between lighthearted commercialism and a darker, more personal style.

Select Discography

Classic Everly Brothers, Bear Family 15618. For completists, some early radio shows, all of their early recordings for Columbia, and their four albums for Cadence, beautifully packaged as a four-CD set.
Songs Our Daddy Taught Us, Rhino 70212. Reissue of the classic LP.

EXILE (1980s lineup: J. P. Pennington [gtr, voc]; Sonny LeMaire [b, voc]; Les Taylor [gtr, voc]; Marlon Hargis [kybds]; Steve Goetzman [drms])

Exile was a glitzy pop-rock group of the 1970s who successfully transformed themselves into a glitzy country-pop group of the 1980s, and brought an arena-rock-sensibility into the country fold.

The band was founded way back in 1963 as The Exiles, a pop-rock group. One of the original members was J. P. Pennington, who actually has impeccable country credentials: his mother was BANJO/FIDDLE player LILY MAY LEDFORD; his dad, the emcee of *The Renfro Valley Barn Dance* radio show; and his uncle, RED FOLEY. However, Pennington showed little interest in country music, admitting to one interviewer: "If somebody would have told me in 1972 that I was gonna be in a country band with a number one record, I would have beat them to death with an Iron Butterfly record." In fact, by 1978 Exile was at the top of the rock charts with the gooey hit "Kiss You All Over." However, they were unable to maintain their lofty position in rock's pantheon, and by the early 1980s they were working as a bar band in The Rebel Room, a Lexington, Kentucky, bowling alley.

It was during their period of artistic "exile" that the band began hearing their songs being covered by country artists, including DAVE AND SUGAR, JANIE FRICKE, and their soon-to-be rivals in the country-band fold, ALABAMA. This led their manager to have the band audition in 1983, in Nashville, for producer Buddy Killen, who had previously worked with Joe South and other R&B acts, as well as mainstream country performers. They scored their first country #1 hit with Pennington's "Woke Up in Love," followed by a string of hits written by Pennington and bandmate Sonny LeMaire. Oddly enough the band was still creating what would have been considered soft-rock or pop-styled songs in the mid-1970s; but by the mid-1980s this music was now called "country." The band also became famous for their lengthy instrumental introductions, as if each song was a miniplay with its own "overture" to set the proper mood.

The band began to fall apart in the late 1980s, beginning with the defection of keyboardist Hargis in 1987, followed by Les Taylor a year later; the final blow was the defection of principal vocalist/songwriter Pennington in 1989 (he released a solo album for MCA). A new Exile emerged, led by LeMaire and new vocalist Paul Martin (who had replaced Taylor), and they moved to a new label, Arista, in 1990 scoring another hit with "Yet." However, in 1993 the band was dropped by Arista, and they fell apart for good.

Exile defies the distinction between pop and country; in fact they actually show that much of country really is just pop, carefully packaged for a different market. Their influence can be felt in the creeping influence of arena rock on other country acts.

Select Discography

Greatest Hits, Epic 40401. 1970s–1980s hits.
Super Hits, Arista 18887. The latter-day group from 1990 to 1993.

FAIRCHILD, BARBARA (b. Knoebel, Ark., November 12, 1950)

Fairchild is a pop-country singer best known for her kiddie-themed hits of the mid-1970s, particularly "The Teddy Bear Song," who subsequently found the Lord and a new career in country-gospel.

Fairchild, whose father was a small-time trucker and farmer, was raised in rural Arkansas; she began singing with two aunts in a GOSPEL trio at an early age. Her father was an early booster of her career, taking her to local bars so that she could sing with the bands. When the family relocated to St. Louis in 1962, her father became increasingly involved with promoting her talents, arranging for her first recording session in 1965 and then, two years later, driving her to Nashville for an audition with Kapp Records. Eighteen-year-old Fairchild had her first hits with the little-tough-gal stance of "Remember the Alimo-ny" and "Breaking in a Brand New Man." These early recordings attracted the attention of Columbia Records, and she soon moved to that label. Fairchild wrote many of her first Columbia releases, including 1970's "A Girl Who'll Satisfy Her Man," reflecting her backcountry conservatism that would manifest itself even more strongly in her hitmaking years.

In 1973 Fairchild had a big hit with the sugary-sweet "The Teddy Bear Song" on both pop and country charts. The song—which related a young girl's wish that she could be held and cuddled like the teddy bear of her youth—led to a spate of similar drivel, including "Kid Stuff," "Baby Doll," and "Little Girl Feeling," that also rocketed up the charts. She recorded the 1975 anti-women's lib anthem, "I Just Love Being a Woman," guaranteed to keep her off of Betty Friedan's list of best-loved singers! At the same time more mature material like 1976's "Cheatin' Is," about infidelity, and 1978's "She Can't Give It Away," about the hard life of an aging streetwalker, failed to dent the charts.

By the end of the 1970s Fairchild was dropped by CBS and her second marriage—to a jazz pianist who had inspired her 1978 megadud LP, *This Is Me*, with its light pop arrangements—was on the rocks. She retired to Texas, where she was born again, and began performing gospel-tinged material. In 1982 she recorded "The Biggest Hurt," an anti-abortion anthem, and two years later returned to Nashville. She formed Heirloom, a gospel trio with Tanya Goodman and Candy Hemphill, in 1990 and a year later recorded a comeback gospel solo album, featuring the minor hit "Turn Right and Then Go Straight."

Through it all Fairchild remained a pleasant-enough pop singer, not so powerful as to blow the tubes out of your stereo, but likably sincere. Unlike many other gospel performers, who send their message home with the subtlety of a sledgehammer, Fairchild lets her material speak for itself, and for this alone is one of the least annoying of the gospel-crooners.

Select Discography

Classic Country, Simitar 5635. All her Top 40 hits.

FARGO, DONNA (b. Yvonne Vaughan, Mount Airy, N.C., November 10, 1945)

Fargo is a mid-1970s chanteuse best known for the ever-perky megahits "The Happiest Girl in the Whole U.S.A." and "Funny Face."

Born in the heart of mountain-music country (the Mount Airy, North Carolina/Galax, Virginia, region is home to countless old-time and BLUEGRASS musicians), Fargo sang as a youngster, but had no ambitions to a musical career. The daughter of a big-time tobacco farmer, she attended college locally, earning a teaching degree, and eventually settled in California to teach. There she met singer/guitarist Stan Silver, who became her biggest booster, manager, and husband; he encouraged her to learn the GUITAR, sing, and write her own material. When she was in her late twenties, she took the stage name of Donna Fargo, recording a single for the Phoenix-based Ramco label; in 1968 she went to Nashville to record the racy (for the time) "Who's Been Sleeping on My Side of the Bed?," which was boycotted by many country stations that thought it too suggestive, particularly for a girl singer.

After recording for a number of small labels, Fargo finally hit pay dirt with her "Happiest Girl in the Whole U.S.A.," picked up nationally by Dot Records in 1972; it rocketed to #1 on the country charts and earned her a Grammy. The follow-up was another sunshiny anthem, "Funny Face," cementing her image as a well-scrubbed eternal optimist.

Fargo remained with Dot through 1976, when she signed a million-dollar contract with Warner Brothers, who were looking to break into the country market. The variety of her material increased, ranging from the perky rocker "Superman" of 1973 to the slightly feminist "A Song with No Music" of 1976, which told of the unhappiness of a woman caught in a difficult relationship. In the late 1970s she moved from her own compositions to covering country-pop standards, including "Mockingbird Hill" and "Walk on By." She also landed her own syndicated TV show, and appeared to be poised for pop-crossover stardom.

In 1978, however, she was tragically afflicted with multiple sclerosis. Although she continued to perform into the 1980s, she was increasingly debilitated by the disease. She did manage a comeback hit in 1986, "Woman of the '80s," which, although more progressive than her earlier material in subject matter (it documented the trials and tribulations of five women struggling with their new roles in a changing world), still managed to bubble forth with the sunny attitude that marked all of her recordings.

Fargo continued to tour through the 1990s, focusing on GOSPEL-tinged material along with her hits. She has written an inspirational collection of "thoughts," available in book form and on her own line of greeting cards.

Select Discography

Best of, Varese 5567. All of her cheerful hits; reissues the 1977 MCA collection (1634).

FEATHERS, CHARLIE (b. Charles Arthur F., near Holly Springs, Miss., June 12, 1932–August 29, 1998)

Fans of 1950s ROCKABILLY have long idolized Feathers, who is best known for his 1950s recordings, particularly "Tongue-tied Jill" and "Get with It."

Feathers was raised on a farm in rural Mississippi and learned to play GUITAR from a black sharecropper and blues musician, Junior Kimbrough. For a while he worked for small petroleum companies in Illinois and

Texas before settling in Memphis around 1950, working in a box manufacturing firm until a bout with spinal meningitis left him bedridden for several months. While he was laid up, he listened constantly to the radio, determined to become a professional singer.

Legendary Memphis producer SAM PHILLIPS was launching a country label, to be called Flip, when he met Feathers. He paired him with two other musicians, Bill Cantrell and Quinton Claunch (two local studio musicians who would later start the Hi label, originally a country-oriented company that later recorded Al Green and other classic Memphis soul singers), and the trio recorded the 1955 release "I've Been Deceived," a powerful country WEEPER in the mold of HANK WILLIAMS. Later in the same year Feathers worked on demos of songs by Stan Kesler, gaining coauthor credit for the classic country song "I Forgot to Remember to Forget (About You)," which was ELVIS PRESLEY's last Sun recording (Feathers later claimed that he taught the King the vocal licks for this number); he also wrote with Kesler "We're Getting Closer to Being Apart." Feathers cut a second country single, but it went nowhere.

By 1956 Feathers had switched to a rockabilly vein, imitating the vocal hiccups and stutters that were a trademark of recordings of this genre. Los Angeles-based Meteor Records issued his single of "Tongue-tied Jill" backed with "Get with It," along with a number of other songs. He then signed with Cincinnati-based King Records, and for a while it looked like Charlie might make it big. He toured with a number of package shows and even appeared at Dallas's Big D Jamboree before his career fizzled out.

Feathers spent much of his final twenty-five years recounting his days in the limelight while performing at small down-and-out bars. A talented country singer, he also occasionally recorded, most notably in 1991 for Elektra's American Masters series. He continued to perform in the Memphis area, often accompanied by his son and daughter, until his death, following a stroke, in the summer of 1998.

Select Discography

Get with It: Essential Recordings 1954–69, Revenant 209. Two-CD set of his classic Sun and other small-label recordings.

FELTS, NARVEL (b. Albert N. F., North Keiser, Ark., November 11, 1938)

Like many country stars of the 1950s, Felts went through a period recording teen-pop and ROCKABILLY before returning to his country roots.

A farm boy, Felts raised enough money through picking cotton to buy a Sears, Roebuck GUITAR when he was a teenager, learning songs from THE GRAND

OLE OPRY. Bitten by the new rock-and-roll bug, he won his town's high-school talent contest aping CARL PERKINS's "Blue Suede Shoes," and was soon performing on local radio, backing local pop-crooner Jerry Mercer.

In his early twenties Felts showed up at the legendary Sun studios in Memphis, where he backed such stars-to-be as CHARLIE RICH and Harold Jenkins (later CONWAY TWITTY) as well as making some recordings on his own. He recorded for MGM in the late 1950s and moved to the tiny Pink label in the early 1960s, still searching for that elusive teenage hit; he did have minor success with the sickly sweet "Honey Love."

By the early 1970s he was back in Memphis, recording for the Hi label (which began as a country outfit but would become famous for its soulful stars like Al Green) with little success. He then switched to an even tinier label, Cinnamon, where he had his first country hits, 1973's "Drift Away" and "All in the Name of Love," and 1974's "When Your Good Love Was Mine." Felts's dramatic vocals—smoothly swooping from high falsetto to low bass notes—combined the excitement of rock and roll with the gentle smoothness that the country audience prized in the mid-1970s. He was signed by ABC in 1975, scoring hits with "I Don't Hurt Anymore," "One Run for the Roses," and "Everlasting Love," in 1977, 1978, and 1979, respectively. Felts continued to record for ABC/MCA into the early 1980s, but was dropped by the label after his hitmaking days ended.

Since the 1980s, Felts has toured through the U.S. and Europe, reviving his career in the rockabilly style while also performing his country hits. His band included his son, Albert Narvel Felts., Jr., known as "Bub," until Bub died in a tragic car accident in 1995. Felts released *Ode to Bub*, a compilation of recordings made with his son along with new songs in his honor, in 1997. He is a member of the Rockabilly Hall of Fame.

Select Discography

Drift Away, Bear Family 156902. Reissues all of his 1970s hits on ABC/Dot.

FENDER, FREDDY (b. Baldemar G. Huerta, San Benito, Tex., January 4, 1937)

Fender is a popular Tex-Mex country star who had a number of mainstream country hits in the mid-1970s. He is the only Hispanic artist who has been able to have country hits while maintaining his ethnic identity, combining elements of Mexican music (particularly instrumentation and rhythms) with traditional country themes.

Born to a migrant farmworker family who roamed throughout the Southwest, Fender took an early inter-est in the GUITAR and sang in Spanish. He dropped out of high school at age sixteen to join the Marines and returned at age nineteen to play local clubs, taking the name Freddy Fender and performing a combination of ROCKABILLY, R&B, and Tex-Mex standards. He hooked up with club owner Wayne Duncan, and the pair wrote "Wasted Days and Wasted Nights," a local hit released nationally on Imperial.

In 1960 Fender was convicted of possession of marijuana, and spent three years in the infamous Angola State Prison in Louisiana (where folksinger Leadbelly had earlier done time). JIMMIE DAVIS, governor of Louisiana and himself a country singer, arranged for his release, with the proviso that he abandon country music as a career! Fender quickly returned to performing, although his recording career was virtually ended.

In 1974 Huey Meaux, a famous Louisiana-based producer of R&B recordings, began to produce Fender's most successful recordings. His biggest hit was 1975's "Before the Next Teardrop Falls," sung half in English and half in Spanish, along with a remake of "Wasted Days." Meaux's productions emphasized Fender's tear-drenched vocals along with an unusual combination of PEDAL-STEEL GUITAR, accordion (from Tex-Mex conjunto music), and harpsichord! Fender's first few singles charted on both country and pop charts, although most of the rest of his hits in the late 1970s appealed primarily to a country audience.

Fender spent most of the 1980s pursuing an acting career, achieving his most high-profile role in 1988, in Robert Redford's film *The Milagro Beanfield War*. Late in the decade he teamed up with longtime bar-band friends Doug Sahm and Augie Meyers, of the Tex-Mex rock band The Sir Douglas Quintet, as well as with Flaco Jimenez, one of the masters of Tex-Mex accordion, to form the supergroup The TEXAS TORNADOS, gaining some new success on the country and pop charts. The band performed and recorded together through the 1990s before officially "breaking up" in 1999.

In 1998 Fender appeared as a member of Los Super Seven, a supergroup of Mexican-American artists put together by Los Lobos' David Hidalgo and Cesar Rosas to record an album of traditional Mexican songs. He also continued to record and tour into the new millennium as a solo artist. In early 2002 he underwent a kidney transplant, and spent the winter months recovering.

Select Discography

Canciones de Mi Barrio: The Roots of Tejano Rock, Arhoolie 366. 1959–1964 Ideal label recordings, Fender's first, mostly in Spanish, showing a rockabilly/Tex-Mex blend.

The Freddy Fender Collection, Reprise 26638. One of many reissues of Fender's mid-1970s hits.

FIDDLE Perhaps the best-known instrument in all of country music, the fiddle has a long-standing place in the traditional musics of the British Isles and Appalachian and southwestern America.

One of the first questions asked by new listeners is "what's the difference between the fiddle and the violin?" Actually the difference does not lie in the structure of the instrument—although many fiddlers modify their violins in several important ways—but in the style of playing the instrument.

The fiddle takes its name from medieval bowed, stringed instruments that were the precursors of the modern violin, known as feydls or viols. The modern violin's story begins in Italy in the late seventeenth and eighteenth centuries. There, famous builders like Antonio Stradivari and Nicolo Amati developed new designs that made the instrument easier to play and sound better. Composer/performers like Arcangelo Corelli and Antonio Vivaldi developed new ways of playing the instrument. By the late eighteenth century these innovative instruments and playing styles had reached the British Isles.

With the introduction of the violin family, a new virtuoso musician developed. One of the most active centers for fiddle composition in the British Isles in the late eighteenth and early nineteenth centuries was Scotland, where the Baroque Italian style of variation was applied to traditional and new compositions. The Scottish fiddle tradition developed its own unique dance form, the strathspey (literally meaning "valley of the river Spey"), which featured a unique rhythm known as the "Scotch snap" (a sixteenth note followed by a dotted eighth). The last in the line of these great Scottish fiddlers was J. Scott Skinner (1843–1927), who lived long enough to make some stunning recordings and also composed many famous dance tunes.

The nineteenth century was also marked by a series of dance crazes that swept Europe. Many originated in Eastern music and moved rapidly west, like the waltz (of Austrian/German origin) and the polka (of Polish origin). These tunes, along with the traditional jigs, reels, and hornpipes, rapidly entered the fiddle repertoire, particularly in Scotland and Ireland. By the early twentieth century a school of virtuoso Irish fiddlers came to the fore, rivaling and surpassing their Scottish forebears. Noteworthy among this group of musicians was Michael Coleman, who made many recordings in the 1920s and 1930s that were popular on both sides of the Atlantic. The English fiddle tradition seems never to have reached the virtuosic heights of the Irish, although many bread-and-butter musicians played for country dances.

English, Irish, and Scottish immigrants came to the United States in several different waves, beginning in the early eighteenth century and continuing through the twentieth century. Each new wave brought their music with them, and new, home-grown fiddle styles also developed, particularly in the South and Southwest. Tunes came from the various British traditions but also from MINSTREL SHOWS and from the popular classical music of the day. There was also a wealth of composers who added an American sound to the fiddle tradition.

The first fiddle tune collections were issued in the early 1800s by music publishers like Elias Howe. However, beginning in the Civil War period, American dance music became increasingly popular, leading to more widespread publication. In landmark instruction books written for fife players, who accompanied the troops to battle, dance tunes were collected and notated in standard versions. The war itself inspired the composition of many tunes, or older tunes were given a new association (named for a battle or event in the conflict). After the war "mammoth" collections of dance tunes began to appear, to meet the needs of amateur fiddlers.

Several regional fiddle traditions have been well documented in the U.S. In the South the area of northern West Virginia bordering the Kanawha River has spawned several well-known fiddlers, including CLARK KESSINGER, Ed Haley, Franklin George, and the Hammonds family. With perhaps the exception of Kessinger, these players seem to share a unique repertoire of tunes, a more modal sound, and a less refined or polished manner of playing the instrument.

Another region that has been much studied is the Mount Airy, North Carolina–Galax, Virginia, nexus. Galax plays host to one of the oldest fiddlers conventions in the country. Fiddlers conventions—where fiddlers compete for prize money and get a chance to exchange tunes—originated sometime in the early twentieth century, and perhaps go back further than that. They are often organized by a particular local organization as a way to raise funds for schools or charitable groups. The Galax fiddlers meeting is one of the best known, and it was there in the mid-1960s that an important fiddle player, TOMMY JARRELL, was "discovered" by FOLK-REVIVAL musicians. Jarrell's fiddle style has been much copied and studied; he was in the middle of a fiddle dynasty, because his father, Ben, recorded in the 1920s and his son, B. F., played in a more modern, BLUEGRASS style.

Texas has been the home of some of the greatest "show" fiddlers. They have developed a flashy style of playing improvisations on traditional tunes, tinged with jazz and other more modern, syncopated dance musics. Texas has a long tradition of virtuoso fiddlers, beginning with ECK ROBERTSON, usually named as the first Southern fiddler to make a record (in 1922). His version of "Sally Goodin" and "The Brilliancy Medley" set the standard for elaborate and breathtaking variations. Over the years Texas has spawned many other virtuoso fiddlers, so that fancy fiddling in general is known as "Texas style" or "contest style."

The fiddle survived as the key melody instrument in both old-time string bands and in the more modern bluegrass band. But its true imporance in country music was its role as the main melody instrument on countless Nashville recording sessions, beginning in the early 1950s. All of HANK WILLIAMS's recordings featured a prominent fiddle part played by TOMMY JACKSON; the bluesy, lonesome sound of Williams's voice was perfectly echoed by the fiddle. Jackson would go on to become a major player in Nashville's "A team" of session musicians through the 1950s and 1960s. The fiddle was thus established as a must-have instrument on almost any country recording, even surviving the dreaded days of the new NASHVILLE SOUND of the 1960s and the COUNTRYPOLITAN movement of the 1970s.

When country musicians announced a return to their roots in the early 1980s, it was natural for the fiddler to return to the fore. Meanwhile, young bluegrass and old-time revivalists were learning to play the instrument, mostly through recordings of earlier musicians. One musician who became particularly prominent as both a Nashville session player and a soloist on his own was MARK O'CONNOR, who began his career as a teen bluegrass champion. ALISON KRAUSS has opened a new chapter in bluegrass fiddle history by playing the instrument as leader of her band, Union Station. Prior to her success the instrument was rarely played by a woman as a bandleader (or even as a backup musician).

Today no reputable country act would tour without a fiddler, although the fiddle player's style may owe as much to electric guitar riffs as it does to traditional fiddle tunes. Amplified instruments and special effects abound; often the fiddle is limited to an occasional fill here or there. But the fiddler has to be on stage—and very few country artists risk the wrath of the audience by failing to deliver.

FIDDLE FEVER (c. 1977–1982: Jay Ungar, Matt Glaser, Evan Stover [fdls]; Russ Barenberg [gtr]; Molly Mason [b])

A loose-knit band led by fiddler Ungar, Fiddle Fever performed a wide variety of music, from CAJUN to WESTERN SWING to pure and old-time country. Their unique use of three fiddles, each with a distinct personality, made them one of the more versatile of the old-time revival bands.

Ungar had first gained exposure through performing with folk-blues guitarist David Bromberg in the early

1970s, and then cofounded the short-lived Putnam String County Band, along with ex–NEW LOST CITY RAMBLERS member JOHN COHEN. In the mid-1970s he performed as a duo with his then-wife, Lynn Hardy, for a while, before forming Fiddle Fever. Glaser, Stover, and Barenberg had all performed with the various permutations and combinations of progressive bands that grew out of COUNTRY COOKING in the early-to-mid-1970s, including Breakfast Special, as well as working as soloists and backup artists.

In the group Ungar had the more traditional sound; even his own compositions, like "Ashokan Farewell" (which became a major FM-radio hit a decade later, when it was used prominently in the PBS *Civil War* series), sounded like ancient, roots fiddling. Stover and Glaser, on the other hand, were much more influenced by the jazz styles of Stephane Grappelli and BLUEGRASS players like KENNY BAKER. Thus, although the band was fiddle-dominated, it was still able to explore many different styles and moods of music.

By the early 1980s the band had pretty much fizzled out, although it was always rather informal to begin with. Ungar and Mason were married and performed as a duo sporadically through the next decade, while also running a series of summer music camps in Ashokan, New York; Barenberg resumed a solo career and has since relocated to Nashville, where he has been performing most recently with ace Dobroist JERRY DOUGLAS; Stover was fiddler in the Broadway production of ROGER MILLER's *Big River*, an adaptation of the Huck Finn story, while continuing to work in various New York bands; and Glaser teaches music at the Berklee School in Boston.

Select Discography

Best of: Waltz of the Wind, Flying Fish 303. Compilation of their albums, including the "hit" tune "Ashokan Farewell" from the Ken Burns/PBS Civil War documentary series.

FINK, CATHY (b. C. Ann F., Baltimore, Md., August 9, 1953)

A FOLK-REVIVAL BANJO player and vocalist, Fink has been performing both children's music and feminist country material since the mid-1980s.

Raised in a suburb of Baltimore, Fink was first exposed to old-time country music while a student at Montreal's McGill University. She hooked up with fellow student "Duck" Donald (1951–1984), and the duo toured Canada through the 1970s as well as releasing three albums, mostly focusing on old-time duets in the spirit and style of classic 1930s duos like THE BLUE SKY BOYS. Around 1981 the duo broke up and Fink relocated to Washington, D.C., where she pursued a solo career.

Through the early 1980s Fink performed as a soloist while recording both children's LPs and landmark feminist collections, such as 1985's *The Leading Role*, featuring BLUEGRASS and country-styled numbers answering age-old stereotypes promulgated through more typical songs in these styles. She also formed a number of loosely knit performing groups, first with Marcy Marxer, another children's performer who had previously played with Boston's all-female old-time band, Bosom Buddies, and later Blue Rose, an all-female country band featuring Marxer, fiddler LAURIE LEWIS, Dobroist Sally van Meter (of San Francisco's Good Ol' Persons), and Molly Mason (late of FIDDLE FEVER). Their album got some attention on country radio, and they were featured performers on The Nashville Network.

Fink continues to perform as a soloist and as a duo with Marxer. The pair have also produced a number of instructional videos aimed at children interested in playing old-time musical instruments.

Select Discography

Doggone My Time, Sugar Hill 3783. Her old-time songs.

Cathy & Marcy Collection for Kids, Rounder 8029. Best of their children's recordings from the early 1990s.

FLATT AND SCRUGGS (Lester Raymond Flatt, b. Duncan's Chapel, Tenn., June 14, 1914–May 11, 1979, and Earl Eugene Scruggs, b. Flint Hill, N.C., b. January 6, 1924)

Flatt and Scruggs are the two most famous names in BLUEGRASS, thanks to their long association with Columbia Records and the use of their music in the 1967 hit film, *Bonnie and Clyde*. Scruggs single-handedly created bluegrass BANJO picking, and Flatt's smooth lead vocals and creative guitar runs have been widely imitated.

Flatt came from a musical family; both of his parents played the banjo in the old-time or frailing style, and he soon learned the instrument, along with GUITAR and MANDOLIN. A big fan of BILL and CHARLIE MONROE, Flatt formed an amateur duo in which his wife played guitar and sang lead while he took the harmony and mandolin parts; at the same time he worked in a textile mill. By 1939 he had settled near Roanoke, Virginia, where he performed on local radio as a member of The Harmonizers; a few years later he was also playing with The Happy-Go-Lucky Boys, a group that included guitarist CLYDE MOODY. Moody was an alum of bands led by both Monroe brothers, and introduced Flatt to Charlie Monroe, who hired him and his wife to be members of his group, The Kentucky Pardners, in 1943. Soon tiring of life on the road, Flatt settled in North Carolina, where he worked for a while as a trucker. In 1944 he received a telegram inviting him to join Bill Monroe's new band, The Blue Grass Boys.

Scruggs, too, came from a musical family. He took up the banjo at an early age and, inspired by the picking of local banjo whiz Snuffy Jenkins, began playing in a three-finger picked style. He quickly developed the capability to play syncopated melody parts and chord

Earl Scruggs (center with banjo) and Lester Flatt (with guitar) c. mid-1950s. Photo: University of North Carolina, Southern Historical Collection, Southern Folklife Collection, University Archives

rolls, the rudiments of what would become the bluegrass style. He was performing as early as age six with his brothers, and had a radio job with The Carolina Wildcats by the time he was fifteen. During World War II he worked in a textile mill, but by the war's end had hooked up with "Lost" John Miller, who broadcast out of Nashville. When Miller quit touring, Scruggs was hired to join the Monroe band, just after Flatt had come on board.

The Bill Monroe Blue Grass Boys of 1946–1948 is a legendary band, in many ways serving as the archetype of all bluegrass bands that followed. Because mandolinist Monroe had a high, tenor voice, he switched Flatt to singing lead and playing guitar, with Scruggs prominently featured playing his new style of banjo; the group was rounded out by fiddler CHUBBY WISE and bassist Howard "Cedric Rainwater" Watts. When the band began broadcasting over Nashville's Grand Ole Opry, listeners were astonished by their power; many couldn't believe that Scruggs was playing a five-string banjo! Their recordings of Monroe standards like "Blue Moon of Kentucky" and "Molly and Tenbrooks," along with new instrumentals like "Bluegrass Breakdown" that prominently featured Scruggs, were immediate sensations. Monroe preferred high-energy, fast-paced music, often pitching the tunes up a key or two (from D to E, for example) to give them a brighter sound. Flatt, a more laid-back vocalist and guitarist, had trouble keeping up with the rest of the band; it was for this reason, some say, that he developed his characteristic bass runs (as a way to keep up with the frantic pace!).

Monroe was a difficult taskmaster who worked his band long and hard hours. In 1948 Flatt and Scruggs quit the band, taking with them bassist Watts and recruiting a young singer/guitarist named MAC WISEMAN along with fiddler Jim Shumate (another Monroe alum). They signed a deal with Mercury Records and took the name The Foggy Mountain Boys, after the CARTER FAMILY song "Foggy Mountain Top." Curly Seckler took Wiseman's place almost immediately, playing mandolin (although this instrument was rarely featured prominently in the band's recordings, perhaps because they did not wish it to compete with Monroe). Their most famous recording of this period is the 1949 instrumental "Foggy Mountain Breakdown," which was used eighteen years later as the theme for *Bonnie and Clyde*.

The group was signed to a radio job in Bristol, Virginia, where their broadcasts influenced local musicians like The STANLEY BROTHERS and DON RENO to play in the new bluegrass style. They signed with Columbia Records in 1950 (leading Monroe to leave the label, because he felt that they had stolen his sound). One of their first recordings for the new label was 1951's "Earl's Breakdown." By quickly turning the pegs on the banjo, Scruggs was able to drop a note a full pitch after he had struck it. A few years later he developed special tuners, now known as Scruggs's pegs, to automatically drop or raise a string's pitch.

In 1953 the band signed with flour maker Martha White, who was their sponsor for many years on the radio, TV, and tours. They were invited to join *The Grand Ole Opry* in 1955, the same year they launched their first syndicated television program. Through the later 1950s they toured widely on the bluegrass circuit.

In the early 1960s Columbia started to market the group to the FOLK-REVIVAL audience. They were assigned a younger producer and began recording songs by BOB DYLAN and PETE SEEGER, among others. They also were hired to perform the theme for *The Beverly Hillbillies* TV program, resulting in their first pop hit, 1962's "Ballad of Jed Clampett." They made guest appearances on the show, further promoting the group. Their big break came in 1967 when several of their songs were used in the film *Bonnie and Clyde*, which attracted a hipper, younger audience. However, as their recordings moved increasingly in a pop direction, Flatt became disillusioned with the new sound. Always a traditionalist, he wanted to return to recording the music that had made them famous. Scruggs, on the other hand, had two young sons who played contemporary music, and wanted to broaden his musical horizons. This led the duo to split in 1969.

Flatt formed The Nashville Grass with old friends Curly Seckler and Mac Wiseman; Scruggs formed The Earl Scruggs Review with his sons Randy and Gary, along with Dobroist. "UNCLE" JOSH/BUCK GRAVES. Sadly, Scruggs took a backseat to the other musicians in the Review, playing less and less of his distinctive banjo, while the material they chose to perform was among the weaker folk-rock songs. By the mid-1970s the band had pretty much run out of steam, and Scruggs went into retirement, performing only on occasion. In 2001 his son Randy produced a new album by the veteran picker, bringing him together with many young Nashville stars.

Flatt's Nashville Grass lacked the spark of the original Flatt and Scruggs bands of the 1950s but was a serviceable bluegrass unit; he introduced a hot young picker named MARTY STUART, who has since broken into the new-country market. As his health deteriorated through the 1970s, the quality of his lead singing and the band's recordings faltered, although he continued to record and perform until his death in 1979.

The duo was inducted into the Country Music Hall of Fame in 1985.

Select Discography

The Mercury Sessions, Vols. 1 and 2, Mercury 512644. Reissues all of their Mercury recordings made between 1948 and 1950. Also available on two CDs from Rounder with more complete notes.

Don't Get Above Your Raisin', Rounder 08. Fine early Columbia recordings from the 1950s.

Blue Ridge Cabin Home, County 102. More Columbia recordings from the 1950s.

1949–1958, Bear Family 15472. Four-CD set of all of their classic 1950s recordings.

1959–1963, Bear Family 15559. Five-CD set picking up the chronology from 15472.

1964–69, Plus, Bear Family 15879. Completes the recording career of the duo.

Songs of the Famous Carter Family, Columbia 08464. Recorded in the 1960s during the folk revival.

Foggy Mountain Banjo, County 100. 1961 all-instrumental album that was highly influential on the budding bluegrass revival. Originally issued as Columbia 23392.

FLECK, BELA (b. B. Anton Leos F., New York City, July 10, 1953)

A progressive BANJO player closely associated with his onetime teacher TONY TRISCHKA, Fleck has had a career moving from progressive BLUEGRASS to bebop-flavored jazz to an amalgam of funk and jazz with his group, The Flecktones.

Fleck's playing is very much in the style of Tony Trischka in its explorations of the outer limits of five-string banjo technique. Unlike Trischka he uses silence as a suggestive element in his music (influenced by some of the great jazz improvisers of the 1950s and 1960s), so that there are often large gaps in his solos that combine rapid-fire bursts of melody and choppy chords.

Fleck made a series of solo albums for Rounder Records in the late 1970s, including some interesting instrumentals that combined a bebop feeling for melody and harmony with traditional bluegrass instrumentation (particularly on his LP *Crossing the Tracks*). A

frequent session mate of these days was Sam Bush, who was also one of the founder-leaders of NEW GRASS REVIVAL; when the band's original banjo player quit in the early 1980s, Fleck came on board and performed with the group for several years.

In 1989 he formed his progressive funk-jazz group, The Flecktones, featuring brothers Victor (bass) and Roy (drumitar, a drum-machine synthesizer in the shape of an electric guitar) Wooten along with Howard Levy (harmonica, keyboards). The group was signed by Warner Brothers Records, and marketed as a new-acoustic/jazz ensemble, not to the country audience. The band's sound was dominated by the Wooten brothers' electronics, which tended to overwhelm Fleck's banjo. The band's attempt at a bluegrass-jazz-funk fusion was only somewhat successful, both commercially and musically.

In 1993 harmonica/keyboard player Levy quit the band, leaving it a trio (although often augmented with scores of others on their recordings). Through the 1990s Fleck alternated between recording and touring with his jazz-fusion group and recording acoustic albums, mixing traditional bluegrass tunes and instrumentation with his own unique compositions. In 2000 he left Warner Brothers to sign with Sony as both bandleader and solo artist. He released his first "classical" album of original compositions in 2001.

Select Discography

Places, Rounder 11522. Compilation drawn from his various Rounder LPs of the 1980s.

Greatest Hits of the 20th Century, Warner Bros. 47301. Compilation of the band's 1990s recordings; a good introduction with a tongue-in-cheek title.

Tales from the Acoustic Planet, Warner Bros. 45854. 1994 release, mixing originals and traditional tunes.

The Bluegrass Sessions, Warner Bros. 47332. 1999 album that makes a nod toward the traditional audience with a supergroup of newgrass pickers in the band.

Bela Fleck (left with banjo) and the band, Tasty Licks, c. 1980. Photo courtesy Rounder Records

FLORES, ROSIE (b. Rosalie Durango F., San Antonio, Tex., September 10, 1950 [some sources give 1956])

Flores, a talented ROCKABILLY-revival singer/guitarist, has had a long career in rockabilly, alt-country, and country-punk. Born in Texas, she moved with her family to southern California when she was twelve. Flores was influenced by a wide range of popular musical styles, but unlike many other women musicians, focused on developing her guitar-playing skills. Her first band was a local group called Penelope's Children; an all-female outfit, it played soft rock and opened for the Turtles on a West Coast tour. In 1978 she moved into the cow-punk field with her group

Rosie and The Screamers, a band that lasted about five years and played the California alternative music circuit. 1983 saw her joining her first successful band, The Screaming Sirens, another all-girl outfit that mixed heavy guitar work with country and rockabilly riffs; in 1987 the band was featured in the TV film *The Running Kind*, gaining them some national notoriety.

Flores went solo in 1987, signing with Warner Brothers Records. DWIGHT YOAKAM's lead guitarist and close associate Pete Anderson served as the producer for her first album, which not surprisingly had the sound and feel of Yoakam's neo-rockabilly recordings. A second album was recorded, but Warner Brothers dropped Flores before it could be released (it eventually appeared in 1996 on Rounder). Flores spent the early 1990s recording for Hightone and increasingly focusing on her guitar work. In 1995 she released an album, *Rockabilly Filly*, that featured duets with two of her rockabilly idols, WANDA JACKSON and JANIS MARTIN; a tour with Jackson followed. After settling in the Austin, Texas, region, Flores released *Dance Hall Dreams* in 1999, featuring several alt-country stars; it reached #1 on the Gavin alt-country charts (before the charts were discontinued).

In 2000, besides her own solo touring, Flores teamed up with several other female new-country artists to form Henhouse, which played some gigs in Nashville. In the fall of 2000 Eminent Records announced they were signing the artist, pairing her with pop producer Rick Vito. The resulting album, *Speed of Sound*, appeared in April 2001.

Select Discography

Honky Tonk Reprise, Rounder 3136. Best of her early-through-mid-1990s recordings.

Speed of Sound, Eminent 25090. Flores returns to a harder-rocking style on this 2001 release, with rockabilly, WESTERN SWING, and Tex-Mex sounds all thrown into the mix.

FLYING BURRITO BROTHERS (1969–1971, sporadically thereafter; original lineup: Gram Parsons [gtr, voc]; Chris Hillman [gtr, mdln, voc]; Chris Ethridge [b]; "Sneaky" Pete Kleinow [pedal-steel]; Jon Corneal [drms])

The Flying Burrito Brothers were a seminal turn-of-the-1970s COUNTRY-ROCK band, featuring GRAM PARSONS's emotional lead vocals and excellent original songs (at least until he left the group in 1970). After their initial demise, they remained popular in Europe for years, with many different lineups touring through the mid-1980s.

After recording *Sweetheart of the Rodeo*, the BYRDS' move into country-rock, Byrds founder CHRIS HILLMAN and newcomer Parsons left the band to pursue country-rock to its logical conclusions. In forming the Burritos they were among the first to incorporate a PEDAL-STEEL GUITAR into a pop-rock band (the pedal steel being a hallmark of most country recordings of the era). It's interesting to note that POCO, formed out of the remnants of Buffalo Springfield in 1969, also employed a pedal steel player (Rusty Young), and MICHAEL NESMITH's First National Band, another pioneering country-rock outfit, had Red Rhodes on steel.

The original Burritos' classic debut album, *The Gilded Palace of Sin*, featured Parsons's update of the country HONKY-TONK ballad "Sin City." The band announced their nouveau country look with the cover photo, in which bandsmen were garbed in traditionally lavish Nudie suits (crafted by famous Nashville tailor NUDIE Cohen), although instead of country motifs the suits featured hand-stitched marijuana leaves as a design element! Other notable songs popularized by the band included a countrified cover of The Rolling Stones' "Wild Horses"; the ever-popular "Devil in Disguise," written by Hillman and Parsons and covered by progressive bluegrass bands through the 1970s; and "Hot Burrito #2 (I'm Your Boy)," an Ethridge-Parsons composition.

While the group's first album was being made, drummer Corneal left and was replaced by ex-Byrds drummer Michael Clarke; soon after, Ethridge left, replaced by Hillman on bass (an instrument he had played with the Byrds). They added Bernie Leadon on guitar and vocals (he had previously performed with Doug Dillard and GENE CLARK in their early country-rock band). The second album was completed and released as *Burrito Deluxe* in 1970. Arguments among Parsons and the rest of the band, due to Parsons's increasing drug use and unreliability, led to another shake-up, with Parsons embarking on a solo career and replaced by Rick Roberts. The more-or-less original group released one more album, but it suffered from Parsons's absence.

Further defections came in mid-1971, when Leadon left to form THE EAGLES and Kleinow retired; Al Perkins (pedal steel), BYRON BERLINE (fiddle), Roger Bush (bass), and Kenny Wertz (guitar) joined, forming a touring band. This ensemble lasted until late 1971, when Hillman and Perkins joined ex–Buffalo Springfield leader Stephen Stills to form the short-lived country-rock outfit Manassas; the balance of the band, without Roberts, became the nucleus of COUNTRY GAZETTE, a bluegrass-oriented band. Roberts enlisted yet another group to make a final European tour before forming the rock group Firefall in 1972.

The legend and legacy of The Flying Burrito Brothers would not die; original members Ethridge and Kleinow revived the name for two mid-1970s Columbia albums, featuring the duo of Gib Guilbeau (fiddle) and Gene Parsons (drums; no relation to Gram) along with bassist Joel Scott-Hill. Ethridge quickly bowed out, replaced by latter-day Byrdsman Skip Battin. The group held on until the mid-1980s with varying personnel, but none of these later "Burrito" recordings were anywhere near as good as their original albums. Surprisingly, in 1999 Pete Kleinow paired with SINGER/SONGWRITER John Beland (along with an all-star studio cast) in a revived Burritos, producing a single album and then disappearing, once again, into the mist.

Although they enjoyed only marginal success on either pop or country charts during their heyday, The Flying Burritos Brothers became a model for almost every country-rock group that followed. Their understanding of the basic affinity between hippie rebellion and country attitudes would finally bear fruit in the mid-1980s when a number of Southern new-country bands, as well as solo acts, picked up their musical cues. Although the Eagles had greater success (and perhaps more influence on the next generation), it can be said that without The Flying Burrito Brothers there would have been no Eagles.

Select Discography

Hot Burritos, A&M 490610. Two-CD set reissuing their first three albums in their entirety, plus "rare" other tracks.

FOLEY, RED (b. Clyde Julian F., Blue Lark, Ky., June 17, 1910–September 19, 1968)

Although best remembered as a smooth-voiced singer of GOSPEL and country ballads, Foley had a career that took him through a variety of styles, from string-band vocals through R&B, ROCKABILLY, and jump sides to his mainstream Nashville outings. A pioneer performer on radio and television, Foley did much to popularize country sounds for a mainstream audience.

Foley spent most of his high school and college years on the athletic field, winning numerous awards. He won an amateur singing contest at age seventeen, and three years later he was hired by country radio producer JOHN LAIR to be the vocalist with the WLS *Barndance* radio program's house band, The Cumberland Ridge Runners. His smooth-voiced vocals of old-time ballads and songs made him an obvious candidate for wider radio exposure; seven years later Lair built the very popular *Renfro Valley Barn Dance* radio program around Foley. Foley became a big star thanks to this radio exposure, which continued through the 1940s on WLS, on THE GRAND OLE OPRY, and finally, in 1954–1961, on the early country-music television program *The Ozark Jubilee*, based in Springfield, Missouri.

In 1941 Decca Records signed Foley to a lifetime contract. His first recordings were in a sentimental vein, including 1945's "Old Shep" (later covered by ELVIS PRESLEY) and 1947's "Foggy River." In the early 1950s he showed an interest in rockabilly and bop, laying down "Sugarfoot Rag" with guitarist Hank Garland; the two would make many other rockabilly-flavored recordings, often accompanied by the (ghastly) ANITA KERR Singers. His bop-flavored numbers include "Birmingham Bounce" from 1950 and the square-dance favorite "Alabama Jubilee" from 1951. Foley was also interested in R&B, and recorded covers of "Shake a Hand" (an early ode to integration originally recorded by Faye Adams) and "Hearts of Stone" (originally by The Charms) in the early 1950s. Yet his biggest hit was 1951's "Peace in the Valley," a clever combination of country sentimentality with a religious message, said to be the first gospel song to sell a million copies on disc. (Others claim the honor for Mahalia Jackson's "Move On Up" issued in 1946.)

Foley spent most of the 1950s bouncing between styles, although his gospel recordings were the ones that seemed to do best. Meanwhile, he increasingly changed from a jazzy country singer into a pop-styled crooner, and the accompaniments on his recordings became knee-deep in the swelling choruses and killer strings that were typical of Nashville at its most grotesque.

In the 1960s Foley continued to be a popular attraction, and even appeared for one season on a network TV show, *Mr. Smith Goes to Washington*, costarring with Fess ("Davey Crockett") Parker. He died in 1968, of a heart attack after a performance, one year after being inducted into the Country Music Hall of Fame.

Foley's daughter, Betty (1933–1990), was featured on *Renfro Valley Barn Dance* in the early 1950s, and she also recorded several hit duets with her father, including "Satisfied Mind" in 1955. She continued to perform and record through the 1950s, before retiring from the musician business to invest in Kentucky Fried Chicken. Another Foley daughter, Shirley, married teen popster Pat Boone, and they in turn produced white-bread country queen DEBBIE BOONE.

Select Discography

Complete Recordings, Vol 1: 1937–39, Document 6024. Early recordings by Foley with just guitar and vocal.

Stay a Little Longer, Jasmine 3523. 1950s radio airchecks, featuring many hits and novelties from the era, without the heavy-handed studio accompaniment that sometimes marred his recordings.

Country Music Hall of Fame, MCA 10084. Selections from his Decca recordings, many featuring overblown arrangements.

FOLK REVIVAL (c. 1958–1965)

For a brief period in the late 1950s and early 1960s, folk music was tremendously successful on the pop music charts. Granted, these hits were mostly produced by professional or at least semiprofessional musicians (not the "folks" themselves), and were often watered-down versions of the true folk styles. Nonetheless, the folk revival had a profound impact on the future direction of pop and country music styles.

There has always been a fascination in the city with the culture of the country, dating back at least to the time when cities first emerged out of the rural background. In the nineteenth century Romantic poets and philosophers idealized country life, and so influenced the first folklorists to go into the field to collect the traditional songs, dances, and legends of the ordinary "folk." At the turn of the twentieth century, folklorists like Francis James Child, out of Harvard University, and JOHN LOMAX, working out of Texas, published influential collections: Child, of literary ballads, and Lomax, of the COWBOY songs that he collected throughout the Midwest. The recording and radio industries that blossomed in the 1920s further spread folk musics to the city; it was now possible for a resident of Manhattan to buy a recording of New Orleans jazz or Tennessee string-band music. Traditional folk musicians like WOODY GUTHRIE and AUNT MOLLY JACKSON were brought to major urban areas to perform, sometimes as curiosities and sometimes to support various political causes.

After World War II the first "folk boom" occurred when The Weavers, a group led by banjoist PETE SEEGER, had a massive pop hit with a version of Leadbelly's "Goodnight, Irene," orchestrated by pop producer Gordon Jenkins. The Weavers' success was unexpected, but short-lived; because many of its members had been involved in radical political causes in the 1930s, the group was effectively silenced during the early 1950s Communist scare. By the late 1950s and early 1960s a new generation of more freshly scrubbed (and less politically adventurous) groups arose to pick up the Weavers' style, beginning with the blandly innocuous Kingston Trio (who had a big hit with a traditional banjo blues number, "Tom Dooley"), The Rooftop Singers, The Chad Mitchell Trio (who specialized in more politically oriented and satirical material), and, of course, Peter, Paul, and Mary. More sophisticated groups like THE NEW LOST CITY RAMBLERS were able to ride the crest of the popularity of the mainstream groups, though never achieving quite the commercial success that these other groups enjoyed.

In this same period country music also took a turn toward a return to its folk roots. The popularity of the "saga songs," newly composed songs that were written in the manner of traditional ballads, was one reflection of this new folk emphasis. JOHNNY CASH's series of albums on folk themes, the renewed popularity of traditional-styled performers like Mother Maybelle Carter, some country acts' attempt to cross over into pop-folk (like The BROWNS, who began recording folk-oriented material), and a renewed interest in and popularity of BLUEGRASS music all showed the effects of the folk revival.

More important to the development of popular and country music in the long run was the emergence of the SINGER/SONGWRITER. Traditionally, in pop and country music professional songwriters wrote songs that were recorded by trained singers. A songwriter who couldn't sing up to professional standards would never have dreamed of recording his or her own material. Nor was the material itself necessarily an expression of personal feelings; it often was written to meet the needs of a specific audience or market. However, in folk circles (and in early country music) the artists often wrote and performed their own material; musical ability or lack thereof (in terms of mainstream musical talent) was not a deterrent to performing.

Woody Guthrie pointed the way, showing how a singer could be the best interpreter of his own material, despite his rudimentary guitar style and nasal voice. During the folk-revival days BOB DYLAN expanded the notion of singer/songwriter, and thousands more arose in his wake. WILLIE NELSON was perhaps the first country songwriter to realize that despite his perceived lack of "musical" abilities, he could be the best performer for his own material.

By the mid-1960s the energy of the folk revival was pretty much absorbed by rock and roll. Interest in folk music reemerged in the mid-1970s; at this time a more sophisticated revival occurred, with various regional musics, from WESTERN SWING to CAJUN to old-time string band to Tex-Mex, coming to the fore.

FORD, TENNESSEE ERNIE (b. Ernest Jennings F., Bristol, Tenn., February 13, 1919–October 17, 1991)

Finger-snappin', pencil-moustached TV star and singer, Ford is best remembered for his (melo)dramatic rendition of MERLE TRAVIS's "Sixteen Tons," a mid-1950s hit. Ford was as much a personality as a country singer, and became a well-recognized icon of 1950s and 1960s TV variety shows.

Ford did not have a particularly rural upbringing; he was raised in Bristol, Tennessee, a Southern mill town, where he sang in the high-school choir and played in the school band. When he was eighteen, he got his first job as an announcer at a local radio station, and then enrolled in the Cincinnati Conservatory of Music for classical training. After serving in World War II he returned to radio work in Pasadena,

California, and began working as a vocalist with West Coast COWBOY-styled bands, most notably with CLIFFIE STONE, a prominent musician/bandleader/promoter who quickly took Ford under his wing. As an executive of the newly formed Capitol Records, Stone got Ford his recording contract and went on to manage his lengthy career.

Signed by Capitol Records in 1948, Ford had a number of hits with pseudo–Western numbers, beginning with 1949's "Mule Train," "Smokey Mountain Boogie," and "Anticipation Blues," jazz-flavored renderings of pop songs written in the style of country blues and cowboy numbers. A year later he scored big with his own composition, "Shotgun Boogie," leading to his own network radio show.

In 1955 Ford covered Merle Travis's "Sixteen Tons," a song about the life of a coal miner that Travis had written in the folk style. Ford's rendition became a massive hit, decked out with its crooning chorus and poppish instrumental arrangement. Following its success on pop and country charts, Ford had his own TV variety show on NBC, lasting until 1961, besides regular appearances on a number of other shows.

In the early 1960s Ford turned to more conservative material, in 1963 recording country's first million-selling album, *Hymns*, the first in a series of all-religious recordings. Balancing this with remakes of patriotic material like "America the Beautiful," Ford became a leading conservative voice in the country hierarchy. His smooth-voiced, nonthreatening renditions of mostly time-worn material cemented his 1960s popularity. Although he had a chart hit in 1971 with "Happy Songs of Love," Ford's career had pretty much ended by that time, although he was still performing live into the 1980s.

In 1990 he was inducted into the Country Music Hall of Fame. A year later he collapsed at a White House dinner, and died of liver disease soon after.

Select Discography

Sixteen Tons of Country Boogie, Rhino 70975. Compilation of his better earlier recordings.
Ultimate Collection, 1949–65, Razor & Tie 2134. Two-CD compilation of all his best-known recordings.

FORESTER SISTERS (1984–1996: Kathy [b. January 4, 1955]; June [b. September 22, 1956]; Kim [b. November 4, 1960]; and Christy Forester [b. December 21, 1962]; all b. Lookout Mountain, Ga.)

Well-scrubbed and perky, the singing Foresters combine true country roots with a progressive attitude that made them consistent chart-toppers during the mid-1980s.

Born in Lookout Mountain, Georgia, to a farmer father and millworker mother, the four children were stars at their local church from the mid-1970s. They formed their first "band" in 1978 to play local clubs, while Christy and Kim were still in college, and June and Kathy were working as grade-school teachers. A demo tape landed them a contract with Warner Brothers in 1984, and their first hit came a year later, the up-tempo "(That's What You Do) When You're in Love," a traditional stand-by-your-man song with a twist. Although the man has cheated on his sweetheart and is forgiven for his transgressions, the lyrics imply that perhaps she was doin' a little cheatin', too, in the wake of his two-timing. They followed this a year later with the play-on-words of "Lyin' in His Arms Again," the story of a spunky girl who has cheated on her man (a reversal of the typical country sex roles).

The Foresters' first recordings were produced by Wendy Waldman, who had had a career as a folk-rock SINGER/SONGWRITER in the 1970s, and supplied them with one of their most moving early hits, 1988's "Letter Home." This simple narrative about a woman who was the high-school prom queen, married young and foolishly, and then was deserted by her husband and left to raise the kids, again focuses on issues traditional country songs avoided. While there was always infidelity in country music, the effects of that infidelity on the family—and particularly on the woman left behind—were rarely described.

The Foresters' early-1990s hits continued to emphasize their spunky, female point of view. Their recordings took a more jazzy, almost WESTERN SWING approach with 1991's scornful "Men," directed right at their target audience of young female boot wearers, and the not-quite-over-the-hill, older woman's anthem, 1992's "I Got a Date," with its playful video (the protagonist of the video is a single mom going out on a date for the first time in a long time, reflecting Nashville's realization of the changing demographics in American society, where more women were older and single again). However, a four-year gap followed while the band turned to recording GOSPEL music. Their last country-pop album appeared in 1996, but produced no hits.

The Foresters' sunny harmonies and golly-gosh-gee personalities made them perfect country performers. While they championed a woman's point of view in their music, they were so wholesome-looking that they could hardly be considered threatening to men, who could enjoy the frothy, up-tempo songs without listening too closely to the words.

Select Discography

Talkin' About Men, Warner Bros. 26500. Concept album focusin' on the troubles boys create for gals.

FORRESTER, HOWDY (b. Howard Wilson F., Vernon, Tenn., March 31, 1922–August 1, 1987)

Forrester did much to popularize the so-called Texas or show fiddle style, a tradition that began with players like ECK ROBERTSON and continues today in the hands of players like MARK O'CONNOR. It is characterized by rich melodic variation, a slight jazz influence, "long-bow" rather than short-bow playing (playing several notes per bow stroke rather than changing bow direction for each note), and flashy, high-speed execution.

Forrester was not a native of Texas, however, having been born in Tennessee to a long line of fiddlers; both his father and grandfather played, and his uncle, Bob Forrester, had competed on the fiddle contest circuit. Forrester did not begin playing fiddle until the early 1930s, after his father had died; he spent several months bedridden recovering from a bout of rheumatic fever, during which time he taught himself to fiddle. The family moved to the big city of Nashville when Forrester was a teenager, and he began playing locally with his brothers. In 1938 he got his first professional job working on THE GRAND OLE OPRY with the popular singing group THE VAGABONDS. A year later he followed Vagabond lead singer Herald Goodman to a new job in Tulsa, Oklahoma, working on the *Saddle Mountain Roundup* radio show.

Forrester next spent a year in Dallas before returning to Nashville in 1940–1941 to work with BILL MONROE's new outfit, The Blue Grass Boys. His stint with Monroe was cut short when he was drafted. (His wife, Sally, remained with Monroe, playing accordion on several of his early 1940s recordings.) Although at this time the band had not matured into the legendary BLUEGRASS outfit it would become, Forrester's jazz-influenced fiddle style left its mark on Monroe's style. His smooth playing, rich with double-stops and melodic variation, would become a model for bluegrass fiddlers to come.

After the war Forrester returned to Dallas for three years, working as a duo with Robert "Georgia Slim" Rutland. He then worked with COWBOY COPAS for a year around 1950, before taking a job with ROY ACUFF's Smoky Mountain Boys, which would lead to a long association with the popular entertainer. Forrester got wide exposure through his recordings and radio work with Acuff, and gave the band a slicker, more modern sound. He also freelanced with other groups, including appearances on recordings by FLATT AND SCRUGGS. In 1964 he retired from performing with Acuff and moved into the business end of music, joining Acuff-Rose Artists Corporation, a part of Acuff's country-music publishing empire. He continued working for Acuff until his death.

Besides working as a sideman, Forrester recorded and performed on his own, although less frequently after the mid-1960s. He cut some bluegrass-styled albums in the 1970s and one in the 1980s. Forrester composed several original tunes and also created variations on standards like "Grey Eagle" that have been widely copied. He was sometimes called "Big Howdy" Forrester.

FOSTER AND LLOYD (1987–1990: b. Radney F., Del Rio, Tex., July 20, 1959, and Bill L., Bowling Green, Ky., December 6, 1955)

Foster and Lloyd brought Beatles-styled harmonies and pop-rock sensibilities to new-country music.

Typical of mid-1980s country acts, this duo brought myriad influences to their music, from COUNTRY-ROCK sounds inspired by POCO and THE EAGLES to the smooth harmonies of THE EVERLY BROTHERS and John Lennon and Paul McCartney of the Beatles, to the HONKY-TONK blues of HANK WILLIAMS. Their biggest hit was their first single, 1987's "Crazy over You," which combined an intelligent lyric with a solid beat. Their sound was halfway between the cutting edge of new country and a pleasant, Hall and Oates (or perhaps BROOKS AND DUNN, although they came later) pop sound.

Radney Foster went solo in 1992, projecting the image of a yuppie country singer with his wire-rim glasses and well-starched suits. His first album featured support from other nouveau-country acts, including MARY CHAPIN CARPENTER and JOHN HIATT. Two further albums followed through the mid-1990s, but he was unable to duplicate his earlier success as half of Foster and Lloyd. After a few years off record, he returned in mid-2001 with the live album *Are You Ready for the Big Show?* The first single, "Texas in 1880," received a heavy push on Country Music Television.

Select Discography

Essential, BMG 66825. Two-CD compilation of the duo's biggest hits.
Del Rio, TX, 1959, Arista 18713. Radney Foster's 1992 solo album, named (pretentiously) for his birthplace and year of birth.

FRANCIS, CLEVE (b. Cleveland F., Jr., Jennings, La., April 22, 1945)

Son of a sharecropper, Francis had a brief period of popularity as a country crooner in the mid-1990s, enjoying some novelty coverage thanks to his being African American and his prestigious background as a cardiologist.

Francis grew up influenced by country, GOSPEL, and soul music. Like many other rural musicians before him, he crafted his first "guitar" out of a cigar box, and was given a fancy Sears Silvertone guitar by his parents when he was a teen. Pursuing music in church and local venues, he attended the College of William and Mary and then gained a medical degree in 1973. Still, he longed to be a musician, and one of his heart patients recommended him to a small label, Playback Records, which released his first single in 1990. The doctor pumped $25,000 of his own cash into a video to promote the song; Nashville producer JIMMY BOWEN caught the clip on Country Music Television and quickly signed Francis to a contract.

In 1991 Francis released his major-label debut album, which produced a major country hit, "Love Light," and two moderate follow-ups. He was heavily promoted because of his anomalous background as a successful cardiologist and an African American who performed country music. His sound and style were similar to much other mid-1990s country-pop; with a smooth voice he could easily "pass" audibly for white. Francis followed up with another minor hit, "Walkin'," the title track of his next album, in 1993. However, after one more album, the label dropped him due to poor sales.

Francis returned to medicine full-time after his brief major-label success. However, he was a major force behind a three-CD set commemorating black artists in country music released in 1998. He has continued to perform, mostly in the Washington, D.C., area (his home), particularly for benefit concerts.

Francis—like Charley Pride before him—was a rare figure in country music: a black performer who emulated "white" country sounds. But, unlike Pride, he never achieved great success on the charts and was unable to overcome the "novelty" of being a doctor-turned-crooner. Still, his presence in the mid-1990s helped break the color barrier in the primarily lily-white field of country performers.

FRAZIER, DALLAS (b. Spiro, Okla., October 27, 1939)

Frazier is a powerful vocalist and songwriter in pop and country styles who is better known for his songs than for his performances.

Born in rural Oklahoma, Frazier migrated with his family to California, settling, like many other Okies, in the town of Bakersfield. There, as a teenager, he won a talent contest sponsored by FERLIN HUSKY, earning him a place in Husky's road show. He was signed by Capitol Records in the early 1960s, and moved to Nashville to work as a songwriter. One of his first hits was the pop novelty "Alley Oop" (based on the antics of the comic-strip hero), recorded by The Hollywood Argyles, although he also had solid country hits with Husky's recording of "Timber (I'm Fallin')," followed by O. C. Smith's "Son of Hickory Holler," "California

Cottonfields" by MERLE HAGGARD, "Then Who Am I?" by CHARLEY PRIDE, and "Mohair Sam" by CHARLIE RICH.

His mid-1960s recordings for Capitol were only somewhat successful; he had a minor hit with his song "Elvira," which became much more successful when it was covered in 1981 by THE OAK RIDGE BOYS. Other contemporary country singers have revived Frazier's material, including EMMYLOU HARRIS, who recorded his "Beneath Still Waters." In the early 1970s Frazier recorded for RCA, again with only moderate success. In 1976 he was inducted into the Nashville Songwriters Hall of Fame. He spent the 1980s attending Bible college, earning a master's degree in theology in 1989. He has since worked as a fundamentalist minister.

FRICKE, JANIE (b. J. Marie F., South Whitley, Ind., December 19, 1947)

Moderately successful, Fricke is an all-around professional who began her career as a backup singer and had some success as a pop-flavored vocalist from the late 1970s through the mid-1980s.

Inspired by FOLK REVIVALISTS Joan Baez and Judy Collins, Fricke took up playing the guitar in her teen years, eventually relocating to Memphis, where she began working as a backup singer for jingles. She made her way to Nashville, where she worked many country sessions as an anonymous vocalist. She also sang with the Lea Jane Singers, who backed country acts like neo-OUTLAW JOHNNY RODRIGUEZ. Fricke was signed to a solo contract by famed producer BILLY SHERRILL in 1977, supposedly because country deejays had sent in letters asking "Who was that girl" they heard singing backup on many hit records.

Because of Fricke's wide range of experience singing everything from pop-rock to soda-pop jingles, Sherrill had difficulty deciding what direction to take her career. Meanwhile, he invited her to overdub a harmony part on CHARLIE RICH's "On My Knees," giving her her first label credit as a backup singer; the song shot to #1, helping to launch Fricke's career. After a few more singles produced by Sherrill, she hooked up with producer Jim Ed Norman, who gave her more upbeat, danceable songs, including her first #1 hit, 1982's "Don't Worry 'Bout Me, Baby," with backup vocals by soon-to-be new-country star RICKY SKAGGS. A third producer, Bob Montgomery, brought her another 1982 hit, "It Ain't Easy Bein' Easy," and her follow-up 1983 hit "He's a Heartache (Looking for a Place to Happen)." These bubbly numbers were in the ALABAMA-EXILE mode of rock-flavored country, launching Fricke on a glitzy career as a pop singer.

Fricke's success lasted through the mid-1980s. She cut one more session as an overdub singer, accompanying MERLE HAGGARD on 1985's #1 "A Place to Fall

Apart," another one of Merle's songs of a relationship gone bad. She signed with new producer Norro Wilson to create a bluesier, gutsier sound, yielding her last #1 hit, 1986's "Always Have, Always Will"; at this time she added an "i" (Frickie) to her last name, because people were always mispronouncing it as "Frick," but then reverted to the original spelling. After 1989 she ceased recording for Columbia. In 2000 she released her first album in seven years, aptly titled *Bouncin' Back*, on her own JMF label.

The popularity of new-country stars has made Fricke's pop approach sound decidedly old-fashioned. Meanwhile, she has moved into the apparel business, introducing fashions based on her own designs for her stage outfits (the kind of show wear that make Vegas acts shine) with some success.

Select Discography

Anthology, Renaissance 206. Twenty-six of her big chart hits from the 1970s and 1980s.

FRIEDMAN, KINKY (b. Richard F. F., Palestine, Tex., October 31, 1944)

Friedman and his band, The Texas Jewboys, were popular on the folk, rock, and comedy circuits in the early 1970s for their musically literate satires of WESTERN SWING and other popular country forms.

Friedman is an anomaly: a well-educated man of Jewish descent who hails from a small Texas town. His father was a university professor, and Friedman grew up developing a sardonic sense of humor. When he had just finished college, he and his close friend Jeff Shelby formed their first band, a send-up of pop-rock bands known as King Arthur and The Carrotts, specializing in satires of surf music. The two later formed The Texas Jewboys, and by the end of the decade they had a recording contract with the folk-rock label Vanguard.

The Jewboys' biggest hit was 1973's "Sold American," a social-protest song that was later covered by country star GLEN CAMPBELL. Friedman also created a number of tongue-in-cheek Western songs, including "Ride 'Em Jewboy," the unofficial theme song of the band, and "Carryin' the Torch," a satire of the typical country WEEPER, except that the much-put-upon and long-suffering female in this song is the Statue of Liberty (this number was produced by WAYLON JENNINGS). The band folded in 1977, but Friedman continued to perform into the 1980s as a solo act. His career took another unusual twist beginning in the mid-1980s, when he wrote the first in a number of successful mystery novels, many of which have plots that deal with the ins and outs of the music industry.

Friedman's irreverent look at country clichés helped broaden the audience for the real McCoy, while it also appealed to younger country musicians who hoped to break free from the pop-schlock that was dribbling out of Nashville in the 1960s and 1970s.

References

Sold American, Vanguard 79333. 1974 album, featuring original recordings of many of his classic songs.

FRIZZELL, DAVID (b. Corsicana, Tex., September 26, 1941)

Much younger brother of legendary HONKY-TONK wailer LEFTY FRIZZELL, David became a COUNTRYPOLITAN star in the early 1980s, thanks to his successful duets with SHELLEY WEST and a few solo recordings.

Frizzell had a long, arduous climb to success, beginning in the late 1950s when he joined his brother Lefty in California. In 1958 he was signed to Columbia by producer Don Law, releasing a few singles that barely grazed the bottom of the charts before enlisting in the Army for a couple of years. He was back with Columbia in the late 1960s, scoring minor success with 1970's "I Just Can't Help Believing." He toured with BUCK OWENS in the early 1970s, also signing with Capitol and scoring a few minor hits in 1973–1974. He recorded for RSO and MCA, again without much luck, and then in 1977 opened his own nightclub in Concord, California, where he began performing with Shelley West, daughter of legendary country chanteuse DOTTIE WEST.

The duo had one release on the disco-oriented Casablanca label before moving to Viva Records, co-owned by actor Clint Eastwood; their song "You're the Reason God Made Oklahoma," released in 1981, was featured in Eastwood's film *Any Which Way You Can*, becoming a big hit. They continued to record as a duo through 1985, with the hits "Another Honky-Tonk Night on Broadway" in 1983 and 1985's "Do Me Right." Meanwhile, Frizzell had a solo hit with 1982's comic novelty "I'm Gonna Hire a Wino to Decorate Our Home" and "A Million Light Beers Ago" from the following year, along with more mainstream countrypolitan numbers like 1985's "Country Music Love Affair."

Frizzell pretty much dropped off the charts after the mid-1980s; his melodramatic pop-oriented style was supplanted by the new-country movement. In 2001 he issued his first new album in many years, featuring both remakes of his 1980s hits and some new ballads.

FRIZZELL, LEFTY (b. William Orville F., Corsicana, Tex., March 31, 1928–July 19, 1975)

One of the most influential of all the HONKY-TONK singers, Frizzell brought the barroom sensibility into a more mainstream country setting. His vocal manner-

FRIZZELL, LEFTY

isms have been widely imitated, both by traditional country performers such as GEORGE JONES and MERLE HAGGARD, and new-country stars such as GEORGE STRAIT (who recorded "Lefty's Gone" in tribute to Frizzell) and RANDY TRAVIS, to name just a few.

Frizzell was the son of a footloose oil-field worker. A common PR myth was that he gained his nickname thanks to a teenage career as a Golden Gloves boxer; however, Frizzell never actually boxed. He began performing in Dallas and Waco-area honky-tonks, covering the hits of his two idols, JIMMIE RODGERS and ERNEST TUBB. His first hit came in 1950 with "If You Got the Money, Honey, I've Got the Time," a classic honky-tonk song noteworthy for its simple accompaniment (although featuring prominent tinkling piano, rather than FIDDLE or steel guitar, an early sign of the coming NASHVILLE SOUND), forthright lyrics, and Lefty's incomparable vocalisms. 1951 brought four records that all made the country Top 10 at the same time, a feat never since repeated by any artist. Lefty was poised to be more popular than HANK WILLIAMS, but then his hits dried up. In 1953 Frizzell moved to Los Angeles and became a regular on the popular TV show *Town Hall Party*.

In the late 1950s Nashville was swept by a craze for story songs, mini sagas that, ballad-like, told stories of the mythical old South. Frizzell abandoned his beer-soaked honky-tonk sound to make a number of popular records in this mold, including 1959's "Long Black Veil" and 1964's "Saginaw, Michigan." Sadly, this was his last hurrah as a charting performer; alcohol took its toll on his recordings and live performances, although he continued to perform until his death in 1975. By then he was more or less forgotten by mainstream Nashville, although his recordings would influence the next generation of country performers.

Select Discography

Look What Thoughts Will Do, Columbia/Legacy 64880. 1950–1963 recordings, with all the hits and some alternate takes, on a two-CD set.

Life's like Poetry, Bear Family 15550. Haul out the checkbook and put a second mortgage on your home; this twelve-CD set gives you 330 songs, including everything Lefty recorded between 1950 and 1975, with a 153-page book by Charles Wolfe.

FROMHOLZ, STEVE (b. Temple, Tex., June 8, 1945)

Texas, with its rich individualistic tradition, seems to nurture oddball country stars who combine the sensibilities of 1970s SINGER/SONGWRITERS with the raucousness of the OUTLAW movement. Fromholz is another in this pantheon of musical eccentrics, whose combination of rock, BLUEGRASS, country, and God

knows what else has made him a legendary performer with a loyal, if small, following.

After enrolling in Texas State University in 1963, Fromholz met future country star MICHAEL MARTIN MURPHEY and the twosome became a duo, later forming The Dallas Country Jug Band. After college and a brief stint in the Navy, Fromholz formed a close relationship with singer/songwriter Dan McCrimmon, and the two took the colorful name of Frummox, recording a COUNTRY-ROCK LP for the tiny Probe label in 1969; two years later they briefly worked with Steve Stills as his backup band. During this period Fromholz recorded an album for MIKE NESMITH's Countryside label, but it never saw the light of day.

After struggling for a few more years on the West Coast, Fromholz returned in 1974 to Austin, where a vibrant outlaw music scene was brewing. He was befriended by WILLIE NELSON and appeared on Nelson's *Sound in Your Mind* album as a backup singer, as well as providing original material for Nelson to record. In 1976 he finally made an album that was released, aptly called *A Rumor in My Own Time*, featuring many friends, including Nelson, banjoist Doug Dillard, steel GUITARIST Red Rhodes, and folksinger John Sebastian. Although a cult success, the album was not a commercial one, and Capitol dropped him after he released an even more far-out collection of original material in the following year.

In 1979 Nelson had his own label, Lone Star, distributed by Columbia, and invited old friend Fromholz to make an album, titled *Jus' Playin' Along*. This also failed to generate much in the way of sales, and Fromholz has since been one of many "local heroes" who play regularly in the greater Austin area. In 2001, he issued his first new album in many years on a local label, followed shortly thereafter by a live CD.

FRUIT JAR DRINKERS, THE (c. 1927–mid-1970s: George Wilkerson [fdl]; Tommy Leffew [mdln]; Howard Ragsdale [gtr]; Claude Lampley, [bnj])

Although promoted as a group of backwoods rubes, The Fruit Jar Drinkers, an early string band popular on *The Grand Ole Opry*, were solidly working-class Nashville residents, all involved in the thriving lumber business by day and making music by night. The band's leader was George Wilkerson, a fiddler who originally hailed from Stevenson, a town in Northeast Georgia. His two brothers, Charlie and Brownie, were also musicians, and the youngsters soon formed their own band. The family moved to Nashville when Wilkerson was sixteen, and he was soon working in a local lumberyard. Along with his brother Charlie on MANDOLIN, he began playing locally, and he may have played on WSM as early as 1926. The earliest documented appearance of Wilkerson as a FIDDLE player on the station was January 1927.

At WSM, Wilkerson met another performer who had been an occasional soloist on the air: mandolinist Tommy Leffew, who worked in a flooring factory. Leffew brought on board his fellow worker Claude Lampley, who came from a small rural town in Hickman County, about fifty miles southwest of the city. Finally guitarist Howard Ragsdale, also from Hickman County and another woodworker, joined up. Not only did the four men share similar occupations, they lived within four blocks of each other and held weekly rehearsals at their homes. The band was originally nameless, but sometime in early 1927 they hit on The Fruit Jar Drinkers as having the appropriately rural sound to it.

The history of the band is somewhat complicated by the fact that their name was either borrowed or stolen by the flamboyant BANJO player UNCLE DAVE MACON. His label, Vocalion, noting the popularity of string bands, asked Macon to assemble one for his May 1927 recording session. He brought his sometimes accompanists, Kirk and SAM MCGEE along with fiddler Mazy Todd, to these sessions. These records were issued as by "Uncle Dave Macon and His Fruit Jar Drinkers." Whether Macon knew of the earlier band is unclear; according to the band members' descendants, GEORGE HAY, the announcer for the *Opry*, scolded Macon for taking the name without permission.

Despite their popularity on the *Opry*, where they were often featured as the closing act, the original Fruit Jar Drinkers never recorded. Even at the 1928 Victor Nashville sessions—where several of their friends and competitors, such as The CROOK BROTHERS and The GULLY JUMPERS, were recorded—they were mysteriously overlooked. According to Charles Wolfe, who has heard homemade acetate recordings of the band, they were an energetic unit, propelled by Wilkerson's somewhat archaic fiddling and Lampley's rhythmic frailing.

The Fruit Jar Drinkers continued to play on the *Opry* for decades. By the mid-1930s the band had "modernized" only to the extent that they added a bass player. By this point Wilkerson had earned the nickname "Grandpappy" from Hay, because of his constant on-air bragging about his first grandchild. Wilkerson retired from performing in 1953, shortly before his death, but the band soldiered on with various members until the mid-1970s. In later years—like other veterans the Crook Brothers and The Possum Hunters—their appearances were limited to accompanying staged square dances on the *Opry*, but nonetheless they maintained an original Tennessee string-band style for generations of listeners.

G

GATLIN BROTHERS (Larry [b. L. Wayne G., Seminole, Tex., May 2, 1948, gtr, voc]; Steve [b. Steven Daryl G., Olney, Tex., April 4, 1951, gtr, voc]; Rudy [b. R. Michael G., Olney, Tex., August 20, 1952, b, voc])

The Gatlins were a popular three-part harmony group of the 1970s and 1980s who combined Las Vegas glitz with down-home appeal.

Larry, the eldest brother, is the brains behind the group and its main songwriter. All three brothers performed together as children, beginning in church, which led to a stint as a GOSPEL group on Slim Willet's Abilene-based TV show when they were in their teens; they also recorded a religious LP for the tiny Sword & Shield label. Soon after, Larry went into music full-time, working originally with The Imperials, a gospel-harmony outfit out of Las Vegas that accompanied many major country artists, including ELVIS PRESLEY. In 1972, DOTTIE WEST encouraged him to move to Nashville, where, a year later, he signed with the Monument label, scoring his first hit in 1976 with his song "Broken Lady."

Meanwhile, brothers Steve and Rudy finished their education at Texas Tech, and along with sister LaDonna and her husband, came to Nashville to audition as backup singers for CHARLEY PRIDE; they eventually worked for TAMMY WYNETTE, leaving her to rejoin their elder brother as a group after his first single hit. Larry continued as a solo act backed by his siblings until 1978, when "I Just Wish You Were Someone I Love" hit #1, credited to "Larry Gatlin with Brothers and Friends." Their next single went to #2 as by "The Gatlin Brothers Band," and by the end of the year the major labels were pounding down their door. They also began appearing on TV variety shows, spreading their appeal well beyond the country audience.

In 1979 they scored their next #1 hit, "All the Gold in California," their first for new label Columbia, inspired by the bidding war that had ensued among the big-time record execs for the rights to the band. The next three and a half years had their ups and downs as Larry battled alcohol and drug addiction, turning out only a few minor hits. In 1983 they hit #1 again with "Houston (Means I'm Closer to You)," although Larry was at a personal low. The swinging number was an immediate sensation, and was followed by another city ode, "Denver." Then Larry checked himself into drug rehab, finally breaking a decade-long pattern of abuse. He became a spokesperson for Members Only, a maker of fancy men's jackets who also sponsored drug-education advertisements. The Gatlins continued to record for Columbia through 1988, scoring hits with "The Lady Takes the Cowboy Every Time" and "Talkin' to the Moon." They signed with the smaller Universe label in 1988, reflecting the fact that their close harmonies and pop arrangements were becoming old hat in the face of the onslaught of new country.

The Gatlins still remain a big draw at Vegas and other lounge venues. Larry scored points as a Broadway star, taking over the lead in *The Will Rogers Follies* in 1992. In 1993 the brothers took refuge in their own theater in BRANSON, MISSOURI, which became their main performing venue. They continued to appear there and in vacation spots like Las Vegas through the 1990s, recording for the small Branson Sound label.

Select Discography

Best of, Columbia/Legacy 64760. Eighteen hits recorded from 1975 to 1988.

GAYLE, CRYSTAL (b. Brenda Gail Webb, Paintsville, Ky., January 9, 1951)

One of the most successful female vocalists of the 1970s, Gayle brought an easy-listening sensibility to country music. Gayle's vocal style is the antithesis of the gutsy sound of many of Nashville's most famous

Crystal Gayle at the dawn of her career, c. mid-1970s. Photo: Raeanne Rubenstein

women, favoring a soft sexuality that is decidedly unthreatening. Her image, with her long, straight hair and earth-mother clothing, suggests a 1970s post-hippie look, while her style is so middle-of-the-road to be almost antiseptic.

The youngest sister of country star LORETTA LYNN, Gayle began her career when she was sixteen, backing her sister and CONWAY TWITTY. Lynn gave her her stage name, perhaps inspired by the country chain of Krystal hamburger stands! She made her first solo recordings at age nineteen with her sister's country WEEPER, "I Cried (The Blue Right out of My Eyes)," but did not crack the country charts again for five years.

Resisting the efforts of Nashville to mold her into a younger Loretta Lynn, Gayle finally hooked up with producer Allen Reynolds, who supplied her 1975 hit "Wrong Road Again." Three years later she scored a major pop crossover hit with the bar-lounge favorite "Don't It Make My Brown Eyes Blue." The tinkling piano prominently featured on this cut, along with Gayle's purring vocals, has earned it a rightful place in middle-of-the-road heaven. She had a few more pop successes in the late 1970s.

In the 1980s Gayle returned to her roots as a country chanteuse, having country hits with a cover of JIMMIE RODGERS's "Miss the Mississippi and You" in 1981 and 1986's "Cry." However, by the late 1980s, when "new country" was in full swing, Gayle's more relaxed vocal style and the mainstream production values of her recordings made her sound decidedly old-fashioned, even to country listeners. Still, she continues to be a steady concert draw and regular performer, although limiting herself primarily to friendly venues in BRANSON, MISSOURI, and tours of Europe.

Select Discography

Certified Hits, Capitol 34499. 2001 CD reissue of her 1970s recordings.

GENTRY, BOBBIE (b. Roberta Streeter, Chickasaw County, Miss., July 27, 1944)

Gentry was a slinky-voiced, sultry songstress who had one megahit with 1967's "Ode to Billy Joe."

Raised in the Mississippi delta, Gentry first learned piano by imitating the sounds she heard in church; after the family relocated to southern California when she was thirteen, she took up a number of other instruments, including GUITAR, BANJO, bass, and vibes. She had always written her own songs, beginning with an ode to the family dog when she was seven, and continued to write new material through her teen years.

While studying philosophy at UCLA, Gentry performed an occasional club date; her love of music led her to enroll at the Los Angeles Conservatory of Music, and she began performing with local acting troupes and made a demo tape of her songs that she circulated among local record labels. Los Angeles-based Capitol Records signed her in 1967, and her first record, "Ode to Billy Joe" (which she wrote), was an immediate sensation on country and pop charts. The "mystery" of exactly what Billy Joe threw off the Tallahassee Bridge made the song a cult item, and Gentry's smoke-gets-in-your-eyes delivery seemed to put more meaning in the lyrics than perhaps were there. An album followed, with several more songs inspired by her backwoods childhood, including "Okohona River Bottom Band" and "Chickasaw County Child" (released as a single in 1968). She recorded an album of duets with GLEN CAMPBELL, another Capitol artist, in 1969, scoring hits with "Let It Be Me" and "All I Have to Do Is Dream," both originally recorded by The EVERLY BROTHERS.

Gentry spent the early 1970s performing as a Las Vegas lounge star, and her records pretty much disappeared from the charts. Her career was temporarily revived in 1976 when a film based on her famous song was released, but her marriage to songwriter/performer JIM STAFFORD two years later pretty much led to her retirement as a performer, although she remained active in song publishing.

Select Discography

Greatest Hits, Curb 77387. Mid-1960s Capitol recordings.

GEORGIA YELLOW HAMMERS (active c. 1924–1929; primary members: Uncle Bud Landress [b. George Oscar L., bjo, fdl, voc]; Bill Chitwood [b. William Hewlett C., fdl, voc]; C. E. Moody [b. Charles Ernest M., uke, bjo, gtr, voc]; and Phil Reeve [gtr, voc])

A popular Georgia string band of the 1920s—second in popularity only to Gid Tanner and His SKILLET LICKERS—the group is best remembered for their tight harmony singing on GOSPEL and original composed songs.

The nucleus of the group came from northern Georgia's Calhoun County, where they were all active as musicians and songwriters, and had played in various combinations in local bands. "Uncle Bud" Landress and Bill Chitwood had played together on occasion, often in a trio with banjoist Fate Norris (later of The Skillet Lickers). In 1924 the duo traveled to New York and recorded twelve sides for the Brunswick label. Sometime after, they met local music promoter and player Phil Reeve, who put together the first Georgia Yellowhammers group and arranged for them to record in February 1927. C. E. Moody was a local SINGER/SONGWRITER, still remembered for his gospel songs that have become BLUEGRASS and country favorites, such as "Kneel at the Cross" and "Drifting Too Far from the Shore." He became the group's final member.

The group's name was concocted by an employee of their record company in early 1927. From the start the group emphasized quartet singing over rousing fiddle tunes, although through their career they recorded everything from comic songs and skits to gospel numbers. (Landress and Moody had attended local singing schools, and were trained in SHAPE-NOTE singing.) Their biggest seller was Landress's composition "The Picture on the Wall," a Victorian-styled tearjerker about mother and home that is said to have sold over 100,000 copies on 78.

Between 1927 and 1930 the group recorded for a variety of labels under a number of names—including Bill Chitwood and His Georgia Mountaineers and The Turkey Mountain Singers—sometimes recording the same songs under each new pseudonym. It is unclear whether all four attended every session; there is evidence that other musicians participated, and on later sessions Chitwood seems to have dropped out entirely, replaced on FIDDLE by the smoother-sounding Landress.

The Depression put an end to most early country recording, and the various Yellowhammer combinations could no longer find an outlet for their music. Of all the players Landress remained a "professional" longest, working locally through the 1940s.

GERRARD, ALICE (b. Seattle, Wash., July 8, 1934)

Long active on the Baltimore-Washington country-BLUEGRASS scene, Gerrard has performed as a soloist and in a variety of groups, as well as working as a folklorist and journalist.

Gerrard first recorded in the mid-1960s as a duo with country/bluegrass SINGER/SONGWRITER HAZEL DICKENS on albums for Verve/Folkways (although only one was issued at the time), accompanied by a bluegrass band featuring banjoist Lamar Grier and mandolinist DAVID GRISMAN. In the mid-1970s the duo reunited, making two albums for Rounder Records that featured Hazel's original compositions in a feminist vein, including the classic "Don't Put Her Down (You Helped Put Her There)." Meanwhile, Alice had married folklorist/performer MIKE SEEGER, and in 1974 the two, along with Dickens, formed the short-lived Strange Creek Singers with Seeger's NEW LOST CITY RAMBLERS bandmate Tracy Schwartz and banjoist Grier, performing a mix of old-time and bluegrass music. Gerrard and Seeger also toured as a duo and cut an album together in the late 1970s.

Also in the late 1970s Gerrard hooked up with Jeanie McLerie and Irene Herrman to form The Harmony Sisters, a feminist old-time trio that performed a mix of CAJUN numbers, songs of the CARTER FAMILY, and Alice's own compositions featuring working-class women heroes, such as "Payday at the Mill." This informal group lasted until the early 1980s. Gerrard also produced a film on the life and music of legendary fiddler TOMMY JARRELL, *Sprout Wings and Fly*.

In 1987 Gerrard relocated to North Carolina, where she founded *The Old Time Herald*, a quarterly magazine that addresses both traditional old-time country music and the second-generation revivalists, often in an outspoken way. She also formed another band, The Herald Angels, with Gail Gillespie and Hilary Dirlam. In the late 1990s she performed with fiddler Brad Leftwich.

Gerrard's strong voice and her affinity for topical material were an inspiration to many other old-time music revivalists, including musicians like CATHY FINK.

She has also been important in the preservation and documentation of many fine traditional musicians.

Select Discography

Pieces of My Heart, Copper Creek 134. 1996 solo album.

GIBSON, DON (b. Donald Eugene G., Shelby, N.C., April 3, 1928)

Gibson is a deep-voiced SINGER/SONGWRITER who is best remembered for his many hit compositions, including the immortal "I Can't Stop Lovin' You" and "Sweet Dreams."

Gibson was already a fine guitarist during his school days, playing local dances and radio jobs. He signed on with *The Tennessee Barn Dance* out of Knoxville in 1946, and began recording soon after. His earliest recordings were made with the COWBOY band The Sons of the Soil, recalling the style of the popular SONS OF THE PIONEERS, but he soon switched to a HONKY-TONK country style. His mature vocal style really didn't jell until he linked up with NASHVILLE SOUND guru CHET ATKINS, who signed him to RCA in 1957. For the next seven years the pair produced some of the more listenable of the pop-oriented Nashville recordings, with many of the famous session players who helped craft the slicker Nashville Sound. Meanwhile, Gibson's career as a songwriter also took off, with the success of KITTY WELLS's cover of "I Can't Stop Lovin' You" in 1957 and the posthumous release of "Sweet Dreams" by PATSY CLINE in 1963.

Gibson's 1950s recordings showed the influence of both contemporary country stylings and pop, thus ensuring him a broader audience than many other country artists. His specialty became the tearjerkin' country ballad, although many of his recordings were so drenched in self-pity that they crossed the line into pure bathos. For this reason his songs are often better known in other artists' cover versions than in his own recordings.

Gibson's own first hit was the double-sided "Oh, Lonesome Me" backed with "I Can't Stop Lovin' You" of 1958. That same year he made his first appearance on THE GRAND OLE OPRY. His follow-up hits included further deep-voiced WEEPERS, notably "Blue, Blue Day," "Give Myself a Party," and "Lonesome Number One." His last big hit was 1961's "Sea of Heartbreak," written by P. Hampton and Hal David, a hanky-wringer that appealed to the pop as well as the country charts.

In 1964 Gibson gave up his *Grand Ole Opry* membership; like other artists he found the demands of playing regularly on the *Opry* restrictive. Gibson con-

tinued to record through the 1960s, as a soloist and in duets with DOTTIE WEST, although an increasing dependence on pills and alcohol slowed his career. He made a comeback in the 1970s, most notably as a duet partner with Sue Thompson, scoring a #1 country hit with "Woman (Sensuous Woman)" in 1972. In 1975 he returned to the *Opry* as a member, and scored minor country hits through 1980. Gibson continues to be an attraction on tour and performs on *The Grand Ole Opry*. In 2001 he was elected to the Country Music Hall of Fame.

Select Discography

A Legend in My Time, Bear Family 15401. Classic RCA recordings originally made between 1957 and 1964, lovingly remastered, with excellent documentation.

All Time Greatest Hits, RCA 2295. Similar to the Bear Family set, although less lavishly produced.

The Singer, the Songwriter, Bear Family 15475/15664. Two megasets (four CDs each) giving you all of Gibson's recordings through 1966.

GILL, VINCE (b. Vincent Grant G., Norman, Okla., April 12, 1957)

Coming out of a pure BLUEGRASS background, Gill has graduated to be one of the more traditionally oriented of the new country stars.

The son of a judge, Gill began playing GUITAR and BANJO in his early teens, joining The Bluegrass Alliance (forerunners of NEW GRASS REVIVAL) after high school. He then teamed with RICKY SKAGGS in the short-lived progressive bluegrass band Boone Creek. Later he performed with COUNTRY-ROCK outfits including Sundance and THE PURE PRAIRIE LEAGUE before joining RODNEY CROWELL's backup band, The Cherry Bombs. Although he began recording as a solo artist in 1984, he didn't break through until 1990 with his hit ballad, "When I Call Your Name," leading to his induction into THE GRAND OLE OPRY a year later. Gill has maintained his bluegrass roots, performing with MARK O'CONNOR and Skaggs as The New Nashville Cats as well as continuing to record with California bluegrassers BYRON BERLINE, DAVID GRISMAN, and others for special projects.

Gill's greatest chart success occurred between 1994 and 1996, often with sentimental ballads, including his song written in honor of his father, "Go Rest High on That Mountain" (winner in 1997 of a BMI Most-Performed Song award, along with his #1 hit of that year, "Pretty Little Adriana"). In the later 1990s Gill became the subject of intense tabloid coverage when he left his wife, Janis (who, incidentally, is half of the vocal duo The SWEETHEARTS OF THE RODEO), to wed Christian rock singer Amy Grant. While this might have sunk the career of a lesser country star, Gill was able to ride out the storm, and continued to be in demand as a host of award programs and other events. A popular figure on the music scene, he has scored fourteen Grammys out of a total of thirty nominations; his fourteen wins put him in a league with Eric Clapton and ahead of Michael Jackson and Paul McCartney.

Besides being a classy tenor vocalist, Gill is an excellent flat-picker on the guitar, a legacy of his bluegrass training. His recordings tend to incorporate bluegrass instrumentation and vocal harmonies into the more progressive productions typical of the New Nashville. He has also remade several country/bluegrass standards, including his hit update of the WESTERN SWING classic "Liza Jane." During the 1990s his handlers tried to turn him into a weepy balladeer, and songs like "When Love Finds You" set many a heart a-flutter. But Gill is at his best on sprightly up-tempo numbers like "One More Last Chance," a classy revival of the Western Swing sound and a 1993 #1 song, showing that there's money to be made even in more traditional country music.

Select Discography

Essential, RCA 66535. Collects his early 1980s tracks, before he was a major hitmaker.

Souvenirs, MCA 11394. His later 1980s and early 1990s hits.

GILLEY, MICKEY (b. M. Leroy G., Natchez, La., March 9, 1936)

As owner of Gilley's Bar, Mickey Gilley rode the mechanical bull to country stardom in the late 1970s and early 1980s, following a long career in ROCKABILLY, country, and R&B.

Gilley makes much of his pedigree, and he ought to; his mother, Irene, was the sister of JERRY LEE LEWIS's dad, making Gilley and Jerry Lee first cousins (another first cousin is Jimmy "I Have Sinned" Swaggart). Born in Natchez, Louisiana, Gilley was raised in Lewis's hometown of Ferriday, and knew the older songster well. Both were pianists, and Gilley's mature style is, frankly, derivative from his more famous piano-poundin' relative. In fact, Gilley didn't try for a musical career until his older relative had a hit with "Crazy Arms" on Sun Records in 1956.

By then Gilley was living in Houston, and he began recording for a number of small Texas labels, sounding an awful lot like old Jerry Lee. Gilley spent much of the 1950s and 1960s laboring as a local favorite, with an occasional moderate hit, primarily limited to Texas radio. By the early 1970s, tired of comparisons with you-know-who, Gilley gave up playing the piano for a while, to try to create a more countrified persona; he also opened his own club, Gilley's Bar, which eight

years later would inspire the "urban cowboy" movement, first in an article in *Esquire* magazine and then in the 1980 film *Urban Cowboy*.

Gilley's career, meanwhile, had ticked upward a little. A local deejay asked him to record his composition "She Calls Me Baby," and he backed it with a remake of GEORGE MORGAN's 1949 hit "Room Full of Roses"; the B-side, heavy with an echoey steel guitar (supposedly to hide the fact that the steel player was out of tune), became Gilley's first certifiable hit, leading to a contract with Playboy Records. When the record was reissued by Playboy, it shot to #1 in 1974. "I Overlooked an Orchid," Gilley's second single and another flower-themed song (with a similar Jerry Lee-styled piano introduction), did equally well, and was followed by a string of COUNTRYPOLITAN recordings, including 1975's "Roll You like a Wheel" (a duet with ex-Playmate Barbi Benton), 1976's "Don't the Girls All Get Prettier at Closing Time," and 1977's "Honky-Tonk Memories."

In 1979 Gilley signed with Epic Records, just in time to cash in on the urban cowboy craze. His remake of the Ben E. King classic "Stand by Me" was featured in the *Urban Cowboy* film, becoming an immediate hit, and was followed by more standard early 1980s country fare, including several #1 hits: 1980's "True Love Ways" and "That's All That Matters," 1981's "A Headache Tomorrow (or a Heartache Tonight)" (the song was somewhat controversial, not because it describes a typical night of heavy drinking but because the singer also mentions taking "a pill"; Gilley insists that this was aspirin as a remedy for a walloping hangover!), 1982's "Put Your Dreams Away," and 1983's "Fool for Your Love."

Gilley faded from the charts in the face of new-country music, and his club went into a tailspin, a victim of the excesses of the 1980s; it closed its doors in 1989, two years after Gilley sued his ex-partner in the venture. A "new" Gilley's has arisen out of the ashes in the ersatz-country capital, BRANSON, MISSOURI. Gilley himself had one further hit, 1986's "Doo Wah Days," a nostalgic look at 1950s rock.

Select Discography

10 Years of Hits, Epic 39867.

GILMAN, BILLY (b. William W. G., Westerly, R.I., May 24, 1988)

By the time you read this, Billy Gilman will have become either a forgotten novelty hitmaker or a major Nashville star . . . or perhaps something in between.

Gilman's main claim to fame is his young age: he made it big just after his eleventh birthday. The pint-sized country crooner is otherwise not terribly distinguished; he sings standard-issue pop country in a little kid's voice while sporting leather pants and a junior-sized cowboy hat.

Gilman was drawn to country after seeing a PAM TILLIS music video at age three; two years later his parents gave him his very own karaoke machine. At age eight he began vocal training; his teacher introduced him to the venerable Ray Benson, leader of ASLEEP AT THE WHEEL, who recorded the tyke's first sessions in Austin when he was ten. He also showcased the singer in front of the band at Nashville's Wild Horse Saloon. Soon little Billy had a bevy of managers and a record deal with Sony/Nashville.

Gilman debuted on the Academy of Country Music Awards show in 2000, singing the BOB WILLS standard "Roly Poly," again with Asleep at the Wheel. But his first single was hardly WESTERN SWING; instead, "One Voice" was a generic NEW NASHVILLE ballad, with a slight social message. (Appropriately, it gave a child's view of the world's problems, with the predictable moral that we should all follow "the Golden Rule.") The song hit #1 on the country charts in July 2000, and stayed there for five weeks.

Meanwhile his debut album, from which the song was drawn, entered the charts in the Top 5, making him the youngest artist ever to reach that spot, and only the third to have the first album debut so high. The single and album quickly went gold, and then the album went platinum; Gilman is the youngest artist in any musical genre to have a debut album sell over a million copies. Knowing a cash cow when it saw one, his label rushed out a Christmas album, and by November 2000 Billy was the biggest selling artist in all of country music.

And, naturally, the awards piled on: in early 2001 he was given an American Music Award as Favorite New Country Artist (again, he's the youngest ever to win this honor), and in June won the Discovery Award at the TNN/CMT *Country Weekly* awards. In February 2001 he issued another uplifting single, "There's a Hero," donating profits to the St. Jude's Hospital fund.

In May 2001 Gilman issued "She's My Girl," drawn from his third album, *Dare to Dream*, his first tentative step into adult romantic material. Billy gamely dances and sings (sporting leather pants) in the song's video, but the content of the song seems a little mature for him. The album also includes the uplifting ballad "Elisabeth," about a young girl overcoming disease and misfortune, a piece of sentimental mush very much in keeping with his earlier image.

Gilman has racked up the hits quickly, and so far has terrorized anybody with even a shadow of a beard in Nashville with his baby-faced good looks. Whether he can survive as a pop singer—let alone mature into an important artist—is yet to be seen.

Select Discography

One Voice, Sony 62806. 2000 debut album.

GILMORE, JIMMIE DALE (b. Amarillo, Tex., May 6, 1945)

The ultimate "cosmic cowboy," Gilmore is another eccentric SINGER/SONGWRITER out of Texas who has been more legendary than well known in even the die-hard circles of country fans.

Gilmore came out of Lubbock, Texas, where his first band, The Flatlanders, was financed by BUDDY HOLLY's father. This near-mythic group, featuring JOE ELY (now one of COUNTRY-ROCK's big shakers) and BUTCH HANCOCK (another erratic singer/songwriter), recorded one album in 1971 that went unreleased for nineteen years, finally appearing on Rounder Records. Gilmore spent the mid-1970s on the move, first relocating to Austin, the center of Texas's hippie-country music community, and then giving up music altogether to pursue a degree in Oriental philosophy at the University of Colorado.

Gilmore returned to Austin in 1980, and recorded two albums for the small Hightone label in the mid-1980s, introducing his combination of high-falutin' lyrics with a steady, rockin' beat. He even managed a #72 country hit with one of his best-known songs, "White Freight Liner Blues."

Gilmore's career got a kick in the pants when he was selected to be part of Elektra Records' American Explorers series in 1991; these were recordings by lesser-known singer/songwriters in country, ROCKABILLY, and rock who deserved more attention. In 1993 he was signed by Elektra itself as a regular-label act, and embarked on a nationwide tour. Still, Gilmore failed to win a large country audience, and he was also unable to crack the alternative charts. By the end of the decade he was releasing his own recordings on his Windcharger imprint, distributed by Rounder. But after over three years off disc, his 2000 album, *One Endless Night*, was mostly covers of other Texas songwriters, and odd choices like a cover of "Mack the Knife."

Select Discography

After Awhile, Elektra/Nonesuch 61148. 1991 "comeback" album.

GIMBLE, JOHNNY (b. John Paul G., near Tyler, Tex., May 30, 1926)

One of the greatest fiddlers in the WESTERN SWING style, Gimble began his career as a protégé of BOB WILLS, and also was a member of WILLIE NELSON's band, as well as guesting with Western Swing revival bands like ASLEEP AT THE WHEEL.

Raised in rural Texas, Gimble showed an early facility for music, playing BANJO and MANDOLIN. He joined his brothers' group, The Rose City Hipsters, in his early teen years; the band played locally for dances and parties, as well as broadcasting over Tyler's radio station. When he was seventeen, he was hired to play with THE SHELTON BROTHERS, leading to work with JIMMIE DAVIS.

After World War II, Western Swing master Bob Wills hired Gimble, originally to play mandolin, although soon his talents as a fiddler showed through. He remained with Wills through the 1950s, and his jazz-influenced fiddling, with its rich tone, became a hallmark of Wills's later recordings. In the 1960s and early 1970s Gimble worked as a Nashville studio musician; he rejoined Wills in 1973 for The Texas Playboys' reunion LP that was inspired by MERLE HAGGARD's love for Western Swing; he then performed through the 1970s with several alumni of Wills's band, recording several albums.

From 1979 to 1981, Gimble worked with Willie Nelson's touring band. He achieved his greatest chart success accompanying RAY PRICE on the single "One Fiddle, Two Fiddle," drawn from Clint Eastwood's 1982 film *Honkytonk Man*. He has since recorded as a solo artist, leading his own band, Texas Swing, and also working with various Texas Playboys reunion bands. He has also sessioned with new-country stars like GEORGE STRAIT and older traditionalists like Haggard. In 1993 his work on MARK O'CONNOR's *Heroes* album garnered him a Grammy nomination, and a year later he won the award for his arrangement of "Redwing" that was featured on Asleep at the Wheel's *A Tribute to Bob Wills and The Texas Playboys* album. Over the 1990s he hosted "Swing Week" in his native Texas as a learning workshop for young fiddlers, as well as producing instructional videos.

Select Discography

Texas Fiddle Collection, CMH 9027. Mid-1970s recordings with many of the old Texas Playboys on hand.

GIRLS OF THE GOLDEN WEST (Mildred Fern "Millie," April 11, 1913–May 3, 1993 [gtr, voc], and Dorothy Laverne "Dolly," December 11, 1915–November 12, 1967 [gtr, voc], Goad [later Good], both b. Mount Carmel, Ill.)

A popular close-harmony Western-styled duo of the 1930s, the Girls brought an Andrews Sisters sensibility to COWBOY-styled singing.

Although born in rural Mount Carmel, Illinois, the Goad sisters were raised primarily in Midwestern cities, where their father unsuccessfully tried his hand at a variety of occupations, from storekeeper to insurance salesman to, finally, factory worker. Mama Goad was a talented singer of old-time songs, and it was younger sister Dolly who showed the greater musical ability, learning to play GUITAR early on from her mother. Dolly also was the more interested in a professional career, dragging her fourteen-year-old sister to an audition for St. Louis's KMOX radio station. They got the job, took the name Girls of the Golden West, and changed their last name from Goad to Good; after a period of radio work in Kansas and on the Mexican-border radio station XERA, they returned in 1933 to St. Louis, where they were "discovered" by scouts for the Chicago-based *National Barn Dance* show.

In 1934 they made their first appearance on the *Barn Dance* and also their first recordings. The girls were an immediate sensation with their sweet harmonies, precision harmonized yodeling, and novelty sound effects (such as vocally imitating the sound of a Hawaiian slide guitar). Their first recording was a remake of Belle Starr's risqué hokum number "My Love Is a Rider," cleaned up to fit the Girls' wholesome image. It was followed by a number of cowboyesque numbers, many written by Millie, including "Two Cowgirls on the Lone Prairie" and "Will There Be Any Yodelers in Heaven?" Lucille Overstake, another popular *Barn Dance* performer, wrote their most popular number, "I Want to Be a Real Cowboy Girl," which, like most of their songs, was slightly ahead of its time in its theme (the lyrics implied that a girl could be just as macho as a rootin', tootin' cowboy).

The girls left Chicago for New York in 1935, and two years later relocated to Cincinnati's *Midwestern Hayride* program, where they remained into the 1950s. Millie eventually retired to raise a family, but Dolly continued to perform on local radio, hosting a children's show and a pop hit-parade program.

Select Discography

Songs of the West, Old Homestead 143. This out-of-print LP reissues 1930s recordings, plus a 1963 reunion cut with BRADLEY KINCAID.

GLASER BROTHERS, THE (Tompall [Tom Paul G., b. September 3, 1933]; Chuck [Charles G., b. February 3, 1936]; and Jim [James William G., b. December 16, 1937], all b. Spalding, Neb.)

The Glasers were a vocal harmony group who recorded both as backup vocalists and on their own without much success; in the mid-1970s Tompall became a member of the Texas-based OUTLAW movement.

Led by eldest brother Tompall (a nickname derived by running together his first and middle names), the group first worked as backup singers in Nashville, accompanying MARTY ROBBINS on his hit "El Paso" in

1959 and four years later working with JOHNNY CASH on "Ring of Fire." Brother Jim wrote "Woman, Woman," a hit for the pop group Gary Puckett and the Union Gap in the 1960s. The Glasers began recording as a group in the mid-1960s, took a break between 1973 and 1979, and had minor hits in 1971 with "Rings" and in 1981 with "Lovin' Her Was Easier (Than Anything I'll Ever Do)." They also became involved in music publishing.

All three pursued solo careers as well, Jim beginning in 1968 and Tompall and Chuck soon after. Tompall became associated with WAYLON JENNINGS and WILLIE NELSON in the mid-1970s, appearing on the famous *Outlaws* anthology album issued by RCA, which gave his career a small boost. He made a couple of LPs for ABC/Dot in the late 1970s, but they went nowhere. Chuck had his biggest solo hit in 1974 with "Gypsy Queen," but a year later a stroke limited his ability to record and perform. Jim struggled along trying to make it, finally scoring a #1 hit in 1984 with "You're Gettin' to Me Again" for producer Don Tolle, on Tolle's Noble Vision label. Unfortunately, the label folded due to lack of funding, and Glaser ended up working as a backup singer with such COUNTRYPOLITAN stars as RONNIE MCDOWELL and SYLVIA.

From 1978 to 1981 the brothers were once again a group, recording for Elektra. They scored some minor hits—particularly with KRIS KRISTOFFERSON's "Lovin' Her Was Easier (Than Anything I'll Ever Do Again)." However, personal problems again arose, and Jim left the group. In 1983 he scored his greatest solo success with the song "When You're Not a Lady," released on the small Noble Vision label; since then he has performed regularly on *The Grand Ole Opry*.

Tompall made a final solo album in 1986, and then concentrated on working as a producer through the end of the decade. He subsequently sold his studio, and by the late 1990s was once again on the road, performing in smaller venues at home and in the United Kingdom, where he still has a strong following. After years of acrimony the brothers no longer speak and so a future reunion is unlikely.

Select Discography

The Outlaw, Bear Family 15606. Combines two LPs made for ABC/Dot in the late 1970s by Tompall Glaser.

The Rogue, Bear Family 15596. Another ABC LP from the late 1970s by Tompall, along with more recent recordings.

GOINS BROTHERS (Melvin, b. M. Glen G., December 30, 1933 [gtr, voc, b]; Ray, b. R. Elwood G., January 3, 1936 [bnj]; both b. Bramwell, W.Va.)

Influential early BLUEGRASS musicians of the 1950s, the Goins have maintained a traditional style for many decades.

The brothers were raised in rural West Virginia, where they heard groups like THE STANLEY BROTHERS and BILL MONROE over local radio in the late 1940s, and became immediate converts to bluegrass. Older brother Melvin joined a local band, The Lonesome Pine Fiddlers, around 1949, and Ray followed in 1951. They recorded with the group for RCA in 1952 and then formed the first Goins Brothers band in late 1953, after the rest of the Fiddlers packed up to move to Detroit.

Neither The Fiddlers nor the Goins were successful during their year apart, so when The Fiddlers returned to West Virginia, the Goins were back in the lineup. They worked with the band sporadically through the 1950s and early 1960s, recording with them and appearing on local radio.

In the mid-1960s Ray temporarily retired from music making and Melvin worked with a number of bands, including his idols, The Stanley Brothers. Besides playing bass with the Stanleys, Melvin performed classic COUNTRY-RUBE comedy on stage, going by the name "Big Wilbur."

The Goins were reunited in the late 1960s and have since performed with a variety of backup musicians. Some of their best recordings were made in the 1970s for Jessup and Rebel Records. They have also hosted their own radio show since 1974, broadcasting out of Hazard/Lexington, Kentucky. Associated groups include The Woodettes, a female GOSPEL quartet featuring Melvin's wife, Willia, and her sisters; and The Stedhouse Trio, a group-within-the-group led by Melvin to perform pure country material.

One of the last of the old-style bluegrass bands, the Goinses' style and repertoire has changed little over the decades. Although not as distinctive as their idols, The Stanley Brothers, they produce solid music in a traditional style.

GOOD OL' PERSONS (Kathy Kallick [gtr, voc]; Laurie Lewis [fdl, voc]; Bethany Raines [b, voc]; John Reischman [mdln]; Sally van Meter [Dobro])

The Good Ol' Persons were a mid-1980s San Francisco Bay-area-based BLUEGRASS/country band with a strong feminist twist, thanks to the strong lead vocals and original songs of Kallick and Lewis.

The name of course is a play on "good ol' boys," here expanded in politically correct terms to include women. The cofounders—Kallick and Lewis—made this band special; they performed a combination of classic country material by THE CARTER FAMILY and THE DELMORE BROTHERS, among others, laced with their contemporary recastings of traditional country themes in their original songs. The band was also unusual in that it featured so many talented females as instrumentalists, including Lewis's fine fiddling (she was later replaced by Paul Shelasky and Kevin Wimmer, in succession) and van Meter's new-acoustic-influenced DOBRO playing.

Even after the band folded in the late 1980s, Kallick and Lewis remained closely aligned, recording a duo album in the early 1990s. In 1993 Kallick recorded her first solo album, featuring all original material, in an attempt to capture the mainstream country market.

GORDY, EMORY, JR. (b. Atlanta, Ga., December 25, 1944)

Talented bass player, producer, and husband of singer PATTY LOVELESS, Gordy began playing bass in his late teens, and within two years was working professionally in teen popster Tommy Roe's band (a bandmate was Joe South). South introduced him to the world of the session musician, and the two worked steadily in the Atlanta area. In 1970 Gordy relocated to Los Angeles to join Neil Diamond's band, and also worked sessions for ELVIS PRESLEY (his bass playing is heard on a number of Presley's later hits, most notably "Burning Love") and GRAM PARSONS. In 1975 Gordy began touring and recording as a member of EMMYLOU HARRIS's Hot Band, and in the late 1970s worked as a member of RODNEY CROWELL's group, The Cherry Bombs. In that group he met future country producer TONY BROWN and future crooning star VINCE GILL.

After Brown relocated to Nashville in the early 1980s, he called Gordy to work for him at MCA Records. Gordy became a much-in-demand country producer and session artist. While working for MCA he met label star Patty Loveless, whom he produced, and the two married in 1989. He also produced STEVE EARLE's seminal album *Guitar Town*, and even worked with bluegrass legend BILL MONROE.

Gordy left MCA in 1996 to join the fledgling Rising Tide operation, where he continued to produce and sign artists; however, the company was out of business by early 1998. Gordy has continued to work as a producer on a freelance basis, in early 2001 overseeing two albums by his wife, including a traditional BLUEGRASS outing, *Mountain Soul*, along with a more mainstream-commercial album, and also working with veteran country singer GEORGE JONES.

GOSDIN, VERN (b. Vernon G., Woodland, Ala., August 5, 1934)

A country crooner who has had a checkered career, thanks to almost constant label-hopping, Gosdin has a voice that recalls the mournful side of GEORGE JONES.

Raised in rural Alabama, Gosdin performed locally with his brother in a duet act that was reminiscent of THE LOUVIN BROTHERS, whom they heard weekly on THE GRAND OLE OPRY broadcasts. He also sang in a GOSPEL group over local radio station WWOK. By the mid-1960s the brothers had relocated to California, where they were members of The Hillmen, a BLUEGRASS band led by CHRIS HILLMAN (who later helped form THE BYRDS). In 1966 they recorded an album with GENE CLARK after he left the Byrds, but it went nowhere. The Gosdin Brothers recorded by themselves for Bakersfield International, scoring a hit with "Hangin' On" in 1967, then moving to Capitol a year later for a follow-up, "Til the End," a minor hit. By 1972 work had dried up, and Gosdin had returned to Alabama and abandoned the music business.

Thanks to his Byrds connection Gosdin had a reputation among 1970s COUNTRY-ROCKERS, and was encouraged by EMMYLOU HARRIS to resume his recording career. In 1976–1977 he rerecorded his two earlier hits, which both went Top 10, and followed them with a series of recordings through the mid-1980s for a variety of labels. He made a comeback in the late 1980s on Columbia with his LP *Chiseled in Stone*; while the production is a bit heavy-handed, the title song and "Who You Gonna Blame It on This Time" are both fine country WEEPERS, made even more compelling by Gosdin's achy vocals. Gosdin continued to record and perform, releasing albums on the small American Harvest label through the 1990s, beginning in 1995 with an all-gospel album.

Select Discography

The Best of, Warner Bros. 25775. Late-1970s recordings that were reissued after Gosdin's success in the late 1980s.
Chiseled in Stone, Columbia 40982.

GOSPEL MUSIC

Country gospel music is another genre—like old-time and BLUEGRASS styles—that is the outgrowth of the rich interplay between black and white traditions in the South.

It also is a unique product of commercial forces—from song publishing through record production and radio and television broadcasts—that have helped to quickly disseminate new styles and innovations throughout its century and a half of existence.

SHAPE-NOTE SINGING had been known throughout the original U.S. colonies and was the original "folk" gospel music, taught by traveling singing masters. By the end of the Civil War a new wrinkle was introduced to this tradition when the Ruebush-Kieffer Publishing Company was founded in Virginia. The firm was the first prolific Southern producer of shape-note hymnals and, more important, also established a network of singing schools to teach music to ordinary folk.

The most influential graduate of the Ruebush-Kieffer schools was James D. Vaughan of rural Lawrenceburg, Tennessee. He began his own publishing empire in 1903, and within a decade was dominating the market. Vaughan hit on the happy idea of employing traveling singing groups to promote his books, employing the standard soprano-alto-tenor-bass lineup of barbershop quartets. These groups became popular on their own, and by the early 1920s Vaughan had expanded his empire to include a radio station and a record label. Several of Vaughan's songs became staples of early country acts, ranging from THE CARTER FAMILY (who adopted his "No Depression in Heaven") to THE MONROE BROTHERS (who scored a major hit with his "What Would You Give [In Exchange for Your Soul]?").

Country gospel groups became a mainstay of country radio and recording from the late 1920s on. Shows like THE GRAND OLE OPRY began to feature their own quartets (most notably, the ex-Vaughan employee group, The John Daniel Quartet). Groups like THE CHUCK WAGON GANG made long careers out of performing gospel material. BILL MONROE was particularly fond of gospel music, and—as the father of bluegrass music—made it a part of the standard bluegrass vocal repertoire.

In 1926 Vaughan's business faced a new, and powerful, competitor in the Stamps-Baxter Publishing Company. Virgil Oliver Stamps was a successful singing-school teacher who on his own published a best-selling hymnal, *Harbor Bells*, in the early 1920s. Strapped for capital, he partnered with J. R. Baxter, Jr., another singing master. The two positioned their songbooks as featuring more "snappy" (ragtime and pop-song influenced) melodies than Vaughan's more staid publications. In 1927 the Stamps Quartet, led by Virgil's brother Frank, produced a major hit in this more contemporary mold, "Give the World a Smile Each Day," furthering the company's success. Stamps-Baxter became so big that they opened their own printing plant in Dallas, Texas, to meet the demand for their annual songbooks and also to produce customized books for individual groups.

The white gospel quartet tradition was not untouched by the parallel growth of gospel in the black community. Spurred by songwriter Thomas A. Dorsey—previously a blues performer who had recorded as "Georgia Tom"—dozens of black gospel groups had sprung up throughout the South, singing Dorsey's and others' original compositions. Dorsey's songs—most notably "Precious Lord" and "Peace in the Valley" (later a major hit for RED FOLEY)—became staples of both black and white traditions, and introduced more modern, blues-influenced melodies and themes.

Another major gospel composer and entrepreneur was ALBERT E. BRUMLEY. He also combined modern themes with age-old sentiments. His greatest song—"I'll Fly Away"—has become a country and bluegrass standard. It combines an upbeat message with a modern melody and harmonies that wouldn't sound out of place on the pop chart.

Gospel quartets continued to be popular after World War II, although many began to cross over into the pop marketplace. THE STATLER BROTHERS began their lives in the gospel medium before succumbing to the siren call of commercial success. THE BLACKWOOD BROTHERS, founded in 1934 and briefly employed by Stamps-Baxter, became major hitmakers in the early 1950s when they were living in Memphis, Tennessee, influencing a young singer named ELVIS PRESLEY. Presley later emulated their gospel arrangements on his own recordings, using the pop vocal group THE JORDANAIRES, who had crossed over from gospel to being Presley's number-one choice for vocal accompaniment (although they never totally abandoned their gospel identity). Elvis continued to feature gospel material in his act until his death. Other mainstream country stars would often feature a gospel song as a closing number in their acts, as a way of acknowledging their ties to God and community (two favorites among the country audience).

Gospel-tinged songs have continued to be popular on the country charts, even when they are not directly "religious" in content. Such upbeat numbers as RAY STEVENS's perennial hit "Everything Is Beautiful" recall gospel sentiments and sound without actually addressing biblical or religious subjects.

Bluegrass gospel has continued to be popular. Many groups have recorded "secular" albums with the full band and then cut "sacred" ones, sometimes omitting instrumentation that might be associated with the devil's doings (such as FIDDLES and BANJOS, strongly associated with dance music—and thus the bane of religious folks). Some later groups, like DOYLE LAWSON's Quicksilver, specialized in country gospel, but most simply featured it as part of their acts. RALPH STANLEY has been a major proponent of old-style gospel harmony singing, and made semireligious songs like "Rank Strangers to Me" signature pieces in his act.

In the 1980s and 1990s it was very popular for mainstream and new-country performers to thank "the Man Upstairs" when receiving awards, but less popular to include gospel songs in their acts. Nonetheless, by this time religious-tinged material was so much a part of country that the songs continued to pop up on albums and at concerts, and occasionally even became hits. Country gospel also was made somewhat outmoded by Christian pop, with singers like Amy Grant taking a more contemporary, mainstream sound to preach a familiar message.

GRAND OLE OPRY, THE (1925–present)

The Grand Ole Opry was not the first country music radio program, but it became the most popular and the one most closely associated with country music. It helped establish Nashville as a center of country music recording and also introduced country music to countless listeners over its long existence.

The *Opry* was given its name by announcer GEORGE D. HAY, nicknamed "The Solemn Old Judge." Hay originally worked for Memphis and Chicago radio stations; he had hosted *The Chicago Barn Dance* in 1924 (later called THE NATIONAL BARN DANCE, which was among the first country-music radio programs (it remained on the air until 1960). He came to the fledgling station WSM, run by Nashville's National Life and Accident Insurance Company (the initials stand for "We Shield Millions"), in early 1925. A program hosted by Hay featuring the elderly fiddler UNCLE JIMMY THOMPSON in November 1925 proved the popularity of country music, and a few weeks later *The Grand Ole Opry* was launched.

Early stars of the *Opry* included harmonica-playing DOCTOR HUMPHREY BATE and his Possum Hunters string band; the flamboyant banjoist UNCLE DAVE MACON, who often was accompanied by Kirk and SAM MCGEE; and the blues-tinged harmonica player DEFORD BAILEY. In the mid-1930s the *Opry* launched a booking agency to send its acts on the road; this not only spread the sound of the *Opry* stars throughout the South and West, it also enriched WSM, which took a hefty commission on the acts it booked.

The second key figure in the Opry's history was Harry Stone, who was hired to book more modern acts onto the show. In 1931 he brought THE VAGABONDS, a vocal trio who had previously appeared on Chicago's *National Barn Dance* (which always took a more pop-oriented direction). Stone would be central in establishing the booking agency, and also in attracting more pop-oriented acts. In the mid-1930s COWBOY-styled acts like PEE WEE KING's Golden West Cowboys appeared on the program, and in 1938 a young fiddler/vocalist named ROY ACUFF was invited to join the show, after many years of trying to get on it. Acuff changed the direction of the *Opry* from being primarily an instrumental broadcast to one focusing on vocals; his crooning helped lay the groundwork for future stars like EDDY ARNOLD. A year later the *Opry* joined the NBC "red" network, bringing it to a national audience, and future BLUEGRASS star BILL MONROE joined the cast.

During the 1930s and 1940s hundreds of similar shows blossomed on local radio stations, giving many country acts their first important exposure. Perhaps the most important radio producer was JOHN LAIR, who worked for WLS in Chicago, followed by a stint in Cincinnati, and then, in 1937, created the *Renfro Valley Barn Dance*, both a tourist attraction in the hills of Kentucky and a popular broadcast featuring a popular young singer/emcee, RED FOLEY. Lair specialized in packaging bands and singers to fit a specific image, based heavily on a nostalgic (and perhaps exaggerated) sense of what life in the backwoods was like a century earlier.

In 1940 the *Opry* cast was invited to appear in a movie produced by budget studio Republic Pictures. Acuff, young and handsome, was made the lead, but the film also showcased older stars like Uncle Dave Macon. In the same year Eddy Arnold joined the show's cast as featured singer with Pee Wee King. In the summer of 1940 the first *Opry* tent show hit the road, and country comic MINNIE PEARL made her debut on the radio program.

For many years the *Opry* had various homes, from the original one in a tiny radio studio (that could not accommodate the crowds of listeners who came to see it) through various auditoriums in Nashville. Finally it found its most famous home in 1943, at the legendary Ryman Auditorium. This would serve as the home of the *Opry* for thirty years, and is still an important tourist attraction for *Opry* fans.

In the post–World War II years Nashville blossomed as a country music center. Although Victor Records had come on a "field trip" to record country stars in the late 1920s, no permanent studio opened there until 1947, when WSM engineers opened the Castle Studio. In the same year an ex–*Opry* announcer named Jim Bulleit started his Bullet label, and soon after, RCA opened its Nashville division, hiring CHET ATKINS to be its staff producer.

Meanwhile, the *Opry* was bowing to change. In 1943 ERNEST TUBB shocked *Opry* management when he appeared playing an electric guitar; it took several years for this radical departure, along with his HONKY-TONK repertoire, to find a place on the program. A year later BOB WILLS's Texas Playboys appeared on the air, the first group allowed to use drums in its act (although just a snare drum, and the drummer had to be hidden behind a curtain so the audience wouldn't be shocked). In 1949 a young singing sensation named HANK WILLIAMS popularized the steel guitar on the *Opry*, as well as his blues-tinged repertoire. He would remain a popular act until he had to be fired three years later, when he became increasingly unreliable due to his alcoholism.

George Hay finally retired in 1953, and the *Opry* spent much of the 1950s, 1960s, and early 1970s becoming a bastion of conservative music making. Though new acts continued to be signed, the show became highly predictable. Meanwhile, the NASHVILLE SOUND, which turned mainstream Nashville music recording into a mushy amalgam of purling piano and cooing choruses, was also taking its place on the *Opry* stage. In the 1960s and 1970s the *Opry* had become the voice of conservative America, so much so that when SKEETER DAVIS publicly criticized the Nashville police for brutality from the *Opry* stage, she created a scandal that derailed her career.

In 1973 the old Ryman was closed and the *Opry* moved to its current home in the glitzy theme park Opryland USA complex. Appropriately enough, the new theater was opened by President Nixon, himself a big fan of country music. Its new 4,400-seat auditorium was built to accommodate the large crowds who come to see the show, but it has none of the intimacy of the Ryman. The show increasingly took on a manufactured-for-TV look, with its live aspect incidental to the proceedings.

Not surprisingly the new country music of the 1980s and 1990s helped revitalize the *Opry*. Many of these stars saw performing on the show as a major career validation. Performers still must be invited to "join" the Opry, and must commit to playing a certain number of Saturdays a year on the show, forgoing more lucrative opportunities on the road. However, "guests" (particularly big hitmakers) are increasingly allowed to play the show without committing to full membership. But the tradition of *Opry* membership—with the luster it gives to an act—makes it still one of the most coveted badges of achievement in Nashville.

In the fall of 2000 a gala seventy-fifth anniversary celebration was held for the *Opry*, including several concerts and a TV broadcast. The *Opry* is now part of Gaylord Entertainment, a major player in Nashville that owns music recording, publishing, and broadcasting properties.

GRANT, BILL AND DELIA BELL (Grant, b. Billy Joe G., Hugo, Okla., May 9, 1930 [?] [mdln, voc], and Bell, b. D. Nowell, Bonham, Tex., April 16, 1930 [?] [gtr, voc])

A BLUEGRASS duo with country-flavored vocal harmonies, Grant and Bell achieved some success with their recordings for a number of labels in the 1970s and 1980s.

Grant and Bell were exposed to bluegrass music through radio and records, particularly the late 1940s and early 1950s recordings of BILL MONROE and THE STANLEY BROTHERS, which helped establish and popularize the style. Grant was born and raised on a ranch near Hugo, Oklahoma, and took up the MANDOLIN in emulation of Monroe. In the late 1950s he befriended

Bobby Bell, who introduced him to his future wife, Delia, who was playing GUITAR and singing at home. Bill and Delia began playing together and soon established a local following, thanks to appearances on radio and TV throughout Oklahoma.

In 1969, while traveling through the area, Bill Monroe heard them perform and invited them to appear at his annual bluegrass festival held in Bean Blossom, Indiana. This appearance helped broaden their popularity among bluegrass fans, and they decided to take to music making full-time. They formed a backup band, The Kiamichi Mountain Boys, and Grant established a record label to issue their material, also with the colorful Kiamichi name. Grant established a major bluegrass festival in his home town of Hugo, which has become one of the biggest west of the Mississippi.

In the late 1970s it looked like Delia Bell might establish a solo career. In 1978 she cut an album on her own for County Records, featuring Grant in a supporting role. On it she recorded Grant's song "Roses in the Snow," which EMMYLOU HARRIS would cover as the title track for her influential 1980 bluegrass album. Through Harris, Bell was signed to Warner Brothers, but her resulting 1983 solo album for the label was not a success. From this album Bell scored a minor country hit in a duet with JOHN ANDERSON on "Flame in My Heart."

Meanwhile the Grant-Bell duo continued to perform and record for various bluegrass labels, notably Rounder and Old Homestead. Grant has written a number of songs that have achieved popularity among bluegrass musicians, including "Rollin'," "Cheer of the Home Fires," and "Stairway to Heaven" (not to be confused with . . .). A strong vocal duo who perform a mix of bluegrass standards and more contemporary country, Grant and Bell both look back toward traditional country and reflect more modern trends. Since the mid-1990s the duo have hosted the Oklahoma Bluegrass Festival.

GRAVES, BUCK/UNCLE JOSH (b. Burckett K. G., Tellico Plains [some sources give Tellico Springs], Tenn., September 27, 1928)

Graves, one of the most talented DOBRO players in the BLUEGRASS style, is famed for his work with FLATT AND SCRUGGS. He was also a fine country comedian, taking "Uncle Josh" as his comedic name.

Graves was nine years old when he heard country musician Cliff Carlisle of THE CARLISLE BROTHERS playing an exotic instrument: the Dobro. Carlisle's command of the instrument and his bluesy playing were immediately attractive to him, and he soon befriended the elder musician. However, Graves's first professional work was as a bass player with various country bands. By the early 1950s he had joined with the country/bluegrass duo WILMA LEE AND STONEY COOPER, playing bass and Dobro.

In 1957 the Coopers were invited to play on THE GRAND OLE OPRY. Graves was quickly spotted by Flatt and Scruggs, and invited to join the band—as a bass player. However, within a month he was playing Dobro with them. Emulating Scruggs's three-finger bluegrass BANJO style on the Dobro, Graves soon was playing lightning-fast solos that fit perfectly into the bluegrass instrumental style, while also offering bluesy accompaniments to Flatt's repertoire of songs.

Although not the first to play Dobro in a bluegrass band, Graves was one of the most influential, and dozens of other groups added the instrument after hearing its dynamic role in the Flatt and Scruggs band. In addition to displaying his instrumental skills, Graves played the comic foil to bass player Jake Tullock ("Cousin Jake") as the COUNTRY-RUBE "Uncle Josh."

In 1969, when Flatt and Scruggs disbanded, Graves initially stayed with the more traditional band led by Flatt. However, in 1971 he rejoined with Scruggs in the COUNTRY-ROCK band the Earl Scruggs Revue, recording with them through 1974. At the same time he sessioned widely on bluegrass and country recordings, including some of the best early records by KRIS KRISTOFFERSON.

In 1974 Graves embarked on a solo career while continuing to pursue both bluegrass and country session work. Through the 1970s and 1980s he recorded a number of solo albums in both bluegrass and more jazz-oriented styles, with musicians including guitarist JOE MAPHIS and fiddler VASSAR CLEMENTS. Graves established himself as a regular presence in Nashville studios, on radio, and on TV, appearing for a while in the early 1990s as a member of the *American Music Shop* television program's house band, led by fiddle virtuoso MARK O'CONNOR. He continued to work through the 1990s, often in partnership with fiddler KENNY BAKER. His health began to decline in the early 2000s; in 2001 and early 2002 he had two operations to amputate his legs. A benefit concert was held to help pay his medical bills in the autumn of 2001.

Select Discography

Sultan of Slide, OMS 2504. 2000 CD with all-star cast.

GREENBRIAR BOYS (1962–1964; original members: Ralph Rinzler [mdln, voc]; Bob Yellin [bnj, voc]; John Herald [gtr, voc]; Frank Wakefield [mdln, voc] replaced Rinzler 1965–1967)

One of the most popular of New York's BLUEGRASS revival groups, The Greenbriar Boys did much to popularize bluegrass and country sounds in the early-to-mid-1960s.

Originally formed by guitarist John Herald and banjo player Eric Weissberg (later famous for his recording of "Duelin' Banjos" that became the theme for the 1972 film *Deliverance*) and other New York-area folkies, the band solidified around 1962 with the addition of Yellin and Ralph Rinzler, who had a more academic bent than the other musicians. The group's first few albums were fairly accurate re-creations of traditional bluegrass sounds, much as THE NEW LOST CITY RAMBLERS had earlier "revived" old-time country music by studiously re-creating earlier recordings. When Rinzler left the group in 1964, he was replaced by Frank Wakefield, who brought a looser style and his unique high-tenor vocals to the group. Herald's vocals also straddled the line between traditional bluegrass and HONKY-TONK country.

Rinzler went on to become a noted folklorist who headed the Smithsonian Institution's Department of Folklife until his untimely death in 1994. Herald recorded as a solo artist in the early 1970s, performed with Happy and Artie Traum and other Woodstock-area musicians on the informal *Mud Acres* albums, and then led his own bluegrass band from the mid-1970s through the 1990s. Wakefield has recorded sporadically as a solo artist and bandleader, and Yellin has pretty much disappeared into the woodwork.

GREENE, JACK (b. J. Henry G., Maryville, Tenn., January 7, 1930)

Greene was a successful country crooner of the mid-1960s very much in the pop/NASHVILLE SOUND mold.

Greene began his career as an instrumentalist with the GUITAR (which he took up at age eight), then added bass and drums. By the time he completed high school, he was living in Atlanta and playing with a number of COWBOY-flavored groups. After a stint in the Army in the early 1950s, he returned to Atlanta (via Alaska), playing local clubs with a group called The Peachtree Cowboys. It was there that laconic singer ERNEST TUBB discovered him in the early 1960s and asked him to join his backup band, The Troubadours.

In the mid-1960s, discovering Greene could sing as well as pick, Tubb invited him to contribute vocals to an album track, "The Last Letter," and soon country deejays were requesting more from the smooth-voiced vocalist. He was signed separately to Decca, and under the hand of veteran producer OWEN BRADLEY cut his first hit, a cover of DALLAS FRAZIER's "There Goes My Everything," complete with the JORDANAIRES providing backup harmonies. His next hit, 1967's "All the Time," featured a neoclassical piano break by ace sessionman FLOYD CRAMER and led to Greene's engagement as a regular on THE GRAND OLE OPRY.

Greene's hitmaking days continued through 1969, with a couple more #1 solo hits and a duet with JEAN-

NIE SEELY, 1969's "Wish I Didn't Have to Miss You." Seely remained with Greene's road show through the early 1980s. His career steadily declined through the 1970s, although he continued to tour and record for Decca/MCA; he moved to smaller labels in the 1980s. In a bizarre twist, although he was now known primarily as a touring star, Greene suffered through the 1980s at the hands of a mysterious impersonator who passed himself off as the country star, running up huge bills at hotels across the country and bilking investors out of a considerable amount of cash. Finally this impersonator (who turned out to be named Lawrence Irving Taylor) was apprehended in 1988 when he tried to buy a nearly $750,000 horse farm, using Greene's name.

Select Discography

Twenty Greatest Hits, Deluxe 7808. Budget cassette-only release.

GREENE, RICHARD (b. Beverly Hills, Calif., November 9, 1942)

Greene is a far-out fiddler who began his career in BLUEGRASS, moved into contemporary rock, and has returned to play a music that combines classical, jazz, folk, bluegrass, and rock influences.

Raised by a musical family in swanky Beverly Hills, Greene was a classically trained violinist who was named concertmaster of the Beverly Hills Orchestra while still in high school. When he enrolled at the University of California at Berkeley, he was introduced to folk music, and soon turned his attention to bluegrass, thanks to the influence of local fiddler Scotty Stoneman, son of legendary country star ERNEST STONEMAN.

In the mid-1960s Greene was hired by bluegrass legend BILL MONROE to play in his band; there he met PETER ROWAN, another young musician who had his sights on a new, more progressive style of bluegrass. Greene left Monroe to tour briefly with Jim Kweskin's Jug Band, which featured another Monroe alum, BILL KEITH, and then returned to California to form the rock band Seatrain with Andy Kulberg, formerly of The Blues Project; Rowan later joined the band as a vocalist/songwriter/guitarist.

In 1972, discouraged with the world of rock, Greene left Seatrain to work as a session musician in southern California. He performed with Rowan, DAVID GRISMAN, Keith, and Clarence White in the group MULESKINNER, one of the first progressive bluegrass "bands" (they performed together only once, for a TV special, and recorded one album, but they never really stayed together as a band). A year later he and Grisman formed the short-lived Great American Music Band, featuring blues guitarist Taj Mahal, which performed a mixture of different musics. Later in the 1970s he

performed in the first incarnation of Grisman's Quintet.

Greene recorded sporadically through the 1980s as the leader of various loosely formed groups, including his own Greene String Quartet, which performed everything from classical material to jazz and pop. His combination of bluegrass, rock, and jazz elements in his playing style was quite influential on younger progressive bluegrass fiddlers in the 1970s and 1980s, and he continues to enjoy a loyal, if small, following. During the late 1980s and early 1990s he worked primarily with his quartet, playing a mix of bluegrass, jazz, and classical-flavored originals. In the later 1990s he returned to playing bluegrass music, recording for the Rebel label.

Select Discography

Sales Tax Toddle, Rebel 1737. 1997 CD featuring primarily bluegrass tunes played by an all-star supporting cast.

GREENWOOD, LEE (b. Melvin L. G., near Sacramento, Calif., October 27, 1942)

One of the last of the glitzy Nashville singers, smoky-voiced Greenwood had his biggest success in the early-to-mid-1980s with a series of ballads culminating in the patriotic showstopper "God Bless the U.S.A."

Raised by his grandparents on a chicken farm outside of Sacramento, Lee was already playing sax and piano as a youngster in a local band called My Moonbeams. By 1958 he was performing with local country artist Chester Smith and then playing for DEL REEVES, serving as a backup musician on GUITAR, BANJO, and bass as well as sax. In 1962 he formed a pop-oriented band called Apollo, working primarily out of Las Vegas. By 1965 the band had signed with short-lived Paramount Records, under a new name, The Lee Greenwood Affair. The band dissolved without making much of a dent on the pop charts, leaving Greenwood working as a card dealer by day and lounge singer by night.

Larry McFadden, who worked as bandleader for MEL TILLIS, heard Greenwood in Vegas in 1979 and urged him to take a more country direction. After a few unsuccessful trips to Nashville to market demos, Greenwood finally landed a contract in 1981, scoring his first big hit with "It Turns Me Inside Out." It's said that his husky voice was caused by years of heavy vocalizing and overuse of his vocal cords; he was at first compared with KENNY ROGERS because of his frog-in-my-throat delivery. Soon, though, he got out of Rogers's shadow by scoring a series of hits, mostly in a schmaltzy-ballad mold, including "Ring on Her

Finger," "Time on Her Hands," "IOU," "Somebody's Gonna Love You," and "Going, Going, Gone." In 1984 he penned "The Wind Beneath My Wings," a big hit in England that later became a chart-topper stateside for Bette Midler after it was featured in her film *Beaches*.

After the 1985 release of "God Bless the U.S.A.," Greenwood concerts became increasingly patriotic, flag-waving affairs, with the overdone anthem a centerpiece of every performance. He began the 1990s with Capitol Records, but was soon forgotten amid the wave of new-country artists. By mid-decade he had stopped recording, but attempted a comeback on the small Free Falls label. In 2001 Greenwood made a radio comeback after the World Trade Center attack, when his song "God Bless the U.S.A." was once more in great demand.

Select Discography

Greatest Hits, MCA 5582.

GRIFFIN, REX (b. Alsie G., Gadsden, Ala., August 12, 1912–October 11, 1959)

Griffin was a bridge between the blues style of JIMMIE RODGERS and the HONKY-TONK of HANK WILLIAMS and ERNEST TUBB; in fact he helped launch Williams's career.

Griffin began performing professionally as one of many Jimmie Rodgers imitators, working radio stations throughout the South in the early 1930s. While performing on the air in Birmingham, he gained his stage name of "Rex" because the announcer found "Alsie" impossible to pronounce; Rex also had more of a COWBOY ring to it.

In 1935 Griffin was signed to the then-new Decca label, remaining with it for four years. Although none of his recordings were major hits, his own songs quickly entered many singers' repertoires, including 1936's upbeat "Everybody's Trying to Be My Baby" and 1937's classic WEEPER, "The Last Letter." This song was supposedly based on a suicide note that Griffin wrote after his wife left him; whether that was true or not, the stark realism of the lyric had immediate appeal, and the song was covered by countless performers.

In 1939 he recorded a song originated by the Southern blackface performer EMMETT MILLER, "Lovesick Blues." In turn he taught it to Hank Williams when the young singer was beginning his career (and often touring as a support act with Griffin). Williams later scored big imitating Griffin's vocal style on this number.

Despite his solid start as performer and songwriter, Griffin's career rapidly declined in the 1940s, due to his increasing alcoholism. During this time he was working radio out of Dallas, Texas, but his performances lacked the vitality and quality of his earlier work. By the 1950s he was pretty much forgotten, although his songs continued to live on. Old friend Ernest Tubb did much to champion his work, and EDDY ARNOLD had a hit with his "Just Call Me Lonesome" in 1955. Griffin died of alcohol-related problems in 1959.

Select Discography

Last Letter, Bear Family 159112. Three-CD set collecting all of Griffin's 1935–1946 recordings, including radio transcriptions and sixteen tunes by his brother, Buddy.

GRIFFITH, NANCI (b. Seguin, Tex., July 16, 1954)

Griffith is a Texas-based chanteuse/songwriter who has made some attempt to crack into the country market. With her quavering voice, quiet and intense stage presence, and confessional repertoire, Griffith would have been definitely "classified" as a folk, or at most folk-rock, artist in the 1960s or 1970s. Today she is often placed in the "country" rack for lack of a better category. She is one of those genre-bending artists who have been lumped into the "new-country" category, even though she has little in common with the other boot-wearin' stars of this genre.

Griffith was still working as a schoolteacher when she began issuing her music locally on her own label, starting with *There's a Light Beyond These Woods* in 1978 (she called her label B. F. Deal). The folk label Philo Records picked up her recordings in the early-to-mid-1980s; her haunting vocals and combination of original material and covers of other SINGER/SONGWRITERS made her a popular figure on the folk scene of the day. She was signed to MCA's country division in 1987, recording the LP *Lone Star State of Mind*, including her cover of "From a Distance," the Julie Gold ballad that was to be a hit for Bette Midler a few years later.

After a few commercially disappointing LPs aimed at the country market, MCA attempted to market Griffith to a pop audience, moving her to the Los Angeles division of the label. At about this time, ironically, new-country stars KATHY MATTEA and SUZY BOGGUSS had hits covering Griffith's songs, Mattea with "Love at the Five and Dime" and Bogguss with "Outbound Plane." In 1993 Griffith abandoned the pop sheen of her previous two releases to record an entire collection of covers of folk-rock standards, in homage to the singer/songwriters who influenced her most; the success of this collection inspired a second outing in 1997. Her production of new material slowed in the later 1990s, and she failed to find success among either country or more pop audiences. Some of her choices seemed odd, such as 1999's *Dust Bowl Symphony*, an attempt to wed her intimate songs with lush string accompaniments.

Griffith has drawn on influences beyond music, including the literature of Southern writers like Flannery O'Connor and Fannie Flagg. Some of her earlier albums were arranged almost like mini-novels, with each song forming a "chapter" in the overall story. For this reason her appeal tends to be strongest among an urban, intellectual audience, who probably were Joni Mitchell fans in the 1970s. This makes her one of the most unusual of all "country" artists, and may account for her limited success on her own in this field.

Select Discography

There's a Light Beyond These Woods, Philo 1097. Reissue of her first album, recorded live in 1977–1978.

Once in a Very Blue Moon, Philo 1096. Her 1984 breakthrough Nashville album produced by country folkie JIM ROONEY.

Lone Star State of Mind, MCA 31300. Her 1987 big-label debut.

Other Voices, Other Rooms, Elektra 61464. 1993 album of folkie standards, her most commercially successful to date.

GRISMAN, DAVID (b. D. Jay G., Hackensack, N.J., March 17, 1945)

Grisman is a BLUEGRASS MANDOLIN player who has created his own genre of music that he playfully calls "dawg music," a form of acoustic jazz.

Grisman began his career performing in the New York area with both traditional bluegrass musicians (RED ALLEN and Don Stover) and younger innovators (BILL KEITH). He formed The New York Ramblers in 1965 with banjoist Winnie Winston and Jerry and DEL MCCOURY on bass and guitar/vocals, respectively. Although the band did not issue an album during its short period of existence, they achieved a near-legendary status on both the FOLK-REVIVAL and bluegrass circuits. Grisman relocated to California in the late 1960s, joining with eccentric guitarist/vocalist/songwriter PETER ROWAN to form the folk-rock band Earth Opera, and then moved on to The Great American Music Band. In 1973 he was a member of MULESKINNER, a special band put together for a single album to perform traditional and progressive bluegrass that featured Rowan, hot guitarist Clarence White, fiddler RICHARD GREENE, and banjoist Bill Keith. He also did session work for many popular mid-1970s SINGER/SONGWRITERS.

In the mid-1970s Grisman was invited to record a traditional bluegrass album for Rounder Records, as a return to his roots performing this music. At about the same time, in 1976, he formed his first quintet, featuring TONY RICE (guitar), Darol Anger (fiddle), Todd Phillips (second mandolin), and Bill Amatneek (bass). The group sounded like an updated version of Django Reinhardt's and Stephane Grappelli's 1930s-era Quintet of the Hot Club of France, and performed Grisman's own jazz-influenced compositions. Their first album on the California-based Kaleidoscope label almost single-handedly launched what is now called "new acoustic music."

Grisman soon moved to A&M, and then Warner Brothers Records. Later versions of his quintet featured mandolinist Mike Marshall and whiz-kid stringbender MARK O'CONNOR (now one of Nashville's premier session players). He also recorded with his idol, Stephane Grappelli, and his more recent recordings show an even stronger jazz and blues influence than previous work. At the same time he continued to perform in traditional bluegrass settings, usually for one-time recording projects, and also formed an acoustic duo with head Grateful Deadman, Jerry Garcia.

Grisman founded the Acoustic Disc label to issue his own and other acoustic-oriented recordings in the early 1990s. The latest Grisman quintet features fiddler Joe Craven, flutist Matt Eakle, guitarist Rick Montgomery, and bassist Jim Kirwin. They have more of a light-jazz feel than previous Grisman groups. He has also recorded several albums of duets with musicians from various genres, including Tony Rice and jazz pianist Danny Zeitlin.

Grisman's mandolin playing tends to be light and highly melodic, rather than the guttural, heavy chord-chopping often heard in traditional bluegrass work. He also tends to avoid much use of vibrato, another trademark of bluegrass mandolin picking that is often overdone, particularly on slower numbers. Grisman's playing is energetic but not hard-driving like the work of BILL MONROE; instead the energy of the music comes through complex melodic variations and the excitement generated by this invention.

Select Discography

Early Dawg, Sugar Hill 3713. Compilation of previously unissued 1960s and early 1970s recordings.

Quintet, Kaleidoscope 5. This is the album that started it all, defining "dawg" music and launching one strand of "new acoustic" music.

Rounder Compact Disc, Rounder 610069. A return to his bluegrass roots; reissues the LP of similar name (Rounder 069).

DGQ 20, Acoustic Disc 20. Three-CD retrospective of the Grisman quintet, with live recordings drawn from its entire career.

GUITAR (c. 1850)

The American guitar is an instrument different from its Spanish forebears. Its history has been shaped by a combination of technological advances and new musical styles.

The common Spanish or "classical" guitar features a wide fingerboard, gut strings, a slotted peg head, and, most important, a fan-shaped bracing system under the instrument's wooden top, giving it a sweet sound; it dates back to the early nineteenth century. The American guitar has its roots in a group of talented Viennese instrument builders who developed a new way of building guitars. Most notably in 1833 a German immigrant named Christian Friedrich Martin began making instruments in New York City, moving six years later to Nazareth, Pennsylvania, where the company is still located.

Martin either developed or perfected a new form of bracing called an X-brace. This allowed for greater volume and, eventually, the introduction of steel strings (fan bracing will not support the increased tension that steel strings create on the face of a guitar). He also redesigned the guitar's body shape, exaggerating the lower bout (or half) of the instrument's body so that it was no longer symmetrical in appearance. By the late 1800s the Martin style had been copied by mass producers like Lyon and Healy in Chicago, and guitars made by the hundreds were available inexpensively through mail-order catalogs. Among the middle and upper classes in major cities, the instrument became popular among young ladies, and instruction books and pieces written for the instrument in this delicate style (called "parlor guitar," because the instrument was associated with the formal front room of many middle-class homes) proliferated.

It is difficult to point to a specific time period or musician who was responsible for introducing the guitar to country music. Certainly the instrument had found its way into the backwoods of American society as early as the 1860s. The image of the guitar-toting COWBOY is not entirely a work of fiction. Solo guitarists were soon finding a chair in bands; as the guitar entered the traditional BANJO-FIDDLE ensembles of the South, it flattened out modal melodies (because guitars are oriented toward standard, Western chordal accompaniment) and also gave the music increased power and drive. Early recording guitarists like RILEY PUCKETT and, of course, JIMMIE RODGERS helped popularize the instrument as the ideal accompaniment for the solo vocalist.

The second great technological innovation occurred from the 1920s through the 1940s. As a band instrument the guitar was hampered by its relative lack of projective power, the ability to cut through other instruments. Steel strings helped, but didn't answer the problem entirely. Martin developed a new body style it labeled the "Dreadnought," after the great battleship (the original Dreadnought model was custom-made by Martin, to be sold by the Ditson Company in the late 1910s). This squarer and larger-bodied instrument was an immediate success among country and BLUEGRASS musicians. Meanwhile, rival guitar makers like Gibson developed "Jumbo"-bodied guitars, which looked like regular guitars on steroids and were highly regarded by cowboy stars like GENE AUTRY.

Amplified instruments were the next logical step, although they were slow to win acceptance in country music circles. The first musicians to use amplification were the players of lap steel guitars in WESTERN SWING bands. They had to be heard over large brass sections and drums, so they had little choice but to turn to amplification. Next, HONKY-TONK singers like ERNEST TUBB began using electric guitars to cut through the noisy atmosphere of these tiny bars. Traditionalists were horrified, but could do little to stem the tide of the eventual amplification of all country instruments. CHET ATKINS helped popularize the smooth-sounding, jazz-influenced, hollow-bodied electrified guitar by working with the Gretsch Company on designing the Country Gentleman model of the early 1950s; meanwhile younger players like BUDDY HOLLY espoused the harder sound of the solid-bodied instruments designed by Leo Fender in the middle years of the decade.

The FOLK REVIVAL of the 1960s brought renewed interest in acoustic instruments, and Martin had its best sales year toward the end of the decade thanks to the popularity of folk-derived music. Today the line between acoustic and electric instruments has been blurred by the prevalence of built-in pickups on acoustic guitars and the increasing use of effects, such as reverb and chorusing, that used to be limited to electric instruments. But whether acoustic or electric, the guitar remains the primary instrument for all country stars, even if they just carry it as a prop.

GULLY JUMPERS (c. 1927–c. 1960; original lineup: Paul Warmack [leader; mdln, gtr, voc]; Charles Arrington [fdl]; Roy Hardison [bnj]; Bert Hutcherson [gtr])

Paul Warmack was born and raised in Goodlettesville, Tennessee, a farming community north of Nashville, and was established in the city at least as early as 1921, when he opened an auto-repair shop there. Blessed with an Irish tenor voice, he began performing as early as May 1927 on radio station WSM, the city's most powerful outlet. Warmack gathered a bunch of other local musicians—guitarist Hutcherson had previously worked with a popular band led by harmonica player DR. HUMPHREY BATE—to create his own band. The band made its GRAND OLE OPRY debut on June 30, 1927, under the name Paul Warmack and His Barn

Dance Orchestra. By December the group had earned the more rural-sounding Gully Jumpers moniker, and was off and running.

The band's most talented members were Warmack and Hutcherson. They performed separately as a duo on early-morning shows for WSM, earning the nickname The Early Birds. Hutcherson was an influential guitarist, giving lessons in Nashville, and performing on radio and at local events as a soloist. The band gained great popularity on the *Opry*, so not surprisingly they were among the groups recorded at the historic September–October 1928 sessions organized by Victor in Nashville. They recorded sentimental songs, featuring Warmack's warm vocals, as well as a number of instrumentals, including Oliver Stone's "Stone's Rag." (Oliver Stone was the lead fiddler for a rival group, The Possum Hunters; his "Stone's Rag" became a country favorite, later revived by Western Swing king BOB WILLS as "Lone Star Rag.")

In the early 1930s the Gully Jumpers' *Opry* segment was so popular that the station charged significantly more for advertisements during their performance. Nonetheless, they never recorded again after 1928, and although remaining on the *Opry* through the early 1960s, never had as wide a following as groups like CHARLIE POOLE's North Carolina Ramblers or THE SKILLET LICKERS. Warmack died in 1954, but the band continued, drawing on musicians associated with various other *Opry* string bands.

GUNTER, ARTHUR "HARDROCK" (b. Sidney Louis G., Jr., Birmingham, Ala., February 27, 1925)

Gunter was an early performer in what would become known as the ROCKABILLY style, as well as the composer of the COUNTRY-ROCK perennial "Baby, Let's Play House."

After finishing his education Gunter entered the music business at age twenty-one as a deejay; soon after, he was recording for a number of small labels. He worked for a while as a RUBE comedian under the name "Goofy Sid," and also played children's shows in the Birmingham area. The "Hardrock" nickname does not refer to his style but to a time when he was accidentally hit on the head by the trunk lid of an automobile; his fellow musicians marveled at his seemingly unfazed endurance, noting that his head was "hard as a rock," and the nickname stuck.

Gunter's 1950 small-label recording "Birmingham Bounce," an upbeat country-swing number, was successfully covered on the country charts by RED FOLEY and on the R&B charts by Amos Milburn. Gunter's follow-up record, "Gonna Dance All Night," even mentions the words "rock 'n' roll" in connection with the music, making it one of the earliest records to do so. Gunter also covered risqué blues numbers like "Sixty

Minute Man," forecasting the rockabilly style by nearly half a decade. After serving in the Army from 1951 to 1953, he returned to recording for MGM and then for Sun, as well as performing on radio out of Wheeling, West Virginia.

Despite his early prominence Gunter quickly faded into obscurity, emerging in the early 1960s with the Chubby Checker knockoff "Hillbilly Twist," and again in the early 1970s with a tribute album to HANK WILLIAMS. He performed sporadically through the 1990s, in Europe and the U.S., as part of the rockabilly revival.

Select Discography

I'll Give 'Em Rhythm, Hydra 27108. 1950s Decca and King recordings.

GUTHRIE, WOODY (b. Woodrow Wilson G., Okemah, Okla., July 14, 1912–October 3, 1967)

Guthrie was a topical SINGER/SONGWRITER whose songs have become favorites among FOLK REVIVALISTS. Guthrie's songs, from "This Land Is Your Land" to "Pastures of Plenty," have become American classics; he did much to popularize the talking blues; and he even worked as a COWBOY singer early in his career, penning one country classic, "Philadelphia Lawyer," later covered by singers from ROSE MADDOX to WILLIE NELSON.

Guthrie's family were pioneers in Oklahoma when it was still part of Indian Territory. His father ran a trading post and real-estate office, prospering during the first Oklahoma oil boom. The elder Guthrie was also a part-time guitarist and BANJO picker, and Guthrie's mother, Nora Belle Tanner, was a fine ballad singer. The young Guthrie grew up surrounded by music, including not only his family's singing and playing but also the music of Native Americans and African Americans, all of whom lived and worked in his hometown.

Guthrie's family life dissolved with the end of the real-estate boom in the mid-1920s, when his father took to heavy drinking. His mother began to show the symptoms of Huntington's chorea, a disease that would eventually lead to her institutionalization. His sister died in mysterious circumstances, in a fire accidentally started by her mother, who was slowly losing her coordination and her mental stability. By his early teens Woody had quit school and relocated to Texas, where he bummed around, taking odd jobs and living on and off with his father's half-brother in the small town of Pampa. He received a few guitar lessons from his relative, and the two played locally. He married Mary Jennings and took up work as a sign painter, still singing at night.

In the early 1930s disastrous dust storms swept through upper Texas and Oklahoma, the result of years of poor land management. Thousands of family farmers were ruined, and took to the road in search of better living conditions. Like many others Woody abandoned his home and traveled to California. There he began performing in a cowboy duo with Maxine Crissman, known as "Lefty Lou." The two had a popular Los Angeles-based radio show, performing the kind of Western/cowboy material that was popular at that time thanks to the horsy escapades of actor/singers like GENE AUTRY.

Through the mid-1930s, Woody traveled around much of the Southwest as an itinerant painter and singer. He was hired by the Works Progress Administration to memorialize the building of the Bonneville Dam in Oregon in 1937, writing a series of classic songs including "Roll on, Columbia." By the end of the decade he had settled in New York City, where he encountered performers like PETE SEEGER and other young members of the first folk revival. Their leftist political philosophy appealed to Guthrie, who had been radicalized by the suffering of rural Americans that he had experienced firsthand during the Depression. Guthrie's quick wit appealed to them, and his ability to compose a song on almost any topic at the drop of the hat (often by fitting new words to time-honored traditional melodies) made him a favorite performer. At this time he recorded his famous *Dust Bowl Ballads* for RCA, as well as lengthy sessions organized by Alan Lomax for the Library of Congress. Although Guthrie's commercial recordings were not terribly successful at the time, they resurfaced in the 1950s and early 1960s during the next folk revival.

In the early 1940s Guthrie performed with a loose-knit group known as the Almanac Singers, along with Seeger, Lee Hays, and Millard Lampell. He supplied the group with many of their popular songs, including "Union Maid," that encouraged workers to fight unfair management practices and unionize.

After serving in World War II, Guthrie settled in Brooklyn, New York, with his new wife, a modern dancer named Marjorie Mazia. However, symptoms of Huntington's chorea were already manifesting themselves, making his behavior increasingly erratic. Guthrie continued to record and perform through the early 1950s, often playing with Cisco Houston, until his health deteriorated to the point that he had to be hospi-

talized. By the early 1960s, when he was a legend among younger singer/songwriters like BOB DYLAN, he was confined to a hospital bed and unable to perform.

Guthrie's contributions to American popular music are immense. He never tried to hide his Southwestern roots, letting his nasal twang and Okie accent shine through his singing (in fact, he may have intentionally heightened these qualities to try to appeal to an urban audience as an "authentic" folk performer). His simple guitar accompaniments, appropriations of popular tunes, and songs that addressed topical issues simply and directly greatly expanded the possibilities for popular singer/songwriters. The young Bob Dylan was virtually a Guthrie clone; but Guthrie's influence has also been felt by country singer/songwriters, from the OUTLAWS of the 1970s through today's more progressive country writers. Guthrie showed that songs could be both topical and popular, and that a songwriter could be his own best interpreter, even if his musical skills were not great.

His brother Jack (b. Leon Gerry G., Olive, Okla., November 13, 1915–January 15, 1948), a cowboy-styled performer in California, wrote the classic song "Oklahoma Hills" with Woody; severely injured in World War II, he never fully recovered, and his career was forgotten in the wake of his older brother's success. Woody's son, Arlo (b. July 10, 1947, New York City), a prominent performer on the folk-rock circuit since the late 1960s, is famous for his half-recited, half-sung comic opus "Alice's Restaurant."

Select Discography

Columbia River Collection, Rounder 1036. Recordings made in the late 1930s for the Works Progress Administration that were never previously available.

Dust Bowl Ballads, BMG 57839. Reissue of Guthrie's RCA recordings.

Library of Congress Recordings, Rounder 1041/1042/1043. Three-CD collection of recordings made by Alan Lomax for the Archive of Folksong in 1940.

Struggle, Smithsonian/Folkways 40025. Late 1940s recordings, commissioned by MOSES ASCH, on political themes.

Asch Recordings, 1–4, Smithsonian/Folkways 40112. Four-CD set collecting 105 recordings, made by Moses Asch, in the mid-to-late 1940s. Also available as individual CDs.

H

HAGGARD, MERLE (b. M. Ronald H., Bakersfield, Calif., April 6, 1937)

The mythic life of Merle Haggard—born in grinding poverty, a stint in prison, rehabilitation and success achieved through hard work and harder livin'—is as much responsible for his success as his songs. Like WOODY GUTHRIE, Haggard is an Okie who took his real-life experiences and molded them into his music. Also like Guthrie he has been uncompromising in producing records which reflect that experience. Unlike Guthrie, though, Haggard has enjoyed great success on the country charts, nearly ruling the Top Ten from the mid-1960s through the mid-1970s.

Haggard's parents were displaced Okies from the small town of Checotah (halfway between McAlester and Muskogee); like many others, they were driven off their land by the ravaging dust storms of the mid-1930s and moved west to California in search of a better life. They found living conditions tough there, and jobs few; the family was living in a converted boxcar when Haggard was born. They fared better after Merle's father got a job with the Santa Fe Railroad, but this brief period of prosperity ended with his premature death when Merle was nine.

Haggard attributes his troubled teenage years to his father's passing. He became difficult and unruly, constantly running away from home. He ended up serving time in reform school, and then, when he reached age seventeen, ninety days in prison for stealing. Merle hung with a tough crowd, and when he was released, he was soon in trouble again. One night Haggard and a drunken friend tried to break into a restaurant that they thought was closed; it turned out to be earlier than the boys thought, and the owner greeted them at the back door just after they had removed the hinges to break in. Haggard spent two and a half years in prison following his arrest. While in prison he heard JOHNNY CASH perform, which renewed his interest in country music and his desire to write songs that would reflect his own experiences.

Upon his release in early 1960, Haggard was determined to turn his life around. He began working for his brother, who was an electrician, while performing at night in local bars and clubs. In 1963 he was hired by WYNN STEWART to play in his backup band in Vegas; there Fuzzy Owen heard him play and signed

Merle Haggard, c. 1995. Photo: Raeanne Rubenstein

him to his Tally record label. Haggard had his first solo hit with "Sing Me a Sad Song," followed by a minor hit with a duet with BONNIE OWENS on "Just Between the Two of Us." (Owens was married to BUCK OWENS at the time, although she would soon leave him to marry Haggard and join his road show.) 1964 brought his first Top 10 hit, "(My Friends Are Gonna Be) Strangers," written by BILL ANDERSON, which also gave Merle the name for his backup band.

Haggard was signed to Capitol Records by producer KEN NELSON, who was in charge of the label's growing country-music and folk rosters. His first hit for the label, "I'm a Lonesome Fugitive," written by Casey and LIZ ANDERSON, defined the classic Haggard stance: a man who has been in trouble with the law but now rues his rough-and-rowdy earlier days (although still subject to temptation). More prison ballads followed, including Merle's own compositions "Branded Man" and his first #1 hit, "Sing Me Back Home," a true story of a man who was about to be executed and asked to hear, one last time, a country song to remind him of his youth. Although this song literally drips with sentiment, Haggard's dry-as-dust delivery and unquestioned tough-guy credentials made it (and many more like it) instantly credible to his audience. His 1968 hit, "Mama Tried," told of the difficulty his mother had in raising him and expressed regret for his difficult teenage years.

Unlike many other country artists of the day, who were often backed with tons of strings and smothering vocal choruses, Haggard formed a lean, tough backup band he named The Strangers, after his 1964 hit. The original band included Roy Nichols (lead guitar), Norm Hamlet (steel guitar), Bobby Wayne (guitar), Dennis Hormak (bass), and Biff Adam (drums). The band's pared-down sound became a hallmark of Haggard's recordings, and he also wrote songs with its members, including Nichols and drummer Roy Burris (who replaced Adam in 1968).

Haggard gained his greatest fame for his 1969 recording of "Okie from Muskogee," a song that enraged hippies and the antiwar movement while it cemented Haggard's position in mainstream, conservative country circles. Haggard was inspired when drummer Burris spotted a road sign for Muskogee during a tour through Oklahoma; the drummer commented, "I bet the citizens of Muskogee don't smoke marijuana." The song inspired many loony parodies, including Pat Sky's immortal remake (with the ending of the first verse changed to "Love me, or I'll punch you in the mouth") and The Youngbloods' "Hippie from Olema." Haggard feels his message was misinterpreted, although he followed the song with the equally jingoistic "The Fightin' Side of Me," full of old-time American bravado, and began hanging out with President Richard Nixon.

One of Haggard's heroes from his youth was BOB WILLS, who regularly performed in southern California at the time. So great was his admiration for Wills that Haggard began to rigorously practice the FIDDLE, seeking to emulate the swinging style of Wills's best lead fiddlers. He paid homage to the master fiddler in 1970 with an album of Wills's standards, recorded with many of Wills's then-retired sidemen, including mandolinist TINY MOORE, who soon joined Haggard's traveling show. It was quite a gutsy move to record this decidedly "noncommercial" album, showing Haggard's considerable clout at the height of his career. (Six years later he had a hit with Wills's "Cherokee Maiden," arranged by Moore.)

By the mid-1970s Haggard's life and career were in disarray; his marriage to Bonnie Owens was on the rocks, and he broke with his longtime record label, Capitol, in 1977. He took a brief break from the music business, hinting that he would no longer perform, although he quickly reemerged as a performer and recording artist (with ex-wife Bonnie still singing in his show). He recorded a duet, "The Bull and the Bear," in 1978 with LEONA WILLIAMS (who also cowrote the song); the two were married soon after. (The marriage lasted only until 1983.)

Haggard's recording career has been more sporadic since the 1980s. He had his greatest success in 1983 when he recorded a duo album with WILLIE NELSON, yielding the #1 hit and title track, "Pancho and Lefty" (written by Texan TOWNES VAN ZANDT, and introduced to the pair by Haggard's daughter). Since then he has had occasional chart hits while continuing to tour with one of the tightest country revues on the road, stubbornly performing his own brand of country balladry. He has also had a few roles on TV and in films, most notably appearing in Clint Eastwood's *Bronco Billy*, which yielded the 1980 hit "Barroom Buddies," a duet with the equally grizzled actor that really made his day.

In 1990 Haggard moved to Curb Records, who tried to repromote his career. In 1994 he had his last chart single, "In My Next Life," although it only grazed the Top 50. In the late 1990s he signed with the punk label Ansi/Epitaph, releasing an acoustic-flavored album, *If I Could Only Fly*, in 2000. The following autumn came *Roots, Vol. 1*, spotlighting songs by LEFTY FRIZZELL and including Norm Stephens, Frizzell's original guitarist, in the backup band.

The winner of many awards, Haggard was elected to the Songwriters Hall of Fame in 1977 and the Country Music Hall of Fame in 1994.

Select Discography

Merle Haggard, Capitol 93181. Part of the Capitol Collector's Series, this CD gives a good overview of his career from the early 1960s through the 1970s.

More of the Best, Rhino 70917. Programmed to complement the Capitol release, this includes rarer tracks from Haggard's oeuvre.

Same Train: Different Time, Bear Family 15740. Reissues Haggard's wonderful tribute to JIMMIE RODGERS, along with some additional tracks not originally included.

Merle Haggard's Greatest Hits, MCA 5386. Budget-priced compilation of 1980s recordings.

Pancho & Lefty, Epic 37958. Reissue of Haggard's famed duet album with Willie Nelson.

If I Could Only Fly, Ansi/Epitaph 86593. 2000 acoustic album, his best in over a decade.

HALE, THERON, AND DAUGHTERS (Theron Hale, b. Pikeville, Tenn., 1883–January 29, 1954 [fdl]; Mamie Ruth Hale [fdl, mdln]; Elizabeth Hale [pno])

Fiddler Theron Hale was of another time and place; he was born in 1883 in rural Pikeville, Tennessee, 100 miles southeast of Nashville. His father and uncle were both active in the Baptist Church and noted SHAPE-NOTE singers. Hale took up the FIDDLE and BANJO at an early age, playing as an avocation. After attending religious school in Johnson City, Tennessee, Hale married and settled in his hometown, working as a farmer. For a brief period he moved his family to Iowa, but by 1915 he had returned to Tennessee, settling in Nashville, where he initially worked on a dairy farm. When he first played on THE GRAND OLE OPRY, he was a traveling salesman for a sewing machine company.

Hale's two daughters were highly educated: Mamie Ruth was classically trained on the violin and would eventually teach at Vanderbilt, and Elizabeth taught music in the Nashville schools. From childhood they had played with their father at home. Elizabeth later recalled that sometime in 1926 they were approached by GEORGE HAY, who was scouting for talent for the new *Opry* program. The family band—Ruth played a second, alto part to her father's lead, and both were accompanied by Elizabeth's piano—had a distinctive sound, much less ragged around the edges than many of their more rural contemporaries. This made them a successful addition to the *Opry*, where they were initially featured on a monthly basis from 1927 to 1929, and then as regulars every week until 1934, when the band broke up.

Their signature tunes were nineteenth-century parlor favorites—not surprising, given the origins of the group. "Listen to the Mocking Bird" was a particular hit. The band's twin-fiddle harmonies caught the ear of audiences, who were unused to such sophisticated music making. Because of their popularity they were included in the 1928 Victor sessions held at Nashville,

recording eight numbers, among them "Listen to the Mocking Bird." The other numbers focused on late-nineteenth-century waltzes and even an adaptation of a ragtime piece.

Theron Hale apparently was also a talented banjo player, although he rarely played the instrument in public. He is said to have taught the instrument to his nephew, Homer Davenport, who later recorded and performed in and around Chattanooga in the 1920s and 1930s. Davenport played in a three-finger, picked style—quite a novelty for the time—and Hale may have also used this style. Hale's banjo was inherited by SAM McGEE after his death.

By 1934 Mamie Ruth had married and left Nashville. Tired of returning for the *Opry*, she dropped out of the band. Theron and Elizabeth tried to continue with other musicians, but no one could replace the close, harmonized fiddle part that Ruth had provided. Although the band ended, Theron continued to fiddle locally, working in the 1940s with Sam McGee. In the early 1950s the duo made some local recordings for use in teaching square dancing. Theron also operated a used-piano business for a while. He died in 1954.

HALL, CONNIE (b. Walden, Ky., June 24, 1929)

Country singer championed by promoter HAROLD "PAPPY" DAILY who was most successful during the early-through-mid-1960s.

Hall was born in Kentucky but raised in Cincinnati, Ohio. As a teenager she got a job in a local music shop managed by singer JIMMIE SKINNER. After hearing her on local radio, Skinner hired her to perform on his popular radio show broadcast out of Newport, Kentucky, beginning in 1954. She also cut her first recording as a duet with Skinner, "We've Got Things in Common," in 1957.

A year later she came under the wing of Houston, Texas-based promoter/producer Harold "Pappy" Daily. Daily produced her first solo recordings, issued by Mercury, including her first major chart hit, "The Bottle or Me" which went Top 20 in 1960.

Following that success Hall switched to Decca, and had a series of chart hits for the next four years, mostly in the suffering female style that was popular at the time. Among her bigger hits were 1960's "Poison in Your Hand," "Sleep, Baby, Sleep" from the next year, and 1963's "Fool Me Once," her last country chart hit. Daily enticed her to return to working with him at his new label, Musicor, in 1964, but although the topics of her songs and style of her performances stayed the same, the hits dried up.

By the early 1970s Hall had retired from music making to her native Kentucky.

HALL, ROY (b. R. Davis H., Waynesville, N.C., January 6, 1907–May 16, 1943)

Guitarist-vocalist Roy Hall led The Blue Ridge Entertainers, one of the finest of the transitional bands that transformed old-time country music into BLUEGRASS.

Hall, from a large musical family, was raised in western North Carolina. Like many from the region he began working at a young age in the local textile mills, but continued to play music on the side with his family. Inspired by the success of other brother acts, Roy and his brother Jay Hugh (1910–1972) formed a duo called The Hall Brothers in the mid-1930s; they recorded for Bluebird from 1937 to 1939.

When the act dissolved, Roy formed his first version of The Blue Ridge Entertainers, featuring noted fiddler Tommy Magness. The tonic/soft drink company Dr. Pepper became the group's first and only sponsor when they were hired to perform on station WAIR out of Winston-Salem, North Carolina. Longtime country producer ART SATHERLEY signed them to the ARC family of dimestore labels in 1938; among their first recordings were "Wabash Cannonball" and "Lonesome Dove," both of which became country and bluegrass standards.

A year later the group expanded with the addition of the Hall Twins—no relation—and moved to a bigger radio market, hosting *The Virginia Jamboree* out of Roanoke, Virginia. They enjoyed their greatest popularity there, and soon had so many bookings that Roy had to form two bands to meet the demand. Brother Jay Hugh came back into the fold in 1940. Also members of one or another version of the group during this period were young singer/guitarist JIM EANES and soon-to-be-actor Andy Griffith.

On their radio broadcasts the group performed a repertoire that straddled old-time country, pre-bluegrass, and even COWBOY and WESTERN SWING material. This potent combination would come together very quickly in the late 1940s to form the basis of BLUEGRASS music, and many of the early bluegrass acts, including BILL MONROE and THE STANLEY BROTHERS, covered Hall's recordings.

In 1940–1941 the group returned to the recording studio, this time cutting discs for RCA's budget Bluebird label. Again the songs they recorded would become favorites in bluegrass circles, including "I Wonder Where You Are Tonight" and Magness's fiddle tune, "Natural Bridge Blues."

By 1942, however, the band was decimated by the draft. A year later, Hall died in an automobile accident. After the war his brothers Jay Hugh and Rufus (b. 1921) attempted to revive the band but were unsuccessful. In the late 1970s County Records reissued a number of Hall's best recordings, reintroducing the group to the old-time and bluegrass revival community.

HALL, TOM T. (b. Thomas H., Olive Hill, Ky., May 25, 1936)

A SINGER/SONGWRITER best known for his narrative songs, Hall wrote the megahit "Harper Valley P.T.A.," recorded by JEANNIE C. RILEY in 1968.

Not surprisingly for a songwriter who loves to tell a story, Hall is a preacher's son who began playing music when he was eight years old, on an old Martin guitar that his dad gave him. He hooked up with an older local musician named Clayton Delaney (immortalized in his 1971 hit "The Year Clayton Delaney Died"), who impressed the young musician with his stories of his successful band that featured shirts with "puffed sleeves that glowed in the dark," according to Hall. Hall's mother died when he was eleven, and three years later his father was hurt in a gun accident. Hall had to quit school, and began working in a local garment factory, a job he held for a year and a half.

Hall began his professional career when he was sixteen, as an announcer for a small-time local promoter who had a traveling movie theater mounted on the roof of his car! As an added attraction Hall put together his first band, The Kentucky Travelers, to perform before the movies were shown. They were hired to play on the local radio station out of Morehead, Kentucky, sponsored by the Polar Bear Flour Company, for whom Tom wrote a theme song. After the band broke up, Hall remained at the station as a disc jockey.

In 1957 Hall joined the Army and was stationed in Germany, where he performed over the Armed Forces Radio Network and at NCO clubs. He began writing comic songs, including "3,000 Gallons of Beer" and "36 Months of Loneliness," commenting on his experience in the service. In 1961 he was discharged and returned to radio work in Morehead, as well as opening a small grocery store. He performed briefly with another band, The Technicians, out of Indiana, while moving from station to station as a deejay.

Hall's big break came in 1963 when country singer JIMMY NEWMAN recorded his song "DJ for a Day," which went to #1 on the country charts. His song "Mad" was a hit for DAVE DUDLEY the next year, encouraging Hall to relocate to Nashville. Hall was not anxious to record himself, but eventually was talked into recording his first single, "I Washed My Face in the Morning Dew," which was a minor 1967 hit.

1968 was the banner year for the songwriter. Jeannie C. Riley's recording of "Harper Valley P.T.A." sold 6 million copies; Hall compared the experience to "walking down the street and suddenly bending over and finding $100,000." His own recording career soon took off, his hits beginning with 1969's "A Week in the County Jail" and continuing to "Old Dogs, Children and Watermelon Wine" and "Ravishing Ruby," both from 1973. He recorded an album of BLUEGRASS standards in the mid-1970s, scoring a hit with Tony Hazard's "Fox on the Run," which soon became the number most played to death by bluegrass bands, amateur and professional.

Hall's aw-shucks backwoodsy narratives were immensely popular through the mid-1970s, but then his popularity waned. He made his last significant recordings with banjoist Earl Scruggs in 1982, on the album *The Storyteller and The Banjoman*. Although he had further hits in the mid-1980s with "Everything from Jesus to Jack Daniels" and "Famous in Missouri," Hall mostly coasted on his reputation.

Hall branched out during this period, recording two albums of children's songs, and also hosting the syndicated show *Pop Goes the Country*, out of Nashville, from 1980 to 1983. His commercial endorsement activity ranged from a longtime relation with Tyson chicken products to promoting pickup trucks. He has published several collections of fiction, inspirational writings, and "how-to" books on songwriting. Hall has continued to record and perform, signing briefly with Mercury Records in the mid-1990s, but has not enjoyed the same level of success as in his heyday.

Hall took the tradition of country balladry to new and contemporary heights in his best compositions. He was unafraid to attack the small-mindedness of traditional country society, and championed the rights of the "little guy" against the system. Although he wrote some jingoistic songs in the mid-1960s and early 1970s in support of the Vietnam War (including the rabble-rousing "Mama, Tell Them What We're Fighting For"), in general Hall's sympathies are with the downtrodden. In songs like "America the Ugly" and "The Promise and the Dream," he attacks a country that allows its people to go hungry and poor.

Select Discography

Greatest Hits, Vol. 1, Mercury 824143, and *Greatest Hits, Vol. 2*, Mercury 824144. Cassette-only, two-volume overview of his Mercury years. (Also, strangely enough, packaged on a single cassette as Mercury 810462; go figure.)
Ballad of Forty Dollars/Homecoming, Bear Family 15631. His first two Mercury LPs reissued on a single CD.
I Witness Life/100 Children, Bear Family 15658. His third and fourth Mercury LPs.

HAMBLEN, STUART (b. Carl S. H., Kellyville, Tex., October 20, 1908–March 8, 1989)
Hamblen started out as a 1930s COWBOY singer and film actor, then became a mainstream country song-

smith, and finally "saw the light" and became a GOSPEL star, in many ways tracing the increasingly conservative trends of country music from the 1930s to the 1960s.

Raised in rural Texas, Hamblen was naturally introduced to cowboy lore and legend, participating in amateur rodeo events as a teenager. He enrolled in a teachers college in Abilene, planning a career as a schoolmaster, but soon his love of music swayed him to switch majors. When he was twenty, he traveled to Camden, New Jersey, where the studios for Victor records were located, becoming one of the first performers to record cowboy material. Soon after, he headed for southern California, and soon was performing on the radio on a series of colorful cowboyesque programs, including *The Covered Wagon Jubilee*. His backup band was a swinging ensemble he called THE BEVERLY HILL BILLIES (a name borrowed by TV sitcom producers in the 1960s). His cowboy compositions included the popular "My Mary" and "Texas Plains," both issued in the mid-1930s.

In the 1930s and 1940s Hamblen was a popular "heavy," appearing as the bad guy in many of the low-budget horse flicks that featured white-hat stars ROY ROGERS and GENE AUTRY. He also developed a heavy thirst for liquor, giving himself a bad-boy reputation on screen and off.

After World War II, when the cowboy craze gave way to HONKY-TONK music, Hamblen wrote some of his best-loved songs, including 1949's "But I'll Go Chasin' Women" and "(Remember Me) I'm the One Who Loves You," from a year later, a big hit in a cover version by ERNEST TUBB. 1949 was a banner year in Hamblen's life for another reason: he attended a Billy Graham crusade and was "born again," giving up alcohol and eventually giving up secular music making as well.

Hamblen's biggest 1950s hit was the sentimental "This Old House," issued in 1954; Rosemary Clooney successfully covered it in the same year for the pop charts. A year later HANK SNOW had a hit with Hamblen's "Mainliner." However, Hamblen was soon producing more gospel material, including biblical tub-thumpers like "Open Up Your Heart and Let the Sun Shine In," "Be My Shepherd," and the colorfully titled "When the Lord Picks Up the Phone" (let's hope he's not calling collect!).

Hamblen married in the 1950s, and he and his wife hosted a Los Angeles-based country music TV show for a while. He retired from performing during the 1960s, but returned to radio at the invitation of a local station to begin a gospel hour that was eventually given the colorful title *The Cowboy Church of the Air*. This show, featuring Hamblen's homespun philosophizing, was syndicated and became quite popular in the 1970s.

A talented horseman, Hamblen appeared through the 1970s in the annual Rose Bowl Parade.

Select Discography

I Gotta Feeling, Roots of Country 211011. Gospel recordings of unknown vintage.

HAMILTON, GEORGE IV (b. Matthews, N.C., July 19, 1937)

Hamilton has been most successful bringing American country and folk-rock to foreign audiences, particularly in Canada and England, and on the Continent. Like many 1950s stars he began recording in the teen-pop mold before moving into country and then contemporary folk.

Born and raised in central North Carolina just outside the commercial center of Winston-Salem, Hamilton first fell in love with country music thanks to the popular COWBOY flicks shown at the local movie theaters. He formed a pop-country band in high school and, through producer Orville Campbell, met the famous COUNTRY-ROCK songwriter JOHN D. LOUDERMILK, who gave him his "A Rose and a Baby Ruth" to record in 1956. The song raced up the pop charts, and Hamilton found himself a teenybopper star. For three years he performed with the likes of THE EVERLY BROTHERS, BUDDY HOLLY, and Gene Vincent.

After his pop career fizzled, he relocated to Nashville in 1959, signing with RCA Records to record mainstream country material. He had a couple of minor hits between 1959 and 1963, including "If You Don't Know, I Ain't Gonna Tell You," "Ft. Worth, Dallas or Houston," and his #1 country hit, 1963's "Abilene." In the early 1960s he joined THE GRAND OLE OPRY, remaining with that institution throughout the decade.

In 1965, while touring Canada, Hamilton met young SINGER/SONGWRITER Gordon Lightfoot, who introduced him to other new Canadian songwriters, including IAN AND SYLVIA, Leonard Cohen, and Joni Mitchell. Hamilton became a champion of their material, recording several albums devoted to these new styled folksingers. Although the material did not fare well on the conservative country charts of the day, Hamilton was well received in Canada and then in England.

In 1971, tired of the commercialism of Nashville, Hamilton retired from the *Opry* and moved back to his home state of North Carolina. From there he began broadcasting a show for Canadian state television, focusing on singers and songwriters from north of the border; this show was syndicated around the world, influencing country music fans in the South Pacific (New Zealand, Australia), the Far East (Hong Kong), and South Africa. Hamilton also continued his peripa-

tetic touring, being the first country star to perform behind the Iron Curtain, as well as in many other far-flung corners of the globe.

In the late 1970s Hamilton tried to revive his stateside career, signing with Dot, but he remains known and loved primarily abroad. During the 1980s he switched to GOSPEL material, which he continues to record and perform. His son, George Hamilton V, had a single chart success in 1988, and has toured with his father.

Select Discography

1954–65, Bear Family 15773. Six-CD set of all of his recordings from this period, for the diehard fan.
Country Boy, BMG 39340. Reissue of budget-priced hits collection from his RCA years.

HANCOCK, BUTCH (b. George Norman H., Lubbock, Tex., July 12, 1945)

Along with boyhood friends JOE ELY and JIMMIE DALE GILMORE, Hancock is a semilegendary, eccentric Texas SINGER/SONGWRITER. Born and raised in BUDDY HOLLY's hometown, Butch heard FIDDLE and square-dance music as a youth; he also attended junior high and high school with Ely and Gilmore. The trio would form the seminal group The Flatlanders to showcase their own material around 1970; two years later they recorded a "legendary" album for a tiny Texas label that quickly disappeared (it was reissued in England in 1980, and ten years later by Rounder Records in the U.S.).

After studying architecture in college, Hancock began a sporadic solo career while pursuing an interest in photography. He recorded several albums on his own label from the 1970s through the mid-1980s, then semiretired from music making. In the early 1990s two anthologies of these homemade recordings were issued by Sugar Hill Records, which led to Hancock's return to touring and recording.

Since then he has veered between his own minimalist recordings (often taped live, featuring just him and his [sometimes out-of-tune] guitar, and available only on cassette) and more heavily produced albums. He has also recorded a duet album with Gilmore. The Flatlanders "reunited" to record a song for *The Horse Whisperer* (1997) sound track; they subsequently played some tour dates around the country.

Hancock's songs share the wry sense of humor and generally skewed outlook on life that mark the works of the entire Austin, Texas, school. He is best known via his songs covered by other artists, including EMMYLOU HARRIS ("If You Were a Bluebird") and THE TEXAS TORNADOS ("West Texas Waltz"). Hancock is neither a stunning vocalist nor a great guitarist; in the tradition of BOB DYLAN he makes the most of his limited capabilities. As with Dylan, listeners find him either captivating or irritating.

Select Discography

Eats Away the Night, Sugar Hill 1048. Hancock's most "produced" album, an attempt to earn mainstream success.

Own & Own, Sugar Hill 1036/*Own the Way Over Here*, Sugar Hill 1038. Compilations of earlier recordings released by Hancock.

No 2 Alike, self-produced. Fourteen-cassette (only) issue of an entire week's performances at Austin's Cactus Café; Hancock never repeated a song during the entire week.

HARGROVE, LINDA (b. L. Ann H., Tallahassee, Fla., February 3, 1949)

Hargrove was a country SINGER/SONGWRITER/guitarist of the mid-1970s who was considerably ahead of her time; by the time country caught up with her melding of rock, blues, and country styles, she had become "born again" and retired from music making.

During her Florida childhood Hargrove was unaware of country music; instead, pop and rock were her first loves, and by her teenage years she was playing GUITAR and writing her own brand of pop songs. However, BOB DYLAN's *Nashville Skyline* (1969) showed her the possibility in country styles, and she traveled to Nashville to try to make it as a songwriter. While cutting a demo session for Epic in the early 1970s, she met producer/pedal steel guitarist PETE DRAKE, who became her champion and introduced her to many of the more progressive figures in country and rock music, including singer/songwriter MIKE NESMITH, who signed her to his short-lived Countryside label (the album she recorded was never released after Countryside was dropped by its parent company, Elektra/Asylum). Other COUNTRY-ROCKERS like Leon Russell recorded her material; her big break came in 1975 when JOHNNY RODRIGUEZ had a hit with her song "Just Get Up and Close the Door." She had a minor solo hit a year later with "Love Was (Just Once Around the Dance Floor)," followed by a couple of singles. In 1978 she was "born again," and turned her back on secular singing and songwriting to pursue her mission of spreading the GOSPEL, recording under her married name of Linda Bartholomew. Faced with health problems in the early 1980s, she slowed down touring and recording, and has not appeared on record since 1987, although she made an attempt at a comeback during the later 1990s.

HARMAN, BUDDY (b. Murrey M. H., Nashville, Tenn., December 23, 1928)

Harman was one of the best-known session drummers of the 1950s and 1960s in Nashville, part of the "A Team" of session musicians who defined the NASHVILLE SOUND. He was also the first house drummer for THE GRAND OLE OPRY radio show.

Harman's parents were both amateur musicians. His mother played drums with his dad's dance band. Through her he met several jazz drummers when they passed through the city, most notably the showmen Buddy Rich and Gene Krupa, both early influences. Harman honed his skills during his high-school years, working with the school band, and then enlisted in the Navy, where he continued to play drums. On his release in 1949 he spent three years in Chicago furthering his drum studies at the Roy Knapp School of Percussion.

Harman returned to Nashville in 1952. Soon he was playing regularly around town, and began working sessions. Two years later CARL SMITH brought him to the *Opry* as part of his accompanying group; he was forced to perform behind the curtain (so as not to offend the country audience). Soon, though, the *Opry* management allowed Harman to appear on stage, but only with a snare drum. By the late 1950s he had established himself among country producers as a reliable and tasteful drummer through his work with artists like RAY PRICE. He played on numerous hit recordings, including JOHNNY CASH's "Ring of Fire," PATSY CLINE's "Crazy," and BRENDA LEE's "I'm Sorry." Soon Harman was also working with the nascent rock artists in Nashville, including THE EVERLY BROTHERS, JERRY LEE LEWIS, Johnny and DORSEY BURNETTE, and ROY ORBISON. His work with these stars has made him as much of a legend among fans of early ROCKABILLY as among country fans.

By the early 1960s Harman was said to be working 600 sessions a year. He appeared on almost all of Elvis's film sound-track recordings made after Elvis returned to civilian life in 1959. He also worked with other pop artists, including Simon and Garfunkel ("The Boxer") and Ringo Starr (the *Beaucoups of Blues* album). Nonetheless, his meat and potatoes continued to be country music, and he worked with dozens of Nashville artists through the 1960s and early 1970s.

Harman has worked less frequently since then, although he continues to perform and record. In 1991 he returned to the *Opry* as house drummer. At last count he claims to have appeared on over 17,000 recordings.

HARRELL, KELLY (b. Crockett K. H., Drapers Valley, Va., September 13, 1889–July 9, 1942)

Harrell was a popular old-time vocalist of the 1920s who recorded with a subdued string-band accompaniment, somewhat in the style of his contemporary, CHARLIE POOLE.

Harrell was discovered by legendary country producer RALPH PEER when he was living and working in Fries, Virginia, as a mill hand. Like VERNON DALHART he had a semitrained voice with clear enunciation that made him instantly appealing to rural audiences. He began recording in 1924 and continued through the rest of the decade, usually accompanied by FIDDLE (played by Posey Rorer, who also performed with banjoist Charlie Poole), GUITAR, and sometimes BANJO, in the relaxed string-band style of the upper South.

Harrell recorded many traditional songs, including the popular late-nineteenth-century ballad "Charles Guiteau," about the assassin of President James Garfield, and composed "Away Out on the Mountain," later covered by JIMMIE RODGERS, and "The Story of the Mighty Mississippi," a hit for ERNEST "POP" STONEMAN. Like many other early country artists Harrell received little (if anything) in the way of royalties from these successes, and his career ended when the Depression knocked the wind out of country music recording. He returned to mill work in the 1930s and died of a heart attack in 1942.

Select Discography

Complete Record Works, 1 & 2: 1925–29, Document 8026/8027.

HARRIS, EMMYLOU (b. Birmingham, Ala., April 2, 1947)

A pioneering COUNTRY-ROCK vocalist of the 1970s who made a successful transition into mainstream country in the 1980s, Harris has been an influence on many new-country female vocalists, including KATHY MATTEA, SUZY BOGGUSS, and MARY CHAPIN CARPENTER.

Harris came from a solid, middle-class background. She attended the University of North Carolina and formed a folk duo there with a classmate. In 1969 Harris hit the road for Greenwich Village, then the mecca for folk-styled singers, and recorded her first solo LP on the tiny Jubilee label. In the early 1970s she moved to California and hooked up with GRAM PARSONS, the influential country-rocker who had helped transform THE BYRDS into a more country-oriented group and also founded THE FLYING BURRITO BROTHERS. The two became romantically and musically involved, and Harris added harmony vocals to Parsons's solo LPs and performances, her clear, bell-like tones perfectly complementing his lived-in lead vocals.

After Parsons's death from a drug overdose, Harris became a champion of country-rock appealing to a primarily urban, college-educated audience. She formed her first backup group, The Angel Band, and had sev-

Emmylou Harris in concert, 1998. Photo: Raeanne Rubenstein

eral hits on the country and pop charts through the 1970s. Harris's repertoire was heavy on classic country songs of the 1930s, 1940s, and 1950s (she was a particular fan of THE LOUVIN BROTHERS), along with material by contemporary folk, rock, and country SINGER/SONGWRITERS. Changing her backup band's name to The Hot Band in the late 1970s, Harris employed many musicians who would later become well known on their own, including RODNEY CROWELL, RICKY SKAGGS, ALBERT LEE, and VINCE GILL. Skaggs was particularly influential in moving Harris in a more pure-country direction, shaping her BLUEGRASS-homage album of 1980, *Roses in the Snow*. (Harris, in turn, encouraged Skaggs to become a solo act.)

In the 1980s, Harris focused on the country audience almost exclusively. She created a country song cycle on the 1985 recording *The Ballad of Sally Rose*, her most ambitious project to that date as both songwriter and performer. In 1987 she released *Trio* in collaboration with LINDA RONSTADT and DOLLY PARTON, which yielded her biggest commercial hits. Into the early

1990s Harris continued to be active on the country charts, although she never reached the stratosphere of big-selling records that defines a marketable star.

Harris made an abrupt career change in the mid-1990s when she began working with producer Daniel Lanois. The resulting album, *Wrecking Ball*, returned her to a more mainstream pop/rock sound, but failed to win her a wider audience while alienating her country base. She followed with a live album, *Spyboy*, including backup musicians who had worked with her on the Lanois album, plus Nashville session guitarist Buddy Miller. This was followed by a duet album with old friend Linda Ronstadt, which received critical acclaim but had small sales.

In 2000 Harris released her first album of her own songs, *Red Dirt Girl*. Not exactly country music—and also way outside the realm of mainstream pop—this album reasserted Harris's independence from any industry labels. If anything, she combines several American musical genres to create her own highly personal material.

Just as important as her musical output is Harris's image. She is the first successful female country singer to come out of a country-rock background, and has done little to change her style. She has let her hair go naturally gray, dresses plainly (although occasionally she wears rhinestone-encrusted cowgirl outfits in homage to country stars of the past), and wears little makeup, in marked contrast to most country female recording stars, who sometimes look like exaggerated Barbie dolls. Today's more natural-looking female country singers owe a debt to Harris for this change.

Select Discography

Profile: The Best of, Warner Bros. 3258.
Profile II: The Best of, Warner Bros. 25161.
Blue Kentucky Girl, Warner Bros. 3318. One of her better early albums.
Roses in the Snow, Warner Bros. 3422. Her most traditionally oriented album, with arrangements by Ricky Skaggs and picking by Skaggs, JERRY DOUGLAS, TONY RICE, and other progressive bluegrassers.
The Ballad of Sally Rose, Warner Bros. 25205. A song cycle composed by Harris.
Wrecking Ball. Atmospheric pop-rock album recorded with producer Daniel Lanois.
Red Dirt Girl, Elektra/Nonesuch 79616. 2000 album of all-original songs.

HART, FREDDIE (b. Frederick Segrest, Loachapoka, Ala., December 21, 1926)

Freddie Hart's life is one of those rags-to-riches stories, complete with an eighteen-year struggle to make it big, that all country fans love.

One of fifteen children born to a sharecropping family, Hart got started on the wrong road early, running away from home when he was twelve and enlisting in the Marines (by lying about his age) at age fourteen, then serving in the Pacific in World War II. After being released from the service, he took a number of odd jobs on the East Coast, gravitating toward Nashville; he even worked as an unofficial roadie for HANK WILLIAMS for a while in 1949. Finally Hart relocated to Los Angeles in 1951, in search of a musical career.

His break came two years later in Phoenix, Arizona, where he was working in a cotton mill. He met legendary HONKY-TONKER LEFTY FRIZZELL, who admired his songwriting abilities and hired him as a member of his backup band, a position Hart held for eleven years. Frizzell also arranged for Hart's debut recording for Capitol Records, 1952's "Butterfly Love," and got him a steady job on the *Town Hall Party* radio show, Los Angeles's answer to THE GRAND OLE OPRY.

Hart had more success as a songwriter than a performer in the 1950s. CARL SMITH covered his "Loose Talk" in 1955 to earn a solid hit; the song has since been covered more than fifty times. Two years later Hart had a minor hit with "Keys in the Mailbox." PATSY CLINE recorded his "Lovin' in Vain" as the flip side to her smash "I Fall to Pieces." GEORGE JONES had a minor 1964 hit with his "My Tears Are Overdue," and PORTER WAGONER had a #3 single with 1966's "Skid Row Joe." Still, Hart's solo career was going downhill as he moved from label to label through the 1960s.

Finally, in 1969, he re-signed with Capitol, delivering a couple of albums. In 1971 the label was ready to drop him when a deejay out of Atlanta, Georgia, began playing one of his album tracks, "Easy Loving," on the radio. The song took off after Capitol had already dropped Hart, but they hastily renewed his contract after the song made #1. The slick production, with parallel GUITAR and STEEL GUITAR parts and a slightly racy topic (the song is said to be the first country hit to have the word "sex" in the lyric), made it a natural hit. A follow-up was rushed out, a veritable "Easy Loving" clone right down to the guitar/steel guitar riff, called "My Hang-up Is You."

Hart recorded through the 1970s, with his hits coming early in the decade (and featuring his backup band—called The Heartbeats, naturally). Many of them had a similar sexy undertone, including "If You Can't Feel It (It Ain't There)" from 1974 and 1975's "The First Time," along with the standard barroom angst of songs like 1977's "When Lovers Turn to Strangers."

Capitol dropped Hart in 1979 and he moved on to smaller Sunbird Records, with a few more saccharine hits. Although he continued to perform in the 1980s, even turning up on late-night TV ads on the Nashville

Network to plug mail-order reissues of his big hits, Hart's hitmaking days were over.

Select Discography

Best of, CEMA 19030. Budget-priced, ten-song collection of his Capitol label hits.

HARTFORD, JOHN (b. J. Cowan Harford, New York City, December 30, 1937–June 4, 2001)

John Hartford was an anomaly in country music: a talented instrumentalist (primarily on BANJO, but also GUITAR and FIDDLE), songwriter, and eccentric performer who managed to carve out his own career, following the path of earlier country stars such as UNCLE DAVE MACON in writing and performing material that combines earthy humor with social commentary and pointed wit.

The deep-voiced Hartford was born in New York but raised in St. Louis, and was soon an active figure in the city's BLUEGRASS scene, performing with artists Doug Dillard (later of THE DILLARDS) and BYRON BERLINE. An early love of the Mississippi River led to a brief career as a deckhand on one of the last great steamboats, as well as part-time work as a local deejay. In 1965 he moved to Nashville in search of a country-music career.

John Hartford, c. 1975, playing the fiddle and piloting a steamboat. Photos courtesy the artist

Hartford signed with RCA Records (and added a "t" to his last name), recording a series of almost unclassifiable LPs. Although RCA produced him with typical Nashville backup, his songs were highly personal, ranging from the comic "Old-Fashioned Washing Machine" (in which he imitated the sound of an ancient washer on its last legs) to the wordy, anthemic "Gentle on My Mind" and "Natural to Be Gone." Hartford's big break came with the 1967 hit recording of his "Gentle on My Mind" by singer/guitarist GLEN CAMPBELL; he subsequently moved to Los Angeles, where he wrote for the Smothers Brothers and Glen Campbell TV programs, as well as recording his last record for RCA (*Iron Mountain Depot*), an early stab at COUNTRY-ROCK including a cover of The Beatles' "Hey, Jude."

In 1970 he returned to Nashville and signed with Warner Brothers, releasing his classic LP, *Aeroplane*. Hartford established a band bringing together the most talented and progressive of Nashville's musicians, including TUT TAYLOR (DOBRO), NORMAN BLAKE (guitar), VASSAR CLEMENTS (fiddle), and RANDY SCRUGGS (bass). The album ranged from Hartford's classic celebration of his steamboat days on "Steamboat Whistle Blues" to an elegy for the Ryman Auditorium, the longtime home of THE GRAND OLE OPRY, on "They're Gonna Tear Down the Grand Ole Opry."

Hartford soon dissolved his band and spent most of the 1970s and 1980s touring as a solo musician. Accompanying himself on banjo, guitar, and fiddle, Hartford rigged up a plywood board with a microphone to enable him to clog dance while singing and playing. His love of the Mississippi River was expressed most deeply in the concept LP *Mark Twang*, released by Flying Fish Records in 1976, which earned him a Grammy.

In the late 1980s Hartford briefly re-signed to a major record label (MCA) and began performing with his son. In the early 1990s he issued his recordings on his own colorfully named label, Small Dog A-Barkin'. He also took an interest in West Virginia fiddler Ed Haley, documenting his life and recording several albums of tunes that he had performed. In 2000 he performed on the sound track for the Coen Brothers' film *O Brother, Where Art Thou?*, and emceed a concert of traditional music at the Ryman Auditorium in Nashville that was featured in a documentary film by D. A. Pennebaker, titled *Down from the Mountain*.

In the mid-1990s Hartford was diagnosed with cancer, which he had battled some twenty years earlier. Determined to continue performing, he played concerts until about two months before his death.

Select Discography

Aero-Plain, Rounder 366. Reissue of classic 1971 Warner Bros. album (#1916) that was highly influential on 1970s newgrass bands.

Me oh My, How Time Flies, Flying Fish 70440. Compilation of his mid-1970s through early-1980s recordings.

Good Ol' Boys, Rounder 462. Hartford's last studio vocal album, a collection of new songs including a wonderful story song about the life of BILL MONROE, "Cross-Eyed Child."

HAWKINS, HAWKSHAW (b. Harold Franklin H., Huntington, W. Va., December 21, 1921–March 5, 1963)

The third figure tragically killed in the plane wreck that took the lives of PATSY CLINE and COWBOY COPAS, Hawkins had a checkered career from the mid-1940s through the 1950s, gaining his greatest success just before his death.

Winning a talent contest as a teen, Hawkins performed on radio in his hometown of Huntington, West Virginia, until he enlisted in the Army in 1942. Four years later, on his discharge, he returned home and began performing on the popular *Wheeling Jamboree* radio show and recording for the King label out of Cincinnati. Early minor hits included 1949's "I Wasted a Nickel," 1951's "Slow Poke," and the first recording of "Sunny Side of the Mountain," which was to become the theme song for BLUEGRASS singer JIMMY MARTIN.

He was signed by RCA in 1955 and became a member of THE GRAND OLE OPRY a year later, but the hits just didn't come. It wasn't until 1963, when he recorded Justin Tubb's "Lonesome 7–7203" that he finally had a #1 country hit; but two days after the song charted, Hawkins was dead.

Select Discography

Volume 1, King 587. CD reissue of 1958 LP that included recordings made from the late 1940s through the early 1950s, including his hit "Sunny Side of the Mountain."

Hawkshaw Hawkins, Bear Family 15539. His mid-1950s recordings for RCA, which pale in comparison with his earlier King sides.

HAY, GEORGE D. (b. G. Dewey H., Attica, Ind., November 9, 1895–May 8, 1968)

Hay was the famous "Solemn Old Judge" who was the founder of and announcer for THE GRAND OLE OPRY, country music's best-known radio program.

Hay began his career in real estate, working as a salesman until 1920, when he decided to switch to being a newspaperman. He was hired as a reporter for the *Memphis Commercial Appeal*. The paper branched out into the new field of radio, opening its own station, WMC, where Hay worked as an editor and announcer.

George D. Hay at the WSM microphone, c. mid-1930s. Photo courtesy Bob Carlin

At this station he began to develop his character, calling himself "The Solemn Old Judge" and opening his broadcasts by tooting on "Hushpuckena," his name for the steamboat whistle that became his on-air signature. In 1924 Hay was hired by WLS in Chicago to be the announcer for their popular NATIONAL BARN DANCE program. He gained national exposure on this program, and within a year won a popularity poll as the top radio performer in the U.S.

In October 1925 the National Life Insurance Company of Nashville opened a small, 1,000-watt radio station, WSM (after the company's slogan, "We Shield Millions"). Hay joined the new station as an announcer and newsman. On November 28, 1925, he invited local old-time fiddler UNCLE JIMMY THOMPSON to perform on the station, inaugurating a program Hay called *The WSM Barn Dance*. In January 1926 the show was renamed, following a famous quip by Hay. The radio station carried the NBC Symphony Orchestra, a program picked up from New York. When Hay's *Barn Dance* program followed a symphonic broadcast, the announcer said: "You've been up in the clouds with grand opera; now get down to earth with us in a . . . Grand Ole Opry." The name stuck.

Hay was responsible for booking many of the early *Opry* stars, and he did much to bring the best local talent to the station. He was particularly anxious to book UNCLE DAVE MACON, who was already a well-loved performer in the area. He also introduced black harmonica player DEFORD BAILEY, The McGee Brothers, THE DELMORE BROTHERS, and countless other acts to the *Opry*.

Hay also was central in building WSM into a regional powerhouse. In 1929 the station gained "clear-channel" status, allowing it to jump to 50,000 watts by 1932, meaning it could be heard throughout the South and Midwest, and even as far north as Canada. Hay formed the WSM Artists Bureau in the 1930s, arranging tours for many of the radio performers. Through the influence of this powerful booking agency, the station could make or break a performer's career (and also was able to pocket a percentage of the profits performers made on the road).

Although Hay continued to be an *Opry* presence until his retirement in 1951, he was less than pleased with the new direction country music was taking. He was annoyed when BOB WILLS's band appeared on the program in 1943 with amplified instruments; he had always banned electric instruments from the *Opry* stage. A staunch traditionalist to the end, Hay was unhappy with the hotter new styles, particularly WESTERN SWING and HONKY-TONK music. Still, Hay's presence on the show, though diminished, maintained its links to the past, a key element in its continuing success.

HAYES, WADE (b. Bethel Acres, Okla., April 20, 1969)

This hunk-in-a-hat, western-styled country star of the mid-1990s was the son of a local country performer who encouraged his son to take up the GUITAR; by age fourteen Wade was playing second guitar in his father's band. In 1992 he traveled to Nashville to establish himself as a working musician, and was quickly hired by JOHNNY LEE. Two years later Wade was simultaneously signed as a songwriter by Sony/Tree music and as an artist by Columbia Records. His debut single, "Old Enough to Know Better," released in the fall of 1994, was hailed as a return-to-roots country sound and reached a chart-busting #1 ranking; his second single release, "One Good Night," also fared well. This led his first album to gold status, and the usual awards and media attention. His label wasted no time in releasing follow-ups. However, like many new artists, the second-album slump dogged Hayes, although he still managed to score a few moderate hits. His next major hit came from his third album, the playful "The Day She Left Tulsa (in a Chevy)."

Through the 1990s Hayes's career was carefully molded by producer/managers Don Cook and Chick Rains; Rains has also written many of Hayes's hits with the singer. His sound is derived largely from the great Bakersfield, California, stars of the 1960s, including more than a tip of the hat to BUCK OWENS and MERLE HAGGARD. However, the music is given a 1990s sheen that makes it attractive to a new audience, and Hayes's he-man-in-a-hat good looks don't hurt, either. Hayes's attractive, although somewhat bland, vocals are nicely accompanied by his prowess on the guitar; in fact his lead playing is probably his strongest suit as a performer.

Hayes's last minor hit of the 1990s was 1998's "When the Wrong One Loves You Right," a classic HONKY-TONK WEEPER. He then took a two-year breather from recording, and also broke with Cook and Rains. In 2000 Hayes returned with a new single, "Up North," as a teaser for a new album coproduced by Hayes and singer Ronnie Dunn (one half of the famed duo BROOKS AND DUNN). As a publicity stunt Sony Nashville invited Hayes's fans to "name the album" by sending suggestions to their Web site. The winning title, *Highways and Heartaches*, could be the name of half a dozen or more country albums; and the less-than-memorable album and single did little to revitalize Hayes's career as a hitmaker.

Select Discography

Old Enough to Know Better, Columbia 66412. His first, and still his best.

HAYWIRE MAC (b. Harry Kirby McClintock, Knoxville, Tenn., October 8, 1882–April 24, 1957)

Haywire Mac, a SINGER/SONGWRITER/union organizer best remembered for writing "The Big Rock Candy Mountain," was a real hobo who in later life became a professional one, glorifying the life of cowboys and migrant workers of the West. He was born and raised in a middle-class home where he learned to play GUITAR as a youth. At age fourteen he left home to join a traveling show, working his way to New Orleans. Longing to see the world, two years later Mac was working as a mule driver in the Philippines, delivering supplies to the American troops, and then, in 1899, worked as a journalist's assistant during the Boxer Rebellion. From China he worked his way to Australia, and then South Africa, where he again served as a mule driver, this time in the Boer War. By 1902 he was in London, and then South America and the Caribbean, finally returning around 1905 to San Francisco.

After returning to the U.S., McClintock first worked as a railroad brakeman. Sympathizing with his fellow workers, and left-leaning in his politics, he became an early organizer for the International Workers of the World. He wrote a rousing theme song for his fellow workers, "Hallelujah, I'm a Bum," around the early 1910s. Still working as an amateur singer, he began to attract attention singing on the streets, eventually getting his own daily radio show, which began broadcasting out of San Francisco in 1925. Three years later he made his first recordings for Victor Records. He cut forty-one sides over the next three years, including his "Hallelujah, I'm a Bum" and two follow-ups, and "The Big Rock Candy Mountain," along with COWBOY and novelty numbers.

The Depression slowed Mac's recording career, but he made a strong comeback in 1938 for Decca, rerecording his earlier hits. That same year he moved to Hollywood to appear in a number of B Westerns with GENE AUTRY. He also built on his myth by writing stories, plays, and nonfiction pieces for various publications, including his popular column, "The Railroad Boomer," which appeared from 1943 to 1953 in a railroad-enthusiast publication. His homespun humor resembled that of Will Rogers and also WOODY GUTHRIE's newspaper work, and he achieved similar fame among folk-music and liberal readers.

In 1953 McClintock returned to San Francisco to host his own radio/TV show, *The Breakfast Hour.* Two years later he "retired," although he continued to perform until his death. However, McClintock's songs—and legend—lived on after his death. Burl Ives repopularized "The Big Rock Candy Mountain" as a children's song in the 1950s and 1960s, achieving a minor hit with it. The song was included in McClintock's 1928 recording on the sound track of the Coen Brothers' film, *O Brother, Where Art Thou?*, in 2000, bringing renewed attention to the cowboy/hobo singer.

In the mid-1980s the Boston-based bluegrass/folk label Rounder Records issued an album of McClintock's 1928–1929 recordings, reintroducing him to the folk audience. McClintock was also one of the artists selected to be featured on Harry Smith's legendary *Anthology of American Folk Music* box set, first issued in 1952, which was influential on the FOLK REVIVAL of the late 1950s and early 1960s. The set was reissued in 1997, again drawing attention to McClintock's artistry.

HEAD, ROY (b. R. Kent H., Three Rivers, Tex., September 1, 1941)

Head is a Texas rocker who turned to country after his teenybopper years were over.

Born in Three Rivers, Head was raised in a one-room shack in the tiny Texas border town of Crystal City. After performing country material with his older brother Donald, he gravitated to R&B and rock in his high-school years, when he formed a local band called The Traits. They had a regional hit in 1958 with "Baby, Let Me Kiss You (One More Time)," leading to lots of work throughout the South. In the early 1960s Head came under the influence of legendary record producer

Huey Meaux, who produced The Traits' biggest pop hit, 1965's "Treat Her Right," making Head something of a legend as an early blue-eyed soulster. Breaking from the rest of the band, Head began touring on his own, although still using The Traits' name; the other members sued him for six-sevenths of all his income, which ended the tour. Soon after, Head developed nodes on his vocal cords, and his career hit the skids.

Head switched to a country repertoire in the late 1960s, encouraged by Houston club owner Lee Savaggio, who gave him a regular place to perform plus a recording contract with his Shannon label. After a couple of regional hits, Head's contract was picked up by ABC/Dot, and he had a Top 10 country hit with 1976's "The Door I Used to Close." A year later Head covered Rod Stewart's "Tonight's the Night" for the cowpoke crowd; in 1979 he moved to Elektra and then, two years later, to smaller Churchill Records, scoring moderate success with a combination of revivals of his rockin' hits and more hard-core country material. Although popular on the ROCKABILLY revival circuit, Head has not been as active since the mid-1980s.

Select Discography

Treat Her Right, Varese 5618. His 1960s blue-eyed soul hits.

HEBB, BOBBY (b. Robert von H., Nashville, Tenn., July 26, 1938)

One of the few black country stars, Hebb is best remembered for his crossover hit, 1966's "Sunny," which made him (for a while, anyway) a favorite lounge act.

When he was twelve, Hebb was discovered by producer ROY ACUFF, who hired him to perform on THE GRAND OLE OPRY as a spoons player. Two years later he made his first recordings for the tiny Rich label, including "Night Train to Memphis." In 1961 he and Sylvia Shemwell teamed up as the R&B/pop duo Bobby and Sylvia, performing together for two years.

In 1966 Hebb was recording again as a solo artist, now for Philips, and scored his big pop and country hit with "Sunny." He followed this with a cover of "A Satisfied Mind" in a more country vein, then disappeared off the charts. By the early 1970s he was back to recording for small country labels, having a minor hit in 1972 with "Love, Love, Love." Hebb again disappeared from the scene, but was "rediscovered" in 2000–2001, making a few club appearances and drawing renewed press interest for his work as a soul SINGER/SONGWRITER.

HEE HAW (1969–1993)

Hee Haw was originally a network television program featuring country music and humor in a variety-style format. Broadcast for two seasons nationally by CBS, the program was hosted by BUCK OWENS and ROY CLARK, and featured a wide variety of mainstream country performers. The show's combination of corn-ball humor and teary-eyed country music dated back to the old style minstrel and tent shows that had toured the South beginning in the mid-nineteenth century; the quick editing from joke to joke was borrowed from a popular TV series of the day, *Laugh-In*. The network dropped the program after two years, but the producers refused to let it die, taking it into syndication, where it lasted for another two decades.

Set in "kolorful Kornfield Kounty," *Hee Haw* mixed straightforward musical performances with the kind of RUBE HUMOR that had been entertaining country audiences since the days of the minstrel shows. Add to this a couple of buxom blonds, and you had a surefire formula for long-lasting success. Besides hosts Clark and Owens, the show featured many regular guests, including BANJO-playing comedians STRINGBEAN and GRANDPA JONES; Roni Stoneman, the big-voiced daughter of ERNEST "POP" STONEMAN; famed backwoods comedienne/monologist MINNIE PEARL; and even *Playboy* Playmate Barbi Benton. Famed harmonica player CHARLIE McCOY served as co-musical director for the original program, ensuring that many fine Nashville session players appeared on the show, along with Buck Owens's regular backup band, The Buckaroos, and the NASHVILLE SOUND vocal groups The Inspirations and Nashville Addition.

Although it was in many ways a throwback to the old stereotypes of country music as something produced by dim-witted hayseeds, the show did provide valuable exposure for its stars. In 1992 a last-ditch attempt was made to modernize the show, but it finally died as an original production, although it lived on in reruns.

HENDRICKS, SCOTT (b. Clinton, Okla., July 26, 1956)

Along with college buddy TIM DuBOIS, Hendricks was one of the most successful producers and record label executives in Nashville—until he tussled with GARTH BROOKS.

Hendricks attended Oklahoma State University, where he met DuBois and future RESTLESS HEART singer Greg Jennings. All three would end up in Nashville, with DuBois and Hendricks producing Restless Heart's debut album in 1985. Hendricks was much in demand as a producer through the 1990s, and is said to have been responsible for over thirty #1 country hits. He also groomed new artists, including FAITH HILL, SUZY BOGGUSS, and TRACE ADKINS.

In 1995 Hendricks was hired to head the Capitol Nashville label. About a year later he got into a battle with Garth Brooks, the label's biggest-selling artist at the time. Brooks saw his sales declining on his newer releases, and blamed Capitol for poor marketing; Hendricks felt that Brooks was merely maturing from a phenomenon to an artist who was continuing to sell a very respectable number of albums while not dominating all of the music charts. Brooks held up the release of his album, *Sevens*, because of his anger with Hendricks; in the resulting power struggle Hendricks was relieved of his position in the fall of 1997, although he was quickly reassigned to Capitol's sister label, Virgin Nashville (both are part of the EMI conglomerate).

Hendricks got off to a good start at Virgin, signing two of the biggest artists of 2000, Clay Davidson and Chris Cagle. Despite this success, however, the Virgin label was closed in a cost-cutting measure by Capitol in late February 2001.

HERNDON, TY (b. Boyd T. H., Meridian, Miss., May 2, 1962)

Herndon, a pleasant-voiced country hitmaker of the mid-1990s, was born in Mississippi but raised in Butler, Alabama. He showed musical talent at age five, when he began playing GOSPEL music on piano. In 1979 he was hired as a singer at Nashville's Opryland theme park, where he worked off and on for the next decade. He became a member of the vocal group The Tennessee River Boys, there; other members later formed the group DIAMOND RIO. In 1983 he took first-place honors on Ed McMahon's *Star Search* TV show, but it didn't help boost his career much. Reduced to singing jingles while trying to find a label interested in him, he finally left Nashville to try the greener fields of Dallas, Texas. After five years of club performances in Texas, he attracted the attention of producer Doug Johnson, who signed him to Epic Nashville.

Herndon's first single, issued in 1995, was an instant smash, reaching #1 on the country charts and launching his career. Herndon was immediately showered with awards, and hit the road. However, while touring in June 1995, he was arrested following a bizarre incident in Fort Worth, Texas. He was charged with indecent exposure—it was claimed that he had masturbated in front of a police officer—and a substantial amount of a "powdered narcotic" was found in his possession. Rumors that Herndon might be gay—something rarely discussed in country music circles—were rampant, but strongly denied by the married singer.

This might have derailed the career of a lesser star, but Herndon bounced back with his 1996 second album. The title track, "Living in a Moment," was another #1 hit, and the fans—much to his publicists' relief—seemed to have forgiven his transgression. Oddly, it wasn't his unusual behavior of 1995 that slowed his career, but rather the cooling of the country marketplace in the later 1990s. Although he was still a pleasant-voiced balladeer, his songs were heard on the radio less often and failed to see much action. In 1999 he tried a new tack by releasing the album *Steam*, featuring more hard-rocking numbers, but again failed to stir much chart attention. Nonetheless, he continues to be a regular second-tier performer on the country circuit.

Select Discography

What Mattered Most, Epic 66397. His debut album from 1995.

HIATT, JOHN (b. Indianapolis, Ind., 1952)

Hiatt is a gravelly voiced SINGER/SONGWRITER who has supplied hits for other artists but has yet to find a niche for his own performances. Combining country, R&B, and rock sounds, Hiatt has created a strong body of highly personal songs for which he is the perfect interpreter, even though chart success has eluded him.

Hiatt began playing during his high-school years with a local R&B outfit known as The White Ducks; his love for R&B continues to show in his own songs and performances. In 1970 he moved to Nashville, and by mid-decade had hooked up with Epic Records, where he recorded two LPs, followed by two more for MCA; none sold well, although they helped establish his reputation. Folk-rocker Ry Cooder was looking for material when his manager suggested he listen to Hiatt's records; he liked what he heard, and hired Hiatt as his backup guitarist in 1980 (the two would continue to make music together on and off through the next decade). In the mid-1980s Hiatt recorded a number of albums for the Geffen label, and his reputation as a songwriter grew. His own songs were marked by an often ironic, sometimes cruel portrayal of the foibles of human relationships. However, his increasing dependence on alcohol, plus his records' poor sales, put an end to his recording career for a while.

Hiatt returned magnificently with 1987's *Bring the Family*, accompanied by Cooder along with British punk-country singer Nick Lowe on bass, and session drummer Jim Keltner. Although still sharply focused and humorous, Hiatt's songs and attitude seemed more forgiving than in the past, while the band provided the perfect rocking foil to his songs that combined elements of soul, GOSPEL, country, and ROCKABILLY. Bonnie Raitt scored her first comeback hit with Hiatt's "Thing Called Love" from this album, a bluesy rocker that provided the title for Peter Bogdanovich's 1993 film about a young singer trying to get a break in Nashville.

Hiatt formed a touring band called The Goners, with whom he produced a follow-up LP, his most "country"

in flavor, called *Slow Turning*. This featured "Drive South" (a 1993 hit for SUZY BOGGUSS), a hymn to the joys of Southern living, along with his humorous take on a demented Elvis fan ("Tennessee Plates"), and the HONKY-TONK lament "Icy Blue Heart," a modernized version of boy-meets-(deadly)-girl-at-the-saloon (covered by EMMYLOU HARRIS).

Although both albums were critically acclaimed, Hiatt still was a slow seller in the stores. An attempt to glitz up his sound on his next album (*Stolen Moments*, 1991) was a total failure, and it was followed by an odd reunion with Cooder, Lowe, and Keltner, who were now calling themselves Little Village. The album they produced featured songs that were jointly composed by the band, and although Hiatt provided most of the lead vocals (and, one suspects, the ideas for some of the better songs), the entire album had a tossed-off quality that didn't quite make it.

In 1993 Hiatt released a new solo album, *Perfectly Good Guitar*, which attempted to meld his offbeat writing personality with a more hard-rock sound. The album features more excellent songs, including (not surprisingly) the most countryesque number, "Buffalo River Home." His next album, *Walk On*, featured some of his most searing country-flavored songs, including the understated breakup song "Dust on a Country Road." Bass player Davey Faragher and multiple instrumentalist David Immerglück, the core members of Hiatt's touring and recording band since the early 1990s, are prominently featured on this album.

In 2000 Hiatt released *Crossing Muddy Waters*, a fine collection of country and blues-tinged originals. It was recorded with Faragher and Immerglück quickly, like his earlier *Bring the Family*, and mostly with acoustic instruments. The title track is perhaps the strongest, but the album as a whole was a welcome return to form for the singer/songwriter after some lackluster late-1990s output. It also marked his first independent production; major label Capitol had dropped him, and Hiatt produced the album on his own, licensing it for CD and on-line release. 2001 saw a return to a harder-rocking sound with the release of *The Tiki Bar Is Open;* the album also reunited him with his mid-1980s touring guitarist, Sonny Landreth.

Hiatt's vocal style is an endearing mix of R&B and country mannerisms, although his husky singing takes some getting used to, and may account for his lack of popularity among the fans of Nashville's more photogenic and smoother-sounding hunks. Hiatt looks as wrinkled and worn as he sounds, showing the evidence of many years of hard living. His songs share an authenticity and humor that are definitely unique and hard-won in a music scene that is often populated by singers who are no more than a clever marketing plan packaged in a cowboy hat.

Select Discography

Y'All Caught, Geffen 24247. Anthology of his 1979–1985 Geffen recordings, many poorly produced but featuring some good songs nonetheless.

Bring the Family, A&M 5158. 1987 comeback album with great backup by Ry Cooder and company.

Greatst Hits, Capitol 7 2438 59179 2 9. 1998 compilation mostly drawn from Hiatt's 1987 to current recordings, with some remakes of earlier songs.

Crossing Muddy Waters, Vanguard 79576. 2000 album of acoustic country and blues numbers; a standout in Hiatt's discography.

HI FLYERS (1929–1946)

During the 1930s Texas was a hotbed of swinging string ensembles, usually founded to play sponsored shows on radio, and then hitting the local circuit of HONKY-TONKS and dance halls. The Hi Flyers, a jazz-oriented Texas string band that was among the pioneers of WESTERN SWING, were one of the more distinctive and successful of these groups, going through varied styles (and band members) during their approximately fifteen-year heyday.

The band, originally christened The High Flyers, made its debut on Fort Worth, Texas, radio in 1929, the brainchild of announcer Zack Hurt. The original group was a more conventional string band, featuring Kentucky fiddler Clifford Gross playing a mixture of popular and dance tunes, particularly waltzes. By 1932 the band was rechristened with the more concise name Hi Flyers, and was now led by guitarist Elmer Scarborough. Influenced by the success of MILTON BROWN and BOB WILLS, Scarborough changed the band's emphasis toward jazzy instrumentals and modern instrumentation. The band was still FIDDLE lead, but new fiddler Pat Trotter was far more jazz-oriented than Gross. In 1936 Trotter and several others were hired away by an Amarillo radio station, and were rechristened The Sons of the West. Nonetheless, a year later The Hi Flyers made their recording debut, now featuring Scarborough, fiddler Darrell Kirkpatrick, steel guitarist Billy Briggs, and Landon Beaver, a jazz-styled pianist, as the key players.

1937–1938 saw the band in transition, leaving Fort Worth and moving for a while to a smaller Texas station. After a brief period of inactivity, Scarborough reactivated the band, now operating out of Oklahoma City. From 1939 to 1941, this version of the band—featuring the jazzy electric guitar leads of Sheldon Bennett and (on session work only) pianist Beaver—made the group's most memorable and best-loved recordings. Their signature number, "Hi Flyer Stomp," became a classic of Western Swing recordings. The group also added Buster Ferguson, a smooth-voiced vocalist, in order to compete with Wills's band, which featured the noted crooner TOMMY DUNCAN. Ferguson's vocals looked forward to the popular, post-war honky-tonk ballads of beer and betrayal.

The band members scattered during World War II as various players were inducted into the armed services. Following the war, Scarborough once more tried to revive the group, working back in their original home base of Fort Worth, but this band lasted only about a year before The Hi Flyers were no more.

HIGHWAY 101 (1987–1995; sporadically thereafter; original members: Paulette Carlson [b. Northfield, Minn., October 11, 1953, voc]; Curtis Stone [b. North Hollywood, Calif., April 3, 1950, voc, b, mdln, gtr]; Cactus Moser [b. Scott Moser, Montrose, Calif., May 3, 1957, voc, drm, gtr]; Jack Daniels [b. Choctaw, Okla., October 27, 1949, voc, gtr]; Carlson was replaced by Nikki Nelson [b. San Diego, Calif., January 3, 1969, voc] in 1989; Jack Daniels left in 1993 and was not replaced; Nelson left in 1994; Carlson rejoined in 1995)

Highway 101 was a hard-rockin' country outfit, formed originally to accompany smoky-voiced singer Carlson.

Carlson is definitely a new-country star, recalling the style (musically and as a fashion plate) of rocker Stevie Nicks in her choice of material and its presentation. She first came to Nashville in 1978, when she was twenty-four, working on the staff of THE OAK RIDGE BOYS' publishing company and backing GAIL DAVIES. Solo recordings for RCA in 1983–1984 failed to chart, and she moved back to her native Minnesota in 1985, disappointed with her career progress.

Although Carlson was in semiretirement, her manager, Chuck Morris, felt that she could be successful if packaged correctly. Noting the increased interest in COWBOY-flavored bands, he enlisted the help of a trio of California COUNTRY-ROCKERS/session musicians to form Highway 101, showcasing Carlson in a cowgirl-meets-New-Nashville getup. The group's hits capitalized on her raspy singing by portraying her as a tough broad who is not to be slighted, from their first charting record, 1987's "The Bed You Made for Me" (a song Carlson wrote, addressed to an ex-boyfriend who had cheated on her), to "Whiskey if You Were a Woman," portraying the havoc brought to a marriage by a husband's dependency on alcohol, and 1988's "All the Reasons Why," telling of a woman who is unafraid to end an unhappy relationship (cowritten by Carlson) and "Just Say Yes," in which the woman frankly and unabashedly pursues her man.

Carlson left the band in 1989 to pursue a solo career. Her first solo recording continued the sassy-girl-with-an-attitude trend with her minor hit "Not with My Heart You Don't." Nikki Nelson, a young, fire-breathing redhead, replaced Carlson as the band's focal point, visually and vocally, singing lead on their up-tempo 1991 hit, "Bing Bang Boom." However, the band could not follow this success, and after a failed 1993 album, Nelson was gone.

Neither Carlson nor the reconstituted Highway 101 enjoyed as great a success on their own as they did when they were together. By 1995 Carlson rejoined for a reunion tour and new album. Since then the group has appeared on the road and on two more albums issued on small labels. However, they have never been able to recapture their original commercial success.

Select Discography

Highway 101, Featuring Paulette Carlson, Warner Bros. 25608. Their debut LP from 1987.
Greatest Hits, Warner Bros. 26253. Best of the original band.
Bing Bang Boom, Warner Bros. 26588. 1991 release with new vocalist Nikki Nelson.
Love Goes On, Liberty 97711. Carlson's 1991 debut solo LP.

HIGHWOODS STRING BAND, THE (c. 1973–1978: Walt Koken [fdl]; Bob Potts [fdl]; Mac Benford [bnj]; Doug Dorschug [gtr]; Jenny Cleland [b])

The Highwoods String Band was one of the most popular revival string bands of the 1970s. Modeled after Gid Tanner's SKILLET LICKERS, they took a twin-fiddle sound and high-powered backup, and wed it with a humorous approach to FIDDLE tunes and old-time songs. They were also influenced by the recordings of traditional fiddle and BANJO players who were "rediscovered" in the 1960s, particularly fiddler TOMMY JARRELL.

The band originated in the Berkeley, California, old-time music community of the 1970s, and several members appeared on the seminal anthology *Berkeley Farms*, recorded by MIKE SEEGER. Group members relocated to Ithaca, New York, where the final lineup stabilized around 1973. Their first LP, *Fire on the Mountain* (Rounder), was recorded outside, in an attempt to capture the spontaneous sound of the band; their next two LPs, *Dance All Night* and *Radio Special #3*, were more professionally recorded. However, none of their albums captured the excitement of the band's live performances. Mac Benford's hoarse vocals, the ragged-but-right sound of the twin fiddles, and Dorschug's RILEY PUCKETT-influenced GUITAR runs made for a sound that was both contemporary and nostalgic. The band influenced countless other outfits, amateur and professional, particularly The Plank Road String Band, The Chicken Chokers, and The Tompkins County Horseflies.

After the band broke up, Benford recorded a solo banjo LP and briefly formed a new band, The Backwoods Band, in the style of Highwoods; Dorschug went to work as a record producer for June Appal Records; Koken recorded two solo banjo records for Rounder during the 1990s. The other band members faded from the performing scene.

Select Discography

Feed Your Baby Onions: Fat City Favorites, Rounder 11569. CD compilation of their three LPs from the 1970s.

HILL, FAITH (b. Audrey F. Perry, Jackson, Miss., September 21, 1967)

Perky, blond-haired Hill is a SINGER/SONGWRITER who had almost immediate success once she was "discovered."

Raised in rural Mississippi, Faith sang in church and at local functions. Determined to make it as a singer/songwriter, she moved to Nashville in her late teens but it was difficult to find a job in the music business. Eventually she was hired by the Gary Morris Publishing Company for a desk job; this led to singing on demo recordings, which in turn led to being a backup singer for Gary Burr. Burr had a production deal with Warner Brothers, and subsequently produced Hill's first album.

Hill's first single, "Wild One," promoted by a sexy video, shot to #1; the only previous female vocalist to score a #1 hit right out of the box was JEANNIE C. RILEY with the sultry "Harper Valley P.T.A." Her second single, a countryesque cover of "Piece of My Heart" (the same song that Janis Joplin used to wrap her lungs around), also hit #1. Hill's debut album, *Take Me as I Am*, went gold in 1994, and subsequently double platinum.

Hill's second album was somewhat less successful, and she took some time off after marrying country singer TIM MCGRAW. She scored a minor hit with her duet with McGraw, "It's Your Love," in 1997, and then came back strong in 1998 with her big hit song, "This Kiss." Her third album, *Faith*, from which the single was drawn, went platinum a little over a month after its release.

Hill crossed over from country superstardom to pop divadom in 1999 with the release of her album *Breathe*. The title track became Hill's first single platinum-seller, topping country, pop, and adult contemporary charts. Taking a page from SHANIA TWAIN's book, Hill's style was even more mainstream, and her videos even sexier. The album produced four major hits, including "The Way You Love Me," a pop song with a video featuring multiple costume changes. Hill hit the road, and produced the obligatory concert video to promote "If My Heart Had Wings," a sentimental ballad sung, like all of Hill's material, as if she were trying to launch her tonsils into the upper tier of seats at Yankee Stadium. The *Breathe* album was a massive best-seller, remaining on the top country list for seventy-one weeks, and selling over 6 million copies by mid-2001.

Her pop success led to further exposure: on magazines covers, TV (including a notable invitation to appear in *Diva's 1999* concert, on VH-1), and in the general gossip/celebrity media. She won numerous awards, both from the music industry and from just about everyone else, including one readers' poll that found her "most kissable" and a group of hair stylists who pronounced her hair style "most admired."

Hill has been living off the success of *Breathe* into the twenty-first century. She suffers from a classic diva problem; her range is somewhat limited, and her tendency to overdramatize is nearly unquenchable. In many cases it seems to be a case of Faith versus her material, with the song crying "uncle" under the assault of her powerful voice. Whether she will be able to maintain her phenomenal pop presence is unknown; but, like many other country performers, she can look forward to years on the country circuit once her flash-in-the-pan pop stardom dissipates.

Select Discography

Faith, Warner Bros. 46790. 1998 album featuring "This Kiss."

Breathe, Warner Bros. 47373. 1999 album featuring several massive mainstream hits.

HILL, GOLDIE (b. Argolda Voncile H., Coy City, Tex., January 11, 1933)

Hill, a 1950s country-ROCKABILLY star who briefly enjoyed chart and touring success, was born in tiny Coy City, near Kerrville, Texas, the youngest sibling of a musical family; her elder brother, Tommy, was particularly talented, and helped introduce her to local HONKY-TONKS and their music. She began singing with her brother's band as a teenager, and in the spring of 1952 both she and Tommy joined WEBB PIERCE's stage band. When Pierce went to Nashville that July to record, Decca executive Paul Cohen heard Goldie sing and immediately signed her.

Country music was just learning the allure of female singers when Hill was signed to Decca. Like many other female artists, she was often given the task of recording "answer songs" to earlier country hits, usually sung by men. In this way the "female" point of view could be given, and it was easy to ride the coattails of a previous hit. (The most successful example had come just months earlier, in May 1952: KITTY WELLS's "It Wasn't God Who Made Honky-Tonk An-

gels," a response to HANK THOMPSON's hit "Wild Side of Life.")

Hill's first answer disc was 1952's "Why Talk to Your Heart?," a response to RAY PRICE's earlier hit, "Talk to My Heart." She followed that year with an answer to "Don't Let the Stars Get in My Eyes," a country hit written and sung by SLIM WILLETT and then covered for the pop charts by Pat Boone; her response was the regretful "I Let the Stars Get in My Eyes," written for her by brother Tommy.

Thanks to her initial success Hill moved to Nashville in the fall of 1953 and joined THE GRAND OLE OPRY. While continuing her solo career Hill was paired with other country stars—also a common practice for females at that time. With RED SOVINE she cut the tearjerker "Are you Mine" (Sovine's first charting hit), and with Justin Tubb the more upbeat "Surefire Kisses," "Fickle Heart," and "Looking Back to See." She also briefly worked with Justin's father, ERNEST TUBB, as a radio host of *Country Tune Parade* in 1954.

In January 1957 she toured with the Philip Morris Country Music Show, a package tour that promoted country singers and cigarettes. Also on the tour was singer CARL SMITH, who had recently divorced June Carter. Goldie married Smith, and like many other women of the day, ended her career to raise her family. Although she sporadically recorded thereafter, her days as a 1950s country femme fatale were over.

HILLMAN, CHRIS (b. Los Angeles, Calif., December, 4, 1944)

Hillman is a seminal figure in the California COUNTRY-ROCK scene, a founding member of THE BYRDS, THE FLYING BURRITO BROTHERS, and THE DESERT ROSE BAND.

Born in southern California, Hillman was raised in the ranch country in the northern part of the state, where he had his first exposure to country-styled music. His first group was the colorfully titled Scottsdale Squirrel Barkers, a BLUEGRASS ensemble that became better known in the early 1960s as The Hillmen; the band featured the Gosdin brothers and Don Parmley. In 1964 Hillman returned to southern California to participate in the rich folk music scene in and around Los Angeles; there he met ex-folkies Jim (later Roger) McGuinn and David Crosby. Influenced by The Beatles, they first formed a group called The Jet Set, then changed their names to the very twee The Beefeaters before settling on The Byrds. The group was one of the most successful folk-rock ensembles of the 1960s, and they recorded the seminal country-rock fusion album *Sweetheart of the Rodeo* in 1968 with SINGER/SONGWRITER GRAM PARSONS.

Hillman and Parsons left the Byrds to pursue country-rock music, forming The Flying Burrito Brothers, which went through many permutations in its short existence, in 1969. After the Burritos, Hillman performed with Stephen Stills's short-lived country-rock band Manassas, and then with singer/songwriters J. D. Souther and Richie Furay in an equally short-lived supergroup. Two solo albums for Asylum records fell dead on the charts, and then Hillman reunited in the early 1980s with McGuinn and GENE CLARK to form an acoustic trio, with critical, if not much commercial, success.

A reunion album for the Hillmen and two more solo albums on the country-folk label Sugar Hill followed. In 1985 Hillman and old friend Herb Pedersen were invited to form a backup band for soft-folkie Dan Fogelberg; the band stuck together after the tour was over and became The Desert Rose Band, scoring hits on the country charts into the 1990s. After the band folded in the mid-1990s, Pedersen and Hillman recorded a duo album for Sugar Hill, and then Hillman made a solo album in 1998, his last studio release as of this writing.

Select Discography

The Hillmen, Sugar Hill 3719. Reunion album for this fabled group.
Desert Rose, Sugar Hill 3743. Comeback solo LP from the mid-1980s.

HINOJOSA, TISH (b. Leticia H., San Antonio, Tex., December 6, 1955)

Hinojosa is a country/alt-rock crossover artist who, like statemate NANCI GRIFFITH, straddles the gap between various traditions, including 1970s SINGER/SONGWRITER, country, and her own take on her Latino heritage.

Raised in a working-class family in the multiethnic city of San Antonio, Hinojosa began playing guitar in high school, influenced, as many others were, by the early 1970s soft-rock of Joni Mitchell, Judy Collins, James Taylor, and BOB DYLAN. She began writing her own material soon after, and recorded a few singles in Spanish for the local market. Relocating to New Mexico, she issued her cassette *From Taos to Tennessee* (which she produced) in 1987, staking out her territory as a new-country artist with Southwestern roots. Soon after, major label A&M picked her up, in 1989 releasing an album called *Homeland*, produced by Los Lobos' sax player, Steve Berlin. A second LP was recorded (under the guiding hand of soulster Booker T. Jones) but was not released; in a management shuffle Hinojosa was dropped from A&M.

Picked up by specialty label Rounder Records, Hinojosa released *Culture Swing*, a mostly acoustic album reflecting Mexican, Spanish, country, and even Caribbean sounds. Strangely enough, the smaller label was able to get her more attention than the conglomerate, and she had a minor hit with her ode to migrant workers, "Something in the Rain." During the later 1990s Hinojosa veered between producing Spanish-language recordings, records for children, and her own material, failing to build on the critical success of *Culture Swing*. After a three-year recording hiatus, she returned in 2000 with *Sign of Truth*, with twelve new songs that she wrote or cowrote.

In the early 1970s Hinojosa would have been marketed as a singer-songwriter; today she is considered "country," which shows how broad the category has become.

Select Discography

Culture Swing, Rounder 3122. Her best recording.
Sign of Truth, Rounder 613172. 2000 album of new songs returns Hinojosa to solid ground.

HOFNER, ADOLPH (b. Moulton, Tex., June 8, 1916–June 2, 2000)

Pioneering WESTERN SWING singer and bandleader, Hofner had a six-decade career, mostly in his native Texas.

Hofner and his brother Emil were raised in a Czech-German family who lived in a small, primarily Czech community located between Houston and San Antonio. When he was ten and his brother was eight, the family moved to San Antonio, where both boys were exposed to a variety of musical styles. The first music that really caught their ears was Hawaiian songs; they quickly got a mail-order ukulele, which led to lessons on GUITAR for Adolph and STEEL GUITAR for Emil. Along with local musician Simon Garcia, they formed The Hawaiian Serenaders in the late 1920s, to play at local picnics and clubs.

In the early 1930s the first Western Swing records by MILTON BROWN and BOB WILLS were released, and immediately were tremendously successful. Like many others the Hofner brothers were bitten by the swing bug, as was another local singer/guitarist, Jimmie Revard. Revard formed his own group, The Oklahoma Playboys (although they were based in Texas) around 1934. He heard Emil playing the steel guitar in a local bar and hired both brothers to join his group. Revard kidded the teenage Emil about his bashfulness around women, which earned him his nickname of "Bash." Revard and his Playboys recorded in San Antonio in the fall of 1936, and the brothers played on record, radio, and in local appearances with the group through 1938.

By the spring of 1938 Adolph was recording for Bluebird as a solo artist, and also working locally with Tom Dickey and The Showboys. With the Showboys he had a hit with FLOYD TILLMAN's song "It Makes

No Difference Now." Putting together a full band later in the year (including his brother), Hofner returned to the studios in October to cut his first swing material. The band had various names; at first billed as Adolph Hofner and His Boys, they were going to call themselves The Texans until they discovered another band had claimed the name, so they settled on The San Antonians.

From the start the band played music to appeal to the diverse ethnic groups in the region; it was natural for the Hofners to play Czech waltzes and polkas, but they also performed Spanish-flavored material to appeal to the considerable Hispanic community in Texas. In fact Hofner's biggest success was the record "Maria Elena," cut in early 1940. He also is credited with cutting the first Western Swing version of the popular old-time FIDDLE tune/song, "Cotton-eyed Joe," in 1941.

During World War II, sensitive to anti–German sentiment, Hofner performed under the name of Dolph (some sources also say he alternately used the name Dub). Immediately following the war, like many other Western Swingers, Hofner and the band relocated to southern California, where many displaced Okies, Arkies, and Texans had moved. Returning to Texas in the early 1950s, Hofner's band gained a radio sponsor, the Pearl Beer Company, and so took a new name, The Pearl Wranglers. They toured to promote the brew, and often appeared at local events.

Up through the mid-1990s Hofner remained active in his native Texas, mostly recording for the local Sarg label. As his health began to fail later that decade, he was forced to leave the stage. He died in San Antonio in mid-2000, just short of his eighty-fourth birthday.

The Hofner band reflects the crazy quilt of American traditional music. What other band could record hot swing numbers like "Yes Sir!" and "Dirty Dog," segue into "Spanish Two-Step" and "Joe Turner Blues," and then perform the Czech favorites "The Prune Waltz" and "Shiner Song"?

Select Discography

South Texas Swing, Arhoolie 7029. Classic recordings from the late 1920s through the 1950s, mostly centering on his swing material.
Texas-Czech, Bohemian & Moravian Bands, Arhoolie/Folklyric 7026. Five tracks feature Hofner and the group, singing in Czech.

HOLCOMB, ROSCOE (b. Daisy, Ky., 1913–February 25, 1981)

Holcomb was an intense, high-voiced mountain vocalist and BANJO/GUITAR player who was "discovered" by folklorist JOHN COHEN in the late 1950s and became a central figure in the old-time music revival.

Roscoe lived and worked near Hazard, Kentucky, the center of the state's coal-mining region. His earliest memory was of someone playing the harmonica (which he called the mouth harp, as many country people do). His brother-in-law gave him a homemade banjo when he was ten, and he was soon playing for local dances. By his late teen years he was working in the mines and married to a religious woman who urged him to give up music as the devil's work. He abandoned playing for a while, but soon was back to making music as a sideline to his mining career.

By the late 1950s, when John Cohen first heard him play, Holcomb was working odd jobs around his home. Even after he was recorded by Cohen and began appearing at folk festivals, he continued to do hard labor, including paving work on many of the superhighways that were then being put through the mountains. Holcomb never viewed music making as a "profession," although he was deadly serious about maintaining a high level of performance.

Holcomb once said, "If you cut my head off at the throat, I'd go on singing." This is an apt description of his vocal quality, which Cohen described as a "high lonesome sound" (a term that has come to be used to describe much of traditional country and BLUEGRASS vocal music). Holcomb's high-pitched falsetto singing was perfectly suited to his repertoire of bluesy songs. He played the banjo in a two-finger, picked style, and used a similar style when picking the guitar (achieving a unique, banjo-like style when playing this instrument). Holcomb's intensity as a performer was legendary; he lived the songs, sometimes crying during performances on stage, even if he was performing a song that he had sung countless times before.

Holcomb is one of those performers whose recordings truly transcend genre; he is said to have been a favorite musician of everyone from BOB DYLAN to electric blues guitarist Eric Clapton. In the best country music, even music produced by performers who never heard Holcomb, there is a small echo of the intensity that made his performances so breathtaking and pure.

Select Discography

Mountain Music of Kentucky, Smithsonian Folkways 40077. Anthology featuring Holcomb and other musicians from the area.
The High Lonesome Sound, Smithsonian Folkways 40079. Drawing from all of Holcomb's Folkways recordings, a beautifully produced reissue with great notes and photographs by John Cohen.

HOLLY, BUDDY (b. Clarence Hardin H., Lubbock, Tex., September 7, 1936–February 3, 1959)

The songs and performance style of Holly, one of the founding fathers of COUNTRY-ROCK, have greatly influenced the growth of country, pop, and rock music since the late 1950s.

Holly was exposed to a wide variety of music in Texas, including WESTERN SWING, R&B, and country and western. His first musical group, formed in high school with classmate Bob Montgomery, performed as Buddy and Bob over the local radio station. Montgomery was the songwriter of the duo, mostly writing in ROCKABILLY and straight country styles (he would later become a leading Nashville writer/producer, penning "Misty Blue," a 1972 hit for Joe Simon, and working with EDDY ARNOLD, B. J. THOMAS, and SLIM WHITMAN). When FERLIN HUSKY and ELVIS PRESLEY came to town in 1955, the duo was hired as the opening act, leading to Holly's first record contract. He traveled to Nashville to work with legendary country producer OWEN BRADLEY, but Bradley was not sympathetic to Holly's unique blend of rock and country, and these first recordings were a failure.

Returning to Lubbock, Holly formed a new group that he named The Crickets. In 1957 the band hooked up with producer Norman Petty, who operated a studio in Clovis, New Mexico. It was there, over the next two years, that the classic Holly recordings were made, including hits "That'll Be the Day," "Peggy Sue," "Oh Boy," "Words of Love," and "Not Fade Away." Holly split from The Crickets by the end of 1958, settling in New York and recording more pop-oriented tracks accompanied by a thick string section.

In 1959 he toured with a new band, featuring bassist WAYLON JENNINGS (whose first single, a cover of the Cajun classic "Jole Blon'," had been produced by Holly) and guitarist Tommy Alsup. It was on this tour that Holly died in the famous plane crash that ended his short career.

It may seem strange to include Holly in an encyclopedia of country music, but his influence was not limited to rock. Many of his songs have been covered by country artists. His hiccupy vocal style is often imitated, and itself can be traced back to the YODELING of country singers like JIMMIE RODGERS and GENE AUTRY. The rockin' sound of Holly's band was a natural outgrowth of earlier rockabilly recordings, and was influential on the return-to-roots country sounds of the 1980s and 1990s.

Select Discography

From the Original Master Tapes, MCA 5540. Twenty of his most famous hits.

HOLY MODAL ROUNDERS (c. 1964–1969; sporadically thereafter: Pete Stampfel [fdl, bnj, voc] and Steve Weber [gtr, voc])

The Holy Modal Rounders, an urban old-time revival duo with a unique sense of humor, are best re-membered for two LPs they cut for Prestige in the mid-1960s.

Unlike THE NEW LOST CITY RAMBLERS and other FOLK REVIVALISTS who were deadly earnest in their attempts to re-create the country music of the 1920s and 1930s, the Rounders brought a New York, tongue-in-cheek humor to their performances. This sense that a performer could interact with the culture, rather than just studiously re-create it, was very liberating for an entire generation of revival musicians. Stampfel was the more energetic of the pair, with a high, nasal voice and rough-hewn FIDDLE style that were perfectly suited to the material; Weber was quieter, playing a blues-influenced GUITAR and providing low harmony vocals.

The Rounders came into contact with New York's growing underground art scene, and soon joined forces with the avant-garde rock band The Fugs. Their later albums, with a growing cast of supporting characters, combined avant-garde noise with electrified fiddling, a musical marriage that went nowhere. The group soon disappeared into the haze of late 1960s drug culture. They were reunited in the late 1970s by Rounder Records, the folk label named in their honor, although by then Weber was a sad shadow of himself. Stampfel performed sporadically in the 1990s with numerous "bands" (loose conglomerations of different musicians), sometimes using the name The Holy Modal Rounders and sometimes using other names (such as The Bottlecaps). Against all odds the duo reunited in the late 1990s and began performing in New York City at small folk clubs, reviving much of their mid-1960s repertoire.

Select Discography

Holy Modal Rounders, Fantasy 24711. Reissues their first two (and best) LPs.
Too Much Fun, Rounder 3163. The 1999 reunion of Stampfel and Weber produced this recording, which features remakes of some of their 1960s recordings along with new "old" (traditional) material.
I Make a Wish for a Potato, Rounder 611598. Compilation of several Rounder albums by the Rounders and their disciples and spin-off bands.

HOMER AND JETHRO (Homer, b. Henry D. Haynes, Knoxville, Tenn., July 27, 1920–August 7, 1971 [gtr, voc]; Jethro, b. Kenneth C. Burns, Knoxville, Tenn., March 10, 1920–February 4, 1989 [mdln, voc])

Homer and Jethro were one of country music's greatest comedy duos—and, incidentally, were also fine musicians. The pair specialized in satires of country and pop numbers. After Homer's death Jethro enjoyed a second career as a swing-style MANDOLIN player.

The two players were thrown together when auditioning for a talent show on radio station WNOX in Knoxville. At age twelve mandolinist Jethro was performing with his brother, and guitarist Homer was playing with a trio. Program director Lowell Blanchard heard both groups jamming together backstage, immediately disqualified them from the talent contest, and hired four out of the six on the spot to be a house band for the station! He named them The String Dusters, and the group specialized in playing the popular swing music of the day. For comic relief Homer and Jethro worked up a few comedy numbers to perform while the band took a break; reaction was so positive that four years later they permanently separated from the group to perform strictly as a parody act.

They appeared on a variety of radio programs between the late 1930s and the mid-1950s, including *The Renfro Valley Barn Dance* and Chicago's *Plantation Party* before the war, and Cincinnati's *Midwestern Hayride* (where they worked from 1945 to 1947, while also making their first recordings for the local King label), then moving on to RED FOLEY's program out of Springfield, Missouri, and finally Chicago's prestigious NATIONAL BARN DANCE from 1949 to 1958. A year before signing with WLS, they had their first country and pop chart hit, a satire of "Baby, It's Cold Outside" featuring young June Carter on vocals. In 1953 they had their biggest chart hit with the crossover satire "Hound Dog in the Winder." The duo were also early pioneers of jazz-country fusion, recording a country all-stars jazz album in the early 1950s, and worked many RCA sessions.

Through the 1950s the duo continued to record satirical singles and albums. They graduated from the backwoods circuit to the glitzier Vegas arena in the 1960s, also becoming popular performers on network television. Their 1962 LP, *Playing It Straight*, an all-instrumental homage to the swing music that they both loved to perform, underscored the fact that they were more than just a comedy act. They also got a job promoting Kellogg's corn flakes in the mid-1960s.

After Homer's death in 1971, Jethro was inactive for a while. Chicago-area SINGER/SONGWRITER Steve Goodman lured him out of retirement, and he performed on many of the singer's recordings and toured with him. The BLUEGRASS and new-acoustic music revivals of the mid-1970s brought renewed interest in his mandolin playing, and Jethro was soon recording solo albums as well as working with jazz instrumentalists like Joe Venuti. Jethro's mandolin style was hardly bluegrass- or country-influenced at all; he picked up on the techniques of the great 1930s jazz guitarists and, like "TINY" MOORE (who played five-string electric mandolin with BOB WILLS), took a highly melodic approach to his playing.

Homer and Jethro were inducted into the Country Music Hall of Fame in 2001.

Select Discography

America's Favorite Song Butchers, Razor & Tie 2130. Nice compilation of twenty of their best parodies.

HONKY-TONK MUSIC (c. 1935–1955)

In the days before the jukebox, the honky-tonk—a small bar often located on the outskirts of town—became a center of musical creation. Employing hundreds of small-time performers (many of whom would later become big-time stars), these local watering holes nurtured a new style of music that would become, in the late 1940s and early 1950s, country music's mainstream voice.

Previously country musicians had performed at local gatherings, often sponsored by schools or churches, and played for a mixed audience including women and children. For this reason the repertoire tended to emphasize mainstream values: religion; home; faithfulness to wife and mother. This strong moralistic tone reached its apex in the songs of the brother acts of the 1930s, who popularized songs like "The Sweetest Gift (a Mother's Smile)" and "Make Him a Soldier."

Honky-tonks came to the fore in response to the lifting of the restrictive liquor laws during the early years of the Depression. However, because Southern towns tended to be conservative, and drinking was still frowned upon, these bars tended to be located either on the outskirts of town or in the no-man's-land between towns. Here men could gather after work to enjoy a few beers, play pool, and listen to music. The music was frequently provided by a lone guitar player who often could be barely heard above the racket. For this reason newly introduced electrified instruments (such as the STEEL GUITAR in the 1930s and electric guitars and basses in the 1950s) and drums became necessary equipment for the small-time country band, along with microphones to amplify vocals.

Besides this change in presentation, the subject matter of church-mother-home was hardly appropriate for a rough bar atmosphere. Songwriters responded by creating lyrics that reflected the realities of honky-tonk life. Songs about drifting husbands, enticed into sin by the "loose women" who gathered in bars, and the subsequent lyin', cheatin', and heartbreak created by their "foolin' around," became standard honky-tonk fare, particularly in the late 1940s. Songs like "Dim Lights, Thick Smoke (and Loud, Loud Music)" celebrate the honky-tonk lifestyle while at the same time taking a moralistic tone, warning against the allure of cheap drinks and equally cheap women. Typically in the sexist world of country music, the "fallen women" were often blamed for dragging down their hapless victims, the hardworking country men; in songs like THE STANLEY BROTHERS' "She's More to Be Pitied Than Scolded," the moralistic singer reminds his listeners that, after all, it was "the lure of the honky-tonk" that "wrecked" the life of the so-called honky-tonk angel. (The song was based on the nineteenth-century tearjerker "She's More to Be Pitied Than Censured," which tells of an earlier era of fallen, female barflies.)

In the period from about 1948 to 1955, honky-tonk music became the predominant country form, thanks largely to the contributions of HANK WILLIAMS. In songs like "Honky-Tonkin' " he contributed a more upbeat, less moralistically dour view of life in the small bars; his backup combo of crying steel guitar and scratchy FIDDLE became the model for thousands of honky-tonk bands. The honky-tonk style reached its apex in HANK THOMPSON's 1952 recording of "The Wild Side of Life," another one of those songs that both celebrate and criticize the honky-tonk life; it inspired the wonderful answer song, "It Wasn't God That Made Honky Tonk Angels," which made a major star out of KITTY WELLS.

The coming of the jukebox, allowing bars to offer music without paying for live performers, pretty much spelled the end of the golden era of honky-tonk. That, and the popularity of younger performers like ELVIS PRESLEY, who launched the brief ROCKABILLY fad (as well as the longer-lasting white rock and roll), pretty much put honky-tonk music in its grave. Still, the musical style continues to have a strong influence on country music making today, with the proliferation of dance halls in some way replacing the original honky-tonks as centers of socializing and music making. And songs like JOE DIFFIE's "Prop Me Up Beside the Jukebox (When I Die)" pay homage to classic honky-tonk attitudes.

HOOD, ADELYNE (b. South Carolina, 1897–1958)

Hood was a fiddler, pianist, and vocalist who originally recorded with VERNON DALHART and CARSON ROBISON and then made a series of tough-gal recordings. She specialized in semiclassical fiddling and dialect numbers, eventually originating the Aunt Jemima character on radio for Quaker Oats in the late 1930s.

Hood was a classically trained musician from a genteel Southern family when she met popular recording artist Dalhart around 1917. Some ten years later they joined with country guitarist Carson Robison to make the famous Dalhart-Hood-Robison trio recordings, primarily of minstrel-era songs. In 1928 Robison quit, feeling that Dalhart was unfairly milking him of his traditional repertoire, and a year later Hood and Dalhart recorded a series of duets, beginning with their biggest hit, 1929's "Calamity Jane." This highly successful recording led to a series of songs profiling

tough Western women, on which Hood took the lead with support from Dalhart, quite unusual for a female artist of the day.

In the early 1930s Dalhart and Hood briefly hosted *Barber Shop Chords*, a syndicated radio show featuring Hood in the role of saucy manicurist; in early 1931 they toured England and made some recordings there. The duo continued to work through 1933, and then reunited around 1938 in upstate New York for radio work and appearances. Meanwhile, in 1936, Hood had begun broadcasting for the NBC network as a "folksinger," taking the name of Betsy White (which she used through the late 1930s when working alone or with Dalhart). She continued to perform on radio through the mid-1940s, increasingly focusing on portraying "mammies," then wed a wealthy Pittsburgher and retired from the business.

Although Hood's "country" background, like Dalhart's, did not run very deep, she was unmistakably Southern in her accent. Her flair for comic novelty numbers, and her ability to portray different "characters" through her music, made her tremendously popular in the country market right up to World War II.

HOOSIER HOT SHOTS (founding members: Kenny "Rudy" Trietsch [tenor gtr, tuba]; Paul "Hezzie" Trietsch [washboard, slide whistle]; Charles Otto "Gabe" Ward [clarinet]; Frank Delaney Kettering [b])

The Hoosier Hot Shots, a novelty country act of the 1930s and 1940s, got their training portraying country RUBE characters and playing hepped-up country music in Ezra Buzzington's touring vaudeville troupe, known as The Rube Band or Rustic Revellers. Four Trietsch brothers, along with Paul Trietsch's wife, were members of this troupe from about 1923 through the company's folding in 1929 due to the Depression. Clarinetist "Gabe" Ward had previously led his own group, The Hoosier Melody Five, before joining with Buzzington in the early 1920s. Buzzington's outfit made one record for Gennett in 1925, including the upbeat "Brown Jug Blues." Around 1927 Frank Kettering joined the troupe, and the four original members of the Hot Shots—now just two Trietsch brothers, Ward, and Kettering—were brought together.

After Buzzington shut down his operation, the four Hot Shots got a nonpaying radio job on WOWO out of Fort Wayne, Indiana, and scraped along as best as they could. In 1933 they got their big break when they were hired to join the popular NATIONAL BARN DANCE out of Chicago. Their combination of rube humor and jazzy novelties made them an immediate success, and they recorded for dozens of dime-store and major labels through the mid-1940s. The group often began each number by asking, "Are you ready, Hezzie?," which was their trademark and also became a popular slang expression.

In 1944 Frank Kettering left the group and was replaced by Gil Taylor, and the group relocated to Hollywood. They had their only country hits in the mid-1940s, and also starred in dozens of B- and C-grade Western films, providing—what else?—the comic relief. The group soldiered on through the late 1950s, often working Las Vegas and other nightclub venues, with various members. They also recorded three albums during the early 1960s FOLK REVIVAL. Ward was the key man holding them together, and continued to perform with various Hot Shots as late as the mid-1970s.

The Hot Shots were mostly a novelty act, but an extremely popular one. Their role in preserving nineteenth-century stereotypes of country rubes in the country-comedy tradition was important, but they also helped promulgate a more syncopated, swinging sound and harmony singing in country music—although they were hardly alone in this effort. Still, they were an enjoyable band—and who else could get away with recording "From the Indies to the Andes in His Undies"?

Select Discography

Rural Rhythm, Columbia/Legacy 52735. Twenty-song compilation.

HOPKINS, AL, AND THE HILL BILLIES (c. 1924–1931: Al [bert Green] Hopkins [pno]; Charlie Bowman [fdl]; [Alonzo Ellis] Tony Alderman [fdl]; John Hopkins [gtr]; Frank Wilson [Hawaiian gtr])

Al Hopkins and The Hill Billies were an old-time string band from the North Carolina/Virginia border area who popularized the term "hillbilly" as something other than a pejorative name for folks from the backwoods.

The group was groundbreaking in many ways. Although from rural western Virginia, they were performing in Washington, D.C., on major radio station WRC as early as 1925; this led to auditions with Victor and Okeh records. They were signed by Okeh, and their first session was supervised by legendary producer RALPH PEER. When Peer asked Hopkins for the group's name, he is said to have replied, "Call the band anything you want. We are nothing but a bunch of hillbillies from North Carolina and Virginia anyway." A publicity photo from the time emphasizes this hillbilly image; the band members are decked out in worn coveralls, bandannas, and floppy hats (Hopkins wears his fashionable Stetson sideways), and they all stand with wide-mouthed grins, emphasizing the country-RUBE look. However, the strength of their music making and the quality of their recordings also gave new

meaning to the word "hillbilly," making it a term of pride as well as scorn (much as in the previous decades Southern black musicians had embraced the term "jazz," which originally also had negative connotations).

The Hill Billies were so popular that they landed a job in New York in 1927; within the next few years they performed for President Calvin Coolidge and appeared in an early Vitaphone fifteen-minute "soundie" (short film). The band was also unusual in featuring piano accompaniment, played by leader Hopkins, as well as Hawaiian-styled slide guitar. Some of their sides were issued under the equally colorful name of The Buckle Busters. However, the Depression brought an end to the group's short ride of fame, and they returned to life in the mountains.

Select Discography

Complete Recordings, Vols. 1–3, 1925–28, Document 8039–8041. All of the recordings issued by Hopkins.

HOPKINS, DOC (b. Howard H., Harlan County, Ky., January 26, 1899–January 3, 1988)

Hopkins was a popular country singer who is best remembered for his radio work from the 1930s to the mid-1940s.

Hopkins did not set out for a musical career, although he learned to play BANJO, MANDOLIN, and GUITAR as a child. He served in the Army in World War I, and then in the Marines after the war ended. Settling in Mount Vernon, Kentucky, he began playing banjo in the late 1920s with two younger high-school kids, Karl Davis and Harty Taylor (later famous as KARL AND HARTY) in a band they called The Krazy Kats. The band landed a job on a Louisville radio station, and within a year was hired by Chicago's NATIONAL BARN DANCE. Producer JOHN LAIR enlarged the band and renamed them The Cumberland Ridge Runners; they became the house band in 1930.

By 1931, though, Hopkins had left the band and was performing solo on WLS—mostly traditional country songs and ballads delivered in a relaxed, smooth voice, accompanying himself on the banjo. He made his first solo records in late 1931, and also recorded later in the decade for the dime-store American Record Company (ARC) family of labels. In 1935 he joined the popular *Suppertime Frolic* show, also broadcast out of Chicago and a major rival to the *National Barn Dance*. Hopkins made his final recordings of this period in 1941 for Decca. A year later he rejoined WLS, where he was given his own morning show in addition to his *Barn Dance* duties.

By 1949, however, Hopkins's old-time style of ballad singing and banjo playing was fairly dated, and he retired from music making. Except for a brief period when he lived in Los Angeles, he remained in Chicago, and was "rediscovered" during the 1960s FOLK REVIVAL. He made some final recordings for the small Birch label, and also played the folk festival circuit for a while into the 1970s and early 1980s.

HORTON, JOHNNY (b. J. LaGale H., East Los Angeles, Calif., April 30, 1925–November 5, 1960)

Horton was a mid-1950s HONKY-TONKER who single-handedly launched the early-1960s craze for pseudo ballads with his hit recording of JIMMY DRIFTWOOD's "Battle of New Orleans."

Horton was born while his family was residing in southern California, but the family regularly moved between rural Texas, where his father had a small farm, and California. Johnny eventually finished high school and made a few stabs at college, then, in the late 1940s, followed one of his older brothers to California, where he worked in the mail room of a movie studio. The brothers rambled between Seattle, Florida, and California before Johnny took a trip to Alaska.

In early 1950 Horton was back in Texas, where he was inspired to try a career in music after winning a local talent contest. By year's end he had returned to California, where he was heard by country producer Fabor Robison, who had him signed to the small Cormac label and arranged for him to appear on local radio and TV. One of Horton's day jobs was working for a fishing tackle maker; hence Robison promoted him as "The Singing Fisherman." Cormac quickly folded, and Robison moved his talent to Abbott Records, a label he owned with a drugstore owner. More Horton releases followed through 1951, when Johnny married and relocated to Louisiana in order to appear on THE LOUISIANA HAYRIDE radio show. In 1952 Robison managed to interest Mercury Records in Horton, but his first big-label release was only a marginal seller.

At the *Hayride*, Horton had befriended HANK WILLIAMS, who was on the last alcohol-soaked legs of his career. After Williams died, Horton—whose wife had previously left him—married Williams's widow, a gorgeous young redhead named Billie Jean. His career, though, was quickly going nowhere, and took an even greater blow in 1954 when he parted with manger Robison, who was now more successfully promoting JIM REEVES. Horton left both *The Louisiana Hayride* and Mercury Records in late 1954, and it seemed his career was over.

But then a new force came into his life and career, manager/performer Tillman Franks. Though Franks had been a big-time manager following World War II, with acts like WEBB PIERCE, he was now as down on his luck as Horton. However, through old friend Pierce, he was able to get Horton a contract with Columbia.

Horton's first big hit was the first record he made for Columbia, 1956's "Honky-Tonk Man," a song with the upbeat power of ROCKABILLY. A string of hits followed, but then, as if jinxed, Horton's career took another nosedive from early 1957 to late 1958. Then, miraculously, he bounced back with his first country #1 hit, "When It's Springtime in Alaska," the first of the "saga" songs; it tells a Robert Service-like story of tough times in the gold prospecting days, complete with a swelling country-string section. The ever-popular "Battle of New Orleans" followed in the same year, leading to a slew of folky-styled "ballads," including 1959's "Johnny Reb" and 1960's "Sink the Bismarck" and "North to Alaska."

While enjoying this newfound success Horton began to have strange premonitions of his own death. He made preparations for his passing and even took steps to avoid his death, practicing driving his car off the road, in the belief he would be killed while driving. Nonetheless, toward the end of 1960, Horton was in fact killed in an automobile accident while en route from Texas to Nashville. He continued to be a popular country artist even after his death, and his songs have been covered by everyone from Claude King to DWIGHT YOAKAM.

Select Discography

American Original, Columbia 45071. All your favorite hits on one CD.
1956–60, Bear Family 15470. Four CDs giving you 127 of his Columbia recordings along with demos. The hits and so much more!

HOT MUD FAMILY (c. 1972–1982: Dave Edmundson [fdl, voc]; Suzanne Edmundson [gtr, voc]; Rick Good [bnj, voc]; Tom "Harley" Campbell [b, voc])

The Hot Mud Family was an Ohio-based old-time string band who were active on the FOLK-REVIVAL scene in the 1970s.

The Family centered on the husband-wife team of the Edmundsons along with banjoist Rick Good, who originally as a trio performed material in THE CARTER FAMILY mold; they viewed themselves as an organic family, if not a blood one, and took their name from a combination of their astrological signs (earth, fire, and water equaling, in their minds, Hot Mud). They were one of the few old-time bands to feature a female as a lead vocalist, and Edmundson played a number of instruments as well, although she most often limited herself to GUITAR on stage. The group recorded a number of albums for JIMMIE SKINNER's Ohio-based Vetco label in the mid-1970s before moving on to the larger Flying Fish label. However, as the old-time revival fizzled out, so did the band (and the Edmundsons' marriage), and by 1982 they had called it quits.

The group's repertoire focused on old-time fare and some straight HONKY-TONK country, thanks to Suzanne's affinity for country WEEPERS. Good was able to re-create the BANJO and vocal style of legendary performer UNCLE DAVE MACON, which became a feature of their stage show. Campbell was a fine bass vocalist, and in the 1980s formed an acoustic-folk trio with fiddler Tom McCreesh and hammer-dulcimer player Walt Michael. He is also the author of the fine BLUEGRASS-GOSPEL number "The Man in the Middle," which was covered by a number of 1980s newgrass bands.

HOT RIZE (c. 1977–1989: Pete Wernick [bnj]; Tim O'Brien [mdln, gtr, voc]; Charles Sawtelle [gtr, voc]; Nick Forster [b, voc])

Founded by BLUEGRASS banjoist Pete Wernick, Hot Rize was one of the more traditional of the "newgrass" bands of the 1980s.

Wernick began his career playing second banjo to TONY TRISCHKA in the all-instrumental, progressive COUNTRY COOKING band from Ithaca, New York, in the mid-1970s. He then moved to Colorado and recorded a solo album, featuring a more traditional bluegrass sound and vocal numbers (although he did play his BANJO through a phase shifter!). Shortly thereafter Hot Rize was formed; its name is taken from a brand of flour made by the Martha White bakeries, FLATT AND SCRUGGS's radio sponsors, and therefore is a nod toward traditional bluegrass. The group recorded several albums through the 1980s, drawing on the traditional repertoire of country songs from the 1930s and 1940s, bluegrass standards, and their own compositions in a traditional style.

Unlike Trischka, whose noodling solos favor melodic improvisation and far-out chord progressions, Wernick has maintained close ties with traditional bluegrass banjo techniques, particularly making the "Scruggs roll" (a method of playing chords in a rapid arpeggio originated by Earl Scruggs) a central element of his technique. O'Brien's high tenor vocals recall a more mellow BILL MONROE, as does his MANDOLIN playing, which tends to be sweetly melodic rather than encompassing the raw power other players have developed. Sawtelle was a fine flatpicker on the guitar, somewhere between DOC WATSON and TONY RICE in style.

In the early 1980s Hot Rize added a new element to their live show, introducing themselves as another band entirely, called Red Knuckles and The Trailblazers. This parody country bar band specialized in the HONKY-TONK WEEPERS of the 1950s, and was both an homage to and a subtle satire of the best (and worst) in this style of music. As an alter-ego band, Red Knuckles

made two separate albums, and became almost as popular as the original group.

By the late 1980s, O'Brien had moved to Nashville in search of a career as a SINGER/SONGWRITER; he has recorded solo albums of soft-country songs, as well as a duo album with his sister Mollie, who sounds like a countrified LINDA RONSTADT, and he has recently been leading an acoustic trio called The Oh Boys that performs his own compositions plus country standards. Wernick reemerged in 1993 with his second solo album, a collection of bluegrass-styled instrumentals along with original compositions recorded with a light-jazz trio (clarinet, vibes, and drums). Sawtelle died in the late 1990s after a long struggle with cancer; a collection in his honor was issued following his death.

Select Discography

Red Knuckles/Hot Rize Live, Flying Fish 70107. CD reissue of two 1980s LPs featuring both Hot Rize and their alter-ego band, The Trailblazers.
Take it Home, Sugar Hill 3784. 1990 release, the last from the band.

HOUSTON, DAVID (b. Bossier City, La., December 9, 1938–November 25, 1993)

Houston was a popular country star of the mid-1960s, best remembered for his hits "Mountain of Love" and "Almost Persuaded."

Coming from distinguished lineage (his father was a descendant of famous Texan Sam Houston and his mother of Confederate general Robert E. Lee), Houston showed musical talent early on. He was encouraged in his singing career by a family friend, Gene Austin (who was himself a crooning star of the 1920s, famous for his recording of the pop classic "My Blue Heaven"). Houston auditioned for the famed LOUISIANA HAYRIDE radio show when he was twelve, and was a regular cast member within a few years. While working there he gained the attention of promoter/musician Tillman Franks, who would play a key role in his career.

After a few years of college, Houston returned home to work with his father and brother in their house-building business. Franks called Houston in the early 1960s, asking him if he was interested in recording a new song called "Mountain of Love." Franks supervised the recording and took it to Epic Records in Nashville, who immediately signed the singer. The song was a big 1963 crossover hit, and Houston followed it with even bigger hits, including 1965's "Livin' in the House of Love" and the song most closely associated with him, 1966's "Almost Persuaded," a classic HONKY-TONK tale of a man hovering on the edge of cheatin' on his wife, for which he won a Grammy.

A year later Houston was offered a role in the grade-D country flick *Cottonpickin' Chickenpickers*, certainly not one of cinema's finest moments. Meanwhile he continued to churn out the hits through the early 1970s, including two duets with BARBARA MANDRELL, 1970's "After Closin' Time" and 1974's "I Love You, I Love You," plus numerous solo hits. In 1972 he was made a member of THE GRAND OLE OPRY, where he remained a performer for twenty-one years, until his death.

By the mid-1970s Houston's career began a free fall from which it never recovered. He bounced from small label to smaller label, scoring a couple of minor hits along the way. Meanwhile he continued to tour and perform on the lower end of the country circuit, often accompanied by his manager/friend Franks, who played guitar in his backup band.

Select Discography

American Originals, Columbia/Legacy 45074. 1963–1970 recordings, including all the big hits.

HOWARD, HARLAN (b. H. Perry H., Detroit, Mich., September 8, 1929–March 3, 2002)

One of Nashville's most prolific and well-loved songwriters, Howard has over 400 songs to his credit, and many of them have become country standards.

Although Howard later claimed to have been born in Lexington, Kentucky, he was actually born in Detroit. His Southern family were devoted listeners to WSM's GRAND OLE OPRY, and Howard's first idol was HONKY-TONK singer ERNEST TUBB. Although he began composing his own songs at age twelve, he didn't really begin playing GUITAR until after high-school graduation, while he was stationed as a paratrooper at Fort Benning, Georgia. While there he made weekly pilgrimages to Nashville on his days off, and began aspiring to a country-music career.

After completing his military service Howard bummed around the country, eventually ending up in the vibrant music scene of Los Angeles, centered on the famous *Town Hall Party* radio show. There he met JOHNNY BOND and TEX RITTER, both of whom took an interest in his career and began publishing his songs. He also met and married a young singer named Lulu Grace Johnson (aka JAN HOWARD), who would later have a career on her own. WYNN STEWART was the first person to record a Howard song, "You Took Her off My Hands," followed by Charlie Walker's classic 1958 recording of "Pick Me Up on Your Way Down," Howard's first certifiable hit.

During the late 1950s and early 1960s Howard compositions dominated the charts, including 1958's WEEPER classic "Mommy for a Day," recorded by KITTY WELLS; PATSY CLINE's 1961 hit "I Fall to Pieces" (written with ex-rocker HANK COCHRAN); 1963's moralistic

"Don't Call Me from a Honky-Tonk," recorded by Johnny and Jeanie Mosby; "Busted," a hit for JOHNNY CASH on the country charts and for RAY CHARLES on the R&B/pop charts in the same year; and "Streets of Baltimore," written with Tompall Glaser of THE GLASER BROTHERS, a 1966 hit for BOBBY BARE. In the late 1960s Howard recorded a couple of albums for Monument and smaller labels, although his own performances didn't equal others' interpretations of his songs. He was divorced from Jan in 1967.

Howard was more active in the business end of things in the 1970s and 1980s. New-country star RODNEY CROWELL lured him out of retirement to cowrite "Somewhere Tonight," a 1987 hit for HIGHWAY 101, and Howard had a few other late-career hits, including PATTY LOVELESS's "Blame It On Your Heart." In the later '90s, Howard helped champion the career of newcomer SARA EVANS. He died suddenly at his Nashville home in early 2002.

HOWARD, JAN (b. Lulu Grace Johnson, West Plains, Mo., March 13, 1930)

Howard was the wife of the famed songwriter HARLAN HOWARD during her biggest hitmaking days, although she was most closely associated with the country-pop singer BILL ANDERSON, with whom she recorded many successful duets.

Raised in Missouri, Jan was one of eleven children of a down-and-out farm family. She was exposed early on to country records and radio, and began performing locally while still in high school. After two failed marriages she moved to Los Angeles in the early 1950s, in search of a musical career; there she met up-and-coming songsmith Harlan Howard, to whom she was soon married. Harlan used her as a demo artist for many of his songs, and soon record execs were as interested in her as an artist as they were in Howard's songs. Also through her husband she met and befriended JOHNNY CASH and his wife June Carter, and began touring with their road show.

The Howards relocated to Nashville in 1960 to further both of their careers; Jan signed with Challenge Records, cutting a duet with WYNN STEWART on "Yankee, Go Home," followed by a successful solo single on "The One You Slip Around With," a wife's teary answer to her husband's wild and reckless ways. She then moved to the Wrangler label, and finally in the mid-1960s to the major label Decca, where she was paired with the smooth-voiced baritone of Bill Anderson, beginning with 1966's "I Know You're Married," and continuing for five years with a number of Top 10 hits, from 1967's "For Loving You" through 1971's "Dissatisfied."

Howard also had solo hits, starting with 1966's "Evil on Your Mind" (a #5 hit written by her husband). Jan was divorced from Harlan in 1967; though previously she had relied on her husband for original material, she now began recording her own songs, beginning with her maudlin composition "My Son," written in the form of a letter to her son in Vietnam—who, ironically, was killed two weeks after the song was released in 1968. Other Jan Howard originals include "It's All Over but the Crying," a 1966 KITTY WELLS hit, and her own playfully titled "Marriage Has Ruined More Good Love Affairs," from 1971.

Howard's hitmaking dried up by the mid-1970s, and she went into semiretirement. She recorded sporadically, including briefly for the revived Dot label in 1985, and toured with Johnny Cash road show and TAMMY WYNETTE. By the late 1980s she was married again and working in real estate.

HUSKY, FERLIN (b. Flat River, Mo., December 3, 1927)

Ferlin Husky is two performers in one: country singer Husky and country comic Simon Crum (not to mention his earliest incarnation, HONKY-TONKER Terry Preston)!

Husky was raised on a farm in central Missouri, where he first heard country music and learned to play the GUITAR. After serving in the merchant marine, he began working as a country deejay, eventually settling in the vibrant country scene centering around Bakersfield, California. There he was discovered by CLIFFIE STONE, TENNESSEE ERNIE FORD's manager, who encouraged him to begin performing on his own. Thinking his name was too rural-sounding, Husky took the stage name of Terry Preston on his first recordings. He also took on the comic persona of Simon Crum for his stage act, a standard backwoods RUBE character. Initially it was this comic character that attracted record executives to him, although his first hit, the hanky soaker "A Dear John Letter" from 1953, was recorded under the Preston persona (in duet with JEAN SHEPARD; it inspired the follow-up "I'm Sorry, John").

Husky had his first minor hit under his own name with the HANK WILLIAMS tribute song "Hank's Song," also from 1953, followed by "I Feel Better All Over" from 1955. In 1957 he remade the song "(Since You're) Gone," which he had cut as Preston five years earlier, scoring another solid hit, followed by "Fallen Star." A year later alter ego Crum had a hit with the novelty number "Country Music Is Here to Stay." Husky also made some wonderful satires of ROCKABILLY and early rock-and-roll sounds under the Crum name.

Husky hit a dry spell in the early 1960s but returned to the charts during the period 1967–1975 with middle-of-the-road country sounds, beginning with 1967's "Once" and ending with 1975's "Champagne Ladies and Blue Ribbon Babies," written with DALLAS FRAZIER. Two years later he suffered a stroke and retired from performing.

Select Discography

Ferlin Husky, Capitol 91629. Overview of his country career.

HUTCHISON, FRANK (b. Logan County, W. Va., March 20, 1897–November 9, 1945)

Hutchison was a country-blues vocalist and guitarist who is best remembered for his 1926 recording of "The Train That Carried My Girl from Town." He played the GUITAR using open tunings and a bottleneck slide, in imitation of black blues-guitar styles, and sang in a nasal style reminiscent of blues performers.

Born and raised in the coal belt along the West Virginia–Kentucky border, Hutchison was early exposed to blues music thanks to an influx of black laborers who came to the area to lay track for the railroads that serviced the coal mines. One worker who was particularly influential was Henry Vaughn, who, according to Hutchison family legend, taught the boy the rudiments of playing slide-guitar, using a knife to dampen the strings, when Hutchison was eight years old. Another early influence was Bill Hunt, described by Hutchison as "a crippled Negro living back in the hills"; along with blues, Hunt was a repository of ragtime-era novelty songs, ballads, play-party songs, and other items popular in the hills around the turn of the century. Hutchison absorbed much of this repertoire, and was performing locally by the early 1920s. The tall, red-headed guitarist of Irish stock specialized in performing the blues, quite a novelty for a white musician at the time.

Somehow, Okeh Records of New York heard about Hutchison and brought him to the big city to record two songs in late 1926: his most famous number, "The Train That Carried My Girl from Town," featuring train-whistle sound effects performed on the guitar, and "Worried Blues." The success of this first recording led to more sessions in 1927, producing a series of blues-tinged recordings, including the traditional badman ballad "Stackalee," a reworking of the black ballad "John Henry" as "K. C. Blues," a song about the hard times in the coal mines ("Miner's Blues"), and a half-spoken narrative record based on the sinking of the *Titanic* ("The Last Scene of the Titanic"). After 1927 Hutchison recorded sporadically through 1930, and told friends that he would have recorded more blues numbers if Okeh had let him (by the end of his recording career, the company was pushing him to record more mainstream country material for a white market, urging him to work with a country fiddler). In

1930 the company stopped recording Hutchison, probably because of the onset of the Depression.

Hutchison gave up music making, which was always at best an avocation for him, sometime in the 1930s. He became a storekeeper in Columbus, Ohio, where he died in 1945. Hutchison's recordings, however, had a large impact on performers who followed him. Doc Watson, for one, re-created his recording of "The Train That Carried My Girl from Town" on one of his first records after he was "discovered" during the early days of the FOLK REVIVAL, attesting to its popularity some thirty-five years after it was originally released, and MIKE SEEGER created a compelling version, accompanied by his own FIDDLE and harmonica, that he performed and recorded in the mid-1970s.

Select Discography

Complete Recorded Works, 1926–29, Document 8003. Just about everything Hutchison recorded, a treasure trove of white country blues.

IAN AND SYLVIA (Ian Tyson, b. Victoria, British Columbia, Canada, September 23, 1933 [gtr, voc], and Sylvia Fricker Tyson, b. Chatham, Ontario, Canada, September 19, 1940 [voc])

Originally a FOLK-REVIVAL duo of the mid-1960s, the Tysons formed one of the first COUNTRY-ROCK bands—Great Speckled Bird, named for the ROY ACUFF classic—and have since been active as nouveau country singers. The duo began performing together in 1961 in their native Canada, then moved to New York in search of a more sympathetic audience. They hooked up with folk music's most masterful manager, Albert Grossman, who at the time also handled BOB DYLAN and Peter, Paul, and Mary. He got them a contract with Vanguard Records, and they had their first hit with Tyson's bilingual "Four Strong Winds," sung in English and French, which was a favorite of sensitive, long-haired college girls through the 1960s.

The duo were quite popular through the mid-1960s, helping to introduce new Canadian songwriters, including Gordon Lightfoot and Joni Mitchell, to the American market. Increasingly interested in blending country music with their own form of folk-pop, they recorded an album titled *Nashville*, which featured a strange blend of country and improvisational jazz. They then formed a country-rock group Great Speckled Bird, but the reaction of their fans was hardly enthusiastic; the audience expected to hear sensitive folk-rock, and instead were greeted with the unusual (for the time) sound of mainstream country. The group's debut album, produced by seminal rocker Todd Rundgren, went nowhere.

After the pair divorced in 1974, Ian hosted his own Canadian TV show, originally called *Nashville North*, while Sylvia pursued a solo career. More recently Ian has recorded a couple of albums of Western and COWBOY-flavored songs, both his own compositions and covers of old standards.

Select Discography

Best of the Vanguard Years, Vanguard 79516. Remastered recordings drawn from their classic albums, including live tracks from Newport that were previously unavailable.

ISAACS, BUD (b. Bedford, Ind., March 26, 1928)

Isaacs, a pioneering player of the PEDAL STEEL GUITAR, helped popularize the instrument in postwar country music.

Isaacs was influenced early in his life by hearing Jerry Byrd on country radio, and took up the Hawaiian guitar in his early teens. He was working on local radio by his mid-teens, and had acquired and was playing one of the first Gibson "Electra-Harps," an early form of the pedal steel guitar.

In 1944 he got a radio job in Texas, and then worked in various capacities as a sideman until the end of the decade, when he was hired to accompany "LITTLE" JIMMY DICKENS. He was hired for THE GRAND OLE OPRY house band in 1950, remaining there through the early 1960s, except for the period from 1954 to 1957, when he worked for the rival *Ozark Jubilee*, hosted by RED FOLEY.

In 1953 he was hired to accompany WEBB PIERCE for a recording session that produced the major hit "Slowly." This one song is generally credited with introducing pedal steel to country fans, and was an immediate sensation. Issacs is credited with creating the technique whereby the pedal is manipulated while the steel bar is slid across the strings, creating the weeping sound that has become the instrument's trademark. By this time Isaacs was playing a custom instrument, made for him by West Coast guitar maker Paul Bigsby, that featured two necks.

Isaacs was signed by RCA in 1954, and recorded a number of seminal instrumentals for the company, including the much-copied "Bud's Bounce." In 1956 the Gibson Company hired him to consult on the development of their pedal steel instrument, which was introduced a year later as the Multiharp.

Primarily doing session work, Isaacs remained active on the Nashville scene through the 1960s. He has since partnered with his wife, Geri Mapes, and the duo perform as the Golden West Singers. In 1984 he was inducted into the International Steel Guitar Hall of Fame.

J

JACKSON, ALAN (b. A. Eugene J., Newnan, Ga., October 17, 1958)

One of the best of the new-country hunks, Jackson is a talented songwriter as well as a performer in the GEORGE JONES school of honky-tonks and heartaches.

Jackson's story is a typical rags-to-riches odyssey that Nashville loves. Marrying young, he worked as a forklift driver while writing songs in his spare time. His wife was his biggest supporter, and urged him to relocate to Nashville. His first job was in the mail room of cable's Nashville Network. A chance meeting with GLEN CAMPBELL at the Nashville airport led to a job as a songwriter with Campbell's publisher; the company later sponsored his first tour. In 1989 he released his first album on Arista, featuring nine of his original songs, including his first hit, "Here in the Real World." 1991 brought his spunky "Don't Rock the Jukebox," a ROCKABILLY-flavored number declaring Jackson's allegiance to traditional country sounds.

Jackson's vocal style owes much to his mentor, George Jones, and the other great 1950s HONKY-TONK singers. His recordings are tastefully produced in a new-country style (plenty of FIDDLE and twangin' electric guitars, along with occasional DOBRO or PEDAL STEEL), and range from old-fashioned WEEPERS to modern dance numbers. His summer of 1993 hit, "Chattahoochee," is a perfect example of Jackson's appeal; the video features him water-skiing and performing in front of a campfire (for sex appeal), while the song itself is vaguely CAJUN-meets-rockabilly in flavor. Like many new-country hits, it is suited for dancing as well as listening, and the lyrics offer a nostalgic reminiscence of a country adolescence.

Unlike other early-1990s stars who have faded from the scene, Jackson has managed to continue to produce hits without changing his style much. Although he did not record between 1997 and 1999, he remained active on the road, and his earlier hits continued to be aired on radio and country TV. His 2001 hit, "It's Alright

Alan Jackson in a characteristic "hunk in hat" pose, 1995. Photo: Raeanne Rubenstein

to Be a Redneck," could have been featured on his first album. He has a knack for a catchy tune with simple lyrics that can be easily remembered. Plus, his boyish good looks remain pretty much unchanged, as frozen in time as his style and sound.

Jackson came roaring back in late 2001 with his song "Where Were You (When the World Stopped Turning)?," hastily written and recorded following the attacks on the World Trade Center and Pentagon. Propelled by the song's success, his 2002 album, *Drive*, debuted at the top of both *Billboard*'s Hot 200 and country charts, a career first for Jackson. This success was undoubtedly fueled by the patriotic mood of the song.

Select Discography

Don't Rock the Jukebox, Arista 8681. His second album, from 1991.
Greatest Hits, Arista 18801. The hits through the mid-1990s.

JACKSON, AUNT MOLLY (b. Mary Magdalene Garland, Clay County, Ky., 1880–September 1, 1960)

Jackson was a union organizer and balladeer who wrote and performed some of the most stirring songs of the 1930s. She became a spokesperson for the coal miners in their struggle to obtain better working conditions, particularly among Northern, urban audiences, for whom she often performed in the mid-1930s and 1940s.

The daughter of a coal miner, Jackson was politicized by the many disasters that she witnessed in the small mining communities. As a professional midwife she worked with many mining families, and her own life was affected by many personal tragedies, including serious injuries to her father and a brother and the deaths of another brother, her husband, and her son. She was first jailed for union activities when she was ten years old, and in 1936 was run out of her mountain home by vigilantes. She was befriended by the folklorist Alan Lomax and the novelist John Steinbeck, who helped organize concerts in New York and Washington to raise money for miners' causes. In the 1940s she was recorded by Lomax for the Library of Congress.

Jackson took the powerful vocal style of mountain singing and wed it to topical subjects. Her most famous song is "I Am a Union Woman (Join the CIO)," which became a battle cry for unions in a number of industries. Many of her songs were tinged with a bluesy undertone, reflecting not only the many tragedies in her life but also a defiance of fate. Although Jackson was idolized by urban listeners, she made only one commercial record, and was not well known by country performers. Her sister Sarah Ogan Gunning (June 28, 1910–October 14, 1983) and brother Jim Garland continued to perform topical songs on the folk circuit through the 1960s and 1970s.

Select Discography

Library of Congress Recordings, Rounder 1002. Wonderful collection of recordings of the singer in her prime, made by Alan Lomax.

JACKSON, CARL (b. Louisville, Ky., September 18, 1953)

BLUEGRASS BANJO player closely associated with GLEN CAMPBELL in the 1970s.

Jackson learned the banjo at age five, and was performing with his family's band when he was thirteen. He also toured during his teenage years with JIM AND JESSE, and recorded his first solo album at age eighteen for the local Prize label. One year later he replaced Larry McNeely in Glen Campbell's touring band, an association that would last twelve years.

Jackson's second solo album, produced by Campbell, was released in 1973, and was followed by more traditional outings on the small bluegrass-specialty label Sugar Hill. In the early 1980s he signed with Columbia, and scored some minor hits as a new-country singer, covering LEFTY FRIZZELL's "She's Gone, Gone, Gone" in 1984. Through the later 1980s he worked as a session player and vocalist, often performing with EMMYLOU HARRIS.

Jackson's banjo playing is more traditionally oriented than that of many of the younger pickers. For this reason he is more comfortable playing mainstream country sessions.

Select Discography

Banjo Hits, Sugar Hill 3737. 1970s solo album with Jim and Jesse in the backup band.

JACKSON, SHOT (b. Harold Bradley J., Wilmington, N.C., September 4, 1920–January 24, 1991)

Jackson was a pioneer player of the DOBRO and an instrument builder/designer.

Raised in North Carolina, he earned the nickname "Buckshot" as a youth; it was later shortened to "Shot," which became his professional name. He began playing guitar as a teen, but quickly switched to Dobro and steel guitar. He got his first professional work in 1937, working with George Smith's Rhythm Ramblers out of Jacksonville, Florida.

In 1944 his big break came when he was hired by Cousin Wilbur, a GRAND OLE OPRY star, to join his backup group. However, his career was short-lived; he was drafted into the Navy in 1945 and served for one year. On his return he joined THE BAILES BROTHERS, playing electric steel, and recorded with them on their early King and Columbia sessions in 1946–1947. He also played with them on the first LOUISIANA HAYRIDE broadcast in 1948.

In 1949 he teamed with JOHNNIE AND JACK, joining their backup band and accompanying them along with singer KITTY WELLS, Johnnie's wife. He played steel on her classic 1952 "It Wasn't God Who Made Honky-Tonk Angels." He also recorded with WEBB PIERCE during this period. He remained with Johnnie and Jack for about six years.

In 1955 Jackson was hired by country legend ROY ACUFF to join his Smoky Mountain Boys as a Dobro player. He remained with Acuff for about a decade, except for a brief period in 1962 when he left to manage young singer MELBA MONTGOMERY. He was hurt in the car accident that nearly killed Acuff in 1965, and decided to retire from performing soon after. He opened a music shop in Nashville and began experimenting with instrument design. He was the original partner with BUDDY EMMONS in the Sho-Bud company, which made steel guitars and later developd the Sho-Bro, a seven-stringed Dobro. In 1983 he retired due to ill health, and died eight years later.

Jackson is considered one of the best players of the Dobro. He helped keep the instrument current in country music at a time when most players were switching to pedal steel.

JACKSON, STONEWALL (b. Tabor City, N.C., November 6, 1932)

Stonewall Jackson was a minor country star of the late 1950s who had one crossover hit, 1959's "Waterloo."

Jackson came from a poor, rural background. When he was ten, he swapped a beat-up bicycle for a GUITAR, and immediately began to play. He served in the Navy in the early 1950s and then worked as a farmhand until 1956, when he moved to Nashville. He was signed by Acuff-Rose Publishing and, thanks to his good looks and pleasant voice, immediately landed TV work.

His first country hit was 1958's "Life to Go," followed by his pop crossover, "Waterloo." This novelty song told the story of a love affair, comparing the hapless man's defeat to Napoleon's rout. Early 1960s hits included "A Wound Time Can't Erase," "Don't Be Angry," and the novelty hit "B.J. the D.J." He also had some minor chart hits with his covers of the GOSPEL standard "Mary, Don't You Weep" and the prison song "I Washed My Hands in Muddy Water." Jackson continued to score minor successes through the 1960s, with one final burst of chart activity in 1967 with the two-hanky "Stomp Out Loneliness."

Jackson continued to perform through the 1970s with his group, The Minutemen, and made a comeback recording in 1981 without much further success. He has been fairly inactive musically since then, although he did write his autobiography, *From the Bottom Up*, which was published in 1991.

Select Discography

American Original, Columbia 45070. Selected recordings cut between 1958 and 1987.

JACKSON, TOMMY (b. Thomas Lee J., Jr., Birmingham, Ala., March 31, 1926–December 9, 1979)

One of the greatest and most popular Nashville session musicians of the 1950s and 1960s, Jackson helped create the modern country FIDDLE style and also made instrumental recordings that fueled the popularity of Western square dancing.

Jackson was born in Alabama, but his family moved to Nashville just before his first birthday, so he was raised in the country capital. A child prodigy on the violin, he quickly absorbed traditional fiddle stylings, listening to ARTHUR SMITH on radio and assimilating his modern techniques. He was already a professional by age twelve, when he was touring with Johnnie Wright and KITTY WELLS. As a slightly older teen he formed his own band, The Tennessee Mountaineers, and they found radio work and played for local events in Nashville. By the time he was seventeen, Jackson was a regular on THE GRAND OLE OPRY, working both with the Georgia Peach Pickers, led by Curly Williams, and Paul Howard.

Jackson's career was put on hold for two years when he enlisted in the Navy in April 1944. On his return to civilian life in 1946, he began working with a variety of musicians in Nashville. He quickly broke into studio work, appearing on a number of HANK WILLIAMS's classic recordings, including "I Saw the Light" and "Lovesick Blues." He also began a long association with RED FOLEY, playing in his backup band, The Cumberland Valley Boys. Other band members included Zeke Turner and Louis Innis on guitars and JERRY BYRD on steel guitar. The foursome often worked together on early country sessions, besides accompanying Foley.

Foley fired his band in 1948, but they remained together and moved on to Cincinnati, where they established themselves as The Pleasant Valley Boys (also known as The String Dusters). There they worked local radio and did session work for King and other labels. While recording with REX ALLEN for Mercury that year, Jackson made his first solo recordings of the traditional fiddle tunes "Black Mountain Rag" and "Fire on the Mountain." The disc sold surprisingly well, so much so that Mercury signed him as a solo artist. He remained with Mercury until 1953, when he signed with the new Nashville label, Dot. Recognizing the growing popularity of square dancing, Dot issued an LP of Jackson playing traditional tunes aimed at that market; it was a huge success, and Jackson eventually cut ten more albums of music for this audience. He eventually added a full, modern rhythm section to the recordings, bringing square dance music firmly into the Nashville Sound of the 1950s and 1960s.

Besides his solo work Jackson was in demand as a session fiddler. Working out of Nashville from the early 1950s, he recorded with just about every major country singer. RAY PRICE used him religiously for eleven years, beginning in 1956—when he made a splash with his solo on Price's megahit, "Crazy Arms"—and others were equally devoted to him, including ERNEST TUBB and FARON YOUNG. Jackson is credited with incorporating more modern fiddle techniques, such as smoothly played double stops, into country accompaniment styles.

By the early 1970s Jackson's health was failing, and many of the artists he had accompanied in the past had retired from the business. He appeared on a few more albums, including a Ray Price band reunion recording, but basically retired from playing. He died in 1979.

JACKSON, WANDA (b. W. Lavonne J., Maud, Okla., October 20, 1937)

Wanda Jackson is a country/GOSPEL belter best remembered for her ROCKABILLY hits of the 1950s and her spunky delivery.

Jackson was the daughter of a small-town barber who played piano on the side and encouraged her to take up music at an early age. She was a prodigy on GUITAR and piano, and was performing on radio as early as age ten. In 1954 she toured with country star HANK THOMPSON, impressing Thompson's bandleader, who recommended her to Decca Records. Her early records were standard-issue WEEPERS, including 1955's "Tears at the Grand Ole Opry." Later that year, however, a tour with ELVIS PRESLEY turned Wanda's musical life around. She signed with Capitol, who packaged her as "the female Gene Vincent," scoring teen-pop hits from 1956's "Honey Bop" through "Fujiyama Mama" (1958) to her biggest number, 1960's "Let's Have a Party." On many of these sides Wanda was sympathetically backed by the cream of Nashville musicians, including guitarists MERLE TRAVIS and JOE MAPHIS and country-boogie pianist Merrill Moore; "Let's Have a Party" featured R&B superstar BIG AL DOWNING (with whom Jackson toured) on piano and guitarist BUCK OWENS. Like BRENDA LEE, Wanda was one of the few girl singers of the 1950s to capture the power of rock and roll.

In the early 1960s Wanda switched directions back to country hankie-soakers, beginning with her own composition, 1961's "Right or Wrong," arranged by her bandleader, ROY CLARK. She followed this with a second crossover hit, "In the Middle of a Heartache,"

replete with NASHVILLE SOUND strings and choruses. She was given her own syndicated TV show, and continued to churn out sugary hits through the 1960s.

In 1973 Wanda made another transition, now devoting herself to gospel material. She left Capitol and recorded for small religious labels, including Word and Myrrh. Although the message changed, the musical arrangements were still heavy-handed.

In the early 1980s Wanda returned to performing rockabilly live, particularly on tours of Europe, where the style was enjoying renewed popularity. She continues to perform a mixture of pop, country, and gospel.

Jackson's best material remains her 1950s rockers. With sympathetic backup musicians and her own excellent vocals, Wanda proved that women could rock with the best of them.

Select Discography

Rockin' in the Country: The Best of, Rhino 70890. Her greatest rock and country hits.
Right or Wrong, Bear Family 15629. Four-CD set of all of her recordings, from her very first in 1954 through the early 1960s.
Tears Will Be the Chaser for Your Wine, Bear Family 16114. Picks up with her complete 1960s and early 1970s recordings.

JAMES, SONNY (b. James Loden, Hackleburg, Ala., May 1, 1929)

Raised in a country family, James had his first hits as a teen-pop crooner, then emerged as a country performer from the mid-1960s through the late 1970s.

Born into a family of musicians, Sonny appeared with the Loden Family band as early as age four. He took up the FIDDLE at age seven, and then the GUITAR, becoming proficient enough as a musician to win a job as a staff player on a Birmingham, Alabama, radio station in his teen years. He was drafted into the Army during the Korean War, serving for fifteen months and performing throughout his military service. On his return he met legendary producer/guitarist CHET ATKINS, who introduced him to house producer KEN NELSON of Capitol Records. He was signed by Capitol, who initially marketed him as a teen popster, and he scored hits in 1956–1957 with "Young Love" and "First Date, First Kiss, First Love," accompanied by thick vocal choruses.

James's career stalled out until 1963, when he returned to the charts with "The Minute You're Gone," followed by a string of mainstream country hits through the mid-1970s. His 1960s successes gained him a role in the howlingly bad D-film *Hillbilly in a Haunted House*, featuring Lon Chaney, Jr., and Basil Rathbone, a true kitsch classic. His rich baritone voice made him a natural for crossover possibilities, and he

Sonny James in the mid-1970s after he made a transition to playing country music. Photo: Raeanne Rubenstein

drew not only from the country repertoire but also pop, light rock, and even R&B catalogs. Most of his recordings suffered from the NASHVILLE SOUND/COUNTRYPOLITAN production values that were prevalent during the heart of his career.

James's career has stalled out since the mid-1970s, although he continues to work as a proficient musician and singer. He has occasionally taken a producer's role, most notably on MARIE OSMOND's 1973 recording of "Paper Roses," her first notable country success.

Select Discography

Young Love, Razor & Tie 2150. His big hits, from 1950s ROCKABILLY through 1960s country.

JARRELL, TOMMY (b. Thomas Jefferson J., Round Peak, N.C., March 1, 1901–January 28, 1985)

Jarrell was one of the great old-time fiddlers and singers, whose "discovery" in the mid-1960s, followed by recordings, festival appearances, and a documen-

tary film, did much to spur on the old-time music revival. His style was much imitated, but it could never be equaled.

Jarrell came from a musical family; his father, Ben, was a fine fiddler well-known in the Galax, Virginia–Mt. Airy, North Carolina, region. Along with BANJO players Da Costa Woltz and Frank Jenkins and child prodigy musician Price Goodson, Ben recorded as a member of Woltz's Southern Broadcasters; they recorded a single session for the Gannett label in 1927. Tommy took great interest in his father's playing: "Any time he'd take his FIDDLE out, I'd take a strong interest in it. I'd pay close attention to how he'd use his bow arm and I'd watch just exactly how he'd note. I was young, about thirteen, and it would sink in back then." In later life he could duplicate his father's style, performing the novelty fiddle number "The Drunken Hiccups" in a version remarkably similar to the one his father recorded in 1927. Tommy also learned from older fiddlers in the area, including two Civil War veterans, Pet McKinney and Zack Paine, and banjoist Charlie Lowe, who was also associated with his father.

While many other fiddlers were influenced by more modern styles heard on records and radio, Tommy seems to have learned most of his repertoire in his young days, and did not seek to emulate more modern fiddlers. Also unlike more recent players, he used a wealth of different tunings; in fact, he hadn't heard a fiddle tuned to "standard tuning," he claims, until he was in his twenties.

Tommy was "discovered" in the 1960s after years of working as a manual laborer in the mountains and performing locally. When he was recorded, he was often paired with Oscar Jenkins, the son of the banjoist Frank who had recorded with his father. However, Tommy was more sympathetically accompanied by another banjo player, FRED COCKERHAM, who is featured on many of his recordings. While Tommy also played a simple style of old-time banjo, Fred also doubled on fiddle, but his fiddling was strongly influenced by more modern players like FIDDLIN' ARTHUR SMITH, and so had a jazzier feel to it.

When the old-time revival blossomed in the 1970s, Tommy became a role model for many aspiring young musicians. He opened his home to hundreds of players, appeared regularly at festivals, and recorded widely. Besides his excellent fiddle playing, Tommy was a talented singer whose expressive vocals added much to his performances. Tommy's son, B. F. (for Benjamin Franklin, named for his grandfather), has performed as a BLUEGRASS fiddler, carrying the family's musical tradition into a third generation.

Select Discography

Legacy of, Vols. 1–3, County 2724–2726. Reissues of Jarrell's classic County recordings, beginning with his great solo fiddle album (Vol. 1), through his duets with Fred Cockerham (Vol. 2), and his solo banjo album (Vol. 3).

JENKINS, REVEREND ANDREW (b. Jenkinsburg, Ga., November 26, 1885–April 25, 1957)

A musician, entertainer, and preacher, Jenkins is best known for the many country songs he composed, particularly "The Death of Floyd Collins," a massive hit for country-styled songster VERNON DALHART in the 1920s.

Little is known of Jenkins's early life. Although born partially blind, he apparently mastered a number of musical instruments by his early twenties, including GUITAR, MANDOLIN, BANJO, and harmonica. He became a Holiness minister in Atlanta in 1910, and nine years later married his second wife, who came from a musically talented family. By this time he had lost his sight entirely. Jenkins and his family were regular performers on Atlanta's WSB from the time it began broadcasting in 1922 (they were among the very earliest country performers on radio), and then recorded for a number of years.

Jenkins composed much of their material, including many songs that have entered the country tradition, such as "God Put a Rainbow in the Clouds" and "Billy the Kid." His most popular composition was "The Death of Floyd Collins," which furniture-dealer-turned-talent-scout Polk Brockman of Atlanta (who also discovered FIDDLIN' JOHN CARSON) asked him to write. It was based on the true story of a young man who was exploring the caverns near Mammoth Cave in 1925 when he tragically died in a cave-in. The song was sold by Brockman to pioneering record producer FRANK WALKER, who selected it for Dalhart's next recording session. It became one of the most popular of all country 78s, long after the actual event was forgotten.

Jenkins and his family performed in a typical parlor style of the day, with subdued instrumentation and pretty harmonies typical of family groups such as THE CARTER FAMILY. They were the first country family band to record, setting the stage for countless other conglomerations to come.

JENKINS AND SHERRILL (DeWitt "Snuffy" Jenkins, b. Harris, N.C., October 27, 1908–April 30, 1990 [bnj, gtr, voc] and Homer Lee "Pappy" Sherrill, b. Sherrill's Ford, near Hickory, N.C., March 23, 1915–November 30, 2001 [fdl, voc])

A very popular North Carolina-based radio duo, Jenkins and Sherrill performed under the stage name The Old Hired Hands. Additionally, Jenkins's three-finger BANJO work was highly influential on BLUEGRASS pickers Earl Scruggs (of FLATT AND SCRUGGS) and DON RENO.

Jenkins started playing banjo to accompany his fiddler brother, Verl, and claimed to have been playing in a three-finger style as early as 1927. The two added a guitarist cousin to their duo and became The Jenkins String Band, broadcasting on radio out of Charlotte beginning in 1934. Two years later Snuffy joined the successful group led by J. E. MAINER, The Mountaineers, recording with them through 1938 and performing over station WIS in Columbia, South Carolina.

Mainer took a more lucrative radio job elsewhere in 1939, leaving his backup group to fend for themselves. Announcer Byron Parker, who went by the moniker "The Old Hired Hand," took over the band's leadership that year, and a new player, Homer Sherrill, joined the band on FIDDLE. Sherrill had played the fiddle since age seven, making his radio debut six years later, and had since worked with a number of popular local groups, including THE BLUE SKY BOYS and THE MORRIS BROTHERS.

Under Parker's leadership the group was renamed The WIS Hillbillies. With various members they continued to perform over the radio, and made recordings in 1940 and 1946. In 1948 Parker died, and Jenkins and Sherrill took over the band, which they named The Hired Hands in Parker's memory. Along with ex-medicine show comedian Julian "Greasy" Medlin, the group expanded its range to country comedy, and the RUBE characters of "Snuffy" (Jenkins) and "Pappy" (Sherrill) were born.

The group continued to work on WIS radio and then television through the 1950s. With the FOLK REVIVAL of the early 1960s they were "discovered" and recorded by Harry Oster on his Folk Lyric label. This led to engagements at folk and BLUEGRASS festivals, and further recordings in the early 1970s for Rounder. Although the band continued to work through the 1980s, Snuffy's health began to deteriorate, and vocalist/guitarist Harold Lucas, along with his banjoist son Randy, took over as leaders of the band. A final Old Homestead album was issued in 1989, but it was a sad shadow of the duo's earlier work.

Jenkins and Sherrill were important "transitional" artists, bridging the gap between traditional old-time country string-band style and the new bluegrass picking. Jenkins was certainly a key player in the transformation of the banjo into a lead instrument.

Select Discography

Snuffy Jenkins: Pioneer of the Bluegrass Banjo with Homer Sherrill, Arhoolie 9027. 1962 sessions.

JENNINGS, WAYLON (b. Littlefield, Tex., June 15, 1937–Feb. 13, 2002)

Jennings was a baritone-voiced singer who was a leader of the 1970s OUTLAW movement, a reaction to

Waylon Jennings during his outlaw days, c. 1980. Photo: Raeanne Rubenstein

the stodginess of the NASHVILLE SOUND. Along with SINGER/SONGWRITERS KRIS KRISTOFFERSON and WILLIE NELSON, Jennings expanded the subject matter of country music while returning to a more primal, stripped-down recording sound that honored the roots of the great HONKY-TONK records of the 1950s.

Jennings came from a musical family, and was performing over local radio by the time he was twelve years old. He got his first work as a deejay at the radio station in nearby Lubbock, Texas, where he met pop-rocker BUDDY HOLLY. Holly produced Jennings's first single, a cover of Harry Choates's CAJUN classic, "Jole Blon," and invited the young singer to be his bass player on what would turn out to be his last tour. Following Holly's death, Jennings continued to work as a deejay and recorded ROCKABILLY for the small Texas label, Trend.

In the mid-1960s Waylon hooked up with CHET ATKINS at RCA Records, where he was initially packaged as a folk singer. Although he had some minor country hits, he was unhappy with the way RCA was handling him, and began introducing different material into his recordings. In 1970 he recorded a couple of songs by a then unknown writer named Kris Kristofferson, including "Sunday Morning Coming Down," and a year later released an album titled *Ladies Love Outlaws*, featuring more contemporary songs by HOYT AXTON and Alex Harvey. In 1972 he renegotiated with RCA, gaining artistic control over his recordings. The first album made under this new contract was 1973's *Honky-Tonk Heroes*, featuring Waylon's road band, The Waylors, on a set of hard-driving songs mostly written by BILLY JOE SHAVER. In 1976 RCA released an anthology album featuring Jennings and his wife, JESSI COLTER, along with Willie Nelson and Tompall Glaser (of THE GLASER BROTHERS); titled *The Outlaws*, it became the definitive collection for this new style of music. In 1978 he recorded the classic album of duets with Nelson, *Waylon and Willie*.

Although Jennings continued to produce hits well into the 1980s, he was starting to sound like a parody of himself. He recorded the theme song for TV's redneck comedy, *The Dukes of Hazard*, in the early 1980s, followed by a lackluster album of rock oldies. In the mid-1980s he reunited with Kristofferson, JOHNNY CASH, and Nelson for the concept LP *The Highwaymen*, which showed how all four of these formerly innovative performers had gotten awfully long-in-the-tooth; there would be two more albums and various tours through the early 1990s for the quartet.

Jennings left RCA for MCA in the late 1980s, but the quality of his recordings continued to drop, although his late-1980s LP *Full Circle* at least showed him reaching for his past glories. In 1995 he signed with the small Justice label, releasing two albums by the end of the decade. In 2001 Jennings was inducted into the Country Music Hall of Fame. Later that fall, suffering from diabetes, he underwent surgery for the amputation of a foot.

Jennings at his best embodied the outlaw image both physically and aurally. His accompaniment was tough, bass-driven, and reduced to the bare essentials, the perfect complement to his rough baritone. In choosing to perform songs by innovative, younger Nashville songwriters, Jennings championed songs that went beyond the pop-schlock posturing that was then being produced by Nashville's establishment. And, in relocating to Austin, Texas, with his buddy Willie Nelson in the mid-1970s, he helped establish an alternative center for country music, paving the way for the new-country revival of a decade later.

Select Discography

The Outlaws, RCA 5976. The anthology that started it all.
Only Daddy That'll Walk the Line, RCA 66299. Two-CD set documenting Jennings's recordings from the mid-1960s through the 1990s.

Waylon and Willie, RCA 8401. Cassette-only reissue of a classic collaboration.

JIM AND JESSE (b. James Monroe McReynolds, Coeburn, Va., February 13, 1927 [voc, gtr], and Jesse Lester M., Coeburn, Va., July 9, 1929 [voc, mdln])

Jim and Jesse are something of an anachronism in the country and BLUEGRASS worlds. They sound like a typical brother duet of the 1930s, right down to their homey harmonies and emphasis on simple MANDOLIN and GUITAR accompaniments. On the other hand, they scored a series of mid-1960s mainstream country hits, and they usually perform with a full bluegrass band accompanying them. For this reason their sound is both nostalgic and contemporary, an amalgam of the 1930s, 1950s, and 1990s.

Their musical pedigree is impressive: their fiddling grandfather led The Bull Mountain Moonshiners, who recorded for RCA in 1928. The young boys, Jim on guitar and tenor vocals and Jesse on mandolin and lead vocals, first performed over local radio in 1947; they also made some recordings, signing with Capitol in the early 1950s. Their career was briefly interrupted when Jesse was drafted to serve in the Korean War, but picked up steam after his discharge in 1954. They returned to radio work, this time on Knoxville's famous *Tennessee Barn Dance* program, leading their group, The Virginia Boys, which featured fiddler VASSAR CLEMENTS and banjoist Bobby Thompson.

After signing with Epic in 1962, they had a series of chart successes beginning with 1964's "Cotton Mill Man," followed by their biggest chart hit, "Diesel on My Tail." These recordings prominently featured the traditional harmonizing of the brothers, along with Jesse's distinctive mandolin playing, but otherwise were drowned in typical NASHVILLE SOUND productions. Still, they were the most traditional of any hit-making country act of the era, which was no small achievement. And their recordings were much more funky than those made by THE LOUVIN BROTHERS a few years earlier, which were drenched in vocal choruses.

Through the 1970s, 1980s, and 1990s Jim and Jesse rode the crest of the BLUEGRASS revival, returning to more traditional instrumentation on their recordings and performing at festivals throughout the United States and other parts the world. In 1994 the brothers became members of THE GRAND OLE OPRY, and began adding band backing—including electric guitar, bass, and drums—from the house band to their numbers. This backup is reflected on their most recent recordings, for the small Pinecastle label.

Select Discography

1952–1955, Bear Family 15635. Fine Capitol recordings, their first for a major label.

Y'All Come, Epic/Legacy 65076. 1960s hits for Epic, in bluegrass and HONKY-TONK country style.

JOHNNIE AND JACK (Johnnie Robert Wright, b. Mount Juliet, Tenn., May 13, 1914 [gtr, voc], and Jack Anglin, b. Columbia, Tenn., May 13, 1916–March 7, 1963 [gtr, voc])

Johnnie and Jack were a popular 1950s vocal duo who often performed with Johnnie's wife, Muriel Deason (aka KITTY WELLS).

Both musicians came from musical families, with Wright descended from a long line of champion musicians, including his fiddling grandfather and BANJO-picking father. He came to Nashville from rural Tennessee when he was nineteen years old; there he met young Muriel Deason, who was working as a singer, and the two were married in 1938. Meanwhile, he hooked up with another singer/guitarist named Jack Anglin, and the Johnnie and Jack duo was born.

In the early 1940s, Johnnie, Jack, and Kitty toured and performed extensively with their backup band, The Tennessee Mountain Boys, performing on radio stations in Greensboro, North Carolina, and Knoxville, Tennessee, among other smaller markets. They joined THE GRAND OLE OPRY briefly after World War II, but then left to become featured acts on Shreveport, Louisiana's, popular LOUISIANA HAYRIDE radio program, before returning to the *Opry* in 1952. The duo initially cut sides for Louisiana-based Apollo records, better known for its R&B acts, and then signed with RCA in the late 1940s. They had a string of hits, beginning with 1951's "Poison Love," mostly in a blue-and-lonesome style, featuring their tight-knit harmonies. They also backed Wells on her break-through recording, "It Wasn't God That Made Honky-Tonk Angels." Other heartbreakin' hits that they recorded include "Oh, Baby Mine (I Get So Lonely)" and "Goodnight, Sweetheart, Goodnight" from 1954, 1958's "Stop the World," and 1959's "Sailor Man." They had their last hit in 1962 with "Slow Poison."

Jack Anglin died in 1963—ironically, in a car crash on the way to the funeral service for PATSY CLINE. Wright went out on his own, having a hit with the patriotic "Hello, Vietnam" in 1965. Son Bobby began performing with Wright and Wells in a family roadshow in the late 1960s, and in 1977 he recorded a tribute album to his dad's famous duo for Starday.

Select Discography

and the Tennessee Mountain Boys, Bear Family 1553. Six-CD set featuring all of their recordings made between 1947 and 1962, 180 tracks.

JOHNSON MOUNTAIN BOYS (c. 1982–1988; sporadically thereafter: Dudley Connell [lead voc, gtr];

David McLaughlin [mdln]; Eddie Stubbs [fdl]; Richard Underwood [bnj]; Marshall Wilborn [b])

There was something eerie about watching this acclaimed mid-1980s retro-BLUEGRASS group perform; decked out in string ties, suit jackets, and white cowboy hats, they looked like an archetypal bluegrass ensemble out of the mid-1950s come back to life. Though some charged them with the worst type of ersatz recreation of the classic bluegrass sound, they gained a wide audience and helped revive many lesser-known classic songs and instrumentals. As the band became more mature, they let their personalities flavor the music more, as well as showing off to good effect their instrumental and vocal virtuosity. Although they officially disbanded in 1988, they came out of retirement in the later 1990s to perform again.

Select Discography

Favorites, Rounder 11509. Selections from their Rounder recordings of the 1980s.

JONES, GEORGE (b. G. Glenn J., Saratoga, Tex., September 12, 1931)

George Jones, c. 1960s. Photo: University of North Carolina, Southern Historical Collection, Southern Folklife Collection, University Archives

The ultimate HONKY-TONK singer, Jones is the one artist that today's new-country male vocalists consistently cite as a key influence on their style. Indeed, his distinctive singing style, often jumping from a grumbling bass to a falsetto hiccup within the same measure, is immediately recognizable. Jones is also one of those artists whose legend (as a rabble-rousing, hard-drinking, hard-living performer) has more than once threatened to engulf him, yet somehow he survives and maintains his popularity.

Jones began performing honky-tonk material after his discharge from the Marines in the early 1950s. In 1954 he hooked up with HAROLD "PAPPY" DAILY, who served as his manager and also ran Starday Records, which issued his first recordings. His early records showed the strong influence of HANK WILLIAMS, although he also briefly jumped on the ROCKABILLY bandwagon, recording under the names Thumper Jones and Hank Smith and The Nashville Playboys. His first big hits came with United Artists in the early 1960s with songs drenched in honky-tonk heartache, including 1962's "She Thinks I Still Care." He also recorded his first duets with MELBA MONTGOMERY at this time.

In the mid-1960s Jones's recordings suffered from the typical girly chorus and mushy strings that were among the worst excesses of the NASHVILLE SOUND. He married TAMMY WYNETTE in 1969, and moved to her label, Epic, in 1971, hooking up with producer BILLY SHERRILL. There he recorded a series of hugely successful duets with his wife, beginning with 1973's "We're Gonna Hold On," and continuing after their divorce through the 1970s. He also recorded a number of solo hits, all custom-tailored to his legendary status as a heartbroken, heavy drinker: most notable were 1981's "If Drinking Don't Kill Me (Her Memory Will)" and 1986's "The One I Loved Back Then." In the late 1980s Jones branched out to cut a series of duets with unlikely younger partners, from LINDA RONSTADT to Elvis Costello and James Taylor. Through the 1980s he had a tendency to coast on his reputation, both in the choice of his material and in often lackluster (or missed) performances.

The revival of the honky-tonk sound among the mid-1980s New Nashville vocalists is largely credited to the influence of Jones. Every time RANDY TRAVIS dramatically drops his voice to a low bass note, he's emulating the style pioneered by Jones. Although none of the new singers can match his unique vocal style, many try to emulate his image.

In 1992 Jones was elected to the Country Music Hall of Fame. In 1993 he made yet another comeback (although he's never really gone away) with "I Don't Need Your Rockin' Chair," a good-natured but defiant statement of where this old fella's coming from. In 1995 Jones reunited with ex-wife and duet partner, Tammy Wynette, for the *One* album and tour; Wynette was very ill by this time, but nonetheless the reunion brought new attention to Jones. A year later he published his autobiography, a somewhat sanitized version of his rags-to-riches-to-drug-abuse-to-renewal life story.

Jones's rough and rowdy ways were not entirely a thing of the past, however; in March 1999 he was involved in a bad accident, crashing his car into a bridge, and was charged with driving under the influence. Luckily for Jones he was not seriously injured, and he returned to recording and performing. In 2001 he released a new album, *The Rock: Stone Cold Country 2001*, which included a duet with GARTH BROOKS on "Beer Run (B Double E Double Are You In?)," which was intended to be a comeback single for both singers. However, Brooks canceled its release after the terrorist attacks on September 11, 2001. Jones subsequently complained to the press, saying Brooks failed to live up to his bargain to help promote the record. Either Jones, a longtime alcoholic, or his record label added this unusual note to the back of the album: "George Jones does not in any way condone drinking and driving, and the inclusion of the song 'Beer Run' is not an endorsement of such behavior. Historically, drinking songs have been an integral part of country music. George asks: If you do drink, do so responsibly." Jones substituted a solo single, "The Man He Was," as his first new release, but it failed to see much action, and the album was largely ignored.

Jones has had trouble getting his more recent recordings played on country radio, despite the plaudits of many of today's country stars. He was so dismayed when he was told that he could perform only part of a recent release on the 1999 Country Music Association awards show that he refused to attend, a gesture symbolic of old Nashville's rejection of the more pop-oriented younger acts.

Select Discography

The Best of, Rhino 70531. 1955–1987 recordings in a hard-country vein.

Live at Dancetown USA, Ace 156. Wonderful 1965 live recordings with BUDDY EMMONS on steel guitar. Not great fidelity, but a lot of fun.

Greatest Hits, Vols. 1 and 2, Epic 34716/48839. George with Tammy Wynette on their greatest WEE-PERS and honky-tonkers.

I Love Country, Epic 54941. Sixteen tracks from the mid-1970s to early 1980s, including remakes of earlier hits.

Walls Can Fall, MCA 10562. 1993 recording reveals that The Possum can still put 'em away like few others.

Cold Hard Truth, Elektra 62368. 1999 returns-to-roots album, with Jones in good voice on a nicely produced selection of honky-tonk songs.

JONES, GRANDPA (b. Louis Marshall J., Niagara, Ky., October 20, 1913–February 19, 1998)

A country comedian and BANJO player who portrayed an eighty-year-old hayseed beginning when he was just twenty-two, Jones was a featured performer on the HEE HAW TV show.

The youngest of ten children of a sharecropping family, Jones grew up listening to his father's FIDDLE playing and his mother's accordion playing. He got his first GUITAR from his brother, and before he was fifteen, he was performing locally for dances and get-togethers.

After moving from farm to farm throughout Jones's early childhood, the family settled in Akron, Ohio, in 1928, where Pop Jones hoped to get a job in a tire plant. Marshall, as Grandpa was then known, entered a talent contest at the local Keith-Albee theater and won $50.00, enough to buy a pretty fancy guitar. He hooked up with harmonica player Joe Troyan, and the duo began performing on local radio; Jones was billed as "The Young Singer of Old Songs." From Akron they moved to Cleveland, where they were heard by talent scouts for the radio show *Lum and Abner*, broadcast out of Boston. This corn-pone serial hired them to be staff musicians, and in Boston Jones linked up with country balladeer BRADLEY KINCAID.

Although he was only twenty-two at the time, the gruff-voiced Jones already sounded like an elderly backwoodsman. Seeking to cash in on the image, Kincaid had him outfitted in oversize clothes, old boots, and a comic brush-handle mustache. He renamed him "Grandpa" Jones, and from then on, the comedian switched to portraying an energetic old-timer. He even switched to playing the banjo, more often associated with old-time music than the guitar. Jones took UNCLE DAVE MACON as a role model, emulating the older performer's energetic approach to music making.

After touring with Kincaid, Jones had jobs on a number of West Virginia-based radio stations. In 1942 he signed on with *The Boone County Jamboree*, broadcast out of Cincinnati. There he met THE DELMORE BROTHERS and MERLE TRAVIS; the four formed The Brown's Ferry Four, which sometimes featured RED FOLEY. Jones also hooked up with Syd Nathan, a local record-shop owner who later formed King Records, for which Jones made his first recordings.

After serving in World War II, Jones returned briefly to Cincinnati, but felt his talents were not appreciated enough by the radio station there. In 1947 he joined THE GRAND OLE OPRY, remaining a favorite performer there for decades. Through the 1950s and 1960s he toured with *Opry* package shows, often accompanied by his wife, Ramona. Besides performing traditional mountain songs and energetically playing the banjo, Grandpa and Ramona performed the kind of country comedy dialogues that audiences love.

In 1969 Jones signed on with *Hee Haw*, and his old-time, cornball humor became a permanent feature of this ever-popular program. His autobiography, *Everybody's Grandpa*, a chatty memoir, appeared in 1984. During the later 1980s and 1990s Jones was less active as a performer, due to declining health. He died in 1998.

Select Discography

Grandpa Jones Story, CMH 9007. Cassette-only reissue of 1970s recordings, with wife Ramona on a couple of cuts.

JORDANAIRES, THE (Original members: Gordon Stoker [1st ten], Neal Matthews [2nd ten], Hoyt Hawkins [bar], Hugh Jarrett [b])

Most famous of all the Nashville vocal groups, The Jordanaires have backed hundreds of country and pop performers. Their greatest fame comes from their association with ELVIS PRESLEY on his first RCA recordings.

Formed in 1948 in their hometown of Springfield, Missouri, the group first sang in pure barbershop style. In the early 1950s they came to Nashville, where they emulated groups like The Golden Gate Quartet in creating a GOSPEL-harmony hybrid. They began recording spirituals for Decca, backing RED FOLEY on his recording of "Just a Closer Walk with Thee." In 1953 they joined the cast of EDDY ARNOLD's TV show, the first network program to feature Nashville musicians (although it was broadcast from Chicago). They also toured with Arnold, in 1954 performing at Memphis's Cotton Carnival, where supposedly a still-green Elvis first heard them.

The Jordanaires were popular at Nashville sessions, and CHET ATKINS, who supervised Elvis's first RCA recordings, undoubtedly brought them in to fatten his sound. They provided everything from pop-sounding "ooh wahs" to sophisticated gospel harmonies and even some doo-wop on 1956's "I Was the One" (the B-side to "Heartbreak Hotel"). They went on to record many sides with The King, and are an integral part of the sound of his mid-1950s hits, including "All Shook Up," "A Fool Such As I," "Are You Lonesome Tonight?," and "It's Now or Never." Their own solo hit, "Sugaree," was a Top 10 country song in 1956.

There's hardly a major country artist of the 1950s or 1960s who was not associated, at least in the studio, with these smooth vocalists. Everyone from PATSY CLINE to MARTY ROBBINS worked with them (along with popsters like Steve Lawrence and Julie Andrews). They appear on all of RICK NELSON's classic recordings, as well as on JOHNNY HORTON's late 1950s and early 1960s hits. They also are featured on all twenty-eight of Elvis's film sound tracks.

The group continued to work into the 1990s with various members. It was inducted into the Country Music Hall of Fame in 2001.

JUDDS, THE (Wynonna, b. Christina Ciminella, Ashland, Ky., May 30, 1964 [gtr, voc], and Naomi, b. Diana Ellen Judd, Ashland, Ky., January 11, 1948 [voc])

The Judds were a popular mother-daughter duo of the 1980s who came out of the new-country movement but became one of the most successful mainstream acts. Emulating the vocal harmonies of the brother acts of the 1930s and 1940s, they scored many hits combining a repertoire of sexy up-tempo numbers with ballads dripping nostalgia for "the good old days." Oddly enough, Naomi hardly played the role of a country mother; her sex appeal was always much greater than that of her often dour-looking daughter, although Wynonna musically was the heart of the act.

Much has been made of the Judds' story, beginning with Wynonna's birth in rural Kentucky; the family's move to California, where Naomi tried unsuccessfully to become a model; their return in the mid-1970s to a

Wynonna Judd, after embarking on her solo career, 1995. Photo: Raeanne Rubenstein

"simple country life" in Kentucky, where Wynonna began to show her budding talent on the guitar; Wynonna's "wild teenage years," when only her music would soothe her; their discovery that they could relate to each other through their music; their relocation in 1979 to Nashville, where Naomi pursued a nursing degree while the duo recorded demo tapes on a $30.00 recorder purchased at K-Mart; and their final successful audition, performing THE BLUE SKY BOYS' "The Sweetest Gift (a Mother's Smile)" for RCA executives, which won them a recording contract.

The Judds' first recordings were very much in the mold of traditional country harmony singing, and the arrangements emphasized acoustic instruments without too much clutter. Their first #1 hit played off their mother-daughter relationship in "Mama, He's Crazy." A string of hits through the 1980s, including the sentimental "Grandpa (Tell Me 'Bout the Good Old Days)," the up-tempo "Rockin' with the Rhythm of the Rain," and the anthemic "Love Can Build a Bridge," showed the talents of Wynonna as a gutsy lead singer, tempered by her mother's sweet harmonies. As their career grew, their recordings became more heavily produced, and their act more elaborate, reflecting country music's tendency to smother their best acts in glossy productions.

The Nashville music world was stunned by the announcement of Naomi's retirement from active performing, due to chronic hepatitis, in 1990; the duo undertook a yearlong "farewell tour," culminating in a pay-per-view concert at the end of 1991. Wynonna came out from under her mother's shadow with her first solo LP, showing the influence of pop-rock singers, particularly Bonnie Raitt, on her style. In fact her solo LPs show a much more blues-rock orientation than a straight country one, while her stage show is geared more toward a pop audience.

Without her mother on board to provide sex appeal, Wynonna was put in the uncomfortable position of being gussied up by her handlers, who even tried to give her a few dance steps, but she clearly remained most comfortable singing and playing the guitar without having to provide the "visual excitement" audiences seem to expect in this day of music videos. Wynonna continued to release albums through the 1990s, although her later efforts failed to garner much attention.

Despite her "retirement," Naomi continues to show up at various Nashville events, looking none the worse for wear. She also gives inspirational talks (for a fee) to people facing illness.

Select Discography

The Judds, RCA 8402. Their debut album, and their most traditionally oriented recording.

Greatest Hits, Vols. 1 and 2, RCA 8318/61018. All their biggies. The first volume takes you to 1987; the second, through the rest of their chart-toppers.

Collection, MCA 11583. Hits from Wynonna's first three solo albums from the 1990s.

K

KARL AND HARTY (Karl Victor Davis, b. near Mount Vernon, Ky., December 17, 1905–May 29, 1979 [mdln, voc], and Hartford Connecticut Taylor, b. near Mount Vernon, Ky., April 11, 1905–October 1963 [gtr, voc])

Karl and Harty, although not related by blood, were an influential duo in the brother-act mold who were members of the cast of the popular NATIONAL BARN DANCE radio show in the 1930s, influencing other acts such as THE BLUE SKY BOYS.

Childhood friends from rural Kentucky, Karl and Harty took up music early in life. Karl picked up the MANDOLIN after hearing local mountain songster DOC HOPKINS play the instrument, and Harty taught himself to play the GUITAR. Their schoolmaster for at least part of their early teen years was JOHN LAIR, who would later be the main force behind *The National Barn Dance* radio show. Lair brought them to Chicago to perform on the show as part of a larger band he assembled, The Cumberland Ridge Runners, which also featured Doc Hopkins. They performed on this show, and Lair's related *Renfro Valley Barn Dance* out of Kentucky, for many years, as well as recording for the budget American Record Corporation (ARC) label in the 1930s, and Capitol after World War II.

Besides playing mandolin, Karl wrote a number of sentimental songs that entered the repertoire of many other country entertainers, beginning with 1934's "I'm Just Here to Get My Baby Out of Jail," later covered by both The Blue Sky Boys and THE EVERLY BROTHERS. His 1938 hymn to his home state, "Kentucky," was another favorite for the many brother duos who followed. Karl and Harty's smooth, pop-styled harmonies and relaxed performance style were highly influential as well.

Karl and Harty retired from full-time performing in the early 1950s. Karl continued to work as a songwriter until his death from cancer in 1979; Harty had predeceased him in 1963, after suffering a stroke.

Select Discography

Karl & Harty, Old Homestead 137. Out-of-print LP reissuing some of their better material from the 1930s.

KAZEE, BUELL (b. Burton Fork, Ky., August 29, 1900–August 31, 1976)

A college-educated BANJO player and collector of traditional mountain songs, Kazee recorded a number of sides in the late 1920s and again in the early 1960s, during the FOLK REVIVAL.

Unlike many other mountain musicians, Kazee was well-educated, eventually becoming an ordained minister. His banjo playing was fairly restrained, as were his vocals, but he did record many classics of the American folk repertoire from 1926 to 1930, including the folk ballad "Wagonner's Lad." He also recorded two series of humorous skits, one recounting a typical backwoods election day and the other, called "A Mountain Boy Makes His First Record," that played up his rural roots. Perhaps because Kazee was more educated, his singing style was fairly simple, without much of the ornamentation or intensity that marked other mountain performers. His relaxed vocals and clear enunciation were two factors that made his records popular, particularly among other folk music collectors. An ordained Missionary Baptist minister, Kazee abandoned his career as an entertainer when the Depression led his record label, Brunswick, to close down.

Kazee was "rediscovered" during the folk-revival years, and made an album for Folkways Records that showed his style was little changed over the decades. He also occasionally performed at folk festivals.

Select Discography

Buell Kazee Sings and Plays, Folkways 3810. Early 1960s recordings, now available on special-order CD/cassette.

KEEN, ROBERT EARL (b. Houston, Tex., January 11, 1956)

Another of Texas's eccentric storytellers, Keen is a noted songwriter whose own recordings have yet to find a mainstream audience.

Keen is the son of an attorney and oil speculator, and grew up in upper-middle-class luxury in Houston. His parents had a large collection of folk and country recordings, including MARTY ROBBINS's *Gunfighter* album, which inspired the teenage Keen to begin writing narrative poems. While attending Texas A&M University in the mid-1970s, he met LYLE LOVETT and began setting his poems to music. Both Lovett and Keen went to Nashville in the early 1980s, but only Lovett found major-label interest. Keen worked menial jobs while he recorded a series of albums for the country-folk label Sugar Hill.

Not to be dissuaded, Keen returned to his native Texas, where he had a strong cult following. His career was given a significant boost when the Highwaymen (aka JOHNNY CASH, WILLIE NELSON, WAYLON JENNINGS, and KRIS KRISTOFFERSON) selected his "The Road Goes on Forever" as the title cut for their third album. In 1996 he was signed by Arista Texas, a new label trying to cash in on the "alt-Texas" country phenomenon. He recorded several albums, including a song cycle called *Walking Distance* in 1998. In early 2001 Keen moved to the Mercury subsidiary Lost Highway, and a new album was released, *Gravitational Forces*.

Keen's songs focus on Texas-type drifters, blue-collar losers, and near-criminals. He shares with Lovett a wry sensibility that colors his material. Known for his rowdy concertizing, so far Keen has been more popular as an act around Texas A&M than on disc.

Select Discography

A Bigger Piece of the Sky, Sugar Hill 1037. 1993 debut album on the small folk label.
Walking Distance, Arista Texas, 18876. 1998 song cycle.

KEITH, BILL (b. William Bradford K., Brockton, Mass., December 20, 1939)

Keith was one of the first city-born pickers to take up BLUEGRASS-style BANJO, introducing a new, melodically oriented playing style he called chromatic picking.

Born in a suburb of Boston, Keith first took up tenor banjo to play Dixieland-style music in his high-school years, but soon was sucked into the vibrant FOLK-REVIVAL scene of the Boston area. While attending Amherst College he befriended another young folknik, JIM ROONEY, and the pair were soon performing as a duo. Keith switched to five-string banjo, influenced by PETE SEEGER, and learned to pick in what was then called Scruggs style (after bluegrass banjoist Earl Scruggs of FLATT AND SCRUGGS), acquiring the rudiments from Seeger's book. Whereas Scruggs's style centered on playing sequences of chord rolls (quickly played arpeggios, or the grouping of notes from particular chords), Keith developed a melodic style in which he picked out the melody notes of traditional FIDDLE tunes, such as "Devil's Dream." This became his trademark.

In the early 1960s Keith and Rooney were active figures in the Boston folk-music scene. A 1962 locally produced album was picked up by the national folk/jazz label Prestige a year later and helped put them on the map. Keith briefly played with bluegrass legend BILL MONROE and his band in 1963 (along with young fiddler RICHARD GREENE) Monroe was impressed with his innovative banjo picking, and recorded his arrangement of "Sailor's Hornpipe" (although he insisted on calling the young picker "Brad," because, after all, there could be only one Bill in his band!). Soon after, Keith gave up bluegrass to play with Jim Kweskin's Jug Band, a 1960s folk-revival group, and then took up pedal steel guitar, reuniting with Rooney to record as The Blue Velvet Band, featuring fiddler Greene and banjoist Eric Weissberg, on an album of country standards.

Keith returned as a banjo player in 1972 when DAVID GRISMAN formed the group MULESKINNER to perform on a television program with Bill Monroe; the band ended up recording an album that was highly influential on the progressive bluegrassers of the 1970s. Keith pretty much faded into the woodwork after that album, recording occasionally with other old folkies (such as on the *Mud Acres* album), as well as occasionally issuing a solo bluegrass outing and performing with younger pickers like TONY TRISCHKA. He also issued a couple of solo albums in the 1980s and 1990s.

Although chromatic-style picking was quite revolutionary when it was new, few have followed Keith's lead in totally eliminating chord work from their playing. As an accompaniment technique chromatic picking is a dead end, and it seems that there is a limit to the number of fiddle tunes that can be arranged in this style. Still, Keith was the first picker to show urban folks that bluegrass wasn't just for cowboy-hat-wearin' backwoods pickers.

Select Discography

Banjoistics, Rounder 0148.
Fiddle Tunes for Banjo, Rounder 0124. Also includes Tony Trischka and BELA FLECK.
Beating Around the Bush, Green Linnett 2107. 1992 recordings.

KEITH, TOBY (b. Clinton City, Okla., July 8, 1961)

A heartthrob country-pop singer noted for chart-topping hits and his songwriting abilities, Keith spent high school working summers in a rodeo and school years on the football team, and, after graduation, worked on oil rigs. Only when the oil boom began to slow in the mid-1980s did he take up music, working in a bar band covering mainstream country acts like ALABAMA. Although the band was locally successful, Keith continued to divide his time between oil-field work, semi-pro football, and music. His band, which eventually became known as The Easy Money Band, put out a few independent albums and cassettes, and Keith made a few unsuccessful trips to Nashville, but nothing much was happening with his career.

In 1988 Alabama's former producer, Harold Shedd, heard a tape of Keith's band and was impressed enough to fly to Oklahoma City to hear them live. He signed them to a production deal, and produced Keith's self-named debut album in 1992. The album was an immediate success, thanks to its first, #1 hit single, "Should've Been a Cowboy." In short order Keith had hits with the WEEPER "He Ain't Worth Missing" and the HONKY-TONK boogie "A Little Less Talk and a Lot More Action."

Keith followed Shedd to a new label in 1994, but then broke free, beginning to coproduce and cowrite much of his material (usually with songwriter Chuck Cannon). Keith showed a knack for writing the kind of tongue-in-cheek honky-tonk material that has long been a staple of country music, such as his 1996 hit, "You Ain't Much Fun (Since I Quit Drinkin')." In 1997 he had a hit with a vocal duet with pop star Sting on Sting's song "I'm So Happy I Can't Stop Crying," an unusual move for a Nashville denizen. In 1998 he moved to the new Dreamworks label, which was seeking to establish itself in the country market. He hit big with the title cut of his 1999 album, *How Do You Like Me Now?*, which topped the country charts for five weeks. "You Shouldn't Kiss Me Like This" was the successful follow-up.

Pull My Chain followed in 2001. The lead single, the #1 hit "I'm Just Talking About Tonight," shows Keith's continuing allure. Although ostensibly about a man looking for a one-night stand, the song is promoted by a humorous video that in effect makes fun of barroom pickup lines. It was followed by "Talk About Me," a country-meets-rap number that ruffled some Nashville feathers but ultimately also shot up the charts, propelled by another clever video showing Keith, in a variety of roles, arguing with the women in his life. Keith has shown GARTH BROOKS-like acting abilities in the videos, and his success certainly makes him the latest pretender to the Brooks throne. The album debuted at #1 on the country charts.

Keith's warm baritone and songwriting abilities set him a notch above many of the other young COWBOY studsters, and his career has shown he is willing to stretch beyond the confines of New Nashville.

Select Discography

Greatest Hits, Mercury 558962. The hits through 1998.

KENDALLS, THE (Royce Kykendall, b. St. Louis, Mo., September 25, 1934–May 22, 1998, and Jeannie K., b. St. Louis, Mo., November 30, 1954)

The Kendalls were a father-daughter HONKY-TONK harmony duet who were most popular in the late 1970s and early 1980s.

Royce Kendall was a minor country star of the 1940s and 1950s, performing with his brother, Floyce, as The Austin Brothers. They began playing together when Royce was just five, performing on local radio. In the 1950s Royce also worked with HANK COCHRAN and CAL SMITH, without much success. By the 1960s, he was running his own barbershop in his native St. Louis.

Royce began singing with his only child, Jeannie, and the pair hit the road for Nashville when she was nineteen. They were signed by producer PETE DRAKE, who produced their first recordings for his own label and employed Jeannie as a backup singer for Ringo Starr's *Beaucoups of Blues* album.

The duo continued to record through the 1970s, without much success. Their first big success was "Heaven's Just a Sin Away," released by the small Ovation label in 1977. This led to further hits through 1981, including 1978's #1 country hit "Sweet Desire," 1979's "You'd Make an Angel Wanna Cheat," and 1981's "Heart of the Matter." They then moved to Mercury, where they had further hits with more love-'em-and-leave-'em ditties like "Teach Me How to Cheat." Their last major hit was 1984's "Thank God for the Radio."

From the mid-1980s the duo recorded for various smaller labels. They continued to employ the close-knit harmonies, simple accompaniments, and songs about love affairs gone wrong that had been the heart of their repertoire. It's unusual for a father and daughter to be singing together about boozin', lovin', and losin', but the Kendalls were a hard combination to beat in the heart-wrenching honky-tonk category.

While touring in 1998 Royce suffered a stroke. Two days later he was dead, and the duo's career ended.

Select Discography

Twenty Greatest Hits, Deluxe 7777.
Heaven's Just a Sin Away, Richmond 2294.

KENTUCKY COLONELS, THE (c. 1962–1967: Clarence White [gtr, voc]; Roland White [mdln, voc]; Billy Ray Latham [bnj, voc]; Roger Bush [b])

Thanks to the later success of superpicker Clarence White, The Kentucky Colonels have become one of the most revered of all the 1960s progressive/FOLK-REVIVAL BLUEGRASS bands, although they performed together for only a few years. White single-handedly transformed the role of the bluegrass guitarist from accompanist (who occasionally played a bass run) to a full-fledged soloist, influencing every bluegrass guitarist who came after him.

The White brothers were born in rural Lewiston, Maine, but the family relocated to California in 1954. There Clarence began performing with his elder brothers Eric and Roland; they even had a local TV show, billed as "The Three Little Country Boys." By 1958 banjoist Billy Ray Latham had joined the group, now simply known as The Country Boys. Five years later the group was known as The Kentucky Colonels, featuring the final lineup of the two Whites, Latham, and Roger Bush, sometimes along with fiddler Bobby Sloan; the group was now based in the Los Angeles area. Later Scotty Stoneman (son of the legendary ERNEST STONEMAN, an early country-music star) performed with the band, playing a highly ornamented, flashy, show-style FIDDLE.

White's life was changed when he heard DOC WATSON perform at a California folk club, The Ash Grove. Watson had developed a unique style of flatpicking fiddle tunes, his signature piece being the flashy "Black Mountain Rag." White quickly learned the piece, and adapted the flatpicking style to other traditional tunes and ballads. His lightning-fast picking was featured on the Colonels' third album, *Appalachian Swing*, an all-instrumental outing released by the West Coast label World Pacific. The album quickly went out of print, becoming one of the most collectible of all early bluegrass recordings (it has been reissued on CD by Rounder Records).

The group's act was a fascinating mixture of old and new. Billy Ray Latham and bassist Bush performed corny country comedy routines straight out of the hokiest bluegrass stage show, as if they had just fallen off a hay wagon at the country fair. The band's repertoire was mostly made up of hoary country and HONKY-TONK classics, along with traditional fiddle tunes. But, thanks to Clarence White's guitar picking, the band earned a well-deserved reputation as a cutting-edge outfit.

The group folded by 1967–1968, when Clarence became increasingly interested in COUNTRY-ROCK. He performed on THE BYRDS' legendary *Sweetheart of the Rodeo* album, and soon after joined the second incarnation of the group, remaining with them through 1972. When mandolinist DAVID GRISMAN and fiddler RICHARD GREENE were asked to form a bluegrass band to perform on a TV show with BILL MONROE, they enlisted White and singer/guitarist PETER ROWAN to form MULESKINNER. The band recorded one album that was highly influential on the development of newgrass later in the decade.

By 1973 White was again performing with his brother Roland in a more traditional bluegrass setting. Sadly, while they were touring, he was struck down by a drunk driver and killed. Roland White soon joined forces with Alan Munde to form COUNTRY GAZETTE, a band that went through many incarnations through the mid-1980s; he performed with THE NASHVILLE BLUEGRASS BAND through the '90s. Billy Ray Latham and Roger Bush performed in a number of folk-rock ensembles, including Dillard and Clark and one of the many later versions of THE FLYING BURRITO BROTHERS.

Select Discography

Appalachian Swing!, Rounder 31. Reissue of their classic all-instrumental World Pacific album from 1964, with fiddler Bobby Sloan and DOBRO picker Leroy Mack.

Long Journey Home, Vanguard 77004. 1964 live recordings from the Newport Folk Festival.

KENTUCKY HEADHUNTERS, THE (Original lineup: Richard Young, b. Glasgow, Ky., January 27, 1955 [gtr, voc]; Greg Martin, b. Louisville, Ky., March 31, 1954 [lead gtr]; Ricky Lee Phelps, b. Paragould, Ark., October 8, 1953 [lead voc]; Doug Phelps [b. Calvin Douglas P.], b. Leachville, Ark., February 16, 1960 [b, voc]; Fred Young, b. Glasgow, Ky., July 8, 1958 [drms, voc]; the Phelpses left the band in 1992 and were replaced by Mark Orr, b. Charlotte, Mich., November 16, 1949 [voc, gtr]; and Anthony Kenney, b. Glasgow, Ky., October 8, 1953 [b]; Doug Phelps returned in 1996, replacing Orr)

The Kentucky HeadHunters are the closest thing in country music to 1990s grunge rock. Dressed in suitably ragged clothing, they combine a sound cribbed from the great Southern rockers of the 1970s like the Allman Brothers with a true love of traditional country material. Their biggest hit so far is a cover of the TV theme "Davy Crockett."

The Young brothers are from the backwoods town of Glasgow, Kentucky, and along with their statemate guitarist Greg Martin, have been playing together since their early teens, often using the name Itchy Brother for the band (named after a cartoon character that Fred Young particularly admired). By the early 1980s Richard Young had located in Nashville, where he was working as a songwriter for Acuff/Rose; his drummer brother Fred was backing up the squeaky-clean vocalist SYLVIA, and guitarist Martin was working for Elvis clone RONNIE MCDOWELL. While playing with McDowell, he met bandmate Doug Phelps who was bassist in the backup group; he brought his brother Ricky Lee into the nascent HeadHunters, and the group's sound was born.

The group's stage act combined 1970s arena-rock antics with good-natured backwoods goofiness. The two Young brothers are the visual highlight of the band, with shaggy Fred noteworthy for his near-bald pate and long sideburns, while Richard specializes in the "haven't-showered-in-a-year" look with long, scraggly locks; Ricky Lee Phelps, with his HONKY-TONK-flavored vocals was the most conventionally handsome in the outfit, bringing some sex appeal to their otherwise anarchic stage show.

The group released two albums, the aptly titled *Pickin' on Nashville* in 1989 (the band recorded it on their own for a total cost of $4500) and *Electric Barnyard* two years later, the latter spawning their biggest hit with their yuppie-nostalgia re-creation of "Davy Crockett." They also covered country tunesmiths like BILL MONROE and DON GIBSON, showing that they had a true understanding of country's roots. The two Phelps brothers, perhaps in search of more mainstream success, left the group in 1992 to strike out on their own as Brother Phelps, recording a mainstream album that sounds like much of the day's blandest pop-country. The HeadHunters drew in old friend Mark Orr and another cousin, Anthony Kenney, to fill out the ranks. Although Orr, their new lead vocalist, lacked Ricky Lee Phelps's charisma or overall talent, they soldiered on with their characteristic heavy-duty approach to the country repertoire. Their 1993 hit, "Honky-Tonk Walkin'," drew on the latest craze for country line dances, while at the same time (typically) having its tongue firmly in cheek.

In 1994 the band paid homage to an early idol by recording an album backing pianist Johnnie Johnson, who is most famous for his work on Chuck Berry's classic recordings. In 1996, with Brother Phelps having failed to make much of a mark, Doug Phelps returned to the group, replacing his replacement, Orr. They issued a new album in 1997, and another in 2000 (moving to the small Audium Entertainment label), but could not regain their original success.

Select Discography

Pickin' on Nashville, Mercury 838744.
Electric Barnyard, Mercury 848054.
Rave On, Mercury 512568. 1993 release with new band members.

KERR, ANITA (b. A. Jean Grilli, Memphis, Tenn., October 31, 1927)

Anita Kerr was the leader of the syrupy-sweet Anita Kerr Singers, Nashville's answer to a Muzak chorus, who were featured on hundreds of country and pop-rock sessions of the 1950s and 1960s.

Kerr, a multitalented musician who has worked as a pianist, vocalist, and producer, was one of the first female record producers in Nashville. She began singing as a child, on her mother's Memphis-based radio show, and had her own vocal trio by the time she was in high school. She formed the Anita Kerr Singers in 1949, signing with Decca in 1951 and appearing on the famed *Arthur Godfrey's Talent Scouts* TV show in 1956. The Anita Kerr Quartet, with Kerr singing lead, Gil Wright (tenor), Dottie Dillard (alto), and Louis Nunley (baritone) worked on countless Nashville sessions, oohing and aahing behind JIM REEVES, RED FOLEY, THE BROWNS, and countless others. As such, they represent the worst excesses of the NASHVILLE SOUND, when swooning strings and sighing singers drowned legitimate country acts in dreadful audio ooze.

Kerr broke new ground as a Nashville producer, working on SKEETER DAVIS's *End of the World* LP. In the later 1960s she formed a working partnership with "poet" (and I use the term loosely) Rod McKuen for a series of narrated mood albums featuring The Sebastian Strings, and also led the "world music" group The Mexicali Singers.

Anita Kerr deserves much of the "credit" for the success of mainstream country recordings of the 1960s. And for all who love "ear candy," there's nothing like an Anita Kerr LP to take you down memory lane. (Political activists, please note: The Anita Kerr singers were the house vocal group of the "radical" Smothers Brothers TV show in the late 1960s!)

Select Discography

Music Is Her Name, Sony Music Special Products 48979. Budget-priced CD featuring Anita Kerr singing (!) with her group.
'Round Midnight, Bainbridge 6228. Cassette-only reissue of a Kerr homage to jazz.

KERSHAW, DOUG (b. Douglas James K., Tiel Ridge, La., January 14, 1936)

Kershaw is a CAJUN fiddler/vocalist who had a brief period of success on the rock circuit in the early 1970s, and wrote "Louisiana Man," a well-loved country hit. As well known for his energetic stage antics as for his music, Kershaw was one of the first to bring Cajun styles into mainstream country and rock.

Coming from a musical family, Doug was already fiddling at age eight, when he made his professional debut performing with his mother, a talented singer, guitarist, and fiddler, at the Bucket of Blood saloon in

Lake Arthur, Louisiana. Four years later, he formed a family band with his brothers Nelson (Pee Wee) and Russell Lee (Rusty; February 2, 1938–October 23, 2001), called The Continental Playboys; they performed over Lake Charles, Louisiana, TV and at bars and social clubs. By 1953 the band was down to a brother duo, with Rusty and Doug performing on the prestigious LOUISIANA HAYRIDE radio program and recording for a local label.

In 1956 the duo moved to Nashville, where they were signed to Acuff-Rose's Hickory label. They made recordings in mainstream country, country boogie, early ROCKABILLY, and Cajun styles, scoring their first hit with "Hey, Sheriff" in 1958, performed in the close-harmony style of THE EVERLY BROTHERS, followed by their biggest successes, 1960's "Louisiana Man" and "Diggy Diggy Lo" from the following year.

The brothers' chart success was short-lived, and by 1964 they had split up. Doug continued to work as a session musician through the early 1970s, recording with everybody from Earl Scruggs (of FLATT AND SCRUGGS) to heavy-metal rockers Grand Funk Railroad. He signed with Warner Brothers in 1969, recording several albums that ranged from COUNTRY-ROCK fusions to NASHVILLE SOUND, string-laden productions. His most successful recording was 1976's *Ragin' Cajun*, his most roots-oriented outing. Doug's flamboyant performance style made him a favorite as an opening act on the rock circuit as well as on network TV.

Since the mid-1970s Kershaw has continued to record and tour sporadically. He has made several "comebacks," scoring his last country hit in 1981 with "Hello, Woman." In 1988 he cut a duet with HANK WILLIAMS, JR., on the novelty "Cajun Baby." In the early 1990s he made a comeback recording with Nashville session fiddler MARK O'CONNOR, and later in the decade reappeared on two albums issued by specialty labels.

Select Discography

Best of Doug & Rusty Kershaw, Curb 77466. Twelve cuts made by Doug with his brother Rusty in the early 1960s for Hickory Records.
The Best of, Warner Bros. 25964. Kershaw's later solo recordings.

KERSHAW, SAMMY (b. Kaplan, La., February 24, 1958)

Third cousin to fiddler DOUG KERSHAW, Sammy has become a major star in the New Nashville.

Sammy began playing guitar when he was in the fourth grade, and was already working professionally at age twelve as guitarist/road manager for a local country singer, J. B. Perry. Remaining with Perry until

he was twenty years old, Kerhsaw played throughout Louisiana, Texas, and the lower South and Southwest. The band often opened for other country acts, exposing Sammy to a wide variety of styles.

Sammy retired from music after his first marriage, and worked at a variety of menial jobs through the next decade. He also battled drug and alcohol addictions, which did little to further his musical or other career aspirations. In the mid-1980s he played with a local band called Blackwater, which gigged through the Southwest and made a few independent singles. Still, his musical career was going nowhere, so in the late 1980s he took a job as a traveling store remodeler for Wal-Mart.

Luck finally struck in 1991 when Kershaw played a showcase for producer Harold Shedd, who had produced the very successful country act ALABAMA, and would go on to discover TOBY KEITH. Kershaw was signed to a production deal, and his first album gave him a hit right out of the box with 1991's "Cadillac Style" (it also got him a job as a pitchman for Cadillac dealers). The album spawned further hits through 1992, and went gold by that August.

Kershaw's style is definitely middle-of-the-road country, showing little of his Cajun roots. He continued to score successes with WEEPERS like 1993's "She Don't Know She's Beautiful" and more up-tempo numbers like 1994's "National Working Woman's Holiday." Reflecting his working-class roots, Kershaw had minor hits with "Queen of My Double-Wide Trailer" and "Yard Sale," which chronicles the end of a marriage and its messy resolution. Kershaw had a hit with the romantic ballad "Meant to Be" in 1996, but then his career slowed. In 1998 things looked up again when he hit big with another sentimental number, "Love of My Life" (written by his producer Keith Stegall and Dan "Sometimes When We Touch" Hill). However, this was his last major hit to date. By decade's end he released an album of covers of 1970s country and soft-pop hits, not a good sign for the future of his career.

Kershaw is a fine middle-of-the-road country vocalist with a lot of personal charm, but he has never really broken through to superstar status—and probably never will.

Select Discography

The Hits, Chapter 1, Mercury Nashville 528536. His biggest hits through 1998.

KESSINGER, CLARK W. (b. South Hills, W.Va., July 27, 1896–June 4, 1975)

A well-loved fiddler, Kessinger enjoyed two careers, in the late 1920s and again in the 1960s, during the FOLK REVIVAL.

Kessinger was born in the Kanawha River valley, which has spawned so many talented fiddlers, including Ed Haley, Burl Hammonds, and Franklin George. Having learned the FIDDLE as a youngster, Kessinger went professional sometime after World War I, often accompanied by his nephew Luke (b. Luches K., Kanawha County, W.Va., August 21, 1906–May 6, 1944). After working local radio in West Virginia, they were heard by a scout from Brunswick Records who signed them to the label and named them The Kessinger Brothers. They recorded extensively from 1928 to 1930, and many of their instrumentals sold well for the dime store label.

Kessinger's recording career was ended by the Great Depression, which slowed much recording of country musicians (and, indeed, crippled the entire recording industry). He continued to play fiddle conventions and to perform on radio and at dances, but made his primary living by painting houses. He played less frequently after Luke died prematurely in 1944, although he continued to perform occasionally.

In the early 1960s he was "discovered" by folklorist/record label owner Ken Davidson, who championed the music of West Virginia on his small Kanawha label. Kessinger began performing again, taking prizes at major fiddlers conventions, including those at Galax, Virginia, and Union Grove, North Carolina. He eventually recorded four albums for Kanawha and one for Rounder. Kessinger remained active until a stroke in 1971 left him unable to perform; he died four years later.

Select Discography

Legend of, County 2713. CD reissue drawn from various 1960s recordings.

KETCHUM, HAL (b. H. Michael K., Greenwich, N.Y., April 9, 1953)

A country-styled SINGER/SONGWRITER with a strong flavor of a Texas OUTLAW, Ketchum has had a varied career trying to fit into the Nashville mold.

Ketchum grew up in the Adirondack Mountains, then moved to Florida when he was seventeen. After working as a carpenter and a drummer in bar bands there, he then relocated to Austin, Texas, where he was influenced by the nascent singer/songwriter community. In 1986 he went to Nashville, hoping to establish himself as a songwriter, and recorded ten of his original songs for the independent Watermelon label. This got him a songwriting contract, and eventually led to a deal with Curb Records.

In 1991 Ketchum's first album was released and was an immediate success, going gold by February 1992. The debut single, "Small Town Saturday Night," propelled the album's success, with its mixture of thoughtful lyrics and a jaunty beat. However, Ketchum's second album was not as successful, and fearing that he did not fit into the Nashville mold, he returned to Austin, which he felt was more open to his songwriting. While there he became dependent on drugs and alcohol, and his career floundered.

In 1997, working with producer Stephen Burton (formerly guitarist with Bonnie Raitt), Ketchum attempted to dig himself out of his career hole by pursuing a more blues-rock sound. However, when Ketchum presented the finished record to his label, they refused to release it. Meanwhile, Ketchum finally admitted his drug dependency, and went into rehab over the Christmas holidays that year.

In 1998 Ketchum rerecorded much of his 1997 Austin album along with more mainstream-oriented material for the album *I Saw the Light*, reflecting his newfound sobriety. *Awaiting Redemption* followed a year later, and then in 2001 the RODNEY CROWELL-produced return, *Lucky Man*.

Select Discography

Greatest Hits, Curb 77797. The major hits through 1996.

KILGORE, MERLE (b. Wyatt M. K., Chickasha, Okla., August 9, 1934)

Kilgore was a country SINGER/SONGWRITER who later had some success as an actor in B-Westerns.

Though born in Oklahoma, Kilgore was raised in Louisiana, and took up the guitar at an early age. He was already working as a deejay and guitarist in his late teen years, scoring his first hit with his own composition "More, More, More."

He was featured guitarist on THE LOUISIANA HAYRIDE radio program from 1952 through the end of the decade. In 1959 he scored a hit on his own with "Dear Mama," and his song "Johnny Reb" was a massive hit for country balladeer JOHNNY HORTON. His best-known songs are 1962's "Wolverton Mountain," written with CLAUDE KING, whose recording of the number was a worldwide pop hit, and "Ring of Fire," which he wrote with June Carter, a megahit for JOHNNY CASH in 1963. He also wrote the classics "Seein' Double, Feeling Single" and "It Can't Rain All the Time."

Kilgore managed to score only on the lower ends of the country charts, and by the mid-1960s he was pursuing an "acting" career in such "classic" films as *Nevada Smith* and *Five Card Stud*.

Select Discography

Teenager's Holiday, Bear Family 15544. Includes both his early ROCKABILLY and later straight country recordings.

KINCAID, BRADLEY (b. William B. Kincaid, Point Leavell, Ky., July 31, 1895–September 23, 1989)

Kincaid was a smooth-voiced singer who was immensely popular in the 1930s, thanks to his radio and personal appearances and recordings, as well as his series of best-selling songbooks. His repertoire was largely made up of traditional mountain ballads and songs, along with the sentimental songs and hymns that he learned in his childhood in Kentucky. His singing style, however, was greatly influenced by his advanced schooling and exposure to other forms of classical and popular music.

Kincaid was born in the backwoods of Kentucky, and was already playing music as a young child. His father, a talented singer and musician, traded a hunting dog for a guitar for his young son. Traditional songs, ballads, and hymns were performed by all the members of his immediate family, and Kincaid could remember performing the MINSTREL-SHOW song "Liza Up in the 'Simmon Tree" when he was just three years old!

Educational opportunities were poor in rural America when Kincaid was young. However, a school in Berea, Kentucky, was dedicated to educating mountain youth as well as preserving the traditional arts and crafts of the Appalachians. Kincaid enrolled in the school at age nineteen, entering at the sixth-grade level and, except for two years during World War I when he served in the Army, remained there until he earned his high-school degree. During his Berea years he met his future wife, who served on the music faculty, and became involved with the Young Men's Christian Association (YMCA). In the late 1920s he relocated to Chicago to attend the YMCA college.

It was through the YMCA that Kincaid had his first radio job, as a member of a close-harmony quartet performing on Chicago's largest radio station, WLS. At that time WLS was home to THE NATIONAL BARN DANCE, a leading producer of "old-time" entertainment. When the station manager heard that Kincaid knew many traditional folk songs, he invited him to appear on the program to present his traditional repertoire. Kincaid was an immediate success, and he became a show regular in 1928.

WLS was owned and operated by Sears, Roebuck, who were immediately besieged by requests for copies of Kincaid's songs. At Sears's urging, Kincaid compiled a series of songbooks, mostly drawing on his memories of the songs that were popular in his youth. Kincaid's education made him look askance at "composed" or popular songs, although he did include some parlor and sentimental numbers among the traditional ballads and songs. The books were tremendously popular, and many of Kincaid's arrangements were adopted by professional and amateur singers.

Sears arranged for his first recording sessions with the Gennett Company in the late 1920s. These were sold on a variety of licensed labels through Sears, Montgomery Ward, and dime stores, reaching thousands of rural listeners. Kincaid would continue to record for a number of different labels through the late 1930s.

From the late 1920s through the mid-1950s, Kincaid performed on a variety of radio programs, including Nashville's famous GRAND OLE OPRY from 1944 to 1949. He also had a touring show, which in the late 1930s featured a young country comedian named Marshall Jones, whom Bradley named GRANDPA JONES. Bowing to the popularity of singing COWBOYS in the 1930s, 1940s, and 1950s, Kincaid took to wearing cowboy attire, although he continued to perform basically the same repertoire of mountain songs.

Kincaid was a tireless performer, even buying his own radio station in 1949 so he could continue performing out of what would be his retirement home in Springfield, Ohio. When he "retired" in 1954, he bought a local music store, and soon was performing again. He made recordings in the early 1960s and 1970s, and continued to perform until an automobile accident slowed him down in the mid-1980s. He died in 1989.

Kincaid's importance was twofold. As a smooth-voiced, accessible singer, he helped introduce a broad audience to the traditional music of the mountains. As a prolific collector and arranger of folk songs, he made available a wide variety of material in arrangements that even a beginning musician could master.

KING, CLAUDE (b. Shreveport, La., February 5, 1923)

A master of the country-saga song, King had great success through the 1960s on the pop and country charts.

Born and raised in Louisiana, King began playing GUITAR in his early teen years, but did not intend to be a professional musician; he attended college and business school in the 1950s, although at the same time he began to get work performing in local clubs. In 1961 he signed with Columbia Records, right at the beginning of the craze for pseudo ballads composed on country themes. King churned out a number of these macho songs of the old West, beginning with 1961's "Big River, Big Man" and "The Comancheros," through his biggest number, 1962's "Wolverton Mountain," written with MERLE KILGORE, and "The Burning of Atlanta" from the same year. The songs gained considerable success on both pop and country charts, thanks to the vogue for folkish, Western-flavored numbers in the early 1960s.

By the mid-1960s King was recording more straightforward country material, including 1965's "Tiger Woman" and "Friend, Lover, Woman, Wife" from

1969; by the early 1970s his style of music was pretty much passé, although he managed to have a few more hits sporadically through the decade, including his last minor hit, "Cotton Dan," from 1977. In 1982 he appeared in the TV Civil War miniseries *The Blue and the Gray*. Although he has performed occasionally since, primarily at the Johnny Horton Days festival in Shreveport, Louisiana, King has been more or less retired since the 1980s.

Select Discography

More Than Climbing That Mountain, Bear Family 15619. All of his Columbia recordings from 1961 to 1972 and other rarities; for the devoted fan.
16 Original Classics, Collectables 6041. More manageable collection of King's best-known recordings.

KING, PEE WEE (b. Julius Frank Kuczynski, Milwaukee, Wis., February 18, 1914–March 7, 2000)

Perhaps the only Polish COWBOY, King is best remembered for leading the popular Golden West Cowboys and cowriting "The Tennessee Waltz," a 1950 pop hit for Patti Page that has become a country and pop standard.

Many Eastern Europeans settled in the upper Midwest in the late nineteenth century, and were quickly absorbed into their communities. Many were musicians, including King's father, who played concertina and FIDDLE for local dances and parties. There was a wealth of different ethnic groups living in and around Milwaukee, including Poles like the Kuczynski family, Germans, Swedes, Italians, and Anglo-Saxons. Like many regional musicians King's father played a mix of traditional ethnic dance tunes and the country and square-dance tunes that were indigenous to the region. King's parents encouraged him to learn the violin ("not the fiddle," King pointed out, making the distinction between the classical repertoire performed on violin and folk tunes played on the fiddle). In his high-school years he bought a secondhand accordion and took the name of Frankie King for local performances; he soon had his own radio show out of Racine, Wisconsin, on which he played popular tunes.

GENE AUTRY is credited with "discovering" King and bringing him to Louisville, Kentucky, to accompany him on his radio show in 1935. Autry had always featured an accordion player, and hired King to fill the shoes of a musician who was leaving his backup group, known then as The Log Cabin Boys. It so happened that the other three musicians in the band were also named Frank; since King was the shortest, he was rechristened Pee Wee, a name he later legally adopted. When Autry packed up his boots for Hollywood, King remained in Louisville, renaming the band The Golden West Cowboys and maintaining the radio program.

King soon had his own radio show out of Knoxville, and joined THE GRAND OLE OPRY in 1937, appearing on that program through the early 1940s. King's group was the first to perform on the *Opry* with drums, something bitterly opposed by the traditionalists in the audience.

During World War II, King toured with his band (then featuring an unknown singer named EDDY ARNOLD), along with comedian MINNIE PEARL, as part of what was called The Camel Caravan, thanks to its cigarette-maker sponsor. This outfit toured U. S. military bases along with outposts in Central and South America, performing an increasingly pop-oriented repertoire that included the patriotic tub-thumpers typical of the day, along with pop-harmony numbers like "Don't Sit Under the Apple Tree," sung sweetly by the Camel Cigarette Girls.

After World War II, Pee Wee resettled in Louisville, where he spent most of the late 1940s and early 1950s. His big hit, "Tennessee Waltz," was written with his new lead vocalist, REDD STEWART, in 1946, but didn't chart for him until 1948 on the country charts; it was also covered by COWBOY COPAS. Patti Page took the song to #1 on the pop charts two years later; in 1965 it was made the state song of Tennessee, and is said to have been recorded in over 500 different versions. King continued to record his own compositions, scoring several modest country hits. He also hosted his own syndicated TV program out of Louisville, which was broadcast nationally in the late 1950s.

King's activities slowed somewhat in the 1960s. He cut out his TV work and cut back on recording, although he still toured extensively through the next decade. His sound and style, a blend of late-1930s pop, changed little over the years, with his bouncy accordion playing and upbeat vocals a trademark. In 1969 he retired from performing altogether, becoming a promoter packaging and booking minor country acts on the county-fair circuit. He died in early 2000.

Select Discography

Rompin', Stompin', Singin', Swingin', Bear Family 15101. Great swinging sides from the mid-1940s through the mid-1950s.

KOSTAS (b. K. Lazarides, Salonika, Greece, 1949)

An unlikely, but highly successful, Greek-born country songwriter, Kostas penned many of the biggest hits of the 1990s.

Raised in the northwestern U.S. from the age of seven, Kostas originally played a mix of American popular music, working through his twenties and thirties in a regional rock band that gained a small following. He also cut a solo album for a tiny Seattle label in 1980, but it went nowhere.

In the mid-1980s Nashville power producer TONY BROWN discovered Kostas and urged him to focus on songwriting. Despite his lack of background in country music, Kostas quickly assimilated themes that would appeal to the country audience, setting his lyrics to catchy melodies. He began penning material primarily for PATTY LOVELESS, including her first #1 hit, "Timber, I'm Falling in Love" in 1989. This began a long string of hits, including "Ain't That Lonely Yet" for DWIGHT YOAKAM in 1994 and "Blame It on Your Heart," written with HARLAN HOWARD and a major hit for Loveless. He also provided the early TRAVIS TRITT blue-collar anthem, "Lord Have Mercy on the Working Man." Kostas worked closely with Raul Malo of THE MAVERICKS, authoring many of the songs on the group's second album with the bandleader.

In 1994 Kostas cut a solo album, *XS in Moderation*, marred by a high-gloss pop production, which barely sold beyond members of his immediate family. Nonetheless, Kostas continued to be a major hitmaker for other artists. JO DEE MESSINA had a major hit with the power ballad "Because You Loved Me," written by Kostas and John Scott Sherill, in the fall of 1999.

KRAUSS, ALISON (b. Decatur, Ill., July 23, 1971)

Krauss was a whiz-kid fiddler who as a teenager formed her own band, Union Station, a BLUEGRASS-country unit that has brought a traditional style to the mainstream charts.

Krauss is another in a line of annoying (to those of us who are musically butterfingered) prodigies who begin playing when they are still riding tricycles, and start racking up prizes when most of us are struggling with acne. She won her first FIDDLE contest at age ten in the traditional Western contest category (i.e., highly ornamented and ornate fiddle solos featuring fleet fingering and fast bow work). She was signed to the bluegrass label Rounder when she was just fourteen, and won her first Grammy when she was nineteen.

Her fourth Rounder album, 1990's *I've Got That Old Feeling*, saw a change in direction, away from emphasizing her fiddle skills to playing up her country singing. It turns out that Krauss is a good vocalist who combines bluegrass inflections with sounds that owe much to EMMYLOU HARRIS and many other new-country divas. She had two hits as a singer, "I've Got That Old Feeling" and "Steel Rails." Another innovation was adding Alison Brown to her backup band; this Harvard-educated BANJO player quickly gained a reputation as one of today's leading progressive pickers. However, Brown quickly resumed a solo career after touring briefly with Krauss.

A slew of awards came to Krauss in the early 1990s, including a Country Music Association Single of the Year award for her hit recording, "When You Say

Nothing at All" in 1993. She was also invited to join THE GRAND OLE OPRY that year, the first bluegrass-oriented act to be so honored in twenty-nine years. In 1995 a "hits" retrospective album, *Now That I've Found You*, reached the Top 20 on both country *and* pop charts, and sold double platinum, propelled by the title cut.

Like the careers of other new-bluegrass stars, Krauss's career was given a boost in 2000 by her inclusion on the sound track to the film *O Brother, Where Art Thou?* The album was an unexpected best-seller, and Krauss participated in several concerts featuring performers from the film. She has continued to record a mix of contemporary songs with a bluegrass-flavored accompaniment, and despite her increasing fame, still works with her original backing band, Union Station. Through the later 1990s she had released both solo albums and "Union Station" recordings (the major difference is that the band recordings feature lead vocals by other group members, most prominently guitarist Dan Tyminski, who provided the voice for "Man of Constant Sorrow" in *O Brother, Where Art Thou?*). In 2000 she added ace DOBRO player JERRY DOUGLAS to the group. Early in 2001 she released a new Union Station album, featuring the country hit "The Lucky One."

Krauss's instrumental skills, well-scrubbed girl-next-store looks (she's hardly a glamour-puss), and authentic Midwest twang have made her a role model for many other aspiring bluegrassers and mainstream country acts. Not surprisingly, many more young women are showing up on Country Music Television, and on the road, grasping a fiddle under their arms.

Select Discography

I've Got That Old Feeling, Rounder 275. 1990 "breakthrough" album.
Every Time You Say Goodbye, Rounder 285. 1992 album of contemporary and traditional vocals and instrumentals.
Now That I've Found You: A Collection, Rounder 285. Her first megaseller album.

KRISTOFFERSON, KRIS (b. Brownsville, Tex., June 22, 1936)

Kristofferson is a country music SINGER/SONGWRITER who enjoyed a few hits in the early 1970s and contributed to the nascent OUTLAW movement. He came from outside of the Nashville establishment, and was never really comfortable in it. Kristofferson abandoned his music career pretty much for a successful career in film acting, although he continues to perform sporadically.

An Army brat who is probably the only country star to be a Rhodes Scholar at Oxford University, Kristof-

Kris Kristofferson, David Allan Coe, and Neil Young at the first Farm Aid concert, 1986. Photo: Raeanne Rubenstein

ferson began performing while living in England, linking up with shameless impresario Larry Parnes, who marketed him as a teen-popster under the name Kris Carson. In 1960 he joined the Army, and five years later, on his discharge, he moved to Nashville. He first gained success as a songwriter when ROGER MILLER recorded the original cover of "Me and Bobby McGee" and JOHNNY CASH covered "Sunday Morning Coming Down," both in 1969. One year later SAMMI SMITH had a big hit with his "Help Me Make It Through the Night," a particularly forthright and controversial love song for the time.

Janis Joplin's cover of "Me and Bobby McGee" just before her tragic death in 1971 helped catapult Kristofferson to pop-star status. Two years later Gladys Knight scored a pop hit with her version of "Help Me Make It Through the Night." In the same year Kristof-

ferson wed RITA COOLIDGE, a folk-pop warbler. The marriage lasted five years and produced two duo albums.

From the late 1970s on, Kristofferson was more or less absorbed with his film career. He did record as one of The Highwaymen, a loose-knit group of old friends and fellow outlaws including WILLIE NELSON, Johnny Cash, and WAYLON JENNINGS, through the 1980s. He made some solo LPs in the late 1980s that featured somewhat bitter ruminations on the state of contemporary America, but failed to make much of an impact on the charts. In the 1990s he cut a few solo albums, including one in 1993 with pop producer Don Was, but was unable to regain much commercial momentum. In 1999 he recut his earlier hits with an all-star supporting cast on the album *The Austin Sessions*, a pleasant enough, if not exactly groundbreaking, release. Kristofferson made a comeback as an actor in the late 1990s, thanks to his appearance in John Sayles's film *Lone Star*. This led to a few more film roles through 2000.

Kristofferson's late 1960s/early 1970s songs helped update traditional Nashville subject matter. "Me and Bobby McGee" brought a hippie sensibility ("Freedom is just another word/for nothing left to lose . . .") to a traditional "buddy" song, while "Help Me Make It Through the Night" was unusual in its direct invitation for a one-night stand. Kristofferson served as a bridge between folk-rock singer/songwriters, such as BOB DYLAN and James Taylor, and mainstream country.

Select Discography

Me and Bobby McGee, Monument 44351. His "breakthrough" early-1970s album.
Jesus Was a Capricorn, Monument 47064. Another early album that shows Kristofferson at his best.

L

LAIR, JOHN (b. J. Lee L., Renfro Valley, Ky., July 1, 1894–November 12, 1985)

Lair was the influential scout and producer who helped build Chicago station WLS's influential NATIONAL BARN DANCE program and then founded *The Renfro Valley Barn Dance*.

Lair was born in Renfro Valley, which is located about fifty miles south of Lexington, Kentucky, and remained devoted to its music and lore throughout his life. He began participating in amateur theatrics, and wrote a show, *Atta Boy*, that toured the trenches as part of a Special Services unit during World War I. After the war he settled in Chicago, initially working for an insurance company. But the show biz bug had bitten him, and he began performing on WLS's *Barn Dance* show. Soon he was recruiting traditional musicians from Kentucky to form the house band, The Cumberland Ridge Runners. The station's management rewarded him with the position of music director for the program.

By the mid-1930s, Lair was dismayed at the influx of smooth vocal acts and COWBOY singers into country music. In 1937 he accepted the invitation from Cincinnati-based station WLW to begin a new barn dance show there that would focus on more traditional music. Lair named it *The Renfro Valley Barn Dance*, after his home. He brought with him announcer/musician RED FOLEY, who became the voice of *Renfro Valley*, and comedian Whitey Ford. He even wrote a theme song for the program, "Take Me Back to Renfro Valley." After mounting the show in the Cincinnati area for two years, Lair achieved a lifelong dream by opening a large theater in his native Renfro Valley. The show became an enormous success among both listeners and tourists. At various times the national NBC, CBS, and Mutual networks picked up the show, which until 1941 was broadcast over WLW, and then moved to Louisville's WHAS.

Lair continued to build the Renfro Valley complex into a kind of living museum of rural life. Besides presenting the shows he published a local paper, and opened a museum and general store. However, by the mid-1950s the fad for barn dance shows was very much a thing of the past, and the show lost its network broadcast in 1957. The stage show and park continued to draw tourists, and Lair continued to operate it until selling it, briefly, to another producer in 1968. By 1972 Lair was back with a new set of partners, and he continued to be active in the business until his death. In 1989 his partners sold to a management group that incorporated as Renfro Valley Entertainment. At that time they undertook a massive updating and expanding of the facilities, and still operate it as a tourist attraction open ten months a year. The Saturday night show returned to syndicated radio in the 1990s, and is currently heard across the country on over 125, mostly smaller and rural, stations.

LANG, k.d. (b. Kathryn Dawn L., Consort, Alberta, Canada, November 2, 1961)

Lang is a gender-bender new-country star who draws heavily on the sound and repertoire of PATSY CLINE. Lang's audience has been drawn primarily from punk, rock, and even adult-pop; her mix of outrageous Western wear, brush-cut hair style, and aggressive stage presence made her an anomaly even in the realm of progressive country music. Never totally entrenched in "country," lang recorded an LP of pop oldies in 1992, crossing over into the realm of pop chanteuse as her idol Cline had done later in her career. Since that time her work has been primarily in a retro pop mold.

Lang came to country music thanks to a college dramatic production based on the life of Patsy Cline; in preparing for the role she fell in love with Cline's music, even believing she was Cline reincarnated. She formed her band, "the re-clines," in punning homage to her idol, and recorded a successful album of country covers for the Canadian market in 1984. Two years later she won a Nashville contract, recording a combination of late-1950s heartthrob ballads and her own often goofy takeoffs on Nashville conventions. Her second Nashville LP, *Shadowland*, was produced by the legendary OWEN BRADLEY, who had worked with Cline. Her big breakthrough came with 1989's *Absolute Torch and Twang*, which, as the title suggests, weds her twangy country persona with her aspirations to be a pop diva. A mild stir was created a year later when she threatened to launch an anti-meat campaign, and two years later when she "came out" as a lesbian in the gay publication *The Advocate*. Her 1992 recording *Ingenue* took her firmly into the area of femme fatale popster, complete with a video featuring lang sporting a 1950s ball gown while a bubble machine worked in the background. Her follow-up albums were in a modern pop style that had a distinctly retro flavor.

Lang's big-voiced approach to country music, her combination of reverence for and ironic detachment from country traditions, and her willingness to confront her audience all made her the ideal country anti-star of the late 1980s. However, country was never her only milieu, and she has focused primarily on crafting a unique blend of old and new pop sounds since 1992.

Select Discography

Angel with a Lariat, Sire 25441. 1987 debut album.
Shadowland, Sire 25724.
Absolute Torch and Twang, Sire 25877. Her "breakthrough" album.
Ingenue, Sire 26840. 1992 album where k.d. goes for the mainstream pop market.

LASSES AND HONEY (Lee Roy "Lasses" White, b. Wills Point, Tex., August 28, 1888–1949; Lee Davis "Honey" Wilds, b. Betton, Tex., August 23, 1902–March 29, 1982)

The Amos 'n' Andy of THE GRAND OLE OPRY, this well-loved act brought elements of MINSTREL humor and stereotypes to country radio.

Lee Roy "Lasses" White was a farm boy from rural Texas. When he was a teenager, his family relocated to Dallas, where he performed in amateur theatricals. Around 1912 he became an assistant/understudy to latter-day minstrel star William George "Honeyboy" Evans, a Welsh-born singer (he cowrote "In the Good Old Summertime") who led a large minstrel troupe. White remained with Evans until his sudden death while the group was touring in February 1915. White led the company to complete the tour after his mentor's death.

After performing with other companies, White returned to Dallas, where he published "Nigger Blues," a stringing together of standard blues verses. (It opens with the oft-repeated, "The blues ain't nothin' . . . but

a good man feelin' bad.") By the early 1920s he was leading his own minstrel troupe, which recorded for Columbia. In 1923 he settled in Memphis, where he met newspaperman GEORGE D. HAY, later the founder of *The Grand Ole Opry*.

In 1932 Nashville radio station WSM invited White to bring his act to the radio. He arrived with a partner in tow: "Honey" Wilds. The two were so popular that by April 1934 they were being featured both in their own Friday night "minstrel show" and on *The Grand Ole Opry*. They specialized in "Negro" dialect and parodies of country songs, often on topical, Depression-era subjects. In this way they foreshadowed the successful comic song adaptations of later acts like HOMER AND JETHRO.

In May 1936 Lasses left for Hollywood, where he found a new career as a character actor in the B-grade Western "horse operas" then being churned out by minor-league studios. Wilds formed a new duo known as Jamup and Honey, featuring various partners, through the mid-1940s.

LAW, DON (b. London, England, February 24, 1902–December 20, 1982)

Law was a legendary country-music producer whose career began in the 78 era and extended into the NASHVILLE SOUND years of the 1950s and 1960s.

Oddly enough for a man who would be famous for producing blues and country records, Law was born and raised in England. As a teenager he sang with the London Choral Society, his only musical education. At age twenty-two he emigrated to the U.S., working wherever he could. Sometime in the later 1920s he settled in Dallas, Texas, and took a job as a bookkeeper for the Brunswick label. In 1931 the label was purchased by the American Recording Company (ARC), and later that decade ARC was absorbed into Columbia Records. In 1936–1937, while working for ARC, Law oversaw the sessions of legendary bluesman Robert Johnson.

In 1942 Columbia brought Law to New York to manage their children's recordings. Soon after World War II, Law was reassigned to comanage their country music roster, along with legendary producer ART SATHERLEY; Law handled acts living east of El Paso, Texas, and Satherley took care of the rest. Law oversaw BOB WILLS's mid-to-late-1940s recordings for Columbia, as well as the HONKY-TONK sounds of AL DEXTER and LEFTY FRIZZELL, one of his discoveries. In 1952 Satherley retired, and Law had the country roster to himself.

Law worked mostly out of Texas studios until 1956, when he made the move to Nashville, which was quickly becoming the major center for country recording. Unlike CHET ATKINS and OWEN BRADLEY, Law's productions did not for the most part employ lush choirs, strings, and tinkling pianos. Instead he launched a semi-FOLK REVIVAL with songs like MARTY ROBBINS's "El Paso" and JOHNNY HORTON's "Battle of New Orleans" in the late 1950s. He also oversaw JOHNNY CASH's famous theme albums of the early 1960s.

Law remained at Columbia until 1967, although he was already considered somewhat out of touch with more recent musical trends by the mid-1960s. He continued for a while as an independent producer, most notably scoring a hit with "Skip a Rope" by Henson Cargill, a #1 country hit in 1968. Law retired in the early 1970s and returned to Texas, living outside of Galveston, where he died in 1982. He was inducted into the Country Music Hall of Fame in 2001.

LAWRENCE, TRACY (b. Atlanta, Tex., January 27, 1968)

A pleasant-voiced and pleasant-looking singer/guitarist who had a string of #1 country hits through the mid-1990s, despite some personal problems, Lawrence was born in Texas but raised in rural Arkansas. A performer since his teenage years, he spent two years in college before quitting to become lead vocalist with a Louisiana-based band from 1988 to 1990. He left the band to seek his fortune in Nashville, where he supported himself by day as a telemarketer and ironworker, and by night by winning amateur talent contests. After one contest he was offered his own radio show out of Daysville, Kentucky, netting him $25 a performance. Lawrence's luck changed after a showcase performance at Nashville's well-known Bluebird Café in 1991, leading to a management contract with Wayne Edwards and a recording deal with Atlantic Records.

After completing his first record, *Sticks and Stones*, Lawrence was shot three times during a mugging. He quickly recovered, just in time to see the title track from the album hit #1. Through 1992 and early 1993 he had more chart success with three other songs taken from his album, and garnered *Billboard* and Academy of Country Music Best New Male Vocalist awards. It took only seventeen days for his second album, 1993's *Alibis*, to go gold, and all three singles from the album hit #1. In 1994 he took over his own management and opened a management firm, and also expanded into music production.

Lawrence's good-guy image, fostered by his favoring slower ballads over the more aggressive HONKY-TONK of some of his peers, has taken several hits. In 1994 Lawrence claimed a group of teenagers fired at his car while he was driving with his brother on the interstate outside of Nashville. Lawrence fired back, using an unregistered gun. He claimed he fired into the air, in self-defense, but was later charged with aggravated assault and carrying an unlicensed weapon. Charges were dropped when he agreed to pay all court costs, spend a year on probation, and surrender his weapon. Nonetheless, he had a major hit with "Renegades, Rebels and Rogues," which he recorded for the popular Western film *Maverick*, as well as "If the Good Die Young," released earlier that year.

In 1996 Lawrence divorced his wife of three years to marry an ex-Dallas Cowboys cheerleader. In mid-1998 he was accused of spousal abuse after allegedly hitting his wife several times. The couple filed for divorce that fall, and Lawrence's good-guy image took another beating. LORRIE MORGAN threatened to cancel appearing with him at a cystic fibrosis benefit because of the alleged incident, but later relented. Meanwhile his record label delayed releasing any new product, besides a "greatest hits" album, until 2000, the aptly titled new release, *Lessons Learned*. However, this lukewarm collection of WEEPERS and honkers did little to revive the singer's career. A new album for a new label, Warners, was released in fall 2001.

Select Discography

Best of, Atlantic 83137. The hits through 1998.

LAWSON, DOYLE (b. D. Wayne L., Kingsport, Tenn., April 20, 1944)

A MANDOLIN player and vocalist, Lawson has established a strong reputation leading his progressive BLUEGRASS group, Quicksilver.

Lawson's father was a GOSPEL singer who encouraged his young son to sing and play music. The family relocated to Sneedville, Tennessee, when Doyle was nine, and there he befriended a neighbor, JIMMY MARTIN, the great bluegrass guitarist/vocalist. Lawson's first love was the mandolin, but he also learned GUITAR and five-string BANJO, and it was as a banjo player that he first worked professionally, joining Martin in his Sunny Mountain Boys in 1963. After working with Martin for seven months, he relocated to Louisville, Kentucky, where he worked with various bands. In 1966 he joined J. D. CROWE, working as a guitarist with Crowe's Kentucky Mountain Boys and singing tenor harmonies; he remained with Crowe through 1971.

In 1971 he joined the second incarnation of THE COUNTRY GENTLEMEN, led by original member Charlie Waller. Lawson finally got to play mandolin, and helped establish the new version of this venerable band as one of the best on the bluegrass circuit through the late 1970s. In 1977 he also recorded his first mandolin solo record, supported by many other well-known names in bluegrass and newgrass, including JERRY DOUGLAS, KENNY BAKER, and Crowe.

In 1979 Lawson formed the first version of his own band, Quicksilver. The group originally included Terry Baucom on banjo, Jimmy Haley on guitar, and Lou Reid on electric bass, along with Lawson on mandolin and lead vocals. Unique among progressive bluegrass bands, they decided to alternately issue secular and gospel albums; surprisingly, the gospel albums were far more popular, and the group became known for their a cappella renditions of traditional and newly written gospel songs.

In 1982 Rounder Records organized a kind of bluegrass "Super Session," enlisting Lawson, Crowe, guitarist/vocalist TONY RICE, fiddler Bobby Hicks, and bassist Todd Phillips to rerecord classic bluegrass songs. Issued as *The Bluegrass Album*, it was a very successful offering, and was followed up by several more albums and tours through the 1990s.

Through the 1980s and 1990s Quicksilver had various personnel lineups while maintaining its mix of gospel and bluegrass material. Lawson's imaginative mandolin playing and strong tenor lead made him one of the most distinctive voices in the bluegrass revival. And his love of gospel hymns set him apart from many others, winning him an audience beyond the limits of bluegrass.

Select Discography

Gospel Collection, Vol. 1, Sugar Hill 9104. Thirteen tracks recorded through 1993.
Just over in Heaven, Sugar Hill 3911. A cappella and accompanied gospel material, released in 2000 with the latest version of Lawson's band.

LEDFORD, LILY MAY (b. Pilot, Ky., March 17, 1917–July 14, 1985)

Ledford was a fiddler/banjoist who led The Coon Creek Girls, the first all-female country band, popular in the 1930s. She was "rediscovered" during the 1970s old-time music revival.

Born in tiny "Pinch-'em-Tight Holler," Ledford began performing on a homemade BANJO with a groundhog hide for a tone head when she was seven. She took up the FIDDLE at age eleven, and by the time she was seventeen, was fiddling for tips at the local train station, some eight miles from her home. A local businessman arranged for her to travel north, where she won a talent contest in 1936 and a place on the influential WLS NATIONAL BARN DANCE. Producer JOHN LAIR encouraged the youngster to switch to banjo, adapt her wardrobe to stereotypical "mountain garb," and perform the older traditional songs of her youth. Ledford commented years later, "Mr. Lair discouraged my buying clothes, curling my hair, going in for makeup or improving my English. 'Stay a mountain girl, just like

you were when you came here. Be genuine and plain at all times,' he said."

A year after Ledford came to Chicago, Lair moved to Kentucky to produce the new *Renfro Valley Barn Dance* radio program, taking most of his major performers with him. He had the brainstorm of creating an all-women's band in a backwoods mold. He christened the group The Coon Creek Girls, featuring Ledford on fiddle and banjo, her sister Rosa Charlotte "Rosie" (1915–1976) on guitar, mandolinist Esther "Violet" Koehler, and fiddler/bass player Evelyn "Daisy" Lange. The group was an immediate sensation, becoming one of the most popular acts on the new program. By 1939 Lily's sister Minnie Lena (1922–1987), known as "Black-Eyed Susan," joined the act, which was now a family trio because Koehler and Lange had quit. The group continued to perform with various personnel for another eighteen years.

Ledford was married to Glenn Pennington from 1945 to 1967; son J. P. led the pop group EXILE in the 1970s, scoring a major hit with 1978's "Kiss You All Over," and then switched to a country sound in the 1980s with hits "She's a Miracle" and "Woke Up in Love." Ledford herself returned to performing in the 1970s on the old-time music circuit, reintroducing her theme song, the traditional mountain song "Banjo-Picking Girl." She performed sporadically through the end of the decade.

Select Discography

Banjo-Pickin' Girl, Greenhays 712. Late 1970s recordings.

LeDOUX, CHRIS (b. Biloxi, Miss., October 2, 1948)

If ever there was an act that earned its COWBOY hat, it has to be Chris LeDoux, a genuine lover of cowboy material and a onetime rodeo star.

Born in Mississippi but raised in Austin, Texas, LeDoux began riding horses and competing in rodeos in his early teens. Later he competed on the high school and college rodeo circuit, becoming a professional in 1970. For the next decade he seriously worked the rodeo circuit, attaining his greatest success in 1976, when he earned the World Championship Bareback Rider buckle at the National Finals.

In 1980 LeDoux retired from rodeoing, and for the next ten years recorded both his own and traditional cowboy songs, released on the Lucky Man label, owned by his father. LeDoux made a good living touring and selling songbooks and cassettes out of the back of his car. Then-fledgling country star GARTH BROOKS heard about LeDoux, giving passing mention to "a worn-out tape of Chris LeDoux" in his 1989 song "Much Too Young (to Feel This Damn Old)."

Brooks's label, Liberty, paid heed, and signed LeDoux in 1990.

LeDoux's 1991 first album and singles were critically well-received but did not see much in the way of sales. They were too pure-cowboy to motivate a country audience that likes its artists to wear boots and hats, but not necessarily to sing "Home on the Range." Brooks decided to give LeDoux's career a boost by appearing on the title cut of LeDoux's next album, guaranteeing radio play and chart action for the song, "Watcha Gonna Do with a Cowboy."

Through the 1990s LeDoux continued to tour and record. With hard-core fans he has been able to make a good living, even though his songs rarely appear above the Top 50 line in the country charts. LeDoux relies so little on being a part of the Nashville scene that he is one of the few current country artists to live outside of town, making his home in cowpoke country in Wyoming. In 1998 LeDoux took a controversial step among the hats-and-spurs crowd by recording "Bang a Drum," a duet with hard rocker Jon Bon Jovi.

Select Discography

20 Greatest Hits, Capitol 99871. Most of his best-known songs to 1999.

LEE, ALBERT (b. Leominster, Herts., England, December 21, 1953)

Although British by birth, Lee has become one of the leading exponents of modern country GUITAR, particularly since his days as a member of EMMYLOU HARRIS's Hot Band. His electric guitar playing shows the influence of such earlier country pickers as CHET ATKINS and MERLE TRAVIS, yet also reflects British bluesters like Eric Clapton and folk-rockers like Richard Thompson. Lee's background in rock but sympathy for country makes him the ideal session guitarist for the New Nashville.

Lee began his professional career associated with British pop-rocker Chris Farlowe, performing in his backup group, The Thunderbirds, from 1965 to 1967. He joined Joe Cocker's backup band after leaving Farlowe, and then became a member of Country Fever, a British folk-rock ensemble. In 1971 he was a featured member of Head, Hands, and Feet, a band that gained a solid reputation on both sides of the Atlantic for its COUNTRY-ROCK style. After that band folded in 1973, he performed with the re-formed Crickets (BUDDY HOLLY's original backup band), who remained a popular concert draw in the U.K., and then moved to the U.S.

From 1976 to 1978 Lee performed with Emmylou Harris on tour and record. His skills on guitar and MANDOLIN made him a popular session player who performed with a wide variety of performers from rock,

blues, and country. In 1979 he released a solo album produced by Harris's husband, Brian Ahern, and has since sporadically released other solo efforts. In the early 1980s he returned to rock as a member of Eric Clapton's backup band, but has since worked primarily on country sessions, backing artists from RICKY SKAGGS to RODNEY CROWELL. In the later 1980s he released a handful of solo albums for MCA. From the mid-1990s he worked as musical director for the revived EVERLY BROTHERS touring band.

Select Discography

Black Claw and Country Fever, Line 9.01057. Reissues of two late-1960s albums.
Gagged but Not Bound, MCA 42063.
Speechless, MCA 5693. Two late-1980s solo outings.

LEE, BRENDA (b. B. Mae Tarpley, Lithonia, Ga., December 11, 1944)

"Little Miss Dyn-a-mite," as she was known in the 1950s, Brenda Lee is a big-throated chanteuse who has passed through careers in ROCKABILLY, tear-jerkin' country-pop, cabaret, and then country.

Lee was performing on country radio in and around Atlanta as early as age seven. When she was eleven, RED FOLEY's manager convinced Decca to sign her to a contract, and she had her first hit with "Dynamite" a year later, earning her her nickname. She continued to record in the rockabilly mold through the early 1960s, including the novelty Christmas classic, "Rockin' 'Round the Christmas Tree."

In the early 1960s Lee hooked up with producer OWEN BRADLEY, who had been nudging country singers like PATSY CLINE in a more mainstream-pop direction. Together the duo produced a string of classic country WEEPERS, including 1960's "I'm Sorry," "Dum Dum" and "Fool No. 1" from 1961, "All Alone Am I" and "Break It to Me Gently" from 1962, and 1963's "Losing You." Lee wrapped her powerful lungs around the sappy sentiments expressed in these often formulaic songs, managing to find depth in even the tritest lyric. However, by the mid-1960s, although the hits continued to come, Lee's recordings became increasingly predictable.

Following her last country hit in 1966, Lee made an abortive attempt to break into the Las Vegas/cabaret market by recording more mainstream material. However, she returned to the country fold in the early 1970s, beginning with "If This Is Our Last Time" in 1971 and going through 1975's "He's My Rock." She recorded more sporadically from the mid-1970s onward, scoring a minor hit in 1984 with "Hallelujah, I Love You So," featuring GEORGE JONES and RAY CHARLES. She continues to perform, primarily around Nashville. She has also been very active in charities around her hometown. In 1997 she was inducted into the Country Music Hall of Fame.

Lee's feisty early recordings were undoubtedly her best work. Her powerful singing and rockin' repertoire have been emulated by contemporary retro rockabilly artists, including CARLENE CARTER.

Select Discography

Anthology, MCA 10384. Two-CD set that gives a good overview of her career, and a great booklet.

LEE, BUDDY (b. Joseph Lioce [some sources give his name as Joseph Pino], Brooklyn, N.Y., October 7, 1932–February 13, 1998)

Buddy Lee was the founder of one of the most successful talent agencies in Nashville, Buddy Lee Attractions.

Lee was born in Brooklyn, and by the time he was eighteen was traveling the country as a professional wrestler. He spent fourteen years in the sport, picking up how to promote sporting events by osmosis. After he retired, Lee moved in 1955 to Columbia, South Carolina, where he kept a hand in wrestling by managing female stars, including his wife, Lillian Ellison, who was known as "The Fabulous Moolah" thanks to her winning ways. Lee also began managing musical acts, primarily in the R&B style. In the later 1950s he happened to attend a country music show and, recognizing an opportunity, started to work with country performers.

By 1963 Lee was working out of Boston, where he put on a show for HANK WILLIAMS, JR. His work impressed Hank's mother, Audrey, who encouraged him to move to Nashville to manage the young singer. The two formed Aud-Lee Attractions in 1964, and four years later Lee took over the business, renaming it Buddy Lee Attractions.

From the start Lee built an impressive roster of contemporary Nashville stars, new up-and-comers, and older traditional acts. He was among the first to recognize that the state fair circuit could be a rich ground for country performers, and soon was providing entertainment for many fairs. His agency is generally credited as the first "modern" agency in Nashville that used public relations to promote country-music performers effectively.

The agency managed to remain a prime mover through the many changes in country music from the 1960s to the 1990s, and still has an impressive talent roster. In 1982 Lee moved beyond simple talent management to form Mainstage Production Enterprises to manage entire large-scale events, such as state fairs. He also played a key role in the first Farm Aid concert, arranging for most of the acts.

Lee continued to run the agency until his death from cancer. In 2001 the agency had three offices—in Nashville, Kansas City, and New Waverly, Texas—with twenty-one agents handling a diverse range of artists, including retro cowpokes RIDERS IN THE SKY, new-country stars THE DIXIE CHICKS, and sultry balladeer LORRIE MORGAN. In 2001 Lee's son Joey was appointed head of the agency, after a three-year period when the firm was led by Tony Conway, a longtime employee.

LEE, DICKEY (b. Royden D. Lipscombe, Memphis, Tenn., September 21, 1936)

Moving from COUNTRY-ROCK to teen pop to pure country, Lee's career summarizes about thirty years of American musical history as he has brushed up against success, occasionally scoring a big hit and then dropping back into obscurity.

Born in the blues-country-rock hotbed of Memphis, Lee formed his first group—a country trio—while still a teenager. After being befriended by local radio dee-jay Dewey Phillips, he was introduced to "COWBOY" JACK CLEMENT, who was then working as a recording engineer at the fabled Sun label. Lee cut a couple of country-rock sides for Sun and its affiliated Phillips International label in 1957, including the classic "Good Lovin'" (later a hit for the Young Rascals), before winning a wrestling scholarship to Memphis State University.

After college Lee signed with the Smash label as a teen-pop artist, scoring his biggest pop hit with 1962's tear-stained "Patches" as well as other frighteningly bad teen-angst fare such as "I Saw Linda Yesterday" from the same year, the follow-up "Don't Wanna Think About Paula" from 1963, and 1965's "Laurie (Strange Things Happen)." Lee is best remembered for his 1962 song "She Thinks I Still Care," first a hit for GEORGE JONES and later covered by many others.

By the late 1960s Lee's pop career had fizzled, and he signed with RCA as a country artist under veteran producer CHET ATKINS. His first country record was "The Mahogany Pulpit" in 1971, followed by the #1 "Never-Ending Song of Love." He hit it big again four years later with a remake of the pop hit "Rocky" and then 1976's "9,999,999 Tears." Lee left RCA for Mercury in 1979, but his career as a performer fizzled out. In the early 1980s Lee cowrote a number of hits for new-country artists, including REBA MCENTIRE's second #1 hit, 1983's "You're the First Time I've Thought About Leaving," a throwback to earlier HONKY-TONK sounds written in a country-waltz time, as well as GEORGE STRAIT's 1984 hit "Let's Fall to Pieces Together." In 1995 he scored an Academy of Country Music Song of the Year with "Keeper of the

Stars," a major hit for TRACY BYRD. Meanwhile, Lee has continued to tour on both the country and ROCKA-BILLY revival circuits.

LEE, JOHNNY (b. John L. Ham, Texas City, Tex., July 3, 1946)

The "urban COWBOY" himself, Lee got a big career boost when his song "Looking for Love" was selected for the popular early-1980s flick *Urban Cowboy.*

Raised in rural Alta Loma, Texas, Lee formed his first band in high school, a country-pop outfit called The Roadrunners. He enlisted in the Navy, and then worked in California after his discharge, eventually returning to Texas, where he hooked up with MICKEY GILLEY, the famous country barkeep, leading Gilley's band when Gilley was on the road. By the mid-1970s Lee had recorded a number of singles for a variety of small labels, having minor chart hits with "Sometimes," the venerable "Red Sails in the Sunset," and "Country Party."

Gilley's club was selected as the locale for the John Travolta-Debra Winger romance *Urban Cowboy,* and Lee's baritone warbling on the pop-flavored "Looking for Love" gained him a #1 country hit as well as a Top 10 pop single. An album was quickly released, with three more tracks hitting the charts. Lee soon graduated from performing in beer-soaked clubs, moving up to glitzy venues in Vegas, often performing with Gilley under the name The Urban Cowboy Band. He made tabloid heaven when he married TV soap star Charlene Tilton of *Dallas* fame in the early 1980s, a marriage that lasted through mid-decade (he even contributed a love ode to his bride called "Lucy's Eyes," after the character she portrayed on the popular melodrama). After a few more country-pop hits in the early 1980s, Lee faded from the charts. He has nonetheless continued to tour without making any new recordings since then.

Select Discography

The Best of, Curb 77322. Later hits.

LEHNING, KYLE (b. Cairo, Ill., April 18, 1949)

Lehning is a Nashville-based producer and record executive, most famous for producing RANDY TRAVIS from the beginning of his career.

Lehning was educated in Illinois, where he began playing keyboards. Coming to Nashville in 1971, he hoped to make it as a session musician, but ended up working behind the boards for THE GLASER BROTHERS at their studio. He also did some session work around town. In 1975 he got his big break as a producer, working with the pop-country duo of England Dan and John Ford Coley and producing their 1976 megahit "I'd Really Love to See You Tonight." He continued to work with the duo through their breakup in 1979, and then with DAN SEALS as a solo artist. With Seals he racked up an impressive twenty-four country hits from 1983 to 1992.

Meanwhile, in 1985 Lehning was hired by Warner Brothers to produce the debut album of a new country artist, Randy Travis. The two molded Travis's back-to-roots country sound, and worked together through the mid-1990s on all of Travis's major hits. He also produced TRACY LAWRENCE's first major hit in 1991. These successes led to Lehning's being offered a job as executive vice president of Asylum Records in 1992, a position he held through 1998. At Asylum he helped launch the careers of BRYAN WHITE and MANDY BARNETT. After leaving Asylum, Lehning founded his own recording studio, Morningstar, located in Henderson, Tennessee. Among his late '90s productions are the roots-country band The Derailers and young singer Lila McCann.

LEWIS, BOBBY (b. Hodgenville, Ky., May 9, 1946)

Lewis, a minor country star of the mid-1960s and early 1970s, is best remembered for strumming on a lute instead of a GUITAR.

Bobby started playing the guitar at age nine, when his older brother taught him his first chords. He was soon showing talent as a picker, although he had difficulty handling the jumbo-sized guitar that his brother used. Small for his age, Lewis searched in a local junk shop to find a smaller guitar. What he found was an old lute, which he strung and tuned like a guitar.

When Lewis was eleven, he made his performing debut on the *Kentucky Barn Dance* radio show out of Lexington, where he continued to appear for three years. He broke into television in the late 1950s, and by the early 1960s was appearing regularly on the *Hi-Varieties Show.* At the same time he moved to Nashville, where he recorded an original composition, "Sandra Kay," on a small, local label; it gained him an appearance on THE GRAND OLE OPRY and a contract with United Artists Records. His 1960s hits included a slew of country WEEPERS, from 1964's "How Long Has It Been" to his biggest hits: 1967's "Love Me and Make It Better," "From Heaven to Heartache" from a year later, and the rockin' "Hello, Mary Lou" from 1970.

Lewis was dropped by United Artists in the early 1970s, and moved to the smaller Ace of Hearts label, scoring one more Top 20 hit with "Too Many Memories" in late 1973. The hits pretty much dried up after that, although he did reemerge briefly on the short-lived revived Capricorn label with 1979's "She's Been Keeping Me Up Nights."

LEWIS FAMILY (c. 1950–the present; various membership)

The Lewis Family is one of the longest-running BLUEGRASS GOSPEL groups still performing. Beginning with a group of brothers in the 1950s, the ensemble has embraced three generations of Lewises, continuing to perform gospel harmonies with bluegrass-styled accompaniments.

Roy "Pop" Lewis, Sr. (b. Pickens, S.C., September 22, 1905), and his wife Pauline are the patriarch and matriarch of the Lewis family dynasty. Their four sons—Wallace (b. Lincoln County, Ga., July 6, 1928), Talmadge, Esley, and "Little Roy" (b. February 24, 1942)—the original group members, began to perform locally in the late 1940s as The Lewis Brothers. Eventually Roy, Sr., joined in on bass, Esley and Talmadge retired, and various Lewis daughters joined the act.

The group first recorded for the tiny Sullivan label in 1951, and then hooked up with legendary country promoter/record executive Don Pierce. Pierce would bring them to his Starday label in 1957, and they would continue to record for him through 1970. They have since recorded primarily for Christian-oriented labels.

In 1954 the family launched a live bluegrass/gospel TV show, broadcast out of Augusta, Georgia, which continued on the air for thirty-eight years, making it probably the longest-running gospel show. In 1990 they began a tradition of a family homecoming bluegrass festival that they sponsor in their hometown of Lincolntown.

Select Discography

16 Greatest Hits, Hollywood 217. Compilation of recordings originally made for Starday.

LEWIS, HUGH X. (b. H. Brad L., Yeaddiss, Ky., December 7, 1932)

Hugh X. Lewis was a minor-league recording star/performer of the 1960s better known for the hits he wrote for others.

After working as a coal miner and steel-mill foreman through the 1950s and early 1960s, while strumming the guitar in local clubs and bars on the side, Lewis slowly built up a reputation as a talented SINGER/SONGWRITER. He finally made the break from his day job in 1963, moving to Nashville, where he had his big break when STONEWALL JACKSON recorded his novelty song, "B.J. the D.J.," which became a #1 country hit in 1964. The song was quickly covered by KITTY WELLS and CARL SMITH (Smith later recorded Lewis's "Take My Ring Off Your Finger"), and other big-name Nashville stars had hits with his material, including MAC WISEMAN, who recorded "Heads You Win, Tails I Lose," and GEORGE MORGAN, with "One Rose."

Lewis quickly signed a contract with Kapp Records and released the single "What I Need Most." He stayed with Kapp through the late 1960s, then moved to GRT with the novelty hit "Blues Sells a Lot of Booze," followed by recording with a string of smaller labels. He even appeared in the "full color" film *Forty Acre Feud*, a typical C-grade Western potboiler of the period.

Lewis's songs were a mix of novelties, up-tempo HONKY-TONK numbers, and standard "you-left-me-and-I'm-blue" WEEPERS. Not a particularly distinctive performer, he produced material that was better served when covered by more successful acts.

LEWIS, JERRY LEE (b. Ferriday, La., September 29, 1935)

The "Ferriday Fireball," the original wild man of ROCKABILLY and country, Jerry Lee has his career divided into two major parts in standard biographies: his original 1950s hits, in a rockabilly/pop-rock style, followed by his "comeback" in the 1960s, 1970s, and 1980s as a country star. Actually, Jerry Lee has always recorded country songs, often as B-sides to his original rock hits, and his sensibility is as pure country as you can get.

The Lewis family were farmers in Louisiana. Much is made of the fact that Lewis is related to country crooner MICKEY GILLEY and the fallen TV evangelist Jimmy Swaggart (both are cousins), as if these represent polar sides of Lewis's own personality. His musical influences are diverse, from the WESTERN SWING/jazz piano stylings of MOON MULLICAN to the rockin' style of Fats Domino; even the great showman Al Jolson is said to have had an influence on young Lewis. Having played piano since the age of nine, he won a Ted Mack *Amateur Hour* show, leading to a gig at a Natchez, Mississippi, radio station. After a brief stint at Bible college he worked his way to the legendary Sun studios headed by SAM PHILLIPS.

At Sun, Lewis first worked as a sideman, backing CARL PERKINS; it was at a Perkins session that he encountered ELVIS PRESLEY and JOHNNY CASH in an impromptu jam session primarily of old hymn tunes, which has become known as "The Million Dollar Quartet" session. Lewis's first hit was "Whole Lotta Shakin' Goin' On" from 1957; originally radio stations were wary of the song, fearing its obscene subtext, but Lewis's wild performance on a Steve Allen TV show catapulted the song—and the star—to fame.

Lewis's rock career came to a grinding halt in 1959 with his scandalous (for the time) third marriage to a thirteen-year-old cousin. He struggled through the 1960s, recording in a number of different styles, including his first "pure country" recordings. In the late 1960s and early 1970s he broke through on the country charts with hits in a HONKY-TONK style, including

"Another Place, Another Time," "What Made Milwaukee Famous (Has Made a Loser Out of Me)," and "She Even Woke Me up to Say Goodbye." In 1978 he made yet another country comeback with the humorous "39 Years and Holding."

The 1980s brought continuing personal problems, including tax problems (in 1993 the IRS would seize Lewis's home for back taxes) and the mysterious murder of his fifth wife. Still, Lewis continues to perform regularly, particularly in Europe, drawing on both his rock and country repertoires, while making periodic well-publicized comebacks.

Lewis is important to country music for a number of reasons. His high-voltage personality has made him a legendary performer, although he can be just as unreliable in his stage manner as he is in his lifestyle. His pounding piano style, combining elements of honky-tonk, jazz, R&B, and rock and roll, is as distinctive as his engaged, dynamic vocals. As a country crooner Lewis has perfectly captured the slightly ironic, world-weary tone of a man down to his last beer (and sinking fast). It is this perfect melding of personality and material that makes Lewis, at his best, a pure country performer.

Select Discography

Pretty Much Country, Ace 348. Mid-1980s country sessions, remastered with new lead guitar parts added by Eddie Jones.

Up Through the Years, 1956–1963, Bear Family 15408. Twenty-four of his greatest Sun sides, including rockabilly, straight rock, and country.

Killer: The Mercury Years, Mercury 935/938/941. Three-volume set covering his 1960s country, rock, and GOSPEL recordings for Mercury and its subsidiary, Smash.

Milestones, Rhino 71499. Includes his great Sun hits, plus his better later recordings for Mercury.

Rockin' My Life Away, Warner Bros. 26689. Late-1970s sessions originally issued by Elektra; these are fine "comeback" performances primarily in country style, including the hit "39 Years and Holding."

LEWIS, LAURIE (b. Long Beach, Calif., September 28, 1950)

BLUEGRASS fiddler, vocalist, and songwriter, Lewis is a veteran of several bluegrass bands, including San Francisco's GOOD OL' PERSONS, as well as an accomplished solo artist.

Coming out of the rich Bay Area FOLK REVIVAL scene, Lewis was first introduced to bluegrass music in 1965 through the early progressive band THE DILLARDS. In 1973 she formed her first band, The Phantoms of the Opry, playing bass, and was fiddler for the

Good Ol' Persons from 1975 to 1977. Through the rest of the 1970s she was a studio musician for a number of Bay Area folkies, including feminist SINGER/SONGWRITER Holly Near, besides running her own instrument-repair shop.

In 1983 Lewis formed a new backup band, The Grant Street String Band, issuing her first solo album with this group three years later. A number of her original compositions were recorded by new-country artists, including "Love Chose You," which was covered by KATHY MATTEA. Legendary cowpuncher PATSY MONTANA recorded her "The Cowgirl's Song," which was selected as the official theme song of the Cowgirl Hall of Fame.

Lewis's albums featured her new-styled HONKY-TONK singing of her own country-folk ballads, along with her bluegrass-flavored fiddling. In 1988 she was a member of the all-female Blue Rose band along with CATHY FINK and other "all-star" women musicians, and she has continued to perform as a duet with Kathy Kallick, another Good Ol' Person alum. In the early 1990s, Lewis began doing session work in Nashville for a number of new-country acts. In 1994 Lewis was involved in a bad automobile accident while touring with Grant Street, but luckily recovered, and continued to record and tour through the decade's end.

Select Discography

Earth and Sky: Songs of, Rounder 610400. Gathers material from her 1980s Flying Fish albums in a country-folk-pop vein.

And Her Bluegrass Pals, Rounder 610461. All-star bluegrass album.

LEWIS, "TEXAS" JIM (b. James L., Meigs, Ga., October 15, 1909–January 23, 1990)

COWBOY star of the 1930s and 1940s who recorded for a variety of labels in a pseudo-Western style.

Lewis's family was on the move from the time he was two years old, when they relocated from Georgia to Florida. His mother died when he was six years old, and from that point on, the family moved throughout the South. Both his father and grandfather were old-time fiddlers, and his father also worked as an evangelist following the death of his first wife. Jim's siblings (and later half siblings) were also musical.

Around 1919 the Lewis family settled in Fort Myers, Florida, where Jim was raised until the age of nineteen, when he relocated to Texas. There he began his musical career in his early twenties, working in local medicine shows and on the radio. Around 1931 he moved to Detroit, to join his half brother guitarist/singer Jack Rivers (actually named Rivers Lewis). The two worked together in a loose group called The Purple

Gang. A year later Jim was in Houston, Texas, where he found radio sponsorship from the Swift meatpacking firm. He formed the first Swift Jewel Cowboys, hiring a sixteen-year-old steel guitar player named LEON MCAULIFFE for the group (he would later gain great fame with BOB WILLS). Later versions of the Swift Jewel group would make records in a jazzy style.

Following a tonsil operation in 1934, Jim lost his ability to YODEL; he also ran into what he described as "women problems" around Houston. He decided to return to Detroit, where he rejoined his brother both in The Purple Gang and on radio as members of Jack West and His Circle Star Cowboys. Jim quickly formed his own group, The Lone Star Cowboys, with other disaffected members of West's outfit.

From 1935 to 1937 Lewis worked at New York's famous pseudo-Western club, the Village Barn. From 1936 to 1939 the band broadcast over the Mutual Network nationwide, usually playing hot swing numbers and novelties. In 1937 Lewis made his first recording for Vocalion, and continued to appear on disc through the early 1950s. Like the HOOSIER HOT SHOTS and other novelty Western acts, his recordings focused on Western-themed pop songs, often "enhanced" by sound effects produced by his "Hootin' nanny," a noisemaking instrument that was a big part of his act. Lewis described it as a cross between a "hoot owl and a nanny goat"; the contraption included washboards, bells, sirens, and even guns loaded with blanks. He also composed a number of country standards, including the wartime hit "Squaws Along the Yukon." His " 'Leven Miles from Leavenworth" became an unofficial theme song for the Women's Air Corps (WACs), who trained at that base.

In the 1940s Lewis worked out of Hollywood, appearing in many of the popular B-Westerns of the day. Many members of Lewis's pre–World War II band joined with SPADE COOLEY after Lewis was drafted in 1942. After the war Lewis formed a new band, featuring young GUITAR picker MERLE TRAVIS. He also opened a series of dance halls in southern California that catered to the hillbilly crowd.

In 1950 Lewis settled in Seattle, where he performed on a local children's TV show, *Sheriff Tex's Safety Junction*, for the next seven years. One of his last professional appearances was in 1962 at the Seattle World's Fair, where he premiered yet another new band, The Apple Knockers. Lewis continued to perform in and around Seattle through the mid-1980s, although he was retired from full-time music making. In 1985 a concert was held to honor his "55 years in show business." He died five years later.

Select Discography

Western Swing Nostalgia, Cattle Compact CCD 221. Selection of his 1930s–1940s recordings, mostly focusing on novelty numbers.

LIGHT CRUST DOUGHBOYS, THE (Original lineup, 1931–1932: Bob Wills [fdl, voc]; Milton Brown [voc]; Durwood Brown [bnj]; Herman Arnspiger [gtr]; Clifton "Sleepy" Johnson [steel gtr]; W. Lee "Pappy" O'Daniel [emcee])

The Light Crust Doughboys, the first true WESTERN SWING band, introduced two enormous talents: fiddler/vocalist BOB WILLS, who would soon be leading his own Texas Playboys, and vocalist/bandleader MILTON BROWN, who went on to form his Musical Brownies.

Wills had been touring Texas with guitarist Arnspiger when they got a radio job in Fort Worth. They soon hooked up with vocalist Brown, who brought along his brother Durwood, forming a quartet first known as The Wills Fiddle Band and then the Aladdin Laddies (because their radio show was sponsored by the Aladdin Lamp Company). The show was picked up by the Texas Quality Network, a string of radio stations throughout the state. Searching for a sponsor to replace the lamp company, Wills approached PR man W. Lee O'Daniel at the Burrus Mills Company, makers of Lightcrust Dough. O'Daniel liked the idea, and the group, renamed The Lightcrust Doughboys, made their home base in Fort Worth. After a few recordings for Victor, the original group disbanded.

O'Daniel was enthusiastic about continuing the group, and soon enlisted his own "Doughboys" to carry forward the name. They recorded for Vocalion from 1933 to 1935, waxing a mix of up-tempo fiddle tunes, sentimental ditties, and COWBOY numbers. O'Daniel left the group in 1935, when he formed the Hillbilly Flour Company and hired his own group of country musicians. The Doughboys were then led by Western Swing legends Eddie Dunn and Cecil Brower, among others, maintaining their link with Burrus Mills until 1942; then the Duncan Coffee Company took over their sponsorship, and suddenly they were known as The Coffee Grinders. However, the Doughboys name was so well-loved that by the end of World War II they had reverted to their former name, even though they were no longer sponsored by the mill. They continued to work on the rodeo/country fair circuit into the 1960s, with varied personnel, including many alums of the great Western Swing bands of the 1930s, 1940s, and 1950s.

LILLY BROTHERS (Everett, b. Charles E. L., Clear Creek, W. Va., July 1, 1924 [voc, mdln, bnj, fdl], and B, b. Mitchell Burt L., Clear Creek, W. Va., December 15, 1921 [voc, gtr])

The Lilly Brothers were a transitional act between the brother acts of the 1930s and the BLUEGRASS bands of the 1950s and 1960s. They were very important in popularizing bluegrass in Boston, far from their home, beginning in the mid-1950s.

The brothers grew up in rural West Virginia, where they heard traditional mountain music from birth. They were also exposed to the popular brother acts of the 1930s, particularly THE BLUE SKY BOYS and The Monroe Brothers, on recordings and the radio. Emulating the sound and style of these acts, B took up the GUITAR and Everett the MANDOLIN; they made their professional debut on *The Old Farm Hour*, broadcast out of Charleston, West Virginia, in the late 1930s. They continued to work as a duet and in various groups through the mid-1940s on radio stations in the South.

In 1945 they were hired by a major radio station, WNOX out of Knoxville, Tennessee, to play on a show hosted by Lynn Davis and MOLLY O'DAY. Three years later they moved up further in the country world by joining WWVA's *Wheeling* [West Virginia] *Jamboree*, where they met a young Texas-born FIDDLE player, Benjamin "Tex" Logan, who would later work with them when they were based in Boston.

After two years with the *Jamboree*, the brothers quit in a financial dispute and for a while gave up their act. Everett joined the new FLATT AND SCRUGGS group in 1951, recording and touring with them as mandolinist and harmony singer for about a year. A call from old friend Tex Logan, who had relocated to Boston, where he was working with a young banjo player named Don Stover, convinced the brothers to reunite and move to that city in 1952.

The group eventually became the house band at a club that catered to both country and bluegrass fans as well as young college students who were to make up the core of the FOLK-REVIVAL audience. Albums on the folk labels Folkways and Prestige International helped broaden their audience base and made them one of the most influential groups in the first bluegrass revival. It helped that the Lilly Brothers maintained an older-style repertoire and manner of singing, making them sound more "authentic" to the urban purists who were dismayed by any commercial influence on bluegrass music.

The Lilly Brothers continued to perform with Stover and Logan through early 1970, making them one of the most stable lineups in bluegrass history. In 1970 Everett's son died in a car crash, and he decided to leave Boston. From that point on, the band would reunite occasionally for tours and recordings through the late 1970s. In the 1980s Everett worked primarily with another son, Mark, in a band called Clear Creek Crossin'. B retired from music making.

Select Discography

Have a Feast Here Tonight, Prestige 9919. Reissues two early 1960s albums by the brothers, with Don Stover on banjo.

LINE DANCING Line dancing is to country music what the Hustle was to disco: the main reason people flock to clubs, and perhaps one reason that so many "more sophisticated" listeners disdain country music.

Traditional square dances are performed in sets of four couples; "reels" (such as the Virginia reel) are performed in lines of facing couples. The traditional dance of the HONKY-TONKS is the two-step, which is very simple to perform but also requires a partner. Line dancing has the advantage of not needing a partner to get out on the dance floor. This makes it ideal for a society where divorced and single people outnumber the happily married. And line dances are simple to perform; they involve walking steps performed in easy-to-remember sequences, so that you don't need to be a world-class dancer to participate.

Line dancing seems to have grown up in the glitzy country clubs that followed in the wake of disco's popularity in the mid-1970s. Like disco dancing, line dancing is performed to records spun by deejays, often on a dance floor that is garishly lit with moving colored lights. One of the first line dances to gain wide acceptance was the Texas Freeze; not surprisingly, it spawned many variations including the colorfully named Slappin' Leather, Bus Stop, and, most popular of all by the early 1980s, the Electric Slide. Also big in the early 1980s was the Tush Push, which adapts a watered-down cha-cha step to the line.

Recognizing the growing line-dancing phenomenon, country music television (on cable stations TNN and CMT) regularly featured line-dance programs from the get-go, in the tradition of the old *American Bandstand* show, and they were popular shows among viewers through the mid-90s. When Mercury Records wanted to launch a young, then-unknown studly singer named BILLY RAY CYRUS, they hired a choreographer to create a new line dance, the Achy Breaky, to accompany his debut single. It was a clever marketing move, propelling the single to the top of the country charts and making Cyrus the poster boy for the new manufactured stardom in Nashville. However, this feat was never repeated, and today's line dancers tend to follow the charts, dancing to whatever songs are currently "hot."

LITTLE TEXAS (c. 1990–c. 1997; Porter Carleton Howell, b. Longview, Tex., June 21, 1964 [lead gtr; voc]; Dwayne Keith O'Brien, b. Ada, Okla., June 30, 1963 [gtr, voc]; Timothy Ray Rushlow, b. Arlington, Tex., October 6, 1966 [lead voc, gtr, mdln]; Brady Seals, b. Hamilton, Ohio, March 29, 1969 [kybds, voc]; Duane Carlisle Propes, b. Longview, Tex., December 17, 1966 [b, voc]; Del Anthony Gray, b. Hamilton, Ohio, May 8, 1969 [drms]; Seals left in mid-1994 and was replaced by Jeffrey Howard Huskins, b. Arlington, Tex., April 26, 1966)

Little Texas was another in a long string of 1990s "new-country" bands who were heavily influenced by pop-rock bands like THE EAGLES, while their vocal harmonies recall mainstream country-schlock stars like ALABAMA. While the group is among the few to feature five-part vocal harmonies, their general sound (kick-ass rock and roll moderated with the occasional weepy country ballad) is generic to many bands making their debut in the late 1980s and early 1990s.

The group originated around the quartet of Rushlow, O'Brien, Howell, and Propes. Signed to a development deal by major label Warner Brothers, they spent most of the late 1980s on the road, honing their sound. They hooked up with keyboardist Seals and drummer Gray, completing their transformation into a more pop-oriented sound. Finally deemed ready for the recording studio, they produced the album *First Time for Everything* in 1992, yielding five gold singles. This album and their 1993 follow-up, *Big Time*, featured a mix of rough-and-rowdy dance numbers, including the Texas-ophile's favorite "God Blessed Texas," which won them the praise of then Governor Ann Richards, along with sentimental ballads like "What Might Have Been," featuring a full orchestral backup. The group scored patriotic brownie points by singing a five-part a cappella version of "The Star-Spangled Banner" for candidate Bill Clinton, later performing their hit "What Might Have Been" in a show for the president featuring other mainstream artists like easy-listening saxophone tooter Kenny G and R&B diva Whitney Houston.

After their last major hits in 1994, the band went for three years without a new record. They finally produced a new album in 1997, but by then their fan base apparently had disappeared. The group has not released any new material since then.

During the group's heyday lead singer Rushlow said (in all seriousnessness): "I feel like we're the first country band that was influenced by 'young country.' Sure, we love bands like The Eagles and POCO, but our real influences were Alabama, RESTLESS HEART—country's *new* sound." These spiritual forebears shine through in their every slick note, although a less passionate critic might hope that this is not going to become country's dominant style.

Select Discography

Greatest Hits, Warners 46017. The band's best-loved hits.

LOCKLIN, HANK (b. Lawrence Hankins L., McLellan, Fla., February 15, 1918)

A pioneering smooth-voiced country vocalist, Locklin created a pleasant, middle-of-the-road style about a decade before it became the predominant NASHVILLE SOUND, scoring his biggest hit with 1960's "Please Help Me, I'm Falling."

Growing up on a small family farm, Locklin played GUITAR from an early age, playing for local dances and parties. By the 1930s he was doing road work for the Works Progress Administration while occasionally performing on local radio and still dreaming of being a singing star. His big break came after World War II, when he earned a spot on the prestigious LOUISIANA HAYRIDE radio program; he was signed by Four Star Records, and had a minor hit with 1949's "The Same Sweet Girl" (unusual for a HONKY-TONK ballad, in that it told of a husband's *devotion* to his wife), followed by a bigger one with 1953's "Let Me Be the One." The success of this second single led to a spot on THE GRAND OLE OPRY and a contract with major country label RCA Victor.

At RCA his mature crooning style came to full flower, and he had a number of hits with poppish numbers like 1957's sappy "Geisha Girl," the mushy "Send Me the Pillow You Dream On" and "It's a Little More Like Heaven," both from 1958, and his chart-buster "Please Help Me, I'm Falling" from 1960, which he rerecorded a decade later with the cloying accompaniment of the Nashville Brass for yet another trip up the charts. (SKEETER DAVIS provided an answer song to this million seller with "[I Can't Help You] I'm Falling, Too.") The bathetic "Happy Birthday to Me" followed in 1961. Locklin also recorded albums of standards, including the Irish pop song "Danny Boy," which he cut in 1963; it became a later career signature for him. Although he continued to record through the 1960s and early 1970s, his hits grew fewer. He became a popular touring act, known throughout the U.S., Canada, and Europe, and was a big star in Ireland, where his crooner-styled vocals won a huge audience.

By the early 1970s Locklin had returned triumphantly to his hometown, buying up his boyhood farm and building a lavish ranch, and even was elected mayor. In the mid-1970s he was back to performing in the Houston area, and in 1975 recorded, with little success, for the MGM label.

From the 1980s through the close of the century, Locklin continued to perform on *The Grand Ole Opry*, but mostly limited his playing to around the south Georgia/north Florida region. In 2001 he released his first new record in twenty years, *Generations in Song*, on his own label. Produced by his son, it featured many of the famed Nashville Sound musicians who recorded with Locklin in the 1950s and 1960s, along with new-country artists like VINCE GILL. To market the record he sponsored a time slot on the *Opry*. As his Web site proclaims, "It is a mark of distinction to own a Hank Locklin record."

Select Discography

Send Me the Pillow You Dream On, Bear Family 15953. Three CDs of all his recordings made between 1946 and 1954, for a variety of small labels.

Please Help Me, I'm Falling, Bear Family 15730. Four-CD set of all his RCA recordings from the mid-1950s through the 1960s.

LOGSDON, JIMMIE (b. Panther, Ky., April 1, 1922–October 7, 2001)

The son of a Bible-thumpin' minister, Logsdon recorded some country obscurities in the 1950s, but is best remembered for his classic ROCKABILLY side "I've Got a Rocket in My Pocket" from 1957, issued by "Jimmy Lloyd."

Logsdon spent much of his childhood moving from town to town as his father pursued the life of an itinerant preacher. The family finally settled in Cincinnati; soon after, Logsdon was drafted into the Air Force, where he was trained in electronics; after the war he opened an electronics store in nearby Louisville, Kentucky. After hearing HANK WILLIAMS's first recordings, he took up the GUITAR, and quickly earned a local following, performing over the radio.

In 1952 he opened for Williams on a local radio show, and Williams was so impressed that he introduced Logsdon to Decca producer Paul Cohen; Logsdon recorded a series of Williamsesque numbers, including his best-known country blues recording, "The Death of Hank Williams," backed by the original DRIFTING COWBOYS. A move to the Dot label did little to boost his career, for the Williams HONKY-TONK style was quickly going out of favor. In 1957 he moved to Roulette Records and a new persona as "Jimmy Lloyd," jumping on the popularity of rockabilly with the classic "Rocket in My Pocket." Although this became a collector's item in later years, it did little for him at the time, and by the early 1960s he was back to recording country for the King label. Logsdon continued to work sporadically, mostly in the Kentucky area, as performer, deejay, and local TV announcer, until 1976, when he gave up music for a job with the state's Department of Labor.

LOMAX, JOHN (b. J. Avery L., Goodman, Miss., September 23, 1867–January 26, 1948), and Alan L. (b. Austin, Tex., January 15, 1915)

One of the most famous folklorists of our time, John Lomax virtually created the vogue for COWBOY songs with his famous 1910 collection *Cowboy Songs and Other Ballads*, as well as conducting pioneering fieldwork throughout the South, often accompanied by his son, Alan.

Raised in the Southwest, Lomax was fascinated with the songs and legends that he heard from his neighbors, family, and friends. When he entered Harvard, he met folklorist George Lyman Kittredge, a noted collector of folk ballads who, unlike other early collectors (who relied on written sources), encouraged his students to conduct fieldwork, that is, to go among the people and collect their songs. Lomax followed Kittredge's example, and published his first collection of what he called "cowboy songs" in 1910, with an introduction by ex-President Teddy Roosevelt. This became the source for many "cowboy" recording stars from the 1930s on, introducing songs that have become veritable chestnuts, such as "Home on the Range."

After working for a while in banking and as an amateur academic, Lomax took to the road again in 1933, bringing along one of the first portable recording machines (it recorded on discs, and was powered off the battery of his car); his eighteen-year-old son, Alan, accompanied him. One of their most famous stops was the notorious state prison farm in Angola, Louisiana, where they discovered a convicted murderer and talented guitarist named Huddie Ledbetter, later famous as "Leadbelly." Ledbetter became the Lomaxes' driver, and was later brought to New York to become one of the stars of the first FOLK REVIVAL.

Meanwhile, the Lomaxes published several more collections, including 1934's *American Ballads and Folk Songs*, 1941's *Our Singing Country*, and 1947's *Folk Song, U.S.A.* The two became codirectors of the Library of Congress's Archive of American Folk Song in 1937; Alan Lomax was active in producing radio programs and recordings of traditional folk musicians beginning in the late 1940s. The elder Lomax starred in his own radio series, *The Ballad Hunter*, shortly before his death. In the late 1950s Alan was among the first to take stereo equipment into the field, producing two large series of recordings of traditional country and blues music from the South, issued by Atlantic and Prestige.

From the mid-1960s on, Alan Lomax was increasingly involved in the study of what he called "cantometrics," the links between traditional musics from around the world. Working out of Columbia University, he became more active in the academic field than in popular folklore. In the early 1990s he produced a series of programs on world music and dance for public television, and wrote his memoirs of recording blues musicians in the South in the 1930s, 1940s, and 1950s. Later in the decade the Lomax Archives arranged for Rounder Records to issue his complete field recordings; dozens of CDs have appeared, with more to come.

Select Discography

Sings American Folksongs, Folkways 3508. John Lomax recorded these songs in the late 1940s; although he was not a great performer, they are of some historical interest.

LONZO AND OSCAR (Lonzo, b. Lloyd L. George [aka Ken Marvin], Haleyville, Ga., June 27, 1924–October 16, 1991 [gtr, voc], and Oscar, b. Rollin Sullivan, Edmonton, Ky., July 7, 1917–June 5, 1967 [mdln, voc])

Lonzo and Oscar were a classic country-comedy duo who had their biggest hit in 1947 with "I'm My Own Grandpa," later a theme song for comedian GRANDPA JONES.

Rollin Sullivan grew up in central Kentucky in a family of ten, and began performing for local dances with his brother, John (July 7, 1917–June 5, 1967). Rollin was the more ambitious of the two, and found work as a RUBE comedian on radio in 1939, when he gained the nickname of Oscar; he joined Nashville's prestigious WSM in 1942, as a backup musician. When a new singer named EDDY ARNOLD joined THE GRAND OLE OPRY two years later, Sullivan was enlisted to play rhythm GUITAR in his backup band. His brother also joined the group, as did Lloyd George, who took the stage name of Ken Marvin and played bass.

Arnold asked Rollin and Lloyd to perform a standard country cutup act for his stage show, because he was uncomfortable handling comic material. Originally they were known as Cicero and Oscar, but Marvin was uncomfortable with the high-falutin' Roman name, and wanted to switch it to something a little more authentically backwoodsy. It is said that an exasperated hotel clerk, on seeing Marvin haul his laundry through the main lobby of the hotel, berated him by calling him "Lonzo," and the name stuck. The duo hit pay dirt with their recording of "I'm My Own Grandpa" in 1947, and broke with Arnold to become *Grand Ole Opry* stars on their own.

When Marvin tired of the comic routine, he was replaced by Sullivan's older brother John as a new Lonzo; the brothers continued to perform together until John's death in 1967, recording for Victor, Columbia, and the bluegrass Starday label and continuing the act in all of its corn-pone style pretty much unchanged for almost twenty years. Dave Hooten (b. February 4, 1935) was brought on board as the third Lonzo in 1968, and the duo continued to perform into the 1970s, carrying the tradition of hayseed comedy into a new era. They expanded their sound into a BLUEGRASS band inspired by the sound and style of the popular OSBORNE BROTHERS. They continued to perform on the *Opry* and in and around Nashville through the remainder of the decade, when they finally retired.

LOUDERMILK, JOHN D. (b. Durham, N.C., March 31, 1934)

One of the most famous country songwriters of the 1950s and 1960s, Loudermilk supplied hundreds of songs to Nashville's establishment while also recording his own material, mostly in a folksy manner.

The son of a carpenter who had worked on the Duke University chapel, Loudermilk began his musical career in church, becoming a member of the local Salvation Army band in his teens and quickly mastering a number of instruments. When he was twelve, he won a Capitol Records-sponsored talent contest run by a Durham radio station and hosted by country music legend TEX RITTER. As a teen he was employed by the local radio station, where he was a bass player for the noon-hour band and did odd jobs around the office. Influenced by the popularity of R&B and teen-pop, he wrote a song called "A Rose and a Baby Ruth," premiering it on the station. A local producer heard the song and had his protégé, GEORGE HAMILTON IV, from nearby Winston-Salem, record it; the record became a 1956 million-seller, launching Hamilton's and Loudermilk's careers.

Loudermilk still hadn't settled on music as a career; hedging his bets, he entered college, at the same time releasing his first recording of his own material, "Sitting in the Balcony," under the nom de disc of Johnny Dee; in 1957 rocker Eddie Cochran covered the song, for another big hit. By the late 1950s Loudermilk had moved to Nashville, where he hooked up first with Cedarwood Music and then the country powerhouse Acuff-Rose. One of his first country hits was "Waterloo," recorded by STONEWALL JACKSON, one of those saga songs that were so popular in the late 1950s. In 1959 Loudermilk made another solo recording, now taking the name Tommy Dee, on the minor hit "Three Stars," a bathetic attempt to cash in on the death of BUDDY HOLLY. Loudermilk's other big teen-pop hit was "Ebony Eyes," a 1961 hit for THE EVERLY BROTHERS.

Meanwhile, Loudermilk was blossoming as a country tunesmith. He supplied SUE THOMPSON with her big 1961 hit "Sad Movies (Make Me Cry)," followed a year later by "Norman." He began recording on his own in the folk-pop style that was then coming into vogue, and had minor hits with 1961's "The Language of Love," and "Thou Shalt Not Steal" and "Road Hog" from the following year. When George Hamilton's teen-pop career faded, he also turned to country, and naturally asked old friend Loudermilk to supply him with some material; the results were the 1963 hit "Abilene" and "Break My Mind" from four years later. "Tobacco Road," one of Loudermilk's most realistic and moving portrayals of the tough times faced by rural folks, was a hit for the British country-rock outfit The Nashville Teens in 1964. By the late 1960s he had turned his attention more to record production, as the producer on the first album by the Southern rockers The Allman Brothers. In 1971 he had his last major pop hit with "Indian Reservation," recorded by Paul Revere and the Raiders.

In the early 1970s Loudermilk became interested in academic ethnomusicology, the study of folk and traditional musics. Since that time he has been more or less inactive on the country music scene as a songwriter, although he has served on the boards of several country music organizations, and his songs continue to be covered by new Nashville artists.

Select Discography

Sittin' in the Balcony, Bear Family 15875. His earliest recordings, made 1957–early 1960s, mostly in a ROCKABILLY vein.
Blue Train, Bear Family 15431. RCA recordings from the 1960s.

LOUISIANA HAYRIDE
In its heyday second only to THE GRAND OLE OPRY, the *Hayride* was one of the most influential of all country-music radio programs, launching the career of HANK WILLIAMS.

The show was born in 1948 when Dean Upson, one-time member of THE VAGABONDS and a former talent coordinator for the *Opry*, joined forces with the management of Shreveport, Louisiana's, clear-channel station, KWKH, to break the *Opry* monopoly. Opening with a cast that included THE BAILES BROTHERS, JOHNNIE AND JACK, and KITTY WELLS, the show was given an enormous boost in August 1948 when SINGER/SONGWRITER Hank Williams joined the roster. Williams, like many after him, stayed only a little over a year before moving to the more prestigious *Opry*, and the *Hayride* would be plagued by its second-class status throughout its lifetime. Lacking a booking agency (the backbone of the *Opry*'s hold on its acts and a great moneymaker for the station), the *Hayride* was unable to hold on to its talent.

Nonetheless, through the mid-1950s a number of stars got their start on the program, including RED SOVINE, SLIM WHITMAN, WEBB PIERCE, FLOYD CRAMER, JOHNNY HORTON, and JIM REEVES. In an ironic twist Hank Williams returned to the *Hayride* in 1952, after he was fired from the *Opry* due to his drunkenness, but by this time his performances were pretty eratic in quality (he died on New Year's Eve 1953). Both Pierce and Reeves served as announcers on the show, which was broadcast nationally over the CBS network in the early 1950s as well as on Armed Forces Radio in Korea.

The *Hayride*'s biggest coup occurred on October 6, 1954, when ELVIS PRESLEY, a young ducktailed star out of Memphis, joined the cast. Initially promoted as a country artist, Elvis remained with the Hayride for eighteen months; he could never find acceptance at the *Opry*. When Elvis left the program in 1956 and signed with RCA as a teen-pop star, the program began its long decline.

Although the *Hayride* continued on the air under its original ownership through 1973, and thereafter through 1987 under new hands, the show never really regained its stature or audience. In 1987 it was reintroduced as a television show, but made little impact on the country music world.

LOUVIN BROTHERS, THE
(Ira and Charlie Loudermilk; Ira, b. Rainesville, Ala., April 21, 1924–June 20, 1965 [mdln, voc]; Charlie, b. Jefferson City, Mo., July 7, 1927 [gtr, voc])

Influenced by the popular brother acts of the 1930s, the Louvins were big stars on THE GRAND OLE OPRY from the mid-1950s through the early 1960s with their brand of GOSPEL-influenced harmonies and songs.

Raised in Henegger, Georgia, the duo began singing at an early age, particularly influenced by traditional balladry, old-time gospel, and the sounds heard over the radio and on records, particularly acts like The

Ira (left) and Charlie (right) Louvin performing on *The Grand Ole Opry*, c. mid-1950s. Photo: University of North Carolina, Southern Historical Collection, Southern Folklife Collection, University Archives

Monroe Brothers, THE DELMORE BROTHERS, and THE BLUE SKY BOYS. Their big break came in 1943, when they won a position on early-morning radio in Chattanooga, Tennessee, thanks to a local talent show; by the late 1940s they had moved to WNOX in Knoxville and the popular *Midday Merry-Go-Round* program. They recorded briefly for MGM and Decca in the late 1940s, then signed with Capitol in 1951, under the management of FRED ROSE.

Their hits began in the mid-1950s with "I Don't Believe You've Met My Baby" and "You're Running Wild" in 1956, leading to a regular spot on *The Grand Ole Opry*. At the same time they issued *Tragic Songs of Life*, a combination of traditional ballads and modern sentimental songs with sparse, primarily acoustic backup, which Capitol issued with a strange cover that resembled the tacky art on pulp fiction of the day. Still, this remains one of their finest recordings, for its fine singing, tasteful accompaniments, and sympathetic production values; their later-1950s and early-1960s sessions were marred by heavy-handed NASHVILLE SOUND productions, although their tasteful and distinctive singing shines through the acoustic sludge. About half of their albums were all-gospel recordings, and they also paid tribute to their roots on an entire LP tribute to The Delmore Brothers.

The brothers had an increasingly stormy relationship, and Charlie finally broke with his brother in 1963 to pursue a solo career, beginning with the hit "I Don't Love You Anymore." Ira continued to appear with his wife, Florence, who performed under the stage name Anne Young; they were killed in an automobile accident in 1965. In 1970–1971 Charlie formed a partnership with vocalist MELBA MONTGOMERY, who had previously recorded with Gene Pitney and GEORGE JONES, and continued as a solo artist on the *Opry* and the road through the 1990s. In late 2001, after the brothers' induction into the Country Music Hall of Fame, Charlie was hospitalized following a serious automobile accident.

Charlie and Ira together are credited with writing some 400 songs, including the perennial standard "When I Stop Dreaming" (covered by EMMYLOU HARRIS, among many others). Their trademark high-vocal harmonies, with a plaintive sound reminiscent of backwoods gospel music, makes almost all of their recordings worth hearing, even when they are awash in syrupy strings. They were one of the few modern country duos able to preserve a true country sound into the early 1960s.

Select Discography

Close Harmony, Bear Family 15561. Eight CDs giving 220 songs recorded for Capitol and MGM, cut between 1947 and 1965. Great notes (by Charles Wolfe) and rare pictures accompany these classic sides, some of which suffer from Nashville Sound production.

Greatest Hits, Capitol 57222. Nine 1950s and 1960s hits on this cassette-only release.

Radio Favorites, 1951–1957, Country Music Foundation 009. Air checks from the 1950s.

Fifty Years of Makin' Music, Playback 4505. Charlie Louvin joined by country stars WILLIE NELSON, WAYLON JENNINGS, CHARLIE DANIELS, TANYA TUCKER, George Jones, and more.

LOVELESS, PATTY (b. P. Ramey, Pikeville, Ky., January 4, 1958)

Loveless is a big-throated HONKY-TONK-styled new-country singer who became a major star in the late 1980s. She is a fine singer who recalls performers like PATSY MONTANA, ROSE MADDOX, and LORETTA LYNN (who, incidentally, is her cousin), to name just a few, while still having a contemporary edge.

Born in rural Kentucky, the daughter of a coal miner, Loveless was introduced to country music through her older brother, Roger, who later managed her career. She began performing as a duo with him at age twelve. Two years later he took her to Nashville, where she was hired to replace cousin Loretta in THE WILBURN BROTHERS' summer touring show. She toured for several summers with them, eventually wedding their drummer, Terry Lovelace. After her wedding she went into semiretirement (although she continued to sing rock and pop music locally), leading the life of a housewife in North Carolina.

She returned to Nashville in the mid-1980s after her marriage failed, changing her stage name to Loveless because it was easier to pronounce and also because she didn't want to be associated with the soft-core porn star Linda Lovelace. Her brother got her an introduction to MCA Records and producer EMORY GORDY, JR., who has been associated with her ever since (and later became her husband). From her debut LP she has recorded a mix of new-country styles by leading SINGER/SONGWRITERS of the Nashville scene. Some of her early hits included the ballad "I Did," from her first LP, and up-tempo numbers like "Timber, I'm Falling in Love" and "I'm That Kind of Girl" (both with a rocking edge). Vocal troubles waylaid her career in the early 1990s, but she returned triumphantly in 1993 with her hit single, "Blame It on Your Heart," an up-tempo, ROCKABILLY-esque number, along with the country swing of "Mr. Man in the Moon."

Loveless had a hard time producing hits through the later 1990s, as younger (and more videogenic) female singers came to the fore. 1995 saw her last major country hits with "Lonely Too Long" and "You Can Feel Bad." Nonetheless, she remains a solid concert draw and continues to record critically well-received albums. In 2001 she issued her first acoustic-BLUEGRASS album, *Mountain Soul*, joining singers like DOLLY PARTON and ALISON KRAUSS in a return to their bluegrass roots.

Loveless's recordings have always featured the finest traditional musicians (such as fiddler Stuart Duncan of THE NASHVILLE BLUEGRASS BAND, guitarist ALBERT LEE, and multiple-instrumentalist MARK O'CONNOR), wed with a contemporary big drum sound to make them palatable to pop radio. Her voice is unaffected country; she manages to honor the stylings of the greatest country singers without aping them shamelessly. In other words, she is a unique vocalist who is mindful of tradition while continuing to create her own personal style.

Select Discography

20th Century Masters, MCA 112352. Her hits recorded for MCA from the mid-1980s through early 1990s.
Classics, Epic 69809. Hits of the Epic label years (1993–1999).
Mountain Soul, Epic/Jahaza 85651. 2001 release featuring all-star bluegrass accompaniment, including RICKY SKAGGS and Earl Scruggs (of FLATT AND SCRUGGS).

LOVETT, LYLE (b. Klein, Tex., November 1, 1957)

Lovett is a Texas-bred songster as well known for his tall hairdo and craggy features as for his music that is just quirky enough to draw attention on both pop and country charts.

Born and raised in the small town of Klein, Lovett had his musical tastes formed by a mixture of Texas HONKY-TONK, BOB WILLS's classic WESTERN SWING, and the neo-hipster attitude of pop singers like Tom Waits. His career was slow getting off the ground, so for a while he was an assistant to his mother, who taught motivational training courses for businesspeople, while pursuing his musical career at local clubs at night. Finally he raised enough for the fare to Nashville, where he landed in the early 1980s, seeking a recording contract.

Lovett's half-spoken vocals, wordy songs, and wacky looks got him some initial attention, including a recording contract with Curb Records (an MCA affiliate), producing his first single, "Farther Down the Line," which drew on and skewed the classic image of the rodeo cowboy. This was followed by further Western-flavored numbers, including his only Top 10 hit, "Cowboy Man." And who else but Lovett would have the audacity to title a song "An Acceptable Level of Ecstasy," addressing issues of upper-class racism?

Lovett hit his stride with his third album, *Lyle Lovett and His Large Band*, melding Western Swing and jazz

influences. Oddly enough, the minor hit off this record was an acoustic cut, "Nobody Knows Me (Like My Baby)," a tender, offbeat love song rich with the kind of hip wordplay that makes Lovett's best compositions so intriguing to his fans.

Lovett fits in with the other great Texas country songwriters—ranging from WILLIE NELSON through BILLY JOE SHAVER and JERRY JEFF WALKER to NANCI GRIFFITH—in his literate, witty lyrics, offbeat melodies, and myriad influences, from Dylanesque poetry to HANK WILLIAMS- and Bob Wills-styled arrangements. Also like the other Texans, he is somewhat of an anomaly in an industry that prizes predictable product. For this reason he is destined to have a strong cult following while widespread commercial success will probably be rare.

Lovett's career got an odd boost in 1993 with his surprise marriage to Hollywood honey Julia Roberts, splashing his droopy jowls across supermarket tabloids as the world's most unlikely husband for the troubled sexpot. (Ironically, he had a minor hit in 1992 with his swing-band version of "That's No Lady [That's My Wife].)" Not surprisingly, the marriage was not long-lived, and Lovett's first album following his divorce was widely interpreted as an ode to his lost love. Also in the 1990s, Lovett established a movie career, often portraying offbeat characters in films by his mentor, Robert Altman.

Lovett made a bold move in 1998 by releasing an album of songs written by other Texas songwriters, *Step Inside the House*, that includes many of his longtime friends and heroes, such as GUY CLARK, TOWNES VAN ZANDT, Walter Hyatt, ROBERT EARL KEEN, and STEVE FROMHOLZ. A critically acclaimed work, it failed to do much on the charts, and Lovett lacked the clout of an artist like Nanci Griffith to bring these artists the attention they deserved. Still, it showed how closely linked the Texas school of songwriting is.

Select Discography

Lyle Lovett, MCA 5748. 1986 debut album.
Pontiac, MCA 42028.
And His Large Band, MCA 42263. 1989 third album, with a more Western Swing feel to it.
Joshua Judges Ruth, MCA 10475. A more confessional album from 1992.
Step Inside This House, MCA 11831. 1998 release featuring songs by his favorite songwriters.

LULU BELLE AND SCOTTY (Lulu Belle, b. Myrtle Eleanor Cooper, Boone, N.C., December 23, 1913–February 8, 1999; Scotty, b. Scott Greene "Skyland Scotty" Wiseman, November 8, 1909–January 31, 1981)

Country duos were immensely popular in the 1930s, thanks to the proliferation of "brother" acts. Husband and wife Lulu Belle and Scotty added a down-home, family image to the mix while introducing several songs written by Scotty that have become country standards, including the sentimental "Remember Me" and "Have I Told You Lately That I Love You?" (Scotty also authored with BASCOM LAMAR LUNSFORD the perennial favorite comedy number, "Mountain Dew.") Their smooth vocal harmonies helped move country music toward a more mainstream, pop orientation.

Lulu Belle began performing as a soloist in her teen years, successfully auditioning for the popular NATIONAL BARN DANCE radio show out of Chicago when she was nineteen. She first performed country comedy bits (playing a backwoods hayseed in the manner of MINNIE PEARL) with popular entertainer RED FOLEY, and then the station paired her with another newcomer, Scott Wiseman, nicknamed "Skyland Scotty." Their radio partnership blossomed into a romance, and the duo married. They became one of the most popular acts on the *Barn Dance*, and thanks to their considerable exposure, recorded prolifically for many different labels. They performed a mix of traditional and more recent compositions, leaning toward sentimental and heart songs, many composed by Wiseman to suit the duo's romantic image. Their early recordings featured spare accompaniments, with solo GUITAR augmented with second guitar and BANJO, and sometimes harmonica and FIDDLE; the emphasis is on their beautiful harmony singing, and justly so. From the late 1940s through their retirement from performing in 1958, they expanded on their radio work to host a Chicago-area musical-variety television program.

In the late 1950s, sensing the onslaught of rock and roll, the duo retired to North Carolina, where Lulu Belle became a successful local politician and Scotty took up teaching. After Scotty's death Lulu Belle remarried and took the name Lulu Belle Wiseman Stamey; she died in 1999.

Select Discography

Sweethearts of Country Music, Hollywood/IMG 289. Cassette-only issue of recordings of unknown vintage.

LUMAN, BOB (b. Robert Glynn L., Nacogdoches, Tex., April 15, 1937–December 27, 1978)

In his career Luman, ROCKABILLY-turned-country star of the 1950s and 1960s, traces the many changes in country music during this era.

The son of a talented old-time fiddler, guitarist, and harmonica player, Luman got early exposure to country music, and was playing GUITAR by the time he was in high school. After playing local clubs and winning a

slew of talent contests, he was hired to replace JOHNNY CASH on the popular LOUISIANA HAYRIDE radio program, taking on a more teen-pop sound. In the mid-1950s he recorded in a rockabilly style on small Texas labels, including one recording with a band led by legendary stringbender JAMES BURTON; his "A Pink Cadillac and a Black Mustache" is a legendary recording among fans of classic rockabilly, although it did little on the charts at the time.

In the late 1950s, THE EVERLY BROTHERS took an interest in his career, encouraging their new label, Warner Brothers, to sign him in 1959. In 1960 he had his one and only pop hit, BOUDELEAUX BRYANT's "Let's Think About Living," which also charted on the country listings. Lesser pop hits followed, including "Why Why Bye-Bye," from the same year, and 1961's "The Great Snowman." His pop career was cut short when he was drafted into the military; by the time he returned in 1963, the British invasion was beginning to sweep older American acts off the radio, and he turned to country.

In 1964 he signed with Hickory, the label run by Nashville starmakers ROY ACUFF and WESLEY ROSE, scoring a minor country hit with "The File" in the same year. He moved to Epic in 1966, and had a slew of Nashmopolitan hits in the style of the day, beginning with 1968's "Ain't Got Time to Be Unhappy" and running through 1974's "Still Loving You." He moved to Polydor in 1977, and under the guidance of Johnny Cash had one last hit with "The Pay Phone." Ironically, his last album was called *Alive and Well*; a year after its release Luman died of pneumonia in a Nashville hospital.

Select Discography

Loretta, Sundown 68. Hickory label recordings from the 1960s.
10 Years, 1968–77, Bear Family 15989. Beautifully produced, comprehensive chronicle of his last ten years of recording, for the Epic and Polydor labels. Five CDs are probably a lot for the casual listener, but a must for fans.

LUNN, ROBERT (b. R. Rainey L., Franklin, Tenn., November 28, 1912–March 8, 1966)

An ex-vaudevillian who worked on THE GRAND OLE OPRY stage for over twenty years, Lunn's claim to fame was the "talking blues," a long, often comic, spoken narrative accompanied by a simple blues chord pattern.

Lunn began performing in vaudeville as a teenager, and then worked on radio during the early 1930s. Besides singing and playing the GUITAR, he did imitations and worked as a ventriloquist. In late 1933 Lunn came to Nashville, where he began performing at the posh Hermitage Hotel. His signature number was "Talking

Blues." Although he became most closely associated with this song, it probably was originated by an earlier singer/comedian named Chris Bouchillon, who recorded a "Talking Blues" in 1926 for Columbia that was a strong seller, leading to several follow-ups. Lunn was heard by a WSM executive, and invited to perform on *The Grand Ole Opry* in early 1934.

Lunn joined the *Opry* in that March, remaining with the show for twenty-four years (with a break for service in World War II). Despite the popularity of his act, he rarely recorded, perhaps because most of his material was fairly similar. However, his regular radio appearances were quite influential on other country performers, most notably WOODY GUTHRIE, who transformed the talking blues into an effective, and often ironic, form of commentary on social conditions during the Depression and World War II. He retired from the *Opry* in 1958.

Select Discography

Original Talking Blues Man, Starday 228. Out-of-print 1962 album.

LUNSFORD, BASCOM LAMAR (b. Mars Hill, N.C., March 21, 1882–September 4, 1973)

Lunsford was one of the few folklorists to come from within the mountain culture. Founder of the Asheville Folk Festival in 1928, he was also a fine BANJO player, singer, and teller of traditional mountain stories.

Although he learned to play banjo and FIDDLE as a child, Lunsford did not initially pursue a career in music. His first job was as a rural fruit-tree salesman, and he traveled throughout the Appalachians selling his product to the landlocked mountain farmers. Along the way he became interested in the traditional songs, dances, and tales that he heard and saw. He returned to school to study folklore and law, eventually becoming a full-time lawyer and an amateur folklorist. In 1928 he was instrumental in starting what was officially known as the Mountain Dance and Folk Festival in Asheville, a community on the edge of the Appalachians where the Vanderbilts had a palatial summer estate. He also made a few commercial recordings in the 1920s but, like BUELL KAZEE, he never pursued a professional performing career.

In the 1930s, Lunsford became a close friend of Scotty Wiseman, one half of the famous mountain-music team of LULU BELLE AND SCOTTY. He wrote the original lyrics for the pseudo folksong "Good Old Mountain Dew," which Scotty set to music. This has since become a favorite of the FOLK REVIVAL. Also in the 1930s he began recording for the Library of Congress, becoming an important informant for folk-

lorists JOHN AND ALAN LOMAX, and helped in the founding of the National Folk Festival.

After World War II, Lunsford recorded sporadically for folk-revival labels and continued to perform in the Asheville area. He possessed a clear-as-a-bell singing voice; like other singers from the region, DOC WATSON and JEAN RITCHIE, he sang in a relaxed style, unlike the intense vocalizing of deep mountain singers like ROSCOE HOLCOMB, making his music much more accessible to an urban audience. He used the banjo as a simple but effective accompaniment to his repertoire, which was made up mostly of traditional ballads, nineteenth-century play-party songs and folk songs, and more recently composed compositions.

Select Discography

Ballads, Banjo Tunes and Sacred Songs of Western North Carolina, Smithsonian/Folkways 40082. Collection of 1950s and 1960s recordings.

LUTHER, FRANK (b. F. L. Crow, Larkin, Kan., August 4, 1899–November 16, 1980)

Luther was an early city entertainer who entered the country-music field, primarily working with CARSON J. ROBISON, and later became a popular performer of children's music.

Educated in music in college, Luther performed with several local vocal quartets of the mid-1920s, including The DeReszke Singers (for whom he provided piano accompaniment) and The Revellers, who were minor Midwestern radio stars. In 1928 he came to New York, where he hooked up with fellow Kansas native Robison, and the duo recorded many pop, novelty, and countrified songs for the urban market, often under the names of Bud and Joe Billings. Ethel Park Richardson, a New York radio hostess who specialized in presenting "country" music for city dwellers, used them regularly on her popular radio broadcasts. With Robison, Luther took songwriting credit for his adaptations of traditional humorous and COWBOY numbers, including "Barnacle Bill the Sailor" and "Home on the Range," both of which existed long before the duo "wrote" them. Luther also recorded as a solo artist, picking up on the cowboy fad in the 1930s.

In the mid-1930s he formed a radio group with his wife, Zora Layman (1900–1961), a fiddler who had previously worked with Carson Robison, replacing ADELYNE HOOD on his recordings; the duo were sometimes accompanied by Ray Whitley (a singing cowboy star of the era). Layman also recorded as a solo artist; her "Seven Years with the Wrong Man" was an early abused-wife saga that was phenomenally popular. By the decade's end Luther was writing and performing children's material with his wife, and the two became popular children's artists on record; although they divorced in 1940, they continued to perform together for another eight years. In the 1950s he moved into record production before finally retiring from the music business.

LYNN, LORETTA (b. L. Webb, Butcher Hollow, Ky., April 14, 1935)

One of country music's pioneering female performers and songwriters, Lynn has a classic country voice that is perfectly suited to her to-the-point lyrics reflecting a uniquely woman's point of view. Perhaps the only country singer who has taken on a wide variety of issues, from birth control to the Vietnam War to wife abuse, Lynn has made an important contribution to widening the subject matter and audience for country music.

Lynn was born in a small coal-mining community, as she emphasized in her biography, *Coal Miner's Daughter* (1976; later a feature film). When she was thirteen, she married Oliver "Mooney" Lynn, who later became her manager. The couple relocated to Washington state, where Lynn raised four children while she began performing her own material. Her first single

Loretta Lynn, c. mid-1970s. Photo: Raeanne Rubenstein

was in the classic barroom mold, "I'm a Honky-Tonk Girl," released in 1960 on the tiny Zero label. This brought her to the attention of OWEN BRADLEY, the legendary producer who had worked with PATSY CLINE.

Her early 1960s recordings showed the influence of KITTY WELLS in their brash lyrics of lovin' and losin'. Soon, however, her vocal style softened and her original material turned to unusual (for the time) topics, including "Don't Come Home a-Drinkin' (with Lovin' on Your Mind)," "You Ain't Woman Enough (to Steal My Man)," and "The Pill," a song in support of birth control. All of the songs were written from a woman's point of view; although their sound was classic HONKY-TONK, their message was unusually liberated for the mid-1960s and early 1970s. It is also noteworthy that Lynn wrote her songs from the point of view of a wife, a figure not often encountered on the honky-tonk landscape (primarily peopled by wayward husbands and "honky-tonk angels," the unattached women who lure them to their doom). This heavy dose of reality in a medium that seemed to thrive on fantasy pointed the direction for many of the more progressive songwriters of the 1970s and 1980s. Her autobiographical song, "Coal Miner's Daughter," from 1970, perfectly expressed the pride and anguish of growing up dirt-poor in the mountains.

The early 1970s also saw her teamed up with CONWAY TWITTY on a series of successful duets, including "After the Fire Is Gone" and "Louisiana Woman, Mississippi Man." Her autobiography, published in the mid-1970s, was instrumental not only in cementing her image as a "true country woman" but also in reasserting country music's roots at a time when many acts were trying to cross over onto the pop and rock charts.

Sadly, the success following by her autobiography and the subsequent film of her life seemed to encourage Lynn in the 1980s and early 1990s to move in a more mainstream direction. She less frequently wrote her own material, and the material selected for her was weak. Her live show leaned heavily on her early hits, and her many fans seemed content to hear her perform the same repertoire of well-known numbers.

In 1988 Lynn was elected to the Country Music Hall of Fame. From 1990 to 1996 she more or less withdrew from performing in order to nurse her ailing husband, who finally succumbed to diabetes in August 1996. She returned to performing on a limited basis thereafter, although she suffered from time to time with health problems of her own. In 2000 she released her first new album in over half a decade, on the small Audium label.

In the mid-1990s Loretta's twin daughters Patsy Eileen and Peggy Jean (b. 1964) began performing as The Lynns. In 1998 they released their debut album, which consisted primarily of their own material, featuring upbeat tunes graced by their perky harmonies.

Select Discography

Coal Miner's Daughter, MCA 936. Early 1970s collection released to cash in on the movie of the same name; representative of her work when she was at her peak.

Honky-Tonk Girl, MCA 11070. Three-CD set covering her career from 1960 to 1988; the best introductory collection.

LYNNE, SHELBY (b. S. Lynn Moorer, Quantico, Va., October 22, 1968)

A torchy balladeer in the K.D. LANG mold who, like lang, has tried to cross over into pop vocalizing, Lynne has not had an easy life. Her father was a violent ex-Marine who beat his wife and two daughters. His wife, who left him to protect her children, dreamed of forming a Judds-like duo with her elder daughter, Shelby. However, that dream died when her husband tracked the family to Mobile, Alabama, in 1986 and killed his ex-wife, then committed suicide.

Still recovering from this family tragedy, Shelby got her big break on the cable program *Nashville Now* just a year later. She was immediately signed to a recording contract, and began touring as an opening act for RANDY TRAVIS. She specialized in love-gone-wrong songs, including her first hits "The Hurtin' Side" and "I Love You So Much It Hurts," as well as tear-jerkin' classics like "Heartbreak Hotel" and "I Can't Stop Lovin' You."

Her 1993 album, *Temptation*, found her dipping even further into middle-of-the-road heartbreakers. Although she sounds somewhat uncomfortable singing the more upbeat numbers, her big voice and gutsy delivery are perfectly suited to the more bluesy ones. She returned to more mainstream country with the 1995 album *Restless*, but still failed to see much success. She would not release another album for five years.

Lynne never achieved much success in the country arena, so in the late 1990s she began working with producer Bill Bottrell, who had previously worked with pop-rocker Sheryl Crow. The outcome was the 2000 album *I Am Shelby Lynne*, which moved her squarely into the pop market. Ironically, the album won her a Best New Artist Grammy in 2001 (under the theory, one supposes, that she is *new* to pop music). She followed up with *Love, Shelby,* also in a mainstream pop vein, in 2001.

Select Discography

Sunrise, Epic 44260. 1989 debut album.
Temptation, Morgan Creek/Mercury 2959–20018–2. WESTERN SWING-styled recording from 1993.

M

MAC AND BOB (Lester McFarland, b. Gray, Ky., February 2, 1902–July 24 1984 [mdln, voc], and Robert Alexander Gardner, b. Oliver Springs, Tenn., December 16, 1897–September 30, 1978 [gtr, voc])

Mac and Bob are famous for creating the MANDOLIN-GUITAR accompanied vocal duet; if they were not the first to perform in this style, they were certainly the first to record in it, beginning in 1926 and continuing on radio through the early 1950s. As such, they were influential on many of the "brother" acts that followed, from THE BLUE SKY BOYS to The Monroe Brothers and THE DELMORE BROTHERS.

McFarland, a Kentucky native, and Gardner, from Tennessee, met in their teens at the Kentucky School for the Blind, where they were both enrolled. They began performing together immediately, soon gaining local popularity. They started broadcasting over Knoxville's KNOX in 1925, and were signed to Brunswick Records a year later. They got their widest exposure through a number of appearances on the popular NATIONAL BARN DANCE program out of Chicago (from 1931 to 1934 and again from 1939 to 1950). Their records were issued and reissued throughout the period on a number of bargain labels marketed through mail-order outlets like Sears and Montgomery Ward, making them highly influential throughout the South.

The Mac and Bob style was greatly influenced by the light, popular parlor music that they heard as youths. Their biggest hits were sentimental songs, including "When the Roses Bloom Again" and " 'Tis Sweet to Be Remembered"; they even recorded the popular 1919 hit "I'm Forever Blowing Bubbles." They did manage to wax a few more traditional numbers, including the ever-popular hymn "This Little Light of Mine," but their repertoire was primarily drawn from what was called "old-time" music, the popular hits of the Victorian era and early twentieth century.

In 1951 Bob retired, while Mac continued as a solo artist for another two years.

MACK, WARNER (b. W. McPherson, Nashville, Tenn., April 2, 1938)

Mack is a minor-league country SINGER/SONGWRITER who had a decade's success beginning in the mid-1960s.

Born in Nashville, Mack was raised in Vicksburg, Mississippi, where he began his performing career in high school. In the late 1950s he was a regular on the famous LOUISIANA HAYRIDE radio show and also worked on RED FOLEY's *Ozark Jubilee*. His first record, a minor teen-pop hit from 1957, "Is It Wrong?," was issued as by "Warner Mack," and the name stuck. He followed with some ROCKABILLY-flavored sides, including the controversial 1958 release "Roc-a-Chica," which was banned after one deejay complained that the background singers were chanting the "F" word.

Mack came to Nashville in search of a new career in the early 1960s, first charting in 1964 with the moderately successful "Surely." A year later he produced the big seller "The Bridge Washed Out," followed by lesser hits through the decade's end, including 1966's "Talkin' to the Wall" and "How Long Will It Take?" from a year later. Mack's popularity faded in the early 1970s, and his last charting single was 1977's "These Crazy Thoughts," issued by the tiny Pageboy label. He has since taken to the barroom and country fair circuit, as well as playing regularly in Europe for both country and rockabilly fans.

Select Discography

Early Years: Southern Rockabilly 1957–1962, Lost Gold 51497. As the title says; rockabilly sides and demos, not his later country hits.

MACON, UNCLE DAVE (b. David Harrison M., Smart Station, Tenn., October 7, 1870–March 22, 1952)

Uncle Dave Macon appeared on THE GRAND OLE OPRY's stage from its opening days into the early

Uncle Dave Macon (left) and his son Dorris, c. 1944, on the set of the Grand Ole Opry movie. Photo courtesy Bob Carlin

1950s, when he was in his early eighties, performing a combination of traditional BANJO songs, sentimental songs, and his own compositions, often commenting on contemporary trends.

Macon was born outside of Nashville, but the family soon relocated to the big city, where his father operated a rooming house located on downtown's main street. The rooming house was popular with vaudeville performers, and the young Macon was particularly impressed by the stunt banjo playing of one traveling star, Joel Davidson. He began to learn the instrument and to play locally, mostly in informal settings. When Macon was a teenager, his father was stabbed in a brawl outside the rooming house, and the family moved once again. Macon's mother opened a rest stop for stagecoaches in rural Readyville, and Dave took on the task of providing water for the horses.

As a young man Dave established his own freight-carting business, using teams of mule-drawn wagons. He was an established businessman working mostly between Murfreesboro, in the northeastern part of the state, and Woodbury. However, the coming of motorized trucks began to threaten Macon's business. In his fifties he decided he could not adapt to new times, and let his business go.

Throughout this period Macon had continued to play the banjo, mostly to amuse his customers and family. In the early 1920s, while visiting a Nashville barbershop, Macon was playing for customers when he was heard by a scout for Loew's vaudeville houses. Macon was soon performing on stage, and in early 1924 made his first recordings. A year later he was invited to be the second member of WSM's *Barn Dance* program

in Nashville, which would soon be renamed *The Grand Ole Opry*.

Macon played both clawhammer and two-finger banjo styles. He was an exceptionally talented musician, but it was his ability to perform stunts like playing the banjo while swinging the instrument between his legs, and other tricks he learned through years of informal entertaining, that really won over his audiences. Macon's hearty vocals, good humor, and energetic banjo playing influenced an entire generation of musicians, including STRINGBEAN and GRANDPA JONES. He recorded many 78s, often accompanied by the talented McGee Brothers and fiddler Sid Harkreader, going under the name The Fruit Jar Drinkers (illegal moonshine liquor was often dispensed in used fruit jars, hence the name). In the 1940s and early 1950s he was often accompanied by his son, Dorris, in *Opry* appearances.

Like other early country performers Macon had a repertoire consisting of a mix of traditional songs and dance tunes, sentimental and popular songs of the late nineteenth and early twentieth centuries, and his own offbeat adaptations of these songs, along with original compositions. Macon's presentation of his material showed the influence of years of performing on the tent-show circuit; his recordings often began and ended with a lusty shout of "Hot dog!" Macon's biting social commentary is illustrated in songs like "In and Around Nashville," in which he criticizes, among other things, women who chew gum and wear "knee-high" skirts. In the 1950s one of his popular songs, "The Cumberland Mountain Deer Chase," describing a deer hunt back in the mountains, was transformed by PETE SEEGER into a long story-song for children that he called "The Cumberland Mountain Bear Hunt."

Select Discography

Go Long Mule, County 3505. 1926–1934 recordings, among Macon's best, with excellent sound quality.
Travelin' Down the Road, County/BMG 115. Bluebird sessions from 1935.

MADDOX, ROSE (b. Roselea Arbana Brogdon, Boaz, Ala., August 15, 1925–April 5, 1998)

Maddox was a HONKY-TONK singer of the late 1940s and early 1950s who performed with her family band as The Maddox Brothers and Rose, then switched to recording in a traditional BLUEGRASS setting. Maddox was one of the earliest powerhouse female vocalists, setting the stage for the success of KITTY WELLS a few years later.

Rose's family, like many other Southerners and Westerners who had worked on farms, emigrated to southern California in search of a better life in the early 1930s. Her five older brothers had a band, in a

Western/COWBOY style, that performed at local rodeos and parties. In 1937 the group was approached by a Modesto radio station to put on a cowboy music show, with the stipulation that they have a female singer. Twelve-year-old Rose was enlisted, and The Maddox Brothers and Rose was born.

The band temporarily broke up during World War II, but returned with a vengeance in the late 1940s, signing with southern California's Four Star label and producing a series of hilarious, high-energy recordings melding WESTERN SWING with early honky-tonk. Rose's big-throated vocals were ably accompanied by the band, along with her brothers' good-natured horse-play (they provided many shouted asides, jokes, and other interjections, particularly on the up-tempo numbers). The group's biggest hit was a 1946 cover of WOODY GUTHRIE's "Philadelphia Lawyer," introducing the song to the country repertoire. They also recorded a range of music from boogie-woogie and jazz-influenced numbers like "Milk Cow Blues" to sacred songs like "Gathering Flowers for the Master's Bouquet" to country WEEPERS like "Tramp on the Street" and "Blue Eyes Crying in the Rain."

In 1951 the group, still maintaining their high-energy style, was signed by Columbia. However, the label saw more potential in Rose's more serious side, and began playing down their antics on the recordings. The band was featured on the popular LOUISIANA HAYRIDE radio program in the early 1950s, and continued to record and perform through 1957; one of their last hits featured Rose's brother Don on vocals on "The Death of Rock and Roll," one of country's first reactions to the latest trend in pop music.

Rose switched to Capitol Records in 1959 as a solo artist, and continued to have hits through the early 1960s with her gutsy recordings of "Down, Down, Down" and "Sing a Little Song of Heartache," and duets with BUCK OWENS, another southern California-based Capitol star, on "We're the Talk of the Town," "Loose Talk," and the classic "Mental Cruelty." In 1963 bluegrass star BILL MONROE suggested to Capitol that Rose's style was perfectly suited to his style of music, and since the FOLK REVIVAL was in full swing, the label decided to release an album of Rose singing bluegrass standards accompanied by Monroe and Reno and Smiley. This album was way ahead of its time, becoming a collector's item a decade later during the bluegrass revival and launching an entirely new career for Maddox.

After a period of inactivity from the mid-1960s through the mid-1970s, Maddox returned as a bluegrass vocalist, recording a number of records for folk-revival labels and performing on the bluegrass circuit. Maddox's strong vocals still set her leagues apart from even younger female bluegrass singers. However, a number of heart attacks slowed her down, and she

pretty much retired from performing in the early 1990s, although she made one last album in 1996. She died of kidney failure two years later.

Maddox was important in pointing women in country music in a new direction: they could be gutsy and strong while remaining acceptable to a predominantly male (and conservative) audience. She also was a pioneering woman in bluegrass, at a time when women in the field were few and far between. As such she served as an inspiration to later female bluegrass/country stars, such as ALISON KRAUSS.

Select Discography

America's Most Colorful Hillbilly Band, Arhoolie 391. Reissues wonderful Maddox Brothers and Rose recordings cut between 1946 and 1951; good clean fun! Originally reissued on two Arhoolie LPs in the mid-1970s.

The One Rose: The Capitol Years, Bear Family 15743. 112 tracks recorded between 1959 and 1965, with a beautiful booklet. Includes many previously unreleased tracks; fine singing and playing throughout.

MAINER, J. E. (b. Joseph Emmett M., Weaverville, N.C., July 20, 1898–June 12, 1971)

Mainer was an old-time country fiddler and bandleader who led a variety of groups under the name Mainer's Mountaineers from the 1930s through the 1960s. Mainer's group enjoyed popularity during the FOLK REVIVAL, thanks to recordings made by folklorist Alan Lomax in the late 1950s.

Mainer and his younger brother, BANJO player Wade (b. April 21, 1907) were both cotton-mill workers who began working semiprofessionally as musicians in the late 1920s. In 1934 they were hired by WBT out of Charlotte, North Carolina, and formed their first band, a quartet originally known as The Crazy Mountaineers, featuring yodeler/guitarist "Daddy" John Love and mandolinist/guitarist Zeke Morris (later one half of THE MORRIS BROTHERS duo). A year later they were signed by Bluebird and made their first recordings, including their 1935 hit, "Maple on the Hill." The group's sound was fairly primitive even for this time, recalling the string bands of the 1920s, although Lowe's YODELING and COWBOY repertoire looked forward to the nascent singing-cowboy craze.

The Mountaineers existed in various forms through the 1930s. At times Wade and J. E. would split, each leading his own Mountaineers, while at other times they came back together. Wade formed his own group, The Sons of the Mountaineers, in 1937, taking Zeke Morris and fiddler CLYDE MOODY with him. They scored a hit with "Sparkling Blue Eyes" two years later, one of the last string-band-accompanied songs to achieve this level of success. His recordings were a little more modern-sounding, particularly in his duets with Zeke Morris that were patterned after the very successful mid-1930s recordings of THE BLUE SKY BOYS.

After a period of inactivity during World War II, the brothers turned up again in the late 1940s as recording stars on the King label. Their stage show and recordings were a hodgepodge of old-time string-band music, re-creations of MINSTREL and medicine show material, and sentimental and heart songs of the turn of the century. Toward the end of the decade folklorist Alan Lomax "discovered" Mainer's band, recording them for two large projects he was producing at that time, *The Sounds of the South* series (issued by Atlantic Records in the late 1950s) and a similar series for the Prestige label. This led to renewed interest in the group, and some bookings on the folk-revival and BLUEGRASS circuits. Later in the 1960s Wade was leading a more bluegrass-oriented outfit, while J. E. was in semiretirement, repairing fiddles.

Select Discography

J. E. Mainer's Crazy Mountaineers, Old Timey 106/107. Two out-of-print LPs reissuing early recordings by Mainer's band.
Run Mountain, Arhoolie 456. 1963 recordings by a later group of Mountaineers.

MANDOLIN The mandolin, of Neapolitan origin, has become a key voice in BLUEGRASS and country music. Its odyssey into country music is a typical American story of experimentation and innovation.

The eight-stringed instrument, tuned like a fiddle, originally was made with a bowl-shaped back, like a lute. In the late nineteenth century American musical instrument designer Orville Gibson came up with a new idea: a carved-body instrument, to emulate the design of the great violins. The back of the instrument had a slight arch, but sat more comfortably against the player's body than earlier bowl-backed instruments. Gibson came up with two basic designs, one a pear-shaped instrument with a sweet sound that he called his "A" series, and the other a more fancy design with scrolls and points that he called the "Florentine" or "F" models. Mandolin clubs sprang up on college campuses and in small towns, many organized by the Gibson Company. And just after World War I an inexpensive "Army and Navy" model was introduced specifically for sale at military bases. Other makers—notably mass-marketers Lyon and Healy—entered the fray, and soon inexpensive instruments were readily available.

The first popularity of the mandolin came in the "brother acts" of the 1930s, although there had been a couple of mandolin players in earlier string bands. The sweet-voiced instrument, perfect for playing short

Gibson "A" mandolin, c. mid-1930s. Although not the fanciest mandolin made, it enjoyed a long life thanks to its low price and general playability. Photo courtesy George Gruhn, Gruhn Guitars

melodic fills, became a favorite after it was popularized by duos like THE BLUE SKY BOYS. Then, in the mid-1930s, a new brother act with a much higher-powered sound hit the radio: The Monroe Brothers. Bill Monroe played a Gibson F-5, the fanciest of the Florentine models introduced in the 1920s, which had a biting sound; his melodic parts were intricate, high-powered, and flashy. After the brothers broke up, Bill formed his first Blue Grass Boys, and became the pioneer of bluegrass-style mandolin. For this reason most bluegrass pickers prefer the F-series Gibson instrument because it is the one most closely associated with Monroe, and dozens of companies have copied the design.

The mandolin enjoyed a further resurgence in popularity in the 1970s when a group of ex-bluegrass players took the instrument into the realm of a blend of new-acoustic and jazz music. DAVID GRISMAN pioneered what he called "dawg music," performing in a quintet with two mandolins; soon others were forming similar outfits. Earlier pickers like "TINY" MOORE (who had played for BOB WILLS) and Jethro Burns (one half of the famed HOMER AND JETHRO comedy act) gained new popularity as masters of a jazz-flavored style of picking. The instrument, which was rarely heard on country recordings outside of bluegrass records, enjoyed new popularity thanks to session work by Grisman and others. Most recently Sam Bush (an original member of NEW GRASS REVIVAL) has been Nashville's busiest session picker.

MANDRELL, BARBARA (b. B. Ann M., Houston, Tex., December 25, 1948)

Mandrell is a multitalented country queen of the mid-1970s and early 1980s whose glitzy act hides her real talents as an instrumentalist and vocalist.

Barbara Mandrell in a high-fashion shot, 1996. Photo: Raeanne Rubenstein

Mandrell, from a musical family, was born in Texas but raised in southern California. She began playing with the family band at a young age, and was adept on a number of instruments, particularly the difficult-to-master PEDAL STEEL GUITAR. When Mandrell was eleven, she was already playing the instrument in Las Vegas shows, and two years later she toured with JOHNNY CASH, performing in military shows in Vietnam and Korea.

After a minor hit as a vocalist on "Queen for a Day," released by the small Mosrite label, Mandrell and family moved to Nashville, where she was signed by Columbia in 1969. Her first success was covering R&B standards, beginning with "I've Been Loving You Too Long," originally recorded by Otis Redding, followed with such chestnuts as "Do Right Woman-Do Right Man" through 1973's "Midnight Oil." At mid-decade she signed with ABC/Dot, and her first period of major success occurred, including 1977's "Married (but Not to Each Other)" and the 1978 #1 country hit, the cleverly titled "Sleeping Single in a Double Bed."

Mandrell continued to be a major star in the early 1980s, thanks to increased exposure hosting a network variety program with her sisters, Irlene and Louise. A combination of HEE HAW and *The Bell Telephone Hour*, the show offered the girls' sweet harmonies and musical talents, as well as decidedly lo-tech comedy routines. Mandrell continued to churn out solo hits, including 1981's "I Was Country When Country Wasn't Cool," 1983's "One-of-a-Kind Pair of Fools," and 1984's duet with LEE GREENWOOD, "To Me."

Barbara's life and career were dealt a severe blow in 1984 when she was involved in a head-on car collision, leading to a long period of hospitalization and some doubts that she would recover. She came back full steam a year later, with the hit "Angels in Your Arms," although her popularity on the country charts was already eroding due to the influx of new-country stars.

Through the mid-1990s Mandrell continued to pack 'em in at Vegas (or Branson, Missouri) like few other stars, but her chart-topping days were over, perhaps because her older style of country-meets-pop crooning seems somewhat outdated in today's return-to-roots renascence. In 1997 she gave a well-publicized farewell show, saying she wished to focus on her acting career.

Select Discography

Super Hits, Sony 68507. Early 1970s recordings.
The Best of, MCA 31107. Her best mid-1970s recordings.

MANDRELL, LOUISE (b. Corpus Christi, Tex., July 13, 1954)

FIDDLE- and bass-playing sister of pop chanteuse BARBARA MANDRELL, Louise enjoyed some spillover popularity in the early 1980s thanks to her exposure on her big sister's TV program.

Originally the bass player of the Mandrell family band, The Do-Rites, Louise graduated to playing with Nashville crooner Stu Phillips in the early 1970s, then for a time was the girl singer in MERLE HAGGARD's Strangers. In 1978 she signed with Epic as a solo act, and a year later married country singer R. C. BANNON, with whom she had her first major hit, the duet "Reunited." The pair signed with RCA in 1981, and Louise also had a solo hit with "Where There's Smoke, There's Fire." Beginning in 1983 she appeared with Barbara and sister Irlene on network TV, spawning hits with "Save Me" and "Too Hot to Sleep," followed by her last major charting song, 1984's "I'm Not Through Loving You Yet."

Louise's career slowed after the Mandrell sisters' TV show was canceled. Although she has a perky personality and is a talented musician like her sister, she failed to cross over into the lucrative middle-of-the-road pop market that embraced Barbara. Besides having less musical personality than her elder sister, Louise performed music whose pop leanings went out of style during the return-to-roots movement that swept the country charts in the late 1980s.

Select Discography

The Best of, RCA 6714. Cassette-only reissue of her early-1980s hits.

MANN, LORENE (b. Huntland, Tenn., January 3, 1937)

Mann was a popular SINGER/SONGWRITER of the mid-1960s who penned some unusual country songs.

Born on a farm near the Alabama-Tennessee border, Mann started playing GUITAR at age twelve, learning the instrument from her older brothers. She came to Nashville at age nineteen in search of a career as a songwriter. She began performing in the mid-1960s, dueting with Justin Tubb (ERNEST TUBB's son) and Archie Campbell. Her solo recordings include the unusual "Don't Put Your Hands on Me," on which she tells off a two-timer, and, perhaps most radical of all, "Hide My Sin," about a woman's mixed feelings after having an abortion. (This is probably the only Nashville-produced recording that features the backup singers, the famous JORDANAIRES, spelling out "A-B-O-R-T-I-O-N," the singer's unnameable crime.) After these mid-1960s successes, Mann faded from the music scene.

MAPHIS, JOE (b. Otis Wilson M., Suffolk, Va., May 12, 1921–June 27, 1986)

A multiple instrumentalist most famous for his lightning-fast GUITAR picking, Maphis revolutionized country and pop guitar music through his creative acoustic and electric picking.

Raised in Cumberland, Maryland, Joe began performing with his father in the family band, The Railsplitters, in 1932. Not content simply to play chord accompaniments to the band's up-tempo readings of traditional square-dance tunes, Maphis developed his unique approach to finger-picking the melody. When he was seventeen, Maphis went professional, eventually performing on country radio shows such as Chicago's NATIONAL BARN DANCE. He took up the newly introduced electric guitar in 1947, and in the same year hooked up with vocalist Rose Lee (b. Baltimore, Md., 1922), who was to become his musical partner and, five years later, his wife. The duo wrote the HONKY-TONK classic "Dim Lights, Thick Smoke (and Loud, Loud Music)," still one of the favorites of this genre. In 1952 they were invited to star on the *Town Hall Party* TV program, where Joe helped launch the career of junior stringbender Larry Collins of THE COLLINS KIDS.

In 1954 Maphis became one of the first performers in any musical style to play a twin-necked guitar, recording the classic "Fire on the Strings," his adaptation of the country FIDDLE classic "Fire on the Mountain." He also began performing as a session musician on MANDOLIN and BANJO in addition to guitar, as well as recording and performing with the other great country guitar ace of the day, MERLE TRAVIS. Maphis's distinctive picking can be heard on the early pop hits of RICKY NELSON, as well as on such classic bits of yuppie nostalgia as the theme songs for TV's *Bonanza* and *The FBI*.

Maphis and his wife continued to record through the 1960s, 1970s, and 1980s, first for mainstream Capitol Records and later for BLUEGRASS (Starday) and GOSPEL (World) labels. He also encouraged his young niece, BARBARA MANDRELL, another multiple-instrumental talent, to enter country music as a profession. (Mandrell returned the favor by featuring Maphis and buddy Travis on one episode of her TV variety show in the 1970s.) Always a heavy smoker, Maphis succumbed to lung cancer in 1986. Sons Dale and Jody carried forward his sound as Nashville sessionmen.

Select Discography

Fire on the Strings, Sony 62148. Reissue of 1957 Columbia album (1005), with six additional cuts.
Flying Fingers, Bear Family 16103. Columbia recordings from the mid-to-late 1950s.

MARTIN, BENNY (b. Benjamin Edward M., Sparta, Tenn., May 8, 1928–March 13, 2001)

Legendary country and BLUEGRASS fiddler and a genuine country-music character, Martin was a well-loved and talented multiple instrumentalist.

Benny was already enamored of country music as a youngster, religiously listening to Knoxville's *Midday Merry-Go-Round* radio program, which featured stars like CHARLIE MONROE and MOLLY O'DAY. At age thirteen he traveled to Nashville, and began his professional career as a member of the backup band for Big Jeff and Tootsie. Tootsie was the owner of the legendary Tootsie's Lounge in downtown Nashville, and became a kind of surrogate mother to the young fiddler. Benny appeared on radio with the duo, and recorded with them beginning in 1944; in 1946 he cut his first solo record, "Me and My Fiddle." He also began to perform on THE GRAND OLE OPRY. Sometime during this period Martin gained his nickname "The Roarin' Tiger," supposedly bestowed on him by HANK WILLIAMS.

After meeting the young fiddler at the *Opry*, legendary bluegrass bandleader BILL MONROE hired him to join his group in 1947. Two years later Martin left Monroe to join FLATT AND SCRUGGS, remaining with the band on and off for the next four years. He appeared on the classic instrumentals that the band recorded in 1952–1953, including "Dear Old Dixie" and "Flint Hill Special." In 1954 Martin joined JOHNNIE AND JACK's road show, accompanying them and KITTY WELLS. He also signed with Mercury Records as a solo act, and contracted with legendary country manager "COLONEL" TOM PARKER. Parker urged Martin to feature his vocals over his fiddling. Martin scored hits with his own songs, including "Ice Cold Love" and "Lover of the Town," the latter featuring his impressive lead GUITAR work.

In the later 1950s, Martin's popularity faded, as did many country acts, in the face of the onslaught of rock and roll. He also began a long descent into alcoholism, an addiction he was unable to conquer until the late 1970s. Martin nonetheless continued to score vocal hits through the mid-1960s, now recording for the Starday label. 1963 brought the sentimental hit "Rosebuds and You," and then he recorded the somewhat maudlin "A Soldier's Prayer in Vietnam," appealing to the conservative country market, in 1966.

Martin was less active from the late 1960s through the late 1970s. However, with a new generation of bluegrass fans arising, and the reissue of many classic recordings that featured Martin's fiddling, he returned to performing both on his own and as a studio musician in the 1980s and 1990s, particularly working with JOHN HARTFORD. Martin was a master of a number of instruments besides FIDDLE and guitar, and often appeared at bluegrass festivals sporting nothing but a ukulele. Unfortunately, he suffered from a rare disease that affected his vision and speech in his later decades, limiting his ability to tour. Nonetheless he remained a familiar figure around Nashville, sometimes spotted on the street busking for quarters. Martin issued a few albums on small labels in the 1980s and 1990s; his last offering featured several "guests" from the world of new country and bluegrass. He died in 2001.

Select Discography

Tennessee Jubilee, Flying Fish 70012. 1970s recordings with John Hartford and Lester Flatt.
Big Tiger Roars Again, OMS 25010. 1999 release, with Earl Scruggs, John Hartford, Jesse McReynolds, Bobby Osborne, and many other legendary players.

MARTIN, GRADY (b. Thomas G. M., Chapel Hill, Tenn., January 17, 1929–December 3, 2001)

Martin was one of the best-known studio guitarists in Nashville, appearing on thousands of recordings cut in the 1950s, 1960s, and 1970s.

Martin played FIDDLE and GUITAR as a youngster; in fact he debuted on THE GRAND OLE OPRY as a fiddler at age seventeen, two years after moving to Nashville from his small hometown. He cut the jazzy guitar instrumental "Chattanooga Shoeshine Boy" on his own in the late 1940s, and then moved into a steady stream of session work, beginning with HANK WILLIAMS and continuing with most of the big-name country acts of the 1960s. Martin was a member of the group of studio musicians who worked under the guidance of producer CHET ATKINS, including tinkling pianist FLOYD CRAMER, and like Cramer he developed a pleasant, adaptable, middle-of-the-road style. In 1979 he joined WILLIE NELSON's road band, with which he performed for the next sixteen years. In 1995 he retired from performing. Martin was the author of the country/pop hit "Snap Your Fingers," recorded by DICK CURLESS, DON GIBSON, pop crooner Dean Martin, and RONNIE MILSAP.

MARTIN, JANIS (b. J. Darlene M., Sutherlin, Va., March 27, 1940)

Martin was one of the few 1950s female ROCKABILLY stars who was promoted by RCA as a clean-cut teenager with a decidedly sexy delivery.

Appearing on Richmond, Virginia, radio as a diminutive country star in 1954, Janis was, like many teens of the time, an avid fan of R&B. At age fifteen she made a demo cover version of "Will You Willyum" that was heard by RCA's director of A&R, STEVE SHOLES. She was brought to Nashville to record under the guiding hand of CHET ATKINS, producing a series of minor rockabilly hits including 1956's "My Boy Elvis" and "Let's Elope, Baby," 1957's "Cracker Jack" and a cover of the hoary old folk chestnut "Billy Boy, Billy Boy" (rocked up for the teenie-pop market), and her last hit, 1958's "Bang Bang" (covered by new-country cutie KELLY WILLIS). Already married at age fifteen (a fact that RCA's PR department kept carefully under wraps), Martin's career was ended when she became pregnant in 1958; she attempted a comeback on the smaller Palette label in 1960, with little success. After her second marriage ended in 1970, she returned to touring sporadically, reviving her trademark "female Elvis" persona.

Select Discography

The Female Elvis, 1956–1960, Bear Family 15406. All of her recordings.

MARTIN, JIMMY (b. James Henry M., Sneedville, Tenn., August 10, 1927)

Jimmy Martin is a country vocalist who wed the sensibilities of BLUEGRASS and mainstream country to make a series of classic recordings in the 1950s and 1960s. His vocals combine the smoothness of a pop crooner with characteristic, YODELING vocal breaks that are pure traditional country, making him one of the most easily recognized vocalists in all of country music.

Martin's career began on the radio in 1948; a year later he was invited to join BILL MONROE's Bluegrass Boys as lead vocalist to replace MAC WISEMAN. He performed with Monroe on classic recordings until 1953, and was probably Monroe's second greatest lead vocalist. (Lester Flatt [of FLATT AND SCRUGGS] would have to take the highest honors.) In 1951–1952 he briefly broke from Monroe to record with country MANDOLIN picker Bobby Osborne, making a series of classic vocal-duo recordings.

In 1954 Martin, Bobby Osborne, and his banjo-playing brother Sonny performed as THE OSBORNE BROTHERS band for a year; two years later Martin formed the first of his Sunny Mountain Boys, performing on both THE GRAND OLE OPRY and THE LOUISIANA HAYRIDE radio programs. Martin was the first of the pure bluegrass stars to "cross over," attempting to create what he called "good 'n country music," a kind of less hard-driving, more vocally oriented bluegrass music. This led to mid-1960s hits with songs like "Widow Maker" and "Sunny Side of the Mountain," which became his theme song. He also began performing novelty numbers, chasing the elusive chart hit.

Martin nurtured many talents in his band, including banjoists J. D. CROWE, BILL EMERSON, and Alan Munde, and mandolinists Paul Williams and DOYLE LAWSON. His career was given a gigantic boost when he was invited to perform on the NITTY GRITTY DIRT BAND's landmark 1971 recording, *Will the Circle Be Unbroken*; he contributed fine vocals on his upbeat reading of "I Saw the Light" and "Sunny Side of the Mountain." Despite the introduction to a rock audi-

ence, Martin continued to perform on the country and bluegrass circuit, where he felt most at home.

Martin formed his own label in the 1990s, and his career got some renewed attention thanks to Tom Piazza's article, "True Adventures with the King of Bluegrass," which appeared in *The Oxford American* in the late 1990s; it was subsequently issued as a book. In it Martin is portrayed as a somewhat eccentric survivor. Unlike Bill Monroe and Ralph Stanley, he has not cashed in on the bluegrass revival of the last few decades, and seems happy to continue to perform for his longtime fans.

Select Discography

You Don't Know My Mind, Rounder 21. Great 1950s recordings in a bluegrass style.
Twenty Greatest Hits, Deluxe 7863. 1970s recordings from the Gusto label.

MASSEY, LOUISE, AND THE WESTERNERS (b. Victoria L. M., Hart County, Tex., August 2, 1902–June 22, 1983)

Louise Massey was the motivating force behind her family band of Western-styled musicians. She is famous for composing the country-pop hit "My Adobe Hacienda."

The family, originally from Texas, relocated in 1914, when Massey's father purchased a farm in the then sparsely populated new state of New Mexico. The father, mother, and eight children were musically inclined, with dad playing old-style Western FIDDLE, and daughter Louise a talented pianist and vocalist. Louise married bass player Milt Mabie in 1919, and he quickly became a member of the group. They began performing on the local vaudeville circuit in the early 1920s, and then began longer tours across the U.S. and Canada, with the elder Massey finally retiring because of the rigors of life on the road. The rest of the band settled into a five-year stint on KMBC radio out of Kansas City, which led to a network broadcast on the station's parent network, CBS. In 1933 a talent scout for the WLS BARN DANCE out of Chicago heard the group and signed them to this influential show.

The center of attention of the band was the glamorous Louise, who besides providing lead vocals was also something of a fashion plate, wearing Spanish-styled costumes for their south-of-the-border numbers and pioneering sequined cowboy suits for herself and members of the band (she wore satin boots). The group, now known as Louise Massey and the Westerners, moved east to broadcast out of New York for a couple of years before returning to Chicago and then going to Hollywood to appear in the C-grade flick *Where the Buffalo Roam*, starring TEX RITTER.

Like most of the COWBOY bands of the day, the group played a wide range of material, mostly filtered through a soft, pop sound. Besides the obligatory cowboy and sentimental numbers, they could perform dance music from fiddle tunes to Eastern European polkas, waltzes, and schottisches through novelty numbers, ragtime, and light jazz, and even an occasional jazzed-up traditional mountain song. Louise wrote many of the group's hits, including their early 1934 disc "When the White Azaleas Start Blooming," featuring her honey-voiced vocals, and their biggest number, 1941's "My Adobe Hacienda," a crossover country and pop hit after the war. Other major hits for the group were 1939's "South of the Border (Down Mexico Way)" and "I Only Want a Buddy (Not a Sweetheart)," a typical tough-girl, I-don't-need-no-man ditty.

In 1948 Louise and husband Milt retired to New Mexico. Brother Curt went to Hollywood, where he would gain fame as the writer of two of the most memorable TV themes of all time: for *The Beverly Hillbillies* and the spin-off series, *Petticoat Junction* (that's him singing the *Petticoat Junction* song).

MATTEA, KATHY (b. Cross Lanes, W. Va., June 21, 1959)

Originally a BLUEGRASS singer/guitarist, Mattea became one of the most successful of the new traditional artists, without selling out either to slick commercialism or to upscale, Las Vegas country-pop.

Mattea began playing music in her teens, and joined her first bluegrass band, Pensboro, while a college student. She left college to move to Nashville, where she got a job as a tour guide at the Country Music Hall of Fame, and occasional work as a backup and demo vocalist, most notably on sessions for Bobby "Honey, I Miss You" Goldsboro.

New-country producer Allen Reynolds signed her to Mercury in 1983, but she failed to produce any hits until three years later, when she scored big with a cover of NANCI GRIFFITH's "Love at the Five and Dime." The hits, as they say, just kept coming through the 1980s, including the modern-day TRUCK DRIVIN' SONG "Eighteen Wheels and a Dozen Roses" from 1988, "Come from the Heart" and "Burnin' Old Heart" from a year later, and "She Came from Fort Worth" in 1990. Mattea suffered from vocal cord problems in 1992, but she came through surgery and returned to the charts a year later.

Mattea's music strikes a balance between mainstream country and her own traditional roots. Possessing a powerful voice, with a hint of country flavorings, Mattea is just pop enough to appeal to a mass audience. Mattea is best defined by what she is not: she's not a pure folkie like Nanci Griffith, or a Southern cutie pie

like SUZY BOGGUSS; she's also not a glitzy, ready-for-Vegas belter like LORRIE MORGAN. Mattea simply puts the music out there, with a minimum of fuss, and for that she deserves plenty of kudos.

Part of the dilemma she faces is illustrated by her 1991 experiment with a melding of Scottish folk influences and contemporary country on her album *Time Passes By*. A courageous career step, in that it went against the grain of the slicker Nashville productions of the time, the album ultimately did not sell very well, and Mattea was chagrined to find her own *A Collection of Hits* LP outstripping it in sales. In 1992 she returned with a more mainstream album, in an attempt to balance her artistic goals with the necessity of maintaining a mainstream career. However, although she continued to record and tour through the rest of the decade, she never achieved the chart-topping success that she had in the 1980s. Still, she continues to produce thoughtful, interesting albums, such as 2000's *The Innocent Years*, which depicts her sadness as she witnessed her father's final years of life.

Select Discography

A Collection of Hits, Mercury 84230. The hits up to 1990.
Time Passes By, Mercury 846975. Concept album based on folk-flavored influences.

MAVERICKS, THE (c. 1990–c. 1999: Raul Malo, b. Miami, Fla., August 7, 1965 [lead voc, gtr, pno]; Robert Reynolds, b. R. Earl R., Kansas City, Mo., August 30, 1962 [b, gtr]; David Lee Holt, b. Lubbock, Tex. [lead gtr]; Paul Deakin, b. P. Wylie D., Miami, Fla., September 2, 1959 [drms]; in 1993 Holt left and was replaced by Nick Kane, b. Nicholas James K., Jerusalem, Ga., August 21, 1954 [lead gtr, drms])

The Mavericks were a popular and eclectic COUNTRY-ROCK band of the mid-1990s. Lead singer Malo is the son of Cuban refugees who came to Florida in 1959, following the revolution, and settled in Miami. By the time he was in high school, Malo was a rabid ELVIS PRESLEY fan, and formed many bands to perform The King's music (despite the fact that Elvis was somewhat out of fashion at this point in his career). Malo was also a major Elvis record collector, and he met fellow band founder Robert Reynolds at a big collectors' show. Reynolds had played in a number of bands that specialized in 1950s rock and country, particularly BUDDY HOLLY and BUCK OWENS. He had befriended another local musician, Paul Deakin, while both were at the University of Miami. In the late 1980s the trio formed a band and began playing local clubs.

In 1990 the group financed their first recording, and managed to convince the local rock station to give it some airtime. A regional promo man for MCA heard the tape and recommended the group to the label. The group was quickly signed, and the label convinced them to add a lead guitarist, David Lee Holt, who had previously worked with CARLENE CARTER, JOE ELY, and ROSIE FLORES. Recorded in Miami, their first album consisted primarily of Malo's own songs, although only a cover of HANK WILLIAMS's "Hey, Good Lookin' " saw any chart action.

The group fared better with their second album. This time they recorded in Nashville, and Malo was paired with professional songwriter KOSTAS for a number of cuts. Guitarist Nick Kane joined the group as a full-fledged member, replacing hired-hand Holt and giving the band a more stable lineup. The title track, "What a Crying Shame," was a Top 30 hit. The band scored their biggest chart hit in 1996 with "All You Ever Do Is Bring Me Down," which peaked at #13 and featured the Tex-Mex accordion of Flaco Jimenez. The band won the Country Music Association's Best Vocal Group award in 1995 and 1996.

The group's later 1990s albums showed a more eclectic mix of material and instruments, reflecting Malo's wide-ranging interests. Although Malo is an effective singer, he can go overboard with the histrionics, sometimes sounding like he's trying to outcry ROY ORBISON. Malo left the band in 1999, and after extricating himself from contractual problems, began work on his first solo album. The album, *Today*, was released in 2001, and continued to push the boundaries of country music, featuring Latin rhythms and themes as well as some songs with Spanish lyrics.

Selected Discography

Super Colossal Smash Hits of the 90's: The Best of the Mavericks, MCA 170112. Let's hope the title is tongue-in-cheek; the album includes eight of their chart hits, plus four new numbers as fan bonus tracks.

McAULIFFE, Leon (b. William L. M., Houston, Tex., January 3, 1917–August 20, 1988)

One of the pioneers of the steel guitar, McAuliffe is best known for his "Steel Guitar Rag," which he first recorded as a member of BOB WILLS's Texas Playboys.

McAuliffe was a protégé of BOB DUNN, the steel guitarist who is most famous for his jagged-edged solos with MILTON BROWN. Leon joined THE LIGHT CRUST DOUGHBOYS in 1933, then moved on to Wills's band two years later. He recorded "Steel Guitar Rag" (an adaptation of Sylvester Weaver's country-blues recording "Guitar Rag") in 1936. His electrified steel guitar lines, often in duet with electric guitarist Eldon Shamblin, helped mold Wills's sound throughout the 1930s. McAuliffe also sang lead vocals on many of the more bluesy numbers. Wills's joyful shouts of "Take

it away, Leon!" are heard on many of these classic recordings.

McAuliffe spent World War II in the Navy, but returned in 1946 to form his own band, The Cimarron Boys. His 1949 recording of "Panhandle Rag," also his own composition, became a much-imitated standard in the WESTERN SWING repertoire. He stayed with Columbia through the 1950s and then recorded for a variety of smaller labels in the 1960s, including his own Cimarron label. By the late 1960s he owned two small radio stations near Rogers, Arkansas, but the mid-1970s Western Swing revival brought him out of retirement as a leader of the Original Texas Playboys, featuring many players from Wills's bands. The band was active for about a decade, until age and ill health caught up with many of the members. McAuliffe died of heart disease in 1988.

McAuliffe was one of the first to electrify the lap steel guitar. Unlike his mentor Bob Dunn, whose playing was noted for its sharp, almost abrasive sound, McAuliffe developed a sweeter, more flowing, and lyrical style. Still, he managed to pack considerable punch, and his sliding chords often propelled Wills's band. He was also an important composer, with "Blacksmith Blues" and "Cozy Inn" to his credit along with his more famous instrumentals.

McBRIDE AND THE RIDE (Terry McBride, b. Taylor, Tex., September 16, 1958 [voc, gtr]; Ray Herndon, b. Phoenix, Ariz., July 14, 1960 [voc, gtr]; Billy Thomas, b. Fort Myers, Fla., October 24, 1953 [b, voc])

McBride and the Ride are one of many 1980s groups that were put together to serve a specific market niche; their style is kind of an update on the vocal harmonies of groups like ALABAMA, spiffed up a bit to fit in a contemporary sound.

As a group of studio musicians, McBride and Herndon were brought together by MCA producer TONY BROWN to create a new band. Thomas, who had a background in COUNTRY-ROCK from his work in RICK NELSON's Stone Canyon Band and then in the backup bands for EMMYLOU HARRIS and VINCE GILL, was brought along to fill out the sound. Their pleasing vocals were married with an upbeat, neo HONKY-TONK sound (perfect for new-country radio), and they had a hit out of the basket with "Can I Count on You." Although they were not consistent hitmakers, they were a popular group on the road and on country music television. Like many other manufactured bands, they were competent if not exciting, making music that sounded more manufactured than heartfelt.

Founders Herndon and Thomas left in early 1994, and were replaced by studio hands; the new group was billed as Terry McBride and the Ride, but had little success.

Select Discography

Sacred Ground, MCA 10540. 1992 album.

McBRIDE, MARTINA (b. M. Mariea Schiff, Sharon, Kan., July 29, 1966)

A perky video starlet with a number of hits under her belt, McBride combines the gutsy vocal stylings of LINDA RONSTADT with a sweeter, country side.

Raised in a small Kansas farming community, the diminutive McBride has been a musician nearly since birth. Her father, Daryl Schiff, led the family in a band called The Schiffters, which featured Martina on lead vocals and keyboards, and her younger brother on guitar; mother Jeanne served as official roadie and soundman. They worked local clubs, benefits, and parties until 1984.

Martina briefly attended community college while continuing to work as a singer with local bands. Through one of her bands she met John McBride, a Wichita, Kansas, native who owned a rehearsal studio and worked as a sound engineer. The two married in 1988, and relocated to Nashville in search of careers. Within a year John was hired as a soundman for GARTH

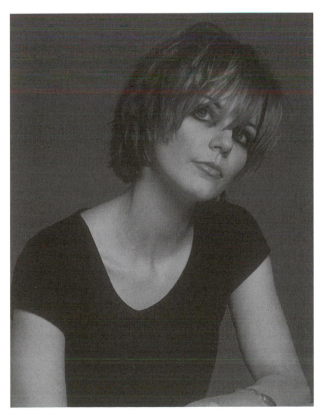

Martina McBride, 1996. Photo: Raeanne Rubenstein

BROOKS, and landed his wife a job with Brooks's concession stand. Meanwhile he also passed around Martina's demo tape to anyone who would listen. In late 1991 she was signed by RCA Nashville.

McBride's first album and single releases were not terribly successful, but her career took off in 1993 with her second album, *The Way That I Am*, buoyed by the video-friendly hit "My Baby Loves Me." The next year McBride shocked some listeners with her hit "Independence Day," which depicted an abusive relationship. Instead of "standing by her man," the wife in the song ends up torching the family home. In 1998 she had another hit on a similar topic with "A Broken Wing," although this time the abused woman concentrates on rebuilding her own life rather than taking revenge on her husband. McBride has used both songs to build a more serious image for herself, and has since raised money for abused women and children.

1999 saw the album *Emotion*, continuing with a mix of socially conscious songs and the more usual love ballads. "Love's the Only House" was promoted with a clever video portraying McBride as a sympathetic checkout girl at a supermarket who treats a young (presumably unwed) mother to a free carton of milk. The album's biggest hit was the ballad "I Love You," which spent five weeks at #1 on the country charts and won McBride a Grammy nomination for Best Country Song. As part of a "hits" album in 2001, she released a new single, "When God-Fearing Women Get the Blues," somewhat of a change of pace for her. This humorous song was supported by a clever video in the form of a "late breaking" newscast.

McBride has a powerful voice and is talented at handling a wide range of material, from upbeat rockers to more thoughtful social-commentary songs. Although some of her material borders on the bathetic, she manages to convey it with a solid feeling of commitment.

Select Discography

Greatest Hits, RCA 67012. 2001 compilation album.

McCALL, C. W. (b. William Fries, Audubon, Iowa, November 15, 1928)

McCall is an ex-advertising executive-turned-country star who rode the mid-1970s craze for TRUCK-DRIVING SONGS, his biggest hit being 1975's "Convoy," made into a popular film by blood-and-guts director Sam Peckinpah three years later.

Fries was a fine-arts major at the University of Iowa who went into advertising. In the early 1970s he created the character of C. W. McCall for an ad campaign for a local bakery. His spoken monologues on behalf of the goodness of old-time baked goods soon were drawing lots of attention on local radio; in 1974 he adapted the routine successfully to his first record (and first commercial hit), "The Old Home Filler-Up and

Keep on A-Truckin' Cafe." Follow-up monologues included "Wolf Creek Pass," "Classified," "Black Bear Road," and his biggest hit, "Convoy." McCall continued to churn out minor hits, including 1976's "There Won't Be No Country Music (There Won't Be No Rock 'n' Roll)" and the comic novelty "Crispy Critters," followed a year later by "Roses for Mama." In 1982 he was elected mayor of the small Colorado town of Ouray, and retired from both advertising and music making, although he attempted a comeback in 1990.

Select Discography

Greatest Hits, Polydor 825793. Cassette-only reissue of mid-1970s and early-1980s recordings.

McCLAIN, CHARLY (b. Charlotte Denise M., Memphis, Tenn., March 26, 1956)

McClain is a middle-of-the-road country-pop chirper who had her greatest success in the early-to-mid-1980s.

Born in the R&B capital of the South, McClain began performing early, playing bass in her brother's COUNTRY-ROCK band from the age of nine, and becoming a regular performer on the Memphis-based *Mid-South Jamboree* radio show in her teen years. She hooked up with the local pop-rock band Shylo, and their producer Larry Rogers made a demo tape of her singing that he passed along to famed country producer BILLY SHERRILL. This led to a contract with Epic in 1976, and her first single, "Lay Down," was followed by her first hits two years later, "Let Me Be Your Baby" and "That's What You Do to Me."

McClain formed her own country-pop backup band, Bluff City, and became a popular touring attraction in the early 1980s. Chart-toppers included the suggestive "Who's Cheatin' Who" from 1980 and 1981's "Surround Me with Love" and "Sleepin' with the Radio On." She also cut duets with JOHNNY RODRIGUEZ ("I Hate the Way I Love It," 1979), MICKEY GILLEY ("Paradise Tonight" from 1983 and "Candy Man" from the next year), and Wayne Massey ("With Just One Look in Your Eyes," from 1984, and "You Are My Music, You Are My Song" from a year later), who became her husband in 1984.

The new-country boom pretty much ended the popularity of pop-oriented artists like McClain, although she continued to record through the 1980s.

Select Discography

Biggest Hits, Epic 40186.

McCLINTON, O. B. (b. Obie Burnett M., Senatobia, Miss., April 25, 1942–September 23, 1987)

McClinton is perhaps best known in pop circles for the many R&B hits that he penned, including James Carr's "You Got My Mind Messed Up" and Otis Redding's "Keep Your Arms Around Me." But, his first love was HANK WILLIAMS-styled country music, and this is the type of music that he recorded on his own, showing once again the cross-fertilization between black and white cultures that occurred in the South.

The son of a landowning reverend in rural Mississippi, O. B. was exposed early on to country radio, particularly favoring the bluesy sounds of Hank Williams. At seventeen he ran away from home and landed in Memphis, where he got his first GUITAR. After working odd jobs in the big city, he returned to Mississippi to attend Rust College on a choral scholarship, performing with the a cappella choir there. In 1966, after graduation, he returned to Memphis and worked as a deejay for a while, and then enlisted in the Air Force at the end of the year. He appeared in several talent shows and was discovered by the owner of Memphis's Goldwax Records, Quinton Claunch. His songs became popular among many Memphis-based soul artists, and in the early 1970s he attracted the attention of Stax Records executive Al Bell, who signed him to Stax's country label, Enterprise.

O. B.'s first hit was 1972's "Don't Let the Green Grass Fool You," followed by a cover of the MERLE HAGGARD classic "Okie from Muskogee" remade as "Obie from Senatobia." He had a 1974 hit with "Something Better," and a year later, after Stax folded, he moved to several other labels before landing at Epic, where he was produced by country producer Buddy Killen, who had discovered Joe Tex. O. B.'s Epic hits included the 1978 single "Hello, This Is Anna." He moved to the smaller Sunbird label in the early 1980s, and then the even smaller Moonshine label for a minor hit with 1984's "Honky-Tonk Tan," before being diagnosed with cancer. The disease took his life in 1987.

McCOURY, DEL (b. Delano Floyd M., Bakersville, N.C., February 1, 1939)

A talented BLUEGRASS guitarist and vocalist, McCoury came into his own in the 1990s, leading a band featuring his sons Ronnie and Rob.

McCoury was raised in a musical family; his mother was an amateur singer/guitarist. The family relocated from North Carolina to rural southeastern Pennsylvania soon after his birth. When he was a teenager, McCoury heard a recording of FLATT AND SCRUGGS and decided to take up the BANJO. In the late 1950s he was playing banjo in the Baltimore area with Jack Cooke's (later bass player for Ralph Stanley) Clinch Mountain Boys.

From 1963 to 1964 McCoury was lead singer with BILL MONROE. Although hired as a banjo player, he ended up playing GUITAR after BILL "BRAD" KEITH came on board. McCoury's distinctive mountain-flavored vocals returned Monroe's sound to his Kentucky roots. In 1964 McCoury relocated to California, where he formed The Golden State Boys, but by 1968 he was back in Pennsylvania, leading his Dixie Pals.

The band became a family affair in 1981 when son Ronnie joined on MANDOLIN, followed eight years later by son Rob on banjo. In 1989 McCoury recorded with DAVID GRISMAN on his bluegrass album, *Home Is Where the Heart Is*, and subsequently toured with Grisman to promote the album. In 1992 McCoury left Pennsylvania for Nashville. Thanks to a series of albums released on Rounder Records beginning in the early 1990s, he established a strong following in the bluegrass community.

In 1999 McCoury's band accompanied STEVE EARLE on his bluegrass-flavored album of originals, *The Mountain*, and Del sang tenor vocals to the raspy-throated SINGER/SONGWRITER. McCoury's band subsequently toured with Earle. McCoury is also a talented songwriter, and his songs have been covered by many bluegrass groups. The rock group Phish recorded his "The Beauty of My Dreams," which helped bring him a new group of fans. In 2000 the group was signed by the Hollywood label.

Select Discography

Classic Bluegrass, Rebel 1111. 1970s recordings.
Del, Doc, and Mac, Sugar Hill 3888. With DOC WATSON and MAC WISEMAN; released in 1998.
Del and the Boys, Hollywood 902006. 2000 album brings Del and his band to a major label; a typical mix of contemporary songs and some older traditional numbers performed in straight-ahead bluegrass style.

McCOY, CHARLIE (b. Charles Ray M., Oak Hill, W.Va., March 28, 1941)

McCoy is the best-known session harmonica player of the 1960s and 1970s; his style virtually defined how the instrument would be used on mainstream country releases.

Born in rural West Virginia, he began playing the harmonica at age eight, and had some musical training as both a vocalist and an arranger in his teen years. In the late 1950s he starting performing on both rock and country circuits as a backup artist; MEL TILLIS heard him playing at a local gig and introduced him to his Nashville agent, who brought McCoy to the country capital, where he began working sessions, tours, and THE GRAND OLE OPRY radio show. He gained a great deal of exposure by joining country star STONEWALL JACKSON's touring band.

In the early 1960s McCoy signed a contract as a vocalist, with little success, although he did have a minor hit in 1961 with "Cherry Berry Wine," issued on the small Cadence label. He subsequently led his own pop-rock lounge group, The Escorts, in Nashville, and also sessioned for various artists, appearing prominently on ROY ORBISON's single "Candy Man." He was much in demand as a studio musician through the 1960s, impressing folk-rocker BOB DYLAN, who used him on his *Blonde on Blonde* and *Nashville Skyline* sessions. This led to work with other pop stars interested in the country sound, including Ringo Starr, Joan Baez, and ELVIS PRESLEY. He joined the Nashville-based "supergroup" AREA CODE 615, and his harmonica playing was featured on their instrumental hit, "Stone Fox Chase."

In 1972 his solo recording of "Today I Started Loving You Again," originally recorded as an album track four years earlier, started getting airplay on country radio, and it was followed by a series of covers, including HANK WILLIAMS's "I'm So Lonesome I Could Cry" and the perennial BLUEGRASS FIDDLE-festival favorite, "Orange Blossom Special." He recorded "Boogie Woogie" with Barefoot Jerry in 1974, and in the early 1980s formed a partnership with Laney Hicks, including minor hits on 1981's "Until the Night" and "The State of Our Union" from two years later. McCoy served as musical director for the country comedy show HEE HAW from 1977 until 1996. He also enjoyed success touring and recording in Europe, where he remains a legendary figure.

Select Discography

The Fastest Harp in the South, Monument 44354. Reissue of 1960s recordings.
Harpin' the Blues, Monument 47087. Tribute to Chicago blues harp masters.

McCOY, NEAL (b. Hubert N. McGauhey, Jr., Jacksonville, Tex., July 30, 1958)

Born of Irish and Filipino parents, McCoy is another young hunkster-in-hat who enjoyed success in the mid-to-late-1990s.

Raised in East Texas, McCoy began singing in clubs as a teenager, initially spelling his name as "Neal McGoy" (representing the actual pronunciation of his last name). The "G" gave way to a "C" by the early 1980s, when country singer JANIE FRICKE caught his act and recommended him as an opening act to her friend CHARLEY PRIDE. McCoy spent six years on the road with Pride.

Toward the end of the 1980s McCoy was recording for the small 16th Avenue label. In 1991 he was signed by Atlantic, and released two moderately successful albums before finally hitting pay dirt with his third release, *No Doubt About It*, in 1994. The title track was a #1 hit for the singer, as was a second single release, "Wink." More hits followed in the later 1990s, including 1995's "You Gotta Love That" (also the title track of his next album), a remake of JOHN D. LOUDERMILK's song "Then You Can Tell Me Good-bye" in 1996, and "Shake" in 1997.

In 1999 McCoy released *The Life of the Party*, an album primarily of new songs but written in a 1960s pop/soul vein. The album produced a moderate hit, "Lipstick on the Radio," which was more reminiscent of Motown than Cowtown. McCoy returned to a more country sound on 2000's *24–7–365*. Although his big hitmakers have slowed, McCoy continues to be popular on the road and has taken to playing more upscale venues, including Vegas lounges, as well as the more usual state fairs.

Select Discography

Super Hits, Atlantic 83375.

McCREADY, MINDY (b. Malinda Gayle M., Fort Myers, Fla., November 30, 1976)

A flash-in-the-pan newcomer in 1996, McCready never regained that level of success.

Raised in Florida, McCready was a musical child, beginning to sing as early as age three. She took voice lessons, particularly focusing on opera, and also sang locally in bars and clubs. At age eighteen, she moved to Nashville, vowing to have a record deal within a year; her dream came true when she signed with BNA Records exactly fifty-one weeks later (at least according to her myth). Discovered by producer Norro Wilson, McCready recorded a first album that was an immediate sensation, featuring four Top 10 hits, including the #1 "Guys Do It All the Time." It didn't hurt that McCready wore skin-tight outfits and was among the first female country stars to bare her midsection for video.

McCready's fans were predominantly young and female, so she decided to tackle more "serious" themes on her second album, *If I Don't Stay the Night*. By "serious," she apparently meant "should-I-or-shouldn't-I" songs about sex. She also posed for her cover shot without heavy makeup (although dressed in a flimsy white chemise). Whether it was her decision to downplay her fashion-plate looks, or simply a lack of strong material, this album failed to go very far, although it was more successful in Europe, where the song "Oh Romeo" was a minor hit. In 1998 McCready contributed a vocal to the soundtrack of Disney's *Prince of Egypt*. A year later *I'm Not Tough*, her third album, put the nail in the coffin, sinking with barely a (chart) trace. *Super Hits* followed in 2000, a last attempt by her label to cash in on her onetime fame.

McCready offered an attractive package to Nashville: good looks; teen appeal; perky, upbeat material.

But it took SHANIA TWAIN to really grab the gold ring when she took this formula to all-new heights.

Select Discography

Super Hits, BNA 67920. All the hits from her first two albums.

McDANIEL, MEL (b. Checotah, Okla., September 9, 1942)

McDaniel is a country SINGER/SONGWRITER who had his biggest success in the early 1980s with a number of pop-country hits.

The Oklahoma native took a while to establish himself, beginning as a 1950s rocker and then relocating to Nashville; moving to Alaska, where he worked as a lounge singer; and finally returning to Nashville, where he performed in the Holiday Inn while pushing his songwriting career. His big break came in 1976 when his comic novelty "Roll Your Own" was covered by COMMANDER CODY AND HIS LOST PLANET AIRMEN, as well as by HOYT AXTON and Arlo Guthrie. This led to a contract with Capitol Records, and a minor hit with a cover version of "Have a Dream on Me" in 1976, followed by a couple more minor successes through the late 1970s.

In the early 1980s McDaniel's luck took a turn for the better. His 1981 releases "Louisiana Saturday Night" and "Right in the Palm of Your Hand" were major successes, followed by a number of Top 20 hits through the mid-1980s. He was made a GRAND OLE OPRY member in 1986, but after that the hits dried up. He remains a performer on the second-string road circuit where old country stars appear, it seems, forever.

Select Discography

Greatest Hits, Alliance 46867. Reissues 1970s Capitol recordings.

McDONALD, SKEETS (b. Enos William M., near Greenway, Ark., October 1, 1915–March 31, 1968)

McDonald was an early COWBOY star who is best remembered for his self-penned 1952 hit "Don't Let the Stars Get in Your Eyes."

After being raised on a small farm, in 1932 he moved with his family to Michigan, where he formed his first band, The Lonesome Cowboys, a high-energy outfit specializing in a blend of country, pop, and jazz. They performed on Michigan radio through the early 1940s, until McDonald was drafted into the Army in 1943. He revived the band in 1946, and then made a couple of solo recordings, including the hanky-soaker "Please, Daddy, Don't Go to War" in 1950. He was hired as lead singer for the Michigan-based Johnny

White and His Rhythm Riders soon after, returning to an up-tempo country boogie sound with a couple of minor hits, including "Mean and Evil Blues" and "The Tattooed Lady." By 1952 he was living in Los Angeles and had signed with Capitol Records, where he had his big hit with the schmaltzy "Stars."

By the mid-1950s he was jumping on the ROCKA-BILLY bandwagon, with some early recordings that are much prized among collectors of this genre, including "You Ought to See Grandma Rock and Roll." He was signed as a country act by Columbia in the early 1960s, having minor hits in the mid-1960s with "Call Me Mr. Brown" and "You Took Her Off My Hands," both in the pop-country style then prevalent. He died of a heart attack in 1968.

Select Discography

Don't Let the Stars Get in Your Eyes, Bear Family 15937. Complete 1950s Capitol recordings in a lavish boxed set.

McDOWELL, RONNIE (b. Portland, Tenn., March 26, 1951)

McDowell is a small-time country star who boosted his career by crooning over poor old ELVIS PRESLEY's bones with the 1977 hit WEEPER "The King Is Dead."

After being raised on a farm, McDowell enlisted in the Navy, where he had his first experience as a performer. On his discharge in 1969, he formed his first band, The Nashville Road, which became popular on the bar circuit through the South. He struggled through the early 1970s in search of a record contract, with little success. After the death of Elvis, McDowell was moved to write "The King Is Dead"; his demo tape of the song was picked up by tiny Scorpion Records, who rushed it out to cash in on the Elvis mania. He had a couple of follow-up hits on Scorpion, and also provided Elvis sound-alike vocals for the 1979 ABC TV documentary on the Memphis hipshaker.

His 1979 recording of his original composition "He's a Cowboy from Texas" announced a new countrified direction for his career, and soon after the song charted, he left Scorpion for Epic Records, where he quickly produced another self-penned hit, "World's Most Perfect Woman." He hooked up with soulful producer Buddy Killen, and the duo wrote "Lovin' and Livin'," his first hit of 1980. In 1981 he had two hits with songs written by young songwriter Jamie O'Hara (later of THE O'KANES), and he followed these with the 1983 tongue-in-cheek #1 hit "You're Gonna Ruin My Bad Reputation." The hits slowed up in the mid-1980s, and by 1987 he had moved to the Curb label, where he had his last hit, a remake of CONWAY TWIT-TY's "It's Only Make-Believe." Since then McDowell

has taken his Elvis show on the road, reverting to lip-curlin' imitations of The King.

Select Discography

Older Women and Other Greatest Hits, Epic 40643. Early 1980s recordings, including his best-known hits.
The Best of, Curb 77254. Late 1980s and early 1990s recordings.

McENERY, RED RIVER DAVE (b. San Antonio, Tex., December 15, 1914–January 15, 2002)

McEnery rode the COWBOY wave in the 1930s to become a permanent fixture in country music circles, and is best known for his story-songs based on people in the news.

After performing through the South on a variety of small radio stations, McEnery hit it big when he hooked up with New York City's radio station WHN in 1938, remaining there for three years. Before returning to his native Texas, he released his recording of "Amelia Earhart's Last Flight" in 1941, the first in a long string of topical songs based on current events. After returning to San Antonio, Dave began performing on a string of Tex-Mex border radio stations; these unregulated stations could be picked up throughout much of the U.S., further spreading his fame. After the war he appeared in a couple of C-grade Westerns, including 1948's *Swing in the Saddle*.

Dave's career went into an eclipse in the 1950s, but he came back with a vengeance in the early 1960s with "The Ballad of Francis Gary Powers," recounting the story of the shooting down of the famous U-2 pilot over Russia. (Earlier in the decade he had expressed his anticommunist feelings in his reworking of T. TEXAS TYLER's 1948 hit, "Deck of Cards," as "The Red Deck of Cards.") He followed this with such perishable topical numbers as "The Flight of Apollo Eleven" and even "The Ballad of Patty Hearst." In his later years Dave was more of a personality than a performer, well known for his long white hair and pointy goatee, gold-colored boots, and glittering, NUDIE-styled cowboy duds.

McENTIRE, REBA (b. Chockie, Okla., March 28, 1954)

This ropin'-and-ridin' sweetheart began her career very much in a new-country/cowgirl mold, but has since veered increasingly—and very successfully—into being the ultimate country diva and an industry power broker.

McEntire comes from an authentic rodeo family; her grandfather was a celebrity on the national rodeo circuit, and her father was a talented roper. Her brother,

Pake, and two sisters, Alice and Susie, all performed in rodeos, as did young Reba, and the four formed a family singing group, scoring a local hit in 1971 with a ballad memorializing their grandfather, "The Ballad of John McEntire." Country star RED STEAGALL heard Reba belt out "The Star-Spangled Banner" at the National Rodeo Finals in Oklahoma City in 1974, and invited her to come to Nashville to make a demo. Reba, her mother, and brother all ended up in Music City, and both brother and sister made their first albums in late 1975.

Reba's first recordings were in a traditional style, and although they forecast the new-country trends of the next decade, they failed to find much chart action. Meanwhile, she married bulldogger Charlie Battles (a bulldogger is a steer wrestler) and got her teaching certificate just in case her singing career failed to take off. In the late 1970s and early 1980s she finally began to see some chart action, covering PATSY CLINE's "Sweet Dreams" and "A Poor Man's Roses"; her first #1 record came in 1983 with "Can't Even Get the Blues." McEntire's producer insisted she record the song, although she resisted cutting yet another ballad, preferring to try some more up-tempo material.

But it was as a balladeer that Reba reached her greatest popularity in the mid-1980s. Her highly emotional, charged vocals were perfectly suited to the often melodramatic material she recorded. She did, however, maintain a country-influenced technique, using bends, twirls, trills, and even a slight yodel—all found in traditional mountain singing—to give her vocals added depth and authenticity. Meanwhile, her image was constantly being made more upscale by her handlers, who were steering her in the direction of becoming a Vegas-style diva.

In 1987 McEntire divorced her husband, and two years later wed her steel guitarist/road manager, Narvel Blackstock. The duo began building McEntire's empire, taking over the responsibility of managing and booking her act, working with the record company and producers to shape her image, and even becoming involved in the nuts and bolts of song publishing and transporting equipment for tours. Although McEntire took a more active hand in her career, there was not much change in the music that she produced; she continued to turn out finely crafted pop ballads, with the occasional more spirited number thrown in for variety. She also began to pursue an acting career, landing some minor TV roles in miniseries and movies, but her best acting remained in her videos, in which she continued to project a feisty, if down-home and lovable, personality.

The 1990s saw McEntire continue to be a strong concert draw, and her recordings consistently sold well. In 1999, celebrating her 40 millionth record sold, the Recording Industry of America named her Female Country Artist of the Century. In 2001 McEntire made a splash when she appeared on Broadway in the revival of Irving Berlin's *Annie Get Your Gun*, showing that her perky performance style translated well to the musical stage. That summer she headlined the Girls Night Out tour, featuring established and up-and-coming female country stars, including MARTINA MCBRIDE and SARA EVANS. She also starred in a sitcom on the WB network beginning in the fall of 2001.

Select Discography

Greatest Hits, MCA 5979. The hits through 1987.
Greatest Hits, Vol. 2, MCA 10906. The hits from 1987–1993.
Greatest Hits, Vol. 3, MCA 170202. The hits from 1994–2001.
Whoever's in New England, MCA 31304. One of her better 1980s recordings.

McEUEN, JOHN (b. Long Beach, Calif., December 19, 1945)

McEuen, a founding member of the folk-rock-country NITTY GRITTY DIRT BAND, has since had some success as a solo artist.

Growing up in Long Beach, John was first exposed to rock and roll and R&B via his older brother Bill, who was a local deejay and concert promoter. While he was still in high school, John formed a folk band with a couple of friends, originally taking the name The Illegitimate Jug Band (because they didn't have a jug player). This group evolved into the Nitty Gritty Dirt Band, and brother Bill soon became their manager. McEuen primarily played BLUEGRASS-styled BANJO in the group, although he also played GUITAR, MANDOLIN, and sometimes even FIDDLE.

After leaving the Dirt Band in the late 1980s, McEuen was signed as a solo artist by Vanguard Records. He produced a couple of solo albums in a style that melds bluegrass with Irish traditional music, old-time country, and jazz, similar to other performers in the PROGRESSIVE BLUEGRASS/newgrass styles, such as TONY TRISCHKA. He also produced and hosted a special on the music of the old West for TNN. Through the 1990s he continued to record, mostly in a progressive bluegrass style. In 2000 he reunited with Nitty Gritty Dirt Band singer Jimmy Ibbotson for a duet album, *Stories and Songs*.

Select Discography

String Wizards, Vanguard 79462. His first 1991 solo album, with contributions by VASSAR CLEMENTS, BYRON BERLINE, JERRY DOUGLAS, and Earl Scruggs (of FLATT AND SCRUGGS).

Stories and Songs, Planetary 9023. Duet album with Ibbotson features a group of contemporary COUN-TRY-ROCK songs, along with the "stories" behind them.

McGEE, SAM (b. S. Fleming M., Franklin, Tenn., May 1, 1894–August 21, 1975)

McGee was a country guitarist with blues influences who worked for many years with his brother, Kirk (November 4, 1899–October 24, 1983), and as an accompanist for UNCLE DAVE MACON and FIDDLIN' ARTHUR SMITH.

McGee came from a musical farming family; his father was a fiddler and the McGee boys were playing music early on in the family band. Both Sam and Kirk could remember the playing of local black musicians as highly influential on their playing; Sam said that the sound of traditional blues would "just ring in my head." The brothers were discovered by Uncle Dave Macon in 1924; Sam was thirty years old at the time and working as a blacksmith. Soon the two brothers were touring with the flamboyant banjoist, with Sam playing GUITAR and Kirk playing FIDDLE. They became members of THE GRAND OLE OPRY in 1926, and made their first solo recordings at the time, including Sam's unusual fingerpicked guitar instrumental, "Franklin Blues," showing the influence of black blues guitarists. Macon and the McGees were joined by fiddler Mazy Todd in a 1927 recording session as "The Fruit Jar Drinkers," recording some of the most high-spirited string-band music of the era. (Macon's group is not to be confused with the *Opry* string band of the same name.)

Although both McGees would continue to perform with Uncle Dave through the 1930s, they also hooked up with a more modern performer, Fiddlin' Arthur Smith, early in the decade to form The Dixieliners. Kirk switched to banjo in this group that featured Smith's more modern, jazz-influenced fiddling and his smooth vocals. The group disbanded by the decade's end, but would reunite in the 1960s to record and perform at folk festivals.

In the 1940s the McGee Brothers toured with BILL MONROE's new band, The Blue Grass Boys, joining Monroe's traveling tent shows. During the 1950s they continued to perform on the *Opry*, often as members of a revived Fruit Jar Drinkers featuring various other *Opry* old-timers. The 1960s FOLK REVIVAL brought them an entirely new audience of young, urban pickers; MIKE SEEGER produced two albums of the McGees with Arthur Smith, as well as a solo album by Sam, in the early 1970s.

Sam McGee continued to perform on the *Opry* until his death in a farming accident in 1975. At that time his brother Kirk pretty much retired from playing. All in all, they had nearly fifty years of *Opry* membership, and were among the last early cast members still performing on the program.

McGee's unique guitar style influenced a generation of pickers. His syncopated instrumentals, including the oft-copied "Buck Dancer's Choice," became test pieces for any would-be fingerpicker. The McGees brought an authentic appreciation for syncopated music into the country repertoire, and were a key link between black and white country traditions.

Select Discography

1926–34, Document 8036. Complete recordings from this period, some featuring brother Kirk.
Grand Dad of the Country Guitar, Arhoolie 9009. Reissue of 1969–1970 recordings produced by Mike Seeger (Arhoolie 5012).

McGRAW, TIM (b. Timothy Samuel M., Delhi, La., May 1, 1967)

Half of New Nashville's late 1990s power couple, along with wife FAITH HILL, McGraw dominated the country charts for the second half of the decade, as well as crossing over into the pop market.

Tim McGraw reflects on his career, 1995. Photo: Raeanne Rubenstein

McGraw descends from baseball royalty: his father, Tug McGraw, had an affair with his mother, a fact that was not revealed to Tim until he was a teen. Up to that point he was raised as Tim Smith, the son of a trucker. McGraw at first focused on a possible sports career, but a knee injury in college sidelined his goal, and he turned to music and the GUITAR. Arriving in Nashville in 1989, he scuffled around until Tug arranged for a friend at Curb Records to listen to his son's audition tape. The deal was made, and McGraw was signed to the label in 1991.

After releasing a debut album in 1992 that saw little action, McGraw leaped to prominence with the release of 1994's aptly titled *Not a Moment Too Soon*. The best-selling country album of the year, it yielded two gold singles ("Indian Outlaw" and "Don't Take the Girl") in less than three months, a feat not yet beaten. The hits kept coming with his third album release, *All I Want*, in 1995, with Tim balancing romantic ballads (the title track) with more up-tempo rockers ("I Like It, I Love It"). Following its release McGraw made a summer tour, selecting up-and-coming country chanteuse Faith Hill as his opening act. A romance blossomed, and the two were wed in 1996. McGraw also coproduced singer JO DEE MESSINA's first album that year, launching her chart career.

Cashing in on their romantic attachment, the duo released their first vocal duet, "It's Your Love," which was the lead release from McGraw's fourth album, 1997's *Everywhere*. The song spent six weeks in the #1 spot, a record for *Billboard*'s country charts, and launched further McGraw mania.

In 1999 McGraw released his next album, *A Place in the Sun*, which continued the formula of bad-boy up-tempo numbers and tearful ballads, producing five hit singles, including two #1 hits ("Please Remember Me" and "Something Like That"). The album debuted at #1 on both pop and country charts, no small achievement. Meanwhile, the publicity machine around his storybook marriage continued to yield results, including a Father of the Year award from the National Fatherhood Initiative. That summer's tour brought McGraw together with the New Nashville honeys THE DIXIE CHICKS and also with GEORGE STRAIT.

Not wishing to rest on his moneybags, McGraw issued a *Greatest Hits* set in 2000 that brought further cash to the hunky superstar. Another duet with Hill—"Let's Make Love"—brought McGraw his first Grammy. While touring with Kenny Chesney and George Strait that summer, McGraw was involved in a minor backstage scuffle with the police following a New York state show; Chesney apparently tried to appropriate a policeman's horse, and the other two came to his aid when the police objected. Brought to trial a year later, McGraw escaped unscathed when all three were found not guilty of assault and related charges.

Keeping product flowing, McGraw released *Set This Circus Down* in April 2001, with the leadoff single, "Grown Men Don't Cry," a tearful WEEPER. All signs indicate more multiplatinum sales. As of mid-2001, McGraw has sold over 19 million albums and nearly 5 million singles.

By 2001 McGraw had easily eclipsed GARTH BROOKS as the biggest male name in country music. Taking a page out of Brooks's playbook, he crossed over to the pop charts and—thanks to his association with Hill—the supermarket tabloids as well. How long his career will go depends on the sometimes fickle taste of the country-pop audience.

Select Discography

Greatest Hits, Curb 77978. Fifteen big ones from the 1990s.

MESSINA, JO DEE (b. Holliston, Mass., August 25, 1970)

A Massachusetts-bred cutie who has become a major country star in the late 1990s and early 2000s, Messina began her career at age thirteen at the local Holiday Inn, belting out "Stand by Your Man." As an older teen she formed her own country band, which gained some popularity around New England. At age twenty she abandoned hopes of attending law school and relocated to Nashville to try to make it as a singer. She became a regular at a local bar/showcase, the Pink Elephant, and won the grand prize, which gained her a radio job in Kentucky. Meanwhile, a young producer named Byron Gallimore was developing his own new artist, TIM McGRAW. Hearing Messina, he signed her to a development deal, initially with RCA, but then his relationship with the label went south. Finally, Gallimore brought her to Curb Records in 1995, and soon she was in the studio, with Gallimore and singer Tim McGraw producing.

In 1996 Messina's debut album was released, yielding two hits, the up-tempo #1 "Heads Carolina, Tails California" and the #5 "We're Not in Kansas Anymore." It took Messina two years to produce a follow-up, but her next album, *I'm Alright*, produced several hits, including the #4 "Bye-Bye" and the #2 title track. In 1999 she won the "Horizon" Award for Best New Artist from the Country Music Association, and *Billboard* named her the Most-Played Female Artist of the year.

In 2000 Messina released *Burn*, a pop-flavored collection that launched her big time as a pop, as well as country, superstar. The album's first single, "That's the Way," held the #1 spot for four weeks, earning Messina her first Grammy nomination for Best Female

Country Performance. The title track was promoted by a steamy (and smoke-laden) video, featuring a very Vegas-like set. Powered by Messina's strong live appearances and a relentlessly upbeat message, the album enjoyed strong sales in country and pop charts. 2001 saw her undertake a very successful summer tour. She was also tapped to cohost the pre-awards show broadcast of the Country Music Awards that spring.

Messina's strong vocals, perky attitude, and video-attractive looks make her the perfect package for country and pop stardom. By early 2001 she was the dominant female performer, second perhaps only to FAITH HILL, in country music.

Select Discography

Burn, Curb 77977. Her breakthrough third album of 2000.

MILLER, BOB (b. Memphis, Tenn., September 20, 1895–August 26, 1955)

Miller was a country songwriter and record producer who began his career producing topical material that was covered by many early country artists.

Raised in Memphis, a melting pot of black jazz and blues and white country music, Miller got his first job as a pianist working on a Mississippi riverboat. This led to an early career in jazz and pop music as a conductor, arranger, and music publisher. He joined the staff of Irving Berlin's publishing company in New York in 1928, and soon after founded Bob Miller Music Company, becoming a force in New York's Tin Pan Alley.

In 1931 producer ART SATHERLEY hired him to work for the American Recording Company (ARC) label. ARC specialized in producing material for catalogs like those of Montgomery Ward and Sears Roebuck, along with discount labels sold through dime stores. As such they had a vibrant line of "hillbilly" recording artists, including VERNON DALHART and CARSON ROBISON. Miller began writing material for them, ranging from topical laments like "Eleven Cent Cotton, Forty Cent Meat," focusing on the squeeze that farmers felt in trying to make a living, to more sentimental numbers like "Rockin' Alone (in an Old Rockin' Chair)." In the mid-1940s he produced his biggest hit, the patriotic "There's a Star-Spangled Banner Waving Somewhere," also a major hit for ELTON BRITT.

In the postwar years Miller spent most of his time administering his copyrights and living off royalties from his songs, until his death in 1955.

MILLER, BUDDY AND JULIE (Buddy, b. Steve Miller Princeton, N.J.; Julie, b. Waxahachie, Tex.)

Buddy and Julie are SINGER/SONGWRITERS and a new-country power couple. Buddy began playing rock

music as a teenager, performing locally with his own band in the early 1970s. By the mid-1970s he had moved to Austin, Texas, and had become interested in the "new country" movement centered on that city. He joined a local COUNTRY-ROCK band, Partners in Crime, which included a local singer named Julie. Born in the small town of Waxahachie, Texas, Julie settled in Austin just as the new folk-country-rock-blues style was developing there. Buddy and Julie were married in 1981, and began looking for work as performers and songwriters, working through the 1980s in New York and Los Angeles. During this period Buddy was guitarist for country-pop singer Jim Lauderdale, and Julie recorded four contemporary Christian albums.

In 1993 the couple settled in Nashville, just as the alt-country movement was growing. Julie's songs and Buddy's GUITAR playing attracted the attention of EMMYLOU HARRIS. Buddy was soon a member of her early 1990s touring band, Spyboy, and Harris covered Julie's song "All My Tears." Buddy released his first solo album, *Your Love and Other Lies*, soon after the couple settled in Nashville; from that point forward the two have collaborated on a series of albums, although they have been issued as either Buddy or Julie "solo" discs. In 1997 they both issued solo albums, his second (*Poison Love*) and her first (*Blue Pony*). Both received strong reviews from critics.

Julie followed up in 1999 with *Broken Things*, an album of all original songs, with the exception of the traditional ballad "Two Soliders," recorded as a duet with Emmylou Harris. A critical and artistic success, it featured several songs that are destined to be new-country classics, including "I Know Why the River Runs," later covered by LEE ANN WOMACK. Buddy followed with his next solo album, *Cruel Moon*, featuring the hard-country romp "Does My Ring Burn Your Fingers," also covered by Womack. The regular backup team of vocalists Emmylou Harris, Jim Lauderdale, and Julie Miller, along with instrumentalists drawn from Harris's and STEVE EARLE's touring bands, appear on the album. In 2001 they released their first true duo album, featuring a more hard-rocking sound than some of their earlier efforts.

The Millers have been described as the "yin and yang" of new country: he has a gruff, low voice, somewhat reminiscent of BOB DYLAN or Tom Petty, and has developed a more bluesy style; she has a reedy, sweeter voice, and is more of a sentimentalist and balladeer. They have quickly developed a strong following among artists and the alt-country underground; whether they will break through into mainstream country success is anybody's guess.

Select Discography

Buddy and Julie Miller, High Tone 8035. 2001 duet album.

MILLER, EMMETT (b. E. Dewey M., Macon, Ga., February 2 1903–March 29, 1962)

Miller was a blackface singer and vaudevillian whose recordings were highly influential on country singers, most notably HANK WILLIAMS.

Miller began his performing career as a teenager, performing with a traveling MINSTREL troupe led by Dan Fitch; he later would tour with the A. J. Fields troupe, another traveling show that at one time had been quite popular but was now suffering from the popularity of more modern entertainment. By the early 1920s he was settled in New York, where he began appearing in vaudeville theaters, often working with Cliff Edwards (aka Ukulele Ike). Through Edwards he got his first opportunity to record in 1924, cutting his first hit, "Anytime." From the start Miller's unique singing style was featured on his recordings; he would suddenly break from his normal voice into a crying falsetto, an effect described (when it was featured by JIMMIE RODGERS) as a "blue yodel." Contemporary critics described Miller as having a "clarinet voice," perhaps because of its reedy quality and his ability to improvise short melodic embellishments in the manner of a jazz clarinetist. Miller's falsetto yodel would also become a vocal trademark for Hank Williams.

In August 1925 Miller was appearing in Asheville, North Carolina, where he again had the opportunity to record. RALPH PEER, an executive for Okeh, had set up a makeshift studio in the city's hotel. His "Lovesick Blues" was recorded here, complete with his warbling yodels. On a later trip to Asheville in 1927, Miller met THE CALLAHAN BROTHERS, who learned "St. Louis Blues" from him (it was among their first recordings). According to his partner Turk McBee, Miller also met and influenced Jimmie Rodgers in Asheville, although there is some question whether the two ever met, or if Rodgers simply heard Miller's recordings.

Although he continued to tour the South, Miller spent the balance of the 1920s back in New York. In 1928 he rerecorded his early hits, and also cut "St. Louis Blues" and "I Ain't Got Nobody" for the first time. The latter was noted for his drawing out, and YODELING, the first word "I-ai-yi-ya-yi-ya-yi . . .," which would be imitated by many others (including Louis Prima in his famous recording of the song). He cut a total of twenty-eight sides during 1928–1929, all of them accompanied by "The Georgia Crackers" according to the records' labels; in fact they were a crack band of New York studio musicians, including leading jazz players like Tommy Dorsey and Eddie Lang. He also cut blackface minstrel dialogues, reflecting his long experience in minstrel-type traveling shows.

Miller remained committed to vaudeville and traveling shows through the 1930s and 1940s, making his last recordings in 1936. In 1951 he appeared in the film *Yes Sir, Mr. Bones*, an anthology of older acts. Meanwhile many country artists were emulating his style. Besides Williams and Rodgers, BOB WILLS greatly admired Miller's recordings; one of his first recordings as a bandleader was a direct cover of "I Ain't Got Nobody," yodels and all. Rex Stewart cut his own version of "Lovesick Blues" in 1935, modeled after Miller's original; both discs served as models for Hank Williams's recording in the late 1940s. EDDY ARNOLD covered "Anytime," Miller's signature song.

Miller remained a shadowy figure in country history until the 1980s, when researcher Charles Wolfe finally documented his true story. Previously Nick Tosches had written an "imaginary biography" of the singer, based on his recordings, that was one of the most inspired chapters in his book *Country*. Tosches remained obsessed with the elusive performer, and in 2001 published *Where Dead Voices Gather*, documenting his search for information on the singer, and making a strong case for Miller's importance in the history of American popular music. Miller's recordings are marred somewhat by his minstrel-like "accent," and the somewhat dated accompaniments, but remain important because of their influence on later country and WESTERN SWING artists.

Select Discography

Minstrel Man from Georgia, Columbia Legacy 66999.

MILLER, JODY (b. Myrna J. M., Phoenix, Ariz., November 29, 1941)

Jody Miller is a minor-league country artist who began her career in folk-pop, and had a fluke crossover hit in the mid-1960s before becoming a mainstream country artist in the 1970s.

The daughter of an old-time fiddler, Miller was born in Arizona but raised in Oklahoma, where she developed an early love of horseback riding. She formed a pop vocal trio while still in high school, and on graduation headed for California in search of a music career. However, soon after, she broke her neck in a riding accident and returned home to recuperate. It was during this period of recovery that she began performing on the local coffeehouse circuit. She befriended folksinger/songwriter Tom Paxton, appearing on his syndicated television program along with actor Dale Robertson, who gave her demo tape to Capitol Records. The label signed her as a young "folksinger" in 1963.

Two years later Miller had a fluke pop and country hit with her cover of Mary Taylor's "Queen of the House," a pre-women's liberation answer song to ROGER MILLER's famous "King of the Road." This led to several albums of country covers, but Miller was unable to duplicate her initial hit, and was dropped by the label in 1968.

Miller dropped out of the music industry for two years, but then returned to performing when she was signed by Epic in 1970, working with legendary Nashmopolitan producer BILLY SHERRILL. He provided her with a hit straight out of the gate, "Look at Mine," and followed it with other hits in a sprightly manner through 1972. Miller also recorded a duet with JOHNNY PAYCHECK, "Let's All Go Down the River," which was a moderate hit in 1972.

Through the 1970s Miller continued to record for smaller labels, achieving less success as her perky style began to wear thin. She still performs occasionally, although she has more or less retired to pursue horse farming in Oklahoma. In 1987 she made a comeback album of patriotic songs, and in 1990, with her daughter Robin, she tried unsuccessfully to launch a Juddslike duo. She then retired again from performing.

Select Discography

Anthology, Renaissance 226. Twenty-four-track summary of her career.

MILLER, ROGER (b. R. Dean M., Fort Worth, Tex., January 2, 1936–October 25, 1992)

Miller was a SINGER/SONGWRITER best known for his string of mid-1960s pop and country hits, including the novelty songs "Dang Me" and "Chug-a-Lug" and the classic trucker's anthem, "King of the Road."

Although born in a large city, Miller grew up in tiny Erick, Oklahoma. His father died when he was an infant, and Miller was raised by his aunt and uncle, who had a small cotton-and-chicken farm there. Like many other future country stars, Miller was exposed to the music through the radio, and also through an in-law, country comic SHEB WOOLEY.

After completing the eighth grade, Miller worked as a ranch hand and small-time rodeo star for several years before enlisting in the army during the Korean War. By this time he was an adept guitarist, and could play the FIDDLE, BANJO, piano, and drums as well. After the war, while stationed in South Carolina, Miller served with a sergeant whose brother was Jethro of the famous HOMER AND JETHRO comedy act. He encouraged Miller to go to Nashville, and arranged an audition for him at RCA Records. Although Miller's initial audition was not successful, he did eventually get session and band work, playing the fiddle for comedian MINNIE PEARL and joining FARON YOUNG's backup band as a drummer.

In the late 1950s Miller began achieving success as a songwriter, first with "Invitation to the Blues," covered by RAY PRICE (with whom he played as a backup musician) and, later, pop crooner Patti Page. Further hits included "Half a Mind" for ERNEST TUBB and "Billy Bayou" for JIM REEVES. Miller had his first hit as a performer with 1961's "When Two Worlds Collide," which he wrote with BILL ANDERSON.

Miller was still frustrated with Nashville's failure to take him seriously as a solo act, so in 1963 he relocated to Hollywood, where he signed with the MGM subsidiary Smash Records. It was at this label that he had his biggest success, including his first two novelty songs, 1964's "Chug-a-Lug" and the perennial favorite "Dang Me." 1965 was his most productive year, including, besides the monster hit "King of the Road," "Engine Engine No. 9" and "Kansas City Star." Smash, a label more oriented toward the pop scene than country, successfully marketed Miller as a pop star—and, oddly enough, his songs reached #1 on the pop charts but settled only in the Top 10 on the country listings. In 1966 mellow-voiced Andy Williams had a big hit with Miller's "In the Summertime," leading him to invite the country performer to appear on his high-rated TV show.

Miller was a talented comic vocalist whose gentle twang betrayed his country roots, but whose vocal styles were subdued enough to win a mainstream audience. Although Nashville executives found his voice "unusual," it was the perfect vehicle for expressing his often ironic, slightly skewed vision of the world. His success as a crossover artist on the pop charts was mainly thanks to his easygoing vocals and amusing songs. And, unlike other acts who were buried by the NASHVILLE SOUND of the 1960s, Miller's best records were made in Hollywood, and had the stripped-down sound of BUCK OWENS and other California country stars.

From the late 1960s through the mid-1980s, Miller's career was spotty at best. He mostly lived off his big hits, while continuing to record erratically. His big comeback came in the mid-1980s with the Broadway hit *Big River*, a musical based on Mark Twain's *Huckleberry Finn*, which he scored. Miller's good-humored countryesque songs were a perfect fit for this informal musical, and his success on the Broadway stage brought renewed interest in his country-music career. Sadly, Miller died soon after, although his classic recordings continued to sell into the 1990s.

Select Discography

The Best of, Vols. 1 and 2, Mercury 848977/512646. His Smash label recordings of the 1960s, with the first volume focusing more on country styles and the second on his pop hits, including "King of the Road." These tracks are duplicated, along with some lesser numbers, on the three-CD box *King of the Road* (Mercury 526993).

MILSAP, RONNIE (b. Robbinsville, N.C., January 16, 1943)

Milsap is a pop country singer who was most popular from the late 1970s through the mid-1980s. His voice is similar in timbre to James Taylor's, and Milsap's performances share with the pop singer a sugar-coated romanticism.

Blind from birth, Milsap was a musical prodigy, becoming proficient on several instruments by the time he was ten years old. In high school he formed his first rock group, and after an abortive attempt at college, decided to pursue music making full time. He performed with blues rocker J. J. Cale before going out on his own, recording his first singles for the Scepter label in an R&B style. Through the 1960s Milsap toured with other R&B performers.

In 1969 he settled in Nashville, and began writing and performing in a mainstream country style. Although he had some minor hits, his career didn't really take off until he signed with RCA in 1973. His recordings were given the standard strings-and-choruses production, making them immediately popular not only on the country but also on the mainstream pop charts. From 1975's "Daydreams About Night Things," Milsap scored chart-busters through the mid-1980s, primarily focusing on smooth ballads. Perhaps his biggest crossover pop/country hits were 1981's "(There's) No Gettin' Over Me" and "I Wouldn't Have Missed It for the World," and his 1982 remake of Chuck Jackson's 1962 hit, "Any Day Now." His stage act grew increasingly glitzy, and he became a fixture on country and pop television shows.

Ronnie Milsap, c. mid-1970s, during his hit-making days. Photo: Raeanne Rubenstein

Milsap's career pretty much petered out when the new-country movement made his brand of sentimental love songs sound increasingly passé, although he continues to be a strong concert draw.

Select Discography

40 Greatest Hits, Virgin 48871. Actually has forty-three tracks (two newly recorded), drawn from his RCA recordings.

MINSTREL/TRAVELING SHOWS (c. 1830–1950s)

Classic minstrel shows—in which white entertainers performed in blackface—are a rich source of country-music traditions, including musical instruments (BANJO, FIDDLE), humor (the classic Interlocutor/Mr. Bones dialogues), skits, and songs. Although often criticized as degrading to blacks (for good reason), the shows were tremendously popular, and eventually embraced black entertainers as well as white. They served as models for touring and tent shows that later regularly crisscrossed the South.

The classic minstrel era is usually defined as running from the late 1840s through the 1880s, when minstrelsy gave way to other forms of entertainment. Originally individual performers such as banjo player J. W. Sweeney toured with traveling circuses or other informal entertainments. Early performers like George Washington Dixon and Thomas Dartmouth Rice ("Jim Crow") developed their own specialties, as well as a group of stock characters, including the archetypal backwoods man (Jim Crow) and the uptown dandy (Old Zip Coon).

As instrumentalists began to pair up with dancers or comedians, they developed individual acts that could be integrated into an evening of song and dance. In 1843 in New York City, four early performers decided to stage an evening's entertainment: violinist Dan Emmett, banjo player Billy Whitlock, bones player Frank Brower, and tambourinist Dick Pelham. They called themselves the Virginia Minstrels, and they were an immediate phenomenon, touring Britain and the U.S., and developing the typical cast and format for the minstrel show.

Minstrel troupes—large and small—toured throughout the country, bringing a new musical instrument—the FIVE-STRING BANJO—and repertoire of jokes, songs, and dances to the hinterlands. Banjo tunes that are still collected from traditional players today, such as "Boatman's Dance," and fiddle tunes including "Turkey in the Straw," among dozens of others, all can be traced to the minstrel repertoire. Moreover, the character of the dim-witted Jim Crow is an obvious model for hundreds of country-RUBE humorists, who make hay out of malapropisms and punning. Sketches where the country rube outwits the city slicker—such as the comic dialogue of "Arkansas Traveler"—are derived from similar minstrel routines. Performers like STRINGBEAN, HOMER AND JETHRO, and MINNIE PEARL all carried forward traditions of rube humor that can be traced, in part, to the minstrel past. (Rube humor is a rich vein in American cultural life, and was promulgated as well through newspapers, literature, and monologists, all of them sources for later comedians.)

Blacks were not the only figures caricatured in minstrelsy. America was being flooded with new ethnic populations beginning with the immigration of Germans, Slavs, and Irish in the mid-nineteenth century. The Irish came to escape the crushing poverty—and the infamous potato famine—and soon became a new working class, often maligned in the popular press. Irish step dancers became popular entertainers, and step dancing undoubtedly influenced the growth of traditional Appalachian flat-foot or clog dancing, as well as African-American tap-dance styles. Several dance styles imitating animal movements—such as the buck and wing—had African sources and became part of the folk repertoire.

Many songs that are considered "folk" or "traditional" today were in fact minstrel songs. Stephen Foster was the most famous composer in the genre, contributing "Camptown Races," "O! Susannah," and dozens more to the country repertoire. James Bland, an African-American songwriter of the later nineteenth century, also composed sentimental songs in the Foster vein, notably "Carry Me Back to Old Virginny," another classic popular song of the era. Moreover, sentimental popular songs—first introduced on the minstrel and then traveling show stages—entered the repertoire of country singers, sometimes preserved for decades. FIDDLIN' JOHN CARSON made the first country-music 78 featuring a sentimental song ("Little Old Log Cabin in the Lane" that dated to the 1870s) which was backed with a fiddle-novelty tune ("Old Hen Cackled") that could have been performed as a instrumental tour de force by a traveling musician. Early collectors often mistakenly labeled this music as "folk song," not realizing that it was merely the (by then forgotten—at least among city dwellers) popular music of a previous era.

Although the minstrel shows "died" in the later nineteenth century, their format of humorous skits, dazzling instrumental solos, dances, and sentimental numbers lived in numerous tent and traveling shows. "Medicine shows"—usually selling some remedy of dubious quality and usefulness—often employed individual or groups of musicians, dancers, and comedians to hawk their wares. As late as the 1940s HANK WILLIAMS was sponsored by the makers of Hadacol, a patent medicine that promised "Health and Happiness" to its users. Many musicians were "sponsored" by commercial concerns; early WESTERN SWING stars MILTON BROWN and BOB WILLS's band was sponsored by the Light Crust Dough company, and FLATT AND SCRUGGS spent several decades peddling Martha White flour. All of these sponsors expected their acts to travel around, usually as part of an effort to attract consumers to try or purchase the company's products.

WSM's GRAND OLE OPRY radio program began sending out tent shows on the road in the 1930s, featuring the more celebrated members of their staff. Musicians themselves soon realized that—for a small investment in equipment—they could mount their own touring shows. During the later 1940s BILL MONROE sponsored several successful tent shows that featured not only musical performances but also a traveling baseball team, which would challenge locals to a game.

Even today major corporations sponsor "caravans" of country artists on tours. In 1957 the Philip Morris Company sponsored a famous caravan that played over sixteen months to 4 million people throughout the Southeast. During the 1970s, 1980s, and 1990s Marlboro cigarettes continued this tradition, sponsoring a touring show, and makers of liquor and blue jeans, among other consumer goods, have also gotten into the act. These shows more closely resemble today's concerts, although they still present a variety of entertainers, often augmented by comedians.

MONROE, BILL (b. William Smith M., Rosine, Ky., September 13, 1911–September 3, 1996)

Justifiably known as the "Father of BLUEGRASS Music," mandolinist Bill Monroe was a highly influential composer, vocalist, and instrumentalist.

Monroe was the youngest in a family of farmers and musicians. Elder brother CHARLIE MONROE played GUITAR, and Birch, the FIDDLE. The family farmed 655 acres of prime Kentucky land, and Bill was raised working the land. Because he was the youngest by a wide gap (Charlie, the second in line, was eight years older), and also because of poor eyesight, Monroe grew up a shy loner who sought refuge in his music. He often cited two important musical influences from his youth: one was his mother's brother, Pendleton Vandiver (known as "Uncle Pen"), who was a champion fiddler. Young Monroe often accompanied him to play at local dances, and absorbed his repertoire of traditional fiddle tunes. The second influence was black blues guitarist Arnold Shultz; Monroe claims that Shultz, although unrecorded, was a fine interpreter of the blues, and it's undoubtedly from him that he picked up his own "blue and lonesome" sound. Young Monroe also heard recordings of traditional country performers, including JIMMIE RODGERS and CHARLIE POOLE.

Charlie and Birch left home to search for employment in the North in the mid-1920s, settling in East Chicago, Indiana. Bill joined them there when he was eighteen years old, staying for five years. They worked in the local oil refineries by day, playing music nights and weekends. In 1934 Chicago radio station WLS offered them full-time employment; Birch quit the group, but Charlie and Bill continued as The Monroe Brothers. They relocated to the Carolinas in 1935, performing on radio out of Greenville, South Carolina, and Charlotte, North Carolina, sponsored by Texas Crystals, a popular if somewhat dubious over-the-counter home remedy.

In 1936 Bluebird Records (a division of RCA Victor) made the brothers' first recordings. Although these were in the style of the popular brother duets of the era, you could already hear the difference in Bill's intense singing and lightning-fast MANDOLIN playing. They recorded traditional songs and hymns, including their first hit, "What Would You Give (in Exchange for Your Soul)." Their recording of the folk standard "Nine Pound Hammer (Roll on Buddy)" was widely imitated, and shows how they could take a traditional song, and modernize and energize it. Charlie's laconic delivery was a good foil to his brother's highly charged tenor vocals, and their records and radio appearances were very successful.

The brothers split up in 1938, with Bill relocating to Arkansas and forming his first band, The Kentuckians. He was then hired by an Atlanta station and formed his first group known as The Blue Grass Boys. In 1939 he auditioned for legendary GRAND OLE OPRY announcer GEORGE D. HAY, who hired him on the spot; Monroe's first performance on the *Opry* was of Jimmie Rodgers's classic that he made his own, "Mule Skinner Blues."

In the early 1940s Monroe was still searching for a sound. He hired banjo player Dave Akemann (aka STRINGBEAN) primarily to provide comic relief for his stage act; the BANJO is barely heard on the group's recordings. He also hired fiddler CHUBBY WISE and accordionist Sally Ann Forrester (fiddler HOWDY FORRESTER's wife); Monroe's mother had played the accordion, and it was a popular instrument in WESTERN SWING bands of the day. Monroe's early Blue Grass Boys was a swinging outfit, although still rooted deeply in country sounds.

In 1945–1946 Monroe's greatest band was assembled, featuring Wise on fiddle, Lester Flatt (guitar, lead vocal), Earl Scruggs (banjo), and Cedric Rainwater (b. Harold Watts; bass, vocal). This lineup would become the classic Bluegrass ensemble. The group recorded some of Monroe's first compositions, including the classic "Blue Moon of Kentucky," "Footprints in the Snow," and "Will You Be Loving Another Man?" They also recorded fine instrumentals, with "Bluegrass Breakdown" introducing Earl Scruggs's new banjo style, the model for all bluegrass banjo playing to come. The group also recorded as a GOSPEL quartet,

with Scruggs taking the bass vocal part and playing guitar, on some absolutely stunning country gospel numbers that combined the modern sound of bluegrass with the ancient modalities of SHAPE-NOTE SINGING. Flatt's laconic lead vocals (like Charlie Monroe's before him) were a perfect foil to Monroe's intense high tenor, and the band had the power of twice to three times the number of pieces. Their Columbia recordings made between 1946 and 1948, along with their appearances on the *Opry* and on the road, made them legends in their own time.

Flatt and Scruggs left the band to form their own group in 1948; Monroe would never again feature the banjo as prominently as he had before, perhaps an indication that he realized Scruggs could not be replaced, perhaps out of anger with his sidemen who had deserted him. In the early 1950s he signed lead guitarist/vocalist JIMMY MARTIN, along with a number of banjo players, including young Sonny Osborne and fiddlers VASSAR CLEMENTS and Buddy Spicher. He composed a series of high-powered instrumentals featuring his mandolin playing, including "Rawhide" and "Roanoke." He also composed his homage to his fiddling uncle, "Uncle Pen," which has become a bluegrass standard. By the mid-to-late 1950s Monroe was experimenting with a twin-fiddle sound, composing the instrumental "Scotland" using one fiddle as a drone to try to capture the modal sound of the traditional music that was at the roots of his Appalachian heritage (the original recording featured fiddlers KENNY BAKER and Bobby Hicks).

In the early 1960s Monroe linked up with Ralph Rinzler, a young mandolinist who became his connection to the FOLK-REVIVAL world. Rinzler encouraged Monroe's label, Decca, to reissue his 1950s recordings on LP (many had previously been available only on hard-to-find 45s), giving them the careful annotation that they deserved; he also acted as Monroe's agent, booking him into many prestigious folk festivals. Most important, Rinzler introduced Monroe to younger musicians who were invited to join his band, including fiddler RICHARD GREENE, innovative banjoist BILL KEITH, and SINGER/SONGWRITER PETER ROWAN, with whom Monroe wrote "The Walls of Time." Keith was particularly important; his melodic banjo playing, in which single notes were picked with no chord accompaniments, was prominently featured on Monroe's instrumental recordings, including his famous rendition of "Sailor's Hornpipe." This was the first time since Scruggs was in the band that Monroe had featured the banjo; typically he refused to call the younger picker "Bill" (there was room for only one Bill in his band), so he nicknamed him Brad, from his middle name, Bradford.

By the late 1960s and early 1970s Monroe was an established legend in the bluegrass and country worlds.

Fiddler Kenny Baker, who had originally played with Monroe in the late 1950s and early 1960s, became a fixture in the band from 1967 through the early 1980s, and his sympathy for traditional fiddle styles, along with a more modern swing, made him the perfect fiddler for Monroe's band. Son James Monroe, born in 1941, was often featured in the band on bass and vocals, although he also formed his own group, The Midnight Ramblers. New-country star RICKY SKAGGS, who got his start in bluegrass, did much to revive Monroe's songs for a new audience, as well as featuring the older picker in his video *Country Boy* and on his recordings. While Monroe had more recognition thanks to the bluegrass revival, his bands became less innovative, and particularly in the 1980s and 1990s, as he got older, his playing became less energized and his singing flatter. Monroe continued to perform until shortly before his death.

Monroe's contribution to bluegrass music is so great that it is difficult to summarize. First and foremost, he formed the first great band, which became a model for all others. His mandolin playing included melody picking with a chopping chord style for accompaniment that helped propel the beat forward. His high tenor voice is an immediately recognizable feature of his recordings; perhaps because he had a high voice, he tended to pitch his music up a key or two (explaining that this gave it a "brighter" sound). His compositions, both instrumental and vocal, have become the standards both as tests for young pickers and as the backbone of the bluegrass repertoire.

Select Discography

Monroe Brothers, Vols. 1 and 2, Rounder 1073/1074. First two volumes of projected reissue of all of the brothers' RCA/Bluebird recordings of the 1930s.

Essential Bill Monroe and The Monroe Brothers, RCA 67450. Twenty-five RCA/Bluebird recordings from the 1930s and early 1940s featuring the Monroe Brothers and Monroe's early Bluegrass Boys band.

Essential, 1945–48, Columbia/Legacy 52478. Two-CD set of all of the Columbia recordings, although sixteen of the forty tracks are represented by alternate takes rather than the better-known originals. Includes the classic Flatt and Scruggs/Chubby Wise band.

Blue Moon of Kentucky, Bear Family 15423. Four CDs reissuing everything Monroe recorded for Decca between 1950 and 1958, with notes by Charles Wolfe and Neil Rosenberg.

Bluegrass 1959–69, Bear Family 11529. Complete Decca/MCA recordings from this period on four CDs.

1970–79, Bear Family 15606. Continues the saga.

Off the Record, 1945–1969, Smithsonian/Folkways 40063. Live tracks lovingly assembled by Monroe protégé/manager Ralph Rinzler.

Live Duet Recordings, 1963–1980, Smithsonian/Folkways 40064. Monroe had a special relationship with blind guitarist DOC WATSON, who performed with him several times over the years to re-create the classic Monroe Brothers sound.

MONROE, CHARLIE (b. Rosine, Ky., July 4, 1903–September 27, 1975)

Elder brother of BILL MONROE and one half of The Monroe Brothers duo, Charlie went on to have a minor career leading older-styled bands through the late 1950s.

A lower-keyed guitarist and singer than his very highly energized brother, Charlie split from Bill in 1938, leading first a trio known as The Monroe Boys and then a band called The Kentucky Pardners. Alumni of his band include many well-known names in BLUEGRASS and country music, including Lester Flatt of FLATT AND SCRUGGS (who was hired away by his brother, Bill), Ira Louvin of THE LOUVIN BROTHERS, and fiddler Curly Sechler. The band recorded for Victor from the mid-1940s through the early 1950s, when they switched to Decca, also home to brother Bill.

Charlie ended the band in 1957, although he continued to make personal appearances and a few recordings into the early 1960s for the small Rem label. In 1972, after a decade of working for Otis Elevator and Howard Johnson's in Indiana and Tennessee, he was lured out of retirement by JIMMY MARTIN to perform at a bluegrass festival. Until his death three years later, Monroe returned to performing primarily on the festival circuit.

Select Discography

Vintage Radio, Rebel 4302. Radio transcriptions from 1944, featuring Monroe and his band.

MONTANA, PATSY (b. Rubye Blevins, Jessieville, Ark., October 30, 1908–May 3, 1996)

The first female country vocalist to have a million-seller, Montana laid the groundwork for women to enter country music in a big way after World War II.

A talented fiddler, vocalist, and yodeler, Montana originally partnered JIMMIE DAVIS in the early 1930s before joining The Prairie Ramblers, a four-piece Western band featured on Chicago's *WLS Barn Dance* program, the main rival to the famous WSM GRAND OLE OPRY. Their 1935 recording of "I Want to Be a Cowboy's Sweetheart" was Montana's million-selling

Patsy Montana, still a cowboy's sweetheart, during the mid-1970s. Photo: Raeanne Rubenstein

Select Discography

Columbia Historic Edition, Columbia 38909. Reissues her classic 1930s recordings.
The Cowboy's Sweetheart, Flying Fish 90459. Cassette-only reissue of 1970s recordings.

MONTGOMERY, JOHN MICHAEL (b. Danville, Ky., January 20, 1965)

A hunky roots-country hitmaker of the 1990s, Montgomery was raised on music, playing since he was a child with his father, a singer/guitarist, and mother, a drummer, in the family band. They continued to work as a group until his parents' divorce, when he was seventeen; even after that Montgomery continued to perform locally with his father and brother. By his early twenties he was working as a solo act in Lexington, Kentucky, where he befriended a local bar owner who became his manager. Through showcases and demo tapes, Montgomery's music reached Atlantic Records in Nashville, and he was signed by the label in 1991.

From his debut album Montgomery's roots-country sound was a great success. Both the title track, "Life's a Dance," and the follow-up single, "I Love the Way You Love Me," were major country hits, and the album even placed in the Top 30 on the pop charts. His second album immediately went to #1 on the country charts, and produced the #1 hit "I Swear," leading to Montgomery's winning numerous awards, including Single of the Year and the Horizon Award for Best New Talent, both given by the Country Music Association.

In 1995 Montgomery underwent vocal surgery to remove a swollen gland that had troubled his singing for a few years. Afterward rumors spread that he had lost his voice, fueled by his decision to remain inactive through 1996. A few of his hits released in this period, such as "Angel in My Eyes," were said to be doctored in production to hide vocal problems. However, Montgomery returned to his usual style with his 1998 album *Leave a Mark*, with its debut single, "Love Working on You," charting in the Top 20 on the country listings. In 2000 he followed up with *Brand New Me*, which, despite its title, was pretty much the "same old" mix of ballads and up-tempo country-rockers.

A likable singer with an appreciation for traditional country vocal stylings, Montgomery will probably have a long career, even if he stops being a chart-topper, simply because of his strong audience following and his genuine vocal talent.

Select Discography

Greatest Hits, Atlantic 83060. Collects his hits from his first four albums, through 1996.

breakthrough, setting the stage for a series of Western-themed novelty numbers (including the nod to big-band sounds on "Swing Time Cowgirl"). She remained with the Ramblers through 1941, recorded sporadically as a soloist through the 1940s, and appeared on radio on the ABC network program, *Wake Up and Smile*, right after World War II. She retired from active recording and performing in the 1950s, although she continued to appear on occasion through the 1980s.

Montana's gutsy, powerful lead vocals and strident YODELING flew in the face of the stereotype that women should be demure and limit their activities to the home. Recording executives may have feared that featuring a female in a country band or as a soloist would offend listeners who were basically conservative. Montana's big hit, which had her asserting that she wanted to "rope and ride" just like her cowboy sweetheart, was as assertive in its message as its delivery. Her success paved the way for other big-throated females, particularly 1950s stars KITTY WELLS and PATSY CLINE.

MONTGOMERY, MELBA (b. Iron City, Tenn., October 14, 1938)

Montgomery is best known as a duet partner for other country artists, including GEORGE JONES and Charlie Louvin (of THE LOUVIN BROTHERS).

Born in Tennessee but raised in rural Alabama, Montgomery was introduced to music as a young girl by her father, who taught singing at her hometown's Methodist church, as well as played FIDDLE and GUITAR at parties. Along with her brothers she formed a family harmony band, performing at fairs, talent contests, and local charity events.

In the late 1950s Montgomery relocated to Nashville in search of a singing career, and won a talent contest in 1958 sponsored by WSM, the home station of THE GRAND OLE OPRY. One of the judges was ROY ACUFF, who added her to his road show. In 1962 she broke with Acuff, and a year later was linked with George Jones for a series of successful duets, beginning with "We Must Have Been Out of Our Minds" and followed in 1964 by "Let's Invite Them Over." She continued to record and perform with Jones until 1967, although she also made solo recordings with some success, including 1963's "Hall of Shame," as well as dueting with other pop and country stars, including Gene Pitney in 1966.

In the early 1970s Montgomery moved to Capitol Records, where she was paired with producer PETE DRAKE and singing partner Charlie Louvin. When Drake was invited to start a country division for the folk/rock label Elektra Records in 1973, he took Montgomery with him, and she scored her biggest solo hits under his hands, including the 1974 #1 cover of HARLAN HOWARD's "No Change," a drippy, sentimental recitation record. By 1977 the hits had dried up, but Montgomery continued to record for smaller labels into the early 1980s, scoring only sporadic success. She reunited with Louvin for some lackluster recordings in the early 1990s.

Montgomery is the ideal partner for a stronger male vocalist; her solo recordings lack enough power and presence to make them memorable, and thus she has been unable to maintain a career on her own.

Select Discography

Golden Moments, Classic World 2100. Ten-song, budget compilation of hits.

MOODY, CLYDE (b. Cherokee, N.C., September 19, 1915–April 7, 1989)

Moody, a vocalist best known for his work with the original Blue Grass Boys under BILL MONROE, gained popularity after World War II as a sentimental country crooner.

Moody got his start when he was twenty-one, performing with country bandleader J. E. MAINER, with whom he performed from 1936 to about 1938. He then moved to a more modern radio outfit, The Happy-Go-Lucky Boys with singer Jay Hugh Hall, before joining with Bill Monroe to handle lead vocal chores with the first incarnation of The Blue Grass Boys in the early 1940s. Moody contributed the traditional song "Six White Horses" to Monroe's repertoire, but left the band to work briefly with GRAND OLE OPRY star ROY ACUFF before striking out on his own. He scored hits with the fledgling King label, beginning with "Shenandoah Waltz," literally dripping with sentimental goo, followed by similar tear-dripping numbers, including "Carolina Waltz," "Next Sunday, Darling, Is My Birthday" (later covered by THE STANLEY BROTHERS), and "I Know What It Means to Be Lonesome." He spent the late 1940s through early 1950s in the Washington, D.C., area before returning to his native North Carolina, where he continued to perform and record occasionally until his death in 1989.

Select Discography

White House Blues, Rebel 1672. 1962 recordings by this country stalwart, originally issued on the Wango label.

MOONSHINE KATE (b. Rosa Lee Carson, Atlanta, Ga., 1909–1994)

BANJO and GUITAR player Rosa Lee "Moonshine Kate" Carson is best known as the accompanist for her father, FIDDLIN' JOHN CARSON. Serving as a foil to her father on a number of classic country-comedy recordings, Kate established the character of the sassy, wise-cracking mountain woman who could hold her own against her lazy, heavy-drinking father, thus setting the stage for the next generation of female country comics. Kate also made some excellent solo recordings from 1924 to 1935, with her slow, drawling, blues-influenced vocals forecasting the HONKY-TONK gals of the 1950s. Her best-known recording was of the topical ballad "Little Mary Phagan," retelling the story of the 1913 murder of an innocent factory girl, supposedly at the hands of her employer, Leo Frank. She also recorded the melodramatic "heart songs" that were a favorite part of many singers' repertoires, including "The Poor Girl's Story" and "The Lone Child." She even covered JIMMIE RODGERS's "T for Texas," complete with YODELING and fancy guitar licks, forecasting the popularity of the yodeling cowgirls of the mid-1930s and 1940s.

MOORE, "TINY" (b. Billie M., Hamilton County, Tex., May 12, 1920–December 15, 1987)

WESTERN SWING pioneer and MANDOLIN virtuoso "Tiny" Moore was "rediscovered" during the mandolin craze of the late 1970s and early 1980s.

Moore was raised in Port Arthur, Texas, and initially studied violin. He began playing mandolin after hearing Leo Raley, then mandolinist for Cliff Bruner's Western Wanderers. Raley was perhaps the first mandolinist to play an amplified instrument, inspiring "Tiny" to take up an electrified instrument. He joined the band of Western Swing pioneer BOB WILLS in 1946, remaining with him during his stay in southern California through the early 1950s. During this time he wed Dean McKinney, one half of the singing McKinney sisters who often fronted Wills's band. Working with Wills, he played a single-note style inspired by jazz guitarist Charlie Christian; he often played in close harmony with Wills's guitarist, Eldon Shamblin, who was also a Christian disciple. From 1952 to 1954, he was a member of the band of Bob's brother Billy Jack.

Around 1952 Moore purchased a five-string electric mandolin from pioneering maker Paul Bigsby. Unlike other mandolins the strings were not doubled, and the instrument included an extra bass string. The body shape was based on MERLE TRAVIS's design for an electric guitar also built by Bigsby. The sound Moore got was closer to an electric guitar than a traditional mandolin, and it became his trademark.

After working with Wills, Moore remained in southern California, opening his own music store and playing occasionally. In the 1970s avid Bob Wills fan MERLE HAGGARD brought Moore out of semiretirement for his Bob Wills tribute album. Moore subsequently joined Haggard's touring band. In 1979 Moore paired with Jethro Burns (one half of the legendary country duo HOMER AND JETHRO) for an album of jazz-flavored instrumentals; this brought him renewed attention, and he subsequently recorded a solo album. Moore remained active until his death in 1987.

Select Discography

Back to Back, Kaleidoscope F–9. With Jethro Burns; recorded in 1979.
Tiny Moore Music, Kaleidoscope F–12. Solo album from 1982.

MORGAN, GEORGE (b. G. Thomas M., Waverly, Tenn., June 28, 1924–July 7, 1975)

Morgan was a smooth-voiced country crooner and songwriter in the EDDY ARNOLD style who had his greatest successes in the late 1940s.

Morgan spent his high-school years in rural Ohio. On completing his schooling, he worked part-time as a performer while holding day jobs in truck driving and sales. After World War II he was hired as a regular vocalist on Wheeling, West Virginia's, *WWVA Jamboree* radio program, which won him the attention of Columbia Records. In 1947 they released his first re-

cording, his self-penned schmaltz classic "Candy Kisses," which raced to #1. He became a member of THE GRAND OLE OPRY in 1949, and had a few lesser follow-up hits with the equally sentimental "Rainbow in My Heart," "Room Full of Roses," and "Cry-Baby Heart."

Although he continued to be popular on radio and in personal appearances, Jones never equaled his early hitmaking days. By the mid-1960s Columbia had dropped him, and he moved to Starday, where his recordings were literally drenched in strings. By the early 1970s, he was moving from label to label, scoring a minor hit with 1973's "Red Rose from the Blue Side of Town" on MCA. In 1975, while working on the roof of his house, he suffered a heart attack, and died soon after.

His daughter, LORRIE MORGAN, who performed with her father from her early years on the *Opry*, is now a successful new-country balladeer.

Select Discography

Candy Kisses, Bear Family 158512. Everything recorded by Morgan for Columbia between 1949 and 1966 on eight CDs.
Roomful of Roses, Razor & Tie 82109. Good introduction to Morgan's hits of the 1940s and 1950s.

MORGAN, LORRIE (b. Loretta Lynn M., Nashville, Tenn., June 27, 1960)

Blond bombshell Morgan is a true daughter of Nashville (her father was country crooner GEORGE MORGAN), whose trials and tribulations in life are the stuff of country music legend. A belter of big-throated ballads and jumpy up-tempo numbers, Morgan is in danger of becoming the kind of glitzy lounge singer who ends up performing in Vegas.

A tumultuous adolescence quickly led to a singing career, first as a backup singer for GEORGE JONES's traveling company. She was briefly married to Ron Gaddis, who played steel guitar for Jones, and the two had a daughter in 1979. She found life on the road with the hard-drinkin', high-livin' Jones tough, and temporarily retired from performing. In 1984 she joined THE GRAND OLE OPRY, where she had sung as a child, and in 1987 met new-country singer KEITH WHITLEY backstage; he was to become her second husband. Whitley was a heavy drinker, and died of alcohol poisoning two years later. Ironically his death propelled Morgan to country stardom with the WEEPER "Dear Me," which in retrospect seemed to reflect her own turbulent life.

Morgan enjoyed her greatest success in the early 1990s with a series of perky up-tempo numbers and the requisite weepers. While Morgan's close-cropped bleached hair and aggressive performance style

Lorrie Morgan enjoys life, 1995. Photo: Raeanne Rubenstein

aligned her with the more progressive elements in new country, her repertoire was pretty much standard country fare. Although the lyrics to the snappy "Watch Me" tell of a brassy girl who is quite prepared to leave her two-timing boyfriend, the video for the song ends with Morgan melting in the arms of the snake. Her biggest hit was the lushly romantic "Something in Red," the kind of classic "chanteuse" number that places her squarely in the tradition of middle-of-the-road country queens like PATSY CLINE. However, her star faded beginning in the mid-1990s, although she still recorded new material. The soap opera of her life continued when she fell in love with singer SAMMY KERSHAW in the late 1990s; the duo produced a duet album in 2001.

Select Discography

Greatest Hits, BNA 66508. Her best-known recordings through 1995, which in essence amount to all of her hits to date.

MORRIS BROTHERS, THE (Wiley Andrew Morris, February 1, 1919–September 22, 1990 [gtr, voc], and Zeke Edward Morris, May 9, 1916–August 5, 1999 [mdln, voc]; both b. Old Fort, N.C.)

The Morris Brothers are a North Carolina brother act who are the "missing link" between the 1930s close-harmony acts and the BLUEGRASS bands of the later 1940s.

Elder brother Zeke first worked professionally as a guitarist and vocalist with J. E. MAINER's Mountaineers, a nostalgic country string band of the mid-1930s. He participated in the band's 1935 recording sessions, singing lead on the country best-seller "Maple on the Hill," later a bluegrass favorite. A year later he left the band with Mainer's brother Wade to form a vocal duo, and in 1937 his brother Wiley joined them to make a trio. Wiley also played GUITAR, so Zeke switched to MANDOLIN.

Later in 1937, Wade Mainer left, and was replaced by fiddler Homer "Pappy" Sherrill, and the trio became The Smiling Rangers, broadcasting out of Raleigh, North Carolina. In 1938–1939 the brothers recorded with Sherrill for the Victor budget label Bluebird, their most popular number being "Let Me Be Your Salty Dog." From 1939 to 1944, the Morrises were working out of Asheville, North Carolina; future bluegrass BANJO greats Earl Scruggs (of FLATT AND SCRUGGS) and DON RENO were among the musicians who passed through the band. Reno was only sixteen years old when he worked with the Morrises, but was already showing a distinct style that would set him apart from the dozens of Scruggs imitators in the late 1940s and early 1950s. During this period the Morrises also played in CHARLIE MONROE's band.

Briefly separating in 1944–1945, the Morrises were reunited by Victor country producer Eli Oberstein, who oversaw their last classic-period recordings in 1945. They recut "Let Me Be Your Salty Dog" as "Salty Dog Blues," and also recorded "Tragic Romance," a WEEPER that was often covered by bluegrass groups in the years to come. However, this was pretty much the end of their professional careers. In 1964 the brothers appeared at the Newport Folk Festival, having been "rediscovered" during the FOLK REVIVAL of the early 1960s. In 1972 the Morrises were lured out of retirement by the bluegrass-revival label Rounder Records, recording with old friend Homer Sherrill.

MORRIS, GARY (b. G. Gwyn M., Fort Worth, Tex., December 7, 1948)

Morris, a hunky country star of the early 1980s, has also had success as a stage and TV actor.

Classically trained as an opera singer, Morris got his musical start in the church choir before forming a

273

pop-country trio in high school; after graduation the threesome successfully auditioned for a job in a Denver country music club, where they performed for several years. In the early 1970s Morris returned to Texas, where he hooked up with pop tunesmith Lawton Williams (who wrote Bobby Helms's hit "Fraulein"), who actively promoted the singer's career. Williams was active in the presidential campaign of Jimmy Carter, and arranged for Morris to perform at Carter rallies; this led to a performance at the White House in 1978, followed by some demo recordings for MCA, and finally a contract with Warner Brothers in 1980 under the hands of producer Norro Wilson.

Morris's greatest success came in the early 1980s, beginning with 1981's COUNTRYPOLITAN ditty "Headed for a Heartache," through 1983's "Velvet Chains," and then a string of #1 country hits beginning with "Baby Bye-Bye" in 1985 and its follow-up, the R&B-flavored "I'll Never Stop Loving You." In 1984 Morris appeared off-Broadway, costarring with LINDA RONSTADT in an updated version of Puccini's *La Bohème*; he asked Ronstadt to record "Makin' Up for Lost Time," a song he wrote with Dave Loggins, as a duet with him, but since she was signed to another label, the record was eventually made with his labelmate, CRYSTAL GAYLE, producing a 1986 #1 hit. Although Gayle had recorded her part separately from Morris and had never met the singer, the success of this song led a year later to their recording an album of duets.

Morris's TV career blossomed in 1986, when he was hired to portray a blind country singer in several episodes of ABC's soap-sudsy *Dynasty II: The Colbys*; on the show he premiered his last #1 single, 1987's "Leave Me Lonely," from his album *Plain Brown Wrapper*, a more simplified, roots-oriented effort than his earlier Nashville-pop work. Later that year he appeared in the Broadway production of *Les Miserables*. He continues to perform on THE GRAND OLE OPRY and to tour; his country recording career fizzled out in the late 1980s, although he has continued to record.

Select Discography

Greatest Hits, Vols. 1 & 2, Warner Bros. 25581/26305.

MULESKINNER (1973: David Grisman [mdln, voc]; Peter Rowan [gtr, voc]; Clarence White [gtr]; Richard Greene [fdl]; Bill Keith [bnj])

One of the first revival BLUEGRASS "supergroups," Muleskinner lasted only long enough to appear on a single TV special and make one album, but was quite influential on the growth of PROGRESSIVE BLUEGRASS.

All of the group's members had originally performed in bluegrass bands: PETER ROWAN, RICHARD GREENE, and BILL KEITH were early 1960s alumni of BILL MONROE's band; White had been a founding

member of THE KENTUCKY COLONELS; and DAVID GRISMAN, a founding member of The New York Ramblers, as well as performing with RED ALLEN and DEL MCCOURY. In the mid-to-late 1960s and early 1970s, they had all pursued different musical directions, with Keith joining Jim Kweskin's Jug Band and The Blue Velvet Band (a country ensemble led by Boston folkie JIM ROONEY), White playing lead guitar for THE BYRDS, Greene fiddling with the rock-jazz fusion band Seatrain, and Grisman and Rowan forming the progressive rock band Earth Opera. Muleskinner was their first "return" to their bluegrass roots.

The band was formed at the invitation of a California public television station that had booked BILL MONROE's Blue Grass Boys and wanted to have a young band as a second act to provide a "fathers and sons" angle to the show. Their performance was so successful that they were given a one-record deal with Warner Brothers; this album was reissued several times through the 1970s and 1980s, influencing subsequent generations of bluegrass pickers. Besides reworkings of traditional material, it featured the first appearance on record of a David Grisman original composition as well as Rowan's unique original songs. (His "Blue Mule" is a retelling of the traditional "Molly and Tenbrooks" story, this time with Molly beating her opponent by flying into outer space.) The album also introduced Clarence White's excellent acoustic-guitar picking to a new generation (his earlier bluegrass recordings were virtually unavailable at the time).

Although the band never toured, band members (with the exception of White, who was killed in a hit-and-run accident soon after) have reunited from time to time. The record set the stage for 1980s and 1990s bluegrass supergroups with various members, as well as forecasting the blend of rock, jazz, and bluegrass that would become known as progressive bluegrass (or newgrass).

Select Discography

Muleskinner, Warner Bros. 2787. The 1973 album.
Live: Original Television Soundtrack, Sierra 6001. Not the album that made them famous, but the actual sound track from the local public television program that was the impetus for forming the band.

MULLICAN, MOON (b. Aubrey Wilson M., near Corrigan, Tex., March 29, 1909–January 1, 1967)

Mullican, one of the first great HONKY-TONK songsters and pianists, had a swinging style that influenced an entire generation of keyboard ticklers, particularly the Ferriday Fireball, JERRY LEE LEWIS.

Raised in a religious household, Mullican began his keyboard career playing the family's pump organ, although his secular bluesy style was not pleasing to his fundamentalist family. Around age twenty-one he worked his way to the Houston area, where he was a pianist in several unsavory nightspots, earning the nickname "Moon" because he worked all night and slept all day. He soon was leading his own band, performing throughout the Louisiana-Texas area, and by the end of the 1930s was also working with several prominent WESTERN SWING ensembles, most notably one led by swinging fiddler Cliff Bruner, as well as performing on radio out of Beaumont, Texas. In 1939 he made his way to Hollywood to appear in the "classic" film *Village Barn Dance*, and began performing in the Los Angeles area.

Returning to Texas in the 1940s, Mullican continued to perform and opened his own nightclubs in Beaumont and Port Arthur. His big break on the country charts came in 1947 with his cover of the CAJUN classic "Jole Blon" on the King label, called "New Jolie Blon." He had a series of hits on King with folk and boogie numbers, including a cover of Leadbelly's "Goodnight, Irene" (popularized by the FOLK-REVIVAL group The Weavers on mainstream radio) and his own "Cherokee Boogie," written with W. C. Redbird.

Mullican stayed with King through 1956, although the hits pretty much dried up in the early 1950s; still, his recordings featured many of the greatest hillbilly jazz pickers, including steel guitarist SPEEDY WEST and fiddler JIMMY BRYANT, running the gamut from hanky-soakin' WEEPERS to upbeat country to full-fledged rock and roll. When he signed with Decca and came under the hands of producer OWEN BRADLEY, the quality of his recordings suffered greatly, because Bradley tried to mold him into just another mainstream Nashville act. (Bradley later admitted that he just didn't know what to do with Mullican.) Mullican continued to broadcast and perform through the 1960s, and died of a heart attack in 1967.

Although there had been other, earlier Western Swing pianists who blended blues and jazz influences into the country mix, Mullican combined a bluesy vocal style and a great command of piano styles into his playing, as well as a unique performing personality. He was the first pianist to really stand out from the pack, and as such was highly influential on the next generation of performers.

Select Discography

Showboy Special, West Side 800. His first recordings for King cut in 1946, mixing Western Swing with honky-tonk weepers.
Moonshine Jamboree, Ace 458. 1946–1954 King recordings, a great introduction to Mullican's best work.
Sings His All-Time Hits, King 555. Various recordings from the King archives.

MURPHEY, MICHAEL MARTIN (b. Dallas, Tex., March 13, 1945)

SINGER/SONGWRITER Murphey has always showed a strong affinity for COWBOY material and, since 1990, has recorded primarily traditional and newly composed songs celebrating life on the range.

Born in urban Texas, Murphey was educated at UCLA, and quickly became part of the burgeoning California folk-rock scene. He was a member of the COUNTY-ROCK band The Lewis and Clark Expedition, scoring minor success on the pop charts, while his songs were recorded by diverse southern California groups including THE NITTY GRITTY DIRT BAND and TV's The Monkees. Returning to Texas in 1971, Murphey scored his first hit with "Geronimo's Cadillac" in 1972, an Indian rights anthem. Four years later he had his biggest successes on the pop-rock charts with "Wildfire" and "Carolina in the Pines," followed by country hits with "Cherokee Fiddle" and "A Mansion on the Hill" in 1977. In 1978 he settled on a ranch in Taos, New Mexico, a move furthering his interest in songs of the West.

In the 1980s Murphey charted primarily as a country singer/songwriter, beginning with 1982's "What's Forever For" through a number of other love-gone-wrong hits, including "Will It Be Love by Morning," "I'm Gonna Miss You, Girl," and "Talkin' to the Wrong Man." Unlike the other Texas OUTLAWS, Murphey's songs were fairly accessible, not delving into the deep metaphysics of JIMMIE DALE GILMORE or the hard rock of STEVE EARLE.

In 1990 Murphey recorded his first all-cowboy song album, including such venerable old chestnuts as "Home on the Range," "When the Work's All Done This Fall," and "Old Chisholm Trail," combined with newer hippie-cowboy anthems like Ian Tyson's "Cowboy Pride." This album was the first in a trilogy of releases for Murphey, all in the cowboy vein. The albums have become increasingly bombastic; while still including old chestnuts from the cowboy songbook, Murphey has introduced his own epic-length songs—including on his 1993 album a seven-minute retelling of the life of Belle Starr. This album also features an annoying tribute to MARTY ROBBINS, featuring a "duet" with Robbins on "Big Iron" (his 1960 pseudo-cowboy hit) created through the miracle of overdubbing. (Robbins has moved on to the great cow palace in the sky.) Murphey has also been the moving force behind West Fest, an annual cowboy song/story gathering.

For fans of the myth of the West as much as the starker reality, Murphey offers a nostalgic re-creation of the old days when men were men and cows were cows. If you drive a Jeep Wrangler but live in Scarsdale, you should keep a Murphey tape handy when you hit the ol' Chisholm Trail.

Select Discography

Best of Country, Curb 77336. His early-to-mid-1970s hits.

Cowboy Songs, Warner Bros. 26308. 1990 album of horsy favorites.

MURPHY, JIMMY (b. Republic, Ala., October 11, 1925–June 1, 1981)

Murphy was a country-blues and ROCKABILLY SINGER/SONGWRITER whose unique GUITAR style and often tongue-in-cheek songs are some of the most unusual in postwar country music. Despite a lack of commercial success, Murphy's recordings have become prized collectors' items, and his 1978 "comeback" LP, one of the best of the country-music revival.

Murphy, the son of a coal miner, was exposed early on to the music of THE GRAND OLE OPRY and classic blues performers like Blind Boy Fuller and Leadbelly through 78 recordings. He learned to play the GUITAR from local musician Bee Coleman, who showed him an open E tuning that was ideally suited to the blues. (Coleman's father recorded country blues under the name Dutch Coleman in the late 1920s and returned to recording in the 1950s, now focusing on GOSPEL material.) Murphy first performed on radio in Birmingham, Alabama, and then, after finishing school, joined his father as an apprentice bricklayer. Sometime around 1950 he arrived in Knoxville, where he eventually ended up as a featured performer on the local radio station's *The Midday Merry-Go-Round*. About the same time he was introduced to CHET ATKINS, who arranged for his first recordings for RCA.

Murphy's recordings were unique among postwar records in that they featured just his bluesy guitar with the accompaniment of Anita Carter on bass and background vocals. They also were made up of his own compositions, which had unusual themes (aging, wayward children) and imagery. For instance his song "Electricity" is a fast-moving blues with lyrics that compare the power of God's love to the invisible force of electrification.

Murphy's 1951–1952 recordings for RCA were unsuccessful, and he did not return to the studio until 1955, when he recorded some new compositions in a rockabilly style for Columbia, including his take on the classic "Sixteen Tons," renamed "Sixteen Tons Rock and Roll" (with the immortal chorus "Go, cats, go, dig that coal!"). These records also failed in the marketplace, and although Murphy continued to perform on radio and to appear locally, his recordings were more sporadic through the late 1950s and 1960s.

Musicologist Richard K. Spottswood rediscovered Murphy in 1976 when he was assembling a set of recordings for the Smithsonian in honor of the bicentennial. He arranged for the recordings that were issued by bluegrass revival label Sugar Hill in 1978 that brought Murphy back into the limelight. These sensitively produced sessions (produced by RICKY SKAGGS) introduced a new generation to Murphy's dry vocals, hot guitar licks, and unique songs.

Murphy disappeared again after making his "comeback," preferring to avoid even the margins of the mainstream musical world for a life of day labor and part-time music making. His recordings remain a provocative indication of the direction postwar country could have taken had the Nashville A&R men stuck closer to the roots of the country sound.

Select Discography

Electricity, Sugar Hill 3702. Out-of-print, fine album; reissued briefly on CD.

MURRAY, ANNE (b. Spring Hill, Nova Scotia, June 20, 1945)

Canada's gift to Nashville-pop, Murray is one of those smooth-voiced crooners who combines good-girl looks with golly-gosh material, making her a consistent country as well as pop hitmaker.

Murray was raised in the coal mining/fishing village of Spring Hill, Nova Scotia, where country music was fairly typical radio fare, although her mother and father preferred the light pop of Perry Como and Rosemary Clooney, which perhaps explains Anne's later affinity for similar music. She began singing pop and folk music in high school, although she didn't intend to pursue a musical career; instead she enrolled in teachers college, majoring in physical education. However, she continued to perform in local clubs and auditioned for local TV programs, including the popular folk-pop show, *Sing Along Jubilee*. Although her initial audition in 1964 was a failure, producer and cohost William Langstroth was sufficiently impressed to invite her to audition again two years later, when she finally made the mark. She remained with the show for four years.

Another producer associated with the show, Brian Ahern (who would later produce EMMYLOU HARRIS's successful 1970s recordings), encouraged her to pursue a full-time musical career, and produced her first album for the Canadian Arc label in 1968. Canadian Capitol was impressed, and signed her to a contract in 1969; its U.S. sister label picked up her single, "Snowbird," which became a U.S. gold record in 1970.

Capitol immediately brought her to Los Angeles, and vigorously promoted and showcased her as a pop recording star. But the hits dried up for a while, and Murray felt somewhat lost in the big California city. In 1973 she finally returned to the pop charts with a cover of Kenny Loggins's "Danny's Song," and a year later had her first country hit, again produced by Ahern, a cover of DICKEY LEE's "He Thinks I Still

A young Anne Murray, c. mid-1970s. Photo: Raeanne Rubenstein

Care" (originally a 1962 hit for GEORGE JONES). Murray had learned this song during her *Sing Along Jubilee* days, and recorded it as something of an afterthought; it established her as a country star.

In the mid-1970s Murray tired of the endless touring and decided to wed longtime friend William Langstroth and retire for a while. Although Capitol had plenty of material in the can, Murray actually did little recording until she returned from her self-imposed exile in 1978. She made a big splash on pop and country charts with the cloyingly sentimental "You Needed Me," following it with a #1 country hit with a cover of "I Just Fall in Love Again." Now working with mainstream country producer Jim Ed Norman, Murray churned out the hits in the late 1970s and early 1980s, including 1980's "Could I Have this Dance?" featured in the film *Urban Cowboy*, which launched an early-1980s country music renaissance. Murray became one of the most popular of the early 1980s divas, even

though her musical output was no more "country" than it was "easy listening." She gained further attention with her 1983 hit "A Little Good News," which pleased such political conservatives as Vice President George H. W. Bush, who quoted from its lyrics during campaign speeches.

In 1986 Murray decided to move in a more pop-oriented direction, working with new producer David Foster (known for his middle-of-the-road production style). Despite this attempt to storm up the pop charts, Murray scored another country #1 with "Now and Forever (You and Me)" from these sessions. A follow-up album continued with this new emphasis on mainstream pop, but Murray managed to alienate her core country audience while failing to cross over into the more lucrative mainstream market. Murray had one final hit in 1990, "Feed This Fire," a surprise Top 10 country song, and then performed primarily on the country fair and Vegas circuit. In the later 1990s, she turned to performing religious and inspirational material.

Select Discography

The Best . . . So Far, Capitol 31158. Twenty-song collection of hits.
What A Wonderful World, StraightWay 20231. 1999 two-CD set of inspirational/religious songs.

MUSIC PUBLISHING In the music business the owners of song copyrights often make more money than the composers or performers. Publishers play a key role in promoting individual songs because they make their livelihood from the income that these songs generate. Also, the publishers are a key element of two very powerful groups—ASCAP (The American Society of Composers, Artists, and Publishers) and BMI (Broadcast Music, Inc.)—that regulate the performance of music.

Music publishing's profitability is based on the ability to copyright a song as an original creation. In early country music, much of which was based on folk sources, many musicians would claim to have "written" songs that clearly were performed long before they were on the scene. For folk or traditional material, there were few people who could legitimately complain, although competing versions of the same song would occasionally raise a copyright storm. This was further complicated by the age-old music-industry practice of bandleaders claiming to have "written" any song developed by band members, as well as agents, managers, DJs, and others claiming "pieces" of a song in order to promote it. Publishers were not above giving themselves coauthor credit as a means of siphoning off royalties.

Recording executives often encouraged performers to bring "original" material to sessions. A. P. Carter of THE CARTER FAMILY seemed to have few qualms about claiming songs like "Bury Me Beneath the Willow" or "Storms Are on the Ocean," which have traditional roots, as "original" works. The notion of "composing" a song may have been different among traditional performers, who felt that by changing a song to suit their particular style or delivery—or perhaps by introducing different verses, melodies, or harmonies—they were creating a "new" composition. Record company executives didn't make any real attempt to verify such claims, because it was usually in their interest to release "new" material.

Record producer RALPH PEER, who was key in discovering many early country performers, was also a savvy businessman. He encouraged his artists to perform their "own" material—or at least to perform standards that they could claim as their own. His deal with Victor Records allowed him to own the music publishing rights for his artists' works, and thus he formed Southern Music in 1928. When Victor realized how Peer was profiting from this arrangement, they complained to him; subsequently he sold Southern to Victor, but by the early 1930s had purchased it back (after leaving the label). Southern's catalog is rich in classic country material from this era.

However, country publishing really took off in 1940, when radio broadcasters got into a war with the music licensing firm, ASCAP, which wanted to increase fees for performance of its material over the air. A rival organization, BMI, was formed, and soon was aggressively signing country songwriters (previously unwelcome in ASCAP). Peer formed Peer International to be his BMI link, keeping Southern Music as an ASCAP-affiliated firm.

Performer ROY ACUFF and his manager FRED ROSE were the next major players in the music-publishing business. They formed Acuff-Rose in 1942 to work with the newly formed BMI. Six years later they came up with a unique arrangement to benefit country songwriters; Acuff-Rose would give a portion of its BMI income to the writers themselves, and BMI would reimburse them. Known as the "Nashville Plan," it helped make it possible for many songwriters to support themselves.

The second major player after World War II was Hill and Range Songs, formed in 1944. Owned by the Aberbach brothers, who had previously worked with Chappell Music, the firm initially made its mark in the popular COWBOY genre. The firm came up with a unique arrangement to attract talent; they would give large advances to songwriters and form subsidiary firms "co-owned" by the publishing firm and the composer. Most major Nashville artists were interested in what promised to be a more profitable arrangement, and Hill and Range developed a roster that was a vir-

tual Who's Who of 1950s country. The company reached the height of its power in 1955 with the signing of ELVIS PRESLEY, which directly led to RCA's signing him to record. RCA benefited from the Aberbachs' considerable clout in promoting Presley; Hill and Range benefited by having primarily songs it controlled recorded by the new hip-swiveling sensation.

In 1953 Cedarwood Publishing was established, one of the first to open its doors on Music Row. It was the brainchild of JIM DENNY, who had been the longtime manager at THE GRAND OLE OPRY, and singer WEBB PIERCE, who wanted to control his own songs. Like Peer at Victor, Denny was criticized for operating the publishing firm by his employers at the *Opry*, who feared he was favoring his own acts. In response Denny left the *Opry* in 1956, and added a booking agency to Cedarwood's publishing operations. When Denny died in 1963, the company was taken over by his sons, who ran it for the next two decades. Cedarwood employed a stable of songwriters to supply it with hits through the 1960s, including JOHN D. LOUDERMILK, CARL PERKINS, and MEL TILLIS (Tillis purchased the catalog from the Denny family in 1983), among many others. Its back catalog is now controlled by PolyGram Music.

Another ex-WSM employee, Jack Stapp, was the founder of Tree International in 1951, with bankrolling by CBS quiz-show producer Lou Cowan. (Cowan sold his interest to Stapp in 1956 when he was promoted at CBS.) Two years later Stapp hired Buddy Killen to serve as a song scout; among their signings was Mae Axton, who wrote the song "Heartbreak Hotel," a major hit in 1956 for Elvis Presley. The next key signing came two years later, when songwriter ROGER MILLER joined the firm. He would become a major hitmaker in the early-through-mid-1960s. Cementing its powerful position in Nashville, the publisher moved to quarters on Music Row in 1964. Tree began aggressively purchasing other catalogs, first Pamper Music in 1969, and would continue to buy other firms until it owned over fifty lists. In 1980 Killen became full owner of Tree following Stapp's death, and nine years later sold to Sony Music.

As country grew, more publishers came on the scene, often founded by a songwriter seeking independence and greater financial stability, and bankrolled by businessmen. Pamper Music was formed in 1959 by popular country artist RAY PRICE, his manager Hal Smith, and businessman Claude Caviness. Located outside of Nashville in rural Goodlettsville, the firm hired HANK COCHRAN to be its manager for songwriters a year after its birth. In 1961 WILLIE NELSON was signed as a songwriter, and a year later HARLAN HOWARD; both would provide classic country hits through the 1960s. The firm was purchased in 1969 by Tree International.

In 1963 publishing executive Al Gallico formed his own music publishing company in Nashville, after having run Painted Desert Music (a Nashville-based subsidiary of the pop publishers Shapiro-Bernstein). He brought with him songwriter MERLE KILGORE, and the two formed partnerships with other Nashville players, including songwriter/producer BILLY SHERRILL, who would become a major power at Epic Records in the late 1960s–early 1970s. With Gallico, Sherrill formed Algee for his own songs and Altam, with additional partner TAMMY WYNETTE, for material that she recorded. Meanwhile, many members of Gallico's stable of songwriters became stars as recording artists, including JOE STAMPLEY, DAVID HOUSTON, and JOHN ANDERSON. Gallico's major holdings are now owned by EMI Publishing.

New-country and "alternative" country have brought new publishers into the field, some of which do not focus solely on country music. One of the most aggressive is Bug Music of Los Angeles, which was founded in 1975 by Del Shannon's then-manager Dan Bourgoise. In 1985 they opened their first Nashville office, and signed SINGER/SONGWRITER John Prine; younger songwriters like JOHN HIATT, ROSANNE CASH, and NANCI GRIFFITH would follow.

N

NASHVILLE Although today recognized as the capital of country music, Nashville was only one of many centers of country performance prior to World War II. With the exception of THE GRAND OLE OPRY, the country music industry had no real presence in the city before the late 1940s. Only a combination of geography and luck made Nashville the important center it has become today.

While there were many other "barn dance" RADIO shows, the *Opry* grew into a powerful outlet in the 1930s thanks to the strength of its Artists Bureau, which served as a clearinghouse for booking members' acts. Nashville's central position in the South—with its proximity to the rich musical regions of North Carolina, Kentucky, and rural Tennessee—also helped establish it as a center for music making. However, through the 1930s only one recording session by Victor had been held in the city, as opposed to the dozens or more that were held in Atlanta, Chicago, Dallas, and other major centers.

After the war a number of factors came together to make Nashville a candidate for country recording. The formation of BMI in 1940 led to a new interest in musical styles not already dominated by the older ASCAP organization, including country music and blues. The introduction of a "Country and Western" chart in *Billboard* helped draw attention to the popularity of the music.

Savvy country performers, like ROY ACUFF, were beginning to recognize the value in their music and taking steps toward forming MUSIC-PUBLISHING firms; Acuff-Rose was among the first, formed in 1942. And the labels themselves were looking for a place where a stable of talented musicians could be found to serve as accompanists.

WSM, the station that broadcast the *Opry*, had a financial stake in seeing the program remain successful. In stiff competition during the 1930s with Chicago's NATIONAL BARN DANCE and then, beginning in 1948, with the LOUISIANA HAYRIDE out of Shreveport, the station hoped to establish its program as the premier the country showcase. In 1950 a WSM announcer coined the phrase "Music City U.S.A." to describe the town, and the name stuck. Although there were yet to be many music companies active in the town, by the mid-1950s the "Music City" nickname had taken on a life of its own, appearing in trade publications and in chamber of commerce press releases. By staking claim to this title, Nashville willed itself to become a major player in the industry.

The center of music making in Nashville from a commercial standpoint is Music Row, the small, tree-lined neighborhood located about two miles from downtown. Originally a neighborhood of well-to-do lawyers and doctors, by the mid-twentieth century its mansions were in disrepair, with many converted to inexpensive boardinghouses. It took OWEN BRADLEY and his brother Harold to recognize the neighborhood's potential (and dirt-cheap commercial land); they opened their first studio there, and convinced Decca Records to let them be their house studio. The Bradleys first opened their studio in a renovated home, but then purchased an Army-surplus Quonset hut for $7500, originally placing it behind their main property to use as an ancillary facility for sound-track work. However, they found the hut had excellent acoustics, and the building became a legendary recording center.

In 1957 RCA opened their legendary Studio B on Music Row along with their Nashville headquarters. (The studio remained in operation for two decades, then was taken over by the Country Music Foundation and transformed into a museum.) Five years later Columbia purchased the Bradleys' Quonset hut and surrounding properties for their studios. By 1963 one trade publication estimated that half of all recording in the U.S. was being done in Nashville. With the other major labels quickly moving to the area, it made sense for music publishers and talent agencies to follow suit, so they could be near the center of the action. BMI and SESAC (Society of European Stage Actors and Composers), two major country-music licensing agencies, also moved to the neighborhood for the same reason. And the area's importance was cemented in 1967 when the Country Music Hall of Fame opened on its northern end. Still, Music Row was limited to modest, two- or three-story buildings until the mid-1970s, when the first modern office towers were built.

After decades of neglect, downtown Nashville began to enjoy a renaissance in the later 1980s and early 1990s. The old Ryman Auditorium, which had been the principal home of *The Grand Ole Opry* until 1974, when Opryland, U.S.A. was opened outside of town, was renovated and reopened for concerts and performances. The venerable Hatch Show Print, the country's last wood-block printer of advertising materials, was purchased by the Country Music Foundation and maintained as a working business/museum. And in 2000 the Country Music Hall of Fame and Museum opened a lavish new exhibition space and library downtown. (Its space on Music Row had long been coveted by its neighbor, BMI.)

Although Music Row is the center of the music business in Nashville, it is not the center of music performance. Several clubs have played important roles in the town's history. Among the most venerable is Tootsie's Orchid Lounge, a downtown watering hole that was purchased by Hattie Louise "Tootsie" Bess in 1960. Located across the back alley from the Ryman, it attracted a crowd of *Opry* performers and would-be performers. The Lounge is famous for its crowded wall of framed photographs that runs behind the bar, and its general seedy atmosphere. However, when the *Opry* moved in 1974, the Lounge suffered along with the rest of downtown; Tootsie died in 1978, and the property went through several hands. During the mid-1990s downtown revival the bar became a popular performance spot, helping to launch new-country artists like TERRI CLARK and the early versions of the retro country band, BR4-59.

Another downtown institution is Robert's Western Wear. Actually a clothing store, in the later 1990s it began featuring performances by BR4-59, among others. These concerts helped launch the group's career, and also brought new pedestrian traffic to the area known as Printers' Alley, a historic area that had fallen into disrepair.

For several decades Nashville's premier BLUEGRASS club has been the Station Inn. For many years the house band was led by Roland White, the ex-KENTUCKY COLONELS mandolinist who has made Nashville his home. Located near Vanderbilt University, the club has drawn a more upscale, educated audience typical of the bluegrass revival.

The most important club for new country has been the Bluebird Café. Opened in 1982 and located (improbably) in a strip mall well outside of the central district, the club became the premier showcase for new-country artists. In 1987 a group of young songwriters including DON SCHLITZ and his partner, PAUL OVERSTREET, began a series of informal, round-robin concerts there where performers would sit in a circle and swap songs. About a year and a half later PAM TILLIS organized a similar night for female performers. Since then the café has become a popular place to showcase new performers, thanks to its small, intimate atmosphere. Performers who got their start there range from KATHY MATTEA and The Indigo Girls to GARTH BROOKS.

Only a few miles from downtown lies the mammoth Opryland U.S.A. complex, a combination *Grand Ole Opry* concert hall/shopping mall/conference center/office complex/golf course. Owned and operated by Gaylord Entertainment, the complex has become a major tourist attraction, although many criticize it for its overt commercialism. The original Opryland U.S.A. theme park, opened in 1974, was shut down in 1997 and remade into Opry Mills, a shopping mall with a few rides (including a paddle-wheel steamboat attraction). Gaylord runs its radio and TV operations from the complex, although it sold off its major cable holdings (TNN/CMT) to CBS (now CBS/Viacom) the same year the theme park was closed.

The premier country museum and center of academic study is the Country Music Hall of Fame and Museum. In 1964 the Country Music Association (CMA), a group of radio broadcasters determined to promote country music, formed a spin-off organization, the Country Music Foundation (CMF), as a nonprofit organization with the express purpose of promoting the study of country music. In 1967, when the CMA opened the Country Music Hall of Fame, the CMF finally came into its own, operating a library and mounting exhibits in the museum. The museum was expanded several times, but because of the need for additional exhibition and library space, a new building was planned and opened in 2000 in downtown Nashville. The museum's collection includes everything from historic musical instruments to a large collection of recordings to cars and NUDIE suits. When its new building opened, CMT began broadcasting its *Total Request Live* program from its glass-walled lobby.

NASHVILLE BLUEGRASS BAND (1984–present)

This group of players has been together for over a decade and a half, playing traditional-style BLUEGRASS.

The original group was centered on the vocals of Pat Enright (GUITAR) and Alan O'Bryant (BANJO). Specializing in performing straight-ahead bluegrass, they were augmented by the BILL MONROE-influenced MANDOLIN playing of Mike Compton. The final original band member was bassist Mark Hembree. Soon after they formed, fiddler Stuart Duncan joined, making the group a quintet.

The group became quite popular on the bluegrass circuit, thanks to a repertoire that focused on traditional and contemporary songs (including some strong originals) performed in a style that was strongly rooted in tradition while still having a contemporary edge. With a repertoire of a cappella GOSPEL numbers and strong instrumentals, the group became the premier "young" bluegrass band of the 1980s.

In 1988 an accident while on tour left bass player Hembree injured; he and Compton left the band soon after. Compton was replaced by legendary mandolinist Roland White, of THE KENTUCKY COLONELS and, more recently, COUNTRY GAZETTE. The new bass player was Gene Libea. During the 1990s the band's reputation grew, and individual band members—particularly Stuart Duncan—became in-demand session players for mainstream country acts. The band won several International Bluegrass Music Association honors, and their albums have been nominated for several Grammys. In early 2000 Roland White retired from the band, and Mike Compton filled his shoes. They continue to record and tour in the new century.

Select Discography

Waiting for the Hard Times to Go, Sugar Hill 3809. 1993 album that combines contemporary and traditional bluegrass songs and stylings.

NASHVILLE SOUND, THE (c. 1957–1970)

In an attempt to "broaden" the appeal of country music, several producers—mostly notably CHET ATKINS and OWEN BRADLEY—developed a more pop-oriented style of recording that almost completely eliminated traditional country instrumentation and molded the careers of singers away from a country or HONKYTONK orientation to a more bland, middle-of-the-road repertoire of pop ballads (for men) and tearjerkers (for women).

In the mid-1950s there was some embarrassment among younger Nashville-based musicians with the "old-fashioned" musical styles and hillbilly routines employed by older acts. They thought the clichéd image of the FIDDLE-sawing, BANJO-whomping backwoodsman was holding back country music; many were more interested in playing jazz, which they felt was a more "progressive" musical style. A leader of this movement was Chet Atkins, whose elder brother was a talented jazz guitarist and who himself had a great love for the chamber-styled jazz that was popular in the 1950s. An informal group of musicians began

jamming with Atkins at the Carousel Club in Nashville to play this wedding of Nat King Cole and Dave Brubeck-styled jazz, including pianist FLOYD CRAMER, sax master "BOOTS" RANDOLPH, Bob Moore on bass, and BUDDY HARMAN on drums. Because Atkins was working as assistant head of A&R at RCA (he became head of the country division in 1957), the leading Nashville studio, he was in a position to hire these musicians for session work; Cramer was particularly popular, playing piano on hundreds of sessions, including accompanying ELVIS PRESLEY on classics like "Heartbreak Hotel." Along with this "modern," light-jazz-styled instrumentation, Atkins introduced vocal choruses, particularly the JORDANAIRES and the ANITA KERR Singers, again to soften the rough edges of country recordings.

In a similar move producer Owen Bradley worked through the 1950s at Decca to change country music into a more popular style. His biggest achievement was in molding the career of singer PATSY CLINE, who started out as a big-lunged honky-tonker but was transformed into the kind of dreamy, pop chanteuse that makes middle-aged men's hearts go pitty-pat. Cline hated the more pop-oriented material, but her cold-as-ice, gliding vocals became the model for hundreds of future country singers, who gave up the old mountain dew for the bubbly champagne of mainstream pop.

Nashville had become a professional music-making center by the early 1960s. Slews of session musicians prided themselves on their ability to accompany anybody, and thus to sound like nobody. Although some developed a distinctive style (such as Cramer's "slip-note" piano playing), the emphasis was on a homogenized, one-sound-fits-all style of playing that was bound to take the character out of the music. Plus, with the advent of large MUSIC-PUBLISHING houses (beginning with Acuff-Rose), Nashville became the last bastion of professional songwriting, a Tin Pan Alley of the South. Unlike folk and rock, which were moving toward songwriters performing their own material (and becoming stars), in country the music was still dominated by "professionals" who carefully molded the music to fit the often conservative audience.

Naturally, as country instrumentation was eliminated, the repertoire was watered down until country acts were covering the same kind of lame, mainstream pop that dominated the white-bread charts of the 1950s and early 1960s. Pretty soon you couldn't tell JIM REEVES from Perry Como, and if you could, who cared? When THE BROWNS hit the country charts singing the Edith Piaf remake "Les Trois Cloches" (The Three Bells), the spirit of HANK WILLIAMS was surely grieving in his grave. Although Atkins always argued that the Nashville sound was a compromise, a way of preserving country music during a time when its popularity was in decline, it is undoubtedly his greatest sin against the music. It was up to a select band of pioneers—like BILL MONROE in BLUEGRASS and the renegade ROCKABILLY stars like CARL PERKINS and JERRY LEE LEWIS—to keep the true spirit of country alive during the dark days of the Nashville Sound.

The Nashville Sound naturally matured into the 1970s phenomenon known as COUNTRYPOLITAN, where middle-of-the-road pop music flooded the country charts.

NATIONAL BARN DANCE (1924–1971)

The *National Barn Dance* was the first successful country music program, beating THE GRAND OLE OPRY to the airwaves by a year. The *Barn Dance* was most successful in the 1930s, and spawned a slew of talented performers.

The first show was broadcast on April 19, 1924, over the Sears, Roebuck & Company's Chicago-based station, WLS (named for Sears's slogan, "World's Largest Store"). The first program was an experiment, and simply featured a fiddler and square-dance caller, literally re-creating a Saturday night barn dance. Listener reaction was very positive, and the show was off and running; one of its first announcers was GEORGE D. HAY, later the founding genius behind the *Opry*.

The show expanded to over five hours by 1928, when Sears sold the station to Burridge D. Butler, owner of an agricultural newspaper, *The Prairie Farmer*. The show became a cornerstone of the station's broadcast, reflecting Butler's down-home philosophy and conservative, Midwestern values. In 1931 he was able to increase the station's power to 50,000 watts, which effectively meant its signal blanketed the midsection of the country.

Two years later the NBC "blue" network picked up national syndication rights, and the show became *The National Barn Dance*. A new stomach-soothing product with the unusual name of Alka-Seltzer was the show's sponsor, and it soon became as successful as the fiddlers, comedians, and singers. Star names of the 1930s included COWBOY crooners GENE AUTRY, RED FOLEY, and PATSY MONTANA; the comic novelty act THE HOOSIER HOT SHOTS; and more traditional singers like LULU BELLE AND SCOTTY. The show had a more contemporary sound in its heyday than did the *Opry*; this made it tremendously successful for a while, but when tastes changed, listeners left. The brains behind the show's 1930s success was performer/producer JOHN LAIR, who left (along with popular star Red Foley) to found the *Renfro Valley Barn Dance* in 1937.

From 1946 to 1949 the show went sponsorless and dropped off national radio. It picked up a new sponsor in 1949, and continued on the national airwaves through WLS's sale in 1960, when the station was converted to a teen-pop format. The cast moved to competitor WGN soon after, and a companion syndicated TV show went on the air in 1964. However, by about 1971 the *Barn Dance* was no more, a victim of changing tastes.

Although the *Barn Dance* was the first, it was never able to grow beyond its 1930s success in promoting smooth-voiced cowboy acts. Unlike the *Opry*, which expanded into a multimillion-dollar business, the owners of the *Barn Dance* did not expand their empire into other areas, such as music publishing or tourism. And after World War II, Chicago ceased being a center of country-music performance, while Nashville rose to become the music's capital.

NELSON, KEN (b. Kenneth F. N., Caledonia, Minn., January 19, 1911)

Nelson is a country producer best remembered for his work with the Capitol label in the 1950s and 1960s.

The Nelson family moved to Chicago when Ken was a young boy. At age twelve he became a stockboy at Chicago's Melrose Music Company, working there for five years. He then was an announcer at several Chicago radio stations. He made his reputation not in country but as the chief announcer for the Chicago Symphony Orchestra. However, like most radio employees of the day, he had to wear many hats, and found himself put in charge of his station's *Suppertime Frolic* show, a competitor to the very successful NATIONAL BARN DANCE. As a talent scout for the program, he became well acquainted with the best country stars. He also befriended Lee Gillette, who would join the fledgling Capitol label after World War II.

Gillette recommended Nelson to his Capitol bosses, and Nelson moved to Hollywood to work for the label in 1946. In December 1951 he produced HANK THOMPSON's megahit, "The Wild Side of Life," establishing himself as Capitol's country expert. Luckily for Nelson, a number of prominent country performers had relocated to California following the war. He tapped into this talent pool, helped along by promoter CLIFFIE STONE, signing many notable West Coast acts, including WANDA JACKSON and FERLIN HUSKY. Like other canny producers Nelson augmented his cash flow and power by founding with Stone a publishing company, Central Songs, that held the copyrights to the music that they recorded.

In 1957 Nelson jumped on the nascent rock-and-roll bandwagon, bringing Gene Vincent to Capitol while still working with their major country acts. He also began to do some work in Nashville in addition to his California activities, producing 1960s recordings for earlier stars like the LOUVIN BROTHERS, including the celebrated *Satan Is Real* album. His two strongest signings from the late 1950s and early 1960s were BUCK OWENS, who previously was a session guitarist for

Nelson, and MERLE HAGGARD, who came to the label in 1962. Nelson had a special relationship with Haggard, crafting a hard-edged, stark sound for the singer. Even after Nelson stepped down as head of country production for Capitol, he continued to produce Haggard through the early 1970s. Nelson retired in 1976.

Nelson was always an active figure in the music industry. In 1964 he encouraged the National Academy of Recorded Arts & Sciences (NARAS) to open a Nashville chapter. He was also a founding member of the Country Music Association, serving for two terms as its president, and has served on the board of trustees of the Country Music Foundation. In 2001, at the age of ninety, he was inducted into the Country Music Hall of Fame.

Compared to other country producers of the era, like CHET ATKINS and OWEN BRADLEY, Nelson is applauded for maintaining a grittier, "true-country" sound, although as his productions in Nashville for the Louvins and others showed, he was not immune to the lure of swelling strings and vocal choruses. Nonetheless, perhaps because of his California focus, he tended to produce recordings that have a more traditional honky-tonk flavor. His recording style used for Buck Owens and Merle Haggard laid the blueprint for retro country artists like DWIGHT YOAKAM.

NELSON, RICK(Y) (b. Eric Hilliard N., Teaneck, N.J., May 8, 1940–December 31, 1985)

The son of well-known bandleader Ozzie Nelson and singer Harriet Nelson, who later created a successful family comedy on radio and television, Nelson was originally a teen-pop star in the late 1950s who became an innovative performer of COUNTRY-ROCK before the music reached its greatest popularity.

Nelson got his start when his girlfriend admitted that she had a heavy-duty crush on ELVIS PRESLEY; stating that he, too, could play the guitar, Ricky found himself pushed into the role of teen idol thanks to his frequent appearances on the family's TV show. Many of his early pop recordings had a fine, stripped-down flavor, thanks to the dazzling string work of JAMES BURTON, who would continue to work with Nelson after he made a career switch to country.

In the mid-1960s, after his teen idol career had fizzled, Nelson began recording country music, featuring the works of the most progressive young songwriters, including WILLIE NELSON, and with James Burton playing GUITAR and DOBRO. To mark this change, he changed his name from the juvenile Ricky to the more mature Rick (he would return to Ricky later in life, when he once again began performing his earlier pop hits). After hearing BOB DYLAN's crossover country LP, *Nashville Skyline*, Nelson formed The Stone Canyon Band in late 1969, probably the first country-rock

band in Los Angeles. Joining him was ex–POCO bassist Randy Meisner (who later formed THE EAGLES) as well as other floating members, including Tom Brumley, a pedal steel-guitarist who had previously worked with BUCK OWENS's Buckaroos. They did a mix of covers of SINGER/SONGWRITER material by Dylan, Tim Hardin, and Randy Newman, as well as Nelson's own compositions.

Nelson's career got a shot in the arm in 1973 when he had a hit with his ironic "Garden Party," a song commenting on his audience's unwillingness to let him escape his teen-idol past (it was inspired by an experience he had performing in an oldies show at Madison Square Garden). Oddly enough, Nelson would embrace his earlier hits by the end of the decade, even referring to himself once again as "Ricky Nelson." Remaining a solid road act, Nelson died en route to a gig in 1985.

Select Discography

Best of Rick Nelson, MCA 10098. His more "mature" recordings, cut after the teen-pop years were over, 1963–1975.

In Concert: The Troubador, MCA 25983. Reissue of 1969 important Decca LP that showed Nelson in the early phases of his country-rock career; features Randy Meisner and Tom Brumley.

All My Best, MCA 6163. Originally released in 1985 by Rick on his own Silver Eagle label and hawked on late-night television, this is a nice collection of remakes featuring THE JORDANAIRES on backup vocals.

NELSON, WILLIE (b. W. Hugh N., Abbot, Tex., April 30, 1933)

Willie Nelson was one of the most influential country songwriters (in the early 1960s) and performers (from the mid-1970s to the mid-1980s). A leader of the "OUTLAW" movement, Nelson abandoned the slick Nashville Sound of the 1960s to forge his own unique style, laying the groundwork for the explosion of "new" country in the 1980s. His reedy, sun-beaten voice and bluesy songs reflecting romantic love gone awry have become an integral part of American popular culture, beyond the confines of strictly "country" music.

Nelson, the son of a farmer, began performing while still in high school. He served in the Air Force until 1952, and worked in Texas and briefly in Vancouver, Washington, as both a performer and a country deejay. After publishing his first song, he moved to NASHVILLE, where he hooked up with RAY PRICE, working as bassist in his backup band, The Cherokee Cowboys. His first success was as a songwriter, penning such #1

Willie Nelson at the CMA awards, 1996. Photo: Raeanne Rubenstein

country classics as "Crazy" for PATSY CLINE and "Hello Walls" for FARON YOUNG, both in 1961.

He signed with Liberty and then RCA Records in the 1960s as a solo artist, but his unique style was ill-suited to the heavy-handed strings and syrupy choruses typical of Nashville production of the day. When his house burned down in 1970, he returned to Austin, Texas, turning his back on the country-music community. Influenced by younger performers who also were weary of the NASHVILLE SOUND, including KRIS KRISTOFFERSON and WAYLON JENNINGS, Nelson began to experiment with writing song cycles, or groups of related songs, that would be issued on a series of seminal LPs, including 1973's *Shotgun Willie*, 1974's *Phases and Stages* (telling the story of the breakup of a relationship from both the man's and the woman's perspective), and 1975's landmark *Red Headed Stranger*, a romantic story set in the nineteenth-century West. Given artistic control over his recordings, he pared down his sound, often just to his own vocals and guitars, as on his first hit, 1975's cover of FRED ROSE's "Blue Eyes Crying in the Rain," from the *Stranger* concept LP.

The outlaw movement was given a strong push by RCA when they released the compilation album *Wanted: The Outlaws* in 1976, featuring Willie, Jennings, JESSI COLTER (then Jennings's wife), and Tompall Glaser (of THE GLASER BROTHERS). In typical contrary fashion, Willie followed this success with an album of covers of 1930s and 1940s pop standards,

Stardust. He proved what country audiences had long known: that there was a strong following for these pop songs among country-music fans, as well as among the rock and "yuppie" audiences who were attracted to Willie's straight-ahead approach to music.

Through the late 1970s and early 1980s Willie performed as a soloist and in duets with Jennings, Leon Russell, and MERLE HAGGARD, and in the informal group The Highwaymen, with JOHNNY CASH, Kristofferson, and Jennings. He even cut a duet with Spanish crooner Julio Iglesias on the saccharine "To All the Girls I Ever Loved." A brief movie career also developed, including a remake of the classic tearjerker *Impromptu*, about a classical musician's love affair with his student, improbably reset in the world of country music as *Honeysuckle Rose* (1980, yielding the hit, "On the Road Again," which has become a theme song for Nelson), and a TV version of *Red Headed Stranger* (1987).

Tax problems with the IRS led to one of the most unusual deals in music history: Willie recorded two solo LPs that featured just him and his guitar performing his "old songs," then marketed them directly through late-night TV ads; the proceeds were used to pay off back taxes. He returned to more mainstream recording on his sixtieth birthday with a new album produced by mainstream pop producer Don Was and a TV special. Nelson continued to record through the 1990s, moving to Island Records in 1996, and working with a variety of producers (including Daniel Lanois, who had jump-started BOB DYLAN's career), as well as producing more theme albums, among them another collection of standards and an album of blues covers.

Nelson's success in broadening the country market in the 1970s and early 1980s opened up the field to influences such as COUNTRY-ROCK, WESTERN SWING, and HONKY-TONK sounds. He proved, along with Bob Dylan, that a songwriter could be the most expressive performer of his own material, even if his vocals were not as "polished" as those of more commercially oriented performers (although Nelson, unlike Dylan, is a talented guitarist). In a culture oriented toward youth, Nelson's well-lined face and laidback performances showed that artistry could overcome imagery.

Select Discography

Early Years, Scotti Bros. 75437. Demos made in the early 1960s, before Nelson had a recording contract.
Nite Life, Rhino 70987. Early, hard-to-find tracks.
Essential, RCA 66590. His RCA label recordings made between 1965 and 1971.
Red Headed Stranger, Columbia Legacy 63589. Reissue of the 1975 concept album (Columbia 33482).
To Lefty from Willie, Columbia 34695. Wonderful 1977 tribute album featuring songs associated with LEFTY FRIZZELL.

Revolutions of Time, Sony 85667. Three-CD compilation of Columbia recordings made between 1975 and 1993, Nelson's most successful years.

Classic and Unreleased Collection, Rhino 71462. Recorded between 1957 and the mid-1980s, a three-CD set of "rarities" originally marketed through the Home Shopping Network. For true fans.

NESMITH, MICHAEL (b. Houston, Tex., December 30, 1942)

One of the original "pre-Fab Four," a member of TV's The Monkees, Nesmith was a creative SINGER/SONGWRITER who was one of the founders of COUNTRY-ROCK.

The son of a secretary who invented Liquid Paper, and thus earned a small fortune, Nesmith learned to play the guitar after serving in the Air Force in the early 1960s. After a successful audition he became the only star of *The Monkees* TV show who actually played his instrument and wrote songs. Although Nesmith provided country-rock originals for the group, he was dismayed by the hype surrounding them, and left soon after the TV show was canceled.

Nesmith's fame as a songwriter grew steadily in the late 1960s. His "Different Drum" was covered by LINDA RONSTADT as a member of The Stone Poneys and was a 1967 hit; The NITTY GRITTY DIRT BAND had a minor hit with his "Some of Shelley's Blues," and middle-of-the-road meister Andy Williams had a big hit with his early 1970s composition "Joanne."

Meanwhile, Nesmith formed a series of loose-knit country-rock bands, called The First (or Second) National Band, often in cahoots with pedal steel guitarist Red Rhodes, recording an eccentric mix of Nesmith's own compositions and psychedelized adaptions of country standards. In the early 1970s Elektra Records invited him to form the Countryside label to record Los Angeles's burgeoning country-rock scene, but the label was short-lived due to a change in management of the parent company.

In the mid-1970s Nesmith became increasingly interested in experimentation with video, suggesting the original idea for MTV and becoming one of the first and most inventive creators of music videos through his company, Pacific Arts. He more or less retired as a performer, although he still occasionally produces new material in a style that is distinctly his own.

Select Discography

The Older Stuff, Rhino 70763. His great country-rock sessions from 1970 to 1973.
The Newer Stuff, Rhino 70168. On which our hero ventures into territories only he would explore.

NEW GRASS REVIVAL (c. 1972–1990: Sam Bush, b. Bowling Green, Ky., April 15, 1952 [fdl]; Curtis Burch [gtr, Dobro, 1972–1981]; Pat Flynn, b. Los Angeles, May 17, 1952 [gtr, voc, 1981–1990]; Courtney Johnson, b. Barren County, Ky., December 20, 1939–June 7, 1996 [bnj, 1972–1981]; Bela Fleck, b. New York City, July 10, 1959 [bnj, 1981–1990]; Harry "Ebo Walker" Shelor, b. Louisville, Ky., October 19, 1941 [b, 1972–1973]; Joel Cowan, b. Evansville, Ind., August 24, 1952 [b, voc])

One of the most influential of the PROGRESSIVE BLUE-GRASS groups, The New Grass Revival were born out of an earlier group known as The Bluegrass Alliance, featuring hot guitarist Dan Crary as its leader. When Crary left the band in 1970, he took the name with him; he was replaced by Sam Bush, who along with Johnson, Burch, and Walker brought a rock-and-roll sensibility to their performance of traditional instrumentals and songs. Walker was soon replaced by powerful singer Joel Cowan, who had previously performed in a rock-and-roll band. This first version of the band, which lasted through the early 1980s, helped popularize the newgrass sound. Their stage act and performance style were geared to appeal to young listeners who grew up on rock, though they still performed with acoustic instruments and drew on the traditional bluegrass repertoire to some extent.

Burch and Johnson tired of the endless touring that is the life of a bluegrass outfit, and were replaced by progressive banjoist BELA FLECK and singer/guitarist Pat Flynn. Fleck brought a more jazz-influenced sound, particularly in his approach to harmonies and his sparse, melodic improvisations. The band scored their greatest success with 1988's *Hold to a Dream*, their sole LP to have much action on the country charts. However, they were quite a successful performing band, touring on the bluegrass, college-campus, and, to some extent, traditional country circuit.

The band fizzled out in the early 1990s. Bush continues to be a much-in-demand session musician, and Fleck formed his jazz-country fusion band, The Flecktones, who have had some success on both the pop and the country charts.

Select Discography

Fly Through the Country/When The Storm Is Over, Flying Fish 70032. Reissues two classic 1970s albums by this influential group.
Best of, Liberty 28090. The latter-day band, with Bela Fleck, taken from their Capitol/Liberty albums.

NEW LOST CITY RAMBLERS, THE (1958–c. 1970, sporadically thereafter: Mike Seeger, b. New York City, August 15, 1933 [fdl, bnj, gtr, hca, mdln, voc]; Tom Paley, b. New York City, March 19, 1928

[1958–1963: bnj, gtr, voc]; John Cohen, b. New York City, August 2, 1932 [bnj, gtr, mdln, voc]; Tracy Schwartz, b. New York City, November 11, 1938 [1964–thereafter, fdl, bnj, gtr, mdln, voc])

The first and perhaps greatest of the old-time string-band revivalists, The Ramblers introduced the classic sounds of CHARLIE POOLE, THE SKILLET LICKERS, DOCK BOGGS, and many other recording artists of the 1920s and 1930s to a new, urban audience. Taking an almost academic approach (perhaps as an antidote to the slick commercialism of FOLK-REVIVAL groups like The Kingston Trio), they reproduced the sound of these early recordings almost note-for-note. As the years went by, the group loosened up somewhat, taking a more interpretive role in their re-creations.

MIKE SEEGER, the son of folklorist Charles S. and half brother of folk revivalist PETE SEEGER, was enamored of BLUEGRASS and country music in the Washington, D.C., area, where he grew up. Yale-educated JOHN COHEN was active in the New York folk scene in the 1950s, and Paley, a mathematician, was from the Boston area. The trio's academic background is reflected in their approach to the music, particularly on their first few albums released by Folkways in the late 1950s and early 1960s. They often focused on a single theme—such as Prohibition or songs of the Depression—and presented the music with meticulous documentation, including information on their sources. Their appearance at the 1959 Newport Folk Festival introduced them to the folk-revival audience, and led to many years of popularity on the college and small folk-club circuit.

Paley left the group in 1963 to form another short-lived old-time band, The Old Reliable String Band, with New York-based musician Arnie Rose; he then relocated to England, where he recorded a duet album with Mike Seeger's sister Peggy. In the late 1960s he formed The New Deal String Band with British musicians Janet Kerr on FIDDLE and Joe Locker on BANJO, and in the late 1970s he recorded a solo album.

To replace Paley, Seeger recruited his friend Tracy Schwartz, who brought a more modern sound to the group. Schwartz's background in bluegrass widened the group's repertoire to include re-creations of 1950s country recordings as well as the older styles they had previously performed. The band recorded an all-instrumental album, perhaps the first to emphasize this side of the old-time music tradition, as well as accompanying legendary country performer COUSIN EMMY on a 1967 recording. 1968's concept album, *Modern Times*, was perhaps one of their best recordings; while still centering on a general theme (country folks' reaction to the changes in their lives brought about by industrialization), the band took a freer approach to the music, giving it their own personal musical stamp.

By the early 1970s, the Ramblers were performing together only sporadically. Seeger was pursuing a solo career and also performing with his wife, ALICE GERRARD, as a duo and in the bluegrass/country band The Strange Creek Singers, which also featured Tracy Schwartz. Cohen formed The Putnam String County Band, one of the more innovative revival bands of the early 1970s, with fiddler Jay and guitarist/vocalist Lynn Ungar and cellist Abby Newton. Schwartz performed with Seeger in The Strange Creek Singers for a while, and then began performing with his wife, Eloise, and eventually his children as well, while pursuing an interest in CAJUN music.

Although the Ramblers never officially disbanded, they have performed together only on and off for over two decades, mostly for special occasions such as reunions, or at festivals. They issued their first new album of studio recordings in over two decades in 2000, for the Smithsonian/Folkways label.

Select Discography

The Early Years, Smithsonian/Folkways 40036. Selections from their albums cut between 1958 and 1962 with Tom Paley.

The Later Years, Smithsonian/Folkways 40040. The band's best recordings from 1963 to 1973.

NEW RIDERS OF THE PURPLE SAGE (c. 1971–1978; primary lineup: Dave Torbert [gtr, voc]; Buddy Cage [steel gtr]; Skip Battin [b]; Spencer Dryden [drms])

In the wake of The Grateful Dead's two successful COUNTRY-ROCK albums of the early 1970s, The New Riders of the Purple Sage (taking their name from a Zane Grey dime-store Western novel) were formed as a spin-off band for lead Deadhead Jerry Garcia to pursue his interest in making country music and playing the PEDAL STEEL GUITAR. The original band members included other Deadsmen Mickey Hart (drums) and Phil Lesh (bass), along with the husband-and-wife team of Keith (keyboards) and Donna (vocals) Godchaux; this same aggregation also toured in the mid-1970s under the name of The Jerry Garcia Band.

New steel guitarist Buddy Cage came on board after Garcia's interest waned, and along with guitarist/vocalist Dave Torbert, led the group through most of its recordings. They recorded two fairly decent country-rock albums for Columbia in 1972 and then disbanded for a while. By the mid-1970s they were back as a true band, now joined by ex-BYRDS bassist Skip Battin and ex-Jefferson Airplane drummer Spencer Dryden. However, their later recordings were fairly lame blends of pop and rock, and the band fizzled out by the decade's end.

Select Discography

Before Time Began, Relix 2024. Attention Deadheads!
Here's Jerry and crew kickin' up the sawdust on
early, never previously issued recordings.

Best of, Columbia 34367. Skimpy, ten-track overview
of the band's official recordings, graced with a
shameless cover photo (not of the band, but of a
close-up of a tank-topped woman, emphasizing her
two selling points).

NEWBURY, MICKEY (b. Milton N., Houston, Tex., May 19, 1940)

Better known as a songwriter than as a performer,
Newbury has written solid hits for country, pop, and
R&B artists.

After graduating from high school Newbury
bummed around for a while in the Houston-South
Texas-Gulf Coast region, playing piano in small bars
and clubs. He joined the Air Force, where he discov-
ered a skill for songwriting, and began seriously work-
ing on songs when he was twenty-four. Moving to
Nashville in the mid-1960s, he had his first hit when
DON GIBSON covered his "Funny Familiar Forgotten
Feeling." He then hit the pop charts with KENNY ROG-
ERS and The First Edition's smash version of "Just
Dropped In (to See What Condition My Condition Was
In)." He had another hit with the country WEEPER "She
Even Woke Me Up to Say Good-bye," recorded by
JERRY LEE LEWIS in his mid-1960s country phase, and
R&B hits for Bobby Bland ("You've Always Got the
Blues") and Solomon Burke ("Time Is a Thief").

In the early 1970s Newbury was signed to Elektra
Records' new country division. His biggest solo hit
was 1972's "American Trilogy," based on three traditional Civil War songs, which did even better when it
was covered by ELVIS PRESLEY. Newbury's recording
career quickly fizzled, although he continued to write
highly literate country hits through the 1970s. His recording output since has been sparse: two albums in
the 1980s, and one in 1994.

Select Discography

Lulled by the Moonlight, Mountain Retreat 8653.
Twenty tracks from the late 1950s through the early
1960s.

NEWMAN, JIMMY "C" (b. Big Mamou, La., August 27, 1927)

Newman brought CAJUN sounds to the country
charts in the late 1950s and early 1960s, and has continued to be one of the few artists who can perform
successfully in either style.

An authentic Cajun, Newman began performing in
the Lake Charles, Louisiana, area, and was already
performing the mix of country and traditional Cajun
dance numbers that would become his trademark. He
recorded for several small local labels beginning in
1949, and quickly gained a strong regional following.
Hired for the popular LOUISIANA HAYRIDE radio program, he was quickly signed by Dot, where he had a
rockin' country hit with "Cry, Cry, Cry" (1954). He
was invited to join THE GRAND OLE OPRY in 1956, and
had his biggest country-pop hit a year later with "A
Fallen Star." He remains a performing member of the
Opry.

After a couple of lackluster years at MGM, Newman
returned to the country charts under the hands of producer OWEN BRADLEY at Decca Records, beginning
with 1961's "Alligator Man" (playing off his Cajun
heritage) and the half-spoken "Bayou Talk." Although
Bradley managed to cover Newman's distinctive style
in the same schlocky instrumentation he employed on
all of his NASHVILLE SOUND sessions, the essential regional character of Newman's music was not lost. In
1962 he recorded *Folk Songs of the Bayou Country* to
appeal to the nascent FOLK-REVIVAL crowd; this featured many songs sung in his native Cajun French,
and wonderful instrumentation by noted Cajun fiddler
Rufus Thibedeaux and "Shorty" LeBlanc on accordion. Unfortunately, most of Newman's later Decca
recordings were pitched at the mainstream country audience, and much of his Cajun heritage was lost.

In the mid-1970s Newman returned to his roots with
a new band called Cajun Country. Although no longer
a strong chart presence, he continues to record and
perform, mostly focusing on traditional material.

Select Discography

Bop a Hula—Diggy Liggy Lo, Bear Family 15469.
Two-CD compilation of his Dot recordings made
between 1953 and 1958, featuring Cajun-flavored
country and ROCKABILLY.

Alligator Man, Rounder 6039. 1991 recording in a
more traditional Cajun style.

NEWTON, JUICE (b. Judy Kay N., Lakehurst, N.J., February 18, 1952)

Newton was a COUNTRY-ROCK-pop star of the late
1970s and early 1980s, best remembered for her cover
of the 1960s soft-pop hit "Angel of the Morning."

Born in New Jersey, Newton was raised in Virginia,
where she began performing folk songs as a teenager.
After attending college in North Carolina and working
in local coffeehouses, she moved to California, where
she met guitarist Otha Young; they formed a light folk-
rock band called Dixie Peach that evolved into Silver
Spur. The group stayed together for about two years,
recording a couple of albums and scoring a minor hit
with 1976's "Love Is a Word."

Newton went solo in the late 1970s, signing with Capitol in 1981 and immediately scoring on the pop charts with her remake of the 1960s pop hit "Angel of the Morning," followed by "Queen of Hearts." From 1982 to 1987 she was marketed as a country act, although little about her sound had changed. Her first country hit went straight to #1; it was "The Sweetest Thing (I've Ever Known)," written by her longtime associate Otha Young, which had originally been recorded by Silver Spur in 1975. She had a final pop hit with "Love's Been a Little Hard on Me," followed by her countrified cover of BRENDA LEE's "Break It to Me Gently." A remake of the Little Anthony and the Imperials' hit "Hurt" was a big country hit for her in 1986, as was a duet with EDDIE RABBITT on "Both to Each Other (Friends and Lovers)."

In 1986 Newton broke with her longtime boyfriend Young, and wed a polo player. As if in reaction to this life change, she moved from recording country-pop to an attempt at more glitzy, mainstream material, with little success. She has since become a staple of the Vegas circuit. She did not record again until 1998, and has since issued two albums, one featuring remakes of her older hits.

Select Discography

The Early Years, RCA 61142. Reissue of recordings originally made by Silver Spur, featuring Newton as lead vocalist.
Greatest Country Hits, Curb 77367.

NICKEL CREEK (1990–present: Sara Watkins [fdl, voc]; Shawn Watkins [gtr, mdln, voc]; Chris Thiele [bnj, mdln, voc]; Scott Thiele [b], replaced by Derek Jones in 2001)

Nickel Creek is a photogenic new BLUEGRASS band championed by ALISON KRAUSS.

Like many bluegrass groups, Nickel Creek is a family affair. The Watkinses and Thieles were raised in southern California, long a country-music mecca. Both families were patrons at a Carlsbad pizzeria that featured the newgrass band Bluegrass Etc., associated with the well-known fiddler BYRON BERLINE. The young Watkinses and Chris Thiele began studying with band members, and a local promoter recognized their talent—and young, well-scrubbed looks—and encouraged them to hit the road, taking along Chris's father, Scott, on bass. They hit the bluegrass trail, playing festivals big and small, while attracting an audience among the traditional music set. Meanwhile, they garnered awards, particularly Thiele, who became a noted MANDOLIN player, and began sessioning in Nashville, recording his own solo albums and working with DOLLY PARTON.

They also met nineteen-year-old ALISON KRAUSS, herself a prodigy on the bluegrass circuit. Krauss became the band's unofficial fourth member and advocate, promoting them as the next wave in bluegrass-acoustic music. Signed by the Sugar Hill label in 1999, the band produced their debut album in 2000, drawing great media attention. After discreetly dropping the elder Thiele—to play up their young good looks—the band was showcased on video and special programs on CMT, and also named one of five Music Innovators of the Millennium by *Time* magazine. Their album was also nominated for a Grammy. Its leadoff single, "Reasons Why," was #1 on the Americana chart (before the chart was discontinued); the follow-up, "When You Come Back Down," was a major hit in 2001 on the country charts and in heavy rotation on CMT.

Like Krauss's Union Station, Nickel Creek's repertoire bridges bluegrass and country pop, as well as rock and jazz. Their youthful good looks are bringing a new audience to bluegrass. Adept instrumentalists, strong vocalists, and attractive to boot, they are a publicist's dream. However, how long the bluegrass fad lasts in mainstream country is anybody's guess—and, long-term, like many other bluegrass acts, they face a life of one-nighters and festivals, something they know all too well from their first decade of performing.

Select Discography

Nickel Creek, Sugar Hill 3909. 2000 debut album, heavily promoted on Country Music Television.

NITTY GRITTY DIRT BAND (c. 1965–1999: Jeff Hanna, b. Detroit, Mich., July 11, 1957 [gtr, voc]; John McEuen, b. Oakland, Calif., December 19, 1945 [1965–1986: bnj, mdln]; Jimmy Ibbotson, b. Philadelphia, Pa., January 21, 1947 [gtr, voc, 1971–1999]; Jimmy Fadden, b. Long Beach, Calif., March 9, 1948 [drms]; Lee Thompson [1965–1975, mdln]; Bob Carpenter, b. Philadelphia, Pa., December 26, 1946 [1984–1999, kybds])

The Nitty Gritty Dirt Band was a California COUNTRY-ROCK band that crossed over into being a pure country band in the mid-1970s. Formed out of the California folk-rock community, the original band wed the sensibilities of a traditional jug band with a electric-folk sound. They initially scored hits with the late-1960s pop song "Buy for Me the Rain" and a remake of the 1910s standard "The Teddy Bears' Picnic." They disbanded in the late 1960s only to re-form in the early 1970s, scoring their biggest pop hits with country-rock versions of "Mr. Bojangles" and MIKE NESMITH's "Some of Shelley's Blues."

In 1973 the band organized sessions in Nashville that brought together traditional country stars (Earl Scruggs [of FLATT AND SCRUGGS], Maybelle Carter,

JIMMY MARTIN, MERLE TRAVIS, and DOC WATSON) to perform a set of country standards. The result was the landmark three-LP set *Will the Circle Be Unbroken*, which helped popularize these country stars among rock audiences, and also made the band heroes of both the country and the rock communities.

By the mid-1970s the band was performing country-rock material under the name The Dirt Band. They were down to a quartet (Thompson had left the group), but they continued to try to appeal to both their rock and their country constituencies. In the mid-1970s they backed the comic-novelty "King Tut" recorded by Steve Martin (who, incidentally, was managed by McEuen's brother, Bill, who had handled the band since its inception), going by the name of Toots Uncommons. They also scraped near the bottom of the Top 10 with their 1979 recording of "An American Dream."

By the 1980s, the "Nitty Gritty" was back in their name, and they were recording as a pure, new-country act. They scored a number of hits performing a combination of original songs and Nashville songwriters' products, with just a hint of traditional flavorings. In 1984 they had their first country #1 with RODNEY CROWELL's "Long Hard Road (the Sharecropper's Dream)." In 1985–1986 in time for their twentieth anniversary, they hit #1 again with "Modern Day Romance," a pure new-country song cowritten by Kix Brooks (later of BROOKS AND DUNN). Founder-member John McEuen left after the band's anniversary year to pursue a career as a solo banjo performer; the quartet of Ibbotson, Hanna, Fadden, and country/rock keyboardist Bob Carpenter further pulled the band in the "new country" direction. A follow-up to the famous *Will the Circle Be Unbroken* was released in 1989, with a cast drawing on more contemporary country figures (ROSANNE CASH, JOHN HIATT, and so on), although it was not as much of a landmark effort as the first set. That same year the band produced a streak of Top 10 country singles, solidifying their position as more consistent hitmakers than in the past.

The band's final decade saw them touring and producing a handful of albums, although without the success they had enjoyed on the country charts in the 1980s. In 2001 Ibbotson and John McEuen rejoined the band for a series of reunion concerts.

Select Discography

Twenty Years of Dirt, Warner Bros. 25382. "Best of" collection covering recordings from 1966 to 1986.
Will the Circle Be Unbroken, EMI 46589. Reissue of the famous three-LP set on two CDs.
Will the Circle Be Unbroken, Vol. 2, Universal 12500. Less exciting follow-up to the original cut in 1989.

NOACK, EDDIE (b. Armond A. N., Jr., [some sources give his birth name as D. Armona Noack], Houston, Tex., April 29, 1930–February 5, 1978)

Noack was an active recording artist from the late 1940s through 1960, moving between country, HONKY-TONK, and ROCKABILLY, as well as a country songsmith who is best remembered for HANK SNOW's mid-1950s hit, "These Hands."

Born in Houston, Noack received a degree from the university there in English and journalism. An amateur musician, he won a talent contest in 1947 at the Texas Theatre; it led to local radio work and, two years later, to a contract with the local Gold Star label. His first hit was a cover of the pop hit "Gentlemen Prefer Blondes," but he soon was label-hopping, scoring his biggest country hit to date in 1951 with "Too Hot to Handle" on the TNT label; this led to a contract with the Nashville-based Starday label that ran through the mid-1950s. In 1958 he moved to HAROLD "PAPPY" DAILY's "D" label, recording rockabilly and teen-pop under the pseudonym of Tommy Wood, and having another minor country success under his own name with "Have Blues, Will Travel." He soon became active in Daily's music-publishing operation, and retired from performing in the early 1960s to focus on the business side of Nashville.

During the 1950s Noack's songs were covered by many mainstream country acts following Hank Snow's success with "These Hands," including honky-tonkers ERNEST TUBB and GEORGE JONES. Jones covered many of Noack's songs in the early 1960s, including "Barbara Joy," "No Blues Is Good News," and "For Better or Worse."

Noack made several abortive "comebacks" as a recording artist from the late 1960s until his death in 1978. Perhaps his most interesting recording was *Remembering Jimmie Rodgers*, featuring sparse, acoustic instrumentation (unusual for the time) in a program of material that had been made famous by the Yodelin' Brakeman. His recordings were issued by a variety of tiny labels, here and abroad, but with little success. Ironically, after Noack's death his earlier recordings were rediscovered, particularly among country rock and rockabilly fans.

NORMA JEAN (b. N. J. Beasler, Welliston, Okla., January 30, 1938)

Norma Jean was a popular country singer of the 1960s who is best known as PORTER WAGONER's duet partner (until she was replaced by young DOLLY PARTON in 1967) and for her series of solo recordings celebrating the life of the working poor.

Influenced by KITTY WELLS, whom she heard performing on THE GRAND OLE OPRY as a child, Beasler began singing on the radio when she was thirteen years old, and was touring as a vocalist with various WESTERN SWING bands two years later. She made her way to Nashville, where she hooked up, emotionally and professionally, with Wagoner, who molded her "just folks" image. She recorded a number of brassy songs, including her first hit, 1964's suggestive "Let's Go All the Way." 1967 brought her first working-class anthem, "Heaven Help the Working Girl (in a World That's Run by Men)." After parting with Wagoner, she recorded the concept LP *I Guess That Comes from Being Poor*, featuring hokey crowd pleasers like "The Lord Must Have Loved the Poor Folks (He Made So Many of Them)."

After her marriage to a fellow Oklahoman, Norma Jean retired from the music business from 1974 to 1984. She returned to Nashville in the latter year, and has since performed her old hits as a nostalgia act.

Select Discography

Best of, Collectors Choice 102. Twenty-one-cut anthology drawn from her RCA recordings.

NUDIE "THE RODEO TAILOR" (aka Nudie Cohn/Cohen, b. Nutya Kotlyrenko, Kiev, Ukraine, December 15, 1902–May 9, 1984)

Although not a performer, Nudie suited up Nashville stars in clothes that came to symbolize Nashville's 1950s and 1960s success and excess.

Nudie got his nickname from an immigration official on New York's Ellis Island when his family emigrated from the Ukraine around 1914. After a career as a boxer and a Hollywood extra, Nudie settled in New York City around 1932 to begin a new life as a tailor, crafting eye-catching G-strings and pasties for burlesque stars during the mid-1930s. In 1940 Nudie returned to the West Coast, where he tried to break into sewing for the stars. Western performer TEX WILLIAMS gave him his first big commission in 1947, ordering eleven cowboy suits. Soon Nudie had his own North Hollywood store, suiting up the many celluloid cowboys of the era.

In 1951 HONKY-TONK country star LEFTY FRIZZELL ordered a rhinestone-encrusted cowboy shirt from Nudie, and his signature, over-the-top style was born. Soon every wanna-be country star had to have flashy Nudie suits; even ELVIS PRESLEY got into the act in 1957, ordering a $2500 gold lamé outfit. Nudie's suits were flamboyant and often outrageous, designed to catch the eyes of audience members. But they also included many subtle symbols, particularly in their embroidery: symbols associated with a star (such as wagon wheels for PORTER WAGONER) were cunningly worked into the stitchery.

But it took GRAM PARSONS to make Nudie hip. In 1968 he asked the tailor to make suits for his new band, THE FLYING BURRITO BROTHERS. Nudie obliged, embroidering a design replete with marijuana leaves onto their coats. The band sported the outfits on the cover of their justly celebrated first album. Suddenly it was hip to be flashy, and *Rolling Stone* placed the diminutive tailor on its cover in June 1969.

Nudie became something of a legend following his media exposure, and played the part to the hilt. He usually dressed in his own designs, and sported highly decorated, although never matching, cowboy boots. He also had a famous silver-dollar-encrusted Cadillac convertible, notable for the pair of steer horns that sat perched above the grill.

Nudie continued to work until ill health sidelined him in the early 1980s. Much of his later work was done by his associate, Manuel, who has carried on the Nudie tradition. Nudie's wife kept the Hollywood store going through 1994. In 1997 The Gene Autry Museum of Western Heritage purchased what was left of Nudie's business records.

"Nudie suits," as they came to be known, symbolized the sometimes excessive gaudiness of postwar Nashville. They were tasteless, tacky, and strangely wonderful: so ugly that they are beautiful. They have become valuable collectibles; musician and country-music archivist MARTY STUART has built up one of the most impressive collections, now part of the Country Music Hall of Fame.

OAK RIDGE BOYS (c. mid-1960s–present); best-known lineup: Duane Allen, b. Taylortown, Tex., April 29, 1943 [lead voc, gtr]; Joe Bonsall, b. Philadelphia, Pa., May 18, 1948 [tnr]; William Lee Golden, b. Brewton, Ala., January 12, 1939 [bar]; Richard Sterban, b. Camden, N.J., April 24, 1943 [b]; in 1987, Golden left and was replaced by Steve Sanders, b. Richland, Ga., September 17, 1952–June 10, 1998; Golden returned in early 1996 after Sanders left)

Originally a country-GOSPEL quartet, the Oak Ridge Boys gained their greatest success in the late 1970s and early 1980s as a pop-vocal group; their biggest hit was 1981's crossover, "Elvira."

Tracing their roots to a gospel quartet that performed in and around the Oak Ridge, Tennessee, nuclear facility, the group went through many personnel changes from its founding in the late 1940s to today. Walter Fowler, a country SINGER/SONGWRITER who crossed over into gospel music and promotion, founded the Oak Ridge Quartet in 1948.

Fowler was a member of The Georgia Clodhoppers, a country-gospel quartet based in Oak Ridge, Tennessee, in the late 1940s. Inspired by the success of EDDY ARNOLD, Fowler recorded as a soloist for Decca and King, writing and performing such sentimental country favorites as "I'm Sending You Red Roses" and "That's How Much I Love You, Baby." The Clodhoppers eventually took the more elegant Oak Ridge Quartet name, but Fowler left the band by the early 1950s to become a gospel music promoter.

The Oak Ridge personnel soldiered on through the 1960s, and the lineup stabilized by the mid-1970s. All of the group's members were educated musicians, and they all had long histories in other gospel or pop-vocal groups. Lead singer and guitarist Duane Allen, who joined in 1966, had a music degree from East Texas State, and had previously sung baritone in the popular group The Southernaires. Tenor Joe Bonsall, a native of Philadelphia and an Oak Ridge Boy since 1973,

performed with many local street-corner harmony groups and was a regular dancer on Dick Clark's *American Bandstand* show. Baritone Bill Golden, who joined in 1964, had performed with his sister as a country duo in his native Alabama and had also worked in a paper mill. Distinctive bass Richard Sterban, a New Jersey native who came to the group in 1972, had performed with the gospel groups The Keystone Quartet and The Stamps (who recorded and toured with ELVIS PRESLEY).

The Oak Ridge Quartet, as they were known in their gospel incarnation, were successful gospel recording artists and performers by the mid-1970s. However, their iconoclastic attitude, including their long hair and beards and use of drums and electrified instruments in the backup band, was upsetting to some of the more traditional members of the gospel audience. Meanwhile, they longed to cross over to the more lucrative pop market. Their first break came when they were invited to provide vocal backups on Paul Simon's mid-1970s hit "Slip Slidin' Away." They were signed by ABC in 1977, and also began performing at upscale venues in Vegas, opening for ROY CLARK. Mainstream hits came through the early 1980s, along with dozens of appearances on TV variety shows as well as dramatic parts on country-oriented shows like *The Dukes of Hazzard*. Among their better-known wax is 1981's gazillion-selling "Elvira" (with the distinctive "oom-papa-mow-mow" bass line borrowed from the early 1960s teen-pop hit), the patriotic gut-thumper "American Made" from 1983 (picked up as a jingle by Miller beer), 1985's cover of The Staple Singers' gospel favorite "Touch a Hand, Make a Friend," and 1988's "Gonna Take a Lot of River," featuring new leader singer Steve Sanders (William Lee Golden had been forced out of the band in 1987, and subsequently sued the group for forty million dollars). However, in a reversal of fortune, Sanders left in 1995 and was replaced by Golden; in 1998 Sanders committed suicide. The

Boys continued to tour and record sporadically through the decade's end.

The Oak Ridge Boys' combination of traditional gospel harmonies with doo-wop and early rock influences, plus their dramatic stage presentation, were highly influential on the new-country harmony groups that followed, including ALABAMA.

Select Discography

Greatest Hits, Vols. 1–3, MCA 5150/5496/42294.

O'BRIEN, TIM (b. Timothy Page O., Wheeling, W. Va., March 16, 1954)

O'Brien is a BLUEGRASS/country vocalist and songwriter who has performed as a member of the band HOT RIZE and also in duets with his sister, blues/folk singer Mollie O'Brien.

Raised in Wheeling, West Virginia, O'Brien first learned GUITAR at age twelve, then mastered MANDOLIN and FIDDLE as well. By his late teens, he was leading a local bluegrass band. At around age twenty he moved to Boulder, Colorado. In 1978 he was one of the founding members of the group Hot Rize, formed by banjoist Peter Wernick. He remained with the band for its twelve-year run, writing a number of their best-loved songs. He also portrayed "Red Knuckles" in the group's parody/homage HONKY-TONK band, Red Knuckles and the Trailblazers.

O'Brien launched a solo career in 1990, initially signing with mainstream label RCA. However, the album was abandoned by the label, so he moved to a smaller bluegrass label, Sugar Hill. O'Brien formed a backing band, the Oh Boys, which featured well-known bluegrass bassist Marc Schatz. He has recorded albums of his own songs, as well as a Grammy-nominated 1996 album of BOB DYLAN covers.

O'Brien has a sweet, high tenor voice, in many ways reminiscent of the vocal style of VINCE GILL (another ex-bluegrass vocalist who has crossed over into country-pop). O'Brien's songs are typical of today's mainstream country hits: they have a SINGER/SONGWRITER flavor, with a warm edge of sentiment. A talented mandolin player, he was active on the NASHVILLE bluegrass-traditional country scene through the 1990s. However, O'Brien has yet to break through in the commercial country marketplace, lacking either the teen appeal of younger performers or the creative management that is necessary to make it in the big time. He has continued to experiment, in 1999 releasing an album called *The Crossing* that traces the Celtic roots of bluegrass music, and an interesting, living-room album of duets recorded with multiple instrumentalist Darrell Scott on the independent Howdy Skies label in 2000.

Select Discography

Red on Blonde, Sugar Hill 3853. 1996 album of Bob Dylan material that garnered O'Brien a well-deserved Grammy nomination.

O'CONNOR, MARK (b. Seattle, Wash., August 5, 1961)

A child virtuoso on a number of instruments, O'Connor was a championship fiddler in the 1970s who became, in the mid-1980s, the most in-demand session musician in NASHVILLE. He has recorded with hundreds of artists in country and pop, besides his own solo albums.

O'Connor showed jaw-dropping capabilities on a number of musical instruments by the age of eleven; he started playing classical GUITAR at age six, and won a flamenco competition four years later. He soon turned his attention to country music, quickly mastering bluegrass guitar, MANDOLIN, BANJO, and DOBRO. But his true capabilities were first revealed when he picked up the FIDDLE at age eleven (he was inspired to take up the instrument after seeing DOUG KERSHAW performing on JOHNNY CASH's TV show); eighteen months after his first lesson, he won the Junior Division of the National Old-Time Fiddlers Contest in Weiser, Idaho. He was signed by Rounder Records, a BLUEGRASS label, soon after, and released his first album at age twelve; he recorded five more albums for the label in the 1970s, including a solo guitar record that showed his capabilities as a flatpicker. Over the next decade he won every major U.S. fiddle championship, including the open competition at the National Festival four times before retiring undefeated.

Like many other contest winners, Mark's original style was very flashy, designed to bring a crowd to its feet. However, in his late teens he came under the influence of PROGRESSIVE BLUEGRASSERS and acoustic-jazz musicians like DAVID GRISMAN, whose group he joined in the early 1980s (as a guitarist). His fiddling began to pick up a sweeter tone and a sophistication and subtlety that is not usually heard in championship fiddling circles. After a year with Grisman, O'Connor played briefly with The Dregs, the original country/grunge-rock fusion group, and also toured with DOC and Merle WATSON, PETER ROWAN, and JERRY DOUGLAS. In 1983 he relocated to NASHVILLE, where he soon was working as a studio musician.

O'Connor's dexterity on a number of instruments, and his ability to quickly fashion an appropriate style for an accompaniment, led him to be a major session player, recording with country stars as well as pop-rock singers like James Taylor and Paul Simon. In the late 1980s, he signed with Warner Brothers as a solo artist, producing the *New Nashville Cats* LP as an homage to his bluegrass roots with popular country stars

RICKY SKAGGS, VINCE GILL, and STEVE WARINER as his informal bandmates. In 1989 he was named the musical director of *American Music Shop*, an acoustic-music concert series on cable's Nashville Network; he composed the theme song for the program and leads the band, which included Dobroist Jerry Douglas. However, the show was broadcast only briefly.

As O'Connor's fame has grown, so have his musical ambitions, although he has been less successful outside of the pure country realm. He composed a violin concerto that was premiered by the Sante Fe and Nashville Symphony Orchestras in 1993, taking the solo chair himself. In 1995 he signed with Sony Records, continuing to produce an eclectic mix of albums featuring jazz, classical, and bluegrass-styled performances. In 1998 he issued an album of his own classical-flavored solos, *Midnight on the Water*, and three years later, *Hot Swing*, in homage to famed jazz fiddler Stephane Grappelli.

Select Discography

The Championship Years, Country Music Foundation 015. Mark as a young fiddle-burner performing in various contests.

National Junior Fiddle Champ, Rounder 0046. Cassette-only reissue of his first album, cut when he was twelve.

Retrospective, Rounder 11507. Best of his many Rounder albums.

New Nashville Cats, Warner Bros. 26509. Fine bluegrass/HONKY-TONK country outing with Skaggs and Gill.

O'DAY, MOLLY (b. LaVerne Williamson, McVeigh, Ky., July 9, 1923–December 5, 1987)

O'Day was a gutsy HONKY-TONK wailer who abandoned her career for evangelical preaching.

O'Day was the daughter of a coal miner. Her family was musically talented, and Molly listened to the NATIONAL BARN DANCE radio program out of Chicago as a child, particularly admiring the singing of PATSY MONTANA and TEXAS RUBY, two cowgirl stars. In 1939 her older brother Skeets got a radio job in West Virginia and invited his sixteen-year-old sister to be his vocalist, under the stage name of Mountain Fern. In 1940 she broke with her brother and joined Lynn Davis's group, The Forty-Niners; a year later she married Davis. The two spent the World War II years working radio in West Virginia, Alabama, and Kentucky; it was on their last job, in Louisville, that Williamson gained the stage name of Molly O'Day. She also met a young singer/guitarist, HANK WILLIAMS, who impressed her with his sincerity and powerful songs.

The duo's greatest success came in 1945, when they joined Knoxville's WNOX. A year later Molly was signed by Columbia, and had hits with "Tramp on the Street," her best-loved song, as well as the honky-tonk anthem "I Don't Care if Tomorrow Never Comes" (which she learned from Hank Williams) and the tear-jerking ballad "The Drunken Driver." Molly's music was also spread through her popular songbooks that she sold on her radio show and at personal appearances throughout the South and Midwest.

As her career progressed, O'Day showed a growing propensity for religious material, particularly songs that emphasized man's failures and his need to seek solace in God. In 1949 she was hospitalized, apparently following an emotional breakdown, and after her release she and her husband joined the Church of God. Although she continued to record through 1951, she was no longer interested in being an entertainer. In 1954 Lynn was ordained a minister, and for the next three decades the duo preached in small West Virginia coal-mining towns. Although O'Day made some religious recordings for small labels in the 1960s, she never again returned to commercial country music. She died of cancer in 1987.

O'Day could have become a major star in the 1950s; her powerful singing, coupled with a highly emotional delivery, set the stage for the next generation of female country stars on the honky-tonk side of the aisle.

Select Discography

and the Cumberland Mountain Folks, Bear Family 15565. Two CDs of O'Day's Columbia recordings made between 1946 and 1951. Includes duets with husband, Lynn Davis.

O'KANES, THE (Kieran Kane, b. New York City, October 7, 1949 [gtr, voc]: Jamie O'Hara, b. Toledo, Ohio, August 8, 1950 [mdln, voc])

A popular vocal duo of the mid-1980s, the O'Kanes performed a roots-oriented music with a unique twist on traditional country harmony.

The duo were songwriters for NASHVILLE's Tree Music when they began performing together. O'Hara had written many hits for mainstream country acts, most notably "Grandpa (Tell Me 'Bout the Good Ol' Days)" for THE JUDDS, and Kane had written "Let's Have a Party," a hit for ALABAMA. Kane brought a more rock-oriented sound to the group, having grown up in the borough of Queens in New York City, while O'Hara had a soft-country orientation.

The duo were most noteworthy for their unorthodox approach to harmony; they often traded harmony and lead parts several times in a single song, while each vocal line maintained its own special quality (because each singer had a very distinctive voice). They also used spare, almost minimalist, accompaniments, shunning the arena-rock or glitzy-pop styles of many of their country contemporaries. Kane played MANDOLIN from his BLUEGRASS days, while O'Hara played simple guitar, and their accompanists often included accordion, FIDDLE, subtle electric guitar, and bass, recalling bluegrass instrumentation without using these acoustic instruments in a bluegrass style. Their unusual sound can be heard from their first hits, including their only #1 country disc, 1987's "Can't Stop My Heart from Lovin' You." They had a couple more hits later in 1987 and in 1988, but their acoustic, laid-back style was not as popular as more up-tempo groups.

After their successful debut in 1986, the duo lost steam with each successive release, and finally called it quits in 1990. Three years later O'Hara released his first solo effort, reflecting a continuation of the O'Kanes' philosophy of soft-country sounds presented in sparse settings; he has not released any more recordings. Kane released a solo album in 1994. He formed his own label, Dead Reckoning, in 1995, and has since released a handful of albums, appealing mainly to his core fans.

Select Discography

The Only Years, Sony/Lucky Dog 61489. Not a greatest-hits package, as you might expect, but a budget-priced, ten-song sampler.

OLD AND IN THE WAY (1973: Jerry Garcia [bnj, voc]; David Grisman [mdln, voc]; Peter Rowan [gtr, voc]; Vassar Clements [fdl]; John Kahn [b])

In the beginning, before God created The Grateful Dead, there was a young, BLUEGRASS BANJO picker named Jerry Garcia working around San Francisco in a jug band. Garcia's love for bluegrass music did not end after he became the ultimate hippie rocker, and he formed the informal group Old and in the Way as a means to express his love for this music (the name comes from the words of a sentimental old-time song). He joined forces with an obscure West Coast session player named DAVID GRISMAN on MANDOLIN and PETER ROWAN, who had previously played together in another one-off group, MULESKINNER. Fiddler VASSAR CLEMENTS was an alum of JOHN HARTFORD's early 1970s band, and had played with many other FOLK REVIVALISTS, including David Bromberg. They recorded one album, released by the Dead's own Round record label, featuring many Rowan originals that have since become newgrass standards: "Panama Red" and "Land of the Navajo," two of his mythic Western ballads, are the best known. Garcia revived the band from time to time with various personnel; he teamed up again with Grisman in 1993 to record an acoustic duo album for children, and then cut another album of old-time country standards. Other informal sessions were recorded by the duo before Garcia's untimely death in August, 1995.

Select Discography

Old and in the Way, Sugar Hill 3746/Grateful Dead 4104. Reissue of their first album, recorded live.
High Lonesome Sound, Acoustic Disc 19. A second album of live recordings, recorded in 1973 but not issued until 1996.

ORBISON, ROY (b. Vernon, Tex., April 23, 1936–December 6, 1988)

Orbison exists in that mythical region somewhere between country and rock; indeed, though he has recorded and been successful in both genres, he is most famous for a series of early 1960s pop ballads that exist in their own special world, propelled by his operatic, unearthly singing voice.

Orbison began performing as a teenager, leading the country band The Wink Westerners, who performed on his tiny hometown radio station. After finishing high school, he enrolled at North Texas State, where he met soon-to-be-teen-popster Pat Boone, who encouraged him to adapt to the new sound of rock and roll. In the mid-1950s Roy formed the Tune Wranglers, attracting the attention of JOHNNY CASH, who recommended that he send a demo tape to SAM PHILLIPS's Sun Records.

At Sun, Roy hit it big with the novelty "Ooby Dooby" in 1956, a teen rocker written specifically with that audience in mind. A year later Orbison was working in NASHVILLE as a songwriter for legendary promoter WESLEY ROSE. He penned "Claudette" for THE EVERLY BROTHERS, a big pop hit named for his wife.

In 1959 Rose arranged for Orbison to record for Monument Records, where he had his greatest success with a series of balladic pop tunes that defy categorization. These include 1961's "Crying," 1962's "Dream Baby," 1963's "Blue Bayou" and "In Dreams," and the classic 1964 recording of "Oh, Pretty Woman," featuring Roy's trademark growl. Orbison became a huge success, not only in the U.S. but also in England, where he was revered by British Invaders like The Beatles and The Rolling Stones. Orbison, whose vision had been terribly limited since childhood, forgot to bring his regular glasses to a show in England and was forced to wear his prescription sunglasses; these dark glasses, along with his jet black hair and black suit, became trademarks for the singer. Ironically the success of British acts on the U.S. pop charts beginning in 1964 did much to end Orbison's popularity at home.

In the mid-1960s, in search of broader horizons as an actor as well as a singer, Orbison signed with MGM, which had both a record label and a major film studio. He appeared in the lame B-grade film *Fastest Guitar Alive*, and also provided the sound track. Tragedy struck with the death of his wife in a 1965 motorcycle accident and, two years later, a freak fire at his home that killed two of his children. LINDA RONSTADT scored a huge success in 1977 with her cover of Roy's "Blue Bayou"; this brought the singer out of retirement and back into the studio for two albums, although neither was particularly successful.

The 1980s saw a continued interest in Roy's music, and he made a series of duet recordings, including one with EMMYLOU HARRIS on "That Lovin' You Feelin' Again" and an intense duet with Canadian punk-country star K.D. LANG on his "Crying." Roy's biggest triumph came at the end of his life when he was invited to join the looseknit pop band The Traveling Wilburys, along with George Harrison, Jeff Lynne, BOB DYLAN, and Tom Petty. A comeback solo LP was produced by Lynne, featuring the upbeat "You Got It" and the dramatic "Mystery Girl," which was released just after Orbison's death from a heart attack.

Although Orbison was not a pure country star by any means, his impact was felt in country as well as pop music. His unique musical personality inspired countless others to follow their own musical inspiration.

Select Discography

The Sun Years, Rhino 70916. Includes previously unreleased material.
For the Lonely, Rhino 71493. Great recordings cut between 1956 and 1965, Orbison's primo years.
The Legendary Roy Orbison, Sony Music Special Productions 46809. The ultimate gift for your friends in dark glasses; four CDs covering thirty years of recordings from 1955 to 1985, with an illustrated booklet.

OSBORNE BROTHERS, THE (b. Robert Van [Bobby] O., Hyden, Ky., December 7, 1931; Sonny O., b. Hyden, Ky., October 29, 1937)

The Osborne Brothers are PROGRESSIVE BLUEGRASS/country musicians who have pioneered the use of amplified instruments in bluegrass, as well as drums and PEDAL STEEL GUITARS. They are noted for their innovative harmonies and high-powered recordings.

The brothers performed together from childhood, and were already working professionally in the early 1950s, when Bobby was drafted to serve in the Korean War. Sonny was an accomplished BANJO player at age fourteen in 1952, so good that he was invited to join BLUEGRASS legend BILL MONROE's band for touring and recording during that summer. When Bobby returned from Korea in 1953, the brothers began performing together as a duo over local Knoxville radio. In 1954 they relocated to Michigan to perform and record with JIMMY MARTIN, another Monroe alumnus. Their output included the classic sides "Chalk Up Another One" and "20/20 Vision."

A year later they were in Dayton, Ohio, where they hooked up with another bluegrass legend, RED ALLEN, at the beginning of his career. The group signed with MGM Records in 1956, scoring with their cover of COUSIN EMMY's classic reworking of "Reuben/Train 45," renamed "Ruby." Their dramatic harmonies—Red on lead; Bobby, with his distinctive high tenor; and Sonny on baritone—highlighted on the a cappella introduction, made the single a standout. The use of drums on these recordings made them controversial among pure bluegrass fans, although they clearly fit in with the high-energy music that the brothers created. They also pioneered the use of twin harmony BANJOS, an innovation later copied by progressive bands like COUNTRY COOKING.

After Allen left the group, the brothers began performing on the *WWVA Jamboree* radio program in Wheeling. In 1959 Sonny Birchfield took over the lead vocal chores. A year later the band was booked into Antioch College in Yellow Springs, Ohio, introducing bluegrass music to a young, educated audience. They were soon in demand on the college and folk festival circuit, though they maintained strong ties to country music. In 1964 they were invited to join THE GRAND OLE OPRY, one of the few bluegrass groups at that time on the *Opry* stage, and signed with Decca. Their mid-1960s recordings broke further barriers in instrumentation, including their use of piano on "Up This Hill and Down," electric bass on "The Kind of Woman I Got," and pedal steel guitar on their big 1967 hit "Rocky Top," which has become perhaps the most overplayed song in all of bluegrass.

In 1976 the Osbornes left Decca for the more traditional bluegrass label CMH, and then began recording for Sugar Hill in the early 1980s; since the mid-1990s they have recorded for Pinecastle, a small bluegrass label. Their music remains as high-powered as ever, although in today's world of progressive bluegrass and newgrass, they hardly sound as revolutionary as they had some thirty years earlier.

Select Discography

Bluegrass, 1956–68, Bear Family 15598. All their MGM and Decca recordings from this period, totaling 114 tracks.
1968–74, Bear Family 15748. Four-CD set covering their later Decca recordings.
Once More, Vols. 1 & 2, Sugar Hill 2203. CD reissue of remakes of their favorite bluegrass numbers, originally issued on two LPs in 1985–1986.

OSLIN, K. T. (b. Kay Toinette O., Crossett, Ark., May 25, 1941)

Oslin is a SINGER/SONGWRITER with a feminist slant who had her first success in the late 1980s, when she was already in her forties, after a career that spanned folk to theatrical music to recording TV jingles.

From rural Arkansas, Oslin relocated with her family first to Mobile, Alabama, and then to the Houston area. In 1962 she formed a folk trio with singer/songwriter Guy Clark and local radio producer Chuck Jones. She moved to Los Angeles soon after, joining forces with another folksinger, Frank Davis; together they issued an LP that went nowhere. She switched to theatrical singing, touring with the road company of *Hello Dolly!* and ending up in New York City in 1966.

After a few more bit parts on Broadway and off, as well as work cutting commercial jingles, Oslin began experimenting with songwriting. By 1978 she had built up an impressive portfolio, and attracted the attention of Nashville publishing executive Dianne Petty. However, Nashville didn't seem ready for her more liberated themes, although she did briefly record under the name Kay T. Oslin for Elektra in 1981–1982. She then returned to New York for more commercial work.

Finally, in 1987, Oslin signed with RCA in Nashville, scoring a hit with her own "80s Ladies," an ode to her generation of women who had "burned our bras and burned our dinners." A series of spunky country chart-toppers followed, including "Didn't Expect It to Go Down This Way" (with the immortal couplet "I'm overworked and overweight/I can't remember when I last had a date") and her 1990 #1 hit, "Come Next Monday."

Through the 1990s Oslin was less active, returning with an album of covers of her hits in 1996 (playfully titled *My Roots Are Showing*), and then, five years later, attempting a comeback with an album of pop-flavored numbers produced by The Mavericks' headman, Raul Malo. However, only her longtime fans were left to buy these albums.

Oslin's Broadway background is evident in all of her recordings, which are more middle-of-the-road pop than country in their orientation. Despite the feminist message of her best-known hit, she was really a fairly conservative performer, appealing to Nashville's older guard.

Select Discography

Greatest Hits: Songs from an Aging Sex Bomb, RCA 662277. Compilation of her best-known work from the late 1980s.

OSMOND, MARIE (b. Ogden, Utah, October 13, 1959)

The only female member of the Osmond clan, Marie represents the apotheosis of the sickly sweet, primly neat girl singer who appeals to the most conservative elements in the country audience. A marginally talented singer, she trades on her wholesome image and made-for-TV personality.

The Osmonds are a pop phenomenon that defies explanation or even description. Whiz producer Mike Curb had shaped pop careers for brothers Donny and "Little Jimmy"; in search of another star, he turned to the Osmond matriarch and asked her if thirteen-year-old Marie had any talent. Mom assured him she did, although she preferred country music, not the cloying teen-pop that her brothers performed. Curb hooked her up with veteran ex-rockabilly star Sonny James, who produced her first #1 success, a cover of the 1960 "classic" by Anita Bryant, "Paper Roses," which Osmond cut in 1973; not only was it a #1 country hit, it hit #5 on the pop charts, proving once and for all that you can't account for America's musical taste. As a teen Marie joined with brother Donny, performing pop-flavored material on the Vegas/lounge-club circuit. From 1976 to 1979 the duo were paired on a variety TV show, which opened with good-girl Marie sweetly singing "I'm a little bit country," while leather-pants-wearin', pseudo-tough-guy Donny thrilled pre-adolescent America by chiming in "I'm a little bit rock 'n' roll." By country, it seems that her handlers meant she was the less threatening of an already sugar-coated duo; Marie's career has been built on this all-American image.

Fortunately for fans of true country, Osmond's career faded after the TV show went blank, although she made a comeback in the mid-1980s both as a soloist with the cloying "There's No Stopping Your Heart" (written by Michael Brook, aka Bonagura, who would later form the group Baillie and the Boys) and in duets with popsters Dan Seals and Paul Davis. Neither her vocal style (which is a mixture of mid-1970s rock, pop, and schlock) nor her accompaniments are particularly country, but that's OK with her audience, who prize her primarily because of their memories of her teenage success. Anyone who makes Karen Carpenter sound like a reasonably talented vocalist has a role to play in music history; and, after dwelling in Osmond country, even Crystal Gayle sounds like she deserves a spot in the country rack.

Select Discography

The Best of, Curb 77263.

OUTLAW COUNTRY (c. 1975–1985)

The "outlaws"—led by Willie Nelson and Waylon Jennings—were frustrated by the Nashville Sound and countrypolitan transformations of country music into a light pop, mainstream style. Influenced by traditional country sounds, particularly Western Swing and Texas honky-tonk, as well as the breakthroughs of singer/songwriters like Bob Dylan who proved that pop songs could have a message, the outlaws made a highly personal music that helped revive interest in true country sounds.

The movement took its name from a 1975 RCA anthology called *Wanted: The Outlaws* that featured recordings by Jennings and Nelson. However, it dates back to Nelson's frustration with working as a songwriter and performer in mid-1960s NASHVILLE. Although he had provided major hits for other artists, Nelson felt that Nashville's producers didn't understand his own approach to making music.

Influenced by Bob Dylan and the other 1960s singer-songwriters, Nelson was beginning to write more personal music that he felt only he could perform. But Nashville's producers were burying his music in the same Nashville-Sound, hyperslick commercial production that they applied to all country acts. Fed up with his inability to make music his own way, Nelson left Nashville to live in Austin, Texas, in 1968.

Texas is a breeding ground for an unusual sort of country singer/songwriter. With its strong streak of independence and its musical mix of honky-tonk, Mexican, Western Swing, and COWBOY traditions, Texas has been fertile ground for innovative musicians. Already a group of songwriters were gathering in Austin, including JERRY JEFF WALKER, JOE ELY, and JIMMIE DALE GILMORE. Nelson's arrival on the scene helped further invigorate it; he began sponsoring an annual picnic/festival that brought younger NASHVILLE songwriters and performers like KRIS KRISTOFFERSON and Waylon Jennings to the region.

The outlaw musicians appealed not only to a core country audience but also to COUNTRY-ROCK fans and fans of singer/songwriters. Nelson left RCA to record for Atlantic, a company more famous for its jazz releases than for pure country, and then moved to Columbia; these labels promoted his music in the college, FM market as well as to country enthusiasts. Nelson's success making music in his own way had a profound influence on Nashville. For one thing, it showed that returning-to-roots country sounds could be a way for country music to survive, rather than simply pandering to the latest pop styles. For another, it showed that the strong tradition of eccentric, highly individual musicians who had created country music needed to be honored and developed if the music was to grow. This led directly to the revolution that has come to be known as the new traditionalists.

Select Discography

Wanted: The Outlaws, RCA 5976. The compilation album that gave the movement its name.

OVERSTREET, PAUL (b. Antioch, Miss., March 17, 1955)

Overstreet is a SINGER/SONGWRITER who is better known for providing other folks with hits—particularly nouveau country hunk RANDY TRAVIS—than for his own recordings.

He originally came to NASHVILLE in 1973, but it took him about ten years of struggle to get to the top of the heap. By the early 1980s, however, he was producing a string of hits, including Randy Travis's first biggie, "Diggin' Up Bones," a clever, honky-tonkesque song about old true loves who return to haunt the song's narrator. It was followed by a slew of other Travis hits, "On the Other Hand" (an on-the-edge-of-cheatin' song), "Forever and Ever Amen," and "Deeper Than the Holler"; THE JUDDS' sappy "Love Can Build a Bridge"; GEORGE JONES's hit "Same Ole Me"; TANYA TUCKER's bad girl song "My Arms Stay Open All Night"; "Houston Solution" for RONNIE MILSAP . . . the list goes on and on.

As a performer Overstreet first appeared with two other songwriters who longed to be performers, Thom Schulyer and Fred Knobloch, forming S.K.O. The trio had a few 1987 hits, including the #1 "Baby's Got a Brand New Band." Overstreet left the group to pursue a solo career, and had his biggest hit in 1990 with "Daddy's Come Around." In the meantime he had found God, a particularly nasty thing to happen to a good ol' HONKY-TONKER, and since the early 1990s has forsaken his mainstream career to perform religious material.

Select Discography

Best of, RCA 66040. Drawn from his RCA recordings made between 1990 and 1994.

OVERSTREET, TOMMY (b. T. Cary O., Oklahoma City, Okla., September 10, 1937)

Overstreet was a minor-league country performer of the early 1970s who is best known for his work on TV's HEE HAW.

Born in Oklahoma City, Tommy was raised in Houston and became interested in a musical career thanks to his parents, who bought him a GUITAR when he was fourteen, and an uncle, Gene Austin, who had been a successful pop crooner in the 1920s, famous for his hit recording of "My Blue Heaven." In high school Tommy performed in a teen-pop style on the local radio station, and then, when his family moved to Abilene, he began performing as Tommy Dean of Abilene, again in a pop-rock style.

In 1967 he moved to NASHVILLE in search of a country career, and was hired to manage the country label Dot. He signed with Dot in 1969, scoring his first country #1 with 1971's "Gwen (Congratulations)," and continued to hit the Top 20 of the country charts through 1977. His recordings were typical COUNTRYPOLITAN fare of the day, as much influenced by Neil Diamond and other pop-schlock acts as they were by any country roots. In fact, Overstreet admits that he was hardly a country-music fan, although he saw country as an area that would support his watered-down mainstream pop style in the early 1970s. In 1979 he signed with Elektra/Asylum, which made a brief attempt at starting a country division, and then recorded for A&M and smaller labels in the early 1980s. Since then Overstreet has mostly stuck to the country fair and rodeo circuit.

Select Discography

Greatest Hits, Hollywood 390.

OWENS, BONNIE (b. B. Campbell, Blanchard, Okla., October 1, 1932)

Bonnie Owens is a fine country-styled vocalist in the female-WEEPER mold who has been overshadowed by her association with two of country's megastars, first husband BUCK OWENS and second husband MERLE HAGGARD.

From a dirt-poor family, as a child Owens picked cotton to help her family survive. The family relocated to Arizona when she was a young teenager, and things looked up for a while. She got her first job in Mesa, Arizona, working on the *Buck and Britt* radio show, where she met future husband, Buck Owens. The two-some worked for a while in a touring country band, eventually making their way in the mid-1950s to new-country mecca Bakersfield, California, where Herb Hensen hired Bonnie to sing on his locally broadcast *Trading Post* TV show. The Owens marriage soon dissolved, and Bonnie's mother came west to care for her two children while Bonnie began building her career as a solo artist. She had her first local hit with the early 1960s "A Dear John Letter," released on the tiny Marvel label, as well as her tribute to PATSY CLINE, "Missing on a Mountain."

In the early 1960s she befriended an up-and-coming country singer named Merle Haggard, and the two began making demo recordings together, attracting the attention of local producer/record label owner Fuzzy Owens (no relation). Owens signed Bonnie and Merle to his Tally label, and Bonnie had solo hits with 1963's "Daddy Doesn't Live Here Anymore," a classic weeper, and the more feisty "Don't Take Advantage of Me" from a year later; in 1964 Bonnie teamed with Merle, and the duo scored a big hit with "Just Between the Two of Us," leading to a contract with Capitol Records for them both.

Bonnie had a couple more hits through the 1960s as a solo artist, but in 1970 pretty much retired from performing, at least on her own. She divorced Haggard in 1975, but by the early 1980s she was back in his backup band, working as a singer as well as continuing to manage his business affairs.

One of Bonnie's sons from her marriage to Buck Owens is Buddy Allan, who has had some success as a solo country performer, as well as appearing with his dad in the early 1970s.

OWENS, BUCK (b. Alvis Edgar O., Jr., Sherman, Tex., August 12, 1929)

One of the creators of the southern California country sound, Buck Owens is best known for his early 1960s hits, including his first #1 country tune, "Act Naturally," later covered by The Beatles.

Born in Texas, Buck was the son of a sharecropper. The family moved to Arizona in search of a better standard of living, but to little avail, and Buck had to leave school after the ninth grade to help support his family. Already a talented musician playing both MANDOLIN and GUITAR, he was performing on local radio out of Mesa, Arizona, when he was just sixteen; he met future wife BONNIE CAMPBELL OWENS there, and married her a year later.

In 1951 he relocated to Bakersfield, California, which was a center of California's country-music community in the 1950s, thanks to its military base. There he formed his first band, The Schoolhouse Playboys, a swingin' ensemble in which he played sax and trumpet, and also worked as a guitarist on numerous country and pop-rock sessions. He also recorded some ROCKABILLY tunes under the name of Corky Jones. Local country star TOMMY COLLINS gave Owens his first big break in the mid-1950s, when he hired him to be lead guitarist in his band and featured him on many of his early hits. Owens formed his own band, The Buckaroos, in the late 1950s, and signed with Capitol as a solo performer. The Buckaroos helped define the

Buck Owens in front of his recording studios, c. mid-1970s. Photo: Raeanne Rubenstein

"modern" country-band sound; rather than acoustic guitars and MANDOLINS, the band featured stinging electric-guitar leads played by Don Rich on the newly introduced Fender Telecaster (Rich also provided wonderful harmony vocals), along with "crying" PEDAL STEEL GUITAR licks played by Tom Brumley. Both of these elements would become standard on country recordings of the 1960s.

Owens's first hit was "Second Fiddle," followed by "Under Your Spell Again" from 1959, "Excuse Me, I Think I've Got a Heartache" from a year later, and 1961's "Fooling Around." From the first, Owens established himself as a purveyor of upbeat, HONKY-TONK flavored material, with a distinctive vocal style that showed the influence of Western COWBOY yodelers as well as the beer-soaked honky-tonk vocalizing of HANK WILLIAMS. Owens was rarely off the charts in the 1960s, including wonderful hits such as 1963's "Act Naturally" and "I've Got a Tiger by the Tail," "Buckaroo" from 1965, "Waitin' in Your Welfare Line" from a year later, and 1969's "Tall Dark Stranger." He also made some fine duet recordings in the early 1960s with WESTERN SWING-turned-BLUEGRASS vocalist ROSE MADDOX.

After his 1960s hits Owens hooked up with a new-country music TV show, HEE HAW. The success of the show made Buck one of the most instantly identifiable of all country stars, even though the quality of his recordings had declined. His career hit a nadir in 1974 when he issued the junky novelty number "Monster's Holiday"; by the early 1980s he was focusing on his business interests and had pretty much retired from music making. In the mid-1980s nouveau-country star DWIGHT YOAKAM took Owens's characteristic 1960s sound and reintroduced it to a new generation of listeners. Owens rerecorded "Act Naturally" as a duet with Ringo Starr (who popularized the song with The Beatles), and cut a duet with Yoakam, as well as continuing to play live dates. In 1996 he was given his rightful spot in the Country Music Hall of Fame.

Select Discography

The Buck Owens Collection (1959–1990), Rhino 71016. Three CDs covering Owens's entire career; great sound and seventy-six-page illustrated booklet by country authority Rich Kienzle.

OWENS, TEX (b. Doye Hensley O., Killeen, Tex., June 15, 1892–September 9, 1962)

Owens was a Western SINGER/SONGWRITER best known for penning "Cattle Call," a hit for EDDY ARNOLD in the late 1940s and for LEANN RIMES in the mid-1990s.

Owens was one of thirteen children raised on a small farm in Texas. (His younger sister, Ruby Agnes, would become well known as a cowgirl performer, TEXAS RUBY.) As a teenager he worked in a MINSTREL SHOW, and then held a number of jobs, including police officer. All the while he continued to play GUITAR and perform on the side.

In 1932 he got his first break when he was given his own time slot on a Kansas City, Missouri, radio station. He was given the handle "the Texas Ranger" for this broadcast. Two years later he made his only issued recordings, including his most famous song, "Cattle Call." Another session in 1936 did not result in any released records. Meanwhile Owens remained with the Kansas City station until 1943.

From the mid-1940s through 1960, Owens continued to work at radio stations in Cincinnati, Oklahoma City, and Hollywood, California. In 1960 he retired to his native Texas, and died two years later.

His daughter, Laura Lee McBride, was lead vocalist with BOB WILLS's Texas Playboys in the late 1940s and early 1950s, the first female vocalist that Wills employed.

Select Discography

Cattle Call, Bear Family 15777. Twenty-two tracks drawn from home demos, 1934 Decca recordings, and a handful of early 1950s small label tracks.

OXFORD, VERNON (b. Larue, Ark., June 8, 1941)

Oxford is a traditional, HONKY-TONK vocalist who has been more popular in Europe than in the U.S., although he was reintroduced to the American audience through a series of albums for the BLUEGRASS label Rounder in the early 1980s.

The son of a FIDDLE player, Oxford was raised in a music-making atmosphere, both at home and in church. After the family moved to Kansas, he took up the fiddle and became a state champion, forming his own band and touring through the West. He eventually made it to NASHVILLE in the mid-1960s, and was briefly signed by RCA at the height of the NASHVILLE SOUND era. Oxford's sound was far too traditional for the times, and he was dropped by the label. He began touring Europe, where his popularity was so great that RCA re-signed him in the mid-1970s, and he had one big hit with 1976's "Redneck." Soon after, he moved to the more traditionally oriented Rounder label, which heavily promoted his recordings as examples of the true country sound. Unfortunately the new-country movement was yet to take root, and these recordings again proved more popular abroad than at home.

In 1978 Oxford was born again, but nonetheless has continued to perform "sinful songs." As he explained in an interview for the BBC, "I do cheating songs, but now I do them to represent what sin is: I use them to make a point about Jesus Christ. 'Redneck!' shows what I used to be before I was saved. I sing GOSPEL songs at the end of every show and tell them about the Truth. Sometimes I combine singing with preaching. When I called a girl out of the audience once, the power of God knocked her down and she slithered like a snake across the floor. I have found peace and happiness, and I would like to help others to find it too." He has remained popular in Europe, where he toured and recorded during the 1990s.

Select Discography

Let Me Sing You a Song, West Side 849. Compilation of 1960s recordings made for RCA.
Keeper of the Flame, Bear Family 15774. Five-CD set of his mid-1970s RCA recordings, along with miscellaneous other material. For the diehard fan.
Keepin' It Country, Rounder 156. Cassette-only reissue of early 1980s recordings.

P

PARKER, "COLONEL" TOM (b. Andreas Cornelis van Kuijk, Breda, The Netherlands, June 26, 1909–January 21, 1997)

One of country music's first great promoters, Parker did much to professionalize the management and promotion of country acts. He was also the notorious long-time manager of ELVIS PRESLEY, carefully controlling the singer's career.

Parker's life has long been shrouded in rumor and mystery. Born in The Netherlands, he came to the United States in the late 1920s, settling here permanently in 1929. In 1930 he joined the Army and was stationed in Hawaii, serving until 1933. The commander of American troops there was Thomas R. Parker; this may have been an inspiration to the young Dutchman to take a new name and identity after his discharge: Thomas A. Parker, who gave his birthplace as Huntington, West Virginia. (His "Colonel" title came later, when Governor JIMMIE DAVIS of Louisiana gave him this honorary title, and had nothing to do with his military career.)

In the mid-1930s Parker began working as a carnival advance man, learning how to pack in the crowds, and also performed as a fortune-teller, palmist, and emcee. Parker was a shameless promoter who would do literally anything to drum up an audience; these techniques would serve him well in later years. By 1935 he was living in Tampa, Florida, booking shows for a variety of performers.

Parker met up-and-coming country crooner EDDY ARNOLD in mid-1945. Through artful promotion he built Arnold into one of the first great postwar country stars. Arnold was soon seen in films and had his own radio show. The two remained close partners until Arnold mysteriously dropped his manager in 1953; he never spoke ill of Parker after the breakup, but he would never explain why he decided to break with his successful manager.

Parker replaced Arnold with Canadian HANK SNOW in 1954, and the two were soon business partners.

While handling Snow, Parker saw the audience's reaction to Snow's opening act, ELVIS PRESLEY, and discovered his life's vocation: managing the hip-swiveling singer. In 1955 he purchased Elvis's management contract for a paltry $2500, and soon arranged for an enormous advance of $40,000 (a princely sum for a pop act) from RCA Records. He also set up a publishing company, promoted Elvis on television, and arranged for a movie deal with producer Hal Wallis.

Parker remained devoted to Elvis through the singer's career ups and downs and his eventual decline. Many have faulted him for the unusually high fees that he charged the singer; not only did he claim a full 25 percent for management, but he also took cuts from Elvis's publishing, recording, and concertizing. After Presley's death Parker retired, but not before exacting a $2 million fee from RCA for his rights to the singer.

The epitome of the big-mouthed, pushy publicist/manager, Parker has been blamed for pushing Elvis into his ill-fated 1960s film career, as well as for insulating him from current trends in music. But Elvis was as devoted to Parker as Parker was to his charge; and it's undoubtedly true that Parker was a master at whipping up publicity for the singer. Parker's techniques have been copied in the worlds of pop, rock, and country by countless other promoters, both scrupulous and not so scrupulous.

PARKER, LINDA (b. Genevieve Elizabeth Meunich, Covington, Ky., January 18, 1912–August 12, 1935)

Linda Parker was an early star of WLS's popular NATIONAL BARN DANCE, specializing in sentimental ballads sung in a clear, professionally trained voice.

Parker was born across the river from Cincinnati and raised in Gary, Indiana, where as a teenager she began performing on radio and in clubs. JOHN LAIR, the enterprising producer of Chicago's *National Barn Dance* radio show, discovered her there, and gave her a new name, a little-girl sweetheart image, and a country repertoire. She was made the featured singer of the show's house band, the Cumberland Ridge Runners, and given the cutesy-poo nickname "The Little Sunbonnet Girl." (In publicity photos she wore a sunbonnet and gingham dress; backwoods dress became the standard uniform for female country performers after her.) Although she was often pictured holding a BANJO or GUITAR, Parker did not play either instrument; again the publicity machinery molded her image to include the accoutrements that fans expected to see.

From 1932 until her death from appendicitis three years later, Parker was a favorite act, dividing her repertoire between nineteenth-century WEEPERS like "I'll Be All Smiles Tonight" and the occasional brassy traditional song like "Single Girl." She sang in a clear, soothing style that reflected her pop music roots, and became a model for country radio stars through the 1930s. Her death at age twenty-three cemented her appeal to Depression-era listeners; in her honor WLS stars KARL AND HARTY rewrote the old standard "Bury Me Beneath the Willow" to become "We Buried Her Beneath the Willow."

PARNELL, LEE ROY (b. Abilene, Tex., December 21, 1956)

Parnell serves up a heaping portion of good-time Texas-styled musical stew, including a dash of BUDDY HOLLY rock, a hearty dose of BOB WILLS WESTERN SWING, and the zest of R&B and Tex-Mex music.

Parnell formed his first band at age nineteen, playing in and around his home town of Abilene. He came to Nashville at age twenty-one, and was one of many young singers showcased and discovered at the Bluebird Café, where he first performed in 1987. Signed with Arista in 1988, he produced his first album a year later, scoring immediately with his tough-minded blend of country, rock, and soul. His first success was the rockin' "Oughta Be a Law," followed by the country-gospel "The Rock," and his own song "Road Scholar."

In 1992 Parnell's second album produced a #2 hit, "What Kind of Fool Do You Think I Am," but then it was three years until he scored another Top 10 hit, "A Little Bit of You." Like many other early 1990s hat acts, Parnell had difficulty matching his early success in the later 1990s, releasing his last major label album of new material in 1997. He was dropped by Arista in 1999, then returned in 2001 on the smaller Vanguard label.

Select Discography

Hits and the Highway Ahead, Arista 18889. 1999 collection.

PARSONS, GRAM (b. Ingram Cecil Connor III, Winterhaven, Fla., November 5, 1946–September 19, 1973)

A seminal figure in the birth of COUNTRY-ROCK, Parsons embraced a fast-lane lifestyle that led to his premature death, but not before he influenced a generation of new-country singers.

Parsons was born in Florida but raised in Georgia, the son of country SINGER/SONGWRITER "Coon Dog" Connor, who took his own life when his son was thirteen. An early love for the GUITAR led Parsons to form his first professional band, the FOLK-REVIVAL trio The Shilohs, in 1962 (the band also included Jim Stafford, who later had country hits including 1973's "Spiders and Snakes," and Kent LaVoie, who later formed the pop band Lobo and had hits with bubble-gum anthems like 1971's "Me and You and a Dog Named Boo").

Parsons was admitted to the Harvard Divinity School in 1966, and while in the Boston area he formed the short-lived International Submarine Band. This group is generally credited with being the first to record what would become country-rock music. He then joined the folk-rock group THE BYRDS, and participated in their seminal country album, *Sweetheart of the Rodeo*. Parsons's original "Hickory Wind" is a high point of the album, which includes many country standards.

In 1969 Parsons and Byrds bass player CHRIS HILLMAN formed THE FLYING BURRITO BROTHERS, along with ex-Byrds drummer Michael Clarke, "Sneeky" Pete Kleinow on PEDAL STEEL GUITR, and bassist Chris Ethridge. Their first album, *The Gilded Palace of Sin*, featured the Parsons classic "Sin City," a country song for a new generation of hippie country singers. In 1970 banjoist Bernie Leadon joined the group (he would later be a founding member of THE EAGLES). A second album followed, featuring a cover of Mick Jagger and Keith Richards's "Wild Horses." Parsons left the group soon after to pursue a solo career.

Parsons introduced a new singer as a member of his backup band on his first solo album: EMMYLOU HARRIS. The duo recorded some of the most compelling country-rock, particularly on Parsons's second solo disc, *Grievous Angel* from 1974, featuring a remake of "Love Hurts" by the famous country songwriting duo of BOUDELEAUX AND FELICE BRYANT. JAMES BURTON, a guitarist who had previously recorded with ELVIS PRESLEY and RICK NELSON, and whose trebly sound was a defining one in country-rock, also performed with Parsons.

Years of drug and alcohol abuse caught up with Parsons, and he died soon after the release of his second solo album. In a bizarre move his manager kidnapped the singer's corpse from the funeral parlor, in order to carry out Parsons's last request to be cremated. Since his death numerous tapes (including early recordings by The Shilohs and live concert material and outtakes) have been issued, furthering his legend as a martyred singer. Emmylou Harris has made it a point to credit Parsons for her own career, and to mention his name whenever she is asked about the roots of her music.

Parsons's influence was great: He took country themes and modernized them so that a younger audience could sympathize with the material. He showed how the nostalgic sadness of country music could be wed to the power of rock and roll. Incidentally, he introduced country instrumentation—BANJO, FIDDLE, pedal steel guttar—into the world of rock, paving the way not only for countless other rock bands (from POCO to The Eagles) but also for rockin' country bands (such as SAWYER BROWN).

Select Discography

Warm Evenings, Pale Mornings, Bottled Blues, Raven 24. Covers Parsons's entire career, from The Shilohs through The Byrds to his solo work.
GP/Grievous Angel, Reprise 26108. CD reissue of both of Parsons's early 1970s albums on one disc.
Live 1973, Sierra 6003. With Emmylou Harris.

PARTON, DOLLY (b. D. Rebecca P., Locust Ridge, Tenn., January 19, 1946)

A larger-than-life-size figure (in more ways than one) on the American cultural scene, Dolly Parton is hardly the "aw-shucks," country-bred, dumb blond personality that she often projects. A talented singer and songwriter, she has shown a unique ability to market herself and mold an image, at the same time producing unique, personal music that continues the great traditions of previous generations of SINGER/SONGWRITERS.

The fourth of twelve children raised in poverty in rural Tennessee, Dolly first made recordings in 1959 for Goldband; in 1964 she traveled to Nashville, signing with Monument Records and scoring her first hit with "Dumb Blonde" in 1967. The same year she joined forces with country legend PORTER WAGONER, a savvy businessman who ran a large country revue. He recorded a string of duets with the younger singer, beginning with a cover of Tom Paxton's "Last Thing on My Mind" that helped launch her career.

Dolly's solo recordings for RCA in the late 1960s and early 1970s established her as a sensitive singer/songwriter who could reflect on her own rural heritage. In songs like 1971's "Coat of Many Colors" she honored the memory of her mother, who made her a patchwork coat out of fabric remnants. Many of her songs were based on childhood memories, presenting in a straightforward, unembarrassed way the often hard times that she endured as a child. In 1974 Parton permanently split from Wagoner, who was bitterly jealous

Dolly Parton in concert, c. 1995. Photo: Raeanne Rubenstein

of his younger protégée's talent and success, and her songs began to be covered by folk-rock artists from LINDA RONSTADT ("I Will Always Love You," later a 1992–1993 #1 hit for pop singer Whitney Houston) to Maria Muldaur ("My Tennessee Mountain Home").

This encouraged Parton to attempt her own crossover recordings for the pop charts, beginning with the bouncy 1977 hit "Here You Come Again."

In 1980 Parton's everywoman personality was perfectly exploited in the working-class/feminist movie *9 to 5*. This depiction of a group of secretaries' revenge on their domineering and sexist boss appealed to working women and helped cement Parton's image as "just another gal." Her title composition for the film was a pop and country hit. This success led to a decade of minor and major film roles, plus continued recordings in a pop-country vein. A longtime friendship with pop stars Linda Ronstadt and EMMYLOU HARRIS resulted in the 1987 LP *Trio*, a rather subdued folk-country outing that produced a minor hit in their cover of Phil Spector's "To Know Him Is to Love Him." In 1989, in an attempt to return to her roots, she recorded *White Limozeen*, a more country-oriented LP produced by new-country star RICKY SKAGGS, an artistic if not a great chart success.

Parton also showed savvy as a businesswoman, opening her own theme park, Dollywood, to celebrate Tennessee mountain crafts and culture. This somewhat ersatz re-creation of an idealized mountain life has proved to be quite successful, helping the economic revitalization of her childhood region and, not incidentally, making a good deal of money for the singer.

In 1993 Parton partnered with LORETTA LYNN and TAMMY WYNETTE on the *Honky-Tonk Angels* album, a nice collection that showed all three were still in fine voice (despite Wynette's failing health). She continued to record mainstream country through the later 1990s without enjoying much success. In 1999 Parton was finally recognized by the country world by being elected to the Country Music Hall of Fame. That same year she issued an album accompanied by a BLUEGRASS band, working with new bluegrass star ALISON KRAUSS. She followed up in 2001 with a second all-acoustic, bluegrass album, setting yet another new course for her career. The song "Shine" from the second album had some airplay, and its accompanying video was popular on Country Music Television.

Dolly's sister Stella (b. 1949) had some minor country hits in the mid-1970s, including 1975's "Ode to Olivia," in which she defended Olivia Newton-John against her country music critics.

Select Discography

The World of, Vols 1. and 2, Monument 44361/44362. Her first, mid-1960s solo recordings, including the hit "Dumb Blonde"; of interest to Partonophiles.
The RCA Years, 1957–1986, RCA 66127. Two-CD set featuring thirty tracks taking her from her early tracks to her COUNTRYPOLITAN heyday.

Trio, Warner Bros. 25491. With Ronstadt and Harris; pleasant, if understated.
White Limozeen, Columbia 44384. Nice 1989 album produced by Ricky Skaggs.
Grass Is Blue, Sugar Hill 3900. 1999 acoustic-bluegrass album that launched a new phase of Parton's career.

PAUL, LES (b. Lester William Polsfuss, Waukesha, Wis., June 9, 1915)

One of the pioneers of electric-guitar playing and design, Paul is best remembered for his sugary pop hits of the 1950s, accompanying his wife, Mary Ford.

From his earliest days Paul was an amateur inventor, tinkering with radio sets and early forms of amplified guitars. He took up harmonica and piano when he was nine, followed soon after by GUITAR. He began performing as a guitarist/country comedian under the name Hot Rod Red, the Wizard of Waukesha, appearing before local Lions clubs and playing on local radio. He then moved to Chicago to perform over WLS with the Western group Rube Tronson and His Texas Cowboys, now taking the stage name of Rhubarb Red. By the mid-1930s he was broadcasting as Rhubarb Red, performing country music in the mornings and then switching to jazz pickin' under his new stage name, Les Paul, in the afternoons. He had a hit record with a countrified cover of "Just Because" that was released on the dime-store Montgomery Ward label.

In 1936 he formed a light-jazz trio with second guitarist Jim Atkins (half-brother of CHET ATKINS) and bassist Ernie Newton; they were hired to tour with the popular Fred Waring's Pennsylvanians dance band. In 1939 he returned to Chicago, and two years later perfected a solid-body electric guitar design, the first of its kind; also in 1941 he relocated to Los Angeles.

After serving in the Army, Paul returned to civilian life and hooked up with girl singer/guitarist Colleen Summers, who had previously played with COWBOY star JIMMY WAKELY; she took the stage name of Mary Ford by the late 1940s. The new duo began recording the jazzy pop songs that would make them famous. Meanwhile Paul's fascination with electronics led him to experiment with multiple overdubbings of the guitar and vocal parts, creating some of the earliest overtracked recordings. Their 1950s pop hits included jazzy versions of "How High the Moon," "Nola," "Lover," and "The World Is Waiting for the Sunrise."

In 1952 the Gibson Company issued the first Les Paul guitar, an electric, solid-body instrument based on his earlier designs. This has remained one of the most popular electric guitars, although it has been somewhat overshadowed by Leo Fender's 1950s guitar designs, including the Telecaster and Stratocaster models that are favored by rock musicians.

Paul and Ford divorced in 1962, and Paul retired from performing. However, interest in his recordings and his phenomenal guitar technique led him to return to performing in the 1970s. His album of duets with Chet Atkins (*Chester and Lester*), released in 1976, brought out the best of both guitarists. Paul continues to perform regularly, primarily in the New York area.

Select Discography

Complete Decca Trios—Plus, MCA 11708. All of his Decca recordings, including some previously unissued tracks, made between 1936 and 1947, on two CDs. Also includes some tracks where he accompanies other pop singers.

The Best of Capitol Masters, Capitol 99617. Reissues late-1940s and early-1950s pop hits with Mary Ford.

16 Most Requested Songs, Columbia/Legacy 64993. Their later hits, cut between 1958 and 1961.

PAYCHECK, JOHNNY (b. Donald Eugene Lytle, Greenfield, Ohio, May 31, 1938)

One of the orneriest of the OUTLAWS, Paycheck had a megahit in 1977 with the worker's anthem "Take This Job and Shove It."

Exposed to country music from his youth in Ohio, Paycheck began playing GUITAR and bass as a teenager,

Johnny Paycheck, c. mid-1970s. Photo: Raeanne Rubenstein

as well as writing countrified songs. He was working as a bass player in PORTER WAGONER's Wagonmasters backup band in the late 1950s, followed by stints with FARON YOUNG, GEORGE JONES, and RAY PRICE; he also took up PEDAL STEEL GUITAR. In the late 1950s he cut some ROCKABILLY-styled sides under the name of Donny Young, having a minor hit with "Shakin' the Blues."

In the early 1960s he returned to performing and writing country material, and in 1965 was signed by Mercury, taking his new stage name of Johnny Paycheck (the original Paycheck was a little-known boxer who unsuccessfully bouted with Joe Louis in 1940). He had a couple of modest hits in the mid-1960s, including 1965's "A–11" and "Heartbreak Tennessee" from a year later, as well as writing hits for TAMMY WYNETTE ("Apartment Number 9") and Ray Price ("Touch My Heart"). In 1966 Paycheck cofounded the Little Darlin' record label, scoring a hit with his own "The Lovin' Machine." However, by the late 1960s his career was derailed by his increasing dependence on alcohol and drugs.

Famed producer BILLY SHERRILL gave Johnny a chance to make a comeback in the early 1970s, and he scored a couple of hits with the Sherrill-produced "Song and Dance Man" from 1974 and "I Don't Love Her Anymore" from a year later. But Johnny's bad-boy ways caught up with him again in 1976, when he declared bankruptcy after several questionable business dealings went sour. However, a year later he was back on the charts with the appropriately titled "I'm the Only Hell (Mama Ever Raised)" and the DAVID ALLAN COE-penned "Take This Job (and Shove It)," his sole country #1 hit. Paycheck continued in the humorous vein in 1978 with the self-mocking "Me and the IRS" and the gushy "Friend, Lover, Wife" that he wrote with Sherrill. Meanwhile, in 1977 he received a Career Achievement Award from the Country Music Association.

Paycheck teamed up with his old boss George Jones in 1979 for a series of successful duets, beginning with a countrified cover of Chuck Berry's classic, "Maybelline." The duo produced a rockin' album with the tongue-in-cheek title *Double Trouble*. Next he teamed with another country legend, MERLE HAGGARD, with the appropriately titled duet "I Can't Hold Myself in Line," a 1981 hit. However, Paycheck's rough and rowdy ways got the better of him again, and by 1983 he had moved to the tiny AMI label. Two years later he was convicted of aggravated assault following a barroom brawl in his native Ohio, and sentenced to nine and a half years in prison, a case that he appealed successfully until 1989, when he finally was sent to prison (he was paroled after two years).

In 1987 Paycheck returned to recording, now for Mercury, producing some of the best music of his career, although the hit from these sessions, "Old Violin," was a tearjerker of the first order. However, he was dropped by the label within a year, and then became a born-again Christian. Since his release from prison in 1991, he has performed primarily in BRANSON, MISSOURI, recording occasionally for small labels. He also changed the spelling of his name to "PayCheck," perhaps to leave behind an unpleasant chapter in his life. In the late 1990s he was seriously ill with emphysema but has since recovered, although his performing has been limited.

Select Discography

Biggest Hits, Columbia 38322.
Take This Job and Shove It, Richmond 2300. Reissue of his most famous album, with the big hit title cut.

PAYNE, LEON (b. Alba, Tex., June 15, 1917–September 11, 1969)

A blind multiple instrumentalist and singer, Payne is famous for his compositions, including "Lost Highway," a major hit for HANK WILLIAMS.

Payne was born blind and, like many blind children of the day, was encouraged by his teachers at the Texas School for the Blind to take up music as a means of supporting himself. It turned out that he had unusual musical capabilities, and by his early teens he had mastered a number of instruments: GUITAR, piano, and drums, to name a few. He also had a pleasant, smooth voice, reminiscent of the successful pop crooners like Bing Crosby.

By the mid-1930s he was working with a number of popular WESTERN SWING bands, most notably Bill Boyd's Cowboy Ramblers. After World War II he was a member of Jack Rhodes's Rhythm Boys, and in 1949 formed his own band, The Lone Star Buddies. In that same year he had his only hit on his own with the sentimental valentine he wrote for his wife, "I Love You Because."

From the late 1940s through the 1950s, numerous artists had hits covering Payne's material. Some of his better-known songs include "Lost Highway," "Blue Side of Lonesome," "They'll Never Take Her Love from Me," and "You'll Still Have a Place in My Heart." Meanwhile, Payne continued to record as a solo artist, for labels big and small, until a heart attack in 1965 led him to cut back on his performing activities; four years later a second attack took his life.

PEARL, MINNIE (b. Sarah Ophelia Colley, Centerville, Tenn., October 25, 1912–March 4, 1996)

Minnie Pearl, probably the best-known and one of the greatest of all country comedians, offered time-honed, cornball humor that appealed to generations of country-music fans.

A very young and demure Minnie Pearl, before she attached a tag-sale label to her country hat. Photo: University of North Carolina, Southern Historical Collection, Southern Folklife Collection, University Archives

Like many other rural comedians who played hayseed parts, Pearl was not as dumb as she acted. In fact, she was raised in an educated family, exposed to classical music and literature (and only vaguely aware of the country music around her); her mother, known as "Aunt Fannie" Colley, led a book circle and played organ at the local church. The young Sarah Ophelia aspired to be an actress, and attended the tony Ward-Belmont College, a high-class finishing school, in Nashville, where she also showed talent as a dancer.

After graduating and teaching dance locally, Pearl was hired as a dramatic coach for a small company out of Atlanta that specialized in sending directors into small Southern towns to mount amateur productions. She held this job for five years. While working in the tiny town of Baileyton, Alabama, she was put up by a local family; the family's grande dame was a great teller of tales, and became the model for Colley's new creation, Minnie Pearl. She began performing monologues based on this backwoods character as a way of raising interest in the plays that she was directing.

Pearl's father died in the late 1930s, and she returned to her hometown to take care of her ailing mother.

Asked to entertain a local bankers' meeting, she revived her hayseed character, taking as her hometown the nearby railroad crossing, Grinder's Switch. One of the bankers recommended that she audition for THE GRAND OLE OPRY; the *Opry* liked her act but there was concern that some of the rural listeners might be offended by it. They scheduled Minnie's first broadcast well after the prime listening time, at 11:05, but their fears proved to be groundless; Pearl soon became one of the *Opry*'s most popular attractions. Made a permanent member in 1940, she continued to perform until 1991, when she suffered a massive stroke. She died five years later, having spent her last years in a nursing home.

The Pearl persona—complete with a flowered hat from which a price tag dangled and a thrift-store cotton print dress—and her signature greeting of "How-dee" are instantly recognizable even by people who rarely listen to country music. Her typical monologue was made up of a string of corny old jokes, set as "true events" from the little town of Grinder's Switch; this trick of incorporating dusty old jokes into what purport to be real stories was appropriated by monologuist Garrison Keillor, whose monologues are set as "news" from his fictional hometown of Lake Wobegon.

Select Discography

Country Music Hall of Fame, King 3808. Varied material from Starday sessions, including comic routines and songs, with little documentation.

PEDAL STEEL GUITAR What would a classic country recording of the late 1950s and early 1960s be without the sound of a crying pedal steel guitar? The instrument has become an integral part of country music-making, and for many people its sound defines a country recording.

The steel guitar has its roots in the lap-played Hawaiian styles of the 1920s. It's called a "steel guitar" because the player uses a steel bar to note the strings (not because the body of the instrument is made of steel, although some do feature metal bodies). Standard guitars originally were adapted for lap playing by raising the nut (giving a higher action) and lowering the frets. However, because the sound hole was facing up rather than out, it was difficult to produce an instrument that could be heard easily, particularly in a band setting.

In a search for greater volume, instrument builders like the Dopyera brothers introduced models with built-in resonators, marketed as National steel guitars and later as DOBROS. In the mid-1930s electric amplification came in, and players like BOB DUNN in WESTERN SWING ensembles began playing electrified instruments for greater volume and a cutting, hard-edged sound. In the late 1940s the amplified steel guitar became a part of HONKY-TONK ensembles, thanks to the radio appearances and recordings of HANK WILLIAMS, whose backup band featured the instrument. The bluesy sounds that could be created on the instrument were a perfect accompaniment to the sad-and-lonesome music that Williams made.

With amplification there was no longer a necessity for the guitar to have a large and bulky body that had to be balanced on the player's lap. One of the first innovations was the electrified instrument nicknamed the "frypan"; this tiny-bodied instrument was easily transportable, sat comfortably on a player's lap, and still had all the power that amplification offered. Later, musicians began mounting these instruments on legs. Because lap players work with open tunings, it is often necessary to retune their instruments many times during a performance, a time-consuming annoyance. To alleviate this problem, someone came up with the idea of mounting two separate necks on a stand, each tuned to a common, but different, open chord. More strings were added, again to expand the range of the instrument. Ancillary pedals and levers eventually were added to the instrument, giving the player greater control over volume, retuning individual notes, and other special effects.

One of the first country musicians to embrace the new so-called pedal steel was SPEEDY WEST, who began using the instrument in 1948. His wide-ranging session work on the West Coast helped popularize the instrument among other players. In the mid-1950s BUDDY EMMONS began playing with popular singer "LITTLE" JIMMY DICKENS, and he also became a leading innovator in instrument design and manufacture when he founded the Sho-Bud company. BUD ISAACS was another innovative player, whose appearance on WEBB PIERCE's recording "Slowly" in 1953 is generally credited with introducing the modern pedal steel sound to country music. During the 1950s Isaacs also served as a consultant to Gibson in the development of their early pedal steel guitars. By the early 1960s the pedal steel was firmly established on all of Nashville's recordings, despite the fact that more traditional instruments like FIDDLE and BANJO had been eliminated by producers working in the new NASHVILLE SOUND.

When COUNTRY-ROCK groups were first formed in the late 1960s, the pedal steel was eagerly embraced by a new generation. GRAM PARSONS's first country-rock outfit, The International Submarine Band, featured a young steel player named J. D. Maness, whose style was widely copied. POCO centered on steel player Rusty Young, THE FLYING BURRITO BROTHERS featured "Sneaky" Pete Kleinow, and MICHAEL NESMITH's First National Band had Red Rhodes. These groups eliminated the excesses of the Nashville Sound but kept the pedal steel as a vital link to country's past.

The 1970s saw a revival of interest in the pedal steel's ancestors, including the Dobro and earlier electrified steel instruments. But the pedal steel continues to be found in most major country stars' backup bands, and individual players have evolved diverse styles that take the instrument far beyond the clichéd, trademark whining sound that used to be its limit.

PEER, RALPH (b. R. Sylvester P., Kansas City, Mo., May 22, 1892–January 19, 1960)

Peer was one of the first great producers of country music as well as the founder of Peer-Southern Music, among the first publishers of country songs.

Peer was born to the music business; his father sold phonographs and had a link with the Columbia Company, for which Peer worked in his native Kansas City from 1911 to 1919. He was hired by a rival firm, the General Phonograph Company, in 1920 to run their Okeh division. His first job was to oversee the recordings of blues singer Mamie Smith; her "Crazy Blues" of 1920 is said to be the first blues recording by a black singer. In 1923 he was contacted by an Atlanta furniture dealer who wanted him to record a local fiddler named FIDDLIN' JOHN CARSON. The resulting record—Carson's rendition of "The Little Old Log Cabin in the Lane" backed with "The Old Hen Cackled"—is generally credited as the first successful country-music recording.

In 1925 Peer moved to Victor Records, which offered him a unique arrangement: Instead of paying him a salary, they offered him the publishing rights to any of the material that he recorded. Because there were no publishing rights to traditional songs or tunes, Peer began to encourage his artists to write their own material. In 1928 Victor and Peer founded Southern Music, which became a leading publisher of blues and country material.

In the summer of 1927 Peer made a field trip to Bristol, Tennessee, that would become legendary in recording circles. At this session he "discovered" both JIMMIE RODGERS and THE CARTER FAMILY, overseeing their first recordings. His music-publishing arm would naturally become the outlet for both of these acts' prolific compositions.

In 1932, foreseeing the change in musical tastes, Peer branched out in his publishing business to sign popular songsmiths like Hoagy Carmichael and also explored the international market. He was central in the founding of Broadcast Music International (or BMI) in 1940, which challenged the more conservative ASCAP (American Society of Composers, Artists, and Publishers) in its dominance of the music-licensing field.

In the 1940s and 1950s Peer left the day-to-day operations of his company increasingly to his son while he pursued a lifelong interest in horticulture, becoming a world-renowned authority on camellias.

PENNY, HANK (b. Herbert Clayton P., near Birmingham, Ala., September 18, 1918–April 17, 1992)

Penny was a WESTERN SWING-styled bandleader who turned to upbeat country and HONKY-TONK in the 1950s.

Inspired by pioneering bandleaders BOB WILLS and MILTON BROWN, Penny formed The Radio Cowboys, gaining fame over station WWL in New Orleans as well as a number of other stations in the South. He first recorded for Vocalion in the late 1930s under the direction of ace producer ART SATHERLEY. At that time his band featured fiddler BOUDELEAUX BRYANT (who later became one of country's and rock's greatest songwriters), as well as master musicians Noel Boggs and Eddie Duncan.

Penny relocated to the West Coast after the war, and his greatest recordings were made from 1945 to 1950 for the Cincinnati-based King label. By then Penny's band featured hot stringbender MERLE TRAVIS, along with Boggs, ace steel guitarist SPEEDY WEST, and girl chanteuse Jaye P. Morgan. Their instrumental work was outstanding, reflecting the influence of the new chamber jazz that was coming out of the West Coast, although they also began recording novelty numbers that would increasingly form the backbone of Penny's repertoire.

In the 1950s Penny moved to RCA and Decca, but the quality of his work suffered at the hands of unsympathetic producers. By decade's end he was working out of Las Vegas with a new band, featuring young hotpicker ROY CLARK as well as steel guitar legend Curly Chalker. Penny spent most of the 1960s performing as a country comedian, then retired in the early 1970s, in Los Angeles.

Select Discography

Hollywood Western Swing, Krazy Kat 25. 1944–1947 recordings.
Crazy Rhythm: The Standard Transcriptions, Bloodshot 808. 1951 radio transcriptions.

PERKINS, CARL (b. C. Lee P., Tiptonville, Tenn., April 3, 1932–January 19, 1998)

One of the greats of early rock and roll, Perkins had a career that crisscrossed genres from ROCKABILLY to country and back to jazzy rock. He is, of course, well remembered for his 1950s compositions, most notably "Blue Suede Shoes," the first song to top the country, R&B, and pop charts, establishing rock and roll as a dominant pop style.

Born to a poor farming family, Perkins was exposed to music from his youth. His father was an avid fan of THE GRAND OLE OPRY, and it was one of the few radio shows he would allow the family to listen to on their radio. A second important influence was black sharecropper "Uncle" John Westbrook, who played guitar in a rural, fingerpicking blues style.

After World War II the family relocated to Bemis, Tennessee, where Carl's uncles were working in a cotton mill. They settled in their first home with electricity, and soon Carl was practicing on a second-hand Harmony electric guitar in the attic. He cited as inspirations for his single-string guitar lead work ARTHUR "GUITAR BOOGIE" SMITH and "Butterball" Paige, who played lead in ERNEST TUBB's backup band in the 1940s.

In the early 1950s Carl talked his brothers Jay and Clayton into forming a country trio, and they began performing in local HONKY-TONKS as The Perkins Brothers. After a while it became clear to Carl that the group would need drums if they were to provide a danceable beat for their customers. After a trial drummer joined in 1953, Clayton brought on board schoolmate W. S. "Fluke" Holland, who had a keen appreciation for R&B as well as country music. Carl, meanwhile, was moving the music in an up-tempo direction to suit dancing, thus forming the seeds of rockabilly. At the same time they were playing honky-tonks at night, the brothers worked by day in Jackson's Colonial Bakery.

In 1954 Perkins heard ELVIS PRESLEY's recording of "Blue Moon of Kentucky" on the radio and realized that someone else was experimenting with up-tempo country music. He took his brothers to Memphis in search of Sun Records, which recorded Presley, and met legendary producer SAM PHILLIPS. In October, Phillips recorded Perkins's first song, the country honky-tonk ballad "Turn Around." A second session yielded another HANK WILLIAMS-esque number, "Let the Jukebox Keep on Playing," complete with crying PEDAL STEEL GUITAR and FIDDLE. The flip side revealed another side of Perkins's personality; the song "Gone, Gone, Gone" had only muted steel guitar and no fiddle, with Perkins right up front in the mix, featuring a rocking beat along with scat vocals. This was his first recording in his new R&B-influenced style.

In late 1955 Perkins returned to the studio to record two boppin' numbers and two more standard country WEEPERS. Although in the past Phillips had issued the country songs as the A-sides, keeping the up-tempo material for the less often played flip sides, he decided to issue the two rockabilly numbers on one single; they were "Blue Suede Shoes" backed with "Honey Don't." "Blue Suede Shoes" would establish Perkins's reputation; it also saved Phillips from bankruptcy and made Perkins an instant star.

Sad to say, Perkins's new success was short-lived. While on the road to New York for a taping of Perry Como's TV show in early 1956, his manager fell asleep at the wheel, and all three Perkins brothers were injured. Carl lost key national exposure and momentum; another hillbilly rocker, Elvis Presley, would soon be grabbing the spotlight. Perkins's next releases came out in the summer of 1956; both were country-flavored numbers, "Boppin' the Blues" followed by "Dixie Fried." The latter is one of Perkins's best songs, although its Southern-oriented lyrics limited its mass-market appeal.

In late 1956 Perkins returned to the Sun studios for another session. This time young session pianist JERRY LEE LEWIS was on hand, and Elvis Presley showed up at the studio to say hello to his old friends. Later in the session another newcomer, JOHNNY CASH, stopped by. Phillips happily recorded the jam session that resulted, which was released as *The Million Dollar Quartet*.

By 1957 Perkins was a has-been at Sun. Newer artists Johnny Cash and Jerry Lee Lewis were successful on the country and rock charts, respectively, and Perkins was pretty much ignored by Phillips. Producer DON LAW of Columbia Records signed the frustrated singer in 1957, and the following year began issuing teen-oriented pop with him, including "Pink Pedal Pushers" and "Pop Let Me Have the Car." However, Perkins sounded somewhat uncomfortable in the role of teen idol. Tragedy beset his life when his brother Jay died of a brain tumor in 1958; Perkins and his other brother both became alcoholics (Clayton eventually died of alcoholism); drummer W. S. Holland quit the group in early 1959.

In the early 1960s Perkins was disillusioned with the music business; dropped by Columbia in 1963, he recorded country material briefly for Decca before being dropped again. He went into retirement for a while, then early in 1964 he was approached to tour England with another rock-and-roll legend, Chuck Berry. Perkins was surprised to discover that he was venerated in England, particularly by a young guitarist named George Harrison, who had learned many licks from Perkins's recordings. The Beatles' recordings of Perkins's songs—including "Honey Don't," "Matchbox," and "Everybody Wants to Be My Baby"—revitalized the singer's career in Europe, where he quickly became a favorite touring artist.

In the late 1960s Perkins was a featured artist in Johnny Cash's touring group. He wrote the nostalgic 1968 country hit "Daddy Sang Bass," about a backwoods country band, for Cash. He recorded a comeback album with the rock revivalists NRBQ in 1979, producing a minor hit with "Restless," and then recorded sporadically through the 1980s, primarily in Europe, waxing a mix of country and early rock. In

1986 he reunited with Cash and ROY ORBISON for the *Class of '55* album, an attempt to recapture the glory days of Memphis. He continued to perform and record into the 1990s, although he was slowed by a series of strokes that eventually took his life in early 1998.

Perkins brought a country sensibility to rhythm and blues. His combination of soulful vocals, hot guitar picking, and a powerful band set the stage for countless other acts in rockabilly, mainstream rock and roll, and new country. His influence can be heard throughout American popular music.

Select Discography

Original Sun Greatest Hits, Rhino 75890. Sixteen of his classic Sun recordings.

Restless, Columbia/Legacy 48986. Mostly teen-pop material from Columbia cut in the late 1950s and early 1960s, although it also includes tracks from late 1970s sessions with NRBQ.

Jive After Five, Rhino 70958. His best cuts between 1958 and 1978, after the Sun years.

Country Boy's Dream: The Dollie Masters, Bear Family 15593. Mid-1960s recordings in the then-current country style. Includes previously unreleased material.

PHILLIPS, SAM (b. Samuel Cornelius P., near Florence, Ala., January 5, 1923)

Phillips was the legendary recording engineer/owner of Sun Records who discovered, among others, ELVIS PRESLEY and made him a star.

Phillips's father owned a large tenant farm on the Tennessee River just outside of Florence, Alabama, and was fairly well-to-do until the stock market crash decimated his savings. In 1941 his father died, and Phillips left high school, taking jobs at a grocery store and then a funeral parlor to help support his mother. Meanwhile he studied engineering through a correspondence course, and got his first chance to work on radio at WLAY in Muscle Shoals, Alabama. After marriage and further radio jobs in Decatur, Alabama, and Nashville, in 1945 Phillips settled in Memphis to work for WREC, where his brother Jud was already working in a singing group. Five years later he opened Memphis Recording Service as a means of supplementing his income.

Originally Phillips recorded local R&B performers, including Howlin' Wolf, B. B. King, and Jackie Brentson, licensing the recordings to established companies like Chess out of Chicago and Modern out of Los Angeles. In 1952 he founded Sun Records, scoring his first hit with "Bear Cat," his own rewriting of the popular Big Mama Thornton song "Hound Dog," which was recorded by local deejay Rufus Thomas. Other R&B acts, along with the doo-wop group The

Prisonnaires (the novelty was that all of the members were real prisoners), were quickly added to Sun's roster.

In 1953 a local boy came into the studios to make a recording as a birthday present for his mother; his name was Elvis Presley. Sometime over the next year the young singer made an impression on Phillips, who was said to be looking for a white singer who could sound black (Phillips recognized the popularity of R&B music among white teenagers, but realized that a white singer would be more acceptable to radio programmers, parents, and the teens themselves). Phillips teamed Elvis with guitarist Scotty Moore and bassist Bill Black, and shaped his first recording, the blues standard "That's All Right Mama," learned from Big Boy Crudup, backed with BILL MONROE's "Blue Moon of Kentucky."

The great success of Elvis swamped the tiny Sun label, and within a year Phillips sold his contract with the hip-shaker to RCA for the then-enormous sum of $35,000. Attempts to mold CARL PERKINS, JOHNNY CASH, and JERRY LEE LEWIS into the "next Elvis" were only partially successful; Perkins's career was dogged by bad luck, Cash had little sympathy for the teenybop material that Phillips had him record, and Lewis made the mistake of marrying his thirteen-year-old cousin. Besides these country rockers, Phillips recorded some pure country acts (usually issued on the Phillips International label rather than Sun), but by the early 1960s the label had pretty much run out of steam. The Sun masters were sold to country producer SHELBY SINGLETON in 1969, and since that time Phillips has been active primarily in other business interests, including radio stations and Holiday Inns. He was inducted into the Country Music Hall of Fame in 2001.

Select Discography

The Sun Story, Rhino 75884. Two-CD set featuring R&B and country acts originally recorded by Phillips.

PICKARD FAMILY, THE (c. 1924–c. 1950s: Original lineup: Obed "Dad," Leila May [Wilson], Ruthie, and Ann Pickard [vocs])

The Pickards were early vocal stars on THE GRAND OLE OPRY who specialized in sentimental songs of family and home.

Led by multiple instrumentalist Obed "Dad" Pickard and his wife Leila May, the group began performing on the *Opry* in 1926 and then moved to over forty other radio stations. Dad specialized in the sentimental ballads of the late nineteenth century that had been popular in suburban parlors and then spread to the country, such as "Poor Kitty Wells"; evergreen classics like "She'll Be Comin' 'Round the Mountain"; and

COWBOY standards like "Bury Me Not on the Lone Prairie." The group eventually worked in major cities like Detroit, New York, and Philadelphia, spreading the country-music style into urban areas, and also published popular songbooks that became the basis for many artists' performing repertoires. The group recorded about forty sides during the height of the country-music craze from 1927 to 1930. By the late 1930s, the Pickards (like THE CARTER FAMILY) were broadcasting on the famous border radio stations out of Mexico. In 1940 the family moved to California, making a few appearances in C-grade films and then starring on a live television variety program out of Los Angeles from 1949 to 1954.

PIERCE, WEBB (b. West Monroe, La., August 8, 1921–February 24, 1991)

Pierce was one of the most successful and popular of the HONKY-TONK singers of the 1950s and 1960s, second only to EDDY ARNOLD in placing chart hits during that period.

Born in rural Louisiana, Pierce began playing guitar as a teenager and got his first radio job after the war in Monroe. He went to Shreveport, then the center of country music in the state, thanks to the popular LOUI-SIANA HAYRIDE radio program that originated there. After a couple of unsuccessful years, during which he was reduced to working at the local Sears, Pierce finally attracted the attention of Horace Logan, the program's producer, and was hired to join its cast in the early 1950s.

Webb made recordings as a vocalist with Tillman Franks's band (including the minor hit "Hayride Boogie") for the local Pacemaker label, and then was signed on his own to Four Star; his band at the time featured future big names in country circles, including pianist FLOYD CRAMER and guitarist FARON YOUNG. In 1951 he was signed by Decca, where he had his first hit, "Wondering," followed quickly by the #1 record "Back Street Affair." Between 1952 and 1958 all of his releases made the country Top 10; in 1952 he left the *Hayride* to join the more prestigious GRAND OLE OPRY. Some of Pierce's best-known recordings include classic barroom numbers such as 1953's "I'm Walking the Dog," "That's Me Without You," and "There Stands the Glass"; 1954's up-tempo "More and More" and the classic "Slowly" (featuring BUD ISAACS's classic weeping PEDAL STEEL GUITAR solo that helped popularize the instrument in country circles); 1956's "Teenage Boogie" (a remake of his first recording, "Hayride Boogie"); a cover of THE EVERLY BROTHERS' "Bye Bye Love" and "Honky Tonk Song" from 1957; and two songs written with MEL TILLIS, 1958's "Tupelo County Jail" and "A Thousand Miles Ago" from the following year.

Although he was no longer dominating the charts, Pierce continued to produce solid hits through the mid-1960s, including 1961's "Sweet Lips"; "Crazy Wild Desire" from 1962, also written with Tillis; and his last major hit, 1964's "Memory Number 1." In the mid-1960s Pierce switched his attention to the business end of publishing and promoting, and became a symbol of country-music excess when he had a custom, guitar-shaped swimming pool installed at his home and began tootling around Nashville in a silver-dollar-encrusted Pontiac. Although he continued to record for Decca/MCA through the mid-1970s, Pierce's hits became fewer and fewer after the mid-1960s. In 1977 he moved to the tiny Plantation label and then semiretired, although he was lured out of retirement for a duet session with country OUTLAW WILLIE NELSON in a 1982 remake of his 1955 recording of "In the Jailhouse Now."

Pierce died of pancreatic cancer in 1991. A tribute album, produced by SINGER/SONGWRITER GAIL DAVIES, was released in the fall of 2001, at the same time the singer was inducted into the Country Music Hall of Fame.

Webb Pierce on the diving board of his (in)famous guitar-shaped swimming pool, c. mid-1970s. Photo: Raeanne Rubenstein

Select Discography

Wondering Boy, 1951–58, Bear Family 15522. All of his classic recordings on four CDs.

King of the Honky-Tonk, Country Music Foundation 19. Compilation of his biggest Decca hits from the 1950s.

POCO (1968–1982; original lineup: Richie Furay, b. Yellow Springs, Ohio, May 9, 1944 [gtr, voc]; Jim Messina, b. Harlingen, Tex., December 5, 1947 [gtr, voc]; Rusty Young, b. Long Beach, Calif., February 23, 1946 [pdl. steel gtr]; Randy Meisner, b. Scottsbluff, Nebr., March 8, 1946 [b, voc]; George Grantham, b. Cordell, Okla.), November 20, 1947 [drms, voc]

Poco was among the first COUNTRY-ROCK bands. They never achieved much popular success, but several band members would be influential in the next generation of country-rock and mainstream pop.

Furay and Messina had met as members of the last incarnation of Buffalo Springfield, which had fallen apart early in 1968. Determined to pursue a more countrified sound, they formed a new group originally called Pogo, after the popular comic strip; however, when the owners of the strip objected, they changed their name to Poco. The band favored soft folk-rock harmonies with just a dash of countrified flavor, particularly emphasized by Young's tasteful PEDAL STEEL-GUITAR work, a novelty for a rock-and-roll ensemble.

The group seemed to be in a constant state of flux when it came to its personnel. Bassist Meisner was the first to go, after about a year, joining RICK NELSON's seminal country-rock outfit, The Stone Canyon Band, and then cofounding THE EAGLES; he was replaced by Timothy B. Schmidt. Messina left in the early 1970s to pursue a career as a record producer; he ended up producing a new SINGER-SONGWRITER named Kenny Loggins and soon returned to performing in the very popular 1970s duo of Loggins and Messina. Messina was replaced on guitar by Paul Cotten, who had previously played with the country-rock ensemble The Illinois Speed Press. Furay left to form a country-rock trio with CHRIS HILLMAN (previously of THE BYRDS and THE FLYING BURRITO BROTHERS) and singer/songwriter J. D. Souther; he was not replaced.

The band soldiered on through the 1970s, led by original member Rusty Young and scoring some minor chart successes. Schmidt left in 1977 to replace Meisner in The Eagles, and Grantham left at the same time; they were replaced by Charlie Harrison on bass and Steve Chapman on drums, and keyboardist Kim Bullard was added. This group lasted until about 1982, when they finally bit the dust. The original members have reunited from time to time, first in 1984 to make a comeback album and again in 1991, with little success.

Select Discography

The Forgotten Trail, Epic 46162. Two-CD set of recordings from 1969 to 1974, with historical booklet.

20th Century Masters, MCA 112224. Hits from 1975 to 1982 by the later incarnations of the band.

POOLE, CHARLIE (b. Charles Cleveland P., Randolph County, N.C., March 22, 1892–May 21, 1931)

Influential North Carolina banjoist/vocalist/band leader, Poole had a short, but extremely prolific, career as a recording artist. He is the Buster Keaton of traditional music; he even looked like Buster, with a large, flat face and protruding ears. If Buster Keaton had sung, he would undoubtedly have sounded like Charlie Poole, whose slightly droll, but deadpan, vocal style is immediately recognizable.

Born in rural North Carolina, Poole developed a unique BANJO style based on the traditional styles around him. Unlike banjoists from the deeper South, who brush against the strings in a style known as "frailing," Carolina pickers have tended to pick the strings using two or three fingers; eventually this style evolved into what is now called BLUEGRASS banjo picking, developed by two Carolinians, "Snuffy" Jenkins and Earl Scruggs (of FLATT AND SCRUGGS). Poole also credited as an influence ragtime banjoist Fred Van Epps, who made many recordings in the first decades of the twentieth century; Poole even made a few instrumental recordings in emulation of the ragtime banjoist's style. There were also stories that Poole had damaged his right (picking) hand while playing baseball, leading to the creation of his unique style; in any case, as an adult he picked the banjo with his thumb and two fingers.

Poole worked most of his life in the textile mills, as did many other country musicians of that time. He

Charlie Poole (left with banjo), with his North Carolina Ramblers, Posey Rorer (fiddle) and Roy Harvey (guitar), c. 1928, from a Columbia Records catalog. Photo: University of North Carolina, Southern Historical Collection, Southern Folklife Collection, University Archives

was working in the small textile town of Spray, North Carolina, when he began his performing career. He first formed a duo with fiddler Posey Rorer, a coal miner from Tennessee who had been injured in a mining accident and so had taken to working in the mills. They were joined by guitarist Norman Woodlieff to form the first version of what would become The North Carolina Ramblers. In 1925 the trio got jobs in Passaic, New Jersey, working for a car manufacturer. Poole went to New York and arranged for them to record for Columbia Records; in 1925 they made their first recordings, which were immediately successful. The first record issued by the Ramblers was "Don't Let Your Deal Go Down," a blues-influenced song that remained in print for years and became Poole's signature number.

The band had a unique style centering on Poole's wry, uninflected vocals, and intricate chordal work on the banjo. Poole sang a combination of sentimental heart songs and comic novelty numbers, many from the late nineteenth and early twentieth centuries. Although his vocal style was not highly ornamented like other Southern singers', he did possess a deadpan humor, jazzy phrasing, and, most important for early recordings, clear enunciation, which made these discs extremely popular. Unlike other string bands, The North Carolina Ramblers were a subdued group, focusing on Poole's banjo and vocals accompanied by discreet GUITAR and FIDDLE. Poole's versions of many songs, including "Jay Gould's Daughter," "Ramblin' Blues," "Hungry Hash House," and "If I Lose (Let Me Lose)," have become standards in the old-time country repertoire. Poole made jazz-influenced recordings of old-time numbers, such as "Goodbye, Liza Jane," which would indirectly influence such artists as WESTERN SWING fiddler BOB WILLS, who also adopted old-time fiddle tunes to a new, jazz-and-blues-influenced style.

The band went through several personnel changes in its short life; West Virginia guitarist Roy Harvey replaced Woodlieff on their second Columbia session in 1926, and fiddler Rorer left the band in 1928, to be replaced by Lonnie Austin, who two years later was succeeded by Odell Smith. Like many recording units of the day, the band was not a fixed ensemble, but probably had a set of floating members who would come together for specific recording dates or local jobs.

In 1929 Poole decided to enlarge The Ramblers to include many of the other musicians who had been performing with them. However, producer FRANK WALKER at Columbia was unwilling to change the successful Ramblers formula. The group then went to the budget Paramount label, recording under the name of The Highlanders. This group featured a much richer ensemble sound, including piano played by Roy

Harvey's sister, Lucy Terry, and the twin fiddles of Austin and Smith. They also made a series of comic-novelty dialogue recordings, "A Trip to New York," perhaps to answer the popularity of THE SKILLET LICKERS' series of mini-playlets.

In 1931 Poole was so popular that he was invited to come to Hollywood to provide background music for the movies. However, he died of a massive heart attack before he could make the trip west. Although he hardly looked the part, Poole was the first in a line of high-living country stars whose lives were tragically cut short by a love of heavy drinking. His recordings sold very well throughout the South, and continued to sell after his death, so that his influence was deeply felt decades later. When County Records, a New York old-time revival label of the 1970s, began reissuing these sides, they found a new and enthusiastic audience.

After Poole's death many of the musicians associated with him continued to record, often in bands formed to mimic the sound of the original group; Roy Harvey even formed his own North Carolina Ramblers in the early 1930s with fiddler Posey Rorer and Bob Hoke, followed by a second Poole-like group.

Select Discography

Vols. 1–3, County 3501/3508/3516. All of Poole's classic recordings, in pristine sound; County originally issued this material on three albums during the 1970s.

PRAIRIE RAMBLERS (c. 1930–1956; original members: Charles Gilbert "Chick" Hurt, b. Willowshade, Ky., May 11, 1901–October 9, 1967 [mdln, bnj]; Floyd "Salty" Holmes, b. Glasgow, Ky., March 6, 1909–January 1, 1970 [gtr, hca, jug]; Shelby David "Tex" Atchison, b. Rosine, Ky., February 5, 1912–August 4, 1982 [fdl]; Jack Taylor, b. Summerdale, Ky., December 7, 1901–August 4, 1962 [b])

The Prairie Ramblers were an influential COWBOY WESTERN SWING ensemble of the early 1930s who performed on WLS's powerful NATIONAL BARN DANCE radio program out of Chicago.

Originally a traditional string band influenced by the jazz craze, the four members came from rural Kentucky and called themselves The Kentucky Ramblers. They got their first radio job in the early 1930s in Davenport, Iowa, where they were heard by talent scouts for the *National Barn Dance*. They joined the *Barn Dance* in 1932 and remained there for nearly two and a half decades. At first they accompanied popular cowgirl vocalist PATSY MONTANA, but they soon began recording on their own, originally for the budget ARC label. Their repertoire became increasingly urbanized and pop; they even recorded hokum double-entendre blues numbers under the pseudonym of The Sweet Violet Boys.

The band went through many personnel changes, beginning in 1937 when Atchison jumped ship to head west, where he appeared in C-grade Westerns and fronted many popular California cowboy bands; he had several replacements. Holmes came and went from the band through its long existence, performing for a while on THE GRAND OLE OPRY with his wife, Mattie (whose sister was the popular country vocalist MARTHA CARSON), as the duo of Salty and Mattie. Taylor and Hurt somehow stuck it out through the band's entire run; after the band ended, they were absorbed lock, stock, and barrel into Stan Wallowick's Polka Chips dance band, where they continued to play into the 1960s.

The Prairie Ramblers' Western-jive style has been often copied, most recently by the popular neo-cowboy ensemble RIDERS IN THE SKY.

PRESLEY, ELVIS ARON (b. Tupelo, Miss., January 8, 1935–August 16, 1977)

Although best remembered as a teen idol and rock star, Presley maintained a strong connection with country music throughout his career, and his singing style, repertoire, and myth had as large an impact on country music as they did on pop in general. It is a rare artist whose music transcends categorization, and an even rarer one who remains influential over two decades after his death; yet Presley undoubtedly will remain just such a performer, becoming more legendary as the years go by.

The son of a white sharecropper, Presley named as his earliest musical influences the white church and black field hands. He undoubtedly was exposed to country radio, which at the time was a mix of white "mainstream" country (including JIMMIE RODGERS-styled country blues and HANK WILLIAMS-styled HONKY-TONK) and the nascent R&B music (including jive, blues, and swing recordings, along with early "rockin'" sides). His family relocated to Memphis, where Elvis was somewhat of a loner in high school; after completing his education he worked as a truck driver and also made an amateur recordings at SAM PHILLIPS's legendary Sun studios. It was here that he was to make his first commercial recording, launching an entirely new sound.

Sam Phillips's genius was in recognizing that Elvis could mimic the bluesy phrasing of popular black singers, yet (thanks to his skin color) would be acceptable to a mainstream white audience. On his first recording Elvis bridged the gap between R&B and country by recording on the A-side "That's All Right, Mama," originated by bluesman Big Boy (Arthur) Crudup, backing it with the BLUEGRASS standard "Blue Moon

of Kentucky" by BILL MONROE. Elvis's Sun recordings were marketed as "hillbilly bop" rather than rock, and Elvis was booked onto THE LOUISIANA HAYRIDE, a popular country radio program. His first tours were pretty much limited to the South, and his primary market was country/ROCKABILLY.

When Elvis hooked up with COLONEL TOM PARKER, who had successfully marketed country legend HANK SNOW, he made the first step toward mainstream acceptance. Parker arranged for Presley to record for RCA, a label better equipped than Sun to market him to the nascent teen-pop crowd. At RCA, Elvis's initial recordings were produced by CHET ATKINS, and were glossed up with production values that Atkins brought to his other NASHVILLE SOUND recordings. THE JORDANAIRES, a popular white gospel harmony group, were employed as backup singers, providing the "bop-bops" on "Don't Be Cruel" and countless other Presley recordings. Although Presley was marketed (and successful) as a teen popster, the sound of his recordings was not much different from RCA's other Nashville output of the day.

Elvis's 1950s career ended with his induction into the Army; some believe that his first (and last) golden age ended at this time as well. He spent much of the early-to-mid-1960s, after his return from service, in Hollywood, producing lackluster recordings and starring in C-to-D-grade films. However, in 1968 a rock comeback was staged as an NBC TV special; this was followed by some classic recordings made in Memphis with a tougher, COUNTRY-ROCK sound, producing hits like "In the Ghetto" (penned by MAC DAVIS) and "Suspicious Minds," which has become a country standard. Unfortunately the 1970s would find Elvis mostly working in Vegas, where his weight and dependence on drugs increased while his talent fizzled away. He died of heart failure due to drug abuse in 1977.

Elvis maintained a lifelong love of GOSPEL music, another link with his country roots. The now famous "Million Dollar Quartet" sessions at the Sun studios occurred in 1956 when Elvis stopped by to visit CARL PERKINS during a recording session; an impromptu jam, joined by JERRY LEE LEWIS and JOHNNY CASH, occurred. Not surprisingly the session was almost entirely gospel favorites that they all knew from their youth. Elvis recorded several gospel LPs, which sold primarily in the country market.

It would be impossible today to find a performer in any type of popular music uninfluenced by Elvis. His energetic stage performances (proving, definitively, that white men *can* dance), his sneering demeanor, and his intense vocals that combined sweet crooning with blues inflections and a gospel fervor all have found their place in country music.

Select Discography

Million Dollar Quartet, RCA 2023. The legendary sessions with Perkins, Cash, and Lewis. This is mostly a program of standards, particularly hymns, and many tracks last a minute or less. Great notes by Colin Escott.

Twenty Great Performances, RCA 2277. Just about everything you'd like to have.

The King of Rock and Roll: Complete '50s Masters, RCA 66050. Five CDs and lavish booklet (with excellent documentation by Peter Guralnick) including all of the lip-curler's classic recordings.

PRICE, KENNY (b. Florence, Ky., May 27, 1931–August 4, 1987)

Known affectionately as "the round mound of sound," Price gained his greatest popularity through his appearances on the HEE HAW TV program in the late 1960s and early 1970s.

Raised in rural Kentucky, he got his first GUITAR from the Sears, Roebuck catalog and began playing for local functions. After service in the Korean War, he returned home to study music at Cincinnati's Conservatory of Music. In 1954 he joined WLW out of Cincinnati as a regular performer on the *Midwestern Hayride* radio show, serving as lead singer with his band, The Hometowners. On the *Hayride* he met Bobby Bobo, who would later move to Nashville and open Boone Records, Price's first label. In the mid-1960s Price followed Bobo to Nashville and signed with Boone, recording a couple of hits, including 1966's "Walking on New Grass" and "Happy Tracks," both written by Ray Pennington.

A couple more hits followed, and in 1969 Price was signed by RCA, where he had hits in 1970 with "Biloxi" and "Sheriff of Boone County." At about this time he joined *Hee Haw*, where his likable personality and smooth singing style fit in perfectly with the show's upbeat tone. After leaving RCA in 1974, Price recorded for the smaller MRC and Dimension labels through the early 1980s without achieving much success, although he continued to be a popular performer on the country fair and rodeo circuit. He died in his hometown in 1987.

PRICE, RAY (b. R. Noble P., Perryville, Tex., January 12, 1926)

Ray Price has had a long career in country music, from his beginnings as a HONKY-TONK singer in the HANK WILLIAMS mold in the early 1950s, through the height of the NASHVILLE SOUND in the 1960s, when he transformed himself into a histrionic crooner. Still, Price has always been somewhat controversial, pushing the envelope of country music—sometimes in a decidedly pop-schlock direction. Along the way he nurtured the careers of many younger country innovators, including WILLIE NELSON and KRIS KRISTOFFERSON.

Born in rural East Texas, Price was raised on a small farm. As a youngster he developed a love for animals—including raising fine horses—that would remain throughout his life, and began to play the GUITAR. The family relocated to Dallas when Price was a teenager, and he began performing locally. Intending to be a veterinarian, he went to Abilene to enter college; his college career was interrupted by a four-year stint in the Marines during World War II. On his return he began performing on Abilene radio, taking the name The Cherokee Cowboy.

In 1949 Price was invited to join Dallas's prestigious *Big D Jamboree* radio show, which was broadcast both locally and, in part, nationally by CBS Radio. This led to one release on the small, Nashville-based Bullet label. Coming to Nashville in 1951, he met his idol, Hank Williams, with whom he briefly lived and toured, often standing in for the older singer when he was too drunk to perform. At the same time he signed with Columbia, achieving his first hit with 1952's "Talk to Your Heart."

After Williams's death, Price began performing with THE DRIFTING COWBOYS, Hank's old backup band, which by the mid-1950s he enlarged into a new group that he called The Cherokee Cowboys; alums would include Willie Nelson and pedal steel guitarist BUDDY EMMONS. Price created a stir in Nashville by including a drummer in his group (for years drums were forbidden on THE GRAND OLE OPRY's stage). In these early recordings Price used the drummer and rhythm section to create what is now known as the shuffle beat, which became a standard for country-music recording (most recently revived by young country stars like GEORGE STRAIT).

Price's first big hits were 1954's "I'll Be There" and his signature tune, "Release Me," which has become a country classic. From that point on, he was rarely off the charts. A list of Price's 1950s and 1960s hits reads like an encyclopedia of country standards, from 1956's "Crazy Arms," 1958's "City Lights," 1959's "Heartaches by the Number," 1963's "Make the World Go Away," 1965's "The Other Woman," 1970's "For the Good Times" (written by a then relatively unknown songwriter named Kris Kristofferson), to 1973's "You're the Best Thing That Ever Happened to Me," all released by Columbia. As Price matured, his tear-in-the-throat style changed to a more pop-crooner style. He also challenged country fans by introducing full string sections on his 1960s recordings, a revolutionary move for the time, and abandoned his stage cowboy suit for a suit-and-tie look, emphasizing his ambition to become a mainstream star.

Price continued to record through the 1970s, although he also took considerable time off to pursue his first love, raising horses. Many of his recordings were marred by excessive, heavy-handed orchestrations and Price's own increasing pretensions to being a pop warbler. One of his best later works was 1980's *San Antonio Rose*, reuniting him with Willie Nelson and bringing forth a hit with their cover of BOB WILLS's classic "Faded Love." During the later 1980s Price recorded for the Step One label, usually in his all-out pop mode, although occasionally with more tasteful acoustic instrumentation, then returned to Columbia in 1992 for the album *Sometimes a Rose*. He has recorded sporadically since, focusing his energy primarily on performing at his own theater in BRANSON, MISSOURI.

Select Discography

The Essential, Columbia Legacy 48532. His best recordings cut between 1952 and 1961, before he went nuts with the string sections.

PRIDE, CHARLEY (b. Sledge, Miss., March 18, 1938)

One of the best-selling country performers of the 1960s and 1970s, Pride is noteworthy for being one of the few blacks to break through to true country stardom. Pride's interest in country music reflects the fact that in the rural South, traditional country (and blues) audiences crossed racial lines; and his success reflects both the slickness of Pride's recordings and the smooth-as-silk quality of his vocals.

Pride was one of eleven children born to poor tenant farmers. Like many other black families in rural Mississippi, they made their living by picking cotton, for which they were paid $3.00 for each hundred pounds picked. Early on, Pride became a fan of country radio, particularly emulating the bluesy sounds of HANK WILLIAMS, and taught himself the GUITAR. At the same time a talent for athletics manifested itself, and he began playing baseball in the Negro League in the late 1950s.

After serving in the military, Pride was hired to play for a minor-league team in Helena, Montana. He continued to perform in local bars in his free time, and also worked off-season for Anaconda Mining as a smelter. In 1963 RED SOVINE was passing through and heard Pride perform; he encouraged Pride to come to Nashville to audition for RCA. Pride stalled for a year while pursuing his dream of playing big-league baseball as a member of the New York Mets' farm team. In 1964 he traveled to Nashville to audition for famed country producer CHET ATKINS, who signed him to RCA.

Charley Pride, 1998. Photo: Raeanne Rubenstein

Pride's recording career was blessed with early success. His first single, "The Snakes Crawl at Night," was an immediate Top 10 country hit, and was followed by another hit, "Just Between You and Me." Atkins smothered Pride's vocals in the blend of echoey guitars and girly choruses that Nashville was becoming (in)famous for, and the country audience ate it up. Little emphasis was placed on Pride's racial identity by RCA, and no one in the audience seemed to mind that he was a lone black star among a white (and relatively conservative) group of musicians.

Pride enjoyed his greatest success in the late 1960s and early 1970s, winning numerous Grammy, CMA, and gold record awards. In addition to the standard songs of lovin' and losin', Pride also was a popular GOSPEL recording artist, bringing the same smooth, pop delivery to his gospel recordings that he did to his songs of heartache.

A longtime resident of Dallas, Pride pretty much retired from performing in the 1980s, although he continued to record sporadically, issuing a couple of albums late in the decade for the small 16th Avenue label. His 1993 comeback single, "Just for the Love of It" is typical 1960s Nashville in its conservative message, and Pride's voice still sounds smooth as silk, even though the backing is simpler than on his earlier recordings, reflecting the influence of new country. He has continued to perform and record through the '90s.

Select Discography

Super Hits, RCA 66947. Budget compilation (only eleven tracks) giving an overview of the hits.

PROFFITT, FRANK (b. Laurel Bloomery, Tenn., January 1913–November 24, 1965)

Proffitt was a traditional BANJO player and instrument maker who was active during the 1960s FOLK REVIVAL.

Proffitt was born in Tennessee, but his family soon migrated to North Carolina, and he was raised in the Tennessee–Carolina border town of Reese. His father was a farmer who made traditional-style banjos, fabricating the rims and necks out of solid wood, with an animal-skin head set into the wooden body of the instrument. His father also sang traditional songs and ballads, which Frank heard from an early age. In 1932 Frank married Bessie Hicks, from a noted storytelling family of the region, and settled on his own farm in the colorfully named Pork Britches Valley. The Hickses had been "discovered" in the mid-1930s by folklorists Anne and Frank Warner, who asked the family if they knew other traditional musicians. Frank's in-laws recommended that the Warners visit him, and they began notating his songs during the early 1940s, eventually collecting over 120 local songs. One of these songs, a ballad about a love affair gone wrong between locals Tom Dula and his beloved Laurie Foster, would change Proffitt's life.

The Warners were active on the folk circuit in the 1950s, and began performing the ballad of "Tom Dula." A young folk-revival group called the Kingston Trio heard the Warners' version, and issued it as a single in late 1958 under the name "Tom Dooley"; within a year it had sold over a million copies. A local newspaper tracked down Proffitt, and he was invited to appear at the first University of Chicago folk festival in 1961. This led to a flurry of concerts on the folk circuit through the mid-1960s; two albums were released during this period. Proffitt also continued the family tradition of banjo making, and his soft-voiced, traditional wooden banjos became much sought-after and copied by other makers.

Like fellow Carolinian DOC WATSON, Proffitt sang in a relaxed, baritone voice. His banjo accompaniments were simple and rhythmic, a perfect complement to his unassuming manner. Although he was not as dynamic a musician as some of the more high-powered old-time players who found favor in the 1970s (such as FRED COCKERHAM and TOMMY JARRELL), Proffitt's banjo playing and singing represented an important thread in the Southern tradition.

Select Discography

High Atmosphere, Rounder 0028. Anthology of 1960s recordings by JOHN COHEN, featuring several fine performances by Proffitt. Proffitt's two albums—on Folkways and Folk Legacy—are currently available only on special order.

PROGRESSIVE BLUEGRASS (c. 1975–present)

The mid-1970s BLUEGRASS revival spawned a number of groups that used traditional bluegrass instrumentation but were influenced by other types of music, from swing and jazz to rock and progressive music. Known at the time as either "progressive" or "newgrass" bands (the latter name coming from the popular group NEW GRASS REVIVAL), these bands met with some hostility from traditionalists while they greatly helped expand the bluegrass style and the market for bluegrass music. Many of the newgrass pioneers have returned to playing more traditional bluegrass styles in later years.

Undoubtedly the group most important to the growth of progressive bluegrass was New Grass Revival. While there had been groups in the 1960s that sought to stretch the bluegrass repertoire (THE COUNTRY GENTLEMEN, THE GREENBRIAR BOYS, and the Charles River Valley Boys, to name a few) by drawing on a wider range of musical influences, New Grass Revival was the first to try to introduce the energy of rock and roll, as well as pop and rock songs, into their repertoire. Their use of electric bass and electrified BANJO and FIDDLE was distressing to bluegrass traditionalists.

Another important early progressive band was COUNTRY COOKING. The original instrumentals by band members TONY TRISCHKA and Peter Wernick were based on jazz harmonies and unusual rhythms. Trischka also produced a number of even more far-out solo albums in the 1970s, beginning with *Bluegrass Light*, which took the banjo far beyond the usual bluegrass repertoire. The music was so experimental that some people mockingly called it "spacegrass," a name that stuck.

In the mid-1970s mandolinist DAVID GRISMAN expanded progressive music to encompass acoustic jazz. This hybrid form of music—which he called dawg music—was often played in small ensembles featuring just MANDOLIN, fiddle, and GUITAR, but mainstream bluegrass bands were also influenced by Grisman's work to venture into jazz and swing territories. This movement was called "jazzgrass" by some, although it didn't last very long. Soon, Grisman's lighter, swinging style of picking the mandolin was incorporated into mainstream progressive bluegrass, although he continued to produce his own quirky brand of music into the 1990s.

Like most progressive music, the best elements of progressive bluegrass—advanced harmonies and rhythms, electrified instruments, a broader range of songs—have more or less been incorporated into mainstream bands. Meanwhile, artists like Sam Bush (originally of New Grass Revival) and Trischka have returned to playing more traditionally oriented music, so that progressive and traditional bluegrass have met on a new common ground. While progressive bluegrass was undoubtedly an important trend in the expansion of bluegrass both as a style and in reaching a broader audience, it has not survived as a separate genre.

PRUETT, JEANNE (b. Norma Jean Bowman, Pell City, Ala., January 30, 1937)

Pruett was one of the most popular SINGER/SONGWRITERS of the 1970s, scoring a string of hits beginning with 1973's "Satin Sheets."

Music was an integral part of the Bowman household, whether it was at church or at local play-parties. Norma Jean, one of ten children, began playing piano and GUITAR at an early age, and soon was well known for her talents. In the early 1950s she married guitarist Jack Pruett, who brought her to Nashville in 1956 when he was hired to be MARTY ROBBINS's guitarist, a position he held until 1970. At first she was a housewife, caring for her children and singing only socially. However, Robbins urged her to turn professional, and arranged for her first, not terribly successful, recordings for RCA in 1963–1964. He did, however, give a big boost to her career in 1966 when he had a hit record with her song "Count Me Out."

In 1969 Decca signed Pruett. Unlike many other artists of the day, Pruett shunned the NASHVILLE SOUND, relying on a simpler production style featuring tasteful GUITAR, bass, and her own double-tracked harmony vocals. Her first minor hit was 1971's "Hold to My Unchanging Love," but she really made it big in 1973 with "Satin Sheets." This was followed by her first in a string of stand-by-your-man-type ditties, "I'm Your Woman." (She eventually took a more liberated outlook in her 1983 hit, "Lady of the Eighties.")

Pruett continued to score hits through the 1970s, but her career slowed when she left MCA in 1981 for the smaller Paid label. She began turning her attention to her love of cooking, opening a successful restaurant and limiting her performing and touring. In 1986 she was instrumental in establishing the first segment of THE GRAND OLE OPRY program dedicated solely to female musicians, a milestone in the history of this rather conservative institution.

Select Discography

Satin Sheets: Greatest Hits, Varese 5967. Sixteen hits originally recorded in the 1970s for Decca/MCA.

PUCKETT, RILEY (b. George R. P., Alpharetta, Ga., May 7, 1894–July 13, 1946)

One of the first great country singers, Riley Puckett also was a member of the legendary SKILLET LICKERS string band. His smooth vocal style, coupled with his innovative although sometimes erratic GUITAR playing, made him highly influential on BLUEGRASS and mainstream country artists who followed.

Puckett was born sighted, but when he was three months old, a mistreated eye ailment caused him to become almost totally blind. Trained at the Macon School for the Blind, he first took up the BANJO, then switched to the guitar, quickly evolving a unique style featuring bass-note runs as bridges between chord changes. While other guitarists doubtless had used bass runs previously, Puckett's runs were more elaborate and fully worked out than those of others who were recording at the time or immediately after.

When Georgia fiddler James Gideon Tanner was invited to record for Columbia Records in 1924, he took Puckett as his accompanist to the New York sessions. Soon after, when Columbia urged Tanner to form a string band to cash in on the popularity of that format, Puckett and Tanner formed The Skillet Lickers. Puckett's vocals were an integral part of the band's popularity during its heyday from the mid-1920s through the mid-1930s. His fine baritone voice, with just a slight country inflection, made him immediately appealing not only to a country audience but also to the broader pop market. He made many solo recordings while he was working with Tanner's band, including 1924's "Rock All Our Babies to Sleep," on which he engages in YODELING, thought to be the first country recording featuring this unique vocal style.

Puckett's repertoire was typical of the mountain musicians of his day, made up of traditional songs and dance tunes, along with songs from the MINSTREL SHOW tradition, blues, topical songs, and recent popular and sentimental songs. Puckett was not a distinctive singer, in that he did not imbue his vocals with deep feelings, but took a straightforward approach to "telling the story" of the song.

From 1934, when The Skillet Lickers folded, through 1941 Puckett recorded primarily for RCA Victor (he also briefly recorded for Decca in 1937) while performing on radio stations in Georgia and bordering states. His vocal style became increasingly smooth, showing the influence of pop crooners like Bing Crosby.

During the string-band revival of the 1970s, The Skillet Lickers' early recordings were rediscovered, renewing interest in Puckett's solo recordings as well. His guitar playing—with its intricate bass runs that were sometimes executed with a unique sense of rhythm—led to some discussion among revivalists and scholars alike as to whether Puckett intentionally played arhythmically or whether he simply lacked the technique to execute his advanced ideas. Needless to say, his unique playing style was never duplicated.

Select Discography

Red Sails in the Sunset, Bear Family 15280. Bluebird recordings from 1939 to 1941, featuring mostly pop numbers remade in Puckett's unique style.

PURE PRAIRIE LEAGUE (Original lineup, c. 1972: Craig Fuller [lead voc, gtr]; George Powell [gtr, voc]; John David Call [gtr, voc]; Jim Caughlin [b]; Jimmy Lanham [drms])

Pure Prairie League was a popular Western-flavored COUNTRY-ROCK outfit of the 1970s and early 1980s that had varied personnel through a long and tumultuous life. Though they never really stormed the charts, the group did establish a strong regional following.

Originally from Ohio, the group first performed in Columbus, centering on songwriter/guitarist George Powell and lead singer Craig Fuller. After recording a single LP for RCA, they recruited local drummer Billy Hinds to take the place of Jimmy Lanham, who had left the group; Hinds would bring his friends Michael Connor on keyboards in 1972 and, soon after, Mike Reilly on bass (to replace Caughlin). The band recorded a second album (with a studio bassist, not Reilly) but, like the first, it saw little action and RCA threatened to drop the group. However, in late 1973 "Amie," a song from the group's first album, started to get regional airplay. It eventually hit the national charts, leading RCA to rerelease the second album, and the group had a second hit, Powell's "Leave My Heart Alone."

Just as it looked like the group would break through to bigger success, Fuller got into trouble on a draft-evasion charge. It took the League eighteen months to regroup, hiring Cincinnati-based singer Larry Goshorn to take over for Fuller. Goshorn brought his brother, Timmy, to replace John David Call; both brothers brought a love of BLUEGRASS, the music of THE EVERLY BROTHERS, and early rock and roll to the group. This new lineup remained stable through 1977, producing a series of successful albums.

At the end of the summer of 1977, Powell left the group along with the Goshorns; the brothers formed a family band with a third sibling that was more country-oriented, while Powell decided to leave the grueling life of a touring musician to spend more time with his family. Now based in Los Angeles, the band recruited two new members, SINGER/SONGWRITER and multiple instrumentalist VINCE GILL, who came from a traditional bluegrass background, and singer/songwriter/reedsman Patrick Bolin, who had a rock background. This band lasted from 1979 through 1980, having hits with Bolin's and Gill's compositions. Then Bolin was replaced with singer-guitarist Jeff Wilson, and the band moved to Casablanca Records from their original label. In 1980 they had their biggest hit, "Let Me Love You Tonight," a Top 10 pop entry, then faded from the scene.

Throughout these many personnel changes, the basic sound of the band, remarkably enough, remained pretty much the same: an amalgam of soft rock and a tinge of countryish influences. In fact, it seems that the new members were melded into the band, rather than remolding its sound.

Select Discography

Greatest Hits, RCA 67821. Their 1970s hits, most of the songs that made them famous.

R

RABBITT, EDDIE (b. Brooklyn, N.Y., November 27, 1944–May 7, 1998)

Rabbitt was a hunky, ersatz country star of the mid-1970s and early 1980s who personified the COUNTRYPOLITAN sound of country-pop.

Rabbitt was born to an Irish fiddler father. His family relocated to East Orange, New Jersey, where Eddie learned to play the GUITAR from his scoutmaster, Tony Schwickrath, who had a minor career performing as Bob Randall. Rabbitt won an amateur contest while still a high-school student, as a result landing a radio job broadcasting live from a Paterson bar. This led to further work in local clubs in the New York City–northern New Jersey area.

Rabbitt relocated to Nashville in search of a career as a performer. He immediately placed his song "Working My Way Up to the Bottom" with ROY DRUSKY, and soon was a staff writer at Hill & Range. His "Kentucky Rain" was covered by ELVIS PRESLEY, earning the old hipshaker his fiftieth gold record. This was followed by RONNIE MILSAP's cutting his "Pure Love" in 1973; one year later Eddie got his own recording contract with Elektra Records.

Eddie had a couple of hits in the mid-1970s, mostly written or cowritten by him, and mostly in a neo-HONKY-TONK vein ("Drinking My Baby Off My Mind," "Two Dollars in the Jukebox," "We Can't Go On Living Like This"). In 1978 he was asked to perform the title song for Clint Eastwood's comic Western, *Every Which Way but Loose*. This led to another movie job in 1980, singing the title song for *Roadie*, "Driving My Life Away"; this was Rabbitt's first crossover hit.

In the early 1980s the good-looking, smooth-singing star was rarely off the pop and country charts. He had a series of hits with the pop-rock songs "I Love a Rainy Night," "Step by Step," and "Someone Could Lose a Heart Tonight," all in 1981. All of these songs were produced in a manner not too different from typical mainstream pop recordings of the era; in fact there is little to distinguish Rabbitt from his pop counterparts.

From the mid-1980s on, Rabbitt's career as pop crooner faded, though he continued to tour and perform for his loyal country fans. His life was cut short by cancer in 1998.

Select Discography

All Time Greatest Hits, Warners 26467. His biggest 1970s hits.
Greatest Hits, CEMA 18263. Budget-priced, ten-track compilation of hits from his Liberty recordings of the 1980s.

RADIO Along with recordings, radio has played a key role in the dissemination of country music. In the early days of broadcasting, small local stations, hungry for talented performers, had little problem inviting local musicians to fill airtime. Although initially classical performers were preferred, the strong reaction when local folk artists performed (usually in the form of follow-up mail), quickly led the stations to recognize a market for country-style music among their listeners. Many artists viewed radio as an ideal means of promoting local appearances, and could "work" an area by basing themselves at one station and playing as far as its signal reached. Once the market was saturated, the musician could move to another station and begin the entire process all over again.

The first major program devoted to country music was the WLS NATIONAL BARN DANCE, broadcast out of Chicago. It went on the air on April 19, 1924, supposedly re-creating a "down-home" evening of music and comedy. A roster of artists was developed to perform regularly on the program, so that listeners would come to recognize their favorite performers. The WLS model was quickly imitated, most successfully by Nashville's WSM, which hired announcer GEORGE D. HAY away from WLS in October 1925. A little over a month later Hay hosted the first evening of old-time music on the station, featuring old-style fiddler UNCLE JIMMY THOMPSON. The *WSM Barn Dance* took the GRAND OLE OPRY name by the end of the 1920s, and an institution was born.

At this time radio was not regulated in the same way it is today. Stations that could afford 50,000-watt transmitters—like WLS and WSM—could blanket not only an entire region but large areas of the country, particularly at night, when local, less powerful stations were off the air. These "clear-channel" stations were given their own frequency that could not be used by any other stations. In this way shows like the *Opry* could have an impact far from Nashville. Also, both the *National Barn Dance* and the *Opry* were picked up—at least partially—by the national networks during the 1930s.

The major difference between the *National Barn Dance* and the *Opry* came down to subtle differences in musical styles. The *Barn Dance* was always more oriented toward popular sounds; COWBOY music was popular on the show in the 1930s, with vocal harmony groups performing the light-pop, "Western" material of the day. Hay at the *Opry* insisted on keeping things more "traditional"; he banned modern instrumentation and was not interested in modern vocal groups. Nonetheless his second-in-command, Harry Stone, managed to bring along some more modern-sounding groups in the 1930s, including the popular vocal trio THE VAGABONDS.

In 1933 WWVA out of Wheeling, West Virginia, introduced its weekly *Jamboree* program to feature country musicians. Like the *Opry* it came live from a local theater. George Stoner, the station's manager, built his own roster of country performers, most notably the young GRANDPA JONES and banjo player COUSIN EMMY. After World War II the show reached the peak of its success with acts including HAWKSHAW HAWKINS and STONEY AND WILMA LEE COOPER. The show lost its luster in the later 1950s when rock and roll and TV took bites out of the country-music and radio markets, but nonetheless it has managed to survive, under the name *Jamboree U.S.A.* since 1969.

Another announcer/programmer who got his start on Chicago's *National Barn Dance* was JOHN LAIR. A native of Kentucky, he longed to return to his home region of Renfro Valley, so in 1937 he took several leading performers from Chicago and established the *Renfro Valley Barn Dance*. The show took a more down-home tone in music and presentation than the Chicago model, with an emphasis on folksy humor and acts. In 1957 the original radio show was taken off the air, but it has continued to operate as a stage show and tourist attraction.

Besides these major barn-dance shows, most Southern radio stations featured country music during at least part of each broadcast day. In the days before DJs and records, stations used local performers, who were also called upon to find their own sponsors. These sponsors usually included flour makers (BOB WILLS was originally sponsored by Burrus Mills, and FLATT AND SCRUGGS famously were sponsored by Martha White flour), makers of patent medicines and "miracle cures," meat producers, farm-supply firms, or even local drugstores or groceries. A typical fifteen-minute program might be aired daily in the early morning (before farmers went to work), or at noontime. HANK WILLIAMS's "Health and Happiness Shows," now available on CD, are typical of these fifteen-minute mixes of music, low comedy, and shilling for the product. This practice continued well into the era of DJs and records; for example, THE STANLEY BROTHERS continued to perform fifteen-minute radio spots into the early 1960s as a mainstay of their performing careers.

A largely unregulated part of the radio world in the 1930s was the "border" stations. Located just across the U.S. border in Mexico, these extremely powerful stations would blanket the country with their signals. Some were as powerful as 90,000 watts (nearly twice as powerful as the strongest signal legally allowed in the U.S. at the time), and humorous stories circulated of people picking up the signals in their dental work without the benefit of a radio set! XERA, founded by patent medicine promoter Dr. John R. Brinkley, was among the most famous. These stations featured many country acts who couldn't find work on U.S. stations, including THE CARTER FAMILY and PATSY MONTANA. After World War II the border stations still held sway, but primarily in the Texas region. They were less influential in the following decades, and the deathblow came in 1986 when the U.S. and Mexico signed a treaty that eliminated the "clear-channel" frequencies for high-powered stations.

In 1940 radio broadcasters across the country—dissatisfied by the stranglehold on song licensing exercised by ASCAP, which charged radio stations fees for the broadcast of its members' compositions—formed a rival group known as Broadcast Music, Inc. (BMI). Because ASCAP members were drawn primarily from mainstream popular music, BMI had its first success organizing composers not traditionally represented by that organization, including country-music performers. BMI aggressively signed country performers and set up their royalty system to take account of airplay on local stations (ASCAP focused more on national networks), where BMI's music was more likely to be played. In 1953 BMI began presenting country music awards, and five years later opened its Nashville office. In 1963 BMI was the first licensing organization to open offices on Music Row (ASCAP and the European SESAC followed later). Many of the major country publishers are affiliated with BMI, although since the country boom of the mid-1980s, ASCAP has more aggressively pursued this market.

After World War II the disc jockey increasingly replaced live performers on radio. In country this meant a new emphasis on playing records rather than featuring live acts. In 1953 the country DJs formed their own organization, the Country Music Disc Jockey Association (CMDJA), inspired by the first DJ convention held at Nashville in November 1952. WSM was behind the celebration, tied in with the anniversary of *The Grand Ole Opry*, and the convention was so successful that it attracted 100 attendees. In 1953 the second convention featured the first awards for Best Country DJs. By 1958 membership had grown to over 2,000, but grumblings about problems in the organization—and a recognition that a broader mission was needed to advocate country music—led to the end of the CMDJA and the formation of the Country Music Association (CMA). The CMA made its goal the growth of country radio and general recognition of country music. In 1961 it was a prime force behind the establishment of the Country Music Hall of Fame, and later helped raise funding for its permanent home, which opened in 1967. A year later it hosted the first CMA awards show. In 1972 the CMA launched the annual Fan Fair to bring artists and their fans together; a wildly successful event, it has become an annual event that draws over 25,000 people.

In 1969 the growing corporate influence in country radio was reflected by the formation of the CRB (Country Radio Broadcasters). It held a meeting in February, and promoted a more centrally controlled format over the looser, local control advocated by the CMA. In 1975 it established the Country Music DJ Hall of Fame, and in 2001 added the Country Radio Hall of Fame.

Perhaps the most famous country deejay is RALPH EMERY. Signed to the "graveyard" shift (10 P.M. to 3 A.M.) at WSM in 1957, Emery took advantage of his late-night time slot to bring in acts who might be returning from a late-night gig. Emery quickly built a following, and he became a champion of the late 1960s–mid-1970s COUNTRYPOLITAN movement, particularly through his syndicated *Pop Goes the Country* show. Later, his move into cable television on TNN made him a household face in country circles, and he parlayed his radio and TV success into a series of best-selling memoirs.

The next generation of smooth-voiced DJs is represented by the highly successful Charlie Chase, half of the popular CROOK AND CHASE duo. Chase had developed his chops as a radio announcer from his early teen years, joining the staff of WSM in 1974, when he was twenty-two years old, and remaining with the station for eleven years. He then was paired with the perky Lorianne Crook on a Nashville morning TV show, and the duo have since become the biggest cheerleaders for contemporary country.

But country radio is made up primarily of many hundreds of small stations, each with its own local DJ and, despite corporate pressures, usually with its own programming. The growth in country radio since the 1960s has been breathtaking: in 1961 there were only eighty-one country stations, representing about 1.75 percent of the entire radio market; by the late 1990s the number had swelled to almost 2,400, nearly one-fifth of all radio stations in the U.S. With satellite and Internet radio on the rise, a new generation of stations focusing on specific country genres and artists is undoubtedly just around the corner.

Nonetheless, WSM AM made waves in early 2002 when hints were dropped that a format change was coming to the venerable station, and that *The Grand Ole Opry* might lose its longtime home (although presumably it would not go off the air). The economics of AM radio are such that stations featuring music—even Top 10 popular music—were giving way to all-talk and news formats through the 1990s. For sentimental reasons, if nothing else, fans have objected to the proposed change, although the issue remains unresolved.

RAILROAD SONGS The railroad played a key role in opening up rural America to outside influences between the mid-nineteenth century and the first decades of the twentieth century. It, and the workers who manned the trains, also became the subject of many country songs.

In the early days of railroading, when timetables were at best approximations and time zones were not clearly established, accidents caused by two trains being on the same track at the same time (and heading in opposite directions) were frighteningly common. In the sentimental literature of the day, as well as in song, the "honest trainman" who stayed with his train as it hurtled into another locomotive became a hero, like the captain who bravely goes down with his ship. One of the most popular of these sentimental stories was retold in "The Wreck of the Old 97," the tale of a tragic train derailment. It was recorded by VERNON DALHART and became country music's first million-selling hit.

The image of the trainman was so beloved in country culture that one of the first great country stars, JIMMIE RODGERS, was promoted as "The Singing Brakeman." Rodgers had indeed worked on the trains, but when he first began performing, he dressed in natty clothes and horn-rimmed glasses, looking very much like a well-scrubbed, urban college graduate. But when he was signed by Victor Records, one of the first publicity shots that was released by the company showed him in full railroader's regalia, including striped overalls and hat. It was important for the PR folks at the label to establish Rodgers as "one of the folks," and clearly his well-pressed suits would not do the trick. Rodgers's railroad image was emulated by other performers, just as the COWBOY image would become standard for country performers a decade later.

The train had a more subtle influence on rural music. The "high, lonesome sound" of the train whistle, echoing across the mountains, has been celebrated in many country songs. The whistle came to be a symbol for life beyond the small rural communities, and the train, a symbol of escape and freedom. Where once rural folks were condemned to a life of hard labor on small, often isolated farms, now they could travel to the big cities in search of higher-paying jobs and more social freedom. BILL MONROE was just one of many Southerners who escaped the backwoods of Kentucky by taking a train to East Chicago, Indiana, to join his brothers as a laborer in the oil industry. One of his most famous songs ("Blue and Lonesome") celebrates the feeling he got as a youth when he heard the train whistle: "When I hear that whistle blow/I want to pack my suitcase and go."

Train sound effects were often imitated by master instrumentalists, who could make a career out of reproducing the various sounds of the chugging locomotives. One of the first GRAND OLE OPRY stars, harmonica player DEFORD BAILEY, specialized in re-creating these sounds in his very popular showpiece "Pan American Blues," named after the famous long-distance train. In the 1930s THE ROUSE BROTHERS created a classic train number, "Orange Blossom Special," featuring imitations of train whistles played on the fiddle, that has become one of the most imitated (and overplayed) pieces in BLUEGRASS and country music.

Eventually the automobile (and later still the airplane) would replace the train as a popular means of transportation. The TRUCK DRIVER would replace the trainman as the hero of many country songs during the 1960s.

RAINWATER, MARVIN (b. M. Karlton Percy, Wichita, Kan., July 2, 1925)

Rainwater is a SINGER/SONGWRITER of Indian descent who had his greatest success in country and ROCKABILLY-styled recordings in the late 1950s.

Raised in Kansas, Rainwater was actually named Marvin Percy (Rainwater was his mother's maiden name); he grew up in a fairly well-to-do family and originally trained to be a veterinarian. After serving in the Navy in World War II, he took up a career in music, getting his first break in 1946 when he was hired to perform on the popular *Ozark Jubilee* radio show. Taking his "Indian" name, Rainwater had immediate success that led to early-1950s recordings on the small Four Star and Coral labels. His second break came in

1955 when he appeared on the popular *Talent Scouts* TV show, hosted by the affable, ukulele-teasin' Arthur Godfrey; this led to a contract with MGM Records.

MGM cranked up the publicity machine, promoting Rainwater as a "full-blooded Cherokee brave" and having him appear in full Indian regalia, including headdress. His recordings were a mix of country and rockabilly, beginning with his first hit, 1957's "Gonna Find Me a Bluebird," which he also wrote. His biggest record was "Whole Lotta Woman," a rockabilly classic that, oddly enough, was too racy for pop radio (programmers thought the lyrics were "too suggestive"), but was acceptable to the normally more conservative country stations. His last hit was a cover of JOHN D. LOUDERMILK's "Half Breed" in 1959.

Rainwater label-hopped through the 1960s, without much success. In the mid-1960s he had to have throat surgery and was out of commission for about four years, then made a comeback in 1971. He has remained popular in Europe, where fans of vintage country and rockabilly continue to come to his concerts in droves.

Select Discography

Classic Records, Bear Family 15600. Four CDs with illustrated booklet including all of his MGM, Brave, UA, and Warner Bros. recordings.

RANCH ROMANCE (1987–1994: Jo Miller [gtr, voc]; Barbara Lamb [fdl, voc]; Lisa Theo [mdln, voc]; Nancy Katz [b, voc])

It had to happen: an all-female COWBOY quartet! If the novelty of Doug Green's RIDERS IN THE SKY is wearing thin, how about giving this Seattle-based quartet of neo-cowgirls a try?

The group was formed in 1987 by Jo Miller as "an all-star cowgirl revue." They were featured on the Nashville Network a year later, and released their first record on their own label soon after. A soon-to-be-out-of-the-closet K.D. LANG invited them to perform as her opening act on her 1989 tour (while she was still in her own cowgirl phase), and the band was signed by Sugar Hill Records, issuing their first album in 1991. They cut two more records through 1993, and then disbanded.

Essentially a novelty band, Ranch Romance faced the same problem as their male cowpoke counterparts: Within the limits of the hokey cowboy style, how far could a band go? Once you've recorded "Back in the Saddle Again" as a kind of sophisticated homage to (and at the same time a satire of) country-western conventions, there's a limit to what you can achieve. Still, bands like this make for pleasant entertainment—at least for the occasional listener.

Select Discography

Blue Blazes, Sugar Hill 3794. Their first album for Sugar Hill.

RANDOLPH, "BOOTS" (b. Homer Louis R. III, Paducah, Ky., June 3, 1927)

Randolph, one of the most popular Nashville session musicians—perhaps the "world's only hillbilly saxophone player," as he claims—has had a number of crossover hits, beginning with 1963's classic "Yakety Sax."

Born in rural Kentucky, Boots came from a musical family. He began playing ukulele in the family band as soon as he could hold the instrument; other members included his fiddler father, guitar-playing mother, older brothers Earl (BANJO) and Bob (MANDOLIN), and bass-playing sister Dorothy. The group was quite active in the mid-1930s, when farm or industrial work was hard to find, thanks to the Depression. The family settled in Cadiz, Kentucky, where Boots entered elementary school. His father traded an old revolver for a trombone, which he gave to Boots when he was ready to enter high school, and Boots played in the high-school band in his new hometown of Evansville, Indiana. He switched to saxophone because he tired of carrying the cumbersome trombone in the school's marching band, and soon formed a combo with his brother Bob that played on local Army bases in the early years of World War II.

After serving in the Army from 1945 to 1946, he returned to Evanston, where work was hard to find. By the early 1950s he was playing in a bar in Decatur, Illinois, where he was heard by the country comedy duo HOMER AND JETHRO. They recommended Randolph to country producer CHET ATKINS, who invited him to come to Nashville to work as a sessionman. He recorded with many of RCA's country acts, as well as popsters like Perry Como, folk singer Burl Ives, and even ELVIS PRESLEY. Randolph was hired by OWEN BRADLEY to play on BRENDA LEE's early rockin' sessions, where his jazzy stylings were an immediate sensation.

In the early 1960s RCA dropped Randolph as a solo artist, and he signed with Monument. In 1963 he had his big pop hit with "Yakety Sax," an instrumental he had composed almost a decade earlier with another member of his combo, James Rich. This was followed by "Mr. Sax Man" a year later, and then by schlocky covers of current pop hits including 1966's "Shadow of Your Smile." Randolph continued to churn out the easy-listening material through the 1970s and 1980s.

In 1977 he opened his own Nashville nightclub, Boots Randolph's, where he headed the house band for the next seventeen years. After briefly retiring he founded another club with hornsman Danny Davis,

which remained open through 1999. Since then Randolph has once again hit the road.

Select Discography

Country Boots, Monument 44358. 1974 album featuring contributions from Mother Maybelle Carter, Atkins, JOSH GRAVES, and other premiere Nashville session pickers.
Yakety Sax, Mounment 44356. Featuring his big hit.

RANEY, WAYNE (b. Wolf Bayou, Ark., August 17, 1920–January 23, 1993)

Wayne was a country harmonica player, producer, songwriter, and deejay whose career spanned four decades.

Raney was self-taught on the harmonica, and was already working on Mexican border radio at the age of thirteen. He greatly admired radio/record star Lonnie Glosson, also a harmonica whiz, who was featured on the popular Chicago-based NATIONAL BARN DANCE show in the mid-1930s. The two hooked up in 1936, and would work together in various capacities through 1960. In 1941 they began a long run on Cincinnati radio with a show that by the late 1940s was syndicated nationwide to over 250 stations. Through the show they popularized the humble harmonica, claiming to have sold several million instruments through mail-order.

Postwar Cincinnati was home to King Records, and the two worked sessions there, particularly for THE DELMORE BROTHERS. Their harmonicas can be heard on the hit "Blues Stay Away from Me." Raney's career reached a high point in 1949 with his #1 King release, "Why Don't You Haul Off and Love Me," which led to a guest shot on THE GRAND OLE OPRY radio show.

In 1953 Raney relocated to California, where he worked on the *California Hayride* show. During this period he was also a member of LEFTY FRIZZELL's band and briefly broadcast out of Wheeling, West Virginia. He returned to Cincinnati for more radio work through most of the 1950s, then founded his own studio and record label, Rimrock, in 1958. His last recording appearance was for Starday Records in 1964; he then ceased performing for a while. In the 1970s he made a brief return to the spotlight, blowing his harmonica on the popular HEE HAW TV show. In 1980 he retired for good, selling the remains of his studio business to the Stax label.

Select Discography

Songs from the Hills, King 588. Reissue of late 1950s album that comprised recordings Raney cut in 1948 for King, accompanied by The Delmore Brothers, among others. Good country boogie.

RASCAL FLATTS (c. 1999–present: Jay DeMarcus [voc, gtr, kybds, mdln, b]; Gary LeVox [voc]; Joe Don Rooney [gtr, voc])

Rascal Flatts is a sweet-voiced harmony trio for the new millennium.

Cousins Jay DeMarcus and Gary LeVox were raised in Columbus, Ohio, where their families often joined together to harmonize. In 1992 DeMarcus left town for Nashville, trying to make it as a SINGER/SONGWRITER. Five years later LeVox followed, and the duo were hired to work in minor country singer Charley Wright's band. They also began gigging in small clubs around town, working with a part-time guitarist.

Joe Don Rooney was raised in Picher, Oklahoma, in a musical family. He often visited a country show held in the small nearby town of Grove, improbably (and somewhat grandly) called *The Grand Ole Opry*. He began working there as a guitarist at age nineteen, and then wended his way to Nashville.

DeMarcus and LeVox were looking for a fill-in guitarist for a weekend gig when they encountered Rooney. The trio immediately clicked, and a group was born. They began cutting demos, attracting the attention of producer Dann Huff. He led them to Lyric Street Records (owned by the family-oriented Walt Disney Company), which already was specializing in country-flavored harmony groups, having a hit with the pop singers SHEDAISY. The new group, Rascal Flatts, was more or less a male equivalent of these sunny female harmonizers.

Not surprisingly their first single, "Prayin' for Daylight," zipped up the charts. The band won the 2000 Best Vocal Duo/Group award from the Academy of Country Music, and their subsequent single "This Everyday Love"—much in the style of their first one—was just as successful. Equally unsurprising is the fact that most of the material on their first album was not their original songs but tunes crafted by the usual Nashville "professionals." Although DeMarcus plays bass on the album, the rest of the accompaniment is by studio musicians while the group is relegated to providing the upfront harmonies.

Half New Kids on the Block, half ALABAMA, Rascal Flatts shows how canny Nashville producers have pegged the teen-pop market as the next great opportunity for record sales. Like other groups geared to this market, Rascal Flatts will probably have a short shelf life. But, as of the turn of the twenty-first century, they are riding high on the charts and packing 'em in on tour.

Select Discography

Rascal Flatts, Lyric Street/Hollywood 166011. 2000 debut album that soared up the charts.

RAUSCH, LEON (b. Edgar L. R., Springfield, Mo., October 2, 1927)

Rausch is a Texas vocalist best known for his association with BOB WILLS from 1958 until the veteran fiddler's death.

Born in Missouri, Rausch played several instruments from an early age and performed with his father, beginning at age eleven, at local dances and fairs. After a stint in the Navy in World War II, he returned to Springfield, where he continued performing locally, then relocated to Tulsa, Oklahoma, in 1955, in search of more work as a singer. In 1958 he was hired as lead vocalist for Bob Wills's Texas Playboys, the band's first permanent vocalist since TOMMY DUNCAN had been fired a decade earlier. He worked with Wills through the 1960s, and also with his younger brother, Johnnie Lee Wills, from 1962 to 1964.

After Wills semiretired in the late 1960s, Rausch formed The New Texas Playboys, who had some success on the regional Long Horn label. When Wills was coaxed out of retirement for his "last sessions" in 1973, Rausch came on board again as lead vocalist, and then continued to perform with the revived Texas Playboys through the 1970s after Wills's death. In the 1980s he made two excellent LPs for the Southland label, with a swinging ensemble molded after The Playboys. He has been less active since.

RAVEN, EDDY (b. Edward Garvin Futch, Lafayette, La., August 19, 1944)

Raven is another country star with a long and winding career, beginning in 1950s teen-pop and then coming home to country, with a distinct CAJUN/R&B flavor, originally as a 1970s songwriter and minor recording star, and then as a hitmaker on his own through the 1980s.

Raven's father was a truckdriver and sometime country guitarist who encouraged his son's musical inclinations. By the time Eddy was a teenager, the family was living in Georgia, where he took his stage name and recorded his first discs for the tiny Cosmo label in a teen-rock style. Upon returning to Louisiana, Eddy met local record producer/performer Bobby Charles (best remembered for his hit recording of the peppy "See You Later, Alligator"), who scored a local hit with Raven's "Big Boys Cry." Raven continued to perform as a rocker, working for a while with the young, up-and-coming brothers Johnnie and Edgar Winter out of Texas.

By the late 1960s, though, Raven's rock career was in a shambles and he was at loose ends. Old friend and fellow Cajun JIMMY "C" NEWMAN introduced him to his contacts at Acuff-Rose Publishers, and Raven was soon churning out country hits, beginning with "Country Green" and "Touch the Morning" for DON GIBSON and "Good Morning, Country Rain," a hit for JEANNIE C. RILEY. A showcase performance at Nashville's King of the Road Motor Inn (we don't make these names up, you know) led to a recording contract with ABC in 1974, and a minor hit in the same year with "The Last of the Sunshine Cowboys." Raven continued to supply songs for other country acts, including ROY ACUFF's 1974 single, "Back in the Country," and began appearing at more upscale venues, including Las Vegas.

In the late 1970s he signed with Monument and then, in the early 1980s, Elektra, scoring some minor hits. But he really started churning out the #1 records in 1984 when he signed with RCA, beginning with "I Got Mexico" (which he wrote with Paul Worley) and continuing through the R&B-flavored "Shine, Shine, Shine" (introduced on the syndicated *Dance Fever* TV show in 1987), the Cajun-flavored 1988 hit "I'm Gonna Get You" and the calypso-esque "Joe Knows How to Live" from later in that year, and 1989's "In a Letter to You" and the semiautobiographical "Bayou Boys." Raven explained that he was trying to meld country, R&B, calypso, and Cajun, certainly an unusual marriage. However, after these successes he dropped off the charts again in the 1990s, although he continues to perform.

Select Discography

The Best of, RCA 6815. Hits from 1984 to 1988.
The Best of, Curb 77881. Reissue of 1992 budget compilation of Liberty recordings made from the late 1980s through the early 1990s.

RAYE, COLLIN (b. Floyd C. Wray, DeQueen, Ark., August 22, 1959)

Raye is a middle-of-the-road pop balladeer wrapped in a cowboy suit who scored big through the 1990s with sentimental WEEPERS, all-out rockers, and even social-protest songs.

The son of a ROCKABILLY singer named Lois Wray, Collin was brought on stage at age seven by his mother. He and his brother Scott toured as The Wray Brothers through the 1970s, first in Texas and then in the Portland, Oregon, area after the family relocated there. He took the countryesque name Bubba Wray to front the band The Wrays in the mid-1980s. In this incarnation Wray claimed to be the ultimate bar singer, able to cover over 4000 hits in all genres. The group was mostly a Northwest phenomenon, but they did get signed to a national label, Mercury, and even scored a Top 50 pop hit, "You Lay a Lotta Love on Me," in 1986.

In 1990, taking a new identity as Collin Raye, he moved to Nashville and signed with Epic Records as a country recording artist. A year later he scored his

first #1 hit with the ballad "Love, Me." His next ballad hit, 1992's "In This Life," has become a wedding favorite. These hits set the stage for a number of similar melodramatic weepers, sung in a style that is 90 percent pop, with just a touch of country accent to make it audience-acceptable.

However, unlike other middle-of-the-road balladeers, Raye tackled controversial issues, including domestic abuse ("I Think About You") and racism ("Not That Different"). Some of these songs bordered on the bathetic, but they nonetheless raised issues that are rarely heard on country radio. Raye even ran the 800 number for Alcoholics Anonymous during his video for the song "Little Rock," which supposedly led to hundreds of thousands of calls for help. And, to keep the fans happy, he recorded his quota of upbeat rockers, including "I Want You Bad (and That Ain't Good)" and "My Kind of Girl."

Like other early 1990s hitmakers, Raye had a more difficult time on the charts in the second half of the decade, but soldiered on. In 2000 he attempted to tackle the children's market with *Counting Sheep*, a collection of lullabies for the boot-wearing set. But he has also continued to record the kind of mainstream country that defines his style, a mix of rockers and ballads.

Though many find Raye's ballads overly theatrical and sentimental, he has built a strong and loyal fan base. He's not a particularly distinctive or strong vocalist, but he can belt home a tearjerking ballad with the best of them. And his commercial track record has been strong; his first four albums all went platinum. While Raye may not be the most distinctive of the 1990s stars, he has proved to have a durable career giving fans what they want.

Select Discography

Best of: Direct Hits, Epic 67893. All his hits through the mid-1990s.

RAYE, SUSAN (b. Eugene, Ore., October 8, 1944)

Raye is a pleasant enough singer who had some late-1960s and early-1970s hits thanks to her association with her mentor, BUCK OWENS.

Born in Eugene but raised in the nearby small town of Forest Grove, Raye began performing as a teenager on local radio, as both a singer and a deejay. By the mid-1960s she was a featured performer on Portland's *Hoedown* TV show, and also appeared at clubs throughout the Northwest, where Buck Owens's manager, Jack McFadden, heard her and brought the singer to audition for the Bakersfield star. Owens hired her for his backup band in 1965, and again in 1968. A year later he arranged for her to record her first single for Capitol, "Maybe if I Closed My Eyes," which he wrote for her. This led to a series of hits through the mid-1970s, including the syrupy 1971 disc "Pitty, Pitty, Patter (I've Got a Happy Heart)" and the Top 10 hit "L.A. International Airport," which became a signature song for the artist, 1972's aorta-pumpin' platters "My Heart Has a Mind of Its Own" and "Love Sure Feels Good in My Heart," and a turn away from her good-girl image in 1973 with "Cheatin' Game" and the scolding "Whatcha Gonna Do with a Dog Like That" from a year later. Raye also continued to record duets with Buck, including the minor 1975 hit "Love Is Strange." Raye's solo career dried up after that, although she continues to record occasionally, including a 1984 release on Westexas, "Put Another Notch in Your Belt," which was a minor chart success.

Select Discography

Greatest Hits, Varese 6028. Sixteen Capitol recordings from the early 1970s, all produced by Buck Owens, very much in the country-pop style of the day.

RECORD LABELS Besides RADIO, recordings have played a major role in the growth and dissemination of country music, virtually since the birth of the recording era. Although country music was at first recorded only as a novelty, by the mid-1920s recording executives had discovered the huge market for singers, bands, and instrumentalists catering to the rural, "old-time" market. Major and minor players quickly entered the field to record everything from aging fiddlers to the youngest stringbenders.

Victor, Edison, and Columbia were the major labels of the 78 era (approx. 1910–1950). All three labels occasionally recorded a fiddler or country singer during the first years of sound recording. Often musicians would come to New York or another major center and somehow talk a recording executive into recording them; fiddler ECK ROBERTSON and banjo player SAMANTHA BUMGARNER both made recordings literally by showing up at the studios of Victor and Okeh (a second-tier label), respectively.

Okeh was the label generally credited with discovering the country market, somewhat accidentally, when it issued the first record by FIDDLIN' JOHN CARSON at the request of its Atlanta dealer, Polk Brockman. Carson's record sold so well that within a month he was invited to the company's New York studio, where he quickly recorded more material in a similar style. Columbia, sensing a trend, found its own older Georgia fiddler, Gid Tanner, and brought him to New York to record, along with guitarist RILEY PUCKETT. By the later 1920s many labels had formed special subcatalogs for their country recordings; for example, Columbia created the famous 15000–D series for "old-time"

music, and issued a special catalog to promote these recordings.

The first country "cover" artist was VERNON DALHART; originally a light-opera singer, he had recorded popular material for Edison and Victor. In 1924 he was asked by Victor to record "The Wreck of the Old 97," which had previously been recorded by the rough-hewn country singer HENRY WHITTER. Dalhart's recording was so successful, selling over a million copies, that country singers were suddenly in high demand. Meanwhile, Columbia had encouraged Tanner and Puckett to form a string band, and in 1926 issued the first record by the newly created Gid Tanner and His SKILLET LICKERS. This raucous Georgia group combined the best of Tanner's old-style fiddling and clowning around with young musical hotshots, including fiddler Clayton McMichen, and Puckett's guitar and vocal work. The group's success led many similar bands to be recorded.

Another major record producer of this era was the Starr Piano Company of Richmond, Indiana, which operated the Gennett label. Gennett specialized in issuing recordings under a dizzying number of sublabels, often custom-produced for other vendors, such as Sears, Roebuck, for which it produced the Supertone and Silvertone labels. Artists' names would be changed indiscriminately, partially to avoid paying royalties (although many were paid flat fees for their recordings anyway) but mostly to give the illusion that these budget reissues were "new" recordings. Gennett and rival Paramount (produced by the Wisconsin Chair Company) both had greatly inferior recording studios, clinging to acoustic recording methods longer than the major labels, and often produced poor-quality pressings. Nonetheless they recorded many country and blues artists of the era. In the 1930s many of the smaller dime-store labels were absorbed into the ARC (American Record Corporation) conglomerate; it, in turn, was absorbed by CBS/Columbia by the decade's end.

During the 1920s and 1930s the major labels would send field producers to major centers to advertise for local talent. Perhaps the most famous of these trips was RALPH PEER's 1927 trip to Bristol, Tennessee, for Victor. There he made the first recordings of both JIMMIE RODGERS and THE CARTER FAMILY, representing the two major trends of contemporary country music: the blues-influenced, more modern stylings of Rodgers set against the older, white Appalachian style of the Carters. The Bristol session was just one of many such sessions where countless artists got their first chance to be heard. If the records sold, they would be invited to visit the label's major recording studios to make more recordings; if not, they would disappear back into the semi-anonymity that they had enjoyed before their shot at fame.

The last major label of the 78 era was born during the Depression, making its mark by pioneering lower-priced records. Decca was originally a British firm that in 1934 formed a New York affiliate which was run by Jack Kapp (who had been an A&R man for the Brunswick label) and his brother Dave. Dave was in charge of signing country acts, and he brought a number of popular artists to the label in the 1930s, including JIMMIE DAVIS, ERNEST TUBB, and the Carter Family. The major labels responded to Decca's challenge with their own budget labels, including Victor's Bluebird (which featured country acts like THE MONROE BROTHERS and BILL BOYD's Cowboy Ramblers).

Although it was long the home of THE GRAND OLE OPRY, little recording was done in Nashville during the height of the 78 era. However, after World War II, RCA (the inheritor of the Victor label) established itself in Nashville, and Columbia and other labels soon followed. The availability of talented songwriters, musicians, and music publishers—and its central location in the South—made the city an ideal place to record country music. Nashville also gave birth to several independent studios and labels, notably Bullet Records, founded in 1946 by WSM announcer Jim Bulleit. In 1949 the label established Nashville's first pressing plant.

Still, the major labels were the ones that developed Nashville into the center of country recording. Victor was dominated in the 1950s by A&R man STEVE SHOLES and his studio cohort, guitarist CHET ATKINS. From EDDY ARNOLD in the late 1940s through ELVIS PRESLEY in the mid-1950s, RCA had major hitmaking acts managed out of Nashville. In 1957 it opened its own studio, which was run by Chet Atkins through the 1960s. Atkins was one of the architects of the NASHVILLE SOUND. RCA continued to be a major player in the country market, albeit aimed at the more conservative end of the spectrum, through the mid-1970s. The 1976 release of the "concept" album *Wanted! The Outlaws* on the label (really a marketing ploy to try to stir up interest in artists like WILLIE NELSON and WAYLON JENNINGS) did momentarily put the label back at the forefront of cutting-edge country. The 1980s saw some notable new country successes, including THE JUDDS, VINCE GILL, and CLINT BLACK. In 1986 the label was purchased by the German media conglomerate Bertelsmann, which rechristened the country division RCA Nashville in the 1990s; later in the decade Arista's Nashville division, another part of the Bertelsmann empire, was folded into RCA.

Columbia Records, in its modern form, came together in 1938 when CBS Radio purchased the old American Record Corporation (ARC), a conglomerate of smaller labels, many marketed through five-and-tens. Popular acts like BOB WILLS, cowboy crooner GENE AUTRY, and ROY ACUFF were among ARC's assets that Columbia inherited. Under the new regime country recordings were first issued on subsidiary labels, including Vocalion (in the later 1930s) and Okeh (in the early-through-mid-1940s). From 1945 Columbia featured its country acts on the main label.

A&R man DON LAW had the greatest influence on Columbia's country roster during the postwar era, serving as head of country at the label from 1952 to 1967. New acts developed under his reign included CARL SMITH, LEFTY FRIZZELL, MARTY ROBBINS, and RAY PRICE, as well as BLUEGRASS stars FLATT AND SCRUGGS. In 1953 the company formed the Epic subsidiary, but it did not expand the label into Nashville until 1963. Producer BILLY SHERRILL brought Epic's country line to its highest level of success during the late 1960s through the mid-1970s with acts he handled, including TAMMY WYNETTE, CHARLIE RICH, and GEORGE JONES. In 1987 Columbia, Epic, and the remaining associated labels were purchased by Sony, in an attempt to combine its "hardware" business with the "software" of sound recordings. Since then the Epic and Columbia names have been continued, both featuring contemporary Nashville artists.

Decca has also continued to be a major player, although the Decca name disappeared in 1973. After World War II, Paul Cohen, then working for the firm out of Cincinnati, took over Decca's country roster and oversaw its growth in the late 1940s and 1950s with artists ranging from BILL MONROE to KITTY WELLS and BRENDA LEE; he also secured the distribution rights to PATSY CLINE's recordings (she was under contract to the independent Four Star label). From 1949 Cohen employed producer OWEN BRADLEY, who operated out of his own studio. Bradley put together a house band that helped form the smooth, jazz- and pop-influenced NASHVILLE SOUND. In 1958 Bradley took over as head of Decca's country operations, where he remained until 1976. During his heyday in the 1960s, Bradley brought LORETTA LYNN, BILL ANDERSON, and CONWAY TWITTY, among many others, to the label.

In 1962 the label was absorbed into the MCA Corporation, which continued to use the Decca name until 1973 and then revived it briefly in the 1990s. In 1979 further country artists were brought to MCA with the purchase of ABC/Dot. The label was reinvigorated in the 1980s, first under the leadership of JIMMY BOWEN and then of TONY BROWN, both ex-musicians. New artists including REBA MCENTIRE, PATTY LOVELESS, MARTY STUART, and Vince Gill were all key to the label's growth. In 1990 MCA became part of the Japanese electronics manufacturer Matsushita Electric Industrial. Brown continued through the 1990s, developing more hitmakers, including TRISHA YEARWOOD, MARK COLLIE, and TRACY BYRD.

The Time Warner empire includes several previously independent labels that have joined the country

331

party, primarily in the 1990s. The parent label, Warner Bros., was formed by the movie company in 1958 to release sound-track albums and try to get into the growing record business. It was combined with Frank Sinatra's Reprise label in 1963. Warners paid little attention to country until it opened its Nashville office in 1975. Although it had solid hits in the later 1970s with JOHN ANDERSON, the label really took off when it introduced new-country star RANDY TRAVIS in 1985. Hooking onto the growing interest in cowboy and Western material, a sublabel, Warner Western, was formed in 1992. For about two decades sister label Reprise was home to COUNTRY-ROCK legend EMMYLOU HARRIS and also, in the mid-1980s, introduced DWIGHT YOAKAM.

Elektra Records, previously an independent, New York folk and rock label, was absorbed into the Warner family in the early 1970s. In 1973 it opened a Nashville office, and in 1976 saw great success with new artist EDDIE RABBITT. HANK WILLIAMS, JR. was perhaps Elektra's most successful country artist. In 1978 Jimmy Bowen took over the label's Nashville operation; five years later, when the Elektra name was dropped and the Warner-Elektra offices were combined, Bowen continued at the helm. Asylum, originally distributed and manufactured by Elektra, opened a Nashville office in 1992, under the guidance of KYLE LEHNING. Achieving only moderate chart success, the label surprised the industry in 1998 when Evelyn Shriver replaced Lehning, becoming the first female Nashville label president.

Atlantic, known primarily as a jazz and R&B label, is the third major leg of the Warner empire. It, too, came to Nashville in the wake of the 1980s country boom, first tentatively with the Atlantic America label in the mid-1980s, and then with a full office opening in 1989. Rick Blackburn is the executive who oversaw the label's growth, which has included such mainstream new-country acts as CONFEDERATE RAILROAD and NEAL MCCOY.

But the major labels of Nashville were not the only important outlets for country music in the late 1940s and 1950s. A number of independent labels—often operated by ex-country promoters and/or record-plant owners—helped introduce new acts and document changes in country and early rock and roll. King Records, operated out of Cincinnati by the colorful, cigar-chomping Syd Nathan, took advantage of the popularity of a local radio show, *Boone County Jamboree*, to find talented performers for its roster. In 1943 MERLE TRAVIS and GRANDPA JONES were among the first to record for the label, quickly followed by acts like THE DELMORE BROTHERS and MOON MULLICAN. Country promoters HAROLD "PAPPY" DAILY and Jack Starnes, Jr., founded the Starday label out of Houston, Texas; among their greatest discoveries was singer George

Jones. Starday was then absorbed into the major label Mercury for a while, in order to get a toehold in the country market. In the later 1950s Starday was taken over by label executive Don Pierce, who subsequently turned it into a successful label for second-tier country acts and bluegrass bands.

Mercury was founded in Chicago in 1945 as an outgrowth of a record-pressing business. Early country artists included Flatt and Scruggs, signed in 1948, and CARL STORY. In the early 1950s JOHNNY HORTON was added to the roster. After the Starday deal ended, George Jones remained with Mercury, helping to lay the foundation for its growth in the 1960s and 1970s. Taken over in 1961 by Philips International, a Dutch electronics giant, the country roster grew, particularly on the Smash subsidiary label, which featured successful country satirist ROGER MILLER and rocker-turned-country-star JERRY LEE LEWIS on its list. A&R man SHELBY SINGLETON was an important part of the label's 1960s success, and his cohort, Jerry Kennedy, helped continue the label's growth into the 1970s with TOM T. HALL and THE STATLER BROTHERS. In 1971 Phillips was absorbed into PolyGram, a large Dutch record conglomerate; a year later the country back catalog of MGM Records was added to the list. Mercury's 1980s stars included KATHY MATTEA and JOHNNY CASH (after he was dropped in the mid-1980s by his longtime label, Columbia). BILLY RAY CYRUS was the label's biggest name in the early 1990s, a product of very successful promotion and hype, but quickly faded from the scene. However, SHANIA TWAIN helped bring the label back into contention by the decade's end.

The movie studio MGM had its own label, founded in 1947. Hiring country producer FRANK WALKER to sign talent, the label scored big with HANK WILLIAMS in the late 1940s and early 1950s, as well as recording WESTERN SWING star Bob Wills. Most of its attention was thereafter focused on pop, rock, and jazz, although a Nashville division was opened in 1965 to try to regain a foothold in country. In 1972 MGM's assets were taken over by Polydor, and subsequently Polydor became part of PolyGram.

SAM PHILLIPS, the famous recording engineer who founded Sun Records and subsequently discovered Elvis Presley, recorded many 1950s country artists during their ROCKABILLY phase. Among his most notable signings were Johnny Cash, Jerry Lee Lewis, CARL PERKINS, and Charlie Rich, along with dozens of lesser-known names. He also gave producer/engineers "COWBOY" JACK CLEMENT and Billy Sherrill their starts in the business. In 1969 Sun was sold to eccentric promoter/record executive Shelby Singleton, who continued to reissue and license material from the label through the later 1990s.

Hickory Records was founded in 1953 by Roy Acuff and WESLEY AND FRED ROSE as a means of expanding their very successful Acuff-Rose publishing empire. The label was active through the mid-1970s, recording mainstream country acts including Acuff himself, along with DON GIBSON, MICKEY NEWBURY, and DOUG KERSHAW, at one time or another. It was sold in 1985 as part of the Acuff-Rose empire to Gaylord Entertainment, the owners of *The Grand Ole Opry*.

Monument Records—best remembered for its recordings of ROY ORBISON—was founded by Fred Foster in Washington, D.C. (and named for the Washington Monument). In 1963 he purchased Sun's Nashville studios, thanks to the success the label had with Orbison's many teen-pop singles in the early 1960s. He recorded many country artists at the beginnings of their careers, including Willie Nelson, JEANNIE SEELY, DOLLY PARTON, and KRIS KRISTOFFERSON. After declaring bankruptcy in the early 1980s, the label was sold to CBS in 1987; ten years later Sony (the new owner of Columbia and its assets) brought back the Monument name for a new country label. THE DIXIE CHICKS were the first new act on the revived label.

Another Nashville-based label was Dot Records, founded by record store owner Randy Wood in 1950. Dot signed MAC WISEMAN in 1951 as its first country artist, and subsequently signed others, including JIMMY C. NEWMAN and COWBOY COPAS. The firm was moved to Hollywood in 1957 and then sold to Paramount Pictures, which in turn sold the recording operations to ABC. The Dot name was maintained during the 1960s and 1970s, with later artists including ROY CLARK and BARBARA MANDRELL. In 1977 ABC/Dot became part of MCA, and the Dot name was retired until the late 1980s, when it was briefly revived for a new country line. However, thereafter Dot disappeared once again.

On the West Coast, where a new form of country was developing thanks to the influx of Texans, Okies, and other displaced Southwesterners during the Depression and continuing after World War II, a number of small labels thrived. In 1951 Fabor Robison, a country promoter, formed Abbott Records, named for the drugstore owner who put up the cash. Abbott was formed to release recordings by Robison's key act, Johnny Horton. However, it was JIM REEVES who had the label's major hit, "Mexican Joe." Although located in Hollywood, Abbott drew on the musicians associated with the popular LOUISIANA HAYRIDE radio show. With the money from that release Fabor bought out his partners and rechristened the label Fabor Records. Recordings were now made out of his home studio in southern California, and the label entered into several licensing deals over the years, most notably with Dot Records in the late 1950s. Fabor sold his masters to producer Shelby Singleton in 1965.

Another West Coast label active from 1945 was Four Star, first owned by Dick Nelson (who originally operated an R&B label), but soon controlled by notoriously tightfisted entrepreneur Bill McCall and producer Don Pierce. Located in Pasadena until 1953, when it moved to Nashville (and Pierce left to join Starday), the label had an impressive roster in the late 1940s and early 1950s, including FERLIN HUSKY and WEBB PIERCE. From 1954 to 1960 Patsy Cline was under contract to Four Star (which licensed her recordings to Decca and its subsidiary, Coral). Some critics assert that McCall's insistence that Cline publish songs controlled by his Four Star publishing arm kept her from achieving greater success early on. After moving to Nashville, McCall increasingly focused his energy on publishing; in 1961 he sold Four Star's assets to Gene Autry and Joe Johnson (who owned the Champion label).

But the biggest west coast label would be Capitol Records, founded in 1942 to record pop material. However, that same year the label signed TEX RITTER, recognizing the popularity of Western-flavored music in southern California. In 1951 KEN NELSON came on board to manage the country list, and began building an impressive roster, including FARON YOUNG, Ferlin Husky, and JEAN SHEPARD. In 1955 Capitol was purchased by the British EMI conglomerate. During the 1960s the leading Capitol country acts were BUCK OWENS and MERLE HAGGARD. The label was West Coast-oriented until Nelson's retirement in 1976, when the country division turned its focus to Nashville. The label focused on pop-country in the later 1970s and early 1980s, with artists like ANNE MURRAY. However, the label took a big jump into new country in 1989 with the signing of GARTH BROOKS, along with A&R man Jimmy Bowen, who renamed the label Liberty Records (a label that Capitol had purchased earlier). In 1995 Bowen left, and the label became Capitol Nashville. SCOTT HENDRICKS replaced Bowen, but failed to click with Brooks (who saw the decline in his career as due to Capitol's poor promotion), and Hendricks was forced out in 1997.

The FOLK REVIVAL also saw the birth of several labels, beginning in 1947 with MOSES ASCH and his Folkways family of labels. Operating on a shoestring budget with the goal of recording all types of musical expression, Asch created a model that many others would emulate, even down to his eccentric packaging (featuring an album cover that wrapped around about half of the otherwise plain-black sleeve, with mimeographed song notes and lyrics placed inside). Arhoolie, Folk Lyric, and Folk Legacy were the first to follow in Asch's footsteps in the late 1950s and early 1960s; the early 1970s brought his most important imitator, the Rounder Collective. All of these labels issued bluegrass music among other folk styles, and were instrumental in building the folk revival. County Records, founded by record collector/old-time country fan Dave Freeman in 1963, was another Folkways-inspired label that began reissuing old 78 recordings but then recorded contemporary bluegrass groups; the spinoff Sugar Hill label, founded in 1978 by Freeman and Barry Poss, has since become a major player in acoustic country and bluegrass.

Bluegrass fans have formed specialty labels for their music. Most notable is Charles R. Freeland, who in 1959 formed Rebel Records in suburban Washington to document the thriving bluegrass scene there. In the later 1960s, many prominent traditional bluegrass bands—including Ralph Stanley and THE COUNTRY GENTLEMEN—along with newer groups like THE SELDOM SCENE—were recording for the label. In 1979 the label was sold to County Records, and continues to operate under the Rebel name. Freeland has continued to issue recordings under his own Freeland label.

Smaller labels, including Old Homestead, Puritan, Vetco, and many others, have released recordings aimed at the bluegrass market over the years.

RED CLAY RAMBLERS, THE (c. 1973–present; mid-1970s lineup: Tommy Thompson [bnj, voc]; Jim Watson [mdln, voc]; Bill Hicks [fdl, voc]; Mike Craver [pno, voc]; Jack Herrick [trumpet, b, voc])

The Red Clay Ramblers were one of the most innovative of the 1970s string-band revival groups who melded traditional dance tunes and songs with swing, early jazz, country GOSPEL, and their own unique compositions.

Founded in Chapel Hill, North Carolina, in 1973, its members were interested in pursuing the vocal-music side of the old-time tradition; other local bands, like the Fuzzy Mountain String Band (of which Hicks had been a member) and the Hollow Rock String Band (of which Thompson had been a member) were instrumentally oriented. The group recorded its first album with guest artist Fiddlin' Al McCandless, who is more BLUEGRASS-oriented in his style than the rest of the band. While the band was finishing these recordings, pianist Mike Craver joined the group, and they experimented with adding ragtime and blues to the mix. With the addition of trumpeter Jack Herrick in 1975, the group's best lineup was completed.

The Ramblers made a series of innovative records from the mid-1970s through the early 1980s. Thompson and Craver wrote some amusing novelty songs in the manner of country-jazz, including "The Ace," which tells of a blind date gone seriously wrong, and "Merchant's Lunch," playing off the country clichés of roadside diners and big-rig truckers. Vocalists Thompson, Craver, and Watson also did much to revive the repertoire of THE CARTER FAMILY, recording a trio album in homage to the earlier group. Even when the group recorded a traditional dance tune—like "Forked Deer"—they jazzed it up considerably, adding a ragtime-piano part or muted trumpet. Thompson's comic bass vocals, Watson's gritty country tenor, and Craver's ethereal boy alto combined to make a distinctive group-harmony sound, with a strong nod toward the roots of country harmony (particularly old-time church harmonies).

In the 1980s the band went through several personnel changes while increasingly working with playwright/filmmaker Sam Shepard, scoring his play *A Lie of the Mind* and the film *Far North*. During the mid-1990s they worked with comic mimes Bill Irwin and David Shiner in their Broadway production of *Fool Moon*.

In 1994 last original member Tommy Thompson left the band, after being diagnosed with Alzheimer's disease. Herrick is the last of the classic 1970s ensemble left. After an eight-year hiatus from recording, the band returned in 2001 with a new album, *Yonder*, on their own label.

Select Discography

Twisted Laurel/Merchant's Lunch, Flying Fish 77055.
    CD reissue of two fine albums from the mid-1980s.

REED, BLIND ALFRED (b. Floyd, Virginia, June 15, 1880–January 17, 1956)

Reed was one of the greatest topical songwriters of the 1920s, contributing to the old-time music repertoire such classics as the social-protest song "How Can a Poor Man Stand Such Times and Live?" and the humorous "Why Do You Bob Your Hair Girls (You Know That It's a Sin)."

The coal miner and fiddler was discovered by RALPH PEER at the legendary 1927 sessions held in Bristol, Tennessee, that also produced THE CARTER FAMILY's and JIMMIE RODGERS's first recordings. Reed recorded for Victor, playing fairly simple fiddle parts to accompany his own clearly sung vocals, usually performed with discreet guitar accompaniment. Reed had a clear, powerful voice, and his songs often tackled topical issues in a humorous way, making them immediately popular.

Many of his songs commented on the troubles that women bring to men, although it's not always clear just how serious the fiddler is being in songs like "We Just Got to Have Them, That's All," which traces the problems women have created for their mates all the way back to the Garden of Eden. Reed capitalized on his biggest hit, "Why Do You Bob Your Hair Girls," a semiserious indictment of the craze for short hair, with a second number ("Bob Hair Number 2"), in which he continued to take a fundamentalist approach to the question of coiffure ("Short hair belongs to men," the song warns).

Perhaps Reed's greatest song is the poignant "How Can a Poor Man Stand Such Times and Live?" In a straightforward style Reed outlines how rural Americans are exploited by middlemen and entrepreneurs, benefiting little from their labor. The repeated chorus line (and title of the song) says it all; Reed does not embellish or force the message, but lets the song speak for itself. Perhaps only FIDDLIN' JOHN CARSON's "Taxes on the Farmer Feeds Them All" comes close in its simple eloquence as a great social-protest song of the era.

Select Discography

Complete Record Works, Document 8022. Twenty tracks, all of his Victor recordings cut between 1927 and 1929, with notes by Tony Russell. Supersedes an earlier LP reissue on Rounder (1002), which is worth seeking for its extensive liner notes.

REED, JERRY (b. J. R. Hubbard, Atlanta, Ga., March 20, 1937)

Affable country songwriter/singer/guitarist Jerry Reed has had equal success as a session player, solo artist, and country-fried actor.

Coming from a family of mill workers in Atlanta, Georgia, Reed took up the GUITAR as a youngster, and was a talented picker by the time he reached his teenage years. A friend of the family introduced him to publisher/producer Bill Lowery in 1955, when Jerry was just sixteen, and he was signed to a recording contract with the Los Angeles–based Capitol label. His biggest success, however, came as a songwriter when teen rocker Gene Vincent had a hit in 1956 with his song "Crazy Legs."

After serving for two years in the Army, Reed settled in Nashville, signing with Columbia and having minor hits with the instrumental "Hully Gully Guitars" and a cover of Leadbelly's perennial folk classic, "Goodnight, Irene." However, Reed's real success came as a session player, backing country and pop acts. CHET ATKINS, another talented guitar player, signed him to RCA in 1965, and he had his first major hit two years later with "Guitar Man," which was quickly covered by another RCA act, ELVIS PRESLEY. (Presley also covered Reed's semicomic song "U.S. Male".) Reed continued to score hits through the early 1970s, most notably with his unique blend of CAJUN, rock, and country on 1970's "Amos Moses," his first #1 country hit and a significant pop hit as well.

Reed's work through the 1970s became increasingly erratic, vacillating between powerful, rockin' country recordings and the kind of gooey, let's-all-sing-together records that bring to mind the ANITA KERR Singers at their worst. His last solid country hit was 1971's cover of the HANK SNOW classic, "I'm Movin' On." His best work continued to be as an instrumentalist, particularly in several duet albums with Chet Atkins.

Reed pursued an acting career, beginning in 1974 with the Burt Reynolds country flick *W. W. and the Dixie Dance Kings*; he continued to work with Reynolds in many of his light comedies, including the popular *Smokey and the Bandit* pictures. Meanwhile his recording career continued to suffer, and he was reduced to waxing such comic novelties as "She Got the Gold Mine (I Got the Shaft)" in the early 1980s (although the song did go to #1, proving once again that, in country music, good taste is timeless). Reed has made several abortive comebacks since then, but

Jerry Reed, c. mid-1970s. Photograph by Raeanne Rubenstein

with little success, although he continues to be a popular act on the road.

Select Discography

Here I Am, Bear Family 16306. His mid-1950s recordings for Capitol, during his country-ROCKABILLY years.

RCA Country Legends, Buddha 99776. Sixteen-track compilation of his late-1960s–early-1970s country recordings for RCA.

Pickin, Southern Tracks 106. 1999 album of instrumentals shows Reed still knows how to boogie.

REED, OLA BELLE (b. Lansing, N.C., August 17, 1916–December 3, 2000)

Reed was a banjo-playing songster who gained popularity during the old-time music revival of the 1970s.

Reed was one of thirteen children of a musical schoolteacher named Arthur Campbell. He played FIDDLE, BANJO, GUITAR, and organ, and formed his own traditional band six years before her birth, so she was raised with old-time music all around her. Her grandfather was also a fiddler, and a Baptist preacher. Both her mother and grandmother sang ballads and songs. The Campbells lived on the North Carolina–Virginia border, an area rich in old-time music (the famous Galax fiddlers convention was held close by).

In the 1930s the family relocated to Baltimore, where Ola Belle learned guitar and banjo, and began writing her own songs. Following World War II she and younger brother Alex formed a band that played in an older, traditional country style. They became popular favorites, first on radio out of mid-Maryland and then out of their central Pennsylvania general store, Campbell's Corner.

Ola Belle and Alex were also important promoters of country music in Pennsylvania and Maryland. In 1951, along with Bud Reed, Ola Belle's husband, they founded New River Ranch, a music venue in Maryland. They moved in 1960 to West Grove, Pennsylvania, where they remained for the next quarter-century, producing concerts. Alex and Ola Belle were also talented songwriters, claiming to have written over 200 songs. Some of Ola Belle's songs have become popular among traditional and new-country performers, including her "High on a Mountain."

During the 1970s Ola Belle gained new popularity thanks to a series of albums issued by Rounder and Folkways Records. She often toured and performed with her son, Dave. By the mid-1980s, however, she was confined to her home, and in 1988 a benefit concert was held in Washington, D.C., to help her pay medical bills. In 1986 she was awarded a National Heritage Fellowship by the National Endowment for the Arts. She continued to live in retirement in Maryland, until her death in late 2000.

REEVES, DEL (b. Franklin Delano R., Sparta, N.C., July 14, 1933)

Dubbed the "Dean Martin of country music" thanks to his smooth-voiced 1960s hits, Del began his career in an old-style harmony duet, then recorded HANK WILLIAMS-styled HONKY-TONK and teen-rock before moving on to a successful country career.

Born in North Carolina, a true son of the Depression (he was even named for the new president who promised to pull the country out of the economic doldrums), Reeves began performing country music almost as soon as he could walk; he had his own local radio show when he was just twelve. After a stint at college and in the Air Force, Del settled in southern California, where a vibrant country community was busy creating what would become known as the BAKERSFIELD SOUND.

He hooked up with mandolinist Chester Smith, who had his own country-music TV show, and the two recorded some charming old-style harmony duets for Capitol in 1957. Then Del went solo, and Capitol producer KEN NELSON (who had previously scored big molding the career of Gene Vincent) tried to turn him into a teen-popster; Del did his best, but was not very comfortable with the material. At about this time he met his future wife, Ellen Schiell, and the two began writing country songs, placing hits with mainstream artists from CARL SMITH to SHEB WOOLEY.

Del's first success as a country artist came in 1961 with "Be Quiet, Mind," released by Decca Records; he then moved to Reprise (the first country artist to record for Frank Sinatra's label) and Columbia, but failed to achieve much success until 1965, when he hit it big for United Artists with his song "Girl on the Billboard." This began a string of hits through the early 1970s, including 1966's "Women Do Funny Things to Me" (the same year Del joined THE GRAND OLE OPRY), 1968's "Looking at the World Through a Windshield," and 1971's baseball anthem "The Philadelphia Fillies." Del's mature style was solidly in the pop-country mold, with his laidback vocal style reminiscent of popsters like Dean Martin, to whom he was often compared.

By the late 1970s Del had left United Artists to record for a variety of small labels. He scored little chart action until his fluke 1987 hit "Dear Dr. Ruth," addressed to the diminutive sex therapist from New York. The record was considered "shocking" for a country audience, and got him a little bit of press in his declining years. He has been a member of *The Grand Ole Opry* since 1966, and he continues to perform there.

Select Discography

Greatest Hits, Razor & Tie 2046. Ten of his Capitol hits from the mid-1960s.

REEVES, GOEBEL (b. Sherman, Tex., October 9, 1899–January 26, 1959)

Although from a solidly middle-class background (his father was a Texas state legislator), Reeves became famous as "the Texas Drifter," a hobo performer who wrote the well-known "Hobo's Lullaby" that became a signature tune for WOODY GUTHRIE.

Reeves's service in World War I apparently politicized him, for when he returned to the U.S., he took to a life of rambling, eventually joining the International Workers of the World. He recorded for Okeh and Brunswick in the 1920s and 1930s, and claimed to have written, in addition to "Hobo's Lullaby," such classic RAILROAD and Western songs as "Hobo and the Cop," "Railroad Boomer," "Bright Sherman Valley," and "Cowboy's Prayer." He also performed narrations, spinning tall tales about the life he had lived across the United States. A fine singer and yodeler, Reeves had a pretty large ego; he even claimed to have taught JIMMIE RODGERS to yodel, one of those apocryphal stories that is impossible to disprove. He died in California in 1959, after being inactive for many years.

Select Discography

Hobo's Lullaby, Bear Family 15680. Complete recordings from the 1920s and 1930s, twenty-eight tracks in all.

REEVES, JIM (b. James Travis R., Galloway, Tex., August 20, 1923–July 31, 1964)

Jim Reeves was a smooth-voiced country balladeer who continued to produce hits even after his untimely death in an airplane crash! Although his early recordings had a fine HONKY-TONK style, at least in their accompaniment, later recordings were mainstream pop productions in the spirit of the NASHVILLE SOUND.

Jim came from a single-parent household; his mother worked as a field hand after the death of his father. He showed an early interest in music, and was given a guitar by a construction worker friend of the family when he was five years old. He made his first radio broadcast at age nine, out of Shreveport, Louisiana.

He developed an interest in baseball during his high-school years, and was signed by the St. Louis Cardinals because of his pitching skills. However, he injured his ankle in 1947, ending his career. Meanwhile, he had continued to play music on the side and studied elocution in college. At about the same time as his injury, he met his future wife, Mary White, a schoolteacher who encouraged him to seek a career in music. Thanks to his baritone voice that carried well over the air, Jim landed a job as an announcer at a local radio station. In 1949 he made a few recordings for a small Houston-based label, and by 1951–1952 he was announcing for KWKH, the Shreveport, Louisiana, station that hosted the well-known country radio program LOUISIANA HAYRIDE. While performing on the *Hayride*, he was heard by Fabor Robison of Abbott Records, who immediately signed him.

Reeves's first country hit, "Mexican Joe," came out in 1953. In 1955 he moved to THE GRAND OLE OPRY and signed with RCA, hitting immediately with "Yonder Comes a Sucker." In 1957 he scored his first crossover hit onto the pop charts with "Four Walls," leading to many TV appearances. His 1959 recording of "He'll Have to Go" is typical of the direction Reeves's music was taking; while the accompaniment and subject matter hark back to the honky-tonk tradition, his smooth vocals already forecast the direction his career would take in the early 1960s: pop-schlock balladry.

Indeed, from 1960 until his untimely death in 1964, Reeves was rarely off the charts, beginning with "I'm Getting Better" from 1960 through 1962's "Adios Amigo," 1963's "Is This Me?," to his last single released while he was still alive, "Welcome to My World." The style was now unabashedly romantic, with sighing choruses washing over his baritone burblings.

Apparently Reeves left enough recordings in the can to stock an entire second career, and he continued to have hits on the country charts right through the early 1970s. His wife, Mary, cannily packaged this unissued material, and his popularity grew from the first posthumous single, 1964's "I Guess I'm Crazy" through 1970's "Angels Don't Lie" to 1979's "How I Miss You Tonight." Through the miracle of electronic overdubbing, Reeves was even able to "perform" two duets with dead country star PATSY CLINE.

Select Discography

Singles, 1953–60, BMG 57118. Two-CD set, including all of his hits from the early period cut for RCA.
Gentleman Jim, 1954–59, Bear Family 15439. Four CDs containing 110 recordings cut for RCA during his early tenure with the label.
Welcome to My World, Bear Family 15646. Sixteen (count 'em) CDs with nearly 450 songs, everything Reeves cut for RCA and smaller labels.
Radio Days, Vols. 1 & 2, Bear Family 16274/16282. Two four-CD sets of radio transcriptions, featuring Reeves in less formal settings than on his RCA studio recordings.

REMINGTON, HERB (b. Mishawaka, Ind., June 9, 1926)

One of the pioneers of the steel guitar, Remington helped put the instrument on the map thanks to his postwar recordings with BOB WILLS.

Remington began playing Hawaiian-style guitar as a boy in Indiana, then moved to California as a teenager in search of work as a musician. He hooked up briefly with RAY WHITLEY'S WESTERN SWING band before being drafted in 1944, serving in the Army for two years. On his return he auditioned for Bob Wills's younger brother Luke, who had his own band. The elder Wills, seeing a talented musician, swapped steel players with his brother. In the days immediately following the war, Wills's band was considerably smaller than his prewar outfits, which had featured a full complement of horns; Remington became a key part of this pared-down band, which also featured electric guitarist Eldon Shamblin and mandolinist "TINY" MOORE. Remington wrote and played lead on a number of classic instrumentals with Wills, including "Boot Heel Drag," "Playboy Chimes," and "Hometown Stomp." His best-known instrumental was recorded just after he left Wills's band and joined HANK PENNY'S COWBOY outfit; called "Remington Ride," it's even been covered by blues guitarist Freddie King.

After his marriage Remington relocated to the Houston area, where he appeared on the early 1960s recordings of GEORGE JONES and WILLIE NELSON. He continues to record and perform, often with his son Mark on vocals.

RENEAU, GEORGE (b. Jefferson County, Tenn., c. 1901–December 1933)

A very early country-music star who recorded from 1924 to 1927, Reneau was a blind street musician. He was born in the Smokies, and when he was a teenager his family relocated to Knoxville, where he learned the GUITAR and began playing on street corners. He was heard by a scout for Vocalion Records, who brought him to New York to record. Initially Reneau was used strictly as an accompanist, working with pop singer Gene Austin. They were billed as The Blue Ridge Duo for these country recordings, which included the blues-flavored songs "Lonesome Road Blues" and "Blue Ridge Blues." Austin and Reneau recorded for both Vocalion and Edison.

In early 1925 Vocalion finally recorded Reneau singing and accompanying himself, and the results were several hits, including versions of VERNON DAL-HART's "The Prisoner's Song" and the well-known country songs "Jesse James" and "Wild Bill Jones." In 1927 Vocalion paired him with Lester McFarland (half of the popular duo MAC AND BOB), issuing these recordings under a variety of names, including the Lonesome Pine Twins and The Collins Brothers and The Cramer Brothers. These recordings were available through the early 1930s on a variety of dime-store labels.

The Depression ended Reneau's recording career, as it did for many other country performers. He returned to singing on the streets, where he apparently contracted pneumonia and died in late 1933.

RENO, DON (b. Donald Wesley R., Spartanburg, S.C., February 21, 1927–October 16, 1984)

Reno, one of the first and greatest BLUEGRASS BANJO players, is best known for his recordings with guitarist Red Smiley and the Tennessee Cutups, made between the early 1950s and late 1960s.

Originally playing with THE MORRIS BROTHERS, Reno was almost hired by BILL MONROE to take the banjo spot in his Blue Grass Boys band in 1943; unfortunately, he was drafted, and Earl Scruggs got the job. However, in 1948, when Scruggs left the band with Lester Flatt to form FLATT AND SCRUGGS, Reno came on board, performing with Monroe for about a year; he then met guitarist/vocalist Red Smiley (b. Arthur Lee S., May 17, 1925–January 2, 1972), and the two performed with a couple of other bands before forming their own group in 1951. His unique banjo style, including picking single-string melodies in the style of tenor banjo players of the 1930s, made him an immediate standout. In 1955 Reno joined ARTHUR "GUITAR BOOGIE" SMITH in recording the original version of what was then called "Feuding Banjos" (and is now better known as "Dueling Banjos"), with Smith playing tenor and Reno playing five-string.

The Reno and Smiley group was one of the most respected in bluegrass, slightly more progressive than Monroe and Flatt and Scruggs in outlook, and certainly very prolific. However, Smiley's health began to deteriorate in the early 1960s, and by 1968 he had to leave the band (he died in 1972); Reno then formed a new Cutups with vocalist/guitarist Bill Harrell, and they worked together until 1978. Reno continued to perform until his death in 1984, often accompanied by his sons Ronnie on GUITAR, Dale on MANDOLIN, and Don Wayne on banjo; Ronnie hosted *Reno's Old-Time Music Festival*, a program devoted to acoustic and bluegrass country music, on the Americana cable network in the mid-'90s. The elder Reno's banjo picking was quite influential on the next generation of players, such as Eddie Adcock of THE COUNTRY GENTLEMEN.

Select Discography

Collector's Box Set, Starday 7001. Four CDs giving you 115 classic Reno and Smiley tracks cut between 1951 and 1959.

A Variety of Country Songs, King 646. More 1950s recordings.

RESTLESS HEART (c. 1983–c. 1994; best-known lineup [1987–1990]: Larry Stewart [voc]; Greg Jennings [voc, gtr]; Dave Innis [kybds]; Paul Gregg [b, voc]; John Dittrich [drms])

A manufactured mid-1980s group assembled by producer TIM DUBOIS (who later guided DIAMOND RIO to fast fame), Restless Heart is another in the string of EXILE-styled country popsters who produced a highly professional, if soulless, country-pop music.

The group had its roots in DuBois's desire to find an outlet for his unusual songs, which were too rock to be country and too country to appeal to mainstream rock. From his days as a student at Oklahoma State University in the mid-1970s, DuBois knew both Greg Jennings and SCOTT HENDRICKS, who would work as coproducer on the band's early hits. Hendricks brought bassist Paul Gregg, into the fold, and the remainder of the band—all Okies with the exception of drummer Dittrich—was assembled from the ranks of studio and club players around Nashville in early 1983.

After recording demos of DuBois's songs, they were signed by RCA, and had their first hit in 1986 with the pop-flavored "That Rock Won't Roll." Original lead singer Verlon Thompson remained with the group through their first single, and then was replaced by Larry Stewart, whose smooth pop vocalizing came to define the group's sound. Their biggest hit came in 1988 with "Wheels," the title song of a concept album that celebrated life on the road. Stewart left the band in 1990, and the group soldiered on, now with Jennings, Dittrich, and Gregg as lead singers and songwriters. The group's last studio release appeared in 1994, although they cut three new numbers for a hits collection in 1998.

Select Discography

Greatest Hits, RCA 67628. 1998 compilation of hits from the late 1980s and early 1990s.

RICE, TONY (b. Danville, Va., June 8, 1951)

A talented guitarist and vocalist, Rice began in PROGRESSIVE BLUEGRASS and then moved into more jazz-oriented instrumental music while also performing SINGER/SONGWRITER and folk-country material.

Rice got his start as a guitarist and vocalist in the Bluegrass Alliance and banjoist J. D. CROWE's influential early-1970s progressive band, The New South. Rice's guitar work was heavily influenced by DOC WATSON and Clarence White, although his skills soon outstripped those of his mentors. He recorded progressive bluegrass with DAVID GRISMAN on his 1975 *Rounder Album*, and then joined Grisman's first quintet, dedicated to performing the mandolinist's jazz-influenced compositions. Rice soon struck out on his own, forming a special group to perform progressive string music of his own composition.

In the 1980s he alternated between recording instrumental and vocal LPs. His vocal LPs tended to feature material from singer/songwriters working in both the folk-rock and new-country movements, such as BOB DYLAN, RODNEY CROWELL, Gordon Lightfoot, NORMAN BLAKE, MARY CHAPIN CARPENTER, and James Taylor. In 1980 he recorded an LP of duets with RICKY SKAGGS, in the manner of the brother acts of the 1930s and 1940s. He formed a special group, The Tony Rice Unit, to perform his new-acoustic instrumentals; it has recorded sporadically since then. During the later 1990s Rice lost some of his vocal capabilities, but continued to perform as a guitarist in both bluegrass and jazz/New Age styles. Rice has worked with various "all-star" bluegrass bands, and cut two bluegrass albums with his brother Larry, along with CHRIS HILLMAN and Herb Pedersen, in the late 1990s.

Select Discography

Devlin, Rounder 11531. Compilation of his new-acoustic/instrumental albums for Rounder.
Sings Gordon Lightfoot, Rounder 370. Compilation of tracks featuring Rice's interpretations of the Lightfoot catalog.

RICH, CHARLIE (b. Colt, Ark., December 14, 1932–July 25, 1995)

One of the great wasted talents of country music, Rich gained his greatest successes from his weakest recordings. Prematurely gray and thus nicknamed "The Silver Fox," Rich was an exceptionally talented pianist, vocalist, and songwriter who never reached his full potential.

The son of a heavy-drinking dirt farmer and a fundamentalist mother, Rich was greatly influenced by jazz and blues as a young musician. Unlike many other country performers, he studied music in college, at the University of Arkansas. He joined the Air Force and was stationed in Oklahoma, where he formed his first semiprofessional combo, The Velvetones, a jazz/blues combo in the Stan Kenton mold. His future wife, Margaret, was the group's lead vocalist. After leaving the Air Force, Rich returned to West Memphis, Arkansas, to help his father work his cotton farm. While performing with Bill Justis's band there, Rich was invited to audition for legendary producer SAM PHILLIPS at Sun Records.

Still playing in a jazzy style, Rich was initially dismissed by Phillips, who invited him to listen to early JERRY LEE LEWIS recordings and come back when he had absorbed Lewis's frantic keyboard pounding. Rich would session on many late-1950s Sun recordings, backing ROCKABILLY talents like Billy Lee Riley, Ray

Smith, and Warren Smith. He scored his first hit with 1959's "Lonely Weekends," a song very much influenced by the sound of the early ELVIS PRESLEY, although the girly choruses almost drown his mournful vocals.

In the early-to-mid-1960s Rich struggled to find his sound, moving from the boogie-woogie-influenced "Big Boss Man" of 1963 to the country-novelty of "Mohair Sam," even recording a straight country/HONKY-TONK LP for Memphis's Hi Records, a label later better known for its soul acts. In 1968 he hooked up with Epic Records and producer BILLY SHERRILL, who was instrumental in launching the COUNTRYPOLITAN sound.

It took five years for Rich and Sherrill to hit on a winning formula, but they hit it big in 1973–1975 with songs like "Behind Closed Doors," "The Most Beautiful Girl in the World," "A Very Special Love Song," and "Every Time You Touch Me." Rich won numerous country awards, and at the same time, thanks to their slick production, his songs found a new audience among middle-of-the-road radio listeners. Rich became the epitome of countrypolitan, and many other artists soon jumped on the bandwagon (creating the backlash that would be known as OUTLAW music, popularized by WILLIE NELSON and his coterie). Sadly, though, Rich soon lapsed into a predictable formula, even waxing a schmaltzy version of "America the Beautiful" for the bicentennial. The late 1970s and early 1980s were spent label-hopping. Although Rich continued to have hits, most notably 1979's "I'll Wake You Up When I Get Home," his days of chart-topping success were over. Rich augmented his income by scoring films, including the very popular *Benji* (1974) and *For the Love of Benji* (1977) canine features.

Music critics like Peter Guralnick have lamented that despite his bluesy phrasing, jazz-tinged piano, and smoky, world-weary vocals, Rich never seemed to reach the artistic success that he deserved, despite his commercial popularity in the early 1970s. In fact, it seems that the more commercial recordings, which tended to "sanitize" Rich's musical and vocal delivery, did much to destroy his talent, rather than encourage it.

In 1995 Rich died from a blood clot in the lung, at the age of sixty-two.

Select Discography

Early Years: Memphis Sound, Collectables 6436. Reissues two albums of Sun session material dating from the late 1950s.
Complete Smash Sessions, Mercury 643. Mid-1960s recordings, including the 1965 hit "Mohair Sam." Halfway between rock and country.
Complete Charlie Rich on Hi Records, Hi 250. His mid-1960s Hi recordings, annotated by Colin Escott.
American Originals, Columbia 45073. Drawn from his years with Epic, from the late 1960s through his mid-1970s hits.
Pictures and Paintings, Blue Horizon 26730. 1992-comeback recording.

RICHEY, KIM (b. Zanesville, Ohio, December 1, 1956)
Richey was a country-pop hitmaker and songwriter of the mid-1990s.

Richey began singing in college, performing with the Kentucky-based country band Southern Star. In 1984 she journeyed to Nashville but found little success, and was soon traveling through Europe, Latin America, and the U.S. Returning to Nashville in 1988, Richey got her first break as a songwriter working for a local publisher. She was signed by Mercury Records in the early 1990s, and released three albums through the decade, each progressively more pop-rock in orientation. She is best known for writing two mid-1990s hits: "Nobody Wins" in 1993, for Radney Foster, and "Believe Me, Baby (I Lied)," a 1996 #1 country hit for TRISHA YEARWOOD and a Grammy nominee for Best Song.

In 1999 she released *Glimmer*, her most pop-oriented album to date. She spent much of 2001 touring to support the album, including a long trip to England. Her U.S. tours were in support of SINGER/SONGWRITER Shawn Colvin, whose voice resembles Richey's, and Yearwood.

Select Discography

Kim Richey, Mercury 526812. 1995 debut album, her most country in orientation.

RICOCHET (1993–present; Duane Mack "Junior" Bryant, Jr. [voc, fdl, mdln, gtr]; Perry "Heath" Wright [voc, gtr, fdl]; Jeffrey Park Bryant [drms] through 1999, Tim Chewning thereafter; Greg[ory Charles] Cook [voc, bass gtr]; Shannon Farmer [pedal stl gtr, Dobro, lap stl, gtr] through 1999, Teddy Carr thereafter; Eddie [Edward James] Kilgallon [voc, gtr, kybds, sax])
Ricochet is a 1990s COUNTRY-ROCK band that has enjoyed a series of he-man-themed hits.

The nucleus of the original band, first known as Lariat, was the Bryant brothers, drummer Jeff and fiddler "Junior." Jeff brought his friend singer/guitarist Heath Wright into the original band, which by the fall of 1993 was known as Ricochet. Around that time they showcased for Ron Chancey, a well-known country-pop producer. The band continued to grow through

1994, first adding bassist Greg Cook, and then original PEDAL STEEL GUITAR player Teddy Carr. In early 1995 they signed with Columbia Records.

The band was a commercial success from the get-go, scoring a #5 hit with their first single, "What Do I Know," and then breaking records with "Daddy's Money," a #1 hit that was the top-selling single of the year in any genre (according to Sound Scan). The group began a schedule of rigorous touring, soon becoming state fair, NASCAR racetrack, and concert favorites.

Their second album came in 1997, and continued to produce hits, including the title track, "Blink of an Eye," and the ballad "Connected at the Heart." Around this time they became favorites performing the National Anthem for NASCAR and other sporting events, and their single of the song brought "The Star Spangled Banner" to the charts for the first time since Francis Scott Key wrote it. To capture the seasonal Christmas market, they released a version of "Let It Snow, Let It Snow, Let It Snow" in 1996 that has charted every Christmas since. The band has also written commercial songs for NASCAR ("Get This Show on the Road"), Wrangler (their 2000 tour sponsors), and "Cowboy Up and Party Down," which they are hoping to sell as a theme song for rodeo shows. Founder Jeff Bryant, suffering from carpal tunnel syndrome, retired in August 1999, and was replaced by Tim Chewning. At the same time, steel guitarist Shannon Farmer left and Teddy Carr returned to take his place.

In the fall of 2000 the band released its third album, *What You Leave Behind*. The title track, based on a "true story," was written by lead singer Heath Wright; but true to form it was the rockers' "Seven Bridges Road" and "She's Gone" that had the initial success.

Besides their instrumental abilities, the group is known for its six-part harmony singing, which they often feature in a cappella arrangements.

Select Discography

Ricochet, Columbia 67223. 1996 debut album.

RIDDLE, ALMEDA (b. A. James, lower Cleburne County, Ark., November 21, 1898–June 1986)

Riddle was one of the finest singers of traditional ballads and GOSPEL songs; her clear, powerful delivery represented mountain singing at its finest.

Born and raised in rural Arkansas, where she spent her entire life, Riddle learned a rich repertoire of traditional ballads, children's songs, and religious songs from her family, particularly her father, J. L. James, a descendant of the famous outlaw James brothers and a timber merchant who worked as an amateur singing teacher and also played the FIDDLE. Almeda could remember him singing every morning and evening from his large collection of songbooks; because he could read music, he would often form small singing classes, teaching a ten-day class in sight-singing. Almeda began collecting what she called "ballets" from a young age, including her father's version of the classic English ballad "The House Carpenter." Her mother's brother, Uncle John Wilkerson, was also a strong influence, although he sang many "silly songs" that Almeda's mother objected to his performing, including "Froggie Went a-Courtin'," with its unusual nonsense-word chorus, which Almeda performed for the rest of her life.

In 1916 Almeda married H. P. Riddle, who was a fine singer. The two would often sing together after supper. They lived together happily for a decade in Heber Springs, Arkansas; then a cyclone hit the town, taking the life of Almeda's husband and youngest child, and seriously injuring the other children. Almeda spent four months in the hospital recovering, and then returned to live on her father's farm with the remains of her family.

Riddle was never a professional performer, and probably would have lived and died unknown if she had not been "discovered" by folklorist ALAN LOMAX when he was preparing a series of albums for Atlantic Records in the late 1950s. (They were issued as the Southern Folk Heritage Series.) Riddle's clear-as-a-bell singing and wide repertoire of unusual versions of well-known songs made her the hit of this series, leading to a solo album issued by Vanguard Records in 1966, as well as appearances at folk festivals. In the 1970s she recorded two albums for Rounder Records, as well as a few recordings for smaller labels. Her chilling version of "The Old Churchyard" is one of the greatest recordings of solo singing.

Although not from the deep South, Riddle was one of the finest ballad singers in the tight-throated style that is prevalent throughout the lower Southern Appalachians. She sang with great expression and intensity, fully inhabiting each song in order to "tell the story" clearly to her audience.

Select Discography

Ballads and Hymns from the Ozarks/More Ballads and Hymns, Rounder 0017/0083. Two great albums from the 1970s, now out of print.

RIDERS IN THE SKY (Ranger Doug [b. Douglas B. Green; gtr, voc]; Woody Paul [b. Paul Woodrow Chisman; fdl, voc]; Too Slim [b. Fred LaBour; b, voc])

The Riders are a COWBOY-comedy act who both pay homage to the classic stars of cowboy music and satirize the conventions of cowboy films and radio of the 1940s and 1950s.

They are certainly an unlikely comedy group. Douglas B. Green, the leader, was formerly the aural historian at the Country Music Foundation and a leading scholar who had written widely on the history of country music; Woody Paul was a nuclear engineer with a degree from MIT before he took up cowboy fiddling. The band began its life as a genuine attempt to revive both the hokiness and the goofy charm of early cowboy acts; the threesome appears in the classic rhinestone-encrusted cowboy wear, and their stage show attempts to re-create the charm of the early cowboy acts.

However, as they have continued to perform, the Riders have become a parody of a parody, with their humor wearing thin. Their original compositions have increasingly relied on silly titles ("Concerto for Violin and Longhorns"), and their re-creations have taken on the air of cowboy schtick. Still, they remain popular as performers, with their own radio program—*Riders Radio Theater*, broadcast over National Public Radio—and even briefly their own network Saturday-morning kiddie show. They appear regularly on THE GRAND OLE OPRY, although it has become hard to tell if the audience is laughing at them or with them or both.

Select Discography

The Best of the West, Vols. 1 and 2, Rounder 11517/ 11524. Compilation CDs of their first albums cut for Rounder.

Riders Radio Theater, MCA 42180. 1988 album re-creating the classic cowboy radio shows of the 1930s and 1940s.

RILEY, JEANNIE C. (b. Jeanne Caroline Stephenson, Anson, Tex., October 19, 1945)

Riley is a country one-hit wonder who scored big with her cover of TOM T. HALL's "Harper Valley P.T.A." in 1968. She is probably most responsible for bringing a hipper look to country music, complete with miniskirts and boots, which at the time were certainly daring stage wear for a country artist.

Riley grew up in a small Texas town, where her father was an auto mechanic. She began singing locally while still a teenager, and married a gas-station attendant, Mickey Riley, when she was seventeen. In 1966 they moved from Texas to Nashville, where she worked as a secretary in the music industry and made demo recordings on the side. She was hired by famed producer SHELBY SINGLETON to launch his new country label, Plantation, and scored a megaselling hit right out of the box with "Harper Valley."

With her sexy stage presence and smooth vocals, Riley had follow-up hits—including 1968's "The Girl Most Likely" (telling of a sexy, small-town girl who always got into "trouble," playing into Riley's image

as a hot mama), 1969's "There Never Was a Time," 1970's "Country Girl," and 1971's "Good Enough to Be Your Wife" (in which the heroine of the song refuses to have an affair with the barfly who is making moves on her, because she's too good to be a one-night fling)—before moving to MGM and lesser stardom. She broke up with her husband in 1970 and continued to record occasionally through the mid-1970s, when she became a born-again Christian and gave up secular music (and reunited with husband Mickey). She continues to record and perform as a GOSPEL artist, but will play only dates where alcohol sales are strictly banned.

Select Discography

Harper Valley PTA: The Very Best, Collectables 6022. Twenty-four prime 1968–1974 recordings, including most of the hits.

RIMES, LeANN (b. Margaret L. R., Jackson, Miss., August 28, 1982)

Like BRENDA LEE and TANYA TUCKER before her, Rimes began as a thirteen-year-old sensation whose big voice and sexy poses belied her young years. Also like these child stars, she has matured into an all-around pop-styled singer.

Rimes burst on the country scene in 1996 with the song "Blue," reminiscent of the YODELING vocalizing of generations of country chanters. Rimes was starstruck from an early age, and her parents, particularly her father, Wilbur, became driving forces behind her career. At age seven she was a two-time *Star Search* winner, charming the heart of Ed McMahon, and also was performing regularly in the Dallas area. At age eleven she cut her first album for the small Nor Va Jak label, and two years later signed with Curb Records out of Nashville. Although her first single, "Blue," attracted a great deal of attention, it reached only #10; nonetheless, her fans drove her first album to #1, and her third single, "One Way Ticket (Because I Can)," brought her to the top of the country singles chart as well.

Rushing to cash in on Rimes's notoriety, Curb repackaged some earlier recordings, along with a new remake of "Unchained Melody," for her first 1997 album. It debuted at #1, but was a disappointment to fans looking for new material. Later that year Rimes released *You Light Up My Life: Inspirational Songs*, an album primarily of light-pop hits from the 1970s, along with a few standards. Despite the tired material, the album was the first to achieve the triple crown of opening at #1 pop, country, and contemporary Christian on *Billboard*'s charts. It also produced the #1 hit "How Do I Live (Without You)," a Diane Warren composition, which held the top position for a record-

LeAnn Rimes gets sultry, c. 1998. Photo: Raeanne Rubenstein

had served as producer for her first three albums, was cut out of the picture, and LeAnn and her mother moved to Nashville. A protracted court battle ensued between Rimes and her father, with suits and counter-suits continuing through the early 2000s.

In 1998 she released *Sittin' on Top of the World*, a heavy-handed pop production also helmed by her father (he produced it before his falling out with his daughter). It featured "Looking Through Your Eyes," used in the animated film *The Quest for Camelot*. Again it moved LeAnn more toward mainstream pop than toward country, and some fans were perturbed. To appease her country base, she released a self-titled album in 1999 that consisted entirely of country covers, mostly of classics from the 1950s and 1960s. However, it failed to produce chart hits. Veering back to the pop side of her performing personality, she cut a duet with Elton John, "Written in the Stars," drawn from John's score for the Broadway show *Aida*, which was a major hit. That same year she appeared as one of the "divas" on VH-1's special, *Divas Live*, cementing her position as a pop singer.

2000 saw further forays into popdom. Rimes appeared in the film *Coyote Ugly*, recording four Diane Warren-penned songs for it, including the hit "Can't Fight the Moonlight." She followed with "I Need You," taken from the television miniseries *Jesus*, which was heavily promoted with a sexy video. In 2001 she hosted the Academy of Country Music awards show out of her new hometown, Los Angeles. In the fall of 2001 Rimes sought to be released from her contract with Curb Records, saying that she was underage when she was signed by the label. She briefly joined a coalition of pop artists, including Sheryl Crow and Don Henley, in testifying before Congress about the music industry's abuse of long-term artist contracts. By early 2002 Rimes apparently had settled with the company, because she declined to make further appearances with the coalition.

Select Discography

Blue, Curb 77821. Her 1996 debut disc, and her most country in orientation.

RITCHIE, JEAN (b. Viper, Ky., December 8, 1922)

If one person can be credited with reviving interest in the Appalachian dulcimer, it would have to be FOLK-REVIVALIST Jean Ritchie. Thanks to her series of successful recordings in the early-to-mid-1960s, and her instruction book for the instrument, she introduced thousands of players to this simple instrument. Her quavery-voiced renditions of English ballads—many of which had been in her family for generations—were quite influential on younger folkniks like Judy Collins and Joan Baez, to name just two.

breaking sixty-nine weeks in 1997–1998. The single went triple platinum, placing Rimes in a rarefied club; she and pop singer Whitney Houston are the only artists to achieve such a distinction in any musical genre. Rimes had cut the song to be used on the sound track for the film *Con Air*, but the film's producers decided her version wasn't strong enough and had the song rerecorded by TRISHA YEARWOOD. Both singles were released nearly simultaneously, and Rimes had the last laugh when her version easily trounced Yearwood's on the charts. 1997 saw Rimes winning two Grammys, including Best New Artist.

The Rimes hitmaking machine was shaken badly by her parents' pending divorce in 1997. Her father, who

The Ritchie family were among the first settlers in the Cumberland Mountain region in the late 1700s. Many were known locally as fine ballad singers and musicians, including Ritchie's parents: Balis, a schoolteacher, and her mother, Abigail Hall. The relatives would gather together and play various instruments, including FIDDLE, BANJO, GUITAR, and the three-stringed dulcimer, which became Ritchie's favorite. As a youngster she became deeply interested in the traditional songs passed along by her family, beginning a lifetime of collecting.

Unlike other mountain children, Ritchie was fortunate to be able to attend the University of Kentucky, where she completed a B.A. degree in the mid-1940s. After graduation she won a Fulbright Scholarship to study British balladry in England. On her return to Kentucky in the mid-1950s, she became active in the beginnings of the FOLK REVIVAL and published a collection of songbooks based on her family's song repertoire.

Unlike some mountain singers who sing in a harsh, nasal "twang" that is jarring to urban ears, Ritchie sings in a relaxed style similar to that of DOC WATSON, who hails from nearby Deep Gap, North Carolina. This full-voiced singing style is prevalent throughout the upper South and, along with the region's softer accent, makes singers from this region more easily understood by audiences used to the trained voices of pop crooners. Because she is an educated folklorist, Ritchie was able to present her material to an urban audience in such a way that they could appreciate and understand it.

Ritchie was most popular in the late 1950s and early 1960s, when she recorded for mainstream labels like Riverside and Elektra as well as Folkways. She appeared at the Newport Folk Festival for several years, as well as at most other major festivals. After the folk boom died down in the late 1960s, Ritchie switched her emphasis to her own material, including topical songs addressing the damage done to the Kentucky landscape by strip mining. She continued to record sporadically for larger labels, often saddled with unsympathetic accompanists who played in a soft-rock style clearly not suited to her back-home presentation.

In the early 1980s Ritchie and her husband, George Pickow, formed the Greenhays label to issue her own recordings and those other folk revivalists. By the end of the decade, however, she was seldom heard or seen on the folk circuit.

Select Discography

Live at Folk City, Smithsonian/Folkways 40005. Reissue of early 1960s concert with Doc Watson.
The Most Dulcimer, Greenhays 70714. 1985 recording emphasizing her skills on this instrument.

RITTER, TEX (b. Woodward Maurice R., Nederland, Tex., January 12, 1905–January 2, 1974)

Ritter was a singing COWBOY and country star of the 1940s through the 1960s who was as noted for his acting in horse operas as for his recordings.

Ritter was raised on a 400-acre spread in East Texas that was first settled by his great-grandfather in 1830. He was a true cowboy, raised amid cattle roundups and ranch hands, not just a cowboy-come-lately like other performers. Ritter was introduced to cowboy songs at the University of Texas, JOHN LOMAX's alma mater, where folklorist J. Frank Dobie was still collecting and teaching the material. In 1929 he began performing this material on radio in Houston, and traveled to New York in 1931 to appear as an actor in the play *Green Grow the Lilacs*; during scene changes he performed his cowboy ballads, becoming an immediate sensation. He remained on the East Coast for five years, performing on New York radio stations and giving lecture-concerts in which he introduced "authentic" cowboy material to his audiences. He made his first records for the budget label ARC in 1934. Also

Tex Ritter, c. 1960. Photo: University of North Carolina, Southern Historical Collection, Southern Folklife Collection, University Archives

during his stay in New York he worked on the original *Lone Ranger* radio series as both writer and actor.

In 1936 he traveled to Hollywood to cash in on the singing-cowboy craze in the movies. Although his films suffered from low, low budgets, they often featured good music. Among them was 1940's *Take Me Back to Oklahoma*, featuring WESTERN SWING veteran BOB WILLS as the second lead. After 1943 JOHNNY BOND was his bandleader on film, often appearing with him. All in all, between 1936 and 1945 he made over sixty horse flicks for one-horse operations, including Grand National and Monogram as well as more established B-studios like Universal and Columbia. In 1942, after unsuccessfully recording for ARC and Decca, Ritter was signed by the fledgling Capitol label as its first country act, and recorded a combination of traditional folk songs ("Boll Weevil," "Rye Whiskey"), sentimental ditties ("There's a New Moon over My Shoulder"), and patriotic odes ("Gold Star in the Window").

Ritter's biggest break came in 1952 when he recorded the theme song for the high-class Western *High Noon*. Although he didn't appear in the film, it gave a considerable boost to his career. Along with his friend Johnny Bond he served as host of the popular *Town Hall Party* TV program, which featured guitar wizard JOE MAPHIS, a show that furthered his exposure to a country audience. By the late 1950s and early 1960s he was working as a straight country act, scoring his biggest hit with 1961's unabashedly sentimental "I Dreamed of a Hillbilly Heaven." Following in the footsteps of MARTY ROBBINS and JOHNNY HORTON, who were enjoying success with their newly composed narrative songs in the style of "traditional folk songs," in 1960 Ritter recorded a gooey collection of cowboy numbers called *Blood on the Saddle*, named after the gruesome Western standard. In 1958 he became involved with the movement to form the Country Music Association, and was elected its president in 1963. In 1965 he gained admittance to THE GRAND OLE OPRY.

In the late 1960s Ritter attempted to cross over into politics, running without success for senator in 1970. He served as narrator of the 1971 *Thank You, Mr. President* album, featuring conservative country performers crooning in honor of President Richard Nixon. His son, John Ritter, gained great popularity in the 1970s for his portrayal of the maybe-he's-gay-maybe-he's-not star of the TV sitcom *Three's Company*.

Select Discography

Country Music Hall of Fame, MCA 10188. Sixteen of his Decca recordings from the mid-1930s; not his best-known work, but of interest to fans and collectors.

Blood on the Saddle, Bear Family 16260. Compilation of his earliest recordings from 1932–1947.

High Noon, Bear Family 156348. Twenty-five-track compilation of the best of his Capitol recordings cut between 1942 and 1956. For those who want more, Bear Family offers a 111-track boxed set covering the same period (16356).

ROBBINS, HARGUS "PIG" (b. Rhea County, Tenn., January 18, 1938)

Robbins, a leading Nashville session pianist, has worked since the late 1950s for a number of major stars.

After accidentally blinding himself while playing with his father's pocket knife at age three, Robbins attended the Tennessee School for the Blind, where he was trained in classical piano. However, he was a huge fan of popular piano styles, listening to a wide range of players from country legend FLOYD CRAMER to R&B master RAY CHARLES. His first major Nashville studio job came in 1959, as pianist on GEORGE JONES's hit "White Lightning." In 1963 he cut his first solo album, *A Bit of Country Piano*.

Robbins's career jumped into second gear after he played on BOB DYLAN's famous *Blonde on Blonde* sessions from 1966. His style, however, was comfortably in the NASHVILLE SOUND mainstream; that's his tinkling keyboards on Crystal Gayle's middle-of-the-road hit "Don't It Make My Brown Eyes Blue." In the late 1970s Robbins recorded as a solo instrumentalist, with some limited success. However, he quickly returned to session work, remaining popular among both New Nashville and older stars through the 1990s. He also has played on sessions for COUNTRY-ROCK musicians, as well as for SINGER/SONGWRITERS including NEIL YOUNG, JERRY JEFF WALKER, Joan Baez, and Gordon Lightfoot. He has won the Academy of Country Music's Keyboardist of the Year award eight times, most recently in 1999.

ROBBINS, MARTY (b. Martin David Robinson, Glendale, Ariz., September 26, 1925–December 8, 1982)

A COWBOY-styled SINGER/SONGWRITER, Robbins was both a country and a pop star in the late 1950s, but is best remembered for his long string of country successes from the early 1950s through his death in 1982.

Like many in his generation, Robbins was bitten early by the cowboy bug. Raised in the small town of Glendale, Arizona, he was particularly close to his maternal grandfather, a retired medicine-show performer known as "Texas" Bob Heckle. Heckle was immersed in cowboy lore, much of which he shared with his young grandson. Saturday matinees featuring GENE AUTRY filled out Robbins's cowboy education,

345

and he soon was playing a second-hand GUITAR given to him by his older sister.

When he was twelve, the Robinson family relocated to urban Phoenix, where Marty attended high school and began getting into scrapes with the authorities. He enlisted in the Navy in 1944, and while stationed in the Pacific began to write original songs and perform them for his fellow sailors. On his return to Phoenix after the war, Robbins drifted from job to job while beginning to perform locally in clubs and bars at night. He took the name Marty Robbins because it sounded a little more Western than his real name, and also because he feared his family would disapprove of his aspirations to be a professional singer.

By the early 1950s Marty was performing on local radio station KPHO, hosting his own *Western Caravan* show. "LITTLE" JIMMY DICKENS was a guest on the show, and was so impressed that he recommended that his label, Columbia, sign Robbins. In 1952 Robbins released his first single for Columbia, "Love Me or Leave Me Alone," and a year later joined THE GRAND OLE OPRY, where he remained a member until his death twenty-nine years later. Two months after his first *Opry* appearance, Robbins scored his first Top 10 country hit, "I'll Go On Alone." For the next two years Robbins struggled to place his songs on the country charts.

His big break came in 1956 with "Singing the Blues," followed a year later by "Knee Deep in the Blues," "The Story of My Life," and his own teenybop classic, "A White Sport Coat (and a Pink Carnation)." These jazzy-styled country numbers, with Marty's peppy, smooth vocals, not only scored big on the country charts but also helped him break onto the pop charts. He continued in this pop-influenced vein through the 1950s, turning out 1958's "She Was Only Seventeen" and "Stairway of Love."

Robbins's career took a Western swing with his appearance in the 1958 film *Buffalo Gun*, along with other country stars WEBB PIERCE and CARL SMITH. He recorded his classic album of Western story-songs, *Gunfighter Ballads and Trail Songs*, a year later, producing hits that included "Big Iron" and "El Paso," a song that would become closely associated with him. Propelled by sessionman Grady Martin's Spanish-styled lead guitar, the song ran over four minutes, amazingly long for a hit single on radio. It topped both country and pop charts, gaining the first Grammy ever given to a country song. Robbins followed it with another pseudo-folk number, "Big Iron," based on a story of a Texas Ranger told to him in his youth by his grandfather, as well as "Battle of the Alamo."

Robbins continued to be a force on the country charts through the 1960s, although, like many other Nashville recording artists, his recordings increasingly were buried in schlocky accompaniments including murmuring choruses. While he still produced hits with his own and others' compositions, and he toured extensively throughout the U.S. and Canada, the hits started to thin out by the end of the decade, with his most distinctive recording being 1968's "I Walk Alone," another blues-tinged number in the vein of his earlier hits. In 1969 he suffered the first in a series of massive heart attacks; he claimed to have had a vision of Christ while he was on the operating table, which helped him to a speedy recovery and his first hit of the next decade, the schmaltzy "My Woman, My Woman, My Wife," which introduced the COUNTRYPOLITAN era.

Robbins pretty much coasted along on his reputation through the 1970s, although he did turn out a few further hits, mostly under the hand of seasoned producer BILLY SHERRILL. "El Paso City," a 1976 release, was a follow-up to his earlier hit, filled with references to his best-loved song; it and "Among My Souvenirs" were his last country #1 hits. In the 1970s Robbins suffered many injuries while pursuing his hobby of stock-car racing. In 1981 he suffered a second heart attack, then recovered to make a comeback a year later with his last release, "Some Memories Just Won't Die." In 1982 Robbins suffered a final major heart attack, dying six days later.

Select Discography

1951–1958, Bear Family 15570. Five-CD set covering 136 numbers cut from Robbins's first session in 1951 through 1958; these include his teen-pop tracks.

The Essential, Columbia/Legacy 48537. Two-CD set covering his career from 1951 to 1982.

Gunfighter Ballads and Trail Songs, Columbia 00116. Reissue of his early-1960s Western-flavored hits.

ROBERTS, "FIDDLIN'" DOC (b. Dock Phil R., Madison County, Ky., April 26, 1897–August 4, 1978)

Roberts was a fine Kentucky-styled fiddler who made over eighty recordings during the 1920s and 1930s, and then was "rediscovered" in the 1970s.

Roberts came from a farm family that had settled in the mountains of Kentucky sometime before the Civil War. His older brother, Liebert, was a fine FIDDLE player, and Doc began learning tunes from Liebert and other regional fiddlers at the age of seven. One of the prime sources for both brothers was an African-American fiddler named Owen Walker; folklorist Guthrie Meade believed that nearly three-quarters of Roberts's repertoire came from Walker, who represented a rich (but rarely documented) tradition of African-American string-band music in the region. Roberts himself said of Walker, "He was the fiddlingest colored man that was ever around Kentucky."

Roberts briefly attended school in Berea as a young teenager, then wed a local girl in 1913. They would eventually have eleven children, and Roberts set about supporting them by growing tobacco and corn as a sharecropper on land owned by his mother. A neighbor, Dennis Taylor, recognized Roberts's fiddling talents, and arranged for him to make a trip to nearby Richmond, Indiana, where the studios of dime-store label Gennett Records were located. Along with singer Welby Toomey and guitarist Edgar Boaz, Roberts made his first recordings in October 1925.

Over the next few years Roberts's recordings were released on Gennett and a variety of subsidiary labels with credits including Fiddling Jim Burke, Fiddling Frank Nelson, Uncle Jim Hawkins, the Old Smoky Twins, the Quadrillers, the Lone Star Fiddlers, the Kentucky Thorobreds, Carl Harris, Billy Jordan, and Fiddling Bob White, according to country scholar Charles Wolfe. Adding insult to injury, on properly credited records Gennett dropped the final "k" from Doc's name (he had been christened Dock Phil).

Doc recorded with a variety of accompanists and singers. He is best remembered for his partnership with singer/guitarist Asa Martin, with whom he began recording in September 1927. The record company executives realized that vocal numbers sold better than fiddle tunes, so while Doc was still allowed to record his unique repertoire of material, the addition of Martin's vocals on other tracks was a decided plus. Martin provided the lead vocals on several best-selling records for Doc, including "When the Roses Bloom Again for the Bootlegger" and "The Virginia Moonshiner." Earlier in 1927 Doc had performed in an unusual session featuring an African-American string band, The Booker Family. This was only the second interracial string-band recording (the Bookers had recorded once before, accompanied by a white banjo player), and an important document of the African-American dance band style.

In 1928 country radio star BRADLEY KINCAID brought Roberts to the popular NATIONAL BARN DANCE radio show out of Chicago. After a two-week trial Roberts was offered a weekly slot at the grand salary of $50 a week. However, Roberts found his two weeks in the big city difficult; unable to sleep due to the noise of the elevated trains, he couldn't imagine raising his large brood of farm children in the big city. Plus, he had difficulty finding his favorite brand of chewing tobacco! Nonetheless, Roberts continued to record for Gennett through 1930, with a 1931 session in New York overseen by country producer ART SATHERLEY for the ARC label (which had acquired Gennett's roster of dime-store labels), and then a final session in 1934.

The Kentucky brand of fiddling had its own unique repertoire and sound. Unlike Texas fancy fiddling, it was not showy and fast-tempoed, but sweeter and more relaxed. Nonetheless, the tunes were melodically complex, with many unusual twists and turns. Doc preserved a large number of tunes from the African-American repertoire, including "The Old Buzzard," "Brickyard Joe," "Hawk's Got a Chicken," and "Waynesborough" (a particular favorite of Doc's older brother). Doc is also thought to have composed some of his tunes, including "Drunken Man's Dream" and "Jack's Creek Waltz." He also picked up tunes from contemporary recordings. Roberts became the source for many later Kentucky-styled fiddlers, including Ed Haley and Haley's many disciples.

Roberts "retired" from recording after 1934, although he occasionally appeared on local radio. He was "rediscovered" by folklorists Archie Green and Norm Cohen in the late 1960s, and subsequently was visited by old-time fiddle enthusiasts who wished to learn more about him and his music.

Select Discography

Complete Recordings, Document 8042, 8043, 8044. Just like it says: everything he recorded between 1925 and 1934.

ROBERTSON, ECK (b. Alexander Campbell Robertson, Amarillo, Tex., November 20, 1887–February 17, 1975)

Robertson was a flashy Texas-styled fiddler who is generally credited with making the first recording of an old-time fiddle tune, "Sally Goodin," in 1922. Although he was the first to record, Robertson was a fairly modern-styled fiddler, playing many variations on the tunes that he recorded, using tricks such as double-stops, syncopations, flattened "blue" notes, and drones that have all become hallmarks of the Texas school of championship fiddling.

Raised in the farm country of West Texas, Robertson began fiddling as a youngster, playing for local socials and dances. By the time he reached his teens, he was already traveling around the state, competing at fiddlers' conventions. He is said to have dressed in full COWBOY gear, and later claimed to be the first country performer to adopt this outfit. In 1922 Robertson and a local fiddler, Henry Gilliland, who was thirty-nine years his senior, traveled to Virginia to appear at a Civil War Veterans' reunion; they eventually worked their way up to New York City, where they made some recordings for Victor, including Robertson's legendary solo recording of "Sally Goodin." Robertson returned to Texas soon after, and made only one further recording in 1929, when country producer RALPH PEER recorded him along with members of his family.

Through the 1930s and 1940s Robertson performed locally in Texas, both on radio and at fiddlers' conven-

Eck Robertson from the Victor catalog at the time of his first recording in 1922. Photo: University of North Carolina, Southern Historical Collection, Southern Folklife Collection, University Archives

tions. The old-time music revival brought new attention to his early recordings, beginning with Harry Smith's legendary reissue of early recordings on his *Anthology of American Folk Music*, a six-record set issued by Folkways Records in the early 1950s (and kept in print for over forty years). It featured Robertson's "Brilliancy Medley," which has become a staple for BLUEGRASS bands. In the early 1960s RCA reissued "Sally Goodin" on an anthology of old-time music, which further spread the word about Robertson and his playing. Robertson was "rediscovered" in the early 1960s, and appeared at a number of folk festivals as well as making some final recordings for folklorist MIKE SEEGER that revealed he was still a fine musician in the Texas style.

Almost every Texas contest-style fiddler since Robertson owes something to his style. His ringing tone, clean noting, and talent for improvisation all have become hallmarks for contestants at fiddlers' conventions.

Select Discography

Old Time Texas Fiddler, 1922–29, County 3515. All of his classic era recordings; sound quality is variable, but it's still a "must have" for fans of Texas fiddling.

ROBISON, CARSON J. (b. Oswego, Kan., August 4, 1890–March 24, 1957)

Robison was a songwriter and guitarist noted for his association with pioneering recording star VERNON DALHART, and then made hundreds of recordings on his own.

Robison began his career performing country songs in his native Oswego, eventually moving on to Kansas City, where he worked on local radio. In 1924 he made his first recordings for Victor, as a novelty whistler. In the same year he teamed with Dalhart as his accompanist and occasional accompanying vocalist. Robison provided Dalhart with some of his hit songs, beginning with numbers on hot topics of the day, such as the Scopes trial. After breaking up with Dalhart in 1927, Robison joined forces with another city-bred vocalist, FRANK LUTHER, and later led a series of Western-oriented bands in the 1930s and 1940s.

Robison wrote hundreds of songs, including the country-nostalgia numbers "Blue Ridge Mountain Home" and "Left My Gal in the Mountains," the ever-popular comic novelty "Life Gets Tee-Jus, Don't It" (as well as the sequel "More and More Tee-Jus, Ain't It" and another humorous monologue, "Settin' by the Fire"), and the oft-covered slightly blue "Barnacle Bill the Sailor," to name just a few.

In his later career Robison kept up with changing trends, recording with backup by his own Pleasant Valley Boys in a for-then modern country style. During World War II he churned out patriotic songs with unfortunate names like "We're Gonna Have to Slap the Dirty Little Jap." He took the pseudonym "The Kansas Jayhawk," and even dabbled in the nascent ROCKABILLY style right before his death, with his humorous "Rockin' and Rollin' with Grandmaw."

Select Discography

Home, Sweet Home on the Prairie, ASV 5187. 1996 compilation of 1928–1936 recordings, a mixture of cowboy, novelty, pop, and other styles.

ROCKABILLY (c. 1954–1959)

Literally the wedding of rock and roll with "hillbilly" or country music, rockabilly is a limited style, but one that was highly influential in the mid-1950s. ELVIS PRESLEY's first Sun studio recordings are firmly in the rockabilly style; indeed, it was Elvis's success that helped nail down rockabilly's basic sound: a single guitar, playing jazzy riffs; a heavy, slapped bass; and frantic, pounding drums. Countless country stars jumped on the rockabilly bandwagon, some producing one or two classic sides and others fading into obscurity. The most successful were the brothers Johnny and DORSEY BURNETTE, who led The Rock 'n' Roll Trio.

Perhaps the greatest rockabilly star was CARL PERKINS. His blends of high-energy country sounds with R&B and blues made him an innovative composer and performer. From the sassy attitude of "Blue Suede Shoes" to his cover of Blind Lemon Jefferson's classic "Matchbox," Perkins defined the rockabilly sound and attitude. While some would also place JERRY LEE LEWIS in the style, his music mixed many other elements into the stew, including the jazz tinges of WESTERN SWING piano and the intensity of country GOSPEL.

Needless to say, the success of rockabilly led many country acts to jump on the bandwagon, sometimes for one-off recordings, sometimes for a few years of ceaseless searching for hits. The style was dismissed by older country performers, who felt it represented a sellout to teen-pop trends. Country comedian FERLIN HUSKY took the pseudonym of Simon Crum to record some humorous satires of rockabilly's excesses.

Rockabilly's stripped-down sensibility—including simple instrumentation, basic riffs, and primal lyrics—appealed strongly to the post-punk crowd in the mid-to-late 1970s, particularly in Europe, when the style was revived and many pioneering figures returned to the stage. Meanwhile, groups like The Stray Cats from Long Island picked up on a rockabilly sensibility, enjoying some success in the late 1970s, but like so many others they eventually found the style rather limiting. Today elements of the rockabilly sound can be heard in new-country music, particularly the heavy backbeat and slapped bass, but no star centers his or her act solely on the rockabilly style.

RODGERS, JESSE (b. Waynesboro, Miss., March 5, 1911–December 1973)

A cousin of famed country yodeler JIMMIE RODGERS, Jesse began his career following in his relative's big footsteps, but then established himself up North as a COWBOY singer.

Although born in Mississippi, Rodgers was raised in Texas after his mother's death when he was twelve years old. He began his career around 1932, singing on border radio stations in the familiar style of his successful cousin. After Jimmie passed away in 1933, Victor Records quickly nabbed Jesse to fill Jimmie's YODELING shoes. His first sessions emphasized material in a vein similar to Jimmie's recordings, but he also began performing more cowboy-flavored songs as well. Through the 1930s Rodgers struggled to create

his own career, dropping the "d" from his name and increasingly focusing on cowboy material.

Success came after a 1944 move to Philadelphia, an unlikely spot for a cowboy singer. Nonetheless he landed a job on local station WFIL as the star of its *Hayloft Hoedown*, as well as a kiddie show on which he appeared as "Ranger Joe." He recorded for a variety of labels from 1946 to 1954, emphasizing his cowboy material, and gaining some success on the national charts. In the early 1960s emphysema cut short his performing career, and Rodgers retired to Houston, where he subsequently succumbed to the disease.

Select Discography

Country Boy, Roots of Country 211007. Recordings of unknown vintage.

RODGERS, JIMMIE (b. James Charles R., Meridian, Miss., September 8, 1897–May 26, 1933)

Perhaps the most influential country singer of all time, Jimmie Rodgers in his short career wed black blues and jazz to the traditional country repertoire to form a truly unique type of music that has influenced generations of country performers. Like many country

Jimmie Rodgers in his most-famous pose, dressed in full "Singing Brakeman" regalia, c. 1929. Photo: University of North Carolina, Southern Historical Collection, Southern Folklife Collection, University Archives

stars Rodgers had a gimmick: he yodeled. While undoubtedly his YODELING was a crowd pleaser, Rodgers managed to make it an integral part of his music, so that it would be impossible to think of such standards as "T.B. Blues," "Peach Pickin' Time in Georgia," "Waitin' for a Train," "Muleskinner Blues," and "Blue Yodel Number 1 (T for Texas)" without the yodeling at the end of each verse. Neither a terrific guitarist nor a particularly wide-ranging vocalist, Rodgers, like many other country performers, made a virtue out of his limitations, giving a wonderfully expressive, and often slyly humorous, reading to his songs.

The son of a railroad man, Rodgers worked as a brakeman until tuberculosis cut short his career in 1924. Determined to become a professional performer, he worked the medicine-show circuit of the South, performing in blackface. He also presented more pop-oriented material with his backup band, The Tenneva Ramblers, who would subsequently record without him. He gained an audition with noted producer RALPH PEER in 1927, and was signed by Victor Records at the same time as THE CARTER FAMILY. In his short six-year career, he made over 110 sides, with backings as various as small jazz bands (including Louis Armstrong on trumpet), Hawaiian-flavored groups, and both white and black string bands. Ironically, some of his most moving performances featured just his simple, strummed guitar accompaniments. Victor successfully marketed his recordings by promoting Rodgers as "The Singing Brakeman" (the name of a short motion picture in which Rodgers appeared in 1929) and "America's Blue Yodeler."

Rodgers's recordings enjoyed immediate success; his first "Blue Yodel" sold a million copies, and many of his recordings have remained in print, in one form or another, for more than six decades. Thanks to the tireless promotion of his wife and daughter, Meridian, Mississippi, has had an annual Jimmie Rodgers Day since the 1960s; the star was the first musician inducted into the Country Music Hall of Fame in 1961; and his complete recordings have been reissued in the U.S. on six CDs by the Rounder label.

Rodgers's recordings were primarily made up of blues-influenced numbers, along with Tin Pan Alley standards, jazzy numbers, and the sentimental heart songs that had been popular in the mountains since the 1890s. Rodgers promoted the image of an urbane country performer; he was often pictured wearing a straw hat set jauntily on the back of his head, a polka-dot tie, and a natty suit. Unlike other contemporary acts he did not try to act like a "backwoodsman." However, his music still reflected the lonesome sound of mountain ballads, embodying the yearnings of white and black Southerners for a better life.

Plagued by TB, Rodgers performed and toured as widely as possible, but made his greatest impact through his recordings. He made his last recordings at New York in 1933; two days after this final session, he died in his hotel room. The death of Jimmie Rodgers only added to his legendary status; like HANK WILLIAMS and ELVIS PRESLEY after him, Rodgers became a larger-than-life performer after his death, with record sales continuing unabated for more than six decades.

Select Discography

Singing Brakeman, Bear Family 15540. Lavishly produced six-CD set with notes by Nolan Porterfield; all of his Victor recordings, 145 songs in all. The same material was issued on six individual CDs by Rounder Records (1056–1061), without the lavish booklet.

RODRIGUEZ, JOHNNY (b. Juan Raoul Davis R., Sabinal, Tex., December 10, 1951)

Although of Tex-Mex background, Rodriguez was a mainstream country star of the 1970s and 1980s with a slight OUTLAW image thanks to his association with singer TOM T. HALL.

The eighth son of a Chicano family, Rodriguez began playing guitar at age seven, performing in a local band during his high school years. He made some demo recordings in San Antonio in 1969, but they went nowhere. Meanwhile, Rodriguez began attracting the attention of the local authorities for various minor infractions of the law; he eventually served prison time for the heinous crime of stealing and barbecuing a goat. In prison he became well known for his singing, and one of the guards introduced him to the owner of a country-music bar in Bracketville when he was paroled in 1970. While performing there he was first heard by Tom T. Hall and BOBBY BARE, both of whom encouraged him to pursue a country-music career.

In late 1971 Rodriguez came to Nashville to work as guitarist in Hall's band, The Storytellers, and auditioned as a solo act for Mercury Records. His first single, "Pass Me By," from 1972, went to #9 on the charts, and in the following year he had his first #1 records with "You Always Come Back (to Hurtin' Me)," which he wrote with Tom T. Hall, and his self-penned "Ridin' My Thumb to Mexico." He followed with two covers in 1974, "That's the Way Love Goes," a traditional country WEEPER, written by LEFTY FRIZZELL and Sanger D. Shafer, and The Beatles' "Something," an unusual move for a country artist. The hits kept coming through the late 1970s, when his increasing use of drugs sidetracked his career, although he did manage to make a comeback in 1983 with two recordings featuring backup vocals by LYNN ANDERSON: "Foolin'" and "How Could I Love Her So Much." In 1987 he made a second abortive comeback, this time scoring a minor hit with "I Didn't (Every Chance I

Had).” During the 1990s he released two albums, neither of which did much to further his career.

Select Discography

Hits, Polygram 536221. 1970s hits.
Super Hits, Epic 67129. Ten hits from the late 1970s and early 1980s.

ROGERS, KENNY (b. Houston, Tex., August 21, 1938)

The king of mid-1970s COUNTRYPOLITAN, Rogers did more to drag country music into the pop domain than any other singer of his generation. For this he is to be either glorified or vilified, or perhaps both, but in any case his gruff vocals and washed-in-the-water-of-Vegas stage show have made him a perennial country favorite even after his pop-chartin’ days are over.

Rogers was born to relative poverty in Houston; the lingering effects of the Depression plus his father’s alcoholism (and thus unreliability as a worker) joined to make the family’s life even worse. He had his first exposure to music in the church choir, and then took up the GUITAR, teaching himself to play chords. He often got together with another neighborhood kid, pianist MICKEY GILLEY, to perform the latest pop hits.

In high school Kenny formed The Scholars, a ROCKABILLY outfit, and signed as a soloist with the local Carlton label. In 1959 he recorded an album titled *One Dozen Goldies* (despite the fact that none of his previous singles had reached anywhere near gold-record status). After a brief period at the University of Houston, he joined a light-jazz trio led by Bobby Doyle, who recorded for Columbia in 1962, followed by a stint with Kirby Stone’s pop-jazz group. He relocated to Los Angeles in 1966, hooking up with the folk group The New Christy Minstrels, and made some recordings as a soloist for Mercury in 1966.

Along with fellow Minstrel Mike Settle, he formed the folk-tinged pop vocal group The First Edition, scoring a major pop hit with 1967’s “Just Dropped In (to See What Condition My Condition Was In).” Other hits, in a more country vein, followed, including “Ruby (Don’t Take Your Love to Town)” and the folk anthem “Reuben James.” The group remained together under Rogers’s leadership until 1975, when he embarked on a solo career.

The late 1970s were golden years for Rogers, beginning in 1977 with his monster hit “Lucille,” establishing him as a star on both country and pop charts. He followed it with a hit 1978 duet with DOTTIE WEST on “Every Time Two Fools Collide,” solidifying his position as a country-music star. Later that year he scored on his own with DON SCHLITZ’s “The Gambler,” which has become his best-loved country-flavored

song (and inspired a made-for-TV movie two years later).

Guided by mastermind promoter Ken Kragen, Rogers’s career veered into mainstream mush in 1979 with hits like the hopelessly saccharine “You Decorated My Life,” a duet with popster Kim Carnes on “Don’t Fall in Love with a Dreamer” a year later, and his breathy reading of Lionel Richie’s “Lady,” establishing his gruffness as a mainstream pop star.

After scaling the heights of mainstream pop, Rogers spent most of the 1980s returning to performing for country audiences, although his rhinestone-studded collection of shirts (left open to the navel) still firmly placed him in the Vegas camp. He also took to “acting,” mostly in made-for-TV movies, primarily in parts tailor-made for his personality. Meanwhile, he was often in the tabloids when he wasn’t being interviewed by Barbara Walters, revealing that his real success was as a mainstream artist, not as one who carries the true country flame. His career as a singer slowed considerably in the 1990s; in 1998 he formed his own label to release his new recordings and reissue his classic material.

Select Discography

Through the Years, Capitol 33183. Four-CD, eighty-song compilation covering Rogers’s complete career.
The Gambler, Dreamcatcher 902. Reissue of the 1978 album featuring the monster title hit.

ROGERS, ROY (b. Leonard Franklin Slye, Duck Run, Ohio, November 5, 1911–July 6, 1998)

An influential singing COWBOY and movie star, Rogers founded the Western group THE SONS OF THE PIONEERS, who served as his backup band from 1934 until 1948. This smooth-harmony vocal group did much to modernize the cowboy sound and style.

The son of migrant farm workers, Leonard Slye came to California in 1930 to pick fruit. He began performing with a number of Western bands, founding his own group, The Sons of the Pioneers, in 1934. Their big break came supporting GENE AUTRY in his 1935 epic *Tumbling Tumbleweeds*. Slye decided he could be a singing cowboy, too, and took the names Dick Weston and then Roy Rogers (perhaps in homage to country legend JIMMIE RODGERS). He began starring in B-grade Westerns in 1938, and four years later, when Autry went off to fight in World War II, became the country’s leading cowboy star.

In 1947 he wed Dale Evans (b. Frances Smith, Uvalde, Tex., 1912–2001), a pop chanteuse who had appeared in many of his Westerns and would continue to work with him through the rest of his career. From the 1950s through Rogers’s death, the pair worked on radio, in films, and on TV; Roy also pursued business interests, including franchise fast-food joints. His best-known song is his theme song, "Happy Trails." The duo founded their own museum in their hometown of Victorville, California, where you can visit the stuffed remains of Roy's favorite ride, Trigger (1932–1965). Rogers is the only country performer elected to the Country Music Hall of Fame in two capacities: as a member of The Sons of the Pioneers in 1980, and for his solo work in 1988.

Select Discography

The Best of, Curb 77392. 1950s and 1960s recordings.

RONSTADT, LINDA (b. Tucson, Ariz., July 15, 1946)

Ronstadt is a pop vocalist who was one of the first COUNTRY-ROCK stars to have records charted on both country and pop charts. Ronstadt's combination of the songs and sensibilities of HANK WILLIAMS and BUDDY HOLLY pointed the way to a new marriage of country and rock while reviving sales of the original recordings of both these performers.

Ronstadt was born to a middle-class family in Tucson, where her father, a Mexican-American, operated a hardware store. As a teenager she was a fan of both ELVIS PRESLEY and Hank Williams, and also shared her father's taste for traditional Mexican mariachi music. After one year of college in her native state, she packed her bags for the bustling California folk-rock scene.

In Los Angeles she hooked up with Kenny Edwards and Bob Kimmel to form the Peter, Paul and Maryish trio The Stone Poneys. Their big hit was 1967's "Different Drum," a country-rock ballad penned by MIKE NESMITH. The group soon dissolved, and Ronstadt recorded two straight country LPs, including her cover of "Silver Threads and Golden Needles," which would remain popular with her fans through the 1970s.

In 1974 she hooked up with pop producer Peter Asher (originally half of Peter and Gordon, England's answer to THE EVERLY BROTHERS), and recorded a series of hugely successful albums. Each featured songs in a pop-rock and country vein, including her hit covers of Buddy Holly's "That'll Be the Day," Hank Williams's "I Can't Help It if I'm Still in Love with You," ROY ORBISON's "Blue Bayou," DOLLY PARTON's "I Will Always Love You" (later a hit for soulster Whitney Houston), NEIL YOUNG's "Love Is a Rose," and WILLIE NELSON's "Crazy." She even recorded the traditional "I Never Will Marry" as a duet with Dolly Parton, one of the country SINGER/SONGWRITERS whom Ronstadt admired the most.

The 1980s found Ronstadt searching for a new musical style. She passed through punk rock to Gilbert and Sullivan, then formed an alliance with arranger Nelson Riddle to cover 1940s pop, and finally went whole hog for the Mexican mariachi music that she had loved since her childhood, sung in Spanish (Ronstadt even wore the full Mexican performer's regalia, making her look to some critics like an escaped waitress from Taco Bell). In 1987 she rejoined with old friends EMMYLOU HARRIS and Dolly Parton to release *Trio*, a simple and rather low-key homage to their country roots.

During the 1990s Ronstadt was less active as a performer. She returned to recording in a pop-rock vein, but failed to regain the large audience she enjoyed in the 1970s. A second *Trio* album appeared in 1998, but failed to enjoy the success of the first. She also cut a duo album with Emmylou Harris that was released in 1999 to glowing reviews but small sales.

Ronstadt's strong vocals, sassy image, and mainstream acceptability brought a new level of sophistication to country music. She proved that classic country performed in a simple, reverent fashion could be successful on today's country and pop charts, leading the way for the new-country revival of the mid-1980s and early 1990s. Her independence as a woman, and her promotion of the work of female songwriters, also set the stage for the rebirth of women as movers and shakers in the country world.

Select Discography

Heart like a Wheel, Capitol 46073. Ronstadt combines folk, rock, and country influences on this fine 1974 outing.
Box Set, Elektra 62472. four-CD career retrospective, including one disc of "rarities."

ROONEY, JIM (b. Boston, Mass., January 28, 1938)

A key figure in the Boston FOLK REVIVAL, Rooney has long been involved with country music, and produced a number of SINGER/SONGWRITERS in the 1980s.

Rooney became involved in folk music while attending Harvard, where he met banjoist BILL KEITH. The two began performing together in 1960, about the time that Rooney became manager of the important Boston-area folk club, Club 47. From 1967 to 1969 he ran the Newport Folk Festival, an important institution in the folk revival.

In 1969 Rooney and Keith recorded a one-off country album, *The Blue Velvet Band*. The record also featured fiddler RICHARD GREENE, then a member of the rock group Seatrain, and Eric Weissberg, soon to be famous for recording the theme for the movie *Deliverance*. A year later Rooney moved to Woodstock, New York, to help manager Albert Grossman establish his Bearsville studios and record label. He was involved with recordings made there by The Band, Todd Rundgren, Bonnie Raitt, and many other early 1970s folk-rock artists. He was also a prime mover in the informal *Mud Acres* record and its follow-ups in the 1970s by a group of Woodstock-based folk performers, including Happy and Artie Traum and Maria Muldaur.

In 1976 Rooney relocated to Nashville, where he formed a music-publishing partnership with famous producer/recording studio owner "Cowboy" Jack Clement, and began doing engineering work in Clement's studio. In the early 1980s Rooney became a well-known producer, working particularly with singer/songwriters Nanci Griffith, John Prine, Jerry Jeff Walker, Iris DeMent, Peter Rowan, Townes van Zandt, and many others. Rooney also recorded on his own, primarily for smaller independent labels.

ROSE, FRED AND WESLEY (Fred b. Evansville, Ind., August 24, 1898–December 1, 1954; Wesley b. Chicago, Ill., February 11, 1918–April 26, 1990)

Fred Rose was a pioneering publisher, songwriter, and producer in country music, and his son Wesley built his empire in partnership with Roy Acuff into one of the powerhouses of the Nashville music establishment.

The elder Rose began his career as a Chicago-area pianist, initially recording jazz for the Brunswick label and piano rolls for QRS. In Chicago he wrote many songs for the big-throated chanteuse Sophie Tucker, including her signature tune "Red Hot Mama," " 'Deed I Do," and "Honestly and Truly." After working in Paul Whiteman's band for a while, he joined CBS Radio as a house producer in Chicago and then relocated to the West Coast, where he hooked up with up-and-coming cowpoke star Gene Autry, composing his major hit, "Be Honest with Me."

Anticipating the market for country music, Rose moved to Nashville, where he was hired as staff pianist for WSM, home of The Grand Ole Opry, and quickly befriended a young fiddler/singer named Roy Acuff. Recognizing the value of the acts that he was managing and producing, in 1942 he and Acuff established Acuff-Rose Music Publishing. He also was instrumental in the forming of Broadcast Music International (BMI) as an alternative to the more conservative ASCAP (American Society of Composers, Authors, and Publishers), which was uninterested in representing country or blues composers.

Son Wesley was trained as an accountant and worked for Standard Oil before joining the family business in 1945. Fred left the business to take a more active hand in managing his last great discovery, Hank Williams, for whom he composed "Kaw-Liga." Other popular Rose compositions include "Blue Eyes Crying in the Rain" (revived by Willie Nelson), "Tears on My Pillow," "A Mansion on the Hill," and "Settin' the Woods on Fire." After his father's death Wesley

discovered and helped build the career of acts like The Everly Brothers. In the late 1950s he and Acuff founded the Hickory label, which became the home of many important country acts in the early 1960s.

ROSENBAUM, ART (b. Ogdensburg, N.Y., December 6, 1938)

A folk-revivalist and record producer, Rosenbaum did much to popularize traditional banjo styles through his recordings and instruction books.

Rosenbaum is one of those rare urban artists who does not merely imitate traditional styles; he seems to be able to get to the heart and soul of the sound, so that his performances are both re-creations and new creative works, extensions of the folk traditions into new territory. His high, reedy voice perfectly captures the "high, lonesome sound" of mountain singing without sounding at all condescending, the way some other revival singers do.

Rosenbaum first made an impact on the folk-revival scene in the mid-1960s, when his roots-styled banjo playing was featured on an Elektra anthology of banjo music; because this label catered to city folks (and even folk-rockers), these recordings helped introduce old-time banjo playing to a new audience. For Folkways Records he also recorded and produced a fine collection called *Fine Times at Our House*, featuring fiddler John "Dick" Summers, that became a favorite among young old-time revivalists. In 1968 he authored a banjo instruction book that emphasized mountain styles.

In the early 1970s Rosenbaum relocated to Iowa, where he taught painting. He recorded a duo album with bluegrass-styled fiddler Al Murphy that was released by the tiny Meadowlands label, followed by two solo albums for the folk-instructional label Kicking Mule. In the late 1970s he relocated again, to Athens, Georgia, where he began recording blues, religious music, and old-time string-band music. These field recordings were issued by Flyright Records (a German label) and Folkways. He also authored a book on Georgia's traditional music, illustrated with his own drawings and paintings of musicians, along with his wife's photographs.

Although Rosenbaum does not perform often, his recordings were quite influential, particularly on the old-time string-band revival of the 1970s. His combination of scholarship and creativity makes him one of the most listenable, and enjoyable, of all of the urban revivalists.

Select Discography

Art of the Old Time Banjo, Kicking Mule 519. Cassette-only reissue of a mid-1970s album.

ROUSE BROTHERS (Ervin, b. Craven County, N.C., September 18, 1917–July 8, 1981 [fdl]; Gordon [G. Ernest R.] July 4, 1914–May 17, 1995 [gtr]; Earl B., November 1, 1911–February 1983 [gtr])

The Rouse Brothers were a 1930s country ensemble who bridged the gap between country and BLUEGRASS. Fiddler Ervin was the best known, and is responsible for the ever-popular fiddle contest piece "Orange Blossom Special."

The brothers were raised in coastal North Carolina, where their father farmed tobacco. Of fifteen siblings, eight became musicians of some sort. Ervin learned to fiddle from his mother, and was performing in vaudeville by age five. A seasoned performer by age eleven, Ervin hit the RKO circuit, developing trick fiddling techniques like playing the instrument between his legs and behind his head. His brother Gordon worked with him as a guitarist.

Gordon and Ervin settled in the Jacksonville, Florida, area during the 1920s. However, their work took them as far north as New York, where they played at the famous Village Barn and broadcast over the radio. They also worked in a Miami nightclub.

The brothers first recorded in June 1936 for ARC; they were joined at this time by another sibling, Earl B. In 1938 Ervin composed the song that made the brothers famous; riding on the inaugural run of a new train from Miami to New York, he was inspired to compose "The Orange Blossom Special." Although they were not the first to record it, Ervin copyrighted the piece immediately. The piece has become a standard among bluegrass and contest fiddlers, to the point where it is somewhat hackneyed. Nonetheless, its powerful style helped pave the way for bluegrass-styled fiddling, and it was championed by early bluegrass players including CHUBBY WISE (a friend of the Rouses) and Tommy Magness. The original song featured close harmony singing in the style of the popular brother duos of the 1930s, but the words are rarely used today.

Ervin, a prolific songwriter, tried his best to score another hit by penning more train songs. His next big hit, however, was a sentimental tearjerker, "Sweeter Than the Flowers," first recorded by MOON MULLICAN in 1948 for a #3 country hit.

The brothers' career slowed in the 1950s as Ervin and Gordon apparently battled mental illness and alcoholism. "Rediscovered" in 1965 by JOHNNY CASH, Ervin returned briefly to Nashville, but was unable to relaunch his career. He spent his declining years in Florida, dying in 1981 following a decade of health problems.

ROWAN, PETER (b. Wayland, Mass., July 4, 1942)

One of the pioneers of newgrass and its more spacey offshoots, Rowan is an energetic vocalist/guitarist/MANDOLIN player/songwriter whose sensibility combines traditional BLUEGRASS with Tex-Mex and COWBOY themes.

Rowan was a product of the teeming folk-rock movement of the greater Boston area. Boston hosted a crowd of nascent rockers and social protest singers, but also had a strong tradition of supporting bluegrass and country acts. Rowan was impressed with the energy of bluegrass music, and relocated to Nashville to meet the father of the music, BILL MONROE. By the mid-1960s he was writing with Monroe (the classic "Walls of Time") and recording as a member of The Blue Grass Boys, along with young fiddler RICHARD GREENE. Rowan ultimately was frustrated by Monroe's strict traditionalist approach, and returned to the Boston area to form the eclectic rock band Earth Opera with mandolinist DAVID GRISMAN, also an ex-bluegrasser.

In the late 1960s Greene invited Rowan to join the progressive California rock band Seatrain, and so he relocated to California. After Seatrain reorganized in 1972, Rowan formed several short-lived bluegrass bands, including 1972's MULESKINNER (with Greene, Grisman, banjoist BILL KEITH, and guitarist Clarence White) and OLD AND IN THE WAY, with Grisman, Jerry Garcia (banjo), and VASSAR CLEMENTS (fiddle). Both bands performed traditional bluegrass numbers and Rowan's bluegrass-styled original songs, including "Blue Mule" (which took the story of Tenbrooks and Molly, a Monroe classic, into outer space) and the classic update of a badman ballad, "Panama Red." In the mid-1970s he and his two brothers, calling themselves The Rowans, recorded two folk-rock albums for Asylum Records that gained the group a cult following if not great commercial success.

By the end of the 1970s Rowan was performing as a soloist, leading his own Green Grass Gringos band, featuring a floating membership that included traditional bluegrass fiddler Tex Logan, progressive fiddler Richard Greene, and Tex-Mex accordion whiz Flaco Jimenez. He continued to work with various accompanists over the next decades, recording both his own compositions and more traditional bluegrass songs. Rowan's intense and expressive high-tenor lead vocals were perfectly suited to his songs, which wed New Age sensibilities to classic stories of the Southwest. Rowan created a new mythical cowboy past that reflected his unique sensibilities.

Select Discography

Peter Rowan, Flying Fish 70071. Reissue of late-1970s solo album.

The Walls of Time, Sugar Hill 3722. 1991 bluegrass album with RICKY SKAGGS, Eddie Adcock, and Sam Bush.

RUBE/HILLBILLY HUMOR The stereotypical image of the "hick from the sticks" is a long-lasting one in American culture, and has been exploited by generations of country-music entertainers. Among its earliest manifestations is the famous "Arkansas Traveler" skit, in which a city slicker is outwitted in a series of questions and answers by a clever country "rube." That the supposedly uneducated farmer in fact is smarter than the urbanite is part and parcel of the humor. The fiddle tune and skit date back at least to the early nineteenth century, and variations of the routine have been carried forward through today by BLUEGRASS and country entertainers. (THE STANLEY BROTHERS revived it under the name of "How Far to Little Rock" for a minor hit in 1958.) Nineteenth-century MINSTREL-SHOW portrayals of Zip Coon (the urban "dandy") and Jim Crow (the backwoods slave) draw on the same stock characters, and often incorporate similar situations and dialogue.

Though New England "rubes" are known in American folklore, the classic rube character is a backwoods Southerner. The condescending attitude to both poor white Southerners and their black counterparts was reinforced by years of stereotyped images presented through minstrel, tent, and finally vaudeville shows up until the beginning of the twentieth century. Early country performers often adopted the role of the "hillbilly" in deference to the common image that folk performers had among more "sophisticated" people, like recording company executives and Northerners in general. Thus, professional musician AL HOPKINS, who in the mid-1920s led a popular string band that broadcast and performed out of urban centers like Washington, D.C., and New York City as well as their Southern base, dubbed his band The Hill Billies when recording executive RALPH PEER asked him what to call the group.

Humorous skits—supposedly re-creating "real" backwoods events like fiddlers' contests, picnics, and other get-togethers—were very popular during the mid-1920s. Sometimes skits would be issued over a number of 78s, as a means of selling more records (to hear the end, you had to buy five or more discs). Gid Tanner—himself an old tent-show performer—and his SKILLET LICKERS specialized in these skits, and many other string bands were encouraged to record similar material. "Back-country" activities like fox hunting and bootlegging were popular topics for these records.

Almost every performing country band from the 1920s on featured at least one "rube" comedian among its members. Perhaps as a holdover from minstrel days, this comedian was often a banjo player (like GRANDPA JONES, who at the beginning of his career was a young man bedecked in white false whiskers, wig, and tattered coveralls; eventually he aged into the part). UNCLE DAVE MACON, another ex-tent show performer,

was perhaps the quintessential banjo comedian; he combined both roles, performing tricks on stage like dancing and playing the banjo at the same time, holding the instrument between his legs while still playing it, and other eye-catching routines. Although he recorded and performed everything from Victorian sentimental songs to topical numbers, he is best remembered for his humorous songs and his shouted "Hot Dog!" when completing a particularly satisfying performance.

Not all performers were full-time comedians. Often a musician would carry two identities in a country or bluegrass band: his "serious" role as musician and his "comic" role between numbers, interacting with the band's leader. Thus Dobroist BUCK GRAVES of the 1950s FLATT AND SCRUGGS band would become "Uncle Josh" when it was time for a little horseplay on stage. This not only saved the band having extra (and costly) personnel, but also gave the performer another means of drawing attention to himself and could further his career.

Besides being musicians, rube comics have specialized simply in delivering monologues. The most famous monologuist in country music is, of course, MINNIE PEARL, but there have been many more who deliver mock sermons, "news" from the backwoods (as Pearl did), or other comic material. However, making a living as a full-time comedian is harder, and Pearl was unique in her ability to survive without adding music or song to her act. Pearl was a major influence on Garrison Keillor; his admiration for her monologues broadcast over THE GRAND OLE OPRY (and the *Opry* itself) was highly influential on the development of his popular *Prairie Home Companion* radio series.

After World War II the country comedy tradition was carried forward in a more sophisticated way. The duo HOMER AND JETHRO introduced song satire into their act, taking popular country numbers and reworking them for humorous effect. While they dressed in typical hayseed costumes, they had an appeal as nightclub performers, being easily able to play pop and jazz instrumentals as well as their normal comic song material. These were rubes who winked at the audience, sharing the fact that they weren't as stupid as they appeared. In the 1960s ROGER MILLER took up the mantle of country comic song, drawing on age-old humorous themes such as drinking moonshine ("Chug-a-Lug") and countrified speech ("Dang Me").

The later 1960s saw the institutionalization of country humor in the television show HEE HAW. Although many Southerners were embarrassed by it—and it had only a two-year network run—the show managed to remain in syndication for two decades. Despite the fast pace borrowed from the contemporary hit comedy show *Laugh In*, *Hee Haw* was really just an updated minstrel show, without the blackface but with the same mix of sentiment, song, and corn-pone humor.

Because of the stigma attached to rube humor—and the Civil Rights movement that made blackface humor politically incorrect—very few have tried to revive either the white or the black tradition of this style of comedy. When bluegrass became newly popular among urban performers in the 1970s, many older bands dropped their rube comedy from their repertoire, recognizing that while it appealed to their traditional audience, it did not go over as well with the college-educated crowds they were now drawing.

A few of the young groups tried to revive the humor tradition. The band HOT RIZE even formed an alter-ego band, Red Knuckles and the Trailblazers, to perform HONKY-TONK music as both an homage and a humorous change of pace for their stage show. The alter-ego group became so popular that it issued its own separate album. Sometimes contemporary groups seem to combine humor and affection in their revival of older styles; RIDERS IN THE SKY are a winking tribute to COW-BOY acts of the 1930s and 1940s, and the character of "Ranger Doug" taken by leader Doug Green, for example, is somewhat of a comic alter ego.

RUSSELL, JOHNNY (b. J. Bright R., Sunflower County, Miss., January 23, 1940–July 3, 2001)

Rotund, longtime GRAND OLE OPRY regular, Russell had a minor career as a country songwriter, humorist, and performer.

When he was twelve years old, Russell's family relocated to California, where he was greatly influenced by the BAKERSFIELD SOUND. He got his first big break with the song "Act Naturally," which he cowrote, a 1963 hit for BUCK OWENS (and two years later was covered by the Beatles' Ringo Starr). Following its success he was signed by a Nashville publisher, and relocated there. Russell began his recording career in the later 1950s, but did not chart until 1971, scoring his biggest hits in 1973: "Catfish John," a #12 country hit, and the anthemic "Rednecks, White Socks and Blue Ribbon Beer," which reached #4. He continued to record through the early 1990s, with less success.

Russell's greatest exposure came on *The Grand Ole Opry*; he joined the cast in 1985, remaining at the *Opry* until shortly before his death. His songwriting continued to bring him recognition in the 1980s, when GEORGE STRAIT scored a #1 hit with his "Let's Fall to Pieces Together" in 1984. LINDA RONSTADT, EMMYLOU HARRIS, and DOLLY PARTON recorded his song "Makin' Plans" on their 1987 *Trio* album. Russell was also known as a storyteller and comedian. He died of complications from leukemia and diabetes in 2001.

Select Discography

Greatest Hits, Dominion 3141. Early 1990s remakes of his hits.

SARIE AND SALLY (Edna Earl Umensetter Wilson, b. near Chattanooga, Tenn., July 15 1896–June 27, 1994, and Margaret Faith Umensetter Waters, b. near Chattanooga, Tenn., 1903–November 2, 1967)

Sarie and Sally were a comic duo who foreshadowed the style of country monologuist MINNIE PEARL through their popular GRAND OLE OPRY skits.

Edna Umensetter was a well-educated child of a middle-class carpenter. After moving to Nashville and marrying, she led the life of a housewife and mother until the late 1920s. Then, while the family was living in High Point, North Carolina, Edna began entertaining friends by mimicking an "old mountain lady" who she named Sarie Brown. Sarie became so popular on the local ladies' club circuit that Edna began dressing for the part in a well-worn, long cotton dress, an old bonnet, and old-fashioned spectacles.

In 1930 the family relocated to Lakeland, Florida. There Edna partnered briefly with a local college student, and they performed on the radio as "Sarie and Silas." After returning to Nashville, Edna recruited her sister, Margaret, to join the act to portray Sarie's cousin, Sally Brown. In November 1934 they auditioned for WSM Radio, and were immediately hired for a fifteen-minute broadcast featuring their rural dialogues. The show was so successful that in early 1935 they were invited to join *The Grand Ole Opry*. They continued to broadcast their fifteen-minute show three times a week while appearing nearly every week on the *Opry*, performing shorter dialogues, through 1938.

Edna carefully scripted all of the act's material. The fifteen-minute shows told a continuing story, so listeners would gradually learn more about the two "mountain women" and their activities around their farm homes. Edna had been raised in the mountains, and carefully recreated mountain language, including such colorful expressions as "flutterin' fireflies" and "dear Lesperdeezer!," which became signatures for the act. The duo commented on current events, the en-croachment of city values on rural life, and other topics near and dear to their listeners' hearts.

By 1938 strenuous touring and unending radio work started to take their toll. Margaret's health began to falter, but the sisters continued to work together through early 1941. In 1939 they even appeared in a GENE AUTRY cowboy flick, *In Old Monterey*. After the duo broke up, Edna continued to perform, including a stint from 1943 to 1953 on Memphis radio, where she created a new country character, Aunt Buny (also spelled "Bunie"). She retired in Nashville in the early 1960s.

Though Minnie Pearl is better remembered, Sarie and Sally were trailblazers for the malapropisms and backwoods humor, along with topics drawn from everyday country life, that would be a staple for the later comedienne.

SATHERLEY, ART (b. Arthur Edward S., Bristol, England, October 19, 1889–February 10, 1986)

One of the pioneering producers of traditional country recordings, Satherley worked for the early labels Paramount, Plaza, American Record Company, and finally Columbia, overseeing the sessions of country bluesmen and what was then called hillbilly music.

Satherley came to America when he was twenty-four, initially working in a lumber mill owned by the Wisconsin Chair Company. Like many other furniture manufacturers, the company expanded into producing phonographs in the late 1910s and then into making records on its house label, Paramount. Satherley worked his way up through the ranks, producing landmark recordings for the company's "race" series, beginning with The Norfolk Jubilee Quartet's 1923 recording of "My Lord's Gonna Move This Wicked Race." Discovering the "black" market, he took ads in newspapers that catered to it, and developed the careers of bluesmen Blind Lemon Jefferson and Blind Blake, and cabaret blues star Ma Rainey.

In 1929 Satherley joined the Plaza label, which mostly sold through Sears, Roebuck and other catalog outlets. Soon after, the label, along with other dime-store outfits, was renamed American Record Company (ARC). Satherley became the firm's Southern-music producer, traveling through the South and setting up makeshift sessions to record whatever talent he could unearth. Among his country-music finds were ROY ACUFF, BOB WILLS, and GENE AUTRY; he produced Autry's 1931 recording of "That Silver-Haired Daddy of Mine," a breakthrough hit for the COWBOY star that also brought the company much-needed capital in the depths of the Depression.

In 1938 Columbia Records acquired ARC, and Satherley remained with that label until 1952. He established Columbia's presence in the new country-music recording capital, Nashville, after World War II, overseeing sessions by SPADE COOLEY, ROSE MADDOX, BILL MONROE, and RAY PRICE, to name a few. His assistant, DON LAW, would become a leading country producer in the late 1950s and 1960s. Satherley lived happily in California following his retirement; he was elected to the Country Music Hall of Fame in 1971, and died in 1986.

SAWYER BROWN c. 1984–ongoing: (Mark Miller [lead voc]; Bobby Randall [gtr]; Gregg "Hobie" Hubbard [kybds]; Jim Scholten [b]; "Curley" Joe Smyth [drms]; Bobby Randall left in 1993 and was replaced by Cameron Duncan)

A COUNTRY-ROCK band discovered by Ed McMahon on TV's *Star Search*, Sawyer Brown became progressively more country- (and less rock-) oriented through the 1980s, although they still had the flavor of a mid-1970s arena-rock band.

The band came together as backup musicians for singer Don King. Vocalist Miller and keyboard player Hubbard were high-school friends in Florida; guitarist Randall and bassist Scholten were from Michigan; drummer Smyth had played percussion with the Maine Symphony. While working for King they were impressed by the commercial success of ALABAMA, and after leaving King's employ they formed a band with a similar name (Savannah), in hopes of attracting similar success.

The group soon took the name Sawyer Brown (the names of two roads that cross in Nashville), and got their first break in 1984 when they won first prize on *Star Search*. The prize was a recording contract, and the boys immediately scored with 1985's "Step That Step," written by Miller, their second single and a #1 hit. They followed with more fluffy upbeat numbers, including the too-cute "Betty's Bein' Bad" and a remake of GEORGE JONES's "The Race Is On." Their road show featured smoke bombs, twirling lights, and jazzy

costumes, reflecting their arena-rock leanings and paving the way for similar theatrics from more straight-country acts like GARTH BROOKS.

In the early 1990s, recognizing that new country was making their meld of Alabama and EXILE rock sound passé, the group remade itself in the boot-scootin' mode of a good-time, HONKY-TONK band. It turned out that they could produce watered-down WESTERN SWING in an attractive manner. Miller continued his Mick Jagger-esque stage antics, particularly in their video for "The Boys and Me," an unabashed retro-rocker. The band's popularity declined in the latter half of the 1990s, although they continued to record and tour.

All in all, if not exactly a weighty group, they do provide high-energy entertainment for the masses.

Select Discography

Greatest Hits, Curb 77578. The hits up to 1990.
Greatest Hits, 1990–95, Curb 77689. Picks up with the rest of the band's chart-makers.

SCHLITZ, DON (b. Durham, N.C., August 29, 1952)

Schlitz is one of the most successful songwriters to come to the fore during the country boom of the 1980s and 1990s.

Raised and educated in North Carolina, Schlitz went to Nashville hoping to land a recording contract, or at least to sell a few songs. He recorded a song he wrote, "The Gambler," which was covered by KENNY ROGERS in 1978 as the title track for a theme album. It became a gigantic hit, and launched Schlitz's career. Two years later Schlitz released his first solo album, which failed to see much action.

However, Schlitz's songs became launching pads for many careers. RANDY TRAVIS's first single and hit, "On the Other Hand," was a Schlitz tune, as was the later "Forever and Ever, Amen," both written with PAUL OVERSTREET, a frequent Schlitz collaborator at the time. THE JUDDS found chart happiness with his "Rockin' with the Rhythm of the Rain," TRAVIS TRITT scored with "Deeper Than the Holler," and GARTH BROOKS cut "Learning to Live Again" (written with Stephanie Davis). Teaming with MARY CHAPIN CARPENTER, Schlitz helped push her career to an entirely new level with their songs "I Feel Lucky," "He Thinks He'll Keep Her," and "I Take My Chances," all big hits for her in 1992–1993. Acoustic BLUEGRASS artist ALISON KRAUSS had a major hit with Schlitz and Overstreet's "When You Say Nothing At All" in 1999.

Taking a cue from country songwriter ROGER MILLER, Schlitz composed the lyrics and music for a Broadway show based on Mark Twain's *Adventures of Tom Sawyer*. The project was begun in the mid-1990s, and opened in April 2001. However, the show quickly closed after receiving lukewarm reviews. Nonetheless, Schlitz says he's working on another score for a future Broadway production.

SCHNEIDER, JOHN (b. Mount Kisco, N.Y., April 8, 1960 [some sources give 1954])

Famous for portraying Bo Duke on the TV country corn show *The Dukes of Hazzard*, Schneider parlayed his acting role into a brief career on the Nashville charts, beginning with his cover of ELVIS PRESLEY's "It's Now or Never" from 1981.

Schneider was raised in a suburb of New York City until he was twelve, when his parents divorced and he moved with his mother to Atlanta. After appearing in high-school, summer stock, and amateur productions, he landed the role of the youngest and not-brightest Duke on the popular TV series when he was twenty-four. Three years later he signed with the Scotti Brothers label, having his hit with "It's Now or Never," but was unable to follow it up.

From 1984 to 1987 Schneider produced a string of hits, beginning with "I've Been Around Enough to Know," all cut by whiz-bang Nashville producer JIMMY BOWEN. With his hunky good looks and a voice reminiscent of GEORGE STRAIT, Schneider had a brief run as a new-country star. Then his thespian ambitions got the best of him, and he returned to TV and Broadway work, appearing in the musical show *Grand Hotel*. In 2001, Schneider returned to television in the series *Smallville* as the father of a teenaged Clark Kent.

Select Discography

Greatest Hits, MCA 42033. Lots of 1980s-styled mainstream country songs.

SCOTT, TOMMY (b. T. Lee S., Toccoa, Ga., June 24, 1917)

Known both as Doc Tommy Scott and Rambling Tommy Scott, this longtime country performer led a series of traveling medicine and Western shows for several decades.

Raised in rural Georgia, Scott landed his first job with a traveling medicine show when he was thirteen years old, working for "Doc" M. F. Chamberlain, who developed and sold Herb-O-Lac patent medicine. In 1933 Scott formed his Peanut Band, broadcasting over a small South Carolina radio station. Both on the road and on radio he portrayed Peanut, a blackface character. Three years later Chamberlain passed the recipe for Herb-O-Lac to the young performer, and Scott became the owner/manager of the show. Scott claimed to have made his first recordings for Victor in 1937 (although this claim has not been verified), and he continued to record through the years for King, Bullet, Four Star, and even Folkways (in the 1970s and early

1980s), but never had a major hit. However, he wrote a number of country standards, claiming authorship of the Monroe Brothers' hit "Rollin' in My Sweet Baby's Arms."

By the late 1930s Scott had joined CHARLIE MONROE's original Kentucky Pardners band, broadcasting out of North Carolina. His patent medicine was now being sold under the name of Manoree. However, Scott and Monroe had a falling out over splitting the profits, and by about 1940 Scott was back on his own, selling Herb-O-Lac.

In 1940 Scott moved to Kentucky, where he met future comedy star STRINGBEAN; the two formed the comic duo of Stringbean and Peanut, which lasted about a year. In 1941 Scott briefly joined THE GRAND OLE OPRY, appearing as a ventriloquist with an alter-ego dummy named Luke McLuke. Later that year he was back on the road, now paired with country performer Curly Sechler, working on the radio for yet another herbal remedy, VIM HERB. From 1943 to 1947 he broadcast over the powerful Mexican border radio stations, and also found a national sponsor in the American Tobacco Company, which made the Dental and Garrett brands of snuff.

In the later 1940s Scott headed to Hollywood to look for work in B COWBOY films; he befriended a number of minor-league cowboy stars of the day, including "Colonel" Tim McCoy and Sunset "Kit" Carson, who would continue to travel with him in his road shows during the 1950s and 1960s. Since the late 1940s he traveled throughout the country with his Medicine Show, which featured various performers. His wife, Frankie, frequently appeared as Clarabelle, the Gal from the Mountains, performing magic tricks and comedy. Scott's traveling show was on the road as recently as the late 1990s.

SCRUGGS, RANDY (b. R. Lynn S., Nashville, Tenn., August 3, 1953)

Son of the BLUEGRASS banjo legend Earl Scruggs (half of the famous FLATT AND SCRUGGS duo), Scruggs became a major Nashville producer in the 1990s.

Scruggs began playing the autoharp at age six, having been introduced to the instrument by none other than Mother Maybelle Carter of THE CARTER FAMILY. His father encouraged him to play music, presenting him for the first time, at age nine, on the syndicated Flatt and Scruggs TV show. (The famous bluegrass banjo piece "Randy Lynn Rag" was written by Earl in honor of his secondborn.) Taking up the GUITAR in his early teens, Randy began touring with his father. He briefly came out from under his father's wing to form a partnership with his brother, Gary (b. Knoxville, Tenn., May 18, 1949), who played bass and harmonica, as The Scruggs Brothers in the late 1960s.

When Flatt and Scruggs folded in 1969, the brothers joined with their father to form the COUNTRY-ROCK ensemble The Earl Scruggs Revue. Randy played electric and acoustic guitar in the band, and shared lead vocal duties with Gary. The band stayed together until 1980, eventually taking on one more family member, younger brother Steve (February 8, 1958–September 23, 1992), on piano. The Revue was successful, but controversial, in its day; bluegrass purists were unhappy with Earl's change in musical direction, while the country-rockers never really accepted the band as one of their own. Still, the band's recordings and tours did good business, and only increasing age and back trouble led Earl to fold the group.

Meanwhile, Randy was becoming an important session musician around Nashville. In 1971 he played bass for JOHN HARTFORD recording with Hartford on the influential *Aeroplane* album. Randy also guested on the NITTY GRITTY DIRT BAND's famous 1972 sessions for *Will the Circle Be Unbroken*, a three-record set honoring their country and bluegrass forebears. (Scruggs produced the 1998 follow-up to this landmark recording for the Dirt Band; his lead guitar on "Amazing Grace" garnered him a Best Country Instrumental Grammy the following year.)

After the Scruggs Revue ended, Randy opened his own recording studio, Scruggs Sound. At first he worked mostly with older country acts, such as MOE BANDY, WAYLON JENNINGS, and BOBBY BARE, but soon was nurturing younger talents such as IRIS DEMENT and STEVE WARINER. He produced ALISON KRAUSS's breakthrough single, "When You Say Nothing at All," a 1995 CMA Single of the Year that helped bring Krauss to a bigger audience. Scruggs also has over 100 songs to his credit, including six #1 country hits, among them DEANA CARTER's "We Danced Anyway." He has written songs with many other artists, including Matraca Berg and DWIGHT YOAKAM.

In 1998 Scruggs released a solo album, *Crown of Jewels*, featuring such New Nashville luminaries as MARY CHAPIN CARPENTER, EMMYLOU HARRIS, and VINCE GILL, along with folk-pop singers like Steve Goodman and even Joan Osborne. However, the album sold poorly, and any thought of a solo career was (at least temporarily) abandoned. In 2000 he produced sessions with his father, who had retired in 1980 and had rarely recorded or performed since, pairing the elder statesman with various younger singers and performers, including pop singer Elton John. The album was released in the fall of 2001.

Select Discography

All the Way Home, Vanguard 6538. 1970 second album by Randy and Gary, reissued on CD in 1994.

Crown of Jewels, Reprise 46930. 1998 solo album, with many "special guests."

SEALS, DAN (b. Danny Wayland S., McCamey, Tex., February 8, 1948)

Seals is a 1970s popster most famous for the song "I'd Really Love to See You Tonight," which he recorded as half of the duo England Dan and John Ford Coley. Following the duo's demise, Seals had some success in the mid-1980s as a country artist.

Seals comes from a musical family; his father led a family band that featured older brother Jimmy (who later achieved fame with Dash Crofts, first as a member of The Champs, famous for their early 1960s rock instrumental hit, "Tequila," and then for their late-1960s–early-1970s hippie folk hits, including "One Toke over the Line") with young Dan on bass. Dan heard only country music until he was ten; then the family relocated to Dallas, and some R&B and pop sounds began creeping into the mix. He formed his first band as a teenager, playing country for Lions clubs and rock and roll for teenage dance parties. In 1967 he formed his first recorded group, Southwest F.O.B. (Free on Board) with his friend John Ford Coley, and they scored a freak hit with 1968's flower-child pop song "Smell of Incense."

Like many other pop bands of the 1960s, the band was unable to produce a follow-up, and Seals and Coley relocated to California to perform as a folk duo. There Seals took the stage name England Dan, and the twosome began to record, scoring a hit record in Japan in 1973. Three years later they hit the jackpot with "I'd Really Love to See You Tonight," a soft-rock hit that Seals correctly states would be classified as "country" in today's market. The duo produced a number of follow-up songs, mostly sounding like watered-down clones of their initial hit, all without success.

Seals retired to Hendersonville, Tenn., where he returned to his initial love of country music. He released his first country single in 1984, the self-penned "God Must Be a Cowboy," and had a hit right out of the gate. His biggest year was 1986, when he recorded a duet with MARIE OSMOND on "Meet Me in Montana." Follow-ups were 1988's "Bop," a kind of technopop dance number with a vague country feeling; the rock-tinged "Addicted"; and the weepy ballad "You Still Move Me." In 1991 he signed with Warner Brothers, but failed to produce any hits and was quickly dropped by the label. He continued to tour through the end of the decade. He also released two "just-me-and-my-guitar" albums of acoustic remakes of his hits on small labels during this period.

Seals's success in soft rock-folk-country-pop shows how these styles are in a sense interchangeable; today's country is, in the hands of artists like Seals, really just an extension of 1970s folk-rock. On the folk-pop-country continuum, Seals falls firmly in the middle, creating pop songs with a hint of country feeling.

Select Discography

The Classic Collection, Vols. 1 and 2, Liberty 95952/96384.

SEEGER, MIKE (b. New York City, August 15, 1933)

Folk-revivalist, multiple instrumentalist, folklorist, and record producer, Seeger has played a seminal role in the preservation and popularization of old-time country music. Son of ethnomusicologist Charles Seeger and composer Ruth Crawford Seeger, and half brother of folk revivalist PETE SEEGER, he has been active on the folk scene for over forty years.

Seeger began performing as a BLUEGRASS-styled BANJO player in the Washington, D.C., area in the mid-1950s. In 1957 he produced for Folkways Records one of the first albums of BLUEGRASS music, an important anthology because Folkways catered to a Northern, urban audience that was unfamiliar (at that time) with the diversity of bluegrass styles. About the same time, with Tom Paley and JOHN COHEN, he formed THE NEW LOST CITY RAMBLERS, a band dedicated to performing the old-time music of the 1920s and 1930s in almost literal, note-for-note re-creations.

Seeger made his first solo LP in 1962 (*Old-Time Country Music*, Folkways). By using an Ampex multi-track tape machine, he was able to play all of the parts, in effect creating his own string band. The sound of the album was not much different from the style of The Ramblers at that time. Perhaps most interesting was his re-creation of BILL and CHARLIE MONROE on the tune "Rollin' On."

In this same period he began making field trips to the South. One of the first artists he "discovered" was blues guitarist Elizabeth "Libba" Cotten, who had worked as a maid for the Seeger family. It turned out that she was a talented GUITAR player in the country-blues style, as well as a skilled songwriter. (Her "Freight Train" became one of the hits of the FOLK REVIVAL.) Seeger also sought out performers of the 1920s and 1930s who had stopped recording; one of his most important finds was banjoist DOCK BOGGS. He was also a champion of the autoharp, introducing the country-picking of Maybelle Carter and other important autoharp players to a new audience. His anthology *Mountain Music on the Autoharp* introduced several fine players, including Kilby Snow.

Seeger recorded a second solo album in 1965 for Vanguard, a lower-key affair than his first, and continued to perform with The Ramblers through 1968. Although The Ramblers never officially disbanded, they were less active after 1968. Seeger made two excellent solo albums for Mercury in the mid-1970s: *Music from True Vine*, featuring the charming autoharp song "I Rambled This Country from Early to Late," and *The Second Annual Farewell Reunion*, which featured Seeger performing with traditional performers and revivalists; the most interesting cut on this was his eerie re-creation of "The Train that Carried My Girl from Town," by FRANK HUTCHISON, featuring Seeger on FIDDLE, harmonica, and vocals along with the slide guitar of Ry Cooder.

In the early 1970s Seeger and Ramblers bandmate Tracy Schwartz, Seeger's wife, ALICE GERRARD, HAZEL DICKENS, and bluegrass banjo player Lamar Grier formed a bluegrass-country group called The Strange Creek Singers. This short-lived band played an amalgam of country and bluegrass sounds. Seeger also performed as a duo with Gerrard (the pair recorded an album for Greenhays Records) and also with his sister Peggy. (The two made a 1968 duo recording for British Argo Records, and also performed songs from their mother's collections of children's songs for Rounder Records.)

Through the 1980s and 1990s Seeger continued to perform as a soloist and sometimes as a member of The New Lost City Ramblers. He also was the main force behind the old-time music "exercise" record *A-Robics and the Exertions* (Flying Fish). He continued his fieldwork, in the late 1980s producing the videotape *Talkin' Feet*, a documentary on traditional flat-footed dancing of the upper South. An anthology of his 1950s and 1960s field recordings was issued by Smithsonian/Folkways in 1998.

Select Discography

Southern Banjo Styles Smithsonian/Folkways 40107. 1998 "demonstration" record illustrating various styles of playing old-time banjo.
Close to Home: Old Time Music from Mike Seeger's Collection, Smithsonian/Folkways 40097. Anthology of Seeger's field recordings.

SEEGER, PETE (b. New York City, May 3, 1919)

Son of musicologist Charles Seeger and half brother of country-folk musicians MIKE SEEGER and Peggy Seeger, Pete Seeger has done more to popularize the FIVE-STRING BANJO than perhaps any other performer except Earl Scruggs (of FLATT AND SCRUGGS). He evolved a simplified version of clawhammer-style banjo playing (the traditional banjo strum) that gave just about all folk revivalists of the 1950s, 1960s, and 1970s their first exposure to the instrument, and he has revived traditional mountain folk songs in his performances since the late 1940s.

After attending Harvard for a couple of semesters, Seeger left school in 1938 to accompany folklorist

SEEGER, PETE

ALAN LOMAX on a field trip to the South. There he heard banjoist Pete Steele, who impressed him not only with his energetic playing but also with his repertoire of traditional songs about coal mining and his own compositions, including "Pay Day at Coal Creek." In 1940 he settled in New York, forming The Almanac Singers, one of the first FOLK-REVIVAL groups, with singers Lee Hays and Millard Lampell; WOODY GUTHRIE joined the fold in 1941. They recorded topical songs on unionism and pacifism (before the U.S. entered World War II), and antifascist anthems (while the U.S. was at war with Germany). Seeger enlisted in the Army during the war, and the group disbanded.

After the war Seeger again became involved with progressive musicians in the New York area, helping to found People's Songs, a booking agency for left-wing singers, as well as the folk journal *Sing Out!* In 1949, with Hays, Fred Hellerman, and Ronnie Gilbert, he formed The Weavers. They attracted the attention of Decca Records with their energetic reworkings of world folk songs, and had major pop hits with their arrangements of the African folk song "Wimoweh" (featuring Seeger's high tenor vocals and strummed banjo) and Leadbelly's "Goodnight, Irene." The Weavers were the model for all of the folk-revival groups of the early 1960s, including The Kingston Trio, The Tarriers, Peter, Paul, and Mary, and dozens more. Its members were attacked by anticommunist politicians and groups who were suspicious of their earlier leftist activities. Unable to get work, the group folded in 1952, then reunited triumphantly in 1955. Seeger left permanently in 1958.

During the 1950s Seeger began recording for the small specialty label Folkways. His first solo album, *Darling Corey*, featured mountain folk songs that Seeger had learned during his field trip with Lomax and from other traditional sources. In the mid-1950s he recorded the seminal *Goofing Off Suite*, in which he adapted classical, jazz, and pop tunes to the five-string banjo; this record was highly influential on other banjo players who hoped to expand the repertoire of the instrument. He recorded numerous children's albums, resetting UNCLE DAVE MACON's song "The Cumberland Mountain Deer Chase" into a story-song that he called "The Cumberland Mountain Bear Hunt"; in the early 1960s he encouraged Folkways to reissue an album of Macon's recordings from the 1920s and 1930s. Toward the end of the 1950s he recorded a series of folk ballads (*America's Favorite Ballads*, five albums) as well as traditional industrial ballads. Also in the 1950s Seeger self-published his book *How to Play the Five-String Banjo*, which not only gave detailed instruction in his distinctive frailing style but also introduced BLUEGRASS picking to urban players, highlighting the contributions of Earl Scruggs.

In the early 1960s Seeger became increasingly involved with political causes, and began performing more contemporary material. He also started writing his own songs (he had written the folk classic "If I Had a Hammer" in the early 1950s with his Weavers mate Lee Hays). In the 1960s he set the words of Ecclesiastes to music, producing a hit for THE BYRDS with "Turn, Turn, Turn"; he also wrote the hits "Where Have All the Flowers Gone?" and "Bells of Rhymney." His song "Waist Deep in the Big Muddy" got him into trouble with the censors because it criticized Lyndon Johnson's war efforts in Vietnam. He was invited to perform the song on The Smothers Brothers' television show (the first time he was invited to appear on network television since he had been blacklisted in the 1950s), but it was cut from the program; only after considerable protest was he invited back to perform it on another occasion.

By the late 1960s Seeger was increasingly playing the twelve-string guitar rather than the banjo, emulating the style of Leadbelly. Although he continued to perform in the 1970s (often in partnership with Arlo Guthrie) and 1980s, and up to the early twenty-first century, his more recent performances have lacked the enthusiasm and power that he had as a young player. Increasing hearing problems have limited his performances since the early 1990s.

Select Discography

Darling Corey/Goofin' Off Suite, Smithsonian/Folkways 40018. Two of Seeger's more innovative 1950s recordings, the first dedicated to traditional banjo songs and the second to instrumental versions of everything from fiddle tunes to classical music and pop songs.

Birds, Beasts, Bugs and Fishes, Little and Big, Smithsonian/Folkways 45039. Reissues two LPs from 1955, including his famous children's song "The Cumberland Mountain Bear Hunt."

Essential, Vanguard 97. Compilation of his Folkways recordings of the 1950s and 1960s.

We Shall Overcome, Columbia 45312. Two-CD set drawn from a Carnegie Hall concert in 1963, during the height of Seeger's involvement in civil rights and other contemporary issues.

SEELY, JEANNIE (b. Marilyn Jeanne S., Titusville, Pa., July 6, 1940)

Seely is a smoldering country vocalist best known for her mid-1960s hits and her association with songwriter HANK COCHRAN, who was her husband at the time.

The daughter of a steelworker and sometimes farmer, Seely was performing by age eleven, when she appeared on local radio; five years later she was regularly featured on a country TV show out of Erie, Pennsylvania. After graduating from high school, she enrolled in night school to study banking while working as a secretary by day. With three friends she left Pennsylvania to cross the country in 1961. They ended up in Beverly Hills, where she worked briefly in a bank before taking a job as secretary at Liberty Records, where she met a young country guitarist named Hank Cochran. She began writing songs (soulster Irma Thomas had a hit with her "Anyone Who Knows What Love Is" in 1964), worked as a deejay, and recorded for the tiny Challenge label. Cochran urged her to follow him to Nashville for a career in country music.

Arriving in Nashville in 1965, Seely went into the studio with Cochran, who wrote and produced her first big hit, "Don't Touch Me," a sultry back-room ballad that was a 1966 Grammy winner. The couple married, and Seely continued to produce hits between 1966 and 1969, and also appeared on THE GRAND OLE OPRY, causing somewhat of a stir because she refused to appear in the gingham dress/frilly look of a backwoods girl, instead wearing fashionable miniskirts. In the late 1960s she performed several hit duets with singer JACK GREENE, including "Wish I Didn't Have to Miss You," and appeared in his road show.

In the early 1970s Seely returned to the charts, thanks to her association with country OUTLAW WILLIE NELSON and friends. She had hits with her reworking of traditional folk ballads, changing "Can I Sleep in Your Barn Tonight Mister?" into the definitely racier "Can I Sleep in Your Arms," and transforming the Southern lament "Come All You Fair and Tender Ladies" into the bouncy "Lucky Ladies." By the late 1970s she even recorded the spicy "Take Me to Bed," showing how much mores had changed in country music.

Seely dropped off the country charts in the 1980s, turning her attention to appearing in regional theater productions of popular musicals, publishing a volume of her saucy aphorisms, and still appearing on the *Opry*.

Select Discography

Greatest Hits on Monument, Sony Special Products 28969. Just the first three years of her career are documented here, but it is the only collection currently available; originally issued as Monument 52426.

SELDOM SCENE (c. 1971–present; classic lineup: Mike Auldridge [Dobro]; John Duffy [mdln, voc]; Ben Eldridge [bnj, voc]; John Starling [gtr, voc]; Tom Gray [b, voc])

The Seldom Scene was a Washington, D.C.-based PROGRESSIVE BLUEGRASS band of the 1970s whose popularity transcended the traditional bluegrass field to include pop fans like LINDA RONSTADT and Jonathan Edwards, both of whom recorded with the band.

The group was born out of the remnants of one of Washington's longest-lived and most popular outfits, THE COUNTRY GENTLEMEN, centering primarily on high-tenor vocalist and MANDOLIN whiz John Duffey. With the smooth lead vocals of John Starling, the band from the start focused more on contemporary country and folk-rock songs than on traditional bluegrass fare. Named The Seldom Scene because they began their lives as an informal band playing at Washington's legendary Red Fox Inn, by the mid-1970s they had gathered a large following, particularly among younger bluegrass fans.

The group was not only progressive in their song selection, they featured some of the finest bluegrass players around. Auldridge was the first of many second-generation DOBRO players who transformed the instrument from primarily a background instrument used for special effects to one capable of taking blazing lead solos. (Country trivia fans note: Auldridge's uncle was Ellsworth T. Cozzens, who played Hawaiian guitar on many of JIMMIE RODGERS's classic country 78s) Starling was an energetic lead guitarist whose single-note leads influenced the next generation of new acoustic pickers.

The original band began to run out of steam by the late 1970s. Starling made an abortive attempt at a career as a soloist in the early 1980s and was replaced by SINGER/SONGWRITER Phil Rosenthal. A smoother-voiced singer, Rosenthal led a more pop-oriented band, and for a while it looked like the group might achieve wider commercial success. However, Rosenthal left in 1986 and was replaced for a while by Lou Reid, and when bassist Gray left, his shoes were filled by T. Michael Coleman (who had previously worked with DOC and Merle WATSON) on electric bass, giving them an even more contemporary sound. In 1993 Reid was replaced for a year by original member John Starling, pleasing fans of the 1970s group.

In 1995 it looked like the band was doomed when Auldridge, Coleman, and new lead singer Mondi Klein left to form the band Chesapeake. However, the determined Duffy and Eldridge brought on board former Johnson Mountain Boys lead singer Dudley Connell, along with Dobro player Fred Travers and bass player Ronnie Simpkins, to form yet another new lineup. However, within a year Duffy had died of a heart attack. Although disheartened, the band decided to soldier on, bringing back lead singer Lou Reid to replace Duffy. In 2000 they issued a new album, showing that the spirit of the original band remained pretty much intact, combining BLUEGRASS instrumentation with contemporary songs.

Select Discography

The Best of, Rebel 1101. Drawn from their first three Rebel albums.

15th Anniversary Celebration, Sugar Hill 2202. All-star tribute recorded at the Kennedy Center in 1986.

SHAPE-NOTE SINGING Shape-note singing refers to a method of teaching music to nonmusically literate singers, employed in the late eighteenth and early nineteenth centuries by traveling "singing masters." Originally in New England, and later in the South and West, these itinerant teachers came to towns, mostly at the invitation of the local church, to teach the local choir how to sing. They employed special songbooks that drew on a repertoire of well-known folk and hymn tunes that the congregation presumably would know. The parts were notated using different shapes for the various scale tones (triangles, squares, diamonds, etc.), and were often limited to a five-note (pentatonic) scale, which was common for folk and hymn tunes. The harmonies also were simplified, based on common intervals such as fourths and fifths, giving the music a distinct, archaic sound. By singing the tones associated with the shapes, the congregation could quickly learn new songs and new harmonies.

Although shape-note singing soon died out in the cities, where more sophisticated congregations learned to read music "properly," it lingered in rural areas. Annual conventions were held for the purpose of singing an entire songbook in a single day and evening (this was accomplished by rapidly "reading" each hymn). This helped singers remember the repertoire, and also encouraged them to increase the number of songs they performed throughout the year. These events would also involve communal socializing, and often a large community-prepared meal would be served about halfway through the day.

Even in churches that did not employ shape-note singing, the harmonies from these hymnals could be heard, so that an older style of singing was preserved. When BLUEGRASS groups began incorporating GOSPEL music into their repertoires, they naturally drew on the rich shape-note singing tradition. Many bluegrass singers were raised performing in their local church choirs, and so their vocal styles and harmonies often recall the tonalities of this earlier style. This is particularly true of the more traditionally oriented groups, such as THE STANLEY BROTHERS, although more modern bands ranging from THE RED CLAY RAMBLERS to THE NASHVILLE BLUEGRASS BAND have made this style of singing a part of their performances.

SHAVER, BILLY JOE (b. Corsicana, Tex., August 16, 1939)

The outlaw's OUTLAW, Shaver is best known for writing all of the songs for WAYLON JENNINGS's first great LP, 1973's *Honky-Tonk Heroes*. His ballads celebrating hard-as-nails characters, along with his impeccable Texas heritage, have made Shaver one of the unsung heroes of roots-country music.

Shaver's career has been checkered at best. His parents split up before he was born, so he was raised by his grandmother. He left school after the eighth grade to work for several uncles on their farms, and then served in the Navy, was a broncobuster, and worked in a sawmill (where he lost parts of four fingers on his right hand). In the late 1960s he began making trips to Nashville to try to sell his songs, eventually hooking up with singer/song publisher BOBBY BARE, who put him on retainer and began promoting his material to the first generation of country outlaws.

Shaver's big break came in 1971 when KRIS KRISTOFFERSON covered his "Good Christian Soldier," followed by TOM T. HALL tackling "Old Five and Dimers Like Me." But Shaver's outlaw credentials were solidified when Waylon Jennings decided to record a theme album of his ballads called *Honky-Tonk Heroes*, launching Shaver's songwriting career full swing as well as elevating Jennings to star status. Meanwhile, Shaver had begun recording as a solo artist, first for MGM and then Monument, the latter album being produced by his friend Kristofferson and featuring many of the so-called outlaw musicians. Some of his popular songs from the 1970s include "I Been to Georgia on a Fast Train" and "Ain't No God in Mexico."

Shaver managed to place a few songs with Southern rock groups, including the Allman Brothers, who covered his "Sweet Mama"; this association led to a contract with Capricorn Records in the mid-1970s and some abortive attempts to crack the rock charts. After the label folded, Shaver went unrecorded for a few years, until he signed with Columbia in 1980, recording an album issued in 1981. The title cut, "I'm an Old Chunk of Coal . . .," was immediately covered by JOHN ANDERSON, who had a hit with it.

Through most of the 1980s and the new-country revival, Shaver was without a record label, although his songs continued to crop up here and there. In 1993 he made a comeback album for the small Zoo-Praxis label, featuring old friend Waylon Jennings; Shaver's son, Eddy, who was a fine rock and country-styled guitarist; and even musty old rock-and-rollers like Al Kooper. Undeterred by the move toward arena-rock that has propelled new country into the pop mainstream, Shaver created mythic songs that seem to resonate through the history of country music. Particularly moving is the title cut, "Tramp on Your Street," which tells of his own ten-mile pilgrimage as a young boy to hear the legendary HANK WILLIAMS.

After a live release in 1995, the label dropped Shaver. Undeterred, he continued to record for a variety of labels. In 1998 he signed with the small New West label. 2000 brought two blows to him: the deaths of his son Eddy, his longtime accompanist, and of his wife, Brenda, whom he had wed three times (the first two marriages ended in divorce). Perhaps not surprisingly, Shaver suffered a heart attack in August 2001, and underwent an angioplasty operation in early September. Earlier in the year he had released a new album with a more rock-oriented sound, *Earth Rolls On.*

Select Discography

Restless Wind, 1973–87, Razor & Tie 2082. Compilation of his recordings for various labels through this period.

Tramp on Your Street, Volcano 31063. Reissue of Zoo-Praxis 11063, his 1993 comeback recording.

Earth Rolls On, New West 6025. Rocking album with songs reflecting on the loss of his son and wife.

SHEDAISY (1999–present)

Cross the high fashion of the Spice Girls with the peroxide-induced looks of the DIXIE CHICKS, and what do you get? SheDaisy, Nashville's (latest) attempt to score big bucks off high-gloss makeup.

Well, at least the group wasn't assembled by running an audition announcement in the back of *Savvy* magazine. SheDaisy are in fact "real" sisters, the "kutely" named Kristyn (b. August 24, 1970), Kelsi (b. November 21, 1974), and Kassidy (b. October 30, 1976) Osborn from Magna, Utah (the state that brought us the Osmonds). The group name is supposedly derived from a Native American term meaning "sisters" (so far no Native American has come forward to take the honor for naming the group). After making a name for themselves out West, the spunky girls came to Nashville in search of fame and fortune.

In 1999 the girls signed with Lyric Street Records, and they quickly produced a debut album, coyly titled *The Whole Shebang* (also the title of one of the album's many hits). In videos that looked suspiciously like advertisements for shampoo, shoes, and halter tops, the girls bounced their way through upbeat pop confections including "Little Good-byes" and the will-she-or-won't-she "I Will . . . but." Furthering their middle American credentials, they cut "Deck the Halls" for an animated Disney film, and . . . before you could say seasonal profits . . . released their own Christmas album.

How long lip gloss and good looks can propel a group to chart success is anybody's guess. At least at this turn-of-the-century moment, SheDaisy are queens of Nashville pop.

Select Discography

The Whole Shebang, Hollywood 165002. High-gloss pop from the photogenic trio.

SHELTON BROTHERS (b. Robert Attlesey, July 4, 1909–November 1986, and Joseph Attlesey, January 27, 1911–December 26, 1980, both in Reilly Springs, Tex.)

The Shelton Brothers were hillbilly/WESTERN SWING stars of the 1930s and 1940s, and major radio stars in the Southwest.

Elder brother Bob was a natural comedian but not much of a musician; younger brother Joe was a talented MANDOLIN and GUITAR player. Taking their mother's maiden name, the Sheltons began performing as The Lone Star Cowboys in 1929, broadcasting out of Tyler, Texas. Four years later they recorded two classics of country music: "Just Because," which has become a favorite of BLUEGRASS bands, and "Deep Elum Blues," in honor of a tough Dallas neighborhood where many jazz and blues musicians congregated. They also accompanied up-and-coming country-blues singer (and later Louisiana governor) JIMMIE DAVIS at the same sessions.

The brothers built their popularity over radio, mostly working out of Shreveport, Louisiana, and Dallas, Texas (except for a period during 1935–1936 when they worked with fiddler Curly Fox out of New Orleans). Around mid-1936 they formed The Sunshine Boys, a Western Swing band that featured, from time to time, BOB DUNN on steel guitar and pianist MOON MULLICAN, among other Texas-based musicians. In 1938 younger brother Merle was brought into the band, and Joe switched to electric mandolin, playing in a jazz-influenced style.

During the mid-1940s the brothers began working more on their own, although they officially kept The Sunshine Boys going until about 1948, cutting some postwar sessions for King Records. In 1944 Joe led Jimmie Davis's band during his first election campaign. By 1950 he had retired; brother Bob kept his comedy act going through the 1970s, working on syndicated radio shows like LOUISIANA HAYRIDE.

SHELTON, RICKY VAN (b. Danville, Va., January 12, 1952)

The country-cover king, Ricky Van Shelton has a ROCKABILLY-flavored style and a million-dollar smile that have made him a favorite on the country circuit through the 1990s.

Raised in rural Grit, Virginia, Shelton was first more interested in rock and roll than in country music, although he did sing in a local small church choir. His brother Ronnie played MANDOLIN and had his own BLUEGRASS/country band, and he encouraged his younger sibling to take up country music. Shelton remained in his hometown into his early twenties, working as a pipe fitter by day and a musician by night. Then his wife got a job as a corporate personnel director in Nashville, and the two moved to the country-music capital.

Shelton worked on demos in his basement while performing at night in a small club called The Nashville Palace, where he met another country hopeful, who was washing dishes (RANDY TRAVIS). His wife befriended the wife of a *Nashville Tennessean* reporter, who brought one of Shelton's tapes to Columbia producer Steve Buckingham, who signed the artist in 1986. A year later he had his first hit with his first of many covers, "Somebody Lied," originally recorded by CONWAY TWITTY two years previously. His follow-up hits came from even further back in the country music songbook, including HARLAN HOWARD's "Life Turned Her that Way" (a hit for MEL TILLIS in the 1960s), "Statue of a Fool" (a pop song recorded by JACK GREENE in 1969), and 1989's "From a Jack to a King," which was originally written and recorded by Ned Miller in 1963. In the early 1990s he had a hit covering ELVIS PRESLEY's "Ring Around My Neck," which was featured in the 1992 film *Honeymoon in Vegas*.

Shelton came to a crossroad in his personal life in 1991, when his wife confronted him after years of enduring his heavy drinking and womanizing. He underwent a "born again" experience in 1992, even releasing a GOSPEL album and a series of inspirational children's books. It took Shelton several years to return to more secular material, and he lost his standing on the country charts. In the later 1990s he attempted to resume his more mainstream career, but despite failing to produce many hits, he continues to be a fairly good draw on the country concert circuit.

Select Discography

Living Proof, Columbia 44221. Nice 1988 album.
Greatest Hits Plus, Columbia 52753. The hits to 1992.
Fried Green Tomatoes. 2000 release seeking to return Ricky to mainstream success.

SHENANDOAH (1987–present: Marty Raybon [lead voc]; Jim Seales [gtr]; Stan Thorn [kybds]; Ralph Ezell [b]; Mike McGuire [drms])

Shenandoah were one of the first late 1980s bands to turn away from the glitz-country of ALABAMA, EXILE, and other pop-oriented groups and return to a roots-country sound. With each album they've pro-

duced, they've moved increasingly toward a more hard-country sound.

The group originated as the informal house band of the MGM club in Muscle Shoals, Alabama, where they all worked as session musicians and songwriters. Leader Raybon had a day job as a bricklayer with his father; they also played together in a family BLUEGRASS band. Raybon began hunting for a record deal, finally hooking up with Robert Byrne at CBS, who offered to hire Raybon if he brought along his backup group. Byrne gave them the name Shenandoah.

Their first album was a decided dud as Byrne tried to mold their sound into mainstream country-pop; but they came back with a more roots-oriented second disc, producing their first hits, "The Church on Cumberland Road" and "Sunday in the South." However, their breakthrough into widespread popularity brought legal difficulties in 1991, when three other bands—from Kentucky, Nevada, and Massachusetts—sued the group, claiming that they had prior rights to the Shenandoah name. The lawsuit bankrupted the band by the end of the year, and they were dropped by CBS.

By 1992 they had settled the lawsuits (making the argument that, after all, they had not chosen the name; it was given to them by CBS, so therefore they couldn't be accused of stealing it). Moving to RCA, the group scored new hits with the honky-tonk numbers "Rock My Baby" and "(Your Leavin's Been) A Long Time Comin'." The band began 1993 with the dance-oriented hit "If Bubba Can Dance" and the humorous "Janie Baker's Love Slave." They moved to Capitol Records in 1994.

They scored their last major hit in 1995 with "Somewhere in the Vicinity of the Heart," featuring guest vocalist ALISON KRAUSS. A 1996 album of remakes of their earlier hits showed the band treading water, and then they took a four-year recording hiatus. Their most recent album is the grandly titled *2000*, issued on the small Free Falls label.

Select Discography

Greatest Hits, Columbia 44885. Their Columbia hits (up to 1992).
15 Favorites, Capitol 96392. The group's hits from 1992 to 1996; actually twelve hits and three "bonus" tracks.

SHEPARD, JEAN (b. Paul's Valley, Okla., November 21, 1933)

A no-frills 1950s-style tear-droppin' balladeer, Shepard was one of the first female country vocalists to break through, although it took a while for her career to develop.

Born to an Okie family that relocated to the Bakersfield, California, area in search of a better life, Shepard

Jean Shepard, c. mid-1970s. Photo: Raeanne Rubenstein

began her career as a bass player in the all-female Melody Ranch Girls band in 1948. A few years later she was "discovered" by HANK THOMPSON, who recommended her to his producer, KEN NELSON, at Capitol Records. Her first hits were duets with FERLIN HUSKY, recorded in 1953: "A Dear John Letter," followed by "Forgive Me, John." She toured with Husky in the following year, and also appeared with RED FOLEY on his radio show. In 1956 she was invited to join THE GRAND OLE OPRY thanks to her solo hits "Satisfied Mind" and "Beautiful Lies." At this time she made what was probably the first country-music concept LP, *Songs of a Love Affair*, in which the cycle of twelve songs, all penned by Shepard, tells a wet-hanky story of the breakup and reconciliation of two lovers.

Her career languished after her marriage to HAWK-SHAW HAWKINS, and she remained off the charts until 1964, one year after Hawkins's death in the airplane crash that took the life of PATSY CLINE. Her 1964 recording of "Second Fiddle (to an Old Guitar)" launched a series of hits with equally colorful titles, from 1966's "Many Happy Hangovers to You" through 1967's "Your Forevers (Don't Last Very

Long)" to "Slippin' Away" from 1973, her biggest chart-buster. She continued to record through the late 1970s and early 1980s for a variety of small labels, with little success. Nonetheless, she continues to appear on the *Opry* and remains popular with her core fans.

Shepard created controversy in country-music circles in the 1970s through her outspoken opposition to the COUNTRYPOLITAN movement. She resented the encroachment of pop music into country's terrain, always holding onto the sweet, suffering image that made her famous, as well as her stripped-down HONKY-TONK sound.

Select Discography

Honky-Tonk Heroine, County Music Foundation 21. A good introduction to her Capitol recordings.
Melody Ranch Girl, Bear Family 159052. Five-CD set collecting all her Capitol recordings made between 1952 and 1964, for the serious fan.

SHEPPARD, T. G. (b. William Neal Browder, Humboldt, Tenn., July 20, 1944)

A soulful singer/instrumentalist, Sheppard rode the urban COWBOY craze of the late 1970s and early 1980s for a long string of country successes.

Originally from Tennessee, Browder grew up in a musical household (his mother was a piano teacher and gave her son his first lessons on that instrument). Browder mastered GUITAR and saxophone by his teen years, and formed his first group, a rockin' R&B band called The Royal Tones. He set out for the R&B mecca, Memphis, Tennessee, when he was sixteen. He was hired by producer/guitarist Travis Wammack to play in his band, and even made some rockin' recordings on his own, singing lead on The Embers' minor hit "The Girl Next Door," and taking the nom de disc of Brian Stacey to produce one minor chart-topper, "High School Days." He then worked in the promo department of RCA records out of Memphis.

After leaving RCA, Browder formed his own promotional company, Umbrella Productions. One of his clients was songwriter Bobby David, who had written "Devil in the Bottle." Unable to place it, Browder cut it himself in 1974 for Motown's short-lived country division, Melodyland, taking the name T. G. Sheppard to avoid any conflict of interest with his management business (backup vocals were provided by a young up-and-comer named JANIE FRICKE). The song was an instant hit, and Sheppard continued to produce hit records for Motown until they closed their country division in 1976.

A year later he signed with Warner Brothers and began a long, successful relationship with producer Buddy Killen. Together they produced a string of hits from 1979's "Last Cheater's Waltz," to 1980's pseudo-autobiographical "I'll Be Coming Back for More" (with its spoken first verse) and "Do You Wanna Go to Heaven," 1981's "I Feel Like Lovin' You Again" (originally titled "I Feel You Coming Back Again," but the songwriters worried that "I feel you coming . . ." might be misinterpreted!), "I Loved 'em Every One" (T. G.'s first crossover hit on the pop charts), and "Party Time" (written by Bruce Channel, famous for his pop hit "Hey, Baby!"), and 1982's "Only One You," "Finally," the patriotic tub-thumper "War Is Hell (on the Home Front, Too)," and a duet with KAREN BROOKS, "Faking Love." In 1983 he switched to producer Jim Ed Norman, but the hits slowed, although he did produce the silly "Make My Day" based on the famous Clint Eastwood line (and featuring Eastwood on the record).

In 1985 Sheppard teamed with legendary R&B producer Rick Hall, and had another string of hits, including 1986's "Strong Heart" and 1987's "One for the Money." Since then Sheppard has turned his attention increasingly to his business interests, including an auto racing team, a Smoky Mountain bed-and-breakfast and a nearby Mexican restaurant, and Kansas City's Guitars & Cadillacs nightclub, although he has occasionally issued a new recording.

Select Discography

The Best of, Curb 77545.
Biggest Hits, Columbia 44307. 1985–1987 R&B-tinged recordings.

SHERRILL, BILLY (b. Phil Campbell, Ala., November 5, 1936)

Sherrill was a legendary Nashville producer who nurtured the careers of CHARLIE RICH, TANYA TUCKER, JOHNNY PAYCHECK, TAMMY WYNETTE, and countless others as an A&R man at Epic Records from the mid-1960s through the early 1980s. He also was responsible for the COUNTRYPOLITAN sound of the late 1960s and early 1970s, bringing a more pop-oriented sound to Nashville recordings by downplaying traditional instruments and adding layers of strings and vocal choruses.

The son of an evangelist, Sherrill first took up the piano to accompany the hymns that were part of his parents' revival meetings. As a teenager he switched to saxophone and led a jumping band performing jazz-flavored instrumentals. After a brief career as a solo artist in the late 1950s and early 1960s, he hooked up with legendary producer SAM PHILLIPS, who hired him to operate his Nashville studios. After Phillips's label collapsed, Sherrill joined Epic Records, where he has remained ever since.

From the start Sherrill not only molded artists' sounds but also selected and often coauthored their material, carefully honing their image. Among his classic productions are "Stand by Your Man," Tammy Wynette's famous ode to marital fidelity, which he wrote with her; all of Tanya Tucker's early hits; and Charlie Rich's megahits "Behind Closed Doors" and "The Most Beautiful Girl." Wynette's recordings represent the highest achievement of the Sherrill style; her powerful vocals, recalling the conviction of the great GOSPEL singers, are set against a lush musical backdrop that transforms them into miniature anthems. Among other artists that Sherrill produced during the early through mid-1970s is GEORGE JONES.

Though Sherrill was the most successful producer of the 1970s, the new-country movement of the 1980s made his style seem overblown and tired. During that decade he focused more on administrative duties, although he continued to work occasionally as a producer. One of his last and most interesting projects was a 1981 collaboration with British punk musician Elvis Costello on a country-homage album, *Almost Blue*.

SHOCKED, MICHELLE (b. M. Karen Johnston, Tex., c. 1962)

Another eccentric Texan, Shocked is a SINGER/SONGWRITER of some power who has adapted WESTERN SWING and old-time FIDDLE music to her unique personality.

Shocked reveals little about her life. (She does admit to being raised by a strict Mormon family.) She went to Europe when she was a teenager to perform, but returned to Texas by her early twenties. In 1987 she was singing at an informal session at the Kerrville Folk Festival and was heard by English record producer Pete Lawrence; he issued recordings made informally at the festival as *The Texas Campfire Tapes* in the same year. This led to a major-label signing and her first studio album, *Short Sharp Shocked*, a year later, that focused primarily on her talents as a singer/songwriter. *Captain Swing* was an attempt to modernize Western Swing for a new audience; this produced the minor hit "The Greener Side" (the video for the song featured hunks in skimpy swimsuits dancing around Shocked, perhaps a none-too-subtle reaction to music videos' propensity to feature male rock stars surrounded by adoring, scantily clad babes). Her 1992 album, *Arkansas Traveler*, took as its theme the unusual idea of writing new lyrics to traditional fiddle tunes; it featured many fine acoustic pickers, with mixed results.

After that release Shocked argued with her label, Mercury, proposing to do an album with the group Tony! Toni! Tone!, and, when that idea was rejected, a GOSPEL album. She then recorded for a series of independent and small labels, turning mostly to more "alternative" styles rather than pursuing her explorations of folk and country.

Shocked has had only a cult following at best, and can be considered as much a rock (or punk) performer as a country artist. But her late-1980s/early-1990s attempts to wed country influences to modern, literary lyrics certainly deserve recognition, if only for their sense of commitment, daring, and fun.

Select Discography

The Texas Campfire Tapes, Mercury 834581.
Short Sharp Shocked, Mercury 834924.
Captain Swing, Mercury 838878.
Arkansas Traveler, Mercury 512101.

SHOLES, STEVE (b. Washington, D.C., February 12, 1911–April 22, 1968)

A longtime A&R man at RCA Records, Sholes had a lasting impact on country music through his production work in the postwar years.

Joining the original Victor label in 1929, Sholes worked his way up from a lowly job as a messenger boy. He also attended college and began performing as a traveling dance-band clarinet and saxophone player. By 1939 he was an assistant to RCA producer FRANK WALKER, helping manage sessions in New York and field recordings in Atlanta and Chicago.

In 1945 Sholes was named head of A&R for RCA's country and R&B lines. Four years later he headed the company's new Nashville offices, initially working out of various small studios. Through the mid-1950s he signed a host of artists, including country legends JIM REEVES, HANK SNOW, SKEETER DAVIS, and CHET ATKINS (he also used Atkins as a producer on scores of recordings in the 1950s and put him in charge of RCA's Nashville operations in 1957), and legendary rocker ELVIS PRESLEY. His success with Elvis led the company to reward him by opening the first RCA studios in Nashville in 1957, and promoting him through the ranks. In 1961 he moved to Los Angeles to manage the firm's West Coast operations. That same year he was one of the key forces behind the establishment of the Country Music Hall of Fame, and helped raise funds for its permanent museum. In 1963 he returned to New York to head the company's A&R operation. In 1967 he was among the first inductees into the Country Music Hall of Fame. Sholes died of a heart attack while driving to the Nashville airport in 1968.

SINGER/SONGWRITER It is so common today for pop artists to perform their own material that it's easy to forget that just a few decades ago this was the exception rather than the rule. The revolution that brought forth the singer/songwriter began in the early 1960s and came to its full flowering in the following decade.

In the early days of American popular music, from the mid-nineteenth through the mid-twentieth century, songwriters were professionals who created hit songs; singers were professionals who specialized in performing them. Although there were occasionally songwriters who gained success singing their own material (Fats Waller and Hoagy Carmichael are two examples from the pop world), they were the exception rather than the rule. In country music, of course, songs were often "written" by the performer, but this sometimes had a different meaning than in the pop world; often a singer would take a common folk song, ballad, or blues and reshape it to fit his or her own personality. Many of the songs "written" by A. P. Carter of THE CARTER FAMILY, for example, were simply reworkings of older songs. However, there were many noteworthy songwriters among country and folk recording artists, including the great WOODY GUTHRIE, who would inspire the folk revivalists of the 1960s.

A young singer/songwriter from Hibbing, Minnesota, named Robert Zimmerman, came under Guthrie's spell. He traveled to New York, hoping to meet his idol. When he arrived, he had already transformed himself into BOB DYLAN, and he began writing and performing a string of social-protest songs that were unique in their vivid imagery and power of expression. Dylan's lyrics became increasingly imagistic in the mid-1960s, thanks to the influence of poets like Allen Ginsberg, and he adopted the instrumentation of a rock band for his backup group after hearing THE BYRDS perform his songs (they had a hit with his "Mr. Tambourine Man," among others). Dylan's unconventional (some would say nasal and grating) vocals and limited GUITAR capabilities made it clear that even songwriters lacking traditional performing capabilities could make it big. Despite his "deficiencies," Dylan's performances were often far superior to the many cover versions by more conventional pop singers.

A slew of singer/songwriters appeared on the pop charts in the late 1960s and early 1970s. James Taylor had a hit with his countryesque *Sweet Baby James* album, particularly the autobiographical song "Fire and Rain"; Carole King set new sales records with her *Tapestry* album; and Joni Mitchell created new standards in self-confessional balladry on albums like *Blue*. Even Dylan turned to self-analysis on 1970s albums like *Blood on the Tracks* and *Desire*. Often these performers were accompanied by soft-rock backup—acoustic guitar, with electric bass, drums, and sometimes piano—and the overall sound was pleasantly middle-of-the-road.

The singer/songwriter movement was eclipsed in the mid-to-late 1970s by the emergence of punk and new-wave music. Its influence, however, was strong on the country stars of the 1980s and 1990s. GARTH BROOKS is a longtime James Taylor fan (naming his firstborn daughter Taylor in honor of his idol). Many of today's country songwriters—notably MARY CHAPIN CARPENTER, NANCI GRIFFITH, and LYLE LOVETT—draw on the singer/songwriter tradition, performing their own material with a soft-rock accompaniment. In fact, if Griffith or Carpenter had first recorded in the 1970s instead of the 1980s and 1990s, they would have been classified as singer/songwriters, not country artists. This has made their music somewhat difficult to categorize; while Carpenter had a period of country superstardom, most of her follow-up albums have appealed to her loyal fan base by returning to her singer/songwriter roots. Griffith has been marketed as a singer/songwriter, country star, and pop star, although never too successfully.

SINGLETON, SHELBY (b. Waskom, Tex., December 16, 1931)

Singleton is a legendary rock, R&B, and country producer who was most active from the mid-1950s through the late 1960s.

Singleton was first hired by Mercury in the mid-1950s, and worked with legendary soul acts such as Clyde McPhatter. In 1962 he was made director of the Smash label, a Mercury subsidiary that produced the company's country output. He signed ex-rocker JERRY LEE LEWIS (and oversaw his country sessions), as well as TOM T. HALL and CHARLIE RICH, to the label. In 1966 he formed three of his own labels, Silver Fox and SSS International, focusing on soul music, and Plantation, for the country market. His first discovery was JEANNIE C. RILEY, and he produced her monster hit, "Harper Valley P.T.A."; he also promoted Linda Martell. At the same time he established his own music-publishing operation.

In 1969 Singleton purchased the Sun Records catalog from SAM PHILLIPS, and since then has focused more of his attention on the business side of licensing recordings and songs than on producing new recordings.

SKAGGS, RICKY (b. near Cordell, Ky., July 18, 1954)

Hailing from a musical family, Ricky Skaggs is one of the few artists who has successfully crossed over from traditional BLUEGRASS to mainstream country while maintaining his basic sound and style. He was one of the first new-country stars of the early 1980s who pointed the direction for a return to country's roots in repertoire and style. Although he has not been as consistently popular as some of the more flashy acts who have followed his lead, Skaggs remains an important force in country music.

A multiple instrumentalist, Skaggs began his career while still in high school with his friend KEITH

Ricky Skaggs (mandolin) with his mentor, Ralph Stanley (banjo), 2000. Photo: Raeanne Rubenstein

WHITLEY, performing MANDOLIN–GUITAR duets in a traditional style derived from country's brother acts. The duo were particularly enamored of THE STANLEY BROTHERS' sound, and they soon were members of Ralph Stanley's band. Poor pay and a grueling touring schedule led to Skaggs's retirement and brief employment as a worker in a suburban Washington power plant. He also began performing with a later version of the progressive BLUEGRASS band THE COUNTRY GENTLEMEN.

In the early 1970s he briefly joined J. D. CROWE's groundbreaking bluegrass ensemble, The New South, along with ace guitarist/vocalist TONY RICE. Determined to modernize and popularize the bluegrass sound, he formed his own progressive band, Boone Creek, with DOBRO player JERRY DOUGLAS, who has appeared on many of Skaggs's recordings, and singer/guitarist Terry Baucom. By the late 1970s he was a backup musician for EMMYLOU HARRIS, helping mold her new traditional approach on landmark albums such as *Roses in the Snow*.

Blessed with a high-tenor voice, Skaggs recorded his first solo album in a contemporary country vein for the bluegrass label Sugar Hill; at the same time he made a duet album with Rice featuring just their guitar and mandolin and vocal harmonies, in an homage to the 1930s country sound. He was quickly signed by CBS, and had a string of hits in the early 1980s with his unique adaptations of bluegrass and country standards of the 1950s. In fact, his 1984 cover of BILL MONROE's "Uncle Pen" was the first bluegrass song to hit #1 on the country charts since 1949. He also was one of the first new-country artists to tour Europe, scoring great success in England, where he performed with artists ranging from Elvis Costello to Nick Lowe.

The mid-1980s found Skaggs teetering on the edge of a more pop-country sound, but basically he stuck close to his country roots in choice of material and performance. He married country vocalist Sharon White of THE WHITES, and produced some of their successful recordings of the 1980s. He returned to his bluegrass/country swing roots as a member of MARK O'CONNOR's New Nashville Cats band, which featured another crossover artist from bluegrass, VINCE GILL. After watching his mainstream country career peter out, Skaggs renounced commercial country in the mid-1990s to form a new band, Kentucky Thunder. Recording on his own Skaggs Family label, he has returned to playing acoustic bluegrass music. He oversaw a tribute album to Bill Monroe in 2000, aptly titled *Big Mon*. In 2001 he signed with Hollywood Records.

Select Discography

Family and Friends, Rounder 0151. Charming album with Skaggs's parents and longtime associates playing traditional country and bluegrass material.
Country Gentleman: The Best of, Epic/Legacy 64883. Two-CD set of his Epic recordings made between 1981 and 1991.

SKILLET LICKERS, THE (c. 1925–1931: Gid Tanner [b. James Gideon T., 1885–1960; fdl, voc]; Clayton McMichen [1900–1970; fdl, voc]; Riley Puckett [1890–1946; gtr, voc]; Land Norris [bnj])

Perhaps the greatest of the classic old-time string bands, The Skillet Lickers were also one of the most influential, thanks to their energetic recordings of dance tunes, sentimental and humorous songs, and a famous series of country-humor skits depicting a group of backwoods moonshiners.

Tanner was the elder statesman of the band, a famous solo performer on his own who made fiddle recordings for Columbia in 1924, accompanied by blind guitarist/vocalist RILEY PUCKETT. Tanner sang in a comic, high falsetto voice, and his FIDDLE playing was in the rough, often loose rhythmic style typical of his generation of Georgia fiddlers (including his major rival in fiddle contests, FIDDLIN' JOHN CARSON). The Columbia label urged Tanner to form a band because of the increasing popularity of string bands, and so he

Gid Tanner (far left) with Clayton McMichen (2nd fiddle), Riley Puckett (guitar), and Land Norris (banjo), c. 1928, from a Columbia Records catalog advertisement. Photo: University of North Carolina, Southern Historical Collection, Southern Folklife Collection, University Archives

invited the younger Georgia fiddler Clayton McMichen to join him and Puckett, along with banjoist Land Norris (who can just barely be heard on their recordings).

McMichen looked down his nose at the stage antics and crude style of Tanner. Influenced by the jazz and pop music of the 1920s, he was intent on making The Skillet Lickers a more modern band. As the band gained in popularity, Tanner's role was often reduced to occasional falsetto vocals; McMichen took the fiddle lead, and brought in a second fiddler, a young Georgian named Lowe Stokes, to play harmony. Sometimes McMichen, Stokes, and Tanner all played, foreshadowing the harmony fiddles of later BLUEGRASS recordings. In contrast to other string bands, the BANJO was always kept discreetly in the background, perhaps reflecting McMichen's feeling that the instrument was old-fashioned and not appropriate for his more modern, hard-driving music.

Puckett was the lead vocalist of the band; his rich baritone voice was perfectly suited to the sentimental and old-time dance songs that the group performed. His voice was smoother than those of most country singers of the day, and it carried well on the primitive recording technology used at the time. He was also famous in his day as a guitarist, introducing sometimes wildly erratic bass runs that influenced guitarists from Maybelle Carter of THE CARTER FAMILY to DOC WATSON. Puckett went on to be a minor solo star, and is said to have been the first country vocalist to use YODELING on a record, although he never made it his trademark as JIMMIE RODGERS did.

The high energy of The Skillet Lickers was in marked contrast to Columbia's other big successful string band, The North Carolina Ramblers, led by banjoist CHARLIE POOLE. Their sedate, almost deadpan style was the exact opposite of the exuberant, hell-fire energy of the Georgia band. The Skillet Lickers' sound was emulated by many of the old-time revivalists of the 1970s, including THE HIGHWOODS STRING BAND, as well as The Plank Road String Band and many others.

McMichen left the band in the early 1930s, and the great days of the original Skillet Lickers ended. Tanner continued to use the name with various supporting musicians, including his son Gordon on fiddle. McMichen formed his Georgia Wildcats, a band that recorded pop and jazz as well as country, foreshadowing the WESTERN SWING movement later in the decade. He relocated to Kentucky, where he continued to perform until the early 1950s, when he retired from music making, although he made one appearance during the FOLK-REVIVAL of the 1960s at the Newport Folk Festival.

The Skillet Lickers served as a model for several old-time revival bands, most notably The Highwoods String Band, who adopted their twin lead-fiddle sound and raucous performance style. In turn many others emulated the Highwoods sound, so that The Skillet Lickers' style lived on through the 1990s.

Select Discography

Complete Recordings in Chronological Order, Vols. 1–6, Document 8056–8061. Everything the band recorded between 1926 and 1934. Includes fiddle tunes, songs, and their famous extended group skits. The earlier material is the strongest, but there's much to enjoy on each disc.

SKINNER, JIMMIE (b. Blue Lick, Ky., April 27, 1909–October 28, 1979)

Skinner was a well-known country tunesmith who ran a mail-order country music record business and several small labels out of his Cincinnati, Ohio, home in the mid-to-late 1970s.

Working as a deejay through the 1940s and early 1950s, Skinner had some minor success as a songwriter, beginning with 1941's "Doin' My Time." By the early 1950s he was working out of Knoxville, Tennessee, and his songs were becoming increasingly popular, particularly among BLUEGRASS and more traditional country musicians. JIMMY MARTIN had a mid-1950s hit with Skinner's HONKY-TONK classic "You Don't Know My Mind." At the same time Skinner signed with Mercury Records and had his sole Top 10 hits as a performer in 1957 with "I Found My Girl in the USA" and "Dark Hollow," which has become a bluegrass standard. Although he continued to record through the 1970s for various labels from Decca to Starday and King to his own Vetco, he had little success as a performer. He formed Jimmie Skinner Music in the early 1970s, selling his own and other traditional country records by mail order, and then gave up his business to relocate to the Nashville area. He died soon after, in 1979, following a heart attack in his Hendersonville, Tennessee, home.

Select Discography

Twenty-two Greatest Hits, Deluxe 7814. Cassette-only reissue of Starday/King recordings.

SKYLINE (c. 1982–1992: Tony Trischka [bnj]; Dede Wyland [gtr, voc]; Danny Weiss [gtr, voc]; Barry Mitterhoff [mdln, voc]; Larry Cohen [elec b, voc])

Skyline was an early-1980s New York-based BLUEGRASS band led by BANJO whiz TONY TRISCHKA and his wife, Dede Wyland. They combined progressive instrumentals with pop-country songs, making for an odd musical marriage.

Weiss and Wyland were smooth vocalists who combined folky leanings with a love for the newer country-esque songs created in the 1970s and 1980s. Trischka, ever the spacey banjo noodler, and Mitterhoff (a founding member of New Jersey's Bottle Hill Boys) were both enmeshed in progressive, far-out picking, so that the group's accompaniments were often skittish and disjointed, seemingly at odds with the pop-country flavorings of the songs. Cohen's electric bass playing was often innovative, and he was responsible for many of the group's progressive arrangements. But, on the whole, it must be said that this was one conglomeration that should have gone either one way or the other, becoming a COUNTRY-ROCK band with drums and synthesizers to accommodate the vocalists, or a spacey newgrass outfit, to accommodate the banjo and MANDOLIN parts. However, the group remained somewhere in between, enjoying success on the folk and bluegrass circuits but never breaking out to a wider audience.

Wyland left in 1988, and was replaced briefly by Rachel Kalem. The group died in the early 1990s. Mitterhoff, Weiss, and Cohen continued to perform together as a trio, under the name Silk City, through the 1990s.

Select Discography

Ticket Back: Retrospective 1981–89, Flying Fish 664. Compilation of tracks from their original albums.

SMECK, ROY (b. Reading, Pa., February 6, 1900–April 5, 1994)

Smeck was a fleet-fingered multiple instrumentalist who recorded a slew of novelty instrumentals in the 1920s and 1930s as well as backing country and pop artists. He was particularly well known for his guitar instruction books and his "Hawaiian" style of playing that was quite influential on country steel-guitar players.

Raised in New York, Smeck showed an early talent on a plethora of stringed instruments. He worked on the RKO (Radio Keith Orpheum) circuit in the city, and also appeared in early Vitaphone shorts produced by Warner Brothers to promote talking pictures. He melded a number of influences in his playing, including the jazz single-note picking of guitarist Eddie Lang, the Hawaiian slide work of early recording star Sol Hoopi, and the high-energy tenor banjo work of jazz/novelty musician Harry Reiser.

Besides making solo recordings, Smeck worked as an accompanist on slide and regular guitar for country performers VERNON DALHART and CARSON ROBISON, and sessioned with jazz and dance bands. He led his own group, The Vita Trio, through the 1930s, usually playing slide guitar on instrumental versions of pop numbers. Smeck also issued a seemingly endless stream of instruction books, so-called five-minute methods for guitar, Hawaiian-style playing, ukulele, and tenor banjo, which were sold through mail-order

houses and music shops, influencing countless musicians.

Smeck continued to produce recordings into the 1960s, often playing ukulele on heavily produced sessions for Kapp, ABC-Paramount, and other labels. In the mid-1970s, blues reissue label Yazoo inspired a new round of Smeckomania by reissuing some of his classic 78 recordings, wowing another generation of BLUEGRASS, blues, and jazz pickers.

Although much of Smeck's work is marred by a hot-shot, novelty approach, his truly awesome picking powers are still dazzling fledgling stringbenders today. His masterful handling of the slide guitar, cleanly picking out notes and chords, helped popularize the instrument beyond the strict Hawaiian repertoire featured on many other recordings. He showed how the instrument could be used to take a lead melody part on pop songs, undoubtedly influencing the great WESTERN SWING steel guitarists like BOB DUNN and LEON MCAULIFFE.

Select Discography

Plays Hawaiian Guitar, Banjo, Ukulele and Guitar, 1926–1949, Yazoo 1052. CD reissue of great early sides emphasizing his string wizardry.

SMITH, ARTHUR "GUITAR BOOGIE" (b. Clinton, S.C., April 1, 1921)

Smith was an influential guitarist who was influenced by the single-string jazz work of the legendary French gypsy musician Django Reinhardt. His nickname is drawn from his most famous composition, and is used to distinguish him from FIDDLIN' ARTHUR SMITH.

An adept player on BANJO, MANDOLIN, and GUITAR, Smith was already performing as a teenager in South Carolina, landing his own radio show out of Spartanburg before World War II and recording for Bluebird. While serving in the Navy during the war, he was stationed near Washington, D.C., where he developed his famous instrumental "Guitar Boogie," first issued on the tiny Super Disc label in 1946 and a nationwide hit after it was acquired by MGM in 1947. Recorded on an acoustic guitar with just bass and rhythm guitar accompaniment, the piece was widely influential on country pickers and the nascent ROCKABILLY players, being covered twelve years later by The Virtues as "Guitar Boogie Shuffle."

In the 1950s Smith had his own TV program out of Charlotte, North Carolina, and continued to broadcast for over a decade. He made some excellent jazz-flavored recordings for MGM on guitar and mandolin. As a novelty he cut a piece he composed that he called "Feuding Banjos," featuring alternating parts for four-string (or tenor) banjo, played by Smith, and FIVE-STRING BANJO, played by Don Reno. This piece was covered in the early 1970s as "Dueling Banjos" (now with banjo and guitar) by Eric Weissberg and Marshall Brickman, and became a massive hit after it was used in the film *Deliverance*. Smith had to fight in court to be given composer's credit (and royalties) for this later recording.

Smith's 1960s recordings suffered from a clutter of strings, vocal choruses, and even burbling organ. He more or less retired by the end of the decade, and in the early 1980s was organizing fishing shows in North Carolina.

Select Discography

Here Comes the Boogie Man, Jasmine 3502. Compilation of late-1940s radio transcriptions, including many of his hits.

SMITH, CAL (b. Calvin Grant Shofner, Gans, Okla., April 7, 1932)

An alumnus of the ERNEST TUBB band, Smith had some success from the late 1960s through the mid-1970s, but his career has more or less fizzled out since then.

Born in Oklahoma, Smith was raised in suburban San Francisco, getting his first regular exposure as a performer on the San Jose-based *California Hayride* program in the early 1950s. He worked sporadically through the decade as a deejay and performer, finally hooking up with Ernest Tubb in the early 1960s, joining the famous Texas Troubadours as a vocalist and rhythm guitarist. Thanks to Tubb's recommendation, he was signed by Kapp Records, scoring a minor hit in 1967 with "Drinking Champagne," and began working as an opening act for bigger-name stars on the road. From 1972 to 1975 he had several big country hits, including "I've Found Someone of My Own," the #1 "The Lord Knows I'm Drinking," and a cover of Don Wayne's "Country Bumpkin." His last charting hit was "I Just Came Home to Count the Memories" in 1977. Soon after, he was dropped by MCA (which had taken over the Kapp/Decca catalog in the early 1970s), and occasionally recorded for smaller labels, including remakes of his early hits. He has since faded into the background.

Select Discography

Cal Smith, First Generation 103. Budget hits compilation.

SMITH, CARL (b. Maynardville, Tenn., March 15, 1927)

Carl Smith was an influential country singer of the 1950s and 1960s who modernized the HONKY-TONK sound of HANK WILLIAMS for another generation.

Smith came from the town that gave country music ROY ACUFF, and his sound originally was heavily influenced by the elder musician, as well as by EDDY ARNOLD. He got his first break on radio station WROL in Knoxville after World War II, and then was hired for the WSM morning show in Nashville in 1950. This led to a contract with Columbia Records, and his first hit with 1951's "Let's Live a Little." Through the 1950s he produced myriad hits, mostly beer-soaked classics like "Loose Talk," "Hey Joe," "Kisses Don't Lie," and "If Teardrops Were Pennies." His mid-1950s band, The Tunesmiths, was a classic unit featuring the steel guitar of Johnny Sibert and the bass-twangy guitar of Sammy Pruett (who had previously played with Hank Williams's Drifting Cowboys). Smith was also one of the first bandleaders to feature drums, which were still controversial in country music; his drummer, BUDDY HARMAN, later became a leading Nashville sessionman.

Smith combined a honky-tonker's attitude with flashy Western garb, and borrowed a few choice songs from the Western repertoire, including BOB WILLS's classic "Time Changes Everything." In 1952 Smith wed June Carter, and performed with The Carter Sisters and their famous mother, Maybelle. The two produced a daughter, Carlene, who is now a well-known country-rocker (performing under the name CARLENE CARTER).

By the late 1950s Smith had jumped on another big country bandwagon, capitalizing on the popularity of pseudo folk songs sung in a melodramatic style with his last big hit, 1959's "Ten Thousand Drums," telling a Revolutionary War story in all its guts and glory. In 1957 he married his second wife, Goldie Hill (who also had a minor career as a country singer), and settled down on a large horse farm. Although he continued to record for Columbia through 1974, and then made some more recordings for the smaller Hickory label in the mid-1970s, he never achieved the chart success he had had in the 1950s, and eventually he gave up performing to focus on his home life.

Select Discography

The Essential, 1950–1956, Columbia/Legacy 47996. His best recordings.

SMITH, CONNIE (b. Constance June Meador, Elkhart, Ind., August 14, 1941)

Connie Smith was one of the great throbbin', sobbin' singers of the 1960s who gave it all up for Jesus, her personal heartache mirrored in her choice of material.

Born to an abusive father of a large family (she was one of thirteen siblings), Smith had a troubled young life that culminated in a nervous breakdown at the end

Connie Smith and her daughter, Plastic Rose, c. mid-1970s. Photo: Raeanne Rubenstein

paraded before conventions of usually all-male deejays and music executives for their "enjoyment") led Smith to become increasingly unhappy with her career. In 1972 she wed for a third time, and began incorporating more GOSPEL into her act; she and her husband became evangelists, and by the turn of the decade Smith had retired from performing, except for her weekly spot on the *Grand Ole Opry*, where she continued to share her gospel fervor.

Through the 1980s and the 1990s Smith continued to appear regularly on the *Opry*. From the mid-1980s through the mid-1990s she performed only gospel music. In 1997 she wed the much younger new-country performer MARTY STUART. A year later she returned to secular material on an album produced by her new husband, including many songs that they wrote together.

Select Discography

Super Hits, RCA 67491. Anthology of her mid-1960s recordings.
Born to Sing, Bear Family 16368. Four-CD set focusing on her 1960s through early 1970s recordings.
Connie Smith, Warners 47033. 1998 return to secular music, produced by Marty Stuart.

SMITH, FIDDLIN' ARTHUR (b. Bold Springs, Tenn., April 10, 1898–February 28, 1971)

Not to be confused with his younger, guitar-picking namesake, Fiddlin' Arthur Smith was one of the first modern-styled fiddlers who brought jazz and swing influences to traditional country playing. He was also a smooth vocalist, and his recordings were well loved and influential throughout the old-time music community of the South.

Smith was a railroad worker who, in the early 1930s, joined with the McGee Brothers, early GRAND OLE OPRY stars who had previously worked with UNCLE DAVE MACON. They formed a trio, recording throughout the 1930s and performing over Nashville's powerful WSM. Smith's supersmooth fiddling and crooning vocals made them immediately popular. Working with THE DELMORE BROTHERS, Smith formed a group called the Dixieliners around this time. One of their best-selling recordings is the oft-covered "More Pretty Girls Than One," issued in 1936.

After World War II, Smith relocated to the West Coast, where he worked in low-budget Westerns and accompanied many country artists on tour and recordings. In the early 1960s, thanks to the FOLK REVIVAL, The McGee Brothers were rediscovered and recorded again with Smith, issuing two albums on the Folkways label that were produced by MIKE SEEGER. They also appeared at folk and BLUEGRASS festivals.

of her teenage years. By 1963 she had settled into being a rural housewife when she won a talent contest in Ohio, attracting the attention of GRAND OLE OPRY star BILL ANDERSON, who recommended her to RCA. She made her first recordings under the guidance of producer Bob Ferguson in 1964, including her first hit, "Once a Day," an Anderson-crafted WEEPER.

Through the 1960s and early 1970s Smith was idolized as a pretty-as-a-picture "young lady" who had the ability to pour her heart out through her vocal cords. She made a specialty of singing songs of loneliness and desolation, scoring hits from 1966's "The Hurtin's All Over (Me)" through 1972's "Just for What I Am." She also toured widely with many other country stars, and appeared in a couple of the hilariously bad country flicks of the day, including *Road to Nashville, Las Vegas Hillbillies*, and *Second Fiddle to a Steel Guitar*.

Two failed marriages and a general dissatisfaction with the marketing of female country stars (who were

Smith transformed old-time fiddling, using standard violin tuning (many old-timers used unusual, modal tunings), smoothing out the melody lines, and incorporating elements drawn directly from jazz (such as blue notes and syncopation). He was an enormous influence on contest or show fiddling, particularly as practiced in Texas and the West; he was perhaps the first fiddler to add clean playing, speed, and flash to his instrumental recordings. His vocal style was similarly modern, again influencing a move away from the "backwoods and hollers" sound of older country stars.

SMITH, SAMMI (b. Jewel Fay S., Orange, Calif., August 5, 1943)

Sammi Smith is a soulful, smoky-voiced singer best known for her (at the time shocking) cover of "Help Me Make It Through the Night" in 1971.

Although born in California, Smith was raised in Oklahoma, where she began performing in local clubs when she was twelve years old. As a teen she was heard by Marshall Grant, who was then bassist for JOHNNY CASH in his famous Tennessee Three group. Grant recommended that she come to Nashville, where he introduced her to Cash's label, Columbia, who signed her in the mid-1960s.

After scoring some minor hits for Columbia, including "So Long, Charlie Brown" in 1968 and "Brownsville Lumberyard" a year later, she was dropped by the big label and signed by smaller Mega Records. Her first single, "He's Everywhere," was a moderate hit, but it was her second release, a cover of KRIS KRISTOFFERSON's controversial "Help Me Make It Through the Night," that really set her career ablaze. At the time the thought of a woman inviting her lover to spend the night (particularly in country music circles) was unbelievably risky, but the risk paid off in huge sales.

Smith spent the 1970s label-hopping, scoring minor successes with a number of new songs and covers, mostly sung in the back-room, R&B-colored style that she had perfected. Most memorable was her 1975 recording of "Today I Started Loving You Again"; 1979 brought her last chart hit, "What a Lie." Although her recordings were good, none got higher than the Top 20, and by the early 1980s she was labelless and more or less forgotten by the Music City establishment.

Select Discography

Best of: Help Me Make it Through the Night, Varese 5574. Compilation of her 1970s hits.

SNOW, HANK (b. Clarence Eugene S., Liverpool, Nova Scotia, May 9, 1914–December 19, 1999)

Snow, Canada's greatest country singer, was bitten early on by the country-music bug after hearing the recordings of JIMMIE RODGERS. He composed some classic country songs, and his smooth, clean vocalizing helped popularize the music for a wide audience.

Snow left home when he was twelve to take a job as a cabin boy on a freighter. An early love of Jimmie Rodgers and American COWBOY legends led him to take up the GUITAR, and he was soon a proficient performer, getting his first break at age nineteen when he was hired by the local radio station. He was signed by RCA in Canada in 1936, recording two of his own songs that were closely modeled after Rodgers's recordings. He nicknamed himself "The Yodeling Ranger," combining Rodgers's famous YODELING persona with that of the heroic Royal Canadian Mounted Police; later he changed his nickname to "The Singing Ranger," in recognition of the end of the yodeling fad. Through the 1930s he continued to work in Canada, gaining the attention of American country performers who passed through the local clubs.

One of these performers, ERNEST TUBB, convinced THE GRAND OLE OPRY to hire Snow in 1950. Meanwhile, his 1949 recording of the sentimental "Marriage Vow" was a minor hit, followed by his classic "I'm Movin' On" and "Golden Rocket" in 1950, both million-sellers. Snow produced myriad hits through the 1950s for RCA, including "Rhumba Boogie," "I Don't Hurt Anymore," "A Fool Such as I" (covered in an up-tempo version by ELVIS PRESLEY), "Ninety Miles an Hour (Down a Dead-end Street)," and many more. Snow's recordings were remarkably simple productions, highlighting his fine singing voice that had equal appeal to mainstream and country audiences. In 1953 he was a prime mover behind establishing a Jimmie Rodgers Memorial Day in the singer's hometown of Meridian, Mississippi, thus acknowledging his considerable debt to the earlier singer. Toward the end of the decade he began recording theme albums, particularly of RAILROAD SONGS (again reflecting his love of the songs of Jimmie Rodgers), although many of these recordings were marred by the typical NASHVILLE SOUND productions of the era.

Although Snow continued to work through the 1960s, 1970s, and 1980s, his last big hit was 1962's "I've Been Everywhere," a novelty song featuring a jaw-breaking list of towns to which Snow had traveled. He last made the charts in 1973 with "Hello, Love" (later the theme song of *A Prairie Home Companion's* Garrison Keillor). A staunch traditionalist, Snow became increasingly conservative as time went by, taking to wearing rhinestone-encrusted suits and becoming somewhat of a country cliché. Even in the 1950s he had recorded some teeth-gnashing solo recitation discs, usually telling stories of "Old Doc Brown" or some other crusty character, complete with swelling choruses oohing gently in the background. Still, he remained a popular performer on the *Opry* and on tour, despite his lack of recording success. Snow also became involved in raising money for abused children, a cause close to his heart because he had been abused as a youth.

In 1981 RCA dropped the singer from its roster after a distinguished forty-five-year recording career, reflecting the bottom-line mentality of today's recording executives and their lack of understanding of or appreciation for country's history. Snow was understandably enraged by RCA's move, and RCA, in retaliation, kept his recordings unavailable domestically for many years, although by the late 1980s they had relented.

In 1994 Snow published his autobiography, *The Hank Snow Story*. He suffered from a major respiratory infection in 1997, but recovered and returned to limited performing. He died of heart failure in 1999.

Snow's son, appropriately named Jimmie Rodgers Snow, had a few minor country hits before becoming a full-time evangelist.

Select Discography

Essential, RCA 66931. Twenty of his better-known recordings for the label. If this doesn't satisfy your cravings, check out Bear Family's four multidisc sets of *everything* Snow recorded for RCA.

SOCIAL COMMENTARY AND POLITICS

Country performers and songwriters have commented on politics, current events, and social trends since the earliest days of country recording. And, despite the cliché that all country songs focus on "mother, trucks, and prison," the topics addressed by these songs range from religion to fashion to fear of atomic annihilation. While country performers are often branded as "conservative," these songs have ranged across the political spectrum, sometimes taking a humorous approach to serious issues.

The folk tradition has a long history of songs that comment on local events, from murders to train wrecks. Spreading the news through songs—sometimes originally printed as poems in local newspapers, on ballad sheets, or in songbooks—had a long tradition in the South, and many "folk" songs have been traced to these sources and proven to be based on real events. "The Wreck of the Old 97" was one of the first great country hits, inspiring a slew of RAILROAD SONGS. Floods, fires, and other natural disasters have long been favorite country topics; the famous Johnstown, Pennsylvania, flood of 1889 is long forgotten as a historical event, but songs about the flood continued to be recorded well into the 1930s, and again during the FOLK REVIVAL of the 1960s. Early country recording artist ERNEST STONEMAN was among those who recorded songs about newsworthy events, such as the sinking of the *Titanic* and a famous train wreck on

the C&O line. Stoneman observed the fascination of country listeners with songs based on true events: "Any song with a story will go to the people's hearts because they love stories. They love stories of tragedy, a wreck, or something."

Early country stars often recorded topical material among the fiddle tunes and traditional and popular songs. FIDDLIN' JOHN CARSON commented on the plight of rural farmers in "Taxes on the Farmer Feeds Them All," a popular, late nineteenth-century song that showed how merchants and middlemen profited from the farmer's hard work. Carson was also employed by Eugene Talmadge to draw crowds when Talmadge was campaigning for governor of Georgia. (Carson was rewarded with a job as an elevator operator at the state capitol.) Many other country performers would work the stump circuit, and politicians themselves were not too proud to pick up a fiddle to show their country roots. (Notably, Senator Robert Byrd of West Virginia cut an album of fiddle tunes in the 1970s.)

Often taking a more humorous approach to social commentary—although with a decidedly pointed message—was UNCLE DAVE MACON, the GRAND OLE OPRY star and recording artist. The longtime owner of a mule-and-wagon hauling and carting business, Macon often attacked the newly introduced automobile in his songs. He also took on corruption in Tennessee's government ("Tennessee Gravy Train") and everything from women's clothing styles to the election of Herbert Hoover (in the song "In and Around Nashville"). A slightly more deadpan approach was taken by fiddler/songwriter BLIND ALFRED REED. His most (in)famous song, "Why Do You Bob Your Hair, Girls (You Know It Is a Sin)," is either a tongue-in-cheek satire of the rage for bobbed hair or a deadly serious reaction to women's growing freedom. Part of the fascination of Reed's recording is that it is difficult to determine from his delivery of the lyrics what *he* believes—which probably has contributed to its popularity among folk revivalists who definitely are not alarmed by women's freer hairstyles.

The Depression brought forth a slew of topical songs, mainly focusing on the plight of the hungry and unemployed. THE CARTER FAMILY responded with a call for deeper religious feeling in their famous "No Depression in Heaven." Tramps and hoboes became new song heroes, most notably in "Tramp on the Street," based on a nineteenth-century poem and first recorded in 1936 by Grady and Hazel Cole. Tramp troubadour HAYWIRE MAC (Harry McClintock) popularized "Big Rock Candy Mountain" as a kind of dream to escape from the suffering of the Depression.

SINGER/SONGWRITER BOB MILLER gained fame with his recording of "Eleven Cent Cotton and Forty Cent Meat," which commented on the drop in the price of cotton from 11 cents a pound (hardly a huge amount) to 5 cents, asking pithily, "Five cent cotton and 40 cent meat/How in the hell can a poor man eat?" Uncle Dave Macon returned with "All I've Got's Gone," a song drenched in black humor that contrasts the suffering of the poor with the relative ease of the rich during the 1930s. Songwriter BILL COX extolled the virtues of government programs in his "N.R.A. Blues" and "Franklin Roosevelt's Back Again," and even the usually nonpolitical ALLEN BROTHERS praised Roosevelt in their "New Deal Blues." Early in his career ROY ACUFF reacted to plans for Social Security legislation in the humorous "Old Age Pension Check," envisioning a newly rejuvenated older population enjoying the high life thanks to their new income.

The growing industrialization of the South inspired songs about the cotton mills and coal mines. THE DIXON BROTHERS were best remembered for their critique of life in the mills, "Weave Room Blues." Songwriter Dave McCarn, who worked in the mills from his early adolescence, combined jazzy guitar work and hot melodies for his protest songs, notably "Poor Man, Rich Man" and "Cotton Mill Colic," both revived during the folk and old-time music revivals beginning in the 1960s. Disasters and labor unrest in the coal mines inspired many songs. As early as the late 1920s, VERNON DALHART was recording songs like "The Dream of the Miner's Child"; though admittedly rather sentimental, songs like this did bring home the fact that coal mining was a dangerous and often deadly occupation. Although she was not a commercial recording artist, perhaps the greatest voice of the suffering miners was AUNT MOLLY JACKSON, who penned a series of searing calls for better conditions in the mines, including "I Love Coal Miners, I Do" and her anthemic "Join the C.I.O."

WOODY GUTHRIE was not really a country star; his success came among the urban, FOLK-REVIVAL audience beginning in the late 1930s. However, his landmark collection, *Dust Bowl Ballads*, dramatized the plight of the displaced Okies who fled the ravages of the dust storms to settle in California. The dream of a better life in "sun-filled" California turned out to be something of a cruel myth, as thousands of Southwesterners came to the Los Angeles area and often ended up living in makeshift cities of tarpaper shacks and sewer pipes. Doyle Odell's 1949 WESTERN-SWING-flavored "Dear Okie" captured the ironic gap between the dream and reality in its description of "spouting orange juice fountains" and other supposed comforts that await the refugees.

Changes in religion—particularly the breakdown of "old-time" faith, the closing of country churches (as country folks migrated to Northern cities), and the lack of religious feeling among the younger generation—were often commented on in country songs.

Songs like THE BAILES BROTHERS' "Dust on the Bible" were sharp critiques of what many viewed as a decline in religious feeling. Even seemingly purely religious numbers like "What Would You Give (in Exchange)?," popularized by The Monroe Brothers, implicitly criticize contemporary life. Songs like these called for a return to simpler values. They reflected the anxiety of country folk who moved to the bigger cities; feeling like "rubes" among the "city slickers," they often felt that they were looked down on, if not taken advantage of, by their upscale neighbors. Lowe Stokes's "Wagon Yard," recorded about 1930, was one humorous reflection of this change, pithily warning: "Don't monkey with them city ducks, you'll find them slick as lard/Just go and get you a half a pint, and stay in the wagon yard."

World War II brought a slew of patriotic songs inspired by the battle against Nazi Germany and its allies. An early huge hit was ELTON BRITT's 1942 recording of "There's a Star-Spangled Banner Waving Somewhere" (composed by Bob Miller), which has as its protagonist a "mountain boy" who is "crippled," yet longs to join the roster of American heroes by fighting in the war. The war would bring forth more jingoistic expressions (Carson J. Robison's "We're Gonna Have to Slap the Dirty Little Jap" being among the more offensive), along with a wide range of songs from the sentimental (ERNEST TUBB's "Mother's Prayer") to the topical (BOB WILLS's "Stars and Stripes on Iwo Jima").

The postwar era was one of new anxieties, from fears of atomic attack to Communist infiltration of the United States. THE LOUVIN BROTHERS memorably commented on fears of the newly unleashed power of the atom in their "Are You Ready for That Great Atomic Power?" The song had a predictable moral, urging listeners to prepare for the day they would be swept off to heaven when "the fire rains from on high." The dangers of communism were most famously portrayed in RED RIVER DAVE MCENERY's "The Red Deck of Cards," covered by many other country artists and even pop singer (later game-show host) Wink Martindale (it was based on T. TEXAS TYLER's earlier hit, "The Deck of Cards"). Fear of communism was linked with fear of atheism in "They Locked God Outside the Iron Curtain," recorded by JIM EANES and "LITTLE" JIMMY DICKENS, among others.

The growth of HONKY-TONKS led to several songs commenting on the rise of the "honky-tonk angel," a loose woman who (supposedly) lured married men to their doom. HANK THOMPSON famously set the stage with his "Wild Side of Life," inspiring KITTY WELLS's famous answer song, "It Wasn't God Who Made Honky-Tonk Angels," chastising men for, in essence, creating the situation that gave rise to these women. "She's More to Be Pitied Than Scolded," popularized by THE STANLEY BROTHERS, among others, took something of a middle ground, expressing concern for the plight of the "fallen" woman.

During the 1960s and early 1970s social protest and the Vietnam War were hot topics, as was the growing women's liberation movement. MERLE HAGGARD's "Okie from Muskogee" will always stand as a landmark of the era, a classic song commenting on the clash of "redneck" and "hippie" cultures. Nonetheless, not all country songwriters were pro-war; in 1966 Charlie Moore and Bill Napier recorded "Is This a Useless War?," and THE WILBURN BROTHERS followed a few years later with "The War Keeps Dragging On." ROGER MILLER's "Private John Q." humorously looked at the fears of a typical young man who was hardly anxious to spend a few years overseas serving his country. Similarly, while TAMMY WYNETTE's "Stand By Your Man" is often cited as an antifeminist battle cry, LORETTA LYNN's "The Pill" and "Don't Come Home A-Drinkin' (with Lovin' on Your Mind)" espoused a more feisty, female-centered point of view.

The 1980s and 1990s continued to see country hits on current topics. JOHNNY PAYCHECK's "Take This Job and Shove It" addresses the frustration of the poorly paid laboring man; the title became something of a rallying cry for every disaffected worker. It in turn inspired "Take Your Oil and Shove It" following the Iranian hostage ordeal, and countless other homages and parodies. The hostages' release—and the election of Ronald Reagan—inspired CHARLIE DANIELS's patriotic "In America" (which he revived in the autumn of 2001, following the World Trade Center/Pentagon attacks). LEE GREENWOOD captured the mood of the Reagan era in another generic America-first ballad, "God Bless the U.S.A.," which has reappeared on the charts whenever the country has faced crises through the 1990s and early 2000s. The war with Iraq inspired AARON TIPPIN's "You've Got to Stand for Something," which also was revived in the wake of the terrorist attacks in 2001. ALAN JACKSON was among the first to memorialize this event with his "Where Were You (When the World Stopped Turning)?"

As country has drawn on singers and songwriters from folk, pop, and other styles, more liberal viewpoints have been introduced into the music, although not always consistently. GARTH BROOKS has represented both ends of the political spectrum; his "The Thunder Rolls" graphically attacked spousal abuse, and "We Shall Be Free" called for universal brotherhood and understanding. However, he followed this freedom anthem with the conservative "American Honky-Tonk Bar Association," perhaps as a nod to his core audience. Similarly, in the mid-to-late 1990s MARTINA MCBRIDE recorded a series of more socially conscious (and seemingly liberal) songs, including "Love's the Only House," but did not enjoy great success until early 2000, when she returned to more traditional country fare.

"Redneck values" have long been popular among the country audience, who are unashamed by allusions to hearth, home, and religion (as well as drinkin', cheatin', and fightin'). Alan Jackson tapped into this popular sentiment with his humorous 2001 release, "It's Alright to Be a Redneck." As with many past country songs, it's difficult to say how seriously we're meant to take this ode to fishing and boozing, which again probably makes it more appealing to both sides of the audience.

SONS OF THE PIONEERS (c. 1934–late 1980s; original members: Leonard Slye [aka Roy Rogers]; Bob Nolan; Tim Spencer; Karl Farr; Hugh Farr; and Lloyd Perryman)

One of the most famous Western COWBOY-flavored vocal groups, The Sons of the Pioneers soldiered on for almost six decades with varying personnel, their most influential recordings coming from the late 1930s through the early 1950s. They virtually invented the Hollywoodized image of the cowboy singer who roamed the prairies with a song never far from his lips.

Originally formed as The Pioneer Trio with Slye, Nolan, and Spencer, they became The Sons of the Pioneers around 1934 in southern California with the addition of the talented Farr Brothers on GUITAR and violin. With a swinging, jazzy sound and pop-flavored three-part harmonies, the Pioneers were an immediate sensation on stage and screen. Lead vocalist Slye became better known as ROY ROGERS, going solo by 1937 as a recording artist and actor; the core group of Nolan, Spencer, and the Farrs stuck together through the early 1950s with various additional members. Nolan was a virtual one-man hitmaking machine, creating such classic cowboy tonsil-twisters as "Cool Water," the band's unofficial theme song; "Tumbling Tumbleweeds"; and the immortal "A Cowboy Has to Sing." Spencer was no laggard in the song-making department, turning out "Cigarettes, Whiskey, and Wild Women," "Careless Kisses," and "Room Full of Roses." The Sons combined a sanitized Western image with wide smiles, even wider-brimmed hats, and silky harmonies that were straight from the Rainbow Room. They also popularized smooth, harmonized yodeling, and performed cowboy-type rope tricks and other novelties in their stage show.

The group recorded for Decca and Columbia before World War II, and then began a long association with RCA Victor, from the early 1940s through the late 1960s. During their first RCA years, they recorded with many famous Nashville sidemen, including guitarist CHET ATKINS and legendary PEDAL STEEL GUITARISTS Joaquin Murphey and Noel Boggs, along with the talented Farr brothers. By the early 1950s RCA was covering its bases by having the Sons record with such pop singers as Perry Como, The Fontaine Sisters, and The Three Sons; on a handful of sides, they even accompanied opera superstar Ezio Pinza for some of the most surreal arias-under-the-Western-skies you'll ever hear.

By the mid-1950s the powerhouse vocal/songwriting team of Nolan and Spencer were gone, but the group had acquired a life of its own. By adding new vocalists and musicians as the years went by, they carefully re-created their past hits in a patented style. Unlike their early-1950s recordings, in which RCA sought to modernize their style, their later recordings through the end of the 1960s pretty much emphasized the pure cowboy-meets-cocktail lounge style, slicked up a bit but none the worse for wear. Spencer died in 1974 and Nolan died six years later, but the Pioneers went on, performing in Las Vegas in the winter and in BRANSON, MISSOURI, in the summer as recently as the late 1980s.

Select Discography

Country Music Hall of Fame, MCA 10090. Covers their best recordings from 1934 to 1941.
Columbia Historic Edition, Columbia 37439. Drawn from a single, very fine 1937 session for the budget ARC label.

SONS OF THE SAN JOAQUIN (c. 1988–present: Joe Hannah; Jack Hannah; and Lon Hannah)

These Sons are nouveau COWBOY harmonizers who tip their ten-gallon hats in the direction of the original SONS OF THE PIONEERS, whose style and repertoire they have emulated.

During the Depression the Hannah family, who were Missouri farmers, headed west for better job opportunities in the foothills of the Sierra Nevada. Jack and Joe's dad settled the family on a cattle ranch, and after hours would sing with his sons his favorite music, the slick Western cowboy songs of the hit groups of the day, including The Sons of the Pioneers. Eventually the trio performed locally with some success, although Jack and Joe didn't think of making music a career. Instead both ended up as schoolteachers, although they continued to sing on an amateur basis in local musical theater and opera productions, as well as in church.

Meanwhile, Joe settled down and had his own family, including a son named Lon who showed an interest in vocalizing. Although he, too, became a schoolteacher, Lon performed locally on an amateur level, as well as in the Bennett Consort, a jazzy scat-singing group modeled after the popular Manhattan Transfer.

In the mid-1980s Joe and Jack decided to return to performing the cowboy music of their youth, and in-

vited Lon to join their group. By 1989 they had won the attention of nouveau country cowfellow MICHAEL MARTIN MURPHEY, who asked them to provide backup vocals on his album *Cowboy Songs*, and also produced their debut album for Warner Western records. By 1992 all three had retired from teaching to take up singing full-time. Their second album, *Songs of the Silver Screen*, is a pure homage to the great cowboy acts of the 1930s, 1940s, and 1950s. In 1997 they moved to the smaller Shanachie label.

Like their fellow cowboy revivalists RIDERS IN THE SKY, this group's carbon copy of old-style cowboy music is a little bit eerie. The line between homage and parody can be dangerously razor-thin. One also wonders if the audience comes to admire the music or to laugh at it, particularly when you consider that commercial cowboy music, even in its original incarnation, was a kitschy reflection of the real music of the West. Still, in these times of endless nostalgia, there is room for groups like this one who seamlessly reproduce a past musical style.

Select Discography

A Cowboy Has to Sing, Warner Bros. 26935.

SOVINE, RED (b. Woodrow Wilson S., Charleston, W. Va., July 17, 1918–April 4, 1980)

Sovine was a 1950s honky-tonker who later gained fame thanks to his "touching" country recitations, culminating in the million-seller "Teddy Bear," which should win an award as an all-time hanky soaker.

Raised in West Virginia, Red had his first professional job on his hometown radio station, playing with Jim Pike's Carolina Tar Heels in the mid-1930s; later he performed on radio out of Wheeling. After World War II he formed his first band, The Echo Valley Boys. They were hired in 1949 to replace HANK WILLIAMS on the prestigious LOUISIANA HAYRIDE program, where they remained until 1954. Red also took over Hank's duties as "The Old Syrup Sopper," promoting Johnny Fair syrup on a daily fifteen-minute show for the same Shreveport radio station.

In Shreveport, Sovine hooked up with WEBB PIERCE, and the two began writing and performing together. Moving to THE GRAND OLE OPRY in 1954, they made their first duet recordings with a hit cover of GEORGE JONES's "Why, Baby, Why" followed by Sovine's first recitation record, "Little Rosa," featuring an "authentic" Italian accent by Sovine that will set your teeth on edge. (Despite its hokey text and horrendous delivery, the record hit #5 on the charts.)

Sovine's recording career took a dip in the late 1950s and early 1960s, although he continued to perform. He reemerged in 1964 on the Starday label with two #1 hits, "Dream House for Sale," and "Giddyup Go." This second record was the first in a new series of recitation records, now on the theme of the lonely life of TRUCK DRIVERS, including 1967's hit "Phantom 309." Another period of semi-obscurity followed, with Sovine hitting the performing road but not recording much. About a decade later, when the CB craze swept the land, Sovine scored his biggest hit ever with "Teddy Bear," which tells the touching story of a crippled youth who communicates with truckers via his CB radio, using the handle (you guessed it) "Teddy Bear."

Sovine last hit the charts in 1980 with "It'll Come Back." In the same year he died—appropriately, for a singer who celebrated life on the road—after suffering a heart attack while driving in Nashville. After his death his fans "demanded" that "Teddy Bear" be rereleased, and the disc sold another half-million copies, proving beyond a shadow of a doubt that you can't keep a good song down.

Select Discography

The Best of, Deluxe 7828. Reissue of his better Starday recordings.
16 Gospel Super Hits, Federal 6553. Starday material aimed at the gospel market.

SPEARS, BILLIE JO (b. B. Jean S., Beaumont, Tex., January 14, 1937)

Spears is a blues-influenced belter who has had a spotty career on the country charts.

Born in Beaumont, she appeared on the popular LOUISIANA HAYRIDE radio program when she was just a teenager, already singing sultry material (she debuted with the slightly risqué "Too Old for Toys, Too Young for Boys"). After graduating from high school she worked as a carhop while pursuing a singing career at night. She was discovered by country songsmith Jack Rhodes, who brought her to Nashville to audition for United Artists Records, but these recordings went nowhere. She switched to Capitol Records and had her first hits, including 1969's "He's Got More Love in His Little Finger" and the #4 country song "Mr. Walker, It's All Over." From the start Spears sounded more like a cocktail lounge torch singer than a country queen, even though her recordings were marketed mainly to a country audience.

Spears was unable to maintain the momentum of her initial hits, and dropped off the charts. In the mid-1970s she returned as a countrified disco queen, recording the racy "Blanket on the Ground," a #1 hit in 1975, followed by a couple more chart-busters, including her 1979 remake of Gloria Gaynor's bass-heavy disco hit "I Will Survive" and a duet with DEL REEVES on "On the Rebound."

In the early 1980s she moved to smaller labels with less success. She remains a popular figure in the European market but is less well known in America. In 1993 she underwent coronary bypass surgery, but continued to perform after her recovery through the 1990s, primarily in Great Britain.

SPEER FAMILY, THE (1920–1967; original members: George Thomas ["Dad"] Speer; Lena Brock ["Mom"] Speer; Pearl Claborn; and Logan Claborn)

One of the first and longest-lived GOSPEL singing families, The Speers performed from the mid-1920s to the mid-1960s in a style that harked back to traditional SHAPE-NOTE harmonies. Their greatest popularity came after World War II, when they became leaders of the New Nashville gospel movement, modernizing their sound to fit in better with country's increasingly middle-of-the-road orientation.

The religious Speers got their start when bass vocalist George Thomas Speer wed the talented pianist and singer Lena Brock in 1920; enlisting the help of his sister and brother-in-law, Pearl and Logan Claborn, to sing alto and tenor, George formed a family gospel quartet. The group made their living selling songbooks in rural churches throughout the mid-South, performing the material so that their audience could hear it and, they hoped, be inspired to buy the books.

By the late 1920s the arduous life of traveling musicians began to wear on the Claborns, and the Speers had begun to produce talented offspring. The children, gradually brought on board to replace their aunt and uncle, eventually included eldest brother Brock, followed by Ben, Rosa Nell, and Mary Tom. By the late 1930s Rosa Nell was showing talent on the piano, so her mother switched to the accordion.

After World War II, with the growth of interest in gospel music in the country-music field, The Speer Family settled in Nashville. Their postwar recordings were highly influential, particularly noteworthy for the powerful vocals of "Mother" Speer on her signature song "I'm Building a Bridge." In the early 1950s the Speer daughters were settling down to form families, so Brock's wife was brought on board, as were the first non-Speer members, who became honorary "Speer sisters." In 1954 the family landed a local TV gospel show, gaining further exposure, and by the late 1950s their recordings were awash in the echoey harmonies that were typical of mainstream country. Until her death in 1967, "Mom" Speer remained the motivating force behind the group. Her powerful vocals, with just a hint of jazzy syncopation, gave the group its characteristic sound.

SPRAGUE, CARL T. (b. near Alvin, Tex., May 10, 1895–February 19, 1979)

Sprague was one of the first singing cowboys; his 1925 Victor recording of "When the Work's All Done This Fall" helped start the COWBOY music craze.

Raised on a ranch in South Texas, Sprague learned most of his cowboy material from a singing uncle. However, he did not intend to pursue a musical career; instead, he attended Texas A&M, studying physical education. After hearing VERNON DALHART's successful recordings of folk songs for Victor, he realized a similar market might exist for the songs he learned as a youth. He traveled to New York and had three sessions for Victor in 1925, 1926, and 1927, recording many songs that would later enter the repertoire of the singing cowboys of the 1930s. However, Sprague never performed as a professional; instead he pursued singing as a hobby while working as an athletic coach at Texas A&M.

During the FOLK REVIVAL of the 1960s, Sprague was "rediscovered" and again performed his cowboy material, recording an album of Western songs for the German Bear Family label in 1972.

Select Discography

Classic Cowboy Songs, Bear Family 15456. 1972 recordings.

STAMPLEY, JOE (b. Springhill, La., June 6, 1943)

Best known as half of the comic country duo Moe and Joe (the other half was singer MOE BANDY), Stampley had a career that moved from rock and pop in the 1950s and 1960s, to COUNTRYPOLITAN in the 1970s, and finally to hard-edged HONKY-TONK in the 1980s.

Raised in northern Louisiana near the Texas and Arkansas borders, Stampley heard country music from his early days, particularly the recordings of his father's favorite star, HANK WILLIAMS. He started playing the piano when he was eight, and was performing locally as a teenager when he caught the attention of MERLE KILGORE, then a local deejay. Kilgore arranged for Stampley's first recordings in a teen-pop mold for Imperial Records, cut in 1957–1958, but they went nowhere. A second session for the Chicago blues label Chess in 1961 was also unsuccessful.

Influenced by the success of ELVIS PRESLEY and JERRY LEE LEWIS, and loving the music of R&B vocal groups like The Miracles and The Impalas, Stampley formed The Uniques, who in 1966 had a regional hit with the R&B-flavored "Not Too Long Ago," written by Stampley and Kilgore. After this success the band faded into obscurity.

In the early 1970s Stampley began writing country songs, which he submitted to Al Gallico of Nashville's Algee Music. Gallico signed on as his manager, and arranged for a contract with Paramount Records; Stampley's first minor country hit was 1971's "Take Time to Know Her," followed by the Top 10 "If You Touch Me (You've Got to Love Me)." Stampley continued to have hits with his country-soul recordings through the mid-1970s, including 1973's "Soul Song" and "I'm Still Loving You" from a year later. A switch to Epic Records brought hits in a similar vein, including 1975's "Roll On, Big Mama," and the first of his more honky-tonk-styled material, 1975's "She's Helping Me Get over You" and 1976's "Whiskey Talkin'."

In 1978 ace producer BILLY SHERRILL took over Stampley's recording career, and moved him in a more solid countrified direction. A year later Stampley formed his partnership with Moe Bandy, releasing the #1 hit "Just Good Ol' Boys," which set the pattern for a series of successful tongue-in-cheek numbers, their most famous being 1981's "Hey Joe, Hey Moe." Stampley's solo successes included 1980's "Put Your Clothes Back On" and "Haven't I Loved You Somewhere Before," and the boozy hits "Whiskey Chasin'" (1981), "Back Slidin'" (1982), and "Double Shot of My Baby's Love" (1983).

After the mid-1980s Stampley's chart success pretty much dried up, but he remains a popular attraction on the club and barroom circuit.

STANLEY BROTHERS, THE (Carter Glen S., b. McClure, Va., August 27, 1925–December 1, 1966 [voc, gtr]; and Ralph Edmond S., b. McClure, Va., February 25, 1927 [voc, bjo])

The most traditional-sounding of BLUEGRASS bands, The Stanley Brothers with their group The Clinch Mountain Boys brought the high, lonesome mountain singing style to the new bluegrass style.

The Stanleys were raised in rural western Virginia, where their mother was an old-time BANJO player. Both sons began playing the banjo, learning traditional songs like "Little Birdie" in the drop-thumb or clawhammer style. Carter switched to GUITAR after Ralph became proficient on banjo, and the duo began performing locally. Their first professional work came after World War II with Roy Sykes and The Blue Ridge Boys in 1946; a year later they left the band, along with mandolinist "Pee Wee" (Darrell) Lambert, to form The Clinch Mountain Boys. It was about this time that they heard the legendary performances of BILL MONROE's Blue Grass Boys, and Ralph adopted the finger-picking style of Earl Scruggs (of FLATT AND SCRUGGS) to his banjo playing. The Stanleys' band was hired to perform over the radio in Bristol, Tennessee, and made its first recordings for the tiny Rich-R-Tone label out of Johnson City, Tennessee.

Carter (left) and Ralph (right) Stanley, from an early 1950s songbook. Photo courtesy Gary Reid/Copper Creek Records

In 1949 the group relocated to take a radio job in Raleigh, North Carolina, where they were heard by Columbia talent scout ART SATHERLEY, who signed them to that label. (Supposedly Monroe left that label because he was angered by Columbia's decision to hire another bluegrass group; he signed with Decca in 1950.) The Stanleys recorded for Columbia for three years, featuring their breathtaking harmonies on mountain ballads and Carter Stanley's compositions in a traditional vein, including the classic "White Dove" and "A Vision of Mother." In 1952 guitarist/vocalist George Shuffler, a talented flatpicker who would be featured prominently as a soloist in the band for the next decade, joined the group.

Carter took a job as lead vocalist for Bill Monroe's band briefly in 1952, recording the lead vocals on Monroe's own "Uncle Pen" and the HONKY-TONK song "Sugar-Coated Love." The brothers reunited in 1953, signing with Mercury and remaining with the label through 1958, then recording for King/Starday until Carter's death in 1966. By this time they had solidified their sound around lead guitar and banjo, with Ralph's licks limited to a fairly small repertoire. Carter's expressive lead vocals were perfectly complemented either by Ralph's unearthly high mountain tenor or by Shuffler's more modern-sounding harmonies.

In the late 1950s and early 1960s the market for bluegrass music was fairly small, so the Stanleys relocated to Florida in the winter, hosting a radio program and recording for smaller local labels. The FOLK REVIVAL of the 1960s helped revive their popularity, and they toured the U.S. revival circuit and in Europe. Carter's life was cut short by alcoholism in 1966, and for a while it seemed as if the band would fold.

However, Ralph emerged as an important bandleader by the decade's end. To fill Carter's shoes he first enlisted vocalist Larry Sparks, who went on to be one of the 1970s' most important PROGRESSIVE BLUEGRASS performers, and then the more traditionally oriented Roy Lee Centers, who sounded eerily like Carter. The band signed with Rebel Records, and was popular on both the revival and the traditional bluegrass circuits. Centers's murder in 1974 was another blow to Stanley, but he was soon followed by two high-school-age musicians Ralph had discovered—mandolinist RICKY SKAGGS and guitarist KEITH WHITLEY. Their association with the band helped to launch their careers in bluegrass and, later, the new traditional Nashville music.

The Stanley band centered from the mid-1970s through the mid-1990s on Ralph's banjo, the showy fiddling of Curly Ray Cline, and the bass playing of Jack Cooke, usually augmented by a young guitarist/vocalist and mandolinist. Despite the variability in the talents of the lead vocalists, the sound of the music remains pretty much unchanged. Ralph Stanley's contribution to and influence on Nashville's new-country stars was finally acknowledged by the 1993 release of a two-CD set on which he performs with Ricky Skaggs, VINCE GILL, and other New Nashvillians.

Ralph Stanley's career was given a major boost by the 2000 release of *O Brother, Where Art Thou?* On the film's sound track Stanley is prominently featured singing an a cappella version of the song "O Death."

The Stanley repertoire has remained fairly constant since the late 1950s. The band's theme song is "Clinch Mountain Backstep," an instrumental that combines the modality of old-time mountain banjo tunes with the energy and sheen of bluegrass picking. Its repertoire has always combined traditional mountain ballads, including Ralph's powerful vocals on songs like "Man of Constant Sorrow," with more modern honky-tonk classics, such as "She's More to Be Pitied Than Scolded." Drawing on their experience singing in small local churches, the Stanleys have always included both traditional and contemporary GOSPEL songs in their repertoire, and have recorded some of the most memorable gospel LPs in the bluegrass canon.

Select Discography

and the Clinch Mountain Boys, Bear Family 15564. All of their 1949–1952 classic recordings. Ralph knew about two licks on the banjo (and he uses them in every song), but these are still classic recordings. This material, without two alternate takes, was also reissued on Columbia/Legacy 53798.

Early Starday-King Recordings: 1958–61, King 8000. Four-CD boxed set of everything recorded for these labels; this material has also been issued and reissued on various King and Starday budget CDs.

Long Journey Home, Rebel 1110. Reissue of Wango label recordings from the early 1960s, featuring guitar wizard George Shuffler.

1971–73, Rebel 4001. Four-CD set documenting all of Ralph Stanley's recordings during this classic period, including lead singer Roy Lee Centers and the first recorded appearances of Ricky Skaggs and Keith Whitley with the Stanley band. A selection of all of his 1970s Rebel material is available on *Classic Bluegrass* (Rebel 1109).

Saturday Night and Sunday Morning, Freeland 9001. 1993 two-CD set featuring secular ("Saturday night") and sacred ("Sunday morning") numbers performed with a slew of new country and bluegrass talents.

Songs My Mother Taught Me & More: Clawhammer Style Banjo, Freeland 655. For years Ralph Stanley has preserved the earlier frailing or clawhammer banjo style he learned from his mother, in concert and on occasional recordings; this album highlights this earlier style in a program of mostly well-known banjo songs.

STANLEY, ROBA (b. Gwinnett County, Ga., 1910–June 8, 1986)

Roba Stanley was an early country guitarist and vocalist who made a handful of recordings in her teen years, then retired from the musical scene. Her records were rediscovered in the 1970s by old-time music enthusiasts, and she was belatedly recognized as one of the pioneers of old-time country music.

The daughter of country fiddler Rob Stanley (c. 1859–c. 1935), Roba was raised on a farm in north Georgia. She showed an early talent as a guitarist, borrowing her older brother's instrument while he worked in the fields. Her father soon invited her to accompany him at square dances. Their local performances drew the attention of Atlanta's radio station WSB, and the two debuted on it in early 1924. The novelty of a young, female guitarist playing and singing traditional dance songs led to an offer from Okeh Records.

Roba made a series of recordings in 1924 and again in 1925. On the later date she was accompanied by HENRY WHITTER, one of the pioneering country guitarists. Impulsively marrying at age fifteen, Roba settled with her new husband in Florida; discouraged from performing, she retired from the music business.

Roba was the first in a line of spunky teenagers who sang slightly racy material. In this way she foreshadowed the novelty and popularity of girl singers who were "old beyond their years."

STARR, KAY (b. Katherine LaVern Starks, Dougherty, Okla., July 21, 1922)

Starr was a bluesy, big-throated singer who achieved great success in the late 1940s and early 1950s, paving the way for vocalists like PATSY CLINE.

Born on an Indian reservation, Starr was raised in Dallas, where at age nine she had her own fifteen-minute daily radio show. Her prematurely husky voice won her many fans, and as a teenager she began performing with the popular WESTERN SWING bands of the day, including BILL BOYD's Cowboy Ramblers and one of the later incarnations of THE LIGHT CRUST DOUGHBOYS. In the late 1930s her family moved to Memphis, where Starr found a big audience for her powerful delivery.

Starr spent the war years performing at Army bases; she came down with a severe case of laryngitis due to the overuse of her voice and exposure to cold on Army transport planes. The result was an even sexier, growling delivery that made her a postwar sensation. She first hit it big in 1950 with "Bonaparte's Retreat," written for her by WYNN STEWART and PEE WEE KING, followed in the same year by her duet with TENNESSEE ERNIE FORD on "I'll Never Be Free." She crossed over onto the pop charts with her big-throated delivery of 1952's "Wheel of Fortune" and "Side by Side" from a year later, one of the first recordings to feature a double-tracked vocal. In 1955 she moved to RCA, where she began recording pop-oriented material, including the hit "Rock and Roll Waltz." After a few hitless years she came back big time on the country charts with 1961's "Foolin' Around" and "Four Walls" from the following year. She continued to record country material through the 1970s. In the 1990s she returned on the oldies circuit, performing with veterans Helen O'Connell and Margaret Whiting as 3 Girls 3.

Select Discography

Capitol Collectors Series, Capitol 94080. Her 1950s hits in their original recordings.

Essential RCA Singles, Taragon 1056. Mid-to-late-1950s recordings of standards.

STATLER BROTHERS, THE (1963–present; original members: Lew[is Calvin] DeWitt, b. Roanoke, Va., March 8, 1938–August 15, 1990 [ten]; Phil[ip] Balsley, b. Augusta County, Va., August 8, 1939 [bar]; Harold Wilson Reid, b. Augusta County, Va., August

31, 1939 [b]; Don[ald Sydney] Reid, b. Staunton, Va., June 5, 1945 [lead voc]; DeWitt was replaced by Jimmy Fortune, b. Lester James F., Newport News, Va., March 11, 1955 in 1982)

Not really brothers or named Statler, the Statler Brothers have been one of the most popular smooth-harmony vocal groups in country music for over thirty years.

Originally formed in 1955 as a church-based trio in Staunton, Virginia, by Lew DeWitt, Phil Balsley, and Harold Reid, the group was first called The Kingsmen (not of "Louie Louie" fame; that's another story). In 1960 Harold's younger brother Don joined as lead vocalist, and the group signed on with JOHNNY CASH's road show; they're featured on Cash's recording of CARL PERKINS's classic "Daddy Sang Bass." Soon after, they changed their name to The Statler Brothers, taking their surname from a Massachusetts-based manufacturer of facial tissues (appropriately enough, they would later record some classic hanky-soakers).

In 1964 they signed with Columbia Records (Cash's label), and had their first hit with the DeWitt-penned "Flowers on the Wall" a year later. Follow-up hits included 1967's "Ruthless" and the corny "You Can't Have Your Kate and Edith Too," although Columbia didn't do much to promote their career. In 1970 they switched to Mercury, and had their first solid hit with the crossover success of "Bed of Roses." Many of their 1970s hits were written by the brothers Reid, including 1972's nostalgic "Class of '57," the sentimental tearjerkers "I'll Go to My Grave Loving You" from 1975 and their first #1 single, "Do You Know You Are My Sunshine?," from 1978, and the humorous "How to Be a Country Star" from 1979. Recalling their roots as a GOSPEL quartet, they also recorded all-religious albums, including two based on the Old and New Testaments that were released in 1975.

In 1981 the group established Statler Complex in their base of Staunton, Virginia, which includes a museum housing their many awards and memorabilia. Around this time cofounder Lew DeWitt was forced to retire due to continuing problems from Crohn's disease; he died in 1990. His replacement was Jimmy Fortune, who contributed many of the group's 1980s hits, including "Elizabeth" from 1984, and "My Only Love" and "Too Much on My Heart" from a year later.

Although The Statlers have fallen off the charts, they remain immensely popular in Nashville and BRANSON, MISSOURI, as well as many places in between. For many years they hosted their own variety show on TNN, which was the top-rated show on the fledgling cable network for seven years; however, when CBS purchased TNN and renamed it The National Network in 1999, the show was canceled. Their brand of smooth, church-oriented harmonies and mixture of sentimental and humorous material has always made them one of the most popular—and lasting—of all country quartets. However, citing the pressures of continuing to tour, the group announced that 2002 would be their last year as performers.

Select Discography

Flowers on the Wall: The Essential, Columbia/Legacy 64764. Eighteen tracks from the mid-to-later 1960s, including pop and gospel numbers.
The Best of, Vols. 1 & 2, Mercury 822524/822525. Their biggest hits from the early-to-later 1970s.

STEAGALL, RED (b. Russell S., Gainesville, Tex., December 22, 1937)

Steagall had some popularity in the mid-1970s with his brand of Texas-styled WESTERN SWING and HONKY-TONK.

Raised in Gainesville, Texas, Steagall suffered from polio in his early teens, and used the time during his recuperation to master the GUITAR and the MANDOLIN. He enrolled in West Texas State University to study animal husbandry, and at the same time formed his first country band to play nights and weekends. After graduation he was a soil chemist for a while before being hired by United Artists' West Coast office, to work in A&R. His first big break came when RAY CHARLES covered his song "Here We Go Again," a modest R&B and country hit in 1967.

Steagall formed his own band, The Coleman County Cowboys, and began touring the rodeo circuit, where he has always enjoyed his greatest popularity. He recorded as a solo artist for Dot and Capitol in the early 1970s, scoring modest hits beginning with 1972's "Party Dolls and Wine" and "Somewhere My Love"; his biggest hit came in 1976 with his homage to Western Swing, "Lone Star Beer and Bob Wills Music."

In 1979 Steagall signed with Elektra Records and relocated from Nashville to Forth Worth, Texas. Since that time he has focused on COWBOY-nostalgia material, including poems and recitations as well as songs. Beginning in the 1970s he also pursued an acting career, appearing in popular flicks including *Benji* and *Big Bad John*. In 1991 the Texas legislature conferred on him the title "Official Cowboy Poet of Texas." He signed with Warner Western in 1993, and recorded for the label through the decade. In 1994 he began hosting the syndicated radio show *Red Steagall's Cowboy Corner*, featuring poetry, songs, and stories. In Forth Worth he has hosted the Red Steagall Cowboy Gathering and Western Swing Festival since the mid-1990s.

Select Discography

Lone Star Beer/For All Our Cowboy Friends, Koch 8074. Reissue of two of his better 1970s albums, the first a tribute to BOB WILLS and the second to cowboy singers.

Love of the West, Warner 47423. 1999 album of cowboy love songs.

STEVENS, RAY (b. R. Ragsdale, Clarkdale, Ga., January 24, 1939)

Stevens is a purveyor of the kind of cutesy, annoying country comedy that makes you either laugh hysterically or gag on a spoon, as well as equally nauseating "heartfelt" numbers like his 1970 hit "Everything Is Beautiful."

Trained in classical piano, Stevens formed an R&B dance band in high school, performing material drawn from favorite groups like The Coasters and The Drifters. He also worked as a weekend deejay. In 1956 his family relocated to Atlanta, and a year later Ray made his recording debut, without much success, on Capitol. He then enrolled at Georgia State, majoring in classical piano and music theory.

After graduation he moved to Nashville, where he scored his first novelty comedy hit with 1962's "Jeremiah Peabody's Polyunsaturated Quick Dissolving Fast Acting Pleasant Tasting Green and Purple Pills," followed by the equally "amusing" "Ahab the Arab." After working in record production during the mid-1960s, Ray really came to the fore with a slew of novelty hits, beginning with 1969's "Guitarzan" and "Along Came Jones." In 1970 he turned out the perennial feel-good song "Everything Is Beautiful." He also appeared on many popular TV variety shows, including those hosted by Ed Sullivan and Andy Williams.

Ray moved more into the country-music camp in the 1970s, beginning with "Sunday Morning Coming Down" and "Nashville." He had another pop-novelty hit in 1974 with "The Streak," commenting on the fad of streaking. He moved to Warner Brothers in the mid-1970s, having hits with covers of pop classics like "Misty" and "Indian Love Call" for the country market. In 1979 he had a hit with another tongue-in-cheek ditty, "I Need Your Help, Barry Manilow."

The 1980s saw Stevens returning to the kind of country corn that made him famous, including 1980's "Shriners' Convention," 1984's "Mississippi Squirrel Revival," and "It's Me Again, Margaret" from a year later. He continues to be a popular live attraction at glitzy venues from Vegas to BRANSON, MISSOURI, and his recordings and videos are regularly hawked on late-night TV for insomniacs in need of a good old country belly laugh.

Select Discography

Best of, Rhino 72867. Good compilation of his hits from 1961 to 1971.

STEWART, GARY (b. Letcher County, Ky., May 28, 1945)

Pianist/songwriter Stewart combines country, rock, HONKY-TONK, and R&B into a unique package that has made him a cult figure on the fringes of the Nashville establishment.

One of nine children in a coal-mining family, Stewart moved to Florida with his family when he was twelve, and he was performing at local clubs by his mid-teens. His first recording was the rockin' "I Love You Truly," released in 1964 on the small Cory label, which went nowhere. In the mid-1960s country star MEL TILLIS caught his act and urged him to come to Nashville to work as a songwriter.

In 1967 Stewart teamed with ex-rocker Bill Eldridge, and the duo wrote a number of hit songs for mainstream country acts, beginning with 1969's "Sweet Thang and Cisco," covered by NAT STUCKEY. Meanwhile, Stewart made some unsuccessful solo recordings for Kapp, and by the mid-1970s, discouraged, he returned to Florida after cutting a demo tape of Motown-styled material.

His demo caught the attention of Roy Dea, who signed Stewart to RCA in the early 1970s; he had his first hit there in 1974 with "Drinkin' Thing." This was followed by a couple of years of hitmaking, including his sole #1 country song, the cleverly titled "She's Acting Single (I'm Drinking Doubles)." By 1978, however, Stewart's hitmaking days had ended.

In the early 1980s Stewart found a new songwriting partner in Dean Dillon, and the two had minor hits with 1982's "Brotherly Love" and "Smokin' in the Rockies" from a year later. Dillon was able to make the transition to more mainstream songwriting, but Stewart stuck resolutely to his blend of honky-tonk and R&B. In 1988 he cut a comeback album for the blues-oriented Hightone label, but it was only marginally successful; he turned out two more albums for the label, the last appearing in 1993. Stewart has won praise among progressive rock critics as well as straight country fans, but still his music has not really clicked with a broad public.

Select Discography

Gary's Greatest, Hightone 8030. Traces his career from the 1970s through 1991.

The Essential, RCA 66932. His 1970s recordings for RCA, including some rarities.

STEWART, REDD (b. Henry R. S., Ashland City, Tenn., May 27, 1921)

Stewart is a country crooner best known for his long association with PEE WEE KING, with whom he wrote the ever-popular "Tennessee Waltz."

Born in Tennessee, Stewart wrote his first song when he was fourteen, for a local car dealership. He formed several country bands working out of Louisville, Kentucky, where in 1937 he met ace accordionsqueezer King. Stewart was hired as a musician, but took vocal roles with the band when vocalist EDDY ARNOLD left to pursue a solo career. During World War II, Stewart served in the South Pacific; his experiences there led him to write "Soldier's Last Letter," later a major hit for ERNEST TUBB.

Stewart's greatest success came with the postwar King band. They first produced 1946's reworking of the traditional fiddle tune "Bonaparte's Retreat," the hit that launched the career of KAY STARR, followed by their most famous song, 1948's "Tennessee Waltz," not only a massive country hit but also a top-charting pop number for singer Patti Page in 1950; "Slow Poke" from 1951; and "You Belong to Me," a 1952 pop hit for Jo Stafford.

Stewart remained with King until the mid-1960s. He also cut solo recordings for a variety of labels, although none were as successful as his performances with the King band. He has been more or less retired since the early 1970s.

STEWART, WYNN (b. Wynford Lindsey S., Morrisville, Mo., June 7, 1934–July 17, 1985)

Along with BUCK OWENS, Stewart was one of the pioneers of the HONKY-TONK BAKERSFIELD SOUND whose career never quite reached the heights it deserved.

Performing in church from an early age, Wynn landed a local radio show out of nearby Springfield, Missouri, when he was thirteen. A year later his family relocated to Los Angeles, where he lost no time in forming a band and beginning to perform and record, at first for the tiny Intro label in 1950. In 1953 he put together his first classic country band, featuring ace steel guitarist Ralph Mooney, bassist-singer Bobby Austin, and guitarist Roy Nichols. They recorded his composition "Strollin'," which led to a contract with Capitol and his first hits, including 1955's "Keeper of the Keys." By the late 1950s he had moved to the Jackpot division of the Challenge label, which was owned by a friend, producer Joe Johnson, and scored with the ROCKABILLY-styled "Come On" in 1958. Johnson teamed him with Harlan Howard's wife, JAN HOWARD, for a series of rather tepid duets between 1959 and 1961. In 1961 he scored a regional hit with "Big, Big Love," which was covered nationally by Buck Owens.

In the early 1960s Stewart became resident musician at the country-music haven The Nashville Nevada Club in Las Vegas; he also worked as a deejay and hosted his own local TV show. Capitol producer KEN NELSON heard him performing there, and signed him to the label in 1963, although nothing much happened until 1967's "It's Such a Pretty World Today" hit the charts for twenty-two weeks in a row. Similarly upbeat titles followed through 1970, with Stewart's normally aggressively honky-tonk personality somewhat toned down by the choice of kissy-poo material.

In the 1970s Stewart label-hopped from RCA to Atlantic to Playboy, scoring one comeback hit in 1976 with "After the Storm." After that he turned to producing his recordings himself for his own Win label and various smaller outfits. In the early 1980s his earlier recordings were reissued by the German Bear Family label, renewing interest in him as a pioneering honkytonk and rockabilly star. A revival tour was planned for 1985, but Stewart died of a heart attack before it could begin.

Select Discography

Wishful Thinking, Bear Family 15886. Grab your checkbook! Here are ten CDs of nearly everything Stewart committed to wax, for the true fan.
Very Best of, 1958–62, Varese 066231. Hits from his peak period, nicely annotated and selected by Colin Escott.

STONE, CLIFFIE (b. Clifford Gilpin Snyder, Stockton, Calif., March 1, 1917–January 17, 1998)

Instrumentalist/bandleader Stone, one of the pioneering country music promoters, producers, and songwriters, engineered the careers of mainstream country acts like TENNESSEE ERNIE FORD.

The son of a comedian/BANJO player who performed professionally as Herman the Hermit, Stone showed an early interest in jazz and pop music, taking up the bass and forming his first dance band while in high school. After finishing school he played bass with well-known orchestras led by Anson Weeks and Freddy Slack. However, his interest turned to the blossoming southern California country music scene, and in 1935 he got his first job as a country deejay. From the late 1930s into the 1940s, he was one of the most influential deejays in the area, hosting numerous shows including the CBS network *Hollywood Barn Dance* and the early-morning *Wake Up Ranch*.

After World War II, Stone signed up with the fledgling Capitol label both as a talent scout for their new country and western division and as a recording artist. He recorded from the late 1940s through the mid-1960s in a swinging Western style, having hits with "When My Blue Moon Turns to Gold Again" (now a BLUEGRASS standard), "Blue Canadian Rockies" (later covered by GRAM PARSONS while a member of THE BYRDS), and "Blues Stay Away from Me." Working with younger musicians like MERLE TRAVIS and Eddie

Kirk, Stone coauthored such classic country tunes as "Divorce Me, C.O.D.," "Sweet Temptation," and "So Round, So Firm, So Fully Packed."

In 1947 Stone took a Pasadena-based deejay named Ernie Ford and molded him into Capitol's first big country star, Tennessee Ernie Ford. Ford's likable personality made him a popular figure on early country television, including Stone's *Hometown Jamboree*, broadcast out of Los Angeles. Stone was also an early champion of the careers of HANK THOMPSON and Merle Travis; it was Travis's song "Sixteen Tons" that provided Ford with his biggest hit.

In the 1960s and 1970s Stone was more active behind the scenes than as a recording artist. Besides running a couple of music publishing firms, he continued to produce recordings, forming his own Granite label in 1976, and served on several industry panels. He also was a prominent promoter of bluegrass concerts in southern California into the early 1980s.

In 1989 Stone was elected to the Country Music Hall of Fame. He died of a heart attack nine years later. His son, Curtis, was bass player in the COUNTRY-ROCK band HIGHWAY 101.

STONE, DOUG (b. Douglas Jackson Brooks, Newnan, Ga., June 19, 1956)

Another of the early-1990s hunks-of-the-month, Stone is a solid country crooner whose style is reminiscent of MERLE HAGGARD.

Raised in rural Georgia, Doug was inspired to go into music by his mother, who had aspirations to be a country singer. He formed his first band when he was fifteen, and continued to perform in the Newnan area while holding a variety of factory jobs. In 1987 he was "discovered" by country agent Phyllis Bennett while performing at the VFW hall in his hometown; she arranged for his demo tape to be heard by Epic Records' director of country music, and he was signed by the label. He changed his name to Doug Stone to avoid confusion with country star GARTH BROOKS.

His first hit was 1990's "I'd Be Better Off (in a Pine Box)," with a hard-edged HONKY-TONK sound reminiscent of the early-1960s recordings of Merle Haggard. His next single—"Fourteen Minutes Old"—went to #1, cementing his position as a solid contender in the new-country arena. He followed with "A Jukebox with a Country Song," which trumpets typical redneck values, and "Warning Labels," a more clever send-up of honky-tonk values.

Stone's career was slowed somewhat in 1992, when his hard-livin', good-ol'-boy diet of grits, grease, and gravy led to quadruple-bypass surgery. He released two more albums after recovering, but suffered a heart attack and had a polyp removed from his vocal cords in 1995, leading to four years of inactivity. In 1999 he released his first new album in some time, now recording for Atlantic, that focused on ready-for-radio pop ballads, but it failed to reignite his career. Doug's ill luck caught up with him again in mid-2000; he was seriously injured when the engine of the small plane that he was piloting failed, leading to a crash landing. However, he was soon back on the road, and continues to tour heavily, although he has released no new recordings to date.

Select Discography

Super Hits, Sony/Columbia 67946. Ten-song budget compilation of all the hits.

STONEMAN, ERNEST "POP" (b. Monarat, Va., May 25, 1893–June 14, 1968)

One of the first country artists to record, Ernest Stoneman was also one of those who remained on the scene the longest, returning as the leader of The Stoneman Family Band in the 1950s and 1960s, until his death in 1968.

Hailing from a musical family in western Virginia, Stoneman was a carpenter by trade and a musician by avocation. By his twenties he could play the GUITAR, autoharp, mouth harp (or harmonica), and Jew's harp. He contacted Okeh recording executive and pioneering country music producer RALPH PEER in 1924, and made some test recordings that were released early the next year, including the first recording of "The Sinking of the Titanic." Stoneman continued to record through the 1920s for numerous labels, both as a soloist and as a leader of a string band, The Blue Ridge Corn Shuckers, featuring fiddler Uncle Eck Dunford.

Like many other early stars of country music who actually came from a rural background, Stoneman was not the most "intensely" traditional in his approach to music making; instead of singing in a highly ornamented style, he sang in a relaxed, almost spoken manner, with clear pronunciation. His string-band recordings were more genteel than the rough-and-rowdy style preferred by deep South bands like THE SKILLET LICKERS.

With the coming of the Depression the recording industry was severely crippled, and Stoneman's initial career ended. He worked in a munitions factory through World War II, settling outside of Washington, D.C., and did not return to active performing until the first FOLK REVIVAL of the early 1950s. Stoneman had thirteen children, many talented musically, so he formed a family band that began performing in the Washington area: sons Scotty (FIDDLE), Jim (bass), and Van (GUITAR), and daughters Donna (MANDOLIN) and Ronni (BANJO), plus Pop leading the brood on guitar and autoharp. They recorded for various labels, but their most important and influential album came out in 1957 on the Folkways label, introducing their sound to the urban folk-revival audience. In 1962 they were made members of THE GRAND OLE OPRY, and continued to perform through the 1960s for both country and folk-revival audiences. They also appeared on TV programs ranging from *Shindig* to *Hootenany* to *The Jimmy Dean Show*.

After Pop Stoneman's death, the group moved in a more BLUEGRASS-oriented direction. Son Scotty left the band first, and won fame on the West Coast as a bluegrass fiddler, particularly for his work with the PROGRESSIVE BLUEGRASS band THE KENTUCKY COLONELS in the early 1960s; daughter Ronni became a talented comedian, appearing as a regular on the HEE HAW TV program.

Select Discography

1928 Edison Recordings, County 35102. Twenty-two tracks cut by Stoneman with full string band accompaniment.

STORY, CARL (b. C. Moore S., Lenoir, N.C., May 29, 1916–March 30, 1995)

Story was a BLUEGRASS vocalist and guitarist who recorded a mix of country and bluegrass material.

Story was the son of an old-time fiddler who played local dances, and the FIDDLE was his first instrument, which he took up at age nine. Influenced by recordings of North Carolina string bands like CHARLIE POOLE'S North Carolina Ramblers, Story soon took up the GUITAR and began singing. When he was about twenty-five years old, he moved to Lynchburg, Virginia, where he began his radio career. In 1935 he briefly returned home, hooking up with BANJO player Johnnie Whisnant, who was then only fourteen years old. The two got radio work in Spartanburg, South Carolina, first with an existing band called The Lonesome Mountaineers. The band broke up, and the duo formed their own group, The Rambling Mountaineers. The band lasted through the early 1940s, working out of several Carolina towns; then World War II decimated its membership. Story briefly joined BILL MONROE's band as a fiddle player, but then enlisted in the Navy in 1943.

After the war Carl formed a new Rambling Mountaineers, first working out of Asheville, North Carolina, and then Knoxville, Tennessee, where he broadcast until 1951 and from 1953 to 1957. In 1947 he signed with Mercury Records, making his first recordings, and in 1953 moved to Columbia, where he remained for two years. His bands of this period had various personnel, but he did not have the typical bluegrass lineup because he had no full-time banjo player. Instead he focused on his own guitar work and on strong lead mandolin, often handled by Red Rector.

In 1957 Story formed his first "true" bluegrass band with fiddler Tater Tate and the Brewster brothers. This band recorded for Starday, and led to a second career for Story on the bluegrass circuit. From 1957 to 1960 he had his own local TV show out of Asheville, and then during much of the 1960s out of Charlotte, North Carolina. Story continued to lead bands with various personnel, enjoying his greatest success during the bluegrass revival of the 1960s and 1970s. The group focused on bluegrass GOSPEL, cutting several fine sacred albums. Story worked the bluegrass festival circuit and recorded until his death in 1995.

Story had a pleasant singing voice, in the relaxed style typical of many other North Carolinians, such as DOC WATSON. Never a major country star, he was an important early bluegrass performer, although his recordings have been somewhat overlooked during the bluegrass revival.

Select Discography

16 Greatest Hits, Starday 3004. Bluegrass and country material with various accompanists, from the late 1950s and early 1960s.
Somebody Touched Me, King 5111. Ten-song compilation of gospel numbers.

STRAIT, GEORGE (b. Poteet, Tex., May 18, 1952)

Strait is one of the great HONKY-TONK/WESTERN SWING revivalists, and one of the few new-country acts who—so far, at least—hasn't strayed too far into pop-rock. His recordings have done much to revive the best of the Southwest sound, right down to the trademark twin harmony FIDDLES (often featuring veteran Western Swing fiddler JOHNNY GIMBLE).

The son of a schoolteacher who raised cattle on the side, Strait began, as most of his generation did, by playing rock and pop music. He eloped with his high-school sweetheart, and soon after joined the Army. The Army sent him to Hawaii, where he began performing country music, perhaps to remind himself of home. Returning to the family farm, he began performing locally with the group Ace in the Hole, and recorded for the tiny D label out of Houston. He hit Nashville in the late 1970s but failed to find a contract until 1981, when he signed with MCA.

From his first album Strait established his signature Southwestern sound, scoring a #6 hit with his first single, "Unwound." His sound recalled the best of the early 1950s honky-tonkers, including HANK THOMPSON, RAY PRICE, and FARON YOUNG, before they became buried in the NASHVILLE SOUND of the late 1950s and early 1960s. Strait continued to hit it big through the 1980s, covering BOB WILLS's classic "Right or Wrong" and Whitey Shafer's "Does Fort Worth Ever

Cross Your Mind?" His novelty hit, "All My Ex's Live in Texas," even got some pop radio play.

Beginning in the early 1990s, George recorded more slick, "urban" country material, such as "Ocean Front Property," but his vocal style and arrangements continued to have enough pure country in them to win over the most rabid traditionalists. He gave an unaffected, straightforward performance in the 1992 film *Pure Country* that garnered him minor critical praise. His 1995 career retrospective, the four-CD *Strait Out of the Box*, was a huge seller, and his follow-up album, *Blue Clear Sky*, debuted at #1 country and #7 on the pop charts, an unusual feat even for a New Nashville artist; the title track was a major hit. He continued to produce big hits through the decade's end, including the amusing "Murder on Music Row," a duet with ALAN JACKSON. Strait's track record is amazing; only three out of his sixty-one career singles have failed to chart in the country Top 10.

Select Discography

Does Fort Worth Ever Cross Your Mind, MCA 31032. Strait's fourth LP from 1984, and his first classic one, with stripped-down production and a definite honky-tonk slant.

Greatest Hits, Vols. 1 & 2, MCA 5567/42304. The hits up to the early 1990s.

Latest Greatest Straitest Hits, MCA 170100. 1990s hits.

STREET, MEL (b. King Malachi S., Grundy, Va., October 21, 1933–October 21, 1978)

One of the first new HONKY-TONK singers, Street had his life and career end tragically before the new traditionalist movement of the 1980s, which undoubtedly would have brought him wider fame.

Beginning his career by performing on local radio as a sideline, Street worked for many years in the construction, and auto painting and repair businesses. By the late 1960s he had his own TV show out of rural Bluefield, West Virginia, and in 1970 made his first recording for the tiny Tandem label. The B-side of this single, "Borrowed Angel," his own composition, slowly gained momentum on the charts, finally hitting the Top 10 when it was reissued by Royal American Records in 1972. Despite the success of this hit, and of the follow-up "Lovin' on Back Streets," Street was ignored by the major labels until four years later, when he signed with Polydor. Polydor had the clout to promote him properly, and he had several more hits over the next two years, including 1978's Top 10 "If I Had a Cheatin' Heart." However, the stress of success was too much for the singer, and he committed suicide on his birthday in that year.

Street's emphasis on the traditional honky-tonk sound was undoubtedly ahead of his time. He was one of the first younger artists to appreciate the achievements of GEORGE JONES and other somewhat forgotten stars of the 1950s and early 1960s. He also was among the first to record songs by younger artists like EDDIE RABBITT and EARL THOMAS CONLEY, who would later become hitmakers on their own.

Select Discography

Greatest Hits, Deluxe 7824. Cassette-only reissue of hits from unknown sources.

STRINGBEAN (b. David Akeman, Annville, Ky., June 17, 1915–November 10, 1973)

Akeman, a country comedian and BANJO player, followed in the footsteps of his father, a traditional banjo player, when he made his own first instrument at age twelve. He began performing in the Lexington, Kentucky, area, landing a radio job when he was eighteen as a member of Cy Rogers's Lonesome Pine Fiddlers. Like most country groups at the time, the Fiddlers prominently featured a country-rube comedian as part of their act; the gangly, six-foot-two banjo player seemed a perfect candidate to take this role. Akeman was given the nickname "Stringbean" because of his long, lean appearance.

In the late 1930s he hooked up with CHARLIE MONROE's band, again taking the comic role. At about the same time, BILL MONROE was forming his first Blue Grass Boys, and hired Stringbean away from his brother to be the comedian and banjo player in his new outfit. Stringbean's main role was as a stage comedian; his old-fashioned frailed banjo style did not fit in with even this early version of the Blue Grass Boys, which was a swinging outfit propelled by Monroe's high-powered MANDOLIN playing. (His banjo playing can barely be heard on Monroe's recordings.) Stringbean would be replaced in the mid-1940s by innovative banjoist Earl Scruggs (later of FLATT AND SCRUGGS).

In the late 1940s Stringbean embarked on a solo career as a comic and banjo player in the tradition of UNCLE DAVE MACON (he later recorded a tribute album to the elder banjo player). He was a well-loved member of THE GRAND OLE OPRY for over twenty-five years. His career was given a boost in the late 1960s when the popular TV show HEE HAW was first broadcast; he was an original cast member whose style fit in perfectly with the hayseed humor of the program. Stringbean was murdered along with his wife when the pair encountered burglars robbing their Nashville home in 1973.

Select Discography

A Salute to Uncle Dave Macon, Hollywood 309. Reissue of a Starday LP (215) from 1963, a collection of songs associated with the famous country banjoist.

Front Porch Funnies, King 476. Fifteen minutes and eight songs, probably dating from the late 1950s–early 1960s.

STRIPLING BROTHERS (Charles Nevins "Charlie" S., August 8, 1896–January 19, 1966 [fdl], and Ira Lee S., June 5, 1898–March 1967 [gtr], both born near Kennedy, Pickens County, Ala.)

The Stripling Brothers were a fiddler/guitarist sibling duo who recorded traditional tunes from the later 1920s through the mid-1930s.

Charlie started fiddling at about the age of eighteen, and his brother took up the GUITAR soon after. They became popular at local fiddlers' conventions. In 1926 Charlie took second place at the Dixie Fiddlers Convention, sponsored by industrialist/square dance enthusiast Henry Ford. By then the brothers had their own radio show out of Birmingham, Alabama.

In 1928 they made their first recordings in Birmingham for a mobile unit of the Vocalion label headed by producer FRANK WALKER. They cut two numbers; one, "The Lost Child," is said to be the source for the popular bluegrass instrumental "Black Mountain Rag." Their next session was held a year and a half later in Chicago, producing sixteen sides, including Charlie's own showpiece, "The Kennedy Rag." The traditional tune "Wolves a-Howlin' " also was cut at these sessions; later this unusual local tune would become a favorite of old-time revival fiddlers. This was the brothers' last recording before the Depression slowed the music business. However, in 1934 and 1936 they recorded again, this time for Decca, first in New York and then, their last session, in New Orleans. Their total output was fourteen instrumentals and two vocal numbers.

By the end of the 1930s Ira had retired and Charlie had formed a band with his two sons, Lee and Robert, mostly performing locally. His sons served in World War II, and then Lee settled in Seattle and Robert went to Alabama; neither pursued a musical career at the time. Charlie continued to fiddle until arthritis ended his career in 1958.

Charlie and Ira's work was introduced to the old-time music revival in 1971, when a compilation of their best Vocalion sides was reissued by County Records. This led to renewed interest in their work, and many of their tunes were revived by young bands. In 1999 Lee was encouraged to take up fiddling again, and a year later reunited with his brother. They have performed in the Seattle area, and toured in the spring of 2001.

STUART, MARTY (b. Philadelphia, Miss., September 30, 1958)

Stuart was a child prodigy MANDOLIN and GUITAR player who performed with Lester Flatt (of FLATT AND SCRUGGS) and other traditional bluegrassers before becoming a hip-wiggling new-country star. Stuart's Nashville-based recordings of the late 1980s and early 1990s show a strong ROCKABILLY influence, including the "twangy" guitar sound that is a trademark of early rock.

Beginning as a hot young stringbender, Stuart started performing professionally at the age of twelve, as a member of Lester Flatt's Nashville Grass. After Flatt's death he worked with JOHNNY CASH (he was married to Cash's daughter from 1979 to 1988) and BOB DYLAN, recording his first solo album for Sugar Hill, a bluegrass label, in 1982. He jumped on the new-country bandwagon in 1986, signing with Columbia, but didn't achieve success until his breakthrough single of 1991, "That's Country," along with his duet with

Marty Stuart models his retro-country duds, 1995. Photo: Raeanne Rubenstein

TRAVIS TRITT on his self-penned "This One's Gonna Hurt You," very much in the tradition of HONKY-TONK WEEPERS. In 1993 he was made a member of THE GRAND OLE OPRY.

Stuart's hitmaking slowed in the second half of the 1990s. An avid photographer, he published an interesting collection of his photos, and also began producing other artists. In 1997 he wed country crooner CONNIE SMITH. He is a great collector of country memorabilia, and has contributed to the Country Music Foundation and Hall of Fame, as well as serving as the president of the foundation's board from 1998 to 2001. His last studio album to date is 1999's *The Pilgrim*, which featured an instrumental version of the traditional "John Henry" that won a Grammy in 2000. In 2001 he scored the Billy Bob Thornton film *All the Pretty Horses*, which led to his producing an album with the actor/director.

Select Discography

Once upon a Time, CMH 8000. Actually mid-1970s Lester Flatt and the Nashville Grass recordings, featuring young Marty Stuart when he was an adolescent string wizard.

Busy Bee Cafe, Sugar Hill 3726. 1982 recording, his first toe in the water in contemporary country.

Marty Party Hit Pack, MCA 11204. 1995 collection of his late 1980s through mid-1990s hits.

STUCKEY, NAT (b. Nathan Wright S. II, Cass County, Tex., December 17, 1933–August 24, 1988)

Stuckey was a minor-league country performer of the 1960s who never quite made it; he is best remembered for composing the BUCK OWENS hit "Waitin' in Your Welfare Line."

Trained as a radio announcer and deejay, Stuckey worked in a jazz group in the late 1950s before forming his first country band, The Corn Huskers, which performed on the popular LOUISIANA HAYRIDE radio program. He was signed to the Shreveport-based Paula label, having a hit with "Sweet Thang" in 1966, the same year Owens scored with his "Waitin' in Your Welfare Line." He switched to RCA in 1968, scoring minor hits with the novelty "Plastic Saddle" that year, and a cover of GARY STEWART's "Sweet Thang and Cisco" a year later. He recorded for MCA in the mid-1970s to critical acclaim but little commercial success, and faded into obscurity. He died of lung cancer in 1988.

Select Discography

Sweet Thang, Michele 109. Cassette-only compilation of his hits.

SULLIVAN FAMILY (1949–present: (Enoch [Hugh] Sullivan, b. St. Stephens, Ala., September 18, 1933 [voc, gtr, fdl, mdln]; Margie [Louise Brewster] Sullivan, b. Winnsboro, La., January 22, 1933 [voc, gtr]; Emmett Sullivan, b. St. Stephens, Ala., July 23, 1936–April 10, 1993 [voc, bnj, gtr, b])

The Sullivans are a long-lived BLUEGRASS GOSPEL group.

Enoch and Emmett Sullivan were the sons of a revivalist preacher; their uncle, J.B., was a BANJO player who led local bands. Raised religiously, they were early fans of bluegrass music, listening regularly to BILL MONROE on THE GRAND OLE OPRY. Margie Brewster, born and raised in Louisiana, also loved traditional country sounds and was an avid listener to the LOUISIANA HAYRIDE radio show. She was also an early convert to evangelical religion, beginning to travel the circuit as an assistant to a local evangelist named Hazel Chain when she was a teenager. In 1949 she met Enoch at a revival in rural Alabama, and the couple married and settled in Enoch's hometown of St. Stephens.

After a brief period on the radio out of Mississippi, the two, along with Enoch's brother, Emmett, began working closer to home in 1950, out of Jackson and then out of Thomasville, Alabama, with a daily early-morning, fifteen-minute gospel show. Around this time they met Walter Bailes of THE BAILES BROTHERS, who operated a gospel label, Loyal Records. They began recording for Bailes, and their records became popular among the country-gospel audience. The group featured the robust lead singing of Margie, who was influenced by big-voiced country singers like MOLLY O'DAY.

The Sullivans entered the bluegrass world via their admiration for BILL MONROE. They befriended Monroe, who admired their harmony vocals, and he invited them to appear at his Bean Blossom Bluegrass Festival in 1968. They have since performed on both bluegrass and gospel circuits. The band has included, from time to time, other family members, among them their cousin Jerry, as well as outside musicians.

A young picker from Mississippi named MARTY STUART played with them during 1969–1970 before joining Lester Flatt (formerly of FLATT AND SCRUGGS). Stuart has remained close to the family, and has produced several albums by Jerry and his daughter Tammy Sullivan. In 1989 the family began publishing *Bluegrass Gospel News* as a way of promoting the music and its performers.

Select Discography

A Joyful Noise, Country Music Foundation 16. 1991 album by Tammy and Jerry Sullivan, produced by Marty Stuart.

Tomorrow, Ceili 2005. 2000 release produced by Marty Stuart, featuring father-daughter team Jerry and Tammy Sullivan; Stuart also wrote many of the inspirational songs with Jerry.

SUPERNAW, DOUG (b. Douglas Anderson S., Bryan, Tex., September 26, 1960)

Supernaw is a midlevel "hunk-in-a-hat" hitmaker of the mid-1990s (even Supernaw admits he's not "the world's greatest singer") who has marketed himself as an arrested adolescent in his music and in his life.

Supernaw was raised in Houston, Texas, the son of a research scientist. He began writing and singing his own songs in high school, but his main interest was in golf. After a brief stab at making it as a professional, he discovered he couldn't handle a club well enough to succeed.

By the late 1970s Supernaw was working in a cover band in Florida, and during the early 1980s spent some time on an oil rig off the Texas coast. Later in the decade he came to Nashville, gaining a job as a staff songwriter for one of the many country publishers, but had little success.

In 1991 Supernaw returned to Texas, and soon formed his own band. He was signed by RCA a year later, and released his first album in 1993. From the start Supernaw's songs inspired controversy: His first self-penned hit, "Reno," offended citizens of that fine gambling town when it compared a cold-hearted woman to its (supposedly) equally icy citizens; and the #1, soapy ballad, "I Don't Call Him Daddy," raised the ire of stepfathers everywhere. (The song's protagonist assures his "real" daddy that he will never accept his stepdad as a legitimate father.) Soon after the album's release Supernaw was involved in two major accidents, including a head-on collision, and his first marriage fell into ruins. These events were turned into fodder for his PR machine, on the assumption that country music fans would admire his "bad boy" image.

Although his first album went gold, Supernaw's follow-up album failed to do much business. Nonetheless he managed to offend Mothers Against Drunk Driving in his video for the single release "State Fair" from the album, which some thought encouraged teens to drink and drive. (The song in fact was against drunk driving, but somehow the message got lost in the hoopla.)

In 1995 Supernaw moved to Giant Records, finally returning to Top 10 favor with the love song "Not Enough Hours in the Night." The steamy video featured his new, second bride, adding to Supernaw's manly image. However, the singer continued to be dogged by controversy, thanks to the single "What'll You Do About Me," about a one-night stand gone wrong. The song's protagonist picks up a woman for what she thinks is a temporary fling, but he seems to feel that she's now his property—and he threatens bodily harm to anyone else who casts an eye on her. Unfortunately, the O. J. Simpson trial was then under way, and offered a somewhat creepy parallel to the song, which seemed to be sympathetic toward the abusive man.

Supernaw's career sagged in the later 1990s, although he continued to be popular on the country rodeo-NASCAR-tour circuit. In 1999 he released *Fadin' Renegade*, which continued the combination of tearjerking ballads with up-tempo rockers. The debut single, "21–7," combined the best of both worlds: a syrupy love song set against the sounds of a football announcer. Any true-blue American male could appreciate this combination of love and touchdowns!

Select Discography

Encore Collection, BMG 44518. Hits through 1976.

SWEETHEARTS OF THE RODEO (c. 1984–1996, sporadically thereafter: Janis Oliver Cummins [gtr, voc] and Kristine Oliver Arnold [gtr, voc])

Taking their name from THE BYRDS' COUNTRY-ROCK album, The Sweethearts were a sister act who took California-style country to its next logical stage.

Born in Torrance, California, they were raised in Manhattan Beach, not exactly a country-music capital. (California's country scene was centered in Bakersfield, a dusty inland town northeast of the beach scene.) However, they came of age just as the California country-rock scene was beginning to blossom; groups like The Byrds were flirting on the edges of country, and new bands like THE FLYING BURRITO BROTHERS and POCO, formed in the early 1970s, were dedicated to the country-rock fusion. The girls began playing country and BLUEGRASS in high school, and soon were booked in clubs up and down the coast. In one of these clubs Janis met future husband VINCE GILL, who was also part of southern California's bluegrass scene.

When Gill relocated to Nashville, he took his by-then retired wife with him. The sisters soon reunited and began performing again, and won a national talent contest sponsored by Wrangler jeans, which led to a contract with Columbia Records. The label emphasized their tough-girl image and their sisterly harmony primarily on remakes of 1950s ("Hey, Doll Baby") and 1960s ("I Feel Fine") rock, recast in a countryesque vein. Although their records won critical praise, they were neither traditional enough for the diehard country fans nor mainstream enough to win over a pop audience, so that by 1992 Columbia had dropped the act. Meanwhile, Gill's megasuccess overshadowed his wife and sister-in-law's more modest achievements.

In 1993 The Sweethearts signed with the traditional bluegrass label Sugar Hill; not surprisingly, their two albums for the new label were in a more traditional vein. Their last new album appeared in 1996. Since then they have given an annual show at Nashville's Bluebird Café, and performed occasionally at other clubs. In 1999 Gill left Janis for singer Amy Grant, whom he would wed a year later; Janis also remarried that year, and now is known as Janis Oliver Cummins. Both a solo album by Janis and a new Sweethearts album were said to be in the works during 1999–2000, but neither has yet appeared. The sisters operated a gallery, Gill & Arnold, during the later 1990s, but it closed after they lost their lease in 1999.

Select Discography

Anthology, Renaissance 230. Compilation of their Columbia recordings.

SYLVIA (b. S. Kirby, Kokomo, Ind., December 9, 1956)

In the early 1980s CRYSTAL GAYLE had serious competition in the soulful-long-haired-beauty department from one-named wonder Sylvia. Sylvia was a minor-league vocalist whose good looks and canny pop productions hid her meager talents.

Born and raised in suburban Indiana, Sylvia came to Nashville when she was nineteen years old, looking for a secretarial position. She found one with PiGem Music, where she was both a typist and a demo singer. She went on the road with JANIE FRICKE in 1977, just as that singer was breaking out as a solo act, and later that year auditioned unsuccessfully to join DAVE AND SUGAR as a Sugar replacement, thus showing her pop leanings. RCA was impressed enough with her audition to give her a solo contract, and the label sent her out on the road to open for CHARLEY PRIDE.

Sylvia first hit it big in 1981 with "Drifter," a song that combined a Western theme with a disco beat (if you can believe it). After a second hit in 1982 with "Nobody," the singer continued to produce charting singles through 1985, when she retired from active performing. It was a good thing, too, because her middle-of-the-road country pop would soon go out of vogue, thanks to the resurgence of more traditional country sounds.

Select Discography

Anthology, Renaissance 210. Twenty-four-song compilation of her 1979–1981 RCA hits, for true-blue fans.

T

TALLEY, JAMES (b. Mehan, Okla., November 9, 1943)

Talley is a cult-favorite SINGER/SONGWRITER who melds country with social protest, blues, and R&B. He has a strongly devoted, if small, audience.

Born near Tulsa and raised in Albuquerque, New Mexico, Talley studied at UCLA and the University of New Mexico. After graduation he was a social worker among inner-city Hispanics, and then moved to Nashville, where he worked with urban blacks. In the early 1970s he financed an album of songs based on his experiences growing up in rural Oklahoma, *Got No Bread, No Money, But We Sure Got a Lotta Love*, which was licensed by Capitol Records and became a classic; a second album, *Tryin' Like the Devil*, took a more political bent. His albums had little commercial success, although he did perform at Jimmy Carter's inauguration. After dropping out of sight for a few years to work as a realtor, he returned on the German Bear Family label in 1989 for another fine session. Then he disappeared again for eleven years, returning in 2000 with both an album of Woody Guthrie covers and an album of originals on the small Cimarron label.

Select Discography

Got No Bread . . ./Tryin' Like the Devil, Bear Family 15433. Both of his classic albums on one CD.
The Road to Torreon, Bear Family 15633. Mid-1980s recordings are presented along with a photo booklet by Cavalliere Ketchum.

TASHIAN, BARRY AND HOLLY (Barry b. Oak Park, Ill., August 5, 1945; Holly b. New York City, January 8, 1946)

The Tashians are husband-and-wife SINGER/SONGWRITERS who gained popularity on the "Americana" charts in the mid-1990s.

Barry's claim to fame is that he was guitarist and founder of the Boston-based group The Remains, who opened for the Beatles on their last, 1966 tour. He then moved to California, briefly working with GRAM PARSONS in the original FLYING BURRITO BROTHERS, and later spent most of the 1980s as lead guitarist for EMMYLOU HARRIS's Hot Band. Holly is a classically trained violinist who met her future husband while the two were still in high school. They began working together in the 1970s as members of the New England-based country band The Outskirts.

The duo began performing together in the mid-1980s. They were initially more popular in Europe than at home, releasing an album in 1989 in Germany. Their success abroad led to a recording contract with the bluegrass label Rounder in the U.S. The title track of their second U.S. release, "Straw into Gold," reached #11 on the short-lived Americana chart (this chart was designed to track the sales of "alt-country" artists like NANCI GRIFFITH and LYLE LOVETT). They continued to tour through the 1990s, primarily on the bluegrass and folk circuits. Tashian has also led several Remains reunion tours.

Select Discography

Harmony, Rounder 412. Their third Rounder album, from 1997, produced by JIM ROONEY.

TAYLOR, TUT (b. Robert T., Milledgeville, Ga., November 20, 1923)

Taylor is an influential DOBRO player and instrument maker, best known for his early-1970s association with JOHN HARTFORD.

A talented musician who could play a variety of instruments by his early teens, Taylor began his career as an instrument builder. In the 1960s FOLK REVIVAL he toured with a number of semipopular folk bands, including The Folkswingers and the more BLUEGRASS-oriented Dixie Gentlemen. He hooked up with fiddler VASSAR CLEMENTS, and the duo became the nucleus of John Hartford's backup band in 1969, remaining with him for a couple of years. His tasteful playing with Hartford helped introduce the Dobro to a new generation of pickers. He recorded two solo albums for Rounder Records in 1973 and 1977, and became a popular figure on the bluegrass circuit. In the 1980s Taylor turned his back on performing to focus on building and repairing instruments; his music shop has become a mecca for traditional musicians in the Nashville area.

Select Discography

Friar Tut, Rounder 11. Album originally recorded and released in 1972, with Sam Bush and NORMAN BLAKE.

TEXAS RUBY (b. R. Agnes Owens, Wise County, Tex., June 4, 1909–March 29, 1963)

Texas Ruby was a cowgirl vocalist of the 1930s who became one of the earliest HONKY-TONK wailers of the 1950s. Big-voiced, and larger-than-life in character, Ruby was known for her tough temper and equally tough vocals.

Born to a real COWBOY family, Ruby was raised in the wilds of Texas, performing from an early age with her brothers and sisters (brother Tex would later compose the cowboy standard "Cattle Call," a hit for EDDY ARNOLD). She began singing on her own in her teen years, by 1933 working her way to Cincinnati, where she hooked up with cowboy bandleader ZEKE CLEMENTS, with whom she performed through the 1930s. While they were appearing on WHO out of Des Moines, Iowa, in the middle of the decade, Ruby threw one of her famous fits when she got mad at the young announcer who introduced them, a greenhorn named Ronald Reagan.

In 1936 the couple were booked into New York City's Village Barn, a Greenwich Village nightclub known for its hokey Western decor that gave urban rustlers a country fix. This led to work in Texas and Ruby's first recordings, made with Clements's band The Bronco Busters, for Decca. Ruby and Zeke went from Texas to California, where Ruby's continued ill temper and heavy drinking took its toll on the act; by 1939 they had split up and Ruby had linked up with trick fiddler Curly Fox, who was to become her husband.

Ruby and Fox performed on THE GRAND OLE OPRY from 1944 to 1948, during which time they recorded for Columbia and King. Ruby switched from her earlier cowgirl YODELING act to a more contemporary, honky-tonk girl persona for these records, which included classic he-done-me-wrong songs like "Ain't You Sorry That You Lied," "You've Been Cheating on Me," and "Have You Got Somebody Else on the

String." In 1948 the duo relocated to Houston, where they performed for the next decade, and then moved to Los Angeles in 1960 to appear on the popular *Town Hall Party* TV program. By mid-1962 they had returned to Nashville, where they recorded a comeback album in March 1963. That same month Curly came home to their trailer after an *Opry* performance to discover it engulfed in flames; Ruby apparently had fallen asleep while smoking a cigarette, and died in the blaze.

Ruby was one of the first tough mamas of country music, earning the nickname "The Sophie Tucker of Country" for good reason. Besides her gruff vocals and equally gruff onstage personality, she pointed the direction for an entire generation of honky-tonk gals. Although her backup bands still recalled the saddle-sore country outfits of the 1930s, the themes of her 1940s and 1950s recordings were modern, particularly in her "I-don't-have-to-take-any-more-of-your-cheatin' " attitude.

TEXAS TORNADOS (c. 1989–1999: Doug Sahm [gtr, voc]; Augie Meyers [org, voc]; Freddy Fender [gtr, voc]; Flaco Jimenez [acc, voc])

The Texas Tornados were COUNTRY-ROCK survivors from the 1960s who formed the ultimate superstar bar band to perform a mix of traditional Tex-Mex and modern country compositions.

Sahm and Meyers were legendary members of the pop-rock group The Sir Douglas Quintet, who had a hit with the R&B-flavored 1965 recording "She's About a Mover." After the band splintered, the duo continued to perform together sporadically. Sahm relocated to California, where he scored a hit with the 1969 hippie love ode "Mendocino," introducing Tex-Mex sounds and instrumentation to the psychedelic rock audience. Through the 1970s and 1980s Sahm and Meyers continued to record and perform together and separately, gaining a large cult audience.

FREDDY FENDER was another musician to come out of the rich traditions of Southwestern music; born Baldemar G. Huerta, he recorded in Spanish before scoring his mid-1970s country hits. Like Sahm and Meyers, he was living off his reputation as a hitmaker by the late 1980s, when the Texas Tornados came together.

The final band member was legendary Southwestern accordionist Flaco Jimenez, who comes from a line of talented players of traditional Spanish dance music (his father was a well-known and oft-recorded accordionist, as is his brother). Flaco had sessioned and toured with Ry Cooder for his legendary *Chicken Skin Music* LP, as well as with other country-pop stars.

The group itself was nothing more than a glorified bar band, although these musicians are some of the greatest ever to have played on a beer-soaked stage. They primarily performed either the past hits of individual members or a mix of folk-influenced and new-country material, in a loose-as-a-goose style that reveals years of experience while it also shows an underlying refusal to work hard at their music. The group disbanded in 1992, then got back together for two reunions/tours in 1996 and 1999. Sahm's death in November 1999 spelled the end of the group.

Select Discography

Best of, Reprise 45511. Compilation of their late-1980s–early-1990s recordings.

THOMAS, B. J. (b. Billy Joe T., Houston, Tex., August 7, 1942)

Thomas is a country-pop vocalist best known for his sweet crooning on the 1969 recording of Burt Bacharach's saccharine 1960s anthem "Raindrops Keep Falling on My Head," featured in the film *Butch Cassidy and the Sundance Kid* and a major hit on both country and pop charts.

In the late 1950s Thomas was already rockin' and rollin' as a member of the Houston-based Triumphs, remaining with the group into the mid-1960s. A locally released cover version of HANK WILLIAMS's "I'm So Lonesome I Could Cry" was picked up by the national Scepter label, giving the group their first hit in 1966. Thanks to its success, Thomas left the group and began recording in a soft-pop vein, having minor hits with 1968's "Eyes of a New York Woman" and "Hooked on a Feeling." His big break came with the perennial middle-of-the-road classic "Raindrops," which is still performed wherever tinkling lounge pianists reign.

Thomas continued to record in a pop-rock vein through the early 1970s, then switched to country music, scoring a hit in 1975 with "(Hey Won't You Play) Another Somebody Done Me Wrong Song," recorded in the classic Nashville style, complete with tinkling keyboards and girly choruses. In 1976 he became a born-again Christian, and through the early 1980s recorded GOSPEL-tinged pop material, winning a Grammy in the gospel category for his 1977 album *Home Where I Belong* on the Myrrh label.

Thomas returned to his secular roots in the mid-1980s, continuing to record a mix of pop and country through the early 1990s and periodically making a comeback without putting much of a dent on the charts. During the mid-through-late 1990s he switched his focus again to gospel material. His Vegas-sized histrionics, married to a voice that reeks of pop-schmaltz, makes him at best a minor figure in contemporary country, although fans continue to flock to hear him perform live.

Select Discography

Greatest Hits, Rhino 70752. All the biggies in chronological order with decent, if skimpy, notes.

THOMPSON, ERNEST (b. E. Errott T., Forsyth County, N.C., 1892–1961)

Thompson, a longtime North Carolina-based one-man band and street singer, was among the first to record as a country artist.

Thompson went blind during childhood and also apparently suffered vocal-cord damage in a fire, which led him to have a piercing, high tenor voice. He learned piano tuning at the North Carolina State School for the Blind, and also mastered a number of instruments, including GUITAR and harmonica.

Thompson recorded twice in 1924, the first time on his own in April, and the second time with his niece, Connie Faw Sides, in November. His first release was the most popular, featuring "The Wreck of the Southern Old 97," which had previously been recorded in a different version by HENRY WHITTER, and "Are You from Dixie?," a 1915 vaudeville number written in a "Southern" style. Both were immensely popular in their day.

Thompson never recorded again, but frequently played in his native North Carolina, in the Winston-Salem area, through the 1940s. Like many other street musicians, he performed a mix of traditional and popular songs, as well as hymns and other "favorites." He sometimes worked with his niece and his sister, Agnes, in an informal string band. In 1943 he was photographed by the local paper while entertaining a group of soldiers on leave on the city's streets; he is shown playing a twelve-string guitar, with a harmonica and small tin cup (for tips) around his neck. He wears a bowler hat labeled "Blind."

THOMPSON FAMILY (Joe, b. Cedar Grove Township, N.C., December 9, 1918; Nate, b. Cedar Grove Township, N.C., February 16, 1916–December 22, 1997; and Odell, b. Walter O., near Methane, N.C., August 9, 1911–April 28, 1994)

The African-American Thompson family has a long history of music making in the North Carolina piedmont, according to family lore dating back to Robert Thompson, born in 1849, who was said to be a FIDDLE player. Robert's sons included three musicians: John Arch, who was a fiddler, Jacob A., and Walter E. John Arch and his brothers played for both white and black dances in the region around the family farm. Arch had several sons, among them Nate, a BANJO player, and Joe, a fiddler. Joe began to learn the fiddle at an early age, despite his father's resistance to allowing him even to touch his instrument. He constructed a homemade fiddle, using the wires from a screen door to make strings, thereby impressing his father with his determination.

Joe and Nate played for local dances from the 1930s through the end of World War II. During this time they were sometimes joined by their cousin, Odell

Thompson, a banjo player and guitarist who was the son of their uncle, Walter E. After the war Joe worked in a furniture factory and ceased making music. However, in the 1970s folklorist Kip Lornell "discovered" Joe and encouraged him to begin playing again, usually with his cousin Odell; Nate also recorded and performed on occasion with both Joe and Odell. This led to a series of tours and recordings until Odell's death in 1994. Joe Thompson continued to perform through the 1990s, although increasing age and ill health slowed him toward the end of the decade. As of this writing in the autumn of 2001, he is recovering from a stroke that has left him unable to play music.

The Thompson family represents a little-documented tradition in the South: African-American musicians playing a repertoire of dance music in the old-time string-band style. The Thompsons both performed for white dances and learned many tunes from their white neighbors; in turn they taught many tunes to other musicians, black and white. The survival of the traditional drop-thumb/clawhammer banjo style among African Americans was a surprise to some when these musicians were first documented in the mid-1970s, but new research and fieldwork have shown that a healthy string-band tradition existed among both races in the upper South.

Select Discography

Old Time Music from the North Carolina Piedmont, Global Village 217. Cassette-only issue of Joe and Odell.

Joe Thompson: Family Tradition, Rounder Select 2161. Recordings of Joe, Odell, and Nate Thompson from the 1970s through the 1990s, produced and annotated by Bob Carlin.

THOMPSON, HANK (b. Henry William T., Waco, Tex., September 3, 1925)

Thompson is a Texas singer/guitarist who helped carry on the WESTERN SWING sound for a new generation of honky-tonkers.

Thompson began as a teenage performer on local radio as "Hank the Hired Hand," and also recorded for the tiny, local Globe label. These sides were so successful that they led TEX RITTER to recommend him to California-based Capitol Records, which signed the singer in 1948; he remained with Capitol for eighteen years. His backup band, The Brazos Valley Boys, featured the drive of a good Western Swing outfit; on record and tours they were often augmented by the legendary Capitol session guitarist MERLE TRAVIS. Though the band was swinging in orientation, Thompson's song choices focused on women, booze, and heartbreak, classic HONKY-TONK themes.

Thompson's first big hit was "Humpty Dumpty Heart" from 1948; he followed this with many classics, including 1952's honky-tonk theme song, "Wild Side of Life." In the mid-1950s he helped promote singer WANDA JACKSON by featuring her in his live shows and in recordings.

In the early 1960s, impressed by the success of big-band vocalist Louis Prima in Las Vegas, Thompson hit the trail for the gamblers' capital, recording a fine live LP there in 1961. After leaving Capitol in 1966, Thompson roamed among labels for a while, and began performing mostly with anonymous session musicians. His 1970s recordings are marred by the generic, mainstream Nashville Sound. Thompson continues to record and perform, and is most active around Fort Worth, his current home. He was elected to the Country Music Hall of Fame in 1989. In 2000 he issued the impressive album *Seven Decades*, showing he still has his chops.

Select Discography

And His Brazos Valley Boys, Bear Family 59042. Twelve CDs of everything he recorded between 1946 and 1964. Haul out the checkbook, take a home equity loan, and prepare for hours of classic Hank.

Vintage, Capitol 36901. Twenty of his best sides from 1947 to 1961.

Best of, Varese 5747. His later recordings for MCA, Dot, and Warners, made between 1966 and 1979.

Seven Decades, Hightone 8121. 2000 recordings showing that Hank's picking and singing are undiminished by age.

THOMPSON, SUE (b. Eva S. McKee, Nevada, Mo., July 19, 1925)

Thompson was a pop-country chanteuse of the 1960s famous for her little-girl vocal style.

Thompson was a precocious performer, playing GUITAR and singing on stage by age seven. Her family relocated to California, where she won a San Jose-based talent contest and gained the attention of Dude Martin, who ran San Francisco's *Hometown Hayride* TV show; the two married, and Thompson became a featured performer on the show, as well as recording with Martin's backup band, Round-up Gang. She divorced Martin and then married country singer HANK PENNY, performing with him in Las Vegas until that marriage, too, dissolved in the late 1950s. Through the 1950s she made unsuccessful recordings for a number of labels.

In the early 1960s, when she was living in the Los Angeles area, she was signed to the new Hickory label, led by WESLEY ROSE. She had her first hits on the pop charts with 1961's "Sad Movies (Make Me Cry)" and "Norman," and then moved to countrified material.

Her career wound down by the late 1960s, although she returned to the charts in the mid-1970s with the twosome "Big Mabel Murphy" and "Never Naughty Rosie." She continues to perform in her native Southwest.

Select Discography

Greatest Hits, Curb 77462.

THOMPSON, UNCLE JIMMY (b. James Donald T., Baxter, Putnam County, Tenn., 1848–February 17, 1931)

Born in a small farming town between Nashville and Knoxville, Tennessee, Thompson moved with his family to Texas sometime around his tenth birthday. He learned to fiddle there, absorbing the showy style of Texas contest fiddlers through such virtuoso pieces as "Flying Clouds," a popular late-nineteenth-century dance number. By the mid-1880s Thompson had made his way back to Tennessee, where he settled near his birthplace, married, and worked a farm. Sometime around the turn of the century, he returned to Texas, settling near the Oklahoma border, and began to focus more on his FIDDLE playing.

Jimmy's big moment of fame in his early career came in 1907, when he participated in a famed fiddlers' convention and contest held in Dallas. It is said to have attracted nearly 100 of the time's greatest fiddlers, and Jimmy took first place.

Jimmy returned to Tennessee around 1912, settling outside of Nashville on a small farm. His first wife soon died of cancer, but he was reunited with other family members, including his young niece, a music teacher named Eva Thompson Jones. He also began performing locally with his younger son, a guitarist, and his son's wife, a BANJO player. In 1916 he remarried; he joined his new wife, Ella, in her home on a small farm in Wilson County, Tennessee, near the town of Laguardo. "Aunt Ella," as she was known locally, was a buck dancer who often performed on the streets, accompanied by her fiddling husband. In 1923 Jimmy returned to Texas for another fiddlers' contest, and again took first prize.

But it was Jimmy's appearance on Nashville radio on the night of November 28, 1925, accompanied by his niece on the piano, that would change his life. His playing of the traditional tune "Tennessee Wagonner" brought an incredible response from listeners across the country. This launched the WSM *Saturday Night Barn Dance*, which would become famous as THE GRAND OLE OPRY. Thompson played for the full hour on the first *Barn Dance* broadcast, and continued to be the featured artist for at least a month afterward. When word spread that old-time music was being performed on the air, the show's producer/host, GEORGE D. HAY, was flooded with similar acts, but continued to employ Thompson until 1928; his traditional backwoods fiddle style strongly appealed to the rural audience that the program hoped to reach. Although he was a farmer for most of his life, Thompson had also performed locally at dances and fiddlers' contests and conventions. He recorded for Columbia in 1926 and for Vocalion in 1930. In 1931 he died of pneumonia, at the age of eighty-three.

THREE LITTLE MAIDS, THE (c. 1932–1935: Evelyn, Lucille [January 1, 1915–December 16, 1978], and Eva [d. November 17, 1951] Overstake, all born Decatur, Ill.)

This clean-cut vocal trio were the darlings of WLS's NATIONAL BARN DANCE radio program; all three went on to further careers in country music.

Hailing from Decatur, Illinois, the girls originally sang as a group at home, influenced by their religious upbringing and the family's association with the Salvation Army; a song that became closely associated with them was "I Ain't Gonna Study War No More" (originally a hymn, and then in the 1950s and 1960s FOLK REVIVAL an antiwar anthem).

Eldest sister Evelyn provided the trio's distinctive low voice; when the group dissolved in 1935, she continued to perform on the *Barn Dance* for another twenty years. Middle sister Lucille was the musical brains behind the trio; she played the GUITAR, the only one of the three to play an instrument, and probably was responsible for the group's vocal arrangements. After the group disbanded, she turned to performing slightly "blue" material under the name Lucille Lee, recording with The Sweet Violet Boys, a racy pseudonym for PATSY MONTANA's backup band, THE PRAIRIE RAMBLERS. She wrote a number of suggestive titles, including "I Love My Fruit," about the pleasures of eating in bed. In the 1940s, with the COWBOY/cowgirl phase in full blossom, Lucille transformed herself into Jenny Lou Carson, recording for Decca and writing classics like "Jealous Heart" and "Let Me Go, Lover," and patriotic tub-thumpers like "Dear God, Watch Over Joe" and "When the Boys Come Marching Home." She moved to recording in the cowgirl/folk vein for Mercury Records in the 1950s.

Youngest sister Eva began performing with the group when she was just thirteen; she attracted the attention of WLS star RED FOLEY, who married her in 1935, ending the group. Her daughter, Shirley Foley, wed Pat Boone and became his performing sidekick in the 1950s; Shirley and Pat, in turn, gave the world DEBBIE "You Light Up My Life" BOONE. Eva committed suicide after learning that Red was cheating on her with another (younger) singer.

TILLIS, MEL (b. Lonnie Melvin T., Tampa, Fla., August 8, 1932)

A fine songwriter and performer, Tillis hit his stride in the late 1950s as a writer and in the late 1960s as a performer.

Born in Tampa, Tillis was raised in the small town of Pahokee, Florida, where he learned to play the GUITAR. After serving in the Air Force in the early 1950s and spending two years in college, Tillis went to Nashville in search of a career as a singer. WEBB PIERCE liked his material, and recorded Tillis's "I'm Tired" in 1957. The duo wrote "I Ain't Never" soon after, and also recorded a duet in 1963 on the humorous "How Come Your Dog Don't Bite Nobody but Me?." Tillis was signed by Columbia Records in 1957, who didn't really know what to do with him, and he scored only minor hits, beginning with 1958's sentimental "The Violet and the Rose."

Tillis's next big break came in 1963 when BOBBY BARE had a monster hit with his "Detroit City." He signed with Kapp Records, and had his first hit on his own with 1965's "Stateside" (which became the name of his backup band), followed two years later by a

monster hit with HARLAN HOWARD's classic WEEPER ballad "Life Turned Her That Way" (covered by RICKY VAN SHELTON in 1987). As a songwriter Tillis had another hit with KENNY ROGERS and the First Edition's cover of his "Ruby (Don't Take Your Love to Town)."

Tillis began the 1970s with MGM, recording a fine combination of HONKY-TONK songs and weepers, including 1971's "The Arms of a Fool" and "Brand New Mister Me," a remake of "Sawmill" in 1973 (he had originally cut it for Columbia in 1959), "Midnight Me and the Blues" from 1974, and "The Woman in the Back of My Mind" in 1975. He then switched to MCA, where his recordings took a decided turn toward country-pop after one last fine honky-tonk number, "Good Woman Blues," in 1976. Tillis hit his nadir in 1978 with the maudlin "I Believe in You."

Tillis moved to Elektra in 1980, recorded an album of duets with that old boots-wearin' gal, Nancy Sinatra, in 1981, and then returned to MCA for a couple of minor hits, including 1983's "In the Middle of the Night" and 1984's "New Patches." Although he fell off the charts in the early 1980s, Mel has remained a popular performer on the road and on TV, and operates his own theater in new-country haven BRANSON, MISSOURI. His daughter PAM TILLIS is one of new-country's finest singers; the pair recorded their first duet in 2001.

Select Discography

Greatest Hits, Curb 77482. Recordings of varying quality from the late 1970s and early 1980s.

TILLIS, PAM (b. Plant City, Fla., July 24, 1957)

New-country star (and daughter of SINGER/SONGWRITER MEL TILLIS) Pam broke through on the country charts in the early 1990s with her combination of sassy love songs and humorous takes on country-music conventions.

Tillis is typical of Nashville's new-country performers in that her musical education, while rooted deeply in country traditions, took her through a variety of styles. She performed, sang, and composed in rock, free-jazz, Top 40, disco, 1940s jazz/pop, and even new-wave styles through the mid-1980s. Although these efforts met with limited commercial success, they helped build an eclectic base for her later musical explorations.

In 1986 Tillis formed Twang Night, a mock-country revue that celebrated Nashville's HONKY-TONK glories while building her reputation as a new-country songwriter. In the late 1980s her songs were covered by the trio of DOLLY PARTON, LINDA RONSTADT, and EMMYLOU HARRIS ("Those Memories"), HIGHWAY 101 ("Someone Else's Troubles Now"), and Judy Rodman ("Goin' to Work"). Tillis recorded on her own for

Mel Tillis during his hit-making days, c. mid-1970s. Photo: Raeanne Rubenstein

Warner Brothers, but she didn't chart until switching to Arista in 1990.

Tillis's early-1990s hits include 1991's romantic, steamy love ballad "Maybe It Was Memphis," 1992's softer, more sensual "Shake the Sugartree," and her 1993 tongue-in-cheek "Cleopatra (Queen of Denial)," in which Tillis created the ultimate suffering country female. In 1994 she scored with the Tex-Mex-flavored #1 hit "Mi Vida Loca (My Crazy Life)" and a cover of "When You Walk in the Room." The second half of the decade was more difficult for her, chartwise, although she continued to record and tour. In August 2000 Tillis was made a member of THE GRAND OLE OPRY. A year later she released her first new album since 1999, hoping to regain her chart momentum; it also included her first recorded duet with her father, something that would appeal to the older country crowd.

Tillis is an energetic performer, her strong, assertive vocals showing her background in rock and R&B. Still, she has an identifiably country sound, grounding her music in the traditions of Nashville's great women vocalists of the 1950s and 1960s.

Select Discography

Super Hits, Warners 47789. Late 1980s hits.
Greatest Hits, Arista 18836. Most of her 1990s hits after her Warners years.

TILLMAN, FLOYD (b. Ryan, Okla., December 8, 1914)

Tillman is a legendary HONKY-TONK SINGER/SONG-WRITER who was also a pioneer performer on the electric guitar. In the words of the *Faber Encyclopedia of Popular Music*, "What JIMMIE RODGERS did for railroads in country music, Tillman did for adultery" with his most famous composition, 1949's "Slippin' Around."

Tillman was a multitalented instrumentalist who performed with many of the Southwest's best WESTERN SWING bands in the 1930s, beginning with the band led by German immigrant ADOLPH HOFNER, and eventually hooking up with legendary fiddler Cliff Bruner. In 1938 Bruner recorded his song "It Makes No Difference Now," which has become a country classic thanks primarily to the cover recording by JIMMIE DAVIS, who acquired a half-interest in the song from Tillman for a measly $300. The song was also successfully covered by Bing Crosby, an early example of a country hit crossing over onto the pop charts. Its success led to a solo contract for Tillman with Decca in the early 1940s, and he scored hits with his self-penned "They Took the Stars Out of Heaven" in 1942, followed a year later with "Each Night at Nine."

After the war Tillman enjoyed his greatest success as a recording artist at Columbia with hard-hitting honky-tonk anthems, beginning with 1946's "Drivin' Nails in My Coffin," "I Love You So Much It Hurts" from the next year, and the immortal "Slippin' Around" (with the answer song "I'll Never Slip Around Again," rushed out to capitalize on the original song's success). His jazzy vocal style, influenced by his years of performing Western Swing, would in turn influence a new generation of singer/songwriters, particularly a young Texan, WILLIE NELSON. Tillman continued to record sporadically through the 1950s and 1960s, scoring one more hit in 1960 with "It Just Tore Me Up." He has since lived primarily off the income from his early successful songs, which continue to be performed by both old and new country artists. He was inducted into the Country Music Hall of Fame in 1984.

Select Discography

Country Music Hall of Fame, MCA 10189. Early-1940s Decca recordings.
Columbia Historic Edition, Columbia 39996. Late-1940s Columbia recordings.

TIPPIN, AARON (b. Pensacola, Fla., July 3, 1958)

A hunky hitmaker of the early 1990s, Tippin celebrates the ordinary working man in much of his material, thereby appealing to the core country audience.

Although born in Florida, Tippin was raised in rural South Carolina, where he dreamed of becoming a commercial pilot. He obtained his pilot's license when he was fifteen, and began studying so he could be certified to fly large commercial jets. Music was strictly a sideline at this time, but when the early 1980s brought the energy crisis and recession, Tippin realized that his future as a pilot was limited. Discouraged by the failure of his marriage, he took a job in a cotton mill and temporarily abandoned music.

In 1985 he moved to Nashville, and was hired as a staff writer by Acuff-Rose. After recording demos and writing songs, he was signed by RCA in 1990, producing an immediate sensation with his first single, "You've Got to Stand for Something," released in the wake of the Gulf War. This patriotic gut-thumper set the stage for future Tippin hits celebrating the ordinary man, including "Trim Yourself to Fit the World" and "Working Man's Ph.D." Because Tippin writes his own material, it tends to reflect his concerns; for example, the hit "There Ain't Nothin' Wrong with the Radio" answers critics of country and pop music who think music is leading young listeners astray.

However, like many other early-1990s country stars, Tippin had trouble duplicating his hitmaking after the mid-1990s. In 1998 he left RCA for Lyric Street/Hollywood Records. Also like other 1990s survivors Tippin was able to revive his career in the new century. He scored big in 2000 with the tough-sounding single "Kiss This," which propelled his album *People like Us* to gold status. Tippin's career was revived in the autumn of 2001 with the release of the patriotic "Where the Stars and Stripes and the Eagles Fly," in the wake of the terrorist attacks on the country. Like fellow country artist ALAN JACKSON, Tippin was quick to record and release a number to ride the wave of patriotism.

Select Discography

Greatest Hits . . . and Then Some, RCA 67427. His early-1990s hits.

TRAVIS, MERLE (b. Rosewood, Ky., November 29, 1917; d. Nashville, Tenn., October 20, 1983)

One of the most innovative and influential country guitarists, Travis was also a fine songwriter whose works have the lasting quality of mountain ballads with more than a nod to the sounds of the HONKY-TONK.

Travis's father, a BANJO player, taught him to play the instrument in a two-finger picked style that was common in the upper South in the 1920s and 1930s. When the youngster switched to the GUITAR, he adapted this picking style to the new instrument, playing the bass strings with his thumb while using a flat pick on the upper strings. He damped the strings with the heel of his hand as he strummed, giving a "choked" sound to his music. This technique, which has come to be known as "Travis picking," was highly influential on the next generation of country guitarmen, including CHET ATKINS, DOC WATSON, and scores of others.

Travis hooked up briefly with Clayton McMichen's jazzy band The Georgia Wildcats in the mid-1930s, and soon after was hired by Cincinnati's popular radio program *Boone County Jamboree*, where he worked for a decade as a soloist and accompanist, performing with GRANDPA JONES and THE DELMORE BROTHERS in the informal group known as The Brown's Ferry Four (named after The Delmore Brothers' big hit, "Brown's Ferry Blues"). The group recorded in various configurations for the fledgling Cincinnati-based King label, which in the early 1950s would become a leader in country and R&B recordings.

During the last two years of World War II, Travis served in the military, then returned to civilian life and settled in southern California, where he worked with several transplanted WESTERN SWING bands. He signed with a new label, Capitol Records, and had his first solo hits with his own compositions, the honky-tonkin' "Divorce Me C.O.D.," "So Round, So Firm, So Fully Packed," "Sweet Temptation," and the tongue-in-cheek "Smoke, Smoke, Smoke That Cigarette," which

was written for and recorded by TEX WILLIAMS. In 1947 he cut an album called *Folk Songs of the Hills*, which included his own compositions in a folk style based on his memories of the tough life of the coal miners in his native Kentucky. Two of these songs, "Dark as a Dungeon" and "Sixteen Tons," have become standards in the folk and country repertoires, the latter thanks to TENNESSEE ERNIE FORD's finger-snappin' 1955 cover version.

In the 1950s Travis experimented with developing a solid-body electric guitar; instrument makers Paul Bigsby and Leo Fender both worked on Travis's design, which eventually led to the mass production of the instruments that would become the lead voice in rock-and-roll ensembles. The electric instrument that Travis often played suited his picking style, which emphasized a percussive, rhythmic chop while downplaying the natural "ringing" sound of the acoustic instrument.

Through the 1950s and 1960s Travis was both a soloist and a session artist, although he never regained his popularity of the late 1940s. He was invited to participate in THE NITTY GRITTY DIRT BAND's all-star country tribute album, *Will the Circle Be Unbroken*, in 1971, which helped to revive his career as a performer. After that recording he made a few more albums with Chet Atkins and JOE MAPHIS, as well as returning to his Western Swing roots on an album featuring many alumni of BOB WILLS's bands. His 1981 album, *Travis Pickin'*, was a Grammy nominee.

Select Discography

Folk Songs of the Hills, Bear Family 15636. The great late-1940s folk sessions cut for Capitol and a lesser-known return to the folk style in 1963. The 1947 material is also reissued on Capitol 35810, along with some radio transcriptions.
The Best of, Razor & Tie 82214. Twenty of his best numbers from 1946–1953, including instrumentals and songs.
Guitar Rags and a Too Fast Past, Bear Family 15637. Five CDs, encompassing his Capitol and King recordings, from late 1946 to 1953, accompanied by an eighty-page book.

TRAVIS, RANDY (b. R. Bruce Traywick, Marshville, N.C., May 4, 1959)

Randy Travis was among the most successful of the "new country" performers of the mid-80's–mid-90's because his music paid homage to the country past at the same time it often seemed to be gently poking fun at its conventions. Although he became a more conservative performer as his success deepened, Travis was still able to wring that authentic lonesome sound from his deep baritone vocals and well-chosen, well-crafted country songs.

Born to a poor North Carolina family, Travis was exposed early to the classic country recordings of HANK WILLIAMS, LEFTY FRIZZELL, GEORGE JONES, MERLE TRAVIS, and ERNEST TUBB, all of whom were idolized by his father. He began playing GUITAR at age eight, and six years later was performing as a duo with his brother at local clubs. When he was sixteen, he ran away from home and won a talent contest in Charlotte, North Carolina, which led to his discovery by local bar owner Lib Hatcher, the Svengali manager who would support his career for seven years before he hit it big (later, the two married).

Performing under the name Randy Ray, Travis came to Nashville with Hatcher at the age of twenty-three. He was quickly signed by Warner Brothers Records, recording the classic *Storms of Life* LP. Randy's hits off this first LP have the sly edge of the best of country music; "On the Other Hand" tells the story of a married man who is wavering on the edge of an affair but keeps being reminded of his marital status by the ring he wears "on the other hand." "Digging Up Bones" tells of a man who keeps "digging up the bones" of his failed relationship; the humor is perfectly paired with Randy's deadpan delivery.

Randy scored countless hits through the mid-1990s, but most had retreated from the adventuresome quality of his first recordings. His next big hit, "Forever and Ever Amen," is a touching piece of country corn, but it takes itself too seriously to be believable. Similarly, his early 90's hits echo the country clichés of love that runs "deeper than the hollers, higher than the mountains."

However, by the mid-1990s Travis's career had cooled as newer hunks-in-hats took to the charts. He went hitless through the period, and was dropped by Warner Brothers in 1995. Travis made a couple of appearances in made-for-TV films and series television guest shots, but came across as a rather stiff actor. In 1997 he signed with the new Dreamworks label, and in 1998 scored his first chart-topper in four years with "Out of My Bones." In 2000 Warner Brothers released an "inspirational" album that he had recorded while still with the label but that had gone unreleased, perhaps because of its somewhat lackluster production.

Yet all in all, Randy's quavering bass vocals, his earnest awkwardness as a performer, and even his rudimentary guitar picking make him almost the archetypal country singer. He managed to put forward even the sappiest sentiments with conviction, and never seemed to be stooping for a hit even as his accountants deposit his royalty checks.

Select Discography

Storms of Life, Warner Bros. 25435. 1986 debut LP, still a classic.

Greatest Hits, Vols. 1 and 2, Warner Bros. 45044/45045.

TRICK PONY (1996–present: Heidi Newfield [gtr, hca, voc]; Keith Burns [gtr, voc]; Ira Dean [b, voc])

Trick Pony, a neo-cow-punk/ROCKABILLY band, was formed in 1996. Atlanta-born Burns had previously worked as a backup musician on the road with JOE DIFFIE, and penned Diffie's hit "Whole Lotta Gone" from 1996. Raleigh, North Carolina, native Dean was previously the bassist with TANYA TUCKER's road show. Newfield was a SINGER/SONGWRITER who came to Nashville in the mid-1990s, looking for success as a solo artist. The group has worked up an exciting stage act, complete with flashing headlights mounted in Dean's upright bass, and the stage-diving sex appeal of Newfield.

All of this excitement was successfully captured in the band's first video in 2001, the arch "Pour Me," written by the band members. A neo-rockabilly tune, it starts out as a woman's lament for her lost love, until we realize that "Pour Me" actually means "Pour Me . . . another shot of whiskey." The energetic, good-natured performance of Newfield, the catchy hook, and sprightly three-part harmonies made the song a video hit; it worked its way up the charts. They followed with another hit, "On a Night Like This," a more conventional country-pop ballad.

Newfield's vocals are reminiscent of Tanya Tucker, who projects a similar "baddest good girl" personality. She is obviously the group's strongest asset. The question is whether they can build on the allure of their stage shtick and break out of the novelty mold. There is also a limit to how far rockabilly styles can be stretched. Nonetheless, their debut single and album promised much for the band. At best their hip attitude recalls other new New-Nashville acts, like BR4-59.

TRISCHKA, TONY (b. Anthony Cattel T., Syracuse, N.Y., January 16, 1949)

If one person can be praised (or blamed) for the noodling, spacey BANJO playing that was an integral part of PROGRESSIVE BLUEGRASS bands of the 1970s, it would have to be Tony Trischka, the man who launched a thousand notes.

Trischka originally reached prominence as a member of COUNTRY COOKING, an all-instrumental band that was famous for the twin banjos of Trischka and Peter Wernick. After the band dissolved in the early 1970s, Trischka released his first solo album, *Bluegrass Light*, a kind of Sun Ra-meets-Earl Scruggs outing. Although not exactly easy listening, the album opened up the potential for playing a wider melodic and harmonic range on bluegrass-style banjo. During this period Trischka also performed with the eclectic band Breakfast Special, a more spacey incarnation of Country Cooking.

After a few more avant-garde solo albums, Trischka returned to the fold on the half-traditional, half-modern album *Banjoland* from the late 1970s. He even played in traditional Scruggs style, announcing that the far-out cats were not averse to honoring bluegrass' roots. In the early 1980s he formed the band SKYLINE, which featured an odd wedding of contemporary country songs with his own toned-down original instrumentals.

After Skyline's demise in the early '90s, Trischka performed as a solo artist and as part of the Rounder records banjo tours featuring BELA FLECK, BILL KEITH, and other BLUEGRASS pickers. Though his picking still reflects the influences of jazz, avant-garde, and rock-and-roll styles, his repertoire hews closer to traditional sources, and even his own compositions are nearer to bluegrass roots. During the mid-through-late 1990s he presented "History of the Banjo" concerts, in which he played everything from minstrel-era pieces to his own progressive instrumentals. In 1999 he introduced his latest jazz-fusion outfit, The Tony Trischka Band, on the album *Bend*.

Select Discography

Dust on the Needle, Rounder 11508. Compilation of his many Rounder albums.

Early Years, Rounder 11578. A second compilation, focusing more on his first few albums.

Solo Banjo Works, Rounder 0247. Solos by Trischka and Bela Fleck.

TRITT, TRAVIS (b. Marietta, Ga., February 9, 1963)

Tritt, one of the more distinctive of the new-country vocalists and performers, has a knack for performing and writing interesting material that both honors and extends country traditions. Although, like many other successful country acts, he is in danger of lapsing into glitzy showmanship, Tritt seems rooted enough to last for the long run.

From his first recording, Tritt showed an understanding and appreciation of traditional country genres, particularly HONKY-TONK laments, that set him apart from other crooning wanna-bes. His vocal style has a healthy quaver to it that recalls mountain singers, as well as previous stars like HANK WILLIAMS and GEORGE JONES. Many of his better songs, like 1993's hit "T-R-O-U-B-L-E," recall, perhaps unintentionally, classic country genres (in this case, songs like "S-A-V-E-D" by THE BLUE SKY BOYS and "D-I-V-O-R-C-E" by TAMMY WYNETTE, although it certainly takes a much different slant than either the Bible-thumping of the Boys or Wynette's "let's-not-tell-the-children" theme).

Coming from a middle-class, rural background, Tritt had his first exposure to music in the church choir. He taught himself guitar when he was eight, and wrote his first song at fourteen. Like many other of today's country artists, he was as influenced by mid-1970s folk-rock as he was by pure country, learning songs by groups like THE EAGLES (he participated in a 1993 fund-raising album of Eagles songs released by new-country artists).

After high school Tritt worked for four years on a loading dock, rising through the ranks to be a manager, while performing part-time in local clubs. He was heard by Danny Davenport, a Georgia-based talent scout for Warner Brothers Records, who was as much interested in his songwriting abilities as in his performing skills. They worked together for two years, crafting demo tapes for the label that led to the release of his first album, 1990's *Country Club*, which yielded four hit singles, including the #1 country hit "Help Me Hold On." Mega music manager Ken Kragen, of "We Are the World" fame, came on board to handle Tritt's career, undoubtedly helping to vault him into the upper stratosphere of country stardom.

Tritt's career really took off with his second album, released in 1991. This yielded the barroom anthems "Here's a Quarter (Call Someone Who Cares)" and "The Whiskey Ain't Working Anymore" (the latter a duet with new-country hunkster MARTY STUART). Fans took to throwing quarters at Tritt while he performed, which made him quickly drop his signature song from his concerts for fear of injuries from the flying change!

In 1992 Tritt was inducted into THE GRAND OLE OPRY, at the time the youngest member of this venerable institution. While touring with Stuart he gained exposure, thanks to Kragen, through the placement of his songs in movies, including the theme song for *My Cousin Vinny* ("Bible Belt," a collaboration with the country-rockers Little Feat) and a cover of ELVIS PRESLEY's "Burning Love" for *Honeymoon in Vegas*. In 1993 he appeared with another Kragen client, grizzled country crooner KENNY ROGERS, in a TV movie, *Rio Diablo*.

Tritt's 1993 successes include the topical "Lord Have Mercy on the Working Man," with a clever video showing how the "honest, ordinary citizen" is ignored by the media and politicians; and the bar-hopper's anthem "T-R-O-U-B-L-E," giving his third album its title tune. In the video for this honky-tonk rev up, Tritt appears in tight leather pants, wriggling his way through the number. This is somewhat ironic in light of his criticism of BILLY RAY CYRUS for reducing country music to he-man attitudes, but, as they say, there's no arguing with success.

In 1994 he released the platinum album, *Ten Feet Tall and Bullet Proof*, also the title of his autobiography. It spawned the #1 hit "Foolish Pride," and also marked Tritt's greatest success on both country and pop charts. A year later his *Greatest Hits* package arrived, and also sold strongly.

After a dry period in the mid-through-late 1990s, Tritt left Warner Brothers and signed with Columbia. He returned big time after the turn of the new century. In the summer of 2001 his song "It's a Great Day to Be Alive" reached #2 on the country charts. "Modern Day Bonnie and Clyde" followed as a big hit in 2002.

Select Discography

Greatest Hits—From the Beginning, Warner Bros. 46001. His biggest hits through the mid-1990s.

TRUCK DRIVING SONGS Three subjects have become stereotypes of country songwriting: mother, prison, and trucks. The image of the lone trucker blazing a path through the wilderness has replaced the COWBOY in American folklore as the last hero of the blacktop frontier. An explosion of songwriting from the early 1960s through the CB craze of the 1970s helped make this myth into a subgenre of country music.

Cliff Bruner's recording of "Truck Driver's Blues" from 1939, with a vocal by MOON MULLICAN, is generally credited with being the first truckin' ode on wax. "Truck Driving Man," the best-loved and most often parodied song of the open road, first appeared on a recording by Terry Fell in 1954. However, the song that spurred the movement was DAVE DUDLEY's 1963 megahit, "Six Days on the Road." JIMMY MARTIN leaped on the truckin' bandwagon with his "Widow Maker" from 1964, DICK CURLESS followed with his 1965 hit "A Tombstone Every Mile," and traditional bluegrassers JIM AND JESSE scored a surprise 1967 hit with "Diesel on My Tail." Two small BLUEGRASS/country labels, Starday and King, fueled the truck-drivin' mania, releasing albums with the colorful titles *Super Slab Hits, Truckin' On, Forty Miles of Bad Road*, and *Diesel Smoke, Dangerous Curves*, and equally colorful covers shot "on location" at truck stops showing big rigs, bad dudes, and the gals they love.

Many of these songs incorporated the sentimentality of earlier RAILROAD SONGS celebrating the train engineer. The engineer who bravely piloted his train (even staying at his post through a gruesome train wreck) was replaced in the new truckers' songs by the image of the brave, honest truck driver, who sometimes had to give his own life to save another. A subgenre of trucking recitations, stories supposedly told by the rigmasters themselves about the difficulties of life on the road, reached its nadir in the classic "The Man Behind the Wheel," a recording that falls squarely into the so-bad-it's-good genre of schlock classics.

The 1970s brought a new wrinkle to the truck rage: the CB (citizens band) radio, with its own special jar-

gon. The biggest song to celebrate the new wave of CB outlaws was C. W. McCALL's hit "Convoy." During the '80s, ALABAMA has had hits with "Roll On (Eighteen Wheeler)," and the trucker has been turned into a romantic softie in KATHY MATTEA's 1988 hit "Eighteen Wheels and a Dozen Roses."

A subnote from the hippie culture was the popularity of The Grateful Dead's "Truckin' " from their COUNTRY-ROCK LP of the early 1970s, *American Beauty*. The expression "Keep on truckin'," with its sexual overtones (and reference to the popular 1930s dance style) originated in the world of swing jazz; the Dead melded this groovy image with the traditional country notion of the truckdriver as his own man. Lowell George of the blues-rock band Little Feat wrote two of the most memorable hippie truck-driving anthems, "Willin' " (oft-covered by 1970s guitar strummers) and an answer song to "Truck Driving Man" called "Truck Driving Girl." R. Crumb, a comic-book artist and amateur musician who formed his own country-swing group called The Cheap Suit Serenades in the 1970s, took the motto "Keep on Truckin' " for his comic-book hero, a figure who often appeared painted on the sides of everything from the hippie truck—the VW Microbus—to big rigs.

TUBB, ERNEST (b. Crisp, Tex., February 9, 1914–September 6, 1984)

For those familiar only with Tubb's later performances and recordings, when he was suffering from emphysema, it's difficult to remember how important and groundbreaking an artist he was. Tubb introduced electric lead guitar to country music as early as 1941, and was the first GRAND OLE OPRY member to perform with amplified instruments. He was also one of the greatest performers of HONKY-TONK songs, legitimizing the genre for a broader audience. His slightly off-pitch, relaxed vocals were perfectly suited to the rough-and-tumble honky-tonks where he got his musical training.

Tubb had no ambitions to be a country singer until he heard the recordings of JIMMIE RODGERS. So determined was he to emulate the Rodgers style that he sought out the singer's widow, who gave him her blessing to perform the blue yodeler's material. From the mid-1930s through the early 1940s, Tubb honed his style, beginning as a pure Jimmie Rodgers imitator but slowly transforming himself into a more modern, honky-tonk singer. Undoubtedly his experience performing in small barrooms across Texas helped shape his newer sound; he relied on amplified instruments to cut through the noise, and chose songs that expressed classic barroom sentiments.

The real change came with his signing by Decca Records in 1940 and his enormous hit, one year later, with the loping "Walking the Floor over You," the quintessential honky-tonk anthem that was to become his lifelong theme song and perhaps was the first country recording to feature electric-guitar lead. Tubb's bone-dry delivery wed with the chunky rhythm of the backup band made this recording a country classic. During World War II, Tubb migrated to Hollywood, where he appeared in two B-grade horse operas (among other films) and recorded with pop music's Andrews Sisters.

Tubb made his most influential recordings and radio appearances in the late 1940s and early-to-mid-1950s with his band, The Texas Troubadours, always featuring electric lead guitar. He nurtured the talents of several guitarists, including Fay "Smitty" Smith, Eddie Tudor, Jimmie Short, Butterball Paige, and, later, Billy Byrd and Leon Rhodes, as well as steel guitarists Buddy Charlton and the legendary BUDDY EMMONS. Tubb introduced the electric guitar to the *Opry* when he became a member in 1943; four years later he opened his record store down the street from the Ryman Auditorium, and for many years hosted WSM's *Midnight Jamboree* radio show, broadcast immediately following the *Opry*, from the store. (When Opryland opened, a replica of his store was part of the park, to simulate the original.)

From the early 1960s on, Tubb coasted on his living legend status. His stripped-down sound was augmented on recordings, and the quality of his singing suffered due to his illness. Although he continued to perform until two years before his death in 1984, his recording career pretty much ended in 1975, when he left Decca.

Tubb was followed on the *Opry* by his son, SINGER/SONGWRITER Justin (b. San Antonio, Tex., August 20, 1935–January 24, 1998). Best known as the author of "Lonesome 7-7203," a 1963 hit for HAWKSHAW HAWKINS, Justin was active as a recording star and member of the *Opry* since 1955. While his father was an innovator, Justin took a conservative tack, fighting for the pure honky-tonk sound during the 1970s when COUNTRYPOLITAN ruled the airwaves. Though he continued to appear on the *Opry*, the younger Tubb made few recordings over his final twenty years. He died of an aneurysm.

Select Discography

Country Music Hall of Fame, MCA 10086. Great cuts from 1941 to 1965, all the Tubb you'll probably need.
Let's Say Goodbye like We Said Hello, Bear Family 15498. Every studio cut that Tubb made from 1947 to 1953, 114 in all.
Yellow Rose of Texas, Bear Family 15688. Five CDs give you 150 Tubb thumpers, pickin' up where the last collection ended.

Live 1965, Rhino 70902. One of a thousand nights on the road for Ernest and the boys; although he's a little past his prime, this is a fine document of a country road show.

TUCKER, TANYA (b. Seminole, Tex., October 10, 1958)

Country music has an unending appetite for "bad little good girls," girls who are sexy and slightly dangerous, but also wholesome. Tanya Tucker literally began her career as a little girl who was "wise beyond her years," and has continued to walk the fine line between HONKY-TONK heroine and the girl next door.

Born in Texas and raised in Phoenix, Arizona, Tucker was the daughter of a starstruck country-music fan who was determined to make his daughter a hit. He pushed the youngster on stage whenever a country act came into town. When she was nine years old, convinced he had star material on his hands, he financed a trip to Nashville. After several unsuccessful attempts, her demo tape landed in the hands of ace country producer BILLY SHERRILL, who signed her to

Tanya Tucker as a pre-teen star, c. mid-1970s. Photo: Raeanne Rubenstein

Columbia when she was thirteen. She immediately hit with the slightly suggestive "Delta Dawn" and "Would You Lay with Me (in a Field of Stone)." Tucker was immediately successful at playing up her "sexy-but-sweet" image.

By the end of the 1970s, as she reached her early twenties, Tucker's career took a detour into an ill-advised attempt to cross over into pop/rock with the album *T.N.T.* (she appeared on the cover decked out in leather, in an attempt to give her a more "mature" image). The early 1980s brought duets with her beau GLEN CAMPBELL in a more mainstream country style. After struggling to find a style, she returned to traditional country and honky-tonk sounds in the mid-1980s.

While Tucker continues to record in a variety of styles, from sentimental ballads to hard-edged COUNTRY-ROCK, her best material still plays on her image of a good-girl-gone (slightly)-bad. Her 1992 hit, "It's a Little Too Late," is a classic honky-tonk number that also caters to the craze for country dances. Tucker is one of the few female country stars who could get away with singing this type of song, which would more typically be given to a male artist because of its implicit sexuality. She is able to communicate a nonthreatening good humor to her audience that allows her to cross the line just a little bit beyond what might otherwise be acceptable for a country "lady."

The later 1990s were more difficult for Tucker on the charts, but her touring activity continued unabated. Her last chart single to date was 1997's "Little Things," a Top 10 country hit. That same year she published her autobiography, *Nickel Dreams*, which was a bestseller. She has yet to produce a follow-up album, but remains active on the road.

Select Discography

Super Hits, Sony 69065. The "nymphet" years, when Tucker was a teenage sexpot.

20 Greatest Hits, Capitol 22093. Good career retrospective, although focusing primarily on her hits between 1986 and 1997.

TUNE WRANGLERS (c. 1934–1940; various personnel)

The Tune Wranglers were a wild WESTERN SWING outfit, said to be the first to sport Western-styled costumes.

The band was formed around 1934 by Tom Dickey and Buster Coward, a fiddler and guitarist, respectively, who worked on San Antonio radio. It first recorded in 1936, by which time it was a four-piece group featuring vocalist Red Brown, known for slightly racy numbers like "Red's Tight like That" (an adaptation of Tampa Red's hokum number, "It's Tight

Like That"), and pianist Eddie Whitley. The first Bluebird sessions produced the band's signature number, the COWBOY-flavored "Texas Sand." They also had a hit with the novelty number "Ragtime Cowboy Joe," which has been covered many times. The band also appealed to a Spanish audience, recording a few discs as the Tono Hombres, including "El Rancho Grande," sung in Spanish.

In 1937 Red was replaced by steel guitarist Eddie Duncan, who took over lead vocal duties. Over the next few years other players came and went, including the brothers saxophonist Beal Ruff and tenor banjo player Neal Ruff, and tenor banjo player Joe Barnes, known for his fast, chromatic runs. The band continued to record and perform a mix of novelties, hokum, recent compositions, and "old favorites" (popular songs from the late 1890s through the 1930s), from the vaudeville hit "They Go Wild, Simply Wild over Me" to Duke Ellington's "It Don't Mean a Thing (If It Ain't Got That Swing)." The band's last hit was 1939's "Hawaiian Honeymoon." They then moved to a radio station in Fort Worth, but World War II seems to have ended the ensemble.

Select Discography

1936–38, Krazy Kat CD 28. Representative recordings first issued on LP by the Texas Rose label.

TURNER, ZEB (b. William Grishaw, Lynchburg, Va., June 12, 1915–January 10, 1978)

Turner was a pioneering guitarist in the country boogie style as well as a prolific songwriter, although he remained in the shadows of country-music history through most of his career.

He first performed as a member of the Hi Neighbor Boys, who recorded for the budget American Record Company (ARC) label in 1938. His stage name came from his signature tune, the flashy "Zeb Turner Stomp"; his brother James Grishaw (b. June 18, 1923) took the name Zeke Turner at about this time.

After World War II, Turner was signed by the tiny Bullet label out of Nashville, recording "Mountain Boogie," one of the first "country boogie" instrumentals (i.e., it blended the bouncy feel of boogie-woogie with countryesque guitar licks). The Grishaw brothers worked as studio musicians on recordings by HANK WILLIAMS and RED FOLEY, and in 1947 EDDY ARNOLD had a hit with "It's a Sin," a HONKY-TONK WEEPER written by Zeb. Zeb also wrote the WESTERN SWING standard "Texas in My Soul."

By the early 1950s Turner was working out of the Baltimore/Washington, D.C., area, when he made some excellent recordings in a number of different styles, from R&B to country weepers, for the Cincinnati-based King label. Sometime thereafter, he moved to New Jersey and then, finally, to Montreal, where he last performed as a folksinger before his death in 1978.

TWAIN, SHANIA (b. Timmins, Ontario, August 28, 1965)

Twain is an impossibly perky Canadian songstress who has become a major pop phenomenon.

Twain grew up in relative poverty in the backwoods of Ontario. She has been singing since the age of three, winning talent shows from the age of eight, and performing locally and on national television since her early teens. She trained as a Broadway-style singer/dancer/performer in Toronto, then began performing in the resort town of Deerhurst after her parents were killed in an automobile accident. From singing glitzy Vegas-style material, she decided to jump on the country bandwagon, coming to Nashville in 1991.

Twain was quickly signed by Mercury Records, hitting it big with her sexy video presence on her first single, "Whose Bed Have Your Boots Been Under." The album produced more hits, including "Any Man of Mine" and "(If You're Not in It for Love) I'm Out of Here." All of the songs were marked by a spunky forthrightness in their lyrics that appealed strongly to women, while the sexy underpinning—and basically romantic and nonthreatening message—made the songs attractive to men. The album eventually went nine times platinum, and remained on the charts for nearly 200 weeks.

The album teamed her with pop-rock producer Robert "Mutt" Lange, who coauthored many of her hits and was soon her husband. The duo returned big time with Twain's 1997 album, *Come On Over*. Although a "country" album in name, it was really mainstream pop in the style of singers like Gloria Estefan and Celine Dion. The album was a monster seller, producing many top hits, including the big ballads "You're Still the One" and "From This Moment" (recorded as a duet with BRYAN WHITE on the album, but released as a solo single) and the spunky "That Don't Impress Me Much," "Don't Be Stupid," and "Man! I Feel Like a Woman" (with a video parodying pop singer Robert Palmer's famous "Simply Irresistible" clip, replacing the babes-with-guitars with a set of hunky he-men). This last song was used in an advertising campaign by Revlon that featured Twain. The album has broken all records, selling over 18 million copies to date, spawning eight hit singles, and becoming, by *Billboard*'s estimation, the best-selling recording by a female artist of all time, in any genre.

Twain took some recording time off in 1998 and 1999 after promoting her second megaselling hit through tours and TV appearances. She gave birth to her first child in 2001, and is said to be at work on her much-anticipated follow-up album. Whether she can remain a pop diva is anybody's guess; but with her canny producer/husband and her own catchy, appealing songs, it is probable that her core audience will stick with her at least for one more album.

Select Discography

Shania Twain, Mercury 514422. 1993 debut album.

TWITTY, CONWAY (b. Harold Jenkins, Friars Point, Miss., September 1, 1933–June 5, 1993)

Conway Twitty's career was typical of many country singers of his generation. Although he was born in the backwoods and bred in country and blues, his first

Shania Twain in concert, c. 1998. Photo: Raeanne Rubenstein

Conway Twitty during his mid-1970s return to the country charts. Photo: Raeanne Rubenstein

success was in pop-flavored ROCKABILLY, in the wake of ELVIS PRESLEY's enormous popularity. After the British invasion, when rockabilly fell out of favor, he hewed out a successful career as a country vocalist, enjoying his greatest success in the 1970s on his own and in duets with LORETTA LYNN.

Twitty's father was a captain who operated a tug between Friars Point, Mississippi, and Helena, Arkansas. His father gave him his first rudimentary GUITAR lessons; young Jenkins had his own country band performing on Helena radio by the time he was ten years old. He cited two important influences from his earliest years: the jukebox at the local HONKY-TONK, and the singing at the "little Negro church" across the cotton fields from his home. "I would sit on the ditch bank and listen to them sing for two or three hours," he recalled, and "I'd be singing right along." Like many of his contemporaries, Twitty would wed black and white musical influences in his mature work.

As a teenager Jenkins dreamed of being a professional baseball player; he was talented enough to get an invitation to join the Philadelphia Phillies. He also contemplated a career as a minister. Both plans were put aside when he received his draft notice in the mid-1950s. While he was in the Army, he continued to perform country music. Meanwhile, another country artist, Elvis Presley, was recording his first big hits in a new style: rockabilly.

On Jenkins's return from service, he heard the first Elvis recordings and, inspired by Elvis's success, decided to adopt the new rockabilly sound. He decided that if he was going to be a rock star, he needed a rock star's name. Looking on a map, he hit on the names of two nearby towns: Twitty, Texas, and Conway, Arkansas. He called his band The Twitty Birds. (Later, when he achieved success as a country star, he made his home into a theme park. Its name? Twitty City, of course.)

His first big hit came in 1958 with "It's Only Make-Believe" (which he cowrote), a million-seller on the pop chart. A number of rockabilly/teen pop singles followed on MGM, including 1960's hit "Lonely Blue Boy." His success won him the attention of Hollywood, and, like Elvis, he appeared in a number of forgettable B-flicks, both performing his music and "acting." (These films, like the best country songs, are most memorable for their titles, including *Sex Kittens Go to College* and *Platinum High School*.) After The Beatles broke through the charts in 1964, Conway's pop career fizzled.

After an abortive attempt to be a mainstream pop crooner, he relocated to Oklahoma City and formed a new, country-oriented band, The Lonely Blue Boys. Legendary Decca producer OWEN BRADLEY signed him to the label, where he remained for many years. After appearing on his own local TV show, Twitty relocated to Nashville, where, by the end of the 1960s, he was a major star. His first big country hit came in 1970 with "Hello Darlin'," and was followed by further charting singles through the decade. Most of his best songs were on the subjects of lovin', leavin', and bein' lonely, classic country concerns, from the humorous ("Tight Fittin' Jeans") to the cloyingly sentimental ("After All the Good Is Gone").

At the same time he began a successful collaboration with singer Loretta Lynn. Their duets included sexually suggestive numbers that initially upset mainstream country deejays. Their first hit, 1971's "After the Fire Is Gone," reflected a typical Twitty concern: a relationship on the skids. Other numbers celebrated regional identity ("Louisiana Woman, Mississippi Man") and down-home humor ("You're the Reason Our Kids Are Ugly").

Twitty's distinctive baritone voice had some of the earthiness of JOHNNY CASH, with the same hint of hard living that is more typical of the country blues. His gruff, almost conversational style made a perfect foil for Lynn, helping to create a believable and realistic male–female dialogue.

Twitty became a yeoman performer in the 1980s and early 1990s. Though rarely charting as he had in the past, he continued to perform most months of the year, and his home became a kind of shrine for country-music fans. He had just finished a date in the new-country mecca, BRANSON, MISSOURI, in 1993 when he collapsed from a ruptured blood vessel; he died soon after.

Select Discography

The Best of, Mercury 574. Reissues his 1950s hard rockers.

Greatest Hits, Vols. 1 and 2, MCA 31239/31240. His country recordings from the mid-1960s through the mid-1970s.

Final Touches, MCA 10882. 1993 posthumous album shows that Twitty was in fine form up to his death.

TYLER, T. TEXAS (b. David Luke Myrick, Mena, Ark., June 20, 1916–January 23, 1972)

One of the creators of the country narrative record, Tyler had a string of hits beginning with 1948's "Deck of Cards."

Tyler was born in Arkansas but raised in Texas, where he began performing as a singer/guitarist while a teenager. He went east after high school and appeared on the popular radio show *Major Bowes' Amateur Hour*, which led to further work on radio out of Newport, Rhode Island. By the late 1930s he had moved to Los Angeles, where he played with a couple of the popular COWBOY-type bands of the day.

After serving in the Army during World War II, he returned to Hollywood. Forming his own band, he signed with the small Four Star label, where producer/owner Don Pierce helped shape his initial hits. Tyler's first hit was "Deck of Cards," a sentimental spoken number that described a World War II soldier whose deck of cards helped see him through the tough days of war. This was followed by "Dad Gave the Dog Away," "Remember Me" (which became Tyler's theme song), and "Courting in the Rain" from 1954.

After appearing in the B-grade horse opera *Horseman of the Sierras* in 1949, Tyler hosted his own country TV show, Los Angeles's well-loved *Range Roundup*, beginning in 1950. He continued to record from the mid-1950s through the mid-1960s, following Pierce to his new label, Starday, and also cutting sides for Decca, King, Pickwick, and Capitol, without producing any hits. By the mid-1960s Tyler had given up his secular career to pursue a new career as a minister. He died of cancer in 1972.

Select Discography

The Great Texan, King 689.

T. Texas Tyler, King 721. Reissues of his King label recordings.

U

URBAN, KEITH (b. New Zealand, October 26, 1967)

Urban is an Australian COUNTRY-ROCK SINGER/SONG-WRITER/guitarist who scored major hits in 2000–2001.

Although born in New Zealand, Urban was raised in Australia, where his parents exposed him to country music recordings. A high-school friend introduced him to the guitar work of Mark Knopfler of Dire Straits, and Urban's blend of rock-flavored solos and country themes was born. In the later 1990s he formed his first group in Australia and recorded a very successful album there. In 1998 he came to Nashville, and a year later signed with Capitol. His blond good looks and mix of up-tempo rock-flavored numbers with tearful ballads made him an immediate sensation. Besides racking up the usual award nominations, he scored hits with "It's a Love Thing," a sensitive rocker that Urban wrote with Monty Powell; "Where the Blacktop Ends," a country-themed, retro-rocker composed by STEVE WARINER; "You're Everything," the obligatory heart-felt ballad; and "But for the Grace of God," written with The Go-Gos' Charlotte Caffrey and Jane Wiedlin. Urban even recorded a collaboration with hip-hop producer Stevie J., which he describes as hip-hop meets banjos.

Urban's boyish good looks make him a natural video star. A talented stringbender and a decent enough singer, he should be able to continue to produce hits as long as his youth, looks, and inspiration hold up.

Select Discography

Keith Urban, Capitol 97591. 1999 debut album that produced hits through 2001.

V

VAGABONDS, THE (Herald Goodman [voc]; Curt Poulton [voc, gtr]; Dean Upson [voc])

The Vagabonds were the first "professional" group to appear on THE GRAND OLE OPRY, signaling a turn toward more commercial, pop-oriented music on the show in the 1930s.

Hired by GEORGE HAY's assistant, Harry Stone, the group were neither Southerners nor primarily musicians. Instead they were a vocal trio, with professional music training, who specialized in sentimental novelties like "When It's Lamp Lighting Time in the Valley." The original group was formed by Upson, working out of Chicago's WLS in 1925; three years later Poulton joined, and in 1930 Goodman completed the group, now working out of St. Louis. They were hired by the *Opry* in 1931 and stayed there for seven years, while also recording for the budget Bluebird label.

The group disbanded in 1938, with Upson and Poulton staying at Nashville's WSM, which broadcast the *Opry*; Upson eventually joined the station's management staff and Poulton continued to work as an announcer and guitarist, while Goodman took his talents to KVOO out of Tulsa, where he headed the new *Saddle Mountain Roundup*.

VAN DYKE, LEROY (b. Spring Fork, Mo., October 4, 1929)

Van Dyke was a two-hit wonder country performer of the late 1950s and early 1960s, most famous for his comic novelty, 1956's "The Auctioneer."

Trained in agricultural science, Van Dyke worked as a real-life auctioneer after serving in the Korean War. He developed his "Auctioneer" song from the high-speed patter used at livestock auctions, performing it at a talent contest in 1955 that won him a contract with Dot Records. A year later the song was a massive country and pop hit, and he was invited to join RED FOLEY's *Ozark Jubilee*.

In the early 1960s Van Dyke had his second surge of popularity with "Walk on By," a 1961 pop and country hit issued by Mercury. This was followed by two more charting songs, "Big Man in a Big House" and "If a Woman Answers," both from a year later. However, his hits soon dried up again, and he was dropped by Mercury in 1965. Two years later he appeared in the film *What Am I Bid?* reviving his auctioneer routine.

Van Dyke continued to record for various labels, big and small, through the 1970s and early 1980s, with little success. His last country chart song was 1977's "Texas Tea." He has since continued to work as an auctioneer, motivational speaker, and occasional performer.

Select Discography

The Auctioneer, Bear Family 15647. 1950s recordings for Dot, including his big 1956 hit.
Hits and Misses, Bear Family 15779. Early-1960s recordings for Mercury.

VAN ZANDT, TOWNES (b. Fort Worth, Tex., March 7, 1944–January 1, 1997)

Van Zandt was a moody Texas SINGER/SONGWRITER, part of the 1970s OUTLAW/HONKY-TONK revival in Texas that included his friends JERRY JEFF WALKER and GUY CLARK. Van Zandt's material is somewhat darker and more ominous than the others', and his unique delivery made it difficult for other artists to cover it.

Van Zandt's father was an oil worker who moved frequently, so the young singer was raised in various Western states. He briefly attended the University of Colorado, dropping out to become, in his own words, "a folksinger." In 1966 he returned to Texas, where he played a variety of small clubs. Van Zandt signed with Poppy Records in 1969, producing a series of albums over the next few years.

413

Van Zandt's songs have a heavy blues influence, enhanced by his strained, emotional vocals. Like his fellow Texans, he was equally influenced by the honky-tonk tradition of lonesome balladry and the confessional music of singer/songwriters like BOB DYLAN. Often his songs tell stories with an undercurrent that indicates something more is going on below the surface. His best-known song is "Poncho and Lefty," covered by WILLIE NELSON and MERLE HAGGARD on their duet album of the same title, as well as by HOYT AXTON and EMMYLOU HARRIS. Other story songs from the singer include "Mr. Gold and Mr. Mud" and "Tecumseh Valley."

In 1976 Van Zandt moved to Nashville at the insistence of his manager, and signed with Tomato Records to produce a few more albums before again dropping into obscurity. After almost a decade of inactivity on record, Van Zandt returned to the studio in 1987 for the specialty BLUEGRASS label Sugar Hill. He toured and recorded sporadically until his death; in 1990 he toured with the retro-rock group The Cowboy Junkies. He released his last two albums in 1994, a live disc (actually recorded in 1985) and a studio recording made in Ireland. He died suddenly in 1997, and following his death two more albums of previously unreleased material appeared.

Select Discography

Anthology, 1968–79, Varese 061128. Two-CD compilation of his best early recordings, originally issued by the British Charly label.

Highway Kind, Sugar Hill 1070. Posthumous album of 1990s recordings.

WAGONER, PORTER (b. near West Plains, Mo., August 12, 1927)

Wagoner is a country singer/songwriter who hosted a pioneering syndicated country-music program and boosted the career of DOLLY PARTON. He represented the apex of commercial country music in the 1960s and 1970s, maintaining just enough country twang in his vocals to separate him from mainstream crooners.

The son of a farmer, Wagoner was exposed to country radio from an early age, and soon was singing and playing along with his favorite songs. When he was fourteen, he was hired as a clerk at a West Plains market, where he often entertained customers with his music. The store owner decided that Wagoner's music was good for business, so he sponsored him on a fifteen-minute radio show on the local station. By the late 1940s Wagoner's show was attracting regional attention, and in 1951 he was booked to perform on the radio station in the capital city of Springfield. A year later he signed with RCA Victor Records.

Coincidentally, at about this time RED FOLEY was establishing his *Ozark Jamboree* television program in Springfield. He took Wagoner under his wing, and by the mid-1950s made him a star of the program. This led to Wagoner's first hit, "Satisfied Mind," in 1955. His first GOSPEL recording, "What Would You Do (if Jesus Came to Your House)," followed a year later. In 1957 he was invited to join THE GRAND OLE OPRY, and relocated to Nashville. Soon after, Porter formed his backup band, The Wagonmasters.

Wagoner's career would continue to alternate pop country songs and gospel numbers for over twenty years. His biggest hit was 1965's "Green, Green Grass of Home," which also made a major dent on the pop charts. The swelling choruses and saccharine strings of this recording, along with Wagoner's melodramatic vocals, were typical of the grandiose Nashville productions of the day. Other notable Wagoner outings include "I've Enjoyed as Much of This as I Can Stand" from 1963, "Skid Row Joe" of 1966, and 1968's "Be Proud of Your Man," all expressing typical good-old-boy sentiments.

In 1960 Wagoner began his syndicated television program out of Nashville. Starting with just eighteen

Porter Wagoner, c. mid-1970s. Photo: Raeanne Rubenstein

stations, the program grew to be one of the most popular in syndication, with over 100 outlets in the early 1970s. In the early 1960s Wagoner introduced girl singer NORMA JEAN as his partner, and in 1967 gave Dolly Parton her first career exposure. The pair charted with the duet "Last Thing on My Mind," a Tom Paxton FOLK-REVIVAL standard, and continued to work and record together through 1974. Wagoner felt that he deserved the credit for Parton's later success, and resented her attempts to establish herself as a solo act in the early 1970s; Parton, on her side, felt stifled by Wagoner's old-fashioned musical ideas, and eventually was forced to break with him. A series of lawsuits followed, and Wagoner's career faded while Parton made the crossover to mainstream pop and movie-star status.

Although Wagoner continued to produce minor hits into the early 1980s, his pop-flavored vocal style was something of an anachronism in the New Nashville. RCA dug in the vaults to find unissued Porter-and-Dolly material, and this, along with his more recent solo recordings, kept the fans reasonably happy. Like many country performers before him, Wagoner discovered his core fans were slow to abandon him, so he has been able to continue touring and performing while his recordings continue to sell. In 2000 he issued his first new album in some years, on the small Shell Point label.

Select Discography

The Thin Man from West Plains, Bear Family 15499. Four CDs give you a decade's worth of Wagoner's RCA recordings, beginning with his first session in 1952, when he sounds very much like a HANK WILLIAMS wanna-be, through the birth of his distinctive sound.
Pure Gold, Pair 1991. Ten 1960s RCA recordings, not exactly golden but surely no dross.
Sweet Harmony, Pair 1013. Two-CD set featuring Dolly Parton.

WAKELY, JIMMY (b. James Clarence W., Mineola, Ark., February 16, 1914–September 23, 1982)

Wakely, one of the most popular singing COWBOYS of the postwar era, started the vogue for cheatin' songs with his megahit duet "Slippin' Around," recorded with pop singer Margaret Whiting.

Born in a small Arkansas town, Wakely was raised in Oklahoma. After finishing his education, he held a series of low-level jobs, eventually working his way up to being a local journalist. Meanwhile, he formed his own cowboy trio with JOHNNY BOND and Scotty Harrell, and they landed a job on Oklahoma City radio in 1937. Three years later GENE AUTRY guested on their program, liked what he heard, and urged them to

join him on the West Coast. They subsequently traveled to Los Angeles, where Autry hired the group for his nationally broadcast *Melody Ranch* radio show.

Wakely's exposure on Autry's show catapulted him to cowguy fame; within two years he had formed his own band, nurturing the career of such West Coast master musicians as fiddler SPADE COOLEY, bassist CLIFFIE STONE, and guitarist MERLE TRAVIS. During the war he appeared in a slew of D-grade Westerns, making him nearly as popular as Autry on the silver screen.

In 1948 Wakely had his first major hit with "One Has My Name, the Other Has My Heart," the first in a string of cheatin' songs that would virtually create the genre. This was followed a year later by his duet with Margaret Whiting, "Slippin' Around," and, soon after, the answer song "I'll Never Slip Around Again." Meanwhile he piled on the solo hits with 1949's "I Love You So Much It Hurts," 1950's "My Heart Cries for You," and 1951's "Beautiful Brown Eyes." In 1949 he got his own CBS radio show, which lasted for nine years.

In the mid-1950s Wakely's career began to slow down. His recordings suffered the same fate as those of other country artists with syrupy productions featuring mewing choirs. In the mid-1960s he formed his own record label, Shasta, but by the 1970s he was reduced to playing the ersatz cowboy circuit, appearing in Vegas along with his children, Johnny and Linda Lee. He died in 1982.

Select Discography

Very Best of, Varese 066134. Shasta-label recordings from the mid-1960s.

WALKER, BILLY (b. William Marvin W., Ralls, Tex., January 14, 1929)

Walker was a solid hitmaker in the 1960s who began his career with the gimmick of appearing in disguise, gaining the appellation "The Masked Singer."

Born in Texas, Walker was raised in New Mexico, where he picked up music making at an early age. He won a local talent contest when he was fifteen; the prize was his own fifteen-minute radio show broadcast out of Clovis, New Mexico. Five years later he was hired to perform on the popular Dallas-based *Big D Jamboree* show, where he took on the persona of "The Masked Singer." He was signed by Columbia soon after.

Although active as a performer and recording artist through the 1950s, Walker didn't have his first hit until his country chart-topper "Charlie's Shoes" in 1962. He was quickly invited do join THE GRAND OLE OPRY, and had a string of hits through the 1960s, including remakes of jazz-pop songs ("Willie the

Weeper" from 1962), Western-themed outings ("Cross the Brazos at Waco," 1964), and more traditional country WEEPERS ("Bear with Me a Little Longer," 1966; "Anything Your Heart Desires," 1967; and "Thinking About You, Baby," 1969).

In the 1970s Walker continued to have hits in the prevalent COUNTRYPOLITAN style, including his 1970 hit "When a Man Loves a Woman" (not the same as the R&B classic) and "I'm Gonna Keep On Lovin' You" from a year later. After a few more mid-1970s hits, he turned increasingly toward GOSPEL material, then returned to mainstream country in the mid-1980s in a series of duets with BARBARA FAIRCHILD, including 1986's "Answer Game." He continued to record in a gospel vein through the early 1990s.

Select Discography

Billy Walker, Bear Family 15657. Six CDs and a book, covering all his recordings 1949–1965.

WALKER, CHARLIE (b. Copeville, Tex., November 2, 1926)

Walker is best known for his 1958 hit, "Pick Me Up on Your Way Down," written by ace tunesmith HARLAN HOWARD.

Born and raised in Texas, he began his career as a vocalist in BILL BOYD's Cowboy Ramblers, joining the group in 1943. In the late 1940s and early 1950s he retired from performing to work as a country-music deejay. Signed by Columbia in the mid-1950s, he had a megahit in 1958 with "Pick Me Up on Your Way Down," a song turned down by his labelmate RAY PRICE. He continued to record for Columbia and its subsidiary Epic through the early 1970s, his output including his HONKY-TONK trilogy "Close All the Honky-Tonks" from 1964, 1969's "Honky-Tonk Season," and even a 1970 cover of the Rolling Stones' "Honky-Tonk Women." He had a novelty hit with 1967's "Don't Squeeze My Charmin," based on the TV ads for the popular household product (our polite euphemism for *toilet paper*).

In the 1970s Walker recorded sporadically for RCA, Capitol, and SHELBY SINGLETON's revived Plantation label, with little success. He became a popular performer in Las Vegas, and made an unsuccessful comeback attempt in 1986 with a new album for MCA. He has continued to perform, including regular appearances on THE GRAND OLE OPRY, as well as opening a nightclub in San Antonio.

Select Discography

Pick Me Up on Your Way Down, Bear Family 15852. The usual thorough boxed set from Bear Family, for true Walker fans.

WALKER, CINDY (b. Mart, Tex., July 20, 1918)

Cindy Walker was one of country music's leading songwriters, writing over 500 songs, many of which became hits for artists from ROY ORBISON to GENE AUTRY and BOB WILLS. She also had a brief recording and performing career in the 1940s and early 1950s.

Walker was supported in her love of music by her piano-playing mother, Oree, who wrote all of her daughter's music down and accompanied her in many of her performances. The pair came to Hollywood in the late 1930s, and began pitching Walker's songs; Bing Crosby recorded her "Lone Star Trail" and arranged for her to audition for his label, Decca. Walker was an immediate hit when paired with Gene Autry in the cowflick *Ride, Tenderfoot, Ride*, and started making soundies in the early 1940s. In 1944 she had a hit with "When My Blue Moon Turns to Gold Again," which has since become a BLUEGRASS standard.

After the war Cindy hooked up with legendary WESTERN SWING bandleader Bob Wills. She provided Wills with many of his better postwar hits, including "Bubbles in My Beer," "Miss Molly," "Cherokee Maiden," and "You're from Texas." In 1954 mother and daughter returned to their hometown of Mexia, Texas, where Cindy continued to write hits. Other notable Walker numbers include "Dream Baby," a big hit for Roy Orbison; "I Don't Care," originally cut by WEBB PIERCE and revived by RICKY SKAGGS; "Blue Canadian Rockies," cut by Gene Autry and covered by GRAM PARSONS when he was a member of THE BYRDS; HANK SNOW's "The Gold Rush Is Over"; and JIM REEVES's "Distant Drums." In 1997 she was inducted into the Country Music Hall of Fame.

Select Discography

Words and Music, Sony Special Products 28642. Reissue of Monument 18020 from 1964, featuring Walker performing her own material.

WALKER, CLAY (b. Ernest Clayton W., Beaumont, Tex., August 19, 1969)

Walker is a Texas-born country hitmaker of the 1990s.

Walker has strong musical roots; his grandfather was a semi-professional country singer, and both his father and uncle played GUITAR, although neither made a full-time living out of music. Walker began playing guitar at age nine, then continued his lessons in high school, where he met another soon-to-be country star, TRACY BYRD. Walker began pursuing music as a profession at age sixteen, attending college to study business so he could better manage his career.

In 1992 he signed with Giant Records. His first single, "What's It to You," released in July 1993, was an immediate #1 hit. More hits followed through the mid-

1990s, including an eventual total of 11 #1 hits, following a predictable pattern of boot-scootin' boogie numbers alternating with more heartfelt ballads. His first album produced two other #1s reflecting this dichotomy: "Live Until I Die" (tough guy tells off his girl) and "Dreaming with My Eyes Open" (sensitive guy praises girl). 1994's second album produced "If I Could Make a Living," the rocking title track, and "This Woman and This Man," a tearful ballad. 1995 brought a classic kiss-off number, "Who Needs You, Baby," juxtaposed with the ballad "Hypnotize the Moon." His last #1 to date came in 1999 with "The Chain of Love." All told, his first four albums went platinum. In 2000 Giant Records was closed, and Walker moved to parent company Warner Brothers. In early 2001 he released his seventh album, *Say No More*.

In 1996 Walker was diagnosed with multiple sclerosis. Although the disease didn't slow him down, he became active in raising awareness about the disease and its treatment. Walker has continued to tour and perform on the country music, rodeo, race-car, and sports circuits.

Select Discography

Greatest Hits, Giant 24700. The best from his first four albums.

WALKER, FRANK (b. Fly Summit, N.Y., October 24, 1889–October 15, 1963)

Frank Walker was one of the pioneering country record producers who signed legendary acts ranging from THE SKILLET LICKERS to HANK WILLIAMS.

A World War I veteran, Walker was originally a banker who switched to booking concerts. He was hired by the Columbia Phonograph Company, as it was then known, in 1921. In 1923 he signed blues great Bessie Smith to the label, his first major contracting coup. He was put in charge of the company's country-music catalog in 1925, and traveled frequently through the South, arranging recording sessions primarily in Atlanta and Dallas. After recording the duo of Gid Tanner and RILEY PUCKETT in New York in 1924, he put together The Skillet Lickers band featuring the two musicians. He also scripted and supervised their famous series of musical-comedy sketches, including the twelve-part "Corn Licker Still in Georgia," which were tremendously successful. He arranged for the recordings of the Skillet Lickers' main rival, CHARLIE POOLE and The North Carolina Ramblers, along with more citified country singers like VERNON DALHART. His recordings of CAJUN accordionist Joseph Falcon in 1928 are said to be the first commercial recordings of this style of music.

Walker left Columbia to work in a similar capacity for RCA from 1938 to 1945, then finished his musical career with a bang at MGM, signing a then-unknown country crooner named HANK WILLIAMS.

WALKER, JERRY JEFF (b. Oneonta, N.Y., March 14, 1942)

Walker is a one-hit songwriter who was associated with the mid-1970s OUTLAW scene in Texas, and has had sporadic success as a performer.

Walker came from a musical family: His grandparents played in an upstate New York square-dance band, and his mother and aunt performed in a local tight-harmony trio reminiscent of the Andrews Sisters. He spent most of his high-school years playing basketball, although he quit school when he was sixteen to wander around the country, eventually ending up as a street singer in New Orleans. He returned home to finish his schooling, and became interested in the FOLK REVIVAL music of PETE SEEGER and WOODY GUTHRIE, as well as the reissued recordings of JIMMIE RODGERS.

Walker performed on the folk coffeehouse circuit in the East and Midwest through the mid-1960s, until he met SINGER/SONGWRITER Bob Bruno, who introduced him to the nascent Austin, Texas, folk scene. The two joined forces in a shortlived folk-rock outfit, Circus Maximus, which recorded one album for Vanguard Records and performed sporadically.

In the late 1960s Walker's big break came in the form of a radio appearance on alternative New York radio station WBAI. Accompanied by David Bromberg, he performed his self-penned ballad "Mr. Bojangles," inspired by a cellmate he met one night in Texas while sleeping off a drinking spree. The song was popularized over WBAI, and in 1971 was a big hit for THE NITTY GRITTY DIRT BAND. It also earned Walker his first recording contract with Atlantic.

His first recordings were far from successful, and by the mid-1970s Walker was back in Austin. His homemade recordings were issued in 1973 by MCA Records, introducing a brief period of chart success. His second album from this period featured a cover of GUY CLARK's "L.A. Freeway," which was a minor hit for him.

Walker continued to record and perform through the 1970s, gaining a reputation for high living and erratic performances. His voice grew huskier, probably due at least partially to his increased alcohol intake, although Walker today claims that his boozin' and partyin' image was somewhat exaggerated to fit his outlaw persona.

Walker's career in the 1980s and early 1990s was mostly limited to club dates around Austin and occasional tours. He still is living off his one hit song and his image as an outlaw. His performances, however, continue to be unpredictable, ranging from god-awful to listenable. Since the mid-1990s his recordings have appeared on his own Tried & True label. During the later 1990s Walker's birth month of March has become the occasion for a big celebration in Austin, with Walker performing several concerts. In 1999 he published his autobiography.

Select Discography

Best of the Vanguard Years, Vanguard 79532. Twenty tracks from his Circus Maximus and his first solo albums.

Great Gonzos, MCA 10381. Selected cuts from MCA albums from the mid-1970s.

Live at Gruene Hall, Rykodisc 10123. 1989 live recording.

WARD, WADE (b. Benjamin W. W., Saddle Creek, Va., October 15, 1892–May 1971)

One of the great old-time BANJO players, Ward was part of a historic Virginia family who were active in making music for generations.

Born near Independence, Virginia, in the southwest corner of the state, Ward came from a Scotch-Irish family who had settled in the area at least as early as 1840. When Wade was ten, the family moved to a farm known as Peach Bottom Creek, which was Ward's home for the remaining sixty-nine years of his life. His father, Enoch, was a FIDDLE player who had already stopped playing when his youngest son was born, and his mother knew many of the traditional mountain ballads and songs; however, it was Wade's elder brother, David Crockett Ward (known as Crockett), twenty years his senior, who was the key musical influence on his life. Crockett was a fine fiddle player and began teaching his younger brother the rudiments of banjo and fiddle playing when he was in his early teens.

Although professionally a farmer all of his life, Ward began performing as a part-time musician at an early age. First he worked with his elder brother, playing for dances, festivals, and other special occasions. When he was in his twenties, Ward began a lifelong association with a local auction house; his job was to attract customers with his music. He formed his first band to play at local land auctions with the team of fiddler Van Edwards and his guitar-picking son, Earl. The GUITAR was a relatively new instrument in the region, and it changed the style of music playing from the old-time modal dance music to one more suited to modern chord harmonies. Ward also changed, switching from the older clawhammer banjo style he had learned from his brother to a three-finger picked style most closely associated with popular recording artist CHARLIE POOLE.

In the early 1920s, Ward's elder brother Crockett left the family farm to work in nearby Galax as a carpenter. By the early 1930s Crockett's son Fields Ward was an accomplished guitarist and vocalist, and they began playing as a trio along with Wade. Local fiddler "Uncle" Eck Dunford hooked up with the group to form what would be known as The Bog Trotters Band; a fifth member, Doc Davis on Autoharp, was a friend of Dunford's who joined the group in the mid-1930s. The group was "discovered" by noted folklorist JOHN LOMAX and his son ALAN LOMAX, and recorded for the Library of Congress in 1937; for the next few years they were prominent not only in their home region but also in the budding FOLK REVIVAL, because Alan featured them on his radio broadcasts promoting traditional folk music.

The band continued to play informally through the early 1950s, when Fields left the region for a job in Maryland. At the same time Crockett suffered a stroke, and did not play the fiddle again. In the mid-1950s folklorists interested in The Bog Trotters Band came into the region; they included MIKE SEEGER and the team of Jane Rigg, Eric Davidson, and Paul Newman. Through the mid-1960s the latter group was most instrumental in recording Ward, who was now primarily working with local fiddler Glen Smith. Ward's distinctive, yet simple, banjo style made him an instant celebrity during the folk revival, and his style was widely emulated. His good humor and deep repertoire of traditional music also made him a popular performer, and he continued to record, perform, and appear at festivals until his death in 1971. During the 1970s, Fields Ward sporadically recorded as a singer/guitarist for various folk labels.

Select Discography

Uncle Wade, Folkways 2380. Tribute album featuring fine playing from the 1960s.

WARINER, STEVE (b. S. Noel W., Indianapolis, Ind., December 25, 1954)

The career of Wariner, originally a COUNTRYPOLITAN artist, blossomed in the new-country era of the late 1980s, with his tough, rockin' original compositions complemented by his fine GUITAR work.

Raised in Indiana, Wariner was inspired to play guitar by his father, who had his own amateur country band. The younger Wariner began performing while still in high school; after finishing his schooling he was a bass player for DOTTIE WEST for three years, followed by two and a half years with BOB LUMAN before signing as a solo artist with RCA in 1977. His first release, the self-composed "I'm Already Taken," was a minor hit for him, and later was covered by CONWAY TWITTY.

In the late 1970s and early 1980s, Wariner was produced to sound like a GLEN CAMPBELL clone. He did not perform much of his own material, and his releases were bathed in a pop-country backup that really wasn't suited to him. However, he did manage to break through in 1982 with the #1 hit, "All Roads Lead to You," while still recording in this style.

It was in the mid-1980s, when he changed to more progressive producers, that he finally hit his stride, beginning with a remake of Bob Luman's "Lonely Women Make Good Lovers" in 1984, and his first #1 since 1982, "Some Fools Never Learn," from a year later. With John Hall (lead vocalist for the pop group Orleans) Wariner wrote his next hit, "You Can Dream of Me" from 1986, which had a pop/contemporary sound thanks to the presence of Orleans as backup vocalists, and the glitzy production of TONY BROWN. Wariner's success led to an invitation to write a new theme song for TV's *Who's the Boss?*

Wariner continued to move in a pop-rock direction from 1987's "Small Town Girl," written with session pianist John Jarvis, who had cut his musical teeth as a sideman for Rod Stewart (although his country credentials were strong too; he tickled the ivories on GEORGE STRAIT's novelty hit "All My Ex's Live in Texas," from the same year).

After a couple more poppish hits under the hands of Brown, Wariner switched to producer JIMMY BOWEN and scored a hit in 1989 with the countrified "Where Did I Go Wrong," his second self-written #1 song. This was followed by his jazzy "I Got Dreams," written with Bill LaBounty, which featured Wariner's scat singing (a novelty for a country recording).

In the early 1990s Wariner moved to Arista and further hits, including 1992's #1 song "The Tips of My Fingers" and "Like a River to the Sea" from a year later. His fifteenth album, *Drive*, came in 1993, with a more hard-rocking sound; it scored a Top 10 hit with "If I Didn't Love You." But then Wariner took a three-year recording break, returning with *No More Mr. Nice Guy*, an all-instrumental album featuring a band of super pickers. This was, to say the least, an unusual move for a country pop singer, and, also needless to say, its sales were dismal. Wariner was made a member of THE GRAND OLE OPRY that year.

After this career lull, Wariner came roaring back by returning to big-lunged balladry. He cut a #1 duet with new-country singer/instrumentalist Anita Cochran on "What if I Said" in 1998, followed by his own major hit, the WEEPER "Holes in the Floor of Heaven." Signed by a new label, Capitol, Wariner released *Burnin' the Roadhouse Down*, which scored well on both country and pop charts. His following two albums, through the end of the century, were in a similar mold.

Select Discography

Life's Highway, MCA 31002. 1986 album.
Greatest Hits, Vols. 1 and 2, MCA 42032/10357. The first collection draws on his recordings from 1985 to 1987; the second takes him up to 1991.
I Am Ready, Arista 18691. 1991 album.

WATSON, DOC (b. Arthel Lane W., Deep Gap, N.C., March 2, 1923)

Watson is a talented guitarist whose smooth-voiced singing has won him a wide following in folk, BLUEGRASS, and, to some extent, country circles. Coming from a musical family and blind from birth, Doc early showed capabilities on a number of instruments. Inspired by his idol MERLE TRAVIS, he began playing FIDDLE tunes and elaborate melody fills on the GUITAR. By the late 1950s he was working in a local band, playing electric lead guitar on ROCKABILLY, country, and pop songs.

Folklorist Ralph Rinzler discovered Watson while recording old-time BANJO player TOM ASHLEY. Watson was brought north, and soon began performing and recording with his son, Merle (February 8, 1949–October 23, 1985), on second guitar. He became a major star on the FOLK-REVIVAL circuit, recording with JEAN RITCHIE and also as a duet with bluegrass mandolinist BILL MONROE, although these recordings were never legally released until 1993.

Doc Watson, c. 1978. Photo: A. Maxwell, courtesy Flying Fish Records

Watson's big break came when he was included on the sessions for *Will the Circle Be Unbroken?*, THE NITTY GRITTY DIRT BAND's homage to country-music legends. Watson's vocals were prominently featured, as was his legendary flatpicking. He was immediately signed by the Poppy label, where he recorded two Grammy-winning LPs that suffered from far more cluttered productions than his earlier work for folk-label Vanguard Records.

Watson's repertoire was always a mix of traditional country songs, Tin Pan Alley novelties, country songs from recordings made from the 1920s through the 1950s, and favorite songs from the repertoires of other performers like JIMMIE RODGERS and even bluesman Mississippi John Hurt, whom Watson came to admire while both men were performing at folk festivals in the 1960s. His son Merle added a strong blues influence when, influenced by Southern rockers the Allmann Brothers, he took up slide guitar. Doc's relaxed vocal style, typical of the Kentucky/North Carolina region where he was born, and warm stage presence made him immediately accessible to urban audiences in ways many traditional artists are not.

Although he remains active as a performer, the death of his son Merle in a farm accident in the mid-1980s devastated him and he went into semiretirement. He has continued to perform, often with Merle's son Richard as an accompanist.

Select Discography

Doc Watson Family, Smithsonian/Folkways 40012. Originally issued in 1962, this collection documents Watson and his family before he became a professional musician; excellent notes by Eugene Earle and Ralph Rinzler.

At Gerdes Folk City, Sugar Hill 3934. Doc's first New York appearance, recorded live in 1963. He's joined on some songs by THE GREENBRIAR BOYS.

The Essential, Vanguard 45. Twenty-six tracks recorded for Vanguard between 1964 and 1967. A four-CD set (Vanguard 15558) gives a more thorough overview of his recordings for this label.

Memories, Sugar Hill 2204. Originally issued in 1975 by United Artists (423), this set saw Doc playing many of the traditional songs and tunes that he grew up with.

Pickin' the Blues, Flying Fish 352. 1983 album inspired by Merle's love of the blues.

My Dear Old Southern Home, Sugar Hill 3795. 1992 album, recorded with the NASHVILLE BLUEGRASS BAND, comprising country standards.

Third Generation Blues, Sugar Hill 3893. 1999 recording with his grandson, Richard Watson.

WATSON, GENE (b. Palestine, Tex., October 11, 1943)

Watson is another difficult-to-characterize SINGER/SONGWRITER from the wilds of Texas who has had only minor success on the country charts while developing a cult following.

Born in Palestine, he was raised in Paris, Texas. At sixteen he made his first recordings for Uni Records in a teen-pop style. Four years later he moved to Houston in search of a musical career, singing at night at The Dynasty Club while working as an auto-body repairman by day. After a regional hit with 1975's "Love in the Afternoon," he was picked up by Capitol Records.

He continued to record in a solid HONKY-TONK mold for several labels, scoring hits with 1979's "Farewell Party" (his backup band was renamed The Farewell Party Band in honor of this #3 country hit), the honky-tonk anthem "Should I Go Home (Or Should I Go Crazy)" from a year later, and particularly 1981's "Fourteen Carat Mind," his sole #1 country hit. He continued to record through the 1980s and 1990s with moderate success, but his unwillingness to change his style to fit contemporary tastes has made him mostly a cult figure on the edges of mainstream country.

Select Discography

Greatest Hits, Curb 77393. His first hits, drawn from Capitol recordings made in the mid-1970s.

Greatest Hits, MCA 31128. Hits from the late 1970s and early 1980s.

Back in the Fire, Warner Bros. 23832. 1989 comeback album.

WEAVER BROTHERS AND ELVIRY (Leon "Abner" W. [mdln, gtr, fdl, saw]; Frank "Cicero" W. [bnj, saw]; and Elviry [b. June Petrie, 1891–1977, pno, mdln, uke])

The Weaver Brothers and Elivry were a country-novelty trio who performed in tent and traveling shows, vaudeville, and eventually films.

The two brothers portrayed country RUBES, with Leon beginning the act around 1902, bringing his brother in soon after, and enlisting June Petrie some eleven years later. Leon is thought to have beeen the first performer on the musical saw on the vaudeville stage. While the brothers clowned around, Elviry acted the part of the put-upon wife, her deadpan, exasperated facial expressions the perfect foil to the brothers' broad humor. Around 1927 Elviry formed The Home Folks, a country harmony group made up of various members of their extended families, that toured with the trio. Initially married to Leon, Petrie then married Frank, without apparently breaking up the team.

The group became a model for country comedy acts and, through their extensive touring, were quite influential on establishing the image of "hayseed" characters. Their fame was further spread by thirteen films, beginning in 1937 and continuing through the mid-1940s, most notably *The Grand Ole Opry* (1940). The Weavers performed a wide variety of material, from comic instrumentals and songs to traditional heart songs; Elviry was particularly well known for her rendition of "Just Tell Them That You Saw Me," the tearjerking story of a good woman gone wrong.

WEEPER A weeper is a song dripping with heavy sentiment, often dealing with romantic loss, death, or betrayal.

Overly sentimental songs have long been favorites in country circles, although it's sometimes difficult for the outsider to determine just how seriously these songs are meant to be taken. Songs about orphaned children, lost mothers, betrayed lovers, train wrecks, coal-mining disasters, flood, fire, and famine seem to win the hearts and ears of country audiences, no matter what the decade. Perhaps because life in the rural South was so difficult—with deep poverty, disease, and little opportunity for improvement in daily life—the country audience gravitated toward music that had a strong "blue" or sad component. The very first country hit—VERNON DALHART's recording of "The Wreck of the Old 97"—falls squarely in the category; despite an upbeat tune, the song tells of an unmitigated disaster, a train wreck that took the lives of the devoted engineer and his colleagues. Other classic weepers of the early country era include many of THE BLUE SKY BOYS' hit recordings ("The Sweetest Gift, a Mother's Smile" tells how a prisoner waits anxiously for his mother's visit, not to gain "parole or pardon, no sacks of silver, or any gold, you see," but rather the gift of her smile) as well as many classics by THE CARTER FAMILY ("Bury Me Beneath the Willow" tells of an unrequited lover's request to be buried "under the weeping willow tree" so that "maybe then she'll think of me".)

In the period after World War II, when HONKYTONKS became centers of hard drinkin' and hell raisin', a new crop of weepers arose. HANK WILLIAMS's "Your Cheatin' Heart" is a typical song in the new style; its weepy content is matched by the "crying" sound of the steel guitar and Williams's very emotional delivery (he sounds as if he's about to break down in tears). Often the songs tell of a young man who is lured to his doom by a "honky-tonk angel," a loose woman who hangs out at a bar, hoping to ensnare and lead astray the dedicated, hardworking country boy. (Needless to say, this scenario stretched the truth, because many young boys were looking for trouble in the bars.) One of the many classics in this genre is "She's More to Be Pitied Than Censured," which muses philosophically on the plight of the barroom beauty (with the immortal closing line, "The lure of the honky-tonk wrecked her young life"). HANK THOMPSON's "Wild Side of Life" is a classic of this genre, and it inspired the first great weeper sung by a female, KITTY WELLS's answer song, "It Wasn't God Who Made Honky Tonk Angels," which finally presented the woman's point of view.

The 1960s saw the weeper formula become largely a female domain. Stronger female vocalists, like TAMMY WYNETTE, had hits with big-lunged ballads like "Stand By Your Man," but songs like Wynette's "D-I-V-O-R-C-E," telling of the painful breakdown of a marriage that a mother tries to hide from her children, are more typical of the woman's repertoire of the period.

Although no-holds-barred weepers are not as often heard today, the tradition lives on in various guises, ranging from the upbeat ("Forever and Ever Amen" by RANDY TRAVIS, with its vow of eternal love, verging on the bathetic) to songs mixed with mid-1970s SINGER/SONGWRITER sensibility ("The River," by GARTH BROOKS), to big-throated pop ballads like LORRIE MORGAN's "Something in Red" and LEE ANN WOMACK's "I Hope You Dance."

Following some other critics, I sometimes refer to "two-" or "three-hanky" weepers; these weepers are so sentimental that the listener would need at least that many hankies to make it through the song.

WELCH, GILLIAN (b. New York City, October 2, 1967)

Welch is a paper-thin, neo-Depression SINGER/SONGWRITER whose career was given a significant boost when she appeared on the *O Brother, Where Art Thou?* (2000) sound track and the subsequent Down from the Mountain tours.

Welch's songs sound like they were written by Dust Bowl refugees, though she is from a musically sophisticated background. Her parents wrote music for *The Carol Burnett Show*, and she was raised in Los Angeles. While attending the Berklee School of Music in Boston, she met guitarist David Rawlings, who has become her performing partner. They moved to Nashville in 1992. In 1995 EMMYLOU HARRIS included Welch's song "Orphan Girl" on her *Wrecking Ball* album, which significantly boosted Welch's career. In 1996 Welch released her first album, *Revival*, full of vivid images of people and places that were drawn from the folk-country repertoire. She followed in 1998 with *Hell Among the Yearlings*, a somewhat less focused collection.

Welch's producer, T. Bone Burnett, brought her to the attention of the Coen brothers when he was preparing the sound track for their Southern epic, *O Brother,*

Where Art Thou? She sang on several songs with Harris, and the album surprised nearly everyone by selling over four million copies. Welch made another movie appearance in 2001, singing the traditional ballad "The Wind and Rain" for an independent film about a woman folklorist, *Songcatcher.* She also released her third album, *Time (The Revelator).* While still drawing on older folk themes, this album also featured more personal songs, showing the influence of confessional singer/songwriters like NEIL YOUNG.

Select Discography

Revival, Acony 201. Her 1996 debut album, originally released as Almo Sounds 80006.

Time (The Revelator), Acony 203. 2001 release, covering more personal subject matter.

WELLS, KITTY (b. Muriel Deason, Nashville, Tenn., August 30, 1919)

One of the pioneering female country vocalists, Wells is noted for the 1950s tear-drenched ballads that put women on the country-music map. Previously solo female vocalists were few and far between; most Nashville executives felt the recording-buying public for country music was too conservative to accept a woman singing about lovin', cheatin', and losin'. The popularity of Wells's recordings changed this attitude, and paved the way for PATSY CLINE's great success at the decade's end.

In 1936 Deason began performing on local radio with her sisters and a cousin as The Deason Sisters. A year later she wed Johnnie Wright, a talented musician. Soon after, she began performing with Johnnie and her sister-in-law, Louise Wright, as Johnnie Wright and The Harmony Girls. In 1939 Johnnie added Jack Anglin (who had married Louise) to the band to form The Tennessee Hillbillies (later The Tennessee Mountain Boys). In 1942 Jack was drafted, so Johnnie began performing with his wife as a duo; at this time he christened her "Kitty Wells," taking her stage name from the folk ballad "Sweet Kitty Wells." After the war Jack reunited with Johnnie to form the popular country duo JOHNNIE AND JACK. In 1947 they joined radio station KWKH, becoming members of the new LOUISIANA HAYRIDE show on that station the next year. It made their reputation, bringing them a contract with RCA.

In 1949 Kitty began recording GOSPEL numbers backed by Johnnie and Jack's band, but with little success. Meanwhile the duo's recordings sold well. Semi-retired as a housewife, she was lured back into the studio for one more try at recording in 1952. Paul Cohen, a Decca executive, wanted her to record a woman's answer song to the immensely popular HANK THOMPSON song "Wild Side of Life." "It Wasn't God Who Made Honky-Tonk Angels" rightfully asserted

that men had to share the blame for the "fallen women" who frequented the rough-and-tumble backwoods bars. The song shot up the country charts, making Wells's reputation.

Through the 1950s and 1960s Wells proved she was no one-hit wonder. On solo recordings ("I Can't Stop Loving You," "Mommy for a Day," "Heartbreak U.S.A."), and duets with RED FOLEY ("One by One," "As Long as I Live") she honed her image as the gutsy good girl (sometimes gone wrong). Her vocal style and personality were far more laid-back than those of traditional country female performers like COUSIN EMMY and MARTHA CARSON, who tended to whoop it up on stage and recordings. Her voice embodied a heart-tugging regret that was pure country.

Although Wells continued to record from the mid-1960s through the 1970s, her major hitmaking years were over. She continued to tour and perform for her loyal fans with her longtime husband, appearing occasionally on THE GRAND OLE OPRY, and the duo operate their own museum near their suburban Nashville home. She was elected to the Country Music Hall of Fame in 1976, and won a Grammy Lifetime Achievement Award in 1991, only the third country performer to be so honored, and the first woman.

Select Discography

The Queen of Country, Bear Family 15638. Four CDs featuring all of Wells's RCA and Decca recordings from 1949 to 1958, with an illustrated booklet by Charles Wolfe.

Country Music Hall of Fame, MCA 10081. Reissues Decca recordings cut between 1952 and 1965, including all of her hits in the heartache genre.

WEST, DOTTIE (b. Dorothy Marie Marsh, near McMinnville, Tenn., October 11, 1932–September 4, 1991)

West was one of the popular exponents of the NASHVILLE SOUND during the 1960s and 1970s.

Raised in a tiny farm community, West was inspired to become a musician by her fiddling father. She made her debut on local radio when she was twelve, although she had not yet decided to make music a career. She enrolled at Tennessee Technical College, where she began performing with steel guitarist Bill West on radio and at dances; the couple were married in 1953, and relocated to the Cleveland, Ohio, area. Dottie appeared on Ohio's *Landmark Jamboree*, a Western-styled TV show, during the 1950s, and also performed with singer Kathy Dearth (aka Kathy Dee) as The Kay-Dots, a vocal duo who blended country-styled harmonies with pop material.

In 1958 Dottie began traveling to Nashville on weekends, securing a recording contract with the BLUE-

Dottie West and friend, c. mid-1970s. Photo: Raeanne Rubenstein

GRASS-oriented Starday label a year later, and then with the jazz label Atlantic. She moved permanently to Nashville in 1961, and had her first big break in 1963 when JIM REEVES had a hit with her song "Is This Me?"; the pair teamed up for the 1964 hit "Love Is No Excuse." She was signed by RCA and producer CHET ATKINS, and the duo produced her first hit, the self-written "Here Comes My Baby," a year later, leading to her membership in THE GRAND OLE OPRY. This was followed by other hits in the Nashville Sound, replete with oohing choruses, including 1966's "Would You Hold It Against Me?" and "Paper Mansions" from a year later.

Always a plaintive vocalist, West began turning out a slew of hanky-wringing hits. In 1966 she even recorded a theme album called *Suffer Time*, chronicling, in the words of the liner notes, the story of "an eternal loser." West produced some classic hankysoakers, including 1968's "If You Go Away"; two original songs, the maudlin 1969 hit "Clinging to My Baby's Hand" and 1970's "The Cold Hand of Fate"; and 1971's "Once You Were Mine" and "Six Weeks

Every Summer," telling of the "heart-wrenching" guilt of a single parent.

West's popularity as a singer and songwriter reached its height in 1973 when Coca-Cola invited her to write a series of jingles for the popular brew; one of them, "Country Sunshine," became a big hit that year. Her solo hits came more sporadically after the mid-1970s, although she still managed a couple of #1s, including "A Lesson in Leavin' " from 1980 and "Are You Happy Baby?" and "What Are We Doin' in Love" from a year later, the latter an uncredited duet with KENNY ROGERS.

At the same time, West became a popular duet partner, singing with Jim Reeves, Justin Tubb, and DON GIBSON before forming a very successful partnership with Kenny Rogers, recording several racy titles between 1978 and 1981. However, West's career slowed in the 1980s, culminating in foreclosure on the mortgage of her Nashville mansion in 1990, and several failed marriages (she had divorced Bill West in 1972 to marry several younger musicians and associates in succession); a bankruptcy filing and public auction followed in 1991. Just as she was about to make a comeback, West was killed in an automobile accident on her way to *The Grand Ole Opry*. Daughter SHELLEY WEST was also a popular country singer.

Select Discography

Greatest Hits, Curb 77555.

WEST, SHELLEY (b. Cleveland, Ohio, May 23, 1958)

Daughter of popular chanteuse DOTTIE WEST, Shelley had some hits in the COUNTRYPOLITAN style before fading from the scene.

Shelley got her start as a backup singer in her mother's road show, beginning when she was sixteen years old. She married Allen Frizzell, who worked in her mother's band, in 1978. He came from another country dynasty, with brother LEFTY FRIZZELL a noted country crooner and brother DAVID FRIZZELL an up-and-coming star. In fact, David and Shelley teamed up as a duo by 1979, and began touring on the West Coast.

In 1980 the duo hit it big with "You're the Reason God Made Oklahoma," featured in Clint Eastwood's film *Any Which Way You Can*. Follow-up hits included "A Texas State of Mind," "Another Honky-Tonk Night on Broadway," and "I Just Came Here to Dance," all in the country-pop style that was then prevalent. Shelley went solo in 1983, having another #1 hit with her version of "Jose Cuervo," a song that supposedly boosted sales of the popular tequila by 27 percent. In the same year she divorced Frizzell. In 1985 she remarried and abandoned her career, although she performed some concerts again with David Frizzell in 1988.

WEST, SPEEDY (b. Wesley Webb W., Springfield, Mo., January 25, 1924)

West was a pioneering recording artist on the PEDAL STEEL GUITAR, whose duets with guitarist JIMMY BRYANT, recorded in the 1950s, remain some of the finest country instrumentals of all time.

Born in Missouri, West took up the steel guitar when he was thirteen years old. After serving in World War II he settled in southern California, where he found work with SPADE COOLEY's and HANK PENNY's bands. In 1948 West is said to have been the first steel player to switch to the newly introduced pedal steel guitar. In the early 1950s he became a regular on CLIFFIE STONE's *Hometown Jamboree* TV and radio shows, and also began a long association with Capitol Records as a studio musician and solo artist. After he hooked up with Jimmy Bryant—the two became known as "The Flaming Guitars"—they produced some wonderful instrumentals. It is said that neither had heard the other's work before they entered the studio, and the spontaneous, good-natured fun of 1953's "Speedin' West" and "Stainless Steel" from a year later has made them classics of their kind.

Through the 1950s Speedy was much in demand in sessions for both pop and country acts, and also as a performing artist. Rather than sitting passively at the pedal steel guitar, he developed an energetic stage act that made him one of the more glitzy steel players. In 1960 he helped a young artist named LORETTA LYNN get her start by producing her first record, "I'm a Honky-Tonk Girl," for the tiny Zero label. Later in the 1960s he relocated to Tulsa, Oklahoma, where he worked as a consultant to Fender Guitars while running a recreational vehicle business and playing on the side. In 1981 a stroke ended his performing career, although he continued to be a presence at steel-guitar conventions.

Select Discography

Stratosphere Boogie, Razor & Tie 2067/*Swingin' on the Strings: The Speedy West & Jimmy Bryant Collection*, Vol. 2, Razor & Tie 2192. Two CD compilations of their early-1950s recordings. For completists, Bear Family has issued a 113-track boxed set of everything that they did together (15956).

WESTERN SWING Western Swing is a unique combination of string-band music with jazz styles. It was born in the Texas-Oklahoma region in the late 1920s. Musicians there were influenced by blues and jazz recordings, as well as early pop crooners, to form an amalgam of traditional country sounds with a swinging accompaniment.

The band credited with creating this sound in 1931–1932 was THE LIGHT CRUST DOUGHBOYS, featuring fiddler BOB WILLS and vocalist MILTON BROWN. Wills and Brown soon formed their own bands. Although Brown's band was in many ways hotter than Wills's, it was short-lived (Brown died in the mid-1930s, following an automobile accident); meanwhile, Wills's band mushroomed into a full jazz ensemble, with a large horn section and the crooning vocals of TOMMY DUNCAN. The band's instrumentation also included smooth steel guitar, ragtime-influenced piano, and often twin harmony fiddling (Wills's fiddling was fairly primitive, and he usually took a backseat to the more modern stringmen he employed). Wills's repertoire was made up of popular songs, blues, traditional fiddle tunes (often jazzed up), and big-band standards.

A second wave of Western Swing came in the late 1940s in southern California, where many Western musicians had settled after the war to appear in the countless B-, C-, D-, and F-grade cowpoke films that the lesser Hollywood studios (particularly Republic) were busily churning out. Wills's postwar band returned to the stripped-down sound of his original unit, now featuring electric guitar, steel guitar, and even electric mandolin (played by "TINY" MOORE), with various vocalists (in 1948 Wills had fired Duncan in a fit of anger). Another popular California-based band was led by SPADE COOLEY.

The 1950s and 1960s were lean times for Western Swing. But in the early 1970s new, young bands like ASLEEP AT THE WHEEL began playing the music, introducing a new generation to the Western Swing sound. Meanwhile, country superstar MERLE HAGGARD recorded an entire album in homage to Wills's music, and then brought the star out of retirement for his famous last session in 1973. A slew of reissues of early recordings in the 1970s, 1980s, and 1990s made even the lesser-known bands famous once again.

WHITE, BRYAN (b. B. Shelton W., Lawton, Okla., February 17, 1974)

The mid-1990s brought a new phenomenon to country music: teenage fans. And they demanded performers with lots of teen appeal. Bryan White was one of the first to take advantage of this trend.

He first played drums, starting at age five. Both of his parents were professional musicians: His father sang country music, and his mother performed R&B. Bryan didn't switch to GUITAR or write a song until he was seventeen, but that didn't stop him from moving to Nashville in 1992, seeking fame and fortune. 1994 brought it; his first two singles did moderately well, and then came two #1 hits, "Someone Else's Star" and "Rebecca Lynn." His second album fared even better, yielding the ballad "I'm Not Supposed to Love You Anymore." In 1999 he cut a duet with SHANIA TWAIN, "From This Moment On," for her tremendously successful album, *Come On Over*, although the megaselling single version had his vocal stripped out. White has frequently collaborated with guitarist/singer STEVE WARINER.

Successful because of his boyish good looks, White is actually a talented guitarist, songwriter, and vocalist. Although his material is strictly mainstream modern country, it is well crafted and sincere.

Select Discography

Greatest Hits, Elektra 47890. 2000 compilation of his 1990s hits.

WHITE, JOY LYNN (b. Turrell, Ark., October 2, 1961)

White is a never-quite-made-it country/alternative/HONKY-TONK singer and songwriter of the 1990s.

White's father was a BLUEGRASS GUITAR player, so she was raised in a musical home. When she was very young, the family relocated to Mishawaka, a small-town suburb of South Bend, Indiana. She began singing in church at age four, but her career really began in her late teens, when she worked in local bands around South Bend. In 1982 she went to Nashville, eventually working her way up to singing demos. In 1991 she was signed, among much hoopla, by Columbia Records, and she recorded two albums for the label. Although her music excited critics for its blend of contemporary themes with traditional, honky-tonk sounds, it barely made the bottom tiers of the charts. She was quickly dropped by the label.

In 1997 DWIGHT YOAKAM cohort/producer Pete Anderson signed her to his independent Little Dog label, and she released the album *The Lucky Few*. Again die-hard fans and critics were enthusiastic, but the album saw little action. In 1999 she joined with SINGER/SONGWRITER Walter Egan when he moved his band, The Brooklyn Cowboys, to Nashville. White plays keyboards and sings harmony vocals in the group. They released an album, *Doin' Time on Planet Earth*. The band's style is much influenced by seminal COUNTRY-ROCK outfits like THE FLYING BURRITO BROTHERS. (Egan was a friend of GRAM PARSONS, and wrote some songs with him.)

Select Discography

Lucky Few, Polygram 534642. Her most recent studio album to date, this nicely produced 1997 release showcases a gritty, hard-hitting singer.

WHITE, LARI (b. L. Michele W., Dunedin, Fla., May 13, 1965)

A perky new-country songstress, White comes from a country-GOSPEL background. Her career has been championed by RODNEY CROWELL, who employed her as a backup singer and produced her first successful album.

White has been singing and performing since age four, when she appeared with her parents as a gospel trio (her grandfather was a Primitive Baptist minister). With the arrival on the scene of a younger brother, the group became known as The White Family Singers, performing primarily gospel material for church and community groups. Secular music crept into the act when the two children began performing a medley of ELVIS PRESLEY tunes, and found that the audience enjoyed seeing them ape the master's moves.

In her teen years Lari appeared with a local rock band, performed Broadway tunes at talent shows, and earned a scholarship to the University of Miami in music engineering and voice. She began writing her own material while working in local clubs, and recording background vocals and advertising jingles. She checked out the music scenes in Los Angeles, Chicago, and New York, finally arriving in Nashville in 1988. She appeared on TNN's *You Can Be a Star*, a televised amateur talent contest, winning first prize. Soon after, she signed with Capitol and released a single, "Flying Above the Rain," that had some local popularity; she also signed as a songwriter with RONNIE MILSAP's publishing group and began studying acting.

White spent the late 1980s appearing in Nashville dinner theaters while waiting for her big break. An ASCAP showcase created interest in her songwriting, and in 1991 she was invited by country-rocker Rodney Crowell to sing backup on his summer tour. She signed with RCA in 1992, and Crowell agreed to produce her debut album. It produced some minor hits, but she hit pay dirt with her second release, issued in 1995. She had several Top 10 hits, including "That's My Baby," "Now I Know," and "That's How You Know (When You're in Love)." However, she was unable to follow up this success, and after one further album was dropped by RCA. In 1998 she signed with the Lyric Street/Hollywood label, and issued another album.

In 2001 she announced her new release, *Green-eyed Soul*. In a turn from country material, perhaps in emulation of SHELBY LYNNE, the album featured more pop-rock-oriented material. It is too soon to see if this move will help reignite her career.

Select Discography

Best of, RCA 66994. Compilation of her RCA recordings.

WHITES, THE (1966–present: Buck W. [mdln, gtr, pno, voc]; Sharon W. [gtr, voc]; and Cheryl W. [b, voc])

The Whites are a family band who have gone through many permutations in their nearly thirty-year existence, from BLUEGRASS group to mainstream country to GOSPEL.

Father Buck, Oklahoma-born and Texas-raised, played both HONKY-TONK-styled piano and BLUEGRASS/WESTERN SWING on MANDOLIN, becoming something of a legend in the area; his claim to fame as a recording artist in the 1950s was that he was the pianist on the session that produced Slim Willet's "Don't Let the Stars Get in Your Eyes" in 1952. He retired to take a job as a pipe fitter in Arkansas, but resumed music making when his two daughters, Sharon and Cheryl, began playing guitars and singing as preteens. With his wife, Pat Goza White, they formed The Whites as a bluegrass group in 1966. Five years later Buck retired from his day job, and the family relocated to Nashville in search of success.

They made their first recording in 1972 for the bluegrass/country label County Records as Buck White and the Down Home Folks, a fairly straightforward recording in the progressive bluegrass style that was popular at the time. Buck also made some recordings on his own as a mandolinist in the mid-1970s, thanks to a renewal of interest in the instrument created by the jazz-tinged recordings of DAVID GRISMAN. The trio moved in a solid country direction with their 1978 album, *Poor Folks' Pleasures*, issued by the more pop-oriented division of County, Sugar Hill. When they toured with EMMYLOU HARRIS a year later, Sharon met her future husband, RICKY SKAGGS, who was Harris's musical director.

The Whites had their greatest chart success in the early-through-mid-1980s, beginning with 1981's re-recording of "Send Me the Pillow You Dream On." Most of their hits were remakes of 1950s WEEPERS, prominently featuring Sharon's lead vocals, with Buck and Cheryl limited pretty much to harmonizing. In 1982 they enjoyed their greatest chart success, making the country Top 10 with "Holding My Baby Tonight." In 1984 the group joined THE GRAND OLE OPRY, and four years later switched directions slightly by cutting an all-GOSPEL album (Skaggs and Sharon White have become fundamentalist Christians). The group focused on gospel material through the 1990s.

All in all, the Whites are a sweet-tempered harmony group who, though not enjoying chart-busting success, have brought an element of traditional family harmonizing back to country music.

Select Discography

Greatest Hits, Curb 77498. Their pop-country hits of the early-to-mid-1980s.

A Lifetime in the Making, Ceili 2004. 2000 gospel album, featuring JERRY DOUGLAS.

WHITLEY, KEITH (b. Sandy Hook, Ky., July 1, 1955–May 9, 1989)

One of the finer new-country performers, Whitley had his career cut short when he died of alcohol poisoning at age thirty-three.

Whitley began performing at a young age, working on local radio by the time he was nine. Along with high-school buddy RICKY SKAGGS, he developed a love of the traditional music of THE STANLEY BROTHERS; the two formed a duo that so impressed Ralph Stanley that he asked them to join his band in 1971. Whitley remained with Stanley for six years as lead vocalist, and then performed with J. D. CROWE in his PROGRESSIVE BLUEGRASS band, The New South, from 1977 to 1982. A year later he moved to Nashville and was signed by RCA, one of the first new traditionalists to record.

Unlike Skaggs, who kept one foot in traditional country, Whitley wholeheartedly embraced more mainstream Nashville sounds. He wed LORRIE MORGAN, daughter of well-known country singer GEORGE MORGAN; she would achieve her greatest success as a performer after Whitley's death. His first hit came in 1986 with "Miami, My Amy," which reached #14 on the country charts, followed two years later by his first #1, "Don't Close Your Eyes," from Whitley's third album, the first that he coproduced and the first that he felt really reflected his sound. The same album produced two other hits, "When You Say Nothing at All," written by the popular PAUL OVERSTREET–DON SCHLITZ songwriting team, and "I'm No Stranger to the Rain," which wasn't released until early 1989. Suffering from alcoholism, Whitley was found dead at home in May 1989. His death made him something of a country-music martyr, helping propel his posthumous hits "I Wonder Do You Think of Me," shortly after his death, and "I'm Over You," a year later, to the top of the charts.

Select Discography

I Wonder Do You Think of Me, RCA 9809. His last album, completed just before his death, with fine PEDAL STEEL GUITAR by Paul Franklin and a whole slew of beer-soaked laments.

Essential, RCA 66853. Twenty-song compilation of his major hits.

WHITLEY, RAY (b. Atlanta, Ga., December 5, 1901–February 21, 1979)

A popular singing COWBOY and songwriter, Whitley provided GENE AUTRY with many of his biggest hits, including "Back in the Saddle Again."

After serving in the Navy, Whitley settled in the New York area, where he was an electrician and steelworker while playing music on the side. He successfully auditioned for the New York-based *WHN Barn Dance* in the early 1930s, and by the middle of the decade was cohost of the show with TEX RITTER. He began recording for the budget ARC label as well as bigger Decca Records, producing hits with his "Blue Yodel Blues" (a tip of the cowboy hat, at least in title, to JIMMIE RODGERS) and the topical "Last Flight of Wiley Post." He was among the first cowboy performers to use the newly introduced "jumbo" Gibson SJ-200, which became the standard instrument for cowpokes everywhere.

Whitley was one of the first of the singing cowboys to head west, settling in Hollywood in 1936. Between 1938 and 1942 he made a series of shorts for RKO and appeared as the musical sidekick to cowboy star Tim Holt. His last film appearance was as the ranch manager in James Dean's swan song, *Giant*.

Meanwhile, Whitley hooked up with noted producer FRED ROSE, and the duo wrote a number of horsey classics for Gene Autry, including "Back in the Saddle Again," "Lonely River," "I Hang My Head and Cry," and "Ages and Ages Ago." In the 1950s Whitley gave up performing to become a manager, working for a later incarnation of THE SONS OF THE PIONEERS and popular cowpoke JIMMY WAKELY. His later years were spent appearing at cowboy film festivals. He died in 1979.

WHITMAN, SLIM (b. Otis Dewey W., Jr., Tampa, Fla., January 20, 1924)

Anyone who suffered from insomnia in the late 1970s and early 1980s is surely familiar with the late-late-night TV ads for Slim Whitman, the artist whose records have "outsold Elvis." His wooden demeanor, heavily greased-back hair, and mechanical guitar strumming gave miles of smiles to everyone addicted to country kitsch. Despite the lowball charm of his commercials, Whitman was laughing all the way to the bank, with his direct-mail sales generating enough income to keep him supplied with Brylcream for many years to come.

Beginning as a professional baseball player, in the late 1940s Whitman started singing in local bars to augment his income. This led to a 1949 contract with RCA, where he scored moderate success with Western-flavored numbers like "Casting My Lasso in the Sky." In 1952 he joined Imperial, where he immediately scored with "Indian Love Call," the hoary old chestnut that had been a hit for Jeanette MacDonald and Nelson Eddy. Whitman's high tenor voice, augmented by frequent YODELING on this record, was a novelty on country and pop charts. He continued to record pop songs with a Western theme through the mid-1950s.

Although Whitman's U.S. popularity dried up, he remained tremendously successful in England and Europe, where his lonesome vocals and heavy use of crying PEDAL STEEL GUITAR seemed just the thing for wanna-be Western wranglers. His latter-day fame in the U.S. came with the successful television marketing campaign of the early 1980s.

Select Discography

The Best of, 1952–1972, Rhino 70976. All the Slim you need in one handy package.

Rose Marie, Bear Family 157682. Leave it to Bear Family to issue six CDs of everything Whitman cut between 1949 and 1959. It's up to you whether you have the bucks and the ears for this work, but for the true blue Whitman fan, this is the closest you'll get to Slim heaven.

WHITTER, HENRY (b. William H. W., near Fries, Va., April 6, 1892–November 17, 1941)

Whitter, one of the first to record traditional mountain songs, was most closely associated with "The Wreck of the Old 97," which was covered by citified country singer VERNON DALHART to become country music's first million-seller.

A mill worker, Whitter was also a multiple instrumentalist who was most skilled as a harmonica player, but also played FIDDLE, organ, piano, and GUITAR. Not a particularly talented singer, in 1923 he made some test recordings for the General Phonograph Corporation (which owned the Okeh label) that were considered to be so bad that they were unreleasable. However, when FIDDLIN' JOHN CARSON scored a hit with "Little Old Log Cabin in the Lane," also released by Okeh, the company reconsidered and issued Whitter's recordings, including "The Wreck of the Old 97," in 1924.

Whitter's best recordings were made when he was half of the team of Grayson and Whitter. George Bannon Grayson was a blind fiddler/vocalist, and the duo made some fine recordings between 1927 and 1929, including several songs that have entered the BLUEGRASS repertoire, most notably the instrumental "Lee Highway Blues." The Depression ended their recording career, although the duo continued to work together until Grayson was killed in an automobile accident in the mid-1930s. Whitter also recorded as an accompanist to the female fiddle player ROBA STANLEY, and led recordings of the band The Virginia Breakdowners.

Although Whitter was only a passable guitarist and not the greatest singer, the success of his recordings showed the skeptical New York recording executives that there was a market for country music, and along with pioneers like John Carson, he paved the way for the next generation of performers.

Select Discography

Grayson and Whitter, County 3517. Selection of 1928–1930 recordings by the famed duo. Document Records has released their complete recorded output (8054/8055).

WILBURN BROTHERS (Doyle [b. Virgil D. W., Thayer, Mo., July 7, 1930–October 16, 1982] and Teddy [b. Thurman Theodore W., November 30, 1931])

A kind of watered-down LOUVIN BROTHERS, the Wilburn Brothers had considerable success in the 1950s and 1960s, releasing a series of pleasant if somewhat predictable recordings. They are best remembered for helping launch the career of LORETTA LYNN by featuring her on their mid-1960s syndicated country-music show.

Originally part of a musical family act featuring their parents, brothers, and older sister, the group began performing locally, eventually gaining enough fame to be invited to perform on THE GRAND OLE OPRY in 1941. Soon after, they moved to the LOUISIANA HAYRIDE radio show, remaining there until 1951, when the brothers were drafted into the Army. On their return from service in 1953, they struck out as a duo, linking up with WEBB PIERCE and FARON YOUNG for package tours. They signed with Decca, releasing a series of antiseptic hits ranging from 1956's "Go Away with Me" through the early-1960s discs "Trouble's Back in Town," "Tell Her So," "It's Another World," and "Hurt Her Once for Me." They also recorded covers of country and poppish items, even cutting Nat King Cole's cover of "Answer Me, My Love." Many of their later recordings were marred by the inclusion of choruses and tinklin' keyboards that make mid-1960s Nashville records such a chore to listen to today.

In the early 1960s they founded their own talent agency with Don Helms, the Wil-Helm Agency, complementing their Sure-Fire Music publishing operation. These two businesses made them powerful brokers on the Nashville scene, along with their regular TV appearances on their own variety program. They published many of Loretta Lynn's early classics, until business disagreements led to a nasty parting of the ways in the early 1970s. The pair also "discovered" the young PATTY LOVELESS. The duo continued to perform on the *Opry* until Doyle died of cancer in 1982. Teddy continued to perform for some years after, then turned his focus to the agency.

Select Discography

Country Gold, Longhorn 3007. Reissue of 1965 compilation album, originally Decca 74615.

WILD ROSE (1988–1991: Wanda Vick [voc, many instruments]; Pam Gadd [bnj, voc]; Pam Perry [gtr, voc]; Kathy Mac [b]; Nancy Given [drms])

Wild Rose was a new-country quintet who emphasized their perky good looks and up-tempo harmonies.

The group had a fine pedigree, with each member an accomplished instrumentalist, despite the common stereotype that women are not capable stringbenders. Both Gadd and Perry came out of The New Coon Creek Girls (named in honor of the original 1930s band led by LILY MAY LEDFORD); Vick and Given were alumni of PORTER WAGONER's Right Combination, an all-girl combo featured on his GRAND OLE OPRY performances; and Mac came from a Nashville-based female nightclub outfit known as Tina Carroll and The Nashville Satins. Although they had somewhat more of a traditional flavor than other Nashville-based outfits, they carried forward a strong tradition of Nashville-pop styles in their music.

Although made up of women, the group was not particularly feminist in their choice of material (as was, for example, CATHY FINK's Blue Rose band) or in their dress, which was typical glitzy Nashville stage garb. With their well-puffed hair and cheerful stage manner, they appealed strongly to the traditional values of their audience (i.e., although they are performing women, they didn't threaten their audience by questioning a woman's role as basically being limited to home and hearth). Still, the fact that they all played their own instruments and emphasized their talents as performers has been inspirational to other female performers working their way up through the ranks.

The band was originally called Miss Behavin', but changed the name to the more commercial Wild Rose. They signed with Liberty Records in 1988, and first broke through with "Breakin' New Ground" in 1989. Their second album, produced by well-known new-country producer JIMMY BOWEN, gave them their next hit, "Going Down Swinging." A third album appeared in 1991, but the band broke up soon after.

Select Discography

Breaking New Ground, Liberty 93885. Their debut album.

WILKIN, MARIJOHN (b. M. Melson, Kemp, Tex., July 14, 1920)

Wilkin is a well-known country songwriter, famous for "Long Black Veil" and countless other classics of the late 1950s and 1960s.

Born in Texas, Wilkin came to Nashville when she was in her late thirties, taking a job playing piano in a local bar while signing as a house songwriter for one of Nashville's many music factories. Her big breaks came a year later, when LEFTY FRIZZELL had a major hit with her "Long Black Veil" and STONEWALL JACK-SON was equally lucky with "Waterloo." She wrote "P.T. 109," a 1962 hit for future sausage-monger JIMMY DEAN, the patriotic story song relating President Kennedy's achievements in World War II; the profits enabled her to open her own music publishing house, Buckhorn, the first such Nashville business owned by a woman.

Although Wilkin lapsed into a period of heavy drinking, Buckhorn became a center for young SINGER/SONGWRITERS who were not acceptable to the Nashville establishment, such as KRIS KRISTOFFERSON. Kristof-ferson helped Wilkin out of her slump by writing with her 1974's "One Day at a Time," which was eventually recorded by over 200 artists. Wilkin took this as a sign that the Lord had bigger plans for her, and since the mid-1970s has been writing and performing GOSPEL music exclusively.

Select Discography

Little Bit of Jesus, Moonshine 70035. Gospel record-ings of unknown vintage.

WILLIAMS, DON (b. Floydada, Tex., May 27, 1939)

Williams is nicknamed "The Gentle Giant" for his relaxed, crooning vocal style; he was most popular dur-ing the COUNTRYPOLITAN craze of the 1970s, when pop-styled balladry was big business in Nashville.

The son of an automobile mechanic, Williams was taught GUITAR by his mother, and as a teenager began playing in the rocking country styles that were popular at the time. After finishing high school and serving in the Army, Williams performed in a duo with a friend named Lofton Kline; they hooked up with another local performer, Susan Taylor, to form the Pozo Seco Sing-ers in 1964. A year later they broke through on the pop charts with "Time." The group remained together until 1971, with a few more minor pop hits.

Williams followed Taylor to Nashville to work as a songwriter in support of her nascent solo career in the early 1970s. There he hooked up with producer Allen Reynolds, who worked for noted recording engi-neer/performer "COWBOY" JACK CLEMENT. Clement had just formed his own JMI label, and quickly signed Williams. Williams had minor hits with his first two releases, then hit it big with 1974's "We Should Be Together," leading to a contract with ABC/Dot and his first #1, "I Wouldn't Want to Live if You Didn't Love Me."

The hits continued through the 1970s, all of them characterized by simple productions emphasizing Don's laid-back vocalizing. His resonant baritone voice led him to be compared with JIM REEVES and, like another country hitmaker of the era, KENNY ROGERS, he managed to combine pop schmoozing with enough country sentiments to appeal to a fairly broad audience. Other typical Williams hits include the ba-thetically romantic "Til the Rivers All Run Dry," writ-ten with Wayland Holyfield, from 1976; 1977's "I'm Just a Country Boy," written by Marshall Baker and Fred Hellerman (who was one of the founders of the first great FOLK-REVIVAL group, The Weavers), which became a signature tune for the singer; 1979's upbeat good-ol'-boy anthem "Tulsa Time" (which was cov-ered by Eric Clapton a year later for the pop charts); and his biggest seller, 1980's "I Believe in You."

The 1980s saw a slowing of Williams's career, al-though he continued to turn out records in his patented style. After a successful duet with EMMYLOU HARRIS on "If I Needed You" in 1981, he released "Lord, I Hope This Day Is Good," a 1982 #1 country record. This was followed by 1983's "If Hollywood Don't Need You," given a boost by its references to celebri-ties like Burt Reynolds (with whom Williams had worked in the films *W. W. and the Dixie Dance Kings* and *Smokey and the Bandit II*). His sound changed slightly in 1984 with "That's the Thing About Love," which featured light sax playing by Nashville ses-sionman Jim Horn.

Williams retired for a while in the mid-1980s due to continuing back trouble, but returned to recording for Capitol in 1986. His last #1 came that same year with "Heartbeat in the Darkness," cowritten by AMAZ-ING RHYTHM ACES vocalist Russell Smith. It was an unusual song for Williams, with its slight R&B flavor, but he managed to mold it into his distinctive laid-back, schmoozy style. Williams switched to RCA in 1989, and had a #2 hit a year later with "Back in My Younger Days." In early 1992 he scored his last Top 10 country hit, "Lord Have Mercy on a Country Boy." Dedicated to life on his farm near Nashville, Williams continues to perform and record on occasion, although his hitmaking days are more or less over. His last album of new material to date appeared in 1998.

Select Discography

20 Greatest Hits, MCA 5944. Compilation of his best-known 1970s recordings.
Anthology, Hip-O 112271. Forty-song, two-CD com-pilation of both 1970s and 1980s hits, duplicating some of the material on the MCA disc.

WILLIAMS, HANK (b. King Hiram H. W., Mount Olive, Ala., September 17, 1923–January 1, 1953)

Williams was America's greatest HONKY-TONK per-former. His unaffected singing style and bluesy songs that were tinged with a rough sense of humor revolu-tionized country music after World War II. His early death ensured his permanent place in country music's pantheon of stars.

Hank Williams in full performance garb, c. 1949. Photo: University of North Carolina, Southern Historical Collection, Southern Folklife Collection, University Archives

Williams was born in rural Alabama, to a family of poor farmers who relocated to Greenville, Alabama, Here Williams first heard the blues performed by street singer Rufe Payne; as was true of many other white country artists, his life was changed by this exposure to black traditional music. Around 1937 the family relocated to Montgomery, Alabama, where Williams made his first public appearance; it led to a regular spot on local radio. He formed his first band, The Drifting Cowboys, a name that he would use for his backup band throughout his career. He also composed "Six More Miles (to the Graveyard)," a blues that showed his unique sense of gallows humor.

Williams spent the war years in Mobile, Alabama, shipyards, then returned to music with a new band featuring a young female singer, Audrey Sheppard Guy, who was to become his first wife (and mother of HANK WILLIAMS JR.). In 1946 Williams signed with Nashville power broker FRED ROSE, who became the mastermind behind his successful career. After a brief stint with the small Sterling label, Williams signed with MGM in 1947, charting with his first release, the bluesy and ballsy "Move It On Over," and his first honky-tonk anthem, "Honky-Tonkin'." Williams could even transform religious material into his own unique style, making a hit out of his own "I Saw the Light."

In August 1948 Williams was invited to join the prestigious LOUISIANA HAYRIDE radio program, second only to THE GRAND OLE OPRY in popularity among rural listeners. This spread his sound throughout the Southwest, and helped propel his cover of the 1920s novelty number "Lovesick Blues" into a #1 country hit in 1949. An invitation to join *The Grand Ole Opry* followed, elevating Williams to country stardom.

Despite his increasing dependence on alcohol and painkillers, Williams continued to churn out the hits through the remaining three years of his life. The savvy Rose peddled Williams's songs to more mainstream performers: His "Cold, Cold Heart" was a hit for Tony Bennett, "Hey, Good Lookin'" scored for Frankie Laine, and Jo Stafford made a hit out of the CAJUN novelty number "Jambalaya."

By mid-1952 hard drinking and drug use caught up with Williams. He was expelled from the *Opry* and his marriage ended in divorce. He quickly remarried in a lavish ceremony, but his life was soon over. He died in the back of a car on the way to a performance on New Year's Day 1953. As often happens, his death propelled his final recordings, "Your Cheatin' Heart" and the novelty "Kaw-Liga," to the top of the country charts.

Like many other performers who died young, Williams's death cast a long shadow. His recordings have been in print continuously since his death, and remain staples on jukeboxes across the country. His first wife tried to mold their son into his image, so that Hank Williams Jr. spent his early performing years aping his father's manner and singing his songs. Meanwhile, legends about the life and times of Williams continue to circulate, occasionally making headlines in the tabloids.

Select Discography

40 Greatest Hits, Polydor 233. Good overall introduction to his MGM/Sterling label recordings.

The Original Singles Collection . . . Plus, Polydor 194. Most of the hits in a three-CD package with superior sound.

Complete Hank Williams, Mercury 536077. Ten-CD, 224-track compilation of "all" of Williams's studio recordings and demos; doesn't include some live and other material available on other Mercury/Polydor releases. Beautiful packaging with great annotation by Colin Escott.

Health and Happiness Shows, Polydor 862. Radio shows prepared for broadcast in the early 1950s; some repetition of material across the eight shows, but an interesting document nonetheless. Nicely packaged.

Rare Demos: First to Last, Country Music Foundation 067. Reissues Hank performing with just his own guitar accompaniment, with great notes by Bob Pinson; originally on two LPs, CMF 006 and 007.

WILLIAMS, HANK, JR. (b. Randall H. W., Shreveport, La., May 26, 1949)

Son of the legendary country musician, HANK WILLIAMS, Hank has toiled in the shadow of his famous father for many years, often suffering in more ways than one from the comparison. Following a brush with death in the mid-1970s after an accident while mountain climbing, Williams was reborn as a hell-raising country OUTLAW, an image that by the early 1990s was proving to be somewhat confining.

Williams's career was shaped by his manipulative mother, Audrey, who hoped to make him truly a junior version of his famous father. Even though she had separated from Hank Sr. before his death (and he had remarried), Audrey carried the flame for the elder songster, using his fame to further her own singing career. Hank Jr. was featured in her road shows, always performing his daddy's material. Hank's old record label, MGM, participated in this ghoulish scam by having the younger Williams record almost letter-perfect renditions of his father's songs.

By the late 1960s, Williams was bridling at his mother's management of his career and the limitations of being a clone of his father. He had a number of hits in which he commented on his strange situation, including 1966's "Standing in the Shadows (of a Very Famous Man)." He also began to write songs in a plainspoken, straightforward style, and befriended the Nashville outlaws, including WILLIE NELSON and WAYLON JENNINGS, who were seeking to return country music to its purer roots. In 1974 Williams left Nashville to live in Alabama, and recorded his breakthrough album, *Hank Williams Jr. and Friends*, featuring country-rockers like CHARLIE DANIELS and Chuck Leavell. The album shocked his record label while it announced his new freedom from the slick NASHVILLE SOUND. In 1977 Williams's transformation was completed when he switched from his father's label to Warner Brothers, which marketed him as a hell-raisin' country-rocker.

Williams had a slew of hits for the Warners label, particularly in the late 1970s and early 1980s, starting with 1978's "I Fought the Law" and capped by his "All My Rowdy Friends" single and video in 1981, which featured Hank joined by country, rock, and blues musicians. Hank cultivated a born-to-boogie image, which led to albums that seemed to be recorded in hyperdrive. By the late 1980s the unstoppable party sound was beginning to wear thin, and Williams seemed to be searching for a new direction. One of the strangest career moves was the 1990 "duet" with his dead daddy in the video/single "There's a Tear in My Beer," in which, through the "miracle" of over-dubbing and computer-editing, the son was able to sing and perform along with his long-gone dad. This was followed by the alcohol-drenched "Hotel Whiskey," a duet with new-country star CLINT BLACK, that takes the rowdy imagery of country honky-tonking to new, scary depths.

Williams spent most of the second half of the 1990s coasting on his reputation. In 1996 the embarrassing *Three Generations of Hank* presented Hanks Sr., Jr., and III singing together for the first time thanks to the "miracle" of overdubbing. A more ghoulish exercise could hardly be imagined. In 1999 his first new studio album in three years, *Stormy*, was released, with songs that seemed to parody Hank's once rowdy image. A new CD is scheduled for release in 2002.

Though Williams's rowdy image used to seem to be partially a put-on, it appears that the star has been absorbed by it and can't shake it off, even though its usefulness and relevance have ended. The younger Williams is in danger of becoming a country anachronism or, worse, a country embarrassment, which would be a sad ending to a distinguished career achieved against some difficult odds.

Select Discography

Living Proof, Mercury 320. Traces his MGM recording career from 1964 to 1975, when he finally began to emerge from the shadow of his father and take on his own personality as a redneck rocker.

Bocephus Box 2000, Curb/Carbicorn 77940. His post-MGM career as a rowdy redneck, covering recordings from 1979 to 1999. Originally issued in 1992, the set has been enlarged to cover the rest of the century, although Williams was just barely active during the later 1990s.

WILLIAMS, LEONA (b. L. Helton, Vienna, Mo., 1943)

Leona Williams is a country SINGER/SONGWRITER who was married to MERLE HAGGARD in the late 1970s and early 1980s, performing as his duet partner through that period.

Williams came from a musical family, and performed with her four brothers, seven sisters, and parents as The Helton Family from an early age. At age fifteen she got her own radio show, *Leona Sings*, that was broadcast out of Jefferson City, Missouri, and soon after wed drummer Ron Williams. They were hired by LORETTA LYNN to work in her road band, with Leona playing bass and singing and her husband playing drums.

As a country vocalist Williams was signed by Hickory in 1968, scoring minor hits in 1969 with "Once More" and the novelty "Country Girl with Hot Pants On" in 1971. In 1975 she joined Haggard's road show, replacing his estranged wife, BONNIE OWENS, as his duet partner; the pair were married in 1978. They recorded a duet album, ironically called *Heart to Heart*, in 1983, the same year their divorce became final.

Although Williams went on to record for a number of labels as a solo artist through the 1980s, her music did not chart and she is not active today.

Select Discography

Old Loves Never Die, Bear Family 16411. Duet recordings with Merle Haggard, as well as solo recordings.

WILLIAMS, LUCINDA (Lake Charles, La., January 26, 1953)

Nouveau country SINGER/SONGWRITER, Williams is best known for her song "Passionate Kisses," a 1992 hit for MARY CHAPIN CARPENTER.

The daughter of a college professor/poet, Williams was raised in a number of Southern university towns. She began as a blues and country singer, covering songs by traditional country artists like HANK WILLIAMS. She recorded two albums for Folkways Records in the late 1970s, the first all traditional material, the second all her own songs, which gained some attention. She began focusing on her own brand of semiconfessional singer/songwriter material and by the mid-1980s relocated to Los Angeles, where she recorded her first pop-styled album for the punk-rock label Rough Trade in 1989. In the early 1990s she switched to Chameleon/Elektra, which rereleased her Rough Trade album as well as a new recording, *Sweet Old World*, in 1992.

Between 1992 and 1998 Williams went through a period of label-hopping, attempting to record a follow-up to her previous album. She finally came through in 1998 with *Car Wheels on a Gravel Road*, which had a more produced feeling than her previous recordings. Its roots-rock sound was well received in the music press, and Williams won new fans among the "alternative-country" crowd. In 2001 she released *Essence*, a more personal, and starker, recording, again winning kudos from the music press.

Exactly where Williams falls on the country-music continuum is somewhat hard to say; she is more a singer/songwriter than a country artist, borrowing from sources ranging from traditional blues to Joni Mitchell and NEIL YOUNG. However it is characterized, the music is literate and interesting, and she appeals to an educated audience of college cowboys and (sub) urban outfitters.

Select Discography

Ramblin'/Happy Woman Blues, Smithsonian Folkways 40042/40003. Reissues her two Folkways albums.

Car Wheels on a Gravel Road, Mercury 558338. Her best-received album, its roots-rock sound appealing strongly to listeners of the late 1990s.

WILLIAMS, TEX (b. Sollie Paul W., Ramsey, Ill., August 23, 1917–October 11, 1985)

Tex Williams was a talking-blues singer most famous for his 1947 recording of "Smoke, Smoke, Smoke That Cigarette," which he wrote with guitarist MERLE TRAVIS.

Williams was born in rural Illinois, and by the age of thirteen was performing locally as a one-man band on radio and at local venues. He spent most of the 1930s in a variety of country and COWBOY outfits touring the Western states. By late in the decade he had settled in Hollywood, where he found employment in the movies as a singing cowboy. He joined up with SPADE COOLEY in the early 1940s, playing bass and singing lead on Cooley's biggest hit, "Shame, Shame on You." In 1946 the entire band defected with Williams as their leader, signing with the young Capitol label; a year later they provided Capitol with its first million-seller in "Smoke, Smoke, Smoke That Cigarette." The band produced some exciting sides for Capitol through their last classic hit, 1949's "Bluebird on Your Windowsill."

Although Williams's band was hot and stayed together, with various personnel, through the mid-1960s, he was unable to equal his first hits in subsequent recordings. He opened his own club, The Tex Williams Village, in Newhall, California, while the band toured extensively, backing Tex as well as more pop-flavored vocalists. Many of Williams's late-1950s and early-1960s recordings featured truly dreadful Hollywood orchestra accompaniments, and his singing was reduced to a barely recognizable croak. After closing his club in 1965, Williams went solo, recording sporadically for a number of labels. His last minor hit came in 1972 with "The Night Miss Nancy Ann's Hotel for Single Girls Burned Down."

Select Discography

Best of, Varese 066137. Thirteen of his best-known, late-1940s–early-1950s recordings.

WILLING, FOY (b. F. Willingham, Bosque County, Tex., 1915–June 24, 1978)

Willing was an early COWBOY star who led the often underrated Western band The Riders of the Purple Sage.

Willing began his career while in high school, performing on local radio as a pop crooner and in a GOSPEL quartet. He worked his way to New York by the early 1930s, and had his own radio program sponsored by Crazy Water Crystals from 1933 to 1935. He then returned to Texas, working for a while as a radio announcer, before heading West to the burgeoning Los Angeles-based music scene.

In 1943 the first Riders of the Purple Sage was formed, and by the late 1940s the group grew into a large congregation, featuring two accordions, FIDDLE, clarinet, and some swinging steel guitar. They first recorded for the small Majestic label, having hits with the now classic "Cool Water" and "No One to Cry to," and then moved to Capitol, where they recorded the classic "Ghost Riders in the Sky." Besides appearing in a zillion C-grade Western films, they performed live with ROY ROGERS and the pop trio The Andrews Sisters.

Willing disbanded the group in 1952 and more or less retired from performing, although they did make some "reunion" recordings in the late 1950s. By the 1970s Willing had come out of retirement to cash in on performances at Western film conventions, where he continued to work until his death in 1978.

Select Discography

And the New Riders of the Purple Sage, Simitar 5592. Reissue of 1940s Western recordings, featuring many of his early hits, probably from radio transcription discs.

Cowboy/New Sound of American Folk, Soundies 4108. Reissue of 1958 and 1962 albums, respectively, the first somewhat burdened by backup singers and poppish accompaniments, the second a more "traditional" outing aimed at the budding FOLK REVIVAL.

WILLIS BROTHERS, THE (Guy [b. James Ulysses Harod Lyn W., Alex, Ark., July 5, 1915–April 13, 1981; gtr, voc]; Skeeter [b. Charles Ray Clayton W., Coalton, Okla., December 20, 1917–January 28, 1976; fdl]; and Vic [b. John Victor W., Schulter, Okla., May 31, 1922–January 15, 1995; acc., pno])

The Willis Brothers were a pleasant country trio who scored a few mid-1960s hits, particularly 1964's truckers' anthem "Give Me Forty Acres."

The group began its life performing as The Oklahoma Wranglers, originally on radio out of Shawnee, Oklahoma, and then, in 1940, out of Kansas City, Missouri. With a break for service in World War II, their fame grew steadily, and they performed on THE GRAND OLE OPRY in the postwar years until 1949, when they left to tour with EDDY ARNOLD's road shows. In 1946 they backed a young unknown singer in his first sessions for tiny Sterling records; he was HANK WILLIAMS, and he went on to bigger and better things soon after.

Somewhat unusually for a country trio, the group prominently featured Vic's pleasant pop-flavored accordion, and their stage show played off the personalities of serious Guy, the front man, versus Skeeter, known as the "smilin' fiddler." Like many other outfits of the day, their harmonies and musical orientation drew as much inspiration from mainstream pop as they did from any tenuous connection with country traditions.

In the mid-1960s the group signed with Starday Records, a small BLUEGRASS specialty label out of Nashville that was cashing in big on the craze for truck-driving songs. The Willises provided hits with a few numbers in this vein, along with humorous country songs like 1967's "Somebody Loves My Dog."

In 1976 Skeeter died of cancer and Guy retired, leaving Vic to lead a more pop-influenced trio, that was noted for his burbling accordion and the group's close harmonies.

Select Discography

24 Great Truck Drivin' Songs, Deluxe 7809. Diesel-smokin' mid-1960s Starday cuts. 10-4, good buddy.

WILLIS, KELLY (b. Lawton, Okla., October 1, 1968)

Willis was an early 1990s new traditionalist whose work, loved by critics, did not find an audience. Marketed in her heyday as a perky and sexy singer, she had great eye appeal, and her good looks graced magazines from *Rolling Stone* to *Country Weekly*. Still, Willis struggled to find a niche.

Born in Oklahoma, Willis was raised in Washington, D.C., a hotbed of country and BLUEGRASS music. She began singing at age sixteen in her boyfriend Mas Palermo's band. Renamed Kelly and the Fireballs, they quickly became an area club favorite. Moving to Austin, Texas, the home of new-Texas country, the band lasted another six months before dissolving. The couple formed a new group, Radio Ranch, and began to play local clubs. SINGER/SONGWRITER NANCI GRIFFITH caught their show, and urged her label to sign them. In 1990 the band released their first album, which the label essentially marketed as a Willis solo effort. A second album, *Bang Bang*, followed in 1991, featuring a strong cover of the JANIS MARTIN ROCKABILLY classic title cut. The marketing machine went into overdrive, but the album saw little action. In 1993 pop powerhouse producer Don Was piloted her self-titled third album, but she failed to cross over into the lucrative pop market.

MCA dropped Willis, and she disappeared from the recording scene for a while. The independently produced *Fading Fast* from 1996 was picked up for mainstream release by A&M, but did not produce any hits. In 1997 she married Austin alternative-country singer/songwriter Bruce Robinson and took some time off for her family. Three years later she released *What I Deserve* on the Rykodisc label, remaking herself once again, as a somewhat tortured singer/songwriter. The album was well received in the alternative press, but again didn't do much for her mainstream career.

Select Discography

One More Time/The MCA Recordings, MCA. Compilation of her hits from the early 1990s.

WILLS, BOB (b. Kosse, Tex., March 6, 1905–May 13, 1975)

Wills was the father of modern WESTERN SWING, a hybrid music that combined old-time country fiddling and songs with jazz, blues, boogie-woogie, and even Mexican-American sounds to form a musical dialect that is still strongly identifiable. Although only a moderately talented musician, Wills single-handedly shaped the most important band in this style, The Texas Playboys, and his characteristic "Ah-ha" interjections and introduction of the various instrumentalists made their recordings immediately recognizable and vastly successful.

Wills was the son of an old-time fiddler/cotton farmer who introduced his son to the traditional FIDDLE tunes of the Southwest. Wills also could remember hearing black field hands singing alongside him in the cotton fields, and so his youth was equally influenced by the traditional hollers and blues that they performed, as well as the jazz newly introduced on records and on radio. By 1932 Wills, a passable old-time fiddler, was a member of THE LIGHT CRUST DOUGHBOYS, based in Fort Worth, a band sponsored by Burrus Mills, makers of Light Crust dough, with MILTON BROWN, the other seminal name in Western Swing, as vocalist. By 1934 Wills had his own band, The Texas Playboys, based in Tulsa, Oklahoma, and a year later they signed a recording contract with Brunswick Records.

Wills's new band was defined by two distinctive elements: the newly introduced electric "steel" guitar and the smooth vocalizing of singer TOMMY DUNCAN. Steel guitarist LEON MCAULIFFE was responsible for the group's big hit, "Steel Guitar Rag"; his burbling solos were a trademark of Wills's early recordings, and he was often introduced by Wills's high falsetto shout of "Take it away, Leon!" Duncan blended a mainstream sensibility with an affinity for the blues of JIMMIE RODGERS. The band also featured the fine boogie-influenced piano playing of Al Stricklin, and a loping bass-and-drum rhythm section that predicted the shuffle beat of later country boogie outfits. By the end of

Bob Wills (to the right of the microphone, holding fiddle) and an early version of the Texas Playboys. Photo: University of North Carolina, Southern Historical Collection, Southern Folklife Collection, University Archives

the 1930s the group had grown to include a large brass section, rivaling the big bands of the day in size and sound.

World War II spelled the end of the big bands of the 1930s, and Wills turned to working with a smaller outfit in his new home, southern California, where he moved to appear in a number of forgettable D-grade Hollywood Westerns. Singer Tommy Duncan was expelled from the ranks in 1948, and was replaced by a series of lead vocalists, male and female, who were similarly modern in their approach. The new Wills band featured the swing-influenced fiddles of JOHNNY GIMBLE, Louis Tierney, and Joe Holley; steel guitarists HERB REMINGTON and Noel Boggs; electric guitarist Eldon Shamblin, and electric mandolinist "TINY" MOORE. The pared-down Wills band made an excellent series of recordings for MGM in the late 1940s and early 1950s that in many ways were more exciting than his big-band sides of the late 1930s.

Wills continued to work and record sporadically through the 1950s and 1960s, most notably recording two reunion LPs with singer Tommy Duncan in 1961–1962. Championed by country performer MERLE HAGGARD, who made a tribute LP to Wills in 1970, he came out of semiretirement to supervise one last session, just before his stroke in 1973 and his death two years later.

Different Texas Playboys continued to perform in the 1970s and 1980s, one band led by Leon McAuliffe and another by Wills's brother, Johnnie Lee (September 2, 1912–October 25, 1984), who recorded the original version of "Rag Mop" in 1950 (later a hit for The Mills Brothers). Another brother, Billy Jack (February 26, 1926–March 2, 1991), was a drummer, bassist, and vocalist for Bob's band until 1949, when he and mandolinist "Tiny" Moore formed the group Billy Jack Wills and the Western Swing Band. They had the most progressive sound of any of the Western Swing bands, with a jazz and R&B beat that was rarely heard in Western Swing; the group folded in 1954 when its members rejoined Bob Wills's ensemble.

Wills was also a talented songwriter; his most notable composition was "San Antonio Rose." He also transformed several traditional fiddle tunes ("Liza Jane," "Ida Red," and others) into swinging, pop confections.

Select Discography

Anthology: 1935–1973, Rhino 70744. Two-CD set spanning Wills's entire recording career.

The Essential, Columbia/Legacy 48958. Prewar recordings by Wills and his biggest bands.

Take Me Back to Tulsa, Rounder 11145. Compilation of his Columbia recordings, similar to *The Essential*.

San Antonio Rose, Bear Family 15933. Complete 1935–1947 recordings, 303 cuts in all.

Tiffany Transcriptions, Vols. 1–9, Rhino 71469–71479. Wonderful 1946–1947 recordings made for radio, with a tight combo featuring Herb Remington on steel guitar and vocalist Tommy Duncan. Start with volume 2, *"The Best of. . . ."* Volume 10, with the McKinney Sisters, is only for the hardcore fan; the sisters specialized in saccharine chanting in the 1950s mode. Originally reissued on LP/cassette by Kaleidoscope Records.

Boot Heel Drag: The MGM Years, Uptown/Universal 170206. Fifty tracks recorded in 1947–1954 for MGM in Hollywood, with a great small band. The 1947–1948 tracks feature vocalist Tommy Duncan.

For the Last Time, Capitol 28331. Reissue of 1974 United Artists album (LA216). Wills was present at the session but was confined to a wheelchair, and could do little more than shout encouragement. Still, a good recording by alumni of the various bands.

The Longhorn Recordings, Bear Family 15689. Twenty-three recordings cut by Wills in 1964, including twelve wonderful solo old-time fiddle tunes played by Wills himself.

WISE, CHUBBY (b. Robert Russell W., Lake City, Fla., October 2, 1915–January 6, 1996)

Wise was a famed BLUEGRASS fiddler, best remembered for his early work with BILL MONROE and a long association with HANK SNOW.

Although he started out as a GUITAR player, Wise mastered the FIDDLE by his teen years, working the country-music club scene around Jacksonville, Florida. He befriended THE ROUSE BROTHERS there, particularly fiddler Erwin, composer of the famed fiddle tune "Orange Blossom Special." In 1938 he began playing professionally with a local band, The Jubilee Hillbillies, then was invited by Bill Monroe to join his band in Nashville in the early 1940s.

Wise is best remembered for his recordings with the "classic" Monroe band of 1946–1948, featuring LESTER FLATT and EARL SCRUGGS. Wise's WESTERN SWING-influenced fiddle was the perfect complement to the high energy of Monroe's MANDOLIN and Scruggs's BANJO. Because these recordings established the standard instrumentation and sound of BLUEGRASS bands for years to come, Wise's fiddling became the model for his peers and future generations of bluegrass players. During this period he also partnered with singer Clyde Moody, a Monroe alumnus, composing and recording the popular "Shenandoah Waltz" with him in 1946. Through 1950 he alternated between working for Monroe and with Moody.

In the early 1950s, Wise worked with a number of bluegrass bands, including Flatt and Scruggs. However, in 1954 he began an association with popular country singer Hank Snow that would last until 1970. During this period he continued to session with others, and occasionally recorded on his own. Wise then went solo, working out of Texas through the mid-1980s, when he returned to his native Florida. He continued to record in bluegrass and Western Swing styles until shortly before his death following a massive heart attack, in 1996.

Select Discography

An American Original, Pinecastle 1041. 1994 recordings with Bobby and Sonny Osborne.

WISEMAN, MAC (b. Malcolm B. W., Cremora, Va., May 23, 1925)

Unique among country artists, Wiseman has managed to straddle the division between BLUEGRASS and commercial country throughout his career, maintaining a traditional sound in his arrangements and choice of material. His fuzzy-voiced tenor is immediately recognizable in whatever genre of music he records.

Wiseman was born in rural Virginia, in the Shenandoah Valley, where he was surrounded by old-time country music. He studied classical music at the Shenandoah Conservatory in Dayton, Virginia, and then was an announcer at a small radio station out of Harrisburg, Pennsylvania. His first break as a singer came performing with MOLLY O'DAY after World War II. In the late 1940s he hooked up briefly with LESTER FLATT and EARL SCRUGGS, who had just left BILL MONROE's band. In 1950 Wiseman joined Monroe as lead vocalist.

In 1951 Wiseman was signed as a solo act by Dot Records; six years later he was hired as a house producer for the company, running their country-music division through the early 1960s. Wiseman's first hit recordings were the sentimental " 'Tis Sweet to Be Remembered" and "Shackles and Chains," both accompanied by a hybrid country/bluegrass band featuring two fiddlers playing in harmony (something Wiseman borrowed from the popular WESTERN SWING style). In 1959 he had his biggest hit with the WEEPER "Jimmy Brown the Newsboy."

In the 1960s Wiseman continued to record in a traditional country vein, even though the NASHVILLE SOUND was beginning to encroach on his (and most other) recordings. He left Dot for Capitol in the early 1960s, followed by a stint with MGM and then RCA. When Lester Flatt split with Earl Scruggs (because Scruggs wanted to record more popular music) in 1969, Wiseman teamed up with Flatt, recording a number of traditional bluegrass albums, first for RCA and then CMH. This return to bluegrass won him new friends on the traditional music circuit.

After Flatt died, Wiseman remained a popular touring attraction, returning to performing straight country, but recorded only rarely. In 1986, when MCA revived the Dot label, he returned for an album in the style of his late-1950s recordings. Wiseman continued to be active on the bluegrass circuit through the 1990s. He was inducted into the Bluegrass Hall of Fame in 1993. In 1998 he issued a trio album with DOC WATSON and DEL MCCOURY. In 2000 he issued a similar recording with Bobby Osborne and Jim Silvers, cunningly marketed as *The Three Tenors of Bluegrass*.

Select Discography

Early Dot Recordings, Vol. 3, Rebel 113. Bluegrass-flavored sessions from the 1950s; the first two volumes appeared on LP and are now out of print.

Teenage Hangout, Bear Family 15694. Dot recordings from the 1950s, when the label encouraged him to record in the teen-pop mode; somehow, Wiseman makes these songs sound like traditional bluegrass numbers.

Grassroots to Bluegrass, CMH 9041. 1990 recordings.

Mac, Doc, and Del, Sugar Hill 3888. Nice 1998 recordings with Watson and McCoury, also featuring McCoury's sons and ALISON KRAUSS.

WOMACK, LEE ANN (b. Jacksonville, Tex., August 19, 1966)

Womack is a new-traditionalist SINGER/SONGWRITER who broke through big time in the fall of 2000 with the song "I Hope You Dance."

Womack was exposed to country music at an early age thanks to her father, who was the local high school principal by day and a country deejay at night. She began singing as a teenager, and also wrote her own songs, drawing on country styles. When she was seventeen, she enrolled at South Plains College in Levelland, Texas, one of the few colleges—perhaps the only—to offer degrees in BLUEGRASS and country music. She joined the college's performing group, Country Caravan, appearing with them on tours of the South and West.

At age twenty she moved to Nashville to enroll at Belmont University, where she studied music business. She married songwriter/instrumentalist Jason Sellers, who was touring with VINCE GILL at the time (the couple would later divorce). She also landed a brief internship at MCA Records. Her performing in local showcases brought her a songwriting contract with Tree Music in 1995. She wrote several songs with various Tree staff members, including BILL ANDERSON, who recorded one of their compositions. She also befriended many new traditionalists in Nashville, including RICKY SKAGGS (who employed her husband in his band).

In 1996 she was signed by Decca, a part of MCA. Her solo debut single was the very traditional country-sounding "Never Again, Again." Although it charted only in the country Top 40, the song was hailed as return-to-roots country, and the singer was favorably compared to DOLLY PARTON and TAMMY WYNETTE, among others. Womack's career was launched with her second single, "The Fool," which leaped to #2 on the country charts.

Womack followed up in 1998 with her second album, *Some Things I Know*. Combining classic country WEEPERS with more upbeat pseudo–WESTERN SWING romps, the album produced more hits for the singer, most notably "A Little Past Little Rock." Womack also began recording songs by some of the more progressive Nashville songwriters, including husband-and-wife team BUDDY AND JULIE MILLER, as well as older alt-country icons like RODNEY CROWELL.

Womack's big break came in the fall of 2000 with the release of her third album, *I Hope You Dance*. The title song became a phenomenal hit, shooting to #1. Its upbeat message had strong appeal, and soon the single and album went gold, and shortly after, the album went platinum. Womack was invited to sing the song at the December 2000 Nobel Peace Prize concert in Sweden, and followed that in January 2001 with an appearance at one of the inaugural concerts for President George W. Bush. This success was quickly followed by her next single, "Ashes by Now," a song written by new-country artist Rodney Crowell and originally recorded by him in a much different version in 1980.

Womack's vocal style hearkens back to the throb-in-the-throat of classic country chanteuses including PATSY CLINE, LORETTA LYNN, and Wynette. But she is also a savvy selector of songs, well in touch with contemporary sounds, and has forged her own unique combination of trad country and pop. Not surprisingly, the more pop-sounding she has become, the more successful she has been—her third album is in a much more pop-rock style than her previous releases. Nonetheless, her big lungs will always belong to country.

Select Discography

I Hope You Dance, MCA 170099. 2000 breakthrough album that launched Womack to Shania Twain-level success.

WOOD, DEL (b. Polly Adelaide Hendricks, near Nashville, Tenn., February 22, 1920–October 3, 1989)

Wood was one of the few female instrumentalists to become a major GRAND OLE OPRY star; her 1951

million-selling recording of "Down Yonder" made this ragtime piano piece a country standard.

Wood was born on a farm just north of Nashville, but raised in a working-class neighborhood of the city. A talented pianist by the time she was in high school, she was a song plugger in local music shops during the 1940s and also took a job in state government. In 1951 her recording of "Down Yonder," a ragtime composition of the 1920s that was also turned into a jazzy fiddle tune by Gid Tanner and THE SKILLET LICKERS, was a major hit on both the pop and the country charts. This led to an invitation to perform on *The Grand Ole Opry* in 1953, and she remained there until her death. Her jazzy piano stylings were influential on another young ivory pounder, JERRY LEE LEWIS. She recorded many albums, often with typical Nashville pop backings, but was most popular thanks to her *Opry* appearances.

WOOLEY, SHEB (b. Shelby F. W., Erick, Okla., April 10, 1921)

A country comedian who often recorded as Ben Colder, Wooley is best known to fans of 1950s Westerns as Pete Nolan on TV's *Rawhide* and the hard-drinking villain, Ben Miller, of *High Noon*.

Wooley was born and raised on an Oklahoma farm, and came by his horsemanship skills honestly. After World War II he worked for a short time in Nashville before landing his own radio show out of Fort Worth, Texas. This led, two years later, to an MGM contract and his first successful recordings, many made with excellent West Coast sidemen in a WESTERN SWING/country boogie style. Wooley spent much of the 1950s in Hollywood, appearing in over thirty films and 105 episodes of *Rawhide*. His first major hit was the novelty pop crossover "Purple People Eater" of 1958, followed by "That's My Pa." He began recording as Ben Colder in the early 1960s, having hits with such schlock comedy classics as 1962's "Don't Go Near the Eskimos" (a takeoff on "Don't Go Near the Indians"), a 1968 answer song to JEANNIE C. RILEY's hit "Harper Valley P.T.A.," and 1971's "Fifteen Beers Ago" (based on the earlier hit, "Fifteen Years Ago"). He pretty much faded from the recording scene in the 1970s.

Select Discography

The Best of Comedy, Richmond 2126. Cassette-only reissue of Ben Colder's big country comedy discs.

WORK, JIMMY (b. Akron, Ohio, March 29, 1924)

A fine HONKY-TONK recording artist and songwriter, Work never achieved the success he deserved, although several of his songs have become country classics.

Born in Ohio but raised on a farm on the Kentucky-Tennessee border, Work left home to seek employment in Detroit, where he made his first recordings in the early 1950s. One of his first and best-known songs, "Tennessee Border," was covered by RED FOLEY, and led to a contract with Decca. After a couple of years of unsuccessful recording for a variety of labels, Work signed with Dot in 1954, scoring with his own "Making Believe" a year later, which was also a major hit in a cover version by KITTY WELLS. He also recorded fine up-tempo material including "Tom Cattin' Around," the ever-popular folk classic "Rock Island Line," and his ultimate honky-tonk WEEPER, "That's What Makes the Juke Box Play." Work remained with Dot through 1956, and then retired from music making, returning to the life of a farmer on the Tennessee border.

Select Discography

Making Believe, Bear Family 15651. All of Work's recordings cut between 1945 and 1959.

WRIGHT, MICHELLE (b. Chatham, Ontario, Canada, July 1, 1961)

Wright was a chesty, big-throated singer who hit it big with the pop-glitz ballad "Take It like a Man" in 1992.

Like her countrymate SHANIA TWAIN, Wright was trained as an all-around entertainer; her mother, a Toronto-based lounge singer, raised her daughter to be a performer. From her teen years Wright toured Canada with various pop and country bands, honing her performance skills while developing a bad habit of heavy drinking. Also like Twain, she recognized that country music was a growth business for good-looking singers who could blend girl-next-door wholesomeness with just a tinge of playful bad-girl sass. Wright overcame her drinking problem and in the early 1990s relocated to Nashville, where she was immediately signed to a recording contract. Her first single, "Take It like a Man," was just sultry enough to be a major hit; the video for the song promoted Wright as a sex bomb, with lots of cleavage and pouty lips. Not surprisingly for an ex-showgirl, Wright's road show emphasized costumes and glitter over song and substance.

Despite recording through 1997 for major label Arista, Wright was unable to repeat her initial success and faded from the scene.

Select Discography

Greatest Hits, Arista 18902. Compilation of her 1991–1997 recordings, including her one big hit.

WYNETTE, TAMMY (b. Virginia W. Pugh, near Tupelo, Miss., May 5, 1942–April 6, 1998)

The ultimate 1960s country crooner, Wynette will always be best known for her hit "Stand by Your Man," which set the course of women's liberation back by several hundred years but (nonetheless) remains a classic country song.

Raised by her grandparents in rural Mississippi, Wynette showed early musical talent, learning to play several instruments as well as to sing. She joined her mother in Birmingham, Alabama, during her teen years, and was married for the first time at age seventeen; the marriage ended by the time she was twenty. Wynette worked as a beautician during the day, and a club singer at night, to support her three children. Local

Tammy Wynette, c. mid-1970s. Photo: Raeanne Rubenstein

success led to a regular featured slot on the *Country Boy Eddy Show*.

In the mid-1960s Wynette came to Nashville in search of a career, auditioning for several labels while working as a singer and song plugger. Ace producer BILLY SHERRILL recognized her potential and signed her to Epic, where she had an immediate hit with 1966's "Apartment Number 9," followed by the racy (for the time) "Your Good Girl's Gonna Go Bad." Wynette's good-girl-on-the-edge-of-going-bad image was underscored in a series of hits, including "I Don't Wanna Play House" from 1967 and "D-I-V-O-R-C-E" from 1968 (where a battling husband and wife try to hide "the facts" about their deteriorating marriage from the kids, who apparently are not too swift as spellers). Oddly enough, the same year brought "Stand by Your Man," the ultimate beat-me-whip-me-but-I'll-still-be-true-to-you song, with Wynette's powerful delivery subtly changing the song's message. (It's hard to believe that the big-lunged Wynette would stay home and bake cookies while her husband slept around) 1969 brought more hits with "Singing My Song" and "The Ways to Love a Man."

In 1968 Wynette began a seven-year stormy marriage to hard-drinkin' country star GEORGE JONES that made excellent tabloid headlines. The duo often recorded together, including an album of duets from 1972 (with a hit in 1973 with "We're Gonna Hold On") and again in 1976, hitting it big with "Golden Ring" and "Near You" (even though they divorced in 1975); they teamed up again in 1980, scoring a hit with "Two-Story House." Meanwhile, Tammy continued to record through the 1970s, scoring major hits including 1972's "Bedtime Story" (which sounded like a combination of the instrumental part of "Stand by Your Man" and the gooey children's theme of "I Don't Wanna Play House") and "My Man (Understands)" (which clones the sentiments of "Stand by Your Man"), 1973's "Kids Say the Darndest Things" (perhaps the only country song to take its title from Art Linkletter), 1974's "Another Lonely Song" (which brought Wynette to tears because of the line "I shouldn't give a damn" which she felt was sinful), and her last solo #1 country hit, "You and Me," from 1976. Many of these songs were cowritten by producer Sherrill, and were carefully crafted to fit Wynette's image.

By the early-to-mid-1980s Wynette's career was in the doldrums. The increasingly pop orientation of Sherrill's production was ill-suited to her basically HONKY-TONK style, and she was reduced to singing warmed-over pop songs like "Sometimes When We Touch" (a duet with Mark Gray). An attempt to remake her for the new-country generation in 1987 on her album *Higher Ground*, produced by Steve Buckingham and featuring a duet with RICKY SKAGGS, was a critical, if not financial, success. Wynette even did self-parody, recording with the English-based technorock group KLF and scoring a British hit in 1992 with "Justified and Ancient."

At the end of 1993 Wynette was hospitalized with a serious infection; she recovered but was in a weakened condition. In 1994 she reunited with George Jones for an album and tour, but her health was obviously precarious. Nonetheless the *One* album was a success, showing the enduring allure of the star-crossed couple. Wynette died of a blood clot.

Select Discography

Tears of Fire: 25th Anniversary Collection, Epic 52741. A complete overview of her career, from a 1964 demo of "You Can Steal Me" through her early-1990s comeback with technorockers KLF. There are many other compilations on the Sony labels with varying degrees of completeness.

Higher Ground, Epic 40832. 1987 album featuring new-country stars Ricky Skaggs, VERN GOSDIN, and VINCE GILL in the backup band.

Y

YEARWOOD, TRISHA (b. Monticello, Ga., September 19, 1964)

Yearwood is a talented new-country singer whose career was almost derailed by her being overhyped. A big hit single came right out of the gate, but Yearwood initially had difficulty following it up and her handlers seemed intent on molding her into a more mainstream pop chanteuse. She recovered her core country audience by the century's end, although she never crossed over into the kind of mainstream divadom that SHANIA TWAIN and FAITH HILL achieved.

The daughter of a small-town banker father and schoolteacher mother, Trisha had an ordinary, "whitebread" childhood. She came to Nashville in 1984 after two years of junior college to pursue a music business degree at Belmont University. She interned in the publicity department of MTM Records, and began doing demo and studio work, where she met another young unknown, GARTH BROOKS. Brooks invited her to back him up on his first albums, as well as to tour as his opening act. She was signed to a solo deal in 1991, producing the megahit "She's in Love with the Boy," an up-tempo ballad that Yearwood literally belted out. This was followed by the sultry "Wrong Side of Memphis," along with a duet with Garth on the suggestive "Like We Never Had a Broken Heart."

Mega-agent Ken "We Are the World" Kragen took Yearwood under his professional wing in 1992. He had helped shape KENNY ROGERS's career from pure country into pop superstardom, complete with movie deals, lucrative stays in Vegas, and chart-topping pop records. Kragen urged Yearwood to lose some weight, signed her to a high-visibility contract with Revlon to promote her own perfume, and oversaw the making of her second album. Surprisingly, although the album was well received critically, Yearwood did not achieve the same chart success she had originally, and she was in danger of becoming a one-hit wonder. It may be that her fans felt she was turning away from pure country too quickly, in search of greener fields.

Despite this slight career detour, Yearwood proved her staying power as a country hitmaker through the 1990s. Major hits include 1994's "XXXs and OOOs (An American Girl)" and 1998's "I'll Still Love You More." In 1997 she got into something of a mud fight with fellow chanteuse LEANN RIMES when both recorded Diane Warren's "How Do I Live (Without You)"; eventually Rimes had the bigger hit. Yearwood continued to score hits through the end of the decade; in the fall of 2001 she released a new album, *Inside Out*, with the album's title track and leadoff single featuring her in duet with ex–EAGLES member Don Henley (with whom she had previously recorded the light-pop duet "Runaway Joe").

Yearwood is a powerful vocalist who has a strong core of devoted fans. Although not a crossover sensation, which some may have thought she would become, she has a steady career on the country circuit and regularly scores Top 10 hits on the country charts. She will most likely continue performing for many years to come, with a career that will probably rival those of earlier female country standard-bearers, such as LORETTA LYNN.

Select Discography

Trisha Yearwood, MCA 10297. 1991 debut that was the most important new-artist release since RANDY TRAVIS's first, way back in 1986.

Songbook, MCA 70011. The hits through 1997.

YOAKAM, DWIGHT (b. Pikeville, Ky., October 23, 1956)

Yoakam is a southern California-based country singer who was one of the first "new country" stars. He took traditional country symbols—his oversized cowboy hat, boots, and jeans, and songs about Cadillacs, women, whiskey, and hard livin'—and gave a nostalgic, slightly bemused spin to the material. His

Dwight Yoakam and guitar, c. 1998. Photo: Raeanne Rubenstein

Yoakam's late-1980s and early-1990s hits won him a cult following in rock, pop, and country circles. And, although he has continued to produce minor hits on the country charts, Yoakam stands apart from other new-country acts in his slightly ironic take on the country image. His image is both homage to the urban cowboy and satire of him, and his music has a disturbing underside that seems to question the country ethos.

The height of Yoakam's country and pop chart success came in the late 1980s, with songs like "Little Sister" and "Streets of Bakersfield," a duet with Buck Owens that brought him his first #1 country tune in 1988. That same year "I Sang Dixie" followed at the top of the charts. However, his retrohip style started to stale, and his follow-up releases failed to have the same impact. Yoakam's last major country hit came in 1993 with "Ain't That Lonely Yet." Six years later he had a fluke minor pop hit with a cover of Queen's "Crazy Little Thing Called Love," after recording it for a Gap advertisement. He entered the new century with two albums, an all-acoustic career retrospective and a new country album featuring another rock cover, this time of Cheap Trick's "I Want You to Want Me."

By the way, *Rolling Stone* magazine revealed in 1993 that, under the oversized hats, Yoakam is almost completely bald.

Select Discography

Guitars, Cadillacs, etc., Reprise 25372. His debut LP on a major label that first introduced his sound to a wide audience.
This Time, Reprise 45241. 1993 album.

YODELING Yodeling, a sudden change from a chest voice to a falsetto head voice, originated centuries ago in the Swiss mountains, and probably entered the repertoire of Southern country musicians through traveling tent shows of the nineteenth century.

Country-music scholars commonly believe the first singer to make a record featuring yodeling was RILEY PUCKETT, the popular Georgia country artist. Another early yodeler was the minstrel singer EMMETT MILLER, who in the late 1920s recorded "Lovesick Blues," later a major hit for HANK WILLIAMS. But it was JIMMIE RODGERS who popularized the yodeling style in his famous recordings of the late 1920s and early 1930s. Scores of yodeling COWBOYS came along in the wake of Rodgers's popularity, spearheaded by such famous horsey film stars as GENE AUTRY and ROY ROGERS. During the cowboy craze, a number of cowgirl stars—notably PATSY MONTANA and CAROLINA COTTON—also were popular yodelers, incorporating the sound into their major hits.

In his WESTERN SWING bands BOB WILLS used a kind of modified yodel, an expressive "Ah-ha," to show his

band is a typical pseudo-ROCKABILLY outfit, with a heavy GUITAR-bass-drum sound augmented by country fiddling, based on the country HONKY-TONK sound created by BUCK OWENS and MERLE HAGGARD in the BAKERSFIELD SOUND of the 1950s. Yoakam's biggest hits are "Guitars, Cadillacs, and Hillbilly Music" and his cover of ELVIS PRESLEY's "Suspicious Minds" as part of the sound track for the 1992 film *Honeymoon in Vegas.*

Yoakam does have real country roots; he was born in Kentucky, where his father was serving in the military, and when Dwight was two, the family relocated to Cincinnati, joining many other Appalachian families in search of a better life. The family continued to visit relatives in Kentucky throughout Dwight's childhood, traveling down Route 23, the link between Cincinnati and the upper South immortalized in Yoakam's song "Readin', Rightin', Rt. 23." After completing high school and spending a couple of years as a philosophy major at Ohio State, Yoakam moved to Los Angeles. There he became a fixture in the local punk-rock scene; his retro looks and sound seemed to fit in better with a punk sensibility than with the day's middle-of-the-road country.

pleasure at the band's performance, and BILL MONROE introduced the falsetto break into BLUEGRASS music. The "yee-hay" often shouted out by semi-inebriated fans at bluegrass or country concerts is a kind of mock yodel. Popular R&B vocalist Aaron Neville says he was influenced to create his semi-yodeling vocal technique by listening to Gene Autry when he was a youngster. And GEORGE JONES created a kind of reverse yodel in which he suddenly drops into the low bass from his normal vocal range as a means of adding emphasis to a song, a trick picked up by RANDY TRAVIS and GARTH BROOKS, among others. In a recent twist Wylie and the Wild West had a minor hit with "Yodelin' Fool," featuring traditional yodeling set to a ROCKABILLY beat.

Actually, traditional Southern mountain singing styles have long featured sudden shifts from normal to falsetto voice. For example, North Carolina ballad singer Dillard Chandler often broke into a short falsetto yelp at the end of a stanza, a kind of vocal hiccup that resembles a mini-yodel. Just as yodeling developed as a means of communication in the Alps, so "hollerin'" was used among Southern mountaineers to communicate across vast distances or to call in the animals. The annual hollerin' contests still held in Spivey Corners, North Carolina, feature much vocalizing that could be called "yodeling."

While the Swiss usually yodel for joy, Jimmie Rodgers introduced the yodel as a lonesome or "blue" expression, coming as it did at the end of a verse in songs like "T.B. Blues." Southern musicians have transformed the yodel into one of the most expressive of all musical techniques.

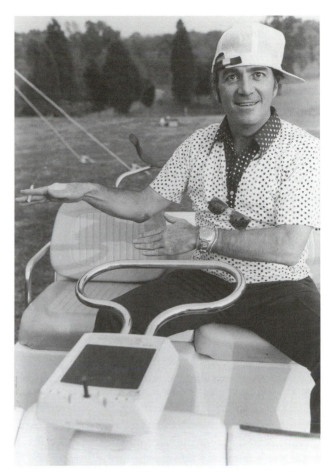

Faron Young mugs for the camera, c. mid-1970s. Photo: Raeanne Rubenstein

YOUNG, FARON (b. Shreveport, La., February 25, 1932–December 10, 1996)

Young was a 1950s honky-tonker who became a 1960s country-music mainstay and industrywide mover-and-shaker.

Born in Shreveport, Young was raised on a small farm outside of town. He began playing GUITAR at an early age, and was a competent country performer by the time he entered high school. After he made a brief stab at college in the early 1950s, Young's musical career interrupted his education. He was signed by the popular LOUISIANA HAYRIDE radio program, where he met another future crooner, WEBB PIERCE, and the duo were soon touring Southern HONKY-TONKS and clubs.

In 1951 Young was signed by Capitol, having hits with the barroom tearjerkers "Tattle-Tale Tears" and "Have I Waited Too Long." Young spent two years in the Army (1952–1954), and in the middle of his service (primarily as an entertainer for the troops) he was invited to join THE GRAND OLE OPRY. After his service

he scored his biggest hits, including 1955's country anthem, "Live Fast, Love Hard and Die Young." More honky-tonk standards followed, including 1956's "I've Got Five Dollars and It's Saturday Night," 1958's "That's the Way I Feel," and 1959's "Country Girl." In 1956 Young made his big-screen film debut in the horse opera *Hidden Guns*, launching a brief film career in Western-flavored flicks that lasted through the early 1960s. *Hidden Guns* also gave him his nickname, "The Young Sheriff," and his band earned the moniker The Young Deputies. When age caught up with him, Young changed his handle to "The Singing Sheriff."

In 1961 Young helped launch the songwriting career of WILLIE NELSON when he recorded Nelson's "Hello, Walls," for a million-selling #1 country hit. However, beginning in the mid-1960s Young entered the mainstream Nashville music-business world with a vengeance. Though his recordings continued, they tended to be conventional middle-of-the-road country crooning (1967's "I Guess I Had Too Much to Dream Last Night" being an example of the excesses of this period). Meanwhile, he founded the influential trade-music paper *Music City News*, and opened his own music publishing company and a Nashville-based race-track.

The 1970s saw Young's activities as a performer trailing off as his importance as a businessman grew. While he still had hits in the first half of the decade, later his music making dropped off. By the 1980s he was recording only rarely, though continuing to make personal appearances.

Young's personal life and his excessive drinking and womanizing (he once quipped, "I am not an alcoholic, I'm a drunk") often made headlines. The strangest occurrence came in 1972 when he was performing in Clarksville, West Virginia. Singing "This Little Girl of Mine," he invited a six-year-old girl in the audience to join him on stage; she refused, and Young reportedly cursed the audience, leaving the stage with the child in tow. Backstage, he gave her an old-fashioned country licking. Subsequent lawsuits were finally settled two years later for the princely sum of $3,400.

Young's later life was not as glorious as his heyday. In 1987 his wife, citing years of abuse and extramarital affairs, divorced him. During the divorce proceedings bizarre stories of Young threatening his daughter with a pistol and subsequently shooting holes in the kitchen ceiling, as well as many tales of womanizing, surfaced, further embarrassing the aging singer. In the 1990s Young's performing career slowed, although he did continue to perform in country hot spots like BRANSON, MISSOURI, where he cut a live album in 1993. In 1996, suffering from emphysema and prostate problems, Young took his own life by a self-inflicted gunshot wound.

Select Discography

The Capitol Years, Bear Family 15493. Five CDs featuring 157 songs, with notes by Colin Escott. All the hits and everything else he waxed for this label.
Live in Branson, MO, USA, LaserLight 137. Young c. 1993 performing his old tunes for his old fans.

YOUNG, NEIL (b. Toronto, Canada, November 12, 1945)

Neil Young is another pop/rock star who, like BOB DYLAN and GRAM PARSONS, has dipped into country music from time to time during a long and often mercurial career. Beginning as a folk revivalist in his native Canada, Young got his first break as a member of the influential folk/rock band Buffalo Springfield from 1966 to 1968. He began a solo career in 1969 while also performing with the popular vocal group Crosby, Stills, Nash, and Young during 1970–1971 and, spo-

radically, over the next few decades, as well as leading the grunge-rock group Crazy Horse.

Young's first solo efforts showed strong country influences, particularly 1972's *After the Gold Rush* with its mournful cover of DON GIBSON's "Oh, Lonesome Me" and Young's own country classic, "Only Love Can Break Your Heart." His follow-up LP was Young's biggest commercial hit, *Harvest*, which featured the Top 40 hit "Heart of Gold." Most of the rest of Young's work in the 1970s was more rock-oriented, although he returned to acoustic folk/rock on 1978's *Comes a Time*.

In the early 1980s a series of mercurial career swings saw Young take on synth-pop, blues-rock, and even ROCKABILLY; a reunion with Crazy Horse followed, with a return to heavy-duty rock and roll with a political edge. Then, in another about-face, Young returned to country on 1992's *Harvest Moon*, with its minor nostalgic title hit. Through the 1990s Young returned to country-tinged material as the mood suited him, when he wasn't leading the ragged-edge band Crazy Horse or reuniting with aging harmonizers Crosby, Stills, and Nash.

Young's reedy tenor vocals, politically edged material, and career-long refusal to fit into a single mold have all influenced country performers who are looking for ways to break the often stifling mold of industry expectations. Young has also been a prime mover behind Farm Aid, the series of concerts masterminded by WILLIE NELSON to aid Middle America's smaller farmers. Still, he has hardly won an appreciable country audience, appealing instead to a core group of aging hippies and yuppies who are attracted to country's primal and highly personal sound.

Select Discography

After the Gold Rush, Reprise 2283.
Harvest, Reprise 2277.
Harvest Moon, Reprise 45057. 1992 release that earned Neil a Grammy nomination.

YOUNG, STEVE (b. Newnan, Ga., July 12, 1942)

An OUTLAW SINGER/SONGWRITER, Young has had a spotty recording career; beloved by WAYLON JENNINGS and his fiercely devoted fans, he has yet to break through to recognized success.

Born in Georgia, Young began performing in a folksinger/songwriter style, recording for A&M, Rounder, and Mountain Railroad records through the mid-1970s; his A&M album featured contributions from California folk-rockers like ex-BYRDS members GENE CLARK and CHRIS HILLMAN, along with legendary country-rocker GRAM PARSONS. His "big break" came in 1976 when he was signed by RCA, thanks to the support of Waylon Jennings, for whom he had provided the 1973 hit "Lonesome, On'ry, and Mean"; his best-known song, "Seven Bridges Road," was a minor mid-1970s hit for THE EAGLES. However, RCA didn't know what to do with him, and he languished at the label. Since then Young has bounced around somewhat, appearing occasionally on smaller labels, while still maintaining his cult following. He recorded a live album and a follow-up studio release for Water- melon Records during the 1990s; in 2000 he released a new album, *Primal Young*, on the small Appleseed label.

Select Discography

Solo/Live, Watermelon 1004. Nice acoustic show from 1991 on which he performs most of his best-known material.

Select Bibliography

Abrahams, Roger, and George Foss. *Anglo-American Folksong Style*. Englewood Cliffs, NJ: Prentice-Hall, 1968.

Ahrens, Pat. *Union Grove: The First Fifty Years*. Union Grove, NC: Union Grove Old Time Fiddle Convention, 1975.

Albert, George, and Frank Hoffman. *The Cash Box Country Singles Chart, 1958–1982*. Metuchen, NJ: Scarecrow Press, 1984.

Allen, Bob. *George Jones: The Life and Times of a Honky-Tonk Legend*. New York: Birch Lane, 1994.

Anderson, Bill. *Whisperin' Bill: An Autobiography*. Marietta, GA: Longstreet Press, 1989.

Artis, Bob. *Bluegrass*. New York: Hawthorn Books, 1975.

Atkins, Chet, with Bill Neeley. *Country Gentleman*. Washington, DC: Regnery, 1974.

Biracree, Tom. *The Country Music Almanac*. New York: Prentice-Hall Press, 1993.

Bufwack, Mary A., and Robert K. Oermann. *Finding Her Voice: Women in Country Music*. New York: Crown, 1993.

Burton, Thomas, ed. *Tennessee Traditional Singers*. Knoxville: University of Tennessee Press, 1981.

Cantwell, Robert. *Bluegrass Breakdown: The Making of the Old Southern Sound*. Urbana: University of Illinois Press, 1984.

Capps, Anita Armstrong. *Not Too Old to Cut the Mustard: "Jumping" Bill Carlisle and Friends Talk About His Life and the Country Music Business*. Overmountain Press, 2000.

Carawan, Guy, and Candie Carawan. *Voices from the Mountains*. New York: Alfred A. Knopf, 1975.

Carlin, Richard, and Bob Carlin. *Southern Exposure: The Story of Southern Music in Pictures and Words*. New York: Billboard, 2000.

Cash, Johnny, with Patrick Carr. *Cash: The Autobiography*. New York: HarperCollins, 1998.

Ching, Barbara. *Wrong's What I Do Best: Hard Country Music and Contemporary Culture*. New York: Oxford University Press, 2001.

Clarke, Donald. *The Penguin Encyclopedia of Popular Music*. New York: Penguin Books, 1990.

Cohen, John, Mike Seeger, and Hally Wood. *Old-time String Band Songbook*. New York: Oak Publications, 1976.

Cohen, Norman. *Long Steel Rail: The Railroad in American Folksong*. Urbana: University of Illinois Press, 1981.

Cooper, Daniel. *Lefty Frizzell: The Honky-Tonk Life of Country Music's Greatest Singer*. New York: Little, Brown, 1995.

Country Music Foundation Staff. *Country Music Hall of Fame and Museum Book*. Rev. ed. Nashville, TN: Country Music Foundation, 1987.

———. *Country: The Music and the Musicians*. New York: Abbeville Press, 1988.

Cusic, Don. *Randy Travis*. New York: St. Martin's Press, 1990.

———. *Reba: Country Music's Queen*. New York: St. Martin's Press, 1991.

Daniel, Wayne. *Pickin' on Peachtree: A History of Country Music in Atlanta, Georgia*. Urbana: University of Illinois Press, 2000.

Davis, Skeeter. *Bus Fare to Kentucky*. New York: Birch Lane Press, 1993.

Dawidoff, Nicolas. *In the Country of Country*. New York: Vintage Books, 1998.

Dellar, Fred, and Alan Cackett. *The Harmony Illustrated Encyclopedia of Country Music*. Rev. ed. New York: Harmony Books, 1986.

Delmore, Alton. *Truth Is Stranger Than Publicity*. Nashville, TN: Country Music Foundation, 1987.

Denisoff, R. Serge. *Waylon: A Biography*. New York: St. Martin's Press, 1984.

Doggett, Peter. *Are You Ready for the Country?* New York: Penguin, 2001.

Eichenlaub, Frank, and Patricia Eichenlaub. *The All American Guide to Country Music*. Castine, ME: Country Roads, 1992.

Ellison, Curtis. *Country Music Culture: From Hard Times to Heaven*. New York: Oxford University Press, 1995.

Eng, Steve. *A Satisfied Mind: The Country Music Life of Porter Wagoner*. Nashville, TN: Rutledge Hill Press, 1992.

Erlewhine, Michael, ed. *All Music Guide to Country*. San Francisco: Backbeat Books, 1997.

Escott, Colin. *Tattooed on Their Tongues: Lives in Country Music and Early Rock and Roll*. New York: Schirmer Books, 1995.

———. *Road Kill on the Three Chord Highway*. New York: Routledge, 2002.

Escott, Colin, and Kira Florita. *Hank Williams: Snapshots from the Lost Highway*. New York: Da Capo, 2001.

Escott, Colin, and Martin Hawkins. *Good Rockin' Tonight: The Sun Records Story*. New York: St. Martin's Press, 1989.

Escott, Colin, with George Merritt and William MacEwen. *Hank Williams: The Biography*. Boston: Little, Brown, 1994.

Ewing, Tom, ed. *The Bill Monroe Reader*. Champaign/Urbana: University of Illinois Press, 2000.

Feiler, Bruce S. *Dreamin' Out Loud: Garth Brooks, Wynonna Judd, Wade Hayes, and the Changing Face of Nashville.* New York: Spike, 1999.

Fong-Torres, Ben. *Hickory Wind: The Life of Gram Parsons.* New York: Pocket Books, 1991.

Fowler, Gene, and Bill Crawford. *Border Radio.* New York: Limelight Editions, 1990.

Gentry, Linnell. *A History and Encyclopedia of Country Western and Gosepl Music.* New York: Scholarly Reprints, 1972. (Reprint of 1961 edition.)

Ginnel, Cary. *The Decca Hillbilly Discography.* Westport, CT: Greenwood Press, 1989.

Greene, Archie. *Only a Miner.* Urbana: University of Illinois Press, 1972.

Gregory, Hugh. *Who's Who in Country Music.* London: Weidenfeld and Nicolson, 1993.

Gruhn, George, and Walter Carter. *Acoustic Guitars and Other Fretted Instruments: A Photographic History.* San Francisco: GPI Books/Miller Freeman, 1993.

Guralnick, Peter. *Lost Highway: Journeys and Arrivals of American Musicians.* Boston: David R. Godine, 1979.

———. *Last Train to Memphis: The Rise of Elvis Presley.* Boston: Little, Brown, 1994.

———. *Careless Love: The Unmaking of Elvis Presley.* Boston: Little, Brown, 1998.

Hagan, Chet. *Country Music Legends in the Hall of Fame.* Nashville, TN: Country Music Foundation, 1982.

———. *The Grand Ole Opry.* New York: Henry Holt, 1989.

Haggard, Merle, and Tom Carter. *My House of Memories.* New York: HarperCollins, 1999.

Haggard, Merle, and Peggy Russell. *Sing Me Back Home.* New York: Timescape Books, 1981.

Hardy, Phil, and Dave Laing. *The Faber Companion to 20th-Century Popular Music.* London: Faber & Faber, 1990.

Hemphill, Paul. *The Nashville Sound: Bright Lights and Country Music.* New York: Simon & Schuster, 1970.

Hoffman, Frank, and George Albert, eds. *The Cash Box Country Album Charts, 1964–1988.* Metuchen, NJ: Scarecrow Press, 1989.

Hood, Phil, ed. *Artists of American Folk Music.* New York: Morrow, 1986.

Horstman, Dorothy. *Sing Your Heart Out, Country Boy.* 3rd ed. Nashville, TN: Country Music Foundation/Vanderbilt University Press, 1996.

Hume, Margaret. *You're So Cold I'm Turning Blue: Guide to the Greatest in Country Music.* New York: Penguin, 1982.

Jensen, Joli. *Nashville Sound: Authenticity, Commercialization, and Country Music.* Nashville, TN: Country Music Foundation/Vanderbilt University Press, 1998.

Jones, Louis M. ("Grandpa"), with Charles K. Wolfe. *Everybody's Grandpa: Fifty Years Behind the Mike.* Knoxville: University of Tennessee Press, 1984.

Jones, Loyal. *Minstrel of the Appalachians: The Story of Bascom Lamar Lunsford.* Appalachian Consortium Press, 1982.

———. *Radio's Kentucky Mountain Boy: Bradley Kincaid.* Berea, Ky: Appalachian Center, Berea College, 1988.

Jones, Margaret. *Patsy: The Life and Times of Patsy Cline.* New York: HarperCollins, 1994.

Kingsbury, Paul, ed. *Country on Compact Disc: The Essential Guide to the Music.* New York: Grove Press, 1993.

———. *The Country Reader.* Nashville, TN: Country Music Foundation/Vanderbilt University Press, 1996.

———. *Encyclopedia of Country Music.* New York: Oxford University Press, 1998.

Klein, Joe. *Woody Guthrie: A Life.* New York: Alfred A. Knopf, 1980.

Kochman, Marilyn, ed. *The Big Book of Bluegrass.* New York: Quill, 1985.

Logan, Horace, and Bill Sloan. *Elvis, Hank, and Me: Making Musical History on the Louisiana Hayride.* New York: St. Martin's Press, 1998.

Lomax, John. *Adventures of a Ballad Hunter.* New York: Macmillan, 1947.

Lornell, Kip. *Virginia's Blues, Gospel and Country Records, 1902–1943.* Lexington: University of Kentucky Press, 1989.

Lynn, Loretta, and George Vesey. *Coal Miner's Daughter.* Chicago: Contemporary Books, 1985.

Malone, Bill C. *Country Music USA.* Rev. ed. Austin: University of Texas Press, 1985.

———. *Don't Get Above Your Raisin': Country Music and the Southern Working Class.* Urbana: University of Illinois Press, 2001.

Malone, Bill C., and Judith McCulloch, eds. *Stars of Country Music: Uncle Dave Macon to Johnny Rodriguez.* Urbana: University of Illinois Press, 1975.

Malone, Bill C., and Wayne Mixon. *Singing Cowboys and Musical Mountaineers: Southern Culture and the Roots of Country Music.* Athens: University of Georgia Press, 1993.

Mandrell, Barbara, and George Vesey. *Get to the Heart: My Story.* New York: Bantam, 1990.

Marshall, Rick. *Encyclopedia of Country & Western Music.* New York: Simon & Schuster, 1988.

Mason, Michael, ed. *The Country Music Book.* New York: Scribner's, 1985.

McCall, Michael. *Garth Brooks.* New York: Bantam, 1991.

McCloud, Barry. *Definitive Country: The Ultimate Encyclopedia of Country Music and Its Performers.* New York: Perigee, 1995.

Milsap, Ronnie, and Tom Carter. *Almost like a Song.* New York: McGraw-Hill, 1990.

Morton, David C., and Charles K. Wolfe. *Deford Bailey: A Black Star in Early Country Music.* Knoxville: University of Tennessee Press, 1990.

Nash, Alanna. *Behind Closed Doors: Talking with the Legends of Country Music.* New York: Knopf, 1988.

Nelson, Willie. *Willie: An Autobiography.* New York: Pocket Books, 1989.

Oermann, Robert, and Chet Flippo. *A Century of Country.* New York: TV Books, 1999.

Paris, Mike, and Chris Comber. *Jimmie the Kid: The Life of Jimmie Rodgers.* New York: Da Capo, 1977.

Piazza, Tom. *True Adventures with the King of Bluegrass.* Nashville, TN: Country Music Foundation/ Vanderbilt University Press, 2000.

Peterson, Richard A. *Creating Country Music: Fabricating Authenticity.* Chicago: University of Chicago Press, 1999.

Porterfield, Nolan. *Jimmie Rodgers: The Life & Times of America's Blue Yodeler.* Urbana: University of Illinois Press, 1979.

Price, Steven D. *Take Me Home.* New York: Praeger, 1974.

———. *Old as the Hills: The Story of Bluegrass Music.* New York: Viking, 1975.

Pruett, Barbara. *Marty Robbins: Fast Cars and Country Music.* Metuchen, NJ: Scarecrow Press, 1990.

Pugh, Ronnie. *Ernest Tubb: The Texas Troubadour.* Durham, NC: Duke University Press, 1996.

Quain, Kevin, ed. *The Elvis Reader: Texts and Sources on the King of Rock 'n' Roll.* New York: St. Martin's Press, 1992.

Riddle, Almeda. *A Singer and Her Songs.* Ed. Roger Abrahams. Baton Rouge: Louisiana State University Press, 1970.

Riese, Randall, and Neal Hitchens. *Nashville Babylon: The Uncensored Truth and Private Lives of Country Music's Greatest Stars.* New York: Congdon and Weed, 1988.

Rinzler, Ralph, and Norman Cohen. *Uncle Dave Macon: A Bio-Discography.* Los Angeles: John Edwards Memorial Foundation, 1970.

Rodgers, Carrie. *My Husband, Jimmie Rodgers.* Nashville, TN: Country Music Foundation, 1975.

Rogers, Jimmie N. *The Country Music Message: All About Lovin' and Leavin'.* Englewood Cliffs, NJ: Prentice-Hall, 1983.

Rooney, Jim. *Bossmen: Bill Monroe and Muddy Waters.* New York: Da Capo, 1989.

Rorer, Clifford. *Charlie Poole and the North Carolina Ramblers.* 2nd ed. NC: Self-published, 1992.

Rosenbaum, Art. *Folk Visions and Voices: Traditional Music and Song in North Georgia.* Athens: University of Georgia Press, 1983.

Rosenberg, Neil V. *Bill Monroe and His Blue Grass Boys.* Nashville, TN: Country Music Foundation, 1974.

———. *Bluegrass: A History.* Urbana: University of Illinois Press, 1985.

Russell, Tony. *The Carter Family.* London: Old Time Music, 1973.

Sandberg, Larry, and Dick Weissman. *The Folk Music Sourcebook.* Rev. ed. New York: Da Capo, 1989.

Schlappi, Elizabeth. *Roy Acuff: The Smoky Mountain Boy.* Gretna, LA: Pelican, 1992.

Scott, Frank, and Al Ennis. *The Roots and Rhythm Guide to Rock.* Pennington, NJ: a cappella books, 1993.

Seeger, Mike, with Ruth Pershing. *Talking Feet.* Berkeley, Calif.: North Atlantic Books, 1992.

Shelton, Robert. *No Direction Home: The Life and Music of Bob Dylan.* New York: Morrow, 1986.

Shelton, Robert, and Burt Goldblatt. *The Country Music Story.* New York: Castle Books, 1971.

Smith, Richard D. *Bluegrass: An Informal Guide.* Chicago: a cappella books, 1996.

———. *Can't You Hear Me Callin': The Life of Bill Monroe, Father of Bluegrass.* New York: Little, Brown, 1999.

Stambler, Irwin, and Grellun Landon. *The Encyclopedia of Folk, Country, and Western Music.* 2nd ed. New York: St. Martin's Press, 1984.

———. *Country Music: The Encyclopedia.* New York: St. Martin's Press, 1997.

Stamper, Pete. *It All Happened in Renfro Valley.* Lexington: University of Kentucky Press, 1999.

Streissguth, Michael. *Eddy Arnold: Pioneer of the Nashville Sound.* New York: Schirmer, 1997.

———. *Like a Moth to a Flame: The Jim Reeves Story.* Nashville, TN: Rutledge Hill Press, 1998.

Stuart, Marty. *Pilgrims, Sinners, Saints, and Prophets: A Book of Words and Photographs.* Nashville, TN: Rutledge Hill Press, 1999.

Tasson, Myron, et al. *Fifty Years at the Grand Ole Opry.* New York: Pelican, 1975.

Tichi, Cecelia. *High Lonesome: The American Culture of Country Music.* Chapel Hill: University of North Carolina Press, 1994.

Tosches, Nick. *Country: The Biggest Music in America.* 3rd ed. New York: Da Capo, 1996.

———. *Where Dead Voices Gather.* New York: Little, Brown, 2001.

Townsend, Charles S. *San Antonio Rose: The Life and Music of Bob Wills.* Urbana: University of Illinois Press, 1976.

Tribe, Ivan M. *Mountaineer Jamboree: Country Music in West Virginia.* Lexington: University Press of Kentucky, 1984.

Tucker, Tanya, and Patsi Bale Cox. *Nickel Dreams: My Life*. New York: HarperCollins, 1998.

Vaughan, Andrew. *Who's Who in the New Country Music*. New York: St. Martin's Press, 1990.

Webb, Robert Lloyd. *Ring the Banjer! The Banjo in America: From Folklore to Factory*. Boston: MIT Museum, 1981.

Whitburn, Joel. *Joel Whitburn's Top Country Singles 1944–1988*. Menomee Falls, WI: Record Research, 1989.

Whiteside, Johnny. *Ramblin' Rose: The Life and Career of Rose Maddox*. Nashville, TN: Country Music Foundation/Vanderbilt University Press, 1997.

Wiggins, Gene. *Fiddlin' Georgia Crazy: Fiddlin' John Carson, His Real World, and the World of His Songs*. Urbana: University of Illinois Press, 1987.

Williams, Jett, and Pamela Thomas. *Ain't Nothing Sweet as My Baby: The Story of Hank Williams's Lost Daughter*. New York: Harcourt Brace Jovanovich, 1990.

Wolfe, Charles K. *Tennessee Strings: The Story of Country Music in Tennessee*. Knoxville: University of Tennessee Press, 1977.

———. *The Grand Ole Opry: The Early Years*. London: Old Time Music, 1978. Enl. and rev. as *A Good Natured Riot: The Birth of the Grand Ole Opry*. Nashville, TN: Country Music Foundation/Vanderbilt University Press, 1999.

———. *Kentucky Country Folk and Country Music*. Lexington: University of Kentucky Press, 1982.

———. *In Close Harmony: The Story of the Louvin Brothers*. Jackson: University Press of Mississippi, 1996.

———. *The Devil's Box: Masters of Southern Fiddling*. Nashville, TN: Country Music Foundation/Vanderbilt University Press, 1997.

———. *Classic Country*. New York: Routledge, 2000.

Wolfe, Charles K., and James E. Akenson, eds. *Country Music Annual, 2000* and *Country Music Annual, 2001*. Lexington: University of Kentucky Press, 2000 and 2001.

Wolff, Kurt, and Orla Duane, eds. *Rough Guide to Country Music*. London: Rough Guides, 2000.

Wright, John. *Travelin' That Highway Home*. Urbana: University of Illinois Press, 1993.

Appendix 1
Selected Entries by Musical Genre

At the request of my publisher, I have listed the entries by musical genre, so fans of a particular style—like Western Swing—can find all of the artists who specialize in this area. Of course, there are many artists—like Dolly Parton—who have moved between various genres, and some may disagree with my decision to place them in one or another category. Also, genre names can mean different things to different people. To clarify what they mean to me, here's a list of the genres along with a rough definition of each:

Alt-country: Country music from the mid-'80s that absorbs singer/songwriter, folk, and traditional styles; sometimes called Americana or Texas-Country.

Bakersfield: The group of performers from the Bakersfield, California, region, active from the mid-'50s through the early '70s, who revived a hardcore, neo-honky tonk country style.

Bluegrass: Pioneered by Bill Monroe in the late '40s, bluegrass music features primarily acoustic instruments (banjo-fiddle-guitar-mandolin-bass, usually), showing the influence of Western swing and honky tonk country, as well as old-time styles.

Comedy: Performers who specialize in portraying classic country comic roles, and comic songwriters.

Country-jazz: Performers who meld elements of jazz and swing in their music.

Countrypolitan: Pop-country music of the mid-'70s through the mid-'80s.

Country-rock: Rock groups that have been influenced by country music, and country groups that incorporate rock instrumentation and rhythms.

Cowboy: Western-styled singers and songwriters who usually sport traditional "cowboy" clothes and primarily sing songs related to the cowboy/Western lifestyle.

Folk: Singers from the folk revival or traditional folk movements, along with folklorists who study these styles.

Gospel: Performers and songwriters specializing in religious-themed songs that show the influence of popular country styles.

Honky tonk: Late '40s/mid-'50s singers and songwriters whose material focuses usually on boozing, cheating, and rambling.

Industry: Record and radio executives; producers and engineers; talent scouts; and others related to the country business.

Nashville Sound: The heavily produced, pop-influenced music coming out of Nashville from the mid-'50s through the early '70s.

New Country: The country revival artists of the '80s and '90s along with the new pop performers, songwriters, and groups.

Old-time: The country performers of the '20s and '30s, and those who emulate or have revived the music that they performed.

Outlaw: Mid-'70s movement of songwriters and singers who rebelled against the popular countrypolitan style of the day.

Rockabilly: Mid-'50s wedding of country and roots-rock styles.

Songwriter: Artist who has primarily made his/her living by composing songs for others to perform.

Western Swing: Mid-'30s-ongoing style that weds elements of swing and jazz with traditional stringband and fiddle repertoire.

ALT-COUNTRY

Allen, Terry
Clark, Guy
DeMent, Iris
Earle, Steve
Ely, Joe
Flores, Rosie
Frumholz, Steve
Gilmore, Jimmie Dale
Griffith, Nanci
Harris, Emmylou
Hiatt, John
Hinojosa, Tish
Keen, Robert Earl
Ketchum, Hal
Lovett, Lyle
Miller, Buddy and Julie
Shaver, Billy Joe
Shocked, Michelle
Talley, James
Tashian, Barry and Holly
Van Zandt, Townes
Watson, Gene
Welch, Gillian
Williams, Lucinda
Young, Steve

BAKERSFIELD

Collins, Tommy
Maphis, Joe
Owens, Bonnie
Owens, Buck
Owens, Tex
Stewart, Wynn
Williams, Leona

BLUEGRASS

Allen, Red
Baker, Kenny
Berline, Byron
Buffalo Gals, The
Clements, Vassar
Clifton, Bill
Cooper, Stoney and Wilma Lee
Country Cooking
Country Gazette
Country Gentlemen, The
Crowe, J. D.
Dickens, Hazel
Dillards, The
Douglas, Jerry
Eanes, Jim
Emerson, Bill
Flatt and Scruggs

Fleck, Bela
Forrester, Howdy
Goins Brothers
Grant, Bill and Delia Bell
Graves, Buck/Uncle Josh
Greenbriar Boys
Greene, Richard
Grisman, David
Hancock, Butch
Hot Rize
Jackson, Carl
Jackson, Tommy
Jenkins and Sherrill
Jim and Jesse
Johnson Mountain Boys
Keith, Bill
Kentucky Colonels, The
Krauss, Alison
Lawson, Doyle
Lewis, Laurie
Lewis Family
Lilly Brothers
Lulu Belle and Scotty
Martin, Benny
Martin, Jimmy
McCoury, Del
Monroe, Bill
Monroe, Charlie
Moody, Clyde
Morris Brothers, The
Muleskinner
Nashville Band
New Grass Revival
Nickel Creek
O'Brien, Tim
O'Connor, Mark
Old and in the Way
Osborne Brothers, The
Reno, Don
Rice, Tony
Rouse Brothers
Rowan, Peter
Seldom Scene
Skaggs, Ricky
Skyline
Stanley Brothers
Story, Carl
Taylor, Tut
Trischka, Tony
Whites, The
Wild Rose
Wise, Chubby
Wiseman, Mac

COMEDY

Bee, Molly
Canova, Judy

Childre, Lew
Clower, Jerry
Duke of Paducah, The
Esmereldy
Friedman, Kinky
Hee Haw
Homer and Jethro
Jamup and Honey
Lonzo and Oscar
Miller, Roger
Pearl, Minnie
Stampley, Joe
Van Dyke, Leroy
Wooley, Sheb

COUNTRY-JAZZ

Bryant, Jimmy
Paul, Les
Turner, Zeb
Wood, Del

COUNTRYPOLITAN

Alabama
Allen, Deborah
Anderson, Lynn
Bailey, Razzy
Bannon, R. C.
Bellamy Brothers
Boone, Debbie
Boxcar Willie
Carver, Johnny
Conlee, John
Coolidge, Rita
Dave and Sugar
Duncan, Johnny
Fricke, Janie
Frizzell, David
Gatlin Brothers
Gayle, Crystal
Greenwood, Lee
Hart, Freddie
Kendalls, The
Lee, Johnny
McClain, Charly
McDaniel, Mel
McEntire, Reba
Miller, Jody
Milsap, Ronnie
Morris, Gary
Newton, Juice
Oak Ridge Boys
Oslin, K. T.
Osmond, Marie
Parton, Dolly
Rabbitt, Eddie

Raven, Eddy
Raye, Susan
Rogers, Kenny
Schneider, John
Sheppard, T. G.
Statler Brothers, The
Sylvia
Thomas, B. J.
Tucker, Tanya
Williams, Don
Wynette, Tammy

COUNTRY-ROCK

Amazing Rhythm Aces
Area Code 615
BlackHawk
Byrds, The
Clark, Gene
Commander Cody and His Lost Planet
    Airmen
Confederate Raliroad
Daniels, Charlie
Dr. Hook and the Medicine Show
Eagles, The
Everly Brothers, The
Exile
Flying Burrito Brothers
Hillman, Chris
Ian and Sylvia
Kentucky HeadHunters, The
Kershaw, Doug
Lee, Albert
Little Texas
Mavericks, The
McEuen, John
Nelson, Rick(y)
Nesmith, Michael
New Riders of the Purple Sage
Nitty Gritty Dirt Band
Parsons, Gram
Poco
Pure Prairie League
Ricochet
Ronstadt, Linda
Sawyer Brown
Shenandoah
Stewart, Gary
Young, Neil

COWBOY

Allen, Jules Verne
Allen, Rex
Allen, Rex Jr.
Allen, Rosalie
Atcher, Bob

Autry, Gene
Bonnie Lou
Britt, Elton
Carolina Cotton
Carson, Martha
Carter, Wilf
Chuck Wagon Gang
Clements, Zeke
Copas, Cowboy
Daffan, Ted
Darling, Denver
Dean, Eddie
Dexter, Al
Edwards, Don
Girls of the Golden West
Griffin, Rex
Hamblen, Stuart
Haywire Mac
Hill, Goldie
King, Pee Wee
lang, k.d.
Lewis, "Texas" Jim
Luman, Bob
Massey, Louise and the Westerners
McDonald, Skeets
McEnery, Red River Dave
Montana, Patsy
Murphey, Michael Martin
Ranch Romance
Riders in the Sky
Ritter, Tex
Rogers, Roy
Sons of the Pioneers
Sons of the San Joaquin
Sovine, Red
Sprague, Carl T.
Texas Ruby
Wakely, Jimmy
Weaver Brothers and Elviry
Whitley, Ray
Willing, Foy

FOLK

Edwards, John
Guthrie, Woody
Lomax, John
Lunn, Robert
Seeger, Pete

GOSPEL

Bailes Brothers
Blackwood Brothers, The
Brumley, Albert E.
Jordanaires, The
Lewis Family

Overstreet, Paul
Speer Family, The
Sullivan Family

HONKY-TONK

BR-549
Bush, Johnny
Drifting Cowboys, The
Edwards, Stoney
Frizzell, Lefty
Gosdin, Vern
Haggard, Merle
Horton, Johnny
Husky, Ferlin
Johnnie and Jack
Jones, George
Mullican, Moon
Murphy, Jimmy
Noack, Eddie
Oxford, Vernon
Pierce, Webb
Reeves, Jim
Smith, Carl
Snow, Hank
Steagall, Red
Street, Mel
Thompson, Hank
Tillman, Floyd
Travis, Merle
Tubb, Ernest
Wells, Kitty
Whitman, Slim
Williams, Hank
Williams, Tex
Work, Jimmy
Young, Faron

INDUSTRY

Acuff, Roy
Asch, Moses
Atkins, Chet
Bowen, Jimmy
Bradley, Owen
Brown, Tony
Clement, "Cowboy" Jack
Crook & Chase
Curb, Mike
Daily, Harold "Pappy"
Denny, Jim
Drake, Pete
Emery, Ralph
Gordy, Emory, Jr.
Hay, George D.
Hendricks, Scott
Lair, John

Law, Don
Lee, Buddy
Nelson, Ken
Nudie "The Rodeo Tailor"
Parker, "Colonel" Tom
Peer, Ralph
Phillips, Sam
Raney, Wayne
Rose, Fred and Wesley
Satherley, Art
Schlitz, Don
Scruggs, Randy
Sherrill, Billy
Sholes, Steve
Singleton, Shelby
Stone, Cliffie
Walker, Frank
Wilburn Brothers

NASHVILLE SOUND

Acuff, Roy;
Anderson, Bill
Anderson, Liz
Arnold, Eddy
Ashworth, Ernie
Atkins, Chet
Bandy, Moe
Bare, Bobby
Blanchard, Jack and Misty Morgan
Bond, Johnny
Browns, The
Butler, Carl and Pearl
Byrd, Jerry
Campbell, Glen
Cash, Johnny
Charles, Ray
Clark, Roy
Cline, Patsy
Coe, David Allan
Colter, Jessi
Cornelius, Helen
Cramer, Floyd
Dalton, Lacy J.
Davis, Danny
Davis, Mac
Davis, Skeeter
Dean, Jimmy
Denver, John
Dickens, "Little" Jimmy
Driftwood, Jimmy
Drusky, Roy
Dudley, Dave
Emmons, Buddy
Fairchild, Barbara
Fargo, Donna

Fender, Freddy
Foley, Red
Ford, Tennessee Ernie
Gentry, Bobbie
Gibson, Don
Gilley, Mickey
Greene, Jack
Hall, Connie
Hall, Tom T.
Hamilton, George IV
Harman, Buddy
Hawkins, Hawkshaw
Houston, David
Howard, Jan
Jackson, Stonewall
Jones, George
Kerr, Anita
Kilgore, Merle
King, Claude
Lee, Brenda
Lewis, Bobby
Locklin, Hank
Lynn, Loretta
Mack, Warner
Mandrell, Barbara
Mandrell, Louise
Mann, Lorene
Martin, Grady
McCall, C.W.
McClinton, O.B.
McCoy, Charlie
McDowell, Ronnie
Miller, Roger
Montgomery, Melba
Morgan, George
Murray, Anne
Newman, Jimmy "C"
Norma Jean
Overstreet, Tommy
Price, Kenny
Price, Ray
Pride, Charley
Pruett, Jeanne
Randolph, "Boots"
Reed, Jerry
Reeves, Del
Rich, Charlie
Riley, Jeannie C.
Robbins, Hargus "Pig"
Robbins, Marty
Rodriguez, Johnny
Russell, Johnny
Seals, Dan
Seely, Jeannie
Shepard, Jean
Smith, Arthur "Guitar Boogie"

Smith, Cal
Smith, Connie
Smith, Sammi
Spears, Billie Jo
Starr, Kay
Stevens, Ray
Stewart, Redd
Thompson, Sue
Tillis, Mel
Twitty, Conway
Tyler, T. Texas
Wagoner, Porter
Walker, Billy
Walker, Charlie
West, Dottie
West, Shelley
West, Speedy
Wilburn Brothers
Willis Brothers, the

NEW COUNTRY

Adkins, Trace
Anderson, John
Baillie & the Boys
Barnett, Mandy
Berry, John
Black, Clint
Bogguss, Suzy
Brooks and Dunn
Brooks, Garth
Brown, ''Junior''
Brown, T. Graham
Byrd, Tracy
Carpenter, Mary Chapin
Carter, Carlene
Carter, Deana
Cash, Rosanne
Chesnutt, Mark
Clark, Terri
Collie, Mark
Cox, Billy
Crowell, Rodney
Cyrus, Billy Ray
Dean, Billy
Desert Rose Band, The
Diamond Rio
Diffie, Joe
Dixie Chicks, The
DuBois, Tim
Dunn, Holly
Emilio
Evans, Sara
Forester Sisters
Foster and Lloyd
Francis, Cleve

Gill, Vince
Gillman, Billy
Hayes, Wade
Herndon, Ty
Highway 101
Hill, Faith
Jackson, Alan
Judds, The
Keith, Toby
Kershaw, Sammy
Lawrence, Tracy
LeDoux, Chris
Loveless, Patty
Lynne, Shelby
Mattea, Kathy
McBride and the Ride
McBride, Martina
McCoy, Neal
McCready, Mindy
McGraw, Tim
Messina, Jo Dee
Montgomery, John Michael
Morgan, Lorrie
O'Kanes, The
Parnell, Lee Roy
Raye, Collin
Restless Heart
Richey, Kim
Rimes, LeAnn
SheDaisy
Shelton, Ricky Van
Stone, Doug
Strait, George
Stuart, Marty
Supernaw, Doug
Sweethearts of the Rodeo
Texas Tornados
Tillis, Pam
Tippin, Aaron
Travis, Randy
Trick Pony
Tritt, Travis
Twain, Shania
Urban, Keith
Walker, Clay
Wariner, Steve
White, Bryan
White, Joy Lynn
White, Lari
Whitley, Keith
Willis, Kelly
Womack, Lee Ann
Wright, Michelle
Yearwood, Trisha

OLD-TIME

Allen Brothers
Arkie the Arkansas Woodchopper
Armstrong Twins
Arthur, Emry
Ashley, Tom
Bailey, DeFord
Bate, Dr. Humphrey and The Possum
    Hunters
Beverly Hill Billies
Binkley Brothers Dixie Clodhoppers
Blake, Norman
Blue Sky Boys, The
Boggs, Dock
Bonnie Lou and Buster
Bumgarner, Samantha
Burnett and Rutherford
Cackle Sisters, The
Callahan Brothers
Carlin, Bob
Carlisle Brothers, The
Carolina Tarheels
Carson, Fiddlin' John
Carter Family, The "Original"
Cohen, John
Cousin Emmy
Cox, Bill
Crook Brothers
Dalhart, Vernon
Darby and Tarleton
Davis, Jimmie
Delmore Brothers
Dilly and His Dill Pickles
Dinning Sisters
Dixon Brothers, The
East Texas Serenaders
Fiddle Fever
Fink, Cathy
Fruit Jar Drinkers, the
Georgia Yellow Hammers
Gerrard, Alice
Good Ol' Persons
Gully Jumpers
Hale, Theron and Daughters
Hall, Roy
Harrell, Kelly
Hartford, John
Hi Flyers
Holcomb, Roscoe
Holy Modal Rounders
Hood, Adelyne
Hopkins, Al, and the Hill Billes
Hopkins, Doc
Hot Mud Family
Hutchison, Frank

Jackson, Aunt Molly
Jarrell, Tommy
Jenkins, Reverend Andrew
Jones, Grandpa
Karl and Harty
Kazee, Buell
Kessinger, Clark W.
Kincaid, Bradley
Ledford, Lily May
Louvin Brothers, The
Lunsford, Bascom Lamar
Luther, Frank
Mac and Bob
Macon, Uncle Dave
Mainer, J. E.
McGee, Sam
Miller, Emmett
Moonshine Kate
New Lost City Ramblers, The
O'Day, Molly
Parker, Linda
Pickard Family, The
Poole, Charlie
Powers, Fiddlin' Cowan
Puckett, Riley
Red Clay Ramblers, The
Reed, Blind Alfred
Reed, Ola Belle
Reeves, Goebel
Reneau, George
Riddle, Almeda
Ritchie, Jean
Roberts, "Fiddlin'" Doc
Robertson, Uncle Eck
Robison, Carson J.
Rodgers, Jesse
Rodgers, Jimmie
Rosenbaum, Art
Scott, Tommy
Seeger, Mike
Skillet Lickers, The
Smeck, Roy
Smith, Fiddlin' Arthur
Stanley, Roba
Stoneman, Ernest "Pop"
Stringbean
Stripling Brothers
The Highwoods Stringband
Thompson, Ernest
Thompson, Joe
Thompson, Uncle Jimmy
Three Little Maids, The
Vagabonds, The
Ward, Wade
Watson, Doc
Whitter, Henry

OUTLAW

Cash, Johnny
Glaser Brothers
Jennings, Waylon
Kristofferson, Kris
Nelson, Willie
Paycheck, Johnny
Williams, Hank, Jr.

ROCKABILLY

Arthur, Charline
Bruce, Ed
Burnette, Dorsey
Burton, James
Cash, Johnny
Cochran, Hank
Collins Kids
Craddock, Billy "Crash"
Curless, Dick
Curtis, Sonny
Downing, Big Al
Feathers, Charlie
Felts, Narvel
Gunter, Arthur "Hardrock"
Head, Roy
Hebb, Bobby
Holly, Buddy
Jackson, Wanda
James, Sonny
Lee, Brenda
Lee, Dickey
Lewis, Jerry Lee
Logsdon, Jimmie
Martin, Janis
Nelson, Rick(y)
Noack, Eddie
Orbison, Roy
Perkins, Carl
Presley, Elvis Aron
Rainwater, Marvin
Yoakam, Dwight

SONGWRITER

Alger, Pat
Axton, Hoyt

Braddock, Bobby
Brooks, Karen
Bryant, Boudleaux and Felice
Conley, Earl Thomas
Davies, Gail
Dylan, Bob
Frazier, Dallas
Hargrove, Linda
Howard, Harlan
Kostas
Lewis, Hugh X.
Loudermilk, John D.
Miller, Bob
Newbury, Mickey
Rooney, Jim
Skinner, Jimmie
Stuckey, Nat
Walker, Cindy
Walker, Jerry Jeff
Wilkin, Marijohn

WESTERN SWING

Asleep at the Wheel
Boyd, Bill
Brown, Milton
Cooley, Spade
Duncan, Tommy
Dunn, Bob
Gimble, Johnny
Hofner, Adolph
Hoosier Hot Shots
Light Crust Doughboys, The
Maddox, Rose
McAuliffe, Leon
Moore, "Tiny"
Mullican, Moon
Payne, Leon
Penny, Hank
Prairie Ramblers
Rausch, Leon
Remington, Herb
Shelton Brothers
Tune Wranglers
Wills, Bob

Appendix 2
Selected Entries by Musical Instrument

My publisher also requested a list of performers by the musical instrument that they play. This is a selective list, focussing primarily on those who are well-known for playing a particular instrument. Although almost every country singer can play the guitar—at least a little bit—I have only listed under "guitar" those who are either lead guitar players or famous/influential as guitarists.

ACCORDION

Pee Wee King

AUTOHARP

Stoneman, Ernest "Pop"

BANJO

Ashley, Tom
Boggs, Dock
Bumgarner, Samantha
Burnett and Rutherford
Carlin, Bob
Cohen, John
Cousin Emmy
Crowe, J. D.
Duke of Paducah, The
Fink, Cathy
Flatt and Scruggs
Fleck, Bela
Hancock, Butch
Hartford, John
Holcomb, Roscoe
Jackson, Alan
Jackson, Carl
Jones, Grandpa
Kazee, Buell
Keith, Bill
Ledford, Lily May
Lunsford, Bascom Lamar
Macon, Uncle Dave
McEuen, John
Poole, Charlie
Reed, Ola Belle
Reno, Don
Rosenbaum, Art
Seeger, Mike
Seeger, Pete
Smith, Carl
Stanley Brothers
Stanley, Roba
Stringbean
Thompson, Joe
Trischka, Tony
Ward, Wade

DOBRO

Douglas, Jerry
Graves, Buck/Uncle Josh
Jackson, Shot
Taylor, Tut

DULCIMER

Ritchie, Jean

FIDDLE

Acuff, Roy
Baker, Kenny
Berline, Byron
Carson, Fiddlin' John
Clements, Vassar
Cooley, Spade
Daniels, Charlie
Forrester, Howdy
Gimble, Johnny
Greene, Richard
Hale, Theron and Daughters
Hood, Adelyne
Hopkins, Doc
Jackson, Tommy
Jarrell, Tommy
Kershaw, Doug
Kessinger, Clark W.
Krauss, Alison
Martin, Benny
O'Connor, Mark
Powers, Fiddlin' Cowan
Reed, Blind Alfred
Roberts, "Fiddlin' " Doc
Robertson, Uncle Eck
Rouse Brothers
Smith, Fiddlin' Arthur
Thompson, Uncle Jimmy
Wise, Chubby

GUITAR

Atkins, Chet
Blake, Norman
Brown, "Junior"
Bryant, Jimmy
Burton, James

Campbell, Glen
Clark, Roy
Collins, Tommy
Delmore Brothers
Gill, Vince
Haggard, Merle
Holly, Buddy
Hutchison, Frank
Lee, Albert
Maphis, Joe
Martin, Grady
McGee, Sam
Nelson, Willie
Paul, Les
Perkins, Carl
Puckett, Riley
Rausch, Leon
Reed, Jerry
Rice, Tony
Rowan, Peter
Smeck, Roy
Smith, Arthur "Guitar Boogie"
Stuart, Marty
Travis, Merle
Turner, Zeb
Watson, Doc
West, Speedy

HARMONICA

Bailey, DeFord
Bate, Dr. Humphrey and The Possum
  Hunters

McCoy, Charlie
Raney, Wayne
Mandolin
Grisman, David
Homer and Jethro
Monroe, Bill
Moore, "Tiny"
Skaggs, Ricky

PIANO

Cramer, Floyd
Downing, Big Al
Lewis, Jerry Lee
Mullican, Moon
Robbins, Hargus "Pig"

SAXOPHONE

Randolph, "Boots"

STEEL GUITAR/PEDAL STEEL GUITAR

Byrd, Jerry
Childre, Lew
Drake, Pete
Dunn, Bob
Emmons, Buddy
Harman, Buddy
Isaacs, Bud
McAuliffe, Leon
Remington, Herb

Name Index

E

H

M

P

X

Y

Z